The Corsini
Encyclopedia *of*
Psychology

The Corsini Encyclopedia *of* Psychology

FOURTH EDITION

Volume 2

Edited by

Irving B. Weiner
W. Edward Craighead

WILEY

John Wiley & Sons, Inc.

Library of Congress Cataloging-in-Publication Data:

The Corsini encyclopedia of psychology / edited by Irving B.
Weiner, W. Edward Craighead.—4th ed.
        v. cm.
    Rev. ed. of: The Corsini encyclopedia of psychology and behavioral science.
3rd ed. New York : Wiley, c2001.
    Includes bibliographical references and index.
    ISBN 978-0-470-17024-3 (cloth, set)
    ISBN 978-0-470-17026-7 (cloth, Volume 2)
    1. Psychology—Encyclopedias. I. Weiner, Irving B. II. Craighead, W. Edward.   III.
Corsini encyclopedia of psychology and behavioral science.

    BF31.E52 2010
    150.3—dc22

                                                        2009031719

Printed in the United States of America

10 9 8 7 6 5 4 3 2 1

PREFACE

The fourth edition of the *Corsini Encyclopedia of Psychology* contains entries whose utility has endured through several editions and entirely new entries written for this first edition of the twenty-first century. The selected previous entries have been updated to reflect recent conceptualizations and research findings; the new entries, which constitute approximately half of the articles, were commissioned to broaden the coverage of the encyclopedia and to capture a full range of contemporary topics in psychology. For readers previously unfamiliar with a particular topic, related articles are intended to be an informative source of what is most important for them to know about it; for readers already knowledgeable about a topic, articles related to it are intended to provide useful, concise summaries of current knowledge.

Numerous features of the encyclopedia are designed to help readers gain information about topics of interest to them. Most entries are referenced to relevant publications in the psychological literature and include suggested additional readings and cross-references to other articles in the encyclopedia on similar or related topics. Many topics are discussed in more than one entry, to provide additional facts about the topic and identify different ways of looking at it. Along with articles on substantive topics in psychology, this fourth edition of the encyclopedia includes detailed biographies of 63 of the most distinguished persons in the history of psychology. Supplementing these biographies is a special alphabetized section in Volume 4 consisting of brief biographies of 543 other important contributors to psychological theory and research.

Among other special topics, the encyclopedia features entries on the history and current status of psychology in various countries from around the world in which there are active communities of psychologists; numerous articles describing the activities and functions of the major psychological and mental health organizations and societies; and attention to topics of psychological significance in related fields of social work and medicine, with a particular emphasis on psychiatry. With further respect to the breadth of coverage in the encyclopedia, the areas in which numerous specific articles appear include the following:

- Child, adolescent, adult, midlife, and late-life development
- Cognitive, affective, and sensory functions
- Cross-cultural psychology
- Forensic psychology
- Industrial and organizational psychology
- Mental and psychological disorders listed in the DSM, the PDM, and the ICD
- Neuroscience and the biological bases of behavior
- Language and linguistic processes
- Personality processes and interpersonal relationships
- Psychological therapies and psychosocial interventions
- Psychopharmacological treatment methods
- Psychological and neuropsychological assessment methods
- Social and environmental influences on behavior
- Statistical procedures and research methods

After selecting the topics for inclusion in this fourth edition, the editors set about to identify and recruit individuals whose scholarly background and professional experience would enable them to give inquiring readers clear and accurate information about topics of their interest. We believe that we were highly successful in this effort, and we are grateful to the approximately 1,200 authors who contributed articles to these four volumes. We appreciate their knowledge, their literacy, and their tolerance of our editing their work to achieve a consistent format across the large number of articles in the four volumes.

An undertaking of this magnitude involves the cooperation and collaboration of a many of individuals in addition to its authors. We would like first of all to express our gratitude to Patricia Rossi, Wiley Executive Editor in Psychology, who brought us together to work on this project. She has been a wonderful editor, leading and supporting us throughout this process beginning with our first meeting to discuss the encyclopedia, what we would include, and the development and implementation of a plan to bring the publication of the encyclopedia to fruition. It is hard to imagine a better editor with whom one could work. For their essential roles in the preparation and production of the encyclopedia, we would like to thank as well Wiley staff members Kim Nir, Senior Production Editor; Kathleen DeChants, Senior Editorial Assistant; and Ester Mallach, Administrative Assistant.

We are especially grateful to Jennifer Moore for her many activities associated with the production of these volumes. She found addresses (especially e-mail addresses), retyped articles, located missing references for articles, and was generally extremely helpful in our completion of the manuscript. We would also like to express our appreciation to Rebecca Suffness and Ava Madoff, who helped with various aspects of the development of the manuscript.

Finally, we would like to thank four librarians who reviewed our plan for the new edition and provided valuable advice concerning its format and content: Barbara Glendenning of the University of California Berkeley Library; Sally Speller of the New York Public Library; Bruce Stoffel of the Milner Library at Illinois State University; and Michael Yonezawa of the University of Calfornia Riverside Library.

Irving B. Weiner, Tampa, FL
W. Edward Craighead, Atlanta, GA
June, 2009

HOW TO USE THIS ENCYCLOPEDIA

Welcome to this fourth edition of the *Corsini Encyclopedia of Psychology*. Like its predecessors, the fourth edition is organized into four distinct parts. Each of the four volumes begins with frontmatter that includes the entire list of entries for all four volumes and a complete list of the contributing authors and their affiliations. The second part of each volume consists of the actual entries, listed in alphabetical order. Included among these alphabetized entries are biographies of 63 of the most important figures in the history of psychology. Alphabetized entries constitute most of Volumes 1 though 3 and some of Volume 4. As a third part of the encyclopedia, Volume 4 contains a section of brief biographies for 543 other important contributors to psychological theory, research, and practice. Finally, Volume 4 concludes with an Author Index and a Subject Index for the entire four-volume set.

Readers looking for information on a particular topic should first check the list of entries in the frontmatter to see if there is an article on that topic. If so, the article can be found in its alphabetical location. If not, the next place to look is the Subject Index in Volume 4. If the topic is mentioned in the encyclopedia, the Subject Index will identify the particular pages on which the topic is discussed. Readers looking for information about a particular person should also first check the list of entries to see if the person is one of the distinguished individuals for whom there is a biography among the alphabetized entries. If not, the next place to look is the section of Brief Biographies in Volume 4. Should the person not appear in either of these locations, the searcher should turn to the Author Index. If the person is mentioned anywhere in the encyclopedia, the author index will identify the pages on which this mention occurs. In most instances in which persons are mentioned in an article, some of their publications are included in a list of references accompanying the article.

An important additional source for locating information is in the cross-referencing that appears at the end of most entries. The following cross-references listed with five selected entries illustrate this guide to further information and also speak to the breadth of coverage in the encyclopedia:

Central Nervous System (See also Brain; Neuroscience; Parasympathetic Nervous System; Sympathetic Nervous System)

Cognitive Development (See also Emotional Development; Intellectual Development; Social Cognitive Development)

Major Depressive Disorder (See also Antidepressant Medications; Depression; Depressive Personality Disorder)

Multivariate Methods (See also Analysis of Covariance; Analysis of Variance; Factor Analysis; Multiple Correlation)

Psychotherapy (See also Counseling; Current Psychotherapies; Psychotherapy Research; Psychotherapy Training)

Each of the cross-references accompanying an article has cross-references of its own to related articles. By pursuing the trail of cross-references related to a topic, readers can maximize the amount of information they can get from the encyclopedia.

CORSINI ENCYCLOPEDIA ENTRIES

CONTRIBUTORS

Norman Abeles, Michigan State University

Jonathan S. Abramowitz, University of North Carolina at Chapel Hill

Lyn Y. Abramson, University of Wisconsin-Madison

Philip A. Ackerman, Georgia Institute of Technology

Thomas G. Adams, University of Arkansas

Wayne Adams, George Fox University, Newburg, OR

Howard Adelman, University of California, Los Angeles

Bernard W. Agranoff, University of Michigan

Muninder K. Ahluwalia, Montclair State University

Leona S. Aiken, Arizona State University

Peter Alahi, University of Illinois College of Medicine, Peoria

Anne Marie Albano, Columbia University College of Physicians and Surgeons

John A. Albertini, Rochester Institute of Technology

Amelia Aldao, Yale University

Mark D. Alicke, Ohio University

Daniel N. Allen, University of Nevada Las Vegas

Lauren B. Alloy, Temple University

Carolyn J. Anderson, University of Illinois, Urbana-Champaign

Corey Anderson, Pacific University

Keelah D. Andrews, Wheaton College

Hymie Anisman, Carleton University

Heinz L. Ansbacher, University of Vermont

Martin M. Antony, Ryerson University, Toronto, Canada

Steven J. Anzalone, State University of New York at Binghamton

Robert P. Archer, Eastern Virginia Medical School

Ruben Ardila, National University of Columbia

Eirikur Orn Arnarson, Landspitali University Hospital, Reykjavik, Iceland

Mark Arnoff, University at Albany, SUNY

Jane Ashby, University of Massachusetts Amherst

Gord, J. G. Asmundson, University of Regina, Canada

John A. Astin, California Pacific Medical Center, San Francisco, CA

Martha Augoustinos, University of Adelaide, Australia

Tatjana Ave, University of Chicago

Oksana Babenko, University of Alberta, Canada

Michael Babyak, Duke University Medical Center

Bahador Bahram, University College London, United Kingdom

Clark Baim, Birmingham Institute of Psychodrama, Birmingham, UK

Tatiana N. Balachova, University of Oklahoma Health Sciences Center

Scott A. Baldwin, Brigham Young University

Michael Bambery, University of Detroit Mercy

Albert Bandura, Stanford University

Marie T. Banich, University of Colorado at Boulder

Steven C. Bank, Center for Forensic Psychiatry, Ann Arbor, MI

Jacques P. Barber, University of Pennsylvania

Daniel Barbiero, US National Academy of Sciences

John A. Bargh, Yale University

Blanche Barnes, Mumbai, India

Sean Barns, Binghamton University

Barnaby B. Barratt, Prescott, AZ

Rowland P. Barrett, Warren Alpert Medical School of Brown University

Tammy D. Barry, University of Southern Mississippi

Jennifer L. Bass, The Kinsey Institute, Bloomington, IN

David S. Batey, University of Alabama School of Medicine

C. Daniel Batson, University of Kansas

Steven H. R. Beach, University of Georgia

Theodore P. Beauchaine, University of Washington

Eric Beauregard, Simon Fraser University

Robert B. Bechtel, University of Arizona

Judith S. Beck, Beck Institute for Cognitive Therapy and Research and University of Pennsylvania

Carolyn Black Becker, Trinity University

Deborah C. Beidel, University of Central Florida

Bernard C. Beins, Ithaca College

Mark Beitel, Yale University School of Medicine

Genevieve Belleville, University of Quebec at Montreal, Canada

J. B. Bennett, Texas Christian University

Shannon Bennett, University of California, Los Angeles

Yossef S. Ben-Porath, Kent State University

Gary G. Benston, Ohio State University

Peter M. Bentler, University of California, Los Angeles

Tanya N. Beran, University of Calgary, CA

Stanley Berent, University of Michigan

Kathleen Stassen Berger, Bronx Community College, City University of New York

Arjan Berkeljon, Brigham Young University

Gregory S. Berns, Emory University School of Medicine

Jane Holmes Bernstein, Children's Hospital Boston and Harvard Medical School

David T. R. Berry, University of Kentucky

Michael D. Berzonsky, State University of New York at Cortland

Jeffrey L. Binder, Argosy University/Atlanta

Andri S. Bjornsson, University of Colorado at Boulder

Danielle Black, Northwestern University

Donald W. Black, University of Iowa Roy J. and Lucille A. Carr College of Medicine

Alberto Blanco-Campal, University College Dublin, Ireland

Ricardo D. Blasco, University of Barcelona, Spain

Sidney Bloch, University of Melbourne, Australia

Deborah Blum, University of Wisconsin-Madison

Mark S. Blum, University of Iowa

Anthony F. Bogaert, Brock University, St. Catharines, Canada

G. Anne Bogat, Michigan State University

Johan J. Bolhuis, Utrecht University, The Netherlands

Trevor G. Bond, James Cook University, Australia

Mark W. Bondi, Veterans Administration San Diego Healthcare System and University of California, San Diego

C. Alan Boneau, George Mason University

Hale Bolak Boratav, Istanbul Bilgi University, Turkey

John G. Borkowski, University of Notre Dame

Robert F. Bornstein, Adelphi University

James F. Boswell, Pennsylvania State University

Lyle E. Bourne, Jr., University of Colorado

James N. Bow, Hawthorn Center, Northville, MI

Christopher R. Bowie, Queen's University, Kingston, ON, Canada

Elza Boycheva, Binghamton University

Michelle J. Boyd, Tufts University

Virginia Brabender, Widener University

Paul Bracke, Mountain View, CA

Rom Brafman, Palo Alto, CA

David Brang, University of California, San Diego

Gary G. Brannigan, State University of New York-Plattsburg

Ann D. Branstetter, Missouri State University

Myron L. Braunstein, University of California, Irvine

Jeremy W. Bray, RTI International, Research Triangle Park, NC

Alisha Breetz, American University

Britton W. Brewer, Springfield College

K. Robert Bridges, Pennsylvania State University at New Kensington

Sara K. Bridges, University of Memphis

Arthur P. Brief, University of Utah

John Briere, University of Southern California

Nicholas E. Brink, Coburn, PA University of Colorado

Martin Brodwin, California State University, Los Angeles

Arline L. Bronzaft, City University of New York

Sarah Brookhart, Association for Psychological Science

Alisha L. Brosse, University of Colorado at Boulder

Ronald T. Brown, Temple University

Sheldon S. Brown, North Shore Community College, Danvers, MA

Caroline B. Brown, University of North Carolina at Chapel Hill

Patricia Brownell, Fordham University Graduate School of Social Service

Timothy J. Bruce, University of Illinois College of Medicine, Peoria

Martin Brüne, University of Bochum, Bochum, Germany

Silvina Brussino, National University of Córdoba, Córdoba, Argentina

Angela Bryan, University of New Mexico

Sue A. Buckley, University of Portsmouth, United Kingdom

Kristen A. Burgess, Emory University School of Medicine

M. Michele Burnette, Columbia, SC

Brenda Bursch, David Geffen School of Medicine at UCLA

William Buskist, Auburn University

James N. Butcher, University of Minnesota

Barbara M. Byrne, University of Ottawa, Canada

James P. Byrnes, Temple University

Desiree Caban, Columbia University

John T. Cacioppo, University of Chicago

David J. Cain, Alliant International University, San Diego

Lawrence G. Calhoun, University of North Carolina Charlotte

Amanda W. Calkins, Boston University

Jennifer L. Callahan, University of North Texas

Joseph Cambray, Massachusetts General Hospital, Harvard Medical School

Jenna Cambria, University of Maryland

Jonathan M. Campbell, University of Georgia

Keith Campbell, University of Georgia

Larry D. Campeau, Clarkson University School of Business

Caroline Campion, Tulane University School of Medicine

Tyrone Cannon, University of California, Los Angeles

Claudio Cantalupo, Clemson University

E. J. Capaldi, Purdue University

Rudolf N. Cardinal, University of Cambridge, United Kingdom

Bernardo Carducci, Indiana University Southeast

Leeanne Carey, National Stroke Research Institute, Melbourne, Australia

Jon Carlson, Governors State University

Laura A. Carlson, University of Notre Dame

Malique L. Carr, Pacific Graduate School of Psychology

Sonia Carrillo, University of the Andes, Bogotá, Columbia

Rachel Casas, University of Iowa College of Medicine

Margaret J. Cason, University of Texas at Austin

Wendy J. Caspar, University of Texas at Arlington

Louis G. Castonguay, Pennsylvania State University

Yoojin Chae, University of California, Davis

Kate Chapman, Pennsylvania State University

Stephanie G. Chapman, University of Houston

Susan T. Charles, University of California, Irvine

Cary Cherniss, Rutgers University

Allan Cheyne, University of Waterloo, Canada

Jean Lau Chin, Adelphi University

Jinsoo Chin, University of Michigan

Nehrika Chowli, University of Washington

Joan C. Chrisler, Connecticut College

Shawn E. Christ, University of Missouri-Columbia

Edward R. Christophersen, Children's Mercy Hospitals and Clinics, Kansas City, KS

Charles Clifton, Jr., University of Massachusetts Amherst

W. Glenn Clingempeel, Fayetteville State University

Sam V. Cochran, University of Iowa

Rosemary Cogan, Texas Tech University

Adam B. Cohen, Arizona State University

Barry H. Cohen, New York University

Karen R. Cohen, Canadian Psychological Association

Lisa J. Cohen, Beth Israel Medical Center and Albert Einstein College of Medicine

Taya R. Cohen, Northwestern University

P. T. Cohen-Kettenis, VU University Medical Center, Amsterdam, The Netherlands

Theodore Coladarci, University of Maine

Raymond J. Colello, Virginia Commonwealth University

Frank L. Collins, Jr., University of North Texas

Lillian, Comas-Diaz, Transcultural Mental Health Institute, Washington, DC

David J. Y. Combs, University of Kentucky

Jessica L. Combs, University of Kentucky

Jonathan Comer, Columbia University

Mary Connell, Fort Worth, TX

Daniel F. Connor, University of Connecticut School of Medicine

Michael J. Constatino, Pennsylvania State University

Frederick L. Coolidge, University of Colorado at Colorado Springs

Steven H. Cooper, Harvard Medical School

Stewart Cooper, Valparaiso University

Tori Sacha Cordiano, Case Western Reserve University

David Cordy, University of Iowa College of Medicine

Stanley Coren, University of British Columbia, Canada

Dave Corey, Portland Oregon Police Bureau

Erminio Costa, University of Illinois, Chicago

Stefany Coxe, University of Arizona

Robert J. Craig, Roosevelt University

Benjamin H. Craighead, Salisbury Pediatrics, Salisbury, NC

Margaret C. Craighead, Emory University School of Medicine

W. Edward Craighead, Emory University School of Medicine

Phebe Cramer, Williams College

Michelle G. Craske, University of California, Los Angeles

Candice E. Crerand, Children's Hospital of Philadelphia

Mario Cristancho, University of Pennsylvania School of Medicine

Pilar Cristancho, University of Pennsylvania School of Medicine

Thomas S. Critchfield, Illinois State University

Paul Crits-Christoph, University of Pennsylvania

Katherine B. Crocker, John College, City University of New York

Jessica M. Cronce, Yale University

Julio Eduardo Cruz, University of the Andes, Bogotá, Columbia

Pim Cuijpers, VU University of Amsterdam, The Netherlands

E. Mark Cummings, University of Notre Dame

David Yun Dai, University at Albany, State University of New York

Melita Daley, University of California, Los Angeles

J. P. Das, University of Alberta, Canada

William Davidson II, Michigan State University

Joanne Davila, SUNY Stony Brook

Samuel B. Day, Indiana University

Edward L. Deci, University of Rochester

Gregory DeClue, Sarasota, FL

Patricia J. Deldin, University of Michigan

Patricia R. DeLucia, Texas Tech University

Heath A. Demaree, Case Western Reserve University

Florence L. Denmark, Pace University

M. Ray Denny, Michigan State University

Brendan E. Depue, University of Colorado at Boulder

Leonard R. Derogatis, Sheppard Pratt Hospital and Johns Hopkins University School of Medicine

Paula S. Derry, Paula Derry Enterprises in Health Psychology, Baltimore, MD

Sreedhari D. Desai, University of Utah

Esther Devall, New Mexico State University

Donald A. Dewsbury, University of Florida

Lisa J. Diamond, University of Utah

Milton Diamond, University of Hawaii

Andreas Dick-Niederhauser, University Psychiatry Service, Berne, Switzerland

Adele Diederich, Jacobs University Bremen, Germany

Marc J. Diener, Argosy University, Washington, DC

Volker Dietz, University Hospital Balgrit, Zurich, Switzerland

Nicholas DiFonzo, Rochester Institute of Technology

Raymond A. DiGiuseppe, St. Johns University

Sona Dimidjian, University of Colorado, Boulder

Beth Doll, University of Nebraska Lincoln

Lorah H. Dom, Cincinnati Children's Hospital Medical Center

Aila K. Dommestrup, University of Georgia

John W. Donahue, University of Massachusetts

M. Brent Donnellan, Michigan State University

William I. Dorfman, Nova Southeastern University

William F. Doverspike, Atlanta, GA

Peter W. Dowrick, University of Hawai'i at Manoa

David J. A. Dozois, University of Western Ontario, Canada

Peter A. Drake, DePaul University

Michelle Drefs, University of Calgary, Canada

Clifford J. Drew, University of Utah

Eric Y. Drogin, Harvard Medical School

Dan Du, Tufts University

Rand A. Dublin, Hofstra University

David Dunning, Cornell University

Francis T. Durso, Georgia Institute of Technology

Donald G. Dutton, University of British Columbia, Canada

Joel A. Dvoskin, University of Arizona College of Medicine

Lutz H. Ecksenberger, German Institute for International Educational Research and Johann Wolfgang Goethe University, Frankfort, Germany

Barry A. Edelstein, West Virginia University

Louisa Egan, Yale University

Howard Eichenbaum, Boston University

Steven M. Elias, New Mexico State University

David Elkind, Tufts University

Brigitte Elle, Roskilde University, Roskilde, Denmark

Robert W. Elliott, Aerospace Health Institute, Los Angeles, CA

Roger E. Enfield , West Central Georgia Regional Hospital, Columbus, GA

Jan B. Engelmann, Emory University School of Medicine

Alyssa M. Epstein, University of California, Los Angeles

Jane Epstein, Weill College of Medicine at Cornell University

Franz Etping, University of Florida

Sean Esbjorn-Hargens, John F. Kennedy University, Pleasant Hill, CA

Chris Evans, Nottingham University, United Kingdom

David R. Evans, University of Western Ontario, Canada

Sara W. Feldstein Ewing, University of New Mexico

Carol Falender, University of California, Los Angeles

Jeanne M. Fama, Harvard University Medical School

Qijuan Fang, University of Hawaii at Manoa

Richard F. Farmer, Oregon Research Institute

Jaelyn, R. Farris, University of Notre Dame

Greg A. Febbraro, Counseling for Growth and Change, L.C., Windsor Heights, IA

Laurie Beth Feldman, University at Albany, SUNY

Eva Dreikers Ferguson, Southern Illinois University Edwardsville

Shantel Fernandez, Medical University of South Carolina

Joseph R. Ferarri, Drake University

F. Richard Ferraro, University of North Dakota

Seymour Feshbach, University of California, Los Angeles

Chelsea E. Fiduccia, University of North Texas

Dustin Fife, University of Oklahoma

Ione Fine, University of Washington

Stephen Finn, Center for Therapeutic Assessment, Austin, TX

Michael B. First, Columbia University

Constance T. Fischer, Duquesne University

Kurt W. Fischer, Harvard University

Kelly S. Flanagan, Wheaton College

Debra A. Fleischman, Rush University Medical Center, Chicago

Gordon L. Flett, York University, Canada

Peter Fonagy, University College London, United Kingdom

Rex Forehand, University of Vermont

Joseph P. Forgas, University of New South Wales, Australia

Blaine J. Fowers, University of Miami

Carol A. Fowler, University of Connecticut

Marcel G. Fox, Beck Institute for Cognitive Therapy and Research, Bala Cynwynd, PA

Lisa A. Fraleigh, University of Connecticut School of Medicine

Norah Frederickson, University College London, United Kingdom

Carolyn R. Freeman, McGill University, Canada

Fred Friedberg, Stony Brook University

Harris Friedman, University of Florida

Regan E. Friend, University of Kentucky

W. Otto Friesen, University of Virginia

Irene Hanson Frieze, University of Pittsburgh

Rober H. Friis, California State University Long Beach

Patrick C. Friman, Boys Town, NE

Randy O. Frost, Smith College

Daniel Fulford, University of Miami

K. W. M. Fulford, University of Warwick Medical School and St. Cross College, Oxford, United Kingdom

Wyndol Furman, University of Denver

Karina Royer Gagnier, York University, Toronto, Canada

Rodolfo Galindo, University of California, Merced

David A. Gallo, University of Chicago

Howard N. Garb, Lackland Air Force Base, Texas

Steven J. Garlow, Emory University School of Medicine

Gareth Gaskell, University of York, York, United Kingdom

Marisa Gauger, University of Nevada, Las Vegas

Kurt F. Geisinger, University of Nebraska-Lincoln

Pamela A. Geller, Drexel University

Charles J. Gelso, University of Maryland, College Park

Carol George, Mills College

Mark S. George, Medical University of South Carolina

Melissa R. George, University of Notre Dame

Kenneth J. Gergen, Swarthmore College

Andrew R. Getzfeld, New Jersey City University

Mary Beth Connolly Gibbons, University of Pennsylvania

Uwe Gielen, St. Francis College, Brooklyn, NY

Howard Giles, University of California, Santa Barbara

Charles F. Gillespie, Emory University School of Medicine

Marika Ginsburg-Block, University of Delaware

Richard G. T. Gipps, University of Warwick Medical School, United Kingdom

Todd A. Girard, Ryerson University, Toronto, Canada

James T. Gire, Virginia Military Institute

Thomas A. Glass, Honolulu, Hawaii

David Gleaves, University of Canterbury, New Zealand

Peter Glick, Lawrence University, Appleton, WI

Laraine Masters Glidden, St. Mary's College of Maryland

Lisa Hagen Glynn, University of New Mexico

Juan Carlos Godoy, National University of Córdoba, Córdoba, Argentina

Maurice Godwin, St. Augustine's College, Raleigh, NC

Hillel Goelman, University of British Columbia, Canada

Jerry Gold, Adelphi University

Peter B. Goldblum, Pacific Graduate School of Psychology

Charles Golden, Nova Southeastern University

Marvin R. Goldfried, Stony Brook University

Tina M. Goldstein, University of Pittsburgh

Robert L. Goldstone, Indiana University

Reginald Golledge, University of California Santa Barbara

Juliya Golubovich, Michigan State University

Emily E. Good, Pennsylvania State University

Jeffrey L. Goodi, Uniformed Service of the Health Sciences

Madeline S. Goodkind, University of California, Berkeley

Gail S. Goodman, University of California, Davis

Amanda Gordon, Sydney, Australia

Robert M. Gordon, Allentown, PA

Bernard S. Gorman, Nassau Community College, SUNY and Hofstra University

William Graebner, State University of New York, Fredonia

James W. Grau, Texas A & M University

Melanie Greenaway, Emory University College of Medicine

Lauren M. Greenberg, Drexel University

Martin S. Greenberg, University of Pittsburgh

William A. Greene, Eastern Washington University, Spokane

Shelly F. Greenfield, Harvard Medical School and McLean Hospital

Gregoire, Jacques Gregoire, Catholic University of Louvain, Belgium

Robert Gregory, SUNY Upstate Medical University

Robert J. Gregory, Wheaton College, IL

Bruce Greyson, University of Virginia Health System

Tiffany M. Griffin, University of Michigan

Vladas Griskevicius, University of Minnesota

Robert J. Grissom, San Francisco State University

Marc Grosjean, Leibniz Research Centre for Working Environment and Human Factors, Dortmund, Germany

James J. Gross, Stanford University

Gary Groth Marnat, Pacifica Graduate Institute, Carpinteria, CA

Corey L. Guenther, Ohio University

Bernard Guerin, University of South Australia, Australia

R. E. Gutierrez, Drake University

Russell Haber, University of South Carolina

Michael N. Haderlie, University of Nevada Las Vegas

William K. Hahn, University of Tennessee, Knoxville

William E. Haley, University of Wisconsin-Milwaukee

Judy E. Hall, National Register of Health Service Providers in Psychology

Mark B. Hamner, Medical University of South Carolina

Gregory R. Hancock, University of Maryland, College Park

Leonard Handler, University of Tennessee

Jo-Ida Hansen, University of Minnesota

Rochelle F. Hanson, Medical University of South Carolina

Lisa A. Harlow, University of Rhode Island

Robert J. Harnish, Pennsylvania State University at New Kensington

Robert G. Harper, Baylor College of Medicine

Anton H. Hart, William Alanson White Institute

Stephen D. Hart, Simon Fraser University, Canada

Chrisopher B. Harte, University of Texas at Austin

Glenn Hartelius, California Institute of Integral Studies

Abby B. Harvey, Temple University

Allison Harvey, University of California, Berkeley

Philip Harvey, Emory University School of Medicine

Nadia T. Hasan, University of Akron

David B. Hatfield, Developmental Behavioral Health, Colorado Springs, CO

Elaine Hatfield. University of Hawaii

Louise Hawkley, University of Chicago

Steven C. Hayes, University of Nevada

N. A. Haynie, Honolulu, HI

Alice F. Healy, University of Colorado

Bridget A. Hearon, Boston University

Pamela Heaton, University of London, United Kingdom

Monica Hedges, University of Southern California

Elaine M. Heiby, University of Hawaii at Manoa

Kathleen M. Heide, University of South Florida

Nicole Heilbrun, University of North Carolina at Chapel Hill

Deborah Heiser, State Society on Aging of New York

Janet E. Helms, Boston College

Lynne Henderson, Shyness Institute, Palo Alto, CA

Scott W. Henggeler, Family Service Research Center, Charleston, SC

James M. Hepburn, Waynesburg University

Gregory M. Herek, University of California, Davis

Hubert J. M. Hermans, Radboud University, Nijmegen, The Netherlands

Adriana Hermida, Emory University School of Medicine

Laura Hernandez-Guzman, National Autonomous University of Mexico

Edwin L. Herr, Pennsylvania State University

M. Sandy Hershcovis, University of Manitoba, Canada

Allen K. Hess, Auburn University at Montgomery

Herbert Heuer, University of Dortmund, Germany

Paul L. Hewitt, University of British Columbia, Canada

Richard E. Heyman, Stony Brook University

Ernest R. Hilgard, Stanford University

Thomas T. Hills, Indiana University

Stephen P.Hinshaw, University of California, Berkeley

Stephen C. Hirtle, University of Pittsburgh

Christine Hitchcock, University of British Columbia, Canada

Kristin Hitchcock, Northwestern University

Julian Hochberg, Columbia University

Ralph Hoffman, Yale University

Thomas P. Hogan, University of Scranton

Ronald R. Holden, Queens University, Canada

Lori L. Holt, Carnegie Mellon University

Ryan Holt, California State University at San Bernardino

Phan Y. Hong, University of Wisconsin Oshkosh

Audrey Honig, Los Angeles Count Sheriff's Department

Burt Hopkins, Seattle University

Adam O. Horvath, Simon Fraser University, Canada

Arthur C. Houts, University of Memphis

Robert H. Howland, University of Pittsburgh School of Medicine

Wayne D. Hoyer, University of Texas, Austin

Jeanette Hsu, Veterans Affairs Palo Alto Health System

Charles H. Huber, New Mexico State University

Samuel Hubley, University of Colorado, Boulder

Daniel A. Hughes, Lebanon, PA

Bradley E. Huitema, Western Michigan University

Olivia Y. Hung, Emory University School of Medicine

Scott J. Hunter, University of Chicago

Steven K. Huprich, Eastern Michigan University

Jena Huston, Argosy University, Phoenix, AZ

Kent Hutchison, University of New Mexico

Pamela Hyde, New Zealand Psychological Society, New Zealand

William G. Iacono, University of Minnesota

James R. Iberg, The Focusing Institute, Chicago, IL

Kaori Idemaru, University of Oregon

Stephen S. Ilardi, University of Kansas

Aubrey Immelman, St. John's University, MN

Mary Helen Immordino-Yang, University of Southern California

Rick Ingram, University of Kansas

Kathleen C. Insell, University of Arizona

Thomas R. Insel, National Institute of Mental Health

David Irwin, Drexel University College of Medicine

James S. Jackson, University of Michigan

Russell E. Jackson, California State University at San Marcos

Safia C. Jackson, University of Washington

Frederick M. Jacobsen, Transcultural Mental Health Institute, Washington, DC

Jacob Jacoby, New York University

Jack James, National University of Ireland, Galway, Ireland

Leonard A. Jason, DePaul University

Sharon Rae Jenkins, University of North Texas

Arthur R. Jensen, University of California, Berkeley

David W. Johnson, University of Minnesota

Deborah F. Johnson, University of Southern Maine

James H. Johnson, University of Florida

Kathryn Johnson, Arizona State University

Roger T. Johnson, University of Minnesota

Sheri L. Johnson, University of Miami

Susan K. Johnson, University of North Carolina-Charlotte

Keith S. Jones, Texas Tech University

Staci Jordan, University of Denver

Anthony S. Joyce, University of Alberta, Canada

Julia I. Juechter, Georgia State University

Barbara J. Juhasz, Wesleyan University

Robert M. Julien, Oregon Health Sciences University

James W. Kalat, North Carolina State University

Thomas Kalpakoglou, Institute of Behaviour Research and Therapy, Athens, Greece

Randy W. Kamphaus, Georgia State University

Jan H. Kamphuis, University of Amsterdam, The Netherlands

Anil Kanjee, Human Sciences Research Council, South Africa

Frank R. Kardes, University of Cincinnati

Georgia Karutzos, RTI International, Triangle Research Park, NC

Nadine J. Kaslow, Emory University

Marina Katz, San Diego, CA

Alan S. Kaufman, Yale University School of Medicine

James C. Kaufman, California State University at San Bernardino

Margaret M. Keane, Wellesley College

Terence M. Keane, Boston University School of Medicine

Christopher A. Kearney, University of Nevada, Las Vegas

Pamela K. Keel, University of Iowa

Michael Keesler, Drexel University and Villanova University School of Law

W. Gregory Keilin, University of Texas at Austin

Ken Kelley, University of Notre Dame

Francis D. Kelly, Greenfield, MA

Joan B. Kelly, Corte Madera, CA

Mary E. Kelley, Emory University

John A. Kenard, Temple University

Carrie Hill Kennedy, Kennedy Naval Aerospace Medical Institute, Pensacola, FL

Ray D. Kent, University of Wisconsin

Roy M. Kern, Vytautus Magnus University, Lithuania

Roy P. C. Kessels, Radboud Unversity Nijmegen, The Netherlands

Ronald C. Kessler, Harvard Medical School

Corey L. M. Keyes, Emory University

Kathryn Kidd, Colorado State University

John F. Kihlstrom, University of California, Berkeley

Bruce A. Kimball, USDA/APHIS/NWRC and Monell Chemical Senses Center, Philadelphia, PA

Gregory A. Kimble, Duke University

Douglas Kimmel, City College, City University of New York

Bruce M. King, Clemson University

Cheryl A. King, University of Michigan

D. Brett King, University of Colorado at Boulder

Roger E. Kirk, Baylor University

Ryo Kitado, Queens University, CA

Karen Strom Kitchener, University of Denver

Elena Klaw, San Jose State University

Daniel L. Klein, Stony Brook University

Dena A. Klein, Albert Einstein College of Medicine

Peggy J. Kleinplatz, University of Ottawa, Canada

E. David Klonsky, Stony Brook University

Tracy A. Knight, Western Illinois University

Kenneth A. Kobak, MedAvante Research Institute, Hamilton, NJ

Carolynn S. Kohn, University of the Pacific

George F. Koob, Scripps Research Institute, La Jolla, CA

Sander L. Koole, VU University, Amsterdam, The Netherlands

Mary P. Koss, University of Arizona

Beth A. Kotchick, Loyola College in Maryland

Chrystyna D. Kouros, University of Notre Dame

Margaret Bull Kovera, John Jay College, City University of New York

Robin M. Kowalski, Clemson University

Eileen M. Kranz, Brandeis University

Alan Kraut, Association for Psychological Science

Dennis L. Krebs, Simon Fraser University, Canada

Tina Kretschmer, University of Sussex, United Kingdom

Ann M. Kring, University of California, Berkeley

Stanley Krippner, Saybrook Graduate School, San Francisco, CA

Radhika Krishnamurthy, Florida Institute of Technology

Joachim I. Krueger, Brown University

Robert F. Krueger, Washington University at St. Louis

Romana C. Krycak, University of Missouri-Kansas City

Kathryn Kuehnle, University of South Florida

G. Tarcan Kumkale, Koc University, Istanbul, Turkey

Robert G. Kunzendorf, University of Massachusetts-Lowell

Jung Kwak, University of Wisconsin-Milwaukee

Virginia S. Y. Kwan, Princeton University

Margie E. Lachman, Brandeis University

Michael Lambert, Brigham Young University

Dominque Lamy, Tel Aviv University, Israel

Frank J. Landy, Baruch College, City University of New York

Brittany Lannert, Michigan State University

Molly Larsen, Emory University

Randy J. Larsen, Washington University

Daniel K. Lapsley, University of Notre Dame

Leah Lavelle, University of Chicago

Michael Lavin, Washington, DC

Patrick F. Lavin, Chattanooga, TN

Foluso M. Williams Lawal-Solarin, Emory University

Jay Lebow, Northwestern University

Susan J. Lederman, Queen's University, Kingston, Canada

Courtland C. Lee, University of Maryland at College Park

Erica D. Marshall Lee, Emory University

Sandra R. Leiblum, Robert Wood Johnson Medical School, University of Medicine and Dentistry New Jersey

Martin Leichtman, Leawood, KS

Jacqueline P. Leighton, University of Alberta, Canada

Michael P. Leiter, Acadia University, Nova Scotia, Canada

Larry M. Leitner, Miami University

Alison P. Lenton, University of Edinburgh, Scotland, United Kingodm

Frederick T. L. Leong, Michigan State University

Richard M. Lerner, Tufts University

David Lester, Richard Stockton College, Pamona, NJ

Richard Lettieri, New Center for Psychoanalysis, Los Angeles, CA

L. Stan Leung, University of Western Ontario, Canada

Ronald F. Levant, University of Akron

Allan Levey, Emory University College of Medicine

Karen Z. H. Li, Concordia University, Montreal

Norman P. Li, University of Texas at Austin

Shu-Chen Li, Max Planck Institute for Human Development, Berlin, Germany

Ting-Kai Li, National Institute on Alcohol Abuse and Alcoholism, NIH, Bethesda MD

Peter A. Lichtenberg, Wayne University

Scott O. Lillienfeld, Emory University

Geoff Lindsay, University of Warwick, Coventry, United Kingdom

Roderick C. Lindsay, Queens University, Ontario Canada

Marsha M. Linehan, University of Washington

Carol F. Lippa, Drexel University College of Medicine

Mark D. Litt, University of Connecticut

Roderick J. Little, University of Michigan

John E. Lochman, University of Alabama

John C. Loehlin, University of Texas at Austin

Jeffrey M. Lohr, University of Arkansas

Richard G. Lomax, Ohio State University

Jeffrey D. Long, University of Minnesota

Julie R. Lonoff, Miami University

David Loomis, California State University at San Bernardino

Christopher M. Lootens, University of North Carolina at Greensboro

Jeffrey P. Lorberbaum, Medical University of South Carolina

William R. Lovallo, VA Medical Center and University of Oklahoma Health Sciences Center

Tamara Penix Loverich, Eastern Michigan University

Kristen Lowell, University of North Dakota

Rodney L. Lowman, Lake Superior State University

Sara E. Lowmaster, Texas A&M University

James K. Luiselli, May Institute, Randolph MA

Katarina Lukatela, Brown University Medical School

Ralph W. Lundin, Wheaton, IL

Robert W. Lundin, The University of the South

Desiree Q. Luong, San Jose State University

Steven Jay Lynn, Binghamton University

Shelley M. MacDermind, Purdue University

William M. Mace, Trinity College, Hartford CT

Armando Machado, University of Minho, Portugal

Maya Machunsky, University of Marburg, Germany

Colin M. MacLeod, University of Waterloo, Canada

Joshua W. Madsen, VA San Diego Healthcare System

Jeffrey J. Magnavita, University of Hartford

Brittain L. Mahaffey, University of North Carolina at Chapel Hill

Robert Malgady, Touro College, New York, NY

Jill Malik, Stony Brook University

Thomas E. Malloy, Rhode Island College

Tina Malti, University of Zurich, Switzerland

Valerie Malzer, University of Chicago

Rachel Manber, Stanford University School of Medicine

Jon K. Maner, Florida State University

Jamal K. Mansour, Queens University, Ontario Canada

Amy Jo Marcano-Reik, University of Iowa

Stephanie C. Marcello, University Medicine and Dentistry of New Jersey

Stephen Maren, University of Michigan

Richard S. Marken, University of California at Los Angeles

G. Alan Marlatt, University of Washington

Ronald R. Martin, University of Regina, Canada

Steve Martino, Yale University School of Medicine

Ana P. G. Martins, Purdue University

Melvin H. Marx, N. Hutchinson Island, FL

Joseph D. Matarazzo, Oregon Health Science University

Kenneth B. Matheny, Georgia State University

Nancy Mather, University of Arizona

David Matteo, Drexel University

Brian P. Max, Boston University School of Medicine

Molly Maxfield, University of Colorado at Colorado Springs

Ryan K. May, Marietta College

Richard E. Mayer, University of California, Santa Barbara

Dan Mayton, Lewis-Clark State College

Randi E. McCabe, McMaster University, Hamilton, Ontario, Canada

Robert McCaffrey, State University of New York at Albany

Barry McCarthy, American University

Elizabeth McCauley, University of Washington and Seattle Children's Hospital

Brook McClintic, University of Colorado at Boulder

Allyn McConkey-Russell, Duke University Medical Center

Bridget L. McConnell, State University of New York at Binghamton

Christine McCormick, University of Massachusetts-Amherst

Barbara S. McCrady, University of New Mexico

Robert R. McCrae, National Institute on Aging

James P. McCullough, Jr., Virginia Commonwealth University

Janet L. McDonald, Louisiana State University

Kate L. McDonald, University of Arizona

William M. McDonald, Emory University School of Medicine

Lata M. McGinn, Albert Einstein College of Medicine, Yeshiva University

Eleanor McGlinchey, University of California, Berkeley

F. Dudley McGlynn, Auburn University

Robert E. McGrath, Fairleigh Dickinson University

Ian McGregor, York University, Toronto, Canada

Laura Gale McKee, University of Vermont

John Paul McKinney, Michigan State University

Kathleen McKinney, University of Wyoming

Patrick E. McNight, George Mason University

Kaitlyn McLachlan, Simon Fraser University, Canada

Richard J. McNally, Harvard University

Neil McNaughton, University of Otago, Dunedin, New Zealand

Kateri McRae, Stanford University

Paul W. McReynolds, University of Nevada, Reno

Stephanie K. Meador, Developmental Behavioral Health, Colorado Springs, CO

Heide Meeke, Pacific University

J. Reid Meloy, University of California, San Diego

Ronald Melzack, McGill University, Canada

Dana Menard, University of Ottawa, Canada

Tamar Mendelson, Johns Hopkins Bloomberg School of Public Health

Jorge Mendoza, University of Oklahoma

Douglas S. Mennin, Yale University

Andrew J. Menzel, Florida State University

Jessie Menzel, University of South Florida

Peter F. Merenda, University of Rhode Island

Stanley B. Messer, Rutgers University

Cindy M. Meston, University of Texas at Austin

Lotte Meteyard, University College London, United Kingdom

Alicia E. Meuret, Southern Methodist University

Andrew W. Meyers, University of Memphis

Kristina D. Micheva, Stanford University School of Medicine

Jesse B. Milby, University of Alabama at Birmingham

Alec L. Miller, Albert Einstein College of Medicine

Andrew H. Miller, Emory University School of Medicine

Carlin J. Miller, University of Windsor, Canada

Catherine Miller, Pacific University

Gloria Miller, University of Denver

Joshua D. Miller, University of Georgia

Mark W. Miller, Boston University School of Medicine

Ralph I. Miller, State University of New York at Binghamton

Cindy Miller-Perrin, Pepperdine University

Glenn W. Milligan, The Ohio State University

Theodore Millon, Institute for Advanced Studies in Personology and Psychopathology, Port Jervis, NY

Jon Mills, International Federation for Psychoanalytic Education

Michael Mingroni, Newark, DE

Hamid Mirsalimi, Argosy University, Atlanta

Victor Molinari, University of South Florida

Ivan Molton, University of Washington

Alexandra Monesson, University of Massachusetts, Amherst

Myriam Mongrain, York University, Toronto, Canada

Timothy E. Moore, York University, Toronto, Canada

Nilly Mor, Hebrew University of Jerusalem, Israel

Marlene M. Moretti, Simon Fraser University, Canada

Leslie C. Morey, Texas A&M University

George A. Morgan, Colorado State University

Robert D. Morgan, Texas Tech University

Charles M. Morin, Laval University, Canada

John W. Morin, Center for Offender Rehabilitation and Education, Fort Lauderdale, FL

Daniel G. Morrow, University of Illinois at Urbana-Champaign

Ezequiel Morsella, San Francisco State University and University of California, San Francisco

Susan M. Mosher, Boston University School of Medicine and Department of Veterans Affairs Healthcare System, Boston Campus

Christohper J. Mruk, Bowling Green State University

Paul M. Muchinsky, University of North Carolina at Greensboro

Kim T. Mueser, Dartmouth Medical School

Michael J. Mullard, Pacifica Graduate Institute, Carpinteria, CA

Ricardo F. Munoz, University of California, San Francisco

Anjana Muralidharan, Emory University

Nancy L. Murdock, University of Missouri-Kansas City

Kevin R. Murphy, Pennsylvania State University

Frank B. Murray, University of Delaware

Lisa M. Nackers, University of Florida

Raymond Nairn, New Zealand Psychological Society, New Zealand

James S. Nairne, Purdue University

Julius Najab, George Mason University

Urs M. Nater, University of Zurich, Switzerland

Francis A. Nealon, Rice Diet Program, Durham, NC

Becca Neel, Arizona State University

Sonya Negriff, Cincinnati Children's Hospital Medical Center

Robert A. Neimeyer, University of Memphis

Rosemery O. Nelson-Gray, University of North Carolina at Greensboro

Cory F. Newman, University of Pennsylvania School of Medicine

Thomas C. Neylan, University of California, San Francisco

Arthur M. Nezu, Drexel University

Christine Maguth Nezu, Drexel University

Michael E. R. Nicholls, University of Melbourne, Australia

Pekka Niemi, University of Turku, Finland

Gil G. Noam, Harvard University and McLean Hospital

Pedro J. Nobre, University of Tras-os-Montes e Alto, Douro, Portugal

Samuel S. Norberg, Pennsylvania State University

Jacob N. Norris, Texas Christian University

Brian A. Nosek, University of Virginia

Raymond W. Novaco, University of California, Irvine

Jack Novick, Michigan Psychoanalytic Institute

Kerry Kelly Novick, Michigan Psychoanalytic Institute

David Nussbaum, University of Toronto Scarborough, Canada

Amy K. Nuthall, University of Colorado at Boulder

Michael S. Nystul, New Mexico State University

William H. O'Brien, Bowling Green State University

Lynn E. O'Connor, Wright Institute and University of California, Berkeley

William T. O'Donohue, University of Nevada, Reno

Daniel O'Leary, Stony Brook University

Thomas Oakland, University of Florida

Carmen Oemig, Bowling Green State University

Christin, M. Ogle, University of California, Davis

Sumie Okazaki, University of Illinois at Urbana-Champaign

Piotr Oles, John Paul II Catholic University of Lublin, Lublin, Poland

Kristina R. Olson, Yale University

Eyitayo Onifade, Michigan State University

Jeanne Ellis Ormrod, University of Northern Colorado and University of New Hampshire

Pamela Orpinas, University of Georgia

Ingrid Osbuth, Simon Fraser University, Canada

Marlene, Boston University School of Medicine and Department of Veterans Affairs Healthcare System, Boston Campus

Frank Oswald, University of Heidelberg, Germany

Michael W. Otto, Boston University

Randy K. Otto, University of South Florida

Willis F. Overton, Temple University

Timothy J. Ozechowski, Oregon Research Institute

Steven R. Pacynski, SRCD Research Associate

David C. Palmer, Smith Colleege

Edward L. Palmer, Davidson College

Josefa N. S. Pandeirada, University of Santiago, Portugal

Joyce S. Pang, Nonyang Technological University, Singapore

Mauricio R. Papine, Texas Christian University

Kenneth I. Pargament, Bowling Green State University

Bernadette Park, University of Colorado

Martin Parker, Northwestern University

Fayth Parks, Georgia Southern University

Christopher J. Patrick, University of Minnesota

Diane T. V. Pawluk, Virginia Commonwealth University

Joshua W. Payen, University of North Texas

Joseph J. Pear, University of Manitoba, Canada

Mary Jo Peebles, Bethesda, MD

Daniel Perlman, University of North Carolina Greensboro

Michael G. Perri, University of Florida

Melissa Peskin, University of Pennsylvania

Christopher Peterson, University of Michigan

Jean Sunde Peterson, Purdue University

John Petrila, University of South Florida

Charles S. Peyser, University of the South.

Bruce E. Pfeiffer, University of New Hampshire

Daniel Philip, University of North Florida

Sheridan Phillips, University of Maryland School of Medicine

John Piacentini, University of California, Los Angeles

Jennifer R. Piazza, University of California, Irvine

Wade E. Pickren, Ryerson University, Toronto, Canada

Ralph L. Piedmont, Loyola College in Maryland

Alison Pike, University of Sussex, United Kingdom

Aaron L. Pincus, Pennsylvania State University

Nancy A. Piotrowski, Capella University

William Piper, University of British Columbia, Canada

Thomas G. Plante, Santa Clara University and Stanford University School of Medicine

Ingrid Plath, German Institute for International Educational Research, Frankfort, Germany

John Porcerelli, Wayne State University School of Medicine

Amir Poreh, Cleveland State University

Nicole Porter, DePaul University

Bruno Poucet, Universite de Provence, Marseille, France

Daniel J. Povinelli, University of Louisiana

Michael J. Power, University of Edinburgh, Scotland, United Kingdom

Judith Preissle, University of Georgia

Jose M. Preito, University of Madrid, Spain

George P. Prigatano, St. Joseph's Hospital and Medical Center, Phoenix, AZ

Mitchell J. Prinstein, University of North Carolina at Chapel Hill

Jerilynn C. Prior, University of British Columbia, Canada

Robert W. Proctor, Purdue University

Dennis Proffitt, University of Virginia

Jean Proulx, University of Montreal

Aina Puce, West Virginia University School of Medicine

Tom Pyszczynski, University of Colorado at Colorado Springs

Sara Honn Qualls, University of Colorado at Colorado Springs

Naomi L. Quenk, Analytical Psychology, Ltd., Albuquerque, NM

James Campbell Quick, University of Texas at Arlington

Mark Quigg, University of Virginia

Karen S. Quigley, Department of Veterans Affairs New Jersey Healthcare System, East Orange, NJ and New Jersey Medical School, University of Medicine and Dentistry of New Jersey

Christine A. Rabinek, University of Michigan

Nosheen K. Rahman, Punjab University, Lahore, Pakistan

Joseph S. Raiker, University of Central Florida

Adrian Raine, University of Pennsylvania

Charles Raison, Emory University School of Medicine

Leo Rangell, University of California, Los Angeles

Mark D. Rapport, University of Central Florida

Richard L. Rapson, University of Hawaii

June Rathbone, University College London, England

William J. Ray, Pennsylvania State University

Tenko Raykov, Michigan State University

Keith Rayner, University of California, San Diego

Robert J. Reese, University of Kentucky

William C. Reeves, Centers for Disease Control and Prevention, Atlanta, GA

Lynn P. Rehm, University of Houston

Holly A. Reich, Wheaton College

Tara C. Reich, University of Manitoba, Canada

Charles S. Reichardt, University of Denver

Scott, A. Reid, University of California, Santa Barbara

Jost Reinecke, University of Bielefeld, Germany

Harry T. Reis, University of Rochester

Sally M. Reis, University of Connecticut

Joseph Renzulli, University of Connecticut

Gilbert Reyes, Fielding Graduate University, Santa Barbara, CA

Cecil R. Reynolds, Texas A&M University

William M. Reynolds, Humboldt State University, Arcata, CA

Soo Hyun Rhee, University of Colorado-Boulder

George R. Rhodes, Ola Hou Clinic, Aiea, HI

David C. S. Richard, Rollins College

Jodie Richardson, McGill University

Margaret W. Riddle, University of Denver

Cedar Riener, University of Virginia

Christopher L. Ringwalt, Pacific Institute for Research and Evaluation, Chapel Hill, NC

Evan F. Risko, University of British Columbia, Canada

Lorie A. Ritschel, Emory University School of Medicine

Rostyslaw W. Robak, Pace University

Gary J. Robertson, Tampa, FL

Richard W., University of California, Davis

George H. Robinson, University of North Alabama

Jennifer L. Robinson, University of Texas Health Sciences Center at San Antonio

Kathryn A. Roecklin, University of Vermont

Karin Roelofs, Leiden University, The Netherlands

Lizabeth Roemer, University of Massachusetts, Boston

Ronald Roesch, Simon Fraser University, Canada

Roger Roffman, University of Washington

Richard Rogers, University of North Texas

Kelly J. Rohan, University of Vermont

Michael J. Rohrbaugh, University of Arizona

George Ronan, Central Michigan University

Elsa Ronningstam, Harvard University Medical School

Steven P. Roose, New York State Psychiatric Institute, Columbia University

Robert Rosenthal, University of California, Riverside, and Harvard University

Alan M. Rosenwasser, University of Maine

David H. Rosmarin, Bowling Green State University

William H. Ross, University of Wisconsin at La Crosse

Joseph S. Rossi, University of Rhode Island

Barbara Olasov Rothbaum, Emory University School of Medicine

Donald K. Routh, Florida Gulf Coast University

Linda Rubin, Texas Women's University

Jerry W. Rudy, University of Colorado, Boulder

Michael G. Rumsey, U.S. Army Research Institute for the Behavioral and Social Sciences, Arlington, VA

Sandra W. Russ, Case Western Reserve University

Alexandra Rutherford, York University, Canada

Bret R. Rutherford, New York State Psychiatric Institute, Columbia University

Richard M. Ryan, University of Rochester

Jeremy Safran, New School for Social Research

Donald H. Saklofske, University of Calgary, Canada

Morgan T. Sammons, National Register of Health Service Providers in Psychology

Trond Sand, University of Science and Technology and Trondheim University Hospital, Norway

William C. Sanderson, Hofstra University

Jerome Sanes, Alpert Medical School of Brown University

Craig Santerre, VA Puget Sound Health Care System, Seattle Division

Craig Santree, VA Puget Sound Health Care System, Seattle Division

Edward P. Sarafino, College of New Jersey

David B. Sarwer, University of Pennsylvania School of Medicine

William I. Sauser, Jr., Auburn University

Lisa M. Savage, State University of New York at Binghamton

Victoria Savalei, University of California, Los Angeles

Mark L. Savickas, Northeastern Ohio Universities College of Medicine

Douglas J. Scaturo, State University of New York Upstate Medical University and Syracuse VA Medical Center

E. Warner Schaie, Pennsylvania State University

Marcia J., Scherer, University of Rochester Medical Center

Dawn M. Schiehser, Veterans Administration San Diego Healthcare System and University of California, San Diego

Elizabeth A. Schilling, University of Connecticut Health Center

Lindsay J. Schipper, University of Kentucky

Kelly Schloredt, University of Washington and Seattle Children's Hospital

Karen B. Schmaling, University of North Carolina at Charlotte

Frank L. Schmidt, University of Iowa

Klaus Schmidtke, University Hospital Freiburg, Germany

Neal Schmitt, Michigan State University

Kirk J. Schneider, Center for Existential Therapy, San Francisco, CA

Michael E. Schoeny, Institute for Juvenile Research and University of Illinois at Chicago

Joseph E. Schumacher, University of Alabama School of Medicine

Julie A. Schumacher, University of Mississippi Medical Center

Dale H. Schunk, University of North Carolina at Greensboro

Alexander J. Schut, Pennsylvania State University

Alan Schwartz, University of Illinois at Chicago

Eliezer Schwartz, Argosy University Chicago

Jonathan P. Schwartz, University of Houston

Marlene B. Schwartz, Yale University

Stephanie Schwartz, Association for Behavioral and Cognitive Therapies, New York, NY

Julie B. Schweitzer, University of California Davis School of Medicine

Lisa S. Scott, University of Massachusetts, Amherst

Gretchen B. Sechrist, University at Buffalo, State University of New York

Daniel L. Segal, University of Colorado at Colorado Springs

Lauren S. Seifert, Malone College

Stephen Seligman, University of California, San Francisco

Edward P. Serafino, College of New Jersey

Ilene A. Serlin, San Francisco, CA

Michael C. Seto, Center for Addiction and Mental Health and University of Toronto, Canada

William R. Shadish, University of California, Merced

Anne Shaffer, University of Minnesota

David L. Shapiro, Nova Southeastern University

Deane H. Shapiro, University of California School of Medicine, Irvine

Francine Shapiro, Mental Research Institute, Palo Alto, CA

Johanna Shapiro, University of California School of Medicine, Irvine

Josh D. Shapiro, University of California, San Diego

Kenneth J. Shapiro, Animals and Society Institute, Washington Grove, MD

Shauna L. Shapiro, Santa Clara University

Brian A. Sharpless, University of Pennsylvania

Richard J. Shavelson, Stanford University

Erin S. Sheets, Brown University Medical School and Butler Hospital

Anees A. Sheikh. Marquette University

Kenneth J. Sher, University of Missouri

Lonnie R. Sherrod, Fordham University

Alissa Sherry, University of Texas at Austin

Stephanie A. Shields, Pennsylvania State University

Robert Shilkret, Mount Holyoke College

Merton M. Shill, University of Michigan

Varda Shoham, University of Arizona

Lauren B. Shumaker, University of Denver

Kristin Shutts, Harvard University

Jerome Siegel, University of California, Los Angeles

Judith P. Siegel, Silver School of Social Work at New York University

David Silbersweig, Weill College of Medicine at Cornell University

Francisco J. Silva, University of Redlands

Doris K. Silverman, New York, NY

Wendy K. Silverman, Florida International University

Louise Silvern, University of Colorado at Boulder

Marshall L. Silverstein, Long Island University

Steven M. Silverstein, University Medicine and Dentistry of New Jersey

Amy M. Smith Slep, Stony Brook University

Frank L. Small, University of Washington

Colin Tucker Smith, University of Virginia

Gregory T. Smith, University of Kentucky

J. Allegra Smith, University of Colorado

Jeffrey K. Smith, University of Otago, New Zealand

Lisa F. Smith, University of Otago, New Zealand

Nathan Grant Smith, McGill University, Canada

Richard H. Smith, University of Kentucky

Ronald E. Smith, University of Washington

Myriam J. Sollman, University of Kentucky

Roger M. Solomon, Buffalo Center for Trauma and Loss, Buffalo, NY

Subhash R. Sonnad, Western Michigan University

Peter W. Sorenson, University of Minnesota

Elizabeth Soucar, Penndel Mental Health Center, Penndel, CA

Susan C. South, Purdue University

Marion Spengler, Saarland University, Saarbrucken, Germany

Dante Spetter, Tufts University

Eric P. Spiegel, James A. Haley VAMC, Tampa, FL

Charles D. Spielberger, University of South Florida

Robert Spies, Buros Institute of Mental Measurements

Frank M. Spinath, Saarland University, Saarbrucken, Germany

Philip Spinhoven, Leiden University, The Netherlands

Bonnie Spring, Northwestern University

Jayne E. Stake, University of Missouri—St. Louis

Jayne M. Standley, Florida State University

Ursula J. Staudinger, Jacobs University, Bremen, Germany

Jeffrey T. Steedle, Council for Aid to Education, New York, NY

Timothy A. Steenburgh, Indiana Wesleyan University

Rebecca Y. Steer, Emory University

Dana Steidtmann, University of Kansas

Axel Steiger, Max Planck Institute of Psychiatry, Munich, Germany

Howard Steiger, McGill University

Emily Stein, Weill College of Medicine at Cornell University

Jennifer Steinberg, Cognitive and Behavioral Consultants of Westchester, White Plains, NY

Melissa K. Stern, University of Florida

Robert M. Stern, Pennsylvania State University

Michael J. Stevens, Illinois State University

Paul Stey, University of Notre Dame

Timothy R. Stickle, University of Vermont

John M. Stokes, Pace University

Stephen Strack, U.S. Department of Veterans Affairs, Los Angeles, CA

David L. Streiner, University of Toronto, Canada

George Stricker, Argosy University Washington

Natalie Stroupe, University of Kansas

Margaret L. Stubbs, Chatham University, Pittsburgh, PA

Sally J. Styles, Yale University

Peter Suedfeld, University of British Columbia, Canada

Alan Sugarman, University of California, San Diego

Jeff Sugarman, Simon Fraser University, Canada

Jennifer A. Sullivan, Duke University Medical Center

Norman D. Sundberg, University of Oregon

Elizabeth Susman, Pennsylvania State University

Lisa A. Suzuki, New York University

Harvey A. Swadlow, Brown University Medical School

Robert A. Sweet, University of Pittsburgh and VA Pittsburgh Healthcare System

Derek D. Szafranski, University of the Pacific

Brian J. Taber, Oakland University

Raymond Chip Tafrate, Central Connecticut State University

Harold Takooshian, Fordham University

Rebecca L. Tamas, University of Louisville School of Medicine

Junko Tanaka-Matsumi, Kansei Gakuin University, Japan

Sombat Tapanya, Chiang Mai University, Thailand

Steven Taylor, University of British Columbia

Richard G. Tedeschi, University of North Carolina Charlotte

Hedwig Teglasi, University of Maryland

Howard Tennen, University of Connecticut

Lois E. Tetrick, George Mason University

Timothy J. Teyler, Washington State University

Michael E. Thase, University of Pennsylvania School of Medicine

Ryan Thibodeau, St. John Fisher College, Rochester, NY

Jay C. Thomas, Pacific University

J. Kevin Thompson, University of South Florida

Scott M. Thompson, University of Maryland

Travis Thompson, University of Minnesota School of Medicine

B. Michael Thorne, Mississippi State University

Shira Tibon, Bar-Ilan University and Academic College of Tel-Aviv, Yaffo, Israel

Jane G. Tillman, The Austen Riggs Center, Stockbridge, MA

Michael Tobia, Temple University

James Toch, State University of New York at Albany

Patrick H. Tolan, Institute for Juvenile Research and University of Illinois at Chicago

David F. Tolin, Institute of Living, Hartford, CT and Yale University School of Medicine

Jessica L. Tracy, University of British Columbia, Canada

Daniel Tranel, University of Iowa College of Medicine

Michael Treanor, University of Massachusetts, Boston

Warren W. Tryon, Fordham University

Ivy F. Tso, University of Michigan

William T. Tsushima, Straub Clinic and Hospital, Honolulu, HI

Larissa Tsvetkova, St. Petersburg State University, St. Petersburg, Russia

Jane Tucker, New York University

Denis C. Turk, University of Washington

Dio Turner II, University of Nevada, Las Vegas

Rachael Unger, Towson University

Annmarie Urso, State University of New York College at Geneseo

Uma Vaidyanathan, University of Minnesota

Mary M. Valmas, Boston University School of Medicine and Department of Veterans Affairs Healthcare System, Boston Campus

Henk T. van der Molen, Erasmus University Rotterdam, The Netherlands

Judy L. Van Raalte, Springfield College

Rodney D. Vanderploeg, James A. Haley VAMC, Tampa, FL and University of South Florida

Susan M. VanScoyoc, University of Phoenix

Myrna V. Vashcenko, Tufts University

Ruut Veenhoven, Erasmus University Rotterdam, The Netherlands

Beth A. Venzke, Concordia University-Chicago

Mieke Verfaellie, Boston University School of Medicine and VA Boston Healthcare System

Philip E. Vernon, University of Calgary, Canada

Ian Verstegen, Philadelphia, PA

Ryan P. Vetreno, State University of New York at Binghamton

Donald J. Viglione, Alliant International University, San Diego, CA

Penny S. Visser, University of Chicago

Jennifer E. Vitale, Hampden-Sydney College, Hampden-Sydney, VA

Ladislav Volicer, University of South Florida

Nora D. Volkow, National Institute on Drug Abuse

Jennifer Vonk, University of Louisiana

Kim-Phuong, L. Vu, California State University, Long Beach

Paul L. Wachtel, City College and CUNY Graduate Center

Nicholas J. Wade, University of Dundee, Scotland, United Kingdom

Harriet Wadeson, University of Illinois at Chicago

Hans-Werner Wahl, University of Heidelberg, Germany

Howard Wainer, National Board of Medical Examiners

Deward E. Walker, Jr., University of Colorado at Boulder

Elaine F. Walker, Emory University

Stephanie Wallio, VA Connecticut Health Care System and University of Kansas

Roger Walsh, University of California College of Medicine, Irvine

Michael R. Walther, University of Wisconsin-Milwaukee

Alvin Wang, University of Central Florida

Philip S. Wang, National Institute of Mental Health Care Policy

William H. Watson, University of Rochester School of Medicine and Dentistry

Adam Waytz, University of Chicago

Stanley Wearden, West Virginia University

Danny Wedding, University of Missouri-Columbia School of Medicine

Bernard Weiner, University of California, Los Angeles

Karen Colby Weiner, Southfield, Michigan

Irving B. Weiner, University of South Florida

Daniel Weisholtz, Weill College of Medicine at Cornell University

Daniel J. West, Pennsylvania State University

Myrna M. Weissman, College of Physicians and Surgeons and Mailman School of Public Health, Columbia University

Julie C. Weitlauf, Veterans Affairs Palo Alto Health Care System and Stanford University School of Medicine

Barbara J. Wendling, University of Arizona

Kathryn R. Wentzel, University of Maryland, College Park

Michael Wertheimer, University of Colorado at Boulder

Donald Wertlieb, Tufts University

Hans Westmeyer, Free University of Berlin, Germany

Michael G. Wheaton, University of North Carolina at Chapel Hill

Mark E. Wheeler, University of Pittsburgh

Mark A. Whisman, University of Colorado at Boulder

Stephen G. White, University of California, San Francisco

Thomas W. White, Training and Counseling Services, Shawnee Mission, KS

Thomas A. Widiger, University of Kentucky

Donald E. Wiger, Elmo, MN

Allan Wigfield, University of Maryland

Ken Wilber, Integral Institute, Boulder, CO

Sabine Wilhelm, Harvard University Medical School

Douglas A. Williams, University of Winnipeg

Paul Williams, Queens University Belfast, Northern Ireland

Rebecca B. Williamson, The Hague, The Netherlands

Hillary D. Wilson, University of Washington

Janelle Wilson, University of Minnesota Duluth

Michael Windle, Emory University

Idee Winfield, College of Charleston

David L. Wolitzky, New York University

Nina Wong, University of Central Florida

Margaret T. T. Wong-Riley, Medical College of Wisconsin

Diana S. Woodruff-Pak, Temple University

Douglas W. Woods, University of Wisconsin-Milwaukee

Robert F. Woolfolk, Rutgers University

J. Brooke Wright, Wheaton College

Jesse H. Wright, University of Louisville School of Medicine

Li-Tzy-Wu, Duke University Medical Center

Robert E. Wubbolding, Center for Reality Therapy, Cincinnati, OH

Yufang Yang, Chinese Academy of Sciences, Beijing, China

William A. Yost, Arizona State University

Larry J. Young, Emory University School of Medicine

Adam Zagelbaum, Sonoma State University

Patricia A. Zapf, John Jay College of Criminal Justice, City University of New York

Tamika C. H. Zapolski, University of Kentucky

Charles H. Zeanah, Tulane University School of Medicine

Moshe Zeidner, University of Haifa, Israel

Elias A. Zerhouni, National Institutes of Health

Eric A. Zillmer, Drexel University

Philip Zimbardo, Stanford University

Grégoire Zimmerman, University of University of Lausanne, Switzerland

Marvin Zuckerman, University of Delaware

Ofer Zur, Zur Institute, Sonoma, CA

The Corsini
Encyclopedia *of*
Psychology

D

DANCE/MOVEMENT THERAPY

Celebrating its 40th year as an organized healthcare profession, dance/movement therapy is one of the original mind/body therapies. Integrating ancient healing practices of movement, meditation, and imagery, it is uniquely suited to take its place as a cost-effective, interpersonal practice in a newly reinvented healthcare system. This article explores the history of dance/movement therapy and its current modes of practice as a psychodynamic, growth-oriented, and international healthcare profession.

History

Dance/movement therapy as an organized profession was born in psychiatric hospitals like St. Elizabeth's in Washington in the 1940s and Camarillo State Hospital in California in the 1920s. Students of the early pioneers of the field in those hospitals and other settings started the American Dance Therapy Association (ADTA) in 1966. Their teacher and model was Marian Chace, a Denishawn dancer who worked with hospitalized patients with psychotic disorders at St. Elizabeth's Hospital and Chestnut Lodge (Sandel, Chaiklin & Lohn, 1993).

There are more than 700 dance therapists in the United States. The mission statement of the ADTA defines dance/movement therapy as "the psychotherapeutic use of movement as a process which furthers the emotional, cognitive, social and physical integration of the individual"; the stated purposes of the ADTA are "to establish and maintain high standards of professional education and competence in the field of dance/movement therapy" and "to stimulate communication among dance/movement therapists and members of allied professions through publication of a Newsletter, the *American Journal of Dance Therapy* (AJDT) and other resources."

Dance therapists provide treatment for people with psychological and physical conditions, including anxiety, depression, psychogenic somatic disorders, heart disease, cancer, and neurological impairment. Dance therapists work with children who are dealing with developmental issues, trauma and separation, anxieties related to hospitalization, and changes in body functioning and image. In settings like cancer support communities and hospices, groups using dance/movement therapy help patients deal with loss, confront mortality, discover hope, and find meaning in their illness.

Other pioneering dance therapists and approaches include Mary Whitehouse, who was a student of Carl Jung and whose students developed an approach called "authentic movement" (Whitehouse, 1958); Alma Hawkins, who developed a method of organic movement at UCLA; Blanche Evan's "dance as creative transformation"; Liljan Espenak's affiliation with the Adlerian school of psychotherapy; and Norma Canner, who believed in going "to the source, your core, the source of your creativity." Elizabeth Polk had roots in folk dance, and Trudi Schoop was a Swiss mime who had her patients dance out their emotions and stories.

With respect to the ancient roots of dance therapy, these are much older than the roots of the modern medical/psychiatric model and go back to ancient healing practices in which circles, rhythm, images, and energy were used for group transformation. Dance therapy in a group setting has powerful precedents as a healing art during times of social breakdown, such as "Bewegungschor" (movement choirs) created by the Hungarian architect and dancer Rudolf von Laban (Bartenieff & Lewis, 1980; Laban, 1971).

Theories of Dance/Movement Therapy

Dance/movement therapy encompasses a range of theoretical approaches and also strong common elements among these approaches, as elaborated by Bernstein (1972, 1984). In brief, the Chace approach uses rhythmic bodily action to mirror clients' actions and establish a relationship. The depth approach, either Freudian- or Jungian-based, uses movement to reach unconscious symbols carried in the body. The developmental approach works with developmental stages in movement and helps clients work through blocks, whereas a systems approach uses dance to explore nonverbal dynamics of the family or group. Medical dance/movement therapy uses movement to work with people with physical or life-threatening illnesses that have a psychological component. An existential/humanistic approach uses movement to explore existential issues like meaning in life, mortality, relationships, freedom, and control. In a Narrative approach to dance therapy, nonverbal narratives of individuals or groups evoke powerful stories of hopes and fears, connections and disconnections, and mythic moments of death and rebirth. The way of knowing in a movement communication comes from the body and from new insights from embodiment theories.

Although distinctly different theoretical schools of dance/movement therapy have developed, they have as just noted strong common elements. Dance therapists are trained in bodily attunement and attachment theories that can open up powerful preverbal experiences. In their work, they provide a safe space to contain, re-experience, and work through bodily held blocks. They understand that movement is a language, an expression of the self that expresses its coping style, defenses, leadership styles, and capacities for intimacy. Movement is a special way of knowing. Kinaesthetic intelligence is one of the multiple modes of intelligence, a way of knowing in the body, a form of active imagination. Movement embodies the creative process. The act of shaping raw material or emotion into symbols or images is healing, as it helps objectify the emotions, creates distance from them, and unleashes a powerful creative force. Movement is healing and transformative. It can unlock primitive feelings and traumas that are stored in the body, restoring our connection to our bodies and the earth. And, in many cultures, dance takes us to the sacred.

New Paradigms of Research and Practice

Dance/movement therapy arose in psychiatric hospitals, and dance therapists were trained in a psychiatric illness model. Times have changed, however, along with medicine and the healthcare system. Dance therapists are now functioning as part of an integrative healthcare treatment team, and the field is establishing itself as an evidence-based modality (Serlin, 2007). Dance therapists often work with physicians to ease some of the fears that patients have about medical treatment, as well as addressing physical and emotional issues like body image.

Research is important to establish dance/movement therapy as an evidence-based treatment method. Research methods that are holistic, as dance therapy is holistic, are appropriate. New research methods include postpositivist, creative, and mixed forms of inquiry. New foundations for dance/movement therapy come from recent research findings in psychoneuroimmunology and neurobiology and studies of attachment, the health benefits of expression, and the awareness of the role of the body in trauma. New exciting developments in dance/movement therapy are happening globally, as well as in the United States, particularly with respect to philosophical, relational, and phenomenological. Significant theory-building, research, and training in dance/movement therapy are taking place in England, Spain, China, Japan, and Israel (Koch & Brauninger, 2006).

The need for a dramatically revised healthcare system is apparent today. Dance/movement therapy speaks to the new understanding of mind/body relationships and can reach necessary layers of healing. Dance/movement therapy can play a valuable role in helping heal symptoms of anxiety, somatic disorders, depression, and deep traumas that will be faced by coming waves of veterans returning from wars and displaced people who have lost jobs and homes. At a time when the healthcare system is going to require an educated and empowered consumer, dance therapy can bring a cost-effective method to the healthcare treatment team. In an age of uncertainty, dance therapy can help us face it with creativity and resilience.

REFERENCES

Bartenieff, L., & Lewis, D. (1980). *Body movement: Coping with the environment.* New York: Gordon & Breach.

Bernstein, P. L. (1972). *Theory and methods in dance-movementtherapy.* Dubuque, IA: Kendall/Hunt.

Bernstein, P. L. (1984). *Theoretical approaches in dance-movement therapy* (Vol. II). Dubuque, IA: Kendall/Hunt.

Koch, S., & Brauninger, I. (Eds.). (2006). *Advances in dance/movement therapy: Theoretical perspectives and empirical findings.* Berlin: Logos Verlag.

Laban, R. (1971). *The mastery of movement.* London: Macdonald & Evans.

Sandel, S., Chaiklin, S., & Lohn, A. (Eds.). (1993). *Foundations of dance/movement therapy: The life and work of Marian Chace.* Columbia, MD: American Dance Therapy Association.

Serlin, I. A. (2007). *Whole person healthcare.* (3 vols.). Westport, CT: Praeger.

Whitehouse, M. (1958). The tao of the body. In Pallaro, P. (Ed.). (1999). *Authentic movement.* London and Philadelphia: Jessica Kingsley Publishers. Reprinted from a paper presented to the Analytical Psychology Club of Los Angeles, 1958.

SUGGESTED READINGS

American Dance Therapy Association. (1984). *Dance Therapy: The Power of Movement* (video). Berkeley: University of California Press.

American Dance Therapy Association, 2000 Century Plaza, Columbia, MD 21044. (ADTA). (2002). *What is dance/movement therapy?* Retrieved July 17, 2002, from http://www.adta.org.

American Journal of Dance Therapy. New York: Human Sciences Press.

ILENE A. SERLIN
San Francisco, CA

DAUBERT STANDARD (See Admissibility of Expert Testimony)

DEAFNESS AND HEARING LOSS

Estimates of the prevalence of hearing loss vary widely within and across countries. As one indicator, over 30 million Americans (10% of the population) have significant, chronic hearing losses, and almost 2 million are deaf in both ears. Variation in the degree of hearing loss, age of hearing loss onset, and the etiologies of the losses influence the way and extent to which deafness affects psychological functioning.

Hearing losses are categorized as *conductive,* involving the middle ear; *sensorineural,* involving the inner ear and auditory nerve; or *central,* involving auditory centers of the brain. Speech perception, which directly relates to ability to interact with others, learn a spoken language, and succeed in school, is most affected by losses at frequencies 500 Hertz (Hz), 1000 Hz, and 2000 Hz. Etiologies of hearing loss range from hereditary losses to adventitious losses that are associated with birth complications, illness, and accidents. Adventitious losses may be accompanied by damage to other sensory systems or related neurological effects. Statistics concerning the academic success of deaf children, literacy rates, intelligence, and so on are based on heterogeneous samples and do not purely reflect consequences of deafness. Similarly, lack of early language exposure, social interaction, and experiential diversity can affect development, but studies involving deaf children of deaf parents reveal them to be indirect effects and not a function of hearing loss per se.

The terms *deaf* and *hard of hearing* refer not only to quantitative descriptions of hearing loss but also to cultural identity. Audiologically, hearing losses from 26 to 40 decibels (dB) in the better ear are categorized as *mild,* those from 41 to 55 dB as *moderate,* from 56 to 70 dB as *moderately severe,* from 71 to 90 dB as *severe,* and greater than 90 dB as *profound.* Whatever the quantitative loss, individuals may consider themselves members of the deaf community, depending on the degree to which they identify with members and institutions in that community and whether or not they prefer to use signed or spoken language. Most countries have such communities, although their visibility varies.

Over 95 percent of deaf children have hearing parents, a situation that significantly influences language, social, and cognitive development. Deaf children of deaf parents reach developmental milestones at rates similar to hearing peers. They also exhibit the same patterns of language acquisition (e.g., errors such as overgeneralizations and pronoun reversals) as hearing children of hearing parents and even have some advantages over their hearing peers (e.g., in vocabulary size, through the one-word stage). Many deaf children of hearing parents, in contrast, show delays in various domains, particularly language and literacy. Developing a sense of identity and self-esteem may be especially challenging, as many deaf children do not have exposure to deaf peers or deaf adults.

Hearing mothers tend toward over-control of their deaf children, but patterns of mother-child attachment generally are similar in deaf and hearing dyads. The quality of hearing parent–deaf child interactions is strongly related to effective communication, often accomplished through sign language. Natural sign languages such as American Sign Language (ASL), British Sign Language (BSL), and Italian Sign Language (LIS) are as difficult for parents to learn as any foreign language; for children with greater hearing losses, however, these sign languages are generally more successful than either spoken language or the various forms of signing based on the vernacular (e.g., Signed English, Signed Mandarin).

Through the early twentieth century, psychologists believed that severe hearing loss predisposed individuals to psychopathology and intellectual inferiority. In fact, distributions in both mental health and intellectual domains are largely comparable for deaf and hearing populations. Although some reports suggest that the prevalence and severity of mental illness among deaf people are greater than in the general population, that situation appears largely due to the lack of mental health services for deaf individuals and poor communication between health personnel and deaf clients. Recent studies suggest that fewer than 2% of deaf individuals who need mental health treatment receive it, a problem particularly acute for deaf individuals from ethnic minorities. Deaf children are still often misdiagnosed as mentally retarded due to communication barriers.

Contrary to assumptions about sensory compensation, hearing loss generally does not result in superior visual processing abilities. Among deaf children and adults who use natural sign languages, however, significant visual processing advantages are seen in domains such as mental rotation, face recognition, visual attention, and image generation. These differences appear to be direct results of various aspects of sign language use (i.e., deaf people who use spoken language do not exhibit them). There also is a more general enhanced sensitivity to visual signals in the periphery as evidenced in both behavioral and neurological assessments and as a result of reliance on visual rather than auditory stimuli in the environment.

Early research indicated that deaf people had shorter memory spans than hearing people, a finding that reinforced assumptions about intellectual deficiency. Recent research has revealed those findings to result not from underlying capacity differences, but from the fact that signs consume more space in the limited-capacity working memory system (the phonological loop) relative to spoken words, a finding with parallels across spoken languages that vary in their pronunciation times for digits and words. Still, deaf individuals tend to remember less than hearing individuals in a variety of memory paradigms. In part, such results reflect more heterogeneous and less well-interconnected conceptual information in semantic memory on the part of deaf individuals, despite considerable overlap in the organizational structure of their knowledge. Deaf adults and children also are less likely to apply conceptual knowledge in various tasks, either due to their educational histories (and lower expectations of parents and teachers) or to differences in their strategic approaches to problem solving. Tasks that require relational processing or the simultaneous consideration of multiple dimensions of a stimulus appear particularly problematic, a result that has general implications for learning and psychological functioning.

Deaf children's educational success depends on early language exposure and effective communication with parents. Early exposure to sign language appears to lead to linguistic and cognitive advantages, but yet acquisition of literacy skills remains a significant challenge to deaf individuals. Many deaf people acquire mental representations functionally equivalent to the phonological codes that underlie reading in hearing individuals, and literacy subskills such as spelling often approach hearing norms. Nevertheless, vocabulary, grammar, and other components of reading and writing in the vernacular remain difficult for deaf children to acquire, even when they are skilled in sign language. Thus far, neither the provision of vernacular-based sign systems nor bilingual programs that involve both spoken and sign language have proven effective in significantly enhancing literacy rates among deaf individuals, and the median reading level for deaf 18-year-olds in the United States remains comparable to that of hearing 9-year-olds. Similarly, high school–aged deaf students in the United States typically write on a par with hearing students in the fourth or fifth grade.

SUGGESTED READINGS

Chute, P. M., & Nevins, M. E. (2006). *School professionals working with children with cochlear implants.* San Diego, CA: Plural.

Emmorey, K., & Lane, H. (Eds.). (2000). *The signs of language revisited: An anthology to honor Ursula Bellugi and Edward Klima.* Mahwah, NJ: Lawrence Erlbaum.

Marschark, M., & Spencer, P. E. (2003). *Oxford handbook of deaf studies, language, and education.* New York: Oxford University Press.

Padden, C., & Humphries, T. (2006). *Inside deaf culture.* Cambridge, MA: Harvard University Press.

Tye-Murray, N. (2004). *Foundations of aural rehabilitation: Children, adults and their families* (2nd ed.). San Diego, CA: Singular.

JOHN A. ALBERTINI
Rochester Institute of Technology

See also: **Auditory Perception**

DECEPTION

Deception is the broadest term used in psychological practice to refer to intentional distortion in self-presentations. Most often deception is discussed in the framework of court-ordered evaluations and adversarial contexts; however, even clients proactively seeking services can be less than completely forthcoming. Moreover, deceptions may occur (see Rogers, 2008) as a result of internal conditions (e.g., cognitive distortions of a sex offender), identity issues (e.g., stigmatization of mental disorders), or external motivations (e.g., impression management for job interviews).

Rogers (2008, p. 5) defined deception as "an all-encompassing term to describe any consequential attempts by individuals to distort or misrepresent their self-reporting." It must be distinguished from nondisclosure, unreliability, and dissimulation. Many nondisclosures are simply refusals to provide requested information. Although potentially frustrating to psychologists, nondisclosures are not necessarily deceptive. When clients actively deny problematic behaviors (e.g., substance abuse), however, they are displaying deception. The term *unreliability* is used to describe reporting of questionable value. Unreliability can also extend beyond the quality of information disclosed to the intended objectives of the communicator in providing the information. Finally, *dissimulation* is a general term for distortions and misrepresentations of psychological symptoms. It is typically used when further specification (e.g., malingering or defensiveness) is not possible.

This article reviews types of deceptions commonly encountered in professional practice. When appropriate, specific methods for the detection of deception are briefly summarized.

Denied Substance Abuse

Denied substance abuse is very common across clinical, community, and forensic settings. As described by Stein and Rogers (2008), either the substance use or its consequences can be purposefully disavowed or grossly minimized by clients. These deceptions are often motivated by either deliberate efforts to create a positive impression (e.g., social desirability) or an attempt to minimize negative consequences such as stigmatization or authority-based penalties (e.g., legal, school, or work-related).

Methods for the assessment of denied substance abuse vary substantially in their cost and effectiveness. Most laboratory procedures are administered by law enforcement personnel or in certain medical settings, such as emergency rooms. The range of effectiveness varies from immediate (e.g., breathalyzer) and short-term (e.g., urinalysis) to long-term (e.g., hair analysis), with the potential for detection sometimes covering months (depending on the length of the hair shafts). Compared to laboratory procedures, psychological measures often have limited value. Many measures are face-valid direct inquiries about the use of illicit substances. Not surprisingly, these methods have minimal utility in assessing denied alcohol and drug abuse. The Substance Abuse Subtle Screening Inventory (SASSI; Miller, Roberts, Brooks, & Lazowski, 1997) is widely used as a measure of unreported substance abuse. However, the empirical data are mixed on its effectiveness and suggest that its subtle items may reflect antisocial content rather than engagement in substance use per se. If correct, the SASSI has limited value in forensic and correctional setting in which antisocial characteristics are common and not discriminating features.

Denial of Sexual Deviations

Williams and Payne (2002) found widespread deceptiveness among sexual partners in their research on nonoffending college students. Common deceptions included critical issues such as infidelities and risk-relevant behaviors (e.g., unprotected sex). Deceiver justifications identified in the study were both self-protective (e.g., saving the relationship) and other-protective (e.g., not hurting the partner). Given the general deceptiveness about sexual practices, practitioners should not be surprised that sex offenders engage in high levels of denial, especially when faced with severe social and legal sanctions.

Lanyon and Thomas (2008) provide a thoughtful analysis of clinical research on denied sexual deviations. As they note, most studies involve admitters of sexual deviance and have limited generalizability to deniers. In critically evaluating measures, Lanyon and Thomas conclude that self-report measures (e.g., Clarke Sexual History Questionnaire and Multiphasic Sex Inventory) have little proven utility for the assessment of denied sexual deviations. Although findings of general defensiveness on the MMPI-2 may have clinical value, they cannot be equated to the specific denial of sexual deviance. Finally, the penile plethysmograph (PPG) lacks standardization (i.e., variations in stimuli and testing procedures). Although group differences are often reported, the PPG's chief limitation lies in its modest accuracy, even among admitters of sexual deviance.

Deception and Eating Disorders

Vandereycken (2006) described the different forms of deceptive behaviors frequently utilized by patients with eating disorders. Although self-deception may complicate what they report, patients often deliberately conceal symptomatic behaviors (e.g., denials of purging or binging) and lie about their current perceptions and distress. Common motivations for deceptions may include the desire to maintain current body image and an avoidance of medical interventions.

Most self-report measures have a high degree of face validity and are thereby ineffective for the assessment of denied symptoms of eating disorders. Interviews are also unlikely to be successful with socially adept, knowledgeable patients who understand the implications of most clinical inquiries. Monitoring for covert behaviors and weight changes can provide some assistance. As noted by Vandereycken (2006, p. 362), the development of reciprocal trust is crucial: "We can trust these patients as far as they can trust us!"

Criminality and Psychopathy

Dishonesty and deception are necessary prerequisites to criminal conduct and behavioral expressions of psychopathy. Historically, mental health professionals have been naïve in their expectations of honest disclosures. In asking face-valid questions and not seeking extensive corroboration, these professionals are making an impermissible leap of faith that persons with antisocial and deceptive histories will suddenly become forthright about their misconduct.

Rogers and Cruise (2000) combined three diverse offender samples to examine patterns of deception associated with psychopathy. Using subcriteria of the Psychopathy Checklist: Screening Version (PCL:SV), three dimensions were revealed via principal axis factoring: (1) implausible presentation of emotions and statements, (2) denial of criminality, and (3) conning and manipulation. High levels of the first two dimensions were almost invariably found among psychopaths, whereas conning and manipulation were less distinguishable. Practitioners may find an examination of these two dimensions useful in assessing deceptive psychopaths.

Measures of psychopathy are susceptible to deception and deliberate distortions. However, very little research has examined the effects on psychopathy assessment of faking prosocial characteristics, despite extensive research on the PCL-R (Hare, 2003). Using the PCL Youth Version (PCL:YV), Rogers et al. (2000) demonstrated that adolescent offenders could manipulate their responses to the extent that their PC:YV scores could be either decreased or increased. Clearly, more research is needed on all psychopathy measures and their vulnerability to manipulation and deception. Similarly, hundreds of empirical studies have been conducted in the last two decades to examine response styles, but they have focused predominantly on malingering and defensiveness. Comparatively fewer studies have grappled with other deceptions and their corresponding methods of assessment. As noted in this discussion of deception in relationship to specific diagnoses and syndromes, these deceptions can markedly reduce the accuracy of assessment and hinder effective treatments.

REFERENCES

Hare, R. D. (2003). *Technical manual for the Revised Psychopathy Checklist* (2nd ed.). North Tonawanda, NY: Multi-Health Systems.

Lanyon, R., & Thomas, M. L. (2008). Detection of defensiveness in sex offenders. In R. Rogers (Ed.), *Clinical assessment of malingering and deception* (3rd ed.; pp. 285–300). New York: Guilford Press.

Miller, G. A., Roberts, J., Brooks, M. K., & Lazowski, L. E. (1997). *SASSI-3 user's guide: A quick reference for administration and scoring.* Bloomington, IN: Baugh Enterprises.

Rogers, R. (2008). An introduction to response styles. In R. Rogers (Ed.), *Clinical assessment of malingering and deception* (3rd ed.; pp. 3–13). New York: Guilford Press.

Rogers, R., & Cruise, K. R. (2000). Malingering and deception among psychopaths. In C. B. Gacono (Ed.), *The clinical and forensic assessment of psychopathy: A practitioner's guide* (pp. 269–284). New York: LEA.

Rogers, R., Vitacco, M. J., Jackson, R. L., Martin, M., Collins, M., & Sewell, K. W. (2002). Faking psychopathy? An examination of response styles with antisocial youth. *Journal of Personality Assessment, 78,* 31–46.

Stein, L. A. R., & Rogers, R. (2008). Denial and misreporting of substance abuse. In R. Rogers (Ed.), *Clinical assessment of malingering and deception* (3rd ed.; pp. 87–108). New York: Guilford Press.

Vandereycken, W. (2006). Denial of illness in Anorexia Nervosa—A conceptual review: Part 2 Different forms and meanings. *European Eating Disorders Review, 14*(5), 352–368.

Williams, S. S., & Payne, G. H. (2002). Perceptions of own sexual lies influenced by characteristics of liar, sex partner, and lie itself. *Journal of Sex & Marital Therapy, 28*(3), 257–267.

RICHARD ROGERS
University of North Texas

See also: **Impression Management; Malingering**

DECLARATIVE MEMORY

Declarative memory involves representations of facts and events that are subject to conscious recollection, verbal reflection, and explicit expression. Sometimes also called explicit memory, declarative memory is contrasted with procedural, implicit, or (simply) nondeclarative memory. The distinguishing features of declarative memory, as just introduced, involve a combination of two major features. One of these features is its mode of expression, characterized by the ability to bring facts and experiences to mind, that is, the ability to consciously recall items in memory. The second feature involves the ability to express a recalled memory in a variety of ways, most prominently by verbal reflection on a learned fact or past experience, but also by using the memory to answer a variety of questions or solve any of a variety of problems.

By contrast, nondeclarative memory is characterized by its inaccessibility to conscious recall and by expression only through implicit measures of performance, typically increases in the speed or shift in choice bias during repetition of a mental procedure. Although several dichotomies of human memory have been proposed, most are consensual in these properties that distinguish a conscious, declarative memory from forms of unconscious memory. Finally, declarative memory is sometimes divided into two subtypes—episodic memory for specific autobiographical experiences and semantic memory for general world knowledge.

Conscious and explicit memory can be dissociated from other types of memory expression in normal human subjects (Schacter, 1987) and in amnesia (Squire et al., 2004), leading several investigators to propose that declarative memory is a distinct form of memory. Studies on normal subjects have shown that manipulation of memory testing demands can differentially affect performance on declarative and nondeclarative memory. For example, study instructions that emphasize semantic processing over superficial phonemic processing of verbal material differentially improves success in declarative, but not in nondeclarative memory, even for the same materials. In addition, manipulation of the retention interval and exposure to interfering information can differentially affect declarative memory as compared to nondeclarative memory performance.

Conversely, changes in the modality of learning materials from initial exposure to memory testing, for example, by a change in the typeface of printed words or by a shift from auditory to visual presentation, can affect nondeclarative memory performance, whereas these manipulations have little effect on declarative memory. Yet other studies have dissociated declarative memory from nondeclarative memory by demonstrating stochastic independence, that is, lack of statistical correlation, between performance success in typical declarative and implicit expression of memory for the same items.

Studies on human amnesia have also revealed numerous dissociations between performance in declarative and nondeclarative memory. In particular, a profound impairment in declarative memory, but not nondeclarative memory, results from damage to the medial temporal lobe region. For example, following removal of most of the hippocampal formation and its associated medial temporal lobe structures, the famous patient H.M. suffered a profound impairment in recall and recognition that was remarkable in its severity, pervasiveness, and selectivity. H.M.'s memory was severely impaired regardless of the form of the learning materials or modality of their presentation (Corkin, 1984). Yet, even the early observations on H.M. indicated that the hippocampal region was important to only some aspects of memory and spared other aspects of memory performance.

With regard to the distinction between declarative and nondeclarative memory, the range of spared learning capacities in amnesia includes motor, perceptual, and cognitive skills, sensory adaptations, and "priming" of perceptual and lexical stimuli. Even learning involving the identical materials may be either severely impaired or fully spared in H.M. and other amnesic subjects, depending on whether they were asked to use conscious recollection to recall or recognize the study phase, as is typical in most memory tasks, or whether memory was assessed by more subtle measures such as changes in response bias or speed after exposure to the test materials (for review see Cohen & Eichenbaum, 1993).

We are only beginning to understand the structure of declarative memory and its neurobiological mechanisms. These mechanisms involve different stages and forms of declarative memory, including working memory, semantic memory, and episodic memory. New information initially enters working memory, a transient form of declarative memory that enables us to retain information about events that have just occurred and to manipulate that information "on-line" in consciousness (Postle, 2006). Working memory depends on the prefrontal cortex, which supports executive functions including selection, rehearsal, and monitoring of information being retrieved from long-term memory. To serve these functions, the prefrontal cortex also interacts with a large network of posterior cortical areas that encode, maintain, and retrieve specific types of information such as visual images, sounds and words, where important events occurred, and much more.

Our permanent warehouse of declarative memories, called semantic memory, also involves a large distributed network of cortical processing systems that are involved in the perception, processing, and analysis of the material being learned. Different cortical networks are specialized for processing particular kinds of material, such as faces, houses, tools, actions, language, and many other categories of knowledge. At the same time many of these same areas also perform different types of processing, for example, distinguishing exemplars within a category or imagining the use of an object. These functional specializations combine so that a large network of cortical areas participates in processing every type of semantic information, and a distinct set of components is engaged in any particular category of semantic processing (Martin et al., 1996).

Structures within the medial temporal lobe areas serve a critical role in the initial processing and storage of episodic memories, our memories of specific personal experiences that happened at a particular place and time. Thus, for example, when you meet a particular person at a particular place and time, information about each of these features of the episode are channeled in parallel into the medial temporal area where the different kinds of information are linked, and those linkages connect the representations of each of those kinds of information in the relevant cerebral cortical areas. Subsequently, interactions between widespread areas of the cerebral cortex and the medial temporal lobe slowly facilitate the interconnections among the representations in different cerebral cortical areas. Over a protracted period, these interactions ultimately cause a substantial reorganization and consolidation of connections among cortical representations to incorporate the key information contained in new episodes into our network of semantic knowledge.

A key feature of declarative memory is the flexibility with which multiple memories are linked and the subsequent network of memories can be accessed to solve new problems in both animals and humans. For example, rats with hippocampal damage can acquire responses to each of a set of particular odors. However, unlike normal rats, rats with hippocampal damage cannot acquire and inferentially express indirect relations among odor memories learned in separate episodes (Bunsey & Eichenbaum, 1996). Under similar circumstances when there is a demand for linking memories and inferring relations between indirectly related items in memory, the hippocampus is strongly activated in humans (Preston et al., 2004). These qualities of hippocampal dependent declarative memory in animals and humans bear similarity with William James (1890) characterization of conscious memory as involving numerous diverse connections among individual memories, allowing memories to be retrieved via many routes. Such a characterization suggests that the fundamental basis of declarative memory involves the networking of memories acquired across distinct episodes, and the consequent capacity to surf such a memory network to retrieve and express memories in a flexible way.

REFERENCES

Bunsey, M., & Eichenbaum, H. (1996). Conservation of hippocampal memory function in rats and humans. *Nature, 379*, 255–257.

Cohen, N. J., and Eichenbaum, H. (1993) *Memory, amnesia, and the hippocampal system.* Cambridge, MA: MIT. Press.

Corkin S. (1984). Lasting consequences of bilateral medial temporal lobectomy: Clinical course and experimental findings in H.M. *Seminars in Neurology, 4*, 249–259.

James, W. (1890). *The principles of psychology.* New York: Holt (1918 edition).

Martin, A., Wiggs, C. L., Ungerleider, L. G., & Haxby, J. V. (1996). Neural correlates of category-specific knowledge. *Nature, 379*, 649–652.

Postle, B. R. (2006). Working memory as an emergent property of the mind and brain. *Neuroscience, 139*, 23–38.

Preston, A., Shrager, Y., Dudukovic, N. M., & Gabrieli, J. D. E. (2004). Hippocampal contribution to the novel use of relational information in declarative memory. *Hippocampus, 14*, 148–152.

Schacter, D. L. (1987). Implicit memory: History and current status. *Journal of Experimental Psychology, Learning, Memory, Cognition, 13*, 501–518.

Squire, L. R., Stark, C. E. L., and Clark, R. E. (2004). The medial temporal lobe. *Annual Review of Neuroscience, 27*, 279–306.

SUGGESTED READINGS

Eichenbaum, H. (2004). Hippocampus: Cognitive processes and neural representations that underlie declarative memory. *Neuron, 44*, 109–120.

Eichenbaum, H., & Cohen, N. J. (2001). *From conditioning to conscious recollection: Memory systems of the brain.* Oxford: Oxford University Press.

Eichenbaum, H., Yonelinas, A. R., & Ranganath, C. (2007). The medial temporal lobe and recognition memory. *Annual Review of Neuroscience, 20*, 123–152.

HOWARD EICHENBAUM
Boston University

See also: **Episodic Memory; Memory Functions; Spatial Memory**

DEFENSE MECHANISMS

A defense mechanism may be defined as a cognitive operation or form of thinking that functions to protect a person from undue anxiety or loss of self-esteem. These mental mechanisms and their function operate outside of awareness, so that people do not realize why they are thinking in a particular way. For example, when Johnny says "Grandma doesn't like me" in the absence of any objective evidence that this is the case, it may well be that Johnny does not like his Grandma, but cannot recognize this emotion in himself, because it would be an unacceptable feeling. In this case, Johnny is attributing his own unacceptable feeling to someone else and would be displaying the defense mechanism of projection to hide his true feelings, while at the same time he is providing an explanation for why he avoids his Grandma.

Given the unconscious nature of defenses, it can be difficult to assess their use. Logically, one cannot ask people to describe something of which they are unaware. Several different approaches have been used to bypass this problem. Questionnaires may ask people to indicate what they would think or how they would behave in different situations, although this approach ignores the problem that people may not be able to self-report unconscious mental processes. Other approaches that avoid this problem include conducting clinical interviews or obtaining extended samples of narrative discourse, which are then coded for indications of the use of defense mechanisms. Descriptions of these methods may be found in Cramer (2006).

There are a number of different defense mechanisms, the most common being denial, projection, displacement, rationalization, intellectualization, repression, reaction formation, isolation, and regression. These and other de-

fenses have been arranged into a hierarchy, depending either on the developmental age at which they become prominent (Cramer, 1987, 1991) or on their immaturity/maturity (e.g., Vaillant, 1993; American Psychiatric Association, 2000). For example, denial is a fairly simple cognitive operation that is characteristic of young children, whereas intellectualization requires more complex cognitive activity and is more frequent among older individuals.

Research has supported this idea of a hierarchy of defenses. Whereas young children (age 5–7) have been found to use the defense of denial frequently, this defense mechanism is infrequent among adolescents and adults (Cramer, 1987; Porcerelli, Thomas, Hibbard & Cogan, 1998). In contrast, projection, which is somewhat more cognitively complex than denial, is used more frequently by adolescents and adults than by children and is infrequent among the youngest children. In this instance, we see a developmental hierarchy. When considering adults, defenses may be ordered in a hierarchy based on the immaturity/maturity of the defense mechanism. For example, denial and projection are considered to be immature defenses, whereas sublimation and altruism are considered to be mature defenses (Vaillant, 1993).

Although the early description of defense mechanisms was linked with the presence of psychopathology (e.g., Freud, 1894/1962), more recently it has been understood that defense use is part of normal, everyday functioning. The particular defenses that characterize different individuals have implications for the way they function in life. For example, young adults who rely on the defense of denial have been found to be self-centered and unpredictable. Those who rely on projection have been characterized as mistrustful and hypersensitive (see Cramer, 2006). Thus, the defense modes of thinking have repercussions beyond their primary function of protecting the individual from anxiety and loss of self-esteem.

These relationships between defenses and personality are found in ordinary people students, homemakers, blue-collar workers, and high-level executives. They may signal personality difficulties, but not psychopathology. In contrast, when defenses are used excessively or are age inappropriate, they may contribute to the presence of severe psychological problems. Thus, in a sample of inner city men, of those with a psychiatric diagnosis of narcissistic personality disorder, 83% made strong use of dissociation/denial. In contrast, of those with a diagnosis of paranoia, 100% made use of the defenses of projection (Vaillant, 1994). Further research has demonstrated that psychiatric patients make greater use of immature defenses, as compared with nonpatients. This research is summarized in Cramer (2006).

In addition to these studies demonstrating the relationship between defense use and personality or between defense use and psychopathology, experimental research has shown that defense use increases when a person is under stress. College students who were erroneously led to believe that they lacked creativity, or that their sex-role orientation was questionable, or that they had a high level of repressed hostility or a tendency toward dishonesty, all showed an increase in their use of defenses, and a greater use of defenses than nonstressed peers. Children also react to stress with an increased use of defenses. For example, those who thought they had been unsuccessful in a perceptual motor task subsequently increased their use of defenses, as compared with children who were told they had been successful. Another study showed that Israeli children who had been traumatized by war at ages 3–5 years showed higher levels of defense use at ages 8–10 than children who had not been thus traumatized. This research is summarized by Cramer (2006).

Overall, the moderate use of defense mechanisms helps keep us on an even keel. Defenses protect us from debilitating anxiety and help us maintain our self-esteem. Only when defenses are used excessively or at a developmentally inappropriate age are psychological problems likely to follow.

REFERENCES

American Psychiatric Association. (2000). *Diagnostic and statistical manual of mental disorders*. (4th ed., text rev.). Washington, DC: Author.

Cramer, P. (1987). The development of defense mechanisms. *Journal of Personality, 55*, 597–614.

Cramer, P. (1991). *The development of defense mechanisms: Theory, research and assessment*. New York: Springer-Verlag.

Cramer, P. (2006). *Protecting the self: Defense mechanism in action*. New York: Guilford Press.

Freud, S. (1894/1962.). T*he neuro-psychoses of defence*. Standard ed., *3*, 45–61. London: Hogarth Press.

Porcerelli, J. H., Thomas, S., Hibbard, S., & Cogan, R. (1998). Defense mechanism development in children, adolescents, and late adolescents. *Journal of Personality Assessment, 71*, 411–420.

Vaillant, G. E. (1994). Ego mechanisms of defense and personality psychopathology. *Journal of Abnormal Psychology, 103*, 44–50.

SUGGESTED READINGS

Freud, A. (1936). *The ego and the mechanisms of defense*. New York: International Universities Press.

Vaillant, G. E. (1993). *The wisdom of the ego*. Cambridge, MA: Harvard University Press.

PHEBE CRAMER
Williams College

See also: Coping Behavior; Psychopathology

DELINQUENCY (See Juvenile Delinquency)

DELUSIONAL DISORDER

Several definitions of delusions have been advanced. Common features of these descriptions include the presence of a false belief or set of beliefs that fall outside of a person's cultural or subcultural values and are held with extraordinary conviction. The beliefs are held in spite of being unsubstantiated, in the face of evidence to the contrary, and/or in opposition to the beliefs of almost all others. Delusions are differentiated from other erroneous thoughts such as phobias and obsessions in that they are illogical, accepted by the individual as true, held with tenacity, and often implausible.

History of Delusional Disorder

Although the term *delusional disorder* was not adopted by the *Diagnostic and Statistical Manual of Mental Disorders* (DSM) until its revised third edition in 1987, its description has been present since the late nineteenth century, most notably in the pioneering diagnostic work of Emil Kraepelin (1921). Kraepelin famously distinguished what later became termed schizophrenia from manic-depressive illness. In later editions, he further distinguished paranoia (now recognized as synonymous with delusional disorder) as a chronic but nondegenerative condition without classical symptoms of schizophrenia, such as hallucinations or thought disorder, and with minimal impairment in general functioning aside from those problems that result from the delusions. Kraepelin's work greatly influenced modern classification of mental disorders, and the current diagnosis of delusional disorder largely resembles his conceptualization more than a century ago.

In the current fourth edition of the DSM (DSM-IV-TR; American Psychiatric Association, 2000) delusions are characterized by the "presence of one or more nonbizarre delusions that persist for at least one month." The person must have never have met Criterion A for schizophrenia (i.e., the presence of two or more psychotic symptoms, negative symptoms, or grossly disorganized behavior; or the presence of bizarre delusions or auditory hallucinations that involve a running commentary or two voices talking to each other). Although the presence of hallucinations does not preclude the diagnosis of delusional disorder, they must not be prominent, as they would be in schizophrenia. The themes of the delusions are not bizarre, thinking is not grossly disrupted, and behavior is not odd or unusual. There is little functional impairment aside from events directly related to the delusions. Persons with delusional disorder may have periods of disturbed mood, but these episodes are brief relative to the duration of the delusions. The delusions must not be caused by the direct effects of a substance, such as amphetamines, or a general medical condition, such as dementia. The distinction between the paranoid type of schizophrenia and delusional disorder can be a difficult diagnostic exercise because the decision largely falls on the interpretation of the bizarreness of the delusion. Delusions are considered bizarre if they are clearly implausible, incomprehensible, and outside of normal human experiences. In contrast, the nonbizarre delusions characteristic of delusional disorder involve circumstances or events that could actually occur in the person's life experiences. The formation of these delusions is typically without evidence or based on incorrect interpretations of real events, and the beliefs are maintained in spite of contradictory evidence or claims by others.

The DSM-IV-TR recognizes several types of delusional disorder. The most commonly observed is a persecutory type. The predominant pattern of thinking in this type involves conspiracies that others intend to harass, cause harm, and/or prevent attainment of desired outcomes. There may be fear of being poisoned, spied upon, or abducted. There is a tendency to exaggerate or conflate innocuous actions of others to fit the belief system. Reactions to the beliefs range from avoiding others to levying criminal charges to acting violently against the supposed perpetrators. A jealous type refers to individuals who hold an unwarranted belief that their romantic partner has been unfaithful. This belief follows from erroneous interpretations of real events or confabulations. There are typically efforts made to collect information and confront the partner. A grandiose type involves believing that one possesses a special ability or power, has accomplished something extraordinary, or has an affiliation with a person of power and prestige. These supposed abilities or achievements go unrecognized by others. Religious beliefs or behaviors that fall outside of the person's cultural norms may have a grandiose quality, such as receiving hidden messages from a god.

An erotomanic type of delusional disorder describes individuals who hold the false belief that some person is in love with them. The object of the delusion is typically someone from a higher class, a person of prestige, or a celebrity. The individual might interpret random behavior of others as amorous advances toward him or her. Correspondence with, stalking, and at times criminal pursuits of the supposedly amorous person may be reactions to the belief. A somatic type is diagnosed when individuals misinterpret bodily sensations or hold false beliefs about the functioning of their organs or systems. Such individuals may claim, in spite of medical evidence to the contrary, that parts of their body are missing or deteriorating. They might interpret normal bodily sensations as being parasitic infections. In the less common case of an individual with more than one delusional theme, the type of delusional disorder is designated according to the most prominent theme, or as a "mixed type" when no single theme is predominant. An unspecified type is assigned when delusions exist but do correspond to any of the specific types.

Historically, a great deal of literature, largely from France, has focused on some of the most bizarre and fascinating delusional themes. Capgras syndrome is characterized by the belief that a loved one has been replaced by an exact replica. Cotard's syndrome is characterized by the belief that one's possessions, organs, and even the entire body, have been lost. A *folie a deux* occurs when an otherwise healthy person adopts the delusional beliefs of another person, with whom he or she is typically in close and rather isolated contact. These particular syndromes are observed less frequently today than in times past, and they typically have a rapid and complete treatment response to pharmacologic intervention.

Etiology and Prevalence

Because delusional disorder is an understudied condition that is seldom seen in clinical practice, its prevalence is poorly understood. Estimates range from 24 to 30 cases per 100,000. There is an overabundance of paranoid personality traits or diagnoses in family members of those with delusional disorder, but little or no increased risk for schizophrenia or other psychotic disorders. The psychotic disorders are increasingly recognized as the interaction of biological risk and environmental triggers. Recent evidence has suggested genetic links of delusional disorder, particularly the persecutory type, with the paranoid type of schizophrenia (Morimoto et al., 2002; Debnath, Das, Bera, Nayak, & Chaudhuri, 2006). Specific mechanisms could involve gene polymorphisms for dopamine receptors and dopamine synthesis, consistent with the dopamine hypothesis of schizophrenia (Morimoto et al., 2002), and/or genes associated with autoimmune functioning, such as human leukocyte antigen (Debnath et al., 2006). Compromised neuropsychological functioning or information processing biases may play causal or maintaining role in the delusional disorders. Impairments in perception and interpretation of external stimuli have been identified in delusional disorder, along with a tendency to be overconfident in conclusions that are based on weak evidence. There is mixed support for a cognitive bias to attribute negative events to external sources.

Clinical Phenomenology

Although delusional disorder was originally described from hospitalized samples by Kraepelin (1921) and Winokur (1977) as a disorder with markedly male predominance, more recent work with a larger number and broader range of subjects, together with an expansion from the concept of paranoia to the other delusional types, has found a slight reversal of gender differences, with females outnumbering males 1.2:1 (Kendler, 1982; de Portugal, Gonzalez, Haro, Autonell, Cervilla, 2008). The average age of onset of between 35 and 55 (Kendler, 1982; de Portugal et al., 2008) is at least a decade later than the age of onset of schizophrenia. Many individuals with a delusional disorder will meet criteria for other mental disorders as well, such as mood disorders, anxiety disorders, or paranoid personality disorder.

Course

The level of functioning during the premorbid period tends to be unremarkable, although most delusional individuals would be described as having a paranoid personality type. The rates of marriage and productive vocational functioning in delusional disorder are generally within the expected ranges. There is evidence for impaired global functioning in delusional disorder, but the impairments are not as broad, severe, pervasive, or deteriorating as are those seen in schizophrenia (Jorgensen, 1995; de Portugal et al., 2008). In spite of this relatively good course, it is important to consider the potential for serious behavioral consequences that stem from delusional beliefs. Problematic areas of functioning tend to be centered on the delusional theme, but this focus might lead to more severe problems in very specific areas. For example, delusions of jealousy are likely to result in marital discord and could progress to abuse or homicidal rage. Delusions of persecution might lead to social isolation and avoidance of situations necessary for effective interpersonal and occupational functioning. There is some evidence that the jealous and mixed types are associated with better functioning, whereas the erotomanic and grandiose types are more likely to have poorer outcomes (de Portugal et al, 2008).

Assessment

The assessment of factors associated with delusional beliefs provides more treatment outcome variables than simply identifying the presence or absence of delusions. One such assessment tool, the Maudsley Assessment of Delusion Schedule, includes factors such as the strength of conviction, the affect related to belief, idiosyncrasy of belief, and insight, among others. Analysis of the components within delusional beliefs will likely yield more valuable phenomenological, prognostic, and treatment response data than traditional rating scales that focus on global severity.

Treatment

Among the psychotic conditions, there is a relative dearth of treatment data for delusional disorder, perhaps as a function of the tendency for individuals with this condition to forgo mental health treatment. The hallmark feature of delusional disorder, an isolated delusion in the absence of other symptoms, suggests that many individuals with the disorder will deny being mentally ill and lack the dysphoria, dangerous behavior, or severe functional deficits that might otherwise lead to treatment-seeking behavior or involuntary treatment. Positive treatment response has been identified in case studies (Morimoto et al., 2002) with antipsychotic medications at lower doses than for schizophrenia, though adequate randomized controlled trials of such treatments do not exist. In contrast, recent randomized controlled trials of cognitive-behavioral therapy (CBT) have demonstrated statistically significant and clinically meaningful reductions in the strength of conviction and behavioral responses in delusional disorder (O'Connor et al., 2007). In CBT, after preparing the patient for the treatment, the therapist helps delusional patients challenge their beliefs and perform reality testing of their thinking patterns.

Future Issues for Research

The low prevalence and unlikelihood of finding delusional disorder in clinical settings have limited our understanding of several critical etiological, phenomenological, and treatment aspects of this chronic and functionally disabling condition. More randomized controlled trials for pharmacologic and behavioral treatments, as well as examinations of interactive effects of these treatment strategies, are needed to better understand gold-standard methods for treating delusional disorder. Its typically late onset might suggest novel causal mechanisms for this psychotic disorder. Future research might examine how the typical age-related changes in the human brain interact with an underlying vulnerability for delusional disorder. From the environmental perspective, studies could examine the accumulation of significant life stressors as a potential trigger for conversion from loosely formed ideas to delusional disorders. It might also be fruitful to search for protective factors in individuals who would be considered at heightened risk for delusional disorders by the presence of paranoid ideation or subclinical idiosyncratic belief systems.

Finally, the functional implications of delusional disorder are still poorly understood. Unlike other psychotic disorders, which show very low correlations between severity of psychosis and functional impairments (Bowie & Harvey, 2005), it might be the case that the hallmark symptom of delusional disorder is the primary predictor of gaps between the individual's capacity to function and achievements in the real world. It will be important to know the severity, chronicity, and treatment-responsiveness of the social, interpersonal, and vocational impairments that are directly or indirectly related to delusional beliefs. Pragmatically, the recruitment of meaningful sample sizes to study delusional disorder will likely require large-scale collaborative efforts.

REFERENCES

American Psychiatric Association. (2000). *Diagnostic and statistical manual of mental disorders*. (4th ed., text rev.) Washington, DC: Author.

Bowie, C. R., & Harvey, P. D. (2005). Cognition in schizophrenia: Impairments, determinants, and functional importance. *Psychiatric Clinics of North America, 28*, 613–633.

Debnath, M., Das, S. K., Bera, N. K., Nayak, C. R., & Chaudhuri, T. K. (2006). Genetic associations between delusional disorder and paranoid schizophrenia: A novel etiologic approach. *Canadian Journal of Psychiatry, 51,* 342–349.

Jorgensen, P. (1995). Comparative outcome of first-admission patients with delusional beliefs. *European Psychiatry, 10,* 276–281.

Kendler, K. S. (1982). Demography of paranoid psychosis (delusional disorder): A review and comparison with schizophrenia and affective illness. *Archives of General Psychiatry, 39,* 890–902.

Kraepelin, E. (1921). *Manic-depressive insanity and paranoia.* Edinburgh: ES Livingstone.

Morimoto, K., Miyatake, R., Nakamura, M., Watanabe, T., Hirao, T., & Suwaki, H. (2002). Delusional disorder: Molecular genetic evidence for dopamine psychosis. *Neuropsychopharmacology, 26,* 794–801.

O'Connor, K. Stip, E., Pelissier, M. C., Aardema, F., Guay, S., Gaudette, G., et al. (2007). Treating delusional disorder: A comparison of cognitive-behavioural therapy and attention placebo control. *Canadian Journal of Psychiatry, 52,* 182–190.

de Portugal, E., Gonalez, N., Haro, J. M., Autonell, J., & Cervilla, J. A. (2008). A descriptive case-register study of delusional disorder. *European Psychiatry, 23,* 125–133.

Winokur G. (1977). Delusional disorder (Paranoia). *Comprehensive Psychiatry, 18,* 511–521.

SUGGESTED READING

Munro A. (1999). *Delusional disorder: Paranoia and related illnesses.* Cambridge: Cambridge University Press.

CHRISTOPHER R. BOWIE
Queen's University, Kingston, ON, Canada

See also: Delusions; Paranoid Personality Disorder

DELUSIONS

There is no widely accepted definition of delusion. Delusions are often described in textbooks as being defined since Karl Jaspers as false, subculturally atypical beliefs, strongly maintained in the face of counterargument. Yet such definitions fail to capture either the rich diversity or key features of delusions.

Common delusions include persecution (there is a plot or conspiracy against the subject; these are the most common delusional beliefs); grandiosity (the subject is an important personage); erotomania (people delusionally believe that someone is deeply in love with them); and control (the belief that one's actions, thoughts, or feelings are being controlled by others). The majority of delusions concern the subjects' position in the social world, or reflect central existential issues in their lives, and these beliefs are indeed often false, atypical, and strongly maintained.

It is however possible that a delusion (such as that of one's partner being unfaithful) may accidentally be true. Levels of conviction in delusions may also vary with time. Some delusions may be paradoxically true rather than false (e.g. the delusion that one is mentally ill), and others may be not beliefs but rather delusional value judgments, thoughts, perceptions, memories, inner experiences, and moods (Sims, 2003). The "delusionality" of delusions of control, for example, arises directly from a disturbed experience of one's own agency, rather than with beliefs about such experiences.

As Jaspers himself reported, to "say simply that a delusion is a mistaken idea which is firmly held by the patient and which cannot be corrected gives only a superficial and incorrect answer" (Jaspers, 1997/1997, p. 93). Delusions instead reflect a fundamental disturbance in our relation to reality and the integrity of the self, which is hard to pinpoint in a definition. Jaspers distinguished between primary delusions, which arise in an ultimately unintelligible way in our contact with reality itself, and secondary delusions, which are intelligible attempts to understand baffling experiences. Although Jaspers' doctrine of the "ununderstandability" of primary delusions has often been criticized, it is important to recognize that his point is not to preclude a reflective understanding of what the deluded person says, what psychodynamics underpin it, or what symbolism it expresses. His point is rather that we always fall short of inhabiting such beliefs or experiences from a first-person perspective.

Psychoanalytic Perspectives

Sigmund Freud described delusions as "applied like a patch over the place where originally a rent had appeared in the ego's relation to the external world" (Freud, 1924/1981, p. 215). He distinguished between neurotic and psychotic conditions as follows. In the neuroses, people attempt to adapt to an incompatible reality by defending against their own feelings. The symptoms that result are the product of the internal conflicts within patients when they try to remodel their desire. In the psychoses, by contrast, people attempt to solve their conflicts with reality not by altering their feelings, but by withdrawing from or disavowing reality and replacing it instead with fantasies that are treated as realities.

In the 1960s the psychiatrist Thomas Freeman extended the psychoanalytic understanding of delusion (Freeman, Cameron, & McGhie, 1966). Although some delusions can be understood as fantasized replacements for lost relationships, others consist of misinterpretations of experiences with others from whom the subject has not become completely detached. Accordingly, the delusional subject attempts to bend or exaggerate reality to make it more tolerable and less threatening of the subject's sense of himself or herself, rather than completely substitute for it, and the delusions are the outcome of such defensive maneuvers.

More recent psychoanalytic thinking on psychosis has been organized not around the concept of delusion, but rather by attempts to understand the nature of omnipotent fantasy, including the mental mechanisms of splitting, projection, projective identification, and symbolic condensation. All of these processes may be implicated in the formation of delusions, but none is specific to it.

Phenomenological Perspectives

Phenomenology aims to elucidate the lived, nonreflective, and immersed experience of being a self in relation to a meaningful environment that includes other selves. Accordingly, the phenomenological understanding of delusions—in particular of schizophrenic delusions—views what is specific to it as already contained in germ in a specific predelusional disturbance of immersed participation. More specifically, most phenomenological psychiatrists track this disturbance back to fragile temporal and corporeal processes that underpin the constitution of the self. Phenomenologists view the delimitation of self from others as arising out of an organism's nonreflective interactions with its social and physical environment. Disturbances of this process result in disturbances in the boundary between self and world, and delusional beliefs and experiences carry this fundamental disturbance in reality contact inscribed within them.

Most phenomenological accounts take their lead from the first two stages of Klaus Conrad's (1958) developmental account of delusion in paranoid schizophrenia. In the initial predelusional "trema" stage, people start to vaguely feel that all is not well with themselves and/or the world. They may complain of an unspecific groundlessness, confusion about or lack of a sense of their own identity, diminished sense of aliveness, and lost automatic connection with reality. The body may become experienced as an object rather than as a living subject, self and others may start to become confused, the objective character of reality may be lost, and the delusional experience of reference—a sense that everything seen has been constructed for the sake of the subject—may begin (Parnas & Sass, 2001).

In Conrad's second stage, "apophany," delusions proper arrive. Now the trema is intuitively resolved into one particular revelatory meaning, and subjects take themselves to now "understand" what had previously only been confusingly signaled. Relief is experienced from the diffuse tension and terror of the trema, and a monothematic reflective grasp of what is happening (e.g. there is a government plot against me) takes the place of the prereflective but destabilized grasp ("something is up") that subjects had on their situation.

Cognitive Science Perspectives

Unlike psychoanalytic and phenomenological theories, cognitive psychological theories are driven by a psychological understanding of the human being as constantly and actively attempting to interpret, or make reflective sense of, their personal situation. Thus Brendan Maher (1974) suggested that delusional beliefs represent rational attempts to make sense of abnormal experiences (e.g. hallucinations or passivity experiences). Phillipa Garety by contrast has suggested that abnormal processes of reflective sense making may be implicated in delusion formation (Garety & Freeman, 1999). She found, for example, that patients with delusions tend to jump to conclusions on the basis of surprisingly little evidence.

Several difficulties confront such cognitive psychological accounts. First, delusions—especially primary delusions—do not present themselves as active interpretive products, but rather as spontaneous and passive revelations in thought, feeling, or perception. Even the delusional explanations that patients offer appear to be more post-hoc rationalization than genuine justification. Second, Garety also found that the hasty reasoning style of delusional patients makes them equally likely to quickly give up their beliefs, which makes it hard to understand the typical intransigence of the delusional subject. It is also important to recognize that the explanatory task, in understanding delusional intransigence, is not merely how unshakeable beliefs arise, but how unshakeable beliefs with the face-value implausibility of delusions could arise. Finally, Maher's theory does not explain why patients fail to accept the obvious explanation that they are hallucinating or experiencing passivity experiences.

Cognitive neuropsychological perspectives, as opposed to cognitive psychological perspectives, are typically not governed by an understanding of the individual as an active reflective sense-maker, and hence they are not restricted to theorizing about delusions in such terms. Hemsley (2005) provides a good example with a speculative model of schizophrenia as being due to a deficiency in the influence of background context on current task performance. This model ties together neurological (e.g., frontotemporal functional disconnections), information processing (e.g., sensory and motor program disturbances), and psychological (a range of symptoms including delusional beliefs and experiences) levels of explanation.

Primary delusions are accordingly theorized by Hemsley as resulting from a mismatch between tacit and automatically deployed frames of reference and the sensory inputs to which they are applied. Delusional experience in the trema is also understood as due to a breakdown in gestalt or context perception. Decontextualized stimuli, including those normally screened out as irrelevant, may appear equally salient, and secondary delusional beliefs may reflect a search for the meaning of stimuli that would not normally have come to conscious attention. Hemsley speculates, for example, that delusional thinking about causal relationships may result from a failure of context to constrain judgments about the relevance of the co-occurrence of stimuli.

Future work on delusion will need to weave together the above approaches. From epistemology we require adequate understandings of what it is that grounds our relation to reality (e.g., reflective thought or bodily praxis) and what it is to lose that relation. From psychoanalysis we require an updating of the theory of delusion in the light of post-Kleinian understandings of the nature of unconscious fantasy. From phenomenology we require a precise understanding of how delusional distortions of reality contact manifest in the various (linguistic, corporeal, behavioral, intersubjective, and reflective) dimensions of human existence. And from cognitive neuropsychology we require theories aptly constrained by the above psychological domains, but informed by the latest neuro-imaging research.

REFERENCE

Conrad, K. (1958). *Die beginnende Schizophrenie. Versuch einer Gestaltanalyse des Wahns*. Stuttgart: Thieme.

Freeman, T., Cameron, J. L., & McGhie, A. (1966). *Studies on psychosis: Descriptive, psychoanalytic, and psychological aspects*. New York: International Universities Press.

Freud, S. (1981). *On psychopathology*. Harmondsworth: Penguin Books.

Garety, P., & Freeman, D. (1999). Cognitive approaches to delusions: A critical review of theories and evidence. *British Journal of Clinical Psychology, 38*, 2, 113–154.

Hemsley, D. R. (2005). The development of a cognitive model of schizophrenia: Placing it in context. *Neuroscience and Biobehavioral Reviews, 29*, 977–988.

Jaspers, K. (1913). *Allgemeine psychopathologie*. Berlin, Springer-Verlag. (Trans. J. Hoenig, & M. W. Hamilton) (1963). *General Psychopathology*. Chicago: University of Chicago Press. New edition (2 vols., paperback), with a foreword by Paul R. McHugh, (1997). Baltimore: Johns Hopkins University Press.

Maher, B. (1974). Delusional thinking and perceptual disorder. *Journal of Individual Psychology, 30*, 98–113.

Parnas, J., & Sass, L. (2001). Self, solipsism, and schizophrenic delusions. *Philosophy, Psychiatry, & Psychology, 8*, 2/3, 101–120.

Sims, A. (2003). *Symptoms in the mind* (3rd ed.). London: Elsevier.

SUGGESTED READINGS

Berrios, G. (1996). Delusions. In G. Berrios, *The history of mental symptoms: Descriptive psychopathology since the 19th century* (ch. 6). Cambridge: Cambridge University Press.

Freeman, D., Bentall, R., & Garety, P. (2008). *Persecutory delusions: Assessment, theory and treatment*. Oxford: Oxford University Press.

Munro, A. (2008). *Delusional disorder: Paranoia and related illnesses*. Cambridge: Cambridge University Press.

RICHARD G. T. GIPPS
*University of Warwick Medical School,
United Kingdom*

K. W. M. FULFORD
*University of Warwick Medical School
and Fellow of St Cross College,
Oxford, United Kingdom*

See also: Delusional Disorder, Disordered Thinking; Irrational Beliefs

DEMENTIA

Dementia is a syndrome characterized by progressive irreversible generalized cognitive decline that must include memory impairment (American Psychiatric Association [APA], 2000). Most symptoms of dementia begin in old age, with varied estimates of its prevalence due to different methodologies and analytic strategies employed, diverse types of assessments used, and disparate screening assessment cut-off points applied. The incidence of dementia is strongly correlated with age; a recent study suggests that 5% of adults over the age of 71 and perhaps 37.4% over 90 have dementia (Plassman, Langa, Fisher, et al., 2007).

Alzheimer's disease (AD) is the most common cause of dementia, accounting for 70% of the cases and costing 80 to 100 billion dollars per year in healthcare expenses and lost wages for both victims and their caregivers (Alzheimer's American Health Assistance Foundation, 2007). AD is a diagnosis most often made by exclusion, in other words, when a person is suffering from cognitive decline and all other reversible causes of this decline have been ruled out. Two types of AD have been identified: a rare type of early-onset dementia and a more common late-onset AD, which occurs after the age of 65. A reduction in the neurotransmitter acetylcholine appears to be associated with a disruption in the intercellular transmission of information leading to cognitive impairment. Chemical changes in the tau protein may be involved in the development of neurofibrillary tangles within the brain cells. These tangles and intercellular beta-amyloidal plaques must be detected for a definitive postmortem diagnosis.

The next most common cause of dementia is vascular dementia. To be diagnosed with vascular dementia there must be evidence of cerebrovascular disease; patchy deficits, executive impairment, and a step-wise disease progression (related to occurrence of multiple ministrokes) are in contrast to the steadier cognitive decline of AD. There are a variety of other causes of dementia including

Huntington's Disease, Parkinson's Disease, Pick's Disease, HIV, head trauma, substance abuse (especially alcohol), Creutzfeldt-Jakob Disease, and Lewy Body Disease (APA, 2000). On autopsy, individuals with dementia often exhibit mixed etiologies.

Multiple conditions can mimic or be comorbid with dementia (but may be reversible) including nutritional deficiencies, severe depression, medication side-effects, localized traumatic brain injury, and a myriad of medical diagnoses. Dementia should be differentiated from delirium, which often has an identifiable underlying reversible cause and is characterized by a waxing and waning of attention and clouded consciousness. Dementia should also be differentiated from amnestic syndromes, which are manifested by memory loss in the absence of other cognitive impairment.

Diverse classifications of severity of dementia have been proposed, with a varied number of stages classified on the basis of increasing functional impairment ranging from mild to severe. Dementia is frequently associated with psychiatric symptoms such as hallucinations and delusions, and with behavioral problems including agitation, wandering, hoarding, and resistance to care. As the disease progresses, persons with dementia (PWDs) are less capable of independently performing instrumental activities of daily living (i.e., shopping, handling finances, making phone calls) and eventually their basic activities of daily living (i.e., eating, transferring, toileting, dressing, grooming).

Persons with dementia must increasingly rely on others for support, and the majority of care falls on family members living in the community, especially spouses and adult children. Placement in long-term care settings is associated with severity of dementia, but also with lack of community support, functional decline, and disruptive behavior especially wandering, incontinence, and resistiveness to care that increase caregiver burden.

There are no cures for dementia, but medications known as acetylcholinesterase inhibitors such as Cognex, Aricept, Exelon, and Razadone boost levels of acetylcholine in the brain. They have been shown to have a modest effect in slowing the progression of the disease for those in its early stages and in prolonging time in the community before nursing home placement. Namenda has more recently received FDA approval for treatment of those with more severe dementia.

Much attention has focused on the pharmacological treatment of the psychiatric and behavioral problems associated with dementia. Although the atypical antipsychotic medications have been shown to be modestly effective in symptom control, use of these agents is controversial and must be weighed against their potential serious side effects including lethargy, falls, and the "metabolic syndrome" elevating cardiovascular and cerebrovascular risk (Martinez & Kunik, 2006). PWDs also frequently suffer from depression that is often underdiagnosed and untreated because the signs of depression and dementia often overlap.

Behavioral protocols have been shown to be promising in the management of undesirable behavior exhibited by PWDs. Most behavioral interventions involve meticulous analysis of the environmental antecedents of disruptive behavior, and of the consequences for the PWD, which may perpetuate the behavior (Allen-Burge, Stevens, & Burgio, 1999). Reduction of stimulation, engagement in appropriate activities, and provision of positive reinforcement for desirable behavior have been shown to reduce behavior problems. Research has shown that formal (e.g., nursing home staff) or informal (e.g., family) caregivers are capable of delivering these interventions.

Because psychiatric and physical symptoms of PWDs are related to the strains of caregiving, attenuation of caregiver stress is thereby an important therapeutic goal (Schulz et al., 2002). Caregivers need to be provided with information regarding the disease process, type of dementia, and prognosis; with education about effective behavioral intervention strategies; and with support to assist them in maintaining their own emotional well-being as they watch their loved one's inexorable decline and as they confront social isolation, vocational impediments, financial losses, and (especially if a spouse is the caregiver) their own physical limitations.

Current research reflects efforts to generate animal models for the development of an AD vaccine; to discover lifestyle modifications or medications with more efficient delivery systems that may maintain or boost acetylcholine levels and prevent accumulation of beta-amyloid deposits in the brain; to establish more refined typologies of dementia and how they relate to specific treatments and prognosis; to delineate screening methods for early detection including testing for mild cognitive impairment (MCI); to generate individualized assessment scales for specific cognitive capacities to assist in the legal determination of competencies; to confirm the adequacy of self-reports for PWDs and the ability to benefit from psychological interventions such as simplified CBT protocols; to identify the specific effective ingredients of multicomponent caregiver interventions; to develop memory enhancement techniques for those with varied levels of dementia; to address thorny ethical dilemmas associated with genetic screening; to investigate positive caregiving experiences, resilience, and their relationship to prior history of family attachments, personality traits, and coping styles; and to explore how to change the culture of long-term care environments to foster improved quality of life and the humane treatment of PWDs.

REFERENCES

Allen-Burge, R. Stevens, A. B., & Burgio, L. D. (1999). Effective behavioral interventions for decreasing dementia-related challenging behavior in nursing homes. *International Journal of Geriatric Psychiatry, 14*(3), 213–228.

Alzheimer's American Health Assistance Foundation (Spring, 2007). The Facts on Alzheimer's disease. http://www.ahaf .org SubIndex/ AD_PDF_FactSheets/ AD_stats.pdf Accessed 12/2/07.

American Psychiatric Association (2000). Diagnostic and statistical manual of mental disorders (4th ed., text rev.). Washington DC: Author.

Martinez, M., & Kunik, M. E. (2006). The role of pharamacotherpay for dementia patients with behavioral disturbances. In S. Loboprabhu, V. Molinari, & J. Lomax. (Eds.). Supporting the caregiver in dementia: A guide for health care providers (pp. 151–168). Washington DC: Johns Hopkins Press.

Plassman, B. L., Langa, K. M., Fisher, G. G., Heeringa, S. G., Weir, D. R., Ofstedal, M. B., et al. (2007). Prevalence of dementia in the United States: the aging, demographics, and memory study. Neuroepidemiology, 29(1–2), 125–132.

Schulz, R., O'Brien, A., Czaja, S., Ory, M., Norris, R., Martire, L. M., et al. (2002). Dementia caregiver intervention research: In search of clinical significance. The Gerontologist, 42, 589–602.

SUGGESTED READINGS

Mace, N. L., & Rabins, P. V. (2006). The 36-hour day: A family guide to caring for people with Alzheimer's disease, other dementias, and memory loss in later life (4th ed.). Baltimore: Johns Hopkins Press.

Reisberg, B., Ferris, S. H., de Leon M. J., & Crook, T. (1982). The Global Deterioration Scale for assessment of primary degenerative dementia. American Journal of Psychiatry, 139, 1136–1139.

Volicer L., Bass E. A., & Luther S. L. (2007). Agitation and resistiveness to care are two separate behavioral syndromes of dementia. Journal of the American Medical Directors Association, 8, 527–532.

VICTOR MOLINARI
LADISLAV VOLICER
University of South Florida

See also: Alzheimer's Disease; Late-Life Forgetting; Memory Functions; Pseudodementia

DEMENTIA PRAECOX (See Schizophrenia)

DENMARK, PSYCHOLOGY IN

Copenhagen University was founded in 1479 and reconstituted in 1539, after the Reformation. Here psychology was established as an independent discipline near the end of the nineteenth century; previously it had been taught in connection with other subjects, such as theology, philosophy, and psychiatry. Through the nineteenth century Danish philosophers pursued psychological studies in connection with such topics as sensory perception, thinking, and the psychology of personality. Among them was the renowned philosopher Søren Kierkegaard, whose writings inspired the existentialists of a later period. It was within philosophy that psychology first had a place, with Harald Høffding (1843–1931) a central figure. In 1882 he published the first Danish textbook in psychology, Psykologi i omrids på grundlag af erfaringer (Outlines of Psychology), which went into 11 editions, the last in 1930, and was also issued in several foreign languages: German, Russian, French, English, Polish, Japanese, and Italian. Høffding's psychology conforms to nineteenth-century positivism and relies on the classical division of the mind into cognition, emotion, and will.

Psychology was introduced as an independent subject at Copenhagen University in 1886, when Alfred Lehmann (1852–1921) founded a psychophysical laboratory that was subsequently taken over by the University in 1892. Lehmann had been on a study visit to Wihelm Wundt's (1832–1920) laboratory in Leipzig, and what he learned there spurred him on to conduct psychophysical experiments, which came to dominate the first phase of psychology in Denmark. Wundt also inspired the development of folk psychology, which used methods similar to those of social psychology and anthropology to investigate the regularities underlying the development of human communities and shared human values in congruence with social relations, language, morality, and religion. In 1912 Lehmann became the first Professor of Psychology at Copenhagen University, and at the same time a Magister degree in psychology was established.

When Lehmann died in 1921, Edgar Rubin (1886–1951) succeeded to the chair in psychology. In the following years, despite the spread of behaviorism to Europe, Rubin adhered to phenomenological psychology and an orientation toward German (Gestalt) psychology as the foundation both for his own work and for psychology at the Danish university. This one-sidedness in Danish academic psychology was finally broken in the period between the two world wars, when a need for psychologists arose in several areas. Psychological tests and measurements were wanted, for example, in educational institutions, in case work and psychiatry, in military psychology, and in occupational psychology. Offices were opened for school psychology and created a great demand for qualified psychologists. University studies in psychology were designed with a view to employment in these areas, especially at the Folkeskole and teachers' training colleges, and in 1944 a curriculum was officially adopted that was largely aimed at training school psychologists.

Up to and during the 1960s, new fields of psychological study and research were formulated, such as cognitive psychology, developmental psychology, neuropsychology, and social psychology, and there was increasing application of psychology in various functions in school psychology, occupational psychology, clinical psychology, and other areas. In 1960 the university study of psychology was thus revised, resulting in the curriculum that by and large is still in place today and leads to a master's degree (cand. psych). The pluralism that is the mark of Danish psychology today is inspired by a broad international field, and its diversity of different theories and methods reflects the general international division of psychology into different perspectives and areas of function. Under the auspices of the Danish Psychology Association, there are today specialized educational programs in psychotherapy, neuropsychology, health psychology, pediatric neuropsychology, geriatric psychology, child psychology, occupational and organizational psychology, psychotraumatology, psychopathology, and educational psychology.

In the course of the 1960s and 1970s, a development took place in Danish institutions that reflected a changed view of the individual's role and relation to the social context. There was a loosening up of previously authoritarian institutions. The educational system, for example, developed in the direction of differentiation, taking account of personal motivation and promoting flexibility, with an emphasis on cooperation. This meant new areas of psychological research within the educational system, and in Danish society a new understanding was opened up of teaching and learning that came to have a great influence on discussion in this context. This is evident in present Danish discussions of evaluation in the education system. These discussions involve a high level of psychological expertise, they extend from internal debates on evaluation to thoroughgoing criticism of new forms of educational management, and they promote particular actions and choices. The interdisciplinary breadth that has characterized Danish psychology will in the future characterize the development of education and training, which will thus be oriented toward the global market with its demands for standardization, individual self-management, and evaluation systems of worldwide comparability. With regard to both content and methods, these developments directly conflict with previous Danish thinking. In general, these developments should be seen in the context of societal changes that today are referred to as globalization and that produce new conditions for the production of knowledge in connection with the resolution of problems arising as a consequence of the developments. Principles pertaining to the global market are now imposed on scholarship and are in opposition to the scholarship that previously was guided by the principle of knowledge for its own sake and as a means of insight into culture, nature, and the human condition, and insight into the preconceptions and power relations which construct knowledge.

It is therefore suggested that, as a consequence of globalization and the adoption of a market mentality, Danish research-based psychology will come to lose some of its individual qualities, perhaps especially those that have characterized it in modern times: interdisciplinarity and an international orientation turned especially toward European discussions.

Since 1968 four new universities have been founded in Denmark, at all of which psychology is an academic discipline. In 2004 the Danish Research School of Psychology (http://www.drsp.dk) was established as a network linking the psychology departments of the universities, enabling them to collaborate on planning and on setting up research courses in research methods and philosophy of psychology, cognitive psychology, neuropsychology, personality and educational psychology, social and cultural psychology, developmental psychology, occupational and organizational psychology, clinical and health psychology, and cross-disciplinary psychology. This course structure will be revised in 2009.

The rate of applications to study psychology at the universities has been high throughout the years. The professional organization for psychologists in Denmark is Dansk Psykolog Forening (the Danish Association of Psychologists), which at the end of 2006 had 7,600 members, of which 1,350 were students. The Association publishes a journal for its members, *Psykolog Nyt* (New Psychologist).

BIRGITTE ELLE
Roskilde University, Roskilde, Denmark

DEPENDENCY

All human beings depend on others: at first for survival and later, for support and companionship. The need to belong and be supported is one of the most basic needs. Some individuals may manifest a more extreme need for support and be intensely preoccupied with obtaining care or being close to their significant other. Dependency refers to a core motivation to obtain and maintain nurturing and supportive relationships (cited in Pincus & Wilson, 2001), and it involves a range of traits that can be either adaptive (e.g., valuing relationships) or maladaptive (e.g., people pleasing or passivity). This personality style is often associated with emotional difficulties and maladaptive relationships (see Bornstein, 2005) and, as a result, has received a great amount of attention from clinicians. Dependent personality disorder is a recognized diagnosis in the DSM-IV. It is important to note that this diagnosis is applied only when the dependent individual's submissiveness, need to be taken care of, and fears of separation interfere with her or his functioning and cause significant distress.

Clinicians have theorized about the roots of this personality orientation, and many emphasize experiences in early childhood that undermine the child's confidence and ability to feel safe in a relationship. According to Blatt (1974), the need to be constantly reassured about the availability of care comes from early experiences when the self was experienced as helpless, ineffectual, and lonely (also see Blatt & Homann, 1992). Real or perceived abandonment could interfere with the development of feelings of safety in a relationship and later create an inordinate preoccupation with maintaining closeness. Dependency has also been attributed to overprotective or authoritarian parenting (see Bornstein, 1997) that undermines the child's ability to acquire confidence and a sense of competence. The combination of temperamental traits (e.g., susceptibility to anxiety) with adverse life circumstances (e.g., loss or overcontrolling parenting) probably accounts for the emergence of dependency.

The dependent person suffers from an insecure attachment, characterized by fears of abandonment, intense needs for support, and the dysfunctional belief that "unless I have someone to lean on, I am bound to be sad" (Zuroff, Santor, & Mongrain, 2005, for a review of the literature on cognitive, developmental, motivational, and interpersonal correlates of dependency). Dependent individuals can be deeply insecure in romantic relationships and may feel quite anxious in response to a partner's lack of availability. In fact, the dependent person's greatest fear is being abandoned, and numerous studies involving both clinical and nonclinical samples have shown that this personality orientation can predispose individuals to depression in the face of loss (see Zuroff et al., 2005, for a review). Dependent individuals are more likely to have difficulties in coping with a breakup, and their insecurities in a relationship can manifest themselves through excessive reassurance seeking. Indeed, research has shown that dependent persons are more demanding of emotional support (Mongrain, 1998) and are more neurotic (Pincus & Wilson, 2001). The need for reassurance, along with the lack of confidence, can create a burden on people in close relationships with dependent individuals.

Research has also shown that dependent individuals can be intensely interpersonally motivated, even at the expense of their own achievements. Highly dependent individuals have a greater number of interpersonal goals involving affiliation and intimacy and fewer achievement and individualistic goals (see Zuroff et al., 2005). Therefore, these individuals are less likely to emphasize their individual achievements, but rather they are motivated to please others. Dependent individuals engage in overly cooperative behaviors and act in ways that benefit friends at their own expense (see Zuroff et al., 2005). In summary, dependent individuals' needs for acceptance and affection may come at the expense of their own success. Indeed, dependency is associated with self-reported interpersonal problems of being submissive and easily exploited by others (see Zuroff et al., 2005). By placating others and undermining their own competence, dependent individuals may reinforce their own sense of helplessness and neediness. An "unhealthy dependence" factor involving submissiveness, nonassertiveness, and neediness has been found to predict major depressive disorder and the diagnosis of a personality disorder (Schulte, Mongrain, & Flora, 2008).

There are desirable traits associated with dependency. These traits have been documented in empirical studies examining the healthy versus maladaptive aspects of dependency (see Schulte et al., 2008, for a review). A healthy form of dependence involving a more connected and loving nature was found to be negatively related to depressive symptoms (Schulte et al., 2008). The fact that some individuals who are dependent are less depressed suggests that there are protective advantages to emphasizing interpersonal relationships. Dependent individuals are often seen as less angry and as trying to keep the peace. They may enjoy and profit from greater social support and are well liked by others. For example, dependent students were found to be more accepted and sought out by their roommates because they were perceived as being more nurturing and loving (cited in Zuroff et al., 2005).

In summary, research has highlighted various manifestations of dependent traits. Valuing and prioritizing relationships can be adaptive and lead to interconnectedness and positive exchanges with others. A healthier form of interpersonal dependence, however, may necessarily involve greater self-confidence, being able to assert one's needs, and being able to cope in the absence of a caring other. These inner resources are underdeveloped in those with unhealthy dependency and may be necessary to deal with the vicissitudes of relationships without undue distress.

REFERENCES

Blatt, S. J. (1974). Levels of object representation in anaclitic and introjective depression. *Psychoanalytic Study of the Child, 29*, 107–157.

Blatt, S. J., & Homann, E. (1992). Parent child interaction in the etiology of dependent and self-critical depression. *Clinical Psychology Review, 12*, 47–91.

Bornstein, R. F. (1997). Dependent personality disorder in the *DSM-IV* and beyond. *Clinical Psychology: Science and Practice, 4*, 175–187.

Bornstein, R. F. (2005). *The dependent patient: A practitioner's guide*. Washington, DC: American Psychological Association.

Mongrain, M. (1998). Parental representations and support-seeking behaviors related to dependency and self-criticism. *Journal of Personality, 66*, 151–173.

Pincus, A. L., & Wilson, K. R. (2001). Interpersonal variability in dependent personality. *Journal of Personality, 69*, 223–251.

Schulte, F. S., Mongrain, M., & Flora, D. B. (2008). Healthy and unhealthy dependence: Implications for major depression. *British Journal of Clinical Psychology, 47*, 341–353.

Zuroff, D. C., Santor, D., & Mongrain, M. (2005). Dependency, self-criticism, and maladjustment. In J. S. Auerbach, K. J. Levy, & C. E. Schaffer (Eds.), *Relatedness, self-definition, and mental representation: Essays in honor of Sidney J. Blatt*. London: Brunner-Routledge.

MYRIAM MONGRAIN
York University, Toronto, Canada

DEPENDENT PERSONALITY DISORDER

Some people are overly dependent, unable to make decisions on their own, needing frequent advice and reassurance, and alienating those around them with neediness and clinging insecurity. Studies show that when dependent personality traits become rigid and inflexible they can have myriad negative effects on social and occupational functioning (Bornstein, 1993, 2005). When dependency is both intense and pervasive, adversely affecting many different aspects of a person's life, it may indicate the presence of dependent personality disorder (DPD).

Evolution of the DPD Diagnosis

Because excessive dependency has pronounced negative effects on adjustment, problematic dependency has been formally recognized in virtually every modern diagnostic system. The most influential early conception of problematic dependency was Freud's (1905) psychosexual stage model, which contended that infants who are frustrated or overgratified during the oral phase of development (the first 6–12 months of life) will become orally fixated, develop an oral dependent character, and continue to show excessive dependency as well as a preoccupation with food, eating, and other oral activities during adulthood.

Although research did not support most aspects of Freud's oral fixation framework, his writings had a strong influence on the DSM-I conceptualization of dependency (Millon, 1996). In the DSM-I DPD was labeled *passive-dependent personality disorder*, and passive-dependent patients were described as being helpless, indecisive, and clinging to others in a childlike way. There was no mention of DPD in the DSM-II, but when the disorder reemerged in the DSM-III it was shorn of its psychoanalytic roots and described in terms of three broad symptoms: (1) pervasive passivity; (2) a tendency to subordinate personal needs to those of others; and (3) lack of self-confidence. The DSM-III-R DPD criteria, though more detailed, continued to emphasize the dependent patient's passivity, external focus, and difficulties with self-esteem and self-confidence.

DPD in the DSM-IV

The essential feature of DPD in the DSM-IV and DSM-IV-TR is "a pervasive and excessive need to be taken care of that leads to submissive and clinging behavior and fears of separation" (American Psychiatric Assocation [APA], 2000, p. 725), which must be present by early adulthood and manifest in a variety of areas. In addition, to receive a diagnosis of DPD the person must show at least five of the following eight symptoms: (1) difficulty making everyday decisions without excessive reassurance; (2) needing others to assume responsibility for most areas of life; (3) difficulty expressing disagreement; (4) difficulty initiating projects or doing things on one's own; (5) going to excessive lengths to obtain nurturance and support

from others; (6) feeling uncomfortable when alone due to fears of being unable to care for oneself; (7) urgently seeking another source of care and support when a close relationship ends; and (8) being preoccupied with fears of having to take care of oneself.

In addition to the essential criterion and eight DPD symptoms, the DSM-IV-TR lists several differential diagnoses—psychological disorders whose symptoms resemble DPD closely enough that the clinician is alerted to possible confusion and misdiagnosis. Differential diagnoses for DPD on Axis I include mood disorders, panic disorder, and agoraphobia; differential diagnoses on Axis II are borderline personality disorder (PD), histrionic PD, and avoidant PD.

The DSM-IV-TR is a bit vague regarding the prevalence rate of DPD, noting only that it is "among the most frequently reported Personality Disorders encountered in mental health settings" (APA, 2000, p. 723). Epidemiological studies suggest that the overall base rate of DPD in the adult population in America is between 1% and 2%, with the prevalence rates of DPD in psychiatric inpatient and outpatient populations averaging 3%–5% and 5%–10%, respectively. These latter prevalence rate estimates vary considerably from sample to sample, however, ranging from a low of 0% in some clinical samples to 20% or more in others (see Bornstein, 2005, for a review of these studies).

Findings regarding gender and cultural differences in DPD are more consistent. Overall the base rate of DPD in women exceeds that in men by about 50% (in other words, for every two men diagnosed with DPD three women receive the diagnosis). Studies further indicate that the base rate of DPD symptoms in people from traditionally sociocentric cultures (e.g., Japan, India) are far higher than that in people raised in more individualistic societies (e.g., America, Great Britain).

Limitations of DSM-IV DPD Diagnoses

Studies indicate that high levels of interpersonal dependency are associated with a broad array of traits and behavior patterns including help-seeking, cooperativeness, compliance with medical and psychiatric treatment, a strong desire to strengthen ties with others (especially figures of authority), fear of abandonment, and acute sensitivity to interpersonal conflict and disruption (see Bornstein, 1993, 2005, for reviews). As Bornstein (1997) noted, the diagnostic criteria for DPD in the DSM-IV, although more consistent with research on dependency than were the DPD criteria in earlier versions of the manual, are limited in at least three respects.

The Passivity Problem

The DSM-IV DPD criteria focus almost exclusively on the passive, helpless features of dependency, but research shows that dependent people—including people with

DPD—can be quite assertive (even downright aggressive) in strengthening ties to others when important relationships are threatened (Pincus & Wilson, 2001). Among the active features of dependency not captured by these criteria are assertive help-seeking in academic and medical settings, frequent pseudo-emergencies (e.g., requests for after-hours therapy sessions), and increased likelihood of perpetrating child abuse (in women) and domestic violence (in men).

The External Validity Problem

The DSM-IV DPD criteria are problematic from a validity standpoint as well. Of these eight diagnostic criteria, four (Symptoms 1, 5, 6, and 8) are supported by the results of published empirical studies, two (Symptoms 2 and 7) have never been tested empirically, and two (Symptoms 3 and 4) have been contradicted repeatedly. Research on the external validity of the DSM-IV DPD symptoms is reviewed by Bornstein (1997, 2005).

The Gender Bias Problem

The third limitation in the DSM-IV DPD criteria concerns the differential base rates of DPD in women and men. Numerous studies have shown that on measures wherein dependency is assessed primarily by self-report (e.g., interviews, questionnaires), women score higher than men do. However, when dependency is assessed via subtler measures that do not rely on self-reports (e.g., free-response tests like the Rorschach), women and men obtain comparable dependency scores (Bornstein, 1995). The degree to which observed gender differences in DPD prevalence rates may be due to overreporting of dependency in women, or underreporting in men, warrants continued investigation.

Relationship of DPD to Other Clinical Syndromes

Research in this area has focused on two issues: (1) the comorbidity (or co-occurrence) of DPD with other Axis I and Axis II diagnoses, and (2) the pathways underlying these observed relationships.

DPD-Axis I Comorbidity

The DSM-IV notes that DPD may be comorbid with three Axis I syndromes: mood disorders, anxiety disorders, and adjustment disorders. For the most part research supports these assertions, although evidence indicates that DPD is actually comorbid with some anxiety disorders (e.g., agoraphobia) but not others (e.g., generalized anxiety disorder; see Ng & Bornstein, 2005). Studies also suggest that the DPD Axis I comorbidity information in the DSM-IV may be underinclusive; in addition to the aforementioned syndromes DPD shows higher-than-expected co-occurrence with substance use disorders, eating disorders, and somatization disorder.

Documenting the comorbidity of DPD with other clinical syndromes is comparatively straightforward; delineating causal links—the underlying psychological and biological pathways that account for observed comorbidity patterns—is more complex. Three pathways appear to account for most (perhaps all) of these links. In some cases DPD represents a diathesis, or risk factor, that when coupled with one or more stressors, leads to the onset of an Axis I syndrome. Evidence suggests that this dynamic underlies the DPD–mood disorders link: When excessive dependency (diathesis) is coupled with relationship conflict or disruption (stressor), depression is likely to ensue (Bornstein, 2005). In other cases DPD and a co-occurring pathology reflect a common underlying factor, or hidden variable. For example, DPD and agoraphobia both stem in part from a view of oneself as helpless, vulnerable, and weak (Ng & Bornstein, 2005). Other DPD-pathology associations reflect a more indirect link. For example, observed associations between DPD and tobacco addiction appear to result from the dependent person's desire to please others and strengthen social ties, which renders them vulnerable to peer pressure during childhood and adolescence (Bornstein, 1993).

DPD-Axis II Comorbidity

Although the DSM-IV indicates that DPD is comorbid with only three Axis II PDs—borderline, histrionic, and avoidant—evidence confirms that DPD actually shows higher-than-expected associations with the majority of Axis II syndromes, including several that bear little resemblance to DPD, either dynamically or behaviorally (e.g., paranoid PD, obsessive-compulsive PD). Because these sorts of nonspecific comorbidity patterns have been found for other Axis II diagnoses as well, they may reflect a more generalized discriminant validity problem on Axis II (Ekselius, Lindstrom, Knorring, Bodlund, & Kullgren, 1994).

DPD across the Life Span

As questions regarding the epidemiology and comorbidity of DPD become resolved, researchers are increasingly examining the precursors of DPD, and the changing manifestations of DPD across the life span. Numerous studies have shown that two parenting styles (overprotective and authoritarian) play a role in the etiology of DPD, in part because these two parenting styles communicate to children that they are fragile and weak, and must look outward for guidance and support. In some instances overprotective and/or authoritarian parenting may be evoked by certain temperament-linked behaviors (e.g., easy startling, difficulty soothing) exhibited by infants and young children; twin and adoption studies indicate that about 30% of the variance in DPD symptom onset can be accounted for by genetic factors (Torgerson et al., 2000).

Because dependency and help-seeking are normative early in life, identifying the childhood precursors of DPD is difficult. Among the earliest behavioral manifestations of DPD are a pattern of insecure attachment, excessive clinginess around teachers, and increased incidence of school refusal. The transition to adulthood is characterized by a change in the objects (or targets) of dependency-related behavior; typically this entails a shift from dependency on parents and other authority figures (e.g., teachers) to exaggerated peer-group dependency, followed by a shift during early and middle adulthood from reliance on peers to dependency on romantic partners, colleagues, and supervisors at work (see Bornstein, 1993, 2005, for a review of relevant research).

There have been no well-controlled studies of DPD in later adulthood, in part because of the difficulty distinguishing excessive dependency from the expectable losses of normal aging. Studies consistently show an increase in functional (but not emotional) dependency during later adulthood, and some investigations suggest that as individuals with DPD age they may express dependency strivings in age-normative, indirect ways. Increases in somatic complaints, and cognitive impairment with no identifiable neurological cause (sometimes called *pseudodementia*) are common manifestations of DPD in later life.

DPD in the DSM-V

As the DPD diagnostic criteria are revised for the DSM-V, two issues warrant attention. First, greater attention must be paid to the active components of DPD, and to situational variability in dependency-related behavior. By doing this clinicians and researchers will capture more completely the range of maladaptive and adaptive behaviors associated with DPD, and can tailor intervention programs to minimizing dependency's problematic aspects (e.g., relationship stress, depression risk) while strengthening its more adaptive features (e.g., conscientiousness during medical and psychological treatment).

Increased focus on the psychological processes that underlie DPD is also needed. Research indicates that a perception of oneself as weak and ineffectual (sometimes called a "helpless self-concept") is central to the etiology and dynamics of DPD (Bornstein, 1996, 1997). This cognitive element of dependency is not present in the DSM-IV DPD essential feature or symptom criteria, however. Inclusion of the cognitive features of DPD would not only lead to more accurate diagnosis and less problematic comorbidity patterns, but would also provide a conceptual and empirical foundation for examining context-driven variations in dependency-related behavior.

REFERENCES

American Psychiatric Association (2000). *Diagnostic and statistical manual of mental disorders* (4th ed., text rev.). Washington, DC: Author.

Bornstein, R. F. (1993). *The dependent personality*. New York: Guilford Press.

Bornstein, R. F. (1995). Sex differences in objective and projective dependency tests: A meta-analytic review. *Assessment, 2,* 319–331.

Bornstein, R. F. (1996). Beyond orality: Toward an object relations/interactionist reconceptualization of the etiology and dynamics of dependency. *Psychoanalytic Psychology, 13,* 177–203.

Bornstein, R. F. (1997). Dependent personality disorder in the DSM-IV and beyond. *Clinical Psychology: Science and Practice, 4,* 175–187.

Bornstein, R. F. (2005). *The dependent patient: A practitioner's guide.* Washington, DC: American Psychological Association.

Ekselius, L., Lindstrom, E., Knorring, L., Bodlund, O., & Kullgren, G. (1994). Comorbidity among personality disorders in DSM-III-R. *Personality and Individual Differences, 17,* 155–160.

Freud, S. (1905). Three essays on the theory of sexuality. *SE 7,* (pp. 125–248). London: Hogarth.

Millon, T. (1996). *Disorders of personality: DSM-IV and beyond.* New York: John Wiley & Sons.

Ng, H. M., & Bornstein, R. F. (2005). Comorbidity of dependent personality disorder and anxiety disorders: A meta-analytic review. *Clinical Psychology: Science and Practice, 12,* 395–406.

Pincus, A. L., & Wilson, K. R. (2001). Interpersonal variability in dependent behavior. *Journal of Personality, 69,* 744–758.

Torgerson, S., Lygren, S., Oien, P. A., Skre, I., Onstad, S., Evardsen, J., et al. (2000). A twin study of personality disorders. *Comprehensive Psychiatry, 41,* 416–425.

SUGGESTED READINGS

Coen, S. J. (1982). *The misuse of persons: Analyzing pathological dependency.* Hillsdale, NJ: Analytic Press.

Huprich, S. K. (Ed.). (2006). *Rorschach assessment of the personality disorders.* Mahwah, NJ: Lawrence Erlbaum.

Pincus, A. L., & Gutman, M. B. (1995). The three faces of interpersonal dependency: Structure analysis of self-report dependency measures. *Journal of Personality and Social Psychology, 69,* 744–758.

ROBERT F. BORNSTEIN
Adelphi University

See also: **Dependency; Personality Disorders**

DEPENDENT VARIABLES

Dependent variable is a term used in research methods and refers to the attribute being measured. In experimental research the dependent variable is what is being assessed to determine the effect of manipulating the independent variable. The term dependent variable is also labeled as the *criterion measure* by some research methodologists. The dependent variable or variables (it is not unusual to record multiple measures in an investigation) may involve behavioral, physiological, or social characteristics, depending on the nature of the study. It may involve assessment of performance, such as the amount of information a participant might learn as measured by the number of correct responses on a test.

A dependent variable is what is being measured to ascertain the effects of some treatment in an investigation or to use as a description of the status of participants in the study. For example, if two methods of math instruction were being compared, the dependent variable might be the number of correct responses on a math test administered after instruction is completed. Alternatively, a demographic investigation may measure household income in dollars per year, the average age of the adult caregivers, or any number of different descriptive characteristics depending on the general nature of the study.

The choice of a dependent measure is a very important step when researchers are designing studies. Selection of an appropriate dependent variable is crucial to the overall strength, outcome, and interpretation of an investigation. A number of matters should be considered in determining the appropriateness of the dependent variable selected.

One important consideration is that a dependent measure should reflect the topic being studied. If a researcher is investigating anxiety, the dependent variable should relate to the construct of anxiety. A dependent variable should also be both sensitive and reliable in the context of the phenomenon under study. From a sensitivity standpoint, the measure should be sufficiently sensitive to accurately detect behavioral or performance changes when they occur. The dependent measure should be able to reflect such changes in a reliable fashion, which means that the level of error in classifying or recording performances should be low. It is very common for investigators to determine how reliable their measure is and reporting measure reliability is typically viewed as a requirement for soundly conducted studies.

Generally, a researcher will select the most sensitive and reliable dependent variable possible. The only circumstance in which this rule of thumb is not appropriate is when such a measure is obtrusive; that is, when the act of obtaining the measure alters a subject's behavior. If a particular measure is adequately sensitive but appears to be obtrusive, another dependent variable may be preferred so that the data obtained are not contaminated. Thus, the measure of choice is one that represents a balance of high sensitivity, highly reliable, and as unobtrusive as possible.

Another consideration related to selection of a dependent variable involves avoiding ceiling or floor effects in the data. A ceiling effect occurs when the performance range of the task is limited so that participants "top out" and their performance reflects the ceiling of the measure rather than their actual ability to perform. A floor effect occurs when a task so difficult that many participants cannot perform the task at all and the data are more reflective of task range limits than the participants' ability to perform. Ceiling and floor effects generate inaccurate results or data that represents an artifact. In circumstances where either ceiling or floor effects exist, the data indicate the limits of the task rather than the participants' ability to perform.

REFERENCES

Colton, D., & Covert, R. W. (2007). *Designing and constructing instruments for social research and evaluation*. Hoboken, NJ: John Wiley & Sons.

Drew, C. J., Hardman, M. L., & Hosp, J. L. (2008). *Designing and conducting research in education*. Los Angeles: Sage Publications.

Mertens, D. M. (2005). Research and evaluation in education and psychology: *Integrating diversity with quantitative, qualitative, and mixed methods* (2nd ed.). Thousand Oaks, CA: Sage Publications.

SUGGESTED READINGS

Christensen, L. B. (2007). *Experimental methodology*. Boston: Pearson/Allyn & Bacon.

Eid, M., & Diener, E. (2005). *Handbook of multimethod measurement in psychology*. Washington, DC: American Psychological Association.

Suter, W. N. (2006). *Introduction to educational research: A critical thinking approach*. Thousand Oaks, CA: Sage Publications.

CLIFFORD J. DREW
University of Utah

DEPERSONALIZATION DISORDER

Depersonalization (DP) is classified in the *Diagnostic and Statistical Manual of Mental Disorders* (DSM-IV-TR) as a dissociative disorder defined as "persistent or recurrent experiences of feeling detached from, and as if one is an outside observer of, one's mental processes or body (e.g. feeling like one is in a dream)" (American Psychiatric Association [APA], 2000, p. 532). DP commonly co-occurs with the phenomena of derealization (DR), defined as "the sense that the external world is strange or unreal" (APA, 2000, p. 530).

These operational definitions, although widely used, are largely confined to feelings of unreality and neglect the phenomenological complexity of DP, which is best conceptualized as a syndrome with five symptom constellations:

1. Depersonalization, which is an alteration in the experience of the self, a distressing sense of being a

stranger to oneself ("as if it wasn't me"). There may be a sense of lacking full control of one's thoughts, voice, or actions (loss of agency) and a heightened and obsessive self-observation ("I check constantly and it's never me"). Some individuals fear their identity is vanishing, looking in the mirror seeking to regain a sense of self.

2. Derealization, in which familiar objects, surroundings, and people are perceived devoid of their former emotional tone leading to a threatening sense of unfamiliarity. The world may appear artificial or 2-D ("everything looks like a replica"). Objects' size and color may become distorted ("as if looking through a goldfish-bowl"), and people may feel like actors ("as if I'm in a film").

3. Deaffectualization, which is an attenuation or loss in the experiencing of feelings (emotional numbing), while affective reactions remain normal, described as just going through the motions, ("I'm laughing but feel nothing").

4. Desomatization, which is a sense of disembodiment, as if parts of the body do not belong to oneself. There is an attenuation or loss of bodily feelings like hunger, thirst, or pain, and a distorted experience of body parts' sizes.

5. Deideation, which consists of anomalous perceptions of time duration, altered experience of autobiographical memories, conjuring episodes without feeling part of them, inability to evoke images or to focus or to sustain attention, and feeling like the mind is empty of thoughts. Insight into the subjective nature ("as if") of each of these experiences remains intact.

DP occurs on a continuum from normal transient experiences in healthy individuals, often under conditions of fatigue or drug-use, to recurrent or persistent episodes in clinical populations. The term symptomatic or secondary DP refers to cases in which symptoms of DP are embedded in the context of some other primary psychiatric disorder (e.g., panic disorder) or a medical condition (e.g., temporal-lobe epilepsy), whereas primary depersonalization disorder (DPD) is reserved for cases in which symptoms of DP are the sole or predominant complaint, independent of other comorbid conditions. The phenomenology of DP symptoms is similar across the continuum, but in DPD they tend to run a chronic course causing marked dysfunction.

Epidemiology

Transient symptoms of DP are common in nonclinical populations, with lifetime prevalence rates 26%–74%. Lifetime prevalence of symptomatic DP was found in 80% of psychiatric inpatients, suggesting that DP might be the third most common psychiatric symptom, after depression and anxiety. Challenging the persisting assumption

that DPD is rare, two large cohorts (204 and 117 persons) have been documented by the two world leading DP research units at the Maudsley (London) and Mount Sinai Hospital (New York) (Baker et al., 2003; Simeon, Knutelska, Nelson, & Guralnik, 2003). Moreover, community surveys revealed 1.6%–1.9% one-month prevalence rates (United Kingdom sample) and a 2.4% current prevalence rate (Canadian sample). Onset is typically in late adolescence and early adulthood and affects men and women equally. Only 5%–10% of cases report a family history of DPD. Onset can be acute or insidious. Although DPD can be suffered episodically or continuously, it tends to run a chronic course. In 10% of cases, DPD emerges episodically and subsequently becomes continuous. Frequent precipitants include drug use (particularly cannabis), an episode of another psychiatric condition, severe and prolonged stress, or a traumatic event. Comorbid anxiety and mood disorders and personality disorders are frequent. The phenomenology, severity, and course of DPD are not determined by type of onset, precipitant, or comorbidity (Simeon, 2004).

Diagnosis

DPD remains underdiagnosed, and it is often misdiagnosed as depression, anxiety, or schizophrenia, with an average duration of misdiagnosis running 7–10 years. Clinicians' restricted familiarity with DP and patients' difficulties conveying their distressing experiences contribute to this situation. The Cambridge Depersonalization Scale is considered the most detailed self-report measure capturing the phenomenological complexity of DPD (Sierra & Berrios, 2000). However, the diagnosis of DPD rests on a thorough clinical interview.

Etiology

The conceptualization of DPD as a dissociative or anxiety disorder remains contentious. Whereas marked alterations in the previously integrated sense of self can be regarded as core dissociative phenomena, other features of dissociative disorders, such as amnesia, are rare in DPD, prompting authorities to distinguish two dissociative types: detachment (DP/DR) and compartmentalization (dissociative amnesia, fugue, and identity disorder). Conversely, comorbid anxiety disorders are frequent in DPD, and transient DP is extremely common in states of extreme anxiety and in life-threatening situations. Two models, one neurobiological and the other cognitive, underscore the role of anxiety in the pathogenesis and maintenance of DPD.

Neurobiological Model

The neurobiological model posits that DP is a "hard-wired vestigial response for dealing with extreme anxiety"

(Sierra & Berrios, 1998, p. 903) that, although protective in its transient form, becomes dysfunctional and abnormally persistent in DPD. A frontolimbic disconnection is proposed involving (1) a left-medial prefrontal overactivation that inhibits limbic regions (e.g., the amygdala), generates a state of hypoemotionality (deaffectualization), disrupts the process of "emotional-coloring" of cognition and perception of the self (depersonalization, desomatization), others, and surroundings (derealization), which experienced as qualitatively changed and reported as unreal; and (2) a right-dorsolateral prefrontal overactivation that inhibits the anterior cingulated and generates a state of hyperalertness and a distressing sense of heightened self-observation and mind-emptiness (deideation). These distressing experiences increase anxiety and generate a perpetuating cycle. Supporting this model, psychophysiological studies revealed attenuated autonomic responses to unpleasant stimuli and facial expressions of disgust in DPD, and fMRI studies showed increased prefrontal activation and limbic suppression in response to aversive scenes and emotionally intense facial expressions.

Cognitive Model

The cognitive model proposes that, whereas most individuals attribute benign transitory symptoms of DP to situational factors (e.g., anxiety), dismissing them and thereby facilitating their natural fading, those developing chronic DPD interpret them as indicative of impending madness or brain dysfunction. This maladaptive appraisal, postulated to depend on underlying assumptions regarding vulnerability to mental illness, increases anxiety and exacerbates and perpetuates the initial symptoms. In seeking to avoid mental health catastrophes, individuals engage in maladaptive behavioral patterns leading to the vicious maintenance cycle of symptoms. These include avoidance of situations believed to aggravate symptoms (e.g., social gatherings), safety behaviors (e.g., acting normal), and cognitive and attentional biases including increased symptom monitoring and heightened self-observation (Hunter, Phillips, Chalder, Sierra, & David, 2003).

Treatments

Pharmacological Treatments

To date, there are no recognized pharmacological guidelines for treating DPD, but some promising treatments are emerging (Sierra, 2008). Selective serotonin-reuptake inhibitors (SSRIs) and benzodiazepines have proved beneficial, particularly for cases with prominent comorbid anxiety or depression, but they have failed to show potent anti-depersonalization effects. More encouragingly, two studies using opioid receptor agonists demonstrated a clinically significant symptom reduction in many cases.

Finally, two open-label trials using lamotrigine as an add-on medication with SSRIs revealed clinical improvements in 50%–70% of cases.

Psychological Therapies

There are no evidence-based psychotherapeutic protocols for DPD. However, single-case reports relying on clinical judgment to evaluate outcome have documented positive effects employing psychoanalytic techniques, family therapy, and behavioral strategies. In a recent open study, 21 DPD patients were individually treated using a cognitive-behavioral protocol encompassing psychoeducation and normalization of the experience, which are known to provide considerable relief; diary keeping of symptoms; reduction of avoidance and safety behaviors; reduction of self-focused attention; and challenging catastrophic assumptions using behavioral experiments. Results showed a clinically significant reduction in symptom severity using reliable and valid self-report measures of DP. Gains were maintained at six-month follow-up (Hunter, Baker, Phillips, Sierra, & David, 2005). Taken together, the findings from pharmacological and psychotherapeutic studies revealed promising lines of treatments to deal with this disabling and treatment-resistant condition.

REFERENCE

American Psychiatric Association. (2000). *Diagnostic and statistical manual of mental disorders* (4th ed., text rev.). Washington, DC: Author.

Baker, D., Hunter, E., Lawrence, E., Medford, N., Patel, M., Senior, C., et al. (2003). Depersonalization disorder: Clinical features of 204 cases. *British Journal of Psychiatry, 182,* 428–433.

Hunter, E. C., Baker, D., Phillips, M. L. Sierra, M., & David, A. S. (2005). Cognitive behaviour therapy for depersonalisation disorder: An open study. *Behaviour Research and Therapy, 43,* 1121–1130.

Hunter, E. C., Phillips, M. L., Chalder, T., Sierra, M., & David, A. S. (2003). Depersonalisation disorder: A cognitive-behavioural conceptualization. *Behaviour Research and Therapy, 41,* 1121–1130.

Sierra, M. (2008). Depersonalization disorder: Pharmacological approaches. *Expert Review of Neurotherapeutics, 8,* 19–26.

Sierra, M., & Berrios, G. E. (1998). Depersonalization: Neurobiological perspectives. *Biological Psychiatry, 44,* 898–908.

Sierra, M., & Berrios, G. E. (2000). The Cambridge Depersonalization Scale: A new instrument for the measurement of depersonalization. *Psychiatry Research, 93,* 153–164.

Simeon, D. (2004). Depersonalization disorder: A contemporary overview. *CNS Drugs, 18,* 343–354.

Simeon, D., Knutelska, M., Nelson, D., & Guralnik, O. (2003). Feeling unreal: A depersonalization disorder update of 117 cases. *Journal of Clinical Psychiatry, 64,* 990–997.

SUGGESTED READINGS

Baker, D., Hunter, E., Lawrence, E., & David, A. (2007). *Overcoming depersonalization & feelings of unreality: A self-help guide using cognitive-behavioral techniques.* London: Robinson.

Blanco-Campal, A. (2006). Depersonalization disorder. In A. Carr & M. MacNulty (Eds.), *The handbook of adult clinical psychology: An evidence-based practice approach.* (pp. 1010–1063). London: Brunner-Routledge.

Daphne, S., & Abugel, J. (2006). Feeling unreal: *Depersonalization disorder and the loss of the self.* New York: Oxford University Press.

ALBERTO BLANCO-CAMPAL
University College Dublin, Ireland

See also: **Dissociative Disorders**

DEPRESSION

Within psychology, the term depression is typically used to refer to a Major Depressive Episode. A depressive episode is most frequently part of a Major Depressive Disorder, but it may also be a part of bipolar or cyclothymic disorders in which there is fluctuation between periods of excessively elevated moods and depression.

In the United States, there are nine symptoms included in the formal guidelines for diagnosing depression. To receive the diagnosis, a person must report experiencing five or more of those symptoms during most of the day and nearly every day for at least a two-week period. In addition, at least one of the symptoms must be either (1) persistent sad mood, or (2) inability to experience pleasure in most or all activities. Additional symptoms include significant change in weight or appetite, significant increase or decrease in time spent sleeping, excessive motor activity (e.g., fidgetiness) or a noticeable decrease in motor activity, fatigue or loss of energy, feelings of worthlessness or excessive/inappropriate guilt, difficulty concentrating or making decisions, and thoughts of suicide or any plans or attempts to commit suicide (American Psychiatric Association, 2000). The number of possible combinations of the listed symptoms makes depression a very heterogeneous disorder. In addition, many people experience subsyndromal depression in which they do not meet full diagnostic criteria of five or more symptoms but report some depressive symptoms. The person must also experience significant impairment or disruption in functioning as a result of the depressive episode.

Epidemiology

Major Depressive Disorder is the most commonly diagnosed mental disorder. Lifetime prevalence rates refer to the percentage of individuals who will, at some point in their lives, experience a major depressive episode. Depending on survey methods, lifetime prevalence rates for depression have ranged from as little as 6% to as high as 25%. There is wide agreement that a lifetime prevalence rate of approximately 17% represents an accurate figure. The percentage of currently depressed individuals, or the point prevalence rate, is estimated to be between 2% and 4% in adults (Kessler, in press). In general, women are diagnosed with depression about twice as frequently as men. Some research also suggests that depression prevalence is increasing with subsequent generations and that lifetime prevalence for current 18- to 25- year olds may be closer to 20%–25%. Depression is seen in childhood but more frequently emerges during or shortly after adolescence. In addition, it is common among those over 65 and frequently co-occurs with other mental disorders including substance abuse and anxiety disorders.

Typically, a depressive disorder will remit, even without treatment, within 6–12 months of initial onset. However, Major Depressive Disorder is frequently conceptualized as a relapsing-remitting disorder, in that occurrence of one major depressive episode renders a person much more likely to experience subsequent episodes of depression. Among individuals with one prior episode, the likelihood of experiencing another episode is approximately 50%, and among those with two prior episodes, the likelihood of another episode increases to approximately 75%. For those with three prior episodes, the likelihood of an additional episode is greater than 90% (Kessler & Walters, 1998).

The nature of the symptoms of depression speaks to the immense suffering of the individuals who experience them (e.g., persistent sadness, loss of pleasure, suicidal thoughts). However, disruption is seen beyond just people who experience depression. Those interacting with depressed people frequently experience added stress, and depression is among the most expensive worldwide health problems in terms of lost productivity (Greenberg et al., 2003).

Causes

Depression has been theorized to result from a variety of causes. The most widespread and empirically supported theories are biological, cognitive, and interpersonal theories of depression. Biological theories are supported by the findings that first-degree relatives of a person who has been depressed are at elevated risk for depression themselves. In the most prominent biological theory, it is believed that depression results from a dysregulation of the neurotransmitters serotonin and norepinephrine. This theory is supported by the finding that a specific variant of a gene implicated in serotonin transport efficiency (termed the "serotonin transporter gene") has been directly linked to increased risk for depression following stressful life events (Caspi, Sugden, Moffitt, Taylor, & Craig, 2003). In cognitive theories, it is proposed that depression results from negative life experiences, which lead to an increased tendency to think negatively about oneself and one's environment. This theory is supported by research showing that among people never previously depressed, a tendency to view the world and the self in a negative way is associated with increased subsequent risk for depression (Ingram, Miranda, & Segal, 1998). In interpersonal theories, it is proposed that depression is a reaction to social rejection. Evidence for interpersonal theories includes the finding that people with lower levels of social support are at increased risk for depression and that tendencies to irritate one's social supports are associated with subsequent depression risk (Segrin & Dillard, 1992). Although each of these theories has been studied individually, and although there is evidence for the validity of each of them, many psychologists recognize that there is no one cause and that the various causes are likely to interact. For example, in diathesis-stress theories it is speculated that the combination of a genetic predisposition and stressful life experiences leads to depression.

Treatments

Consistent with the diversity of proposed causal explanations, there is also a wide variety of treatments used for depression. Medication is the most common treatment, and a variety of classes of drugs are used to treat depression. Selective serotonin reuptake inhibitors (SSRIs) are by far the most widely prescribed class of antidepressants. As the name suggests, SSRIs decrease the reabsorption of serotonin in the brain, thus increasing the presence of serotonin. Some examples of popular SSRIs include fluoxetine (Prozac), paroxetine (Paxil), and sertraline (Zoloft). The newest class of medications approved for treatment of depression is dual serotonin and norepinephrine reuptake inhibitors (SNRIs), which work similarly to SSRIs but also target norepinephrine. Commonly used SNRIs include Duloxetine (Cymbalta) and Venlafaxine (Effexor). Reported side effects of SSRIs and SNRIs are typically mild, with the exception that SSRIs are frequently associated with decreased sexual functioning. Tricyclic antidepressants and monoamine oxidase inhibitors (MAOIs) are older antidepressant medications. They are used much less often than SSRIs due to the frequency and severity of their side effects and some dietary limitations associated with MAOIs. However, they may be especially helpful for depressed persons who do not respond to SSRIs or SNRIs.

Severe cases of depression are sometimes treated with electroconvulsive therapy (ECT), in which electric shocks are passed through the brain. ECT is often quite effective at reducing depressive symptoms in the short term, although symptoms often return within several weeks if additional forms of treatment are not utilized. Although memory loss is a frequent side effect of ECT, refinements to the procedure appear to have minimized the extent of

the memory loss (Loo, Schweitzer, & Pratt, 2006). Transcranial magnetic stimulation (rTMS) and vagus nerve stimulation are recently developed procedures in which brain activity appears to be stimulated by strong magnetic fields. Although they have only been recently developed, initial results show these treatments, especially rTHMS, are effective at decreasing depression in the short term, with minimal side effects reported.

Although numerous types of psychotherapy exist, only two specific forms of psychotherapy, cognitive-behavioral therapy (CBT) and interpersonal therapy (IPT), have been extensively researched and shown to be effective in treating depression. Both therapies are relatively short-term, consisting of 16 to 20 sessions taking place over 12 to 16 weeks. In CBT, therapists work with clients toward the goal of altering negative thinking styles. In IPT, the goal is to help clients manage interpersonal difficulties associated with depression. Possible foci of IPT include life transitions, losses, improving social skills improvement, and role conflicts. Therapists and clients select the most relevant areas from among these options and target the topics in therapy.

IPT, CBT, and antidepressant medications appear to be approximately equally effective for the treatment of depression. Most studies show a significant reduction in depressive symptoms occurring for 50%–65% of people who utilize such treatments. For severe depression, antidepressant medication may be more effective than psychotherapy in targeting acute symptoms. However, psychotherapy appears to be particularly helpful in reducing risk for relapse of depression, especially if medications are discontinued after depression remission. Thus, a combination of medication and psychotherapy is widely recommended as the most effective and longest lasting treatment for depression.

REFERENCES

American Psychiatric Association. (2000). *Diagnostic and statistical manual of mental disorders* (4th ed., text rev.). Washington, DC: Author.

Caspi, A., Sugden, K., Moffitt, T. E., Taylor, A., Craig, I. W. (2003). Influence of life-stress on depression: Moderation by a polymorphism in the 5-HTT gene. *Science, 301*, 386–389.

Greenberg, P. E., Kessler, R. C., Birnbaum, H. G., Leong, S. A., Lowe, S. W., Berglund, P. A. et al. (2003). The economic burden of depression in the United States: How did it change between 1990 and 2000? *Journal of Clinical Psychiatry, 64*, 1465–1475.

Ingram, R. E., Miranda, J., & Segal, Z. (1998). *Cognitive vulnerability to depression*. New York: Guilford Press.

Kessler, R. C. (In press). Epidemiology. In R. E. Ingram (Ed.), *The international encyclopedia of depression*. New York: Springer.

Kessler, R. C., & Walters, E. E. (1998). Epidemiology of DSM-III-R major depression and minor depression among adolescents and young adults in the National Comorbidity Study. *Depression and Anxiety, 7*, 3–14.

Loo, C. K., Schweitzer, I., & Pratt, C. (2006). Recent advances in optimizing electroconvulsive therapy. *Australian and New Zealand Journal of Psychiatry, 40,* 632–638.

Segrin, C., & Dillard, J. P. (1992). The interactional theory of depression: A meta-analysis of the research literature. *Journal of Social and Clinical Psychology, 11,* 43–70.

SUGGESTED READINGS

Gotlib, I. H., & Hammen, C. L. (2008). *Handbook of depression.* New York: Guilford Press.

Ingram, R. E. (2009). *The international encyclopedia of depression.* New York: Springer.

DANA STEIDTMANN
RICK INGRAM
University of Kansas

See also: Adolescent Depression; Culture and Depression; Lifespan Depression; Postpartum Depression

DEPRESSIVE PERSONALITY DISORDER

Since 1994, the American Psychiatric Association has been considering the proposal of Depressive Personality Disorder (DPD) for inclusion in future editions of the *Diagnostic and Statistical Manual of Mental Disorders, Fourth Edition* (DSM-IV; American Psychiatric Association, [APA], 1994). The disorder and related syndromes have had a rich history in the history of philosophy, disease classification, and psychiatry, going back to the Greek philosophers who described melancholic character as one of four basic character types. According to the DSM-IV (APA, 1994) and DSM-IV-TR (APA, 2000), individuals are diagnosed with DPD when they meet five of the seven following criteria: (1) usual mood is joyless, cheerless, and dysphoric; (2) the self-concept centers around feelings of worthlessness and the individual has low self-esteem; (3) the individual is self-critical; (4) the individual broods or worries frequently; (5) the individual is negative or critical of others; (6) the individual is pessimistic; and (7) the individual often feels guilty or remorseful. DSM-IV (APA, 1994) states that this disorder is not to be diagnosed when these criteria "occur exclusively during Major Depressive Episodes" of if they are "better accounted for by Dysthymic Disorder" (APA, 1994, p. 733).

With the formal introduction of DPD into the *DSM* system, there has been much controversy. For instance, it was initially argued that there was not enough preexisting evidence to warrant the creation of this new diagnostic category and that its proposed features overlapped too much with Dysthymic Disorder (Ryder & Bagby, 1999). However, evidence has been gathered that refutes these ideas (Huprich, 2001, 2008). DPD can be reliably distinguished from Dysthymia and other personality disorders, though its overlap with them is considerable. For instance, Huprich (2001) found that approximately 50% of the patients who meet criteria for DPD also meet criteria for Dysthymia. Likewise, when DPD is assessed along with other personality disorders in patient populations, it most often co-occurs with Avoidant, Borderline, and Obsessive Compulsive Personality Disorders.

Part of the challenge in evaluating the validity and ultimate future of DPD in the diagnostic manuals is that existing DPD measures do not converge well, either in their correlations with each other or in their capacity to identify the same individuals as meeting the DPD diagnostic criterion (Huprich, 2008). Yet, evidence exists that each of these measures has construct validity. Obviously, this measurement problem complicates the issue of how to determine whether DPD is a real phenomenon that has clinical utility (Huprich, 2008) if there is no measure of it that is considered the gold standard.

Another present challenge to the future of the DPD category is related to the manner by which personality disorders are diagnosed. It has been suggested by many that PDs should be evaluated and assessed dimensionally, as current categorical models of diagnosis have yielded considerable diagnostic overlap, and their measures have yielded questionable psychometric properties (Widiger & Lowe, 2007). After considering the diagnostic overlap of DPD and Dysthymia, the results of factor analytic studies of DPD and Dysthymia symptoms, as well as research on shared familial vulnerability to mood disorders and DPD, Ryder, Schuller, and Bagby (2006) suggested that the overlap of DPD with Dysthymia is representative of an affective spectrum of psychiatric illness. Even though research, including their own, suggests that the two disorders can be differentiated by the clustering of symptoms, Ryder et al. (2006) suggest that adopting a dimensional orientation to chronic affective disturbance solves the problem of whether DPD and Dysthymia are separate disorders, belonging on different diagnostic axes. They advocate for further research on the overlap of the diagnostic criteria as one way of better differentiating the two disorders. Huprich (2001) has indicated that the use of dimensional models of personality may be useful in better discriminating the two disorders. And indeed, what little research has been done on this idea has found that DPD and Dysthymia may be differentiated empirically on theoretically relevant personality dimensions (Huprich, 2008).

However, much additional research is needed on this issue to demonstrate whether this approach has utility in differentiating these two disorders. The position advocated by Ryder et al. (2006) is reasonable when considering these categories and symptoms in light of the DSM-IV criteria. Yet, it is not clear that Ryder et al. (2006), and those of like mind, will advocate for the inclusion of this diagnostic construct as part of the standard diagnostic nomenclature. A contrary stance has been taken by Huprich (2008), who argues that the diagnosis does merit ongoing consideration. Besides the favorable research on the validity of the disorder, his position is based on the research of Westen and Shedler (1999), who surveyed practicing psychiatrists and psychologists. They found that clinicians often see and treat patients who appear to have DPD. Even more specifically, clinicians report that the DPD prototype was the most commonly observed prototype in their clinical practice. Huprich (2008) states that the ecological utility of this data serves as a testament to the clinical utility of this diagnostic construct.

So, what is to become of DPD in the DSM-V? The answer is not clear at the present time. Huprich (2008) has stated that the research evidence provides sufficient support to continue to consider the inclusion of DPD in the diagnostic manuals. He writes, "... it would be an error at present to conclude DPD is not a valid and useful personality disorder construct that is distinct from Dysthymia. Although some may view DPD as an unwanted bastard child in the diagnostic nomenclature, it appears not to be going away—its empirical voice speaks to us in ways that should not be ignored" (p. 29). Yet, it is the members of the DSM committee that make these decisions, and it can only be hoped that these individuals will give a place in the manual to this interesting, though somewhat perplexing, diagnostic construct.

REFERENCES

Huprich, S. K. (2001). The overlap between depressive personality disorder and dysthymia, revisited. *Harvard Review of Psychiatry*, 9, 158–168.

Huprich, S. K. (2008). What should become of depressive personality disorder in DSM-V? *Harvard Review of Psychiatry*, 17(1), 41–59.

Ryder, A. G., & Bagby, R. M. (1999). Diagnostic viability of the depressive personality disorder: Theoretical and conceptual issues. *Journal of Personality Disorders*, 13, 99–117.

Ryder, A. G., Schuller, D. R., & Bagby, R. M. (2006). Depressive personality disorder and dysthymia: Evaluating symptom and syndrome overlap. *Journal of Affective Disorders*, 91, 217–227.

Westen, D., & Shedler, J. (1999). Revising and assessing Axis II, Part II: Toward an empirically based and clinically useful classification of personality disorders. *American Journal of Psychiatry*, 156, 273–285.

Widiger, T. A., & Lowe, J. A. (2007). Five-factor model assessment of personality disorder. *Journal of Personality Disorders*, 89, 16–29.

SUGGESTED READINGS

McWilliams, N. (1994). *Psychoanalytic diagnosis*. New York: Guilford Press.

Millon, T. (with Davis, R. D.). (1996). *Disorders of personality: DSM-IV and beyond*. New York: John Wiley & Sons.

STEVEN K. HUPRICH
Eastern Michigan University

See also: Depression; Dysthymic Disorder; Personality Disorders

DEPTH PERCEPTION

How do people perceive the three-dimensional qualities of the world and the objects in it? Most investigators believe that the primary information for perception is the images projected onto our retinas. The problem of depth perception would thereby seem to be intractable; our visual system gets information limited to two dimensions (the projected retinal images), which does not uniquely determine any single three-dimensional characteristics of the world. Yet we somehow perceive the three-dimensional world that made those projections, and quite accurately in most circumstances. The two-dimensional images are inherently ambiguous as to size and distance (e.g., large objects that are distant create the same projection as small objects that are close) as well as orientation (a rectangle and a trapezoid can both create the same retinal projection). People solve this problem, called the inverse projection problem, by combining four types of information, or depth cues: (1) oculomotor, (2) stereo, (3) pictorial, and (4) motion cues.

The first type of depth cues is called oculomotor depth cues because they are based on the movement of the eye and the muscles that control eye movement. The first of these is accommodation, or the changing of the shape of the lens. To focus on a distant object, the lens flattens; to focus on a nearby one, the lens becomes more rounded. The visual system uses the thickness of the lens as a cue to the distance of the object from the observer. However, this cue is only valuable for objects approximately within arms' reach; for farther objects, the lens adjustments are very small and are of little informational value. Convergence is the degree to which the eyes rotate in to focus on an object. For close objects, the eyes must rotate more than for far objects. Like accommodation, this cue is most valuable at relatively close distances.

Stereopsis involves using the difference in the images in each of the two eyes, called binocular disparity. For objects close to the observer, the difference between the two retinal images is large, whereas for objects far away, the difference is relatively small. 3-D movies (such as those viewed with red and green glasses) utilize this depth cue by using colored filters to present different images to each eye, thereby evoking depth by artificially providing binocular disparity information.

The third type of depth cues are those that can be seen with one eye, or monocular depth cues. They consist of the pictorial depth cues, or information available in a two-dimensional picture. When one object hides or covers up part of another object, the first is understood to be in front of the second. This depth cue is referred to as occlusion. Relative height, or height in the plane, refers to the fact that objects that are close to an observer appear lower relative to the horizon as compared with far away objects. Depth information is also provided in the form of linear perspective, or the fact that lines that are parallel in three dimensions (like a road receding in the distance) on the ground converge at the horizon. Shadows and shading also provide information about the three-dimensional structure and location of an object. Texture gradient information is based on the fact that visual elements of the same size (such as bricks on the ground), project smaller and more densely packed two-dimensional images when seen farther away.

Motion provides information for depth in several forms. Motion parallax occurs when one's head moves. This motion causes the relative motion (in the retinal image) of near objects and far objects. The retinal projection of near objects moves relatively more than far objects, when viewed by a moving observer. For example, when looking out of the window of a moving car, the nearby trees move past rapidly, whereas the faraway features appear to barely move at all. In other cases, the three-dimensional structure of an object can be deduced by viewing its rotation, if the object is assumed to be rigid. This is known as structure from motion.

An influential review by Cutting and Vishton (1995) highlighted the relative utility of depth cues at different ranges of distance from the observer. They outline three ranges of space: personal space (approximately within arm's reach), action space (that zone of space within which people can fairly immediately walk or act, out to approximately 30 meters), and vista space (beyond 30 meters). In each of these ranges, depth perception is effectively informed by different combinations and weightings of the sources of information, including the cues discussed above.

In addition to the different depth cues available from the eyes and the retinal images, several modern contributions complement this list of depth cues. The first, called the ecological approach to visual perception, put forth by James J. Gibson, lodged influential criticism at the traditional approach outlined above. Gibson's approach emphasizes that three-dimensional information can be immediately recovered by allowing for a freely moving observer and postulating that the eyes maintain a fixed height above the ground. By showing the richness of the information available in motion, Gibson maintained that a unique specification of spatial layout could be extracted from visual information. Gibson also pointed out that the traditional view of depth perception does not account for existing structures in the world, such as the usually constant height of the eye above the reliably present ground plane. Gibson and others adopting his ecological approach maintain that people see a human world and therefore see depth in a way that supports the prevalent mode of human navigation: walking on the ground.

Consistent with Gibson's approach, a second modern contribution promotes an embodied approach to depth perception. Proffitt and colleagues (2006) have found that distances can appear farther, and slants can appear steeper, when more effort would be required to traverse those extents and hills. In these experiments, the physiological state of the body (as well as its anticipated actions) influences the apparent depth relations in the world.

REFERENCES

Cutting, J. E., & Vishton, P. M. (1995). Perceiving layout and knowing distances: The interaction, relative potency, and contextual use of different information about depth. In W. Epstein & S. Rogers (Eds.) *Perception of space and motion.* (pp. 69–117). San Diego, CA: Academic Press.

Gibson, J. J. (1979). *The ecological approach to visual perception.* New York: Houghton Mifflin.

Proffitt, D. R. (2006). Embodied perception and the economy of action. *Perspectives on Psychological Science, 1*(2), 110–122.

SUGGESTED READINGS

Braunstein, M. L. (1976). *Depth perception through motion.* New York: Academic Press.

Gregory, R. (1998) Eye and brain: *The psychology of seeing.* Princeton, NJ: Princeton University Press.

CEDAR RIENER
DENNIS PROFFITT
University of Virginia

See also: **Motion Perception; Perception**

DESENSITIZATION (See Systematic Desensitization)

DEUTSCH, MORTON (1920–)

Morton Deutsch was born, prematurely, in 1920 into a middle-class family in New York City, the last of four sons. He was always eager to be more advanced than his age, so he skipped grades through elementary and high school and entered the City College of New York (CCNY) at the age of 15. He began as a pre-med major with the idea of becoming a psychiatrist. However, after dissecting a pig in biology lab, he switched to psychology. While at college, he was deeply immersed in a student culture that highly valued Marx, Freud, the scientific method, and political activism.

After CCNY, he started graduate work in clinical psychology, obtaining a Masters in 1940 at the University of Pennsylvania. He then had rich, diverse experiences working with mentally ill, individuals with mental retardation, and delinquent individuals in three New York institutions. In January 1942, he entered the Air Force and served as a lead navigator in a bomber group based in England. His war experience shifted his psychological interests toward social psychology. This shift was reinforced in a 1945 interview with K. Lewin, during which Lewin described his exciting plans for the Research Center for Group Dynamics at the Massachusetts Institute of Technology (MIT).

At MIT, Deutsch was fortunate enough to become a part of a creative, innovative group that would mold the development of social psychology for several decades. The MIT Center was an exhilarating atmosphere in which the new ideas and new methods for research bubbled forth in the constantly occurring discussions of social psychology issues. Under the influence of Lewin's dictum that there is nothing so practical as good theory, Deutsch turned his concerns about the possibility of nuclear war arising from the international competition into a theoretical and experimental investigation of the effects of cooperation and competition. This classic study, in addition to being the taking-off point for much of Deutsch's subsequent work, has helped to stimulate the development of a movement toward cooperative learning in schools under the leadership of D. and R. Johnson.

He obtained his PhD from MIT in 1948, and then joined the Research Center for Human Relations headed by S. Cook (at the New School and then at New York University). There, Deutsch worked collaboratively with colleagues on studies of intergroup prejudice and discrimination, on a textbook of research methods, and on a program of theoretical-empirical research factors affecting the initiation of cooperation. During this period, Deutsch also started training in psychoanalysis, at the Postgraduate Center for Psychotherapy, which he completed in 1958. He maintained a small practice during most of the later part of his life.

In 1959, C. Hovland persuaded Deutsch to join and help establish a new basic research group in psychology at the Bell Telephone Laboratories. There, he did research on small group processes and interpersonal bargaining, inventing (with R. Krauss) new gaming procedures. He was also the "peacenik" at the Bell Labs, criticizing the strategic thinking current among established intellectuals and coediting a book on *Preventing World War III* (1962).

In 1963, Deutsch accepted an invitation to establish a new social psychology doctoral program at Teachers College at Columbia University. He emphasized social significance as well as basic theory and research, recruiting "tough-minded and tender-hearted" students. With the help of many students, Deutsch engaged in extensive theorizing and research on conflict resolution and distributive justice. Several basic ideas have emerged from his work, and these ideas had considerable theoretical and practical import and also served to integrate much of the research in these areas. This work is summarized in two books: *The Resolution of Conflict* (1973) and *Distributive Justice* (1985). His other books included *Interracial Housing* (1951), *Research Methods in Social Relations* (1951, 1959), *Theories in Social Psychology* (1965), *Applying Social Psychology* (1975), and *The Handbook of Conflict Resolution* (2000).

His work has been widely honored by such awards as the Kurt Lewin Memorial Award, the G. W. Allport Prize, the Carl Hovland Flowerman Award, APA's Distinguished Scientific Contribution Award, SESP's Distinguished Research Scientist Award, and the Nevitt Stanford Achievement Award; and he was a William James Fellow of APS. He also received a lifetime achievement award for his work on conflict management, cooperative learning, peace psychology, and the application of psychology to social issues. In addition, he has received the Teachers College Medal for his contributions to education, the Helsinki University Medal for his contributions to psychology, and the Doctorate of Humane Letters from the City University of New York. He has been president of the Society for Psychological Study of Social Issues, the International Society of Political Psychology, the Eastern Psychological Association, the New York State Psychological Association, as well as several divisions of the American Psychological Association.

He is currently E. L. Thorndike Professor Emeritus and Director Emeritus of the International Center for Cooperation and Conflict Resolution at Teachers College, Columbia University.

SUGGESTED READINGS

Claire, M. J., Deutsch, M., & Cook, S. W. (1959). *Research methods in social relations.* New York: Holt, Rinehart and Winston.

Deutsch, M. (1965). *Theories in social psychology.* New York: Basic Books.

Deutsch, M., Coleman, P. T., & Marcus, E. C. (2000). *The handbook of conflict resolution: Theory and practice.* San Francisco: Jossey-Bass.

Deutsch, M., & Hornstein, H. (Eds.). (1975). *Applying social psychology: Implications for research, practice and training.* Hillsdale, NJ: Lawrence Erlbaum.

STAFF

DEVELOPMENTAL PSYCHOLOGY

Developmental psychology (DP) may be broadly defined as the scientific study of systematic changes of an organism's behavior and the psychological processes that behavior reflects. Developmental psychology is one of the main branches of psychology, and as such it subsumes a number of subdisciplines including child psychology, adolescent psychology, life-span psychology, and human development.

The field of developmental psychology encompasses the study of several change series such as ontogenesis (development of the individual across the life span), embryogenesis (development of the embryo), phylogenesis (development of the species—evolution), orthogenesis (normal development), pathogenesis (development of psychopathology), and microgenesis (development on a reduced time scale such as development of a single percept). Human ontogenesis/orthogenesis is the most familiar focus of attention of DP, and within this series there are a number of age-related—from conception to death—areas of study including infancy, toddlerhood, childhood, adolescence, adult development, and aging. Both within and across areas, research scientists examine biological, cognitive, emotional, social, motivational, and personality dimensions of development. There is also a strong research focus on various contextual ecological systems that impact on development, including the family, home, neighborhoods, schools, and peers.

Transformational and Variational Change

Change constitutes the fundamental defining feature of DP, but not all change is necessarily developmental change. *Transformational* change and *variational* change have represented the core of developmental change across the history of DP. Perception, thinking, memory, language, affect, and motivation are universal psychological processes, characteristic of the species as a whole; any specific percept, concept, thought, word, memory, emotion, motive represents a particular usage. Transformational change comes into focus with respect to questions concerning the acquisition, retention, or deterioration of universal processes; variational change is the focus of acquisition, retention, or deterioration of particular usages and individual differences.

Transformational change is change in the form or organization of any system—in the case of ontogenesis the systems are the organism's cognitive, affective, and motivational (i.e., psychological) processes. The morphological changes of the embryo; of the caterpillar becoming a butterfly; of the seed becoming a plant, are simple organic examples of transformational change. The transformation of cognitive processes from globally undifferentiated—lacking self-consciousness, thought, or language—to complexly differentiated and integrated—having reflective self-consciousness, formal logical thought, and a complex language system—between infancy and adolescence constitutes one psychological example. Another example is the affective system, which in the newborn begins with the global differences of pleasure and pain and grows to the primary emotions of the toddler and the highly differentiated emotions of the child.

Transformational change has several closely interrelated attributes as necessary features, and these features give further definition to developmental change. First, transformational change is ordered and exhibits a universal sequence (e.g., zygote, embryo, fetus, infancy, childhood, adolescence, adulthood), and any order implies an orientation toward a goal or end state. Thus, it is directional in nature. For example, the development of thinking begins in simple embodied actions and moves toward the mature complexly differentiated and integrated systems of symbols, concepts, and logic found in the adult. Most broadly, the end state of human development—whether called maturity or labeled by some other concept—is defined in terms of adaptation, in the sense of transformations that increase the individual's ability to survive in a complex physical and sociocultural world. As changes of universal processes, transformational changes are relatively permanent and irreversible. For example, the development of thinking is not reversible, except in pathological deterioration.

Transformational change is also epigenetic, defined as increasing system complexity and the emergence of irreducible novel systemic properties (i.e., properties of the system as a system, and not a property of any individual part of the system) and competencies. Systems move from undifferentiated states to highly differentiated and integrated states, and the further differentiations-reintegrations along the way result in the emergence of systemic novelties. For example, early psychological processes entail global sensory-motor action systems that lack both thought and logic. With transformational change the resulting systems exhibit the novel competency of symbolization, while further transformational change involves the emergence of thought and logical competencies. As the novelties emerge, they are often used to characterize the new system as a stage or level of organization of psychological functioning. In the developmental theory of Jean Piaget (1967), for example, the advances from action to thought to logical thought are often termed the development of sensory-motor, pre-operational, concrete operational, and formal operational stages of cognitive development. The emergence of new levels does not imply that earlier levels of competence are eliminated or cease to be available; they are simply subsumed within the higher level. Thus, the adult maintains the ability to function at a sensory-motor level as circumstances warrant.

The emergence of novelty also means that transformational changes cannot be explained as the additive effect of particular causes (i.e., biological and environmental-cultural causes). As a consequence, transformational change is qualitative or discontinuous or nonlinear rather than strictly continuous (additive). Whereas these changes may occur slowly over time, novelty emerges and is not the additive product of other factors. Explanations are given in terms of the actions of individuals as they coact or transact with both the worlds of internal biology and external environment-culture, not in terms of context independent biological and environmental causes.

Variational change operates within the competencies afforded by transformational change. Variational change refers to the degree or extent that a change varies from a standard, norm, or average. Particular changes in adaptive behavior at any level of adaptation constitute the province of variational change. The acquisition of various skills and knowledge content as well as individual differences in these exemplify variational change (e.g., changes in the reaching behavior of the infant, the toddler's change in walking precision, the acquisition of vocabulary, acquiring the social norms of a culture). Like transformational change, variational change is directed toward a goal (adaptation). However, it is not parallel in other ways. Variational change is generally reversible, not permanent. Consequently, variational change is not epigenetic and does not involve stages. This change can be represented as the strictly additive effect of causes—the "interaction" of several causes itself being interpreted additively—and as a result it is said to be quantitative, continuous, linear.

Developmental Issues

Many of the basic issues and controversies in DP arise from a single question: What is the relation of transformational and variational change in the study of development? Historically, two alternative answers to this question have framed the field. The first answer arose from the methodological position of early twentieth-century neopositivism, from psychological theories of behaviorism, including learning theories, and from early social learning theories, as well as from later forms of functionalism, including information processing and artificial intelligence. This has been an exclusionary approach that identifies variational change and only variational change as the true developmental change. The position argues that what may appear to be transformational change must be treated as epiphenomenal, to be explained by variational change. Thus, from this approach, by definition, any observed sequence, order, relative permanence, novelty, stages, or discontinuity must be reduced to (explained by) variational change produced by biological and/or cultural causes.

This position that treats variation as the sole legitimate developmental change in turn establishes what some have considered the overarching issue of DP—the nature-nurture (or heredity-environment or nativist-empiricist) issue. This issue asks whether biological (usually genetic) factors, or environmental-cultural factors, or some combination of the two cause developmental (variational) change. Today, those who follow the "variation only" route generally agree that the answer to the question is that development is the result of one of the two factors. However, this interaction represents the additive combination of these two context-free causes, and not the coaction or transaction described earlier.

The second answer to the transformational-variational change question arises from a postpositivist methodology (Overton, 2006) and from psychological theories that conceptualize organisms together with their biological and cultural contexts as self-organizing, self-regulating, adaptive systems. Developmental theorists who have contributed to this approach include James Mark Baldwin (1895), William Stern (1938), Heinz Werner (1948), Gordon Allport (1955), Jean Piaget (1967), Lev Vygotsky (1978), Erik Erikson (1968), Harry Stack Sullivan (1953), Donald Winnicott (1965), and John Bowlby (1958). Today this approach is identified by the labels *Relational Developmental Systems Theory* (Lerner & Overton, 2008), *Dynamic Systems* (Witherington, 2007), and *Developmental Systems* (Oyama, 2000).

The systems formulation is an inclusive solution that casts transformational and variational change into a relational dialectic (Overton, 2006) in which they operate reciprocally as features of the same organic whole. Acts are embodied. They arise from, and are constrained by, the organic system. Variation arises as an act fails to fully achieve a goal. Successful variations are incorporated by the system and represent the initiation of system transformation (i.e., one differentiation of the many that will eventuate in a reintegration). The cyclical process of system-act-variation-feedback-transformation-system-act represents the pattern of all developmental change across the life span. Acts that are totally successful or unsuccessful, while being relevant to the maintenance and regulation of the system, are developmentally irrelevant.

From the systems perspective a focus on transformational features of change or variational features represents a methodological or pragmatic choice and not an ontological commitment. When focusing on the act in its variational context, the particular, continuous, quantitative, reversible features become foregrounded. When focusing on the act in its transformational context, the universal, the discontinuous (emergence, novelty, stage), the qualitative, and the relatively permanent are foregrounded.

The systems perspective also resolves the nature-nurture issue while preserving the centrality of biology and culture. All development is understood as the product of the co-construction of biology and culture, and hence there are no context independent biological or cultural causes. Heredity and environment cannot be parsed in the explanation of development. All development is 100%

biological because it is 100% cultural, and it is 100% cultural because it is 100% biological. This elimination of the hoary nature-nurture controversy does not, however, eliminate the significance of biology and culture in development. Many questions remain to be addressed from both a biological point of view (i.e., a perspective, not a cause) and as well as from an environmental-cultural point of view.

For example, what environmental and cultural contexts provide the most adaptive or least adaptive opportunities for the growing organism; what forms of parenting, what forms of schooling, what forms of activities, what forms of peer relations, and the like provide such opportunities? Similarly, what biological contexts provide the most and least adaptive opportunities for the growing organism; what features of the genetic system, what features of the hormonal system, what features of the neurological system? These are all important developmental questions, but none entail a nature-nurture issue.

There are two general issues in DP that cut across developmental periods and areas of study—developmental plasticity and the stability/instability of individual differences. Plasticity refers to the organism's ability to change in the face of environmental demands. Thus, questions are raised about developmental times when the organism may be particularly sensitive to environmental-cultural demands. A part of this issue concentrates on the question of the role of early experience in development, and also on the question of whether there are critical periods during which specific environmental events must be present for development to continue properly. The broad question of plasticity has obvious implications for interventions. Individual differences, as noted earlier, become central when the focus is on variational change. In this case investigators are often interested in the question of whether the individual differences remain stable across time. For example, if children are shy and uncertain prior to two years of age, are they likely to timid and cautious in later childhood? Questions of this sort are important to the study of development, but they must be kept separate from the transformational issue of discontinuity.

Models and Theories of the Organism

The study of development, like the study of any facet of psychology, is framed by metaphors that serve as models of the basic nature of the organism. These models in turn operate as the conceptual background to the formulation of theories, issues, and questions. Three metaphors that have been prominent in DP are the empty bucket image, the computer image, and the organic system image. The empty bucket image (or John Locke's *tabula rasa*)—favored by generations of Environmentalists-Empiricists—pictures the organism as psychologically formless and reactive at birth, awaiting an environment that will fill it with knowledge while shaping its cognitive, affective, and motivational architecture. This image formed the background for behaviorism's learning theories and social learning theories.

The computer image—the favorite of Nativists—pictures the psychological architecture as prewired at birth. This architecture awaits an environment that provides the triggers for the activation of inherited modules (e.g., Pinker, 2002) and information that is processed according to the structure of the architecture. This image has served as background for recent functionalist theories, including information processing theories and theories of artificial intelligence. It has also been the context for evolutionary theories of development. In this latter case inherited psychological modules function as the genome, which exhibits random variation, and the environment functions as the agent of natural selection in the formation (development) of a behavioral phenotype.

The organic system image—prominent in system theories—pictures the organism's psychological architecture, environment-culture, and biology as the product of co-constructive processes. As a living self-organizing and self-regulating adaptive system, the organism is inherently active and evidences some degree of organization from its beginning, regardless of whether "beginning" is taken as conception or birth. Through its embodied actions in the world (intra-uterine and extra-uterine), the organism progresses to levels of increased organized complexity and adaptation. At all developmental moments, from conception to death, the biological, the psychological, and the environmental-cultural are understood as being co-constructed processes. As a consequence, each process is necessarily defined in the context of its functioning in an organic whole, and never defined in a context free manner. The most prominent developmental theories formulated within this image have been Piaget and Werner's cognitive theories, Vygotsky's cultural theory, Bowlby's emotional theory, and Erikson's social-emotional-motivational theory. These theories, taken as a whole, represent a triangulated and interwoven perspective of three viewpoints on the major spheres of psychological ontogenesis—the spheres of cognition, affect, and conation. The basic focus of each of these theories is on the developmental of universal processes and on questions related to transformational change. A fourth significant contemporary viewpoint, the ecological perspective (Bronfenbrenner & Morris, 2006), focuses on individual differences in development and the impact of contextual factors on this development.

Methodology

As DP involves the description and explanation of developmental change both within the organism (intra-individual) and between organisms (interindividual), the descriptive, correlational, and experimental research methods employed by DP are broadly the same as those of other branches of psychology. Unique to DP are two research designs that employ methods addressing age specific and developmental questions. Longitudinal designs measure the behavior of interest with the same individuals at several different intervals (e.g., minutes, days, months, or years). This yields a relatively direct measure of developmental change in a process or behavior. Cross-sectional designs measure the behavior at a single time with individuals who are of different ages. This design yields information about age differences in the measured behavior, and hence it is a more indirect assessment of developmental change. At times these two designs are combined, measuring individuals of different ages across several different intervals. This is called a cross-sequential design.

A further important developmental research design feature involves the use of person-centered as a complement to the traditional variable-centered measurement approach. The person-centered approach focuses on the intraindividual structure or organization of systems and subsystems that defines the person, along with developmental changes in this organization. The fundamental assumption of this approach is holistic in its assertion that psychological systems and subsystems are best studied not in isolation, but in terms of patterns of interactive functioning (Magnusson, 1998). As a consequence, this research approach focuses on the discovery of patterns or typologies of psychological systems within the person. This approach is particularly relevant to questions raised by personalistic (i.e., emphasizing the centrality of individuals in their social, political, cultural, intellectual milieu) types of developmental theories, such as those of Werner, Piaget, Vygotsky, and Erikson. The variable-centered approach focuses primarily on interindividual differences and the variables that impact on these differences and changes of differences. This approach is particularly relevant to questions raised by contextual inquiries and ecological theories (e.g., Bronfenbrenner & Morris, 2006).

Applications

Although DP traditionally has been defined by its research orientation, the field is also concerned with the optimization of adaptive developmental change and remediation of maladaptive change. This concern has fostered the growth of the subfield of applied developmental psychology (also referred to as applied developmental science). This subfield "seeks to advance the integration of developmental research with actions that promote positive development and/or enhance the life chances of vulnerable children, adolescents, young and old adults, and their families" (Lerner, in press, p. 4). Some of the mechanisms through which these applied actions take place include the enactment and evaluation of community-based intervention and enhancement programs; the promotion of developmentally appropriate social policies; the evaluation of the effects of developmentally relevant social policies; and the dissemination of developmental knowledge to individuals, families, communities, practitioners, and policymakers.

REFERENCES

Allport, G. (1955). *Becoming*. New Haven: Yale University Press.

Baldwin, J. M. (1895). *Mental development in the child and the race: Methods and process*. New York: Macmillan.

Bowlby, J. (1958). The nature of the child's tie to his mother. *International Journal of Psychoanalysis, 39,* 350–373.

Bronfenbrenner U., & Morris P. A. (2006). The bioecological model of human development. In R. M. Lerner (Ed.), *Theoretical models of human development*. Volume 1 of *The handbook of child psychology* (pp. 793–828). (6th ed.), Editor-in-Chief: William Damon; Richard M. Lerner. New York: John Wiley & Sons.

Erikson, E. H. (1968). *Identity youth and crisis*. New York: W. W. Norton & Company.

Lerner, R. M. (In press). Applying developmental science: Definitions and dimensions. In V. Maholmes and C. Lomonaco (Eds.), *Applied Research in Child and Adolescent Development: A Practical Guide*. London: Taylor & Francis.

Lerner, R. M. & Overton, W. F. (2008). Exemplifying the integrations of the relational developmental system: Synthesizing theory, research, and application to promote positive development and social justice. *Journal of Adolescent Research, 23,* 245–255.

Magnusson, D. (1998). The logic and implications of a person-oriented approach. In R. B. Cairns, L. R. Bergman, & J. Kagan (Eds.), *Methods and models for studying the individual* (pp. 33–63). London: Sage Publications.

Overton, W. F. (2006). Developmental psychology: Philosophy, concepts, methodology. In R. M. Lerner (Ed.), *Theoretical models of human development*. Volume 1 of *The Handbook of child psychology* (6th ed., pp. 18–88), Editor-in-Chief: William Damon; Richard M. Lerner. New York: John Wiley & Sons.

Oyama, S. (2000). *The ontogeny of information: Developmental systems and evolution* (2nd ed.). Durham, NC: Duke University Press.

Piaget, J. (1967). *Six psychological studies*. New York: Random House.

Pinker, S. (2002). *The blank slate: The modern denial of human nature*. Viking: Penguin.

Stern, W. (1938). *General psychology: From the personalistic standpoint*. New York: Macmillan.

Sullivan, H. S. (1953). *The interpersonal theory of psychiatry*. New York: W.W. Norton.

Vygotsky, L. S. (1978). *Mind in society: The development of higher psychological processes*. Cambridge, MA: Harvard University Press.

Werner, H. (1948). *Comparative psychology of mental development*. New York: International Universities Press. (Originally published 1940).

Winnicott, D.W. (1965). *The maturational process and the facilitating environment*. New York: International Universities Press.

Witherington, D. C. (2007). The dynamic systems approach as metatheory for developmental psychology. *Human Development, 50,* 127–153.

SUGGESTED READING

Lerner, R. M. (2002). *Concepts and theories of human development* (3rd ed.). New York: Random House.

WILLIS F. OVERTON
Temple University

See also: **Adolescent Development; Child Psychology; Cognitive Development; Emotional Development**

DEVELOPMENTAL TEST OF VISUAL MOTOR INTEGRATION

The Developmental Test of Visual Motor Integration (VMI), now in its fifth edition, has clearly stood the test of time. Originally developed in 1967 by Beery and Buktenica, its longevity attests to its value to the clinical assessment community. This is not surprising. The VMI is an elegant test that has six critical features whose co-occurrence may be unique in currently available psychological instruments. Its ease of administration minimizes examiner error and maximizes data quality. Its format is enjoyed by (most) children, which promotes rapport and maximizes clinical utility (most children are willing to complete all items—yielding both standard and age-referenced data). It yields qualitative data, in that observation of the child's performance yields insights into psychological processes, deployment of motor skills, and response to increasing load as items increase in complexity. Its quantitative data include standard scores that permit ranking among peers and allow for monitoring of progress over time, and age-referenced achievement levels, provided for each item, that may signal diagnostically relevant within-child discrepancies in capacity when contrasted with standard scores. "Stepping Stones" age norms for tracking the progress of very young children are also provided for gross and fine motor, visual and visual motor development. Last, but by no means least, is an enormously valuable developmental trajectory reference set for each item that allows for evaluation of developmental status.

The VMI is a developmental sequence of geometric forms to be copied. Normative data are available from 2 to 18 years and from 19 to 99 years. A short form can be used with children. Of 30 items, 24 comprise the core set to be copied; where necessary, the first three items are used to prompt marking or scribbling, and the second three forms can be modeled for imitation. The utility of the VMI can be extended with the VMI Visual Perception and VMI Motor Coordination subtests. The former requires identification of line drawings of animals, of body parts, and of "same figure" from a list of distractors increasing in number and detail. VMI Motor Coordination includes observation of gross motor skills, pencil grip, and bilateral hand control, plus a measure of pencil control (staying within a track while connecting dots in increasingly complex figures).

The VMI is widely used (showing more than 50,000 entries in a basic literature search) in clinical, educational, rehabilitation, and research settings for developmental screening, monitoring of change and progress in the course of disease and treatment, and elucidating neurological, psychological, and neuropsychological processes underlying neurodevelopmental and learning disorders and learning disabilities. The validity and reliability of VMI has been evaluated in its various incarnations and deemed adequate by the professional community.

REFERENCE

Bertrand, J., Mervis, C. B., & Eisenberg, J. D. (1997). Drawing by children with Williams syndrome: A developmental perspective. *Developmental Neuropsychology, 13*(4), 41–67.

Foulder-Hughes, L. A., & Cooke, R. W. (2003). Motor, cognitive, and behavioural disorders in children born very preterm. *Developmental Medicine & Child Neurology, 45*(2), 97–103.

Graf, M., & Hinton, R. N. (1997). Correlations for the development visual-motor integration test and the Wechsler intelligence scale for children-III. *Perceptual & Motor Skills, 84*(2), 699–702.

SUGGESTED READINGS

Brassard, M. R., & Boehm, A. E. (2007). *Preschool assessment. Principles and practices*. New York: Guilford Press.

Geisinger, K. F., Spies, R. A., Carlson, J. F., & Plake, B. S. (Eds.). (2007). *The seventeenth mental measurements yearbook*. Lincoln, NE: Buros Institute of Mental Measurements.

Spreen, O., & Strauss, E. (1998). *A compendium of neuropsychological tests. Administration, norms, and commentary* (2nd ed.). New York: Oxford University Press.

JANE HOLMES BERNSTEIN
Children's Hospital Boston and Harvard Medical School

See also: **Motor Control; Neuropsychology; Visual Impairment**

DEVIANCY

Deviancy is a central concept in the study of human behavior and cognition. It underscores the primary focus of personality theory, clinical psychology, and social psychology. Deviancy in psychology describes behavior and thought patterns that are significantly different from what constitutes the norm in a population. These differences in cognition, behavior, and performance can be consistent and fixed or varying over time and situation. They are generally described as too much of an undesirable behavior or too little of a desired behavior. Alternately, these differences can occur as high-intensity isolated events, as in the cases of violence or mental illness.

How one defines the norm of a population has considerable impact on determinations of what actually constitutes deviancy. A popular approach entails statistically determining what behaviors, cognitions, and performances significantly deviate from the greater majority of that population. The second approach adds an additional feature to the determinations of deviancy beyond statistical abnormality to distinguish the concept from nonconformity and pro-social abnormal behaviors and thought processes. This approach suggests that deviance entails some degree of dysfunction or social undesirability of the abnormal behavior or thought. The absolute versus relative nature of these categorizations has long been debated.

The study of deviancy consequently involves multiple approaches and provides several causal explanations of deviance, especially regarding the prevalence of deviance amongst certain social groups. The classic approach suggests that people who are physiologically, psychologically, socially, or culturally different are at greater risk for engaging in maladaptive or undesirable behavior. Deviance in this approach is a result of internal factors intrinsic to the make-up of those individuals. Such individuals can accordingly be classified in a wide array of contexts based on their type of deviancy. The legal system, for example, treats deviance as a separate class of behavior referred to as crime, delinquency, or insanity. A medical perspective refers to deviancy as a mental illness. In the education context deviance from the norm constitutes a learning disability. Members of groups with high levels of deviance are perceived as experiencing outcomes in those regards due to the prevalence of internal person-level differences. Thus differences between groups can be reduced to differences in numbers of deviant individuals with those internal factors.

A second approach to explaining deviance focuses on external factors, which are referred to as social structural differences. The social structural differences perspective suggests that access to opportunity and alienation from society varies between groups as a result of socially constructed barriers and privileges. Consequently, deviance is a manifestation of the inherent conflict between members of society competing for limited resources and stems from differential social structures typical of their respective environments.

A third causal explanation for deviance is referred to as the interactionist point of view, in which deviance is a result of an action-reaction dynamic between individuals and society. Specifically, mental illness, crime, and underachievement are simply labels society assigns to behaviors and performances that society is empowered to treat as undesirable or threatening, and thus there are no objective criteria for determinations of deviance. Rather, deviance better describes the interaction between an individual's behavior and a societal response to this behavior.

A fourth and final perspective for consideration of deviancy is found in learning theory. All behaviors are a product of modeling, reinforcement, and punishment. Deviant behavior is simply a product of differential rewards or punishments of such behavior and modeling of behavior found in one's immediate environment. Therefore, crime, learning disabilities, and undesirable behavior are all learned, whether adaptive or maladaptive.

Deviancy is thus a central subject matter in psychology with a myriad of causal explanations. Alternative perspectives consider internal and external factors, with some focusing on the interaction between the two or on the learning component of all behavior. The process of differentiating deviancy from normalcy is difficult and highly dependent on the perspective from which the determination is made. Ultimately, deviancy constitutes behaviors that deviate from what is considered the norm, whether statistically or conceptually, with the added criteria of being dysfunctional, undesirable, or maladaptive.

SUGGESTED READINGS

Rubington, E., & Weinberg, M. S. (Eds.). (2002). *Deviance: The interactionist perspective* (8th ed.). Boston: Allyn and Bacon.

Thio, A., & Calhoun, T. C. (2004). *Readings in deviant behavior* (3rd ed.). Boston: Allyn and Bacon.

WILLIAM DAVIDSON II
EYITAYO ONIFADE
Michigan State University

See also: **Abnormality**

DEWEY, JOHN (1859–1952)

John Dewey was an American philosopher, psychologist, and educator. He attended the University of Vermont, after which he taught high school and independently studied philosophy. He entered the graduate program at Johns Hopkins University and received his doctorate in philosophy in 1884. He taught at the University of Michigan and the University of Minnesota before going to the University of Chicago in 1894, the same year as James Rowland Angell. Dewey remained at Chicago for 10 years, and his and Angell's influence made the university a center for functional psychology. Dewey started an experimental laboratory school at Chicago, a new approach to educational methods that made him both famous and controversial. When he left, the leadership of the function-alist school passed to Angell. From 1904 to 1930 Dewey was at Columbia University, working on applications of psychology to educational and philosophical problems.

Dewey's paper "The Reflex Arc Concept in Psychology" is usually credited with establishing functionalism as a defined school of psychology, rather than just an orienta-tion or attitude. The paper contained the seeds of all the arguments against the use of the stimulus-response unit as the building block of behavior in psychological theory. In this paper, Dewey attacked the molecular reductionism of elements in the reflex arc, with its distinction between stimulus and response. Dewey felt that behavior reduced to its basic sensory-motor description was not meaningful. He taught that behavior is continuous, not disjoined into stimuli and response, and that sensory-motor behaviors continuously blend into one another.

Dewey understood the organism not as a passive re-ceptor of stimuli but as an active perceiver. He believed that behavior should be studied in terms of its significant adaptation to the environment. The proper subject matter for psychology was the study of the total organism as it *functioned* in its environment. His functionalistic point of view was influenced by the theory of evolution and his own instrumentalistic philosophy, which held that ideas are plans for action rising to reality and its problems. The struggle of the human intellect is to activate conscious responses to bring about appropriate behavior that enables the organism to survive, to progress, to function. "Thus, functional psychology is the study of the organism in use" (Schultz, *History*, 1981, p. 163).

John Dewey wrote the first American textbook of psy-chology in 1886, called *Psychology*, which was popular until William James's *The Principles of Psychology* came out in 1890. But Dewey did not spend many years in psychology proper. After the 1896 paper, his interests turned to practi-cal applications. In 1899, after retiring as president of the American Psychological Association, he became the leader of the progressive education movement. It was consis-tent with the ideas inherent in his functional psychology and his philosophy that he devoted most of his time to American education and its pragmatic development.

Dewey was very much involved in American political and social issues during the latter part of his life, influ-encing education in particular. His positions gradually evolved over the course of his career, and he was concerned with individual rights, including those of minority individ-uals and women. He was one of the few psychologists pictured on a U.S. stamp.

SUGGESTED READING

Dewey, J. (1896). The reflex arc concept in psychology. *Psychologi-cal Review, 3,* 357–370.

N. A. HAYNIE

DIAGNOSTIC AND STATISTICAL MANUAL OF MENTAL DISORDERS (DSM-IV-TR)

The *Diagnostic and Statistical Manual of Mental Disorders*, fourth edition, text revision (DSM-IV-TR) (American Psy-chiatric Association [APA], 2000) is a compendium of mental disorders, a listing of the criteria used to diag-nose them, and a detailed system for their definition, organization, and classification. Put simply, it is the pri-mary diagnostic manual for mental health professionals in the United States and much of the Western world. Diag-nosis refers to the identification and labeling of a mental disorder by examination and analysis. Mental health pro-fessionals diagnose individuals based on the symptoms that they report experiencing and the signs of illness with which they present. The DSM-IV-TR aids professionals in understanding and diagnosing mental disorders through its provision of explicit diagnostic criteria and an official classification system.

General Features of the DSM-IV-TR

In the DSM-IV-TR classification system, mental disorders are grouped into 17 diagnostic categories. The manual increases accuracy of diagnosis because it lists the spe-cific criteria for each mental disorder and the number of criteria that must be met to reach the diagnostic thresh-old. Empirical research and extensive literature reviews have guided refinements in the diagnostic manual and its continued development. Although far from perfect, the DSM-IV-TR functions as one of the most comprehensive and efficient manuals used to diagnose mental disorders in the history of humankind. The only major competitor in the developed world is the World Health Organization's *International Classification of Diseases 10th edition (ICD-10)*, which is widely compatible with the DSM-IV-TR.

According to the DSM-IV-TR, individuals with a par-ticular diagnosis (e.g., major depressive disorder) need not exhibit identical features, although they should present with certain cardinal symptoms (e.g., either depressed mood or anhedonia). In the DSM-IV-TR, the criteria for many disorders are polythetic, meaning that an individual must meet a minimum number of symptoms to be diag-nosed, but not all symptoms need be present (e.g., five of nine symptoms must be present to diagnose depression). Use of polythetic criteria allows for some variation among people with the same disorder. However, individuals with the same disorder should have a similar history in some areas, for example, a typical age of onset, prognosis, and common comorbid conditions.

The DSM-IV-TR aims to provide other important infor-mation about each mental disorder (to the extent that knowledge is available) including prevalence and course data; the extent of its genetic loading (i.e., whether it con-sistently runs in families; the concordance rates among twins); the extent to which it is affected by psychosocial forces; the extent to which the disorder varies according to gender, age, and culture; the subtypes and specifiers of the disorder; and associated laboratory findings, physical examination findings, and general medical conditions. Another important feature of the DSM-IV-TR is that it aids in the process of differential diagnosis by providing guidance about how to discriminate one disorder from another.

The DSM-IV-TR is the latest incarnation of the manual in an evolving process that began with publication of the original DSM (APA) in 1952 followed by DSM-II (APA, 1968), DSM-III (APA, 1980), and a revision of the third edition called DSM-III-R (APA, 1987). The DSM-IV (APA) was published in 1994. In 2000, a "text revision" of the manual was published, which updated slightly some of the content in the manual. With each revision, the scope and magnitude of the manual has grown—DSM-IV-TR now includes 297 mental disorders and encompasses 943 pages. Workgroups have already been organized for DSM-V, which is expected to be published no later than 2012. The current version, DSM-IV-TR, is much improved compared to earlier editions in several ways including the provision of operationalized, behaviorally specific, empirically derived, and standardized criteria for each mental disorder and the manual's attention to multicultural and diversity awareness, which is necessary to diagnose individuals outside the majority culture.

Regarding its multicultural applicability, international experts were involved in the revision process to ensure a wide pool of information on cultural factors in psychopathology and diagnosis. The DSM-IV-TR includes information about cultural factors that may influence some disorders. For example, cultural considerations for conduct disorder include immigrant youth who exhibit aggressive behavior necessary for survival. Perhaps most importantly, a glossary of many culture-bound disorders are described in an appendix of the DSM-IV-TR called "Outline for Cultural Formulation and Glossary of Culture-Bound Syndromes." In this section, information is provided about the names of culture-bound syndromes, the cultures in which it occurs, and a description of the main psychopathological features. For example, a disorder called "susto" occurs mainly in South and Central America and is an illness in which a traumatic event purportedly causes the soul to leave the body. In all, 25 conditions are discussed, which is an important beginning to increasing the cross-cultural validity of the DSM-IV-TR.

The Multiaxial System of the DSM-IV-TR

An important innovation to diagnosis in various earlier editions of the manual and maintained in the DSM-IV-TR is the application of a multiaxial approach. In the multiaxial system, each person is rated on five distinct dimensions or axes, with each axis referring to a different domain of the person's functioning. Although only Axis I and Axis II cover the diagnosis of abnormal behavior, inclusion of Axes III, IV, and V indicates awareness that factors other than a person's symptoms should be considered in a thorough mental health assessment. Each domain is important in that it can help professionals understand the experience of the person more fully, plan treatment, and predict outcome. The multiaxial system also provides a convenient and standard format for organizing and communicating clinical information, captures the complexity of clinical phenomena, and describes potentially important differences in functioning among persons with the same diagnosis.

Axis I: Clinical Disorders and Other Conditions That May Be a Focus of Clinical Attention. All mental disorders experienced by the client are reported on Axis I with the exception of personality disorders and mental retardation, which are coded on Axis II. Axis I is comprised of 16 broad categories under which specific disorders are subsumed. Fifteen of the 16 categories describe the classic mental disorders. Examples include bipolar disorder, obsessive-compulsive disorder, schizophrenia, anorexia nervosa, alcohol dependence, attention-deficit/hyperactivity disorder, adjustment disorder, pathological gambling, and dementia of the Alzheimer's type. The final category called "Other Conditions That May Be a Focus of Clinical Attention" denotes conditions that are not mental disorders but may prompt the need for psychological intervention. Examples include parent-child relational problem, malingering, and bereavement.

Axis II: Personality Disorders and Mental Retardation. Personality disorders are inflexible and maladaptive patterns of behavior reflecting extreme variants of normal personality traits that have become rigid and dysfunctional. Ten personality disorders are standard in DSM-IV-TR: paranoid, schizoid, schizotypal, antisocial, borderline, histrionic, narcissistic, avoidant, dependent, and obsessive-compulsive personality disorder. Personality disorder not otherwise specified is also included as a diagnostic option. Depressive personality disorder and passive-aggressive personality disorder are included in an appendix of the manual devoted to disorders that are deserving of further study, some of which might be included as official disorders in a future edition of the manual should enough research bear out their usefulness. Prominent dysfunctional personality traits can be listed on Axis II when symptoms are noteworthy but below the diagnostic threshold. Defense mechanisms can also be noted on Axis II, although this application is relatively uncommon in clinical practice.

Axis III: General Medical Conditions. On this axis, the professional lists any current physical disorders (e.g., epilepsy, lung cancer, diabetes) that could be relevant to the understanding or management of the client's psychiatric problems. Professionals are advised to list all important medical conditions experienced by the client and be inclusive rather than exclusive.

Axis IV: Psychosocial and Environmental Problems. All significant social and environmental stressors experienced by the client are reported on Axis IV. Examples include: recently divorced, inadequate finances, and recent death of parent. In general, only those stressors that have been present during the year preceding the current evaluation are listed. However, stressors occurring prior to the previous year (e.g., childhood sexual abuse) may be listed if they contribute significantly to the person's current mental disorder or become a focus of treatment.

Axis V: Global Assessment of Functioning. Global Assessment of Functioning (GAF) Scale ratings are recorded on Axis V. On this axis, the professional rates the client's overall level of functioning, described on a 0–100 scale. Higher GAF scores indicate better functioning. Explicit descriptions of functioning in 10 point increments are provided in the DSM-IV-TR. For example, a GAF range of 31–40 indicates "some impairment in reality testing or communication," scores ranging 51–60 suggest "moderate symptoms or moderate difficulty in social, occupational, or school functioning," and scores between 71 and 80 denote mild symptoms that are "transient and expectable reactions to psychosocial stressors" with slight functional impairment (APA, 2000, p. 34). GAF ratings at the current time are typically provided although professionals sometimes include the client's highest GAF within the past year or at some other relevant time, such as at discharge from a psychiatric hospital. GAF scale ratings (albeit subjective) are useful in describing the overall level of impairment of a client, tracking clinical progress over time, and predicting prognosis.

Although the DSM-IV-TR arguably is the most sophisticated and comprehensive diagnostic manual ever created, it is not without significant limitations. Criticisms include a narrow focus on enhancing the reliability or replicability of diagnosis at the expense of improving validity or usefulness of diagnosis; the adoption of a categorical model of diagnosis which assumes a "Yes/No" or "Sick/Well" approach in which individuals either have the disorder (i.e., they meet criteria, they are diagnosable) or they do not (despite possibly having several symptoms but not enough to meet formal criteria) rather than a dimensional approach that classifies clinical presentations based on quantitative descriptions of various domains of functioning; the fact that distinct boundaries between some mental disorders is difficult to determine, and applying such definite categories to mental disorders implies a uniformity that does not exist; the substantial comorbidity of mental disorders, which raises the question of whether or not a single disorder is actually present instead of the co-occurrence of several distinct disorders; the fact that many individuals seen in mental health settings do not fit neatly into any of the categories, suggesting poor clinical utility of some diagnoses; the fact that the classification system is based primarily on descriptive syndromes, which largely ignores etiological and contextual factors; and the improved although still limited cultural applicability of the manual, which still appears to have a false assumption that its primary syndromes represent universal disorders.

For a more complete discussion of strengths and criticisms of the DSM-IV-TR, the interested reader is referred to Widiger and Clark (2000), Widiger and Mullins-Sweatt, (2007), and Segal and Coolidge (2001). It is anticipated that the forthcoming DSM-V will continue to improve upon its predecessors and provide a state-of-the-art manual for the diagnosis and classification of mental illness.

REFERENCES

American Psychiatric Association. (1952). *Diagnostic and statistical manual of mental disorders*. Washington, DC: Author.

American Psychiatric Association. (1968). *Diagnostic and statistical manual of mental disorders* (2nd ed.). Washington, DC: Author.

American Psychiatric Association. (1980). *Diagnostic and statistical manual of mental disorders* (3rd ed.). Washington, DC: Author.

American Psychiatric Association. (1987). *Diagnostic and statistical manual of mental disorders* (3rd ed., revised). Washington, DC: Author.

American Psychiatric Association. (1994). *Diagnostic and statistical manual of mental disorders* (4th ed.). Washington, DC: Author.

American Psychiatric Association. (2000). *Diagnostic and statistical manual of mental disorders* (4th ed., text rev.). Washington, DC: Author.

Segal, D. L., & Coolidge, F. L. (2001). Diagnosis and classification. In M. Hersen & V. B. Van Hasselt (Eds.), *Advanced abnormal psychology* (2nd ed., pp. 5–22). New York: Kluwer Academic/Plenum.

Widiger, T. A., & Clark, L. A. (2000). Toward DSM-V and the classification of psychopathology. *Psychological Bulletin, 126*, 946–963.

Widiger, T. A., & Mullins-Sweatt, S. (2007). Mental disorders as discrete clinical conditions: Dimensional versus categorical classification. In M. Hersen, S. M. Turner, & D. C. Beidel (Eds.), *Adult psychopathology and diagnosis* (5th ed., pp. 3–33). Hoboken, NJ: John Wiley & Sons.

SUGGESTED READINGS

First, M. B., Francis, A., & Pincus, H. A. (2002). *DSM-IV-TR handbook of differential diagnosis*. Washington, DC: American Psychiatric Publishing.

Hersen, M., Turner, S. M., & Beidel, D. C. (Eds.). (2007). *Adult psychopathology and diagnosis* (5th ed.). Hoboken, NJ: John Wiley & Sons.

Thakker, J., & Ward, T. (1998). Culture and classification: The cross-cultural application of the DSM-IV. *Clinical Psychology Review, 18*, 501–529.

DANIEL L. SEGAL
University of Colorado at Colorado Springs

See also: **Diagnostic Classification; Diagnostic Interview Schedule for DSM-IV (DIS-IV); Psychodynamic Diagnostic Manual; Structured Clinical Interview for DSM Diagnosis**

DIAGNOSTIC CLASSIFICATION

The *Diagnostic and Statistical Manual of Mental Disorders* (DSM) is the classification of psychopathology developed under the authority of the American Psychiatric Association (APA). The current version of this diagnostic manual is DSM-IV-TR (APA, 2000), standing for the fourth edition, text revision. Included within are the diagnostic criteria for such mental disorders as major depressive disorder, social phobia, panic disorder, nicotine dependence, alcohol abuse, schizophrenia, mental retardation, pedophilia, attention-deficit/hyperactivity disorder, mathematics disorder, stuttering, dissociative identity disorder, borderline personality disorder, narcissistic personality disorder, pathological gambling, frotteurism, nightmare disorder, and many others.

The primary purpose of DSM-IV-TR is to provide a common language of communication. The first edition of the DSM was published in 1952. Prior to its appearance, confusion reigned. Each major medical center within the United States had its own set of diagnoses. Even if two clinicians were using the same diagnosis, they might still differ substantially in the symptoms that guided their provision of this diagnosis. It was very difficult under these conditions for patients to receive a consistent diagnosis and for scientific research to accumulate.

However, as a common language of communication, DSM-IV-TR is a very powerful document. It provides the authoritative statement as to when particular behaviors, thoughts, or feelings are considered to be a mental disorder. Many important social, forensic, clinical, and other professional decisions are significantly influenced by this diagnostic manual, from deciding whether insurance coverage will be provided for the treatment of a condition to mitigating criminal responsibility for the commission of an illegal act.

In addition, as the common language of communication about mental disorders, DSM-IV-TR governs how psychopathology is taught within undergraduate and graduate programs, and even how persons think about psychopathology. Persons think in terms of their language, and the predominant language of psychopathology is DSM-IV-TR. Nevertheless, DSM-IV-TR is not the final word. Work is in fact underway toward the development of DSM-V. Briefly discussed herein will be the categorical model of classification and the threshold for diagnosis.

Categorical Model of Classification

"DSM-IV-TR is a categorical classification that divides mental disorders into types based on criterion sets with defining features" (APA, 2000, p. xxxi). The diagnostic categories of DSM-IV-TR were developed in the spirit of a traditional medical model that considers mental disorders to be qualitatively distinct conditions. When one is ill, the assumption is that one has a specific disease, with a specific pathology. The intention of the diagnostic manual is to help clinicians determine which particular disorder is present, the diagnosis of which would purportedly indicate the presence of the specific pathology that would explain the occurrence of the symptoms and would suggest a specific treatment that would ameliorate the suffering (Frances, First, & Pincus, 1995). However, as expressed by the chair (Dr. Kupfer) and vice chair (Dr. Regier) of the forthcoming DSM-V, psychiatry's classification system has not been successful in meeting this goal (Kupfer, First, & Regier, 2002). There does not appear to be a qualitative distinction between normal and abnormal psychological functioning; patients often meet diagnostic criteria for multiple disorders, and a lack of treatment specificity is the rule rather than the exception.

Most mental disorders appear to be the result of a complex interaction of an array of interacting biological vulnerabilities and dispositions and environmental, psychosocial events. The symptoms and pathologies of mental disorders appear to be highly responsive to a wide variety of neurochemical, interpersonal, cognitive, environmental, and other mediating and moderating variables that help to develop, shape, and form a particular individual's psychopathology profile. This complex etiological history and individual psychopathology profile are unlikely to be well described by a single diagnostic category that attempts to make distinctions at nonexistent discrete joints (Widiger & Samuel, 2005).

A model for the future might be provided by one of the more well-established diagnoses, mental retardation. The point of demarcation for the diagnosis of mental retardation is an arbitrary, quantitative distinction along continuously distributed levels of intelligence. The current point of demarcation is an intelligence quotient of 70, along with a clinically significant level of impairment. This point of demarcation does not carve nature at a discrete joint. It is simply that point at which the level of impairment appears to warrant professional intervention. Many researchers are now turning their attention away from DSM-IV-TR diagnostic categories to the identification of underlying spectra of dysfunction that cut across the existing diagnostic categories (Widiger & Samuel, 2005).

Threshold for Diagnosis

One of the fundamental purposes of a diagnostic manual is demarcating the boundary between normal and abnormal psychological functioning. Most everyone will at some point have feelings of sadness. Many persons drink alcohol. Many persons have atypical sexual fantasies. At what point would these feelings, behaviors, or fantasies become a mood disorder, alcohol abuse, or a paraphilia, respectfully?

For example, in order to be diagnosed with pedophilia, the prior version of the APA diagnostic manual required only that an adult have recurrent intense urges and fantasies involving sexual activity with a prepubescent child over a period of at least six months and have acted on them (or be distressed by them). The authors of DSM-IV-TR were therefore concerned that these criteria were not providing adequate guidance for determining when deviant sexual behavior reflects a personal preference rather than a mental disorder as every adult who engaged in a sexual activity with a child for longer than six months would meet these diagnostic criteria (Frances et al., 1995). Deviant or repugnant behavior alone has not traditionally been considered sufficient for a diagnosis (Houts, 2002). Presumably, some persons can engage in deviant, aberrant, and even heinous activities without being compelled to do so by the presence of psychopathology. The authors of DSM-IV-TR, therefore, added the requirement that the behavior, sexual urges, or fantasies cause clinically significant impairment in social, occupational, or other important areas of functioning.

Wakefield and First (2002), however, have argued that the presence versus absence of impairment would not actually distinguish between a normal and abnormal sexual interest in children, and may in fact contribute to a normalization of pedophilic behavior by allowing the diagnosis not to be applied if the persons who engaged in these acts were not themselves distressed by their behavior or did not otherwise experience impairment. In response, Frances et al. (1995) had argued that pedophilic sexual "behaviors are inherently problematic because they involve a nonconsenting person (exhibitionism, voyeurism, frotteurism) or a child (pedophilia) and may lead to arrest and incarceration" (p. 319). Therefore, any person who engaged in an illegal sexual act (for longer than six months) would be experiencing a clinically significant social impairment. However, using the illegality of an act as a basis for identifying the presence of disorder is problematic. First, it undermines the original rationale for the inclusion of the impairment criterion (i.e., to distinguish immoral or illegal acts from abnormal or disordered acts). Second, it is inconsistent with the stated definition of a mental disorder that indicates that neither deviance nor conflicts with the law are sufficient to warrant a diagnosis (APA, 2000).

Wakefield (2007) has provided further examples that are less socially controversial than pedophilia and that may also illustrate a failure to make a meaningful distinction between maladaptive problems in living and true psychopathology. For example, the DSM-IV-TR criterion set for major depressive disorder currently excludes most instances of depressive reactions to the loss of a loved one (i.e., uncomplicated bereavement). Depression after the loss of a loved one can be considered a mental disorder if "the symptoms persist for longer than two months" (APA, 2000, p. 356). Allowing only two months to grieve though is perceived by some as a rather arbitrary basis for determining when normal sadness becomes a mental illness. In addition, there are many other losses that lead to depressed mood (e.g., loss of job or physical health) yet these do not warrant a comparable reprieve from becoming classified as a mental illness.

Wakefield and First (2002) argue that the distinction between disordered and nondisordered behavior should require an assessment for the presence an underlying, internal pathology (e.g., irrational cognitive schema or neurochemical dysregulation), and not simply be based on an amount of time or a level of impairment. However, a limitation of diagnosing a disorder on the basis of pathology is the absence of agreement over the specific pathology that underlies any particular disorder. There is insufficient empirical support to prefer one particular cognitive, interpersonal, neurochemical, or psychodynamic model of pathology relative to another.

The concern that the nomenclature is subsuming normal problems in living may itself be misguided. Persons critical of the DSM have decried its substantial expansion over the past 50 years (e.g., Houts, 2002). However, perhaps it would have been more surprising to find that increased knowledge has led to the recognition of fewer instances rather than more instances of psychopathology. In fact, the current manual might still be inadequate in coverage. The most common diagnosis in general clinical practice is often not-otherwise-specified (NOS). The diagnosis of mood disorder NOS, for example, is provided when a clinician determines that a mood disorder is present, but the symptomatology fails to meet criteria for one of the two existing diagnoses of major depressive disorder or dysthymia (APA, 2000). The frequency with which clinicians provide the diagnosis of NOS for mood disorders is a testament to inadequate coverage. In sum, perhaps the problem is not that depression in response to a loss of a job or physical disorder should not be a disorder, analogous to bereavement (Wakefield & First, 2002); perhaps the problem is that bereavement should be a mental disorder when the depression is both impairing and dyscontrolled (Widiger & Sankis, 2000).

Nobody is fully satisfied with or lacks valid criticisms of DSM-IV-TR. Clinicians, theorists, and researchers will at times feel frustrated at being required to use DSM-IV-TR. It can be difficult to obtain a grant, publish a study, or receive insurance reimbursement without reference to a DSM-IV-TR diagnosis. The benefits of an official diagnostic nomenclature do appear to outweigh the costs, however. Despite its significant flaws, DSM-IV-TR does at least provide a useful point of comparison that ultimately facilitates the development of new ways of conceptualizing and diagnosing psychopathology.

REFERENCES

American Psychiatric Association. (2000). *Diagnostic and statistical manual of mental disorders. Text Revision.*(4th ed., text rev.). Washington, DC: Author.

Houts, A.C. (2002). Discovery, invention, and the expansion of the modern diagnostic and statistical manuals of mental disorders.

In M. L. Malik & L. E. Beutler (Eds.), *Rethinking the DSM. A psychological perspective* (pp. 17–65). Washington, DC: American Psychological Association.

Frances, A. J., First, M. B., & Pincus, H. A. (1995). *DSM-IV guidebook*. Washington, DC: American Psychiatric Press.

Kupfer, D. J., First, M. B., & Regier, D. A. (Eds.). (2002). *A research agenda for DSM-V*. Washington, DC: American Psychiatric Association.

Spitzer, R. L., Williams, J. B. W., & Skodol, A. E. (1980). DSM-III: The major achievements and an overview. *American Journal of Psychiatry, 137*, 151–164.

Wakefield, J. C. (2007). The concept of mental disorder: Diagnostic implications of the harmful dysfunction analysis. *World Psychiatry, 6*, 149–156.

Wakefield, J. C., & First, M. B. (2002). Clarifying the distinction between disorder and nondisorder: Confronting the overdiagnosis (false positives) problem in DSM-V. In K. A. Phillips, M. B. First, & H. A. Pincus (Eds.), *Advancing DSM. Dilemmas in psychiatric diagnosis* (pp. 23–55). Washington, DC: American Psychiatric Association.

Widiger, T. A., & Samuel, D. B. (2005). Diagnostic categories or dimensions: A question for DSM-V. *Journal of Abnormal Psychology, 114*, 494–504.

Widiger, T. A., & Sankis, L. M. (2000). Adult psychopathology: Issues and controversies. *Annual Review of Psychology, 51*, 377–404.

SUGGESTED READINGS

Malik, M. L., & Beutler, L. E. (Eds.). (2002). *Rethinking the DSM. A psychological perspective*. Washington, DC: American Psychological Association.

Phillips, K. A., First, M. B., & Pincus, H. A. (Eds.). (2002). *Advancing DSM. Dilemmas in psychiatric diagnosis*. Washington, DC: American Psychiatric Association.

THOMAS A. WIDIGER
University of Kentucky

See also: Diagnostic and Statistical Manual of Mental Disorders (DSM-IV-TR); Psychodynamic Diagnostic Manual; Psychopathology

DIAGNOSTIC INTERVIEW SCHEDULE FOR DSM-IV (DIS-IV)

The Diagnostic Interview Schedule for DSM-IV (DIS-IV; Robins, Cottler, Bucholz, Compton, North, & Rourke, 2000) is a structured interview designed to diagnose in a reliable and valid fashion the major psychiatric disorders according to the *Diagnostic and Statistical Manual of Mental Disorders*, fourth edition (DSM-IV) (American Psychiatric Association, 2000). The DIS-IV is unique among the multidisorder structured diagnostic interviews in that it is a fully structured interview specifically designed for use by nonclinician interviewers, whereas the other interviews are semi-structured. By definition, a fully structured interview specifies clearly all questions and probes and does not permit deviations.

The original DIS was developed in 1978 by researchers at the Washington University Department of Psychiatry in St. Louis at the request of the National Institute of Mental Health Division of Biometry and Epidemiology, which was planning a set of large-scale, multicenter epidemiological investigations of mental illness in the general adult population in the United States. With this purpose in mind, development of a structured interview that could be administered by nonclinicians was imperative due to the prohibitive cost of using professional clinicians as interviewers. As a result, the DIS was designed as a fully structured diagnostic interview, explicitly crafted so that it can be administered and scored by nonclinician interviewers.

Computerized administration of the DIS-IV, called C-DIS, is the current standard, whereas the original paper and pencil version is obsolete. Computerized administration may be interviewer-administered or self-administered. In both formats, the exact wording of all questions and probes is presented to the respondent in a fixed order on a computer screen. Rephrasing of questions is discouraged, although DIS-IV interviewers can repeat questions as necessary to ensure that they are understood by the respondent. All questions are closed-ended and replies are coded with a forced choice "yes" or "no" response format, which eliminates the need for clinical judgment to rate responses. The DIS-IV gathers all necessary information about the person from the person, and collateral sources of information are not used. Notably, the DIS-IV is designed to make diagnoses for many mental disorders as defined in the DSM-IV, which is the predominant classification system in the United States. Because the DIS-IV is closely linked to the DSM-IV, diagnostic criteria for the disorders according to the DSM-IV system have been faithfully turned into specific questions on the DIS-IV. The coded responses to the questions are directly entered into a database during the interview and the diagnosis is made according to the explicit rules of the DSM-IV diagnostic system.

Because the DIS-IV was designed for epidemiological research with normative samples, interviewers do not elicit a presenting problem from the respondent, as would be typical in unstructured clinical interviews. Rather, DIS-IV interviews begin by asking questions about symptoms in a standardized order. The DIS-IV has 19 diagnostic modules or sections that cover different disorders. Each section is independent, except where one diagnosis preempts another. Once a symptom is reported to be present, further closed-ended questions are asked about diagnostically relevant information such as severity, frequency, time frame, and possibility of organic etiology of the symptom. The DIS-IV includes a set of core questions that are asked of each respondent. Core questions are followed by contingent questions that are administered only if the preceding core question is endorsed. DIS-IV interviewers utilize a "probe flow chart" that indicates which probes to use in which circumstances.

For each symptom, the respondent is asked to state whether it has ever been present and how recently. All data about the presence or absence of symptoms and time frames of occurrence are coded and entered into the computer. Consistent with its use of nonclinician interviewers who may not be overly familiar with the DSM-IV or psychiatric diagnosis, the diagnostic output of the DIS-IV is generated by a computer program that analyzes data from the completed interview. The output provides estimates of prevalence for two time periods: current and lifetime.

Due to its highly structured format, full administration of the DIS-IV typically requires between 90 and 120 minutes. The administration time may be significantly increased for respondents who are severely mentally ill with long histories of illness and among those who have multiple diagnoses. To shorten administration time, the modular format makes it possible to drop evaluation of disorders that are not of interest in a particular research study or clinical situation. Another option is to drop further questioning for a particular disorder once it is clear that the threshold number of symptoms needed for diagnosis will not be met. Although designed for use by nonclinician administrators, training for competent administration of the DIS-IV is necessary. Trainees typically attend a one-week training program at Washington University during which they review the manual, listen to didactic presentations about the structure and conventions of the DIS-IV, view videotaped vignettes, complete workbook exercises, and conduct several practice interviews followed by feedback and review. Additional supervised practice is also recommended.

The psychometric properties of the various versions of the DIS are generally solid and such data has been documented in an impressive array of studies. The interested reader is referred to Compton and Cottler (2004) for an excellent summary of the instrument's psychometric characteristics. Overall, the DIS-IV has proved to be a popular and useful diagnostic assessment tool, especially for large-scale epidemiological research. It has been translated into more than a dozen languages and is used in countries across the globe for epidemiological research. The DIS-IV also served as the basis for the Composite International Diagnostic Interview used by the World Health Organization. At present, the DIS-IV is the most popular and well-validated case finding strategy used to make DSM-IV psychiatric diagnoses in large-scale epidemiological research. Like earlier versions, the DIS-IV can be expected to enjoy widespread application in psychiatric research, service, and training for many years to come. For further information on DIS-IV and C-DIS materials, training, and developments, the interested reader may consult the web site devoted to the instrument located at http://epi.wustl.edu.

REFERENCES

American Psychiatric Association. (2000). *Diagnostic and statistical manual of mental disorders* (4th ed., text rev.). Washington, DC: Author.

Compton, W. M., & Cottler, L. B. (2004). The Diagnostic Interview Schedule (DIS). In M. Hilsenroth & D. L. Segal (Eds.), Personality assessment. Vol. 2 in M. Hersen (Ed.-in-Chief), *Comprehensive handbook of psychological assessment* (pp. 153–162). Hoboken, NJ: John Wiley & Sons.

Robins, L. N., Cottler, L. B., Bucholz, K. K., Compton, W. M., North, C. S., & Rourke, K. (2000). *The Diagnostic Interview Schedule for DSM-IV (DIS-IV)*. St. Louis, MO: Washington University School of Medicine.

SUGGESTED READINGS

Antony, M. M., & Barlow, D. H. (Eds.). (2004). *Handbook of assessment and treatment planning for psychological disorders*. New York: Guilford Press.

Rogers, R. (2001). *Handbook of diagnostic and structured interviewing*. New York: Guilford Press.

Segal, D. L., & Coolidge, F. L. (2001). Diagnosis and classification. In M. Hersen & V. B. Van Hasselt (Eds.), *Advanced abnormal psychology* (2nd ed., pp. 5–22). New York: Kluwer Academic/Plenum.

DANIEL L. SEGAL
University of Colorado at Colorado Springs

See also: **Diagnostic and Statistical Manual of Mental Disorders (DSM-IV-TR); Structured Clinical Interview for DSM Diagnosis**

DIALECTICAL BEHAVIOR THERAPY

Dialectical behavior therapy (DBT) is a comprehensive, multimodal cognitive-behavioral treatment developed for clients with complex and difficult-to-treat mental disorders. Originally developed to treat chronically suicidal clients, DBT evolved into a treatment for suicidal clients meeting criteria for borderline personality disorder (BPD). Since its development, DBT has been adapted to treat other problem behaviors in clients with BPD (including substance abuse and eating disorders), suicidal adolescents with BPD features, suicidal behavior in elderly with major depressive disorder, and individuals with antisocial personality disorder in forensic settings. DBT combines basic change strategies drawn from cognitive-behavioral therapy with acceptance-based strategies from Eastern meditative (Zen) and Western contemplative practices. The fundamental dialectical tension in DBT is between an emphasis on validation and acceptance of the client with a persistent attention to behavioral change.

DBT was developed by Marsha Linehan in the 1980s and grew out of a series of failed attempts to apply standard cognitive and behavior therapy protocols in treating chronically suicidal clients. For example, focusing on eliciting client change was often experienced by clients as invalidating and led to client withdrawal from therapy and attacks on the therapist. Because suicidal clients engage in life-threatening behaviors in response to a life of suffering, teaching clients new skills was difficult within a therapy focused on reducing motivation to die. However, the structure and focused agenda needed for skills training made it difficult for therapists to also attend to strengthening clients' motivation to decrease dysfunctional behavior and increase engagement in effective behaviors. Additionally, in times of severe distress, clients had difficulty remembering and employing new behavioral skills.

Linehan accordingly designed a cognitive-behavioral intervention that addressed these issues by incorporating techniques of radical acceptance and validation. This synthesis of acceptance and change-based techniques led to the adoption of the term "dialectical" as a defining characteristic of the treatment. In order to address structural issues, therapy as a whole was divided into four separate components: (1) individual psychotherapy (addressing motivation, strengthening, and generalizing DBT skills and managing crises); (2) highly-structured behavioral skills training (focusing on the acquisition and practice of DBT skills); (3) as-needed telephone consultation (addressing application and generalization of coping skills between sessions); and (4) a therapist consultation team focused specifically on maintaining therapist motivation and adherence to the treatment protocol. DBT is a team-based treatment, and all therapists on the team are responsible for every client, as well as for each other.

In DBT, treatment progresses in stages based on clients' severity and complexity of disorder. In stage 1, treatment focuses on reducing out-of-control client behaviors that are prioritized in the following order: (1) high-risk suicidal behaviors (including suicide attempts, life-threatening suicidal ideation, planning, and urges), non-suicidal self-injury; and other imminent life threatening behaviors, (2) client and therapist behaviors that interfere with the progress of therapy (missing sessions, tardiness, pushing therapist limits, not returning phone calls); (3) behavioral patterns that substantially limit clients from achieving a reasonable quality of life (e.g., Axis I disorders, homelessness, unemployment, legal problems); and (4) acquisition of life skills needed to meet client goals (skills in emotion regulation, interpersonal effectiveness, distress tolerance, self-management, and mindfulness). Once a client has achieved behavioral control as defined by absence of out-of-control behaviors in stage 1, therapy in stage 2 focuses on increasing clients' ability to experience emotions without trauma. Stage 3 focuses on building clients' self-respect and addressing residual problematic behaviors that interfere with achieving personal goals. In the final stage, clients and therapists work to resolve clients' feelings of incompleteness and enhance capacity for freedom and joy.

Treatment strategies utilized in DBT broadly fall under acceptance-based or change-based approaches and are divided into five sets: (1) dialectical strategies, (2) core strategies (problem solving and validation), (3) CBT change procedures, (4) communication strategies (irreverent and reciprocal communication), and (5) case-management (consultation to the client, environmental intervention, supervision/consultation with therapists). DBT also includes specific behavioral treatment protocols covering suicidal behavior, crisis management, therapy-interfering behavior and compliance issues, relationship problem-solving and ancillary treatment issues). These are more fully described in the treatment manuals (Linehan, 1993a, 1993b).

Dialectical strategies are woven throughout all therapeutic interactions. The primary strategy is the balanced therapeutic stance combining acceptance and change in order to increase clients' dialectical thinking. These strategies are used to bring out the opposites present in therapy and in everyday life, while providing an opportunity for synthesis using stories, metaphors, paradox, ambiguity (when therapeutic), and viewing therapy and reality as being in constant change.

Core strategies in DBT consist of the balanced application of problem-solving and validation strategies. The first is a two-stage process starting with a functional behavioral analysis and acceptance of the problem at hand, followed by an attempt to generate, evaluate, and implement alternative solutions that could be used in the future. Behavioral analysis entails a functional analysis of links in the causal chain of events that lead to client behavior, including environmental factors and consequences of client behavior. This exercise, called "chain analysis," is repeated for every instance of targeted problem behaviors until both therapist and client achieve an understanding of the client's response patterns. Generation and evaluation of more skillful responses (i.e., solutions) are woven into the chain analysis.

As noted earlier, problem-solving alone is insufficient to produce positive client change. Validation strategies are used to balance and keep change-oriented problem-solving strategies moving forward. These strategies require therapists to search for, recognize, and reflect the validity and sensibility of clients' patterns of behavior. Validation is required in every therapeutic interaction and is used at any one of six levels: (1) listening to the client with interest;

(2) reflection, paraphrasing, and summarizing; (3) articulating or "mind-reading" that which is unstated by the client, but without pushing the interpretation on the client; (4) acknowledging the role of biology and past learning experiences as factors in the client's current responses; (5) acknowledging the validity of the client's experience and behavior in terms of present circumstances and normal functioning; and (6) relating to the client with radical genuineness, that is, treating the client-therapist relationship as an authentic and real relationship.

DBT change procedures are designed to address problems that may occur when clients try out the new behavioral responses (solutions) identified through behavioral analysis. These strategies are primarily adaptations of CBT techniques that emphasize an emotion-focus. The four formal change procedures are contingency management, cognitive restructuring, exposure-based strategies and skills training.

Two communication strategies are used in DBT: the modal style is reciprocal, marked by warmth, responsiveness to the client's wishes, and self-disclosure of useful information to the client, including reactions to the client's behavior. Reciprocity is balanced by an irreverent communication style that is used to push the client "off balance" when the therapist and client are "stuck" in a dysfunctional pattern. Characterized by a matter-of-fact, or at times slightly outrageous, attitude, irreverent communication is useful in getting clients' attention, changing their affective response, and making a point that they did not consider before.

Case management strategies are designed to guide DBT therapists when interacting with individuals outside the client-therapist dyad. The consultation strategy requires that each DBT therapist meet regularly with a DBT consultation team The primary focus of the team is to support the therapist and assist each other in staying within the DBT treatment model. The consultation-to-the-client strategy is based on the principle that the DBT therapist teaches the client how to interact effectively with their environment, rather than teaching the environment how to interact with the client. Clients are not treated as fragile or unable to solve problems; however, the therapist actively intervenes only when absolutely necessary in order to protect the client or to modify situations that the client does not have the power to influence.

DBT has been evaluated in seven randomized controlled trials (RCTs) conducted across three independent research teams investigating the efficacy of DBT for the treatment of BPD clients with suicidal behaviors, BPD clients with substance dependence, major depression with personality disorder characteristics among the elderly, and binge eating disorder. There have been a number of controlled but nonrandomized trials of DBT in forensic systems, with suicidal adolescents, and on BPD inpatient units and in other outpatient settings. Across these studies, DBT, compared to various control conditions, results in significant reductions in suicide attempts, nonsuicidal self-injurious acts, medical severity of suicide attempts and nonsuicidal self-injury, drug use, treatment drop-out, inpatient psychiatric days, emergency room visits, depression, and anger.

Additionally, clients receiving DBT had significant improvement on scores of global as well as social adjustment. Treatment superiority of DBT is maintained when compared to clients who received only stable individual psychotherapy in the community, even after controlling for number of hours of psychotherapy and telephone contacts, or to those receiving treatment by experts in the community. These findings suggest that common factors of expert psychotherapy are not the critical factors in the efficacy of this treatment. From available evidence, it appears that DBT is a step toward more efficacious treatment for multi-disordered, difficult-to-treat clients, particularly those with suicidal behaviors.

REFERENCES

Koons, C. R., Robins, C. J., Tweed, J. L., Lynch, T. R., Gonzalez, A. M., Morse, J. Q., Bishop, G. K., Butterfield, M. I., & Bastian, L. A. (2001). Efficacy of dialectical behavior therapy in women veterans with borderline personality disorder. *Behavior Therapy, 32*, 371–390.

Linehan, M. M. (1993a). *Cognitive-behavioral treatment of borderline personality disorder.* New York: Guilford Press.

Linehan, M. M. (1993b). *Skills training manual for treating borderline personality disorder.* New York: Guilford Press.

Linehan, M. M., Armstrong, H. E., Suarez, A., Allmon, D., & Heard, H. L. (1991). Cognitive-behavioral treatment of chronically parasuicidal borderline patients. *Archives of General Psychiatry, 48*, 1060–1064.

Linehan, M. M., Comtois, K. A., Murray, A. M., Brown, M. Z., Gallop, R. J., Heard, H. L., Korslund, K. E., Tutek, D. A., Reynolds, S. K., & Lindenboim, N. (2006). Two-year randomized controlled trial and follow-up of dialectical behavior therapy vs. therapy by experts for suicidal behaviors and borderline personality disorder. *Archives of General Psychiatry, 63*, 757–766.

Linehan, M. M., Heard, H. L., & Armstrong, H. E. (1993c). Naturalistic follow-up of a behavioral treatment for chronically parasuicidal borderline patients. *Archives of General Psychiatry, 50*, 971–974.

Linehan, M. M., Schmidt, H., III, Dimeff, L. A., Craft, J. C., Kanter, J., & Comtois, K. A. (1999). Dialectical behavior therapy for patients with borderline personality disorder and drug-dependence. *American Journal on Addictions, 8*, 279–292.

Linehan, M. M., Tutek, D. A., Heard, H. L., & Armstrong, H. E. (1994). Interpersonal outcome of cognitive behavioral treatment for chronically suicidal borderline patients. *American Journal of Psychiatry, 151*, 1771–1776.

Verheul, R., van den Bosch, L. M. C., Koeter, M. W. J., de Ridder, M. A. J., Stijnen, T., & van den Brink, B. W. (2003). Dialectical behaviour therapy for women with borderline personality disorder: 12-month, randomised clinical trial in The Netherlands. *British Journal of Psychiatry, 182*, 135–140.

SUGGESTED READINGS

Koerner, K., & Linehan, M. M. (2000). Research on dialectical behavior therapy for borderline personality disorder. *The Psychiatric Clinics of North America, 23*(1), 151–167.

Linehan, M. M. (1997). Validation and psychotherapy. In A. Bohart & L. Greenberg (Eds.), *Empathy reconsidered: New directions in psychotherapy* (pp. 353–392). Washington, DC: American Psychological Association.

Linehan, M. M. (1998). Development, evaluation, and dissemination of effective psychosocial treatments: Stages of disorder, levels of care, and stages of treatment research. In M. D. Glantz & C. R. Hartel (Eds.), *Drug abuse: Origins and interventions.* Washington, D.C.: American Psychological Association.

Linehan, M. M., Armstrong, H. E., Suarez, A., Allmon, D., & Heard, H. L. (1991). Cognitive-behavioral treatment of chronically parasuicidal borderline patients. *Archives of General Psychiatry, 48*, 1060–1064.

SAFIA C. JACKSON
MARSHA M. LINEHAN
University of Washington

See also: Behavior Modification; Cognitive Therapy; Rational Emotive Behavior Therapy

DIALOGICAL SELF

In its original formulation, the dialogical self is conceived of as a dynamic multiplicity of I-positions in the landscape of the mind. These I-positions are involved in processes of mutual dialogical relationships that are intensely interwoven with external dialogical relationships. In this conception, the I is always bound to particular positions in time and space but has the possibility to move from one position to the other in accordance with changes in situation and time. The I fluctuates among different and even opposed positions and has the capacity to imaginatively endow each position with a voice, so that dialogical relations between positions can develop. The voices behave like interacting characters in a story, involved in a process of question and answer, agreement and disagreement. They all have a story to tell about their own experiences from their own perspective. As different voices, these characters exchange information about their respective Me's, creating a complex, narratively structured self. In this multiplicity of positions, some positions are more dominant than others, so that the voices of the less dominant positions are subdued (Hermans, 1996; Hermans, Kempen, & Van Loon, 1992).

Historical Background

The main purpose behind the work on the dialogical self was to bring together two concepts, dialogue and self, and combine them in such a way that they permit a more extended view on the possibilities of the mind. The theory is rooted in two traditions: the notion of *self* is inspired by the groundbreaking work of William James and George Herbert Mead, main representatives of American pragmatism; the notion of *dialogue* is instigated by the pioneering work of the Russian literary scholar Mikhail Bakhtin, the main representative of the Russian dialogical school.

After the first conceptualization of the dialogical self in the 1990s, further publications appeared primarily in the form of special issues in which authors from different (sub)disciplines addressed a particular topic relevant to the dialogical self. In *Culture & Psychology* (2001, Vol. 7, no. 3), a more detailed theory of personal and cultural positioning was exposed and commented on. In *Theory & Psychology* (2002, Vol. 12, no. 2), dialogical self-theory was discussed from a diversity of perspectives: developmental psychology, psychotherapy, psychopathology, brain sciences, cultural psychology, personality psychology, Jungian psychoanalysis, and semiotic dialogism. In the *Journal of Constructivist Psychology* (2003, Vol. 16, no. 2), authors explored the implications of dialogical self-theory for personal construct psychology, the philosophy of Martin Buber, self-narratives in psychotherapy, and a psychodramatic approach in psychotherapy. The notion of mediated dialogue in a global and digital age was the subject of a special issue in *Identity: An International Journal of Theory and Research* (2004, Vol. 4, no. 4). Finally, in *Counselling Psychology Quarterly* (2006, Vol. 19, no. 1), the dialogical self was applied to a variety of topics relevant to the process of counseling. Recently, the experience of uncertainty in relation to the accelerated processes of globalization and localization was discussed in the context of dialogical self-theory (Hermans & Dimaggio, 2007). Experimental evidence for the multivoiced nature of the dialogical self was presented by Stemplewska-Żakowicz, Walecka, and Gabińska (2006).

In order to stimulate theory, research, and practice, international conferences on the dialogical self are organized biannually, the first in Nijmegen, The Netherlands (2000), the second in Ghent, Belgium (2002), the third in Warsaw, Poland (2004), the fourth in Braga, Portugal (2006), and the fifth at Cambridge University, UK (2008). The sixth conference is scheduled in Kyoto, Japan (2010). The conferences are organized by the International Society for Dialogical Science (ISDS), established in 2002. This Society publishes an electronic, peer-reviewed, open access journal: the *International Journal for Dialogical Science* (*IJDS*) (first issue, spring 2006).

Four Features of the Dialogical Self

Dialogical self-theory can be characterized by four main features: (1) the other-in-the-self, (2) multiplicity-in-unity, (3) dominance and social power, and (4) its spatial and embodied nature. These features are briefly described.

The-Other-in-the-Self

Dialogical self-theory assumes that the other person is not purely outside, but simultaneously part of the self and even constitutive of it. The other is not seen as something that influences or determines an otherwise socially isolated self. Rather, the other is included in the self as an I-position, and social interchange takes place not only between different selves but also between different I-positions in one and the same self.

The concept of otherness is intimately linked to the existence of an actual, physical other. In the tradition of the philosophy of Emmanuel Levinas, otherness is often equated with the expressive face of another human being, whereas the internal sphere of the self is characterized by sameness and identity. However, conceiving the self as sameness would not sufficiently account for the differentiation, diversity, and even oppositions of a multi-voiced dialogical self. The notions of difference, otherness, and alterity can be usefully extended from the interpersonal realm to the intrapersonal while an intersubjective viewpoint is preserved. This preservation implies that otherness exists not only between the self and the actual other, but also within one's own self. Therefore, the concept of *self-otherness* can serve a valuable function in a theory that recognizes the other-in-the-self as one of its defining features (Cooper & Hermans, 2006).

Multiplicity-in-Unity

In psychological discussions, unity is typically considered as a desirable end-state or even as a starting point, rather than a dynamic process. Fragmentation, as its opposite, is generally perceived as an aberration. The term I-position, however, allows the inclusive opposition between unity and multiplicity instead of the exclusive opposition between unity and fragmentation. Whereas the latter opposition bears a strong evaluative connotation (unity is good, fragmentation is bad), the former assumes that the two principles, unity (expressed in the dialogical movements between positions) and multiplicity (expressed in the diversity of positions), are equivalent and even presuppose one another as complementary and dynamic aspects of the self.

The topic of unity is relevant to the distinction between the normal functioning of the multivoiced, dialogical self and the controversial clinical dysfunction, Multiple Personality Disorder (MPD), more recently called Dissociative Identity Disorder (DID). These clinical categories refer to the serious impediments in the dialogical relationships between the host personality and a diversity of alters as rejected parts of the self. The difference between a multivoiced self and dissociative phenomena can only be fully understood when one takes into account the insight that the dysfunctional aspects of MPD and DID are not primarily in the parts but in their organization. In the dissociative self there is an inability to move flexibly from one position to another, with the consequence that the dialogue between positions is impeded. Moreover, in cases of dissociation the different voices are not in line with the requirements of the situation at hand.

Dominance and Social Power

Contemporary theories of the self, particularly those that put a one-sided emphasis on unity, often lack insight into the intense interplay between dominance relations in the society at large and dominance relations in the mini-society of the self. In apparent contrast to theories built on the notion of self-contained individualism, dialogical self-theory proposes a conception of self and dialogue in which social power and dominance play a significant role.

Although there are significant differences between internal and external dialogues (e.g., internal ones are more abbreviated and filled with images), the basic similarity is that voices and their relative dominance play a central role in both forms of dialogue. One voice is stronger, louder, and more influential than another, certainly when differences between voices have a basis in societal and institutional power differences. Like external voices, internal ones may be silenced, suppressed, or marginalized.

The Spatial and Embodied Nature of the Self

A central feature of the dialogical self is its combination of temporal and spatial characteristics. Time and space are of equal significance to the narrative structure of the dialogical self. The spatial nature of the self is expressed in the terms position, and positioning, terms that are, moreover, more dynamic and flexible than the traditional term "role." The spatial term position can only be determined by its relationship with another position. Of particular importance are counter-positions that assume the existence of other positions that are located somewhere else, creating a dynamic field in which dialogical relationships may emerge.

The importance of the functioning of the brain for the dialogical self was emphasized by Lewis (2002), who was interested in the relationship between the dialogical self and the functioning of the (higher) orbitofrontal cortex. This cortex produces, in its linkage to the lower (conservative) subcortical limbic system, an affectively charged, gist-like sense of an interpersonal respondent, which is based on stabilized expectancies from many past interactions. This model has the advantage that shows how relatively stable, sublingual voices put constraints on the linguistic, dialogical processes. Such limits are not necessarily a disadvantage, because the automatic responses, which are inherent to sublingual voices, may contribute in specific situations to our action readiness and behavioral efficiency.

Dialogical self-theory is a relatively young field that explores the self as a society of mind. Crucial for its further development is an exploring attitude and an open mind that is willing and able to deal with uncertainty at the interface of an increasing diversity of voices, so typical of a globalizing society.

REFERENCES

Cooper, M., & Hermans, H. J. M. (2006) Honoring self-otherness: Alterity and the intrapersonal. In: L. M. Simão & J. Valsiner (Eds.), *Otherness in Question: Labyrinths of the Self* (pp. 305–325). Greenwich: Information Age Publishing.

Hermans, H. J. M. (1996). Voicing the self: From information processing to dialogical interchange. *Psychological Bulletin, 119,* 31–50.

Hermans, H. J. M., & Dimaggio, G. (2007). Self, and identity, and globalization in times of uncertainty: A dialogical analysis. *General Review of Psychology, 11,* 31–61.

Hermans, H. J. M., Kempen, H. J. G., & Van Loon, R. J. P. (1992). The dialogical self: Beyond individualism and rationalism. *American Psychologist, 47,* 23–33.

Lewis, M. D. (2002). The dialogical brain: Contributions of emotional neurobiology to understanding the dialogical self. *Theory & Psychology, 12,* 175–190.

Stemplewska-Żakowicz, K., Walecka, J., & Gabińska, A. (2006). As many selves as interpersonal relations (or maybe even more). *International Journal for Dialogical Science, 1,* 71–94.

SUGGESTED READINGS

Hermans, H. J. M. (2009). *The dialogical self: Positioning and counter-positioning in a globalizing society.* Cambridge, UK: Cambridge University Press.

Hermans, H. J. M., & Dimaggio, G. (Eds.). (2004). *The dialogical self in psychotherapy.* New York: Brunner & Routledge.

Oles, P. K., & Hermans, H. J. M. (2005). *The dialogical self: Theory and research.* Lublin, Poland: Wydawnictwo.

HUBERT J. M. HERMANS
Radboud University Nijmegen,
The Netherlands

See also: **Self Psychology**

DISASTER PSYCHOLOGY

Disasters severely disrupt or destroy environments on which people depend for their survival, and they may thus have extensive social and psychological consequences. The origin of a disaster may lie in natural phenomena such as heat, wind, precipitation, fire, tides, and seismic activity (e.g., droughts, famines, tornadoes, hurricanes, floods, blizzards, wildfires, tsunamis, and earthquakes). Disasters may also be brought about by unusually rapid changes in the prevalence and distribution of life forms, leading to infestations of destructive species and epidemics of infectious disease. Human activities may also cause massive destruction, whether inadvertently or by intent. Technological failures are an increasingly worrisome cause of death and destruction, most notably perhaps in the category of failures of transportation conveyances (e.g., aircraft, ships, trains), but failures of architectural structures can also be massively destructive (e.g., dams, levies, pipelines, and large buildings). Manufacturing that involves explosive or toxic substances also requires technological safeguards that may fail (e.g., chemical plants, oil refineries, and nuclear power plants), and major failures can lead to long-term environmental damage and the injury or death of workers or others living nearby.

Although many of the most catastrophic events caused by human activity qualify as unintentional, even if gross negligence was involved, various sources of massive death and destruction originate in intentional acts of violence that involve deliberation by individuals, groups, and government leaders. This last category, which includes among other things terrorism, war, and genocide, has only recently come to be included by some within the category of disasters, and there appears to be little public debate or dissent regarding the inclusion of these events alongside the more customary examples of disaster. This is perhaps partially due to the similarity of outcomes produced by disastrous events, regardless of their origins. Thus, the categorization of events as disasters has come to be determined more by consideration of consequences than of causes. Nevertheless, because the individual and social meaning constructed around disastrous events is influenced by causal attributions and the estimation of human culpability, the intentional infliction of suffering and death carries implications that differ substantially from those ascribed to natural hazards (i.e., acts of God) and errors of human planning and performance.

Psychologists have only recently begun to systematically study how people react to disasters. The earliest studies of reactions to disasters were produced by sociologists (e.g. Prince, 1968/1920), who emphasized the effects on communities, the historical meaning, and the consequences leading to social change. Later psychiatric studies (e.g., Adler, 1943; Lindemann, 1944) focused on clinically significant reactions such as profound grief, depression, and psychological trauma. The terms *disaster* and *crisis* were used almost interchangeably, because of similarities in the psychologically destabilizing aspects of such events and in the symptoms observed in survivors. The approaches to studying the psychosocial effects of disasters can be categorized as clinically focused and community-focused. Clinically focused studies examine just those people who exhibit extreme reactions or who seek treatment for enduring psychological disturbances, whereas community-focused studies examine populations of people affected by a given disaster. The purposes of these studies tend to include the intention of extrapolating some general predictive information about how people are likely to react to disasters, though each approach is prone to a number of confounding conditions that decrease the reliability of generalizations.

The first meta-analytic review of this body of literature (Rubonis & Bickman, 1991) concluded that the studies revealed a significant pattern of global and specific (e.g., anxiety, alcohol abuse) psychopathology among disaster survivors. A later review examining research similar to that covered in the Rubonis and Bickman meta-analysis (Norris, Friedman, Watson, Byrne, et al., 2002) also found significant patterns of specific (e.g., diagnosable posttraumatic stress disorder) and nonspecific (e.g., distress symptoms) forms of disturbance, along with negative effects on health, ongoing problems in adjustment (e.g., relational or occupational difficulties), a loss of psychosocial resources, and some problems specific to the developmental level of younger survivors (e.g., behavioral problems). The latter study also examined risk and protective factors that appeared to influence the degree of exposure to harm and the manifestation of psychosocial disturbances. In a companion article (Norris, Friedman, & Watson, 2002), the researchers linked the empirical findings to their recommendation to implement early psychosocial interventions following disasters, especially in cases in which the disaster is associated with extreme and widespread damage or loss of life.

A less developed line of research in disaster psychology focuses on clinical interventions for those who are exposed to disasters and those who exhibit severe acute reactions or long-lasting mental health impairments. The approaches to intervention can be categorized as preventive (e.g., education for reducing risks and improving coping), immediate (e.g., forms of crisis intervention), or clinical (e.g., treatments for manifest problems with coping and adjustment). Research on disaster-related interventions is mostly confined to clinical interventions, which tend to take place in more stable settings and with populations that are less mobile than those encountered in disaster situations. The interventions delivered during and immediately following disasters tend to be provided by mental health professionals under the aegis of the Red Cross or some other organization involved in disaster relief (Reyes & Elhai, 2004). These interventions have seldom been subjected to empirical evaluation and are instead based on reasoned clinical judgment regarding what can be expected to relieve stress and support adaptive functioning when the existing conditions and population characteristics are given due consideration.

Providers of disaster mental health are expected to gauge the levels of disturbance and resilience among the disaster survivors they encounter and to provide a commensurate degree of support and guidance. This approach is not without controversy, and it has drawn various types of criticism of the premises and assumptions used to support the need for intervention and the approaches to intervention, most notably in response to the widespread application of an approach generally known as psychological debriefing (Litz, Gray, Bryant, & Adler, 2003). A less controversial model of immediate intervention is known as psychological first aid (PFA), which consists of behaviors designed to relieve stress and educate survivors about good coping practices and sources of material and psychosocial support (Vernberg et al., 2008). While PFA and some other approaches to immediate crisis intervention are unlikely to prove harmful and are based on analogous interventions and situations that have received empirical support, there is still a paucity of research on these interventions in the context and populations with which they are being applied. Given that these interventions are being widely disseminated and applied with a limitless variety of disaster survivors in most areas of the globe, research on the effectiveness of these interventions and the contextual and cultural factors that influence their usefulness should become a higher priority.

The future of disaster psychology must include a fuller exploration of the importance of human diversity in understanding psychosocial reactions to disasters and the integration of those findings into the public health and mental health response systems. The American Psychological Association Policy and Planning Board (2006) reviewed that organization's roles and activities in national and international disasters, and included among the challenges immediately facing the disaster mental health system a need to ensure the cultural competence of those who are deployed to provide psychosocial support to disaster affected populations. At the global level, humanitarian organizations have collaborated on the development of an extensive set of guidelines for assessing and responding to the mental health needs of people around the world who are located in emergency settings as the result of disasters and other catastrophic events (Inter-Agency Standing Committee, 2007). These are promising developments, but it will also be critically important to build and improve on the empirical research foundation for the assumptions, policies, and practices of disaster psychology.

REFERENCES

Adler, A. (1943). Neuropsychiatric complications in victims of Boston's Coconut Grove disaster. *Journal of the American Medical Association, 123,* 1098–1101.

American Psychological Association Policy and Planning Board. (2006). APA's response to international and national disasters and crises: Addressing diverse needs. 2005 annual report of the APA Policy and Planning Board. *American Psychologist, 61,* 513–521.

Carr, L. J. (1932). Disaster and the sequence-pattern concept of social change. *American Journal of Sociology, 38,* 207–218.

Inter-Agency Standing Committee (IASC) (2007). *IASC guidelines on mental health and psychosocial support in emergency settings.* Geneva, Switzerland: Author.

Lindemann, E. (1944). Symptomatology and management of acute grief. *American Journal of Psychiatry, 101,* 141–148.

Litz, B. T., Gray, M. J., Bryant, R. A., & Adler, A. B. (2002). Early intervention for trauma: Current status and future directions. *Clinical Psychology: Science and Practice, 9,* 112–134.

Norris, F. H., Friedman, M. J., & Watson, P. J. (2002). 60,000 disaster victims speak: Part II. Summary and implications of disaster mental health research. *Psychiatry, 65,* 240–260.

Norris, F. H., Friedman, M. J., Watson, P. J., Byrne, C. M., Diaz, E., & Kaniasty, K. (2002). 60,000 disaster victims speak: Part I. An empirical review of the empirical literature, 1981–2001. *Psychiatry, 65,* 207–239.

Prince, S. H. (1968). *Catastrophe and Social Change.* New York: AMS Press (1st ed.: Columbia University Press, 1920).

Pynoos, R. S., Goenjian, A. K., & Steinberg, A. M. (1998). A public mental health approach to the postdisaster treatment of children and adolescents. *Child and Adolescent Psychiatric Clinics of North America, 7,* 195–210.

Reyes, G., & Elhai, J. D. (2004). Psychosocial interventions in the early phases of disasters. *Psychotherapy: Theory, Research, Practice, Training, 41,* 399–411.

Rubonis, A. V., & Bickman, L. (1991). Psychological impairment in the wake of disaster: The disaster-psychopathology relationship. *Psychological Bulletin, 109*(3), 384–399.

Vernberg, E. M., Steinberg, A. M., Jacobs, A. K., Brymer, M. J., Watson, P. J., Osofsky, J. D., et al. (2008). Innovations in disaster mental health: Psychological first aid. *Professional Psychology: Research and Practice, 39,* 381–388.

GILBERT REYES
*Fielding Graduate University,
Santa Barbara, CA*

See also: **Crisis Intervention; Trauma Psychology**

DISCRIMINATION

Discrimination is negative behavior directed at individuals or at groups of individuals because of their social group membership. Discrimination is based on social categories to which individuals do not generally choose to belong. Such social categories include gender, race, religion, disability, sexual orientation, stigma, age, and physical appearance. Although it is normal to favor people who are similar to us (e.g., young children frequently play within gender groups and people date and marry primarily within their own race), discrimination involves unfair, unwarranted, and unjustifiable treatment of others.

Discrimination may take a variety of forms, ranging from overt hostility, violence, and genocide to minor everyday hassles. These different forms of discrimination can be classified into explicit and subtle forms of discrimination. Explicit discrimination includes actions such as making negative comments to or about people, excluding individuals from activities, and verbal and sexual abuse or physical harm. Subtle discrimination includes actions that are normally more difficult to detect, such as failing to make eye contact with someone, staring at or avoiding someone, or ignoring them entirely. Explicit discrimination is usually assessed through survey methodology in organizations or through examination of historical records. Subtle discrimination is frequently assessed in laboratory contexts using unobtrusive measures of verbal and nonverbal behavior, such as how much help research participants give to another person, how long they converse with them, or how far away from them they sit.

Discrimination is determined at psychological and sociological levels. At the level of the individual, some people are more likely to discriminate than others. Discrimination is closely related to holding negative stereotypes about members of other groups and to being prejudiced toward them, and occurs when people choose to act on their negative stereotypes and prejudices. Discrimination also occurs in part because it helps maintain individuals' personal esteem and social identity. People may feel better about themselves and their own groups when they put down, insult, or degrade members of another group. People may also assume that individuals from other groups hold different beliefs and values, and therefore dislike them and treat them differently.

At a social level, discrimination is in large part the result of social conformity. If people perceive that the relevant social norms favor discrimination, then they will discriminate themselves; if they perceive that the norms do not allow discrimination, they will not discriminate. Interventions designed to alleviate discrimination frequently attempt to change social norms, with the expectation that this will reduce discrimination. At a societal level, discrimination occurs more frequently when economic conditions are poor. As one example, lynching of Blacks in the South during the early twentieth century was inversely correlated with the price of cotton (an indicator of economic prosperity) (Hovland & Sears, 1940). This relationship is due partly to the frustration caused by hardship and partly to realistic conflict caused by employment scarcity. Discrimination may be socially sanctioned because high status, powerful individuals are motivated to retain their status by discriminating against lower status groups.

It is frequently difficult to identify discrimination (even if it is explicit), because most instances leave room for interpretation. In a case in which a more qualified female is passed over for a position and a lesser qualified male is hired instead, one can be certain that discrimination has occurred only when gender is the sole difference between the two candidates, or if there is a continuing pattern of unequal treatment by the employer over time. However, in many cases there is not enough information to allow an unambiguous attribution (Crosby, Clayton, Alksnis, & Hemker, 1986). Thus even though discrimination may have occurred, it may not be easily interpreted as such and therefore not perceived or reported.

Although members of targeted groups (for instance, women and African Americans) report that there is discrimination directed at their group as a whole, they do not generally report experiencing it personally (Crosby, 1984). People may deny personal discrimination because admitting that they are victims is psychologically costly. There are also many social costs to reporting discrimination (such as embarrassment, ostracism, and employment harassment) that make people unlikely to publicly indicate that they experienced discrimination (Sechrist, Swim, & Stangor, 2004). Researchers have identified several factors related to the likelihood that individuals may report discrimination, including belief in a just world, need for approval, need for control, identification with the in-group, stigma consciousness, and mood (Major, Quinton, & McCoy, 2002; Stangor, Swim, Sechrist, DeCoster, Van Allen, & Ottenbreit, 2003)

If targets or victims are aware of the discrimination they are experiencing, they may make either an internal or an external attribution to discrimination (see Major et al., 2002). In making an internal attribution to discrimination, individuals place the blame for their victimization on themselves. Making such an internal attribution to discrimination may result in lowered self-esteem, self-blame, and disidentification with the in-group. On the other hand, targets may also make an external attribution, placing the blame for their victimization on someone or something else. Attributing their discrimination to an external source can lead to either individual action (such as leaving the negative situation or reporting or confronting perpetrators) or collective action (such as mobilizing political or other organizations).

Discrimination can be both psychologically and physically harmful to those who endure it (see Stangor et al., 2003). Individuals who report frequent exposure to discrimination or unfair treatment also report experiencing more psychological distress, depression, and lower levels of life satisfaction. Discrimination may contribute to the high percentage of minority group members who live in poverty and lack access to high-paying jobs. Discrimination also is responsible in part for higher morality rates, access to less and poorer quality healthcare, delayed diagnoses, or failure to manage chronic diseases for members of minority groups.

The previously discussed harmful effects of discrimination focus on the direct effects of discrimination, which occur as a result of directly experiencing discrimination.

Discrimination also may influence individuals indirectly. Indirect effects of discrimination occur when individuals perceive that they are, will be, or have been targets or victims of discrimination, and their perceptions influence relevant outcomes (Stangor et al., 2003). Individuals' perceptions can have an influence on a variety of behaviors, including the manner in which they interact with other people and even their own task performance. For example, in their research on stereotype threat, Steele and Aronson (1995) demonstrated the potential harmful effects of perceptions about the beliefs of others on individuals' task performance. Thus, discrimination has a variety of negative outcomes, and some of these consequences may have long-term implications for the individuals who experience discrimination.

Political policies in the United States, including the Civil Rights Act of 1964, which established the Equal Employment Opportunities Commission and prohibited discrimination in employment, have reduced the frequency of explicit discrimination in recent years. The courts have ruled that even unintentional discrimination violates equal status laws. If targets are harmed, degraded, or treated differently than others as a function of their group membership, then discrimination has occurred.

These laws have also required reparations for violations of the laws, including awarding employment and promotions and back salary. In some cases, these laws have requested employers to establish practices that require a certain number or percentage of members of victimized social groups to be hired or promoted. Despite a reduction in explicit discrimination, implicit forms of discrimination continue to be common (Dovidio & Gaertner, 2004). In fact, current research shows that women and minorities generally report experiencing discrimination on a weekly basis (Swim, Hyers, Cohen, & Ferguson, 2001). Thus, despite policies directed at decreasing discrimination and regardless of reductions in the occurrence of explicit discrimination (which may stem directly from these policies), discrimination continues to be a problem that many individuals experience in their daily lives.

REFERENCES

Crosby, F. J. (1984). The denial of personal discrimination. *American Behavorial Scientist, 27,* 371–386.

Crosby, F., Clayton, S., Alksnis, O., & Hemker, K. (1986). Cognitive biases in the perception of discrimination: The importance of format. *Sex Roles, 14,* 637–646.

Dovidio, J. F., & Gaertner, S. L. (2004). Aversive racism. In M. P. Zanna (Ed.), *Advances in experimental social psychology* (Vol. 36, pp. 1–51). San Diego, CA: Academic Press.

Hovland, C., I., & Sears, R. (1940). Minor studies in aggression: VI: Correlation of lynchings with economic indices. *Journal of Psychology, 9,* 301–310.

Major, B., Quinton, W. J., & McCoy, S. K. (2002). Antecedents and consequences of attributions to discrimination: Theoretical and empirical advances. In M. P. Zanna (Ed.), *Advances in experimental social psychology* (Vol. 34, pp. 251–330). San Diego, CA: Academic Press.

Sechrist, G. B., Swim, J. K., & Stangor, C. (2004). When do the stigmatized make attributions to discrimination occurring to the self and others? The roles of self presentation and need for control. *Journal of Personality and Social Psychology, 87,* 111–122.

Stangor, C., Swim, J. K., Sechrist, G. B., DeCoster, J., Van Allen, K. L., & Ottenbreit, A. (2003). Ask, answer, and announce: Three stages in perceiving and responding to discrimination. In W. Stroebe & M. Hewstone (Eds.), *European review of social psychology* (Vol. 14, pp. 277–311). Chichester, UK: John Wiley & Sons.

Steele, C. M., & Aronson, J. (1995). Stereotype threat and the intellectual test performance of African-Americans. *Journal of Personality and Social Psychology, 69,* 797–811.

Swim, J. K., Hyers, L. L., Cohen, L. L., & Ferguson, M. J. (2001). Everyday sexism: Evidence for its incidence, nature, and psychological impact from three daily diary studies. *Journal of Social Issues, 57,* 31–53.

SUGGESTED READINGS

Crosby, F. J. (2004). *Affirmative action is dead; long live affirmative action.* New Haven, CT: Yale University Press.

Major, B., & O'Brien, L. T. (2005). The social psychology of stigma. *Annual Review of Psychology, 56,* 393–421.

Swim, J. T., & Stangor, C. (1998). *Prejudice from the target's perspective.* Santa Barbara, CA: Academic Press.

GRETCHEN B. SECHRIST
University at Buffalo, State University of New York

See also: **Interpersonal Perception; Prejudice and Discrimination; Racism**

DISORDERED THINKING

An integrative definition of disordered thinking encompasses a broad perspective that includes traditional concepts such as impaired pace and flow of associations along with such factors as (1) inefficient focusing and attentional processes; (2) deviant word usage; (3) errors in syntax and syllogistic reasoning; (4) inappropriate levels of abstracting; (5) failure to maintain conceptual boundaries; and (6) a breakdown in the discrimination of internal perceptions from external ones (reality testing). A sufficiently broad definition captures the multidimensional nature of disturbances in thought organization (Kleiger, 1999).

Controversies, Problems, and Challenges in Assessment

Measuring disordered thinking is beset with a number of controversies and potential challenges. Making inferences

about the nature of one's thought processes from a sample of speech is controversial and has led some to question the validity of the construct of "thought disorder." Because the construct itself is called into question, instruments that purport to measure disordered thinking, instead of disordered speech, per se, are vulnerable to the criticism that they lack sufficient construct validity to justify claims of their effectiveness as diagnostic tools.

Another difficulty that plagues assessment efforts is the lack of agreement over what constitutes disordered thought. There is general agreement that disordered thinking occurs in a variety of conditions, falls along a continuum of severity, and reflects a number of anomalies in thinking. However, there is no absolute standard for classifying these anomalies of thought. Furthermore, different researchers often employ different techniques to assess different types of disturbed thinking. Although there may be overlap in many of the variables studied by different assessment methods, comparison between the various techniques is often difficult. Different assessment approaches may employ different names for similar variables or use the same name for essentially different types of disordered thinking.

Achieving sufficiently high interrater reliability or clinical sensitivity with the instruments is a challenge, because many of the ratings or scoring systems themselves can be quite intricate, difficult to learn, and subject to interpretation. Research on the most prominent scales and scoring systems demonstrates that significantly high interrater reliability is possible; however, learning some of these rating systems usually requires more than becoming familiar with the manuals. Often consultation with the researchers who pioneered the ratings scales or scoring systems is necessary in order to use the instruments competently.

The impact of phase of illness, medication, and context must be taken into consideration when assessing disordered thinking. The degree to which an individual's thinking is disorganized will depend on whether the person is in an acute phase or in a partial or complete remission. Valid measurement of disordered thinking also requires evaluation of the person's motivation, attitude, and the context in which the idiosyncratic thinking is revealed. Is the person aware of the bizarreness of his or her speech or ideas, and if so, what is the person's attitude toward it? Is idiosyncratic speech used to shock, control, or entertain? The presence of unusual ideas or odd speech does not constitute immediate grounds for inferring the incursion of a psychotic process.

Assessment Instruments

Disordered thinking can be assessed by a variety of instruments ranging from formal psychological tests to structured interview techniques. Chapman and Chapman (1973) reviewed five methods for measuring thinking disturbances in schizophrenia. Included among these were

(1) clinical descriptions of spontaneous verbalizations; (2) clinical interpretation of verbalizations made to standardized stimuli; (3) classification of verbalizations into predetermined categories; (4) standardized tests with formal scoring of deviant verbalizations, and (5) multiple-choice techniques. Simplifying matters, Koistinen (1995) divided assessment techniques into two broad categories: those using structured interview techniques and those based on psychological tests.

One of the most popular interview-based rating scales is Andreasen's Scale for the Assessment of Thought, Language, and Communication (TLC) (Andreasen, 1978). This scale consists of definitions and directions for rating the severity of 20 forms of thought disorder manifestations based on an unstructured sample of the person's speech. The interrater reliabilities of each of the subtypes defined by Andreasen have been shown to be sufficiently high to make the TLC Scale a useful instrument for research and clinical assessment of disordered thought, language, and communication. As a tool to aid in differential diagnosis, Andreasen demonstrated both quantitative and qualitative differences in TLC scores between different groups of psychotic patients.

Traditional personality inventories such as the MMPI/MMPI-2 and MCMI offer the advantages of time-efficiency and ease of administration; however, they provide, at best, crude measures of deviant thinking and psychotic experience. By themselves, these tests cannot provide a detailed assessment of the nature of disturbed thought processes. Even attempting to identify the presence of psychosis with these instruments is usually accompanied by an unacceptably high number of false positives and negatives. True and false or multiple-choice questions, if read carefully, understood correctly, and answered truthfully, might be sensitive to some unusual ideas and experiences; however, without a sample of verbal behavior and an opportunity to inquire into idiosyncratic responses, it is difficult to judge anything about the severity or quality of subtypes of disordered thinking.

Since the Rorschach Inkblot Method was developed more than 70 years ago (Rorschach, 1921), researchers and clinicians have devoted considerable attention to identifying signs of schizophrenia and other forms of serious psychopathology with it. Although early Rorschach studies mirrored general psychiatric diagnostic trends, which assumed an isomorphic relationship between schizophrenia and disordered thinking, sophisticated ways of conceptualizing and measuring thought pathology with the Rorschach have been developed. Virtually all Rorschach systems for assessing disordered thinking are based on the work of Rapaport (Rapaport et al., 1968), who made thought disorder scoring a key aspect of the test.

There are two contemporary Rorschach approaches for scoring thought disorder manifestations. The Special Scores of the Comprehensive Rorschach System (Exner, 1993) and the Thought Disorder Index (TDI; Johnston & Holzman, 1979) both assess a range of deviant thought and speech elements embedded in verbalizations and reasoning used to justify a Rorschach response. Both instruments were developed in the mid 1970s but had relatively separate developments over the last several decades. Exner's Comprehensive System is the most commonly used approach for administering, scoring, and interpreting the Rorschach, while the TDI was developed as a research instrument and, as such, has made few inroads into clinical assessment practice.

The TDI comprises 23 different forms of thought disorder, scored at 4 levels of severity (.25, .50, .75, and 1.0). More complex to learn than the Comprehensive System Special Scores, the TDI is useful for identifying subtle differences among different groups of psychotic persons, which aides in the differential diagnosis of psychotic disorders. Interrater reliability is relatively good for TDI ratings across different severity levels, with interclass correlations ranging from .72 to .77 (Coleman et al., 1993). Apart from its being a difficult scoring system to learn, one drawback of the TDI is that it was developed using the Rapaport method of Rorschach administration, which differs from the standard administration used by the more popular Comprehensive System. Nonetheless, the TDI is viewed as not only a robust measure of thought disorder, but as being sensitive to identifying differential diagnostic patterns among different groups of psychotic subjects.

By contrast, the Special Scores of the Comprehensive System offer a relatively crisp and economical approach to identifying major thought disorder categories. Four major categories comprising eight different scores can be scored according to level of severity (Level 1, mild slippage; Level 2, moderate and severe). By reducing the number of categories, the Comprehensive System ensures better interscorer reliability and ease of learning than characterize the TDI. Different scores are weighted according to their level of severity and entered into a summary index called the Perceptual Thinking Index (PTI).

Future Perspectives

Whereas disordered thinking has traditionally been studied as a psychological construct, researchers are increasingly seeking to understand disordered thinking from a cognitive neuroscience perspective. Cognitive deficits in working memory, executive functions, and information processing have been found to be present in individuals suffering from schizophrenia-spectrum disorders. Cutting-edge research is being conducted to examine the correlation between thought disorder, neuropsychological measures, and neuroanatomical brain characteristics. Increasingly, we might expect neuropsychological studies of thought disturbances in affective, trauma-based, characterological, anxiety-related, and learning disorders.

REFERENCES

Andreasen, N. C. (1978), *The scale for the assessment of thought, language, and communication (TLC)*. Iowa City: University of Iowa Press.

Chapman, L., & Chapman, J. P. (1973). *Disordered thought in schizophrenia*. New York: Appleton-Century-Croft.

Coleman, M. J., Carpenter, J. T., Waternaux, C., Levy, D., Shenton, M. E., Perry, J., et al. (1993). The thought disorder index: A reliability study. *Psychological Assessment, 5*, 336–342.

Exner, J. E. (1993). *The Rorschach, Vol. 1* (3rd ed.). New York: John Wiley & Sons.

Johnston, M. H., & Holzman, P. S. (1979). *Assessing schizophrenic thinking*. San Francisco: Jossey-Bass.

Kleiger, J. H. (1999). *Disordered thinking and the Rorschach: Theory, research, and differential diagnosis*. Hillsdale, NJ: The Analytic Press.

Koistinen, P. (1995), *Thought disorder and the Rorschach*. Oulu, Finland: Oulun Yliopistd.

Rapaport, D., Gill, M., & Schafer, R. (1968), *Diagnostic psychological testing* (rev. ed., R. R. Holt, Ed.). New York: International Universities Press.

Rorschach, H. (1942), *Psychodiagnostics* (5th ed.). Bern, Switzerland: Hans Huber. (Original work published 1921)

SUGGESTED READINGS

Holzman, P. E., Levy, D. L., & Johnston, M. H. (2005). The use of the Rorschach technique for assessing formal thought disorder. In R. F. Bornstein & J. M. Masling (Eds.), *Scoring the Rorschach: Eight validated systems*. Mahwah, NJ: Lawrence Erlbaum.

Weiner, I. B. (1966). *Psychodiagnosis in schizophrenia*. New York: John Wiley & Sons.

JAMES H. KLEIGER
Bethesda, MD

See also: Loose Associations; Schizophrenia

DISSOCIATIVE DISORDERS

The dissociative disorders, as listed in the current (4th) edition of the *Diagnostic and Statistical Manual of Mental Disorders* (DSM-IV-TR; American Psychiatric Association, 2000), include a number of different syndromes, all of which entail an alteration in consciousness affecting memory and identity. Patients with dissociative amnesia (formerly known as psychogenic or functional amnesia) cannot remember certain past experiences (episodic memory), while those with dissociative fugue (formerly known as psychogenic fugue) also lose their personal identities (semantic memory). Patients with dissociative identity disorder (DID; formerly known as multiple personality disorder, or MPD) alternate between two or more separate identities (selves, or "alter egos"), each with its associated fund of autobiographical memory—and an interpersonality amnesia separating at least one alter ego from the others.

Patients with depersonalization disorder feel that they have changed in some profound way—in other words, they do not consciously recognize themselves; in the related syndrome of derealization, they do not consciously recognize their surroundings. There is also a subcategory of "dissociative disorder not otherwise specified," including cases that do not quite fit the diagnostic criteria for amnesia, fugue, or DID, as well as culturally specific cases of "spirit possession," such as *amok*, *latah*, and *ataque de nervios*. These symptoms are "functional" in that they are not associated with demonstrable brain insult, injury, or disease.

The dissociative disorders came to prominence in the late nineteenth century, with the work of Jean-Martin Charcot and Pierre Janet in France, and of Morton Prince and Boris Sidis in America—forming the clinical basis of pre-Freudian ideas about unconscious mental life (Ellenberger, 1970). Throughout the twentieth century, and now into the twenty-first, the dissociative disorders have served as plot devices in countless novels and films, such as *Random Harvest* by James Hilton (novel, 1941; film, 1942), about a World War I veteran who suffered fugue as a result of "shell shock," and *The Three Faces of Eve* (1957), based on an actual clinical case of multiple personality disorder. Despite the high degree of popular interest, however, the dissociative disorders were considered to be extremely rare. For example, fewer than 100 cases were reported in the scientific literature up to 1970.

Following the publication of *Sybil* (1976), another ostensible case of MPD, which was turned (twice) into a television movie, there ensued an "epidemic" of DID cases, and the rise of theories linking dissociative psychopathology to trauma—especially a history of childhood sexual abuse (CSA; e.g., Freyd, 1996), and even "satanic ritual abuse." Although this remains the most popular "psychogenic" theory of the dissociative disorders, the hypothesized link between trauma and dissociation has proved difficult to pin down. In the first place, despite advances in diagnostic criteria and methods, it seems likely that DID has been overdiagnosed in recent years: even the validity of the Sybil case has been challenged. Moreover, while most individuals diagnosed with DID report histories of childhood sexual abuse, many of these reports appear to be based on beliefs shaped by popular culture and "recovered memories" of abuse that may have been distorted by inadvertent suggestion from therapists. Although the role of suggestion in the dissociative disorders remains controversial (Kihlstrom, 2004), the fact remains that no *prospective* study has shown a documented history of childhood sexual abuse increasing an individual's specific risk for DID.

Although impaired memory is the hallmark of the dissociative disorders, clinical and experimental research agree that traumatic and other emotional events are typically well remembered—which is one of the core symptoms of posttraumatic stress disorder (PTSD). When trauma is poorly remembered, the forgetting is usually ascribed to normal memory processes, such as infantile and childhood amnesia, the passage of time, and the like, rather than to any dissociative process. Recent proposals to list DID and other dissociative disorders as forms of PTSD await firm evidence linking dissociation to trauma (McNally, 2003).

Somewhat surprisingly, given the "epidemic" of the 1970s and 1980s, there has been relatively little laboratory research on the dissociative disorders. One line of research has found evidence of "state-dependent" memory in DID, such that one "alter ego" cannot remember items studied by another. Another has uncovered evidence of spared priming and other expressions of implicit or unconscious memory, despite the patient's impairment of explicit or conscious memory. In an attempt to identify attentional correlates of dissociation a third line of research has used the Stroop test and related paradigms with normal subjects (typically college students) who report high levels of dissociative experiences, in an attempt to identify attentional correlates of dissociation.

Until relatively recently, the dissociative disorders were grouped with the conversion disorders under the broad rubric of "hysteria." Indeed, just as dissociative amnesia, fugue, and identity disorder can be described in terms of impairments of conscious memory, so "hysterical" blindness, deafness, paralysis, and the like can be construed as impairments of conscious perception and action (Kihlstrom, 1994). On the other hand, DID, the other dissociative disorders, and the conversion disorders have been given a social-psychological interpretation in terms of role enactment (Lilienfeld et al., 1999). In this view, patients behave "as if" they are amnesic, or blind, or have multiple personalities, as part of a socially sanctioned and goal-directed strategy for expressing personal distress and managing (and manipulating) social relations. A skeptical approach to the dissociative disorders is natural, in view of the excesses of the DID "epidemic" of the 1970s and 1980s. At the same time, we should not let a principled skepticism blind us to genuine cases of dissociative disorder, however few and far between they may be.

REFERENCES

American Psychiatric Association (2000). *Diagnostic and statistical manual of mental disorders* (4th ed., text rev.). Washington, DC: Author.

Freyd, J. (1996). *Betrayal trauma: The logic of forgetting childhood abuse.* Cambridge, MA: Harvard University Press.

Kihlstrom, J. F. (1994). One hundred years of hysteria. In S. J. Lynn & J. W. Rhue (Eds.), *Dissociation: Clinical and theoretical perspectives.* (pp. 365–394). New York: Guilford Press.

Kihlstrom, J. F. (2004). An unbalanced balancing act: Blocked, recovered, and false memories in the laboratory and the clinic. *Clinical Psychology: Science & Practice, 11,* 34–41.

Lilienfeld, S. O., Kirsch, I., Sarbin, T. R., Lynn, S. J., Chaves, J. F., Ganaway, G. K., et al. (1999). Dissociative identity disorder and the sociocognitive model: Recalling the lessons of the past. *Psychological Bulletin, 125*(5), 507–523.

McNally, R. J. (2003). *Remembering trauma.* Cambridge, MA: Harvard University Press.

SUGGESTED READINGS

Crews, F. (1995). *The memory wars: Freud's legacy in dispute.* New York: New York Review of Books.

Ellenberger, H. F. (1970). *The discovery of the unconscious: The history and evolution of dynamic psychiatry.* New York: Basic Books.

Kihlstrom, J. F. (2005). Dissociative disorders. *Annual Review of Clinical Psychology, 1,* 277–253.

JOHN F. KIHLSTROM
University of California, Berkeley

See also: Amnesia; Depersonalization Disorder; Dissociative Identity Disorder

DISSOCIATIVE IDENTITY DISORDER

Dissociative identity disorder (DID) is a psychiatric condition that was formerly known as multiple personality disorder (MPD). DID is viewed as the most complex and severe of the dissociative disorders, a category that also includes dissociative amnesia, dissociative fugue, and depersonalization disorder (see Cardeña & Gleaves, 2007 for a discussion of other dissociative disorders). Although it is controversial and long regarded as exotic and rare, a wealth of research has been conducted on DID in recent years, particularly since the 1980s.

Description

According to the current *Diagnostic and Statistical Manual of Mental Disorders* (DSM; American Psychiatric Association, 2000), DID is defined by the presence of two or more distinct identities or personality states that recurrently take control of the individual. The other essential diagnostic criterion is some degree of psychogenic or psychological amnesia. Although the DSM focuses on the issue of alternate identities, a core set of features of DID has also appeared in research and may be as essential as the diagnostic criteria. These features include severe depersonalization and derealization (feeling as if the self or surroundings are unreal in some way), a variety of memory problems (typically apparent amnesia for childhood or even ongoing events), identity alteration and confusion, and experiences of auditory hallucinations perceived as coming from inside the individual's head. Some researchers (e.g., Dell, 2006) have argued that the DSM criteria should be revised to focus on these features. In fact, the current focus on the issue of alternate identities has probably only fueled controversies about the disorder with respect to its causes, diagnostic validity, prevalence, and treatment.

Etiology/Causes

The central controversy is about the cause of DID; the remaining issues are directly or indirectly related to that controversy. There are two general theories regarding the causes of DID. One is the iatrogenesis or sociocognitive theory (Spanos, 1994). The term *iatrogenic* literally means of physician origin, but it is used more broadly in this context to mean of therapist origin. In other words, proponents of this theory consider DID to be a product of therapy. Because some people with DID have never been in therapy, proponents of the theory may also blame the popular media and use terms such as *mediagenic*. The term *sociocognitive* is adapted from the similar theory of hypnosis, which regards a hypnotic state as a strategic role enactment. Thus, according to this theory DID is something similar to the notion of hypnotic strategic role enactment, and it is caused by therapists suggesting the concept of DID to their patients and inadvertently teaching them how to behave. Such clients are allegedly not lying or purposefully role-playing but have come to believe what they have learned from the therapist.

Although the sociocognitive model seems to be commonly accepted by a subset of the health field and the general population, there are several problems with it, most critically a lack of empirical support. In a review, Brown, Frischolz, and Scheflin (1999) concluded that "these sparse data fail to meet a minimal standard of scientific evidence justifying the claim that a major psychiatric diagnosis like dissociative identity disorder *per se* can be produced through suggestive influences in therapy" (p. 549). It also appears that the model is based on numerous misconceptions regarding the psychopathology, assessment, and treatment of DID (Gleaves, 1996). The model focuses almost exclusively on the concept of multiple identity enactment, which involves behaving as if one had more than one identity, but it does not thoroughly explain the complex dissociative symptomatology described previously.

The second etiological perspective is that DID develops from severe and ongoing childhood trauma. It is thus considered a form of childhood onset posttraumatic stress disorder (PTSD; Spiegel, 1991). According to this perspective, however, it is not trauma alone that causes DID. Kluft (1996) proposed that four factors may be required for DID to develop: (1) the capacity or ability to dissociate (possibly genetic); (2) experiences that overwhelm the child (usually severe trauma but broader than childhood sexual abuse); (3) secondary structuring of the DID alternate identities (typically based on the child's culture); and (4) a lack of soothing and restorative experiences. The last factor implies that, if the child had the resources to help him or her cope with the trauma at the time, the DID would be unlikely to develop. However, the trauma reported by persons with DID is all too often at the hands of their own caregivers.

At least four pieces of information support the posttraumatic model of DID: (1) the vast majority (if not all) of persons with DID report histories of childhood trauma (and the trauma can often be corroborated; Lewis, Yeager, Swica, Pincus, & Lewis, 1997); (2) dissociative symptoms in general are reliably associated with trauma; (3) the vast majority of DID patients also have diagnosable PTSD; and (4) some symptoms of PTSD (flashbacks, emotional numbing, inability to recall) are actually dissociative in nature. Overall, although more research is needed, there is more empirical and logical support for the posttraumatic theory than for competing theories.

Diagnostic Validity

A second area of controversy concerns the diagnostic validity of DID. That is, some authors (e.g., North, Ryall, Ricci, & Wetzel, 1993) argue that DID is not a valid psychiatric disorder, but rather a symptom of another disorder (such as somatization disorder or a personality disorder). A review of the empirical evidence (Gleaves, May, & Cardeña, 2001) suggests otherwise. Although there is no definitive set of criteria for determining if a disorder is valid, DID seems to meet a variety of different criteria fairly well, perhaps more so than do many other disorders whose validity is rarely questioned. Research suggests that the disorder can be reliably diagnosed using structured interviews and that it can be discriminated from other disorders (Gleaves, et al., 2001). The disorder with the most overlap seems to be PTSD, which is not surprising given that DID is considered by many to be a variant of PTSD.

Prevalence

The controversy regarding prevalence is closely tied to the issues regarding its causes. DID was once believed to be extremely rare. Chris Sizemore, the original Eve of the *Three Faces of Eve,* was apparently told that she was perhaps the only person in the world with the condition. As recently as 1980, it was estimated that approximately 200 cases had been reported in the world literature. Now, more recent research suggests that DID may be approximately as common as schizophrenia and more common than anorexia nervosa. Studies in nonclinical samples have found prevalence rates of around 1%, and estimates in clinical samples are in the range of 6% to 10% (see Foote, Smolin, Kaplan, Legatt, & Lipschitz, 2006).

There are two general explanations for this change in the apparent prevalence of the disorder. The first is that the increase is artificial and that most new cases are not real (i.e., are iatrogenic). However, this argument rests on the assumption that the disorder was, in fact, previously rare, when we really do not have any clear evidence that it was, because prevalence studies of DID were not conducted until recently. We only know for sure that the disorder was rarely, if ever, diagnosed. The other explanation of the apparent increased prevalence is that there has simply been an increased recognition of the problem. Although this interpretation is rejected by many skeptics of the disorder, it is noteworthy that the same pattern has been observed for child sexual abuse and incest. That is, as recently as 1975, some psychiatric textbooks stated that incest occurred in one in one million families. We now know that it is much more common and was previously unrecognized (rather than extremely rare). If DID is a secretive condition (related to the abuse itself), it is clearly conceivable that it was previously unrecognized (or perhaps misdiagnosed). There are also many other reasons why an increased recognition of DID is quite plausible, including the inclusion (in 1980) of DID in the DSM, the Vietnam War and subsequent interest in PTSD, the feminist movement and the subsequent recognition of the reality of sexual trauma, and developments in the field of cognitive psychology (e.g., network models of memory and information processing), that may be analogous to the memory subsystems seen in DID (Gleaves, 1996).

Related to concern that the prevalence of DID is artificially increasing is the argument that it is culture bound and restricted to North America. However, this argument is not based on empirical research but rather simply the expressed opinions of clinicians who say they have never encountered cases. There is, in fact, now a growing body of research on the cross-cultural occurrences of dissociative disorders (Şar, 2006). Prevalence studies from clinical samples have come not only from North America, but also from Norway, Turkey, Switzerland, the Netherlands, and Germany. It appears that wherever prevalence studies are done, DID is found to be approximately as common as it is in North America.

Treatment

There are two general approaches to the treatment of DID, each of which is consistent with the theoretical view regarding the nature and causes of the disorder. Proponents of the iatrogenesis model suggest that the dissociative symptomatology should not be actively addressed (North et al., 1993). They believe that doing so shapes and creates the disorder. There is no published empirical research on this approach to treatment, and in the case studies reported by North et al., the clients remained chronic or even worsened. There is also consistent evidence that persons diagnosed with DID have typically spent 7–12 years in the mental health system, without evidence of improvement, prior to receiving the diagnosis. This finding is interpreted by many as *prima facie* evidence that failure to diagnosis and directly treat the disorder is an ineffective overall intervention strategy.

The second general approach, based on the posttraumatic model, involves actively targeting the dissociation and other posttraumatic symptomatology. The treatment is conceptually similar to those designed for treatment of PTSD (e.g., Leskin, Kaloupek, & Keane, 1998), but it takes into consideration the client's perception of separate selves and more severe history of trauma. Treatment guidelines for this approach are published by the International Society for the Study of Trauma & Dissociation (http://www.isst-d.org/). These guidelines refer to a three-phase approach: (1) "Establishing Safety Stabilization and Symptom Reduction"; (2) "Focused Work on Traumatic Memories"; and (3) "Integration and Rehabilitation." Overall, these imply that stability is important before processing trauma memories and that integration, (the bringing together of what were the separated identities) is not an initial goal; rather, it is something that typically only occurs after years of treatment.

Although the treatment for DID is described in these guidelines, empirical research is needed. The evidence that exists comes from several large-case series by clinical researchers and two uncontrolled studies by Ross and colleagues (see Ellason & Ross, 1997). Collectively, the data suggest that persons with DID can make substantial improvements when the disorder is actively treated and that such persons are unlikely to improve when the disorder is not addressed in treatment. However, larger controlled outcome studies are clearly needed, particularly those in which this approach is compared with other active treatments.

In conclusion, what we know about DID has changed dramatically over the last 20–30 years. Evidence now suggests that it is a relatively common although clandestine disorder of posttraumatic origin that does not remit if untreated. Well-established methods of assessment exist and treatment guidelines exist but the treatments need to be better studied.

REFERENCES

American Psychiatric Association. (2000). *Diagnostic and statistical manual of mental disorders* (4th ed., text rev.). Washington, DC: Author.

Brown, D., Frischolz, E. J., & Scheflin, A. W. (1999). Iatrogenic dissociative identity disorder: An evaluation of the scientific evidence. *Journal of Psychiatry and Law, 27,* 549–637.

Dell, P. F. (2006). A new model of dissociative identity disorder. *Psychiatric Clinics of North America, 29,* 1–26.

Ellason, J. W., & Ross, C. A. (1997). Two-year follow-up of inpatients with dissociative identity disorder. *American Journal of Psychiatry, 154,* 832–839.

Foote, B., Smolin, Y., Kaplan, M., Legatt, M. E., & Lipschitz, D. (2006). Prevalence of dissociative disorders in psychiatric outpatients. *American Journal of Psychiatry, 163,* 623–629.

Gleaves, D. H. (1996). The sociocognitive model of dissociative identity disorder: A reexamination of the evidence. *Psychological Bulletin, 120,* 42–59.

Gleaves, D. H., May, M. C., & Cardeña, E. (2001). An examination of the diagnostic validity of dissociative identity disorder. *Clinical Psychology Review, 21,* 577–608.

Kluft, R. P. (1996). Dissociative identity disorder. In L. K. Michelson, & W. J. Ray (Eds.). *Handbook of dissociation: Theoretical, empirical, and clinical perspectives* (pp. 337–366). New York: Plenum Press.

Leskin G. A., Kaloupek D. G., Keane T. M. (1998). Treatment for traumatic memories: Review and recommendations. *Clinical Psychology Review, 18,* 983–1002.

Lewis, D. O., Yeager, C. A., Swica, Y., Pincus, J. H., & Lewis, M. (1997). Objective documentation of child abuse and dissociation in 12 murderers with dissociative identity disorder. *American Journal of Psychiatry, 154,* 1703–1710.

North, C. S., Ryall, J-E., Ricci, D. A., & Wetzel, R. D. (1993). *Multiple personalities, multiple disorders: Psychiatric classification and media influence.* New York: Oxford University Press.

Şar, V. (2006). The scope of dissociative disorders: An international perspective. *Psychiatric Clinics of North America, 29,* 227–244.

Spanos, N. P. (1994). Multiple identity enactments and multiple personality disorder: A sociocognitive perspective. *Psychological Bulletin, 116,* 143–165.

Spiegel, D. (1991). Dissociation and trauma. In A. Tasman & S. M. Goldfinger (Eds.), *American Psychiatric Press annual review of psychiatry* (Vol. 10). Washington, DC: American Psychiatric Press.

SUGGESTED READINGS

Cardeña, E., & Gleaves, D. H. (2007). Dissociative disorders. In M. Hersen, S. M. Turner, & D. C. Beidel (Eds). *Adult psychopathology and diagnosis* (5th ed., pp. 473–503). Hoboken, NJ: John Wiley & Sons.

Dell, P. F., & O'Neill, J. A. (Eds.). (In press). *Dissociation and dissociative disorders: DSM IV and beyond.* New York: Routledge.

Putnam, F. W. (1989). *Diagnosis and treatment of multiple personality disorder.* New York: Guilford Press.

Ross, C. A. (1997). *Dissociative identity disorder: Diagnosis, clinical features, and treatment of multiple personality.* New York: John Wiley & Sons.

DAVID H. GLEAVES
University of Canterbury, New Zealand

See also: Dissociative Disorders; Posttraumatic Stress Disorder; Stress Consequences

DIVORCE, CHILD AND ADOLESCENT ADJUSTMENT IN

Parental divorce has been viewed for many decades as the cause of a wide range of enduring behavioral, emotional, and social problems in children and adolescents. Divorced families have been characterized as flawed structures in which to raise children, whereas married families were assumed to offer healthy and nurturing environments. Such simplistic views regarding these family structures have been abandoned in the past 20 years, as evolving social science research has provided an increasingly complex understanding of both marriage and divorce. Although children and adolescents generally fare better in well-functioning two-parent families than in divorced families, not all married families provide appropriate parenting for their children, and many divorced families offer the nurturance and support necessary for positive outcomes (see Clarke-Stewart & Brentano, 2006; Kelly, 2000).

Child Adjustment in Divorced and Married Families

A large body of empirical research confirms that divorce essentially doubles the risk for adjustment problems in children and adolescents (for reviews, see Amato, 2000; Clarke-Stewart & Brentano, 2006; Emery, 2004; Hetherington & Kelly, 2002; Kelly, 2000). Children of divorce are more likely to have behavioral, psychological, social, and academic problems when compared to children from married families. In continuously married families, 10–12% of children have serious psychological, social, and academic problems, and 20–25% of children from divorced families have similar symptoms (Hetherington & Kelly, 2002). Some of these youngsters are already at high risk when their parents separate, with longitudinal studies indicating that nearly half of the adjustment problems attributed to divorce were evident prior to parental separation (see Kelly, 2000). The magnitude of the differences between divorced and married family children is quite small (see Clarke-Stewart & Brentano, 2006), and the majority of children and adolescents from divorced families fall within the average range of adjustment on objective and standardized measures.

The most consistent adverse effects associated with divorce are conduct disorders, impulsive and antisocial behaviors, and problems with authority figures, peers, and parents. Children from divorced families, compared to those in married families, are also more likely to have symptoms of depression, anxiety, and lower self-esteem, although these findings are less consistent. Divorce has been associated with modestly lower academic performance and achievement test scores, although the differences between divorced and never divorced children are reduced when appropriate socioeconomic controls are used. The school dropout rate of divorced children is more than twice as high as that of never-divorced children. Some of these academic problems existed prior to separation, and parents who later divorced provided less help with homework, talked less about educational achievement, and were less involved in school, compared to still-married parents.

Risk and Protective Factors for Children and Adolescents Following Divorce

One of the more important outcomes of recent empirical research is the identification of factors associated with increased risk for children and adolescents following divorce and protective factors linked to better outcomes (see Amato, 2000; Hetherington & Kelly, 2002; Kelly, 2007; Kelly & Emery, 2003).

Risk Factors

Adjustment of parents. School-age children who live in the custody of mothers with depression, high anxiety, personality disorders, and mental illness are significantly more likely to experience more symptoms of all kinds, compared to divorced children living with better adjusted parents. Parents with such problems are more likely to require substantial emotional support and loyalty from their children following separation and are often emotionally unavailable to their children at a critical time. Adjustment problems in either mothers or fathers not only provide poor role models but are associated with more negative parenting practices and parent-child relationships, which in turn are linked to more symptoms in their children.

Quality of parenting. Quality of parenting has emerged as a critical factor in child and adolescent adjustment following separation and divorce. Parenting is negatively impacted by many parental experiences associated with divorce: sustained high conflict, violence, separation reactions, absorption in dating and new partners, and financial instability. Divorced parents use more coercive and harsh forms of discipline, are angrier, and have less positive involvement and express less affection with their children when compared to married family parents.

Loss of paternal involvement. Loss of important relationships is a major theme in children's divorce experiences, and children report the erosion or loss of the relationship with the father as the most negative aspect of divorce. Traditional "visiting" guidelines and attitudes limiting fathers to every other weekend with their children significantly limit fathers' opportunities to parent, with a diminution in discipline, homework, projects, or providing emotional support. Father-child relationships weaken and deteriorate over time as a result. These one-size-fits-all guidelines are inherently flawed, because they fail to consider children's ages, gender, developmental needs and achievements, the history and quality of the child's relationship with each parent, and family situations requiring special attention. A number of studies indicate that the majority of children and adolescents want more and longer periods of time with their fathers, and many favor substantially equal time (Kelly, 2007). The painful memories and feelings among young adults described as a residue of the divorce experience are in part associated with long-term sadness and longing for more father involvement (Emery, 2004).

High conflict. Although conflict after divorce decreases or stops for the majority of parents, an estimated 8–20% of parents remain angry and highly conflictual in their co-parental relationship 2–3 years after divorce (Hetherington & Kelly, 2002). Continued high conflict is a risk factor for children and adolescents, whether perpetrated by one or both parents. Often those who instigate and sustain conflict have personality disorders or mental illness (Johnston & Roseby, 1997). The most damaging conflict is when one or both parents use their children to express their anger by making demeaning comments or asking intrusive questions about the other parent, asking children to carry hostile messages, and making demands for loyalty and alignments.

Economic decline. Greater economic instability and reduced access to important resources such as better schools, neighborhoods, and extracurricular activities is an additional risk factor. It is estimated that the economic problems of divorced households account for as much as half of the adjustment problems seen in divorced children.

Protective Factors

Good adjustment of parent. As might be expected, when the psychological and social adjustment of residential (custodial) parents is adequate or better, children are significantly more likely to be well-adjusted after divorce than children whose primary parents have significant problems. Better adjusted parents are more capable of dealing with their own divorce-related stress in a timely and effective manner, and they can help their children cope with divorce-related emotional, social and academic difficulties that might arise.

Competent parenting. Effective parenting ameliorates and may prevent the negative impacts of divorce on children and adolescents. Critical components of mothers' effective parenting after divorce include warmth, authoritative discipline (setting limits, noncoercive discipline and control, appropriate expectations), and monitoring of their children's activities. Critical dimensions of fathers' parenting associated with positive outcomes include active involvement, authoritative parenting, and monitoring of child/adolescent activities. Active involvement encompasses help with homework and projects, emotional support and warmth, talking about problems, and involvement in school (Amato & Fowler, 2002; Hetherington & Kelly).

Reduced conflict. When parents cease or diminish their conflict after divorce, children are more likely to have positive adjustment, when compared to children whose parents continue in chronic high conflict. Buffers that protect children from parental conflict include a good relationship with at least one parent, caregiver, or mentor, parental warmth, and sibling support. When high-conflict parents encapsulated their conflict, that is, took their children out of the middle, their children were as well adjusted as children of low conflict parents after divorce (see Hetherington & Kelly, 2002; Kelly & Emery, 2003).

Contact with nonresidential parents. Frequency of contact by itself is not a good predictor of child outcomes, in part because fathers vary in the quality of parenting they provide. When children have close relationships with their fathers and the fathers are actively involved in their lives following separation, then frequent contact is significantly linked to more positive adjustment and better academic achievement in school-age children and adolescents, compared to those with less involved fathers (Amato, 2000; Amato & Fowler, 2002; Hetherington & Kelly, 2002). Greater amounts of paternal involvement, including overnights spent with adequate fathers, are associated with better adaptive behavior skills and communication and socialization skills in very young children as well (see Kelly, 2007).

An extensive empirical literature investigating multiple dimensions of outcomes of children and adolescents following separation and divorce confirm that on average divorced children have twice the risk of behavioral, psychological, and academic problems when compared to children in still-married families. These findings and those regarding risk and protective factors provide valuable guidance to parents, divorce educators, family courts, and others committed to reducing the negative impacts of divorce on children and adolescents. Newer nonadversarial interventions focused on reducing risk for children in separated and divorced families include parent education programs and divorce and custody mediation. Each intervention has shown evidence of reducing parent conflict and promoting more productive coparental relationships, when compared to adversarial divorce processes, and should be widely available, affordable, and encouraged by public policy (see Kelly & Emery, 2003).

REFERENCES

Amato, P. (2000). The consequences of divorce for adults and children. *Journal of Marriage and Family, 62,* 1269–1287.

Amato, P. R., & Fowler, F. (2002). Parenting practices, child adjustment, and family diversity. *Journal of Marriage and Family, 64,* 703–716.

Clarke-Stewart, A., & Brentano, C. (2006). *Divorce: Causes and consequences.* New Haven, CT: Yale University Press.

Cummings, E., & Davies, P. (1994). *Children and marital conflict.* New York: Guilford Press.

Emery, R. (2004). *The truth about children and divorce: Dealing with emotions so you and your children can thrive.* New York: Viking/Penguin.

Hetherington, E. M., & Kelly, J. (2002). *For better or for worse.* New York: Norton.

Johnston, J. R., & Roseby, V. (1997). *In the name of the child: A developmental approach to understanding and helping children of conflict and violent divorce.* New York: Free Press.

Kelly, J. B. (2000). Children's adjustment in conflicted marriage and divorce: A decade review of research. *Journal of Child and Adolescent Psychiatry, 39,* 963–973.

Kelly, J. B. (2007). Children's living arrangements following separation and divorce: Insights from empirical and clinical research. *Family Process, 46,* 35–52.

Kelly, J. B., & Emery, R. E. (2003). Children's adjustment following divorce: Risk and resilience perspectives. *Family Relations, 52,* 352–362.

JOAN B. KELLY
Corte Madera, CA

See also: **Child Custody; Marriage Counseling; Marital Discord**

DOUBLE BIND

Double bind is a concept characterizing an ongoing pattern of communication that imposes painful no-win situations on its victim through two processes: first, through contradictory demands made at different levels of communication, and second, by preventing the victim from either discriminating and commenting on the bind or withdrawing from it. Originally studied in the relationships between schizophrenic adults and their families, the double bind was viewed as having had causal relevance for their schizophrenia through having impaired their capacities to derive clear meaning from communications and to participate in normal social relationships.

The original clinical studies leading to the double bind concept were conducted in Palo Alto, California, in the 1950s and 1960s by Gregory Bateson, Don D. Jackson, Jay Haley, and John H. Weakland (1956), a group of clinicians and scholars who collectively introduced a communication theory approach to the mental health field through pioneering contributions to the development of family therapy. Their work emphasized that there are, within families as within the individual's internal environment, homeostatic or stability-making processes that regulate their functioning and contribute to their survival. Within families, communication serves this function.

A single complex human communication can contain many messages of different logical types, as defined by Bertrand Russell (Whitehead & Russell, 1910), often involving separate modalities that can contradict or reinforce one another. An aggressive utterance might, for example, be qualified by movements, postures, or voice tones conveying that "this is all in fun." Even the relationship of the message to surrounding events or shared past experience may contribute to its meaning. Put entirely into words, which it rarely is, this multilevel message might mean that "I pretend to show aggression in jest because our relationship is such that, under the circumstances, I intend that you will find it funny and feel warmly toward me."

In its regulatory role in human interaction, communication carries substantial responsibility for defining the nature and limits of the relationships between or among people and, therefore, the roles appropriately played by each person in a given interaction. The communicational approach holds that each transaction between the parties to a communication involves a relationship message proffering or affirming a relationship of a particular sort and a response that accepts, modifies, or negates the definition communicated. Thus by the act of scolding, a parent affirms the right to scold in the relationship with that child. The angry transactions between adolescents and their parents may well have less to do with the apparent content of the quarrel than with the relationship changes being forged and contested.

Considerable learning, often nonverbal, is involved in the capacity to decode communications, particularly those involving apparent contradictions between levels, as with angry words said laughingly. When meaning is not apparent, people learn to shift to a more abstract level and to communicate about communication, thereby clarifying the meaning of ambiguous messages. Children initially lack this capacity; if they are blocked from learning how to learn about meaning, serious adulthood disorders may result. The double bind involves a communication style that is pernicious in its reliance upon internal contradictions and blocked learning. As studied in the families of schizophrenics, it appeared often in mother child relationships in which the mothers seemed not to want to be understood: they could accept neither their children nor their rejection of those children. The double bind describes their covert pursuit of distant relationships disguised by reciprocal shows of loving behavior. Such parents appeared to invite closeness at one level while negating it at another. A child who responded by approaching was covertly rebuffed, yet efforts to withdraw were also punished. Efforts to shift levels and to question the meaning of the interactions were also punished, impairing the child's capacity to form and trust impressions of reality.

Although the double bind as an ongoing pattern cannot be fully represented in a single transaction, the following vignette illustrates many of its features. A young woman hospitalized for schizophrenia improved enough to select and purchase clothing for her first hospital leave. When her parents came for her, however, her mother showed immediate distress over her "juvenile taste" in clothing, and agitatedly undressed her and regarbed her in items of the mother's own choosing. "There," the mother said, "now you look all grown up!" The leave went badly, and the woman was soon back in an acutely psychotic condition.

The mother's emphatic behavioral rejection of her adult daughter's independence was belied by the verbal message that she urgently must look grown up, indicating to hospital staff a probable conflict regarding the relationship: the patient must be adult and therefore independent, yet a child and therefore dependent. In responding to movement toward independence, the injunction never to be independent was more emphatic than that to be always independent. Enjoined to be a woman and a child, independent and dependent, close and far, the patient responded with disturbed, psychotic behavior. A woman made childlike by an illness, she was incapable of independence, yet too disturbed to be at home: she was neither too close nor too far. Her relationship to her mother was preserved.

The double bind began as an attempt to understand aspects of the communication of persons with schizophrenia, aspects of their family functioning, and indeed, aspects of the origins of their disorder. As a causal explanation for schizophrenia, it stood in contrast to biological explanations, but it is no longer studied in this context. Today the double bind remains as an exposition of the complex, often contradictory, and sometimes painful nature of human communication, and it continues to serve as a tool in understanding painful paradoxes and contradictions in our intimate relationships and troubled self-concepts.

REFERENCES

Bateson, G., Jackson, D., Haley, J., & Weakland, J. (1956). Towards a theory of schizophrenia. *Behavioral Science, I,* 251–264.

Whitehead, A. N., & Russell, B. (1910). *Principia mathematica.* Cambridge, UK: Cambridge University Press.

SUGGESTED READING

Jackson, Don D. (Ed.). (1968) *Communication, family and marriage*, Vol. 1, 2. Palo Alto, CA: Science and Behavior Books.

ROGER E. ENFIELD
West Central Georgia Regional Hospital, Columbus, GA

See also: **Communication Disorders; Family Therapy; Schizophrenia**

DOWN SYNDROME

People with Down syndrome are first and foremost people. They are men, women, and children who live with the condition and its consequences. They usually enjoy life and want the same things out of life as everyone else. As adults they want and have the right to live with dignity and choices. Increasingly, children with Down syndrome in enlightened communities attend nurseries, preschools, schools, and colleges with their mainstream peers and participate in their communities. As adults, they are increasingly living semi-independently in their own homes, finding work, enjoying leisure facilities, finding partners, and getting married (Buckley, 2000). While this is true in the more developed countries, it is still the case that, in most parts of the world, many children with Down syndrome die young, most of those who survive do not have access to education or health care, and the majority are institutionalized. The point to stress is that, as in the experience of all other human beings, the development of children and adults with Down syndrome is strongly influenced by the care, education, and opportunities available to them. Negative attitudes toward individuals with disabilities and ignorance of what they can achieve are still widespread and diminish their lives and the lives of their families.

Cause and Survival Rates

Fifty years ago, only 45% of infants with Down syndrome survived the first year of life, even in developed countries. Only 40 years ago, most people with Down syndrome were denied essential health care or a decent education and were often subjected to a limited life in institutional care. In many societies today, however, the lives of children and adults with Down syndrome are steadily improving. Advances in medical care, better understanding of the developmental and educational needs of the children, and increasing social acceptance are providing greater opportunities to grow and learn and to participate in society. Down syndrome is a condition caused by the presence of an extra copy of chromosome 21 that influences development from conception. In most cases, an additional copy of the chromosome is present in every cell in the body (trisomy 21). In about 2% of cases, the extra chromosome is only present in some cell lines (mosaic Down syndrome), and in another 2% the extra chromosome 21 is linked to another chromosome (translocation).

Down syndrome is one of the most commonly identified causes of developmental delay and intellectual disability. In Europe and the United States alone, around 9,000 babies are born with Down syndrome each year to parents of all races and from all backgrounds. Improved medical care has increased survival rates for young children dramatically, particularly those born with heart defects. Overall life expectancy has risen in developed countries, with studies indicating an increase from 30 years in the early 1970s to approaching 60 years more recently (Bittles & Glasson, 2004). It is estimated that around 350,000 people with Down syndrome are alive today in the United States, 250,000 in Western Europe, and around 40,000 in the U.K. There are an estimated 3 million people living with Down syndrome worldwide.

A child with Down syndrome can be born to a mother of any age. However, the chance of having a baby with Down syndrome rises quite steeply with age. For a mother of 20 years old, the risk is about 1 in 1,500, at age 30 about 1 in 900, at age 35 about 1 in 350, at age 40 about 1 in 100, and at age 45 about 1 in 30. In countries such as the U.K., where many mothers are waiting to start families until into their 30s, the Down syndrome birth rate is rising, even though screening and termination programs are legal.

Understanding the Biology

The first detailed description of Down syndrome was recorded in 1866, and the genetic cause of the condition—the extra chromosome—was discovered in 1959. Over the past 50 years, our understanding of genetics and our understanding of chromosome 21 have advanced considerably. The genetic, biochemical, and neurological mechanisms influencing development for people with Down syndrome are not yet clearly understood, but good progress has been made in decoding the genes on chromosome 21 and starting to identify their functions (Patterson & Costa, 2005).

Healthcare Needs

Children with Down syndrome are at greater risk for some medical conditions and illnesses than other children. About half of all babies with Down syndrome are born with cardiac defects, some of which require surgical repair, and they have an increased risk of some conditions including conductive hearing loss, visual defects, respiratory infections, sleep disturbance, leukemia, and thyroid disorder. As older children, teenagers, and adults, they are usually as healthy as the rest of the population and less likely to suffer from most solid tumor cancers or heart disease, but they do experience earlier aging and an increased risk of Alzheimer-type dementia (Van Cleve & Cohen, 2006; Van Cleve, Cannon, & Cohen, 2006).

Developmental Needs, Early Intervention, and Education

An accurate picture of the full impact of Down syndrome on development is still unfolding. Developmental research has increasingly shown that, for all children, development is strongly influenced by emotional security and relationships in the family and by the quality of their language and social experience. As we understand more about the developmental trajectories of typically developing children, it has become possible to look more closely at the effects of Down syndrome on development on those trajectories, across social, motor, cognitive, and language domains and practical independence.

In many respects, children with Down syndrome follow developmental trajectories within domains in the same way as their nondisabled peers; that is, they build skills in the same order, though making slower overall progress. However, accumulating evidence points to a specific profile of developmental strengths and weaknesses, with development in some domains progressing faster than in others. In their early years, as infants and toddlers, they show strengths in social relating and nonverbal understanding, while falling behind in motor, spoken language, and verbal working memory development (Fidler, 2005).

In school, reading progress is often a strength and progresses faster than mental age or language might predict, as Down syndrome children have strengths as visual learners. Understanding numbers and mathematics is more of a challenge, however, with number skills often falling two years behind reading skills. Increased understanding of this profile enables early intervention and teaching strategies to be designed to build on strengths while improving and compensating for weaknesses. There is increasing evidence that these targeted strategies significantly improve the developmental outcomes for children with Down syndrome. Inclusive education also plays a part in improving their educational attainments and social behavior (Buckley, Bird, Sacks, & Archer, 2006). There is still a lot to learn about the best ways to teach children with Down syndrome, but at this point there is an even greater need to get what is known and demonstrated to be effective into practice in early intervention services and in education.

In terms of leisure interests and sporting skills, many young people with Down syndrome become competent swimmers, gymnasts, bowlers, and athletes in other sports, especially when their family has an interest in a particular sport or leisure pursuit. Like everyone else, they gain health and social benefits from these opportunities.

Individual Differences

Children and adults with Down syndrome are not all alike. They vary widely in abilities, disabilities, likes, dislikes, and temperament. Some children will have only a mild degree of intellectual disability, although most will have a moderate level and some (about 10%–15%) will be more severely delayed. Those in the latter group usually have experienced additional health or developmental problems, such as a comorbid autism spectrum disorder (in 7%–10% of cases), epilepsy, cerebral palsy, or life-threatening illnesses in infancy. Children with Down syndrome have an extra copy of chromosome 21 along with their own family genes, which means that they will have many of the same attributes as the rest of their family in terms of appearance and aptitudes.

Adult Life

All young adults with Down syndrome want privacy, choice, dignity, independence, and to be treated as adults. This poses a challenge for parents and all service providers. Everyone finds it difficult to remember how old a Down syndrome person is and to treat this person in an age-appropriate way. Adults with Down syndrome have the same rights and needs as everyone else. The level of independence they can achieve as adults depends largely on the facilities offered in their community for work and for supported living. The degree of support they need will vary considerably, but most adults will need at least some support (Brown, 2004).

Aging

People with Down syndrome age faster than adults in the rest of the population, as previously mentioned, with an average life expectancy of around 60 years, although some may now live to 70 or even 80 years of age. The most prevalent aging issue is an increased risk of dementia, with 9% developing it by the age of 49 years, 18% of those aged 50–54, and 35% of those aged 55–59 years (Coppus et al., 2006). It is important to note that dementia may be confused with depression or hypothyroidism, so a careful differential diagnosis is needed. These rates are lower than was suggested in the past, but there remains a need for good care of individuals with Down syndrome as they age.

REFERENCES

Bittles, A. H., & Glasson, E. J. (2004). Clinical, social and ethical implications of changing life expectancy in Down syndrome. *Developmental Medicine and Child Neurology, 46*(4), 282–286.

Brown, R. (2004). Life for adults with Down syndrome. Portsmouth, UK: The Down Syndrome Educational Trust.

Buckley, S. J. (2000). Living with Down syndrome. Portsmouth, UK: The Down Syndrome Educational Trust. Online http://www.down-syndrome.org/information/development/overview/.

Buckley, S. J., Bird, G., Sacks, B., & Archer, T. A. (2006). A comparison of mainstream and special education for teenagers with Down syndrome: Implications for parents and teachers. *Down Syndrome Research and Practice, 9*(3), 54–67. Online http://www.down-syndrome.org/reports/295/.

Coppus, A., Evenhuis, H., Verberne, G. J., Visser, F., van Gool, P., Eikelenboom, P., et al. (2006). Dementia and mortality in persons with Down syndrome. *Journal of Intellectual Disability Research, 50*(10), 768–777.

Fidler, D. (2005). The emerging Down syndrome behavioral phenotype in early childhood: Implications for practice. *Infants & Young Children, 18*(2), 86–103.

Patterson, D., & Costa, A. (2005). Down syndrome and genetics: A case of linked histories. *Nature Review Genetics, 6*, 137–147.

Van Cleve, S. N., & Cohen, W. I. (2006). Part I: Clinical practice guidelines for children with Down syndrome from birth to 12 years. *Journal of Pediatric Health Care, 20*(1), 46–54.

Van Cleve, S. N., Cannon, S., & Cohen, W. I. (2006). Part II: Clinical practice guidelines for adolescents and young adults with Down syndrome: 12 to 21 years. *Journal of Pediatric Health Care, 20*(3) 198–205.

SUE BUCKLEY
University of Portsmouth, United Kingdom

DRAW-A-PERSON TEST (See Figure Drawing Tests)

DREAMS

The study of dreams has moved from a focus on what they mean to attention to the underlying neuroscience mechanisms that are involved in their generation. Current research suggests that cortical areas involved in dreaming reflect those areas associated with emotional and sensory processing and lack the involvement of higher-level logical thinking.

Historical Introduction

Since the beginning of recorded history, dreams have played a role in humans' attempt to make meaning of the world and ourselves. Dreams have represented the other; that is, the aspects of ourselves and our world that stand outside of human knowledge or could not be understood within the current paradigm. As illustrated in a variety of religious texts over the past few thousand years, dreams have foretold future events and allowed as well for communication with the gods. Some writers, including the Roman poet Lucretius in 44 B.C., suggested that dreams are common in all animals. Darwin echoed a similar theme in *The Descent of Man* (1871), in which he suggests that all higher animals including birds have dreams.

Within the past 100 years the understanding of dreams has been brought into a more theoretical perspective within dynamic and analytic psychology and more recently within the context of the neurosciences. Although a topic of heated debate, an initial contribution was Freud's perspective that dreams could be understood within the context of instinctual functioning and the neurology outlined in the *Project for a Scientific Psychology*. As articulated in the Project, dreams were considered to offer an understanding of previously established networks of neurons and pointed to the manner in which ideas and events had come to be associated with one another in the brain. In this way dreams were reflective of an individual's psychology during the waking state. Jung had a more evolutionary perspective in which he viewed specific processes in our environment as triggers for bringing forth action patterns, or *archetypes* as he called them, much in the same manner as described by ethologists. Dreams in this context reflect these evoked archetypical patterns.

Beginnings of Empirical Research

Many view the scientific study of dreams as beginning in 1953 with the discovery by Aserinsky and Kleitman of an association between dreaming and rapid eye movement (REM) sleep. Sleep generally is characterized by four different stages that are reflected in the EEG patterns. In contrast to the high-voltage and more-patterned EEG activity generally found in sleep, REM sleep appears to have an EEG pattern more like that of the waking state. REM sleep is also referred to as "paradoxical sleep" and is characterized by low-voltage and random-appearing EEG activity. Awakening an individual during REM sleep is more likely than any other sleep stage to result in a dream report.

Following the discovery of the association between REM sleep and dreams, the dream state was examined in a number of laboratories. This work included a variety of foci, including the nature of the dream itself, factors involved in dream recall, the influence of external factors on dreaming, and other factors associated with dreaming. For example, following a natural disaster like an earthquake, researchers have found an increase in nightmares, suggesting that trauma can be related to dreaming. Another type of research has shown increased REM sleep when learning a new task in both humans and animals, which suggests that activity during REM may be associated with consolidating new information into long-term memory. Molecular research has also noted the manner in which sleep stages are controlled and in which proteins regulate REM. Dream research has used a variety of theoretical perspectives including a more cognitive one. The main characteristics of dream process include emotionally laden sensory processes and images without a sense of individual control. Less well understood is the so-called "lucid dream" in which individuals while dreaming realize that they are part of a dream and may even experience control of the dream. Lucid dreams are rare and occur in only 1–2% of all reported dreams.

Neuroscience Studies

More recently, dream processes have been examined within the context of current neuroscience work with the goal of determining which brain areas are involved in dreaming and the manner in which dreaming and other cognitive processes (e.g., visual imagery) are related. Early speculation suggested that dreams were related to brain stem functioning, especially the pons with its generators for rapid eye movement sleep. However, neuropsychological case studies have shown that damage to the pons does not stop dream reports, whereas damage to the forebrain areas does.

Current brain imaging studies suggest that a variety of brain areas are active during brain states associated with dreaming. These areas include the brain stem, which is responsible for basic arousal; the limbic system, which is highly involved in emotionality; and forebrain areas involved in sensory processing. Areas involved in higher-level cognitive processes like planning and logical thinking showed decreased activation during these dream periods. Further explorations suggest that pathways between areas involved in emotional processing and those involved in visual processing are active, whereas those between visual processing and higher-level logical thinking are not. This may help to explain the nature of dreams in which emotional and illogical sequencing of imagery are accepted without reflective awareness.

One implication that can be drawn from the brain imaging work is that a variety of processes are involved in the creation of dreams and that such work helps to characterize the nature of the subjective experience of dreaming. For an overview of dreams from a neuroscience perspective, including the role of sleep and dreams in memory, readers are referred to contributions by Domhoff (2003), Foulkes (1996), Jouvet (1999), Payne and Nadel (2004), and Solms (1997). The November 2, 2001, issue of the journal *Science* also has a number of reviews dealing with sleep, dreams, and memory.

REFERENCES

Domhoff, G. (2003). *The scientific study of dreams: Neural networks, cognitive development, and content analysis.* Washington, DC: American Psychological Association.

Foulkes, D. (1996). Dream research: 1953–1993. *Sleep, 19,* 609–624.

Jouvet, M. (1999). *The paradox of sleep: The story of dreaming.* Cambridge, MA: MIT Press.

Payne, J., & Nadel, L. (2004). Sleep, dreams, and memory consolidation: The role of the stress hormone cortisol. *Learning & Memory, 11,* 671–678.

Solms, M. (1997). *The neuropsychology of dreams.* Mahwah, NJ: Lawrence Erlbaum.

WILLIAM J. RAY
Pennsylvania State University

See also: Sleep Cycles; Sleep Cycles

DRUG ADDICTION

Substance dependence can be defined as a chronically relapsing disorder characterized by (1) compulsion to seek and take the drug, (2) loss of control in limiting intake, and (3) emergence of a negative emotional state (e.g., dysphoria, anxiety, irritability) when access to the drug is prevented (defined here as withdrawal). Addiction and substance dependence, as currently defined by the *Diagnostic and Statistical Manual of Mental Disorders* (DSM-IV-TR; American Psychiatric Association, 2000), are used interchangeably in this article to refer to a final stage of a usage process that moves from drug use to abuse to addiction. The term *dependence* has two meanings: (1) an acute withdrawal syndrome (defined here as dependence with a little "d"), and (2) a syndrome in which a subject meets the criteria for substance dependence. In addiction, drug-taking behavior progresses from impulsivity to compulsivity in a three-stage cycle consisting of binge/intoxication, withdrawal/negative affect, and preoccupation/anticipation.

Two sources of reinforcement can be found in drug-taking behavior associated with the use, abuse, and addiction to drugs: positive and negative reinforcement. Positive reinforcement occurs when presentation of a drug increases the probability of a response to obtain the drug. Reward is defined as positive reinforcement with an added positive emotional valence usually associated with pleasure. Positive reinforcement is most often associated with the impulsivity construct that is a key element of the binge/intoxication and preoccupation/anticipation (craving) stages of the addiction cycle. Animal models of the positive reinforcing or rewarding effects of drugs are extensive and well validated and include intravenous drug self-administration, conditioned place preference, and brain stimulation reward. Drugs of abuse are readily self-administered by animals that are not dependent; therefore, positive reinforcement and intravenous drug self-administration have been used to predict abuse liability.

Negative reinforcement occurs when presentation of the drug prevents the aversive consequences of removal of the drug, usually in the context of drug dependence. Negative reinforcement is often associated with the compulsivity construct that is a key element of the withdrawal/negative affect stage and preoccupation/anticipation stage (protracted abstinence) of the addiction cycle. Animal models of the negative reinforcement associated with drug dependence include measures of conditioned place aversion (rather than preference) to precipitated withdrawal or spontaneous withdrawal from chronic administration of a drug, increases in reward thresholds using brain stimulation reward, and dependence-induced increases in drug-taking and drug-seeking behavior. Such increased self-administration in dependent animals has been observed with cocaine, methamphetamine, nicotine, heroin, and alcohol.

A key element of drug addiction is how the brain reward system changes with the development of addiction, and one must understand the neurobiological bases for acute drug reward to understand how the reward systems change with the development of addiction. A principle focus of research on the neurobiology of the positive reinforcing effects of drugs with dependence potential has been on the activation of the circuitry related to the origins and terminals of the mesocorticolimbic dopamine system. Compelling evidence suggests a critical role of this system in drug reward associated with psychostimulant drugs, and all major drugs of abuse activate this system, as measured either by increased extracellular levels of dopamine in the terminal areas (such as the nucleus accumbens) or by activation of the firing of neurons in the ventral tegmental area. However, although selective neurotoxin-induced lesions of the mesolimbic dopamine system block cocaine, amphetamine, and nicotine self-administration, rats continue to self-administer heroin and alcohol in the absence of the mesocorticolimbic dopamine system. Place preference studies also show robust place preferences to morphine and nicotine in the presence of major dopamine receptor blockade. Together these results suggest that activation of the mesolimbic dopamine system is a component of drug-seeking in general, but it is only critical for the rewarding effects of stimulant drugs.

Specific components of the basal forebrain associated with the amygdala have also been identified with drug reward. The reinforcing effects of alcohol in nondependent animals are blocked by administration of γ-aminobutyric acid-A (GABA$_A$) receptor antagonists and opioid antagonists into the nucleus accumbens and central nucleus of the amygdala. As the neural circuits for the reinforcing effects of drugs with dependence potential have evolved, the role of neurotransmitters/neuromodulators also has evolved, and multiple neurotransmitter systems, including mesolimbic dopamine, opioid peptide, γ-aminobutyric acid (GABA), glutamate, endocannabinoids, and serotonin, have been identified to have a role in mediating the acute reinforcing effects of drugs of abuse in these basal forebrain areas.

Neurocircuitry of the Binge/Intoxication Stage of the Addiction Cycle

Electrical brain stimulation reward (or intracranial self-stimulation) has a long history as a measure of activity of the brain reward system and the acute reinforcing effects of drugs of abuse. Brain stimulation reward involves widespread neurocircuitry in the brain, but the most sensitive sites defined by the lowest thresholds involve the trajectory of the medial forebrain bundle connecting the ventral tegmental area with the basal forebrain (Olds & Milner, 1954). Much emphasis was focused initially on the role of the ascending monoamine systems in the medial forebrain bundle, but other descending, nondopaminergic systems in the medial forebrain bundle clearly have a key role (Hernandez et al., 2006). Activity in brain reward pathways measured by brain stimulation reward have provided key validation in animal models of the subjective reward changes reported by humans during the addiction cycle and forms the basis for exploring the underlying neuroadaptive changes in reward systems that occur during the progression to addiction.

All drugs of abuse, when administered acutely to nondependent animals, decrease brain stimulation reward thresholds (Kornetsky & Esposito, 1979). In contrast, measures of brain reward function during acute abstinence from all major drugs with dependence potential have revealed increases in brain reward thresholds measured by direct brain stimulation reward. These increases in reward thresholds may reflect decreases in the activity of reward neurotransmitter systems in the midbrain and forebrain implicated in the positive reinforcing effects of drugs (Koob et al., 2004).

The acute reinforcing effects of drugs of abuse are mediated by the activation of dopamine, serotonin, opioid peptides, and GABA systems, either by direct actions in the basal forebrain (notably the nucleus accumbens and central nucleus of the amygdala) or by indirect actions in the ventral tegmental area (Koob & Le Moal, 2001). Much evidence supports the hypothesis that the mesolimbic dopamine system is dramatically activated by psychostimulant drugs during limited-access self-administration and to some extent by all drugs of abuse. Serotonin systems, particularly those involving 5-hydroxytryptamine-1B (5-HT$_{1B}$) receptor activation in the nucleus accumbens, also have been implicated in the acute reinforcing effects of psychostimulant drugs. μ Opioid receptors in both the nucleus accumbens and ventral tegmental area mediate the reinforcing effects of alcohol and opioid drugs. GABAergic systems are activated pre- and postsynaptically in the amygdala by ethanol at intoxicating doses, and GABA antagonists administered into the nucleus accumbens and central nucleus of the amygdala block ethanol self-administration (Koob, 2006; Nestler, 2005).

Neurocircuitry of the Withdrawal/Negative Affect Stage of the Addiction Cycle

The neural substrates and neuropharmacological mechanisms for the negative motivational effects of drug withdrawal may involve disruption of the same neural systems implicated in the positive reinforcing effects of drugs. These decreases in the activity of reward neurotransmitter systems in the midbrain and forebrain implicated in the positive reinforcing effects of drugs represent what has been termed a "within-system" neuroadaptation. Examples of such changes at the neurochemical level include decreases in dopaminergic transmission in the nucleus accumbens during drug withdrawal measured by *in vivo* microdialysis, decreases in firing of ventral tegmental area dopamine neurons, and changes in signal transduction mechanisms associated with dopamine neurotransmission in the nucleus accumbens during drug withdrawal. The decreases in reward neurotransmitter function have been hypothesized to contribute significantly to the negative motivational state associated with acute drug abstinence and also the long-term biochemical changes that contribute to the clinical syndrome of protracted abstinence and vulnerability to relapse.

Different neurochemical systems involved in arousal and stress modulation also may be engaged within the neurocircuitry of the brain stress systems in an attempt to overcome the chronic presence of the perturbing drug and to restore normal function despite the presence of drug and have been termed "between-system" neuroadaptations. Glutamate, an excitatory neurotransmitter, has been implicated in neuroadaptation to repeated exposure to drugs of abuse. Glutamate hyperactivity in the basal forebrain has been linked to the hyperexcitability associated with ethanol withdrawal, and this hyperexcitability has been observed in slices of the hippocampus, nucleus accumbens, and amygdala. The hyperexcitability is linked to the protracted abstinence state in alcohol dependence and is hypothesized to be a neural substrate for the anti-relapse effects of acamprosate, a medication for the treatment of alcoholism.

Chronic administration of drugs with dependence potential also dysregulate both the hypothalamic-pituitary-adrenal axis and the brain stress system mediated by corticotropin-releasing factor (CRF). Common responses include an activated pituitary adrenal stress response, elevated adrenocorticotropic hormone and corticosteroids, and an activated brain stress response with activated amygdala CRF during acute withdrawal from all major drugs of abuse. Acute withdrawal from drugs of abuse also may increase the release of norepinephrine in the bed nucleus of the stria terminalis and decrease levels of neuropeptide Y in the central and medial nuclei of the amygdala.

These results suggest not only a change in function of neurotransmitters associated with the acute reinforcing effects of drugs (dopamine, opioid peptides, serotonin, and GABA) during the development of dependence, but also recruitment of the brain arousal and stress systems (glutamate, CRF, and norepinephrine) and dysregulation of the neuropeptide Y brain anti-stress system. Thus, reward mechanisms in dependence are compromised by disruption of neurochemical systems involved in processing natural rewards and by recruitment of the anti-reward systems that represent neuroadaptation to the chronic exposure of the brain reward neurocircuitry to drugs of abuse.

The neuroanatomical entity termed the extended amygdala thus may represent a common anatomical substrate for acute drug reward and a common neuroanatomical substrate for the negative effects on reward function produced by stress that help drive compulsive drug administration. The extended amygdala receives numerous afferents from limbic structures such as the basolateral amygdala and hippocampus and sends efferents to the medial part of the ventral pallidum and a large projection to the lateral hypothalamus, thus further defining the specific brain areas that interface classical limbic (emotional) structures with the extrapyramidal motor system. The decreases in neurotransmitter function are paralleled by molecular changes in signal transduction factors such as adenylate cyclase and gene transcription factors such as c-*fos*.

Neurocircuitry of the Preoccupation/Anticipation (Craving) Stage of the Addiction Cycle

Parallel to dysregulation of reward systems are decreases in reward system function and increases in anti-reward system function (Koob, 2008). Shifts in striatal-pallidal-thalamic-cortical function have been hypothesized. Here, drug-seeking moves from corticostriatal loops operating from the ventral striatum to corticostriatal loops operating from the dorsal striatum (Everitt & Wolf, 2002).

Animal models of "craving" involve the use of drug-primed reinstatement, cue-induced reinstatement, or stress-induced reinstatement in animals that have acquired drug self-administration and then have been subjected to extinction of responding for the drug. Most evidence from animal studies suggests that drug-induced reinstatement is localized to a medial prefrontal cortex/nucleus accumbens/ventral pallidum circuit mediated by the neurotransmitter glutamate. For example, glutamate neuroplasticity has been implicated in cocaine-induced reinstatement in which increased glutamate release combined with reduced basal glutamate function in the prefrontal cortex-to-nucleus accumbens core pathway has been hypothesized to explain increased glutamate release in response to repeated cocaine administration. In both models, increased glutamatergic function contributes to increased drug-seeking in addiction. In contrast, neuropharmacological and neurobiological studies using animal models for cue-induced reinstatement involve the basolateral amygdala as a critical substrate with a possible feed-forward mechanism through the prefrontal cortex system involved in drug-induced reinstatement. Stress-induced reinstatement of drug-related responding in animal models appears to depend on activation of both CRF and norepinephrine in elements of the extended amygdala (central nucleus of the amygdala and bed nucleus of the stria terminalis). Again, molecular changes in these circuits that persist into protracted abstinence involve changes that range from cystine glutamate exchange function to gene transcription factors such as ΔFosB that remain increased long past acute abstinence.

In summary, three neurobiological circuits have been identified that have heuristic value for the study of the neurobiological changes associated with the development and persistence of drug dependence. The acute reinforcing effects of drugs of abuse that comprise the binge/intoxication stage of the addiction cycle most likely involve actions localized to a nucleus accumbens-amygdala reward system, dopamine inputs from the ventral tegmental area, and local opioid peptide and GABAergic circuits. In contrast, the symptoms of acute withdrawal important for addiction, such as dysphoria and increased anxiety associated with the withdrawal/negative affect stage, most likely involve decreases in function of the extended amygdala reward system and recruitment of brain stress neurocircuitry. The preoccupation/anticipation (or craving) stage involves key afferent projections to the nucleus accumbens and extended amygdala, specifically the prefrontal cortex (for drug-induced reinstatement) and the basolateral amygdala (for cue-induced reinstatement). Compulsive drug-seeking behavior is hypothesized to engage a transition from ventral striatal-ventral pallidal-thalamic-cortical loops to dorsal striatal-pallidal-thalamic-cortical loops. Molecular neuroadaptations begin with the *binge/intoxication* stage and transition through the addiction cycle with long-term changes in gene transcription that may convey vulnerability for relapse.

REFERENCES

American Psychiatric Association (2000). *Diagnostic and statistical manual of mental disorders* (DSM-IV, text rev.). Washington, DC: Author.

Everitt, B. J., Wolf, M. E. (2002). Psychomotor stimulant addiction: A neural systems perspective. *Journal of Neuroscience, 22*, 3312–3320 [erratum: *22*(16):1a].

Hernandez, G., Hamdani, S., Rajabi, H., Conover, K., Stewart, J., Arvanitogiannis, A. et al. (2006). Prolonged rewarding stimulation of the rat medial forebrain bundle: Neurochemical and behavioral consequences. *Behavioral Neuroscience, 120*, 888–904.

Kornetsky, C., Esposito, R. U. (1979). Euphorigenic drugs: Effects on the reward pathways of the brain. *Federation Proceedings, 38*, 2473–2476.

Koob, G. F. (2006). The neurobiology of addiction: A neuroadaptational view relevant for diagnosis. *Addiction, 101*(suppl 1):23–30.

Koob, G. F. (2008). A role for brain stress systems in addiction. *Neuron, 59*, 11–34.

Koob, G. F., Ahmed, S. H., Boutrel, B., Chen, S. A., Kenny, P. J., Markou, A. et al. (2004). Neurobiological mechanisms in the transition from drug use to drug dependence. *Neuroscience and Biobehavioral Reviews, 27*, 739–749.

Koob, G. F., & Le Moal, M. (2001). Drug addiction, dysregulation of reward, and allostasis. *Neuropsychopharmacology, 24*, 97–129.

Nestler, E. J. (2005). Is there a common molecular pathway for addiction? *Nature Neuroscience, 8*, 1445–1449.

Olds, J., & Milner, P. (1954). Positive reinforcement produced by electrical stimulation of septal area and other regions of rat brain. *Journal of Comparative and Physiological Psychology, 47*, 419–427.

GEORGE F. KOOB
Scripps Research Institute, La Jolla, CA

DRUG THERAPY (See Psychopharmacology)

DSM (See Diagnostic and Statistical Manual of Mental Disorders)

DUAL DIAGNOSIS (See Comorbidity)

DUAL RELATIONSHIPS

In psychotherapy, dual relationships, or multiple relationships, refer to situations in which multiple roles exist between a therapist and a client. These are situations in which therapists have additional relationships with their clients beyond the clinical-therapeutic ones. Examples of dual relationships arise when a therapist's client is also the therapist's student, employee, colleague or friend (Zur, 2007).

There are many types of dual relationships. Although some are avoidable, others, such as those in small rural communities or in sport psychology, are unavoidable

(Schank & Skovholt, 2006). Dual relationships are mandated in certain settings, such as the military and correctional institutions. Dual relationships are considered sequential if, for example, the client was the therapist's student prior to the initiation of therapy, and they are considered concurrent if the added relationships take place simultaneously with therapy. Dual relationships can be unethical, as is always the case with therapists' sexual or other exploitative relationships with current clients, or they can be ethical, when the dual relationships are neither exploitative nor harmful, nor pose a risk of exploitation or loss of objectivity on the part of the therapist.

Dual relationships that are based on familiarity and shared communal or spiritual values can increase trust and therapeutic outcome, and they are considered ethical and clinically appropriate (Herlihy & Corey, 2006; Zur, 2007). Therapist-client concurrent sexual relationships are not only always unethical but also illegal in most states in the United States. Dual relationships present themselves with different levels of intensity or involvement. They can be of low-minimal level when, for example, a therapist runs into a client in the local market or in the theater parking lot, or they can be of medium level intensity when a client and therapist share occasional encounters, as in attending church services every Sunday or occasional PTA meetings. High-intensity dual relationships occur when the therapist and client socialize, work, attend functions or serve on committees together on a regular and highly involved basis.

There are many types of dual relationships. Social dual relationships occur when the therapist and client are also social acquaintances or friends. In professional dual relationships the therapist and client are also professional colleagues in colleges or training institutions. In business dual relationships, the therapist and client are also business partners or have employer-employee relationships. In communal dual relationships the therapist and client live in the same small community, belong to the same church or synagogue, or where the therapist shops in a store that is owned by the client. Institutional dual relationships take place in settings such as the military, prisons, or police department in which complex dual relationships are often an inherent part of the institutional setting. Forensic dual relationships involve clinicians who serve as treating therapists, evaluators, and witnesses in trials or board hearings. Sexual dual relationships occur when the therapist and client are also involved in a sexual relationship. Sexual dual relationships with current or recently terminated clients are always unethical and often illegal (Bennett et al., 2006). An additional and rather rare form of dual relationship is adoption, in which a therapist adopts a former child-client.

In the past, all dual relationships were associated with sexual dual relationships and were therefore frowned upon by ethicists, boards, and ethics committees. However, since the 1990s a deeper and more complex understanding of dual relationships has emerged. Most importantly, it has become apparent that dual or multiple relationships are not only unavoidable but may be normal and healthy aspects of small or interdependent communities (Lazarus & Zur, 2002). Small communities, in this context, do not exclusively refer to remote or rural communities; they also include small communities within large metropolitan areas, such as the LGBT, Hispanic, church, Jewish, or college communities (Schank & Skovholt, 2006; Zur, 2008). In communities where familiarity, interdependence, mutual trust and shared values are held in high esteem, dual relationships are more acceptable and are considered ethical.

The ethics codes of most major professional organizations (e.g., American Psychological Association, American Counseling Association) have recently been revised and clearly recognize that dual relationships may be unavoidable and are not necessary unethical (Bennet, et al., 2006; Zur, 2007). Ethically and clinically, it is important that therapists engage thoughtfully and carefully in dual relationships and avoid relationships that are likely to impair their judgment or objectivity or are likely to negatively effect the treatment. Discussions with clients regarding the risks and benefits are an important part of the process of obtaining informed consent to engage in dual relationships. In determining the appropriateness of dual relationships to each specific situation, therapists must thoroughly consider the context of therapy, which includes the client, setting, therapeutic, and therapist factors. Dual relationships that are appropriate with a certain client in a certain setting may not be appropriate with a different client or in a different setting.

In summary, a new understanding of the nature and complexities of dual relationships has been emerging in the last couple of decades. Appropriate or unavoidable dual relationships are no longer frowned upon by boards and ethicists as it becomes clear that some dual relationships are unavoidable, others are mandated and others can aid the therapeutic process.

REFERENCES

Bennett, B. E., Bricklin, P. M., Harris, E., Knapp, S., VandeCreek, L., & Younggren, J. N. (2006). *Assessing and managing risk in psychological practice: An individualized approach*. Rockville, MD: The Trust.

Herlihy, B., & Corey, G. (2006). *Boundary issues in counseling: Multiple roles and responsibilities* (2nd ed.). Alexandria, VA: American Association for Counseling and Development.

Lazarus, A. A., & Zur, O. (Eds.) (2002), *Dual relationships and psychotherapy*. New York: Springer.

Schank, A. J., & Skovholt, T. M. (2006). *Ethical practice in small communities: Challenges and rewards for psychologists*. Washington DC: American Psychological Association.

Zur, O. (2007). *Boundaries in psychotherapy: Ethical and clinical explorations*. Washington, DC: American Psychological Association.

Zur, O. (2008). *Guidelines for non-sexual dual relationships, multiple relationships & boundaries in psychotherapy and counseling.* Online publication. Retrieved on July 1, 2008 from http://www.zurinstitute.com/dualrelationships.html.

OFER ZUR
Zur Institute, Sonoma, CA

See also: **Ethical Issues in Psychology**

DYNAMIC PSYCHOLOGY

A dynamic psychology considers mental experience and behavior as a function of the interaction of motivational, affective, and cognitive variables of different degrees of intensity or strength. There have been a variety of theories in the history of psychology that fall under the rubric of dynamic psychology. These theories, which have waned in influence in the past half-century, include general systems theory, behaviorist theories (e.g., Hull), Lewin's field theory, cognitive dissonance theory (Festinger), family systems theories, Henry Murray's need-press theory, and a variety of psychodynamic theories (e.g., Freud, Adler, Rank, Horney, Sullivan). Although differing in important respects, these theories have in common a focus on the intensity and direction of motivational forces and conflicts involved in adaptive and maladaptive goal-directed behavior. For example, approach-avoidance conflicts involve the dynamic interaction of competing needs, motives, fears, and goals.

Most dynamic theories emphasize conflicts around tension reduction as well as the seeking of pleasure and the avoidance of pain or negative affect. Some dynamic theories of personality (e.g., object relations theories) focus on the centrality of relationships and the conflicts involved in seeking and maintaining interpersonal connections. Family systems theorists focus on how issues of family roles, alliances, and boundaries preserve or disrupt homeostatic equilibrium in the family (e.g., how a child becoming symptomatic can serve to reduce marital tensions).

Arguably, the most influential of the various dynamic theories of the twentieth century was the one developed by Sigmund Freud (1856–1939) and modified by scores of later theorists. A distinctive feature of Freudian theory is the view of human behavior from the perspective of inner conflict, particularly unconscious conflict. Freud borrowed the term "dynamic" from physics where it refers to the interaction of forces as in thermodynamics or aerodynamics. In a psychodynamic theory, the word "dynamic" is intended to convey the idea of an interplay of forces in the mind. The term "dynamic" had also been used in the late nineteenth century by Leibniz, Fechner, Herbart,

and Hughlings-Jackson to make the distinction between a neurological and a psychological mental impairment.

Freud's Psychodynamic Psychology

Freud began addressing hysterical and other psychological symptoms through the use of hypnosis, at first employing direct hypnotic suggestions to alleviate symptoms. For example, he described a case of a mother of a newborn infant who had an assortment of symptoms, including an inability to nurse her baby (Freud, 1893/1966). After limited and temporary success with direct suggestion (e.g., "your milk will flow"), Freud directed her to emerge from the hypnotic state and express anger toward her family by complaining that she could not be expected to breast-feed her baby if those around her were not attending to her needs. Following this outburst her various symptoms abated and she was able to breast-feed her baby. From a dynamic perspective, Freud was implicitly suggesting that the patient had an unconscious conflict between her conscious desire to nurture her baby and her unconscious desire not to as long as her own needs for nurturance were not met.

The two fundamental, related assumptions of Freud's dynamic theory are unconscious motivation and psychic determinism. Unconscious motivation refers to the idea that the person is strongly influenced by wishes and motives outside of awareness. Psychic determinism refers to lawful regularities in mental life among ideas, feelings, and behaviors that, on the surface, appear unrelated but often are linked by unconscious ideas.

Freud (1923/1961) eventually formulated his conflict model in terms of the interaction of *id, ego,* and *superego.* These terms denote the three major agencies of the mind. The id is the repository of the two main instinctual drives—sex and aggression, both to be understood in the broad rather than the narrow meaning of those terms. For example, when thought of in relation to infantile sexuality, the sexual drive is better thought of as sensual. These instinctual drives are described as having a source, an aim, an impetus, and an object. The source is a bodily one, the aim is to discharge the tension associated with the build-up of the drive, the impetus is the force or strength of the drive, and the object (animate or inanimate), the most variable aspect of the drive, is the means by which drive gratification is sought. In this tension-reduction model, the increase in drive tension is regarded as unpleasurable and decreases in drive tension are regarded as pleasurable. The *pleasure principle* refers to the tendency to seek immediate drive discharge. Because this initial tendency fails to bring more than temporary satisfaction, the organism is forced to turn to reality. Although the *reality principle* supersedes the pleasure principle, it is a necessary delay in the ultimate goal of achieving pleasure. In *Beyond the Pleasure Principle,* Freud (1920/1955) hypothesized that the repetition of traumatic experiences (e.g., in flashback memories) suggested that mastering excessive stimulation was the first goal of the organism. The associated idea of a "death instinct" was never fully accepted.

Mental experience, conscious and unconscious, and behavior are considered as a compromise formation resulting from the interaction of instinctual drives or wishes (the id), reality constraints and opportunities for gratification (as appraised by the ego), and internalized moral standards and ideals (Freud's superego). Identification (the modeling of one's self after significant others) is an important facet of superego and ego development. The ego institutes defenses designed to ward-off perceived dangers. Among the main defense mechanisms are repression (motivated forgetting), reaction formation (expressing the polar opposite of what one truly feels, e.g., saccharin sweetness in lieu of anger), projection (attributing to the other person disavowed, unacceptable aspects of one's self), and isolation of affect (a psychological severing of the links between potentially painful thoughts and their associated affects). Although "defense" has a pejorative connotation, the theory holds that an optimal level of defense aids adaptation. An excessive reliance on defense leads to a marked inhibition of the personality. Insufficient defenses result in symptom formation. Symptoms appear when the underlying impulses are too strong and/or the defenses against them are too weak to contain anxiety and other dysphoric affects. In this sense, symptoms are a second line of defense.

Many accounts of Freud's psychodynamic theory present it as if the id, ego, and superego are concrete entities doing battle with one another. In fact, these terms are hypothetical constructs that refer to aspects of the personality that often are in conflict with one another. In the well-functioning person, these three aspects of personality blend harmoniously into one another. Some theorists (e.g., Brenner, 1994) raise serious questions about the utility of the tri-partite or structural theory of id, ego, and superego. Brenner (1994) prefers to see mental contents and behavior as a compromise formation that reveals aspects of wishes, defenses, and superego factors.

Freud viewed inner conflict in terms of a *drive-defense* model in which mental contents and behavior are the outcomes of a compromise between these two factors. (In contemporary theory one speaks of "wishes" rather than "drives"; wishes are regarded as the mental representations of instinctual drives). A wish reflects a desire to reinstate a previous experience of satisfaction. The drive-defense model applies not only to symptom formation but to virtually every aspect of psychic functioning: the development of character traits and patterns of interpersonal functioning, dreams, slips of the tongue and other parapraxes, and so on.

Freud developed a metapsychology to explain mental functioning on a more abstract level. This approach includes five perspectives for understanding psychic life: (1) the genetic (the historical roots of a given behavior), (2) the dynamic (the interplay of forces in the mind), (3) the adaptive (the effectiveness of different coping and defensive strategies), (4) the topographic (the conscious, preconscious, and unconscious aspects of behavior), and (5) the economic (the degree and transformations of sexual and aggressive psychic energies). Most contemporary psychoanalytic theorists do not embrace Freud's metapsychology, particularly his economic views about so-called psychic energies involving quasi-physicalistic concepts of libido and cathexis.

The genetic viewpoint includes Freud's psychosexual stages of development: oral, anal, phallic, and genital. These stages correspond to developmental shifts in the main psychic focus of the instinctual drives. Each stage is associated with a predominant anxiety: loss of the object in the oral stage, loss of the object's love in the anal stage, castration anxiety in the phallic stage, and guilt in the genital stage.

Excessive gratification or frustration at any of these stages can lead to fixation, which is a tendency to seek the mode of gratification appropriate to that level of psychosexual development, either because of a refusal to relinquish familiar forms of gratification, or the inability to forgo pursuing gratifications one never had. Alternatively, excessive gratification or frustration at any stage can lead to regression, which is a tendency to revert to a prior psychosexual level in the face of conflict or stress.

The therapy based on Freud's view of human functioning focuses on uncovering the patient's warded-off psychological conflicts as they get reenacted in the "transference" to the therapist. Insight into such conflicts and a less self-critical stance toward them are necessary for constructive personality change.

Developments since Freud

Virtually every significant theoretical development since Freud starts from a rejection of his overly strong emphasis on instinctual drive gratification as the major motivational thrust of the organism. In lieu of Freud's biological approach, the so-called Neo-Freudian theorists (e.g., Horney, Sullivan) placed more stress on the family, social, and cultural factors that shape personality development.

Psychoanalytic ego psychology was also a corrective reaction and supplement to Freud's so-called id psychology. Ego psychology focused on the nonconflictual aspects of personality, what ego psychologists (e.g., Hartmann, 1939) referred to as conflict-free spheres of ego functioning. The person came to be seen as having interests and ego functions that were not entirely based on the sublimation of instinctual conflicts. Those aspects of ego functioning that were imbued with conflict could eventually achieve a secondary autonomy, whereas those that developed independently of conflict in the first place were said to have a primary autonomy.

Erik Erikson (1950), in his conception of a life cycle, did much to extend Freudian theory and psychoanalytic ego psychology to the psychosocial aspects of behavior. Thus, the significance of the oral stage was not simply the gratification of oral needs but the development of basic trust (or mistrust). Erikson also included stages of adolescent and adult development (e.g., ego identity versus ego diffusion, generativity versus stagnation) that were not tied directly to Freud's psychosexual stages.

The other two main theoretical developments in psychodynamic psychology in the last several decades were British object relations theories and self-psychology. There are a variety of object relations theorists (e.g., Winnicott, Fairbairn) who stress relationships with others as the building blocks of personality. These ideas were in contrast to Freud's emphasis on libidinal gratification as the person's major motivational goal. The object relations approach is seen most clearly in Fairbairn's (1952, p. 82) famous dictum that "libido is object seeking not pleasure seeking." In this view, one's primary aim is relatedness to others, starting with the primary caretaker. Object relations theories have a strong affinity with Bowlby's (1988) attachment theory in which a secure attachment to a primary caretaker is regarded as essential, although Bowlby's theory has more biological underpinnings.

Object relations theories focus on the internalized mental representations of self and other and the affective coloring of their interactions. Emphasis is placed on the tendency to "split" mental representations of "self" and "other" into "good" versus "bad" and on the difficulty of forming an integrated view of self and other. These theories stress the importance of the pre-Oedipal period in shaping personality, in particular the negative consequences of a failure to experience "good enough" mothering. Such individuals have a difficult time internalizing a soothing introject and are therefore more emotionally vulnerable. Issues of loyalty, even to abusing significant others, and separation and survival guilt figure prominently in this approach.

The self-psychology model, developed by Kohut (1971), centers on the development and maintenance of a cohesive sense of self and the factors that promote or impede the development of healthy narcissism. Chronic failures of empathic responsiveness on the part of the parents prevent the child from using the parents as self-objects. Self-objects are aspects of the other that function as psychological extensions of the self. The two major classes of self-objects are mirroring self-objects (e.g., "You admire me and therefore I feel affirmed as a person of worth") and idealized self-objects (e.g., "I admire you and therefore my sense of self-worth, confidence, and strength are enhanced via my vicarious participation in your strength and power").

Three other developments in dynamic approaches should be noted, all of which stem from a critique of traditional psychoanalysis as a one-person psychology of the isolated mind. First, basing his work on aspects of British object relations theory and Sullivan's (1953) interpersonal theory, Mitchell (1988) has been the leading exponent of American relational psychoanalysis, a view that stresses the centrality of relational configurations as conceptualized from an hermeneutic, constructivist perspective. From this perspective, patient and therapist co-construct a narrative about the patient and the patient-therapist interaction that emerges from the interplay of transference-countertransference. Second, Stolorow and colleagues (1994) have developed an intersubjective perspective that is an offshoot of self-psychology and is also compatible with an object relations view. Their intersubjectivity theory looks at the patient-therapist relationship as centering on the interaction of two subjectivities that reciprocally mutually influence one another. Third, Kernberg (1976) presented an influential synthesis of British object relations theory and Freud's structural theory that has made a major contribution to the understanding of borderline personality disorder.

Although the key phenomena and concepts differ in the several theories mentioned, there is the common ground idea of an organism whose state of dynamic equilibrium is susceptible to disruption by the interplay of intrapsychic and interpersonal forces. These disruptions include anxiety over the expression of forbidden wishes, feared loss of an object's love, conflicts about loyalty to significant others, or the unavailability of mirroring self-objects. The dynamic intrapsychic and interpersonal forces interact with developmental and environmental challenges and stressors.

REFERENCES

Bowlby, J. (1988). *A secure base*. New York: Basic Books

Brenner, C. (1994). Mind as conflict and compromise formation. *Journal of Clinical Psychoanalysis, 3*(4), 473–488.

Erikson, E. H. (1950). *Childhood and society*. New York: Norton.

Fairbairn, W. R. D. (1952). *Psychoanalytic studies of the personality*. London: Tavistock Publications and Kegan Paul, Trench, and Trubner.

Freud, S. (1955). Beyond the pleasure principle. *Standard Edition, 18*, 1–64. London: Hogarth Press. (Original work published in 1920)

Freud. S. (1961). The ego and the id. *Standard Edition, 19*, 1–66. London: Hogarth Press. (Original work published in 1923)

Freud, S. (1966). A case of successful treatment by hypnotism. *Standard Edition, 1*, 115–128. London: Hogarth Press. (Original work published in 1893)

Hartmann, H. (1939). *Ego psychology and the problem of adaptation*. New York: International Universities Press (1958).

Kernberg, O. (1976). *Object relations theory and clinical psychoanalysis*. New York: Aronson.

Kohut, H. (1971). *The analysis of the self*. New York: International Universities Press.

Mitchell, S. (1988). *Relational concepts in psychoanalysis.* Cambridge, MA: Harvard University Press.

Stolorow, R., Atwood, G. E., & Brandchaft, B. (1994). *The intersubjective perspective.* Northvale, NJ: Aronson.

Sullivan, H. S. (1953). *The interpersonal theory of psychiatry.* New York: Norton.

SUGGESTED READINGS

Fonagy, P., & Target, M. (2003). Psychoanalytic theories: Perspectives from developmental psychopathology. New York: Brunner-Routledge.

Greenberg, J., & Mitchell, S. A. (1983). Object relations in psychoanalytic theory. Cambridge, MA: Harvard University Press.

Person, E. S., Cooper, A.M., & Gabbard, G.O. (Eds.). (2005). *Textbook of psychoanalysis.* Washington, DC: American Psychiatric Press

DAVID L. WOLITZKY
New York University

See also: **Personality, Psychodynamic Models of; Psychoanalytic Theories; Psychosexual Stages**

DYSLEXIA (See Alexia/Dyslexia)

DYSTHYMIC DISORDER

Dysthymic disorder is a form of mood disorder that is characterized by mild, chronic depression. The current diagnostic criteria require chronic depressed mood (i.e., depressed most of the day, for more days than not, for at least two years). In addition, the individual must experience at least two of the following six depressive symptoms: (1) low self-esteem, (2) feelings of hopelessness, (3) low energy or fatigue, (4) difficulty concentrating or making decisions, (5) sleep disturbance (insomnia or sleeping too much), and (6) appetite disturbance (poor appetite or overeating). The symptoms must be persistent (i.e., never without depressive symptoms for more than two months at a time during this period), have a gradual (or insidious) onset (i.e., no major depressive episode during the first two years), and cause significant distress or impairment in social or occupational functioning. Finally, the diagnosis cannot not be made if the individual has a psychotic or bipolar (manic-depressive) disorder, or if the symptoms are due to medication, substances of abuse, or a general medical condition (American Psychiatric Association, 2000).

Dysthymic disorder is closely related to the diagnosis of major depressive disorder. Indeed, their symptom pictures are virtually identical. However, episodes of major depression tend to be more severe, have a more rapid (or acute) onset, and the majority are not chronic.

Dysthymic disorder is relatively common, with approximately 2% of adults in the community meeting criteria during the past 12 months, and 3%–6% meeting criteria at some point in their lives (Kessler, Berglund, Demler, Jin, & Walters, 2005). Like many forms of depression, dysthymia is approximately twice as common in women compared to men. It is evident in all age groups, including pediatric and geriatric populations (Kovacs, Akiskal, Gatsonis, & Parrone, 1994). Dysthymic disorder may appear to be relatively mild in cross-sectional assessments at a given point in time. However, the cumulative burden of persistent depressive symptoms and impaired functioning is substantial and can be as great or greater than in major depression.

Approximately 75% of persons with dysthymia experience episodes of major depression that are superimposed on the preexisting dysthymic disorder. This pattern has been referred to as "double depression" (Keller et al., 1995). Although this term implies that such individuals suffer from two different kinds of depressive disorders, it is likely that it is a single disorder that waxes and wanes, often in response to stress. Persons with dysthymia also frequently experience anxiety disorders, substance abuse disorders, and personality disorders (particularly borderline and avoidant personality disorders).

Individuals with an onset of dysthymia in childhood or adolescence are more likely to have other co-occuring psychiatric disorders, a history of childhood adversity, and a greater family history of mood disorders than individuals with an adult onset. In contrast, late-onset dysthymic disorder may be closely associated with stressful life events, particularly chronic stressors related to general medical disorders or the illness or loss of loved ones.

As dysthymic disorder is, by definition, a chronic condition, it is not surprising that recovery rates are low. In "naturalistic" follow-up studies (in which there is no attempt to control treatment), approximately three-quarters of outpatients with dysthymia recover (defined as no or almost no symptoms for at least two consecutive months) during the course of the next 10 years, with a median time to recovery of 52 months. However, almost three-quarters of patients who recover experience a relapse into chronic depression (Klein, Shankman, & Rose, 2006). The naturalistic course of dysthymic disorder in children and adolescents is generally similar to adults (Kovacs et al., 1994). Predictors of a poorer course include comorbid anxiety and personality disorders, a greater familial loading of chronic depression in first-degree relatives, and a history of childhood adversity (e.g., parental rejection, sexual abuse). Chronic stress appears to be an important factor in maintaining dysthymic disorder, particularly in patients with a history of childhood adversity (Klein, Shankman, & Rose, in press).

Dysthymic disorder runs in families, along with major depression. Persons with dysthymia have increased rates of both dysthymia and major depression in their first-degree relatives. There also appears to be a higher rate of some personality disorders in the families of persons with dysthymia (Klein, Shankman, Lewinsohn, Rohde, & Seeley, 2004). Few studies have been conducted to distinguish the role of genetic from environmental factors in the familial transmission of dysthymic disorder. However, there is evidence that persons with dysthymia are more likely to have grown up in adverse early home environments, with increased rates of physical and sexual abuse and poor parenting.

Despite the large literature on the neurobiology of major depressive disorder, little is known about the role of biological abnormalities in dysthymia. However, patients with dysthymic disorder and double depression exhibit many of the same cognitive biases that have been described in major depressive disorder, such as self-criticism and maladaptive cognitive schemas. Indeed, dysthymia may be characterized by even higher levels of maladaptive cognitions than episodic major depression (Riso et al., 2003). In addition, individuals with dysthymia often exhibit dysfunctional interpersonal styles, and have low levels of social support.

Double-blind placebo-controlled trials indicate that antidepressant medications are efficacious in treating dysthymic disorder and double depression. However, it may take longer to achieve a response in chronic than nonchronic depressions. Several large studies have indicated that maintenance pharmacotherapy (i.e., continuing on medication after recovery) for dysthymia and double depression can reduce the risk of recurrences (Kocsis, 2003).

Research on psychotherapy for dysthymia and double depression is more limited, and many commonly used approaches such as cognitive therapy and psychodynamic psychotherapy have not been tested in clinical trials. James McCullough's cognitive behavioral analysis system of psychotherapy (CBASP), a structured cognitive-behavioral approach designed to help patients to develop better interpersonal problem-solving skills, has been tested in one large multisite clinical trial of patients with a variety of forms of chronic depression. At the end of the 12-week (16 session) trial, the response to CBASP and antidepressant medication were equivalent (48% for both), although patients in the pharmacotherapy condition responded more quickly (Keller et al., 2000). There have also been several trials of interpersonal psychotherapy (IPT) in dysthymia and double depression. Although IPT does not appear to be as efficacious as pharmacotherapy, it may help reduce medical and social service costs and increase compliance with medication (Markowitz, Kocsis, Bleiberg, Chritos, & Sacks, 2005).

There is some evidence that the combination of medication and psychotherapy is more effective than either treatment alone. Thus, in the Keller et al. (2000) study, patients receiving the combination of CBASP and medication were significantly more likely to respond than patients receiving either monotherapy.

Few studies have examined the efficacy of psychotherapy in preventing relapse and recurrence in dysthymia and double depression. However, Klein, Santiago et al. (2004) reported that CBASP appears to be effective as a maintenance phase treatment. Chronically depressed patients who responded to 12 weeks of acute phase treatment and 16 weeks of continuation treatment were randomly assigned to continue to receive either one session of CBASP per month or assessment-only for 12 months. Patients who received maintenance CBASP had a significantly lower risk of recurrence than patients who were assigned to the assessment-only condition.

On balance, it appears that antidepressant medication may be somewhat more efficacious than psychotherapy in treating chronic depression. However, some forms of psychotherapy, or psychotherapy administered with sufficient intensity, may be as effective as pharmacotherapy. It is also conceivable that medication and psychotherapy are effective for different subgroups of patients. For example, Nemeroff et al. (2003) found that CBASP produced a significantly higher rate of remission than pharmacotherapy in the subgroup of chronically depressed patients with a history of childhood adversity. In contrast, patients without a history of childhood adversity exhibited a nonsignificantly higher remission rate in pharmacotherapy.

REFERENCES

American Psychiatric Association (2000). *Diagnostic and statistical manual of mental disorders* (4th ed., text rev.). Washington, DC: Author.

Keller, M. B., McCullough, J. P., Klein, D. N., Arnow, B., Dunner, D. L., Gelenberg, A. J., et al. (2000). A comparison of Nefazodone, the cognitive behavioral analysis system of psychotherapy, and their combination for the treatment of chronic depression. *New England Journal of Medicine, 342,* 1462–1470.

Kessler, R. C., Berglund, P., Demler, O., Jin, R., & Walters, E. E. (2005). Lifetime prevalence and age of onset distributions of DSM-IV disorders in the National Comorbidity Study Replication. *Archives of General Psychiatry, 62,* 593–602.

Klein, D. N., Santiago, N. J., Vivian, D., Arnow, B. A., Blalock, J. A., Dunner, D. L., et al. (2004). Cognitive-behavioral analysis system of psychotherapy as a maintenance treatment for chronic depression. *Journal of Consulting and Clinical Psychology, 72,* 681–688.

Klein, D. N., Shankman, S. A., Lewinsohn, P. M., Rohde, P., & Seeley, J. R. (2004). Family study of chronic depression in a community sample of young adults. *American Journal of Psychiatry, 161,* 646–653.

Klein, D. N., Shankman, S. A., & Rose, S. (2006). Ten-year prospective follow-up study of the naturalistic course of dysthymic disorder and double depression. *American Journal of Psychiatry, 163,* 872–880.

Klein, D. N., Shankman, S. A., & Rose, S. (2008). Dysthymic disorder and double depression: Baseline predictors of 10-year course and outcome. *Journal of Psychiatric Research, 42*(5), 408–415.

Kocsis, J. H. (2003). Pharmacotherapy for chronic depression. *Journal of Clinical Psychology, 59,* 885–892.

Kovacs, M., Akiskal, H. S., Gatsonis, C., & Parrone, P. L. (1994). Childhood-onset dysthymic disorder: Clinical features and prospective naturalistic outcome. *Archives of General Psychiatry, 51,* 365–374.

Markowitz, J. C., Kocsis, J. H., Bleiberg, K. L., Christos, P. J., & Sacks, M. (2005). A comparative trial of psychotherapy and pharmacotherapy for "pure" dysthymic patients. *Journal of Affective Disorders, 89,* 167–175.

Nemeroff, C. G., Heim, C. M., Thase, M. E., Klein, D. N., Rush, A. J., Schatzberg, A. F., et al. (2003). Differential responses to psychotherapy versus pharmacotherapy in the treatment for patients with chronic forms of major depression and childhood trauma. *Proceedings of the National Academy of Sciences, 100,* 14293–14296.

Riso, L. P., du Toit, P. L., Blandino, J. A., Penna, S., Darcy, S., Duin, J. S., et al. (2003). Cognitive aspects of chronic depression. *Journal of Abnormal Psychology, 112,* 72–80.

SUGGESTED READINGS

Klein, D. N. (2008). Dysthymia and chronic depression. In W. E. Craighead, D. J. Miklowitz, and L. W. Craighead (Eds.), *Psychopathology: History, diagnosis, and empirical foundations.* Hoboken, NJ: John Wiley & Sons.

Klein, D. N., Shankman, S. A., Lewinsohn, P. M., Rohde, P., & Seeley, J. R. (2004). Family study of chronic depression in a community sample of young adults. *American Journal of Psychiatry, 161,* 646–653.

DANIEL N. KLEIN
Stony Brook University

See also: Depression; Depressive Personality Disorder; Major Depressive Disorder

E

EARLY CHILDHOOD DEVELOPMENT

Childhood is a culturally defined period in human development between birth and adulthood, and, in a historical perspective, is a relatively new social construction. Appreciation of childhood as a "special" time of life began to develop some 400 years ago, marking the beginning of a gradual move toward recognition of children's rights and their special needs for protection. Definitions of early childhood, an important subperiod of childhood, vary as to the ages that mark its beginning and end. The National Association for the Education of Young Children (NAEYC) includes ages from birth to eight, whereas other sources prefer to view infancy as a separate period or to exclude middle-childhood years (school age) from the definition of early childhood. Emerging classifications consider youth as ages 0 to 25 years.

Children undergo dramatic development in early childhood. Marked features of continuity and change have been mapped in addition to individual and diverse group differences. The central accomplishments of this period include physical growth and development, development of the brain and nervous system, sensorimotor and perceptual development, cognitive and intellectual development, information processing development, language and communication development, and emotional development, which includes self-regulation, social understanding, and attachment. These significant and complex advances place early childhood in the center of most theories of human development.

A systematic study of child development began in the early twentieth century, prefaced by Darwin's (1877) observations of his own infant son. Within a short time, major theoretical views of early development began to emerge. Gesell and his colleagues described the steps of physical growth and psychological development, establishing the developmental norms still used by pediatricians and psychologists today. Freud was the first theorist to stress the importance of childhood emotions and conflicts in establishing major personality orientations that persist into adulthood. The tradition of psychoanalytic contributions toward understanding early childhood development include the works of Erikson, Mahler, and Winnicott, all emphasizing the importance of children's relationships with their caregivers. Bowlby and Ainsworth's theory of attachment has become one of the most influential in helping us understand the role of parent-child relationships for personality development, interpersonal relationships, and mental well-being. Young children use the attachment figure as a secure base for exploration of the environment and as a safe haven to which to return for reassurance when distressed (Grossman, Grossman, & Waters, 2006). Sensitive caregiving and consistent responsiveness to the child's signals is fundamental for the development of secure attachment. In contrast, if caregivers are not responsive to children's needs for reassurance and provide insensitive and inconsistent care, children develop alternative strategies for interaction under conditions of stress, which are broadly characterized as insecure attachment.

Cognitive developmental theories espoused by Piaget and his followers also emphasize early childhood development as a period of major steps in a child's construction of her reality and knowledge. An infant in the sensorimotor stage of development begins to make sense of the world through a complex series of interactions with the environment that emphasizes sensory and motor experiences. Most children are born with the capacity to attend and explore, and they are increasingly interested in sights, touch, sounds, and other aspects of the outer world, which are the stimuli and mechanisms for children's motor, sensory, and perceptual development. Through trial and error, infants gradually gain control of their bodies and begin actively assimilating motor schemes (e.g., moving the hand) and sensory schemes (e.g., looking at it), as well as accommodating new schemes they encounter that do not fit into existing schemes (Piaget, 1963). Later, in early childhood, the child achieves preoperational and then concrete operational thinking, being able to think logically about concrete events.

Development of self-regulation is also an important part of early childhood. Self-regulation refers to the capacity to monitor and direct one's activities in order to achieve goals or meet demands imposed by others. It occurs within the brain, is modulated by attachment relationships, and manifests in social behavior. Learning to use the toilet or refraining from grabbing another child's toys are examples of emerging self-regulation and self-control skills. The powerful influence of sociocultural processes on these several lines of early childhood development have been well articulated by scientists such as Bronfenbrenner, Vygotsky, and Rogoff such that contemporary understanding of early childhood development embraces complex and dynamic bio-ecological systems perspectives.

In recent decades, our understanding of young children's behavior and functioning, specifically in the cognitive, linguistic, social, and motor domains of development, has been enhanced by new techniques of brain research. Remarkable discoveries related to synaptogenesis, neural network formation, neurotransmitter action, bioregulation, and linkages between brain structure and function have informed our understanding of the role of the environments in which development takes place (Shonkoff & Phillips, 2000). Development of the brain is highly dependent upon the child's experiences and relies on certain forms of environmental exposure (e.g., light, sounds of speech, touch, and other stimuli) to develop normally. An infant's development is likely to be compromised in environments deprived of the expected external input, as it may lead to arrests of development in areas of the brain that depend on exposure to these inputs. Although neuroscience is far from linking specific types of experiences to specific outcomes, it does expand our understanding of the brain as a dynamic, self-organizing developmental system by pointing out that the evolution of the brain's architecture during the first years of life occurs in the context of the child's transactions with his or her unique socioemotional environment (Cicchetti & Curtis, 2006).

The wide recognition of the importance of the caregiving environment for the development of children can be exemplified by the surge of studies examining parenting (i.e., individual and contextual factors impacting parenting) or the quality of nonparental care as they relate to children's developmental and health outcomes (Bornstein, 2002; Luster & Okagaki, 2005). This perspective has resulted in heightened attention to children's developmental needs and how to best respond to them. This attention has given birth to the field of infant mental health, defined by Zeanah and Zeanah (2001) as "multidisciplinary approaches to enhancing the social and emotional competence of infants in their biological, relationship, and cultural context" (p. 14). This growing field of research and practice is devoted to the promotion of healthy social and emotional development, the prevention of mental health problems, and the treatment of mental health problems in the particularly young children in the context of their families (*Task Force on Infant Mental Health,* 2002). Researchers and practitioners continually seek ways to shape policies that will enable them to support parent-child relationships in adverse environments. Simultaneously, more recent articulations of positive psychology enable the active construction of optimal environments to support and sustain children's healthy development and life success.

REFERENCES

Bornstein, M. (Ed). (2002). *Handbook of parenting* (2nd ed.). New York: Lawrence Erlbaum.

Cicchetti, D., & Curtis, W. J. (2006). The developing brain and neural plasticity: Implications for normality, psychopathology, and resilience. In D. Cicchetti, & D. Cohen, (Eds.), *Developmental psychopathology* (2nd ed.). *Developmental neuroscience* (Vol. 2, pp. 1–64). Hoboken, NJ: John Wiley & Sons.

Damon, W., & Lerner, R. (Eds.). (2006). *Handbook of child psychology* (6th ed.). Hoboken, NJ: John Wiley & Sons.

Darwin, C. (1877). A biographical sketch of an infant. *Mind, 7,* 285–293.

Grossman, K., Grossman, K., & Waters, E. (2006). *Attachment from infancy to adulthood: The major longitudinal studies.* New York: Guilford Press.

Luster, T., & Okagaki, L. (Eds.). (2005). *Parenting: An ecological perspective.* Mahwah, NJ: Lawrence Erlbaum.

McCartney, K., & Phillips, D. (Eds.). (2008). *Blackwell handbook of early childhood development.* New York: Blackwell.

Piaget, J. (1963). *The origins of intelligence in children.* New York: Norton.

Rogoff, B. (2003). *The cultural nature of human development.* New York: Oxford.

Shonkoff, J., & Phillips, D. A (Eds.). (2000). *From neurons to neighborhoods: The science of early childhood development.* Washington, DC: National Academy of Sciences.

Task Force on Infant Mental Health (2002). *Definition of infant mental health. Zero to Three.* Arlington, VA, http://www .zerotothree.org.

Wertlieb, D. (2003). Applied developmental science. In R. Lerner, A. Easterbrooks, & J. Mistry (Eds.), *Developmental psychology* (pp. 43–61). Vol. 6 in I. B. Weiner (Ed.-in-Chief), *Handbook of psychology.* Hoboken, NJ: John Wiley & Sons.

Zeanah, C. H., & Zeanah, P. D. (2001). Towards a definition of infant mental health. In C. H. Zeanah. *Handbook of infant mental health* (2nd ed.). New York: Guilford Press.

MYRNA V. VASHCHENKO
DONALD WERTLIEB
DANTE SPETTER
Tufts University

See also: **Child Psychology; Developmental Psychology**

EARLY CHILDHOOD EDUCATION

The field of early childhood education (ECE) is dynamic and fluid and reflects trends and ideas in education more broadly. Traditional issues in ECE such as curriculum and teacher training are increasingly influenced by current research, interdisciplinary and international perspectives, postmodernism, and multicultural and other diversity perspectives. Whereas ECE has traditionally referred to formal programs for three- to five-year-old children, current definitions now include a wider range of formal and informal settings for children from birth to age eight offered through a wide range of sponsoring auspices.

For example, "preschool education" was usually thought of as half-day enrichment or "education" programs for middle class children and tended to exclude child "care" programs, which grew out of the child welfare movement for children in poverty. Currently, ECE is often referred to by many as "early childhood learning and care" (ECLC) or "early childhood care and education" (ECCE) programs which integrate the features of both "education" and "care." The definition of ECLC now also includes home-based family child care programs as well as group child care programs; early intervention programs for young children facing developmental challenges; and programs for special populations based on language, culture, ethnicity or national origin. The field of ECE is diverse, heterogeneous, and dynamic and is still undergoing rapid development and change.

A comprehensive, detailed examination of the entire field cannot be accomplished in this article, but we can present and discuss some of the most salient issues and developments in ECE. These include (1) the research on neuroscience and on the longitudinal impacts of ECE programs on children; (2) international perspectives on curriculum in ECE; (3) postmodern perspectives on ECE; and (4) the diversity of learners in ECE, in terms of culture, language, and ability.

Current Research on Neuroscience and on the Effects of ECE on Child Development

The traditional "nature" versus "nurture" debate in early child development has been informed by the increasing research on brain-environment interactions. Whereas once the debate was characterized by an either/or argument favoring the impact of either genetic determinism or family and social environments, the research on brain development and the research on the longitudinal effects of ECE points to the importance of the dynamic interaction of biological and environmental determinants. A Canadian report states that "There is powerful new evidence from neuroscience that the early years of development from conception to age six, particularly for the first three years, set the base for competence and coping skills that will affect learning, behavior, and health throughout life" (McCain & Mustard, 1999, p. 5). The authors go on to cite five specific sets of findings that affect ECE: (1) the interaction of nature and nurture; (2) the extensive development of the brain from conception to age five; (3) that care and nurturing has a direct effect on the development of neural pathways; (4) that early environmental and nurturing behaviors can have long-lasting effects on the child into adulthood; and (5) that early negative experiences of abuse or neglect can have negative developmental outcomes.

This growing body of neuroscience research complements and extends the robust research findings on how high-quality ECE environments contribute to short- and long-term developmental outcomes for both special and normative populations. Perhaps the most well known longitudinal research project in this area is the Perry Preschool Study (Schweinhart et al., 2005), which has followed a sample of individuals from poor, inner-city neighborhoods in Ypsilanti, Michigan, from their enrollment in a nursery school program for three-year-old children and with multiple data-collection points until the age of 40. The data included standardized tests throughout their school years, dropout and graduation rates, teen crime and pregnancy rates, employment, incarceration rates, and welfare rates as adults. The study documented a clear pattern of greater educational and social success for those who participated as children in high-quality preschool environments that emphasized play, and guided exploration, facilitated adult-child interactions, and provided high levels of teacher training. Thus, during the preschool years of rapid brain development, these children received the benefit of stimulating educational environments and experiences. The data demonstrated higher rates of success when the children from the Perry Preschool Program were compared to three other groups: a control group of children who attended no preschool; children who attended a preschool characterized by direct instructional techniques; and children who attended a "maturational" program that permitted free play but did not have a coherent curriculum or program philosophy.

The Cost Quality and Outcomes Study (CQO; Kagan, 1999) focused on a larger and more representative sample of children. Conducted in a number of U.S. states, the CQO compared children who participated as preschoolers in child care programs of differing levels of quality. Once more, the findings showed that quality factors predicted higher scores on standardized outcome measures as well as higher levels of school success.

Although the brain research and the longitudinal research tell a story of the benefits of the interaction of biological and environmental factors, there is unfortunately also a downside to this story. Increasingly, entrepreneurs are exploiting the increasing awareness of the importance of the early years by establishing achievement-oriented programs and "academies of learning" that guarantee all kinds of developmental benefits. These programs promise to deliver dramatic child development outcomes through the use of their own specific curriculum models, educational toys, videos, DVDs, and the like. These commercial programs and materials are a far cry from the core vision of ECE as a place where young children could learn through play by exploring stimulating environments that are rich with art, music, blocks, dramatic play, sand, water, and gross motor and fine motor materials, and to do so at their own individual rates of development without the pressure to excel, perform, or achieve to some adult-driven set of criteria.

Curriculum, Teaching, and Learning

The field of ECE has long included a wide range of curricular and teaching approaches. The Child Study movement in the first half of the twentieth century emphasized a more "maturational" approach that allowed for the "natural unfolding" of the child in a relatively stress-free and undemanding environment. For over a century the Montessori approach has focused on individual children's interactions with specific and aesthetically elegant learning materials (blocks, towers, shapes) that were designed to promote children's attention to detail in displays of increasing complexity and challenge. The Perry Preschool Project mentioned previously was based on curricular assumptions that were derived from the child development theories of Jean Piaget. This approach emphasized guided exploration and learning through creative play. Piaget's work has also served as the basis of the Developmentally Appropriate Practice (DAP) created and advocated by the National Association for the Education of Young Children (NAEYC), in which ECE teachers are trained to create learning activities and approaches that are appropriate to an individual child's developmental level.

The Reggio Emilia approach to ECE has been in existence in Italy since the end of World War II but has only come to the attention of North American educators in the past 15–20 years (Edwards, Gandini, & Forman, 1998). This approach, named for the city where it originated, is characterized by a strong emphasis on artistic representations by the children that are constructed in the context of major thematic curricular units. Teachers help to initiate the projects, but the actual implementation is largely determined by the children's interests and abilities. Reggio places a strong emphasis on the careful observation of the children and rigorous and extensive documentation of their work. Another key feature is the strong involvement of the children's parents in all phases of the project.

New Zealand has developed a very interesting and innovative ECE curriculum framework known as "*Te Whāriki*" (pronounced "teh FAH'riki"; the Maori word for "a woven mat"). The approach was developed over many years and draws heavily on the traditions of New Zealand's original inhabitants, the Maori people (Nuttall, 2003; *Te Whāriki*, 1999). As seen in Figure 1, *Te Whāriki* is conceptualized as the interweaving of underlying themes with specific "strands," or approaches, to learning. Although *Te Whāriki*

THE PRINCIPLES

THE STRANDS

Figure 1. *Te Whāriki:* The New Zealand ECE Curriculum Framework

does not prescribe specific learning activities, it is used in virtually all ECE settings in New Zealand to help generate, design, implement, and evaluate curriculum ideas and activities.

The role of technology in early childhood education is becoming a major topic of discussion among practitioners and is of academic interest to researchers. Questions are being raised regarding the efficacy and appropriateness of different kinds of software programs that range from so-called "skill and drill" repetitive readiness exercises versus more creative art or problem solving programs. Many are questioning whether sitting in front of a computer monitor will take away valuable exploratory play with water, sand, clay, and other interactive and tactile materials. The short- and long-term impacts of technological advances in early childhood education are only now beginning to be addressed.

Postmodernism and ECE

Postmodernism, which draws heavily on the work of Foucault, Derrida, and others, has come to ECE primarily through the work of a community of scholars and practitioners who describe themselves as "reconceptualists" (Kessler & Swadener, 1992). They have adopted this term in reference to their efforts to analyze or deconstruct the traditional core concepts of ECE and to propose new ways of conceptualizing ECE in the multiple social, economic, and political contexts that embed ECE research and practice. For example, many postmodernist scholars have criticized DAP and its underlying Piagetian body of theory as social constructions that emerge from attitudes emphasizing universal and invariant rules of child development that can be applied to children in all socioeconomic classes and in all countries. Another example is the postmodern approach to teacher education, which emphasizes personal reflection over direct instruction and the importance of drawing on traditional bodies of knowledge and wisdom and not just the theories of experts.

One of the major contributions of postmodernist approaches to early childhood education has been the entrance into the field by scholars in disciplines beyond education and psychology. Sociologists and anthropologists are studying the cultures of early childhood education. Philosophers and policy analysts have conducted extensive analyses of the nature of childhood and the role of the child as a citizen in Western democracies and in other regions of the world. Art historians and literary critics are studying the ways in which children have been represented in different media over time and in different regions of the world. Indeed, whereas this article on early childhood education appears in an encyclopedia of psychology, it is entirely likely that similar entries will be written in the handbooks and encyclopedias of other disciplines in the not-too-distant future.

Diversity Issues

In years past this section would have been called "multicultural ECE" or "early childhood special education." The term *diversity* is now used to refer to ECE programs that serve diverse ethnic, linguistic, and immigrant populations (e.g., Bernhard, 1995) as well as the ECE needs of children who have special developmental problems (Howard, Williams, Port, & Lepper, 2001). There are similar sets of questions confronting programs that serve both groups of young children. The field is replete with debates over the relative merits of homogeneous programs for children of distinct cultural or developmental abilities versus the perceived advantages of integrated or mainstreamed programs that include heterogeneous groupings of children who come from different cultures and who have a wide range of different abilities.

Some hold that integrated classrooms can foster empathy skills; can introduce new cultural traditions, foods, and customs; and can help to prevent the creation of negative stereotypes of children who differ from the norm. Others maintain that integration leads to mere tokenism and a simplistic "Disney-style" attitude that "it's a small world after all," and they point to research indicating that some children with specific disabilities tend to be marginalized in integrated classrooms. Some have found that the social skills of these children actually improve in homogeneous classrooms with children who share their disabilities. These debates extend to the creation and operation of ECE programs; to the development of curriculum materials; and to the content and implementation of ECE teacher education programs. The debates and the research will undoubtedly continue to enrich and enliven the field of ECE in the future.

REFERENCES

Bernhard, J. K. (1995). Child development, cultural diversity, and the professional training of early childhood educators. *Canadian Journal of Education, 20*(4), 415–436.

Edwards, C., Gandini, L., & Forman, G. (Eds.). (1998). *The hundred languages of children: The Reggio Emilia approach—Advanced Reflections.* Greenwich, CT: Ablex.

Howard, V. F., Williams, B. F., Port, P. D., & Lepper, C. (2001). *Very young children with special needs.* Upper Saddle River, NJ: Prentice-Hall.

Kagan, S. L. (1999). *The children of the Cost, Quality, and Outcomes Study go to school: Executive Summary.* Chapel Hill, North Carolina: Frank Porter Graham Child Development Center, University of North Carolina at Chapel Hill.

Kessler, S., & Swadener, B. B. (Eds.). (1992). *Reconceptualizing the early childhood curriculum: Beginning the dialogue.* New York: Teachers College Press.

McCain, M. N., & Mustard, J. F. (1999). *Early years study: Final report.* Toronto, Ontario, Canada: The Founder's Network.

Nuttall, J. (Ed.). (2003). *Weaving* Te Whāriki: *Aotearoa New Zealand's early childhood curriculum document in theory and in practice*. Wellington, New Zealand: New Zealand Council for Educational Research.

Te Whāriki: *Early childhood curriculum.*(1999). Wellington, New Zealand: New Zealand Ministry of Education.

Schweinhart, L. J., Montie, J., Xiang, Z., Barnett, W. S., Belfield, C. R., & Nores, M. (2005). *Lifetime effects: The High/Scope Perry Preschool study through age 40.* (Monographs of the High/Scope Educational Research Foundation 14). Ypsilanti, MI: High/Scope Press.

Wertlieb, D. (2001). Early childhood education. In W. E. Craighead & C. B. Nemeroff (Eds.), *The Corsini encyclopedia of psychology and behavioral science, Volume 4* (p. 346). New York: John Wiley & Sons.

HILLEL GOELMAN

University of British Columbia, Canada

See also: Early Childhood Development; Head Start

EATING DISORDERS

Anorexia nervosa (AN), bulimia nervosa (BN), and binge eating disorder (BED)—the commonly recognized eating disorder (ED) variants—are all characterized by abnormal thoughts and behaviors surrounding eating, weight, and body image. AN is defined by an intense fear of weight gain, leading to caloric restraint and abnormal thinness. BN occurs in relatively normal-weight or overweight individuals who display recurrent eating binges followed by such compensations as self-induced vomiting, laxative misuse, fasting, or intensive exercise. The most widely known of other ED variants is BED, which involves regular eating binges without compensatory behaviors.

Epidemiology

Findings from diverse geographical regions suggest surprisingly consistent prevalences of EDs among young females: 0.5% to 1% for AN and from 1% to 2% for BN (Hoek & van Hoeken, 2003). Peak prevalences of AN and BN occur in young-adult women (in their 20s), and these disorders occur about one-tenth as frequently in men. BED is believed to affect up to 5% of the general population and a somewhat older age group. BED also appears to have a more even gender distribution, with a prevalence of about two males for every three females.

Comorbidity

Mood disorders (MDs) figure very prominently in the EDs, with one recent large-scale study showing a history of MD in 42% of individuals with AN, 70% of those with BN, and 46% of those with BED (Hudson et al., 2007, cited in Steiger & Bruce, 2008). Studies examining the comorbidity of anxiety disorders (ADs) with EDs have found a history of AD in 47%–83% of individuals with AN, 71%–80% of those with BN, and approximately 65% of those with BED (Steiger & Bruce, 2008). Alcohol and substance dependencies also occur in EDs, in particular in BN, in which roughly a third of affected individuals abuse substances. Arguably, strongest of the comorbid propensities in the EDs is that with personality disorders (PDs), a recent meta-analysis finding 58% of eating-disordered women to have a PD, compared to 28% of a comparison group (Rosenvinge, Martinussen, & Ostensen, 2000, cited in Steiger & Bruce, 2008). AN and BN had equal likelihoods of association with DSM anxious-fearful PDs (45% and 44%, respectively), but in BN there were higher proportions of dramatic-erratic PDs (44% overall) and borderline PD (31%).

Etiology

Sociocultural Factors

EDs are determined by diverse factors. Western cultural ideals promoting thinness certainly play a role. However, a recent review suggests that the incidence of AN has increased surprisingly modestly over the years and occurs often in areas that are untouched by the "culture of slimness" (Keel & Klump, 2003). By contrast, bulimic syndromes appear to have increased dramatically in prevalence in recent years and to be more limited to industrialized cultures. These characteristics argue that bulimic syndromes, more than AN, are expressions of a population-wide exposure to cultural inducements to diet.

Psychological and Family Factors

EDs align themselves with such traits as perfectionism, negative emotionality, and impulsivity. Perfectionism figures strongly in both AN and BN, whereas negative emotionality and impulsivity are more closely associated with binge/purge behaviors. Other psychological factors (e.g., dietary restraint, body-image disturbances) also play a key role in the development and maintenance of EDs (see Steiger & Bruce, 2008).

Empirical studies on the functioning of families in which AN occurs suggest proneness toward enmeshment, overinvolvement, or conflict avoidance. Parallel studies in BN and BED generally suggest families characterized by tension, disengagement, and negative emotional expression. Likewise, available data indicate higher-than-normal rates of childhood sexual and physical abuse in individuals with eating disorders, in particular, those with bulimic variants (see Steiger & Bruce, 2008).

Biological Factors

Recent genetic and neurobiological studies lead to increasing emphasis upon biological determinants in the EDs. Heritability estimates range from 48% to 76% for AN and from 50% to 83% for BN, with 41% for a syndrome including binge eating without compensation (similar to BED) (see Streigel-Moore & Bulik, 2007). Hereditary effects could be enacted through various neurobiological systems. Putative pathophysiological roles have been suggested for several neurotransmitter (e.g., serotonin and dopamine), hormonal (e.g, estrogens), and other brain systems (e.g., brain-derived neurotropic factor)—which could all impact appetitive controls, body weight, anxiety, affect, and impulse controls (Steiger & Bruce, 2008).

Based on effects obtained in our research, we have proposed that vulnerability to bulimic syndromes, and especially to bulimic variants characterized by marked affective or behavioral dysregulation, may reflect the amplification of constitutional (serotonergic) vulnerabilities by developmental stressors (e.g., childhood abuse), and then activation by serotonergic sequelae of too much dieting (see Steiger & Bruce, 2008). With respect to AN, one plausible etiologic gene-environment interaction effect might implicate activation of genetic effects due to malnutrition, dieting, and/ or hormonal influences (Klump & Gobrogge, 2005, cited in Steiger & Bruce, 2008).

Treatment

Available data do not decisively support any one psychotherapeutic strategy for AN. However, findings inconsistently support application of cognitive-behavioral therapy (CBT) and the utility of family-based approaches with adolescent patients, and provide ambiguous indication of the utility of hospitalization (Fairburn, 2005). Overall, outcome indices suggest moderate response to treatment in younger patients, but weak response in older individuals.

Outcome for BN is characterized by moderate to favorable response to various treatments (Shapiro et al., 2007). CBT is the most strongly indicated psychotherapeutic treatment for BN, with use of adjunctive (usually serotonergic) medication suggested in some cases. Other psychotherapeutic approaches (including interpersonal psychotherapy or dialectical behavior therapy) seem also to yield demonstrable benefits. Research examining treatment for BED suggests that individual and group CBT is effective in treating psychiatric and eating symptoms in BED, but has limited or no effect on weight loss (Brownley, Berkman, Sedway, Lohr, & Bulik, 2007).

For BN, selective serotonin reuptake inhibitors (SSRIs) and mood stabilizers have been shown to yield reductions in binge-purge symptoms and associated psychopathological features (Shapiro et al., 2007). In AN, preliminary research suggests that SSRIs may be useful, but only after some weight restoration has occurred (Fairburn, 2005).

Preliminary evidence also suggests that atypical antipsychotic agents (e.g., Olanzepine) may facilitate clinical gains in AN. In the treatment of BED, SSRIs, anticonvulsants, and certain antiobesity drugs have also shown short-term benefits (Brownley et al., 2007).

REFERENCES

Brownley, K. A., Berkman, N. D., Sedway, J. A., Lohr, K. N., & Bulik, C. M. (2007). Binge eating disorder: A systematic review of randomized controlled trials. *International Journal of Eating Disorders, 40,* 337–340.

Fairburn, C. G. (2005). Evidence-based treatment of anorexia nervosa. *International Journal of Eating Disorders, 37* suppl, S26–S30.

Hoek, H. W., & van Hoeken, D. (2003). Review of the prevalence and incidence of eating disorders. *International Journal of Eating Disorders, 34,* 383–396.

Keel, P. K., & Klump, K. L. (2003). Are eating disorders culture bound syndromes? Implications for conceptualizing their etiology. *Psychological Bulletin, 129,* 747–769.

Shapiro, J. R., Berkman, N. D., Brownley, K. A., Sedway, J. A., Lohr, K. N., & Bulik, C. M. (2007). Bulimia Nervosa Treatment: A systematic review of randomized controlled trials. *International Journal of Eating Disorders, 40,* 321–330.

Steiger, H., & Bruce, K. (2008). Eating Disorders: Anorexia nervosa and bulimia nervosa. In T. Millon, P. H. Blaney, & R. D. Davis (Eds.), *Oxford Textbook of Psychopathology* (2nd ed.). New York: Oxford University Press.

Streigel-Moore, R. H., & Bulik, C. M. (2007). Risk factors for eating disorders. *American Psychologist, 62,* 181–198.

JODIE RICHARDSON
HOWARD STEIGER
McGill University

See also: **Anorexia Nervosa; Bulimia Nervosa; Obesity**

ECOLOGICAL PSYCHOLOGY

This article describes James J. Gibson's ecological approach to psychology as it developed. Gibson's system evolved as an approach to visual perception, but the consequences have extended far beyond vision—first to other modalities (Gibson, 1966; Turvey, 1996), then to action, cognition, social psychology, and movement science, to name a few. Part of the range of ecological psychology can be seen in the list of books in the series, *Resources for Ecological Psychology* (see Heft, 2001).

Perception and Reality

In popular speech it is common to hear perception contrasted with reality ("that's only your perception"), as if one can experience reality in some way other than through perception. The research programs of well-known perceptual scientists commonly nourish this attitude by emphasizing illusions and the mismatch between experiences of the world and the "input" for perception. In vision, for example, the physical action on the receptors in the eye is through light and the receptors are arranged as a two-dimensional surface. Nevertheless, we experience a world filled with solid surfaces that reflect light, and the experience is three-dimensional. What gives rise to the extra dimension (depth), and why do we see solid surfaces when the light at the eye is just that, light? This failure of correspondence between what the scientist takes to be "given" and the final, full-blown psychological experience of the world, reinforces the notion that experience must be achieved by a great deal of "filling in" what was not there in the first place and that the perceptual grasp on reality is tenuous indeed. Research on illusions magnifies this attitude.

The ecological approach developed by Gibson takes the opposite approach. It seeks to understand how successful perception and action are possible. The changes required to fashion a science of realism, however, are so fundamental that the consequences ripple through most of psychology and related disciplines.

Very often, theories are built around laboratory experiments and data, without carefully making the connection back to the world and the experiences for which we ultimately want to account. Consider the Müller-Lyer illusion, a frequent topic of laboratory investigation. In this familiar amusement, equal lines do not look equal when they are presented with arrowheads pointing in opposite directions. Our eyes "fool" us. Should we then use this as a caution that "the senses cannot be trusted"? Now consider the laboratory setting more broadly. Why do we think there are two equal lines? To establish this, we need measurements. The measuring process is most commonly done visually by comparing the lines in the illusion to a ruler or to a single line of constant length to show that our two original lines are "really" equal. Thus, vision was used to establish the equality of the lines. The illusion is still present in the illusory context, of course. But the way we sort out what is illusion and what is not is still perceptual. The status of the lines was determined through more than visual perception.

When the experimenter walks through the hallway on the way to the laboratory, this is done by trusting vision, touch, and hearing to indicate walking upright, walking upright through the hallway, through the lab door, and guiding the body into a chair at the table with the computer on it, to a perceived state of being comfortably seated in front of the computer in the laboratory room. In discussing the upshot of the Müller-Lyer experiment, it is not usual to ask how the experimenter perceived his or her surroundings and the pathway through them, or how the experimental observer got to the room. From the standpoint of ecological psychology, these are very pertinent questions. It is important to recognize that perceptual research should address these capacities. Illusions are interesting, but their role in understanding perceiving needs to be incorporated into the understanding of all of perceiving, which must include "normal," unquestioned guided activity in a real (perceived as such) environment.

The ecological approach is distinctive inasmuch as it takes objects of perception to be part of the theory. One fundamental "object," however, is the entire surface of the earth, and its contrast with the sky, meeting at the horizon. This earth-sky pair forms an immense envelope within which all other structures and events of an animal's lifetime occur. As an envelope, it is something that we always are inside of (except for space travelers) and always perceiving to some extent (even when asleep, we are actively adjusting to the surfaces supporting us—and that is an example of perceiving the environment).

Not only is the structure of what there is to be perceived "environing" (called "ambient"), but it has structure at many levels. Some of those levels are too large or too small to be relevant to a given animal, but any material surface has structure at many spatial and temporal scales. This means that what is available in the environment to be perceived is far richer than any animal ever could apprehend in its total lifetime. It makes no sense to say that any part of the environment ever is completely perceived. Perceiving the environment successfully, in the ecological view, means to be "in touch with it," to have a stable orientation to relevant portions of the environment and to be able to explore, in order to extend the portions of the environment apprehended. As with the illustration of the illusion in the laboratory setting, what is tentatively perceived, unclearly perceived, or even incorrectly perceived is brought into a stable awareness by more perceiving.

An area of the desert that looks like shimmering water can be clarified by approaching the area. Real water in a real location can be approached, with more and more detail specific to water coming into view. A mirage will stay in the distance and can be perceived as such. The two can be distinguished if exploration over time is allowed. The perception of persistence is not based on the persistence of a percept.

The key to saying that an extended, persisting, surface can be perceived as such lies in Gibson's analysis of the optics of what he called "the occluding edge." Research reported in Gibson, Kaplan, Reynolds, and Wheeler (1969) shows examples of different ways that something seen can disappear from view. Occlusion occurs when the texture of one opaque surface hides another. The occluding edge is the boundary between the hiding surface and the hidden. In locomoting through a stable, but cluttered, environment, surfaces that previously were hidden come into view, and surfaces that were visible go out of view. Optically, there is a sharp substitution of texture at the boundary. It is important to recognize that the pattern of change itself can be an object of perception. The change specific to occlusion entails that the covered or uncovered surfaces are not going out of existence or coming into existence. There is an optical test for reality. A surface that goes out of sight by occlusion can be brought back into sight by an opposite motion. One could do that repeatedly if necessary. As long as the reversibility holds, the persistence and connectivity of the surface is specified. The significance of occlusion as a type of change is underscored by comparison to other changes—for example, disintegration, explosion, burning, or evaporating. Those are changes that do not preserve surfaces. If one sees those changes, no opposite movement can bring them back into view.

The limiting case of an occluding edge would be an eye socket. The edges of the eyes, face, and body, hide what can be seen at a given moment. Rotations of the head bring parts of a surround into view, and hide previously seen parts. Gibson argued that if a head rotation can be seen as such (which occlusion allows), then the underlying persistence of surrounding surfaces can also be revealed. The stress here is on the fact that the body can be seen at the same time as the scene and that underlying invariances can be separated from specific changes (that also can be apprehended as such). Perceiving is seen as a constant expansion of how much of an environment is perceived.

Scaling to Size and Skill—Affordances

It has been noted that the environment of an animal extends indefinitely in space, time, and scale. Animal life is adjusted to the scales appropriate to the kind of animal it is. Gibson realized that this involved more than mere linear size. An animal's weight and skill will determine what it can stand on, what it can sit on (if it sits at all), and what it can climb on (if it climbs at all). Surfaces must have a certain strength and a certain arrangement to allow these activities. The opportunities for action, for a given animal, in a given environment, are what Gibson called affordances. What an environment affords an animal is an objective feature (an elephant can walk across that surface, or it cannot) of the world. An affordance is an unusual entity because it involves an animal, an environment, and their relation—all considered as a unit. But such entities are not all that mysterious. An occluding edge, including the horizon, has the same logic. They are entities defined as relations between animal and environmental arrangements. Like the occluding edge or the horizon, affordances are perceivable entities if there is structure (say, optical structure) to specify them.

Implications

If perceiving a persisting environment requires exploration over time, what happens to the boundary between perception and memory? Gibson argued that time *per se* was a misleading way to segregate coherent topics. He argued that the perception of persisting surfaces would make for a coherent topic, and could usefully be distinguished from the apprehension of surfaces that previously existed but no longer exist. Surfaces that do not yet exist but can brought into existence. What Gibson argued was that persistence perception depended on the detection of specific structure, invariant over time. Persistence in the mind does not create persistence in the world. By the same token, certain types of meaning can be defined in such a way that they can be said to be objects of perception, where perception is extraction of structure over time, and the structure is specific to the environment and to the self in the environment.

For samples of the range of scientists in vision, movement, comparative psychology, and nonlinear dynamics modeling who were influenced by Gibson's work, see Warren (1998). For social psychology implications, see McArthur and Baron (1983) and Baron and Hodges (2007). For an ecological appreciation of Gibson's impact on film studies, see Anderson and Anderson (2005).

REFERENCES

Anderson, J. D., & Anderson, B. F. (Eds.). (2005). *Moving image theory: Ecological considerations*. Carbondale: Southern Illinois University Press.

Baron, R. M., & Hodges, B. H. (Eds.). (2007). Updating J. J. Gibson's social psychology legacy: Making social psychology more ecological and ecological psychology more social. *Ecological Psychology, 19*, 79–199.

Gibson, James J. (1950). *The perception of the visual world*. Boston: Houghton Mifflin.

Gibson, James J. (1966). *The senses considered as perceptual systems*. Boston: Houghton Mifflin.

Gibson, J., Kaplan, G., Reynolds, H., & Wheeler, K. (1969). The change from visible to invisible: A study of optical transitions. *Perception & Psychophysics, 5*, 113–116.

Gibson, James J. (1986). *The ecological approach to visual perception*. Mahwah, NJ: Lawrence Erlbaum. (Original work published 1979)

Heft, H. (2001). *Ecological psychology in context*. Mahwah, NJ: Lawrence Erlbaum.

McArthur, L. Z., & Baron, R. M. (1983). Toward an ecological theory of social perception. *Psychological Review, 90*, 215–238.

Turvey, M. T. (1996). Dynamic touch. *American Psychologist, 51*, 1134–1152.

Warren, W. H., Jr. (Ed.). (1998). Visually controlled locomotion and orientation. *Ecological Psychology, 10*, 157–346.

WILLIAM M. MACE
Trinity College, Hartford, CT

See also: **Environmental Psychology; Perception; Social Climate Research**

ECT (See Electroconvulsive Therapy)

EDUCATIONAL MAINSTREAMING

The history of educational provision for children with special educational needs (SEN) and disabilities seems extraordinary from a modern perspective. In advanced countries, education is considered a universal right for all children and young people, while in developing countries this is typically an aspiration. Until relatively recently, however, there were children denied this right. For example, it was not until 1970 that children and young people with severe learning difficulties in the United Kingdom were allowed into the education system; previously, they had been cared for in a hospital or at home. This history is relevant today, even in advanced societies, as it lies at the heart of an important question for education policy: How should children and young people with SEN be educated, in special provision or with their typically developing peers? The history has led many to propose policy based upon a *values/rights* perspective (Lindsay, 2003); namely, that all children have the right to be educated in a common system. This is called *mainstreaming*, which is also known as *inclusive education*. Another perspective, however, stresses the importance of the effectiveness of education.

The values/rights perspective has been driven by a desire to prevent the continuation of injustices. Segregated special provision is considered fundamentally inappropriate and discriminatory, a denial of human rights, comparable to segregation on grounds of race/ethnicity. Proponents of this perspective argue that integration of children with SEN into mainstream is not enough, because the child must fit into the relatively unchanging school. Rather, schools should change and become inclusive learning centers for all children.

The values/rights argument has had a powerful effect. In many countries, educational legislation has a clear presumption of mainstreaming and use of special schools and classes has been reduced. There has also been a general social policy shift toward recognizing the rights and wishes of all people with disabilities. For example, in England, more than half of children who require a statement of SEN because they have severe and complex needs are in the education system mainstream (57% in 2008).

However, mainstreaming for all has also been criticized from a values/rights perspective. For example, children have many rights, in addition to the right to be mainstreamed. There is a legitimate debate about a hierarchy of rights including choice, with some arguing that universal mainstreaming removes the choice of specialized provision. Furthermore, who determines the priority right(s): the child or the parent? Parents vary in their values; some actively seek specialized provisions because they consider it more likely to aid their child's development, whereas others seek mainstreaming because they believe in inclusion.

An alternative policy considers the effectiveness of mainstreaming compared with segregated special education. There are substantial methodological difficulties, because mainstreaming is a complex, multifaceted variable. Different types of SEN/disabilities present very different challenges, and mainstream schools vary on many dimensions including their student intake (for example, the social disadvantage profile and the on-entry levels of achievement), thereby providing quite varied contexts. Furthermore, school systems vary according to national and local (e.g., state) laws, and new types of school organizations have been developed including federations of schools working together. Special provisions also vary. For example, the levels of provision and support available in special schools may vary with those in special classes. Also, effectiveness may be measured by one or more different types of academic achievement and/or social development outcomes.

In a classic paper often used to support mainstreaming, Dunn (1968) questioned whether special classes provided a better education than mainstream for students with mild learning problems. However, Dunn's empirical base was limited, and his argument questioning the superiority of special provision was limited to "socioculturally deprived children ... who have been labeled mentally retarded" (p. 5). Later reviews of studies (e.g., Baker, Wang, & Walberg, 1994) indicated a lack of evidence for the superiority of mainstreaming. A more recent review, which distinguished studies by student age group and type of measure, found equivocal evidence for the effectiveness of mainstreaming compared with special provision (Lindsay, 2007).

A forward-looking approach for educational policy and practice requires integration of both the rights/values and effectiveness perspectives. A basic premise may hold that all children have the right to an effective education, including both academic/intellectual and social/affective elements. Mainstreaming provides the opportunity to address these aims, but inherent constraints require the identification of effective elements within this approach. Hence, the current research agenda needs to recognize the social policy reality (pro-mainstreaming) but identify effective practice within this, including studies of the processes and organization features that optimize effectiveness; the use of additional resources both human (e.g., teachers and paraprofessionals), and physical (e.g., optical and auditory aids); and increasingly sophisticated information technology resources with both software and mechanical aids. Fundamental is the need to optimize the curriculum content and its delivery by means of different teaching approaches (Nind & Wearmouth, 2006).

In summary, the challenge is to recognize the values/rights position but carefully and analytically explore and develop optimal education, in its wider sense, for all students with SEN; educational efforts should specifically target the students' varied types, severity, and persistence of need.

REFERENCES

Baker, E. T., Wang, M. C., & Walberg, H. J. (1994). The effects of inclusion on learning. *Educational Leadership, 52,* 33–35.

Dunn, L. M. (1968). Special education for the mildly retarded— Is much of it justifiable? *Exceptional children, 35,* 5–22.

Lindsay, G. (2003). Inclusive education: A critical perspective. *British Journal of Special Education, 30,* 3–12.

Lindsay, G. (2007). Educational psychology and the effectiveness of inclusive education/mainstreaming. *British Journal of Educational Psychology, 77,* 1–24.

Nind, M., & Wearmouth, J. (2006). Including children with special educational needs in mainstream classrooms: Implications for pedagogy from a systematic review. *Journal of Research in Special Educational Needs, 6,* 116–124.

GEOFF LINDSAY
University of Warwick, Coventry, United Kingdom

See also: **Mainstreaming**

EDUCATIONAL PSYCHOLOGY

The discipline of educational psychology, broadly defined, focuses on the application of psychology to the understanding of learners and learning environments. From its inception, the field has reflected a unique interdisciplinary tapestry of interwoven textures and hues representing a balance of psychological theory with respect to learning and application for educational practice. Educational psychology has been defined as the branch of psychology concerned with "the development, evaluation, and application of theories and principles of human learning, teaching, and instruction, and theory-driven educational materials, programs, strategies, and techniques that can enhance lifelong educational activities and processes" (Wittrock & Farley, 1989).

Some authors have referred to educational psychology as a "bi-disciplinary" field, with researchers leaning toward either the educational or the psychological end of the continuum. In a special commemorative volume of the *Educational Psychologist,* O'Donnell and Levin (2001) noted that contemporary educational psychology has prospered from this dualism because it has led to a healthy expansion of mission, methods, and contributions across the fields of education and psychology. Others have called for a more comprehensive definition to unify and advance the field

by referring to educational psychology as "the scientific study of psychology in education" (Wittrock, 1992). Calfee (2006), in a review of changes in the field since 1986, predicted that the lenses of psychology, education, and research used to view contributions of the discipline in the past will continue to frame the essence of the field of educational psychology well into the future.

History of the Field

Educational psychology's historical roots can be traced to some of the major figures in education and psychology at the turn of the past century (Hilgard, 1996). Inspirational leaders who informed as well as moved the field include William James (1842–1910), the founder of the field of American psychology. James was a mentor to James Dewey (1859–1952), another major figure, who established an early laboratory school at the University of Chicago to study the pedagogy and practice of schooling. Most credit E. L. Thorndike (1874–1949) with coining the term "Educational Psychology" in 1903 as the title of a series of influential textbooks that helped firmly establish the field as a distinct discipline within psychology. Central to Thorndike's foundational belief was the contribution of psychological principles and methods to what he called the "science of education."

Historically, research by educational psychologists has influenced major reforms in education and educator preparation. Educational psychology was recognized as a separate subspecialty within the American Psychological Association (APA) in 1946 with the creation of Division 15, which recognizes an outstanding educational psychologist each year through its prestigious E. L. Thorndike Award. An excellent comprehensive overview and review of the founders of the field, historical research trends, and the roots of educational psychology can be found in a chapter by Berliner (2006).

What Do Educational Psychologists Do?

Educational psychologists are dedicated to theoretical study and transmission of information about educationally relevant topics and are sensitive to critical issues facing educators in the field. Michael Pressley, in a provocative 2005 Thorndike award address, identified educational psychology as a "definitely human endeavor" not easily defined by a set curriculum and best viewed as an evolving effort to constructively advance the educational field. The heart of what an educational psychologist does is to create validated instructional approaches informed by research to positively impact students' learning and progress. An informal review of 10 leading textbooks indicated a strong focus on cognition and learning related to memory, thinking, and other intellectual skills; on individual differences related to exceptional abilities such as giftedness, learning disability, and cognitive delays; and on the science of measurement and statistics as it relates to accuracy in the measurement of knowledge, learning, and effectiveness of instruction. More recent editions include greater emphasis on motivation, relational processes, technology, and sociocultural influences.

Professional Training and Employment Opportunities

Today the field of educational psychology is more expansive than ever. Graduate students enrolled in educational psychology programs learn to dissect, plan, and conduct educational research that can help teachers, educators, and others make sound decisions about classroom practice, instruction, and learning. Required coursework varies at top educational psychology programs across the country, but core coursework requirements typically encompass the following domains: learning and cognition, curriculum and instruction, educational measurement and assessment, statistics and research design. Educational psychology graduates have the potential to fulfill many different roles at universities, educational research institutes, testing and evaluation organizations, and school districts. Graduates can be found teaching across many different departments and colleges, including psychology, education, human development, statistics, or measurement.

Educational Psychology Publications

The historical and current research conducted by educational psychologists can be examined through work published in the top journals associated with the field (McInerney, 2005; O'Donnell & Levin, 2001; Pressley & Roehrig, 2002). The *Journal of Educational Psychology,* begun in 1910, is the longest running and most influential publication focused exclusively on educational psychology. The *Educational Psychologist, Educational Psychology Review,* and *Contemporary Educational Psychology* are three other journals that reflect major discipline specific historical and research contributions. Major handbooks devoted to the field also provide a window to current and prior research endeavors. Two handbooks have been sponsored by Division 15 of the APA. The first *Handbook of Educational Psychology* was published in 1996 (Berliner & Calfee, 1996) and the second edition, which includes 41 chapters to synthesize the field, was published in 2006 (Alexander & Winne, 2006). Contributions of educational psychologists also were highlighted in Volume 7 (Reynolds & Miller, 2003) of the 12-volume *Handbook of Psychology* series published in 2003 (Weiner, 2003).

Contributions of Educational Psychologists

Research conducted by educational psychologists has helped inform and transform pre-K through college education as well as educator preparation and training. Educational psychologists employ a wide range of

scientifically valid quantitative and qualitative analyses and have developed sophisticated methodological and statistical approaches to gain new knowledge. The discipline has been refined and redefined over the years, yet many ideas from the past continue to resurface as new, more in-depth, reconstituted insights (Zimmerman & Schunk, 2002). The array of topics found in the literature associated with educational psychology is reflected by at least six content domains.

1. *Learning and knowledge representation.* Research from the field has contributed to critical theoretical knowledge about cognitive processes such as attention, imagery, memory, thinking, and metacognition that has enhanced our understanding of learning and study strategies. Contributions of educational psychologists have been made in the areas of knowledge acquisition, representation, and transfer related to individual learning within and across academic domains such as reading, writing, mathematics, and science. The study of thinking processes, cognitive strategies, and higher order information processing has led to major insights regarding the teaching of critical subject matter in schools.

2. *Educational measurement, statistics, and research.* The work of educational psychologists has been in the forefront of the science of measurement theory and test development. Educators now have valid and reliable measures of background knowledge, aptitude, and individual growth and progress. Applications of test construction principles by educational psychologists have contributed to widely used assessments for intelligence, learning disabilities, social-emotional skills, and early childhood development. This work has led to greater accuracy in individual and classroom assessment and to a greater understanding of the role of high-stakes testing, progress monitoring, and factors that can influence students' test performance and achievement. Advancements in program evaluation and statistics also are attributed to the work of educational psychologists. Educational psychologists employ a range of innovative quantitative and qualitative research methodologies to gather and analyze data. Observations, single case studies, and complex multivariate, longitudinal designs that require advanced hierarchical and structural equation analyses have been developed and verified in relation to important educational outcomes.

3. *Teaching and instruction.* Major advances in the psychology of teaching and learning in real educational settings have been made by educational psychologists. Methods and models of instruction, such as the use of questioning, grouping, cooperative learning, and classroom management have been developed and examined by educational

psychologists. Much has been learned about effective teaching methods that emphasize learner construction of meaning. This work has led to advances in classroom instruction and professional and occupational training. Recently, educational psychologists have directed attention to the study of effective teaching of subjects considered centrally important in a rapidly changing global economy, such as the use and influence of instructional technology, computer-assisted and mediated learning, and other multimedia applications.

4. *Motivation and affective development.* Educational psychologists have made major contributions to the study of the interplay of cognitive and affective processes in complex educational settings. This work has enhanced our understanding of attitudes, attributes, self-concept, and other motivational and social dimensions of learning. Affective processes have been found to interact and mediate how well people attend, comprehend, construct meaning, transfer what they know, and solve problems. Teachers have benefited from a greater understanding about attributions for achievement and feelings of self-efficacy in order to create classroom environments where students are motivated to excel.

5. *Individual differences and special populations.* The work of educational psychologists has been at the forefront of understanding individual differences such as the academic competence and behavior of students with exceptional abilities, including giftedness, learning disability, and cognitive delays. This work has led to increased understanding of successful programs for exceptional learners and inclusive classrooms.

6. *Sociocultural contexts for learning and development.* The understanding of complex sociocultural theories as they relate to instructional and relational processes has been at the forefront of current work by educational psychologists. New insights about education and educational settings have been developed based on cross-cultural research and the study of ecological, cultural contexts for learning. This work has contributed to a greater understanding of family and peer group norms, values, and routines that has led to major insights about how to improve school climate, student engagement, and parental involvement and how to foster successful and collaborative school, home, and community partnerships.

Ongoing Challenges in the Field

Learning, teaching, and educational psychology are intricately entwined, and thus, the continued prosperity of the field depends on how well the next generation of educational psychologists tackles and overcomes important challenges in partnership with educational practitioners.

The first challenge is how to further transform the vast educational psychology research base into instructional practices that can enhance teacher preparation and address today's complex educational issues. This must be done in light of the fact that there has been a steady trend over the last 25 years to reduce the time devoted to educational psychology in teacher preparation programs (Woolfolk, 2000) and the time devoted to advanced methodology and statistical expertise in educational psychology graduate training programs (McInerney, 2005).

A second challenge is that there has yet to be a strong concomitant translation of work within the field of educational psychology to educational policy. Educational psychologists must find new ways to highlight and translate work from the field so that others understand how such research can help guide sound educational policy and influence educational reform (McCombs, 2003). One example of how educational psychology research can help inform educational policy is the widely disseminated set of educational guidelines published in 1997 based on a review by an APA task force and titled *Learner-centered psychological principles: A framework for school reform and redesign.* This document has strongly influenced the current emphasis on evidenced-based intervention and has impacted state regulations and educator licensing standards. A third challenge is the need to address the increased variability and diversification of our schooling communities as well as the longevity of our schooling population. Cross-cultural and intercultural studies that lead to a greater understanding of the sociocontextual nature of learning across the lifespan also are required to examine developmental, motivational, and social transformations that occur as learners gain competence and expertise over time (Greenfield et al., 2006).

Ideas for the Future

Educators as never before can benefit from the substantial progress and contributions within the field of educational psychology. Educational psychologists have unique theoretical and methodological expertise to study new issues and problems facing educators, to assist in the development of state educational standards, to measure progress students make toward meeting standards, and to engage in curriculum enhancement informed by research. In the future, educational psychologists will continue to contribute to the development of unified psychological theory and teaching and learning practices that address real problems in education settings. The pursuit of new knowledge will be balanced with innovative application embedded within foundational educational psychology theory and research (Alexander, 2004).

Future work by educational psychologists also will be instrumental in differentiating general educational principles from those dependent on contextual variables; to identify critical connections between neuro- and biological psychology and learning; and to determine where, when, and how virtual teaching and learning might take the place of direct exposure and experience. Educational psychologists will study teaching and learning in technology-rich environments and advance our understanding of how to evaluate the improvement of skills, application of knowledge, and development of lifelong expertise within the essential framework of accountability (Baker, 2007). Participation in such transformative research will enable educational psychologists to adapt to the educational realities of as well as influence educational practice and reform in the twenty-first century.

Educational psychology is a vibrant, constantly evolving field focused on some of the "most complex, intellectually challenging, and socially significant issues of our time—the education and training of people around the world in and out of schools" (Wittrock, 1992). The work of educational psychologists has much relevance to real-world educational practice. Indeed, work by educational psychologists has led to important insights about learners, learning, instruction, and assessment that will continue to pave the way for more informed educational reforms and policy recommendations in the future (O'Donnell & Levin, 2001). After looking at past contributions of the field, Calfee (2006) offered predictions about where the field might be in 2025, the likely time frame for the third version of the *Handbook of Educational Psychology*. His overall conclusion was that educational psychologists would continue to make substantial reciprocal contributions to education and psychology and would most likely play an even greater future role in the development of solutions to significant educational challenges and the improvement of schooling.

REFERENCES

Alexander, P. A. (2004). In the year 2020: Envisioning the possibilities for educational psychology. *Educational Psychologist, 39*, 149–156.

Alexander, P. A., & Winne, P. H. (Eds.). (2006). *Handbook of educational psychology* (2nd ed.). Mahwah, NJ: Lawrence Erlbaum.

Baker, E. L. (2007). The end(s) of testing. *Educational Researcher, 36*(6), 309–317.

Berliner, D. C. (2006). Educational psychology: Searching for essence throughout a century of influence. In P. A. Alexander & P. H. Winne (Eds.), *Handbook of educational psychology* (2nd ed., pp. 3–27). Mahwah, NJ: Lawrence Erlbaum.

Berliner, D. C., & Calfee, R. C. (Eds.). (1996). *Handbook of educational psychology*. New York: Macmillan.

Calfee, R. C. (2006). Educational psychology in the 21st century. In P. A. Alexander & P. H. Winne (Eds.), *Handbook of educational psychology II* (pp. 29–42). Mahwah, NJ: Lawrence Erlbaum.

Charles, D. C. (1987). The emergence of educational psychology. In J. A. Glover & R. R. Ronning (Eds.), *Historical foundation of educational psychology* (pp. 3–15). New York: Plenum.

Greenfield, P. M., Trumbull, E., Keller, H., Rothstein-Fisch, C., Suzuki, L., & Quiroz, B. (2006). Cultural conceptions of learning and development. In P. A. Alexander & P. H. Winne (Eds.), *Handbook of educational psychology II* (pp. 675–692). Mahwah, NJ: Lawrence Erlbaum.

Hilgard, E. R. (1996). History of educational psychology. In D. C. Berliner & R. C. Calfee (Eds.), *Handbook of educational psychology* (pp. 990–1004). New York: Macmillan.

McCombs, B. L. (2003). Research to policy for guiding educational reform. In W. M. Reynolds & G. E. Miller (Eds.), *Educational Psychology: Vol. 7: Handbook of Psychology* (pp. 583–608). Hoboken, NJ: John Wiley & Sons.

McInerney, (2005). Educational psychology—theory, research, and teaching: A 25-year retrospective. *Educational Psychology, 25*(6), 585–599.

O'Donnell, A. M., & Levin, J. R. (2001). Educational psychology's healthy growing pains. *Educational Psychologist, 36*, 73–82.

Pressley, M. G. (2005). "Oh the places an educational psychologist can go! ... and how young educational psychologists can prepare for the trip (apologies to Dr. Seuss)," *Educational Psychologist, 40*, 137–153.

Pressley, M. G., & Roehrig, A. (2002). Educational psychology in the modern era: 1960 to the present. In B. Zimmerman & D. Schunk (Eds.). (2002). *Educational psychology: A century of contributions* (pp. 333–366). Mahwah, NJ: Lawrence Erlbaum.

Reynolds, W. M., & Miller, G. E. (Eds.). (2003). Educational Psychology, Vol. 7. In I. B. Weiner (Editor-in-Chief). *Handbook of psychology*. Hoboken, NJ: John Wiley & Sons.

Wittrock, M. C. (1992). An empowering conception of educational psychology, *Educational Psychologist, 27*, 139–141.

Wittrock, M. C., & Farley, F. L. (1989). Toward a blueprint for educational psychology. In M. C. Witrock & F. L. Farley (Eds.), *The future of educational psychology* (pp. 193–199). Hillsdale, NJ: Lawrence Erlbaum.

Woolfolk, A. (2000). Educational psychology in teacher education. *Educational Psychologist, 35*, 257–276.

Zimmerman, B., & Schunk, D. (Eds.). (2002). *Educational psychology: A century of contributions*. Mahwah, NJ: Lawrence Erlbaum.

SUGGESTED READINGS

APA Work Group on the Board of Educational Affairs. (1997). *Learner-centered psychological principles: A framework for school reform and redesign*. Washington, DC: American Psychological Association.

What is educational psychology? http://www.cedu.niu.edu/lepf/edpsych/Psychology.pdf.

GLORIA MILLER
University of Denver

CHRISTINE MCCORMICK
University of Massachusetts Amherst

STACI JORDAN
University of Denver

EFFECT SIZE

Most broadly defined, an effect size measures the strength of association between variables or the degree of difference between parameters. If a null hypothesis is false, an effect size measures degree of falseness of that null hypothesis. In the planning of research, the anticipated effect size, or the effect size of minimum interest that the researcher wants to detect, is used in power analysis to estimate needed sample sizes. Estimates of effect size from related studies can be averaged in a meta-analysis in order to yield a better estimate than could be expected from any single study.

A common estimator of effect size for continuous dependent variables is d, the standardized difference between means, which divides the difference between two samples' means by an appropriate standard deviation, such as the standard deviation of a control group or a standard deviation that is based on pooling groups' variances when the population variances are assumed to be equal. Such standardizing of the difference between means renders estimated effect sizes from related studies comparable and valid for averaging in a meta-analysis. Assuming normal distributions, this effect size is analogous to a z-score, so that when $d = +1$ (the percent who score below $+1$ standard deviation), it is estimated that one population's mean exceeds the scores of approximately 84% of the members of the other population. This effect size has an analog, the Mahalanobis D, in multivariate analysis of variance.

Another common measure of effect size for continuous dependent variables is the population POV, which is the proportion of the total variance in the dependent variable that is associated with variation in the independent variable of group membership. In the case of two groups, this strength-of-association measure is known as the coefficient of determination, r^2 in the population, and its square root is the point-biserial correlation measure of effect size. There are also POV effect sizes for multivariate analysis of variance.

A nonparametric effect size for the two-group univariate case is the probability of superiority, $\Pr(Y_a > Y_b)$, which is the probability that a randomly sampled member of population a will have a higher score on Y than a randomly sampled member of population b. In multiple regression, common side effects are the population multiple coefficient of determination (R^2), and the partial and semipartial correlation coefficients and their squares.

There are many measures of effect size for 2×2 as well as larger contingency tables that involve nominal or ordinal dependent variables, such as patient improved versus patient not improved or Agree Strongly/Agree/Disagree/Disagree Strongly (Grissom & Kim, 2005). There are important limitations of the various measures and estimators of effect size. For detailed discussions consult Cohen (1988), Grissom and Kim (2005), and Olejnik and Algina (2000).

REFERENCES

Cohen, J. (1988). *Statistical power analysis for the behavioral sciences* (2nd ed.). New York: Academic Press.

Grissom, R. J., & Kim, J. J. (2005). *Effect sizes for research: A broad practical approach.* Mahwah, NJ: Lawrence Erlbaum.

Olejnik, S., & Algina, J. (2000). Measures of effect size for comparative studies: Applications, interpretations, and limitations. *Contemporary Educational Psychology, 25,* 281–286.

SUGGESTED READINGS

Agresti, A. (2002). *Categorical data analysis* (2nd ed.). Hoboken, NJ: John Wiley & Sons.

Cohen, J., Cohen, P., West, S. G., & Aiken, L. S. (2003). *Applied multiple regression/correlation analysis for the behavioral sciences* (3rd ed.). Mahwah, NJ: Lawrence Erlbaum.

Cortina, J. M., & Nouri, H. (2000). *Effect sizes for ANOVA designs.* Thousand Oaks, CA: Sage.

Fleiss, J. L., Levin, B., & Paik, M. C. (2003). *Statistical methods for rates and proportions* (3rd ed.). Hoboken, NJ: John Wiley & Sons.

Huberty, C. J., & Olejnik, S. (2006). *Applied MANOVA and discriminant analysis* (2nd ed.). Hoboken, NJ: John Wiley & Sons.

Maxwell, S. E., & Delaney, H. D. (2003). *Designing experiments and analyzing data: A model comparison perspective* (2nd ed.). Mahwah, NJ: Lawrence Erlbaum.

Smithson, M. (2003). *Confidence intervals.* Thousand Oaks, CA: Sage.

Robert J. Grissom
San Francisco State University

See also: Cohen's *d*; Significance Testing; Statistical Power

EGO DEVELOPMENT

The ego development concept was first introduced in psychoanalytic thinking. Using Freud's so-called structural model distinguishing between id, superego, and ego, an American group of psychoanalysts developed a branch of theory and practice that came to be known as "ego psychology" (Hartmann, 1964). The term *ego development* has been used with various meanings. Whereas Freud viewed the ego as a weak rider of the powerful id and the strict superego, the more pragmatic line of U.S. psychoanalysis led clinicians and theorists to stress the ego's conscious elements of decision making, choice, and competence. In general, the ego has been utilized as a broad descriptive term for all ego function in the psychoanalytic tradition or, most prominently, as the changing organization of an individual's central frame regarding the psychosocial realm or psychosocial developmental tasks.

Today, ego development seems a dated term and has been substituted with synonyms like the "self." It is important, however, to understand why and how the term ego development historically evolved. Starting in the 1960s, psychologists used the term out of the need to go beyond the predominant theories of cognitive or psychosexual development. This reflected the attempt to capture an integrative, active, meaning-making function that conducts an orchestration of an individual's life narratives, personal concerns, and biographical experiences (McAdams, 1998). The term ego development captured this elastic complexity and developmental vicissitude of the internal world of the self. Ego development nevertheless remains attached to a long-standing theoretical tradition that continues to stimulate research on self- and identity development over the life course.

Theories

The foundational theories of ego development have been most prominently formulated in the tradition of stage development theories. These theories, in general, describe the development of the ego/self (or related concepts such as social cognition) in terms of sequences of increasing levels of complexity, maturity, and differentiation.

Lawrence Kohlberg's cognitive-structural theory of moral development provided in part the foundation for theories of ego development. Basing his approach on Piagetian structuralism and its focus on the rational-epistemic subject, Kohlberg viewed the theory or moral judgment as a cognitive developmental reconceptualization of social development. Outlining the relationship between moral judgment and the broader domain of self, Kohlberg (1969) posited a fundamental unity of personality organization and development that he called self; this generalized, epistemic self is defined in terms of universal structures of justice and cognitive ability. The notion of an epistemic self provided an important foundation for theories of ego development.

Theories of ego development extended the structural dimension of the epistemic self by elaborating on an individual's biographical experiences and meanings that shape the life course and self-development. The greatest contribution that came out of this perspective was Erik Erikson's theory of ego development (1963). Erikson's epigenetic model, a grand synthesis of ego psychology that established the "eight ages of human being," took psychoanalysis into a developmental theory beyond childhood and provided an outline of adaptive mechanisms at each age of the life cycle as well as of typical conflicts and vulnerabilities that arise during that life cycle.

Erikson's theory thus describes an individual's progressions in ego identity development across the lifespan through eight stages from infantile dependency toward increasing individuation. Ego identity is the conscious sense of self that we acquire and develop in our daily interactions with others. At each stage, people experience a typical conflict that serves as a turning point in development. These conflicts are centered on either developing a psychological quality or failing to develop that quality. The successful mastery of normative psychosocial developmental tasks, such as self-control in the toddler years, leads to growth of the ego's strength; as toddlers gain self-control, they begin to feel a sense of mastery. In contrast, unresolved crises are assumed to cause disaffection, identity distortion, and maladaptive outcomes (Erikson, 1963).

An important aspect of this theory is that the ego stages are tied to ages of the lifespan. Age is organized in terms of social tasks and institutional participation, in the form of expectations by society of what has to be worked out at different phases of life. Thus psychological adaptations (e.g., wisdom at late ages), social tasks (grandparenting, retirement), and the historical moment ("cohort effect") come together in Erikson's rich, creative, and influential views on ego development.

Jane Loevinger's theory of ego development is also a major contribution to the substance of this field. According to Loevinger (1976), the ego is the frame of reference or the unity that constructs the meanings that one gives to oneself in relation to the interpersonal world (see Sullivan, 1968). Thus, the active synthesizing or integrative function that aims to make sense of emotions, motives, and interpersonal experiences laid down in a biographic history denotes what ego is. The ego includes content (views, memories, isolated ideas) and structure (the complexity of the relationships between those ideas).

Loevinger distinguished four themes of the ego that run through the stages of ego development: impulse control, cognitive complexity, interpersonal relations, and conscious preoccupations. It is important to study a person from the perspective of domain specificity and to explore the discrepancy between different domains. The simultaneous importance of looking at the overarching self and its developmental path makes ego development theory and measurement very attractive.

In Loevinger's theory, the ego develops along a sequence of eight developmental stages, from the Impulsive stage, where the world is perceived in its dichotomy of black and white (good and bad) and the person is enveloped in his or her own egocentrism; to Self-Protective, where the world is perceived as hostile and threatening; to Conformist, where ideas and behaviors are governed by external rules; to Self-Aware, where self, at last, becomes the focus of its own awareness; to Conscientious, where one's conscience becomes its own judge; to Individualistic, where the value of an individual is fully appreciated; to Autonomous, where the life and the self are perceived in their complexity and interrelatedness; and to Integrated, a stage rarely reached in which people become fully self-actualized. Fuller descriptions of these stages and their characteristics are provided by Loevinger (1976) and Hy and Loevinger (1996). The number of stages was later expanded by Cook-Greuter (2000), who added two further developmental levels called Construct-Aware and Transcendent. Currently, then, the theory acknowledges the existence of stages of maturity extending from Impulsive to Transcendent.

For purposes of measuring level of ego development, Loevinger constructed the Washington University Sentence Completion Test (WUSCT). This test is a semi-projective measure that consists of 36 open-ended partial sentences (stems) that respondents are asked to complete in a way that expresses "your real feelings." Two training manuals developed by Loevinger and her colleagues (Hy & Loevinger, 1996) provide guidelines for scoring WUSCT protocols. Based on hundreds of studies conducted using this instrument since the introduction of the theory, research has brought together evidence in support of the theory and the measure (Hauser, 1993).

Ego Development and Mental Health

It has become a widely accepted trend in psychology and psychiatry that mental health and psychopathology should be understood, at least in part, in developmental terms (e.g., Cicchetti, 1984). There are four theoretical perspectives on the nature of the ego development–mental health relationship. On one extreme is the notion that development and mental health are, in fact, one and the same: Individuals at lower stages of development are less "mentally healthy," and those at more mature stages enjoy better mental health. This relationship is presumed to be especially the case for people who remain in ego development positions beyond the normative age for these positions ("age-stage dysynchrony"). Among the evidence in support of this claim is the fact that the stepwise progression from immature thought and impulsivity to complex, self-reflective, and tolerant forms of maturity consists of many components of mental health. Accepting the contradictory nature of the self, of relationships, and of the world at large is a hallmark of complex development and represents positive adaptation, which clinicians also tend to refer to as mental health. Thus, higher stages promote more stable adaptations to the social world and also indicate more secure mental health.

The second view of the association between mental health and development is that the two are conceptually and empirically distinct phenomena. Anyone can be afflicted with any form of psychopathology at any developmental position. The mechanisms underlying psychopathology and ego development are truly orthogonal. The fact that many people at mature levels of development struggle with mental illness, neurosis, and dysfunctional adaptations to life is strong evidence in support of this view.

A less extreme position than the first two consists of a strong positive relationship between development and mental health, such that people at higher stages of development are better adapted or better able to adapt and, therefore, are more apt to be mentally healthy. This model is quite common in developmental research; for example, a positive association between development and mental health has been stated or implied by researchers in cognitive-moral development (Piaget, 1965). However, this view implies that, although people at more mature developmental levels are not necessarily shielded from psychopathology or dysfunctional adaptations, there is greater probability of mental health. What makes this general view on the relationship between development and mental health more complicated is the multitude of dimensions that underlie psychopathology and maladaptation. Some disorders, such as schizophrenia, are probably quite unrelated to ego development, whereas antisocial behavior problems could be quite strongly related to it.

For those disorders that might be connected to ego development, a fourth model can be introduced. This model suggests key vulnerabilities, risks, and symptom combinations that arise at each ego development position. Each stage brings out new strengths and opportunities to rework past vulnerabilities. However, each new system of self-complexity can also lead to new weaknesses or to more complex forms of old dysfunctions (Noam, Chandler, & LaLonde, 1995). This model is probabilistic; that is, when for example we suggest an association between the Conformist ego stage and depression, what we mean is that the highest risk of depression exists for the people at the Conformist ego development stage, whereas for people close to the Conformist stages, this risk is lower (Noam, Young, & Jilnina, 2006).

Future Directions

Where will ego development go in the future? From one perspective it is possible to see a theory and methodology that has had its prime. The terms are dated, compared with new theories about information processing, executive functioning, and decision-making research, to name just a few. The era of sweeping notions of the self organizing many dimensions of functioning, thought, and emotion has given way to more specific studies of these various domains that do not have to be tied to an overarching organizing principle as the ego. Although these later developments are productive, however, there is still a need to understand a person's attempt to bring unity to experience and superimpose a meaning system and identity that connects the various domains of self.

If ego development is seen as part of the study of self and identity, which is where it should be located scientifically, then there is still much to be learned from these active lines of research. Beyond the specific contributions of the many research findings that come out of ego development, its theoretical sophistication and measurement strengths continue to be very significant. Standing on Erikson's shoulders, we continue to refine our understanding of the lifespan. Standing on Loevinger's shoulders, the idea that personality is evolving throughout development continues to be essential. The next phase of work will be strongly focused on applied areas, such as clinical practice, teaching, parenting, and work force issues. Knowing about ego development means knowing about an individual's frame of reference, abilities to actively make use of interpretations, and understandings of health and illness. In all of these applied domains, the individual differences that these theories and methods on ego development reconstruct developmentally thus have a great utility that has only begun to have an impact.

REFERENCES

Cicchetti, D. (1984). The emergence of developmental psychopathology. *Child Development, 55*, 1–7.

Cook-Greuter, S. (2000). Mature ego development: A gateway to ego transcendence? *Journal of Adult Development, 7*(4), 227–240.

Erikson, E. H. (1963). *Childhood and society.* New York: Norton. (Original work published 1950)

Hartmann, H. (1964). *Ego psychology and the problem of adaptation.* New York: International Universities Press. (Original work published 1939)

Hauser, S. (1993). Loevinger's model and measure of ego development: A critical review, II. *Psychological Inquiry, 4*, 23–30.

Hy, L. X., & Loevinger, J. (1996). *Measuring ego development.* Mahwah, NJ: Lawrence Erlbaum.

Kohlberg, L. (1969). Stage and sequence: The cognitive developmental approach to socialization. In D. A. Goslin (Ed.), *Handbook of socialization theory and research.* Chicago: Rand-McNally.

Loevinger, J. (1976). *Ego development: Conceptions and theories.* San Francisco: Jossey-Bass.

McAdams, D. P. (1998). Ego, trait, identity. In P. M. Westenberg, A. Blasi, & L. D. Cohn (Eds.), *Personality development: Theoretical, empirical, and clinical investigations of Loevinger's conception of ego development* (pp. 27–38). Mahwah, NJ: Erlbaum.

Noam, G., Chandler, M. J., & Lalonde, C. E. (1995). Clinical-developmental psychology: Constructivism and social cognition in the study of psychological dysfunction. In D. Cicchetti & D. Cohen (Eds.), *Developmental psychopathology* (pp. 424–466). New York: John Wiley & Sons.

Noam, G. G., Young, C. H., & Jilnina, J. (2006). Social cognition, psychological symptoms, and mental health: The model, evidence, and contribution to ego development. In D. Cicchetti & D. J. Cohen (Eds.), *Developmental psychopathology* (pp. 750–794). Hoboken, NJ: John Wiley & Sons.

Piaget, J. (1965). *The moral judgment of the child.* New York: Free Press (Original work published 1932)

Sullivan, H. S. (1968). *The interpersonal theory of psychiatry.* New York: Norton. (Original work published 1953)

GIL G. NOAM
Harvard University and McLean Hospital

TINA MALTI
University of Zurich, Switzerland

See also: **Eriksonian Developmental Stages; Identity Formation**

EGO IDENTITY (See Identity Formation)

EGO PSYCHOLOGY

The ego psychological approach to understanding mental life has evolved considerably since Freud created the discipline of psychoanalysis in the latter part of the nineteenth century. Contemporary ego psychologists have a different theoretical and clinical perspective than did Freud or early psychoanalytic theorists. As in all areas of scholarship and clinical practice, ego psychologists have evolved in their understanding of motivation and behavior and have integrated new findings from psychoanalytic practice and research, and from the cognate disciplines. This article relates the early theory of psychoanalysis and ego psychology and then presents its more contemporary edition, referred to as modern conflict theory or modern structural theory.

Early Psychoanalysis: Drive Psychology

Early in his career, Freud discovered that symptoms such as inhibitions, hysteria, and anxiety had psychological meaning. He was deeply influenced by the medical hypnotist Jean-Martin Charcot (1825–1893), who demonstrated that women with seeming neurological symptoms (arm paralysis for example) could be hypnotized and the paralysis transferred from one arm to another. At the time, the latter part of the nineteenth century and early twentieth century, Freud was in private practice, treating middle-class Viennese patients who were sexually repressed and who reported memories of traumatic sexual seduction during their early lives. Freud concluded that neurotic symptoms such as sexual inhibition stemmed from early sexual trauma and/or wishes and desires that were unacceptable and therefore rendered unconscious by a defense mechanism he called repression. During this early phase of psychoanalysis, Freud believed that the patient could obtain relief by freely expressing her innermost thoughts and fantasies, which would then lead the patient to recall the early traumatic event and thus relieve the symptoms. One of Freud's early patients, Anna O., referred to Freud's approach as the "talking cure" (Freud & Breuer, 1893/1955).

Freud initially believed that neurotic symptoms were caused by unacceptable memories, wishes, and emotions that were created by real-life trauma. He saw consciousness as divided into the unconscious, where unacceptably threatening wishes, memories and desires resided and were inaccessible to the person; the preconscious, where memories and feelings were defended against, but could reach consciousness; and the consciousness proper. In his opus, *The Interpretation of Dreams* (1900/1953), Freud developed this topographical model of the mind in its fullest. At this point, consciousness or subjective awareness was, for Freud, synonymous with the self or the ego.

Over time, Freud came to the conclusion that the memories of seduction reported by his patients were in many cases fantasies created by the patient that were repressed and subsequently recalled as actual memories. Although he was well aware that sexual trauma occurred at the turn of the century in upper middle-class Vienna, he felt that the extent of these reports of sexual trauma and consequent symptoms could not be validly accounted for by actual events.

Here it is worth recalling that Freud was trained as a physician and neurologist. As such, he saw himself as a man of science. He formulated a theory of mental life derived from his clinical observations and utilized the contemporary scientific paradigm. He had many intellectual influences, but his thinking was particularly shaped by the evolutionist Charles Darwin and the physiologist Hermann von Helmholtz, who attempted to explain all of nature in physio-chemical terms and through the application of the laws of Newtonian dynamics (Yankelovich & Barrett, 1971.)

By the beginning of the twentieth century, after concluding that many reports of early sexual trauma were not truthful, Freud began to focus his attention on the patient's inner world of sexual wishes, fantasies, and desires. He developed a biological theory of mental life and sexuality that was physio-chemical and mechanical in nature. Viewing sexuality as an instinct, he referred to the energy of this driving sexuality as libido. He believed this libidinal energy pressed for discharge and that an excessive amount of undischarged libidinal energy created psychological symptoms. Later, after witnessing the self-destructive savagery of World War I, Freud added aggression as a second biological drive that, together with sexuality, motivated and influenced mental life and behavior.

Ego Psychology: Early Formulations

During the early part of the twentieth century, psychoanalysis was essentially a drive psychology that focused primarily on the vicissitudes of unconscious and instinctual energy (sexuality and aggression). However, Freud began to appreciate the intractable nature of guilt with its self-defeating and unconscious elements. In his neurotic patients, he observed an inhibition of their impulses, wants, and desires, and not simply an easy discharge of instinctual energy. He realized that not all that resided in the unconscious is instinctual in nature and pressing for discharge, as would be predicted by his Hemholtzian-Newtonian model of mental functioning. He concluded that part of the self or ego also resided within the unconscious along with the instincts and defensively inhibited the discharge of instinctual energy, thereby creating symptoms and undesirable character traits.

With the publication of *The Ego and the Id* (1923/1961a) and also *Inhibitions, Symptoms and Anxiety* (1926/1961b), Freud added the structural model to the topographical model of mental functioning. Recall that with the topographical model, the ego was seen as essentially synonymous with subjective, conscious experience. The structural model brought considerable complexity to Freud's view of mental life in general and the ego in particular. He divided the mind or mental apparatus into three structures. The id is conceived as the seat of sexual and aggressive energy. The ego is now seen as developing from the id via contact with reality and as a "coherent organization of mental processes" (Freud, 1923/1961a, p. 17). It oversees the developing constituent mental processes including attention, reality testing, defense, and perception. The ego is attached to consciousness and discharges excitations from within to the outer world. Part of the ego is split off from its "coherent organization" and is the seed of defense. This part of the ego is unconscious and will " ... exclude certain trends in the mind... " (1923/1961a, p. 17). As the ego derives from the id, the superego, the third of the mental structures, is conceived as a gradient of the ego and as the seat of morality or the conscience, shaped by the internalization of parental and cultural values and by the constitutional strength of the instincts.

The Freudian ego, then, emerged from the id and is the medium of commerce between the inner world of the instincts and outer reality. The ego serves as the executive of the mental apparatus and " ... seeks to bring the influence of the external world to bear upon the Id and its tendencies ... " (Freud, 1923/1961a, p. 25). For Freud, the ego represents reason and common sense (the reality principle), whereas the id represents the passion and the propensity for irrationality (the pleasure principle).

The Freudian ego is energized by the power source of the id (libido and aggression). The instincts were seen as quanta of energy seeking satisfaction and relief of stimulation from both within and outside the organism. The ego as part of the mental apparatus is governed by the nature of the instinctual energy source. Freud saw the ego as a "poor creature" needing to mediate between the inner and outer world. Its function is to discharge and regulate the direction of instinctual energy in an adaptive fashion. The ego attempts to serve its masters, the instincts, reality, and the superego in a way that minimizes internecine warfare and the creation of symptom formation and psychic distress.

Contemporary Ego Psychology: Modern Conflict Theory

The contemporary way of conceptualizing ego in psycho-analysis, known as modern conflict theory, has evolved from the classical ego psychological perspective. The drive theory of mental functioning with its emphasis on psychic energy is deemphasized, and contemporary evolutionary biology serves as a basis for understanding human moti-vation and adaptation. Peskin (1997), utilizing the concept of inclusive fitness and natural selection, noted that the purpose of psychoanalytic theory is to " … capture the adaptive self-enhancing agenda of our species … " (p. 368.) Following Slavin and Kriegman (1992), Peskin notes that, even in close-kin ties, considerable divergence of inter-ests exists, with inevitable interpersonal and emotional conflicts. The ego is the part of the mind that helps to mod-ulate anxiety by effectively reacting to dangers engendered by internal or relational conflicts. Modern conflict theory also utilizes the evolutionary approach (Lettieri, 2005) and the dynamic systems theory (Thelen & Smith, 1994) to conceptualize how the ego orders and reorders percep-tions and reactions to the surroundings so as to synthesize thoughts and feelings, as well as interpersonal and emo-tional conflicts. Adaptive ego functioning is responsive to the unique interests and needs of the person, in a fashion that reduces dissonance and enhances a sense of safety and mastery.

Bachant, Lynch, and Richards (1995) outline a devel-opmental understanding of modern conflict theory. They note that children are faced with a number of fundamental existential questions and calamities and must cope with immature cognitive functions as well as with psychological urges that are self-centered and genuine. Certain wishes and fears become repressed, take on dangerous and pun-ishing characteristics, and become part of the dynamic unconscious. These unconscious fears and wishes consti-tute the raw material of fantasies that are unconscious, but that influence motivation, cognition, and behavior. Again, the ego is viewed here as the executive of ensuing conflicts and defenses, and as the agent responsible for optimal adaptation.

Psychoanalytic treatment involves the establishment of an intimate relationship between the patient and analyst. The therapeutic bond becomes the vehicle through which patients emotionally re-experience and become aware of the underlying sources of their distress. Together, patient and analyst strive to work through and master the patient's anxieties and maladaptive personal patterns created by unconscious and anachronistic fears and fan-tasies.

REFERENCES

Bachant, J. L., Lynch, A. A., & Richards, A. D. (1995). Relational models in psychoanalytic theory. *Psychoanalytic Psychology, 12,* 89–108.

Freud, S. (1953). Interpretation of dreams, Vols. I & II. In J. Strachey (Ed. & Trans.), *The standard edition of the com-pleted psychological works of Sigmund Freud.* London: Hogarth Press. (Original work published 1900)

Freud, S., & Breuer, J. (1955). Studies on Hysteria. In J. Strachey (Ed. & Trans.), *The standard edition of the completed psychological works of Sigmund Freud* (Vol. 2, pp. 21–47). London: Hogarth Press. (Original work published 1893)

Freud, S. (1961a). Ego and the id. In J. Strachey (Ed. & Trans.), *The standard edition of the completed psychological works of Sigmund Freud* (Vol. 19, pp. 3–66). London: Hogarth Press. (Original work published 1923)

Freud, S. (1961b). Inhibitions, symptoms, and anxiety. In J. Strachey (Ed. & Trans.), *The standard edition of the complete psychological works of Sigmund Freud* (Vol. 20, pp. 77–174). London: Hogarth Press. (Original work published 1926)

Lettieri, R. (2005). The ego revisited. *Psychoanalytic Psychology* 22(3): 370–381.

Peskin, M. M. (1997). Drive theory revisited. *The Psychoanalytic Quarterly* 66(3): 377–402.

Slavin, M. O., & Kriegman, D. (1992). *The adaptive design of the human psyche: Psychoanalysis, evolutionary biology, and the thera-peutic process.* New York/London: Guilford Press.

Thelen, E., & Smith, L. (1994). *A dynamic systems approach to the development of cognition and action.* Cambridge, MA: MIT Press.

Yankelovich, D., & Barrett, W. (1971). *Ego and instinct.* New York: Vintage Books.

RICHARD LETTIERI
New Center for Psychoanalysis, Los Angeles, CA

See also: **Personality, Psychodynamic Models of; Psychoanalytic Theories**

ELDER ABUSE AND NEGLECT

Elder abuse does not discriminate. Older adults from all walks of life, regardless of socioeconomic status, reli-gious affiliation, race, or ethnicity, have been mistreated and abused. It is difficult to determine the prevalence of elder abuse. First, it is not a single easily measur-able phenomenon. There are seven types of elder abuse: physical abuse, sexual abuse, emotional abuse, financial abuse, neglect, abandonment, and self-neglect. We do not know the exact prevalence of elder abuse, because it is often underreported and often unidentified. The National

Center on Elder Abuse (2005) estimated that as many as 2 million elders have been mistreated.

Although the way abuse is defined varies, a multidisciplinary approach toward addressing elder abuse is widely employed. Teams may be comprised of professionals such as adult protective service workers, long-term care ombudsmen, police officers, nurses, physicians, lawyers, and mental health professionals. This diverse, multidisciplinary team approach is important for dealing with primary, secondary, and tertiary intervention strategies for elder abuse and mistreatment. The role of the psychologist in the aforementioned strategies is important for delivering services to those at risk, those identified, and those who are in need of psychological services post abuse. Although elder abuse professionals value the role of the psychologist on the team of professionals (Wiglesworth, Kemp, & Mosqueda, 2008), there is little research and literature available on the topic of the role and importance of the psychologist in elder abuse.

Psychological Assessment

Psychologists are able to assess all types of abuse and can assess the elderly, their family and caregivers, and perpetrators of abuse. A high value has been placed on access to psychologists to assess for a myriad of issues that can occur in complex elder abuse cases (Wigelsworth et al., 2008). The most commonly cited reasons a psychologist is brought in for consultation are to assess mental capacity regarding financial exploitation; to assess need for psychological services; to determine capacity regarding conservatorship; to assess capacity as witness or historian; to assess for undue influence; and to determine the capacity to live independently.

The psychologist can assess the cognitive capacity of elderly people in their home or a nursing home and with a physician, case manager, lawyer, or criminal investigator. Such evaluations typically include conducting mental status assessments to determine decision-making capacity, risk for financial abuse, and ability to consent for medical treatment or research, and to determine whether guardianship is needed. A psychologist can also assess elders to determine whether and how they are vulnerable to abuse or mistreatment. Psychological assessments give other professionals, such as caseworkers, lawyers, and physicians, a better understanding of the elder's need for services. This can include helping a caseworker determine the needs of a client, assisting a criminal investigator in determining vulnerability, or establishing for a prosecutor the client's ability to serve as a witness.

Psychologists are not limited to measuring cognitive capacity. They can also help to assess mental health issues. Common examples that affect many elders, especially elders who have suffered mistreatment or abuse, are depression, posttraumatic stress disorder, psychosis,

and anxiety. These appraisals can be useful for appropriately treating an individual suffering from mental health problems, for determining appropriate approaches to care, for determining whether a living environment is safe, and for determining if there is a high risk for abuse or mistreatment.

Referral

Psychologists are able to make referrals to help elders at risk of mistreatment or abuse get the appropriate services or treatment they need before they suffer from abuse or mistreatment, either once abuse is identified, while it is occurring, or after an abuse or mistreatment has occurred. Psychologists can assess and refer family members or caregivers of elders for services or mental health treatment, to reduce risk of abuse, to stop abuse from happening, or to help caregivers deal with abuse that may have already occurred. Referrals can be made to physicians who can help with treatment of medical illness and brain function. Recommendations can be made to social workers and service providers to help the individual receive appropriate services.

Treatment

A variety of interventions are available. Psychoeducation can be offered individually or in a group format, to elders, caregivers, and the workforce (e.g., first responders, medical professionals, nursing home employees, lawyers) to educate them about elder abuse and mistreatment. This is particularly useful in helping elders and others working with or caring for elders learn to identify the types of abuse, how to avoid becoming a victim of abuse and mistreatment, and, for family and caregivers, how to avoid engaging in abusive behavior.

Psychotherapy is a treatment option for individuals who have been abused or mistreated, to help them overcome feelings of helplessness, depression, anxiety, and mistrust. This treatment option is also helpful for individuals suffering from mental health difficulties who are at risk of being abused or mistreated. Psychotherapeutic interventions can include group support, group therapy, family therapy, marriage counseling, or individual therapy. The role of the psychologist is of considerable value in combating elder abuse. The ability of these professionals to be involved in the prevention of abuse, identification of abuse, and treatment of abuse is vital for the welfare of our elder citizens.

REFERENCES

The National Center on Elder Abuse. (2005). Fact sheet: Elder abuse prevalence and statistics. Retrieved October 8, 2008, from http://www.ncea.aoa.gov/ncearoot/Main_Site/pdf/publication/FinalStatistics050331.pdf.

Wiglesworth, A., Kemp, B., Mosqueda, L. (2008). Combating elder and dependent adult mistreatment: The role of the clinical psychologist. *Journal of Elder Abuse and Neglect, 20*(3), 207–230.

DEBORAH HEISER
State Society on Aging of New York

PATRICIA BROWNELL
Fordham University Graduate School of Social Service

See also: **Child Maltreatment; Partner Abuse**

ELECTROCONVULSIVE THERAPY

Electroconvulsive therapy (ECT) is one of the most effective somatic treatments for major depression and mania. For major depression, the remission rates in patients undergoing ECT are as high as 80%, even including those patients who previously failed multiple medication trials. The response to ECT is also faster than with medications, often occurring in the first three to five treatments.

Mechanism of Action

ECT is administered by delivering electrical current to the brain using electrodes placed on the head and inducing a generalized seizure of duration between 30 seconds and 2 minutes. ECT, like antidepressant medications, has been reported to normalize the hypothalamic-pituitary-adrenal axis (HPA), and HPA dysregulation as associated with major depression. ECT also enhances the function of the serotonin system as has been demonstrated with antidepressant medication.

Indications

Research over the past 30 years has confirmed that ECT is an effective treatment in patients with treatment-resistant unipolar or bipolar major depression. ECT has also been shown to be effective in the treatment of mania.

ECT is indicated in patients who have failed or cannot tolerate antidepressant medications and patients who need a more immediate response and cannot wait the four to six weeks (or longer) it would take to respond to an antidepressant. Patients in the latter category include those with active suicidal ideation, psychotic symptoms, or malignant catatonia. ECT is also indicated when a patient has had a prior positive response to ECT and has relapsed subsequent to this previous course of ECT. ECT has also been shown to be safe and effective in pregnancy and has been used to treat intractable depression and mania during pregnancy.

Positive predictors of response to ECT include older age, at least a minimal response after the third ECT treatment, and the presence of psychosis, catatonia, or melancholic depression. Negative predictors include comorbid personality disorders and substance abuse.

Schizophrenia was one of the first illnesses treated with ECT, but with the introduction of antipsychotic medication, its use has become a third-line treatment for this condition. ECT is also effective in treating catatonia and neuroleptic malignant syndrome.

Medical Evaluation

All patients should have a medical evaluation prior to receiving ECT, including lab tests (blood count, electrolytes, pregnancy test) and electrocardiogram. Baseline cognitive status should be determined. Neuroimaging may be ordered before ECT to evaluate for a recent stroke or increased intracranial pressure from conditions such as hydrocephalus.

Although there are no medical conditions that are absolute contraindications for ECT, several clinical conditions may increase the risk of complications. These include recent myocardial infarction or unstable cardiac conditions, any illness that increases intracranial pressure, recent stroke, aneurysm or vascular malformation, and severe pulmonary disease.

Informed consent should be obtained from all patients prior to their receiving ECT. States vary in their legal regulations regarding involuntary administration of ECT.

ECT Administration

ECT is administered on an inpatient or outpatient medical unit. The treatments are scheduled in the morning, because the patient should not eat or drink after midnight prior to an ECT day. The treatments are given under general anesthesia provided intravenously, and ventilation by mask is given throughout the procedure. A muscle relaxant is administered to minimize convulsive motor activity. Other agents are also used during the treatments to modify the cardiovascular response to ECT.

The two electrodes can be positioned in a bitemporal (BT) or right unilateral (RUL) placement. The RUL placement positions the electrodes over the area of the right parietal lobe and the right temple, whereas in the BT placement the electrodes are positioned over both temples. The RUL placement is positioned over the right hemisphere in order to better preserve language-based memory, which is predominantly a function of the left hemisphere. Research has shown that BT ECT is associated with more cognitive side effects than RUL. Many clinicians nevertheless express the opinion that BT ECT is more effective; however, recent evidence indicates that RUL ECT can be as effective as BT ECT. An emerging form of ECT in which the electrodes are placed over the right and left frontal lobes (bifrontal electrode placement) is gaining popularity, as it is felt to have advantages in terms of cognitive side effects over BT ECT while being equally effective. Randomized clinical trials are in process comparing the three electrode placements.

The typical ECT course is 6–12 treatments and is performed with a schedule of two to three treatments per week. Some patients require maintenance treatments to minimize the likelihood of relapse. In fact, the relapse rate for patients who have been successfully treated with ECT is approximately 50% in the six months following an acute ECT course. Many patients and their doctors will choose maintenance ECT every two weeks for at least six months to maintain remission, should the patient relapse on maintenance antidepressant medication alone. Psychotropic medications are usually continued during the treatment and are an important component of maintaining remission following ECT.

Adverse Effects

Headache and nausea are the most common side effects of ECT and can be managed with medications. Cognitive side effects may also occur and limit the use of ECT. Techniques to minimize memory problems include the type of ECT machine used (modern brief pulse machines have much lower frequency of complications than older sine wave machines), the electrode placement (RUL ECT as just noted has fewer side effects than BT ECT), the amount of electrical charge administered (lower charge produces fewer complications), and how often ECT is administered (twice a week causes fewer cognitive side effects than three times a week and has been shown to be equally effective).

Patient variables that are likely to increase cognitive side effects of ECT include dementia, central neurological disorders such as Parkinson's disease, increasing age, and conjoint medications (e.g., lithium). Most patients have a complete return of their baseline cognitive status within weeks of the treatments, although long-term retrograde amnesia has been reported. Memory problems should be monitored closely during the treatments to test both anterograde and retrograde memory problems. Typically anterograde memory loss returns before retrograde memory loss.

Some other possible complications of ECT include acute cardiovascular problems (due to the increased blood pressure and pulse that occur during the seizure), post-ECT agitation, prolonged seizures, prolonged apnea, and confusion between treatments. However complications associated with ECT are minimal when the procedure is done in a hospital setting with an experienced anesthesiologist and psychiatrist administering the treatments. Even though there are several promising future alternatives to ECT (e.g., transcranial magnetic stimulation, deep brain stimulation, and currently approved vagal nerve stimulation), ECT remains the most effective treatment for resistant major depression.

SUGGESTED READINGS

Abrams, R. (1992). *Electroconvulsive therapy,* (2nd ed.). New York: Oxford University Press.

Kellner, C. H. (2001). Towards the modal ECT treatment. *Journal of ECT 17,* 1–2.

Loo, C. K., Schweitzer, I., & Pratt, C. (2006). Recent advances in optimizing electroconvulsive therapy. [Review] [49 refs]. *Australian & New Zealand Journal of Psychiatry 40,* 632–638.

Loo, C. (2008). Cognitive outcomes in electroconvulsive therapy: Optimizing current clinical practice and researching future strategies. *Journal of ECT* Mar. 24(1):1–2.

McDonald, W. M., Thompson T., McCall, W.V., Zorumpski C. Electroconvulsive therapy. In A. F. Schatzberg & C. B. Nemeroff (Eds.), *Textbook of psychopharmacology* (3rd ed.). Arlington, VA: American Psychiatric Publishing.

O'Connor, M. K., Knapp, R., Husain, M., Rummans, T. A., Petrides, G., Smith, G., et al. (2001). The influence of age on the response of major depression to electroconvulsive therapy: A C.O.R.E. Report. *American Journal of Geriatric Psychiatry 9,* 382–390.

Royal College of Psychiatrists. (2004). *The ECT handbook.* Council report CR128 by Royal College of Psychiatrists. London: Royal College of Psychiatrists.

Sackeim, H. A., Prudic, J., Fuller, R., Keilp, J., Lavori, P. W., & Olfson, M. (2007). The cognitive effects of electroconvulsive therapy in community settings. *Neuropsychopharmacology 32,* 244–254.

Weiner, Richard D., & American Psychiatric Association Committee on Electroconvulsive Therapy. (2001). *Practice of electroconvulsive therapy: Recommendations for treatment, training, and privileging.* Task Force Report of the American Psychiatric Association.

ADRIANA P. HERMIDA
WILLIAM M. MCDONALD
Emory University School of Medicine

ELECTROENCEPHALOGRAPHY

First demonstrated by the German psychiatrist and neurologist Hans Berger in 1924 (Karbowski, 2002), electroencephalography (EEG) is the measurement of brain electrical activity via recording electrodes placed on the scalp. Rhythmic variations in this electrical activity assume the form of waves that vary with respect to two key parameters: frequency (the speed of the wave cycles) and amplitude (the size of the wave). A number of distinct rhythms, based on these parameters and denoted using Greek letters, have been identified and are systematically related to variations in consciousness. For instance, the delta rhythm consists of very tall, slow waves that are apparent during deep sleep. The alpha rhythm consists of shorter, faster waves that are apparent during states of relaxation. The beta rhythm consists of short, very fast waves that are apparent during periods of effortful cognitive exertion.

Clinical and Research Applications

Electroencephalography has a number of clinical applications. It is commonly used to inform the diagnosis of epilepsy by determining the nature and anatomical origin of seizure activity in the brain. It is also widely used in the assessment of sleep disorders and organic brain syndromes. In addition, electroencephalography is useful in the confirmation of "brain death," or the complete and irreversible cessation of brain function. Research applications are varied and numerous. Electroencephalography has been fruitfully used to generate important insights into cognitive, attentional, and affective processes.

Strengths and Weaknesses

The main strength of electroencephalography is its excellent temporal resolution; changes in brain activity occur virtually simultaneous to the registration of these changes by the electroencephalogram. Moreover, it is noninvasive and relatively inexpensive.

The main weakness of electroencephalography is its poor spatial resolution; the source of electrical activity recorded from the scalp is difficult or impossible to ascertain using standard equipment and procedures. Use of high-density electrode arrays (which employ up to 256 recording electrodes) may reduce this problem, but they do not totally eliminate it. EEG is also very sensitive to artifact, which is electrical noise that contaminates the electrical activity generated by the brain. Measures to minimize artifact problems are widely available and generally effective.

REFERENCE

Karbowski, K. (2002). Hans Berger (1873–1941). *Journal of Neurology, 249*, 1130–1131.

SUGGESTED READINGS

Davidson, R. J., Jackson, D. C., & Larson, C. L. (2000). Human electroencephalography. In J. T. Cacioppo, L. G. Tassinary, & G. G. Bernston (Eds.), *Handbook of psychophysiology* (2nd ed., pp. 27–52). New York: Cambridge University Press.

Stern, R. M., Ray, W. J., & Quigley, K. S. (2001). *Psychophysiological recording* (2nd ed.). New York: Oxford University Press.

RYAN THIBODEAU
St. John Fisher College, Rochester, NY

EMDR (See Eye Movement Desensitization and Reprocessing)

EMOTION REGULATION

Emotion regulation refers to influencing which emotions one has, when one has them, and how one experiences and expresses these emotions. This includes attempts to change the magnitude and/or duration of behavioral, experiential, and/or physiological aspects of the emotional response. Emotion-regulatory processes may be either automatic or controlled, or conscious or unconscious, and they may dampen, intensify, or maintain positive or negative emotion, depending on one's goals.

History of Emotion Regulation

The idea that emotional responses can be modified in accordance with one's emotional goals is not new. Freud described psychological defenses, or unconscious attempts to subvert emotional responses. An extensive literature on coping has identified techniques that are helpful in attenuating various aspects of the stress response. There is also a tradition of research on self-regulation that encompasses attempts to control one's thoughts, feelings, and behaviors (for a review, see Ochsner & Gross, 2005).

In addition to these forms of intrinsic emotion regulation, emotions can also be regulated extrinsically, via our interactions with others around us. Indeed, developmental and social psychological literatures have explored in some detail the ways that our parents, friends, and spouses can regulate our emotions, and how their emotions in turn can be regulated by our interactions with them (Thompson, 1991).

One enduring challenge for those interested in emotion regulation is how to organize the large number of processes by which individuals regulate their emotions. Our approach has been to conceive of emotions as unfolding over time and to consider the various points in the emotion-generative process at which emotions may be regulated.

In this view, emotions may be seen as arising in psychologically relevant situations that are attended to in some way, which allows one to assess (or appraise) the situation's familiarity, valence, and value relevance (Ellsworth & Scherer, 2003). The emotional responses that follow from these appraisals are reflected in loosely coupled changes in experiential, behavioral, and physiological response systems. Like other responses, emotions often change the situations that prompted them.

The Process Model of Emotion Regulation

This conception of emotion provides a framework for representing the major points in the emotion-generative process

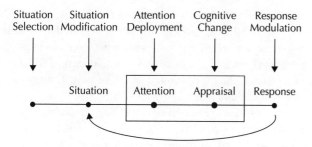

Figure 1. A process model of emotion regulation that highlights five families of emotion regulation strategies (from Gross & Thompson, 2007).

at which one may intervene to shape the trajectory of an emotional response. The process model of emotion regulation (Gross, 1998) organizes regulation strategies according to when in the emotion-generative process the strategy has its primary impact.

At the top of Figure 1, we highlight five points at which regulation can occur. These five points represent five loose-knit families of emotion regulation strategies: situation selection, situation modification, attentional deployment, cognitive change, and response modulation. Although actions often involve multiple regulatory processes, we believe that this process model provides a conceptual framework useful for understanding the causes, consequences, and mechanisms underlying various forms of emotion regulation.

Situation selection is the most forward-looking emotion regulation strategy and involves choosing between situations according to one's own emotional goals. Situation selection requires an ability to predict the likely emotional outcomes of future situations. It also involves balancing the short-term emotional effects of situations with their forecasted longer-term effects, which can often come into conflict with one another.

Situation modification refers to modifying aspects of the environment to meet one's emotional goals. Situation modification requires that one views situations as malleable and sees oneself as an effective agent of change in those situations. Psychologically relevant situations can be external or internal, but situation modification—as defined here—has to do with acting on the external, physical environment.

It is possible to regulate emotions without affecting the external environment. Attentional deployment occurs when one redirects attention in order to influence one's emotions. Depending on one's regulatory goal, attention can be directed toward or away from potentially emotional stimuli or thoughts. In some cases, attentional deployment may be conceived of as situation modification performed upon an internal situation.

Even after a situation has been selected, modified, and attended to, an emotional response requires an evaluation of the situation's meaning and one's capacity to handle the situation. Cognitive change exploits the flexible nature of

appraisal, changing how one evaluates the situation to alter its emotional significance, either by changing how one views the situation or one's capacity to handle it.

Response modulation is a last-ditch effort to change the way an emotional response is manifested. Response modulation refers to attempting to influence responding directly, once the emotion is underway. Examples of response modulation include directly influencing one's physiological state, (e.g., using drugs or exercise) or one's emotional expression (e.g., facial expression, verbal, and nonverbal behavior).

Comparing Consequences of Different Emotion Regulation Strategies

Experimental investigations of different strategies outlined in the process model have begun to reveal important consequences of specific strategies. Cognitive change and response modulation are the most commonly studied forms of emotion regulation. One form of cognitive change that has received particular attention is reappraisal. Several studies have shown that the use of reappraisal can successfully modulate self-reported negative affect, startle eye-blink response, and blood flow to the amygdala (Jackson, Malmstadt, Larsen, & Davidson, 2000; Ochsner & Gross, 2005). One form of response modulation that has received particular attention is the regulation of emotion-expressive behavior. In contrast to reappraisal, decreasing emotion-expressive behavior has mixed effects on emotion experience (decreasing positive but not negative experience) and actually increases activation of the cardiovascular system and amygdala (Gross, 1998; Goldin, McRae, Ramel, & Gross, 2008).

As a complement to experimental studies, individual differences in emotion regulation have been identified as an important link between the immediate consequences of using each strategy and long-term emotional outcomes. Those who report using reappraisal more frequently report lower levels of negative affect, greater well-being, fewer depressive symptoms, and better interpersonal functioning than those who report using it less frequently. By contrast, those who report using expressive suppression more frequently as a regulation strategy report more negative affect, diminished well-being, more depressive symptoms, and poorer interpersonal functioning (Gross & John, 2003).

It bears emphasizing that any one emotion-regulatory process may be helpful in some settings and harmful in others. Although there are some data on the positive and negative ramifications of employing different emotion-regulatory strategies (Gross & John, 2003; Totterdale & Parkinson, 1999), no strategy is likely to be more adaptive than others across all possible contexts. Consistent with a functionalist perspective, regulatory strategies may accomplish a person's own goals but be perceived by others as maladaptive. It seems likely that successful emotion regulation involves the flexible application of a range of context-appropriate emotion regulatory processes.

REFERENCES

Ellsworth, P. C., & Scherer, K. R. (2003). Appraisal processes in emotion. In R. J. Davidson, K. R. Scherer, & H. H. Goldsmith (Eds.), *Handbook of affective sciences* (pp. 572–595). New York: Oxford University Press.

Goldin, P. R., McRae, K., Ramel, W., & Gross, J. J. (2008). The neural bases of emotion regulation: Reappraisal and suppression of negative emotion. *Biological Psychiatry, 63,* 577–586.

Gross, J. J. (1998). Antecedent- and response-focused emotion regulation: Divergent consequences for experience, expression, and physiology. *Journal of Personality and Social Psychology, 74,* 224–237.

Gross, J. J., & John, O. P. (2003). Individual differences in two emotion regulation processes: Implications for affect, relationships, and well-being. *Journal of Personality and Social Psychology, 85,* 348–362.

Gross, J. J., & Thompson, R. A. (2007). Emotion regulation: Conceptual foundations. In J. J. Gross (Ed.), *Handbook of emotion regulation* (pp. 3–24). New York: Guilford Press.

Jackson, D. C., Malmstadt, J. R., Larson, C. L., & Davidson, R. J. (2000). Suppression and enhancement of emotional responses to unpleasant pictures. *Psychophysiology, 37,* 515–522.

Ochsner, K. N., & Gross, J. J. (2005). The cognitive control of emotion. *Trends in Cognitive Sciences, 9,* 242–249.

Parkinson, B., & Totterdell, P. (1999). Classifying affect-regulation strategies. *Cognition & Emotion, 13,* 277.

Thompson, R. A. (1991). Emotional regulation and emotional development. *Educational Psychology Review, 3,* 269–307.

SUGGESTED READING

Gross, J. J. (Ed.). (2007). *Handbook of emotion regulation.* New York: Guilford Press.

KATERI McRAE
JAMES J. GROSS
Stanford University

See also: Coping Behavior; Emotional Development; Emotions

EMOTIONAL DEVELOPMENT

Emotions are a universal and to some extent innate psychological process. Although certain emotions are present at birth, emotions develop and become differentiated throughout the early years of life. Emotional feelings, expression of emotion, and emotional understanding all importantly develop in the first years of life. Emotional development is based on a variety of influences, including cognitive abilities, social interactions, and cultural influences. Although virtually everyone comes to express and experiences a range of emotions, events that elicit emotions and the expression of emotions may differ widely across individuals.

Although the experience of feeling emotions seems familiar, defining what an emotion is has been challenging and lead to differing views among researchers. For example, biological perspectives (e.g., affective neuroscience) emphasize the neural bases of emotions and the belief that each emotion can be defined by a specific neurophysiological substrate. A functionalist perspective on emotion, on the other hand, posits that emotions are elicited on the basis of appraisals of the environment in relation to one's goals. Emotional development is thus affected by cognitive development, including the ability to perceive and appraise the environment. Despite differing perspectives on emotions, at least two points of consensus are evident among emotion researchers: (1) cognitive and emotional processes unfold together in the experience of emotion, and (2) emotions have a function in both self-regulation (i.e., intrapersonal functioning) and in the regulation of social interactions with others (i.e., interpersonal relationships).

The study of emotion in infancy is complicated by the fact that infants do not possess the language capabilities to tell us how they are feeling. Instead, emotions are inferred from infants' facial expressions. Basic emotion expressions are present immediately following birth and develop over the course of the first couple of years of life (Camras et al., 1998). Infants are born with only two general states of arousal, suggesting that emotion is relatively undifferentiated at this point. At birth, infants feel attraction to pleasant stimuli and withdrawal from negative stimuli (Fox, 1991). In the early months following birth infants develop more specific emotions, as inferred from infants' facial expressions. These emotions include happiness, interest, and surprise in response to pleasant stimuli, and fear, anger, sadness, and disgust in response to negative stimuli (Izard et al., 1995).

Infants begin showing interest in pleasant stimuli, such as the human face, during the first 2–8 months of infancy (Langsdorf, Izard, Ravias, & Henbree, 1983). They begin smiling in response to adults' facial expressions and laughing when shown exciting stimuli, like active toys. During these early months infants also begin expressing negative emotion, such as sadness due to disruptions in parent-infant interactions. Expressions of anger begin to develop in infants between four and six months of age, with the frequency of anger increasing over the first year and a half of life (Izard, Hembree, & Huebner, 1987). In addition to anger, infants develop more frequent experiences of other negative emotions throughout these months. Particularly, increases in fear arise as infants are faced with more distressing social situations that increase anxiety, such as the presence of an unfamiliar adult or separation from a caregiver. The development of emotions facilitates exploration of the environment, learning, and affiliative behaviors, which develop simultaneously with changes in children's cognitive abilities and social environment.

Positive emotions (e.g., happiness) can be observed in early development in response to novel circumstances. These emotions also function to communicate pleasure to others and to advance opportunities to gain knowledge and skills in social environments. Infants become aware of their ability to regulate and control their own behavior and their social environment in the context of developing cognitive and motor skills over the first year of life. Both pleasant and negative emotions increase in frequency and intensity throughout the first year. Children are pleased when discovering that they can exert control on objects and other people and are displeased when something prevents them from exerting this control. With further cognitive development and sensitivity to social stimuli, the infant begins to discriminate threatening from nonthreatening situations more effectively, and the frequency of negative emotions begins to decrease.

Children also learn from their social environment when it is appropriate to express particular emotions, and this learning affects the frequency of positive and negative emotional expressions. Throughout toddlerhood, more complex emotions develop, and these self-conscious or social emotions are related to the development of children's sense of self. Toddlers develop a growing repertoire of emotions, including shame, embarrassment, guilt, and pride. The development of these emotions becomes better organized and more clearly contingent on social interaction with caregivers and the surrounding environment. Embarrassment appears to be the earliest of the so-called secondary emotions with the onset of children's recognition of their reflection in mirrors. Other emotions (e.g., shame, guilt, pride) require an additional understanding beyond self-recognition; they involve an appreciation of the standards that are used to evaluate one's conduct (Lewis, Stranger, & Sullivan, 1989). These emotions continue to develop throughout the third year of life. For example, distinctions between types of embarrassment arise, such that simple uneasiness from the attention of others is distinct from a more complex uneasiness over the negative evaluation of one's own behavior.

Parents' reactions to situations contribute heavily to whether children experience certain emotions. A negative response from a parent or having a parent who emphasizes failure may provoke these self-conscious emotions, such as embarrassment or guilt, more readily in children. On the other hand, a positive parental response or a having a parent who focuses on small successes rather than on failure may not elicit these self-conscious emotions in the child (Hoffman, 2000). Children are more likely to display self-conscious emotions when parents are present to observe their behavior, suggesting that their expressions are largely a response to the reactions they anticipate receiving from others. Children do not begin to completely internalize the evaluative standards for their behavior until elementary school. As this internalization develops, they are able to experience these complex emotions regardless of external evaluation.

Another important component of emotional development is children's ability to recognize and understand emotions in others. This ability develops in part based on infants' abilities to recognize and interpret others' emotional cues. In early infancy babies begin detecting others' emotions, as evidenced by infants smiling, laughing, or feeling sad when seeing others express these emotions. Typically between 7 and 10 months of age, infants recognize others' facial expressions. As their cognitive skills improve, infants are able to understand that emotional expressions are meaningful and are elicited in response to a particular occurrence. Following this development, infants begin to look for emotional cues from others, such as caregivers, in uncertain situations. Infants begin evaluating their environment for information to maintain their goal of feeling safe and secure around 8 to 10 months. They often turn to trusted individuals during emotionally arousing situations.

Caregivers' emotional expressions during uncertain situations influence infants' social interaction with unfamiliar objects and individuals. This social referencing helps infants learn about their social world through recognizing and responding to caregivers' emotional cues. For example, infants can learn to avoid harmful situations and to feel safe to explore in unfamiliar environments by referencing their caregiver's signals. This continues developing across toddlerhood, and infants in their second year of life are able to recognize that others' emotions may differ from their own emotional response to the same event. Toddlers utilize this information to develop an understanding of others' preferences and to guide their own interactions with them.

Discussion of emotions between caregivers and toddlers also plays a fundamental role in children's emotional development. Children begin talking about emotions toward the end of the second year of life, and family discussions about emotional experiences can provide children with a rich understanding of their own and others' emotions. Toddlers who have discussions with their families about emotion are more likely to interpret others' emotions accurately.

By kindergarten children are able to recognize others' emotions through gestures and other body language, beyond mere facial expressions. They also begin to understand that emotion may not necessarily be elicited by a current event, but rather by thoughts about past occurrences. School-age children also learn that the same event (e.g., seeing an animal) does not necessarily induce the same emotional reaction (e.g., fear or excitement) in everyone, as well as recognizing that multiple emotions (e.g., joy, sadness) may be experienced at the same time, for example, mixed feelings at the end of a school year. With increases in cognitive development and social experiences across childhood, children begin to integrate the facial, behavioral, and situational cues around them to infer what emotions others might be feeling.

In summary, emotional development is a complex psychological process that develops in conjunction with cognitive and social development. It is a particularly important psychological process, in that the ability to experience, express, and convey emotion has implications for people's functioning in multiple domains, including self-regulatory behaviors and social interactions with others.

REFERENCES

Camras, L. A., Osterm, H., Campos, J., Campos, R., Ujiie, T., Miyake, K., et al. (1998). Production of emotional facial expression in European American, Japanese, and Chinese infants. *Developmental Psychology, 34,* 616–628.

Fox, N. A. (1991). If it's not left, it's right: Electroencephalograph asymmetry and the development of emotion. *American Psychologist, 46,* 863–872.

Hoffman, M. L. (2000). *Empathy and moral development: Implications for caring and justice.* Cambridge, UK: Cambridge University Press.

Izard, C., Fantauzzo, C. A., Castle, J. M., Haynes, O. M., Rayias, M. F., & Putnam, P. H. (1995). The ontogeny and significance of infants' facial expression in the first 9 months of life. *Developmental Psychology, 31,* 997–1013.

Izard, C. E., Hembree, E. A., & Huebner, R. R. (1987). Infants' emotion expressions to acute pain: Developmental change and stability of individual differences. *Developmental Psychology, 23,* 105–113.

Langsdorf, P., Izard, C. E., Ravias, M., & Hembree, E. A. (1983). Interest expression, visual fixation, and heart rate changes in 2- and 8-month old infants. *Developmental Psychology, 19,* 375–386.

Lewis, M., Stanger, C., & Sullivan, M. W. (1989). Deception in 3-year-olds. *Developmental Psychology, 25,* 439–443.

SUGGESTED READINGS

Denham, S. (1998). *Emotional development in young children.* New York: Guilford Press.

Mascolo, M. F., & Griffin, S. (Eds). (1998). *What develops in emotional development?* New York: Plenum Press.

E. Mark Cummings
Melissa R.W. George
Chrystyna D. Kouros
University of Notre Dame

See also: **Affective Development; Cognitive Development; Emotion Regulation; Emotions**

EMOTIONAL DISTURBANCES

Emotional disturbances are found in nearly all disorders in the current version of the *Diagnostic and Statistical Manual* (DSM-IV-TR; American Psychiatric Association, 2000), the official diagnostic system used by mental health professionals. These disturbances span positive and negative emotions and include excesses of emotion (e.g., too much anxiety), deficits in emotion (e.g., lack of self-conscious emotions like embarrassment), disconnections among emotion response components (e.g., strong feelings without outward expression), emotion understanding problems (e.g., misinterpreting the emotional intent of others), and regulation problems (e.g., uncontrollable anger outbursts). Not only are emotion disturbances pervasive, but also many of these disturbances cut across traditional diagnostic boundaries.

For example, excessive irritability can be observed in disorders as diverse as attention-deficit/hyperactivity disorder (ADHD), generalized anxiety disorder (GAD), substance withdrawal, and bipolar disorder. Anhedonia, which refers to a loss of interest or pleasure, can be observed in depression, schizophrenia, posttraumatic stress disorder (PTSD), and Alzheimer's disease. Thus, many emotional disturbances may be transdiagnostic, which suggests the exciting possibility that these disturbances may be similarly treated, even though they are embedded within different disorders (Kring, 2008). Not only are emotional disturbances observed across disorders but also more than one disturbance may be observed in a specific disorder. For example, frontotemporal lobar dementia (FTLD) is characterized by deficits in the experience of certain emotions, such as embarrassment, as well as impairment in the ability to understand others' emotions. In this article, we provide examples of different transdiagnostic emotional disturbances.

In order to more clearly understand emotional disturbances, it is important to first define *emotion*. Broadly speaking, emotions are complex systems that have developed through the course of human evolutionary history to prepare us to respond to a number of environmental stimuli and challenges. Contrary to conventional wisdom that emotions get in the way of rational behavior, contemporary research confirms that under most circumstances, emotions favorably impact our individual functioning and interactions with other people (e.g., Keltner & Kring, 1998). Unfortunately, emotional disturbances can interfere with these helpful functions. For example, the absence of facial expressions in people with schizophrenia may evoke negative responses from others, thus adversely affecting their relationships and interactions.

Typically, emotions are considered to have multiple components, including (but not limited to) expression, experience, and physiological response. The extent to which these components correspond or cohere with one another is a current debate in the field. Thus, although it would make sense that vigorous laughter would correspond to strong feelings of amusement in most situations, there are nevertheless circumstances in which outward expressions may not correspond with our feelings. For example, Olympic athletes may weep upon receiving a gold medal, even though they are probably experiencing great pride and joy. Of course, there are also situations where it is adaptive for us to hide or amplify our emotional expressions, even if they do not correspond to our feelings. For example, if you feel amused in church, it would be in service of polite behavior to suppress the corresponding laughter. Hiding or amplifying our emotions falls under the rubric of emotion regulation (Gross, 1998). Recent affective neuroscience research has greatly advanced our understanding of how the brain is involved in emotion (e.g., Wager et al., 2008).

Types of Emotional Disturbances

Emotional disturbances that reflect too much emotion, or excesses, are exemplified by feeling or showing strong emotions that are not helpful or needed in a particular situation. Although emotions are fundamentally adaptive, at excessive levels, they may interfere with their own adaptive functions. For example, panic disorder involves the extreme experience and expression of fear and its attendant physiological responses (e.g., racing heart rate) in the absence of any life-threatening situation. Similarly, a person with social anxiety can be paralyzed by intense anxiety feelings and physiological responses in a social situation, such as speaking in front of others. Excesses of positive emotions can also have deleterious consequences. For example, an individual with bipolar disorder (formerly called manic depression) may feel intense amounts of euphoria. Although this might seem pleasant, this intense euphoria is often associated with risky behaviors (e.g., excessive spending or sexual behavior), and it can quickly turn into intense negative emotions, such as extreme irritability.

Other emotional disturbances are characterized by too little, or *deficits* in, emotion that may have disadvantageous or damaging consequences. For example, antisocial personality disorder is characterized by little remorse for actions that harm others; however, this does not fully characterize the negative emotional impoverishment believed to be central to this disorder. In the early 1940s, Hervey Cleckley provided a rich description of psychopathy—the precursor to the current diagnostic system's category of antisocial personality disorder—that emphasized diminished emotional reactions and a lack of anxiety. Contemporary research has confirmed that individuals with psychopathy fail to marshal the experiential and physiological responses to negative emotional stimuli (pictures, sounds, cues of imminent punishment) that other people do. Perhaps surprisingly, major depressive disorder can also be characterized by too little emotion. Even though a key symptom of this disorder is persistent sadness, recent research supports the view that individuals with major depressive disorder exhibit dampened positive and *negative* emotional responses that are not consistent with the level of response indicated by the situation (Rottenberg, 2005). Furthermore, apathy, which has been conceptualized as a lack of emotion, commonly occurs in diverse neurodegenerative disorders, such as FTLD and Alzheimer's disease.

Schizophrenia is an example of a disorder that involves disconnections among emotion components. Individuals with this disorder experience strong feelings, much the same as individuals without schizophrenia, yet they do not outwardly display these feelings. Thus, to an observer, individuals with schizophrenia may appear to be emotionless. Studies that assess multiple components of emotion have shown, however, that individuals with schizophrenia do not have a disturbance in the experience or physiology components of emotion. Rather, the disturbance is largely confined to the expression of emotion (Kring & Moran, 2008).

Being able to perceive and understand others' emotions is critical for social interactions. Deficits in emotion understanding are observed in many disorders. For example, individuals with schizophrenia have difficulty perceiving emotion in the faces and voices of others. Individuals with FTLD have difficulty recognizing some (e.g., fearful, sad), but not other (e.g., happy) emotions. Individuals with generalized anxiety disorder or major depressive disorder tend to see negative emotion in other people even when it is not present. Children with autism have difficulty understanding complex social emotions, such as embarrassment or pride, but not other emotions, such as happiness and sadness.

Many current diagnostic criteria explicitly refer to emotion regulation difficulties. For example, difficulty with controlling anger in borderline personality disorder, efforts to avoid feelings in PTSD, difficulty with controlling worry in generalized anxiety disorder, and rapidly shifting expressions of emotion in histrionic personality disorder all point to difficulties in regulating emotions. An important component of emotion regulation is the ability to modulate the time course of emotional responses. Not only are many of the anxiety disorders characterized by too much emotion (anxiety, fear) but also they are associated with a relative inability to regulate or stop these feelings. Appropriate timing of emotional responses also includes the anticipation of things to come, and it appears that individuals with schizophrenia and major depressive disorder have difficulty anticipating situations that will lead to positive emotions.

Frontotemporal lobar dementia is a common type of dementia that impacts areas of the brain known to be involved in emotion, including amygdalae and orbitofrontal cortex, and it appears that individuals with FTLD have difficulties in emotion regulation, but only in situations that are fairly complex (Levenson & Miller,

2008). For example, individuals with FTLD can regulate their feelings when instructed to do so, but they have trouble doing so spontaneously, even when it would be most helpful to implement a regulation strategy (e.g., to dampen the effects of a loud, startling noise; Goodkind, Guryek, & Levenson, 2008).

Treating Emotional Disturbances

There are effective psychosocial and pharmacological treatments for emotional disturbances, some of which hold promise as transdiagnostic treatments. For example, David Barlow and colleagues have developed a unified psychosocial treatment for the mood and anxiety disorders (Moses & Barlow, 2006). The treatment has three main components: (1) altering cognitive reappraisals, a key component in emotion regulation processes; (2) preventing emotional avoidance; and (3) changing emotion action tendencies, or replacing emotion behavior associated with fear and anxiety with behavior related to positive emotions.

Medication is another commonly used form of treatment for emotional disturbances, particularly antidepressant medications. Many medications that were originally approved by the Food and Drug Administration for the treatment of depression have since received approval for the treatment of other disorders. Studies have found that antidepressant medications are effective at reducing the symptoms of several disorders, including specific and social phobia, panic disorder, GAD, obsessive-compulsive disorder, PTSD, some of the personality disorders, and eating disorders.

In summary, emotional disturbances are common yet treatable. In order to clearly identify and treat these disturbances, it is important to specify the nature of the disturbance by indicating which component(s) of emotion are disrupted. An equally important consideration is whether the emotional disturbance is an antecedent, a concomitant, or a consequence of the disorder(s) within which it is embedded. Locating the emotional disturbance in the developmental course of disorders will ultimately help us better pinpoint the causes of such disturbances, identify those disturbances that cut across different disorders, and develop treatments that will help those who struggle with these emotion-related difficulties.

REFERENCES

American Psychiatric Association. (2000). *Diagnostic and statistical manual of mental disorders* (4th ed., text rev.). Washington, DC: Author.

Goodkind, M. S., Guryek, A., & Levenson, R. L. (2008). *Emotion regulation deficits in frontotemporal lobar degeneration and Alzheimer's disease*. Manuscript submitted for publication.

Gross, J. J. (1998). The emerging field of emotion regulation: An integrative review. *Review of General Psychology, 2*, 271–299.

Keltner, D., & Kring, A. M. (1998). Emotion, social function, and psychopathology. *Review of General Psychology, 2*, 320–342.

Kring, A. M. (2008). Emotion disturbances as transdiagnostic processes in psychopathology. In M. Lewis, J. M. Haviland-Jones, & L. F. Barrett (Eds.), *Handbook of emotion* (3rd ed., pp. 691–705). New York: Guilford Press.

Kring, A. M., & Moran, E. K. (2008). *Emotional response deficits in schizophrenia: Insights from affective science*. Manuscript submitted for publication.

Levenson, R. W., & Miller, B. L. (2008). Loss of cells, loss of self: Frontotemporal lobar degeneration and human emotion. *Current Directions in Psychological Science, 16*, 289–294.

Moses, E. B., & Barlow, D. H. (2006). A new unified treatment approach for emotional disorders based on emotion science. *Current Directions in Psychological Science, 15*, 146–150.

Rottenberg, J. (2005). Mood and emotion in major depression. *Current Directions in Psychological Science, 14*, 167–170.

Wager, T. D., Barrett, L. F., Bliss-Moreau, E., et al. (2008). The neuroimaging of emotion. In M. Lewis, J. M. Haviland-Jones, & L. F. Barrett (Eds.), *Handbook of emotions* (3rd ed.). New York: Guilford Press.

SUGGESTED READINGS

Berenbaum, H., Raghavan, G., Le, H.-N., Vernon, L. L., & Gomez, J. J. (2003). A taxonomy of emotional disturbances. *Clinical Psychology: Science and Practice, 10*, 206–226.

Kring, A. M. (2008). Emotion disturbances as transdiagnostic processes in psychopathology. In M. Lewis, J. M. Haviland-Jones, & L. F. Barrett (Eds.), *Handbook of emotion* (3rd ed., pp. 691–705). New York: Guilford Press.

ANN M. KRING
MADELEINE S. GOODKIND
University of California, Berkeley

EMOTIONAL INTELLIGENCE

Interest in emotional intelligence (EI) and related concepts has a long history in psychology. However, the earliest intelligence quotient (IQ) tests focused on cognitive abilities, and research on the social and emotional skills necessary for successful functioning continued to lag behind work on the purely cognitive ones. Then in the early 1980s psychologists like Gardner (1983) and Sternberg (1985) proposed that there are other kinds of intelligences, and in 1990 Salovey and Mayer began publishing on a new form of intelligence that they called emotional intelligence (Salovey & Mayer, 1990).

Current interest in EI has been fueled in part by the realization that the mental qualities measured by IQ tests do not necessarily ensure positive life outcomes.

Anecdotally, there are the stories of high school and college "geniuses" who post perfect scores on the SATs but end up achieving far less than classmates with more modest intellectual ability. And then there are the many examples of smart people who do foolish things. Research has supported these anecdotal observations to a degree. Measures of traditional intelligence have accounted for only a limited amount of the variability in performance. Estimates have differed depending on the measures used and the population studied; however, traditional IQ tests rarely predict more than 25% of the variability in success or effectiveness for key criteria.

Some studies have found that IQ predicts 10% or less (Neisser et al., 1996). At the same time, there is research suggesting that abilities such as being able to handle frustration, control emotions, and get along with other people make the biggest difference in how happy and successful people are (Snarey & Vaillant, 1985). This research eventually led to the notion that EI, which includes the ability to perceive and manage emotions in one's self and others, might be particularly important for positive adaptation.

EI has been defined in various ways. One popular definition is that it is "the ability to carry out accurate reasoning about emotions and the ability to use emotions and emotional knowledge to enhance thought" (Mayer, Roberts, & Barsade, 2008, p. 511). Based on this definition, EI includes a relatively narrow range of abilities, such as the perception, use, understanding, and management of emotional information. However, EI also has been defined more broadly as a set of competencies that enable a person to be effective in a job, successful in life, happy as a person, and a contributing member of society. Using this broader definition, some researchers have included a much larger range of abilities and personality traits, such as stress tolerance, self-regard, and achievement motivation. The question of which definition and model of EI is "right" has led to a lively debate among different researchers in the field.

There also has been a lively debate about the best way to measure EI. One approach is to ask a person to perform a series of tasks, similar to what one might find in a traditional IQ test. For instance, the Mayer-Salovey-Caruso Emotional Intelligence Test (MSCEIT) assesses emotion perception by asking test-takers to identify emotions in faces and landscapes. One problem with ability tests is that, unlike traditional IQ tests, the determination of a right or wrong answer is less clear. Also, like IQ tests, EI ability tests at best only measure a person's potential; they do not indicate the extent to which the person is actually using that potential effectively in real-life situations.

A second approach to measuring EI asks people to describe themselves. This approach is similar to a traditional personality test. For instance, an item designed to measure emotional self-awareness, found in a test called the EQ-i, reads, "I'm in touch with my emotions." A criticism that has been raised about this approach is that people often are not very good judges of their own abilities. A person who was actually low in emotional self-awareness, for example, might think mistakenly that he was "in touch with" his emotions.

A third approach to measuring EI asks a number of people who know the target person to rate the person on various aspects of EI. An example of this approach is the Emotional and Social Competence Inventory (ESCI). A multirater measure avoids the kind of self-deception bias that can hamper a self-report measure; but raters may not be good judges of EI, and relationship dynamics between the raters and the target person can introduce various forms of bias.

The development of different EI tests has been a major focus of research activity. Some of the tests appear to be promising in terms of traditional standards concerning reliability and validity. However, test development efforts still are at a relatively early stage, and at this point there are no EI tests that have the kind of track record that older, established personality and mental ability tests have.

However it is measured, EI seems to be associated with a variety of important life outcomes, even when cognitive intelligence and personality traits are controlled. For instance, children and adolescents who score higher in EI tend to get along better with others. They also are less likely to engage in socially deviant behavior. The same trends have been found for adults. In addition, EI appears to be correlated with better performance and greater success in the workplace, although the magnitude of its impact depends on the type of job and work situation, as well as what measure of EI is used. EI also is correlated with indicators of psychological well-being. The link between EI and academic achievement is less clear; research findings have been mixed (Mayer et al., 2008).

Those interested in practical applications have been especially curious about whether EI can be taught or developed. Unfortunately, there has been much less research on this topic. A number of studies have shown that competencies included in the broader definitions of EI, such as empathy, stress tolerance, achievement motivation, and optimism can be developed in both children and adults (Cherniss & Adler, 2000; Durlak, Weissberg, Taylor, Dymnicki, & Schellinger, 2008). There has been less research examining whether core abilities such as emotion perception can be developed, but a few studies have provided some promising results (Elfenbein, 2006). Some of these studies have used comparison groups with pretests and post-tests, but few have used more rigorous random assignment control group designs.

Much also remains to be learned about important questions such as whether there are gender or cultural differences in EI. Women do seem to perform better on certain aspects of EI, particularly those relating to emotion perception. However, men may perform somewhat better when it comes to emotion management. In any case, these differences appear to be small. Even less is known about cultural differences, but it is likely that this will be an active area of research in the future. In fact, it seems likely that EI in general will continue to be a popular topic for research in the coming years.

REFERENCES

Cherniss, C., & Adler, M. (2000). *Promoting emotional intelligence in organizations.* Alexandria, VA: ASTD.

Durlak, J. A., Weissberg, R. P., Taylor, R. D., Dymnicki, A. B., & Schellinger, K. (2008). *A meta-analysis of school-based social and emotional learning programs.* Manuscript submitted for publication.

Elfenbein, H. A. (2006). Learning in emotion judgments: Training and the cross-cultural understanding of facial expressions. *Journal of Nonverbal Behavior, 30,* 21–36.

Gardner, H. (1983). *Frames of mind.* New York: Basic Books.

Mayer, J. D., Roberts, R. D., & Barsade, S. G. (2008). Human abilities: Emotional intelligence. *Annual Review of Psychology, 59,* 507–536.

Neisser, U., Boodoo, G., Bouchard, T. J., Jr., Boykin, A. W., Brody, N., Ceci, S. J., et al. (1996). Intelligence: Knowns and unknowns. *American Psychologist, 51*(2), 77–101.

Salovey, P., & Mayer, J. (1990). Emotional intelligence. *Imagination, cognition, and personality, 9*(3), 185–211.

Snarey, J. R., & Vaillant, G. E. (1985). How lower- and working-class youth become middle-class adults: The association between ego defense mechanisms and upward social mobility. *Child Development, 56*(4), 899–910.

Sternberg, R. J. (1985). *Beyond IQ: A triarchic theory of human intelligence.* New York: Cambridge University Press.

SUGGESTED READING

Druskat, V. U., Sala, F., & Mount, G. (Eds.). (2006). *Linking emotional intelligence and performance at work.* Mahwah, NJ: Lawrence Erlbaum.

CARY CHERNISS
Rutgers University

See also: Emotions; Intelligence; Social Competence

EMOTIONS

Over the last 10 years, the field of psychology has witnessed an increased interest in emotional processes. This interest has been fueled by considerable advances in (1) understanding and investigating structural components of emotion (e.g., neurobiology); (2) functional roles of emotions in development, cognition, memory, and attention; and (3) the relevance of these processes to health outcomes such as psychopathology and the promotion and treatment of mental health.

Structure of Emotions

Unlike many other processes that are the focus of psychological inquiry, such as cognitions, memory, or attention, emotions are not confined to the brain. Rather, emotional processes are localized throughout our bodies, phenomena we capture when we say that we feel "butterflies in our stomach" or express a need to "catch our breath." Indeed, emotional responses are the result of the orchestrated activity of several components: biological (peripheral physiology and central neurobiology), behavioral (motoric behaviors and facial expressions), and subjective experience (feelings and appraisals); thus we consider emotions to have a multisystemic structure. For example, when we are confronted with a perceived threat, biological indices may involve the sympathetic nervous system preparing the automatic "fight or flight" response, our muscles preparing for this response, and our minds helping us assign linguistic meaning to our experience. However, the exact nature of the relationship between these domains is not yet well understood.

Given the multisystemic nature of emotions, it is possible for these components to often lack convergence in their responses. This potential for lack of convergence has theoretical and methodological implications. Different emotion theorists have argued for different definitions of emotions based on how these components of emotion have converged. The James-Lange theory of emotion focuses on subjective awareness of physiological responses to emotion-eliciting stimuli. In this way, we experience emotion by interpreting physiological responses, so we feel afraid because we startle; it is the perception of our increased heart rate and muscle tension that constitute the startle response that leads to the subjective experience of fear. Strong evidence for this theory comes from studies that have tested the facial feedback hypothesis, which states that making a facial expression actually influences the emotional experience. By placing awareness of the physiological states as central to the experience of emotion, the James-Lange theory makes the experience of emotion dependent on the awareness of physiological states.

Criticism of the James-Lange theory comes from the Cannon-Bard theory, which postulates that the viscera are relatively insensitive structures and that visceral changes are too slow to be the source of emotional feeling. This theory poses that emotion-eliciting stimuli simultaneously trigger both physiological responses and the subjective experience of emotion. Thus, it rejects the notion of awareness of physiological states as the determinant of the emotional experience.

Another view on the relationship between physiological awareness and emotional experience comes from the two-factor theory of emotion developed by Schacter and Singer. These theorists proposed that emotional experience is dependent not only on the awareness of physiological arousal, but also on the label that is adjudicated to that arousal. In a series of classic experiments, they administered norepinephrine to participants in order to produce arousal and modified the context in which the experiment took place. In line with expectations, they were able to show that the same type of experimentally induced arousal took the form of different emotions depending on the appraisals that individuals made in response to the contextual factors to which they were exposed.

Function of Emotions

In addition to structure, emotions have been defined based on their function. Functionalist views are largely based on the evolutionary approach and suggest that if emotions have evolved over time and across species, they must provide organisms with advantages to adapt to their environment. Specifically, these theories state that emotions are comprised of an innate process of motivation that protects us from noxious stimuli and directs us towards appetitive stimuli. In this way, emotions play a role in facilitating adaptation to complex environments.

Functional conceptualizations of emotions establish that emotions provide useful information about the environment (i.e., have an "aboutness" to them) and prepare organisms for action (i.e., action tendencies). Thus emotions are integrally tied to the way we interact with the world around us, and as such, to our thoughts, decisions, motivations, actions, and communication, among others. They are critical to the decision-making process, as they signal adaptive and maladaptive decisions to individuals before they are consciously aware of them (Bechara, Damasio, Tranel, & Damasio, 1997). Emotions are also linked to motivational processes, as they relate to approach and avoidance tendencies. More specifically, emotions are considered to be central to the behavioral approach system (BAS), which is hypothesized to increase goal-motivated behaviors in response to the environment, and the behavioral inhibition system (BIS), which is hypothesized to increase behaviors of avoidance and inhibition (Gray, 2000). Finally, emotions are integrally involved in social interaction, providing not only informational value, but also interpersonal value by facilitating rapid communication among individuals (e.g., facial expressions).

Integrative Perspectives

Recent investigators, such as LeDoux (1996), have emphasized the importance of both structural and functional aspects of emotions. LeDoux has developed a model of emotional processing that posits the existence of two structural systems for emotion processing, namely a "low" and "high" route, that serve different functions. In the low route, sensory information goes through the thalamus and directly reaches the amygdala, bypassing cortical centers. In this way, this pathway allows for a quick detection of environmental cues and the production of fast and automatic responses. In contrast, in the higher route, sensory information passes through the thalamus and reaches the neocortex, where it is contextualized and meaning is assigned. This high pathway allows for a more thorough evaluation of the emotional information, which results in more flexibility in the orchestration of responses. These two routes are, therefore, complementary and are necessary for responses to different contexts. This theory synthesizes different views on the relationship between physiological arousal and subjective experience.

Emotion Dysfunction

Functionalist views of emotions do not maintain that emotions are always adaptive; rather they are useful to the organism insomuch as they provide flexibility to respond to the demands of the environment. For example, when intense fear prevents an organism from reacting to the environment and severely endangers it, the emotion is no longer adaptive. Thus, emotions need to be properly channeled, or regulated, to be advantageous to the organism. Emotion regulation is "the process by which individuals influence which emotions they have, when they have them, and how they experience and express them" (Gross, 1998, p. 275). Emotions not properly regulated can result in emotional experiences or expressions that are either too strong or weak for the situation at hand. This inability to respond effectively to one's emotions according to situational constraints has been termed emotion dysregulation.

Emotion dysregulation has been placed at the core of many psychological disorders, such as generalized anxiety disorder, unipolar and bipolar depression, borderline personality disorder, and substance abuse disorders, among others. The growth in the interest of emotions in psychology has influenced the development of models of psychopathology that not only incorporate emotion dysregulation as the core of disorders, but also as a target for treatment and prevention. This is the case with "third wave" acceptance- and mindfulness-based behavioral therapies, which have placed an emphasis on emotional processes, by advocating awareness and acceptance of emotional states rather than avoidance, distraction, or reappraisal.

In addition to treatment implications, emotions have elucidated prevention efforts and underscored their importance. Central to these prevention efforts has been the construct of emotional intelligence, which involves a set of emotion-related skills, including perceptual processing of emotions, facilitating thought process through emotions, understanding of emotions, and reflective regulation of emotions (Mayer, Salovey, & Caruso, 2004). The concept of emotion intelligence has reached massive audiences through the publication of highly popular books.

Additionally, it has become the focus of school-based interventions, with researchers and educators interested in exploring the relationship between emotional intelligence and academic achievement and social functioning in children and adolescents.

In summary, despite a large body of research produced as a result of increased interest in emotions, many questions still remain unsolved. Of particular interest to both emotion theorists and clinical psychologists is the relationship between the structure and function of emotions. A better understanding of this relationship has the promise of influencing the development of models of emotion that can be used for the prevention and treatment of clinical disorders.

REFERENCES

Bechara, A., Damasio, H., Tranel, D., & Damasio, A. (1997). Deciding advantageously before knowing the advantageous strategy. *Science, 275,* 1293–1295.

Gray, J. A., & McNaughton, N. (2000). *The neuropsychology of anxiety: An enquiry into the functions of the septo-hippocampal system* (2nd ed.). New York: Oxford University Press.

Gross, J. J. (1998). The emerging field of emotion regulation: An integrative review. *Review of General Psychology, 2,* 271–299.

LeDoux, J. (1996). *The emotional brain: The mysterious underpinnings of emotional life.* New York: Touchstone Press.

Mayer, J. D., Salovey, P., & Caruso, D. R. (2004). Emotional intelligence: Theory, findings, and implications. *Psychological Inquiry, 15,* 197–215.

SUGGESTED READINGS

Cornelius, R. (1996). *The science of emotion: Research and tradition in the psychology of emotion.* Upper Saddle River, NJ: Prentice Hall.

Ekman, P., & Davidson, R. J. (1994). *The nature of emotion.* New York: Oxford.

LIA ALDAO
DOUGLAS S. MENNIN
Yale University

See also: **Emotion Regulation; Emotional Development; Emotional Intelligence**

EMPATHY (See Interpersonal Perception)

EMPIRICALLY SUPPORTED TREATMENTS

Empirically supported treatments (ESTs), which were previously known as empirically validated treatments (EVTs) and more recently as evidence-based treatments (EBTs), are psychological treatments that have been shown to be effective in well-conducted controlled research trials. The initial and perhaps most influential effort to identify ESTs was undertaken in 1993 by a task force commissioned by the Society of Clinical Psychology, which is Division 12 of the American Psychological Association (APA) (cf. Task Force on Promotion and Dissemination of Psychological Procedures, 1993).

For a research trial to be considered as evidence for a particular treatment, it must have met the following criteria: (1) characteristics of the sample treated must be clearly specified (e.g., diagnosis such as major depression, or problem such as chronic pain), (2) participants must be randomly assigned to the treatment condition, (3) a control or comparison group must have been used (e.g., alternative treatment such as medication), and (4) clinician's treatment must have been delivered via a manual that specifically describes the treatment protocol. As elaborated by Chambless et al. (1998), it is possible to meet criteria for an EST by using single subject experimental designs.

For a treatment to be labeled as an EST, at least two studies meeting the criteria just listed must demonstrate that the treatment is either (1) equivalent to an already established treatment or (2) superior to a placebo drug or psychotherapy placebo condition. The Division 12 task force further categorized treatments depending upon the strength of existing evidence into one of two levels: well-established and probably efficacious. Well-established treatments were defined as those for which at least two between-group design experiments demonstrate their efficacy in at least one of the following ways: (1) superiority to pill or psychotherapy placebo, or to another treatment or (2) equivalence to already established treatment. It is important to note that, to be labeled as a well-established EST, efficacy must be demonstrated by at least two different investigators or teams. Probably efficacious treatments are those for which there are at least two experiments demonstrating that the treatment is superior to a waiting-list control group (rather than a pill or psychotherapy placebo for well-established treatments) or those that meet the same criteria as well-established treatments, but for which there has not been replication by two different investigators or teams. Treatments not yet tested in trials meeting task force criteria for methodology are considered "experimental treatments."

The Division 12 task force was transformed into a standing committee of Division 12, the Committee on Science and Practice, and it continues its efforts today. The most recent publications containing lists of specific treatments labeled ESTs can be found online at http://www.apa.org/divisions/div12/journals.html).

Other professional efforts to identify ESTs have since been undertaken. Perhaps the most comprehensive effort to date is *A Guide to Treatments that Work*, now in its second edition (Nathan & Gorman, 1998; 2002). In these edited volumes, various content experts review and identify psychosocial and pharmacological treatments meeting criteria independent of but similar to those used by the original Division 12 group. Another effort is contained in a special section of the *Journal of Consulting and Clinical Psychology* in which Kendall and Chambless (1998) report results of EST reviews for adults, children, and marital and family therapies.

ESTs for problems common to the elderly have been offered by Gatz and colleagues (1998), as have ESTs for treatment of chronic pain conditions (Wilson & Gil, 1996). Another task force of Division 12, on Effective Psychosocial Interventions: A Lifespan Perspective, identified ESTs and prevention programs for children (see Spirito, 1999). Outside the United States, EST reviews have taken place in England (Roth & Fonagy, 1996) and Canada (Hunsley, Dobson, Johnston, & Mikail, 1999). Finally, in a "review of reviews," Chambless and Ollendick (2001) discuss the results of many of these efforts and the criteria used to make their determinations.

The EST Controversy

In principle, psychologists and other mental health professionals are likely to agree on the necessity of providing empirical support for treatment interventions they use. It is also reasonable to assume that consumers of mental health treatment expect to receive a proven effective treatment when one is available. Therefore, one would expect clinicians to embrace ESTs. However, psychologists are split on the EST movement. With the exception of the controversy over prescription privileges for psychologists, there is probably no issue more hotly debated among practicing psychologists today. The main arguments against sole reliance on ESTs are as follows.

First, many clinicians argue that EST research favors cognitive-behavioral therapies, because these therapies represent the kinds of standardized treatments that can be tested fairly readily in controlled clinical trials. As a result, these clinicians believe, viable alternative treatments (e.g., psychodynamic therapy) that cannot be as easily standardized will fail to measure up to the EST criteria, even though they may be effective in clinical practice. Second, it has been argued that most studies supportive of ESTs fail to capture the complexity and uniqueness of patients seen in "actual" practice. Consequently, these clinicians question the applicability of such manualized treatments to patients seen in the community. Third, many clinicians have a negative reaction to being "told what to do" by researchers who generate the EST data. This is part of an ongoing tension between scientists and practitioners as to who "knows best" about treatment decisions—those who generate the research findings versus those who provide clinical treatment in actual practice.

The Importance of ESTs in the Evolving Healthcare Environment

Despite the controversy, Division 12's interest in identifying ESTs is part of a larger worldwide movement to make findings from applied medical research more available to clinicians in practice, a movement generally known as evidence-based medicine. The basic aim of this effort is to improve the quality of patient care by making it easier for practitioners to use empirical evidence to inform their choice of medical services. As a result, the issue of ESTs in psychology will need to be resolved if psychologists expect to have their roles as healthcare providers taken seriously within the healthcare community. Consequently, one can expect that the future of the EST movement will primarily be focused on repairing the rift between scientists and practitioners so they can work together to deal with this important issue. In particular, researchers must address the concerns of clinicians noted briefly above. Most essentially, treatments that clinicians believe are effective must be subject to empirical investigations to support (or refute) their legitimacy, and more attention needs to be paid to evaluating ESTs in true clinical settings (which is known as effectiveness research) rather than only in clinical research centers.

REFERENCES

Chambless, D. L, Baker, M. J., Baucom, D., Beutler, L. E., Calhoun, K. S., Crits-Christoph, P., et al. (1998). Update on Empirically Validated Therapies: II. *The Clinical Psychologist, 51*(1), 3–16.

Chambless, D. L., & Ollendick, T. H. (2001). Empirically supported psychological interventions: Controversies and evidence. *Annual Review of Psychology, 52*, 685–716.

Gatz, M., Fiske, A., Fox, L. S., Kaskie, B., Kasl-Godley, J. E., et al. (1998). Empirically validated psychological treatments for older adults. *Journal of Mental Health and Aging, 41*, 9–46.

Hunsley, J., Dobson, K. S., Johnston, C., & Mikail, S. F. (1999). Empirically supported treatments in psychology: Implications for Canadian professional psychology. *Canadian Psychologist, 40*, 289–302.

Kendall, P. C., & Chambless, D. L. (Eds.). (1998). Empirically supported psychological therapies [Special issue]. *Journal of Consulting and Clinical Psychology, 66*(3) 167.

Nathan, P. E., & Gorman, J. M. (Eds.). (1998). *A guide to treatments that work.* New York: Oxford University Press.

Nathan, P. E., & Gorman, J. M. (Eds.). (2002). *A guide to treatments that work* (Vol. 2). New York: Oxford University Press.

Roth, A. D, & Fonagy, P. (1996). *What works for whom? A critical review of psychotherapy research.* New York: Guilford Press.

Spirito, A. (Ed.). (1999). Empirically supported treatments in pediatric psychology [Special issue]. *Journal of Pediatric Psychology, 24*, 87–174.

Task Force on Promotion and Dissemination of Psychological Procedures. (1993). Training in and dissemination of empirically-validated psychological treatments. *The Clinical Psychologist, 48*, 3–23.

Wilson, J. J., & Gil, K. M. (1996). The efficacy of psychological and pharmacological interventions for the treatment of chronic disease-related and non-disease-related pain. *Clinical Psychology Review, 16*, 573–597.

SUGGESTED READING

Bruce, T. J., & Sanderson, W. C. (2004). Evidence-based psychosocial practices: The past, present, and future. In C. Stout & R. Hayes (Eds.), *Evidence-based practice: Methods, models and tolls for mental health professionals* (pp. 220–243). Hoboken, NJ: John Wiley & Sons.

WILLIAM C. SANDERSON
Hofstra University

See also: **Evidence-Based Practice; Psychotherapy Research**

EMPLOYEE ASSISTANCE PROGRAMS

Employee assistance programs (EAPs) are workplace programs offered by employers to employees that assist troubled employees and their family members with a variety of issues, ranging from financial and legal concerns to mental health and substance abuse problems. EAPs traditionally focus on these problems as they affect workplace performance, but EAPs are broadening their focus to include the full range of work-life issues. The EAP movement in the United States grew out of industrial alcohol programs in the 1950s and saw its biggest growth during the 1980s. It was during the 1980s that most EAPs moved from primarily alcohol-focused programs to the multi-issue or broad-brush programs that they are today.

EAPs offer a broad array of services to employees and their family members to assist with their problems. Comprehensive EAPs engage in identification, assessment, motivation, referral, short-term counseling, monitoring, and follow-up activities and help with a variety of personal problems, including family, emotional, financial, legal, and substance abuse concerns. EAPs do not provide long-term treatment or healthcare services. Several attempts have been made to determine a core set of services, or technologies, that define an EAP. The traditional core technologies of EAPs were defined by Paul Roman and Terry Blum in the late 1980s and early 1990s as the following seven activities: (1) identify employee behavioral problems based on workplace performance concerns; (2) provide consultation to supervisors, managers, and union representatives on how to use and refer employees to the EAP;

(3) use constructive confrontation strategies when appropriate; (4) create micro-linkages with treatment, counseling, and community resources; (5) create and maintain macro-linkages between the worksite and treatment, counseling, and community resources; (6) focus on employee alcohol and substance abuse problems as a strategy that offers the most promise for recovery and cost savings to the worksite; and (7) serve as a consultant to the worksite on personal problems affecting employee welfare.

Recently, changes to these traditional core technologies have been proposed by various authors to better match the current role of EAPs in the workplace. Attempts at defining a new set of core technologies have been hampered, however, by the ever-changing role of EAPs. Many EAPs now serve as behavioral healthcare gatekeepers for managed care plans, further complicating efforts to define a core set of EAP services.

Regardless of core services, EAPs fall into two primary types: internal and external. Internal EAPs are owned by the sponsoring employer, and EAP staff members are company employees. Internal EAPs can be housed at the worksite but often have separate offices to increase the perception of confidentiality and independence from company management. External EAPs are separate companies with which the employer contracts to provide EAP services. External EAPs may have on-site representatives, but these representatives are not company employees. Both internal and external EAPs typically offer assessment and referral, but internal EAPs are more likely to offer counseling services. Early on, most EAPs were internal EAPs that evolved from other workplace programs, often through the efforts of a single dedicated employee. More recently, however, large external EAPs have begun to dominate the industry. These EAPs often have affiliate networks that include small providers that service specific employers.

Several studies have attempted to assess the prevalence of EAPs. In the late 1980s, the Bureau of Labor Statistics (BLS) conducted a survey of employer antidrug programs, including EAPs. The BLS estimated that approximately 31% of U.S. employees had EAP services available to them. These employees were concentrated within large worksites, however. Seventy-six percent of establishments with more than 1,000 employees had EAPs, while only 9% of establishments with fewer than 50 employees had EAPs. Two surveys conducted by the Research Triangle Institute (RTI) in the mid-1990s showed that the prevalence of EAPs had grown substantially since the BLS survey. By 1996, EAPs reached well over half of the U.S. workforce, but EAPs were still concentrated within large worksites. Much of the growth in EAPs occurred in external providers, with external EAPs providing approximately 81% of EAP services in 1993. The growth in the prevalence of EAPs has continued well into the twenty-first century. The 2005 National Compensation Survey, conducted by the U.S. Bureau of Labor Statistics, found that

66% of worksites with 100 employees or more offered an EAP to their employees.

Estimates of the extent to which employees use EAP services when they are available are less common than estimates of the prevalence of EAPs. Anecdotal evidence and research conducted at individual worksites suggest that approximately 5%–12% of employees use EAP services annually. Evidence suggests that EAP utilization is slightly lower among females and among minorities, possibly because of confidentiality concerns but also due in part to EAPs' traditional focus on workplace rather than family issues. To date, however, no nationally representative survey has attempted to estimate the rate at which employees use EAP services or examine differences in utilization rates by demographic groups.

Cost estimates of EAP service, which are most often presented as the cost per eligible employee, suggest that EAPs are an affordable workplace program in most cases. The RTI surveys found that, in 1993, the cost of EAP services ranged from about $18 per eligible employee for external EAPs to approximately $22 per eligible employee for internal EAPs. A case study of seven EAPs, however, suggests that cost may vary widely depending on program characteristics and on the number of employees served. Intramarket competition among external EAPs, combined with the movement toward involving EAPs in managed care activities, has kept the costs of external EAPs relatively low over the past decade. Internal EAPs may have seen somewhat more of a rise in costs, but anecdotal evidence suggests that internal EAPs may be even more integrated in managed care and other workplace health promotion programs so that any rise in costs has been accompanied by an increase in services offered. Importantly, however, very little research has been done to estimate the cost per service of EAPs so that EAP services can be compared with other potential providers of comparable services.

Studies on the effectiveness and cost-effectiveness of EAPs suggest that they are effective in addressing employee problems and do so for relatively low cost; however, this literature suffers from several shortcomings that preclude drawing definitive conclusions. Most notable are methodological problems, such as inadequate sample sizes or nonequivalent comparison samples. Perhaps as serious a limitation, however, is that many EAP effectiveness studies are conducted by EAPs themselves in an effort to demonstrate their value to company management.

Historically, most researchers have considered EAP services to be individual level interventions, with most focus being on the effectiveness of EAP counseling on those employees who visit an EAP. Yet this focus does not reflect the current state of EAPs as comprehensive work-life interventions. Modern EAPs are not interventions just for clients. They are purchased, made available, and marketed to the entire workforce. The mix of services offered by EAPs has expanded to include a variety of services that target the workforce as a whole. Although EAPs have long provided supervisor training and health/wellness fairs that are intended to serve the broader workforce, the spread of technology-based services within EAPs has further increased the ability of EAPs to reach the broader workforce. Because technology-based services allow employees to access the EAP anonymously, their spread further emphasizes the need to consider the EAP as a group-level intervention that affects the entire workforce and not just those employees who become formal EAP cases.

From an employer perspective, technology-based services can be appealing because they can easily be offered to widely dispersed or mobile workforces, with every worker having access to exactly the same range of service. They are logistically easy to implement, because services are delivered by the vendor from a centralized location, and they are less expensive than many on-site programs such as child-care centers that address only a narrow group of employees. The employer is not required to hire staff or assume liability for the quality of the services. From a policy or family advocacy perspective, these services are intriguing because they could be easy to implement for workers in smaller workplaces, who at present have little access.

Although more rigorous studies on EAP effectiveness are needed, the realities of workplace research often hamper efforts to design and conduct such studies. First and foremost is the changing role of EAPs. Because both the role of EAPs in the workplace and the services they offer have changed so dramatically over the past decade, EAPs represent a moving target that is very difficult to study. EAPs have moved from providing simple assessment and referral, to providing short-term counseling, and back to assessment and referral but with a gatekeeper or case management role. Another factor limiting EAP research is the willingness of worksites to participate in an extended research study. Even if researchers obtain high-level cooperation, changes in workplace management can often result in workplaces pulling out of studies before adequate data are collected.

In summary, EAPs represent an inexpensive gateway to mental health and substance abuse services. As the behavioral healthcare system in the United States has changed, so has the role of EAPs and the services they offer. These changes have often thwarted attempts to quantify the effectiveness of EAPs in helping with employee problems. Nonetheless, the continuing increase in the number of employers offering EAPs suggests that these employers view EAPs as a beneficial service for their employees.

SUGGESTED READINGS

Arthur, A. R. (2000). Employee assistance programmes: The emperor's new clothes of stress management? *British Journal of Guidance and Counseling, 28,* 549–559.

Masi, D. (2005). Employee assistance programs in the new mil-
    lennium. *International Journal of Emergency Mental Health. 7*(3):
    157–168.

Masi, D. A., Freedman, M., Jacobson, J. M., & Back-Tamburo, M.
    (Eds.). (2002). *Utilization factors and outcomes for EAP and
    work-life programs.* Baltimore: University of Maryland.

JEREMY W. BRAY
RTI International, Research Triangle Park, NC

GEORGIA KARUTZOS
RTI International, Research Triangle Park, NC

SHELLEY M. MACDERMIND
Purdue University

See also: Occupational Stress

ENCOPRESIS

Encopresis is a common, often undertreated, and often overinterpreted form of fecal incontinence. When left untreated, encopresis can lead to serious and potentially life-threatening medical problems and seriously impaired social acceptance, relations, and development. The primary reasons for the medical problems are the possibility of organic disease (some cases have medical causes such as Hirschprung's disease) and the medical risk posed by fecal matter inexorably accumulating in an organ with a limited amount of space. The primary reason for the social impairment is that soiling evokes more revulsion from peers, parents, and important others than other forms of incontinence (and most other behavior problems).

As an example, severe corporal punishment for fecal accidents was still recommended by professionals in the late nineteenth century. The professional approach to encopresis has evolved substantially since then, but the approaches by laypersons (and still some professionals) are not keeping pace. Children with encopresis are still frequently shamed, blamed, and punished for a condition that is almost totally beyond their control.

The definition of encopresis has remained relatively consistent across versions of the DSM; the DSM-IV-TR (American Psychiatric Association, 2000) lists four criteria for encopresis: (1) repeated passage of feces into inappropriate places whether involuntary or intentional; (2) at least one such event a month for at least three months; (3) chronological age is at least four years (or equivalent developmental level); and, 4) the behavior is not due exclusively to the direct physiological effects of a substance or a general medical condition except through a mechanism involving constipation. Approximately 3% of the general pediatric population meets these criteria. The DSM-IV-TR describes two types of encopresis: (1) primary, in which the child has never had fecal continence, and (2) secondary, in which incontinence returns after at least six months of continence. The DSM-IV-TR also describes two subtypes for each type: (1) retentive encopresis, in which constipation and overflow incontinence are present, and (2) nonretentive encopresis, in which they are absent.

A large majority of encropesis cases (80%–90%) are the retentive subtype, the primary cause of which is slow transit of fecal material through the colon. This slow transit is in turn caused by a combination of genetic factors and such behavioral and dietary factors as insufficient roughage or bulk in the diet, irregular eating habits, medications that may have a side effect of constipation, problematic approaches to toilet training (e.g., punitive, unstructured), and toileting avoidance by the child. Any of these factors, singly or in combination, puts a child at risk for reduced colonic motility, actual constipation, and corresponding uncomfortable or painful bowel movements.

Uncomfortable or painful bowel movements, in turn, negatively reinforce fecal retention, and retention leads to a regressive reciprocal cycle often resulting in regular fecal accidents. When the constipation is severe or the cycle is chronic, the child may develop fecal impaction, a large blockage caused by the collection of hard dry stool. Not infrequently, liquid fecal matter will seep around the fecal mass producing "paradoxical diarrhea." Although the child is actually constipated, he or she appears to have diarrhea. Some parents will attempt to treat this type of diarrhea with over-the-counter antidiarrheal agents that only worsen the problem.

Two variables long thought to be causes of encopresis, psychopathology and sexual abuse, are increasingly seen as having no causal role in most cases. Regarding psychopathology, a small number of studies have detected an increase in psychological problems in children with encopresis, but the increase is seldom clinically significant, and it is more likely to be caused by the encopresis than to be a cause of it. Regarding the causal role of sexual abuse, supportive evidence is primarily anecdotal, and empirical attempts to supplement that evidence have been unsuccessful (e.g., Mellon, Whiteside, & Friedrich, 2006).

As indicated, a small minority of cases are of the non-retentive subtype, which involves regular, well-formed, soft bowel movements that occur somewhere other than the toilet. The process underlying these cases is not well understood, except that they tend to be treatment resistant, and it may be that psychopathology plays a much more significant role in this subtype of encopresis than in the retentive subtype.

Accordingly, treatment for the two subtypes of encopresis differs. Treatment for the retentive subtype involves a multicomponent biobehavioral approach that includes colonic evacuation (initiated by physicians and transferred to parents on an as needed basis), stool softeners, a consistent toileting schedule, dietary changes, increased fluid intake, postural support (so the child's feet are on a firm surface), incentives, and eradication of punitive consequences for fecal accidents. The biobehavioral approach has been shown to be successful in well-controlled single subject analyses and randomized clinical trials. It has also been shown to be effective when delivered by a therapist in a group setting (e.g., Stark, Owens-Stively, Spirito, Lewis, & Guevremont, 1990) and by interactive electronic programs on the internet (e.g., Ritterband et al., 2003). The numerous documentations of success have led to the listing of the biobehavioral approach to treatment of encopresis as an empirically supported treatment (McGrath, Mellon, & Murphy, 2000).

In contrast to treatment for retentive encopresis, there appears to be no treatment that is empirically supported, widely accepted, or even well defined for nonretentive encopresis. There are no published reports of randomized trials, quasi-experimental group studies, or even controlled case studies. The relevant literature is composed of a small number of case reports, and treatments vary across these reports. In very general terms, treatment for nonretentive encopresis appears to involve a combination of problem solving, toilet scheduling, psychotherapy, and elements of the biobehavioral approach (cf., Kuhn, Marcus, & Pitner, 1999).

In conclusion, over the past few decades substantial empirical advances have been made in knowledge about encopresis, especially in the areas of assessment and treatment of the retentive subtype. A remaining large gap in the literature involves needed research on the assessment, classification, and treatment of the nonretentive subtype.

REFERENCES

American Psychiatric Association (2000). *Diagnostic and statistical manual of mental disorders*. (4th ed., text rev.). Washington, DC: Author.

Kuhn, B. R., Marcus, B. A., & Pitner, S. L. (1999). Treatment guidelines for primary nonretentive encopresis and stool toileting refusal. *American Family Physician, 59*, 2171–2178.

Mellon, M. W., Whiteside, S. P., & Friedrich, W. N. (2006). The relevance of fecal soiling as an indicator of child sexual abuse: A preliminary analysis. *Developmental and Behavioral Pediatrics, 27*, 25–32.

McGrath, M. L., Mellon, M. W., & Murphy, L. (2000). Empirically supported treatments in pediatric psychology: Constipation and encopresis. *Journal of Pediatric Psychology, 25*, 225–254.

Ritterband, L. M., Cox, D. J., Walker, L. S., Kovatchev, B., McKnight, L., Patel, K., et al. (2003). An Internet intervention as adjunctive therapy for pediatric encopresis. *Journal of Consulting and Clinical Psychology, 71*, 910–917.

Stark, L., Owens-Stively, J., Spirito, A., Lewis, A., & Guevremont, D. (1990). Group behavioral treatment of retentive encopresis. *Journal of Pediatric Psychology, 15*, 659–671.

SUGGESTED READINGS

Field, C., & Friman, P. C. (2006). Encopresis. In J. Fisher & W. O'Donohue (Eds.), *Practitioner's guide to evidence-based psychotherapy* (pp. 277–283). New York: Springer.

Friman, P. C. (2007). Encopresis and enuresis. In M. Hersen (Ed.-in-Chief) & D. Reitman (Vol. Ed.), *Handbook of assessment, case conceptualization, and treatment: Vol. 2: Children and adolescents* (pp. 589–621). Hoboken, NJ: John Wiley & Sons.

Friman, P. C. (2008). Evidence based therapies for enuresis and encopresis. In R. G. Steele, T. D. Elkin, & M. C. Roberts (Eds.), *Handbook of evidence-based therapies for children and adolescents* (pp. 301–323). New York: Springer.

PATRICK C. FRIMAN

Boys Town, NE

See also: **Enuresis**

ENGINEERING PSYCHOLOGY

Engineering psychology is a discipline that aims to improve socio-technical systems: driving cars, working on surgical teams, controlling nuclear power plants, improving consumer products, controlling air traffic, and the like. It does this by considering how human operators interact with technologies, with environments, and with other operators in particular contexts. Engineering psychology contributes to the understanding of human capabilities and limitations and directly or indirectly impacts the design of technologies that operators use. Cognates of engineering psychology include human factors, ergonomics, applied experimental psychology, and cognitive engineering. All have the common goal of improving socio-technical systems, but each does so with a different approach, for example, focusing on the cognitive versus the physical factors that affect the operator. However, differences among disciplines are often subtle, and professionals in separate disciplines often conduct very similar work. In addition to the goal of improving the particular system, inducing general principles from the study of particular systems characterizes the scientific nature of what many engineering psychologists do.

Understanding any scientific paradigm beyond a cursory dictionary definition is aided by consideration of six aspects of the paradigm: its intellectual antecedents, pretheoretical ideas, analogies, concepts and language, methodology, and subject matter (Lachman, Lachman, & Butterfield, 1979).

Intellectual Antecedents

Scholars differ in how far back the origins of engineering psychology should be traced, but there are, at least in hindsight, recognizable features in the field of scientific management of Frederick Winslow Taylor in the late nineteenth and early twentieth century. However, the focus on benefiting humans with engineering psychology probably first emerged in the work of Lillian and Frank Gilbreth, who were pioneers in industrial/organizational (I/O) psychology and industrial engineering. To some extent World War I but certainly World War II led to rapid advances in engineering psychology (Moroney, 1995), and the first textbook appeared shortly thereafter (Chapanis, Garner, & Morgan, 1949).

Like other paradigms within scientific psychology, engineering psychology can lay claim to intellectual antecedents of behaviorism, functionalism, and Gestalt psychology from which the canons of natural science and a focus on perception were inherited. I/O psychology and cognitive psychology helped shape the field's current focus on the social and mental factors critical in performing modern work (Hoffman & Deffenbacher, 1992). There are also intellectual antecedents from outside of psychology proper that influenced modern engineering psychology. Communication engineering lent much to our appreciation of limitations in human processing as well as important methodological tools, and systems engineering spawned appreciation for the system in which the human-technical system is embedded.

Pretheoretical Ideas

Like all disciplines, engineering psychology began with a set of beliefs. Its ideology emerged from its history and the events it addressed, such as the world wars in which it proved its mettle. It also came from the engineering psychologists who transitioned from other areas of psychology, such as cognitive and perceptual branches of experimental psychology. The lynchpin of this ideology is that the human operator is part of a larger system and that the operator, like any other part of the system, has limitations and capabilities that must be considered.

Human behavior is goal directed and variable, and it takes place under specific and sometimes stressful conditions within a particular system. Humans are active information processors well suited to perform some tasks in the system and ill suited to perform others. Failures in the system are multicausal, and the human can contribute to those failures, but engineering psychologists do not believe that focusing exclusively on "human error" and ignoring the system is productive. Engineering

psychologists believe that things can be made better by improving components of the system. There is a preference for trying to bring the technology in line with the human, although it is also possible through selection or training procedures to help bring the human in line with the technology. Engineering psychologists believe that the way to understand the human and the human-technical system is to use the scientific method. They use a variety of empirical methods, including laboratory work, simulations, and field observation, with the goal of producing theories, models, and principles that go beyond the particular system that gave rise to them.

Analogy

Much of the ideology and the inheritance from intellectual antecedents is captured in the engineering psychologist's analogy of the human. Humans are a biological information-processing control structure of the socio-technical system. They are an information sensor, filter, and interpreter; an active judge and decision maker; and ultimately an information transmitter.

Concepts and Language

Although scientists in different disciplines refer to the same phenomena, the concepts and language they use to describe those phenomena often differ. These differences help distinguish one scientific paradigm from another and thus help us gain a better understanding of the paradigm. For example, the use of the term *operator* when referring to subjects or participants in a study reflects the notion that subjects are in control of a larger system and that they have particular goals that are to be maintained or reached. Similarly, calling a display an *automated aid* reflects the collaborative nature of humans and automation in operating the system.

Methodology

In addition to the activities expected from any scientist (see Table 1), engineering psychologists employ a diverse set of techniques to describe and evaluate how people interact with technologies, their environment, and other operators (see Stanton, Salmon, Walker, Baber, & Jenkins, 2005). Techniques for describing such interactions usually require some form of task analysis (Kirwan & Ainsworth, 1992) wherein the engineering psychologist decomposes an activity into its constituent parts. For example, an engineering psychologist working for a telecommunications company might conduct a task analysis to describe the steps required to dial different mobile phones. Alternatively, one working for a large chemical processing plant might conduct a task analysis as part of a human reliability assessment. In that case, the goal would be to

Table 1. Activities performed by the majority of human factors professionals. Numbers are percentage of respondents who acknowledge activity as part of their job. From Van Cott & Huey (1992)

Activity	Percent
Prepare/conduct oral presentations	90
Prepare/contribute to written reports	85
Apply human factors criteria/principles	85
Analyze tasks	81
Prepare/contribute to project proposals	80
Evaluate reports of others	79
Specify user requirements	78
Interpret test and evaluation results	72
Design data collection procedures/questionnaires	68
Review/summarize prior literature	67
Interpret research results	64
Verify conformance to human factors specifications	63
Specify/perform data analysis	61
Collect field data	60
Plan/coordinate evaluations	57
Specify evaluation objectives	56
Design human-equipment interfaces	55
Develop criterion measures	54
Develop hypotheses/theory	52

decompose operators' tasks to identify when and where operators might make mistakes. Historically, such analyses have focused on physical aspects of the task. However, work has become increasingly cognitive and led to an expansion of task analysis to describe cognitive work. A cognitive task analysis might be conducted for the U. S. Army to describe information used by commanders who are making decisions during urban combat.

Techniques include quantitative approaches such as controlled experimentation and simulation and qualitative approaches such as focus groups and usability testing. As a quantitative illustration, an engineering psychologist working for an aircraft manufacturer might conduct a controlled experiment to determine whether a new display leads to better performance than the old display. Alternatively, the engineering psychologist might simulate users interacting with those displays to determine which of them leads to better performance. As a qualitative illustration, an engineering psychologist working for a consulting firm might conduct a focus group to determine whether users prefer a client's software package over their competitor's product. Alternatively, the engineering psychologist might conduct a usability test to identify problematic aspects of their client's software.

In any given situation, engineering psychologists employ a combination of methods. It is usually their responsibility to determine the combination of techniques that will provide the information necessary for the situation at hand.

Subject Matter

Engineering psychologists work on a wide variety of topics ranging from the micro (local or individual) level to the macro (global or systems) level (see Durso, Nickerson, Dumais, Lewandowsky, & Perfect, 2007; Salvendy, 2005). They work to understand the abilities and limitations of the human operator, but they also work from the development of systems to the testing and evaluation of those systems. Engineering psychologists, unlike physical ergonomists, tend to focus on topics that are considered "above the neck" (cognitive) rather than biomechanical; however, whereas this characterizes the prototype of the engineering psychology paradigm, there are exceptions throughout the research areas to be described.

In aerospace, researchers study the socio-technical system in the milieu of aviation and space. They may help develop displays and controls in the modern cockpit of passenger planes with the aim of reducing pilot workload and increasing pilot situational awareness. Indeed, conventional flights require only two pilots to handle what previously required three people in the cockpit, because of engineering psychology. Engineering psychologists may also develop and test flight simulators and their usefulness in pilot training or explore the information needed by air traffic controllers or the work environment helpful to astronauts in the shuttle.

In healthcare environments such as medicine, nursing, hospital, ambulatory and long-term care, engineering psychologists study a variety of socio-technical systems. For example, they may help develop medical devices used by healthcare providers and patients so that the proper dose of medicine is administered. They may also help design the environmental layout of a hospital unit to decrease the time nurses spend on walking and searching and thereby increase efficiency.

In human-computer interaction, engineering psychologists study the interaction between the user and the computer (hardware and software) in contexts from work to recreation. For example, they would help develop websites to make airline reservations on the Internet. Or they may help design screens used on personal digital assistants or cell phones. Finally, engineering psychologists must consider the characteristics of all users and may help design computer devices on multiple levels allowing it to be used by both the young and old and by users with disabilities.

Engineering psychologists in consumer products focus on the design of products from the user's perspective. For example, they would help develop products and tools that are safe and enjoyable for consumers to use. This area would require the psychologists to develop prototypes of the products and test them on pilot groups of users to get feedback in an iterative process.

Engineering psychologists in manufacturing and process control systems study performance in the context of complex control systems. For example, they may help develop the operator components of a nuclear power plant. A recent advance in this area is automation and expert systems. An early example is the cruise control on a car or the autopilot on an airplane. This technology has become more sophisticated and is being considered in more and more systems such as air traffic control. With the air traffic anticipated to double in the next 20 years, automation is considered as a possible solution to monitoring air traffic.

Engineering psychologists in surface transportation study issues pertaining to ground, rail, and water, and pedestrian travel. For example, they may help develop in-vehicle warning systems to alert drivers that they are in danger of a collision or study the distracting effects of using a cell phone. They may assess technologies that measure the physiological reactions of the driver, such as fatigue, and use these measures to control the vehicle directly. To gain a better understanding of research in engineering psychology consider the following example (see also Human Factors Research, this volume) about the centered high-mounted brake light (CHMBL, Malone, 1986) mandated on all passenger cars made since 1985.

The aim of the CHMBL was to reduce rear-end collisions, which account for about 25% of accidents. A number of human factors researchers compared the existing rear brake light system with three alternatives, including the CHMBL, in a field study of taxicabs (Malone et al., 1978). Analyses of accidents over a 12-month period indicated that the CHMBL, but not the other alternatives, resulted in a significantly lower rate of rear-end collisions compared with the existing system. The effectiveness of the CHMBL was replicated in two subsequent studies. In all three studies the accident rate was minimally 50% lower for cabs equipped with the CHMBL compared with the standard rear lighting system. The conceptualization, design, implementation, analysis, and interpretation of this study is a prototypical example of human factors research in which experimental design skills are applied to a real-world problem. In this case it clearly had widespread impact.

In conclusion, engineering psychologists bring their skills and knowledge to a diverse set of topics that vary on multiple dimensions and change over time. This leads to a challenging and interesting field of study.

REFERENCES

Chapanis, A., Garner, W. R., & Morgan, C. T. (1949). *Applied experimental psychology.* New York: John Wiley & Sons.

Durso, F. T., Nickerson, R., Dumais, S., Lewandowsky, S., & Perfect, T. *Handbook of applied cognition* (2nd ed.). Chicester, UK: John Wiley & Sons.

Hoffman, R. R., & Deffenbacher, K. A. (1992). A brief history of applied cognitive psychology. *Applied Cognitive Psychology, 6,* 1–48.

Kirwan, B., & Ainsworth, L. K. (1992). *A guide to task analysis.* London: Taylor & Francis.

Lachman, R., Lachman, J. L., & Butterfield, E. C. (1979). *Cognitive psychology and information processing: An introduction.* Hillsdale, NJ: Lawrence Erlbaum.

Malone, T. B. (1986). The centered-high-mounted brake light: A human factors success story. *Human Factors Society Bulletin, 29,* 1–2.

Malone, T. B., Kirkpatrick, M., Kohl, J. S., & Baker, C. (1978). Field test evaluation of rear lighting systems. *DOT-HS-5-01228.* Washington, DC: National Highway Traffic Safety Administration.

Moroney, W. F. (1995). The evolution of human engineering: A selected review. In J. Weimer (Ed.), *Research Techniques in Human Engineering* (pp. 1–19). Upper Saddle River, NJ: Prentice Hall PTR.

Salvendy, G. (2005). *Handbook of human factors and ergonomics* (3rd ed.). Hoboken, NJ: John Wiley & Sons.

Stanton, N. A., Salmon, P. M., Walker, G. H., Baber, C., & Jenkins, D. P. (Eds.). (2005). *Human factors methods: A practical guide for engineering and design.* Burlington, VT: Ashgate.

Van Cott, H. P., & Huey, B. M. (Eds.). (1992). *Human Factors Specialists' Education and Utilization: Results of a Survey.* Washington, DC: National Academy Press.

SUGGESTED READINGS

Casey, S. (1998). *Set phasers on stun: And other true tales of design, technology, and human error.* Santa Barbara, CA: Aegean.

Cooke, N. J., & Durso, F. T. (2008). *Stories of modern technology failures and cognitive engineering successes.* Boca Raton: CRC Press.

Wickens, C. D., Lee, J., Liu, Y. D., & Gordon-Becker, S. E. (2004). *An introduction to human factors engineering* (2nd ed.). Upper Saddle River, NJ: Prentice-Hall.

Francis T. Durso
Georgia Institute of Technology

Patricia R. Delucia
Keith S. Jones
Texas Tech University

See also: **Human Factors Research; Psychophysics**

ENURESIS

Enuresis is the technical term used for the regular passage of urine into locations other than those specifically designed for that purpose. The diagnostic criteria in the fourth edition of the *Diagnostic and Statistical Manual for Mental Disorders* (DSM-IV-TR; American Psychiatric Association, 2000) include repeated voiding of urine into clothing or bed at least twice a week for at least three months. If the frequency is less than that but the voiding is a cause of significant distress or impairment to social, academic, or occupational functioning, it satisfies diagnostic criteria.

The child must be at least five years of age or exhibit that level of developmental ability if developmental delays are present. The condition cannot be directly due to the physiological effects of a substance (e.g., diuretics) or a general medical condition. The DSM further classifies enuresis into primary cases, in which the person has never achieved urinary continence, and secondary cases, in which incontinence develops after a period of continence. Additionally, the DSM subdivides enuresis into three subtypes—(1) nocturnal, (2) diurnal, and (3) combined nocturnal and diurnal. Nocturnal enuresis is, by a very wide margin, the most frequently presenting type. Prevalence estimates range as high as 25% of six-year-old children and, although it is much less prevalent by the teenage years, as many as 8% of boys and 4% of girls are still enuretic at age 12.

Several causes or correlates of enuresis have been identified, the most prominent of which is family history. The probability of enuresis increases as a function of closeness and number of blood relatives with a positive history of it. Delayed physiological maturation, especially in the areas of bone growth, secondary sexual characteristics, and stature, is correlated with enuresis. A significant association between functional bladder capacity and enuresis has been established. Although the abundant research on sleep dynamics and enuresis has been marred by design flaws, there is modest support for the virtually ubiquitous parental observation that distinctly deep sleep and slowness to arouse typifies their enuretic children. Historically, parents and professionals have attributed enuresis to psychological disorder (e.g., psychopathology) or characterological problems (e.g., laziness), but there is no empirical support for these views. There was initial enthusiasm for a finding of reduced antidiuretic hormone (ADH) in a small number of enuretic children, but subsequent research suggests the finding is not typical of enuretic children in general, and treatments that increase ADH (e.g., DDAVP) have had limited success.

The need for treatment of enuresis predates modern civilization, and the variety of techniques used in antiquity appear to have been limited only by the imagination of the ancient therapists and their tolerance for inflicting unpleasantness on young children in order to secure therapeutic gain. Penile binding, buttock and sacrum burning, and forced urine-soaked pajama wearing are among the many highly aversive treatments reported in a review of ancient approaches to enuresis. In fairness to the ancient therapists, the health-based consequences of prolonged enuresis during their time were severe, due to the limited means for cleaning bedding and ineffective methods for managing infection.

The evolution of treatment for enuresis that began in earnest early in the twentieth century abandoned the physically harsh treatments in favor of approaches that were more humane from a physical perspective but still problematic from a psychological one. Specifically, with the rise of Freudian psychodynamics came psychopathological characterizations of common childhood problems such as enuresis. Although more protected from harsh physical treatment than their ancestral peers, early-twentieth-century enuretic children were often subject to stigma, isolation, and other negative social consequences.

The advent of behavioral theory, and the conditioning type treatments derived from it, inaugurated a paradigmatic shift in the treatment of enuresis. Specifically, behavioral theory rendered psychopathological interpretations obsolete and aversive physical treatments unnecessary. The cardinal conditioning type treatment for enuresis has been the urine alarm. The urine alarm uses a moisture sensitive switching system that, when closed by contact with urine seeped into pajamas or bedding, completes a small voltage electrical circuit and activates a stimulus that is theoretically strong enough to cause waking (e.g., buzzer, bell, light, or vibrator).

Controlled evaluations of the urine alarm indicate that this relatively simple device is 65% to 75% effective with a treatment duration of 5 to 12 weeks, and a six-month relapse rate of 15%–30%. Early alarm-based treatment used bed devices but, over the past two decades, devices that attach to pajamas have become the universal preference. Alarm treatment is often augmented by a range of other components, resulting in behavioral treatment packages. Treatment involving the alarm used alone, or in a package, has been established as effective according to the very strict criteria used to determine that a behavioral treatment is empirically supported (Mellon & McGrath, 2000).

The treatment components that are most often combined with the alarm are retention control training (RCT), over-learning, stream interruption exercises, cleanliness training, waking schedules, and reward systems. RCT requires children to drink extra fluids (e.g., 16 ounces of water or juice) and delay urination as long as possible, which increases the volume of their diurnal urinations and expands the interval between urges to urinate at night. Stream interruption exercises involve purposeful manipulation of the muscles necessary to prematurely terminate urination. They were originally developed for stress incontinence in women and referred to as Kegel exercises. Waking schedules involve waking enuretic children and guiding them to the bathroom for urination. Early use of waking schedules typically required full awakening, often with sessions that occurred in the middle of the night, but present practice merely requires conducting waking sessions just before the parents' normal bedtime.

Over-learning, similarly to RCT, requires that children drink extra fluids—but just prior to bedtime—and is used primarily to enhance the maintenance of treatment effects established by alarm-based means. Cleanliness training involves requiring children to attempt to return soiled beds, bed clothing, and pajamas to a presoiled state (e.g., taking sheets to the laundry room for younger children or actually washing them for older children). Reward systems are used to enhance children's motivation to participate in treatment and usually involve rewards or incentives delivered on a nightly basis (e.g., one small reward for an accident free night or day).

The oldest, best known, and empirically supported treatment package is dry bed training (DBT). Initially evaluated for use with a group of adults with profound mental retardation, DBT has been systematically replicated numerous times across child populations (e.g., Azrin, Sneed, & Foxx, 1974). In addition to the bed alarm, its initial composition includes over-learning, intensive cleanliness responsibility training, intensive positive practice of alternatives to wetting, hourly awakenings, close monitoring, and rewards for success. In subsequent iterations, the stringency of the waking schedule is reduced and retention control training added. Other similar programs were also developed, the best known and empirically supported of which is full spectrum home training (Houts & Liebert, 1985). It includes the alarm, cleanliness training, retention control training, and over-learning techniques.

The preceding description of treatment options pertains to nocturnal enuresis. There is much less literature on diurnal enuresis, and it provides moderate support for an approach that involves scheduled toileting, incentives, and strategic use of the urine alarm.

An additional option for both nocturnal and diurnal enuresis involves medication. Unfortunately, the only two medications that have been shown to effectively reduce urinary accidents, imipramine (Tofranil) and Desmopressin (DDAVP), are also accompanied by serious side effects. In fact, the United States Food and Drug Administration has recently disapproved of DDAVP for use in the treatment of enuresis (United States Food and Drug Administration, 2007), and the use of imipramine has been all but discontinued. Whether imipramine will see a resurgence seems unlikely given its problematic side effects (e.g., Herson, Schmitt, & Rumack, 1979). Hence, until another viable medical option is discovered, behavioral treatment is likely to remain the dominant method for treating enuresis by medical and mental health providers.

REFERENCES

American Psychiatric Association. (2000). *Diagnostic and statistical manual of mental disorders* (4th ed., text rev.). Washington, DC: Author.

Azrin, N. H., Sneed, T. J., & Foxx, R. M. (1974). Dry-bed training: Rapid elimination of childhood enuresis. *Behavior Research & Therapy, 12*, 147–156.

Herson, V. C., Schmitt, B. D., & Rumack, B. H. (1979). Magical thinking and imipramine poisoning in two school-aged children. *Journal of the American Medical Association, 241*, 1926–1927.

Houts, A. C., & Liebert, R. M. (1985). *Bedwetting: A guide for parents*. Springfield, IL: Thomas.

Mellon, M. W., & McGrath, M. L. (2000). Empirically supported treatments in pediatric psychology: Nocturnal enuresis. *Journal of Pediatric Psychology, 25*, 193–214.

United States Food and Drug Administration. (2007). Information for healthcare professionals: Desmopressin Acetate (marketed as DDAVP Nasal Spray, DDAVP Rhinal Tube, DDAVP, DDVP, Minirin, and Stimate Nasal Spray). FDA Alert 12/4/07. Retrieved February 4, 2008, from http://www.fda.gov/cder/drug/InfoSheets/HCP/desmopressinHCP.htm.

SUGGESTED READINGS

Christophersen, E. R., & Friman, P. C. (2004). Elimination disorders. In R. Brown (Ed.), *Handbook of pediatric psychology in school settings* (pp. 467–488). Mahwah, NJ: Lawrence Erlbaum.

Friman, P. C. (2007). Encopresis and enuresis. In M. Hersen (Ed.-in-Chief) & D. Reitman (Vol. Ed.), *Handbook of assessment, case conceptualization, and treatment: Vol. 2: Children and adolescents* (pp. 589–621). Hoboken, NJ: John Wiley & Sons.

Friman, P. C. (2008). Evidence based therapies for enuresis and encopresis. In R. G. Steele, T. D. Elkin, & M. C. Roberts (Eds.), *Handbook of evidence-based therapies for children and adolescents* (pp. 301–323). New York: Springer.

PATRICK C. FRIMAN
Boys Town, NE

See also: **Encopresis**

ENVIRONMENTAL PSYCHOLOGY

Environmental psychology has been called an interdisciplinary science that focuses on the interplay between human beings and the environment. What environmental psychology introduced to the field of psychology was the presence and influence of the physical environment, which up until recently had been largely ignored. In the late 1960s environmental psychology began by a merging of several disciplines: anthropology, architecture, planning, psychology, sociology, and even some aspects of engineering. Environmental psychology also contributed to the area of human factors by showing that choices of methods and objects were not always logical and often followed irrational motives. In order to encompass this diversity, several organizations were formed to establish a more or less concentrated effort.

The first of these organizations was sponsored by the National Institute of Mental Health (NIMH) at the City University of New York (CUNY), which in 1970 produced the first textbook in the field, *Environmental Psychology: Man in His Physical Setting*. The second center was at the University of Utah, where the first conference on the subject was held in 1961. The third center was at the Topeka State Hospital in Topeka, Kansas, and was initially called the Environmental Research Foundation (ERF). Of these three, only the CUNY program survived to the present day, although other similar programs have since been established at the University of California at Irvine and at Georgia Tech University.

The Architecture-Psychology Movement (EDR)

From the beginning in the late 1960s there was an effort on the part of some psychologists and architects to introduce psychological science into the discipline of architecture. This movement has been called by several names. Some call it environmental design research (EDR), some have called it evidence based design, and others have simply called it architecture-behavior research.

Prior to the formation of an Environmental Research Design Association (EDRA) and the beginnings of EDR research, the work of Roger Barker and his colleagues led to some useful and far-reaching consequences for environmental design. Most telling of these findings was the discovery that the mere size of a community or institution has a considerable effect on the behavior of its occupants. Most important was the finding in schools that, as the size of a school increased, the participation level of its students decreased and, consequently, so did the effectiveness of the school. This finding also held true for other organizations, leading to the conclusion that smaller institutions (schools, colleges, factories, etc.) are more effective than larger ones.

Most of the literature from EDR, however, is in the form of post occupancy evaluations (POEs), which constitute the largest body of literature in the field. Unfortunately, most of these POEs lie in architect's or professor's offices and have never been published. The main reason for lack of publication is that many were class exercises in which students would visit a designed environment and report on it. In other cases, architects did their own evaluations and never intended to publish them. Nevertheless, this vast accumulation of POEs remains a potential pool of information for architects and researchers in the field.

The use of POEs led to a more comprehensive approach in which predesign studies involved examining previous POEs and doing research on the building that was anticipated. The goal of these studies was to establish a quality control in the building industry. The POEs would be done in a series after each design so the results would be cumulative over time.

More recently, a new method of design research has been pioneered by such architects as Gehry and is called building information modeling (BIM) (Eastman, Becsley, Chang, & Williamson, 2004). This method uses digital computer technology that allows the designer to "sketch" the proposed building in three-dimensional digital form in a computer and then examine it from any angle. Proponents of this method say that it will make drawing completely obsolete within 10 years. What remains is to show by use of POEs whether this BIM method produces better human habitations than the old pencil drawings method. Since architecture awards are made on a basis of judging drawings, it will be critical to see whether the new system can be applied to the award process.

Another example of the practical uses of EDR is the design of environments to prevent crime, called crime prevention through design (CPTD). Atlas (2008) summarizes these efforts in buildings, organizations, and communities and also describes how environments can be designed to minimize terrorism threats. Kuo (2002) laments the lack of influence that EDR research has had on the building industry compared to the expectations fostered in EDRA and by other researchers.

An interesting aspect of the influence of the designed environment is the impact that the design of schools of architecture has had on the students and faculty. Nasar, Preiser, and Fisher (2008) collected research done on 17 schools of architecture, all of which consisted of POEs. The amount of natural light, the presence of commons areas, the amount of storage space, and many other environmental variables were found to be relevant to the process of learning architecture.

The Environment Behavior Movement (EBR)

A much wider (in subject) body of literature than that on EDR goes beyond the occupation of buildings and encompasses the whole realm of human behavior as it relates to any aspect of the environment. This research can overlap with EDR, but it more often deals with wider issues like global warming, conservation, environmental belief systems, and cultural aspects of the environment. The central stimulus for this research is the universal threat to the environment reflected in the belief that growth is a central cause of human behavior toward the environment. Regardless of most cultural differences, people generally subscribe to the belief that businesses, cities, institutions, and all human endeavors must grow as a sign of health. This belief is enacted irrespective of its effect on the environment. As a result of growth's effects, the term "sustainable development" was coined to create the vision that growth could be pursued in a way that did not exhaust the earth's resources. Thus, sustainable development becomes the goal as a new belief system.

Noise is one of the most difficult environmental problems. From July 29 through July 4, 2008, the European

Union's acoustical scientists met in Paris to discuss a mandate to reduce noise in all European cities with populations of 250,000 or more. It was conceded that all of these cities were lagging in noise reduction except Berlin. Swedish scientists had discovered that using rubber in asphalt paving reduces road noise, and French scientists were proposing to use a "smart" foam as insulation in buildings to reduce noise from the outside. This conference is an example of how European scientists have been more actively engaged in developing sustainable environmental policies than scientists in the United States.

However, the failure of the U.S. to develop environmentally sound policies is also due to a concerted effort on the part of ideologues to convince the public that the environmental threat does not exist. Jacques, Dunlap, and Freeman (2008) investigated 141 English language "environmentally skeptical" books and concluded "... that skepticism is a tactic of an elite-driven counter-movement designed to combat environmentalism, and that the successful use of this tactic has contributed to the weakening of US commitment to environmental protection."

One of the most global instruments used to measure environmental belief is the human exceptionist paradigm versus the new environmental paradigm (HEP-NEP) developed by Dunlap and associates (Dunlap, 2008). The concept of this scale was to measure whether people believed they were outside the environment (HEP) or a part of the environment (NEP), the conclusion being that those who felt they were part of the environment would be more amenable to pleas for conservation and changes in behavior to preserve the environment. When the scale was extended to other cultures, it was discovered that in some cultures the belief that humans were part of the environment could coexist with exploiting it. This was an important lesson in the context of promoting sustainable behavior. An improved version of the HEP-NEP later showed increased acceptance of the NEP among various cultures.

As an example of the great variety of behaviors included in EBR research, Geller and colleagues (Geller, Winett, & Everett, 1982) presented more than 150 studies that were aimed at getting people to change their beliefs and attitudes in order to help preserve the environment. These studies reported particular successes in achieving improved litter control and increased recycling of waste oil, glass, paper, and metals.

The methods used in EBR research often include analyses of data by confirmatory factor analysis, multiple regression, and path analysis, but recently these methods have all been combined in structural equation modeling (SEQ). The SEQ method of analysis allows the simultaneous comparison of theoretical, latent, and observed variables into a model that diagrams the relationship of the variables. This allows inclusion of an ever-widening scope of variables in environmental studies.

The theory of planned behavior is another global view of the environment-behavior interface. This theory predicts actions from attitudes and explains the process by which they are linked. Behavioral intentions, in combination with a favorable attitude toward the behavior, norms, and conventions held about the behavior, and the extent to which the behavior is under the control of the individual, affect the likelihood of adapting a certain behavior related to the environment.

Wilson (1984) proposed the *biophilia* hypothesis as the "innate tendency to focus on life and lifelike processes" as a result of our evolution in the natural environment. This hypothesis was extended by Appleton (1996), who felt that since humans evolved in nature, they would prefer living in a natural as opposed to human-made environment (prospect) and that the natural environment would provide relief from the tensions of the human-made environment (refuge). In this regard, Ulrich (1984) showed that patients in a hospital room who saw a natural environment through their windows got well quicker than those who saw a blank wall. Recent research has also shown that natural environments have a restorative effect of lessening tension.

Stokols and Montero (2002) proposed studying the impact of the Internet by comparing Internet users with those who do not partake, as a way of answering the question whether intensive Internet use reduces the sociability and social skills of the Internet user. Another interesting question is whether the virtual settings of the Internet have a different impact from the settings experienced in "real" life. Still another interesting question is how one measures these differences.

Globalization

The globalization of environmental psychology came before the same phenomenon occurred in economics and began in the countries themselves rather than as an export. Saarinen and Sell (1987) did a review of environmental perception study and reported data from 66 countries. They also reported that the number of researchers in this field grew from 224 in 1967 to 2,951 in 1985.

The International Association for the Study of People and Their Physical Surroundings (IAPS) was founded in 1981 and continues to include all nations in its conferences. Japan began the Man Environment Research Association (MERA) in 1980. Scholars in Australasia founded the People and the Physical Environment Association (PAPER) in 1983. The increasing amount of published international research is reflected in the fact that papers from outside the U.S. accounted for only an occasional article in the journal *Environment & Behavior* in the 1970s, whereas in a recent issue of the journal in 2008, 70% were authored by researchers from abroad. In a very concrete sense, then, environmental psychology has become truly international in scope.

REFERENCES

Appleton, J. (1996). *The experience of landscape* (Rev. ed.). London: John Wiley & Sons.

Atlas, R. (2008). *21st century security and CPTED.* New York: CRC Press.

Dunlap, R. (2008). New environmental paradigm. In Baird, C., Froedeman, R. (Eds.), *Encyclopedia of Environmental Ethics and Philosophy.* Farmington Hill, MI: Thomson Gale.

Eastman, C. M., Becsley, P., Chang, N., & Williamson, S. (Eds.). (2004). Editors proc., ACADIA Conference, Cambridge & Toronto, Canada.

Geller, B., Winett, R., & Everett, P. (1982). *Preserving the environment.* Elmsford, NY: Pergamon.

Jacques, P., Dunlap, R., & Freeman, M. (2008). The organization of denial: Conservative think tanks and environmental skepticism. *Environmental Politics, 17,* 349–385.

Kuo, F. (2002). Bridging the gap: How scientists can make a difference. In R. Bechtel & A. Chruchman, (Eds.), *Handbook of environmental psychology,* Hoboken, NJ: John Wiley & Sons, 335–346.

Nasar, J., Preiser, W., & Fisher, T. (2008). *Designing for designers: Lessons learned from schools of architecture.* New York: Fairchild Publications.

Saarinen, T., & Sell, J. (1987). *International directory of environment-behavior-design.* Tucson: University of Arizona Press.

Stokols, D., & Montero, M. (2002). Toward an environmental psychology of the internet. In R. Bechtel & A. Churchman (Eds.), *Handbook of environmental psychology.* Hoboken, NJ: John Wiley & Sons.

Ulrich, R. (1984). View through a window may influence recovery from surgery. *Science, 224,* 420–421.

Wilson, E. (1984). *Biophilia.* Cambridge, MA: Belknap.

SUGGESTED READING

Bell, A., Greene, T., Fisher, S., & Baum, A. (2001). *Environmental psychology* (5th ed.). New York: Psychology Press.

ROBERT B. BECHTEL
University of Arizona

See also: **Ecological Psychology; Social Climate Research**

ENVY

Envy is an unpleasant blend of discontent and ill will caused by noticing a desired advantage possessed by another person. People often confuse envy with jealousy, but they are distinct emotions (Parrott & Smith, 1993). Envy involves two people and arises when one lacks something enjoyed by another. Jealousy entails three people and arises when one fears losing someone (often a romantic partner) or something to a rival. The confusion derives partly from the dual meaning of "jealous," which can be used to mean either envious or jealous. The term "envy" nearly always refers to the two-person case in which a person lacks a desired thing. Thus, we can say that Salieri was envious or jealous of Mozart's musical talent, but we would not say that he flew into an envious rage if his wife showed interest in Mozart. Jealousy would be the preferred label for his emotion in the latter case.

Some scholars suggest that there are two core types of envy, one admiring and emulative, the other hostile and destructive (Smith & Kim, 2007). This is no small distinction. Depending on which type of envy a person is feeling, the nature of the emotion and its implications for interpersonal relationships and for individual happiness are decidedly different. Admiring envy probably leads to smooth interactions with the envied person and healthy, emulative strivings. Hostile envy can poison interactions and lead to unhealthy competition and unhappiness, especially when it is dispositional and chronic. It is this latter type of envy that most researchers think of as envy proper, and it is the type that is especially important to study.

A final important distinction to make is between envy and greed. Greed involves not only a desire for something, but also an insatiable desire for more and more of the desired thing. Envy involves a desire but, unlike greed, this desire is connected to another person's possession of the desired thing. Also, unlike greed, envy often involves a hostile urge to destroy what is desired if obtaining it is out of reach. Better no one have it, thinks the envious person, if I cannot have it.

Why Do We Envy?

Social psychological perspectives on envy emphasize that relative differences between people have powerful consequences for one's self-evaluation, as superiority in others leads to inferences of personal inferiority in oneself (Alicke & Zell, 2008). Also, suffering inferiority hinders people's chances of obtaining the many important things in life that are apportioned through competition, whether in the workplace or in the realm of romance. Consequently, it is only natural that advantages enjoyed by others might create a painful emotion. In fact, evolutionary perspectives on envy highlight the adaptive nature of envy (Hill & Buss, 2008). Some sort of painful reaction to inferiority may be important in creating a desire for pursuing resources necessary for survival and reproduction.

Whom Do We Envy?

Empirical work shows that people are more likely to envy others who are, except for the advantage itself, similar to themselves in attributes such as gender, age, experience, and background (Salovey & Rodin, 1984). In Biblical text, for example, the Pharisees envied Jesus because he was similar to them in most any appreciable way, except that Jesus was worshipped and they were not. If the individual who possesses the desired attribute is not psychologically similar, the unflattering comparison will lose its capacity to cause psychological pain. These similarities enable people to picture what it would be like to enjoy the desired attribute. However, envy is largely a frustrated desire because, in actuality, the prospects of obtaining the desired attribute are poor when envy arises. Better prospects seem to take the negative edge off the emotion.

What Do We Envy?

Research also shows that people envy others who enjoy advantages in domains that are important to them (Tesser, 1991). The self-relevance of the comparison domain is a key to evoking the emotion. If Salieri envies Mozart's musical gifts, it is because Salieri also fancies himself as a musician and links his self-worth to doing well in this domain. Mozart's superior musical talent diminishes Salieri's sense of self and creates the painful emotion of envy because music is a self-relevant, important domain for Salieri. If Salieri fancied himself as a politician, Mozart's musical success would have little or no effect on Salieri save perhaps feelings of admiration.

The Hostile Nature of Envy

The hostile nature of envy proper is important to emphasize. This hostile element is a likely reason why envy is linked to so many instances of destructive behavior, from internecine conflict on a grand scale, such as between the Tutsi and Hutus in Rwanda, to individual incidents of vandalism, murder, and sabotage. Religious traditions commonly emphasize the aggressive outcomes associated with envy. Jesus was envied by the Pharisees, and in the end, it was they who delivered him to the Romans and demanded his execution. In the Old Testament, Joseph was envied for his coat of many colors and as a result was sold into slavery by his brothers. In literary works, envy is a recurrent theme. In Shakespeare, both Iago and Cassius are examples of characters who commit their deadly acts because of envy. Research shows that envious hostility can emerge in indirect ways as well. For instance, people are likely to feel *schadenfreude*, or malicious joy, when they witness the suffering of an envied person (Smith et al., 1996). A hostile attitude toward the envied person is one reason why the person's misfortune might be pleasing. In competitive settings, so often the breeding grounds for envy, such feelings make even more sense should misfortune for others lead to direct success for the self.

Envy and Transmution

People resist admitting their envy. Some scholars argue that envy is the last emotion that people will acknowledge

(Silver & Sabini, 1978). Envy, because it is hostile in nature and because it undermines the status quo, is a sin in many cultures. Admitting to envy is to admit to being both inferior and hostile, and so it is also shameful. We are taught to feel happy rather than envious over another person's advantage. Envy is so discomforting that people may avoid admitting their envy in private as well as in public. Thus, scholars point out that people will, unawares, repress and then transmute their envy into emotions they can label as more socially acceptable (Smith, 2004). Hostile feelings may be rationalized by coming to view the envied person's advantage as unfairly obtained or the envied person as morally defective. The envied person therefore may seem to deserve a measure of ill will.

Envy and Well-Being

It is often claimed that envy is a frequent cause of unhappiness, especially when it is chronic or dispositional (Smith, Combs, & Thielke, 2008). Some scholars even claim that it might negatively affect physical health. Using comparison with others as a primary basis for determining self-worth is a prescription for disappointment, because the average person is inferior to half of the population. Also, envy can be negatively linked with gratitude, as needing help from others may make the envious person feel inferior and resentful rather than appreciative. Some scholars even suggest that an envious person might reject the help of others because, even in a time of need, the help of others suggests that the envious person is inferior. Envious people are not only subject to a variety of negative feelings and the negative consequences, but they are largely unlikely to benefit from the positive effects derived from optimism and good will directed toward others. Envy may be an adaptive emotion to feel, at least in moderate doses, but it is not an emotion to cultivate in oneself.

REFERENCES

Alicke, M. D., & Zell, E. (2008). Social comparison and envy. In R. H. Smith (Ed.), *Envy: Theory and research*. New York: Oxford University Press.

Hill, S. E, & Buss, D. M. (2008). The evolutionary psychology of envy. In R. H. Smith (Ed.), *Envy: Theory and research*. New York: Oxford University Press.

Parrott, W. G. (1991). The emotional experiences of envy and jealousy. In P. Salovey (Ed.), *The psychology of jealousy and envy* (pp. 3–30). New York: Guilford Press.

Parrott, W. G., & Smith, R. H. (1993). Distinguishing the experiences of envy and jealousy. *Journal of Personality and Social Psychology, 64*, 906–920.

Salovey, P., & Rodin, J. (1984). Some antecedents and consequences of social-comparison jealousy. *Journal of Personality and Social Psychology, 47*, 780–792.

Silver, M., & Sabini, J. (1978). The perception of envy. *Social Psychology Quarterly, 41*, 105–117.

Smith, R. H. (2004). Envy and its transmutations. In L. Z. Tiedens & C. W. Leach (Eds.), *The social life of emotions* (pp. 43–63). Cambridge, UK: Cambridge University Press.

Smith, R. H., Combs, D. J. Y, & Thielke, S. (2008). Envy and the challenges to good health. In R. H. Smith (Ed.), *Envy: Theory and research*. New York: Oxford University Press.

Smith, R. H. & Kim. (2007). Comprehending envy. *Psychological Bulletin, 133*, 46–64.

Smith, R. H., Turner, T., Leach, C. W., Garonzik, R., Urch-Druskat, V., & Weston, C. M. (1996). Envy and *schadenfreude*. *Personality and Social Psychology Bulletin, 22*, 158–168.

Tesser, A. (1991). Emotion in social comparison and reflection processes. In J. M. Suls & T. A. Wills (Eds.), *Social comparison: Contemporary theory and research* (pp. 115–145). Hillsdale, NJ: Lawrence Erlbaum.

RICHARD H. SMITH
DAVID J. Y. COMBS
University of Kentucky

See also: Emotions; Jealousy; Self-Esteem

EPIDEMIOLOGY OF MENTAL DISORDERS

The word epidemiology is derived from the Greek words epidemos, meaning "among the people." Epidemiology is the branch of public health concerned with understanding and controlling disease in the population by investigating correlates of illness that might provide clues about disease-causing agents (Susser, 1973). Because the ultimate goals of epidemiological research are to understand the causes of disease and to prevent disease occurrence, epidemiology is the backbone of public health.

Among the earliest epidemiologic investigations is that of John Graunt, who in 1662 used birth and mortality records collected by parish clerks to study variations in birth and death patterns by sex, urban-rural residence, and seasonality, in hopes that such data could provide clues toward understanding human disease. Early epidemiologic research also includes the work of John Snow, who concluded that the London cholera outbreak of 1848 was associated with the discharge of fecal waste into the water supply, based on the observation that the mortality rate among residents served by a water company whose source was from a heavily polluted part of the Thames River was many times higher than that of other residents. Importantly, Snow reduced the level of mortality by turning off the offending company's pump, thus demonstrating that prevention efforts can be highly successful even if the specific cause of a disease (in this case, a microorganism) is not known.

The principles by which modern epidemiologic studies are now conducted have largely emerged since the end of World War II (Rothman & Greenland, 1998). With the establishment of such principles, large-scale epidemiologic studies on numerous diseases and conditions have proliferated. Results of these studies have had a profound effect on our understanding of diseases (e.g., cardiovascular disease), their risk factors (e.g., smoking), and on public health (e.g., highly successful primary prevention programs for infectious diseases such as poliomyelitis). It is conventional to organize discussion of epidemiology into three broad types of studies: descriptive, analytical, and experimental. Descriptive epidemiology estimates the prevalence and correlates of illness. Analytical epidemiology investigates hypotheses about the causes of illness based on naturalistic studies. Experimental epidemiology tests hypotheses in interventions that manipulate putative causal factors. The latter can include either causes of the first onset of illness or causes of illness severity or persistence.

Important characteristics that distinguish epidemiological research from other types of clinical investigation are the inclusion of representative samples and the application of systematic methods for determining diagnoses and outcomes. In the case of epidemiological studies of mental disorders, the specific types of samples and choice of mental illness measures depend on the goals of the studies. For studies aimed at establishing prevalence and incidence, the population-based survey is the optimal method. Complex sampling procedures have been developed to ensure that samples are representative of the populations from which they were drawn. For rare disorders, identified patients are usually ascertained from registries or a representative set of psychiatric treatment facilities. However, because only a minority of individuals with diagnosable mental disorders is ever treated (Wang et al., 2005), this method is more open to error in studying mental disorders than disorders where the vast majority of cases seek treatment (e.g., in the study of risk factors for heart attacks).

Epidemiological studies of mental disorders are commonly referred to as "psychiatric epidemiology." Psychiatric epidemiology lags behind most other branches of epidemiology because of continuing controversies about how best to conceptualize and measure mental disorders. As a result of these controversies, descriptive studies are the focus of much more research in psychiatric epidemiology than in other branches of epidemiology. These controversies can be traced to confusions about diagnostic criteria, which in the first two editions of the American Psychiatric Association's *Diagnostic and Statistical Manual of Mental Disorders* (DSM) were specified in terms of vaguely-defined etiology-based syndromes that could not be measured in the rigorous way needed for epidemiological research (Mayes & Horwitz, 2005). Epidemiological studies carried out between the end of World War II and the early 1980s consequently defined cases indirectly as scores above some threshold on a general symptom inventory.

This all changed, though, after the publication of the third edition of the DSM in 1980, when for the first time mental disorders were defined in terms of symptom-based categories. This change in diagnostic approach allowed the development of structured diagnostic interview schedules that led to substantial subsequent progress in psychiatric epidemiology, beginning with the implementation of large-scale general population surveys to estimate the prevalence and correlates of mental disorders and following with analytical and, more recently, experimental epidemiological studies. However, due to the fact that the diagnostic criteria for many mental disorders changed in subsequent DSM-III-R (1987) and DSM-IV (1994) revisions (and text revisions were made in DSM-IV-TR; American Psychiatric Association, 2000), descriptive studies continued to be of more importance than in other areas of epidemiology. This remains true even today, as a new edition of the DSM (DSM-V) is scheduled for publication in the next few years, and a new edition of the *International Classification of Diseases* (ICD) is scheduled for publication at about the same time. An added complication is that the diagnostic criteria in the ICD and DSM systems differ in a number of important ways.

Descriptive Psychiatric Epidemiology

Descriptive psychiatric epidemiology studies patterns of mental disorders, including how frequently they occur, their distribution in the population, and their time course (e.g., their onset, duration, and recurrence). Despite the changes in the various editions of the DSM and the differences between DSM and ICD criteria, descriptive studies using modern (i.e., post-1980) criteria find that mental disorders are commonly occurring, seriously impairing, often have a chronic-recurrent course, often begin in childhood or adolescence, and often have significantly adverse effects on life course development. These results hold no matter which of the several sets of modern criteria is used to define cases (Wang, Tohen, Bromet, Angst, & Kessler, 2008). Basic information of this sort is fundamental to the understanding of mental disorders and to the development of effective intervention and prevention programs.

Descriptive psychiatric epidemiological studies have also expanded in recent years to include studies aimed explicitly at evaluating the implications of changing diagnostic criteria. These studies show that most mental disorders represent extreme values on underlying dimensions in which a substantial number of people have subthreshold symptom profiles associated with distress and impairment. A related expansion has been in the subfield of genetic epidemiology, which has documented that scores on the dimensional scales that underlie many mental disorders aggregate in families in ways that strongly suggest the existence of genetic influences. Other recent expansions of descriptive psychiatric epidemiological research include studies of the relationships between physical and mental disorders (documenting that mental disorders co-occur with many physical disorders at levels much higher than expected by chance and precede co-occurring physical disorders in age of onset, raising the possibility that mental disorders might be causal risk factors for some physical disorders) and studies of the use and outcomes of mental health treatments (documenting that mental disorders often go untreated and that much of the treatment delivered is at a sub-optimal level of intensity).

Psychiatric epidemiological studies are increasingly drawing their samples from institutions, such as psychiatric hospitals, general medical facilities, schools, and workplaces. There has been particular recent interest in conducting psychiatric epidemiological studies in primary medical care settings, both because people with mental disorders are relatively heavy utilizers of general medical services and because primary care providers are increasingly being given the responsibility of treating mental disorders. Such studies have focused on the recognition and treatment of mental disorders and the specific patterns of health service use by patients with diagnosable mental disorders. It is likely that these so-called "clinical epidemiological" studies will become more common in the future.

Recent psychiatric epidemiological studies have also been carried out in workplace settings to document the prevalence and workplace costs of untreated mental disorders. A number of epidemiological studies of child-adolescent mental disorders have also been carried out in school settings. Experimental screening, outreach, and treatment effectiveness studies based on the results of epidemiological studies have been carried out in primary care and workplace samples to document the cost-effectiveness of treating mental disorders either as a way of reducing unnecessary primary care visits for vaguely defined physical complaints that are actually due to undetected mental disorders (Hiller, Fichter, & Rief, 2003) or as a way of reducing adverse workplace outcomes (e.g., sickness absence, low work performance, workplace accidents-injuries, disability) due to untreated mental disorders (Simon, Ludman, & Operskalski, 2006).

Promising Areas of Recent Research in Analytical and Experimental Psychiatric Epidemiology

The ability to refine the categorization of cases has been essential for allowing psychiatric epidemiologists to progress from simple descriptive studies aimed at establishing rates to analytical studies aimed both at identifying risk factors and at examining biological and psychosocial variables that mediate or modify the effects of these risk factors. An especially promising area in which there is significant research activity is the investigation of the genetic bases of mental disorders (Risch & Merikangas, 1996) and the modification of these risks by environmental exposures, especially in the prenatal period.

Another area of recent expansion has been clinical epidemiology. Whereas traditional epidemiology has largely been concerned with the occurrence and causes of disease, clinical epidemiology has emerged as a closely related discipline that seeks to identify the occurrence and determinants of clinical outcomes from illnesses (Sackett, Haynes, & Tugwell, 1985). Clinical epidemiological studies employ the same principles and methods as population-based epidemiology, but are usually conducted in clinical samples. Clinical epidemiologic investigations, such as the National Institute of Mental Health Collaborative Program on the Psychobiology of Depression and the Harvard-Brown Anxiety Research Program have provided important information on prognostic factors associated with the natural history of mental disorders. Other important prospective studies include countywide studies of the course of first-admission psychosis that include patients from all facilities in the respective geographical regions, follow-up studies of first-episode psychotic patients to investigate patterns and predictors of illness course, and prospective cohort studies of children and their parents to investigate risk factors for the onset of mental disorders. Pharmacoepidemiology has been an especially fast-growing component of clinical epidemiologic inquiry. Pharmacoepidemiological studies typically focus on description of the patterns and predictors of medications for the treatment of disorders, with a special interest in the unanticipated hazards associated with these medications.

Psychiatric epidemiological research has also begun to evaluate the economic costs associated with mental disorders, both the direct costs for the provision of mental health services and the indirect costs to society secondary to the disability caused by disorders. The World Health Organization Global Burden of Disease (GBD) study (Murray & Lopez, 1996) identified mental disorders as among the most costly diseases in the world. Indeed, major depression was identified by the GBD as the single most burdensome disease in the world among individuals younger than 45 years of age. Another closely related area of inquiry is that of mental health services research, which uses community epidemiological data to investigate the patterns of utilization of mental health services, unmet needs for treatment, barriers to help-seeking, the quality of treatments, and premature dropout from treatment.

The accumulation of information on risk factors for mental disorders, their outcomes, and treatment has led to another important line of inquiry in psychiatric epidemiology: interventional research. In addition to efficacy trials of psychiatric treatments conducted under rigorously controlled conditions, experimental studies have begun to include effectiveness trials of "real-world" treatment strategies (Simon et al., 2006). The proliferation of effective but costly interventions, coupled with growing constraints on healthcare budgets, have also made it imperative to study the cost-effectiveness and cost-benefits of interventions. Economic analyses consequently now accompany most efficacy and effectiveness trials of interventions. Other experimental and quasi-experimental studies have manipulated putative environmental risk factors for the onset of mental disorders, including exposure to childhood family adversities (Kessler et al., 2008) and neighborhood stressors (Leventhal & Brooks-Gunn, 2003). It is likely that intervention studies such as these will become more common as the field of psychiatric epidemiology matures over the next few decades.

REFERENCES

American Psychiatric Association (2000). *Diagnostic and statstical manual of mental disorders* (4th ed., text rev.). Washington, DC: Author.

Hiller, W., Fichter, M. M., & Rief, W. (2003). A controlled treatment study of somatoform disorders including analysis of healthcare utilization and cost-effectiveness. *Journal of Psychosomatic Research, 54,* 369–380.

Kessler, R. C., Pecora, P. J., Williams, J., Hiripi, E., O'Brien, K., English, D., et al. (2008). Effects of enhanced foster care on the long-term physical and mental health of foster care alumni. *Archives of General Psychiatry, 65,* 625–633.

Leventhal, T., & Brooks-Gunn, J. (2003). Moving to opportunity: An experimental study of neighborhood effects on mental health. *American Journal of Public Health, 93,* 1576–1582.

Mayes, R., & Horwitz, A. V. (2005). DSM-III and the revolution in the classification of mental illness. *Journal of the History of Behavioral Sciences, 41,* 249–267.

Murray, C. J. L., & Lopez, A. D. (1996). *The global burden of disease: A comprehensive assessment of mortality and disability from diseases, injuries and risk factors in 1990 and projected to 2020.* Cambridge: Harvard University Press.

Risch, N., & Merikangas, K. (1996). The future of genetic studies of complex human diseases. *Science, 273,* 1516–1517.

Rothman, K. M., & Greenland, S. (1998). *Modern epidemiology* (2nd ed.). Philadelphia: Lippincott-Raven.

Sackett, D. L., Haynes, R. B., & Tugwell, P. (1985). *Clinical epidemiology: A basic science for clinical medicine.* Boston: Little, Brown and Company.

Simon, G. E., Ludman, E. J., & Operskalski, B. H. (2006). Randomized trial of a telephone care management program for outpatients starting antidepressant treatment. *Psychiatric Services, 57,* 1441–1445.

Susser, M. (1973). *Causal thinking in the health sciences: Concepts and strategies of epidemiology.* New York: Oxford University Press.

Wang, P. S., Lane, M., Olfson, M., Pincus, H. A., Wells, K. B., & Kessler, R. C. (2005). Twelve-month use of mental health services in the United States: Results from the National Comorbidity Survey Replication. *Archives of General Psychiatry, 62,* 629–640.

Wang, P. S., Tohen, M., Bromet, E. J., Angst, J., & Kessler, R. C. (2008). Psychiatric epidemiology. In A. Tasman, J. Kay, & J. A. Lieberman (Eds.), *Psychiatry* (3rd ed.). Chichester, UK: John Wiley & Sons.

SUGGESTED READINGS

Kessler, R. C., & Ustun, T. B. (Eds.). (2008). *The WHO world mental health surveys: Global perspectives on the epidemiology of mental disorders*. New York: Cambridge University Press.

Susser, E., Schwartz, S., Morabia, A., Begg, M., & Bromet, E. (2006). *Psychiatric epidemiology: Searching for causes of mental disorders*. New York: Oxford University Press.

Tsaung, M. T., & Tohen, M. (Eds.). (2003). *Textbook in psychiatric epidemiology* (2nd ed.). Hoboken, NJ: John Wiley & Sons.

RONALD C. KESSLER
Harvard Medical School

PHILIP S. WANG
National Institute of Mental Health Care Policy

See also: Diagnostic Classification; Diagnostic and Statistical Manual of Mental Disorders (DSM-IV-TR); Sampling Methods

EPILEPSY

The term *epilepsy* is derived from the Greek word *epilambabein,* meaning "to attack." It is defined by repetitive abnormal cerebral neuron firing that may or may not be accompanied by a disturbance of consciousness or an alteration in perceptual motor functioning. Recurrent seizures are a required manifestation of epilepsy.

It is important to distinguish epilepsy from seizures. A seizure is an event. Epilepsy is a disorder in which seizures recur. In epilepsy, seizures recur exclusively because of a chronic underlying pathology in the central nervous system, such as metabolic abnormality or damage from head trauma. However, a seizure also may occur due to a process, such as fever, external to the central nervous system. Consequently, a person who presents with a seizure as the result of a temporary or correctable condition (e.g., fever) does not necessarily have epilepsy. A person who presents with recurrent seizures as the result of chronic underlying neuropathology, such as tumor or damage from encephalitis, stroke, or head trauma, is correctly diagnosed with epilepsy.

Epidemiology

In the United States, the prevalence of epilepsy is estimated at 8 per 1,000 population. Approximately 30% of epilepsies occur between birth and 5 years of age, and 75% of epilepsies present by age 20. The remaining epilepsies are distributed across adulthood, with a disproportionate share affecting persons older than 65 years. In two thirds of cases, the cause of epilepsy is idiopathic, that is, unknown. The remaining one third of cases are distributed across multiple etiologies, including stroke, head trauma, alcohol, brain tumor, and infection (Banerjee & Hauser, 2008).

Classification

More than 30 different types of seizures have been identified as accompanying epilepsy (Cavazos & Spitz, 2007). These seizure types are classified into two broad categories: (1) partial seizures, which begin at a single site in the brain and typically affect only one sensory or motor system, and (2) generalized seizures, which occur in both hemispheres of the brain at onset and affect the body bilaterally and symmetrically. Approximately 60% of persons with epilepsy experience partial seizures, which also are known as focal seizures.

Partial seizures are further divided into simple and complex varieties. Simple partial seizures may present with motor, sensory, autonomic, or psychic symptoms. Motor symptoms are the classic form of presentation, often beginning as uncontrollable bending (flexion), alternating with extending (extension) around a joint of a distal extremity, such as a finger or wrist, creating a tapping or flailing appearance. Persons with simple partial seizures do not lose consciousness. However, they may experience sudden, unexplained feelings of joy, sadness, anger, or nausea, with or without motor symptoms. They also may experience auras, or the sensation of hearing, smelling, tasting, seeing, or feeling things that are not real.

Complex partial seizures may present in a variety of fashions, with the single requirement that consciousness is altered. The alteration of consciousness may be subtle or dramatic and may affect mood, cognition, memory, and personality traits. The classic presentation of a complex partial seizure involves automatisms, which consist of stereotypic or repetitive activities ranging from eye blinking and lip smacking to marching in circles and disrobing. In some instances, the person continues to engage in an activity, such as washing dishes, but in a repetitive and unproductive manner. Like simple partial seizures, most complex partial seizures are very short-lived, lasting 15 seconds or less. Once a complex partial seizure has concluded, the affected person is often disoriented, tired, and unable to recall the event.

Generalized seizures are a heterogeneous group that includes absence seizures and tonic-clonic seizures. Both of these types involve an impairment of consciousness and bilateral motor symptoms. In the classic tonic-clonic seizure, the person's eyes roll upward into the head, an event that is accompanied by loss of consciousness.

There also may be a grunt or piercing cry, caused by the constriction of the thoracic muscles and forced exhalation through constricted vocal chords. The person then becomes rigid, extending the extremities and arching the back (tonic phase) followed by rhythmic contractions of the extremities (clonic phase). Tonic-clonic seizures are self-limiting and can last from a few seconds to 30 minutes. In absence seizures, there is a brief period of loss of consciousness without the accompanying motor activity. Absence seizures are characterized by momentary lapses of consciousness involving staring, head drooping, loss of facial muscle tone, and in some cases, eyelid fluttering. The onset of an absence seizure is without warning; the seizure typically lasts between 2 to 10 seconds.

Mortality and Morbidity

The risk of death is 2 to 3 times greater for persons with epilepsy compared with the general population. Accidents (drowning), pneumonia, status epilepticus, suicide, and cerebrovascular disease are the leading causes (Morgan & Kerr, 2002). Similarly, the risk of physical injury is higher for individuals with epilepsy. Thirty-five percent of individuals who experienced at least one seizure in the course of a year reported a physical injury related to the seizure. Head injury, burns and scalds, dental injury, and fractures were the most frequently reported (Beghi & Cornaggia, 2002).

Psychological and Social Sequelae

Generalized convulsive seizure activity is frightening to observe, and behavior associated with complex partial seizures may be odd and difficult for the naive observer to reconcile. Children, in particular, may quickly distance themselves from classmates who, during seizures, contort their bodies, urinate, vomit, and/or fall and damage face and head. The child's own embarrassment, when told of the events, may lead to voluntary social isolation and a powerful negative self-image. Regarding adults, approximately 25% of working-age individuals with epilepsy are unemployed as a direct result of their seizure disorder. Others complain that they are underemployed because of driving and work-related safety restrictions. Occupational hardship, social prejudice, the side effects of anticonvulsant medication, and the psychiatric aspects of living with a chronic illness all come to bear on the issue of quality of life for the person with epilepsy (Barrett & Sachs, 2008).

Treatment

Antiepileptic Drugs

Antiepileptic drug therapy is the standard treatment for the vast majority of individuals with epilepsy. Approximately 80% of individuals obtain control of their seizure disorder through the use of medication. Valproic acid is considered the treatment of choice for generalized seizures. It is also effective in the treatment of partial seizures. Similarly, carbamazepine has a well-deserved reputation as an effective treatment for generalized and partial seizures. Ethosuximide is the treatment of choice for absence seizures. Other medications, such as phenytoin, oxcarbazepine, lamotrigine, and gabapentin, also are considered effective antiepileptic drugs (French & Pedley, 2008).

Surgery

Approximately 20% of individuals with epilepsy are resistant to antiepileptic drug therapy. Individuals with mesial temporal lobe epilepsy are the vast majority of the treatment-refractory group. Surgical treatment has emerged as a safe and effective option for these individuals. Approximately 70% of individuals emerge from surgical treatment as seizure-free. An additional 25% of individuals reported a 90% decrease in seizure activity (Cohen-Gadol et al., 2006).

Ketogenic Diet

The ketogenic diet is carefully calculated to simulate the metabolism of a fasting body. The diet relies on burning body fat for energy rather than relying on the intake of glucose from carbohydrates. In the absence of glucose, stored body fat is not burned completely and leaves a residue in the form of ketone bodies that build up in the blood. For reasons unknown, the presence of high levels of ketones in the blood frequently results in the control of seizures. Approximately 30–50% of individuals whose seizures were refractory to the antiepileptic drug therapy were reported as responding favorably to the ketogenic diet (Freeman, Kelly, & Freeman, 1994).

Vagus Nerve Stimulation

Vagal nerve stimulation is an alternative treatment for individuals who have failed antiepileptic drug therapy and who are not candidates for surgery (NINDS, 2006). The procedure involves the subcutaneous implanting of a small generator in the infraclavicular region. The generator is connected to a bipolar platinum electrode placed on the left vagus nerve and programmed by laptop computer to deliver electrical pulses on an intermittent basis. The precise mechanism of action is unknown. However, observations of increased activation of cortical and subcortical pathways secondary to vagal nerve stimulation is thought to result in creating an increased seizure threshold.

REFERENCES

Banerjee, P. N., & Hauser, W. A. (2008). Incidence and prevalence. In J. Engel & T. A. Pedley (Eds.), *Epilepsy: A comprehensive textbook* (pp. 45–56). Baltimore: Wolters.

Barrett, R. P., & Sachs, H. T. (2008). Epilepsy and seizures. In L. Phelps (Ed.), *Chronic health-related disorders in children* (pp. 91–110). Washington, DC: American Psychological Association.

Beghi, E., & Cornaggia, C. (2002). Morbidity and accidents in patients with epilepsy. *Epilepsia, 43*, 1076–1083.

Cavazos, J. E., & Spitz, M. (2007). Seizures and epilepsy: Overview and classification. *eMedicine*. Retrieved November 30, 2007, from http://www.emedicine.com/neuro/TOPIC415.HTM.

Cohen-Gadol, A. A., Wilhelmi, B. S., Collignon, F., et al. (2006). Long term outcome of epilepsy surgery among 399 patients with nonlesional seizure foci including mesial temporal lobe sclerosis. *Journal of Neurosurgery, 104*, 513–524.

Freeman, J. M., Kelly, M. T., & Freeman, J. B. (1994). *The epilepsy diet treatment: An introduction to the ketogenic diet.* New York: Demos.

French, J. A., & Pedley, T. A. (2008). Initial management of epilepsy. *New England Journal of Medicine, 359*, 166–176.

Morgan, C. L., & Kerr, M. P. (2002). Epilepsy and mortality. *Epilepsia, 43*, 1251–1255.

National Institute of Neurological Disorders and Stroke (NINDS). (2006). *Seizures and epilepsy: Hope through research.* Bethesda, MD: National Institute of Health.

ROWLAND P. BARRETT
Warren Alpert Medical School of Brown University

EPISODIC MEMORY

When we think back to a past experience, such as a childhood birthday party, we can bring to mind faces of people in attendance, the appearance and location of the event, the sounds of voices or music, and our mood and thoughts. This contextually rich form of retrieval is the basis for episodic memory. As defined by Endel Tulving (1983), an episodic memory contains three critical elements that delineate it from other forms of memory. The first is that the memories are embedded in a spatiotemporal context in which some aspects of the location and timing of the event are available to consciousness. The second is that they are personal memories associated with a distinct impression of self-involvement. The third is that they are accompanied by a subjective awareness of remembering in which sights, sounds, and other experiences are replayed in the present moment.

These elements of personal and temporal context differentiate episodic remembering from all other types of learning and memory. These other forms of memory include the learning of new motor skills or mental procedures, and the automatic influence of prior habits or experiences on current behavior (sometimes dubbed "implicit" or "nonconscious" memories). To the degree that these forms of memory do not elicit a subjective experience of "thinking of the past," they are not considered to be episodic memories. Episodic memory also can be differentiated from "working memory," which is the temporary activation of information to help us perform ongoing tasks. Rehearsing a phone number while we enter it into our cell phone is a common example. Like episodic memory, working memory involves the conscious access to information, but it is not considered episodic memory because attention is oriented towards present performance as opposed to past episodes.

Semantic memory is another conscious form of memory that is distinct from episodic memory. Semantic memories are factual details or general knowledge about the world that can be retrieved in the absence of the original context in which they were acquired. Knowledge of state capitals, the alphabet and vocabulary, and the names of objects are all examples of semantic memory. Knowledge of some personal facts, such as your name or where you were born, also would be considered semantic memories, because you do not have to think back to the past to retrieve this information. Of course, many aspects of autobiographical knowledge contain elements of both episodic and semantic memories (Conway, 2005).

Encoding: Associative Binding

A fundamental link between the medial temporal lobes (MTL) and episodic memory was revealed nearly five decades ago in the case of the neurosurgical patient H.M. (Corkin, 2002). To alleviate epileptic seizure activity, neurosurgeons removed a large portion of the medial parts of H.M.'s temporal lobes. Postoperatively, H.M. became profoundly impaired in his ability to form new episodic and semantic memories (anterograde amnesia) and lost access to some memories from before the surgery (retrograde amnesia). Other cognitive abilities remained intact. For instance, H.M. could carry on a conversation with visitors, but when they returned later he could not remember the earlier visit. Later research demonstrated that the MTL is critical for forming associations between various contextual details during encoding. For example, using functional magnetic resonance imaging (fMRI), Davachi and colleagues found that the level of hippocampal activity during encoding predicted whether studied information could be consciously recollected at a later test (Davachi, Mitchell, & Wagner, 2003).

Although the MTL is critical for binding information into episodic memories, the details of those memories are thought to be stored in neocortical areas that are involved in the analysis of the event at encoding. Neuroimaging studies have shown that retrieval of sensory and motor details is associated with a reactivation of a subset of cortical areas that were involved when the event was originally perceived (Buckner & Wheeler, 2001). Thus, recalling the face of a friend and the music played at the birthday party involves reactivating parts of the visual cortex that process facial features and parts of the auditory cortex that analyze complex frequency and temporal characteristics of sound.

Attention and working memory have a dramatic influence on the way episodic memories are encoded. Many behavioral studies have shown that dividing attention at encoding impairs subsequent memory, whereas elaborating on encoded events with pre-existing information enhances subsequent memory. Moreover, fMRI studies have found that activity in the prefrontal cortex during encoding, much like activity in MTL, can predict subsequent memory ability (Wagner et al., 1998). These prefrontal regions are involved in attentional control and working memory, and their activation at encoding is thought to reflect the strategic use of rehearsal and elaboration strategies that facilitate subsequent memory.

In addition to processes occurring during the initial event, many researchers believe that memories continue to be "consolidated" for some time afterward, thereby protecting them from subsequent forgetting (see Wixted, 2004). The role of sleep in memory consolidation also is an active area of research, with some theories positing that recurrent activity between MTL and cortical regions strengthen important associations (e.g., synaptic connections), thereby making them easier to retrieve upon awakening. A common finding in support of this idea is that memory is stronger after a period of sleep, relative to the same period spent awake. Of course, sleep also reduces the probability of encoding potentially interfering information relative to a period of wakefulness, so that some of the benefits of sleep on memory may be caused by reduced interference instead of enhanced consolidation.

Retrieval: Associative Reconstruction

The successful retrieval of episodic memories depends on a match between encoded information and retrieval cues. As described in the prior section, information is encoded by a network of brain regions, including cortical regions that code for various details and MTL regions that bind this information into a coherent trace. Retrieval is thought to involve the reverse process, whereby a retrieval cue partially activates some of these cortical details, leading to reactivation of the entire trace via MTL-dependent associations. For instance, the scent of baking cake might reactivate the memory of chocolate cake at the birthday party, leading to memories of the people involved and associated events, but this memory is more likely to be triggered if the retrieval cue overlaps with the original episode (e.g., the scent of chocolate versus vanilla cake).

Episodic memory is not a replaying of information stored in memory, but is rather a dynamic process in which a cue interacts with a memory trace to produce a reconstruction of the original experience. Remembering is dynamic because neither the stored information nor the retrieval process is stable over time. Stored information can be lost due to forgetting and interference, it can be recoded in ways that are not entirely consistent with the original events, and it can become temporarily inaccessible (as when the right retrieval cues are not available). In addition, retrieval of one event can be influenced by the retrieval of other events, as well as by the person's goals at the time of retrieval. To capture this dynamic nature of retrieval processes, Ulric Neisser has likened memory reconstruction to the process of a paleontologist assembling a dinosaur from a few bone fragments (Neisser, 1967).

Because of its reconstructive nature, episodic memory is susceptible to distortion. In order to avoid distorted or false memories, people use various inferential processes at retrieval to monitor the accuracy of memory (Johnson, Hashtroudi, & Lindsay, 1993). In addition to the quality of the retrieved information, these retrieval monitoring processes make use of our expectations about memories. For instance, did you send your friend a birthday card, or did you buy the card and forget to send it? According to the reality monitoring framework proposed by Marcia Johnson and colleagues, if we realize that our memory for sending the birthday card should be relatively rich with details (e.g., having to write a funny message), then the failure to retrieve these details would help us to infer that we had not actually sent the card. Conversely, if we do not take these memory expectations into account, then we might falsely believe that the card was sent, especially if we remember buying the card. Various factors, such as making speeded decisions or being exposed to misinformation, can impair retrieval monitoring and enhance memory distortion.

As was the case with encoding processes, prefrontal regions work in a coordinated fashion with MTL and other cortical regions to reconstruct episodic memory at the time of retrieval. Patients with damage to prefrontal cortex can be more prone to pathological false memories (confabulation), which demonstrate impaired retrieval monitoring. The development of this network of brain regions across the lifespan also influences episodic memory. This network becomes fully developed relatively late in life, leading to more resilient episodic memories in adults than in children. It is also among the first areas to be affected in age-related diseases, as in causing memory impairments in the earliest stages of Alzheimer's disease. Fortunately, the normal aging process does not affect our ability to remember the most important episodic memories of our lives—those that are well rehearsed and laden with emotions or have been incorporated into autobiographical knowledge.

REFERENCES

Buckner, R. L., & Wheeler, M. E. (2001). The cognitive neuroscience of remembering. *Nature Reviews Neuroscience, 2,* 624–634.

Conway, M. A. (2005). Memory and the self. *Journal of Memory and Language, 53,* 594–628.

Corkin, S. (2002). What's new with the amnesic patient H.M.? *Nature Reviews Neuroscience, 3,* 153–160.

Davachi, L., Mitchell, J. P., & Wagner, A. D. (2003). Multiple routes to memory: Distinct medial temporal lobe processes build item and source memories. *Proceedings of the National Academy of Sciences of the United States of America, 100,* 2157–2162.

Johnson, M. K., Hashtroudi, S., & Lindsay, D. S. (1993). Source monitoring. *Psychological Bulletin, 114,* 3–28.

Neisser, U. (1967). *Cognitive psychology.* New York: Appleton-Century-Crofts.

Tulving, E. (1983). *Elements of episodic memory.* Oxford, UK: Clarendon Press.

Wagner, A. D., Schacter, D. L., Rotte, M., Koutstaal, W., Maril, A., Dale, A. M., et al. (1998). Building memories: Remembering and forgetting of verbal experiences as predicted by brain activity. *Science, 281,* 1188–1191.

Wixted, J. T. (2004). The psychology and neuroscience of forgetting. *Annual Review of Psychology, 55,* 235–269.

SUGGESTED READINGS

Roediger, H. L. III,, Dudai, Y., Fitzpatrick, S. M. (Eds.). (2007). *Science of memory: Concepts.* New York: Oxford University Press.

Schacter, D. L. (1996). *Searching for memory.* New York: Basic Books.

Tulving, E., & Craik, F. (Eds.). (2000). *The Oxford handbook of memory.* Oxford, UK: Oxford University Press.

MARK E. WHEELER
University of Pittsburgh

DAVID A. GALLO
University of Chicago

See also: **Episodic Memory and the Hippocampus; Memory Functions**

EPISODIC MEMORY AND THE HIPPOCAMPUS

What did you have for breakfast yesterday? Who went with you to the movies? Who did you see at work today? It is likely that you can answer all questions of this sort. Moreover, if you continue to focus on retrieving information relevant to one or more of these questions, you will recover an amazing amount of contextual detail that surrounded the personal experience. Now answer another question: Did you intend to remember any of these experiences? The likely answer in most cases will be no. Thus, this small exercise reveals that your brain contains a memory system that automatically captures the content of your daily life and stores it in a manner that permits you to intentionally retrieve and replay it.

The term *episodic memory system* is used to describe the system that supports this ability to store and recall personal experiences or episodes (Tulving, 1983). It is contrasted against another system called *semantic memory* that allows us to store factual information and general knowledge that has no personal relevance. A neural system that includes a region in the medial temporal lobes called the hippocampal formation supports the episodic memory. The primary evidence for this statement is that people with damage to this region cannot acquire new episodic memories (Milner, 1970; Squire, 1992). Moreover, if damage to this region is extensive episodic memories acquired before the insult are also lost.

The Hippocampal Formation Index

Virtually all modern theories of how the hippocampal formation supports episodic memory are a variation of a framework called indexing theory (Teyler & DiScenna, 1986; O'Reilly & Rudy, 2002; Rolls & Kesner, 2006). This theory can be understood in relationship to Figure 1. It assumes that the individual features that make up a particular episode establish a memory trace by activating patterns of neural activity in the neocortex. This pattern of activity projects to the hippocampal formation. As a consequence, co-activated synapses in the hippocampus responding to the neocortical inputs are strengthened. The outcome of this neocortical–hippocampus interaction

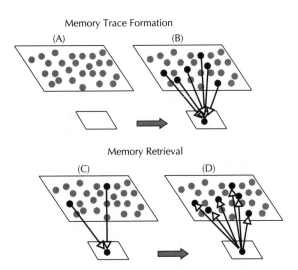

Figure 1. Memory Formation: (A) The top layer represents patterns of neocortical activity, while the bottom layer represents the hippocampus. (B) A set of neocortical patterns (black dots) activated by a particular experience is projected to the hippocampus and activates a unique set of synapses. Memory Retrieval: (C) A subset of the initial input pattern can activate the hippocampal representation. (D) When this occurs, output from the hippocampus projects back to the neocortex to activate the entire pattern. Thus the hippocampus stores an index to neocortical patterns that can be used to retrieve the memory.

is the memory trace represented in B on Figure 1. Note that the experience is represented simply as the set of strengthened synapses in the hippocampus that result from the input pattern. There are no modifications among the neocortical activity patterns. Thus, the memory trace is a hippocampal representation of co-occurring patterns of activity in the neocortex.

The indexing nature of the memory trace can be illustrated in relationship to memory retrieval. Note in C on Figure 1 that a subset of the original input pattern is received by the neocortex. The projections from these input patterns activate the connected neurons in the hippocampus representing the original experience. The activation of this representation then projects back to the neocortex to activate the pattern representing the entire experience (D). It is this projection back to the neocortex that conveys the indexing property to the hippocampus representation. Thus, the index supports a process called pattern completion—the experience of a subset of the features that made up the original experience can activate the neural representations of all the features.

A Neural System that Supports the Index

The indexing properties of the hippocampal formation are possible because of the organization of the neural system in which it is situated. This system is illustrated in Figure 2. Sensory information flows into what are called associative areas of the neocortex and from there to areas of the medial temporal lobes (perirhinal cortex and parahippipcampal cortex, entorhinal cortex) and finally to the hippocampal formation. At each stage

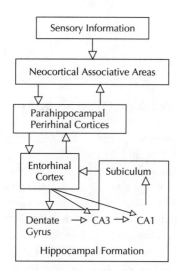

Figure 2. A schematic representation of the neural system that supports indexing theory. Sensory information flows (solid arrows) to the hippocampal formation by way of associative cortices and the medial temporal lobe regions (parahippocampus, perirhinal and entorhinal cortices). Information processed through the hippocampus then flows back (dashed arrows to the cortical sites that initially brought the information to the hippocampal formation).

the information becomes more highly processed. It is important to appreciate that this neural system has a hierarchical organization—information from diverse neocortical areas converges onto the hippocampal formation. So, in a sense the hippocampus "sees" what is happening in these diverse areas and is in a position to bind these inputs together. A second point is that this system has a return loop—the information carried forward to the hippocampal formation is then projected back to the sites lower in the hierarchy that initially brought the information to the hippocampal formation. It is the anatomy of his return loop that makes it possible for the hippocampal formation to provide the index to the neocortical sites that represent the features of a particular episode so that it can support pattern completion.

Synaptic Plasticity and the Hippocampal Index

To create and maintain an index, the connections linking neocortical projections to the hippocampus must be modifiable. Indexing theory capitalizes on the fact that in both intact organisms (Bliss & Lomo, 1973) and in tissue slices taken from the hippocampus (Teyler, 1999) synapses in different regions of the hippocampus are easily modified by input activity synaptic activity—a process called Long Term Potentiation (LTP). Thus, not only does the hippocampus see what is happening in the neocortex, the mechanisms supporting synaptic plasticity are available to support an index.

Our everyday experiences inform us that we have an episodic memory system that automatically captures a record of the many episodes that make up our existence. Episodic memory is made possible by a neural system that includes the hippocampal formation. In this system the hippocampal formation is situated at the end of a hierarchically organized processing stream where it receives information about the neocortical patterns of activity representing the features of particular episodes. It joins together these inputs to create an index that can be activated by some subset of the original episode. This output from the index can then activate the patterns of neocortical activity that represent the whole episode that is perceived as memory.

REFERENCES

Bliss, T. V., & Lomo, T. (1973). Long lasting potentiation of synaptic transmission in the dentate area of the anaesthetized rabbit following stimulation of the perforant path. *Journal of Physiology, 232*, 331–356.

Milner B. (1970). Memory and the medial temporal regions of the brain. In K. P. Pribram & D. E. Broadbent (Eds.), *Biology of memory*. New York: Academic Press.

O'Reilly, R. C., & Rudy, J. W. (2002). Conjunctive representations in learning and memory: Principles of cortical and hippocampal function. *Psychological Review, 108*, 311–345.

Rolls, E. T., & Kesner, R. P. (2006). A computational theory of hippocampal function, and empirical tests of the theory. *Progress in Neurobiology 79*, 1–48.

Squire, L. R. (1992). Memory and the hippocampus: A synthesis from findings with rats, monkeys, and humans. *Psychological Review, 99*, 195–231.

Teyler, T. J. (1999). Use of brain slices to study long-term potentiation and depression as examples of synaptic plasticity. Special issue of *Methods: A Companion to Methods in Enzymology*, entitled Preparation and Use of Brain Slices. A. Schurr, (Ed.), *18*, 109–116.

Teyler, T. J., & DiScenna, P. (1986). The hippocampal memory indexing theory. *Behavioral Neuroscience, 100*, 147–152.

Tulving E. (1983). *Elements of episodic memory*. Oxford, UK: Clarendon Press.

SUGGESTED READINGS

Rudy, J. W. (2008). *The Neurobiology of Learning and Memory*. Sunderland, MA: Sinauer and Associates.

Teyler, T. J., & Rudy, J. W. (2007). The hippocampal indexing theory and episodic memory: Updating the index. *Hippocampus, 17*, 1158–1169.

JERRY W. RUDY
University of Colorado, Boulder

TIMOTHY J. TEYLER
Washington State University

See also: **Declarative Memory; Memory Functions; Spatial Memory**

ERIKSON, ERIK HOMBURGER (1902–1994)

Erik Homburger Erikson was born in 1902 to unmarried Danish parents living in Germany. In 1904, his mother married a pediatrician, Theodor Homburger, who adopted Erik in 1911. Subsequently, and probably following Scandinavian traditions, he changed his name to Erik Homburger Erikson.

He studied and taught art at a private school in Vienna. While there he met Anna Freud and became quite interested in psychoanalysis. He studied psychoanalysis at the Vienna Institute, and he also became quite interested in the study of young children.

In 1933, he left Vienna to escape the Nazis who were then rising to power. With his wife, he first went to Denmark and then to Boston in the United States. He became the first child psychoanalyst in practice in Boston and soon joined the Harvard Medical School faculty. In 1936, he joined the Yale Medical School faculty and the Institute of Human Relations. After two years, he moved west to

study Sioux Indian children, and then took a job at the University of California, Berkeley. He left Berkeley in the early 1950s, during the McCarthy era, because he refused to sign a loyalty oath. Erikson moved to the Austen Riggs Center in Stockbridge, Massachusetts; about 10 years later, he moved back to Harvard's Institute of Public Relations, where he remained until he retired in 1970.

Erikson is known for his work in developmental psychology. He coined the term "identity crisis" and described the human life cycle as comprising eight stages: (1) Trust vs. mistrust; (2) Autonomy vs. shame and doubt; (3) Initiative vs. guilt; (4) Industry vs. inferiority; (5) Ego identity vs. role confusion; (6) Intimacy vs. isolation; (7) Generative vs. stagnation; and (8) Integrity vs. despair. Each stage has its accompanying psychosocial identity crisis, with its desired developmental outcome. For example, the desired outcome of the trust versus mistrust crisis is hope.

Erikson's books included two psychobiographies, *Young Man Luther* and *Gandhi's Truth*, that show how emotional conflicts can be utilized toward constructive social ends. He is best known, however, for his *Childhood and Society*, in which human life cycles are described. In *Identity: Youth and Crisis* he elaborates on the life stages of the individual and the identity crisis. Although his formal training in developmental psychology was limited, Erikson is among the most important of all developmental psychologists.

SUGGESTED READINGS

Erikson, E. (1963). *Childhood and society*. New York: W. W. Norton.

Erikson, E. (1968). *Identity, youth, and crisis*. New York: W. W. Norton.

STAFF

ERIKSONIAN DEVELOPMENTAL STAGES

The developmental theory of Erik Erikson builds upon and extends Sigmund Freud's classical account of psychosexual stages. Noteworthy in this regard is the fact that Erikson was analyzed and influenced by Freud's daughter, Anna. According to orthodox Freudian psychoanalytic theory, personality development is completed by at least adolescence and is relatively independent from positive environmental influences. Moreover, ego development is considered to be defensive in nature; the ego emerges to control and regulate the id, which comprises biologically determined instincts, needs, urges, and the like.

By contrast, Erikson (1950, 1968) provides a life-span account of psychosocial development that emphasizes the autonomous or conflict-free development of an adaptive ego that organizes experience. He postulates that human beings have a need to categorize and integrate their experiences, as well as a need to satisfy their basic biological needs. A consolidated sense of ego identity—a perceived sense of personal wholeness and "continuity of experience"—is considered to be necessary for optimal personal functioning.

The integration and development of personality follows an eight-stage, life-span sequence governed by what Erikson calls the epigenetic principle, which states that "anything that grows has a ground plan, and that out of this ground plan the parts arise, each part having its time of special ascendancy, until all parts have arisen to form a functioning whole." Each stage, from birth to old age, is marked by a normative crisis or challenge that must be confronted and negotiated. These bipolar crises may arise from intrapsychic conflicts (the first five parallel the Freudian psychosexual stages) as well as from societal demands and expectations, but the nature and quality of the social contexts within which they are negotiated and resolved vary. The crises are psychosocial in nature. Crisis resolutions have residual effects on the developing person, with each contributing to the totally formed personality. Ideally, resolutions should not be completely one-sided: A positively balanced ratio of the two poles indicates optimal developmental progress. Too much trust, for instance, may become naïveté or gullibility.

The eight stages, assumed to be interdependent, build upon each other in a cumulative manner. Each stage contributes a unique personal quality of strength or virtue such as hope, faith, or care to the developing personality. The achievement of ego identity during adolescence is central to the developmental scheme; it provides a synthesis and integration of prior experiences and developments, and it serves as the foundation upon which future adult development will proceed.

1. *Trust versus mistrust (infancy).* At birth, infants are dominated by biological needs and drives. The reliability and quality of their relationship with caregivers will influence the extent to which they develop a sense of trust (or mistrust) in others, themselves, and the world in general. The virtue of hope is associated with this stage.

2. *Autonomy versus doubt and shame (early childhood).* Social demands and the imposition of rules for self-control and bodily regulation (toilet training) influence feelings of self-efficacy versus self-doubt. The quality of will, the willful self-discipline to do what is expected and expectable, emerges at this second stage.

3. *Initiative versus guilt (preschool age).* Here children begin to actively explore their environment. Will they sense guilt about self-initiated activities or will they feel justified in forming plans and asserting control over their activities? The virtue of purpose—the

courage to pursue personal goals in spite of risks and possible failure—now ascends.

4. *Industry versus inferiority (school age).* The societal context in which the first three psychosocial conflicts are negotiated is predominantly the home and immediate family. In this fourth stage, however, children begin formal instruction of some sort. Mastery of tasks and skills valued by one's teachers and the larger society becomes a focal point. The quality of competence is said to develop.

5. *Identity versus diffusion (adolescence).* The challenge in this fifth stage is the linchpin in Erikson's scheme, a time when adolescents actively attempt to synthesize their experiences in an effort to formulate a stable sense of their identity. Although this process is psychosocial in nature—a social fit or "solidarity with group ideals" must occur—Erikson emphasizes reality testing and the acquisition of credible self-knowledge. Youth come to view themselves as products of their previous experiences, and a unified sense of temporal self-continuity is experienced. Positive resolutions of prior crises—being trusting, autonomous, willful, and industrious—facilitate identity formation, whereas previous failures may lead to identity diffusion. Fidelity, the ability to maintain commitments in spite of contradictory value systems, is the virtue that emerges during adolescence. Although personality development continues throughout life in Erikson's theory, the three adult stages are directly affected by the identity that is achieved during this adolescent stage.

6. *Intimacy versus isolation (young adulthood).* In this stage, people must be able and willing to unite their identity with that of other persons. Because authentic disclosure and mutuality leave people vulnerable, a firm and coherent sense of identity is prerequisite. The quality that ascends during this stage is love.

7. *Generativity versus stagnation (middle adulthood).* This is the time in the life span when one strives to actualize the identity that has been formed and shared with select others. The generation or production of offspring, artifacts, ideas, products, and so forth is involved. The virtue of care emerges: generative adults care for others through parenting, teaching, supervising, and various other activities, whereas stagnating adults become self-absorbed in self-centered needs and interests.

8. *Integrity versus despair (maturity).* The final Eriksonian stage highlights the integration of life experiences and efforts to come to terms with one's mortality. Mature adults face the challenge of understanding and accepting the completion or fulfillment of their one and only life cycle. Wisdom is the last virtue

to emerge. Wise people understand the relativistic nature of knowledge and accept that their life had to be the way it was.

As a heuristic scheme, Erikson's theory has had a major impact on modern psychology, especially adolescent development. Productive lines of research based on and generally consistent with Erikson's views relevant to particular stages have emerged. Research on adolescent identity formation, in particular, has been voluminous. Consistent with Erikson's writings, these investigations indicate that there are definite advantages to personally achieving a sense of identity, especially in cultural contexts characterized by change and diversity. Adolescents with informed, self-determined identity commitments generally are relatively autonomous, rational, goal-oriented, adaptive, and socially responsible (Berzonsky & Adams, 1999; Marcia, 1993). Investigators have devoted considerable attention to attempting to measure and evaluate Eriksonian stages, including intimacy-isolation (e.g., Orlofsky, 1993), generativity-stagnation (Bradley, 1997; McAdams & de St. Aubin, 1992), and integrity-despair (e.g., James & Zarrett, 2005).

Despite its popularity and apparent face validity, the empirical foundation for the sequential stage theory is relatively weak. There is in particular a need for long-term longitudinal studies to evaluate Erikson's claims about the sequential nature of psychosocial stages and the processes responsible for life-span personality development.

REFERENCES

Berzonsky, M. D., & Adams, G. R. (1999). The identity status paradigm: Still useful after thirty-five years. *Developmental Review, 19,* 557–590.

Bradley, C. L. (1997). Generativity-stagnation: Development of a status model. *Developmental Review, 17,* 262–290.

Erikson, E. H. (1950). *Childhood and society.* New York: Norton.

Erikson, E. H. (1968). *Identity: Youth and crisis.* New York: Norton.

James, J. B., & Zarrett, N. (2005). Ego integrity in the lives of older women: A follow-up of mothers from the Sears, Maccoby, and Levin (1951) patterns of child rearing study. *Journal of Adult Development, 12,* 155–167.

Marcia, J. E. (1993). The status of the statuses: Research review. In J. E. Marcia, A. S. Waterman, D. R. Matteson, S. L. Archer, & J. L. Orlofsky (Eds.), *Ego identity: A handbook for psychosocial research* (pp. 22–41). New York: Springer-Verlag.

McAdams, D. P., & de St. Aubin, E. (1992). A theory of generativity and its assessment through self-report, behavioral acts, and narrative themes in autobiography. *Journal of Personality and Social Psychology, 62,* 1003–1015.

Orlofsky, J. L. (1993). Intimacy statuses: Theory and research. In J. E. Marcia, A. S. Waterman, D. R. Matteson, S. L. Archer, & J. L. Orlofsky (Eds.), *Ego identity: A handbook for psychosocial research* (pp. 111–133). New York: Springer-Verlag.

SUGGESTED READINGS

Erikson, E. (1982). *The life cycle completed.* New York: Norton.

Marcia, J. E. (2002). Identity and psychosocial development in adulthood. *Identity: An International Journal of Theory and Research, 2,* 7–28.

MICHAEL D. BERZONSKY
State University of New York at Cortland

See also: **Human Development; Identity Formation; Personality Development**

ERRORS, TYPE I AND TYPE II

The goal of most social science research is to infer whether variables relate to each other in one or more populations of interest. Statistical tests are a tool used to assist in this inferential process by evaluating data from samples drawn from the population(s) of interest; these statistical tests are, however, by no means foolproof. Occasionally sample information would seem to imply that, for example, variable X is related to variable Y in the population, when in fact no such population relation exists. Such an inaccurate inference is termed a *Type I Error* (or "alpha error"). On the other hand, sample data may seem to imply that X and Y appear unrelated, when indeed those variables do have a relation in the population. This inaccurate inference is termed a *Type II Error* (or "beta error"). These two types of errors are discussed in the context of an illustrative research example.

Consider a biofeedback technique purported to reduce anxiety in academic testing situations. A researcher randomly samples 200 subjects with acute test anxiety, all of whom are college seniors registered to take the Graduate Record Examination (GRE) General Test. She randomly assigns 100 participants to learn how to employ biofeedback in an academic testing situation, while the other 100 participants are given a placebo experience consuming comparable time but unrelated to test anxiety or test performance. Both groups of students then take the GRE as originally intended; for simplicity we will only consider scores from the quantitative section of the examination. The specific question of interest is whether, in the population, average performance for test-anxious students using biofeedback differs from that of test-anxious students not using biofeedback; information from the two samples is used to facilitate the population inference. Put another way, the relation in the sample data between the biofeedback variable (present/absent) and the academic test performance variable (GRE score) will be used to make an inference about the existence and nature of that relation at the population level.

For the current example, one can think of two possible truths existing at the population level, and two possible conclusions derived from the sample information. For the populations, either biofeedback has some average effect or it has none. This latter notion, that there is no average difference between scores from a population of test-anxious students using biofeedback and scores from a population not using the technique, is termed the "null hypothesis" (symbolized H_0). Thus, a genuinely benign biofeedback treatment means that H_0 is true, whereas a biofeedback treatment that affects test performance means that H_0 is false. As for conclusions drawn from samples, if the two sample means are relatively similar (i.e., not differing "statistically significantly"), the guarded inference would be made that H_0 remains tenable. One need not actually believe that biofeedback is completely ineffective in the population; one may merely feel that sufficient evidence has not been gathered to the contrary, thus retaining H_0 as a tenable explanation for the lack of statistical significance associated with the observed difference between the two sample means. Conversely, if the two sample means are statistically significantly different, then one would infer that H_0 is false and that biofeedback has some effect. Specifically, if the biofeedback sample's mean is statistically significantly higher than that of the control sample, then one would infer that the treatment has a positive effect; alternatively, if the biofeedback sample's mean is statistically significantly lower than that of the control sample, then one would infer that the treatment actually has a negative effect.

Crossing the two population and two sample conditions outlined above defines four possible outcomes of a research endeavor, two representing accurate inference and two representing inaccurate inference (i.e., Type I and Type II errors). These are depicted in the Figure 1. Consider first the cells on the left side of the figure, which represent the condition in which H_0 is true; in the context of the example, these cells represent a population truth in which biofeedback has no effect on test performance. The top left cell results when the observed sample relation between biofeedback (present/absent) and test performance is not statistically significant; that is, the observed difference between sample means falls in the realm of what one would comfortably expect by chance if two population means truly do not differ. In this situation the study would lead one to infer that H_0 remains tenable, and in fact the inference would be accurate, because H_0 is true. In short, the study would have gathered no evidence that biofeedback is effective, and in truth it has no effect in the population.

The bottom left cell, on the other hand, results when the observed sample relation between the variables of interest is statistically significant; that is, the observed difference between sample means falls outside the realm of what one would comfortably expect by chance when two population means truly do not differ. In this situation the study would lead one to infer that H_0 should be rejected as false; however, the inference would be inaccurate because H_0 is true, and is thus labeled a Type I error. Such an event would be an unfortunate random occurrence, in which two samples happened to be selected whose quantitative ability was extremely disparate, but this disparity was merely a random occurrence and in no way reflective of any beneficial or detrimental effect of biofeedback. Colloquially speaking, this case could be termed a "false positive."

Now consider the right column of the figure, in which H_0 is false; in the context of the example, these cells represent a population truth in which biofeedback has some effect on test performance. The bottom right cell results when the observed sample relation between the variables of interest is statistically significant; that is, the observed difference between sample means falls outside the realm of what one would comfortably expect by chance if two population means truly do not differ. In this situation the study would lead one to infer that H_0 should be rejected as false, and in fact the inference would be accurate because H_0 is false. Thus, the study would have gathered evidence that the biofeedback is related to test performance, and in truth such a relation does exist in the population.

The top right cell, on the other hand, results when the observed sample relation between biofeedback and test performance is not statistically significant; that is, the observed difference between sample means falls in the realm of what one would comfortably expect by chance if two population means truly do not differ. In this situation the study would lead one to infer that H_0 remains tenable; however, the inference would be inaccurate because H_0 is false, and is thus labeled a Type II error. Such an event would be an unfortunate random occurrence, in which two samples happened to be selected whose quantitative ability was not particularly disparate, but this lack of disparity was not reflective of the actual effect of the biofeedback treatment. Colloquially speaking, this case could be termed a "false negative."

Now looking at the figure from the sample perspective, a study will leave a researcher in either the top row or the

Truth in population

Inference	H_0 is true (X and Y unrelated in population)	H_0 is false (X and Y related in population)
X and Y sample relation not statistically significant; retain H_0 as tenable.	accurate inference	inaccurate inference (Type II error)
X and Y sample relation statistically significant; reject H_0 and infer population relation.	inaccurate inference (Type I error)	accurate inference

Figure 1. Possible outcomes of a research endeavor.

bottom row. In the bottom row the variables of interest appear to be related on the basis of the sample information; the researcher infers that a relation exists in the population, thereby rejecting H_0. This is either an accurate inference or a Type I error, and the researcher never knows which is the case without having direct information about the relevant population(s). Thus, in order to minimize the occurrence of Type I errors, researchers often try to choose a fairly small region ("critical" region; "alpha" region) in which statistical significance will be proclaimed and H_0 rejected. Doing so will help to avoid inferring the existence of a population relation in the event that none truly exists (i.e., it will decrease the Type I error rate, the probability of rejecting H_0 when it is actually true). Choosing too small a region, however, will hinder the researcher from proclaiming statistical significance when the H_0 is false (i.e., will increase the Type II error rate, the probability of retaining H_0 when it is actually false). A common choice is to deem statistically significant a sample relation that is so unlikely as to be observed only 5% of the time or less just by chance, that is, when no such relation exists in the population. This is reflected in common language such as, "The alpha level was set at .05."

In the top row of the figure, the variables of interest do not appear related on the basis of the sample information; the researcher infers (albeit guardedly) that the hypothesis of no relation in the population remains tenable. This is either an accurate inference or a Type II error, and again the researcher never knows which is the case without having direct population information. Thus, in order to minimize the occurrence of Type II errors, and thereby increase the chance of inferring the existence of relations in the population when they truly exist (i.e., increase the "statistical power"), researchers are encouraged to take several preventive steps. Among the many ways to help avoid Type II errors are (1) using the most reliably measured variables possible, (2) using statistical techniques that help to control for extraneous variability in scores, and perhaps most importantly (3) using samples of adequate size in order to ensure sufficient statistical power.

GREGORY R. HANCOCK
University of Maryland, College Park

See also: Null Hypothesis Significance Testing; Significance Testing; Statistical Power

ESCAPE-AVOIDANCE LEARNING

Avoidance learning and extinction are typically studied in rats with electric foot-shock as the aversive stimulus. In active avoidance, the rat is often placed in a runway,

the floor of which is electrified at one end and is, at least temporarily, safe at the other end. The rat must move to the opposite end to escape or avoid shock. Before shock is delivered, the subject has several seconds in which to respond. A naïve subject, however, fails to avoid and is shocked on at least one trial before escaping the shock chamber. Thus traditional avoidance learning always includes escape behavior and is appropriately called *escape-avoidance learning*.

When the situation is arranged so that the subject cannot avoid but can only escape shock, the termination of shock is considered reinforcing (termed *negative reinforcement* by Skinnerians), and learning to escape is usually measured by a reduction in latency with successive shocks (trials). In a one-way situation (described later), a series of, say, 8 or 10 escape trials also can mediate perfect avoidance learning when the opportunity to avoid is provided.

With a two-way, or shutterbox, situation avoidance learning is slow, escape responses prevail, and perfect performance is rarely, if ever, attained. In a shuttle situation, the subject must learn to shuttle from one end of the alley to the other every time a warning signal (buzzer or light) is presented. This is difficult to do because no section of the alley is uniquely associated with either shock or safety. Thus fear is conditioned to the whole apparatus, engendering freezing; the rat has no distinguishable place to go to relax or escape fear, and after each escape trial it must learn to avoid by running right back into the region where it just got shocked.

In a one-way box, however, the rat is placed in a start chamber specifically associated with shock, to which it is conditioned, and the rat avoids by approaching a particular chamber that is consistently safe (i.e., where fear is clearly reduced or relaxation can occur). Some subjects in a one-way box learn to avoid in one trial, and learning to a 100% level in a mean of three or four trials is not unusual. Here the use of distinctive chambers and increasing the shock level up to a point facilitates learning. Presumably fear and safety are thereby segregated better, and reinforcement is enhanced (greater fear reduction), whereas the opposite is true in a shutterbox, where conditioned fear (competition from freezing and the like) is enhanced by these manipulations. The same manipulations that facilitate or hinder avoidance learning have been shown to have parallel effects in pure escape learning by Franchina and associates.

In passive avoidance, the subject avoids shock by not making a particular response. For example, the rat is placed on a small platform surrounded by an electrified grid. If it remains on the platform without stepping down, the rat avoids passively. Because it yields fast learning and is simple to use, many studies of amnesia and other behavioral effects of biological intervention use the passive technique for assessment purposes. Basically, the use of punishment, in which an aversive stimulus is contingent on a particular response, is the same as passive avoidance.

Passive avoidance is impeded if an alternative safe place to approach actively is available after the rat has been shocked for stepping down, and the more so the longer the rat remains in this safe place.

Mowrer's two-factor theory, or fear hypothesis, provides the main explanation of avoidance learning. Fear is conditioned to the shock area or warning signal, and escape from fear or the reduction of fear when the shock area or warning signal is removed as the reinforcement for the avoidance response (this is called *secondary negative reinforcement* by Skinnerians, and the concept of fear is not invoked). Research by Denny and associates indicates that 2.5 minutes away from shock or fear-provoking stimuli on each trial provides a good opportunity to relax, confers optimal approach value to the nonshock safe area, and yields optimal avoidance learning in one-way situations. Also, the concept of relaxation in this context is especially valuable for explaining the extinction of fear-related behaviors such as escape and avoidance. Relaxation is directly incompatible with fear and presumably constitutes the competing response that extinguishes fear. In one-way situations, extinction appears to originate in the safe area, where the longer the subject is confined, the more it relaxes, and the faster fear extinguishes, especially if the safe area is similar to the shock region.

Tortora, working with vicious dogs that had presumably learned to avoid punishment by being aggressive, trained them to avoid shock by promptly following 15 different commands (e.g., down, here, and heel). For many dogs a tone (safety signal) followed each correct response and was associated with a long shock-free, relaxation period. The safety tone clearly facilitated training, producing manageable, prosocial animals. Results from numerous recent escape-avoidance studies indicate that without fear there is no tendency to avoid or to approach safety.

M. RAY DENNY
Michigan State University

See also: Pavlovian Conditioning

ETHICAL ISSUES IN PSYCHOLOGY

Professions share many common characteristics, such as the development of a code of ethics. Ethics codes serve many purposes, one of which is to state the fundamental values of the profession and to bring together the cumulative wisdom of the profession about acting morally toward those with whom the profession works. The 2002 Ethics Code of the American Psychological Association

(APA) is divided into four sections: (1) the introduction, (2) the preamble, (3) general principles, and (4) ethical standards (American Psychological Association, 2002). Kitchener (1984) has argued that the ethical standards are grounded in principles that are more general and fundamental than standards and that serve as their foundation. Although slightly different from those in the 2002 APA Ethics Code, the five principles that seem central to thinking about ethical problems in psychology are (1) beneficence (do good), (2) nonmaleficence (do no harm), (3) respect for persons (treat individuals as autonomous agents, but recognize that those with diminished autonomy or competence need protection), (4) justice (be fair), and (5) fidelity (keep promises, do not lie, be faithful). These principles articulate ethical norms that are central to whatever role the psychologist is in and are quite similar to the principles in the 2002 code.

Covering all of the ethical issues in psychology would involve reviewing all of the ethical standards. However, just as the general principles articulate ethical norms for all the roles the psychologist plays, there are also ethical issues that cut across the same roles. These issues include informed consent, confidentiality, competence, respecting human relationships, sexualized professional relationships, and social responsibility.

Informed Consent

Informed consent has many meanings, particularly ethical and legal ones. Ethically informed consent is tied to the idea that, in order to make a reasonable choice, people must have the information that is necessary to make rational decisions. Having sufficient information allows people to weigh the risks and benefits for themselves or their loved ones. In psychology these decisions may be, for example, whether to enter therapy or to participate in a research project.

Competence has been called the threshold element for consent to occur (Beauchamp & Childress, 1994). In this context, it means the ability to rationally consider alternatives and subsequent choices. In other words, psychologists should ensure that individuals are competent to understand what is being disclosed to them. If they are not competent, they cannot make a reasonable choice about whether to give their consent. The second element is the disclosure itself, since the basic information about the nature of the event should be told to the participants. It is also essential that the information is understood and people voluntarily give their consent.

Confidentiality

Confidentiality is the second core issue. Confidentiality is a commitment made by professionals such as lawyers and psychologists not to divulge private information without a person's consent. Maintaining confidentiality is grounded in autonomy, fidelity, beneficence, and nonmaleficence. Autonomy implies that individuals have the right to make decisions about those with whom they wish to share private information and those from whom they wish to withhold it. Respecting the privacy of intimate interactions is at the core of human relationships, since it is part of being truthful.

When clients or research participants share private information about themselves after a psychologist has extended a promise of confidentiality, the promise carries with it the weight of the psychologist's professional role. Thus, a psychologist has a *prima facie* obligation to respect people's rights to decide what information they wish to disclose and to truthfully divulge the limits of confidentiality. For example, in therapy it would be critical to indicate the limits of confidentiality, because in all 50 states it is legally required to report child abuse, which would involve breaking confidentiality. Allowing a professional to keep information confidential fills a useful purpose for the individual and society. Individuals benefit by getting help for problems that might be embarrassing or, if known, might put them at risk. Fulfilling these ethical obligations helps ensure that harm will not befall the individual because confidential information was revealed. Society may benefit because psychologists may study topics like the transmission of AIDS, which would be unlikely unless the participant were promised confidentiality.

Competence

To incompetently engage in research, practice, teaching, or supervision is a violation of the fundamental obligation to benefit those whom psychologists have agreed to serve. Additionally, disparity in services to a group, for example, those of a particular nationality, because of incompetence is a violation of the principle of justice and may be harmful. In research, incompetence can lead to false claims and a waste of scarce resources. The basic tenet should be that, if you are not competent to adequately fulfill responsibilities associated with a role, do not perform the role unless you are under the supervision of someone who is competent (Kitchener, 2000). This is why the APA Ethics Code requires that psychologists "Provide services, teach, and conduct research with populations and in areas only within the boundaries of their competence . . . ." (American Psychological Association, 2002).

Defining what competence means is difficult. However, in this sense being competent includes having the knowledge, skills, and abilities to perform a role and the ability to recognize when one's knowledge, skills, or abilities are inadequate. Knowledge is the foundation of competence. It involves having the requisite facts or ideas to complete the task successfully. In research, for example, competence would include basic information about research design, interpretation of data, and ethical treatment of

participants, including animals. In other words, for each role the psychologist plays, there is a body of knowledge that competent practice presumes. Although skills are based on knowledge, they also involve the capacity to use the knowledge effectively to perform a task. For example, a psychologist may have read about supervision, but if he or she has never been trained to supervise someone, he or she may not have the skill to supervise. The APA has published several documents that specify the knowledge and skills needed to work with specific groups like women (American Psychological Association, 2007) and those with a multicultural background (American Psychological Association, 2003).

Abilities involve the physical or mental capacity to perform a task. Sometimes psychologists can compensate for their disabilities, however, if they have the necessary knowledge and skills, know their own limits, and are willing to accommodate for these limits. Such self-knowledge may lead some psychologists to choose not to work with certain groups. Lack of self-knowledge is particularly problematic when psychologists become impaired and do not know their limits.

Respecting Human Relationships

Respecting human relationships includes issues like avoiding sexual harassment and entering into multiple role relationships only after careful evaluation. There is high potential for creating harm in both of these situations. Sexual harassment occurs when the psychologist engages in verbal or nonverbal conduct that is sexual in nature, is unwanted, and creates a hostile work or educational environment. Multiple role relationships arise when an individual participates simultaneously or sequentially in more than one relationship with another person. These relationships are often harmful when there is a conflict between the two roles. This is particularly true if a psychologist is playing two or more professional roles with the consumer or is playing a professional role and a nonprofessional one. In both cases there may be a conflict of interest between the roles.

For example, if psychologists' social, financial, or sexual needs conflict with their professional obligations, these needs can compromise their professional judgment. Harmful multiple role relationships arise when roles conflict, because the expectations associated with the roles are different. As the difference in expectations and obligations between the roles increases, so does the probability for the consumer to feel confusion, frustration, or anger. Additionally, as the power differential between the psychologist's position and that of the consumer diverge, the potential for exploitation also increases (Kitchener, 2000).

Sexualized Professional Relationships

Sexualizing professional relationships exacerbates problems that exist in any multiple role relationship. The power differential remains great; the differences in expectations between being a therapist, a supervisor, or a professor and also a lover are huge, and the conflict of interest for the psychologist is profound. One cannot work for the best interests of the consumer or the profession and also try to meet one's sexual needs. The potential for harm when a therapeutic relationship has been sexualized is well documented in the professional literature (Pope, 1990). Furthermore, the psychologist's power does not necessarily dissipate after the explicit relationship is over, for example, when the person is no longer taking a class from the professor. Consequently, the consumer may not be able to autonomously choose to enter a sexual relationship, and the APA Ethics Code accordingly forbids post-therapy sexual relationships for two years and provides explicit guidelines for entering such relationships after that time (American Psychological Association, 2002).

Justice and Issues of Social Responsibility

Issues of justice have to do with deciding how to treat others in a fair, impartial, or equitable manner, including how the benefits and burdens associated with living in a community should be distributed. A variety of issues in research, education, and practice involve these kinds of questions. This includes assigning authorship credit and acknowledging material drawn from other sources, so that investigators can benefit fairly from their own work. Being fair also involves not denying services on the basis of age, gender, gender identity, race, ethnicity, or the like. It also involves the social responsibility to do research on and offer education about these groups, so that competent service can be provided.

Questions about what it means to distribute psychological services fairly are important to raise, because it is often the case that many people who need services are not able to afford them. Similarly, psychologists need to ask who should bear the burden of participation in research, which often falls on populations who have little power to protest (Sieber & Dubois, 2005). Furthermore, being socially responsible includes a duty to challenge injustice when it exists. Since psychology is committed to promoting the welfare of others, psychologists have a duty to challenge unjust social systems and proceed in fair ways.

REFERENCES

American Psychological Association. (2002). Ethical principles of psychologists and code of conduct. *American Psychologist, 57,* 1016–1073.

American Psychological Association. (2003). Guidelines on multicultural education, training, research, practice, and organizational change for psychologists. *American Psychologist, 58,* 377–402.

American Psychological Association. (2007). Guidelines for psychological practice girls and women. *American Psychologist, 62,* 949–979.

Beauchamp, T. L. & Childress, J. F. (1994). *Principles of biomedical ethics.* (4th ed.). Oxford, UK: Oxford University Press.

Kitchener, K. S. (1984). Intuition, critical evaluation and ethical principles: The foundation for ethical decisions in counseling psychology. *The Counseling Psychologist, 12,* 43–55.

Kitchener, K. S. (2000). *Foundations of ethical practice, research, and teaching in psychology.* Mahwah, NJ: Lawrence Erlbaum.

Pope, K. S. (1990). Therapist-patient sexual involvement: a review of the research. *Clinical Psychology Review, 10,* 477–490.

Sieber, J. E., & Dubois, J. M. (2005). *Using best judgment in conducting human research: Ethics and behavior.* Mahwah, NJ: Lawrence Erlbaum.

SUGGESTED READINGS

Bersoff, D. N. (2003). *Ethical conflicts in psychology.* (3rd ed.). Washington, DC: American Psychological Association.

Koocher, G. P., & Keith-Spiegel, P. C. (2007). *Ethics in psychology. Professional issues and cases.* (3rd ed.). Oxford, UK: Oxford University Press.

Pope, K. S., & Vasquez, M. J. K. (2007). *Ethics in psychotherapy and counseling: A practical guide.* (3rd ed.). San Francisco: Jossey-Bass.

KAREN STROHM KITCHENER
University of Denver

See also: American Psychological Association Code of Ethics; Confidentiality and Legal Privilege; Ethical Treatment of Animals; Informed Consent

ETHICAL TREATMENT OF ANIMALS

More than any other single event, the publication of Singer's *Animal Liberation* (1976) reopened examination of contemporary society's many and varied uses of animals other than humans (hereafter, animals). This discussion occurred in three overlapping contexts: (1) governmental regulation and institutional self-regulation and the developments of (2) a major social justice movement, the animal rights movement (ARM), and (3) a field of study, human-animal studies (HAS). It has ushered in numerous policies implementing changes in how we treat nonhuman animals and in public recognition of and changes in attitudes toward the various issues.

Sparked by Singer's seminal work, an emerging subfield of moral philosophy provided a theoretical and conceptual basis of the reexamination of animal-related practices. Regan's 1983 eponymous rights theory ("animal rights movement") and, more recently, feminist, communitarian, contractarian, competency, and performance theories have together assured a secure place for this topic in courses on moral philosophy.

The theories attempt to answer the question of the moral considerability of animals and to infer the policy and practices that follow from the standing claimed for them. For example, beyond that moral consideration due a sentient being, Wise (2000) argues that some animals (e.g., chimpanzees) are persons and this status obligates us to give them legal as well as ethical standing.

In the area of institutional self-regulation and governmental regulation, following the passage of federal legislation in 1966 and subsequent amendments, review committees (Institutional Animal Care and Use Committees) now oversee almost all laboratories engaged in animal research. Although this mechanism is modeled after the successful institutional review boards for research involving human subjects, its adequacy is questionable. Current governing legislation excludes from its purview rodents and birds, although they constitute the predominance of animals used in research. One of the few empirical studies of the animal research review committees (Plous & Herzog, 2001) found low reliability in protocol judgments within and between committees. Committees disapproved or deferred a majority of protocols that had been accepted in the earlier deliberations of other committees.

The emergent field of HAS provided evidence-based information and credibility to the various stakeholders in the debate on our use of animals. Scholars in the social and natural sciences as well as the humanities apply the methods of their respective disciplines to the study of animals and human-animal interfaces. Books and book series published by major university and academic publishing houses, peer-reviewed journals (*Society and Animals* [*S&A*] and *Anthrozoös*), and university programs, courses, fellowships (Animals and Society Institute Summer Fellowship in HAS), and chairs (American Humane Endowed Chair, University of Denver) devoted to HAS constitute an increasingly robust intellectual infrastructure. By featuring the study of human-animal relationships, HAS implicitly elevates the status of animals from models and symbols of human phenomena to subjects in the full sense of that term.

Psychology's Ambivalence

The role of psychology in these developments has been mixed. Plous (1996) found a high level of support for animal research involving observation and even confinement. However, when asked about research involving pain or death to primates and rats, many psychologists (62.1% and 44.4%, respectively, for the two animal groups) indicate that such research is unjustified even when the research is described as "institutionally approved and deemed of scientific merit" (p. 1171).

On the negative side of psychology's role, Singer, in his Benthamite extension of the utilitarian calculus of costs and benefits to apply to animals, singled out psychological animal-based research as particularly unjustified: "Many of the most painful experiments are performed in psychology" (1976, p. 34). Further spotlighting psychology, in the early 1980s a case of abuse involving the use of nonhuman primates in psychological research became a cause célèbre for ARM ("the Silver-Spring monkeys"; Guillermo, 1993) as a psychology laboratory had its major federal support grant suspended. Regarding the field's general response to the issue of psychological animal research, two psychologists chided the field for adopting a "strategic defensive posture" (Gluck & Kubacki, 1991, p. 158).

More positively, two British psychologists contributed conceptual advances in the debate: Ryder coined the term speciesism, and Heim articulated the notion that there are ethical limits on our use of animals that are independent of any beneficial ends. A number of comparative psychologists and cognitive ethologists have conducted noninvasive animal research with primates and other animals that demonstrates the sophisticated capabilities of these animals, such as communication, self-reflection, and attribution of mind. The findings have raised the ethical bar to painful, distressful, injurious, and fatal uses of animals.

Psychologists also have contributed to the critique of animal research by adding science-based evidence and argument to the debate within ethics (e.g., Shapiro, 1998). They also have developed scales to measure degree of pain and harm, and they have provided empirical studies demonstrating the link between violence toward humans and other animals.

Psychologists have been active in the development of the field of HAS. By devoting special issues to the topic, the field of psychology recognized that society's treatment of animals is a major (Plous, 1993) and enduring social issue (Herzog & Knight, in press). A psychologist is the founding editor of *S&A* and two psychologists are co-founding editors of *Journal of Applied Animal Welfare Science*, which began publishing in 1993 and 1998, respectively. Animal Human Interaction, a section-in-formation in the Division 17, Society of Counseling Psychology of the American Psychological Association, held its first organizational meeting in 2007.

Increasingly, clinical psychologists are capitalizing on the empirically demonstrated social support, interpersonal facilitation, and other beneficial and therapeutic effects of involvement in a compassionate and respectful human-animal relationship. Therapists use animals as adjuncts in individual therapy (animal-assisted therapy). Residential group settings also use caring for animals as a vehicle for developing mutual, responsible relationships. A number of psychologists have chosen careers working in organizations in which the mission is the reduction of the suffering and exploitation of animals. In response to legislation in 18 states allowing the judge to require counseling for convicted animal abusers, Jory and Randour (1999) developed a treatment approach for this population.

Through these and other avenues, psychology is moving from a defensive to a constructive and progressive position on the issue of the ethical treatment of animals.

REFERENCES

Gluck, J. P., & Kubacki, S. R. (1991). Animals in biomedical research: The undermining effect of the rhetoric of the besieged. *Ethics & Behavior, 1*(3), 157–173.

Guillermo, K. S., (1993). *Monkey business.* Washington, DC: National Press.

Herzog, H., & Knight, S., (Eds.). (In press). New perspectives on human-animal interactions: Theory, policy, and research. *Journal of Social Issues.*

Jory, B., & Randour, M. (1999). *The AniCare model of treatment for animal abuse.* Washington Grove, MD: Psychologists for the Ethical Treatment of Animals.

Plous, S. (Ed.). (1993). The role of animals in human society. *Journal of Social Issues.*

Plous, S. (1996). Attitudes toward the use of animals in psychological research and education: Results from a national survey of psychologists. *American Psychologist, 51,* 1167–1180.

Plous, S., & Herzog, H. (2001). Reliability of protocol reviews for animal research. *Science, 293,* 608–609.

Regan, T. (1983). *The case for animal rights.* Berkeley, CA: University of California.

Shapiro, K. (1998). *Animal models of human psychology: Critique of science, ethics, and policy.* Gottingen, Germany: Hogrefe and Huber.

Singer, P. (1976). *Animal liberation: A new ethic for our treatment of animals.* New York: Avon.

Wise, S. (2000). *Rattling the cage: Toward legal rights for animals.* Cambridge, MA: Perseus.

SUGGESTED READINGS

Armstrong, S., & Botzler, R. (Eds.). (2003). *The animal ethics reader.* London: Routledge.

Kalof, L., & Fitgerald, A. (Eds.). (2007). *The animals' reader: The essential classic and contemporary writings.* Oxford, UK: Berg.

KENNETH J. SHAPIRO
Animals and Society Institute, Washington Grove, MD

See also: **American Psychological Association Code of Ethics; Ethical Issues in Psychology**

ETHNOCULTURAL PSYCHOTHERAPY

Ethnocultural psychology integrates ethnicity and culture into mental health assessment and treatment. It complements mainstream psychotherapy with cultural values, ethnic/indigenous practices, critical analysis, and empowering approaches. Ethnocultural psychotherapy acknowledges the concept of self as an internal cultural representation.

Ethnocultural therapeutic tools include cultural genograms, transitional maps, narratives, testimonies, psychospirituality, and indigenous healing techniques. One of these tools, the ethnocultural assessment, explores identity development and reformulation (Jacobsen, 1988). Used in diagnosis and treatment, the ethnocultural assessment examines the stages of heritage, myth, niche, adjustment, and relationships. To illustrate, the genetic, biological, and sociocultural familiar heritage provides a backdrop for exploration of the family myth: the circumstances that led to the client's and multigenerational family's cultural transitions. The niche—derived from the post-transition analysis—is based on clients' intellectual and emotional perception of their family's ethnocultural identity in the host society since the translocation. The adjustment stage refers to the client's own perceived adaptation of the host culture as an individual distinct from the rest of the family. This stage involves a therapeutic exploration of the contrasts between the client's ethnocultural identity and that of his or her work and cultural milieu. Finally, the relationships stage examines transference and countertransference (Comas-Diaz & Jacobsen, 1991), considering the therapist's own ethnocultural assessment to determine special areas of similarity and difference. Besides obtaining a wealth of information crucial for the therapeutic intervention, performance of an ethnocultural assessment often opens new channels for the recognition of self in the other.

Ethnocultural psychotherapy facilitates a transcultural analysis that aims at critical consciousness, or the process of transformation that oppressed individuals experience while educating themselves in a dialectical conversation with the world. Through this process clients learn to read their condition as well as to author their own reality. The therapeutic relationship functions as the dialogue that helps clients express their truth, assert their identity, heal, and achieve agency.

Ethnocultural psychotherapy pays special attention to sociopolitical issues prevalent among culturally diverse individuals, such as inclusion/exclusion, power/powerlessness, privilege/oppression, and being the other. Through the use of liberation approaches, ethnocultural psychotherapy addresses coping behaviors to such dynamics. For instance, this therapeutic approach targets ethnocultural allodynia, or the sensitivity to cumulative exposure to ethnoracial trauma (Comas-Diaz & Jacobsen, 2001). With its emphasis on clients' strengths, ethnocultural psychotherapy promotes clients' renewal of their gifts power. Cultural resilience is one of these gifts. Defined as the set of strengths, values, and practices that promote coping mechanisms and adaptive reactions to traumatic oppression (Elsass, 1992), cultural resilience fosters creativity, reconstruction, and evolution.

REFERENCES

Comas-Diaz, L., & Jacobsen, F. M. (1991). Ethnocultural transference and coutertransference in the therapeutic dyad. *American Journal of Orthopsychiatry, 61*(3), 392–402.

Comas-Diaz, L., & Jacobsen, F. M. (2001). Ethnocultural allodynia. *The Journal of Psychotherapy Practice and Research, 10*(4), 1–6.

Elsass, P. (1992). *Strategies for survival: The psychology of cultural resilience in ethnic minorities.* New York: New York University Press.

Jacobsen, F. M. (1988). Ethnocultural assessment. In L. Comas-Diaz & E. H. Griffith (Eds.), *Clinical guidelines in cross-cultural mental health.* New York: John Wiley & Sons.

SUGGESTED READINGS

American Psychological Association. (2003). Guidelines on multicultural education, training, research, practice, and organizational change for psychologists. *American Psychologist, 58,* 377–402.

Freire, P. (1970). *Pedagogy of the oppressed.* New York: Seabury Press.

Freire, P. (1973). *Education for critical consciousness.* New York: Seabury Press.

Sue, D., Capodilupo, C. M., Torino, G. C., Bucceri, J. M., Holder, A. M., Nadal, K. L., et al. (2007). Racial microaggressions in everyday life: Implications for clinical practice. *American Psychologist, 62*(4), 271–286.

LILLIAN COMAS-DIAZ
FREDERICK M. JACOBSEN
Transcultural Mental Health Institute, Washington, DC

See also: **Cross-Cultural Psychology; Culture and Psychotherapy; Multicultural Counseling; Psychotherapy**

ETHOLOGY

The study of animal behavior in their natural environment is termed *ethology* and arose as a consequence of the seminal early works of zoologists and field naturalists, such as Nikolaas Tinbergen and Konrad Lorenz. These researchers stressed the importance of examining the evolution (phylogeny) and development (ontology) of behavior in the context of the animals' unique ecological niche. One goal of ethology is to determine which behaviors are learned and can be modified via an organism's interaction with the environment and which are "built-in" or passed on through genes. A key finding is that very complex behavior patterns are a function of genetics and are instinctive to specific environmental "stimuli" or events.

The ethological approach can be used to study animal behavior in their natural habitat as well as in the laboratory, where parameters are manipulated to resemble those of the natural environment. Researchers that use an ethological approach manipulate features of species-relevant environmental cues to determine how such stimuli modify niche-related behaviors. This approach to the study of animal behavior has aided in the understanding of animal physiology and functional neuroanatomy. The combination of ethology with neuroscience, the study of the brain, has led to the emerging field of neuroethology. In what follows, examples from research on learning, memory, and emotion are used to demonstrate the basic scientific principles of ethological-based research.

Most animals must navigate the environment to search and/or store food. The desert kangaroo rat (*Dipodomys deserti*) appears to have developed the ability to form mental representation of spatial cues, a type of "spatial blueprint," of where food is located in the environment (i.e., foraging patches). This ability allows them to maximize their search patterns and reduces redundancy in path distance (Thompson, 1982). Recently, this spatial capacity has been evaluated in the laboratory on the spatial eight-arm radial arm maze (RAM), which consists of eight arms of equal length radiating out at equal angles from a central arena. Each arm is only baited with food once, so the animal must maintain a working memory of the arms it entered to maximize its foraging strategy. Timberlake and Hoffman (2002) demonstrated that the desert kangaroo rat easily displayed the ability to remember which arms it entered, and thus has the capacity of working memory. However, when these animals were assessed on a floor version of the RAM, in which there were no arm boundaries, they did not use designated paths (i.e., arm locations or trial-following behavior), but rather employed a central-place forging strategy. This method involves remembering food locations while using routes that provide the shortest distance between food locations. The kangaroo rat lives in a desert terrain in which large landmarks and dramatic weather patterns disrupts the ground cover. Thus, central-place forging behavior is the most adaptive for this type of environment, and this behavior persisted in the laboratory maze even though the environmental conditions were quite different.

The study of ethology has also assisted our understanding of the behavioral, neurochemical, and physiological mechanisms underpinning emotion. Behavioral paradigms created in the laboratory that mimic threat situations experienced in the animal's natural environment have allowed scientists to not only study behavioral aspects of emotion but biological ones as well. For instance, studies of aggression commonly use the resident/intruder model to evoke territorial aggression, which is an evolutionary behavior developed to ward off invading predators and rivals from an animal's established home. In this paradigm, the animal is placed inside a single holding cage for a prolonged period of time, allowing the animal to acclimate to its new territory. Introduction of another animal into the home cage, known as the intruder, will evoke aggressive responses from the resident animal. These behaviors mirror the activities of a naturally occurring territorial dispute, including offensive and defensive attack postures, biting, and pinning. As such, the resident/intruder paradigm is a way of eliciting naturally occurring emotive behavior within a controlled laboratory setting.

One study using the resident/intruder paradigm found a functional relationship between norepinephrine (NE) release and offensive aggression (Zagrodzka, Wieczorek, & Romaniuk, 1994). Administration of DSP-4, a drug that damages NE producing neurons, resulted in an increase in offensive aggression that was accompanied by depleted levels of NE in the amygdala, hypothalamus, frontal cortex, and hippocampus. These findings suggest that NE plays an inhibitory role in the emergence of aggressive behavior and may be a functional requisite in modulating social interactions. Thus, this serves as an example of how an ethological approach has aided our understanding of brain function.

In addition to studies of aggression, fear and anxiety research has also benefited from an ethological approach. Ethologically valid animal models such as the elevated plus maze have been used to behaviorally assess fear and anxiety responses in rodents by manipulating particular aspects of the physical environment that are naturally aversive to the animal. Specifically, the rat is placed onto a cross maze that is elevated a few feet above the floor that has two closed arms and two open arms. Due to a rodent's innate affinity for small-enclosed places and its natural aversion to open spaces and heights, the animal tends to spend more time in the closed arms and avoid open areas. Furthermore, anxiogenic responses can be observed when the animal is isolated to the open ends of the maze, displaying various instinctive behaviors such as rearing, freezing, defecation, and instinctive chemical response of increased levels of plasma corticosterone (Pellow, Chopin, File, & Briley, 1985). Unlike conditioning paradigms of fear, which utilize Pavlovian mechanisms to examine fear responses, the elevated plus maze is an unconditioned model of anxiety that utilizes the animals natural predisposition toward specific environmental settings to assess fear behavior. This is important because the induction of fear (and other biologically relevant stimuli) can evoke instinctive behaviors, called "fixed action patterns" in a condition-specific manner. However, some of these innate behaviors can conflict with the demands of the artificial experiment. For example, aversive stimuli (shock) can induce what has been called "vicious circle behavior" in which the behavior elicited by the stimuli conflicts with retreat from the stimulus (see Delude, 1969).

In summary, the preceding examples demonstrate how behavioral, environmental, and genetic factors interact in complex ways. Studying the behavior of animals in their natural habitat provides insight into how specific environmental demands shape a range of physiological responses that then direct behavior.

REFERENCES

Delude, L. A. (1969). The vicious circle phenomenon: A result of measurement artifact. *Journal of Comparative and Physiological Psychology, 69,* 246–252.

Pellow, S., Chopin, P., File, S. E., & Briley, M. (1985). Validation of open: closed arm entries in an elevated plus maze as measure of anxiety in the rat. *The Journal of Neuroscience, 3,* 149–167.

Thompson, S. D. (1982). Microhabitat utilization and foraging behavior of bipedal and quadrupedal heteromyid rodents. *Ecology, 63,* 1303–1312.

Timberlake, W., & Hoffman, C. M. (2002). How does the ecological foraging behavior of desert kangaroo rats (Dipodomys deserti) relate to their behavior on radial mazes? *Animal Learning & Behavior, 30,* 342–354.

Zagrodzka, J., Wieczorek, M., & Romaniuk, A. (1994). Social interaction in rats: Behavioral and neurochemical alterations in DSP-4-treated rats. *Pharmacology, Biochemistry & Behavior, 49,* 541–548.

SUGGESTED READINGS

Gould, J. L. (1982). *Ethology: Mechanisms in the evolution of behavior.* New York: W.W. Norton.

Fox, M. W. (1973). *Readings in ethology and comparative psychology.* Belmont, CA: Wadsworth.

Lorenz, K., & Kickett, R. W. (2004). *The foundations of ethology.* New York: Springer.

RYAN P. VETRENO
STEVEN J. ANZOLONE
LISA M. SAVAGE
State University of New York at Binghamton

See also: Animal Learning and Behavior; Comparative Psychology

EVIDENCE-BASED PRACTICE

Evidence-based practice (EBP) describes a process of decision making for high-quality client care. The idea of basing practice on evidence was introduced in medicine as a way to promote clinical decision making that followed a rational process rather than intuition (Evidence-Based Medicine Working Group, 1992). EBP was defined as "the conscientious, explicit, judicious use of current best evidence in making decisions about the care of individual patients" (Sackett, Rosenberg, Gray, Haynes, & Richardson, 1996). From the outset, EBP was seen as based on more than research alone. Research was depicted as one of three overlapping circles or data streams to be considered in clinical decision making. Sackett and colleagues (1996) defined EBP as "the integration of best research evidence with clinical expertise and patient values."

The forces that gave rise to the evidence-based movement date back to the early 1900s. The 1910 Flexner Report initiated an effort by the medical community to ground medical training and practice on a firm scientific foundation. The randomized clinical trial (RCT), championed by Archibald Cochrane (1972), gradually became accepted as the most valid method to determine which treatments work. Nevertheless, it became recognized that clinical practice too often departs from the ideal, prompting a call for infrastructure to disseminate evidence-based best practices. One tool introduced to help close the gap between research and practice was the systematic review, which is a comprehensive overview of primary research studies conducted according to an explicit, transparent protocol. Systematic reviews offered a means to synthesize and consolidate the evidence across many clinical trials. Dissemination infrastructure emerged via the Cochrane Collaboration, founded in 1992 and now an international network that prioritizes, performs, and regularly updates systematic reviews. An emergent tool even more directly applicable to practice is the evidence-based practice guideline, which applies systematic review methodology to evaluate the management options for a clinical condition or problem. Currently, the National Guidelines Clearinghouse (http://www.guidelines.gov) serves as a repository for more than 2,000 evidence-based practice guidelines, many of which are updated regularly.

Evidence-Based Practice in Psychology

Psychology is a relative latecomer to the evidence-based practice movement, following medicine (Sackett et al., 1996), nursing (Craig & Smyth, 2002), social work (Gibbs, 2003), and public health (Brownson, Baker, Leet, & Gillespie, 2003). Not until 2006 did the American Psychological Association (APA) adopt evidence-based practice as policy for psychology. APA defined EBP as "the integration of best available research with clinical expertise in the context of patient characteristics, culture, and preferences" (American Psychological Association, 2006).

Psychologists expressed some of the same hesitancies about EBP that were voiced in other disciplines, and they expressed some different ones as well. In most fields, a period of debate has preceded general acceptance of EBP. Researchers and practitioners squared off to argue whether greater weight should be given to research or to clinical expertise (Sackett et al., 1996; Spring, 2007; Spring & Pagoto, 2005). Across disciplines, practitioners worried that EBP really meant disguised cost cutting and erosion of professional autonomy (Spring & Pagoto, 2005; Pagoto et al., 2007). A reaction largely unique to psychology was the misinterpretation that performing EBP is entirely synonymous with delivering empirically supported treatments (ESTs) (Luebbe, Radcliffe, Callands, Green, & Thorn, 2007).

The confusion between EBP and ESTs is understandable. Practitioners who engage in performing EBP often do implement ESTs. Presumably, that is because the treatments designated as ESTs by APA Division 12's Dissemination Subcommittee of the Committee on Science and Practice are the ones supported by the best available research evidence. However, what defines clinical practice as evidence-based is not the delivery of any specific treatment but rather the performance of the evidence-based practice process. The EBP process is one whereby the practitioner decides on a course of action by integrating best available research evidence with other specific considerations.

Elements of Evidence-Based Practice

The multidisciplinary Council for Training on Evidence-Based Behavioral Practice (EBBP) proposes a harmonized cross-disciplinary EBP model that is applicable when choosing psychosocial interventions at the individual, community, or population level (Council for Training in Evidence-Based Behavioral Practice, 2008). The council's free online training modules about the evidence-based practice process, systematic reviews, and searching for evidence are available at its web site (http://www.ebbp.org). Its model, depicted in Figure 1, shows three data streams to be integrated when deciding on a clinical course of action: evidence, client characteristics, and resources.

Evidence

Evidence in EBP is research findings derived from the systematic collection of data through observation and experiment and the formulation of questions and testing of hypotheses. Practitioners ask many different kinds of practical questions, not only about the benefits of treatments but also about assessment, prevalence, prognosis, etiology, costs, and even harms associated with treatments. The optimal research design to answer a question depends on the nature of the question being asked. Systematic reviews and meta-analyses can provide high-quality evidence for answering many different kinds of questions. Well-designed cohort studies provide the best evidence to answer questions about prognosis, incidence, or risk factors for a condition. Qualitative studies or sample surveys offer an excellent tool to understand client

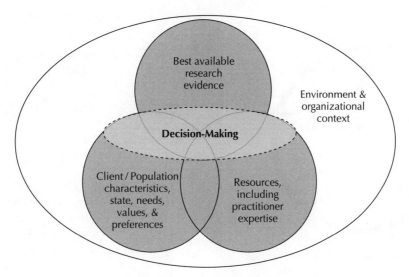

Figure 1. Elements that need to be integrated into EBP (Council for Training in Evidence-Based Behavioral Practice, 2008, http://www.ebbp.org).

or community experiences. Cost–benefit questions call for economic analyses.

The evidence available to answer a question can be arrayed as an evidence hierarchy, with the most comprehensive, systematic, least biased types of data at the top. At the apex of the evidence pyramid for a treatment question is a well-conducted systematic review, followed by randomized controlled trials, followed by observational studies, and finally by anecdote, opinion, or indirect evidence from basic mechanistic research.

Client Characteristics

Except for single case studies, research evidence describes the average responses of individuals or groups. The core challenge addressed by EBP is how to optimize outcomes by applying the averaged data to an individual client. Decision making is needed to contextualize the evidence to the particular circumstances at hand. Client characteristics are one set of key contextualizing factors that need to be taken into account. Relevant client attributes include state and trait variations in condition, needs, history of treatment response, values, and preferences. Contextualizing the evidence by client characteristics is critically important in deciding whether available research evidence is truly relevant to the client. In implementing an intervention, some tailoring to client characteristics (e.g., literacy level of materials) can often be implemented. Such adaptations can enhance treatment feasibility and acceptability, without undermining fidelity to the core treatment elements that make a treatment effective (National Cancer Institute, 2006).

Client preferences warrant special mention as a contextualizing variable. EBP has done much to highlight the importance of shared decision making in the health care delivery process (Krahn & Naglie, 2008). Engaging clients in decision making that acknowledges their preferences is justifiable on sociopolitical grounds of equity. Shared decision making is also justified on evidentiary grounds, because of the association between shared decision making and improved health outcomes (Say & Thomson, 2003; Spring, in press).

Resources

Universally, resources are a contextualizing variable that factors into evidence-based decisions. The most efficacious treatment is irrelevant to any but theoretical EBP if there is no trained practitioner accessible to deliver treatment or no resources to pay for it. The creation of resource-sensitive practice guidelines is a new development in EBP (see Fried et al., 2008). Such guidelines review the quality of evidence supporting alternative practice recommendations. Decision makers can use the guidelines to gauge the level of intervention intensity that makes the best use of available infrastructure, human capital, and financial wherewithal.

Implementing Evidence-Based Practice

The diagram in Figure 1 might make it appear that integration of the three data streams processed in evidence-based practice (evidence, client characteristics, resources) could occur simultaneously, but that is not the case. The evidence-based practice process proceeds through the five clearly defined steps shown in Figure 2: Ask a question; acquire the evidence; appraise the evidence; apply the evidence; analyze and adjust practice.

The steps of the evidence-based practice process are performed in a specific order. After the presenting condition or problem has been assessed, the practitioner begins the EBP process by posing a relevant, well-formulated question and conducting a search for the best research evidence to answer it. The "best available research evidence" refers to relevant findings that have been critically appraised,

Figure 2. Steps in the Evidence-Based Practice process.

either by systematic reviewers with expertise in critical appraisal or by the individual practitioner, using EBP techniques and standards. To find the best evidence to address the target question, the interventionist needs to know which kinds of research evidence best answer different types of questions and how to appraise the quality and applicability of that evidence.

After finding and appraising the evidence, the interventionist assesses what resources, including trained practitioners, are available to be able to offer what the research shows to be the intervention(s) best supported by evidence. The practitioner also considers any stakeholders' characteristics and contextual factors that bear on the likely applicability, acceptability, and uptake of the intervention(s) best supported by evidence. The practitioner also evaluates relevant stakeholders' values and preferences and engages appropriate stakeholders in the process of collaborative decision making.

After interventions have been implemented, the EBP practitioner assesses their impact and engages stakeholders in the process of evaluation and quality improvement. Using an iterative, cyclical process, the practical outcomes of intervention decisions are then used to develop and/or refine local decision-making policies, generate new questions, inform future searches for best evidence, and/or identify needed research.

Evidence-based practice represents a step forward toward rational, systematic, high-quality health care. All major health professions have adopted the principles of evidence-based practice. The Institute of Medicine (IOM) identifies EBP as a cornerstone in the effort to reverse the glacial rate at which research discoveries translate into practice (IOM, 2001). The IOM also characterizes evidence-based practice as a core competency for health professions (Greiner & Knebel, 2003). For the interprofessional health care teams in which psychologists participate, the shared EBP framework supports jointly held foundational assumptions, vocabulary, and practice

principles (Greiner & Knebel, 2003). Continued development of infrastructure remains needed to make evidence accessible at the point of care and to further systematize the EBP decision-making process.

REFERENCES

Brownson, R. C., Baker, E. A., Leet, T. L., & Gillespie, K. N. (2003) *Evidence-based public health*. Oxford, England: Oxford University Press.

Chambless, D. L., & Ollendick, T. H. (2001). Empirically supported psychological interventions: Controversies and evidence. *Annual Review of Psychology, 52,* 685–716.

Cochrane, A. L. (1972). Effectiveness and efficiency: Random reflections on health services. London: Nuffield Hospitals Trust.

Council for Training in Evidence-Based Behavioral Practice. (2008, March). *Definition and competencies for evidence-based behavioral practice*. Retrieved September 19, 2008, from http://www.ebbp.org./Competencies.html.

Craig, J. V., & Smyth, R. L. (2002). *The evidence-based practice manual for nurses*. London: Churchill Livingstone.

Evidence-Based Medicine Working Group. (1992). Evidence-based medicine: A new approach to teaching the practice of medicine. *Journal of the American Medical Association, 268,* 2420–2425.

Fried, M., Quigley, E. M. M., Hunt, R. H., Guyatt, G., Anderson, B. O., Bjorkman, D. J., et al. (2008). Can global guidelines change health policy? *Nature Clinical Practice Gastroenterology & Hepatology, 5,* 120–121.

Gibbs, L. (2003). *Evidence-based practice for the helping professions*. Pacific Grove, CA: Brooks/Cole–Thomson Learning.

Greiner, A. C., & Knebel, E. (Eds.). (2003). *Health professions education: A bridge to quality* (Institute of Medicine Quality Chasm series). Washington, DC: National Academies Press.

Institute of Medicine. (2001). *Crossing the quality chasm: A new health system for the 21st century*. Washington, DC: National Academy of Science Press.

Krahn, M. K., & Naglie, G. (2008). The next step in guideline development: Incorporating patient preferences. *Journal of the American Medical Association, 300*(4), 436–438.

Luebbe, A. M., Radcliffe, A. M., Callands, T. A., Green, D., & Thorn, B. E. (2007). Evidence-based practice in psychology: Perceptions of graduate students in scientist–practitioner programs. *Journal of Clinical Psychology, 63*(7), 643–655.

National Cancer Institute. (2006). *Using what works: Adapting evidence-based programs to fit your needs*. USDHHS, NIH Publication No. 06-5874. Washington, DC: Author.

Pagoto, S. L., Spring, B., Coups, E. J., Mulvaney, S., Coutu, M. F., & Ozakinci, G. (2007). Barriers and facilitators of evidence-based practice perceived by behavioral science health professionals. *Journal of Clinical Psychology, 63*(7), 695–705.

Sackett, D. L., Rosenberg, W. M. C., Gray, J. A. M., Haynes, R. B., & Richardson, W. S. (1996). Evidence-based medicine: What it is and what it isn't. *British Medical Journal, 312,* 71–72.

Say, E., & Thomson, R. (2003). The importance of patient preferences in treatment decisions: Challenges for doctors. *British Medical Journal, 327*, 542–545.

Spring, B. (2007). Evidence-based practice in clinical psychology: What it is; why it matters; what you need to know. *Journal of Clinical Psychology, 63*(7), 611–631.

Spring, B. (in press). Health decision-making: Lynchpin of evidence-based practice. *Medical Decision Making.*

Spring, B., Pagoto, S., Whitlock, E., Kaufmann, P., Glasgow, R., Smith, K., et al. (2005). Invitation to a dialogue between researchers and clinicians about evidence-based behavioral medicine. *Annals of Behavioral Medicine, 30*(2), 125–137.

BONNIE SPRING
KRISTIN HITCHCOCK
Northwestern University

EVOLUTIONARY PSYCHOLOGY

Human psychology is a product of the human nervous system. Neural mechanisms, often clustered in the brain, gather and process information from the environment, interact, and execute actions. All conscious and unconscious mental phenomena, such as motivations, emotions, or planning, derive from neural activity. Even the most mundane behaviors require precise unconscious calculations. Walking, for instance, requires extensive feedback, calculation, and integration in order to coordinate intricate muscle movement.

The only known process resulting in complex biological systems, such as the human nervous system, is evolution by natural selection. Natural selection is the process whereby genetically heritable traits that are more capable of propagating themselves will exist in higher frequencies in the next generation than other traits. Because human psychology is a product of the nervous system and because evolution by natural selection is the only human mechanism that creates complex biological systems, all human psychology is a product of evolution by natural selection.

Natural selection produces adaptations and byproducts of adaptations. Adaptations are genetically heritable traits such as fingers, body hair, or a sneeze reaction, that serve specific purposes, such as object manipulation, warmth, or ridding the respiratory tract of foreign material. Byproducts of adaptations, such as fingerprints, dandruff, or the sound of a sneeze do not serve a specific purpose.

Natural selection tends to eliminate traits that propagate themselves less well than other traits. This means that adaptations exist because they propagated more numerously than other traits or forms of the same trait. Since adaptations derive from genes, the ultimate function of every adaptation is to propagate the gene or genes coding for that adaptation. Adaptations, such as the human nervous system, and thus all psychological mechanisms, are ultimately designed to propagate the genes for which they code.

The adaptations that seem to be designed to facilitate our individual survival, such as eyes that let us see or a gag reflex that prevents choking, could only exist because such survival makes them more likely to make it into the next generation. Traits that do not ultimately facilitate reproduction do not tend to be represented in future generations. Survival is a byproduct of gene propagation.

Success in gene propagation can be subtle; an adaptation that grants 1% reproductive advantage can come to dominate a population after several generations. Gene propagation can be indirect; nepotism toward genetic kin results in propagation of genes shared with the nepotist, even if the act of nepotism was costly. Success in gene propagation is context specific; that which is successful in one context is often unsuccessful in other contexts.

Understanding the context in which humans evolved provides a key insight into human behavior. Humans share an ancestor with our closest genetic relatives, the common chimpanzee, roughly 3 million years ago. Human civilizations have existed for not much more than 10,000 years, and civilization as it is experienced in the developed world, with electricity, plumbing, modern medicine, and the use of petroleum, has existed for less than 100 years. Modern civilization thus accounts for less than one-hundredth of 1% of human evolutionary history. This means that the characteristics that make us uniquely human evolved to solve adaptive problems in environments that were very different from those in which we live today.

For example, we do not have an innate fear of knives, reflexive withdrawal from gamma wave radiation, or nausea from the smell of chemotherapy drugs. Knives, gamma waves, and chemotherapy are present in modern environments but were effectively absent over human evolution. Consequently, we posses no psychological adaptations designed to handle problems associated with these evolutionary novel environmental features. Instead, humans posses a pronounced fear of snakes, reflexively withdraw from a hot fire, and experience nausea from the smell of rotten meat; these threats pose the same risk as knives, gamma waves, and chemotherapy, but were actually present in the environments in which we evolved.

Relatively rapid and inconsistent change typify the last 10,000 years of human existence, yet new adaptations can take thousands of generations (exceeding 15,000 human years) in order to spread throughout a population. Genes for adaptations that are specific to modern environments are thus unlikely because they have not had sufficient time to propagate. As William Allsman suggests, "Our modern skulls house a Stone age mind."

Some adaptations no longer function well in modern human environments. A taste preference for fats once promoted appropriate calorie intake in environments with less reliable and plentiful food sources, now leads to obesity and heart disease in many developed countries. It is difficult to understand psychological adaptations, such as a preference for fats, without understanding their functions in the environments in which they evolved. Evolutionary psychologists, therefore, consider how human ancestral environments might be responsible for seemingly irrational modern human cognition and behavior.

Evolutionary psychology began in the mid-nineteenth century with Charles Darwin, who outlined the evolution of behavioral adaptations in tandem with his better-known work on anatomical adaptations. Since that time, behavioral scientists have utilized evolution as a tool for understanding behavior fields titled as diversely as ethology, sociobiology, and population genetics. Modern evolutionary psychology draws from three key areas: cognitive science used to understand how the mind works; anthropology used to understand the contexts in which psychological adaptations arose; and evolutionary biology used to understand how evolution shapes biological systems. No informed application of evolution to understanding human behavior lacks thorough knowledge of these three key areas.

This deep theoretical background helps unite psychology seamlessly with other sciences. Instead of "theories" applicable only within psychology, evolutionary psychology places the study of cognition and behavior seamlessly within biology, which fits seamlessly within chemistry, physics, and mathematics. For example, instead of viewing incest avoidance as a social construct, scientists utilizing evolution and human behavior have looked at how deleterious genetic effects ultimately motivate incest avoidance and its corresponding cultural taboo (Lieberman, Tooby, & Cosmides, 2003; Westermarck, 1921). This approach has led to novel empirical predictions that are not otherwise obvious to behavioral scientists.

The implications of evolution by natural selection permeate all areas of human behavior. Evolutionary psychology is not a field of psychology per se, but is instead an approach to understanding behavior in any area. Evolutionary psychologists conduct research in all traditional areas of psychology, including social, clinical, and physiological.

The utility of this approach is evident by the inroads it has provided in even the oldest, most thoroughly investigated areas in modern behavioral science. For example, distance perception was the primary topic of investigation of Wilhelm Wundt, the founder of scientific psychology, and distance perception research even predates psychology as a science (Fick, 1851, as cited in Finger & Spelt, 1947; Oppel, 1854, as cited in Hicks & Rivers, 1906). Distance perception research has the longest and one of the largest research records in all of psychology. Nonetheless, evolutionary psychologists recently predicted and then discovered multiple ubiquitous, large magnitude distance illusions in everyday vision by using an *a priori* theory about likely adaptive responses to the environments in which distance perception mechanisms evolved (Jackson & Cormack, 2007). The utility of any scientific approach ultimately rests on its novel empirical contributions, a standard which illuminates evolutionary psychology as a very useful tool.

The indelible marks of evolution by natural selection pervade human psychology. Behaviors, as with all adaptations, evolved in order to solve adaptive problems in the environments in which they evolved. Adaptations ultimately exist because they propagate their genes. This knowledge provides a theoretical framework that unites psychology with other sciences and provides novel empirical predictions that are not otherwise available. Evolutionary psychology provides insight into the design and purpose of behavior across all realms of behavioral science, and many productive advances await evolutionarily informed scientists.

In the end, the first lines of text about evolutionary psychology may summarize it best:

"In the distant future I see open fields for far more important researchers. Psychology will be based on a new foundation, that of the necessary acquirement of each mental power and capacity by gradation. Light will be thrown on the origin of man and his history." (Darwin, 1859)

REFERENCES

Darwin, C. R. (1859). *On the origin of species by means of natural selection, or the preservation of favoured races in the struggle for life.* London: John Murray.

Finger, F. W., & Spelt, D. K. (1947). The illustration of the horizontal-vertical illusion. *Journal of Experimental Psychology, 37,* 243–250.

Hicks, G. D., & Rivers, W. H. R. (1906). The illusion of compared horizontal and vertical lines. *British Journal of Psychology, 2,* 243–260.

Jackson, R. E., & Cormack, L. K. (2007). Evolved navigation theory and the descent illusion. *Perception & Psychophysics, 69*(3), 353–362.

Lieberman, D., Tooby, J., & Cosmides, L. (2003). Does morality have a biological basis? An empirical test of the factors governing sentiments relating to incest. *Proceedings of the Royal Society B: Biological Sciences, 270,* 819–826.

Westermarck, E. A. (1921). The history of human marriage (5th ed.). London: Macmillan.

SUGGESTED READINGS

Barkow, J. H., Cosmides, L., & Tooby, J. (1995). *The adapted mind: Evolutionary psychology and the generation of culture.* New York: Oxford.

Dawkins, R. (1976). *The selfish gene.* Bungay, Suffolk: Oxford University Press.

Ridley, M. (1994). *The red queen: Sex and the evolution of human nature.* New York: Macmillan.

RUSSELL E. JACKSON
California State University at San Marcos

See also: Anthropology; Ethology

EXCITATORY AND INHIBITORY SYNAPSES

Chemical synapses—that is, synapses that use a chemical neurotransmitter to transfer information from one neuron to another—can be excitatory or inhibitory, depending on their effect on the postsynaptic neuron. Synapses releasing a neurotransmitter that brings the membrane potential of the postsynaptic neuron toward the threshold for generating action potentials are said to be excitatory. Alternatively, inhibitory synapses drive the membrane potential of the postsynaptic neuron away from the threshold for generating action potentials.

The effect of a synapse is determined by its neurotransmitter content and the properties of the receptors present on the postsynaptic membrane. For example, in the adult mammalian brain, glutamate synapses are known to be excitatory, while GABA synapses are inhibitory. Meanwhile, synapses containing acetylcholine can be either excitatory or inhibitory, depending on the type of receptors present at a given synapse. Thus, at the neuromuscular junction, acetylcholine produces synaptic excitation by acting on a nicotinic receptor, whereas in the heart it acts on the inhibitory muscarinic receptor resulting in slowing the heart rate. Moreover, acetylcholine can have both excitatory and inhibitory effects in the same region, as described in the hippocampus (Ben-Ari, Krnjević, Reinhardt, & Ropert, 1981; Dodd, Dingledine, & Kelly, 1981).

Even more complex is the case of neurons releasing two neurotransmitters with opposing action, for example, glutamate and GABA in hippocampal granule cells (Walker, Ruiz, & Kullmann, 2001) and dopamine and glutamate in ventral midbrain neurons (Sulzer et al., 1998). Postsynaptic factors may be involved in regulating the differential release of such cotransmitters, as demonstrated in sympathetic neurons, producing both norepinephrine (excitatory) and acetylcholine (inhibitory). In these neurons, BDNF favors the secretion of acetylcholine and its presence can thus transform an excitatory synapse into an inhibitory one within minutes (Yang, Slonimsky, & Birren, 2002).

In many instances, excitatory and inhibitory synapses appear to differ morphologically. In the cerebral cortex, Gray (1959) described two morphological types of synapses, type 1 and type 2, which were later correlated to excitatory and inhibitory synapses (Eccles, 1964). Type 1 synapses have a prominent postsynaptic density and a synaptic cleft about 20 nm wide. They are also called asymmetric synapses, since the postsynaptic membrane specialization is thicker than the presynaptic one (Colonnier, 1968). Most type 1 or asymmetric synapses contain round synaptic vesicles, so they are also termed S-type, (S for Spheroid vesicles). The great majority of type 1 synapses in the cerebral cortex use glutamate as a neurotransmitter, and they are excitatory.

Type 2 synapses are characterized by a less pronounced postsynaptic density and a narrower synaptic cleft of about 12 nm. They are also known as symmetric, since the pre- and postsynaptic membrane specializations have a similar appearance. These synapses contain both round and flat synaptic vesicles after aldehyde fixation; hence the term F-type (F for Flat vesicles). In the cerebral cortex, the vast majority of type 2 or symmetric synapses contain GABA as a neurotransmitter and are inhibitory. Glycine, another major inhibitory neurotransmitter of the brain, is also found in symmetric synapses in the spinal cord, cochlear nucleus, and other regions of the brain (see Legendre, 2001). Although this correlation between morphology and function essentially holds true for the synapses in the adult cerebral cortex, this is not always the case during development or in other regions of the brain. For example, in the very young cerebral cortex, GABA cannot be detected by immunocytochemistry in as many as three quarters of the symmetric synapses (Micheva & Beaulieu, 1996). In some regions of the brain, such as spinal cord, basal ganglia, and inferior olive, GABA terminals have been observed to also form asymmetric synapses.

The excitatory and inhibitory synapses differ in their quantity and distribution in different brain regions. In the cerebral cortex, excitatory synapses represent the majority of synapses (more than 80%) and contact predominantly distal parts of the neuron, such as dendritic spines (which are the protoplasmic protrusions extending from the dendrites of some cells). Inhibitory synapses are less numerous and are most often found on proximal parts of the neuron, such as dendritic shafts and cell bodies (see Beaulieu et al., 1992). These morphological data appear to contradict physiological studies indicating the existence of a balance between excitatory and inhibitory neurotransmission in the cortex. However, even though the excitatory connections are much more abundant, the cortical inhibitory neurons fire at much faster rates than the excitatory pyramidal neurons (see Connors & Gutnick, 1990).

The fact that inhibitory neurons make many more contacts on or near the cell bodies is also important, since the spatial location of a synapse determines its relative contribution to the electrical state of the cell; that is, the closer the synapse to the site of generation of action potentials, presumably the axon hillock, the greater its effect. Therefore, the inhibitory system, by way of its distribution and pattern of activity, can efficiently balance excitatory neurotransmission in the cerebral cortex. The inhibitory system is also in a position to exert a very focused effect on a single excitatory input, since some dendritic spines receive both an excitatory and inhibitory synapse (Jones & Powell, 1969; Qian & Sejnowski, 1990). In this case, the interaction between the two synaptic inputs would occur locally, at the level of the dendritic spine that is relatively isolated from the rest of the neuron.

The strength or efficacy of synaptic transmission at both types of synapses can be modified by activity. This important property, called synaptic plasticity, has been extensively studied at excitatory synapses and has been proposed to form the basis of memory. Recently, the plasticity of inhibitory synapses has also come to attention, at least partly due to the fact that changes in inhibitory transmission have been implicated in a growing number of neurological and psychiatric illnesses like epilepsy, anxiety disorders, and schizophrenia (Fritschy & Brünig, 2003).

It thus becomes clear that studying the distribution and physiology of the excitatory and inhibitory synapses, as well as their development and plasticity, is essential for understanding the overall organization and functioning of the brain.

REFERENCES

Beaulieu, C., Kisvarday, Z., Somogyi, P., Cynader, M., & Cowey, A. (1992). Quantitative distribution of GABA-immunopositive and -immunonegative neurons and synapses in the monkey striate cortex (area 17). *Cerebral Cortex, 2,* 295–309.

Ben-Ari, Y., Krnjević, K., Reinhardt, W., & Ropert, N. (1981). Intracellular observations on the disinhibitory action of acetylcholine in the hippocampus. *Neuroscience, 6,* 2475–2484.

Colonnier, M. (1968). Synaptic patterns of different cell types in the different laminae of the cat visual cortex: An electron microscope study. *Brain Research, 9,* 268–287.

Connors, B. W., & Gutnick, M. J. (1990). Intrinsic firing patterns of diverse neocortical neurons. *Trends in Neuroscience, 13,* 99–104.

Dodd, J., Dingledine, R., & Kelly, J. S. (1981). The excitatory action of acetylcholine on hippocampal neurons of the guinea pig and rat maintained in vitro. *Brain Research, 207,* 109–127.

Eccles, J. C. (1964). *The physiology of synapses.* Berlin: Springer-Verlag.

Fritschy, J.-M., & Brünig, I. (2003) Formation and plasticity of GABAergic synapses: Physiological mechanisms and pathophysiological implications. *Pharmacology & Therapeutics, 98,* 299–323.

Gray, E. G. (1959). Axo-somatic and axo-dendritic synapses of the cerebral cortex: An electron microscope study. *Journal of Anatomy, 93,* 420–433.

Jones, E. G., & Powell, T. P. S. (1969). Morphological variations in the dendritic spines of the neocortex. *Journal of Cell Science, 5,* 509–529.

Legendre, P. (2001). The glycinergic inhibitory synapse. *Cellular and Molecular Life Sciences, 58,* 760–793.

Micheva, K. D., & Beaulieu, C. (1996). Quantitative aspects of synaptogenesis in the rat barrel field cortex with special reference to GABA circuitry. *Journal of Comparative Neurology, 373,* 340–354.

Qian, N., & Sejnowski, T. J. (1990). When is an inhibitory synapse effective? *Proceedings of the National Academy of Sciences, U.S.A., 87,* 8145–8149.

Sulzer, D., Joyce, M. P., Lin, L., Geldwert, D., Haber, S. N., & Hattori, T. et al. (1998). Dopamine neurons make glutamatergic synapses in vitro. *Journal of Neuroscience, 18,* 4588–4602.

Walker, M. C., Ruiz, A., & Kullmann, D. M. (2001). Monosynaptic GABAergic signaling from dentate to CA3 with a pharmacological and physiological profile typical of mossy fiber synapses. *Neuron, 29,* 703–715.

Yang, B., Slonimsky, J. D., & Birren, S. J. (2002). A rapid switch in sympathetic neurotransmitter release properties mediated by the p75 receptor. *Nature Neuroscience, 5,* 539–545.

Kristina D. Micheva
Stanford University School of Medicine

See also: **Central Nervous System; GABA Receptors; Neurotransmitters**

EXHIBITIONISM

Exhibitionism is a psychological disorder listed within the category of sexual disturbances called "paraphilias" in the *Diagnostic and Statistical Manual of Mental Disorders* (DSM-IV-TR; American Psychiatric Association, 2000). Exhibitionism is characterized by "recurrent, intense sexually arousing fantasies, sexual urges, or behaviors involving the exposure of one's genitals to an unsuspecting stranger" (p. 569) that persist over a period of at least six months. A person must have acted on these urges, or the urges or fantasies must cause distress or impairment for the person to be diagnosed with the disorder.

Like all sex offenses, indecent exposure involves the violation of a nonconsenting other person. Historically, exhibitionism has been seen as a mere nuisance behavior that causes little harm to victims. Evidence suggests, however, that many victims of indecent exposure experience traumatizing effects. In most states indecent exposure is now a crime for which individuals can be placed on a sex offender registry.

Exhibitionism is often manifested in highly repetitive and compulsive behaviors, and the presence of exhibitionism has been identified as a risk factor for future sexual reoffending in previously convicted sex offenders (Hanson & Thornton, 1999). Because exposing is so easily and unobtrusively performed, many exhibitionists are successful at eluding detection and sometimes engage in the behavior hundreds or even thousands of times without being caught. Limited evidence indicates that exhibitionist recidivism rates range from 20%–41%. In other words, two to four out of 10 exposure offenders will be rearrested for a new sex crime; they are twice as likely to be arrested for a new exposure offense than for another type of sex offense.

When assessing exhibitionism, it is important to distinguish among (1) true exhibitionists, whose fantasies and behaviors involve exposing their genitals specifically for the sexual excitement they derive from being seen; (2) public masturbators, who masturbate in public places such as cars without a clear desire to be observed; and (3) compulsive masturbators, whose hypersexual behavior usually is kept within the bounds of legal and social acceptability (Kafka, 2001). Because many victims of exhibitionism do not report these crimes to the police, and the offenders themselves do not volunteer such information, the prevalence and incidence of exposure offenses are unknown. However, approximately a third to a half of women surveyed report witnessing an exposure. Contrary to popular belief, no evidence indicates that exhibitionists "escalate" in their behavior. Some exhibitionists, however, will have engaged in a variety of sexually deviant acts or committed other types of sexual offenses.

No accepted theory explains the development of exhibitionism. Some evidence suggests that exhibitionism is related to general hypersexuality, including greater sexual arousability, more frequent masturbation, promiscuity, and dependence on pornography. Treatment for sex offenders has been found to reduce recidivism by about 40%, and cognitive behavioral therapy, combined, in some cases with antidepressant medications, can be helpful for exposers. Other treatment targets for exhibitionists include enhancing social relationships and intimacy skills and identifying strategies for meeting their needs for attention, affection, control, and approval in socially acceptable ways.

REFERENCES

American Psychiatric Association. (2000). *Diagnostic and statistical manual of mental disorders* (4th ed., text rev.). Washington, DC: Author.

Hanson, R. K., & Thornton, D. (1999). *Static-99: Improving actuarial risk assessments for sex offenders*. Ottawa Department of the Solicitor General of Canada.

Kafka, M. P. (2001). The paraphilia-related disorders: A proposal for a unified classification of nonparaphilic hypersexuality disorders. *Sexual Addiction and Compulsivity, 8*, 227–239.

SUGGESTED READINGS

Greenberg, S. R., Firestone, P., Bradford, J. M., & Greenberg, D. M. (2002). Prediction of recidivism in exhibitionists: Psychological, phallometric, and offense factors. *Sexual Abuse: A Journal of Research & Treatment, 14*(4), 329–348.

Morin, J. W., & Levenson, J. S. (2008). Exhibitionism: Assessment and treatment. In D. R. Laws & W. O'Donohue (Eds.), *Sexual deviance* (2nd ed.). New York: Guilford Press.

Murphy, W., & Page, J. (2008). Exhibitionism: Psychopathology and theory. In D. R. Laws & W. O'Donohue (Eds.), *Sexual deviance* (2nd ed.). New York: Guilford Press.

JOHN W. MORIN
*Center for Offender Rehabilitation and Education,
Fort Lauderdale, FL*

See also: **Sex Offenders; Sexual Deviations**

EXISTENTIAL PSYCHOLOGY

Existential psychology is a branch of psychology that studies how people come to terms with the basic givens of human existence. The existential perspective has important roots in philosophy, which has long tried to make sense of people's being in the world. The philosophical tradition most associated with existential psychology is existential philosophy, which was pioneered by such thinkers as Kierkegaard, Nietzsche, and Heidegger. These and other existential philosophers have written about the anxiety that is inherent in human existence, people's need for meaning in a meaningless world, and the importance for people to make their own choices according to their own authentic desires. Existential psychology has also been influenced by artistic expressions of the confusion and alienation that people experience in their confrontation with meaninglessness and absurdity, which can be found in the work of novelists such as Dostoevsky and Kafka and existentialist writers such as Sartre, de Bouvoir, Camus, Ionesco, and Beckett.

Traditionally, existential psychologists have rejected the use of experimental methods in psychology, preferring instead to analyze people's subjective experience and personal phenomenology. This methodological position caused a separation between existential psychology and mainstream academic psychology, which since the early twentieth century has become increasingly experimental and oriented toward the natural sciences. Existential psychologists were more influential in the therapeutic domain, however, where their ideas and methods were incorporated in an emerging existential psychotherapy. Otto Rank, a one-time collaborator of Sigmund Freud, was an important precursor of this therapeutic movement. Rank rejected Freud's emphasis on early childhood experiences, while emphasizing people's personal responsibility in the here-and-now, along with relational themes. Rank's will therapy sought to use the person's creative will as a vehicle for transformation and psychological growth. Rank is credited with having an important influence on Rollo May, a leading figure in the development of existential psychotherapy in the United States. In Europe, a pioneer of existential psychotherapy was Victor Frankl, who developed logo-therapy, which focuses on the importance of finding meaning in life.

A landmark volume on existential psychotherapy was published by Irvin Yalom in 1980. This important work describes the historical background of existential psychotherapy and the main ideas and methods that are used by existential psychotherapists. Existential psychotherapy regards people's existential struggles and their associated anxiety and alienation not as dysfunctional, but rather as an inevitable consequence of the human condition. By allowing clients to face their deepest existential fears, existential psychotherapy seeks to make clients free to appreciate the true significance of life. Existential psychotherapy further encourages clients to search for a new and increased awareness of what matters in the present. This awareness is intended to enable clients to achieve a new freedom and responsibility to act. Various academic programs in Britain offer training in existential psychotherapy and counseling. Publications on existential psychotherapy appear regularly in the journals of the British Society of Phenomenology and the Society for Existential Analysis. In 2006, Emmy van Deurzen and Digby Tantam founded the International Community of Existential Counselors and Therapists.

Since the mid-1980s, there has been a renewed interest in studying existential themes among experimentally oriented psychologists. A major impetus for this development was given by terror management theory (TMT; Greenberg, Solomon, & Pyszczynski, 1986), a theoretical perspective that was inspired by the existential perspective, most notably the work of sociologist Ernest Becker. TMT has emphasized the important role of existential anxiety in social behavior. The theory assumes that people's realization of the inevitability of their own death gives rise to a tremendous potential for death anxiety. To manage this death anxiety, people rely on various social-cognitive constructions that give them a sense of symbolic immortality. Prominent among these constructions are people's sense of self-esteem, which gives people a sense of enduring value, and cultural worldviews, which assure people that their world is meaningful and predictable.

One of the most important scientific innovations of TMT has been to render classic existential thought into a form that can be tested through empirical and even experimental methods. More specifically, one of the key tenets of TMT has been investigated by briefly reminding people of death, a procedure that experimental psychologists refer to as "priming." The effects of death reminders are then observed in people's subsequent behavior. According to TMT, people's needs for self-esteem and stable worldviews are increased by the psychological confrontation with death. Accordingly, reminders of death should lead to increased strivings for self-esteem and increased efforts to uphold one's cultural worldviews. Both predictions have been confirmed in a large number of social-psychological experiments (Greenberg, Solomon, & Pyszczynski, 1997). By thus wedding an existential outlook with sophisticated experimental methods, TMT research has created an important bridge between existential psychology and its scholarly sibling, experimental psychology.

The integration of experimental and existential psychologies has also been extended to other existential themes. Indeed, these developments have given birth to a new subdiscipline of psychology, which is now known as experimental existential psychology (XXP; Greenberg, Koole, & Pyszynski, 2004; Pyszynski, Greenberg, Koole, & Solomon, in press). XXP studies how people are coping with existential concerns through experimental methods. Although existential psychologists originally rejected the use of experimental methods, it is important to recognize that the split between existential and experimental psychology occurred during the 1920s, a time when experimental psychology was theoretically and methodologically more narrow and less sophisticated than it is today. Indeed, modern experimental methods and theories have become increasingly capable of elucidating the high-level cognitive processes that presumably underlie people's existential concerns. The arsenal of modern methods in XXP includes priming, response time measures, and even neuro-imaging techniques. By using rigorous methods of observation and experimentation, XXP aims to complement traditional approaches in existential psychology, which are grounded in the subjective phenomenology of people's existential concerns.

In a review article, Koole, Greenberg, and Pyszczynski (2006) distinguished five major existential concerns that are central to current research in XXP. A first major existential concern is death and refers to the psychological conflict between people's awareness of the inevitability of death versus their desire for continued existence. A second major existential concern is isolation and arises from the conflict between people's need to feel connected to others versus experiences of rejection and the realization that their subjective experience of reality can never be fully shared. A third major existential concern in XXP relates to people's sense of identity and arises from the conflict between people's desire for a clear sense of who they are and how they fit into the world versus uncertainties because of conflicts between self-aspects, unclear boundaries between self and nonself, or limited self-insight. A fourth major existential concern is freedom and originates from people's experience of free will versus the external forces on behavior and the burden of responsibility for their choices. Finally, a fifth major concern in XXP is meaning and stems from the conflict between people's desire to believe that life is meaningful and the events and experiences that appear random or inconsistent with one's bases of meaning.

A host of experimental studies have confirmed that these "big five" existential concerns have a pervasive influence on people's thoughts, feelings, and actions (Koole et al., 2006). Notably, XXP research indicates that existential concerns are often most influential in human behavior when these concerns are activated outside of awareness. This paradoxical set of findings creates an intriguing link between existential psychology and modern theories of unconscious thought. Whereas modern psychologists believed initially that the unconscious consisted strictly of "cold" cognitive computations, XXP research suggests that the unconscious may also harbor motivational conflicts that have existential implications for people (Westen, 1998). In a way, these findings confirm what many classic existential thinkers have long suspected: That existential concerns are a major force in human behavior, and that ignoring these concerns only serves to deepen the psychological conflicts that are associated with them.

REFERENCES

Greenberg, J., Koole, S. L., & Pyszczynski, T. (Eds.). (2004). *Handbook of experimental existential psychology*. New York: Guilford Press.

Greenberg, J., Pyszczynski, T., & Solomon, S. (1986). The causes and consequences of a need for self-esteem: A terror management theory. In R. F. Baumeister (Ed.), Public self and private self (pp. 189–212). New York: Springer-Verlag.

Greenberg, J., Solomon, S., & Pyszczynski, T. (1997). Terror management theory of self-esteem and social behavior: Empirical assessments and conceptual refinements. In M. P. Zanna (Ed.), Advances in experimental social psychology (Vol. 29, pp. 61–139). New York: Academic Press.

Koole, S. L., Greenberg, J., & Pyszczynski, T. (2006). Introducing science to the psychology of the soul: Experimental existential psychology. *Current Directions in Psychological Science, 15,* 212–216.

Pyszczynski, T., Greenberg, J., Koole, S. L., & Solomon, S. (in press). Experimental existential psychology: How people cope with the facts of life. In S. T. Fiske and D. T. Gilbert (Eds.), *Handbook of social psychology*. New York: McGraw-Hill.

Westen, D. (1998). The scientific legacy of Sigmund Freud. Toward a psychodynamically informed psychological science. *Psychological Bulletin, 124,* 333–371.

Yalom, I. (1980). *Existential psychotherapy*. New York: Basic Books.

SANDER L. KOOLE
VU University Amsterdam, The Netherlands

See also: Existential Psychotherapy; Terror Management Theory

EXISTENTIAL PSYCHOTHERAPY

Existential psychotherapy derives from the philosophical and literary writings of such thinkers as Soren Kierkegaard, Friedrich Nietzsche, Martin Heidegger, and Jean Paul Sartre; and from the phenomenological formulations of investigators such as Edmund Husserl, Maurice Merleau-Ponty, and William James (Cooper, 2003; May, Ellenberger, & Angel, 1958). Phenomenology is the art and science of discovering intimate "lived" experience. While the phenomenological basis of existential psychotherapy varies some throughout the world, here our focus will be on the American perspective, which has partly drawn on humanistic psychology (Cooper, 2003).

The basic thrust of existential psychotherapy, as its chief American spokesperson, Rollo May (1981, p. 19), put it, is "to set clients free." Freedom is understood as the cultivation of the capacity for choice within the natural and self-imposed (e.g., cultural) limits of living (Schneider, 2008). Choice is understood further as responsibility; the "ability to respond" to the myriad forces within and about one. Although many forces are recognized as restrictive of the human capacity for choice, which are influences that May (1981) terms "destiny" (e.g., genes, biology, culture, circumstances, and the like), they are nevertheless highly mutative, according to existentialists, in the light of and through the tussle with choice. For existentialists, choice is the key to an engaged and meaningful life (Bugental, 1987; May, 1981).

The second major concern of existential psychotherapy is the cultivation not just of intellectual or calculative decision making, but of decision making that is felt, sensed, or in short, *experienced*. The stress on the experiential is one of the primary areas of distinction between existential and other (e.g., cognitive-behavioral, psychoanalytic) modes of practice. The experiential mode is defined by four basic dimensions: (1) immediacy, (2) affectivity, (3) kinesthesia, and (4) profundity (Schneider, 2008). By immediacy, existentialists mean experience that is fresh, living, or "here and now"; by affectivity, they mean experience that is characterized by feeling or passion; by kinesthesia, they refer to experience that is embodied or intensively sensed; and by profundity, they refer to experience that has depth and impact.

Existential therapists have proposed a variety of means by which to facilitate freedom, experiential reflection, and responsibility. Some, such as Irvin Yalom (1980), emphasize using the support and challenges of the therapist-client relationship to facilitate liberation. Yalom stresses the building of rapport and repeated challenges to clients to take responsibility for their difficulties. Further, Yalom homes in on the immediate and affective elements of his therapeutic contacts, but he refers little to kinesthetic components.

Following the philosopher Martin Buber, Maurice Friedman (1995) also homes in on the interpersonal relationship but stresses the dimension of authenticity or the "I-thou" encounter as the key therapeutic element. The I-thou encounter, according to Friedman, is the dialectical process of being both present to and confirming of oneself, while simultaneously being open to and confirming of another. The result of such an encounter is a "healing through meeting," as Friedman (1995, p. 309) puts it, which is a healing of trust, deep self-searching, and responsibility. Through the therapist's I-thou encounter, in other words, the client is inspired to trust, enhance self-awareness, and take charge of his or her own distinct plight. James Bugental, on the other hand, accents the "intra"personal dimensions of freedom, experiential reflection, and responsibility.

For Bugental (1987), choice and responsibility are facilitated not merely or mainly through therapist and client encounter, but through concerted invitations (and sometimes challenges) to clients to attend to their subtlest internal processes, including flashes of feeling, twinges of sensation, and glimpses of imagination. Via these means, according to Bugental, clients discover their deepest yearnings but also, and equally important, their thorniest impediments to these impulses. By grappling with each side, Bugental maintains that clients learn to negotiate their conflicts, elucidate their meaning, and rechannel them into living fuller and more empowered lives. Similarly, Rollo May (1981) stresses the cultivation of what he terms "intentionality" in the therapeutic relationship. By intentionality, May refers to the "whole bodied" direction, orientation, or purpose that can result from existential therapy. In his case examples, May shows how intellectualized or behaviorally programmed interventions persistently fall short with respect to the cultivation of intentionality, whereas profound struggle, both between the therapist and client and within the client, can, if appropriately supported, lead to such a quality. For May as with most of the existential therapists, the struggle for identity is essential, by virtue of its enhancing clarity, agency, and ultimately commitment or intentionality in the engagement of one's life.

The upshot of this synopsis is that existential therapists use a diversity of means by which to foster a similar result, client empowerment and consciousness-raising. In recent years, and partly as a response to the ethos of financial and scientific accountability, existential therapists have endeavored to reassess and in some cases reform their practices. Kirk Schneider (2008), for example, has developed a "bridgebuilding" approach he calls existential-integrative (EI) therapy. EI therapy draws on a diversity of therapeutic approaches within an overarching existential or experiential framework. The aim of EI therapy is to address clients at the level at which they chiefly struggle—be that physiological, environmental, cognitive, psychosexual, or interpersonal—but all within an ever deepening, ever beckoning experiential context. By experiential, Schneider refers to the availability of an experiential (immediate, affective, kinesthetic, and profound) level of contact.

The degree to which a client can be "met" within the experiential context is a function of his or her desire and capacity for change, but also, according to Schneider, an assortment of therapist offerings. Among these offerings are presence, invoking the actual, vivifying and confronting resistance, and the rediscovering of "meaning and awe." Presence, for Schneider, holds and illuminates that which is palpably (immediately, affectively, kinesthetically, and profoundly) alive, both within the client and between client and therapist. Presence holds and illuminates that which is charged in the relationship and implies the question, "What's really going on here, within the client and between me and the client?" Presence is the "soup" or atmosphere within which deep disclosure can occur, and based upon this disclosure, the client's core battles become clarified.

Invoking the actual refers to the invitation to the client to *engage* that which is palpably alive. By invoking the actual, the therapist calls attention to the part of the client that is attempting to emerge, break through, and overcome stultifying defenses. Invoking the actual is characterized by such invitations (and sometimes challenges) as, "What really matters to you right now?" Or "I notice that your eye moistened as you made that statement." Or "What feelings come up as you speak with me?" At times, invoking the actual calls attention to content/process discrepancies, such as "You say that you are angry but you smile."

If invoking the actual calls attention to that which is emerging in the client's experience, vivifying and confronting resistance call attention to that which *blocks* what is attempting to emerge. These blocks or resistances are seen as lifelines from the existential-integrative point of view, but they are also acknowledged as increasingly defunct. Vivifying resistance "alerts" clients to their defensive blocks, while confronting resistance "alarms" or "jars" them about those blocks. Together, vivifying and confronting resistance serve to intensify and eventually mobilize clients' counter-resistances (or "counter-will" as Otto Rank has put it); and it is these counter-resistances that liberate vital, intentional changes. As a result of this liberation, clients develop new meanings and possibilities in their lives. Throughout EI therapy but particularly in this final stage, therapists help clients to consolidate these new meanings and possibilities, such as the sense of humility and wonder, or in short, "awe" toward life (Schneider, 2004, 2008). The art of this consolidation can be seen in many forms of support—from helping clients to translate their newfound freedom to explore, create, and assert; to assisting them with avenues for spiritual realization, such as in meditative or artistic engagements. Despite the mode of outcome, however, one commonality unites all: a renewed freedom to be.

Notably, the existential emphasis on experiential encounter has been receiving increasing attention from the mainstream therapeutic community. For example, leading therapy researcher Bruce Wampold (2008) has identified the characteristics of existential therapy as exemplary of the common or context factors that appear to underlie all effective therapies. In summary, existential-integrative therapy, like existential therapy generally, assists clients to grapple with their experiences of life, not just their reports about life, and through this illumination, supports their intentional and embodied discoveries.

REFERENCES

Bugental, J. F. T. (1987). *The art of the psychotherapist*. New York: Norton.

Cooper, M. (2003). *Existential therapies*. London: Sage.

Friedman, M. (1995). The case of Dawn. In K. J. Schneider, & R. May (Eds.), *The psychology of existence: An integrative, clinical perspective* (pp. 308–315). New York: McGraw-Hill.

May, R., Angel, E., & Ellenberger, H. (Eds.). (1958). *Existence: A new dimension in psychiatry and psychology*. New York: Basic Books.

May, R. (1981). *Freedom & destiny*. New York: Norton.

Schneider, K. J. (2004). *Rediscovery of awe: Splendor, mystery, and the fluid center of life*. St. Paul, MN: Paragon House.

Schneider, K. J. (Ed.). (2008). *Existential-integrative psychotherapy: Guideposts to the core of practice*. New York: Routledge.

Wampold, B. (2008, February 6). Existential-integrative psychotherapy comes of age. [Review of the book *Existential-integrative psychotherapy: Guideposts to the core of practice*]. *PsycCritiques 53*, Release 6, Article 1.

Yalom, I. (1980). *Existential psychotherapy*. New York: Basic Books.

SUGGESTED READINGS

Laing, R. D. (1969). *The divided self: An existential study in sanity and madness*. Middlesex, UK: Penguin.

Mendelowitz, E., & Schneider, K. (2008). Existential Psychotherapy. In R. Corsini & D. Wedding (Eds.), *Current psychotherapies* (8th ed., pp. 295–326). Belmont, CA: Thompson/Brooks Cole.

Schneider, K. J., & Krug, O. T. (in press). *Existential-humanistic therapy*. (APA Series on Theories of Psychotherapy.) Washington, DC: American Psychological Association Press.

Kirk J. Schneider
Saybrook Graduate School, San Francisco, CA

See also: **Client-Centered Therapy; Humanistic Psychotherapies**

EXPERIENTIAL PSYCHOTHERAPY

Experiential psychotherapy is a meta-theoretical term for a way of conducting therapy, rather than being a specific therapy based on one theory of personality.

The Touchstone

A focus of therapy done experientially is the client's moment-to-moment experiencing. Experiencing is the entry point to productive psychological improvement. It is the primary navigational aid to a fruitful course of therapy.

Therapeutic moves (empathic response, interpretation, suggestion, question, confrontation, chair-work, psychoeducation) can be evaluated by immediate effects on client experiencing: When experiencing becomes more closed, defensive, abstract, or emotionally out of control, the move has had an effect of dubious (or worse) value. When experiencing becomes more open, productively emotional, complex, intricate, and accurately expressible in words or other symbols, the move has had a desirable effect. Positive experiential effects reliably bring a visceral sense of relief and encouragement, opening paths for living that were blocked or nonexistent.

Experiential feedback protects the therapist against selectively perceiving data anticipated by theoretical or personal expectations. The therapist can thereby promptly correct for unhelpful moves, rather than persisting with well-intentioned plans that are unhelpful at the time. Persisting with ill-fitting plans generates problems in therapy.

References to the experiential method are found in the works of many early psychotherapists, including Sigmund Freud, Otto Rank, Sandor Ferenczi, Wilhelm Reich, Frieda Fromm-Reichmann, Harry Stack Sullivan, and Karen Horney (Friedman, 1976). Carl Rogers (1951) was the first to develop a psychotherapy in which the client rather than the therapist was the proper guide of therapy. Whitaker and Malone (1969) may have been the first to use "experiential psychotherapy" to describe their approach. Eugene Gendlin, who worked closely with Rogers, developed a philosophical basis for the experiential method (Gendlin, 1962), and this project continues (*A Process Model* at www .http://www.focusing.org/process.html). Gendlin cites existential and phenomenological philosophers S. Kirkegaard, W. Dilthey, E. Husserl, M. Heidegger, M. Buber, J.-P. Sartre, and M. Merleau-Ponty as precursors.

The proponents of about four dozen later-generation psychotherapies call their approaches experiential (Greenberg, Watson, & Lietaer, 1998, p. 202), but five types of therapy give the experiential method major emphasis: client-centered, existential, Gestalt, process-experiential, and focusing-oriented. These therapies draw on Kurt Goldstein's (1939) observation of an actualizing tendency, found in any organism, to behave to perfect capacities of the organism as a whole. The client's moment-to-moment experiencing is the real-time expression of the actualizing tendency. Experiencing is wider and deeper than conscious experience. Experiencing is considered inherently life-promoting both for the individual and social groups; generally more so with more awareness (Greenberg et al., p. 29). Actualization of healthy potentials implicit in experiencing does not depend only on the individual, but is highly dependent on interpersonal and other environmental conditions with which one interacts.

Why a Need for Therapy?

Things go awry when environmental factors interfere with accurate awareness and symbolization of experiencing, especially if systematically so over a long time. Patterns of relating to experiencing (or avoiding it) result, which shape positive potentials of experiencing into negative forms. "The source of evil and antisocial behavior lies much more in factors that prevent full, accurate, ongoing symbolization of experiencing than it does in the individual personality" (Iberg, 1990, p. 101).

For Gendlin, it is not units such as atoms or personality traits, but interactions that are the basic philosophical givens. Thus experiential therapies give attention to interactions, both interpersonal and intrapsychic. Maintaining an empathic climate has long been recognized as facilitative of personal growth, both in therapy and in normal development. Reflexive attention to patterns of interaction between client and therapist is one thing making therapy different from and more productive of change than other relationships.

Intrapsychically, psychological problems involve

> ... the inability to integrate aspects of functioning into coherent, harmonious internal relations.... At another level ... the inability to symbolize bodily felt constituents of experience in awareness, or symbolizing them in restricted or rigid ways, [is] another source of dysfunction.... A third major source ... involves the activation by minimal cues of core maladaptive emotion schemes. (Greenberg et al., p. 50)

These involve problematic relating to one's "bodily felt sense," which is Gendlin's term for experiencing as felt subjectively.

Outcomes of Experiential Therapy

Therapy corrects problematic attitudes toward experiencing. Leijssen says the generic therapeutic attitude

> ... requires ... waiting, ... quietly ... remaining present with [and being friendly to] the not yet speakable, being receptive to the not yet formed. To achieve this, it will be necessary to suspend temporarily everything that the person already knows about it and to be cognitively inactive. This kind of attention

can also be found in Zen meditation and Taoism, but in therapy it is directed toward a specific object, the felt sense.... The therapist interacts with the client in an attitude of acceptance and empathy; gradually, in the corrective therapeutic milieu the client learns to adopt ... [this] focusing attitude by interacting with the bodily felt experience (the client's inside) in the same friendly and listening way. (Greenberg et al., p. 123)

Developing this attitude is not a short-term or trivial matter, especially for those with troublesome psychological issues. Therapy establishes a climate within which, aided by the expertise of the therapist, the client can adopt healthier attitudes toward experiencing. Many felt shifts occur before lasting change is accomplished:

> When the right symbols that fit the experience are found, the client feels a satisfying sense of rightness. This is a *"felt shift"*: a physical sensation of something moving in the way the problem is experienced. There are many kinds of shifts.... On the continuum of *intensities* at the low end there are "small shifts" which may be very minimal, very subtle; one could easily skip over them if one didn't know about them. At the high end the shift is intense, dramatic, obvious.... There are also different *kinds* of shifts: sometimes the client feels a release or a relief in the body (e.g., a sigh, tears); sometimes it is a sharpening of some vague experience or the sense becomes stronger (e.g., a general feeling of confusion becomes a clear feeling of anger); sometimes the client feels something moving from one location in the body to another (e.g., a choking sensation in the throat becomes a warm feeling around the heart); sometimes it is an experience of more energy, excitement, enthusiasm, personal power, or new life awakening and stirring in some parts of the body or the whole body; at other times it's a feeling more of peace, clarity, groundedness, a warm spacious sense of well-being. The client might also have a new insight about an issue, but we consider this only as a felt shift or a new step if the insight doesn't happen only in the mind but is also in some way a bodily felt resolution. (Leijssen, in Greenberg et al., 1998, p. 138)

When one reliably relates to experiencing so as to get felt shifts, one is said to have a high level of experiencing. There is evidence that high-experiencing work with traumatic experiences has a positive effect on immune function (Lutkendorf, S., Antoni, M., Kumar, M., & Schneiderman, M., 1994). Studies have found psychological benefits associated with high levels of experiencing (Hendricks, 2001).

Recent Developments

Experiential theorists pursued differentiation of ways of relating to experiencing that correspond to contemporary diagnostic categories. Although further work remains, typical processing problems corresponding to some common diagnoses have been defined (Table 1).

Experiential therapists look for structure in repeated patterns of experiencing and interaction, rather than

Table 1. Some Diagnoses and Associated Processing Difficulties (Greenberg et al., ch. 20)

Major depression	excessive self-criticism; unacknowledged emotions; overregulated feelings
Post-traumatic stress	underregulated bodily experiencing needing accurate symbolization
Psychosomatic gastrointestinal disorders	tendency to avoid acknowledging and coping with negative self-image, inconsistent aspects of self
Anxiety disorders	tendency to interrupt the coming into awareness of bodily experiencing; hyperinclination to reflexivity of attention

in the contents of awareness or personality traits. One development has been the identification of "markers" indicating types of processing difficulty calling for differential response. Examples of these markers are (1) problematic reactions: one's view of an experience and emotional reaction don't match; (2) self-evaluative splits: one part of a person negatively evaluates another part; (3) unfinished business: unresolved emotional memories; and (4) a generally vulnerable, fragile sense of self (Greenberg, Rice, & Elliott, 1993). Experiential therapists also minimize diagnostic categorization of clients, out of concern with maintaining respect for and the dignity of the person (Greenberg et al., p. 463).

Recently, proponents of experiential therapy have moderated from extreme positions. In the earlier Rogerian position of "nondirectivity," therapists avoided guiding clients in any way. The earlier Gestalt position involved much "encounter-group-like confrontation" (Yontef, in Greenberg et al.). The more modern position is one of guiding the process, but not the content of client experiencing. Purton (2004) shows how Gendlin's experiential theory facilitates this moderation.

Regardless of theoretical orientation, experiential therapists remain alert for words, images, behavioral strategies, or situational changes having positive resonating power with the bodily felt sense. Different approaches to helping are usable, limited only by what the therapist can apply skillfully. Therapist and client rely on responses from their body senses as a guide toward improvements both uniquely right for the client and in a theoretically and interpersonally desirable direction.

REFERENCES

Friedman, N. (1976). From the experiential in therapy to experiential psychotherapy: A history. *Psychotherapy: Theory, Research, and Practice, 13*, 236–243.

Gendlin, E. T. (1962). *Experiencing and the creation of meaning.* New York: The Free Press of Glencoe.

Greenberg, L., Watson, J., & Lietaer, G., (Eds.). (1998). *Handbook of experiential psychotherapy.* New York: Guilford Press.

Greenberg, L., Rice, L., & Elliott, R. (1993). *Facilitating emotional change: The moment-by-moment process.* New York: Guilford Press.

Hendricks, M. N. (2001). Focusing-oriented/Experiential Psychotherapy. In D. Cain & J. Seeman (Eds.), *Humanistic psychotherapy: Handbook of research and practice.* Washington, DC: American Psychological Association.

Iberg, J. R. (1990). Person-centered experiential psychotherapy. In J. K. Zeig & Munion, W. M. (Eds.), *What is psychotherapy? Contemporary perspectives.* San Francisco: Jossey-Bass.

Lutkendorf, S., Antoni, M., Kumar, M., & Schneiderman, N. (1994). Changes in cognitive coping strategies predict EBV-antibody titre change following a stressor disclosure induction. *Journal of Psychosomatic Research, 38*, 63–78.

Rogers, C. R. (1951) *Client-centered therapy.* Boston: Houghton Mifflin.

Whitaker, C., & Malone, T. P. (1969). Experiential or nonrational psychotherapy. In W. Sahakian (Ed.), *Psychotherapy and counseling: Studies in technique.* Chicago: Rand McNally.

SUGGESTED READINGS

Cornell, A. W. (1996). *The power of focusing: A practical guide to emotional self-healing.* Oakland, CA: New Harbinger.

Gendlin, E. T. (1996). Focusing-oriented psychotherapy: A manual of the experiential method. New York: Guilford Press.

Purton, C. (2004). *Person-centered therapy: The focusing-oriented approach.* New York: Palgrave Macmillan.

JAMES R. IBERG
The Focusing Institute, Chicago, IL

See also: **Client-Centered Therapy; Existential Psychotherapy; Humanistic Psychotherapies**

EXPERIMENTAL CONTROLS

Experimental controls are techniques that researchers utilize to minimize the effects of extraneous experience and environmental variables as well as to strengthen the inference that changes in the dependent variable are due to the independent variable (the ability to infer causality). Does, for example, Treatment X (independent variable) cause a change in Behavior A (dependent variable)? A well-designed, well-controlled, and well-implemented randomized experiment is the best avenue for examining causality.

There are three criteria for causality: time order, where the independent variable precedes the dependent variable; correlation, where there is a statistically significant relationship between the independent and dependent variables; and a nonspurious relationship, where some other factor is not the source of the observed relationship. Let's look for a moment at an experiment that evaluates the impact of an intervention (independent variable) on disruptive classroom behavior (dependent variable) in children. If teachers observe an improvement (decrease) in disruptive classroom behaviors, could they then conclude that the intervention caused the change? Certainly, the intervention precedes the change, and there is definitely a significant relationship between the two. However, there are also a number of other factors that could account for the observed change in behavior.

Two ways in which experiments control for a spurious relationship (i.e., some other factor than the independent variable as the source of the change in the dependent variable) are (1) through random assignment of subjects to groups and (2) through the control of extraneous experience and environmental variables.

Random Assignment of Subjects to Groups

In experimental designs, one way to help determine if the independent variable causes the change in the dependent variable is to have more than one group to compare (either different treatment groups, or a treatment group and a control group). A key question in comparing groups is whether the groups are equivalent on all characteristics prior to the introduction of the independent variable (i.e., treatment). Using random assignment of participants to groups, when there are at least 30 subjects per group, is the best way to ensure equivalence of groups, or at least that the groups are unbiased.

Many studies, however, have small numbers of participants in each group. Other studies may not be able to utilize random assignment of subjects. When either or both are the case, the researcher must use other techniques to strengthen the equivalence of the groups, such as matching or statistical adjustment.

Control of Extraneous Experience and Environmental Variables

Also called contamination, extraneous variables are experiences or environmental conditions (other than the independent variable) that have an effect on the dependent variable during the study. Short of a fully controlled laboratory experience, it is unlikely that any study using human subjects can fully control for all extraneous variables. The researcher can, however, work to minimize the effects of extraneous variables (thus strengthening the study) and must always be aware of the potential limitations to the study's ability to infer causality due to the effect(s) of such variables.

In controlling for extraneous effects, one key aspect is whether the variables or events impact one group more than the other. Morgan, Gliner, and Harmon (2006) discuss several types of questions that the researcher might ask to determine the degree to which the extraneous variables are controlled. These might include (1) Was the study conducted in a controlled environment? (2) If the study was not conducted in a controlled environment, did the groups have the same type of environment? (3) Were the extraneous variables that could affect one group more than another controlled (i.e., held constant)? (4) Was there a control group (i.e., one that received either no treatment or a usual treatment)? (5) Were there controls for extraneous variables that could affect all groups and obscure true effects? (6) Were there adequate attempts to reduce other extraneous influences?

Experimental controls studies often seek to determine the effectiveness of a specific intervention on a specific behavior or set of behaviors. Let us return to the study to evaluate the effectiveness of intervention A on disruptive classroom behaviors in children. In this study, a number of extraneous effects might be of concern and would need to be controlled. The researcher might implement the intervention with one classroom and use another classroom as a control (no intervention) group. As the classroom assignments are already determined, random assignment of subjects to the groups is not possible. But there are other things that could be done to compensate, such as matching the groups.

Often, in such experimental designs, the behaviors are observed and measured for incidence. One possible problem with the study would be instrumentation, differences due to changes in the measuring instrument or to the unreliability of the measuring instrument. In this study, the two classroom teachers might well consider (and therefore measure) different behaviors as disruptive. To control for instrumentation, disruptive behaviors must be clearly defined. If an outside observer is utilized, it would be best to have only one observer. If multiple observers are utilized, it is important to train all observers to ensure that they are measuring the same behaviors in the same way.

Let us say that this study is to be conducted in multiple classrooms, with several teachers administering the intervention. Using different classrooms (and therefore different teachers) might again be problematic. This could produce an experimenter effect, as different teachers would have different styles which might, although unintentional, impact results. By the same token, even when all possible effects are controlled, the children's behaviors might improve as the participants simply move through the school year (maturation effects). In considering and recognizing the potential impact of extraneous experience and environmental variables, the researcher can then work to control and, therefore, minimize (or limit) the impact of those extraneous variables.

In summary, it is important for all experimental designs to control as best as possible for equivalence of groups on participant characteristics and for extraneous experience and environmental variables. The stronger the study in each category, the greater the ability of the researcher to infer causality from the results of the study.

REFERENCE

Morgan, G. A., Gliner, J. A., & Harmon, R. J. (2006). *Understanding and evaluating research in applied and clinical settings*. Mahwah, NJ: Lawrence Erlbaum.

SUGGESTED READINGS

Babbie, E. R. (2007). *The practice of social research* (11th ed.). Belmont, CA: Wadsworth.

Shadish, W. R., Cook, T. D., & Campbell, D. T. (2002). *Experimental controls and quasi-experimental designs for generalized causal influence*. Boston: Houghton Mifflin.

KATHRYN KIDD
GEORGE A. MORGAN
Colorado State University

See also: **Randomized Control Trials**

EXPERIMENTAL PSYCHOLOGY

Experimental psychology is a branch of the broad academic discipline of psychology. As its name suggests, experimental psychology is defined primarily by its methodology. Like all branches of psychology, experimental psychology aims to understand the behavior of organisms, both human and nonhuman. However, it does so exclusively by using the experimental method of science. Experimental psychology includes any aspect of behavior that is amenable to examination by the experimental method.

Experimental Methodology

As noted, experimental psychology relies on its advancement on data collected in experiments, the majority of which are conducted in psychological laboratories. A good general reference for the methodology of experimental psychology is the textbook by Martin (2008). The main feature of a psychological experiment is controlled comparison of behavior of participants (human or nonhuman) under at least two conditions that differ on a variable of interest, but are treated essentially the same in all other ways. A manipulated variable is called an *independent* variable, and the behavior measured is called a *dependent* variable. Variables that are held constant are called *control* variables, and variables that are allowed to vary at random are called *random* variables. If behavioral differences between conditions are large enough to be statistically beyond chance, then the only possible cause of the observed difference is the independent variable. A crucial consideration in the design of any experiment is to avoid a *confounding* variable, which is a variable of no interest that nonetheless co-varies with the independent variable.

Of course, most modern psychological experiments are complex and typically involve more than two conditions defined for a given independent variable and more than one dependent variable. But the principle is always the same: With respect to any comparison of conditions, the cause of behavioral differences can only be the independent variable along which the conditions differ. It is generally accepted that the experimental method is the only scientific method that supports cause-effect conclusions from data.

In the case of two independent variables, a procedure called crossing is often used, which requires that each level on one independent variable occurs in combination with each level on the other independent variable. For example, to study the effects of both font size (e.g., small or large) and font type (e.g., Courier or Arial) on reading speed, all combinations of size and font would need to be included (i.e., small Courier, small Arial, large Courier, large Arial). When there are two or more independent variables that are crossed in an experiment, an evaluation can be made both of their separate effects on the dependent variable, which are called *main effects*, and of whether the effect of one variable depends on the level of another variable, which is called an *interaction* effect. In the example, the effect of font type might depend on font size, such that the difference in reading speed between Courier and Arial fonts might be greater with the larger than with the smaller font size. This is only one example of an interaction, which can take many different forms. In any event, researchers always need to examine the possibility that those variables interact in significant ways when studying multiple variables.

Substantive Areas of Experimental Psychology

Psychology experiments can be conducted on virtually any behavior and in virtually all fields of psychology, including social psychology, clinical psychology, developmental psychology, and neuroscience. However, the label "experimental psychology" has been traditionally limited to a select number of topics that focus on normal adult behavior of individuals. These topics include sensation, perception, attention, learning, memory, cognition, language, motivation, emotion, concept formation, decision making, reasoning, and problem solving. These topics can be grouped into four superordinate categories: (1) input, (2) information processing, (3) affect, and (4) higher mental processes. This grouping should not be taken to imply that the field of experimental psychology is equally divided into these categories. For a more detailed description of the topical areas of experimental psychology, see the handbook volume by Healy and Proctor (2003).

Experimental psychology is a basic science, which aims to elucidate fundamental behavioral processes. The experiments are not completely limited, though, to pure research because applied issues or questions are often addressed by experimental psychologists (e.g., Healy, 2005). In fact, there is a subgroup of experimental psychologists who study human factors in applied settings, including industry, education, and the military. An example of the type of research conducted by experimental psychologists to address applied questions is the work on the relevance of experimental psychology to the classroom, such as McDaniel and Einstein's (2005) demonstrations of ways to use difficult materials to promote students' learning.

Generalizing from Experimental Data

The primary emphasis in experimental psychology is on hard data collected in experiments conducted in the laboratory. Both the average level of performance of a group of participants and the differences among individuals within the group are of interest. Hard data provide a numerical representation of trends attributable to manipulated independent variables, which constitute a description of how behavior is affected under controlled conditions. However, experimental psychologists often strive to go beyond a description of observed behavior and to generalize their observations in more abstract terms. This process of generalization is guided by hypotheses about the specific independent-dependent variable relationship (i.e., cause-effect relationship), by a more abstract model of the relationship, or by a general theory. This generalization process allows the researchers to go beyond their laboratory observations and formulate conclusions concerning a wider range of circumstances. Typically, in modern experimental psychology, there is a tight interaction between theory and data so that most experiments are tests of theoretical ideas. The modern experimental psychologist is not simply a methodologist or data collector but also a theoretician. The same researcher who collects experimental data also contributes to the theoretical description and analysis of them.

Generalization entails methodological as well as theoretical considerations, especially regarding the validity of an experiment. In this regard, there is an important distinction that is made between the internal and external validity of any experiment. The *internal validity* is defined by the certainty that the independent variable is the sole cause of changes in the dependent variable. Thus, an experimenter must control all extraneous variables that might influence the dependent variable and avoid all possible confounding variables that co-vary with the independent variable. But there is a trade-off here, because excessive control can limit the generalizability of the data collected. This consideration relates to the construct of *external validity*, which is defined as the degree to which researchers can generalize from the conditions of their

experiment to broader circumstances. The more variation that is incorporated within the experimental design, the more defensible is generalization, and consequently, the higher is the external validity. For example, the font size experiment described earlier could be tightly controlled in terms of the materials read, so that they are limited to a certain length or difficulty. Such a limitation might allow for enhanced internal validity by ruling out length and difficulty of the materials as potential confounding variables. However, variation in the materials' length and difficulty would be preferable from the standpoint of external validity because they would allow for a wider range of generalization.

History of Experimental Psychology

Prior to the middle of the nineteenth century, psychology was essentially a subdiscipline of philosophy. Questions about human behavior and the human mind were dealt with primarily through intuition and logic. The answers to these questions given by philosophical investigation alone led to unresolved controversy and no consensus on conclusions. What was needed were objective data, which could only be produced under controlled experimental conditions. This movement toward an experimental approach to studying behavior and mind was the beginning of scientific psychology (Boring, 1929).

One of the earliest questions addressed in this movement was about the way in which the mind apprehends physical stimulation from the environment. That is, is there a lawful relationship between dimensions of stimulation and the way in which human beings perceive and respond to those stimuli. Experiments of this type are referred to as "psychophysical" studies to denote the link between the psychological and physical worlds. In the mid-nineteenth century, Gustav Fechner (1860/1966) demonstrated that reported sensations experienced by observers were lawfully related to physical variations in stimuli. He described this relationship as a log function. This law established the possibility of experimental psychology as a quantitative science using the techniques of mathematics, as in more established physical sciences.

The first experimental psychology laboratory was founded in Leipzig, Germany by Wilhem Wundt in 1879. The focal problem addressed in Wundt's laboratory was the analysis of the content of the conscious human mind (Wundt, 1897). The methodological approach was called "introspection," which required trained observers to describe in detail the elemental content of awareness. This approach was a major methodological movement in early psychology, which was named Structuralism by one of its proponents, E. B. Titchener (1910), a student of Wundt who taught psychology in the United States.

Also working in Germany was Hermann Ebbinghaus, who changed the direction of experimental psychology research from introspection, which relies on self-reports by observers, to objective recordings of behavior. The focal questions addressed by Ebbinghaus (1885/1913) concerned human memory. Using himself as the only subject, he employed a study-test procedure, in which he would first study a set of unfamiliar materials and then subsequently test himself for his memory of those materials after different retention intervals. The materials he commonly used were "nonsense syllables," which are short, pronounceable letter clusters with no dictionary definition. He discovered that these items were lost from memory over time, with the rate of loss most rapid initially and declining gradually. He also discovered that even in cases where he could not recall any of the items in a list, subsequent relearning of the items showed significant savings.

Following Wundt and Ebbinghaus, experimental psychology expanded in Europe and, even more dramatically, in the United States. In brief, the work in the late nineteenth- and early twentieth centuries was characterized by various schools of thought differing in their major topics of interest, their methodology, and their theoretical interpretation of data. Among these schools was Structuralism, which, as already described, focused on the conscious content of the mind as revealed by introspection. Functionalism, in contrast, placed an emphasis on performance and the functions or purposes of behavior. Among its most notable adherents were William James (1890), who treated the mind as an organ of the body (like the heart and lungs) whose purpose was to control behavior, and Edward Thorndike (1911), who introduced the notion of stimulus-response (S-R) connections as the building blocks of behavior. Like Structuralism, Gestalt psychology focused on perceptual processes and mental content. However, instead of using an analytical approach designed to reveal mental elements, Gestalt psychologists, including its founders Max Wertheimer, Kurt Koffka, and Wolfgang Köhler, were concerned with perceptual and mental organization, arguing that the whole experience (the Gestalt) is different from, and more important than, the sum of its parts. In contrast to all of these schools, which tried to appreciate the workings of the mind, Behaviorism accepted the recordings of an independent observer as the only real data of experimental psychology and rejected unobservable thoughts. The founder of Behaviorism was John Watson; other notable Behaviorists were Clark Hull, Kenneth Spence, and B. F. Skinner.

Behaviorists were analytic, like Structuralists, but their elements were observable stimuli (S) and responses (R) associated by conditioning. In more recent times starting in the mid-twentieth century, behaviorism became liberalized to include within its theoretical structure the possibility of internal mechanisms, which Neo-Behaviorists referred to as "little" s and "little" r, to denote their status as nonobservables. Neo-Behaviorism set the stage for the cognitive revolution in experimental psychology, which did more than just allow for internal processes; it actually placed primary emphasis on

understanding the mental processes underlying behavior. For psychologists studying both human and animal behavior, cognitive psychology remains the dominant contemporary viewpoint in experimental psychology.

Current State of Experimental Psychology

Experimental psychology today is a burgeoning enterprise involving a large number of researchers in the United States and around the world. This summary cannot cover all of the work that is presently going on. Selected topics representative of the four primary foci are described, with an attempt to include examples of those with general theoretical and practical importance.

Input

For human beings, vision is the primary input modality for information from the environment. Typically, individuals report being aware of everything in their visual world. However, studies of attention have revealed a striking lack of awareness of certain events, even those that are salient and occur in the center of the visual field. For example, if an object or an event is not the focus of attention, it might be missed even though it occurs right before the eyes. This inability to perceive objects is sometimes referred to as "inattentional blindness." A recent striking example of inattentional blindness was reported by Simons and Chabris (1999). In their study subjects watched a video showing an ongoing basketball game and were required to keep a mental count of the number of passes of the basketball between the members of one of the two teams. During the course of this game, unexpected events occurred, including a person dressed as a gorilla walking through the middle of the basketball court. After the conclusion of the video, subjects reported their mental count of the number of passes, and then they were asked whether they saw anything unusual appearing during the video. Nearly half of the subjects (46%) failed to notice or report the gorilla walking through the basketball court during the game. This failure to notice was attributed by the authors not to the visual system per se but rather to a higher-order attention system. This laboratory demonstration suggests the possibility that people miss a lot of important events that occur right before their eyes because they are focusing their attention on one kind of activity and do not expect unusual, irrelevant events to occur. On the basis of experiments with driving simulators, Strayer and Drews (2007) found that memory for objects in the drivers' visual field was disturbed by cell phone conversations. They relate this finding to inattentional blindness caused by focusing on the cell phone conversation rather than the road.

Information Processing

The superordinate category called "information processing" includes research on learning, memory, cognition, and language. Memory tests are usually thought to reflect events that actually occurred. However, studies have shown that sometimes answers on a memory test include events that never occurred, and participants indicate strong confidence in these answers. A classic example of this phenomenon was reported by Roediger and McDermott (1995). In their experiment subjects studied lists of 12 words that were highly associated (e.g., wake, doze, nap) to a given key word (sleep) that was not presented. When asked to recall all the words that had been included on the list, the associated word, which had not been presented, was recalled 40% of the time and, subsequently, recognized as having been presented with high confidence. Roediger and McDermott label this finding as a "memory illusion" because subjects apparently falsely believed that the key word had been presented when it had not. These results are consistent with claims that have been made by Loftus and her colleagues (e.g., Loftus & Bernstein, 2005) that eyewitness testimony in court cases is often based on memories for events that did not actually occur.

Affect

The category of "affect" includes research on the effects of motivation and emotion on behavior. A prominent example of experimental work in this category is research on a phenomenon called "learned helplessness." Learned helplessness is a behavioral effect resulting from exposure of subjects to uncontrollable stressors, such as inescapable shock for rats, which causes emotional disruption leading the subjects to freeze and subsequently to fail to escape a stressful situation even when escape is possible. Learned helplessness has been likened to the psychopathological state of depression in human beings. In the typical learned helplessness paradigm, effects of unavoidable shock tend to be transient and to weaken over a relatively short period of time. Recently, an attempt was made to prolong the learned helplessness effect by introducing periodic reminders to the subjects of the original experience with the uncontrollable stressor (Maier, 2001). In these experiments, after the initial inescapable shock experience, subjects were periodically placed into the same environment where the original shock experience had taken place. It was found that such exposure did indeed prolong the learned helplessness effect indefinitely and at full strength. The reminders are analogous to the ruminations about past events that are typical of human beings suffering from depression or posttraumatic stress disorder. Thus, the learned helplessness paradigm can be viewed as a model for the study of clinical depression.

Higher Mental Processes

Higher mental processes include complex cognitive activities such as categorization and the formation of concepts, planning, decision making, reasoning, and problem solving. These are activities that individuals normally do in their heads, leading eventually to some behavioral output. These processes are thought to run their course in working memory, which is a psychological construct for both the content and the operations occurring in consciousness (e.g., Baddeley, 1986). Mental arithmetic calculations are prototypical examples of a higher mental process. In a series of studies with college students, it has been shown that if working memory is occupied by an irrelevant secondary task, performance even on simple arithmetic problems like addition or subtraction suffers. The adverse effect is stronger when the mental calculation requires carrying over a number from one column to the next (Ashcraft & Krause, 2007). It is well known that students vary in their degree of math anxiety, and math anxiety also adversely affects mental calculation ability. The explanation for the effects of math anxiety are similar to those for the effects of the requirement of a secondary task; in both cases, needed working memory space is occupied either by performance of the secondary task or by worries about performance. Such studies can help educators understand the underlying causes of poor math performance and, thus, develop techniques to counteract math anxiety.

Future Directions of Experimental Psychology

Experimental psychology has been and will continue to be influenced by other related disciplines. The two forces that seem most likely to guide the future of experimental psychology are cognitive science and neuroscience. Experimental psychology will continue its path toward an elucidation of the role of cognition, or mental activities, in behavior. Furthermore, because significant activities take place in the nervous system simultaneously with cognition, it will become increasingly important to examine the relationships between brain processes and the mind as reflected in behavior. As mentioned earlier, there is a tight connection between experimental data, methods, and theory. Theories will continue to dictate the course of experimentation. The theories that are most likely to be influential are those that are quantitative, mathematical, or computational, but also biologically plausible. These models have the advantage over more qualitative theories of giving precise predictions that can be tested experimentally. Modeling is relatively recent in the history of experimental psychology, but over recent years these models have become increasingly complex. That trend is likely to continue in the future.

REFERENCES

Ashcraft, M. H., & Krause, J. A. (2007). Working memory, math performance, and math anxiety. *Psychonomic Bulletin & Review, 14*, 243–248.

Baddeley, A. (1986). *Working memory.* Oxford, UK: Oxford University Press.

Boring, E. G. (1929). *A history of experimental psychology.* Oxford, UK: Appleton-Century.

Ebbinghaus, H. (1885/1913). *Memory: A contribution to experimental psychology* (H. A. Ruger & C. E. Bussenius, Trans.). New York: Teachers College.

Fechner, G. (1860/1966). *Elements of psychophysics* (Vol. 1) (H. E. Adler, Trans.). New York: Holt, Rinehart, and Winston.

Healy, A. F. (Ed.). (2005). *Experimental cognitive psychology and its applications.* Washington, DC: American Psychological Association.

Healy, A. F., & Proctor, R. W. (Eds.). (2003). *Experimental psychology. Handbook of psychology,* Vol. 4 (Ed.-in-Chief: I. B. Weiner). Hoboken, NJ: John Wiley & Sons.

James, W. (1890). *Principles of psychology.* New York: Holt.

Loftus, E. F., & Bernstein, D. M. (2005). Rich false memories: The royal road to success. In A. F. Healy (Ed.), *Experimental cognitive psychology and its applications* (pp. 101–113). Washington, DC: American Psychological Association.

Maier, S. F. (2001). Exposure to the stressor environment prevents the temporal dissipation of behavioral depression/learned helplessness. *Biological Psychiatry, 49,* 763–773.

Martin, D. W. (2008). *Doing psychology experiments* (7th ed.). Belmont, CA: Wadsworth.

McDaniel, M. A., & Einstein, G. O. (2005). Material appropriate difficulty: A framework for determining when difficulty is desirable for improving learning. In A. F. Healy (Ed.), *Experimental cognitive psychology and its applications* (pp. 73–85). Washington, DC: American Psychological Association.

Roediger, H. L., III, & McDermott, K. B. (1995). Creating false memories: Remembering words not presented in lists. *Journal of Experimental Psychology: Learning, Memory, and Cognition, 21,* 803–814.

Simons, D. J., & Chabris, C. F. (1999). Gorillas in our midst: Sustained inattentional blindness for dynamic events. *Perception, 28,* 1059–1074.

Strayer, D. L., & Drews, F. A. (2007). Cell-phone-induced driver distraction. *Current Directions in Psychological Science, 16,* 128–131.

Thorndike, E. L. (1911). *Animal intelligence: Experimental studies.* Lewiston, NY: Macmillan.

Titchener, E. B. (1910). *A text-book of psychology.* New York: Macmillan.

Wundt, W. (1897). *Outlines of psychology* (C. H. Judd, Trans.). Oxford, UK: Engelmann.

SUGGESTED READING

Kantowitz, B. H., Roediger, H. L., III, & Elmes, D. G. (2005). *Experimental Psychology: Understanding psychological research* (8th ed.). Belmont, CA: Wadsworth.

LYLE E. BOURNE
ALICE F. HEALY
University of Colorado

See also: Psychological Science; Scientific Method

EXPERT TESTIMONY

As the world becomes more complex, expert testimony assumes an increasingly important and controversial role in the Anglo-American judicial system. The Federal Rules of Evidence specify that expert testimony occurs when a witness, qualified as an expert by knowledge, skill, experience, training, or education, testifies by providing opinions or facts that assist the judge to understand evidence or to determine a fact in issue. For justice to be served, expert witnesses present unbiased opinions and facts based on sound science or technical knowledge.

To fully appreciate the expert's roles and responsibilities, it is essential to understand the adversary process. During medieval times adversaries resolved conflicts by engaging in trial by combat, with the belief that God's hand determined the winner. Today's adversaries engage in verbal combat, with the judge or jury deciding the outcome according to law. The adversary process is thus based on the theory that each litigant is best able to argue his or her case. The trier of fact—the judge or jury—is then responsible for deciding which argument has the greatest legal merit. In some cases, however, the fact finder is not able to decide the legal issue without considering specialized knowledge that can only be provided by an expert witness.

Legal Basis for Expert Testimony by Psychologists

The case for psychology's worthiness to "take the stand" can be traced to the landmark debate on the value of psychology to the legal system between Harvard University's experimental psychologist, Hugo Munsterberg, and John H. Wigmore, law professor at Northwestern University. Munsterberg authored the first forensic psychology textbook, *On the Witness Stand* (1908), which triggered Wigmore's spirited rebuttal in the *Illinois Law Review* (1909). The issue a century ago is the same today: When is expert evidence probative and when is it junk science? The judicial system has answered by providing evolving guidelines for admitting expert testimony.

For 70 years, the *Frye* test established that, in federal courts, expert testimony needed to be based on scientific theories and methodologies that have "... gained general acceptance in the particular field in which it belongs" (*Frye v. United States,* 1923). However, in 1993, the United States Supreme Court superseded *Frye* with the *Daubert* standard (based on the Federal Rule of Evidence 702) when it held that federal trial judges have an obligation to ensure that scientific testimony is relevant and reliable and would likely assist the trier of fact (*Daubert v. Merrell Dow Pharmaceuticals,* 1993). Regardless of profession or specialty, courts governed by Daubert weigh four factors for admitting expert testimony: (1) whether the procedures and methodology forming the basis of the testimony have been or can be tested (and could be proven false); (2)

whether there is an acceptable known or potential error rate; (3) whether the procedures and methodology have been subject to peer review; and (4) whether there is general acceptance in the relevant scientific community (similar to the Frye standard).

Judges are often lenient about qualifying witnesses as experts, because allowing expert testimony does not mean it will be given weight. Although experts provide opinion testimony to assist the judge and jury, opinions do not establish the facts of a case. Facts originate from physical evidence and from the testimony of lay or nonexpert witnesses, who are customarily restricted to testifying about facts (what they have directly observed or experienced). For example, a lay witness can testify to the fact of having heard Mr. Smith discuss mutual fund purchases with his parrot, but only the expert witness can offer opinions or conclusions as to whether Mr. Smith was mentally ill at that time. Depending upon jurisdiction, however, experts are sometimes barred from offering conclusions about certain legal issues. For example, in federal courts, experts can testify about a defendant's mental state at the time of an alleged offense but cannot conclude whether the defendant was legally insane.

Expert Testimony in Psychology

In the 1962 milestone case of *Jenkins v. United States*, the D.C. Circuit Court of Appeals ruled that clinical psychologists could provide expert testimony regarding criminal responsibility (i.e., insanity). Judge David Bazelon wrote the majority opinion, which subsequently contributed to the legal blueprint for contemporary rules of expert evidence applicable to psychologists. These rules have allowed psychologists to testify on an increasing array of civil and criminal issues. Civil litigation includes matters such as personal injury, malpractice, civil commitment, workers' compensation, testamentary capacity, fitness for duty, disability claims, and child custody. Criminal issues encompass competency to stand trial, criminal responsibility evaluations, diminished capacity, death penalty mitigation, and competency to be executed.

Before witnesses are allowed to testify as experts on case specifics, they testify about their qualifications during *voir dire*—which is an examination of the witness by both attorneys—to determine if they meet the court's admissibility standards. If qualified by the judge as an expert, the psychologist can then offer opinion testimony, provided it is based on reasonable psychological, medical, and/or scientific certainty. Both fact and opinion testimony involve responding, while under oath, to questions posed by an attorney and, at times, the judge. Mental health experts routinely conduct evaluations and then testify about diagnosis, treatment, prognosis, degree of emotional harm, violence risk assessment, standard of care, and research. The unique domain for psychologists is psychological testing. If psychological tests have been administered, the psychologist needs to establish that the tests have psychometric rigor and have been developed to address the case's specific forensic issue (e.g., competency to stand trial) or, if not, that the test can be reasonably applied to the psychological issue (e.g., using the Minnesota Multiphasic Personality Inventory-2 to testify about whether someone meets a statutory definition of mental illness).

Ethical Expert Testimony

Psychologists in the role of expert witness face the complex task of testifying in accordance with legal standards and practice while complying with their discipline's ethics and practice standards (*American Psychological Association's Ethical Principles of Psychologists and Code of Conduct*, American Psychological Association, 2002; *Specialty Guidelines for Forensic Psychologists: Committee on Ethical Guidelines for Forensic Psychologists*, 1991). For example, psychologists are obligated to present all relevant data, even if those data are not consistent with their forensic opinions (Committee on Ethical Guidelines for Forensic Psychologists, 1991, VII.D.). Attorneys, however, are advocates and prefer to enter into the court record only data consistent with their case theory in order to advance the most compelling argument for their client. When, however, psychologists' ethical responsibilities conflict with the law—as distinguished from an attorney's advocacy preferences—psychologists attempt to resolve the impasse by adhering to the principles and standards of the Ethics Code. If the conflict cannot be resolved via such means, psychologists may comply with legal requirements (APA, 2002, 1.02).

It should also be noted that there are many parallels between the standards of psychology and those of the legal system. For instance, Daubert emphasizes the importance of judges considering whether expert testimony is based on theories and methodologies generally accepted in the expert's relevant scientific community. This legal mandate is similar to an Ethics Code standard that states that psychologists base their work "... upon established scientific and professional knowledge of the discipline" (APA, 2002, 20.4). Additionally, courts and the Specialty Guidelines (Committee on Ethical Guidelines for Forensic Psychologists, 1991, III.B) both require that experts possess the specific expertise needed for the case being litigated.

Furthermore, psychologists must be vigilant about ethics issues prior to testifying. Although Daubert established that federal trial judges are the gatekeepers for determining the admissibility of scientific evidence, mental health professionals also have gatekeeping obligations. For example, psychologists, who can be retained by an attorney or by the court, should not become involved in a case if they harbor biases, conflicts of interest, or moral concerns that would compromise objectivity (APA, 2002, 3.06; Committee on Ethical Guidelines for Forensic Psychologists, 1991, III.E).

Expert witnesses prepare for testimony by ensuring that they are knowledgeable about general and case-specific legal, clinical, and ethical issues (Bank & Packer, 2007). For example, it is bad practice for experts to allow attorneys to have unwarranted influence regarding how a client is evaluated. Attorneys should not decide which clinical records are relevant to review, whom to interview, and which test to administer. On the other hand, pretrial preparation with attorneys is invaluable for establishing the psychologist's boundaries of expertise, which then determine the scope of testimony and opinions (e.g., for a personal injury case, a psychologist could testify about a plaintiff's cognitive deficits but should not opine whether one million dollars is an appropriate damage award).

By definition, expert witnesses function in the roles of expert *and* witness. Consequently, they address two professional responsibilities. As experts, psychologists must be knowledgeable about their specialty (Committee on Ethical Guidelines for Forensic Psychologists, 1991, III.A). As witnesses, they have an ethical mandate to "... become reasonably familiar with the judicial or administrative rules governing their roles" (APA, 2002, 2.01[f]). This raises the broader question: What is the proper role of an expert witness? The consensus is that experts should be advocates for their unbiased opinions but not advocates for the biased party retaining them. The integrity of testimony thus depends upon readily admitting valid shortcomings in their opinions, regardless of how this affects the outcome of the case.

Furthermore, psychologists distinguish between the role of an expert witness, who is not part of a legal team, and that of a trial consultant. An expert witness testifies objectively about the case's substantive forensic issues, whereas a trial consultant does not testify but provides advice to attorneys on advocacy issues such as jury selection, witness preparation, and argument strategy. Expert witnesses are, therefore, advocates for their objective opinions, whereas trial consultants facilitate advocacy for the attorney's position. Psychologists who are cognizant of the differences and similarities between the ethics and standards of psychology and those of the legal system are best able to meet the demands of testifying ethically.

Effective Expert Testimony

Expert witnesses need to be effective courtroom communicators in order to accurately convey their specialized knowledge and safeguard the probity of their testimony from distortion by attorneys advocating for their clients. The Courtroom Communications Model (Bank, 2001) provides experts with a conceptual framework and practical guidelines to ethically and effectively navigate the verbal minefield created by the adversary process. The dynamics of courtroom communication are analyzed through the model's three components of the Speaker (expert or attorney), the Message (testimony or attorney question), and the Audience (judge and/or jury). Expert witnesses need to understand that (1) credibility depends on the expert's trustworthiness, expertise, and presentational style; (2) expert testimony is generally given more weight if it is presented logically, rather than emotionally; and (3) psychologists can best convey their message to jurors by explaining their opinions in different ways in order to reach as many jurors as possible.

Whereas experts strive to enhance their credibility and communication, attorneys conducting cross-examinations utilize strategies to discredit them and disrupt the flow of testimony. Some such battle-tested strategies include (1) arguing that the psychologists does not possess relevant expertise; (2) claiming that the methodology used to obtain and analyze data is faulty; (3) demonstrating that the witness made errors in statements of fact; (4) documenting that the psychologist made prior inconsistent statements; (5) characterizing the expert as biased; and (6) assailing the general character of the witness.

Psychologists prepare for cross-examination by anticipating questions and understanding that their court reports (which attorneys scrutinize to develop queries) are to be worded as precisely as testimony. Experts must be vigilant even during direct examination, particularly when attorneys try to elicit a stronger opinion than the expert feels is justified. The most effective testimony is always devised before taking the stand, when experts prepare for both direct and cross-examination.

The Future of Expert Testimony

Although the content of forensic issues will forever evolve, the process of presenting ethical and effective expert testimony will remain the same. Behavioral scientists must possess the requisite expertise and then present it objectively in a manner understood by judges and jurors. To help remain impartial, experts adopt a "forensic perspective," which includes checking their egos at the courtroom door; advocating for their unbiased opinions and not for the party retaining them; understanding that attorneys, not experts, win and lose cases; and realizing that the integrity of the judicial system relies on the credibility of expert witnesses. Correspondingly, an expert's credibility depends on the credibility of everything accomplished before testifying, such as considering all relevant data and case theories; appropriately selecting, administering, and interpreting tests; and understanding how to apply clinical data to legal issues.

Anglo-American courts have utilized expert witnesses for approximately 700 years, with testimony ranging from the effects of leeching to brain wave analysis. No one can predict the future subject matter of expert testimony. However, scientific breakthroughs, medical discoveries, and mental health advancements will undoubtedly give rise to new areas of expertise and admissibility issues for the judicial system. Perhaps the day will come when courts are asked to rule whether a computer or a robot can testify as an expert witness.

REFERENCES

American Psychological Association. (2002). Ethical principles of psychologists and code of conduct. *American Psychologist, 57,* 1060–1073.

Bank, S. (2001). From mental health professional to expert witness: Testifying in court. *New Directions for Mental Health Services, 91,* 57–66.

Bank, S. C., & Packer, I. K. (2007). Expert Witness Testimony: Law, Ethics & Practice. In Alan M. Goldstein (Ed.), *Forensic Psychology: Emerging Topics and Expanded Roles* (pp. 421–445). Hoboken, NJ: John Wiley & Sons.

Committee on Ethical Guidelines for Forensic Psychologists. (1991). Specialty guidelines for forensic psychologists. *Law and Human Behavior, 15,* 655–665.

Daubert v. Merrell Dow Pharmaceuticals, Inc., 509 US 579 (1993).

Federal Rules of Evidence, Rule 702.

Frye v. United States, 293 F. 1013 (1923).

Jenkins v. United States, 307 F.2d 637 (U.S. App. D.C., 1962).

Münsterberg, H. (1908). *On the witness stand: Essays on psychology and crime.* New York: Doubleday.

Wigmore, J. H. (1909). Professor Münsterberg and the psychology of testimony: Being a report of the case of Cokestone v. Münsterberg. *Illinois Law Review, 3*(7), 399–445.

SUGGESTED READINGS

Brodsky, S. L. (1999). *The expert expert witness: More maxims and guidelines for testifying in court.* Washington, DC: American Psychological Association Press.

Faust, D. (2008). *Ziskin's coping with psychiatric and psychological testimony.* (6th ed.). New York: Oxford University Press.

STEVEN C. BANK, Ph.D.
Center for Forensic Psychiatry, Ann Arbor, Michigan

See also: **Forensic Psychology; Psychology and the Law**

EXPOSURE THERAPY

Exposure therapy is used to treat excessive fears, which are central to many anxiety disorders. During exposure therapy, the person is presented with a fear-evoking stimulus in a controlled fashion, until the fear diminishes. Treatment is collaborative, with the patient and therapist working together to decide how and when exposure will take place. Exposure duration depends on many factors, including the type of feared stimuli and the severity of the person's fears. Typically, an exposure session lasts 40–90 minutes, and sessions are repeated until the fear is substantially reduced or eliminated. Sessions may be either therapist-assisted or completed by the patient as homework assignments. In order to ensure that exposure is optimally effective, the patient is exposed to fear-evoking stimuli in a variety of different contexts to promote the generalization of therapeutic effects (Bouton, 2002).

Exposure therapy can be conducted in many ways. The most common form is *in vivo* exposure, in which the person is exposed to real-life fear-evoking events, such as a feared animal. Such exposure can be conducted gradually, which is known as *graded in vivo exposure.* Here, a hierarchy of fear-evoking stimuli is devised; an example appears in Table 1. The person is exposed to stimuli listed in the first step of the hierarchy until fear abates, and then gradually confronts increasingly more distressing stimuli.

An alternative method is known as *flooding,* in which the person is exposed to stimuli at the top of the hierarchy. Graded exposure is more commonly used in clinical practice, because it is more tolerable than flooding. Flooding is used mostly when there is some urgent need for the patient to overcome his or her fear rapidly (e.g., a person with injection phobia might require rapid treatment if she or he is about to undergo surgery).

As an alternative to *in vivo* exposure the person may be exposed to imagined stimuli, such as repeatedly imagining a traumatic event that they experienced. Imaginal methods can be used, for example, when it is not safe or feasible to conduct in vivo exposure (e.g., exposure to traumatic events). Imaginal exposure can be conducted gradually, where mildly distressing images are interspersed with periods of relaxation (a method known as *systematic desensitization*), or the person can progressively move up a hierarchy of increasingly distressing images, in similar fashion to graded *in vivo* exposure (i.e., *graded imaginal exposure*). Finally, the person could be exposed to highly fear-evoking images, which is known as *imaginal flooding* or *implosion.* The considerations for selecting imaginal exposure methods (i.e., gradual vs. intense) are similar to those for *in vivo* exposure.

Another important type of exposure is *interoceptive exposure.* This involves the evocation of feared bodily sensations. An example is aerobic exercises for people who have an excessive fear that rapid heartbeat will result in a heart attack, as is commonly seen in panic disorder (Barlow, 2002).

Conceptual Foundations

The rationale for contemporary exposure therapies has its roots in conditioning models of fear acquisition. An early influential account was Mowrer's (1960) two-factor model, which proposed that fears are acquired by classical conditioning and maintained by operant conditioning. Classical

Table 1. In vivo Exposure Hierarchy for a Patient who was Assaulted while Jogging through a Park

Step	Exposure situation (e.g., place, object, person, or activity)	Anticipated peak level of fear while completing the task (0 = none, 100 = maximum)
1	Wearing the clothes I wore when I was assaulted	15
2	Walking past the park but not going in	35
3	Reading the police report of the assault	55
4	Walking through the park in which I was assaulted, in broad daylight, with a friend.	75
5	Walking through the park in which I was assaulted, in broad daylight, by myself.	90

Note: In clinical practice an exposure hierarchy would contain more steps than are listed here, so that there are smaller gradations between the amounts of distress elicited from one step to the next.

conditioning involves experiences that teach the person to associate a particular stimulus (e.g., a dog) with an aversive outcome (e.g., a painful bite). Clinically, the most important form of operant conditioning is negative reinforcement, in which avoidance or escape from fear-evoking stimuli is reinforced by the avoidance of fear. In turn, avoidance and escape prevent classically conditioned fears from being extinguished.

Subsequent research identified the role of beliefs and expectations in both operant and classical conditioning, leading to more complex (neoconditioning) models in which fear was not directly determined by a stimulus (e.g., driving in the rain), but by the person's expectation of what the stimulus would lead to (e.g., a traffic fatality). According to this view, conditioned fears are strengthened by confirmation of one's expectations (e.g., a "near miss" while driving).

A prominent contemporary theory of the nature and treatment of excessive fear and anxiety is the emotional processing model (Foa, Huppert, & Cahill, 2006). In this model, fears are represented in networks (fear structures) stored in long-term memory. The networks contain representations of feared stimuli (e.g., oncoming trucks, driving at night), response information (e.g., palpitations, trembling, the experience of fear, escape behaviors), and meaning information (e.g., the concept of danger). In the network the three types of information are linked (e.g., links between oncoming trucks, danger, and fear). Fear structures are activated by incoming information that matches information stored in the network. Activation of the network evokes fear and motivates avoidance or escape behavior. According to this model, fears are reduced by modifying the fear structure through the incorporation of corrective information (e.g., safety information acquired during exposure exercises).

Empirical Support for Exposure Therapy

The effects of *in vivo*, imaginal, and interoceptive exposure therapy on reducing various types of pathological fear have been well established in hundreds of studies. Imaginal and *in vivo* exposure are among the most effective known treatments for anxiety disorders, with remission rates typically ranging 60%–80%, depending on the nature and severity of the disorder (Richard & Lauterbach, 2007). Treatment-related gains have been shown to be maintained at follow-up intervals ranging one to five years. Patients who do not fully benefit from exposure may be successfully treated by other psychotherapeutic interventions, such as cognitive therapy, or by augmenting exposure with pharmacotherapy. One of the most promising pharmacologic augments is D-cycloserine. When administered shortly before a session of exposure therapy, this drug enhances the efficacy of exposure (McNally, 2007).

In summary, exposure therapy is the treatment of choice for specific phobia and is an important intervention for use in the psychological treatment of other anxiety disorders. It involves having the person repeatedly confront feared stimuli until fear abates. Patients play an active role in choosing what they will be exposed to and when the exposure will occur. Exposure therapies are often used in combination with other interventions, such as cognitive therapy.

REFERENCES

Barlow, D. H. (2002). *Anxiety and its disorders: The nature and treatment of anxiety and panic* (2nd ed.). New York: Guilford Press.

Bouton, M. E. (2002). Context, ambiguity, and unlearning: Sources of relapse after behavioral extinction. *Biological Psychiatry, 52*, 976–986.

Foa, E. B., Huppert, J. D., & Cahill, S. P. (2006). Emotional processing theory: An update. In B. O. Rothbaum (Ed.), *Pathological anxiety: Emotional processing in etiology and treatment* (pp. 3–24). New York: Guilford Press.

McNally, R. J. (2007). Mechanisms of exposure therapy: How neuroscience can improve psychological treatments for anxiety disorders. *Clinical Psychology Review, 27*, 750–759.

Mowrer, O. H. (1960). *Learning theory and behavior.* New York: John Wiley & Sons.

Richard, D. C. S., & Lauterbach, D. (2007). *Handbook of exposure therapies*. San Diego, CA: Academic.

STEVEN TAYLOR
University of British Columbia

JONATHAN S. ABRAMOWITZ
University of North Carolina at Chapel Hill

See also: **Behavior Modification; Systematic Desensitization**

EXTRAVERSION-INTROVERSION (See Introversion-Extraversion)

EXTREMISM

Moderation has long been identified as a hallmark of virtue. Pythagoras preached virtue from proper proportion among one's feelings, intuitions, and reasons. Plato depicted virtue as arising from reason's skill at bridling the extremes of appetite and spirit. Confucius, the Buddha, and Aristotle all promoted their own versions of a golden mean or middle-way between extremes. Given such praise for moderation, why are people so readily drawn to extremes of thought and action? Extremes seem especially enigmatic when one considers that they are so often self-destructive. For example, in the first century CE a group of religious fanatics who were uncompromising in their opposition to Roman rule carried daggers under their cloaks and killed anyone who did not fully support their views. Their extremism brought reprisals that crushed their "Zealot" sect, but the example of their rabid idealism persists as the origin of the word, "zeal." Zealous extremism has accordingly come to refer to ideological conviction that belligerently insists on consensus, with apparent disregard for practical consequences.

A further puzzling aspect of extremism is that, in addition to being ill-advised and self-defeating, it often seems to defy rationality. Extremist views dismiss conflicting realities and the alternative perspectives that are held with equal zeal by others. Extremists dogmatically assert their version of truth and seem oblivious to limitations of their positions. Such tendencies would be of less social importance if they were reserved for private zeal about innocuous topics. But extremism gravitates toward value-laden social issues and is usually not a private affair. Extremists go public and agitate for social consensus. Their belligerent zeal can accordingly fuel militant conflicts with grave social consequences. What is the psychological motivation for extremism?

In his classic, *The Varieties of Religious Experience*, William James (1902/1958) concluded from interviews with religious converts that "religious rapture and moral enthusiasm incline the sand and grit of self-hood to disappear." At around the same time, Freud observed that his neurotic patients repressed taboo thoughts by rigidly focusing on other, supervalent, or excessively intense trains of thought. Thus, both James and Freud viewed extremism as a tool for quelling conflict and anxiety. Fifty years later, a new wave of psychological research aimed at understanding the atrocious extremes of bigotry, nationalism, and fascism during World War II. In-home interviews about respondents' life experiences and extremist views supported the view that extremism is a motivated reaction to feelings of personal vulnerability (Adorno, Frenkel-Brunswick, Levinson, & Stanford, 1950). More contemporary, cross-sectional research supports the same general conclusion. During wars and threatening times, political leaders tend toward black and white certainty in their speeches, dogmatic religious denominations flourish, and children's books become more moralistic than usual. Accordingly, over the past few thousand years, religious traditions have tended to mutate and foment extremes during periods of social insecurity (Armstrong, 2000; e.g., enthusiasm for the Christian crusades of 1086 CE to 1270 CE spiked under conditions of unprecedented social insecurity in France).

Laboratory research supports the motivated extremism hypothesis. Over the past 20 years, hundreds of studies conducted by dozens of researchers in North America and Europe have found that experimentally manipulated conflicts and vulnerabilities cause people to lurch toward extremes of conviction and pride for their worldviews, convictions, countries, groups, causes, values, opinions, romantic relationships, and important personal goals (McGregor, 2006a). These same threat manipulations also cause increased willingness to fight publicly for moral convictions and to radically overestimate social consensus for them. Extreme conviction reactions to threats occur even in domains that are not related to the eliciting threats. In one study, for example, induced confusion and uncertainty about their own statistical skills caused undergraduate psychology students to become more certain that their religious beliefs were objectively true and more willing to support a war to defend their religious beliefs (McGregor, Haji, Nash, & Teper, in press). Thus, extremism can be regarded as a generalized defensive reaction to self-threat.

Just as the classic ideas of James and Freud proposed, extremes appear to help relieve concern about worries and uncertainties. Laboratory experiments show that expressing strong convictions about worldviews, value ideals, group identifications, opinions, or personal worth, cause previously bothersome conflicts and uncertainties to seem less important. Moreover, even after repeatedly reminding participants of their worries, extreme conviction expression still effectively insulates participants from concern about the worries (McGregor, 2006b). This insulation effect of extremes on salient worries demonstrates that extremism is not simply a form of distraction. It somehow makes distressing thoughts loom less large even when they are in focal awareness. These experimental findings are consistent with James's early observation that moral extremes have the power to make people oblivious to distressing circumstances (James, 1902/1958).

Laboratory research is beginning to demonstrate the related mechanisms for how extreme views can be held with such irrational certainty and for how extremism quells distress. Conflicts and uncertainties activate brain systems that specialize in vigilant scanning for threats and uncertainty detection, while ideological extremes activate brain systems that specialize in eager approach of incentives (Marigold, McGregor, & Zanna, in press). When approach-motivation systems are strongly and unequivocally aroused, stimuli and experiences relevant to the avoidance-system loom less large and seem less vital. The approach-motivated organism becomes like a racehorse with blinders that block out distractions to facilitate eager pursuit of the focal incentive. Preliminary research indicates that this may occur because of reciprocal inhibition between brain areas that are centrally involved in approach processes (left frontal lobe) and those that are centrally involved in avoidance motivation and uncertainty detection (anterior cingulate cortex). This kind of goal-shielding mechanism for facilitating approach-motivation is usually adaptive because it promotes undistracted goal completion. Humans can exploit it, however, for merely palliative purposes. Values and ideals are processed by humans as abstract goals because they guide action. Intense focus on them can accordingly activate the sanguine myopia of unequivocal approach motivation and deactivate neural processes that attend to threat, conflict, and uncertainty. As a result, moral extremes can relieve concern with threats. They can also be dangerously self-sustaining, however, because they insulate the extremist from the conflicts and uncertainties of counterarguments.

REFERENCES

Adorno, T. W., Frenkel-Brunswik, E., Levinson, D. J., & Sanford, R. N. (1950). *The authoritarian personality*. New York: Harper.

Armstrong, K. (2000). *The battle for God: A history of fundamentalism*. New York: Ballantine.

James, W. (1902/1958). *The varieties of religious experience*. New York: Mentor.

Marigold, D. C., McGregor, I., & Zanna, M. P. (in press). Defensive conviction as emotion regulation: Goal mechanisms and relationship implications. In R. M. Arkin, K. C. Oleson, & P. J. Carroll (Eds.), *The uncertain self: A handbook of perspectives from social and personality psychology*. Mahwah, NJ: Lawrence Erlbaum.

McGregor, I. (2006a). Offensive defensiveness: Toward an integrative neuroscience of compensatory zeal after mortality salience, personal uncertainty, and other poignant self-threats. *Psychological Inquiry, 17*, 299–308.

McGregor, I. (2006b). Zeal appeal: The allure of moral extremes. *Basic and Applied Social Psychology, 28*, 343–348.

McGregor, I., Haji, R., Nash, K. A., & Teper, R. (in press). Religious zeal and the uncertain self. *Basic and Applied Social Psychology*.

SUGGESTED READINGS

McGregor, I. (2004). Zeal, identity, and meaning: Going to extremes to be one self. In J. Greenberg, S. Koole, & T. Pyszczynski (Eds.), *Handbook of experimental existential psychology* (pp. 182–199). New York: Guilford Press.

Solomon, S., Greenberg, J., & Pyszczynski, T. (2004). The cultural animal: Twenty years of Terror Management Theory. In J. Greenberg, S. Koole, & T. Pyszczynski (Eds.), *Handbook of experimental existential psychology* (pp. 13–34). New York: Guilford Press.

IAN MCGREGOR
York University, Ontario, Canada

See also: Attitudes; Authoritarianism

EYE MOVEMENT DESENSITIZATION AND REPROCESSING

Eye movement desensitization and reprocessing (EMDR) is an integrative psychotherapeutic approach that emphasizes the role of the brain's information processing system in ameliorating the somatic and psychological consequences of distressing events. Current emotional problems not caused by organic deficit or physical insults are conceptualized as the result of inappropriately processed memories of disturbing or traumatic experiences. EMDR is an eight-phase treatment, including a tripartite protocol that focuses on the memories underlying current problems and those that must be specifically addressed to bring the client to a robust state of psychological health. One of its distinguishing characteristics is its use of bilateral physical stimulation, such as side-to-side eye movements, alternating hand taps, or alternating auditory tones while the person undergoing treatment is mentally focusing on aspects of various life experiences.

Controlled Research

The efficacy of EMDR for trauma treatment has been confirmed by approximately 20 controlled studies. Because it has compared favorably to a variety of pharmaceutical and psychotherapeutic modalities, it was designated efficacious by the practice guidelines of the American Psychiatric Association (2004) and by the Departments of Veterans Affairs and Defense (DVA/DoD; 2004). According to these guidelines, as well as several published meta-analyses (e.g., Bisson & Andrew, 2007), EMDR achieves therapeutic effects that are equivalent to and as long-lasting as those of well-known and -researched cognitive-behavioral therapy methods. A potentially important distinction between EMDR and other trauma treatments is that it does not include the 30–100 hours of prescribed homework characteristic of the latter, and thus its therapeutic effects are accomplished with less exposure to the trauma and require only in-session treatment.

Although it is only one of the treatment elements of EMDR, the bilateral physical stimulation (especially side-to-side eye movements) has attracted the most attention. Component analyses of stimulation using eye movements with clinical populations have shown only marginally significant effects. However, this research has been criticized for its inclusion of clinically inappropriate populations and insufficient treatment doses (Chemtob, et al., 2000; DVA/DoD, 2004). On the other hand, numerous laboratory studies have revealed that these eye movements have distinct effects on memory retrieval, reduction of negative emotions, imagery vividness, and attentional flexibility (Lee & Drummond, in press).

EMDR therapy involves accessing disturbing memories that are relevant to present psychological problems while providing brief applications of bilateral stimulation in the context of a set of standardized procedures. The typical pattern of recovery observed in EMDR treatment sessions is a rapid progression of intrapsychic connections, as emotions, sensations, insights, and memories emerge and change with each new set of bilateral stimulation. Process studies and qualitative analysis have identified distinct treatment effects (including the rapid reduction of emotional distress) that differentiate EMDR from other trauma therapies (Rogers & Silver, 2002). In addition to a decline in trauma symptoms, clients often display evidence of a more comprehensive psychological reorganization. This has been demonstrated by neuroimaging studies, changes in affect regulation and personality characteristics (e.g., Levin et al., 1999), cessation of chronic pain (e.g., Schneider et al., 2008), and cessation of other dysfunctional somatic reactions (e.g., Ricci et al., 2006).

Adaptive Information Processing Model

The theoretical framework that guides EMDR clinical practice, including the rationale for the wide range of therapeutic applications, is referred to as the Adaptive Information Processing (AIP) model. According to this model, the goal of EMDR is to address the experiential contributors to present psychological dysfunction, which can include not only major traumas but the more ubiquitous and chronic experiences of rejection, abandonment, humiliation, and the perceived blame and failure that often underlie negative self-beliefs, negative self-esteem, self-efficacy issues, and attachment difficulties.

Consistent with neurobiological findings, the AIP model posits that new experiences are assimilated into already-existing memory networks, which, in turn, are used to make sense of future experiences. Under normal circumstances, the brain's innate information-processing system easily integrates these experiences with previous ones, gleaning from them the information that is useful and discarding that which is not. This information, along with the appropriate emotional states, is stored in interconnected memory networks that are available to guide the person's future actions (Shapiro, 2001). However, a distressing, traumatic, or otherwise negative event may not be processed and integrated in the normal fashion. Instead, it may be stored in its own neural network, unable to link up naturally with the adaptive information in other networks.

This development lays the foundation for future maladaptive responses, since perceptions of current situations are automatically linked with associated memory networks. When the dysfunctionally stored memory is activated by a present trigger (whether internal or external), the person experiences the previously encoded perceptions, affects, somatic sensations, and cognitions associated with the past rather than simply the present. Hence, a negative self-belief (e.g. "I am not good enough") is not the cause of present dysfunction, but rather the symptom. The cause is understood to be the nonintegrated earlier life experiences that are associated with and contain that affect and perspective. EMDR is distinguished from other forms of psychotherapy by its assumption that present psychological symptoms result from the activation of distressing memories that have been inadequately processed, and by the manner in which these experiences are addressed.

The goals of the procedures and protocols of EMDR are to access dysfunctionally stored experiences and stimulate the innate information-processing system in such a way that these isolated networks are linked up to and assimilated with currently existing functional networks. The event and new perspectives that have been learned can now be recalled and verbalized by clients without the negative affect and physical sensations that characterized their previous psychological condition. It is this processing, or rapid learning, that is at the heart of EMDR treatment. The clinician works to determine which current situations are triggering the disturbance, which experiences have set the current symptom pattern in motion, and what positive experiences and new information/education are needed to overcome any lack of knowledge or skills.

Eight-Phase Treatment Approach

EMDR utilizes an eight-phase approach to address the full range of clinical symptoms caused or exacerbated by past negative experiences. Phase 1 is *client history*, in which the clinician obtains background information, identifies client suitability for EMDR treatment, and identifies processing targets from events in the client's life. Phase 2 is *preparation*, in which clients deemed appropriate for EMDR treatment are prepared to process the targeted memory experiences. The goals in this phase are to establish a therapeutic alliance, educate them about the symptom picture, explain the EMDR process and its effects, and teach them self-control techniques that foster stabilization and a sense of personal self-mastery and control in the face of often very painful memories.

Phase 3 is *assessment*, in which the target memory to be processed by EMDR is identified and accessed. This is achieved by eliciting the mental image, currently held negative belief, desired positive belief, current emotion, physical sensation, and baseline measurements of current reactivity. Phase 4 is *desensitization*, in which past experiences and present triggers are processed. The goal of this phase is to address the dysfunctional aspects of the memories and allow their full integration within adaptive experiential networks. Simultaneous shifts in cognition, emotion, and physical sensation associated with the memory reprocessing demonstrate the in-session treatment effects. Positive templates for adaptive future behavior are also incorporated (see below). Phase 5 is *installation*, in which the client's most desired positive self-belief (initial or emergent) is identified and enhanced to increase its connection with currently existing positive cognitive networks and facilitate generalization effects within associated memory networks.

Phase 6 is *body scan*, in which the client identifies and processes residual physical sensations to complete resolution. Phase 7 is *closure*, which may incorporate methods to return clients to emotional equilibrium, if needed, and ensure client stability. In this phase, clients are briefed about what to expect in between sessions and are instructed to keep a log of their psychological experiences/state of mind. Phase 8 is *reevaluation*, in which clients are assessed at the beginning of a session regarding their current psychological state and the thoughts and feelings that may have emerged since the previous session. This information is used to guide the direction of treatment.

Three-Pronged Protocol (Past, Present, Future)

The reprocessing phases (desensitization, installation, and body scan) are used to address the specific targets that have been identified as contributing to the symptom picture. The generic therapeutic protocol underlying comprehensive EMDR treatment includes a three-pronged approach following appropriate therapeutic stabilization and client preparation. The client is engaged first in processing the past experiences that have contributed to present dysfunction; second in processing present triggers that elicit this dysfunction; and finally in incorporating

positive patterns of behavior for future adaptive actions. The initial targets may include the earliest memories as well as more recent problematic situations. Then, in order to handle any remnants of second-order conditioning, the client imagines and processes the current situations that trigger symptoms (e.g., negative emotions, beliefs, sensations, behaviors).

After processing the past memories and present triggers that have prevented the client from learning adaptive patterns, the clinician needs to assess whether the client has the behaviors necessary for adaptive functioning. To overcome any skill or developmental deficits, the clinician first provides appropriate information and interactive experiences. Then a future template for adaptive behavior is integrated through the additional processing of imagined positive cognitive, emotional, and behavioral responses. Real-world experience and interaction provide feedback to determine what else may need to be processed.

In sum, EMDR views current problems as based in memories that are dysfunctionally stored in the memory networks. During the course of EMDR treatment, past experiences that have not been adequately processed are directly targeted and rapidly integrated within adaptive networks. When adaptive networks are insufficient, these are enhanced through education and additional processing. The EMDR integrative psychotherapeutic approach utilizes an eight-phase, three-pronged (past, present, future) protocol with the goal of liberating the client from the experiential contributors that set the foundation for the current pathology, and incorporating the full range of experiences and stored memories needed to bring the client to a comprehensive state of mental health.

REFERENCES

American Psychiatric Association. (2004). *Practice guideline for the treatment of patients with acute stress disorder and posttraumatic stress disorder*. Arlington, VA: Author.

Bisson, J., & Andrew, M. (2007). Psychological treatment of post-traumatic stress disorder (PTSD). *Cochrane Database of Systematic Reviews*, 2007, Issue 3. Art. No.: CD003388. DOI: 10.1002/14651858.CD003388.pub3.

Chemtob, C., Tolin, D., van der Kolk, B. A., & Pitman, R. (2000). In E. B. Foa, T. M. Keane, & M. J. Friedman (Eds.), *Effective treatments for PTSD: Practice guidelines of The International Society for Traumatic Stress Studies*. New York: Guilford Press.

Department of Veterans Affairs & Department of Defense (2004). *VA/DoD clinical practice guideline for the management of post-traumatic stress* (Office of Quality and Performance publication 10Q-CPG/PTSD-04). Washington, DC: Author.

Lee, C. W., & Drummond, P. D. (In press). Effects of eye movement versus therapist instructions on the processing of distressing memories. *Journal of Anxiety Disorders*, doi:10.1016/j.janxdis.2007.08.007.

Levin, P., Lazrove, S., & van der Kolk, B. A. (1999). What psychological testing and neuroimaging tell us about the treatment of posttraumatic stress disorder (PTSD) by eye movement desensitization and reprocessing (EMDR). *Journal of Anxiety Disorders, 13,* 159–172.

Ricci, R. J., Clayton, C. A., & Shapiro, F. (2006). Some effects of EMDR treatment with previously abused child molesters: Theoretical reviews and preliminary findings. *Journal of Forensic Psychiatry and Psychology, 17,* 538–562.

Rogers, S., & Silver, S. M. (2002). Is EMDR an exposure therapy? A review of trauma protocols. *Journal of Clinical Psychology, 58,* 43–59.

Schneider, J., Hofmann, A., Rost, C., & Shapiro, F. (2008). EMDR in the treatment of chronic phantom limb pain. *Pain Medicine, 9,* 76–82.

Shapiro, F. (2001). *Eye movement desensitization and reprocessing: Basic principles, protocols and procedures* (2nd ed.). New York: Guilford Press.

SUGGESTED READINGS

Shapiro, F., Kaslow, F., & Maxfield, L. (Eds.). (2007). *Handbook of EMDR and family therapy processes.* Hoboken, NJ: John Wiley & Sons.

Stickgold, R. (2002). EMDR: A putative neurobiological mechanism of action. *Journal of Clinical Psychology, 58,* 61–75.

FRANCINE SHAPIRO
Mental Research Institute, Palo Alto, CA

ROGER M. SOLOMON
Buffalo Center for Trauma and Loss, Buffalo, NY

EYEWITNESS TESTIMONY

Eyewitness testimony is a powerful and influential source of information for juries, especially about crimes such as sexual assault in which the victim is the only witness. Because verdicts in these cases often hinge on eyewitness statements, concern over the accuracy of memory for experienced or witnessed events is magnified. Eyewitness testimony is influenced by a complex interaction of cognitive, socio-emotional, and situational factors during encoding, storage, and retrieval of information (Lindsay, Ross, Read, & Toglia, 2006).

During encoding, knowledge base and expectations can affect the interpretation of an event, which may in turn influence the information attended and stored. Longer exposure generally enhances quality of encoding, but details of a specific episode of a recurring event, such as repeated molestation, can nevertheless be difficult to recall. During the storage phase, details tend to fade in memory, although accurate gist may be retained. Forgetting can promote reconstructive memory as well as alteration of recollection by newly presented, sometimes incorrect, information. Regarding the retrieval phase, free recall typically results in the most accurate, albeit not necessarily the most detailed, eyewitness testimony. Consistency in encoding and retrieval contexts elicits more complete memory reports. Nevertheless, some event details stored in long-term memory can be temporarily inaccessible for purposes of recall. Moreover, at retrieval, victims and witnesses might be unwilling to talk about embarrassing or incriminating experiences, despite having accurate memory.

Suggestibility is a critical issue in the study of eyewitness memory (Loftus, 1979). Suggestibility can involve conscious acquiescence to social demands, as well as unconscious alteration of underlying memory, resulting from misinformation presented before, during, or after an incident. When asked a misleading question, witnesses may yield to the misinformation embedded in the question and incorporate incorrect event details into their memory reports. For example, when the erroneous suggestion is plausible and posed by an authoritative interrogator in an accusatory context, memory reports may be adversely affected. Also, different sources of memories can be confused; thus, an interrogator's false suggestions may be misattributed to memory of the actual experience. However, when witness memory for an event is strong, blatantly misleading questioning can bolster resistance to misinformation and enhance memory accuracy.

Eyewitness reports typically concern traumatic events, which are often remembered better than mundane experiences. A variety of factors, such as event distinctiveness, centrality of the to-be-remembered details, and emotional support may facilitate memory for traumatic experiences. For example, memory of a highly stressful incident is more likely to be retained over time because of its distinctive features. Central details directly related to the event are especially well remembered at the expense of memory for peripheral details. Individuals who receive emotional support after the event are better able to cope with stress, which may enhance subsequent memory. Traumatic memories are not immune to distortions and forgetting, however.

Child Witnesses

Given the number of children who provide statements in legal cases, understanding the conditions under which reliable memory reports can be obtained from young people is critical (Goodman, 2006). Eyewitness memory typically improves with age, with older children producing more accurate and complete memory reports than younger children. Although even preschoolers can provide accurate accounts of personally significant incidents, during free recall they generally recount fewer details than do older children and adults. In response to specific and leading questions, younger children compared with older children tend to make more errors. Age differences in free recall may be due in part to young children's relatively limited ability to organize new information during the encoding phase, and to limited use of source monitoring and retrieval strategies in the retrieval phase. Given such limitations, children, on average, are more vulnerable than adults to suggestive questioning. Moreover, without realizing the ramifications of their reports, child witnesses may conform to an authority figure's suggestions to gain the adult's approval. However, individual differences can substantially alter developmental patterns.

Serious crimes, like sexual abuse, are likely to bring children into contact with the legal system. In special forensic interview centers, often called Child Advocacy Centers, children are interviewed by trained professionals who attempt to use nonleading questioning and typically videotape the sessions, thereby reducing the number of interviews children must endure. Repeated interviewing, testifying in formal courtroom settings, facing the accused, and cross-examination may cause anxiety for children that can interfere with memory and heighten suggestibility.

Interview Techniques and Protocols

Several investigative techniques and structured interview protocols have been developed to maximize the amount of accurate information obtained during forensic interviews. It is recommended that interviewers rely primarily on free-recall questions and open-ended prompts and use direct questions only when necessary to obtain more complete accounts. The Cognitive Interview (CI; Fisher & Geiselman, 1992) combines several mnemonic techniques based on theoretical principles of cognitive psychology to enhance witnesses' abilities to report event details. These techniques include (1) reinstatement of the environmental and mental context of the event, (2) the instruction to report everything, including partial information, (3) recounting events in a variety of temporal orders, and (4) reporting the event from various perspectives. Although there is still debate, the CI appears to increase adults' recall of correct information and reduce memory errors compared to standard police interviews. A modified CI has been used to enhance memory reports of child witnesses.

A structured interview protocol specifically designed for use with child victims and witnesses of abuse was developed by the National Institute of Child Health and Human Development (NICHD; Lamb, Hershkowitz, Orbach, & Esplin, 2008). The NICHD Investigative Interview incorporates multiple recommended techniques for forensic interviews including (1) rapport building in a supportive environment, (2) explaining the rules of the interview (e.g., permission to say "I don't know"), (3) practice providing free recall in response to open-ended questions, and

(4) use of open-ended prompts to obtain information about abuse, followed by focused questions only when necessary. Compared to standard police interviews, NICHD protocol interviews can improve the quality of memory reports for children four years of age and older. Other investigative protocols designed for use with children include the Narrative Elaboration Technique, the Step-Wise Interview, the Cornerhouse RATAC Protocol, the Achieving the Best Evidence in Criminal Proceedings protocol, and the NCAC Forensic Interview.

Photo Lineups

During forensic interviews, witnesses may be required to identify the perpetrator from a photo lineup. Correct identification may be influenced by many factors, including lineup bias, presentation style, and witness age. In general, when the perpetrator is included in the lineup (target-present), versus when the lineup contains only innocent individuals (target-absent), the perpetrator is the person most likely to be selected. Witnesses are less accurate at recognizing the absence of the perpetrator, resulting at times in false identification of innocent suspects. False identifications from target-absent lineups are less likely when the witness is warned that the lineup may or may not contain the perpetrator, the option to select no one is stated explicitly, and all lineup members match the suspect's description.

The method of lineup presentation may also influence the rate of false identifications. Witnesses typically view simultaneous lineups in which all photos are presented at once. When the perpetrator is present, correct identification rates are high with simultaneous lineups, arguably because they encourage the use of relative judgments, whereby the witness selects the lineup member who matches most closely the witness's memory of the perpetrator. However, when the perpetrator is absent, relative judgments can lead to error. Under these conditions, witnesses tend to wrongly identify the innocent individual who looks most like the perpetrator.

An alternative method of administration, the sequential lineup, reduces false identifications of innocent suspects from target-absent lineups compared to simultaneous presentation (Steblay, Dysart, Fulero, & Lindsay, 2001). In sequential presentation, the witness views one photo at a time and decides whether each photo depicts the perpetrator before viewing the next photo. The witness is also kept unaware of the total number of photos in the lineup to reduce the cumulative pressure on the witness to make a selection as the end of the photo set is neared. There is currently debate over whether sequential compared to simultaneous presentation reduces false identifications by discouraging relative judgments or by leading witnesses to change their criterion for making an identification (Wells & Olson, 2003).

Sequential presentation is not without limitations, however. For example, sequential versus simultaneous lineups are at greater risk for investigator bias (Phillips, McAuliff, Kovera, & Cutler, 1999). This type of bias occurs when the lineup administrator's knowledge of the suspect's identity unintentionally increases the likelihood that the witness will identify the suspect. Increase in investigator bias with sequential presentation may be due to the fact that there is little doubt as to which photo the witness is viewing at any particular moment. To reduce investigator bias, law enforcement agencies are encouraged to adopt double-blind administration procedures in which the lineup administrator is unaware of the suspect's identity. Furthermore, the benefits of sequential presentation do not extend to child witnesses (Pozzulo & Lindsay, 1998).

In conclusion, eyewitness memory poses crucial issues for psychological theory and legal application. Regarding application, issues of external validity loom large. Although eyewitness testimony varies in veridicality, justice is served as long as fact finders reach the truth.

REFERENCES

Fisher, R. P., & Geiselman, R. E. (1992). *Memory-enhancing techniques for investigative interviewing: The cognitive interview.* Springfield, IL: Charles C. Thomas.

Goodman, G. S. (2006). Children's eyewitness memory: A modern history and contemporary commentary. *Journal of Social Issues, 62,* 811–832.

Lamb, M. E., Hershkowitz, I., Orbach, Y., & Esplin, P. W. (2008). *Tell me what happened: Structured investigative interviews of child victims and witnesses.* West Sussex, UK: John Wiley & Sons.

Lindsay, R. C. L., Read, D., Ross, D., & Toglia, M. (2006). (Eds.), *Handbook of eyewitness psychology,* Vol. 1. Mahwah, NJ: Lawrence Erlbaum.

Loftus, E. F. (1979). *Eyewitness testimony.* Cambridge, MA: Harvard University Press.

Phillips, M. R., McAuliff, B. D., Kovera, M. B., & Cutler, B. L. (1999). Double-blind administration as a safeguard against investigator bias. *Journal of Applied Psychology, 84,* 940–951.

Pozzulo, J. D., & Lindsay, R. C. L. (1998). Identification accuracy of children versus adults: A meta-analysis. *Law and Human Behavior, 22,* 549–570.

Steblay, N., Dysart, J., Fulero, S., & Lindsay, R. C. L. (2001). Eyewitness accuracy rates in sequential and simultaneous lineup presentations: A meta-analytic comparison. *Law and Human Behavior, 25,* 459–473.

Wells, G. L., & Olson, E. A. (2003). Eyewitness testimony. *Annual Review of Psychology, 54,* 277–295.

Christin M. Ogle
Yoojin Chae
Gail S. Goodman
University of California, Davis

See also: Forensic Psychology

EYSENCK, HANS J. (1916–1997)

Educated in Berlin, Hans J. Eysenck left Germany in 1934 for political reasons (opposition to Hitler regime) to study in Dijon, France, and Exeter, England, before enrolling in a psychology course at the University of London in 1935. He obtained the B.A. and Ph.D. in 1940, then joined the Maudsley Hospital and later the Institute of Psychiatry, which is part of the University of London. In the newly formed Institute he founded the Department of Psychology, becoming a Professor at the university and psychologist to the Maudsley and Bethlem Royal Hospitals. He was given the task of establishing clinical psychology as a profession in the United Kingdom, and his newly created department was the first to train clinical psychologists and to use the newly developed methods of behavior therapy.

Eysenck's main research was in the areas of personality theory and measurement, intelligence, social attitudes and politics, behavioral genetics, and behavior therapy. He viewed psychology from a natural science approach, and was hostile to so-called humanistic, psychodynamic, and other more subjective approaches to the study of psychology. He published some 600 scientific papers in psychological, biological, genetic, and other journals, and published three dozen books. He started the first behavior therapy journal, *Behaviour, Research, and Therapy.* His autobiography has been published in *A History of Psychology in Autobiography,* and a book-length biography was published, H. B. Gibson's *Hans Eysenck: A Man and His Work.*

Eysenck's view of humans, which had always governed his thinking and the direction of his research, was that of a biosocial organism whose actions are determined equally by biological factors (genetic, physiological, endocrine) and social factors (historical, economic, interactional). He believed that a one-sided stress on either biological or social factors impeded the development of the science. This insistence on seeing humans as a product of evolution, still bearing traces of millions of years of development from earlier life forms, was not always popular with social scientists who were more inclined to stress social factors, but was regarded by Eysenck as essential for a proper understanding of man.

SUGGESTED READINGS

Eysenck, H. J., & Rachman, S. (1965). *The causes and cures of neurosis.* San Diego, CA: R. A. Knapp.

Eysenck, H. J. (1982). *Personality, genetics, and behavior.* New York: Praeger.

Eysenck, H. J., Eaves, L. J., & Martin, N. G. (1989). *Genes, culture, and personality.* St. Louis, MO: Academic Press.

EYSENCK PERSONALITY QUESTIONNAIRE

The Eysenck Personality Questionnaire (EPQ) is a self-report instrument that is based on Eysenck's theory of personality. The EPQ was developed by Hans J. Eysenck, one of the most influential personality theorists, and Sybil B. G. Eysenck, and is part of a group of scales developed by Eysenck and his colleagues. The first published scale in this line of work was the Maudsley Personality Inventory (MPI; H. J. Eysenck & Knapp, 1962), which measured two personality tendencies, Neuroticism (N) and Extraversion (E). Following the publication of the MPI, a lie scale was added and two alternate forms were devised, forming the Eysenck Personality Inventory (EPI; H. J. Eysenck & Eysenck, 1964). Subsequently, a third personality dimension, Psychoticism (P) was added, creating the Eysenck Personality Questionnaire. The psychoticism subsacle had undesirable psychometric properties and was criticized for having low reliability, a low range of scoring, and a skewed distribution. In response, in 1985 the scale was revised by removing some items from the P scale and adding some items to the P, N, and E scales. The revised measure, the EPQ-R is the currently used form of the questionnaire (S.B.G. Eysenck, Eysenck, & Barrett, 1985) and is a prime measure of Eysenck's personality dimensions.

The EPQ-R contains 100 items that assess the three personality dimensions of neuroticism (24 items), extraversion (23 items), and psychoticism (32 items) and also provide a lie scale (21 items). The items on the scales are dichotomous, and respondents indicate a "yes" or "no" in response to each item. The N scale measures the degree to which the individual is predisposed to experience negative affect. Individuals with high N scores tend to be moody and worried and to experience guilt, loneliness, and sadness. Examples of items on the N subscale include: "are you a worrier?", "would you call yourself tense or 'highly-strung'?", "do you often feel lonely?"

The E subscale assesses the degree to which individuals are sociable, active, and impulsive. Individuals with high scores on the E subscale tend to be talkative, lively, and outgoing, and they often seek out excitement. Examples of the E subscale include: "are you a talkative person?," "are you rather lively?," and "do you enjoy meeting new people?" The P subscale measures behavior patterns that, in their extreme form, were thought to characterize psychotic individuals or to serve as a vulnerability factor for psychoses. Individuals with high P scores may lack empathy, hurt others willingly, and be hostile and inconsiderate. Items on the P subscale include: "Do you prefer to go your own way rather than act by the rules?," "Do you enjoy hurting people you love?," and "Would you like other people to be afraid of you?" Finally, the lie scale examines response bias, social desirability, and people's tendency to "fake good." Items on the lie scale include: "Are *all* your

habits good and desirable ones?," "Do you always wash before a meal?," and "Have you ever cheated at a game?"

The EPQ-R is a reflection of Eysenck's P-E-N biologically based theory of personality. According to the theory, personality can be seen as a hierarchical taxonomy. At the top of the hierarchy are the superfactors of Extraversion, Neuroticism, and Psychoticism, and subsumed under these superfactors are lower order personality factors or facets (e.g., the sociability component of Extraversion) and specific habits and behaviors. The theory postulates that the higher-order factors are each biologically based. Thus, extraversion is thought to be related to arousability of the central nervous system (Eysenck, 2006). Specifically, it was suggested that, whereas introverts are characterized by over-arousal, extraverts are characterized by under-arousal. This pattern may explain why extraverts frequently seek stimulation. These ideas have been tested extensively and received significant empirical support. Similarly, Eysenck hypothesized that the biological basis for neuroticism lies in lability of the limbic system and increased autonomic activation. Indeed, studies have shown that neurotics show increased physiological reactivity in the face of stress. Although Eysenck believed that psychoticism also has a biological basis, study of the nature of the relationship between psychoticism and its physiological substrates has been more limited than research on extraversion or neuroticism.

The EPQ-R takes approximately 30 minutes to complete. In addition to the full scale, a short form of the EPQ-R and a children's version have been devised. The short form has been reported to have similar psychometric properties as the full scale. Although the initial children's version did not have adequate psychometric properties, a revised version corrected the low reliability that characterized the scale. The EPQ-R has been translated into more than 30 different languages, including Japanese, Spanish, Italian, German, Polish, Hindi, and Arabic, and it has been used extensively throughout the world, in varied populations. Across these many countries, the EPQ has shown a similar factor structure. The reliability of the EPQ-R has been examined in multiple studies. In these studies the neuroticism and extraversion scales of the EPQ-R show very good internal consistency (Cronbach alpha between .80 and .90) and good consistency over time (with test-retest reliability ranging from 0.85 to 0.94). The lie scale has shown good sensitivity in identifying individuals who were instructed to fake their responses to appear good.

Although the EPQ-R was developed to overcome psychometric shortcomings of the psychoticism scale, studies continue to demonstrate that the psychoticism scale is characterized by lower internal consistency compared to the extraversion and neuroticism scales. The authors of the EPQ-R claim that the lower internal consistency of this scale can be attributed to the fact that it taps into several different facets (e.g., hostility, cruelty, lack of empathy).

However, other researchers (e.g., Costa & McCrae, 1995) have argued that personality is better captured by five factors rather than three, and that the psychoticism factor encompasses more than one personality factor. Importantly, the psychoticism scale has also been criticized as being unrelated to current or future psychosis, a relationship initially claimed by Eysenck. Instead, it has been argued that psychoticism is more closely linked to aggression and to lack of empathy.

The EPQ-R has been widely used in the prediction of a variety of social, cognitive, personality, clinical, and health-related phenomena. Scores on the scale have been examined in relation to diverse topics such as criminal behavior, migraine headaches, marital dissolution, assertiveness, the tendency to engage in social comparison, cardiovascular effort regulation, ability appraisals, somatic symptoms, depression, anxiety, and many more.

Individuals who score high on the neuroticism scale report higher levels of symptoms of anxiety and depression than people in general, and they are more likely to be diagnosed with depression or with an anxiety disorder. In addition, scores on the neuroticism scale of the EPQ-R have been related to patterns of processing emotional information. These information-processing biases have, in turn, been linked to depression and anxiety. For example, neurotics tend to ascribe more weight to negative aspects of events, they endorse dysfunctional and pessimistic attitudes about themselves and the world, and they are characterized by overly general memory for events.

The predictions associated with extraversion and psychoticism form a somewhat less coherent picture. Extraversion appears to be mostly related to adaptive social behavior and to positive affect. Extraverts tend to show dominant and assertive behavioral patterns. Extraverts appraise their happiness and ability as being significantly higher than introverts, and they ascribe more weight to the positive aspects of events. Psychoticism is often cited in relation to inappropriate social behavior. For example, psychoticism is related to self-reported delinquent behavior and to heavy drinking among both men and women. However, although to a lesser degree, these behavioral patterns are also characteristic of extraversion and are not unique to psychoticism.

In sum, the EPQ is a theoretically driven and psychometrically sound personality measure that has been used extensively in multiple populations and in relation to varied constructs. Although it appears that more research should be conducted on the psychoticism subscale of the EPQ-R to ascertain its reliability and validity, the other subscales of the EPQ-R have clearly demonstrated their utility in the assessment of personality.

REFERENCES

Costa, P. T., Jr., & McCrae, R. R. (1995). Primary traits of Eysenck's P-E-N system: Three- and five-factor solutions. *Journal of Personality and Social Psychology, 69*, 308–317.

Eysenck, H. J., (2006). *The biological basis of personality*. New Brunswick, NJ: Transaction Publishers.

Eysenck, H. J., & Eysenck, S. B. G. (1964). *Manual of the Eysenck personality inventory*. London: University of London Press.

Eysenck, H. J., & Knapp, R. R. (1962). *Manual for the Maudsley personality inventory*. San Diego, CA: EdITS.

Eysenck, S. B. G., Eysenck, H. J., & Barrett, P. (1985). A revised version of the psychoticism scale. *Personality and Individual Differences, 6*, 21–29.

SUGGESTED READINGS

Barrett, P. T., Petrides, K. V., Eysenck, S. B. G., & Eysenck, H. J. (1998). The Eysenck Personality Questionnaire: An examination of the factorial similarity of P, E, N and L across 23 countries. *Personality and Individual Differences, 25*, 805–819.

Caruso, J. C., Witkiewitz, K., Belcourt-Dittloff, A., & Gottlieb, J. D. (2001). Reliability of scores from the Eysenck Personality Questionnaire: A reliability generalization study. *Educational and Psychological Measurement, 61*, 675–689.

NILLY MOR
Hebrew University of Jerusalem, Israel

See also: **Personality Assessment; Self-Report Inventories**

F

F RATIO (See Analysis of Variance)

FACE VALIDITY

Face validity is a characteristic associated with a psychological test and its individual items. Distinct from more technical types of validity, face validity is the appropriateness, sensibility, or relevance of the test and its items as they appear to the persons answering the test. Do a test and its items seem valid and meaningful to the individuals taking the test? More formally, face validity is defined as the degree to which test respondents view the content of a test and its items as relevant to the context in which the test is being administered.

Three components are important to the definition of face validity. First, face validity is not based on the judgments of psychologists or experts in the content area domain being assessed, but rather on the opinions of test takers who may be quite naïve regarding the domain being measured by the test. Second, face validity depends on the obviousness of the test item content (e.g., the test items may imply that a personality trait, such as neatness, is being measured). Third, the situation in which a test is administered will influence face validity.

Most essential, however, is the combination of these three components in determining the face validity of a test or test item. Consider the statement, "Trying something new is scary" to which a test taker must answer either strongly disagree, disagree, unsure, agree, or strongly agree. If this item appeared on an employment test being given to job candidates who were applying to work for a manufacturing company, the applicants might feel that the test item is irrelevant or inappropriate for the testing situation (i.e., the test item is not face valid). Further, if the entire employment test comprised items with content similar to this particular item, then the test as a whole might appear to lack face validity. Now, consider the same specific item being given on a test to patients newly admitted to a psychiatric hospital. For test takers in such a mental health setting, the test item might well seem to be appropriate and contextually relevant (i.e., the test item is face valid).

Should test developers strive to construct tests that are face valid? The answer to this question depends on the test developer's theoretical orientation as well as on considerations of technical validity, public relations, and possible litigation.

The content of face valid tests is readily identifiable by test takers and, some argue (e.g., Bornstein, Rossner, Hill, & Stepanian, 1994), is thus susceptible to faking, either consciously or unconsciously. Test developers who have a theoretical orientation emphasizing test respondent defensiveness (e.g., psychoanalytically oriented test developers), or test administrators who are employed in defensiveness-inducing assessment contexts (e.g., personnel or forensic settings) in which there is an assumption that test respondents cannot or may not present themselves openly and honestly, believe that face valid tests will result in inaccurate responses. Consequently, they argue that such tests should be avoided. Alternatively, test constructors who possess the theoretical perspective that individuals will present themselves openly and honestly believe that direct, transparent (i.e., face valid) tests are those of choice.

Although some regard a concern for face validity as unimportant (e.g., Downing, 2006), research on technical validity (e.g., criterion validity) has shown a significant positive correspondence between face validity and test item accuracy (Holden & Jackson, 1979). Test items having face validity, on average, tend to be more technically valid or accurate (i.e., the items are better because they tend to be more strongly associated with a relevant criterion) than those items not possessing face validity. Further, research also indicates that, in circumstances where test takers have been asked to fake, face valid items (which are putatively more susceptible to faking) are no less accurate than items that are not face valid (Holden & Jackson, 1985). Figure 1 indicates that, although face valid scales may show more of a decline in criterion validity than nonface valid scales as a function of faking, the validity of face valid scales does not fall below that of nonface valid scales. Nonface valid scales' less susceptibility to faking may merely reflect that such scales tend to be less valid to begin with under honest responding conditions.

Although the positive relationship between face validity and technical validity is significant and stable, it is far from perfect and, consequently, cautions are warranted. Face validity may be associated with better test items, but it neither causes nor ensures other more technical and desirable types of validity. That is, the mere appearance

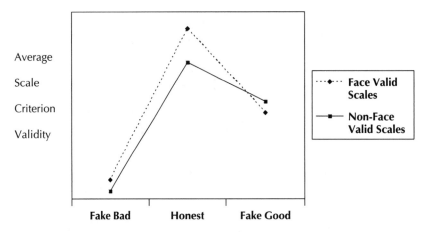

Figure 1. Average Scale Criterion Validity as a Function of Face Validity and Faking Conditions (after Holden & Jackson, 1985).

of relevance or face validity (e.g., as regularly found in tests published in popular magazines) fails to guarantee a test's accuracy. Furthermore, the absence of face validity does not necessarily mean that a test or its items are inaccurate.

The face validity of a test is an important property for issues of public relations and litigation (Nevo, 1985). Psychological testing should not be an antagonistic and seemingly inappropriate exercise for test respondents. Cooperation and good rapport between testers and test takers is sound practice in all assessment contexts. The presence of face validity enhances the perceived relevance of a psychological test and reduces the likelihood of feelings of depersonalization and resentment in the individual being tested. The presence of face *in*validity (Messick, 1989) or the absence of face validity (regardless of technical validity or accuracy) may result in test respondents feeling dissatisfaction and anger, and of being cheated. Such feelings may well be acted on, resulting in negative media publicity, public demands for the cessation of testing programs (e.g., in schools), labor-management conflict, or even costly legal proceedings.

REFERENCES

Bornstein, R. F., Rossner, S. C., Hill, E. L., & Stepanian, M. L. (1994). Face validity and fakability of objective and projective measures of dependency. *Journal of Personality Assessment, 63,* 363–386.

Downing, S. M. (2006). Face validity of assessments: Faith-based interpretations or evidence-based science? *Medical Education, 40,* 7–8.

Holden, R. R., & Jackson, D. N. (1979). Item subtlety and face validity in personality assessment. *Journal of Consulting and Clinical Psychology, 47,* 459–468.

Holden, R. R., & Jackson, D. N. (1985). Disguise and the structured self-report assessment of psychopathology: I. An analogue investigation. *Journal of Consulting and Clinical Psychology, 53,* 211–222.

Messick, S. (1989). Validity. In R. L. Linn (Ed.), *Educational measurement* (3rd ed.). (pp. 13–103). New York: American Council on Education.

Nevo, B. (1985). Face validity revisited. *Journal of Educational Measurement, 22,* 287–293.

SUGGESTED READING

Mosier, C. I. (1947). A critical examination of the concepts of face validity. *Educational and Psychological Measurement, 7,* 191–205.

Ronald R. Holden
Queen's University, Canada

***See also:* Psychometrics; Validity**

FACIAL RECOGNITION

Facial recognition refers to our ability to indicate whether we have previously seen a face. This process involves perceptual, cognitive, and social components. We rely on our facial recognition system for mundane things such as recognizing acquaintances and more infrequent tasks such as identifying criminals from lineups.

Human facial recognition occurs across a variety of environmental conditions (e.g., lighting, obstructions), and the similarity between the initial and recognition viewing context influences recognition accuracy. Additionally, one's viewing experience is affected by situational factors such as viewpoint, pose, and movement and social conditions such as prior knowledge of a person, the own-race bias, and verbal overshadowing. The nature of faces also affects recognition accuracy (e.g., more distinctive faces are recognized better). Face recognition is consistently impaired by manipulations of a tested face image, such as filtering some of the light waves that compose the face, showing the photographic negative of the face, or presenting the face at low spatial frequencies. Other factors improve recognition. These include long presentation durations and in-depth processing of the face.

We recognize faces known to us despite extreme distortions of view (e.g., CCTV footage, changes in lighting, spatial frequency content, viewpoint, expression), but we recognize unfamiliar faces poorly in many circumstances. Bruce and Young (1986) have argued that we initially store the raw image properties of faces (pictorial coding), but after many exposures to a particular face under different circumstances of pose, viewpoint, and the like, a structural code is formed. This structural code is a prototype of the face that allows for recognition under new circumstances. In the absence of such a prototype, recognition is much poorer.

Researchers debate whether and to what degree we process isolated facial features, the spatial relations among features, or both. In support of the featural hypothesis (i.e., we process specific features and then combine them), some brain cells are stimulated by specific facial features, and we use three-dimensional cues to distinguish among features. In support of the configural hypothesis (i.e., we utilize featural and configural processes but configural are more important), we better recognize distorted upright faces than distorted inverted faces, and changing the angle of presentation of a face between learning and test of recognition decreases recognition accuracy. The holistic hypothesis posits that we use featural and configural cues to perceive the face as a single entity, but that configural information is more accessible. Finally, norm hypotheses focus on differences between a currently processed face and facial norms or prototypes developed from experience and schemas.

Four types of models of facial recognition have been developed: (1) functional, (2) multidimensional representation in space, (3) neural network or connectionist, and (4) principal components analysis (PCA) combined with neural networks. Bruce and Young's (1986) functional model suggests that the structural code of a face is compared with structural codes for faces stored in memory and then connected with the identity and name of that matching face. Neural network models are exemplified by Burton, Bruce, and Johnston's (1990) use of the Interactive Activation and Competition model to implement the Bruce and Young (1986) model with a neural network. The model accounts for empirical findings concerning semantic priming, repetition priming, covert recognition by prospagnosiacs, name recall, name recognition, and learning new faces. Burton, Bruce, and Hancock (1999) later incorporated PCA into this model to account for the perceptual component of facial recognition in addition to the cognitive component.

Valentine (1991) utilized multidimensional representation of faces. Each face is represented as a point or vector in multidimensional space. Two faces are considered more similar the closer they are in space. Two models arising from this approach (norm-based coding and purely exemplar-based) successfully model three face recognition effects: (1) distinctiveness, (2) holistic inversion, and (3) the own-race bias.

Other research focuses on the anatomy of facial recognition. Brain injury studies indicate that two paths may be responsible for facial recognition: a ventral visual pathway for overt face recognition and a dorsal visual pathway for covert or affective recognition responses. Some brain-injured patients are unable to overtly recognize people known to them, but show an autonomic response (skin conductance) to them. This suggests that recognition occurs, but without conscious awareness. Others experience the Capgras illusion or delusional misidentification: they recognize they have seen a face before but believe the person is an "impostor." Breen, Caine, and Coltheart (2000) argue that the ventral visual pathway alone can account for the Capgras illusion and other findings with prospagnosiacs.

There are two major accounts of the development of facial recognition over the lifespan. The expertise hypothesis argues that facial recognition is learned similarly to other skills. The modularity hypothesis holds that particular brain systems are responsible for facial recognition and that it is not influenced by experience (Brigham, 2002). There are reliable developmental differences in facial recognition accuracy, involving a consistent dip in accuracy between ages 10 and 14 and a decrease in false eyewitness identifications from childhood to adulthood. However, these differences may not result from facial recognition ability, *per se*, but rather may arise from processes such as working memory capacity (expertise hypothesis). Support for the modularity hypothesis stems from four empirical findings: (1) facial preferences may be innate, (2) there are cortical cells that respond specifically to faces, (3) inversion of faces reduces recognition accuracy, and (4) brain injury can result in the inability to recognize familiar faces while visual recognition of objects and words is relatively unaffected (Brigham, 2002). Thus, some research supports the contention that facial recognition is an innate skill, but other research shows changes over the lifespan suggesting the development of expertise.

In summary, facial recognition is influenced by a number of environmental, situational, and social factors and is clearly superior for familiar faces. Developmental changes occur over our lifespan in our ability to recognize faces, but it is unclear whether this ability is hardwired or learned. Neuroanatomical and brain injury research indicates there are face-specific cells in our brain and similarities between facial and object recognition. Processing of facial information for recognition within the brain clearly occurs in the ventral visual pathway but debate exists over whether the dorsolateral visual pathway also plays a role.

REFERENCES

Breen, N., Caine, D., & Coltheart, M. (2000). Models of face recognition and delusional misidentification. *Cognitive Neuropsychology, 17,* 55–71.

Brigham, J. C. (2002). Face identification: Basic processes and developmental changes. In Eisen, M. L., Quas, J. A., & Goodman, G. S. (Eds.), *Memory and Suggestibility in the Forensic Interview,* pp. 115–140. Mahwah, NJ: Lawrence Erlbaum.

Bruce, V., & Young, A. (1986). Understanding face recognition. *British Journal of Psychology, 77,* 305–327.

Burton, A. M., Bruce, V., & Hancock, P. J. B. (1999). From pixels to people: A model of familiar face recognition. *Cognitive Science, 23,* 1–31.

Burton, A. M., Bruce, V., & Johnston, R. A. (1990). Understanding facial recognition with an Interactive Activation Model. *British Journal of Psychology, 81,* 361–381.

Valentine, T. (1991). A unified account of the effects of distinctiveness, inversion, and race in face recognition. *The Quarterly Journal of Experimental Psychology Section A: Human Experimental Psychology, 43,* 161–204.

SUGGESTED READINGS

Bruce, V., Burton, M., & Hancock, P. (2007). Remembering faces. In R. C. L. Lindsay, D. F. Ross, J. D. Read, & M. P. Toglia (Eds.), *Handbook of eyewitness psychology: Memory for people,* pp. 87–100. Mahwah, NJ: Lawrence Erlbaum.

Kanwisher, N., & Moscovitch, M. (2000). The cognitive neuroscience of face processing: An introduction. *Cognitive Neuropsychology, 17,* 1–11.

Rakover, S. S., & Cahlon, B. (2001). *Face recognition: Cognitive and computational processes.* Amsterdam: John Benjamins.

JAMAL K. MANSOUR
RODERICK C. LINDSAY
Queen's University, Kingston, ON, Canada

FACTITIOUS DISORDER

Factitious disorder is defined in the *Diagnostic and Statistical Manual of Mental Disorders* as "physical or psychological symptoms that are intentionally produced or feigned in order to assume the sick role" (American Psychiatric Association, 2000, p. 513). It is differentiated from somatoform disorders on the basis of involuntary production of symptoms in the latter. However, in clinical practice the two types of disorders can be difficult to distinguish, since many patients present with a mixture of voluntary and involuntary symptoms (Feldman, Hamilton, & Deemer, 2001).

Factitious disorder is differentiated from malingering on the basis of motivation. Malingering involves a conscious intent to obtain tangible benefits, such as drugs or money, rather than an unconscious motivation to remain in the sick role. In practice, however, there are many patients with factitious disorder who appear to have a malingering component (Feldman, Hamilton, & Deemer, 2001).

Another term in the literature is *Munchausen syndrome* (Asher, 1951). This is an older term that is now used to describe more severe cases of factitious disorder with predominantly physical symptoms and characterized by a triad of elaborate false storytelling called *pseudologia fantastica*, wandering from hospital to hospital (peregrination), and bizarre and dramatic presentations.

Diagnosis

Prevalence rates vary widely in different studies, ranging from 0.3% on a neurology ward, to 6% on an inpatient psychiatry unit, to as high as 9% of tertiary care evaluations for fever of unknown origin (Feldman, Hamilton, & Deemer, 2001; Gregory & Jindal, 2006). Perhaps these differences reflect the difficulty in reliably diagnosing this disorder and the general reluctance of clinicians to make the diagnosis. There is an understandable tendency for clinicians to give the patient the benefit of the doubt instead of setting up a potentially antagonistic relationship.

Typical manifestations of factitious disorder with predominantly physical signs and symptoms include lying or exaggerating symptoms such as pain or seizures, intentional self-inflicted symptoms, or conditions such as infection, poor wound healing, hypoglycemia, rashes, anemia, bleeding, diarrhea, vomiting, and fever. The production of physical symptoms is more common in women, many of whom are in a healthcare profession (Feldman, Hamilton, & Deemer, 2001).

Typical manifestations of factitious disorder with predominantly psychological signs and symptoms include depression and suicide ideation or gestures in women and hallucinations in men (Gregory & Jindal, 2006). The suicide gesture typically arises in order to assure inpatient admission or around the time of hospital discharge in order to prolong inpatient care.

A central dynamic of factitious disorder is the need for justification, and this provides an important clue to diagnosis (Gregory & Jindal, 2006). The need for justification reflects an underlying question of "Are my needs legitimate?" Patients typically complain that previous doctors and health care providers have not taken their concerns seriously. They are likely to present with unusual symptoms in order to justify extraordinary care. It is important to realize that patients with factitious disorder truly believe they are very ill, and their distress is genuine. When questioned in depth about their behaviors, such as putting fecal matter in their intravenous line, they will state that it was the only way for their providers to understand how ill they are and how much in need of treatment.

Discharge is typically a difficult time, since it signals that further care is no longer justified. As discharge approaches, patients can become irritable and aggressive, and health-seeking behaviors escalate in order to prolong the hospital stay. Note that the need for justification is also a central dynamic of borderline personality disorder (Gregory, 2008), and this disorder is commonly comorbid with factitious disorder (Feldman, Hamilton, & Deemer, 2001).

Psychological testing can be helpful in confirming a factitious disorder diagnosis. The Minnesota Multiphasic Personality Inventory typically demonstrates either prominent personality disturbance or a "fake bad" profile with elevations across all the subscales (Gregory & Jindal, 2006). However, testers are often reluctant to suggest a factitious disorder diagnosis, since they empathically perceive the patient's genuine distress.

Management

Because of their need for justification, patients with factitious disorder typically have a strongly negative reaction if confronted with the diagnosis and often react by either escalating symptom production in order to prove the legitimacy of their claims or by signing out against medical advice. The provider must keep in mind that these patients strongly believe they are ill and so will seek out providers who are able to give them the treatment that they need.

A better strategy is to attempt to empathically reframe the patient's illness in a biopsychosocial model and provide realistic goals and expectations of treatment while avoiding iatrogenic harm through unnecessary procedures (Gregory & Jindal, 2006). Patients with factitious disorder typically see their illness in a purely biomedical model and are looking for a cure. Providers can attempt to reframe the illness, emphasizing coping rather than curing, and educating the patient regarding the detrimental effects of stress. Referral to psychotherapy should be made in such a way as to help the patient "save face," as by labeling it as "stress management for patients with chronic illness" (Servan-Schreiber, Tabas, & Kolb, 2000).

Hospital staff can often develop polarized perceptions of the patient as either deserving of better care, or as manipulative and attention-seeking, and thus may not provide a consistent and empathic approach. Educating hospital staff regarding this challenging illness is one of the keys to success in treating it.

REFERENCES

American Psychiatric Association. (2000). *Diagnostic and statistical manual of mental disorders* (4th ed., text rev.). Washington, DC: Author.

Asher, R. (1951). Munchausen syndrome. *Lancet, 1,* 339–341.

Feldman, M. D., Hamilton, J. C., & Deemer, H. N. (2001). Factitious disorder. In K. A. Phillips (Ed.), *Somatoform and Factitious Disorders* (pp. 129–159). Washington, DC: American Psychiatric Publishing.

Gregory, R. J., & Jindal, S. (2006). Factitious disorder on an inpatient psychiatry ward. *American Journal of Orthopsychiatry, 76,* 31–36.

Gregory, R. J., & Remen, A. L. (2008). A manual-based psychodynamic therapy for treatment-resistant borderline personality disorder. *Psychotherapy: Theory, Research, Practice, Training, 45,* 15–27.

Servan-Schreiber, D., Tabas, G., & Kolb, R. (2000). Somatizing patients: Part II. Practical management. *American Family Physician, 61,* 1423–1428.

SUGGESTED READING

Eisendrath, S. J., Young, J. Q. (2005). Factitious physical disorders: A review. In M. Maj, H. S. Akiskal, J. E. Messich, & A. Okasha (Eds.), *Somatoform Disorders* (pp. 325–380). Hoboken, NJ: John Wiley & Sons.

ROBERT J. GREGORY
SUNY Upstate Medical University

See also: **Malingering; Somatization Disorder**

FACTOR ANALYSIS

In broad terms, *factor analysis* focuses on the link between a set of intercorrelated variables and their representation by a smaller set of conceptually meaningful megavariables, termed *factors*. Within this all-encompassing umbrella description, factor analysis is more precisely characterized in terms of its function. If used to determine the extent to which the set of variables *can be* adequately represented by a smaller number of factors, then we are describing *exploratory factor analysis*. If, on the other hand, it is used in determining the extent to which a set of variables *are* adequately represented by a smaller number of factors as postulated by theory and/or empirical research, then we are describing *confirmatory factor analysis*. In providing a more comprehensive explanation of factor analysis, I first address the general notion of factor analysis and then follow with a more extensive description of both exploratory and confirmatory factor analysis, together with a comparative summary of these two factor analytic approaches. Finally, I close this article by addressing important issues and caveats associated with the application of these approaches in psychological research.

The General Notion

The key notion underlying factor analysis is that some variables of theoretical interest cannot be observed directly; these unobserved variables are termed *latent variables*, or *factors*. Although latent variables cannot be measured directly, information related to them can be obtained indirectly by noting their effects on the observed variables believed to represent them. The oldest and best-known statistical procedure for investigating relations between sets of observed and latent variables is that of factor analysis. In using this approach to data analyses, researchers examine the covariation among a set of observed variables in order to gather information on the latent constructs (i.e., factors) that underlie them.

Exploratory Factor Analysis

Since its inception more than a century ago (Spearman, 1904), exploratory factor analysis (EFA) has been one of the most widely used statistical procedures in psychological research (Fabrigar, Wegener, MacCallum, & Strahan, 1999). EFA is most appropriately used when links between the observed variables and their underlying factors are unknown or uncertain. It is considered to be exploratory in the sense that the researcher has no prior knowledge that the observed variables, although correlated, actually measure the intended factors. Essentially, the researcher uses EFA to determine the extent to which they do cluster together to form the expected factors; that is, it is used to establish the factor structure.

In reviewing this factor structure, the researcher examines (1) the number of factors that can explain the most variance, (2) the size and statistical significance status of the factor loadings (i.e., correlations between the observed variables and their related factors), (3) the clarity or distinctiveness by which the observed variables cluster around (or load on) their related factors (i.e., the presence of simple structure), and (4) the extent to which the factors themselves are correlated or uncorrelated (i.e., whether they represent an oblique or orthogonal solution respectively). Specific details concerning the attainment of this information can be found in texts addressing this multivariate statistical procedure (e.g., Gorsuch, 1983; Marcoulides & Hershberger, 1997). One logical application of EFA would be in the development of a new assessment measure. Although the developer will have constructed items designed to measure particular constructs underlying this instrument, he or she has no knowledge of the extent to which such scale items do, in fact, meet this expectation.

Confirmatory Factor Analysis

In contrast to EFA, confirmatory factor analysis (CFA) is a more recently developed technique. CFA is based on the analysis of covariance structures, and it was not until Jöreskog (1969) detailed the underlying statistical framework and presented a computer program (COFAMM) capable of performing these analyses that CFA became known and available to the broader academic community. CFA is most appropriately used when researchers have some knowledge of the underlying latent variable structure. Based on theory and/or empirical research, they postulate relations between the observed measures and the underlying factors *a priori* and then test this hypothesized structure in a simultaneous analysis of the entire system of variables to determine the extent to which it is consistent with the sample data. If the goodness-of-fit between the hypothesized structure and the data is adequate, the model argues for the plausibility of postulated relations among variables; if it is inadequate, the tenability of such relations is rejected. For an introduction to the basic concepts and applications of CFA, readers are referred to Byrne (2001, 2006), and for a more mathematical presentation of the topic, to Long (1983).

Exploratory and Confirmatory Analyses: A Comparison

Although both EFA and CFA are based on the common factor model, there are several important differences between them. From a global perspective, one major distinction is that, whereas EFA is primarily a data-driven approach, CFA is theoretically grounded; or, in the words of Bryant and Yarnold, (1995), EFA operates inductively in that the data determine the underlying factor structure *a posteriori*, whereas CFA operates deductively in postulating the factor structure *a priori*. Of the two factor analytic approaches, CFA is by far the more rigorous and, as such, enables the researcher to overcome many limitations associated with EFA; this capability ultimately accounts for several specific distinctions between the two factor analytic techniques.

First, whereas the EFA model assumes that all common factors are either correlated or uncorrelated, the CFA model makes no such assumptions. Rather, the researcher specifies *a priori* only those factor correlations that are considered to be substantively meaningful. Second, with the EFA model all observed variables are directly influenced by all common factors. With CFA, each factor influences only those observed variables with which it is purported to be linked. Third, whereas in EFA the unique factors (i.e., error terms) are assumed to be uncorrelated, in CFA specified covariation among particular error terms can be tapped. Fourth, provided with an ill-fitting model in EFA, there is no mechanism for identifying which areas of the model are contributing most to the misfit. In CFA, on the other hand, the researcher is guided to a more appropriately specified model via indices of misfit provided by the statistical program. Fifth and finally, whereas EFA models provide no mechanism for testing the equivalence of factor loading estimates across groups from either the same or different populations, CFA models can address this issue in a simultaneous analysis of the multigroup data. Furthermore, these tests can be extended to include equivalence of factor variances and covariances, error variances and covariances, and latent factor means.

Issues and Caveats in Using Exploratory and Confirmatory Factor Analyses

Although there are many common misuses of EFA (see e.g., Fabrigar et al., 1999) and of CFA (see e.g., Byrne, 2006), only two are highlighted here for each procedure.

EFA. Most pervasive among these misapplications is the use of principal components analysis (PCA) under the guise of EFA; PCA is not factor analysis. Indeed, EFA and PCA represent two entirely distinct statistical methods designed to achieve distinctly different objectives. Whereas the primary intent of EFA is to explain the pattern of covariance underlying a set of observed variables, thereby identifying the latent construct(s) to which it is linked, that of PCA is simply to reduce a large set of observed variables to a smaller set of composite variables, while concomitantly maximizing the amount of variance accounted for by the original variables.

A second misapplication of EFA involves the typical, almost mechanical use of orthogonal rather than oblique rotation in seeking simple structure. Whereas orthogonal rotation constrains the factors to be uncorrelated, oblique rotation allows for their correlation. Because psychological constructs are typically correlated to some degree, methodologists argue that the use of orthogonal methods is rarely defensible and that researchers should always use oblique rotation. If, in fact, the factors are truly orthogonal, an obliquely rotated factor solution will still reflect these independent factor relations

CFA. One of the most serious misapplications of CFA is failure to test the tenability of the statistical assumptions underlying this procedure; that is, the extent to which the data are multivariate normal, linearly related, and of interval scale. In light of violations, the issue needs to be addressed in accordance with recommended practices and available program options.

A second important misuse of CFA is the conduct of analyses based on samples of inadequate size. Given that the methodology is grounded in large-sample theory, it demands that analyses be based on large samples. Indeed, there is now a rich CFA literature that addresses this topic of sample size. Although sample sizes in excess of 200 have been recommended over the past 40 years, more recently methodologists have suggested that the use of highly reliable and valid measures, together with the specification of relatively simple models, can serve effectively to compensate for smaller sample size. More extensive review and discussion of these misapplication issues and their related caveats are provided for EFA by Fabrigar et al. (1999) and for CFA by Byrne (2006).

REFERENCES

Bryant, F. B., & Yarnold, P. R. (1995). Principal components analysis and exploratory and confirmatory factor analysis. In L. G. Grimm & :. R. Yarnold (Eds.), *Reading and understanding multivariate statistics* (pp. 99–136. Washington, DC: American Psychological Association.

Byrne, B. M. (2001). *Structural equation modeling with AMOS: Basic concepts, applications, and programming.* Mahwah, NJ: Lawrence Erlbaum.

Byrne, B. M. (2005). Factor analytic models: Viewing the structure of an assessment instrument from three perspectives. *Journal of Personality Assessment, 85,* 17–30.

Byrne, B. M. (2006). *Structural equation modeling with EQS: Basic concepts, applications, and programming* (2nd ed.). Mahwah, NJ: Lawrence Erlbaum.

Fabrigar, L. R., Wegener, D. T., MacCallum, R. C., & Strahan, E. J. (1999). Evaluating the use of exploratory factor analysis in psychological research. *Psychological Methods, 4,* 272–299.

Gorsuch, R. L. (1983). *Factor analysis* (2nd ed.). Hillsdale, NJ: Lawrence Erlbaum.

Jöreskog, K. G. (1969). A general approach to confirmatory maximum likelihood factor analysis. *Psychometrika, 34,* 183–202.

Long, J. S. (1983). *Confirmatory factor analysis.* Beverly Hills, CA: Sage.

Marcoulides, G. A., & Hershberger, S. L. (1997). *Multivariate statistical methods: A first course.* Mahwah, NJ: Lawrence Erlbaum.

Spearman, C. (1904). General intelligence, objectively determined and measured. *American Journal of Psychology, 15,* 201–293.

SUGGESTED READINGS

Floyd, F. J. & Widaman, K. F. (1995). Factor analysis in the development and refinement of clinical assessment instruments. *Psychological Assessment, 7,* 286–299.

Kleinbaum, D. G., Kupper, L. L., & Muller, K. E. (1988). *Applied regression analysis and other multivariable methods* (2nd ed.; Chap. 24). Boston: PWS-Kent Publishing.

Preacher, K. J. & MacCallum, R. C. (2003). Repairing Tom Swift's electric factor analysis machine. *Understanding Statistics, 2,* 13–43.

BARBARA M. BYRNE
University of Ottawa, Canada

See also: **Cluster Analysis; Principal Component Analysis**

FACTORIAL DESIGNS

The most basic experimental design is the one-factor analysis of variance (ANOVA). Here there is one continuous dependent variable and one categorical independent variable or factor with two or more levels. For example, to what extent do different therapies (levels of a treatment factor) result in differential recovery from a psychological condition (dependent variable)?

A problem with the one-factor model, due to its simplicity, is that one factor is unlikely to explain or predict much of the variation in the dependent variable. This leads us to consider other types of experimental designs that are more likely to provide better explanation or prediction. Some other designs involve including additional factors (factorial ANOVA designs); a covariate (a variable taken into account statistically in an analysis of covariance, ANCOVA); repeated measures (in which subjects are exposed to all conditions and serve as their own controls); and/or a blocking factor (a variable related to the dependent variable that cannot be manipulated, such as age or IQ). This article provides a basic overview of such factorial designs.

Characteristics

Factorial designs include two or more independent variables or factors, each factor having two or more levels. In a two-factor design, all levels of factor A (e.g., four treatment conditions) occur in combination with all levels of factor B (e.g., three times per day of treatment administration). Individuals are then somehow assigned to these combinations or groups. In a true experiment, individuals are randomly assigned to groups with an equal likelihood of being assigned to any group (e.g., randomly assigned to one treatment condition). In a quasi experiment, individuals are already in intact groups, and thus random assignment is not possible (e.g., the person's age). True experiments are stronger internally as a result of random assignment. Each individual responds to only one such combination; otherwise, a repeated measures design is required.

Main Effects and Interaction Effects

In any factorial design, two types of hypotheses are tested: main effects and interaction effects. Consider the two-factor model. A test of the main effect for factor A is the effect of A, averaged across the levels of factor B, on the dependent variable (i.e., the effect of factor A by itself). The null hypothesis is that the population means of the levels of factor A are equal. There is also a main effect for factor B with a similar null hypothesis. An interaction effect is present when a particular combination of the levels of the two factors produces an effect beyond that of the main effects considered separately. The null hypothesis is that the population mean differences among the levels of factor A are the same across the levels of factor B.

For example, pharmacists are concerned about the possible interaction of two medications. There is a certain benefit of medication #1 (a main effect) and a certain benefit of medication #2 (a separate main effect). When these medications are combined, the benefits may cancel out, or there may be additional benefits, or the combination may even produce a negative consequence. That is why pharmacists ask if you are taking other medications. In psychology, a two-factor design might examine the effects of strength of reinforcement (factor A) and type of reinforcement (factor B) on children's acting-out behavior. Thus an interaction could indicate that a combination of a particular type of reinforcement at a particular strength level reduces acting-out behavior more than other combinations.

If the interaction is not statistically significant, then the findings regarding the main effects can be generalized with greater confidence. Thus we can make a blanket statement about the constant added benefits of two levels of factor A, A_1 over A_2, regardless of the level of B. If the interaction is statistically significant, then the findings regarding the main effects cannot be generalized with such confidence. The effect of factor A depends on factor B. Thus we cannot make a blanket statement about the constant added benefits of A_1 over A_2, because the effect depends on the level of B. Plotting the means is a useful way to interpret interaction effects properly.

Effect Size Measures

Rather than sole reliance on statistical significance, the American Psychological Association (APA, 2001) also recommends reporting an effect size measure to interpret the magnitude of the main and interaction effects. Commonly used effect size measures include Cohen's d, eta squared (η^2), and omega squared (ω^2). According to Cohen's (1988) subjective criteria, effect sizes can be classified into small effect sizes ($d = .20$, η^2 or $\omega^2 = .01$); medium effect sizes ($d = .50$, η^2 or $\omega^2 = .06$); and large effect sizes ($d = .80$, η^2 or $\omega^2 = .14$). The APA also recommends that power (the probability that the null hypothesis has been correctly rejected) be reported.

Assumptions

There are three statistical assumptions necessary in ANOVA: independence among the observations, homogeneity of variance across groups, and normal distribution of variables. Lack of independence increases the likelihood of a decision error, and there is no simple fix. When variances are unequal, it helps to have balanced or nearly balanced designs (in terms of the combination sample sizes) and/or larger sample sizes. Otherwise the likelihood of decision errors is increased. When distributions are nonnormal, the effect is minimal with moderate or less nonnormality, balanced or nearly balanced designs, and/or larger sample sizes.

Statistical Results

The ultimate test statistic in ANOVA is the F ratio. An F statistic is computed for each effect (main effects and interaction effects), and then a probability is determined for the likelihood that the null hypothesis is true. If the null hypothesis is rejected at a specified nominal level of significance (α) and there are more than two levels of that factor, then it is not clear which means are different. This requires some sort of multiple comparison procedure to interpret the significant main and/or interaction effects. For example, if there is a significant main effect for the type of reinforcement factor and there are four levels of reinforcement type, then it is not clear which types are different. A multiple comparison procedure, such as Tukey HSD or Bonferroni, can determine which means or combinations of means are different.

REFERENCES

American Psychological Association. (2001). *Publication manual of the American Psychological Association* (5th ed.). Washington, DC: Author.

Cohen, J. (1988). *Statistical power analysis for the behavioral sciences* (2nd ed.). Orlando, FL: Academic Press.

SUGGESTED READINGS

Huck, S.W. (2008). *Reading statistics and research* (5th ed.). Boston: Allyn and Bacon.

Keppel, G., & Wickens, T.D. (2004). *Design and analysis: A researcher's handbook*. Upper Saddle River, NJ: Pearson.

Lomax, R.G. (2007). *An introduction to statistical concepts* (2nd ed.). Mahwah, NJ: Lawrence Erlbaum.

Myers, J.L., & Well, A.D. (1995). *Research design & statistical analysis*. Hillsdale, NJ: Lawrence Erlbaum.

RICHARD G. LOMAX
Ohio State University

See also: Analysis of Variance; Multivariate Methods

FALSE MEMORY SYNDROME

False memory syndrome (FMS), although not recognized as a psychiatric disorder in either the *Diagnostic and Statistical Manual of Mental Disorders* or the *International Statistical Classification of Diseases and Related Health Problems*, which are the two key reference manuals for mental illness throughout the world, is a term widely used in legal and scientific arenas to describe the hypothesis that recovered memories may at times be partially incorrect or altogether false. The False Memory Syndrome Foundation (FMSF) first coined the term in the 1990s in reaction to an abundance of cases during the previous two decades in which patients claimed to be victims of childhood sexual abuse (CSA) or satanic ritual. These recovered memory cases led to criminal prosecutions of alleged abusers, lawsuits against therapists by former clients and parents, and even legislative reform. The 2008 website of the FMSF supplies the following definition for the syndrome.

[A] condition in which a person's identity and interpersonal relationships are centered around a memory of traumatic experience which is objectively false but in which the person strongly believes ... [T]he syndrome may be diagnosed when the memory is so deeply ingrained that it orients the individual's entire personality and lifestyle, in turn disrupting all sorts of other adaptive behavior.

The FMSF was started as an advocacy group in support of persons against whom victims' claims were directed, predominantly parents of the purported victims. The FMSF largely denies the existence of recovered memories and suggests that FMS in large part occurs through suggestive methods in therapeutic practice that may implant false memories.

Although widespread debate exists as to whether memories can be modified or implanted by therapeutic suggestion, the work of several proponents of FMS, most notably Elizabeth F. Loftus, have used laboratory methods to show that indeed memories are malleable (Loftus, 2005) and that suggestion may lead to implanted memory (Loftus & Pickrell, 1995). Most notably, the "familial informant false narrative procedure," better known as "lost in a mall," shows that false memories can be implanted by telling participants that their relatives have provided information about their being lost in a mall when younger and then suggestively interviewing the individuals to try to elicit memories of the event. Across these studies, an average of 30% of subjects have developed partial or complete illusory memories of the events. These results, as well as others by proponents of FMS, have been used to suggest that such recovered memories are illusory, and that they are largely implanted by therapists using suggestive therapeutic methods.

Although this research has highlighted the malleability and even the fallibility of the memory process, many others, including Pope and Brown (1997), question whether the findings from such contrived studies in the laboratory can be extrapolated to real-world situations. Researchers examining actual cases of CSA suggest that memories of traumatic events may not be recalled at certain points in victims' experience. Empirical studies show that a sizable proportion of women with a documented history of CSA did not report any CSA when interviewed years after the documented abuse. For example, Widom (1997) found that 37% of 94 women with documented histories of CSA denied having experienced CSA when interviewed 20 years later. Similarly, there are also advocates who endorse the idea that memories can be forgotten over long periods of time. With respect to such memories, sometimes termed "delayed memories" as well as "recovered memories," researchers suggest that memories of CSA can be a credible occurrence, in part because of the delay of memories that is associated with posttraumatic stress disorder, an accepted psychiatric condition. Furthermore, delayed memories may result from the power and psychological effects an abuser may exert over child victims, which may help to explain why it is often not until individuals reach adulthood that they are able to address such memories (Kelly, 1988). Moreover, advocates of delayed memories and researchers addressing documented cases of CSA suggest that the work of the FMSF is biased towards disproving recovered or delayed memories and undermines the accounts of victims with actual cases of CSA.

Unfortunately, the extremely sensitive and ethically complex nature of recovered memories, whether false or not, is difficult to study empirically. Because it is unethical to conduct experiments examining the influence of suggestion and how it may lead to false memories of CSA, researchers are left with two general options: either to use (1) ethical methods of suggestion that can plausibly be generalized to false memories of CSA, and/or (2) case-study methodologies to examine whether the individuals involved appear to fit cases of actual false memory recovery. These limitations illustrate why experts on both sides of this issue should be cautious in their claims regarding specific recovered memory cases (Lindsay, 2001).

Whereas FMS engenders considerable polemical debate, there is no divide in the concern for victims of CSA or the victims of accusations revolving around illusory memories. Evidence shows that both illusory and accurate recovered-memory experiences are genuine phenomena. Because of the extremely susceptible nature of false and recovered memories to be highlighted in the media, and their ramifications for legal action, further rigorous yet unbiased empirical investigation is warranted.

REFERENCES

Kelly, L. (1988). *Surviving sexual violence*. Cambridge, MA: Polity Press.

Lindsay, D. S., & Read, J. D. (2001). The recovered memories controversy: Where do we go from here? In G. Davies & T. Dalgleish (Eds.), *Recovered memories: Seeking the middle ground* (pp. 71–94). New York: John Wiley & Sons.

Loftus, E. F. (2005). A 30-year investigation of the malleability of memory. *Learning and Memory, 12*, 361–366.

Loftus, E. F., & Pickrell, J. E. (1995). The formation of false memories. *Psychiatry Annals, 25*, 720–25.

Pope, K. S., & Brown, L. S. (1996). *Recovered memories of abuse: Assessment, therapy, forensics*. Washington: American Psychological Association.

Widom, C. (1997). Accuracy of adult recollections of early childhood abuse. In J. D. Read & D. S. Lindsay (Eds.), *Recollections of trauma: Scientific evidence and clinical practice* (pp. 49–69). Nato Asi Series, Series A, Life Sciences, Vol. 291. New York: Plenum Press.

SUGGESTED READING

Davies, G. M., & Dalgleish, T. (Eds.). (2001). *Recovered memories: Seeking the middle ground*. Chichester, UK: John Wiley & Sons.

BRENDAN E. DEPUE
University of Colorado at Boulder

See also: **Child Sexual Abuse; Recovered Memories; Satanic Ritual Abuse**

FAMILY DEVELOPMENT, THEORIES OF

Family development theory focuses on the stress-induced changes that occur in families over time (White & Klein, 2008). Historically, family development theorists assumed that families move through deterministic, invariant numbers, types, and timing of stages over time consistent with ontogenetic stage theories of individual child development (e.g., Piaget's stages of cognitive development). For example, Duvall's (1957) widely-cited model defined family development in terms of eight developmental stages: (1) married couple without children, (2) childbearing families with the oldest child between birth and 30 months, (3) families with preschool children, (4) families with school-age children, (5) families with adolescent children, (6) launching families (first to last child is leaving home), (7) middle-age families ("empty nest" to retirement), and (8) aging families (retirement to death of both spouses). Whereas Duvall's theory assumes a traditional nuclear family, alternative stage theories describe greater variations in types of family structures (e.g., childless couples, single-parent families, stepfamilies, etc.), but still rely on universalistic assumptions about the number, types, and timing of stages (Laszoffy, 2002).

Beyond Universalistic Stage Theories

Recent advances in family development theory consider the tremendous diversity of family stress-induced changes over time and challenge universality assumptions, or the notion that all families experience similar transitions and stage processes over time (Laszloffy, 2002; White & Klein, 2008). Thus, theoretical refinements take into account different cultures and concomitant changing norms, the social and historical context of transitions in families, linkages of individual and family transitions with transitions in other social institutions (e.g., education, job, and career), intergenerational influences and interdependencies among families, and broad processes of transformation that do not rely upon universal and invariant stages. The two major conceptual frameworks that have driven these revisions in theories of family development are described next.

Systemic Family Development Model

Laszloffy (2002) proposed a systematic family development (SFD) model of family development that emphasizes the process of change from a systems perspective and focuses attention on the complex interdependencies of family changes across multiple generations. She argued that virtually all models of family development have two fundamental weaknesses, including the universality assumption and the bias toward a single generational perspective. The SFD model rejects the universality assumption on the grounds that stage classification systems are limited in their capacity to explain the number, variations, and timing of stressors that impact upon families and the concomitant adaptive or maladaptive transitions that occur in response to normative and non-normative stressful events. Laszloffy reports that most families experience the birth of a child. However, the pile-up of specific stressors coinciding with this birth is highly idiosyncratic among families across generations and in all cultures.

The SFD model emphasizes a common developmental process including the presence of stressors putting pressure on families to make transitions in family norms, roles, and relationships (Laszloffy, 2002). Coping resources and stress management strategies among individual families may determine whether the stressors lead to a crisis in family functioning.

The SFD model also assumes that family development involves changes and transitions across multiple generations. Family changes in one generation may influence adaptation to specific stressors in another generation. The death of a grandparent in the third generation may complicate child care for dual-career parents (second generation) experiencing the birth of a child (first generation) if those parents had been counting on that grandparent for child care services. Laszloffy (2002) elucidates how the labeling of stages often has adopted a single generation bias. For example, the launching stage focuses on the parental generation but ignores the adolescents or young adults who are leaving. She suggests that labeling the stages *launching* and *leaving* would better capture the transitions experienced by two generations.

Laszloffy (2002) uses the metaphor of a multilayered, round cake to illustrate the complex interdependencies of multiple generations in the family development process. The four layers of the cake may represent the four successive generations. At the first generational level, a young adult may be preparing to leave home for college,

the second generation of parents may be preparing to launch their son for college, the third generation of grandparents may have recently divorced and retired, and in the fourth generation the last living great-grandparent may have died. The patterns of change across generations may be diverse, and changes in one generation may influence changes and transitions in another. This metaphor also envisions the cake as revolving in a circular motion over time. This rotating process sheds old layers (older generations) and adds new layers (newer generations).

Family Life Course Development Framework

The family life course development framework (FLCDF) represents an evolution of conventional family development theory that includes an integration of individual life span theory and life course theory (White & Klein, 2008). Whereas family development theory focuses on families as they experience changes over time traversing through predictable and unpredictable life events and stages of the family life career, individual life span theory focuses on social processes including family dynamics that influence individual development, and life course theory, using an event history anaysis, examines how earlier events of family life (e.g., finishing education, starting a first job) influence later life events (White & Klein, 2008). White and Klein (2008) view all three schools of thought as having common features including (1) the influence of family factors on the ontogenetic development of individuals; (2) the impact of the passage of time on change within individuals and families; and (3) the conceptualization of family change within a broader framework of birth cohort, historical period, and age of individuals.

White and Klein describe basic assumptions of the FLCDF. First, change in families over time is inevitable. Family structures, the nature of interactions among family members, norms about family roles, and the behavior of individual family members change with the passage of time. Second, family interaction patterns and structure are affected by factors at multiple levels of analysis that may influence each other in multidirectional ways. Social norms of the larger society and norms of subcultures (e.g., race, social class), as well as interactions and internal rule development within individual families, may influence each other in complex ways. Family dyads or subsystems (e.g., marital, parent-child) may affect other dyads (e.g., sibling) in reciprocal ways and the behaviors of individual family members may affect and be affected by the functioning of specific family subsystems.

Third, the perception of the time often denies orderliness and is multidimensional. A given period of time may be perceived as short for an enjoyable event but long for a boring event. Thus, family experiences as a method of calculating time often abandon the calendar notion of time (e.g., it happened in 1995) in favor of chronicling family events (e.g., when a couple first got married, before a brother was born, after a sister became a parent, just after a grandfather died). Family events may be perceived as more strongly related than calendar dates. For example, when a couple first got married may be more closely linked to finishing school than to any calendar date (White, 1993). In regard to effects on family behavior, it may be the stage of family development that is more important than chronological age of the family member.

According to the FLCDF, family development is a group process regulated by social timing and sequencing norms. These norms vary from culture to culture. For example, premarital births are "off timing" in North America but an expected part of the mate selection process in Polynesian cultures (White & Klein, 2008). Adherence to the sequencing of stages (e.g., finishing education, getting a job, getting married, having a child) is more likely than adherence to a set amount of time between events. Moreover, sequencing of stages may be more important in explaining family behavior than timing (2008).

White and Klein contend that, if a family is out of sequence with social norms regulating the order of family events, the probability of later disruptions in family life is increased. In part, this is due to the importance of synchronization of family events (e.g., getting married, having a child) with norms regarding other social institutions including education (e.g., finishing college) and work (e.g., getting a job). Families who get out of sequence with one institution are more likely to be shifted out of sequence with norms guiding sequencing of other institutions, and most research shows negative consequences of asynchrony of life events across institutions (White & Klein, 2008). Social norms guide when life events are "on timing" or "off timing." Examples of "off timing" events include premarital births and giving birth to a child when a post-adolescent child is leaving home.

White (1991) suggested that the probability of a transition from one family stage to another varies with the current stage and the duration of time in that stage. For example, the probability of a transition to the stage of parenthood is dependent on the current stage (childless marriage) and the duration of time in that stage (probability increases up to five years and decreases thereafter). The effects of duration in a stage depend on the stage involved. For example, the longer the childrearing stage, the greater the likelihood that the family will begin launching children into adulthood (White & Klein, 2008), or the longer the marriage, the lower the probability that a divorce will occur.

Theories of family development have moved beyond universalistic assumptions that all families peregrinate through deterministic, invariant numbers, types, and timing of stages over time. Collectively, Laszloffy's (2002) SFD and White and Klein's (2008) FLCDF emphasize (1) the complexity in the variations, number, and timing of stressors that affect family development; (2) the multigenerational nature of family development; (3) that family changes over time are influenced by multiple factors at multiple levels of analysis; (4) that conformity to sequencing norms regarding family events may be important to family outcomes; (5) the importance of synchronization of family life events with those of other social institutions; and (6) that the probability of a transition from one family stage to another varies with both the current stage and amount of time spent in that stage.

REFERENCES

Duvall, E. (1957). *Family development*. Philadelphia: J.B. Lippincott.

Laszloffy, T. (2002). Rethinking family development theory: Teaching with the systemic family development (SFD) model. *Family Relations, 51*, 206–214.

White, J.M. (1991). *Dynamics of family development: The theory of family development*. New York: Guilford Press.

White, J.M., & Klein, D.M. (2008). *Family theories* (3rd ed.). Thousand Oaks, CA: Sage.

SUGGESTED READINGS

Aldous, J. (1990). Family development and the life course: Two perspectives on family change. *Journal of Marriage and the Family, 52*, 571–583.

Aldous, J. (1996). *Family careers: Rethinking the developmental perspective*. Thousand Oaks, CA: Sage.

Chibucos, T.R., Leite, R.W., & Weiss, D.L. (2005). *Readings in family theory*. Thousand Oaks, CA: Sage.

Klein, D.M., & Aldous, J. (Eds.). (1988). *Social stress and family development*. New York: Guilford Press.

White, J.M. (2004). *Advancing family theories*. Thousand Oaks, CA: Sage.

W. Glenn Clingempeel
Fayetteville State University

Scott W. Henggeler
Medical University of South Carolina

See also: Interpersonal Relationships; Parental Approaches

FAMILY THERAPY

Professional therapists, researchers, and other students of psychotherapy have long been curious about many questions relevant to the field: What constitutes a psychological problem, how could that problem be classified, what differentiates that problem from all others, what is the etiology of the problem, what are developmental sequelae of the problem, what is the most efficacious treatment approach, what is resilience, what is mental health, and many others. One particular question of interest has had to do with the unit identified as the patient. Whereas traditionally this unit was an individual, the emergence of the family therapy movement shifted that focus away from the individual and toward the family as the unit and the focus of study and treatment.

The family therapy movement began as a response to the excitement of some pioneers of this field who observed that contextual issues in the family have tremendous influence on individual functioning. They observed that treatment gains that had taken a long time to achieve in individual therapy were likely to be diminished when the individual patient was returned to his or her family context. Hence, they observed that treating the family, including contextual family issues such as power differentials, structural dynamics, and communication patterns (to name a few), could have a profound impact not only on the mental health of the identified patient, but on the health of the entire family.

The family therapy movement can be traced to three roots. First came the social work, marriage and family life education, and marriage counseling movement of the late 1800s and early 1900s (Kaslow, Kaslow, & Farber, 1999; Mirsalimi, Perleberg, Stovall, & Kaslow, 2003.) The second root was in clinical psychiatry, as many clinicians recognized that problems of their individual patients were better understood in the context of their current family and family of origin dynamics. The third root was in the general systems theory and communications theory.

While the pioneers in this field provided the philosophical and intellectual roots of the movement, a number of organizations and publications helped its growth (Kaslow, 2004; Kaslow et al, 1999; Mirsalimi et al., 2003). Of special note are six organizations: the National Council of Family Relations (NCFR), established in the late 1930s; the American Association of Marriage Counselors, which began in 1942 and was changed to the American Association for Marriage and Family Therapy (AAMFT) in the 1970s; the American Family Therapy Association, established in the mid-1970s and later changed to the American Family Therapy Academy (AFTA); the Division of Family Psychology (Division 41) of the American Psychological Association (APA), established in the mid 1980s; the International Family Therapy Association, established in 1987; and the International Academy of Family Psychology (IAFP), founded in 1990. These organizations have helped promote family therapy in the United States and around the world.

In the past decades since its establishment, the field of family therapy has undergone a number of changes and expansions. For example, new techniques of family therapy and integrated models have been proposed, empirical analyses to establish the efficacy of family therapy techniques have been conducted, ethical guidelines for the practice of family therapy have been established,

subspecialties of family therapy have emerged, and the field has become more sensitive to diversity issues pertaining to race, ethnicity, family structure, sexual orientation, and social class (Mirsalimi, et al, 2003).

Major family systems theories have several common underlying assumptions. First, an individual's behavior is affected by the family context and hence should be viewed and understood within that context; conversely, the individual affects the system and has the ability to cause change in the system. Second, the family is an evolving system in which individual members have interdependent relationships. Third, the family is a dynamic system that goes through changes and moves through different levels of organization and function in the life cycle of the individual and the family. Fourth, the family struggles to establish a balance between change and stability; often some members of the family exert effort to maintain homeostasis in the family while others put effort into causing change. Fifth, there exists a hierarchical structure in the family; this structure is defined by functional roles, implicit rules, degree of responsibility of family members, and family beliefs, rituals, and routines.

Components of the family structure are called family subsystems. These subsystems are maintained and defined by boundaries that can be flexible, rigid, or permeable. Healthy families have boundaries that are clear and are not crossed inappropriately. The subsystems can exert powerful dynamics through healthy or rigid alliances. Sixth, healthy families exhibit flexibility, good communication and problem solving skills, and the ability to utilize feedback in order to bring about positive change. And seventh, some dynamics are transmitted intergenerationally, and understanding of issues experienced by an individual, a couple, or a family is contingent upon careful examination of such intergenerational transmissions (Kaslow, 2004; Mirsalimi et al., 2003).

Kaslow and her colleagues (1999; Kaslow, 2004), in defining various schools of family therapy and identifying their primary treatment methods, provide the following typology: *transgenerational schools* (psychodynamically informed, Bowenian, contextual/relational, symbolic/experiential); *systems models* (communications, strategic, structural, systemic, brief and solution focused); *cognitive and behavioral models* (behavioral, functional, cognitive behavioral); *miscellaneous* (psychoeducational, narrative, social constructionist; integrative).

Some of the above models were proposed and developed by pioneers in the field of family therapy. For example, Ackerman (1938) was an early proponent of psychoanalytic family therapy. His theories view family dysfunction as a failure of role complementarity between family members, as a result of prejudicial scapegoating, and as a result of persistent and unresolved conflicts in the family. His approach to treatment involved disentangling interlocking pathologies among family members.

Carl Whitaker was a founder of experiential-humanistic family therapy (Whitaker & Bumberry, 1988). Whitaker believed in the primacy of choice and the potential of the family and its natural tendency toward growth. Central in this model of family therapy is the importance of here-and-now, the focus on the present as opposed to the past, the fostering of open communication, and the promotion of genuineness and authenticity in family relationships.

Jay Haley was the original theoretician behind strategic family therapy (Haley, 1976). Haley observed that maladaptive family sequences maintain problems that exist in families, and consistent, albeit unsuccessful attempts by family members to resolve such issues are the very source of problem maintenance. Hence, strategic family therapy, which is change oriented rather than growth or insight oriented, involves an active stance by the therapist who uses brief interventions with either the entire family, or a subset of the family, to cause change in maladaptive family interactional patterns.

Salvador Minuchin was the pioneer of structural family therapy (Minuchin, Lee, & Simon, 1996). According to this model of family therapy, healthy family structures allow for, and adapt to changes in structural dynamics; such changes are inevitable because the family changes and evolves with the passage of time. Hence, problematic family structures are viewed as those that are not well defined, are rigid and inflexible, and that do not promote family cohesion. Such problems manifest in the form of unhealthy boundaries, inappropriate alignments among family members, and power imbalances. The structural family therapist joins with the family to evaluate the family structure, to learn about boundaries, to assess the degree of inflexibility of the family in the presence of change or family stressors, the function that the symptomatic family member plays, the impact of contextual issues, and the adaptability of the family to developmental changes in the lifecycle of individuals and the family. The goal is to resolve the presenting problem through altering the family's conceptualization of the problem and through restructuring the family to allow more flexibility.

Murray Bowen was the developer of family-of-origin therapy, a form of transgenerational family therapy (Bowen, 1988). The main tenet of family-of-origin therapy is that dysfunctional patterns in current relationships have their roots in unhealthy family-of-origin dynamics that did not allow for differentiation of the self. If the family-of-origin did not allow for healthy differentiation, the individual was likely to be triangulated and to have found it difficult to express his or her thoughts and feelings in an appropriate manner. Such patterns are often manifestations of rigid relational dynamics that perpetuate across generations and are likely to find their way into current relationships. When they do, similar undifferentiated dynamics tend to manifest in current relationships. Therefore, the role of the therapist is to elucidate such dynamics for the individual, for a dyad, or for the family. This is often achieved through the use of a genogram, a graphic representation of family relational patterns across several generations. It is hypothesized that the awareness of such multigenerational patterns of undifferentiation will lead to better differentiation in current relationships, hence allowing for easier expression of thoughts and feelings; that, in turn, promotes better relationships in the family or a dyadic system.

In addition to the above, other schools of family therapy have made great contributions to the field. Among them are object relations family therapy (the currently dominant form of psychoanalytic family therapy), systemic-Milan family therapy, behavioral and cognitive behavioral approaches to family therapy, and psycho-educational family therapy. Also, several more recently proposed and evolving models of family therapy include narrative family therapy, solution-focused family therapy, solution-oriented family therapy, and postmodern, social constructionist, and integrative approaches (for a review see Mirsalimi, et al., 2003).

Not only have new theories of family therapy been proposed in recent years, but exciting frontiers in family therapy research and practice continue to emerge, as well. For example, there has been a movement toward empirically supported family therapy. One such approach is presented by Friedlander, Lambert, Escudero, and Cragun (2008), who propose a system of observing family therapy alliances (SOFTA) and utilize sequential analysis to examine therapist-client behavior in family therapy. While family therapy research continues to provide important information about the efficacy of certain family therapy techniques, some in the field have cautioned against logical positivistic research approaches that define the truth narrowly (Becvar & Becvar, 2006). Others have questioned certain operational definitions (e.g., what constitutes a family). Such healthy discussions continue in the field.

Family therapy is being utilized in a variety of settings and problem areas. For example, techniques of family therapy are being used to help families in which the medical or psychiatric condition of an individual has brought challenges to the entire family system (e.g., see Fredman, Baucom, Miklowitz, & Stanton, 2008). Family therapy is also being utilized in substance abuse treatment (e.g., see Robbins, Szapocznik, Dillon, Turner, Mitrani, & Feaster, 2008), and in the treatment of families plagued by family violence (e.g., see Pearl, 2008), to name a few.

Multicultural and culturally sensitive family therapies constitute another area of particular interest in contemporary family therapy. As the population of the United States becomes more ethnically and culturally diverse, the need for multicultural and culturally sensitive approaches becomes more evident. For example, it is important to ask whether the same set of family therapy approaches that are traditionally used with a Caucasian family with roots in the United States for several generations, would be effective with a family from Latin America that has recently immigrated to the United States. Additionally, are our conceptions of what constitutes healthy family dynamics universally accepted and practiced? This point becomes particularly meaningful when we consider that most Western industrial nations espouse beliefs that celebrate individuality and value individual freedoms over the interests of the group. Societies that are more group- and community-oriented might have a completely different set of values that dictate, among other things, how family members should relate to one another, and what constitutes appropriate boundaries. Special models and techniques need to be developed to address such cultural differences (see Flicker, Turner, Waldron, Brody, & Ozechowski, 2008; McGoldrick, Giordano, & Pearce, 1996; Nichols, 2004; Pearl, 2008).

It can be argued that the future of our species will be dependent on the health of our families. Healthier families produce healthier individuals and communities that can strive toward better communication, more acceptance, the ideals of freedom, and peace. Hence primary, secondary, and tertiary interventions with families should be promoted and utilized.

REFERENCES

Ackerman, N. W. (1938). The unity of the family. *Archives of Pediatrics, 55*, 51–62.

Becvar, D. S., & Becvar, R. J. (2006). *Family therapy: A systemic integration.* New York: Pearson Education.

Bowen, M. (1988). *Family therapy in clinical practice* (2nd ed.). Northvale, NJ: Jason Aronson.

Flicker, S. M., Turner, C. W., Waldron, H. B., Brody, J. L,, & Ozechowski, T. J. (2008). Ethnic background, therapeutic alliance, and treatment retention in functional family therapy with adolescents who abuse substances. *Journal of Family Psychology, 22*(1), 167–170.

Fredman, S. J., Baucom, D. H., Miklowitz, D. J., & Stanton, S. E. (2008). Observed emotional involvement and overinvolvement in families of patients with bipolar disorder. *Journal of Family Psychology, 22*(1), 71–79.

Friedlander, M. L., Lambert, J. E., Escudero, V., & Cragun, C. (2008). How do therapists enhance family alliances? Sequential analysis of therapist-client behavior in two contrasting cases. *Psychotherapy: Theory, Research, Practice, Training, 45*(1), 75–87.

Haley, J. (1976). *Problem-solving therapy.* San Francisco: Jossey-Bass.

Kaslow, F. W. (2004). Family therapy. In W. E. Craighead & C. B. Nemeroff (Eds.), *The concise Corsini encyclopedia of psychology and behavioral science* (3rd ed., pp. 362–364). Hoboken, NJ: John Wiley & Sons, Inc.

Kaslow, N. J., Kaslow, F. W., & Farber, E. W. (1999). Theories and techniques of marital and family therapy. In M. B. Sussman, S. K. Steinmetz, & G. W. Peterson (Eds.), *Handbook of marriage and the family* (2nd ed., pp. 767–793). New York: Plenum Press.

McGoldrick, M., Giordano, J., & Pearce, J. K. (1996). *Ethnicity and family therapy.* New York: Guilford Press.

Minuchin, S., Lee, W. Y., & Simon, G. M. (1996). *Mastering family therapy: Journeys of growth and transformation.* New York: John Wiley & Sons.

Mirsalimi, H., Perleberg, S. H., Stoval, E. L., & Kaslow, N. J. (2003). Family psychotherapy. In G. Stricker, T. A. Widiger, & I. B. Weiner (Eds.), *Handbook of psychology: Clinical psychology, Vol. 8* (pp. 367–387). Hoboken, NJ: John Wiley & Sons.

Nichols, W. C. (2004). *Family therapy around the world: A festschrift for Florence W. Kaslow.* Binghamton, NY: The Haworth Press.

Pearl, E. S. (2008). Parent-child interaction theory with an immigrant family exposed to domestic violence. *Clinical Case Studies, 7*(1), 25–41.

Robbins, M. S., Szapocznik, J., Dillon, F. R., Turner, C. W., Mitrani, V. B., & Feaster, D. J. (2008). The efficacy of structural ecosystems theory with drug-abusing/dependent African American and Hispanic American adolescents. *Journal of Family Psychology, 22*(1), 51–61.

Whitaker, C. A., & Bumberry, W. M. (1988). *Dancing with the family: A symbolic-experiential approach.* New York: Brunner/Mazel.

HAMID MIRSALIMI
Argosy University/Atlanta

See also: **Couples Therapy; Marriage Counseling**

FEAR

Fear may be the most important emotion for the survival of the human species. The experience of fear is the immediate subjective experience of apprehension marked by activation of the fight or flight response. The experience of fear is best understood on the basis of its principle function. According to Seligman (1971), "the great majority of phobias are about object(s) of natural importance to the survival of the species." In the most severe of circumstances (e.g., in the presence of a fast-approaching predator), fear activates the organism to flee or battle for its life. A less severe illustration of fear function is seen in day-to-day social interactions in which individuals avoid saying or doing embarrassing things in order to prevent social rejection or maintain companionship.

Fear is not a lump (Rachman, 1990), meaning that it cannot be conceptualized as a single entity and must instead be studied as a multidimensional construct and as a collection of related phenomena that differ depending on the experience and on the individual. There are three dimensions of fear involving physiological, behavioral, and cognitive processes (Borkovec, 1976). One or more of these dimensions help characterize an experience as a fearful one. In some cases all three are present in comparable amounts, but in some cases the three dimensions are desynchronized and disproportionate. Thus, the subjective nature of fear can be different in different individuals (Rachman, 1978).

Physiology

Much of the processing of fearful situations is carried out in the limbic system. This is due in large part to the necessity of rapid processing and responding to threatening stimuli (Hope, 1996). Information is first processed in the amygdala where it is then transferred to the basal ganglia for motor processing and then the frontal cortex. In cases where immediate responding is required, the information bypasses further processing and is projected directly from the amygdala to the brain stem.

Changes in the sympathetic nervous system are the most common psychophysiological indices of fearful responding. Activation of the sympathetic nervous system helps the organism protect itself from danger. Increased heart rate, respiration, and perspiration, as well as decreased gastrointestinal function and vascular constriction, are all common changes in the sympathetic nervous system. These autonomic changes are not all required in order for fear to be present, but they are indices that are commonly associated with fearful responding (Rachman, 1990).

Behavior

The acts of escape and avoidance are the most common behavioral indices of fear and represent the most direct survival function. Avoidance is manifest in multiple forms, from overt observable behaviors (e.g., fleeing or refusing to enter a room) to more covert behaviors (e.g., engaging in ritualistic safety behaviors such as hand washing). The motivation of these behaviors is to thwart harm to the self. Although avoidance is the most common behavior associated with fear, the act of freezing is sometimes seen in extremely fear-provoking situations, such as panic attacks or imminent death.

Cognitive

Research on the cognitive dimension of fear has led to a greater understanding of its role in the etiology and maintenance of fear. The most direct form of assessment is through standardized psychological tests. In addition, research on information processing has revealed distinct cognitive biases for fear relevant information (Hope, 1996). Most people display a propensity to allocate large amounts of their attentional resources to fear related stimuli (e.g. threatening words, images, or sounds). Fearful individuals show even greater attentional biases, interpret information related to their fears as more threatening, and evidence biases in memory regarding threatening information.

Acquisition of Fear

Conditioning theory was the dominant explanation of fear acquisition for much of the twentieth century. Mowrer's (1960) two-stage model of fear acquisition and maintenance asserted that fear is first established through classical conditioning and is then maintained via avoidant behaviors. One major limitation of Mowrer's theory was its inability to explain why some fears were so much more common and easily trained (Rachman, 1990). These observations led to the development and support of the biological preparedness theory of fear acquisition (Seligman, 1971). This theory claimed that humans (and other animals) are more prone to acquire fears of certain objects (e.g., spiders) in comparison to others (e.g., sheep) as an evolutionary function. Subsequent study of this theory has yielded mixed results, but the fundamental tenets still play an important role in modern learning theories.

Classical conditioning theory was eventually replaced by more advanced and complete theories of fear acquisition in order to explain indirect or vicarious acquisition of fear (Rachman, 1990). Modern theories of fear acquisition attest that it is possible to acquire fear through three pathways: direct conditioning, vicarious experience, and information transfer (Rachman, 1978, 1990). Vicarious learning results from the modeling of fearful behavior or through the observation of threat or harm impacting others. Fear can also be acquired through exposure to fear-relevant information and subsequent cognitive appraisals of threat and danger. Currently, no one theory explains all of the ways that individuals can acquire a fear. However, substantial improvements have been made in complex models that go into much greater detail to better explain fear acquisition, especially the fear seen in individuals with anxiety disorders (see Foa & Kozak, 1986).

Modification of Fear

The reduction of fear can also occur through multiple pathways. Basic and clinical research have focused largely on the use of behavioral modification for the reduction of fear, specifically exposure techniques. Repeated exposure to feared stimuli in the absence of real harm reduces the intensity of physiological responding through the process of habituation (Barlow, 2002). Oftentimes, appraisals of threat associated with the feared stimuli are corrected and avoidant behaviors extinguished with these techniques. Fear modification can also occur without ever coming into contact with the feared stimuli. Examples of this include exposure to corrective information (e.g., cognitive therapy) about perceived threats, corrective modeling, and imaginal exposures (Foa & Kozak, 1986).

Related Emotions

The experiences of panic, fear, and anxiety are often times used interchangeably in research literature. Panic is a basic and possibly innate alarm system that human beings sometimes call fear (Barlow, 2002). Fear is a functional reaction that results in the flight response to escape and avoid harm. Anxiety is future oriented, usually perceptual, and intended to maintain vigilance for danger (Barlow, 2002). Anxiety may incorporate multiple emotions and result in the experience of distress. Several other emotions co-occur with anxiety and present in ways that are analogous to fear, the most germane of which is disgust. Both fear and disgust mediate several anxiety disorders, such as phobias and some forms of obsessive-compulsive disorder.

REFERENCES

Barlow, D. (2002). *Anxiety and its disorders: The nature and treatment of anxiety and panic* (2nd ed.). New York: Guilford Press.

Borkovec, T. D. (1976). Physiological and cognitive processes in the regulation of anxiety. In J. E. Schwartz & D. Shapiro (Eds.), *Consciousness and self-regulation: Advances in research* (pp. 261–309). New York: Plenum Press.

Foa, E. B., & Kozak, M. J. (1986). Emotional processing of fear: Exposure to corrective information. *Psychological Bulletin, 99,* 20–35.

Hope, D. (1996). *Nebraska symposium on motivation, 1995: Perspectives on anxiety, panic, and fear.* Lincoln: University of Nebraska Press.

Mowrer, H. O. (1960). *Learning theory and behavior.* New York: John Wiley & Sons.

Rachman, S. J. (1978). Human fears: A three systems analysis. *Scandanavian Journal of Behaviour Therapy, 7,* 237–245.

Rachman, S. (1990). *Fear and courage* (2nd ed.). New York: W. H. Freeman.

Seligman, M. E. (1971). Phobias and preparedness. *Behavior Therapy, 2,* 307–320.

SUGGESTED READING

Kleinknecht, R. A. (1986). The anxious self: Diagnosis and treatment of fears and phobias. New York: Human Sciences Press.

JEFFREY M. LOHR
THOMAS G. ADAMS
University of Arkansas

See also: Anxiety; Emotions

FECHNER'S LAW

Gustav T. Fechner (1801–1887), professor of physics at the University of Leipzig, sought to measure the mind quantitatively. In approaching this task he studied stimuli and the sensations they aroused. His interest was in ascertaining how sensations changed with changing stimulation. While lying in bed on the morning of October 22, 1850, he conceived the essential idea of what was later to be called Fechner's law. In his subsequent derivation of the law (which appears at the beginning of the second volume of *Elemente der Psychophysik*), he began with Weber's law (that the just-noticeable difference in stimulation is a constant proportion of the stimulus magnitude, or JND=kI) and the assumption that the sensation (R) of a stimulus is the cumulative sum of equal sensation increments. Translating this into differential form, he started with $dR = dI/I$ and integrated, under the assumption that R = 0 at absolute threshold $(I_\circ)$, to get the equation R = $c\log (I/I_\circ)$.

This equation is Fechner's law, where R is the sensation magnitude, *c* is a constant (which depends on the logarithmic base and the Weber ratio), I is the stimulus increasing intensity, and I0 is the absolute threshold intensity. The law states that sensations follow a negatively accelerated increasing (logarithmic) curve. For example, the increase in brightness experienced in going from 1 to 10 lamps would be the same as the increase in brightness in going from 10 to 100 lamps. This is a special case of the general relationship, algebraically derivable from his law, that stimulus magnitude $(I_\circ)$ is required to generate a sensation midway in magnitude to those sensations generated by stimuli of magnitudes $I\alpha$ and Ic is exactly equal to the square root of the product $I\alpha$ and Ic (i.e., the geometric mean). Sensation magnitude increases arithmetically when stimulus magnitude increases geometrically.

In order to work with his formulation, Fechner needed to know the value of the absolute threshold, $I_\circ$. In the first volume in *Elemente der Psychophsik* Fechner describes methods for measuring differential sensitivity to stimuli (and later suggests their application to absolute sensitivity). These are the classical psychophysical methods that have been used by psychologists and others to determine thresholds (absolute and difference) for the various senses. They have also been used (with modifications) for clinical assessment of hearing, vision, and (to a limited extent) other senses.

Fechner's law influences everyday life through applications in acoustics. A standard measure of sound is the sound pressure level (SPL) scale defined by the (Fecherian) equation SPL = $20 \log (P/P_\circ)$, where P is the pressure of the sound being measured and $P_\circ$ is the absolute threshold pressure. The volume control used in radio and television receivers (among other audio devices) is a variable resistor that has a logarithmic (or approximately logarithmic) variation in resistance in order to provide a positively accelerating audio amplitude output to counteract the negatively accelerated sensation response specified by Fechner's law, thereby resulting in a fairly even increase in loudness as the amplitude in increased by adjusting the volume control.

REFERENCES

Boring, E.G. (1942). *Sensation and perception in the history of experimental psychology.* New York: Appleton-Century-Crofts.

Fechner, G.T. (1964). *Elemente der Psychophysik.* Amsterdam, The Netherlands: E. J. Bonnet. (Original work published 1860.)

Fechner, G.T. (1966). Elements of psychophysics. In D. H. Howes & E. G. Boring (Eds.), *Elements of psychophysics* (trans. H. E. Adler). New York: Holt, Rinehart, and Winston. (Original work published 1860.)

Marks L.E., & Gescheider, G.A. (2002). Psychophysical scaling. In H. Pashler (Ed.-in-Chief) & J. Wixted (Vol. Ed.), *Stevens' handbook of experimental psychology, Vol. 4: Methodology in experimental psychology* (pp. 91–138). New York: John Wiley & Sons.

Uttal, W.R. (1973). *The psychobiology of sensory coding.* New York: Harper & Row.

GEORGE H. ROBINSON
University of North Alabama

See also: Perception; Psychophysics

FEMININITY

Within the psychological literature, femininity is a construct broad in scope with no single agreed-upon definition. It is important to note, however, that psychological femininity, as a type of gender expression, is separate and distinct from female secondary sex characteristics, core gender identity (i.e., one's self-definition regarding gender status), and being biologically female. Females or males can exhibit femininity to a greater or lesser degree, or not at all. Although femininity is thought to be more often expressed by females, there is variability on this dimension. Thus, femininity and identification as female are related, but not identical.

Femininity can be manifest both physically and socially, and it can be expressed through traits, role behaviors, physical characteristics, and even occupations. In the United States, common physical expressions of femininity include the application of make-up, long hair, and certain styles of dress. A nonexhaustive list of social expressions associated with femininity include warmth, communality, and emotionality. Expressions of femininity that are encouraged or condoned are culturally defined and vary according to time period, location, and context. Femininity thus entails more than just acting like a woman; it requires acting like a particular type of woman as prescribed by societal norms.

Origins of Femininity

Various theories have been offered to explain the origins of femininity. Three current views have grown out of influential theoretical traditions in psychology: feminist psychoanalysis, social constructionism, and evolutionary psychology.

According to feminist psychoanalysis, gender and displays of femininity come from the differences in the relationships that girls and boys have with their parents, which lead boys to identify with their fathers and girls to identify with their mothers. This identification leads to the development and reproduction of masculine and feminine traits. According to this theory, gender becomes fixed once this identification occurs (Chodorow, 1978). Although feminist psychoanalysis attempts to explain femininity and masculinity in terms of dynamic internal mechanisms, it also problematically confounds sex and gender and includes the assumption of heterosexuality as a normative feature of femininity.

Social constructionism focuses on factors that shape gender and gender expression through an individual's practice of gender in interactions with others (West & Zimmerman, 1987). Social constructionism argues that gender is continually enacted in the behavioral expression of femininity and/or masculinity; thus, it is continually evolving over the course of one's life. It is through the performance of gender that one's own sense of gender and gender self-presentation are created and sustained. Social constructionism differs from other social explanations of gender and femininity, such as those that emphasize the acquisition of gender-specific behaviors in early childhood (Ruble, Martin, & Berenbaum, 2006) or role theories that view femininity as a by-product of social tasks and positions conventionally viewed as women's domain (e.g., Eagly, 1987). Although social constructionism offers an explanation as to how people create gender at an interactional level, it is criticized for not articulating how biological factors contribute to gender expression.

Finally, evolutionary psychology discusses the origins of gender and gender expression in terms of sexual selection and innate qualities that exist in order to promote and facilitate reproduction. Thus, femininity is construed as an adaptive, biological development that aids in reproduction and child-rearing (Buss, 1999). In the case of evolutionary psychology, gender is viewed as being fixed at birth. Evolutionary psychology is criticized for downplaying the profound effects of social and cultural context on behavior. Indeed, one of the major criticisms of evolutionary theory is that it is unsuccessful in acknowledging variations in gender expression across culture and time.

Femininity and Society

Femininity is commonly viewed as being complementary to masculinity. The problem with a complementary framework, however, is that one side always becomes the standard with which the other is compared (Shields, 1975). Furthermore, this framework ignores the implicit power differentials between women and men in society. The issue of complementarity is significant due to the qualities and social meanings society has attached to femininity and masculinity. Masculinity connotes competence, agency, sexual prowess (heterosexual), and strength; in complementary form, femininity is associated with warmth, communality, sexual passivity, and weakness. In the United States, traits associated with femininity tend to be devalued because they are conceptualized as being incompatible with the competence necessary to successfully participate in jobs and careers in valued (that is, masculine) domains.

Because femininity is often stereotypically associated with being female, societal devaluation of femininity can underlie various forms of gender inequality, such as job discrimination. Such discrimination can arise from women being perceived either as too feminine, and thus not sufficiently competent for the job, or as not feminine enough. For example, in the now famous *Price-Waterhouse v. Hopkins* case, Ann Hopkins sued the firm for which she worked after not making partner. Although she was indeed qualified for the position, the firm believed she was lacking in what they viewed as important expressions of femininity, such as wearing make-up. *Price-Waterhouse v. Hopkins* demonstrates that, although femininity is often devalued in job settings, failure to comply with norms of femininity for women can also lead to negative outcomes. People who do not meet gender-consistent standards of femininity (or masculinity), at least publicly, are labeled as gender deviants, and they face potential negative consequences in the form of economic and/or social sanctions (Rudman & Fairchild, 2004).

Conceptualization and Measurement in Psychological Research

The field of psychology has a long and problematic history of conceptualizing and measuring femininity. At one point, femininity was believed to be a stable framework through which to measure personality, and it was conceptualized as one pole of a unidimensional continuum. Thus, if someone scored high on psychological femininity, they would necessarily score low on masculinity. Self-report instruments adopting this conceptualization of femininity and masculinity began with Terman and Miles' Attitude Interest Analysis Survey (AIAS; 1936). Items on measures such as these were mostly concerned with education

level, projected emotional reactions, issues of morality, and interest in various careers. These measures tended not to predict behavior and were essentially measuring people's conformity to gender norms.

Later, the bipolar notion of femininity and masculinity was abandoned for an approach that conceptualized femininity and masculinity as two independent continua. Adopting this conceptualization, the Bem Sex Role Inventory (BSRI) consisted of various female, male, or androgynous traits (Bem, 1981). However, this scale also failed to predict behavior.

Currently, measures of femininity in the area of social and personality psychology are used to study stereotypic views of women and men, that is, sex differences and similarities regarding cognitive abilities, traits, and social behaviors, as well as self-reported gender expression and gender identity. While the BSRI is still in use, another contemporary measure of femininity (and masculinity) is the Personal Attributes Questionnaire (PAQ; Spence & Helmreich, 1978). Similar to other measures of femininity, the PAQ is a self-report measure of how self-characteristic people find various traits. Higher scores on femininity are characterized by expressive traits and higher scores on masculinity are characterized by instrumental traits. While current measures attempt to avoid the error of over-simplifying femininity as that which females do, there is still debate surrounding what it is the PAQ and BSRI actually measure.

Though femininity is not simple to conceptualize or capture, it is useful in studying gender identity, gender stereotypes, and society's socialization and treatment of women and men more generally. That said, when measuring this construct, it is crucial to take into consideration the limitations of the available psychological tools. Although measures of femininity may never yield the insight into human behavior originally hoped for by early psychologists, such measures could certainly continue to shed light on relations between society, gender, and power.

REFERENCES

Bem, S. L. (1981). Gender schema theory: A cognitive account of sex typing. *Psychological Review, 88*, 354–364.

Buss, D. M. (1999). *Evolutionary psychology: The new science of the mind*. Boston: Allyn & Bacon.

Chodorow, N. J. (1978). *The reproduction of mothering: Psychoanalysis and the sociology of gender*. Berkeley: University of California Press.

Eagly, A. H. (1987). *Sex differences in social behavior: A social-role interpretation*. Hillsdale, NJ: Lawrence Erlbaum.

Ruble, D. N., Martin, C. L., & Berenbaum, S. A. (2006). Gender development. In W. Damon (Series Ed.) & N. Eisenberg

(Vol. Ed.), *Handbook of child psychology* (6th ed., Vol. 3, pp. 858–932). Hoboken, NJ: John Wiley & Sons.

Rudman, L. A., & Fairchild, K. (2004). Reactions to counterstereotypic behavior: The role of backlash in cultural stereotype maintenance. *Journal of Personality and Social Psychology, 87,* 157–176.

Shields, S. A. (1975). Functionalism, Darwinism, and the psychology of women: A study in social myth. *American Psychologist, 30,* 739–754.

Spence, J. T., & Helmreich, R. L. (1978). *Masculinity and femininity: Their psychological dimensions, correlates, and antecedents.* Austin, TX: University of Texas Press.

West, C., & Zimmerman, D. H. (1987). Doing gender. *Gender & Society, 1,* 125–151.

SUGGESTED READINGS

Deaux, K. (1987). Psychological constructions of masculinity and femininity. In J. M. Reinisch, L. A. Rosenblum, & S. A. Sanders. (Eds.), *Masculinity/femininity: Basic perspectives* (pp. 289–303). New York: Oxford University Press.

Lewin, M. (1984). Psychology measures femininity and masculinity 2: From "13 gay men" to the instrumental-expressive distinction. In M. Lewin (Ed.), *In the shadow of the past: Psychology portrays the sexes* (pp. 179–204). New York: Columbia University Press.

EMILY E. GOOD
STEPHANIE A. SHIELDS
Pennsylvania State University

See also: Bem Sex Role Inventory; Gender Roles; Psychology of Women

FERSTER, CHARLES B. (1922–1981)

Charles B. Ferster received the BS from Rutgers University, and the PhD in 1950 from Columbia, where he studied under such well-known behaviorists as Fred S. Keller and William N. Schoenfeld. He served as research scientist at Yerkes Laboratories in Orange Park, FL, at Harvard University, and at the Indiana University School of Medicine. He then became professor of psychology at Georgetown University and then at the American University in Washington, D.C., where he remained until his death in 1981.

Throughout his career Ferster was dedicated to a behavioristic approach to psychology. His writings and research ranged from basic behavioral research to the applications of a behavioral approach to such areas as education and clinical psychology. With B. F. Skinner, Ferster published the results of a long research project in

Schedules of Reinforcement (1957). This work demonstrated the powerful control that various schedules of positive reinforcement could have over the behavior of lower animals such as the pigeon. With Mary C. Perrott he published *Behavior Principles,* which involved the application of the principles of operant conditioning to various species of animals, including man. Other applications of operant conditioning principles involved the modification of the behavior in autistic children.

In the 1950s researchers in operant conditioning often had difficulty in getting their research published in the current journals in experimental psychology, because their methodology involved using small numbers of subjects rather than large groups. As a result Ferster initiated the idea of a new journal to be published under the auspice of SEAB. *The Journal of the Experimental Analysis of Behavior,* which was devoted to the publication of research using operant conditioning techniques, began in 1958. Following its founding, Ferster became the journal's Executive Editor. During the 1960s, Ferster was one of the first scholars to present a behavioral model of Major Depressive Disorder.

SUGGESTED READINGS

Ferster, C. B., & Perrott, M.C. (1968). *Behavior principles.* New York: Appleton-Century-Crofts.

Ferster, C. B., & Skinner, B.F. (1957). *Schedules of reinforcement.* New York: Appleton-Century-Crofts.

RALPH W. LUNDIN
Wheaton, IL

FESTINGER, LEON (1919–1989)

Leon Festinger received his bachelor's degree from the College of the City of New York, in 1939. He then attended the State University of Iowa, receiving the M.A. and the PhD (1942). There Festinger came under the influence of Kurt Lewin's theories and developed them further, earning a reputation in social psychology.

Festinger's major contributions included an expansion of cognitive dissonance theory, social comparison theory, and social network theory. According to cognitive dissonance, people whose behavior is in discord with their thoughts will either structure their thoughts to comport with behavior, or vice versa. Because of psychological pressures toward uniformity, individuals compare their cognitions with others, seeking to convince others of their own position or abandoning their own thoughts for the views of others. A person, for example, who feels hot in a room and wonders whether it is due to a fever or the room temperature, will inquire of others (provided there is no thermometer in the room). Thus social comparison drives us to convert others to our own opinions, or else yield to theirs.

Festinger's books include his classic *A Theory of Cognitive Dissonance: Conflict, Decision, and Dissonance; Theory and Experiment in Social Communications* (with others); *Research Methods in the Behavioral Science* (with D. Katz); *Deterrents and Reinforcement* (with D. H. Lawrence); *When Prophecy Fails* (with H. W. Riecken and S. Schachter); and *Social Pressures in Informal Groups* (with S. Scachter and K. Back).

Before going to the New School for Social Research in 1968, Festinger was at the University of Rochester (1943–1945), M.I.T. (1945–1948), the University of Michigan (1948–1951), the University of Minnesota (1951–1955), and Stanford University (1955–1968).

SUGGESTED READINGS

Festinger, L. (1957). *A theory of cognitive dissonance.* Evaston, IL: Row, Peterson.

Festinger, L., Schachter, S., & Black, K. (1948). *Social pressures in informal groups.* Cambridge, MA: MIT Press.

Festinger, L., Schachter, S., & Black, K. (1950). *Social pressures in informal groups: A study of human factors in housing.* Palo Alto, CA: Stanford University Press.

STAFF

FETAL ALCOHOL SYNDROME

Fetal alcohol syndrome (FAS) is recognized by the World Health Organization as the leading cause of environment-related birth defects and mental retardation in the western world. It results from prenatal alcohol exposure, the consequences of which fall along a continuum ranging from subtle neurodevelopmental and behavioral manifestations to FAS, the most serious outcome. Recently, the term fetal alcohol spectrum disorder (FASD) was coined to encompass all the terms that describe alcohol-related defects, including FAS (Sokol, Delaney, & Nordstrom, 2003). Other terms, such as fetal alcohol effects (FAE), partial FAS (pFAS), alcohol-related neurodevelopmental disorder (ARND), and alcohol-related birth defects (ARBD) describe other effects within the spectrum.

A diagnosis of FAS usually requires a confirmed history of maternal alcohol exposure, evidence of facial dysmorphology (distinctive facial features), growth retardation, and central nervous system (CNS) dysfunction. The "face of FAS" consists of short palpebral fissures (i.e., small eye slits), a smooth philtrum (i.e., the groove between the nose and the mouth), and a flat upper lip. Research

employing magnetic resonance brain imaging techniques has revealed that FAS-related neurological deficits are uncorrelated with facial abnormalities (Bookstein, Sampson, Connor, & Striessguth, 2002). Consequently, children without the distinctive morphological features may be as severely impaired in functional skills as someone with the full range of diagnostic criteria; however, because they may not display any facial deformities, their impairments can easily go unnoticed by healthcare practitioners and legal officials.

The diagnosis of FAS is a complex issue, because a panoply of conditions—such as attention deficit hyperactivity disorder (ADHD), learning disability, and conduct disorder, as well as mood and personality disorders—frequently affect individuals with FAS. Sometimes children with FAS are misdiagnosed with oppositional personality disorder. Early detection is essential to improving the outcome of individuals with FAS, because the facial anomalies tend to become less salient with time and may vary across ethnic groups. However, parents, teachers, and physicians often lack the expertise necessary to identify children with FAS. As a result of these complications, the accurate detection of the syndrome involves the concerted effort of a multidisciplinary team of trained professionals.

Several factors are thought to contribute to the onset of FAS. Although binge drinking and heavy drinking, which tend to make blood alcohol levels peak rapidly, are the drinking patterns most likely to result in FAS, no specific amount of alcohol intake has been deemed safe. The risk of functional impairment in the fetus increases when a pregnant woman drinks five or more drinks at a time at least once a week, and this risk increases with the quantity and frequency of consumption. Furthermore, the risk of birth anomalies increases two- to fivefold when the mother is older than 30 (O'Leary, 2004).

Although the incidence of FAS is greater in Aboriginal and African-American populations, there exists no empirical evidence indicative of an ethnicity-specific genetic vulnerability to FAS. Rather, it is malnutrition, lack of prenatal care, abuse, smoking, drug use, and stress—an array of environmental factors usually associated with a low socioeconomic status—that are most predictive of the development of FAS following prenatal exposure to alcohol (Abel & Hannigan, 1995). In addition to environmental factors, individuals differ with respect to their sensitivity to alcohol. Sensitivity is a function of the type of alcohol dehydrogenase—the enzyme that breaks down alcohol into acetaldehyde—that an individual possesses. Two individuals exposed to the same dosage of the drug will be differentially affected as a result of the rate at which their respective enzyme decomposes alcohol molecules (O'Leary, 2004).

Alcohol is a potent teratogen that hinders the development of the exposed fetus in several ways. The two mechanisms most harmful to cells are hypoxia, which occurs when alcohol in the bloodstream constricts the umbilical cord and thus reduces the flow of oxygen to the fetus, and oxidative stress, in which highly unstable free-radical formations attack the membrane of neighboring cells and lead to mitochondrial dysfunction, cell damage, or cell death. Furthermore, exposure to alcohol during the first trimester can severely disrupt the development of glial cells that typically assist neurons in their migration. Consequently, many neurons lose their way and settle in an improper location, thereby affecting their function (Abel & Hannigan, 1995). In the second and third trimesters of gestation, which is a crucial time for the formation of synapses, alcohol blocks glutamate receptors and activates GABA receptors, causing the death of millions of neurons, mostly in the forebrain. Finally, alcohol delays the development of the serotonin system, thus hindering brain maturation (Welch-Carre, 1995).

The negative effects of alcohol on developing brain structures are reflected behaviorally. Specifically, the FAS brain has been associated with reports of microcephaly, enlarged ventricles, cortical thinning, and reduced white and gray matter, all of which are linked to the low to low average range of intellectual functioning (i.e., IQ ≤ 70, or 70–90) (Mattson, Schoenfeld, & Riley, 2001). Moreover, there is evidence of partial or full agenesis, distortion, or displacement of the corpus callosum, the large bundle of nerve fibers that allows communication between the two hemispheres of the brain. The callosal damage seen in individuals with FAS is consistent with the impairments in attention, learning, verbal memory, and executive control that they often exhibit.

The size of the basal ganglia, and specifically the caudate nucleus, may also be reduced in alcohol-exposed individuals. This group of nerve cell nuclei is linked to motor abilities and cognitive functions, both of which often fail individuals with FAS. Additionally, a small cerebellar vermis, hippocampus, and amygdala may contribute to the many deficits in learning, balance, coordination, memory, and emotional regulation associated with FAS. Finally, alcohol appears to affect dopamine binding and levels of serotonin, which could possibly explain the attention and mood problems observed in alcohol-exposed individuals (Mattson et al., 2001).

The detrimental effects of alcohol are reflected at each stage of life. More specifically, individuals with FAS are more likely than their nonexposed counterparts to have difficulty learning during the school years, to increase their alcohol use in adolescence, to develop a dependence on alcohol in young adulthood, and to suffer from a diagnosable mental disorder in adulthood (Streissguth, Barr, Kogan, & Bookstein, 1997).

More generally, however, individuals with FASD display dysmaturity. In other words, they function socially, emotionally, or cognitively below their chronological age level. They may also exercise poor judgment, because they have difficulty planning, prioritizing, and understanding what is expected of them. Furthermore, due to impairments in executive functioning, many individuals cannot live independently and, most importantly, get lost at one level or another of the criminal justice system. More specifically, their impulsivity and inability to grasp cause and effect relationships render individuals with FAS likely to commit repeat offences and show no remorse. Moreover, the widespread ignorance and lack of awareness of FAS among police officers, lawyers, and judges exacerbate these vulnerable individuals' legal predicaments (Moore & Green, 2004).

The secondary disabilities associated with FAS—such as a having a disrupted school experience, being confined in an institution or prison, having difficulty staying employed, and being unable to live independently—are preventable in theory, when appropriate support is provided. Protective factors include living in a stable and nurturing home, not being a victim of violence, having an IQ below 70, having been diagnosed before the age of 6, and having the facial features associated with FAS. These factors could prevent or at least reduce the frequency of secondary disabilities because they are visible to the people around the affected person and early intervention and accommodations are consequently more likely to be put in place (Streissguth et al., 1997).

FAS is a lifelong disorder, and the objectives of treatment are accordingly to reduce symptoms and increase the individual's ability to function, rather than to achieve a complete relief from symptoms. Interventions for individuals with FAS are scarce and not well documented. They often resemble treatment for ADHD, because they include prescribing stimulant drugs and limiting the number of distractions present in the child's learning and home environments. It is important to keep in mind that individuals with FAS may have specific additional psychological and physical health needs that must also be addressed in the course of treatment.

The most effective prevention tool, however, is to raise awareness among the public, health care practitioners, and government officials. This can be achieved, in part, by educating physicians and sensitizing them to the threat of FAS, by legislating the use of warning labels on alcoholic products, and by shifting attitudes away from normative drinking during pregnancy. While researchers will of course continue to seek ways to reduce the detrimental effects of alcohol, these preventive measures would help ensure that more children receive an accurate diagnosis. In turn, these children could receive treatment early enough to permit the most favorable prognosis.

REFERENCES

Abel, E. L., & Hannigan, J. H. (1995). Maternal risk factors in fetal alcohol syndrome: Provocative and permissive influences. *Neurotoxicology and Teratology, 17,* 445–462.

Bookstein, F. L., Sampson, P. D., Connor, P. D., & Streissguth, A. P. (2002). Midline corpus callosum as a neuroanatomical focus of fetal alcohol damage. *The Anatomical Record, 269*, 162–174.

Mattson, S. N., Schoenfeld, A. M., & Riley, E. P. (2001). Teratogenic effects of alcohol on brain and behavior. *Alcohol Research & Health, 25*, 185–191.

Moore, T. E., & Green, M. (2004). Fetal alcohol spectrum disorder (FASD): A need for closer examination by the criminal justice system. *Criminal Reports, 19*, 99–108.

O'Leary, C. M. (2004). Fetal alcohol syndrome: Diagnosis, epidemiology, and developmental outcomes. *Journal of Paediatrics and Child Health, 40*, 2–7.

Sokol, R. J., Delaney-Black, V., & Nordstrom, B. (2003). Fetal alcohol spectrum disorder. *Journal of the American Medical Association, 290*(22), 2996–2999.

Streissguth, A., Barr, H., Kogan, J., & Bookstein, F. (1997). Primary and secondary disabilities in fetal alcohol syndrome. In A. Streissguth & J. Kanter (Eds.), *The challenge of fetal alcohol syndrome: Overcoming secondary disabilities* (pp. 25–39). Seattle: University of Washington Press.

Welch-Carre, E. (1995). The neurodevelopmental consequences of prenatal alcohol exposure. *Advances in Neonatal Care, 5*, 217–229.

SUGGESTED READINGS

Kyskan, C. E., & Moore, T. E. (2005). Global perspectives on fetal alcohol syndrome: Assessing practices, policies, and campaigns in four English-speaking countries. *Canadian Psychology, 46*, 153–165.

Lang, J. (2006). Ten brain domains: A proposal for functional central nervous system parameters for fetal alcohol spectrum disorder diagnosis and follow-up. *Journal of FAS International, 4*, e12, 1–11.

Premji, S., Benzies, K., Serrett, K., & Hayden, K. A. (2006). Research-based interventions for children and youth with fetal alcohol spectrum disorder: Revealing the gap. *Child: Care, Health and Development, 33*, 389–397.

TIMOTHY E. MOORE
KARINA ROYER GAGNIER
York University, Toronto, Canada

FIBROMYALGIA

Fibromyalgia (FM) is a common musculoskeletal pain syndrome defined by at least three months of generalized bodily pain and tenderness (Wolfe et al., 1990). In addition, an FM diagnosis requires a physical examination finding of at least 11 out of 18 tender points, that is, specific regions of localized pain (e.g., neck and shoulders). The current definition of FM as established by the American College of Rheumatology replaced the previous term "fibrocitis." The literal translation of FM is "pain in the muscles and fibrous tissue."

Ninety percent of the estimated 3–6 million people with FM in the U.S. are women. In addition, FM is the third most common presenting complaint to rheumatologists. Possible reasons for female predominance are early trauma or abuse, hormonal differences, and the higher rate of help seeking in women.

FM is characterized by highly variable symptoms and impairments. Many patients are able to retain full-time jobs and family responsibilities, while others may be generally disabled. Also, a particular patient may experience substantive improvement for weeks or months, only to experience relapse into a debilitated state. Debilitation may be due to severe pain as well as other common FM symptoms including chronic fatigue, cognitive difficulties, sleep disturbance, flu-like sensations, and post-exertional symptom flare-ups. In addition, the common co-morbidities of stress, anxiety, and depression can worsen symptoms.

Individuals affected with FM may report that their symptoms began following physical (e.g., car accident) or emotional (e.g., death of a loved one) trauma or after a prolonged period of intense stress. Once ill, these patients often experience hypersensitivity to loud noises, bright lights, odors, drugs, or chemicals. The disabling effects of the illness may also engender significant stress and adjustment problems (e.g., demoralization). For many patients, FM is a long-term persistent condition.

Theories of Causation

The causes of fibromyalgia are unclear. Although pain is usually experienced in the muscles and joints, no medical abnormalities or derangements have been found in the skeletal muscles or bones. The three theories below represent both biological and psychological explanations of the illness.

Abnormal Pain Processing

This model proposes that hormone abnormalities negatively influence the central nervous system to produce heightened pain perception in FM (Yunus, 1992). For example, FM patients report pain at lower levels of aversive stimulation (e.g., thumbscrew pressure) in comparison to healthy controls (hyperalgesia). In addition, FM patients often experience nonpainful stimuli (e.g., a light breeze) as aversive (allodynia).

Sleep Disturbance Model

This theory postulates that a disrupted sleep/wake cycle triggers chronic pain and fatigue. FM patients commonly report low-quality, unrefreshing sleep. Sleep studies in FM supportive of this theory suggest that (1) poor sleep quality predicts higher pain levels (e.g., Bigatti, Hernandez, Cronan, & Rand, 2008) and (2) deep stage sleep, normally associated with delta brain waves, may be disrupted by the presence of alpha wave light sleep (alpha-delta intrusion).

Pain-Prone Disorder

A psychological model of chronic pain originating in the 1950s (Bluner & Heilbronn, 1982) theorized that the combination of excessive achievement striving, low assertiveness, and an inability to express negative emotion leads to persistent pain and debilitation. For example, an individual with these traits might be overextended with respect to working hours, family responsibilities, social obligations, and volunteer activities, yet feel unable to decline requests from others to do even more. In addition, the patient may not be aware of negative emotions, particularly anger. In support of this model, "action prone" traits, a form of high achievement striving, and alexithymia, an inability to identify and express negative emotions, have been found in FM patients.

With modern advances in mind-body research indicating that both biology and behavior are involved in illness development and persistence, it is prudent to view the above theories as incomplete. Cross-disciplinary evidence for mind-body interactions in FM includes findings of abnormalities in pain-producing hormones (e.g., substance P), stress hormones (cortisol), and neurotransmitters linked to mood states (e.g., decreased serotonin) as well as negative family influences, genetic predisposition, and environmental stress (Okufuji & Turk, 2002).

FM and Depression

FM, as one of a number a medically unexplained illnesses, may be erroneously considered by clinicians to be a type of depression or other psychological disorder. As compared to persons with depressive disorder, FM patients are more likely to present with flu-like symptoms, post-exertional symptom flare-ups after routine activities (e.g., housework, a short walk), and an interest and motivation in pursuing activities, which is not characteristic of people who are significantly depressed.

Treatment Review

Recently, the antidepressant duloxetine (Cymbalta) and the antiseizure medication pregabalin (Lyrica) have been FDA-approved for pain treatment in FM. In addition, selected low-dose antidepressant medications may be helpful for sleep, pain, and depression. Acupuncture treatment studies have yielded mixed results, and evidence is lacking for a variety of alternative remedies such as Glucosamine, Guaifenesin, melatonin, vitamin and mineral supplements, homeopathy, and special diets.

Behavioral interventions including gradual aerobic exercise, relaxation, and cognitive-behavior therapy and patient education programs have shown benefits such as increased tolerance of physical activity and exercise, reduced pain and anxiety, and improved functioning. Symptom reductions have also been shown for water-based exercise and massage. Some FM experts advocate coordinated multidisciplinary treatment, so that both the biological and psychological aspects of the illness can be addressed.

Many physicians are not equipped to provide care for FM patients, given the absence of a definitive diagnosis, limited medical treatment options, and skepticism about the reality of the illness condition. However, medical practitioners who are receptive to these patients can be helpful in providing credibility and support as well as individualized treatments (e.g., certain medications) that may offer benefit (Goldenberg, 2008). In addition, behavioral intervention focused on lifestyle change and stress reduction as administered by a knowledgeable health care provider may produce more sustained benefits in comparison to medications. Treatment, although helpful in many cases, is often inadequate to resolve persistent symptoms and functional limitations over the long-term.

REFERENCES

Bigatti, S. M., Hernandez, A., Cronan, T. A., & Rand, K. L. (2008). Sleep disturbances in fibromyalgia syndrome: Relationship to pain and depression. *Arthritis Care & Research, 59*, 961–967.

Blumer D., & Heilbronn, M. (1982). Chronic pain as a variant of depressive disease: The pain-prone disorder. *Journal of Nervous and Mental Disease, 170*, 381–406.

Goldenberg, D. (2008). Multidisciplinary modalities in the treatment of fibromyalgia. *Journal of Clinical Psychiatry, 69*, suppl. 2, 30–40.

Okufuji, A., & Turk, D. C. (2002). Stress and psychophysiological dysregulation in patients with fibromyalgia syndrome. *Applied Psychophysiology and Biofeedback, 27*, 129–141.

Wolfe, F., Smythe, H. A., Yunus, M. B., Bennett, R. M., Bombardier, C., Goldenberg, D., et al. (1990). The American College of Rheumatology 1990 criteria for the classification of fibromyalgia. Report of the multicenter criteria committee. *Arthritis and Rheumatism, 33*, 160–172.

Yunus, M. B. (1992). Towards a model of pathophysiology of fibromyalgia: Aberrant central pain mechanisms with peripheral modulation. *Journal of Rheumatology, 19*, 846–850.

SUGGESTED READINGS

Friedberg, F. (2006). Fibromyalgia and chronic fatigue syndrome: Seven proven steps to less pain and more energy. Oakland, CA: New Harbinger.

Mease, P., Arnold, L. M., Bennett, R., Boonen, A., Buskila, D., Carville, S., et al. (2007). Fibromyalgia syndrome. *Journal of Rheumatology, 34*, 1415–1425.

Zautra, A. J., Fasman, R., Reich, J. R., Harakas, P., Johnson, L. M., Olmsted, M. E., et al. (2005). Fibromyalgia: Evidence for deficits in positive affect regulation. *Psychosomatic Medicine*, *67*, 147–155.

FRED FRIEDBERG
Stony Brook University

See also: Chronic Fatigue Syndrome

FIGHT/FLIGHT REACTION

The fight-flight reaction can be observed across species and represents a critically important mechanism for survival, no less so in humans than in other living organisms. At the heart of this reaction is fear, which is an immediate response to perceived threat, and anxiety, which is a response similar to fear that can be thought of as anticipation of danger, or even anticipation of fear itself. Put another way, if fear is the sensation people experience with their first bee sting, then anxiety is the emotion they feel thereafter when hearing the buzz of a bumblebee.

Anxiety can be abnormal or normal. It has been estimated, for example, that up to 30% of the population in the United States has at some time experienced an anxiety disorder (Mineka & Zinbarg, 2006). From the perspective of normality, however, anxiety provides us with a means to survive, to avoid the second bee sting, or worse.

From a biological perspective, anxiety, like fear, affects a person's autonomic nervous system, activating some functions (sympathetic arousal) while suppressing others (parasympathetic suppression). Blood is diverted in the affected person from its role in digestion to muscle, heart rate and respirations increase, and pupils dilate. In short, the individual is ready for action, ready to respond to danger.

Two primary actions available for dealing with threat are fighting and fleeing, and the physiological changes just described can be seen as preparing the person, alone or collectively in a group, to do one or both of these actions. Anxiety can vary in intensity, and most people accept that some feelings of anxiety represent consequences of everyday life. In general, greater threat produces a more intense feeling of anxiety and heightened physiological responses and, consequently, more drastic actions in response to that threat. The responses available can be primitive and direct (e.g., engaging in a physical fight to defeat or control the source of danger) or, depending on the organism's capacity for higher intellectual thought, fight and flight can become abstract concepts, leading to responses that reflect analogies to the more basic concepts. A person, for example, might say, "I decided not to see that movie because it doesn't interest me." If, in fact, the true reason for not wanting to go to the movie is social anxiety or a fear of crowds, then the decision not to go may well be a good example of defensive flight rather than a matter of simple lack of interest.

Learning plays an important role in many aspects of fight-flight behavior (Mineka & Zinbarg, 2006), but almost certainly there is also a genetic basis to these behaviors. Some arguments for a genetic basis include the universality of the response across human cultures, both primitive and advanced as well as across species; the demonstrated survival basis for these strategies; their appearance early in life; and evidence for their historical presence. Although this last point may underscore the importance of fight-flight for survival, it is important also to keep in mind that this defense comes with a price. In choosing to fight (whether expressed in efforts to contain or actually to physically eliminate), people accept the risk that they might be injured in the process. Even if a person wins the altercation, there is the risk of infection or other consequence from an injury sustained. There is as well the risk of injury should the person choose instead to flee the danger. He or she might stumble and fall, for instance. Given these various possible consequences, it may be no wonder why so many individuals become indecisive when confronted with a situation that calls for fight or flight.

Adding to the complexity of the seemingly simple concept of fight-flight, a person's autonomic arousal can result in physical symptoms when no physical action follows a signal of threat, including symptoms such as dizziness or a sense of light-headedness. It is no wonder that fight-flight and its underlying anxiety have occupied such a central role in our attempts to understand the human condition, in its normal physical and psychological expressions as well as in medical illness and psychopathology (McEwen, 2004; Reagan, Grillo, & Piroli, 2008).

REFERENCES

McEwen, B. S. (2004). Protection and damage from acute and chronic stress: Allostasis and allostatic overload and relevance to the pathophysiology of psychiatric disorders. *Annals of the New York Academy of Sciences*, *1032*, 1–7.

Mineka, S., & Zinbarg, R. (2006). A contemporary learning theory perspective on the etiology of anxiety disorders: It's not what you thought it was. *American Psychologist*, *61*, 10–26.

Reagan, L. P., Grillo, C. A., & Piroli, G. G. (2008). The As and Ds of stress: Metabolic, morphological and behavioral consequences. *European Journal of Pharmacology*, *585*, 64–75.

STANLEY BERENT
University of Michigan

See also: Anxiety; Approach-Avoidance Conflict; Fear

FIGURE DRAWINGS

The term "Figure Drawings" (FD) describes a variety of drawing tests that tap personality functions, including the Draw-A-Person Test (DAP), the House-Tree-Person Test (H-T-P), and the Kinetic Family Drawing Test (K-F-D), among other lesser-known drawing techniques.

Although ancient drawings of people and animals may be found on the cave walls in Europe and in the tombs of nobles in Egypt, modern day use of figure drawings as personality assessment instruments began in 1926 when Florence Goodenough devised and standardized the Draw-A-Man test as a nonverbal test of intelligence. Clinicians soon noticed that these drawings reflected personality traits and issues, and Karen Machover (1949) devised the DAP as a clinical instrument. Despite concerns regarding the validity of various FD tests, they are still widely used by assessors.

The DAP is said to represent the self, in the subject's perceived environment, but often not directly so. Human beings do not typically draw what they look like; instead they draw figures that reflect how they feel about themselves and how they experience their environment. The drawings might represent "deep unconscious wishes, a frank acknowledgment of physical or psychological impairment, conscious or unconscious compensation for a physical or a psychological defect, or a combination of all of these factors" (see Handler, 1996, p. 219). For example, a tall, assertive, muscular man might draw a tiny figure, expressing underlying feelings of inadequacy, whereas a small, thin, frail man might draw a large, muscular figure, as defensive compensation. Research also indicates that there are major differences in figure drawing content, style, and quality from subjects of different cultures (Handler & Habenicht, 1994; Handler, 1996, p. 229), and clinicians should therefore interpret findings from a subject's cultural perspective.

Advantages of Figure Drawings

Figure drawing tests (DAP, H-T-P, and K-F-D) are simple, easy, and enjoyable tasks for most people. They can be used in assessing children, adolescents, adults, and couples, and they require very little time to administer. They are the only tasks in an assessment battery for which there is no external stimulus. Hence they represent a novel task for the subject, compared to tasks using either explicit or vague stimuli. The assessor can evaluate subjects' functioning without the structure of an external stimulus.

Figure drawings often yield a great deal of information concerning subjects' self-concept, personality style, and areas of conflict. They are also useful with subjects who are inhibited and nontalkative, and with those who are evasive or guarded. Because they are quick and easy to administer, and because they reflect emotional changes in patients, they are instruments for tracking patients'

progress and outcome in psychotherapy and sex therapy (see Handler, 1996, pp. 213–216 for examples). Figure drawings are also excellent springboards for discussion of conflict areas with patients. Figure drawings are especially useful with children in trauma work, in assessing coping skills, as therapeutic tools, and in communicating trauma experiences symbolically (Matto, 2007).

The K-F-D is said to provide a quick understanding of subjects' views of their family dynamics. It also allows clinicians to understand the interaction patterns in the family, and relationship patterns among family members. The K-F-D is useful in sharing with parents their child's feelings about their family. It is also an excellent tool for reflecting cultural and subcultural issues and subjects' degree of acculturation to their predominant culture. Concerning the H-T-P, the house drawing is said to represent the self and also subjects' feelings about family relationships. The tree is also said to represent the self in relation to the environment (Buck, 1948).

Administration

DAP: The examiner gives the subject a standard $8\frac{1}{2} \times 11$ sheet of unlined paper and a #2 pencil with an eraser and asks the subject to "draw a person." Then, another sheet of paper is provided, and the examiner asks the subject to draw a figure of the opposite gender. Typically, the examiner then asks for stories about the figures or asks a series of relevant questions about them (see Hammer, 1958; Handler, 1996, pp. 216–218). Little further direction is given. If subjects draw a stick figure or only the head, they are asked to draw a complete figure, using a new sheet of paper.

H-T-P: The examiner places the paper horizontally and asks subjects to draw as good a house (and then a tree and a person), as they can, on separate sheets of paper. The paper is positioned vertically for the tree and person drawings. The examiner might then also ask for a drawing of the opposite gender. Stories about the drawings, or questions about them, are typically employed to obtain additional information (Buck, 1948; Handler, 1996, pp. 256–257).

K-F-D: The subject is given a sheet of unlined paper, held horizontally, and is asked to "Draw a picture of everyone in your family, including yourself, doing something. Try to draw whole people, not cartoons or stick people. Remember, make everyone doing something—some kind of action" (Burns & Kaufman, 1970, pp. 19–20). Subjects are then asked to identify the figures in the drawing and explain the activity or activities illustrated in it.

Drawing Norms

There are few studies available concerning figure drawing norms for adults. The style and quality of children's and adolescents' drawings depend on age and developmental status, as well as on cultural factors. Koppitz and

Machover have developed age and gender related norms (see Handler, 1996, pp. 222–228).

Validity

There is a considerable controversy concerning the validity of figure drawings. Some researchers report poor validity, and some report excellent validity (see Handler, 1996, pp. 251–252). Some of the negative findings have come from early research that was poorly designed and some from studies in which single drawing variables were studied in isolation, rather than in the context of the entire drawing.

Several checklists encompassing a number of figure drawing variables have been developed and validated (see Handler, 1996). For example, Naglieri, McNeish, and Bardos produced the Draw-A-Person: Screening Procedure for Emotional Disturbance (DAP:SPED) that asks subjects to draw a man, a woman, and themselves, which are then scored on a 55-item checklist of structural and content dimensions (see Matto, 2007, pp. 210–211). The DAP:SPED was standardized on a large sample of children and adolescents (6–17 years). Naglieri and Pfeiffer and McNeish and Naglieri found that the measure demonstrated validity in identifying children and adolescents with emotional and behavioral disorders (Matto, 2007, pp. 210–211). Naglieri also found no significant differences among scores for White, Black, and Hispanic young people. Similar checklists by Koppitz for elementary and middle school students have received moderate support in the literature (see Handler, 1996, pp. 222–225).

Another concern raised by some researchers about figure drawings, mostly the DAP, is that drawing variables are influenced by subjects' artistic ability and that clinicians make diagnostic decisions based purely on the artistic ability of their patients. However, a number of studies and many clinical observations indicate that poor overall quality of figure drawings is related to measures of patients' psychological adjustment. The more emotionally disturbed a patient is, the more there is likely to be a disturbance in body image and reality testing, and these problems are reflected in major distortions of the figures. Robins, Blatt, and Ford evaluated DAPs of patients in long-term psychotherapy. After treatment, the figures improved dramatically (see Handler, 1996, pp. 209–211).

Handler and Reyher (see Handler, 1996, pp. 249–250) reviewed the findings of 51 DAP studies for individual signs of conflict. They found equivocal findings for some variables (e.g., shading, erasure, line reinforcement). Some variables were nonsignificant, and some were very significant (e.g., head and body simplification, omission of major body parts, distortion of head and/or body; very small size and very large size; vertical imbalance).

A review of the K-F-D literature (Handler & Habenicht, 1994) indicates that Burns' formal scoring system lacks validity. However, despite poor validity, the results for

individual patients are often quite dramatic in depicting family problems. The research in the literature indicates that a holistic interpretation rather than an objective scoring approach yields significant results. For example, using the DAP and the K-F-D, Tharinger and Stark (see Handler, 1996, p. 234) compared the ability of an objective scoring system with a holistic approach (much as a clinician would do the interpretation) to differentiate children with mood and anxiety disorders, compared with a control group. They found that the objective scoring system did not differentiate the groups, but the intuitive holistic approach differentiated the groups for both the DAP and the K-F-D. Studies by Yama, and Kot, Handler, Toman, and Hilsenroth found similar results (see Handler, 1996, pp. 232, 234). Handler and Riethmiller (1998) provide an example of a holistic interpretation of the DAP and K-F-D, and Handler, Campbell, and Martin (2004) present a detailed discussion of the reliability and validity of figure drawings.

There are many other figure drawing tests or procedures mentioned in the literature, such as the Kinetic H-T-P, the Draw-A-Person in the Rain, the Chromatic Draw-a-Person Test (Hammer, 1958), the Fantasy Animal Drawing Game (Handler, 2007), the Kinetic School Drawing Test (Handler, 1996), the Silver Drawing Test, and the Diagnostic Drawing Series (Matto, 2007), but these are used infrequently.

REFERENCES

Buck, J. (1948). The H-T-P. *Journal of Clinical Psychology, 4,* 151–159.

Burns, R., & Kaufman, S. (1970). *Kinetic Family Drawings (K-F-D): An introduction to understanding children through kinetic drawings.* New York: Brunner/Mazel.

Hammer, E. (Ed.) (1958). *The clinical application of projective drawings.* Springfield, IL: Charles Thomas.

Handler, L. (1996). The clinical use of drawings: Draw-A-Person, House-Tree-Person, and Kinetic Family Drawings. In C. Newmark (Ed.), *Major psychological assessment instruments,* (2nd ed., pp. 206–293). Boston: Allyn & Bacon.

Handler, L. (2007). The use of therapeutic assessment with children and adolescents. In S. Smith & L. Handler (Eds.), *The clinical assessment of children and adolescents: A practitioner's handbook* (pp. 53–72). Mahwah, NJ: Lawrence Erlbaum.

Handler, L., & Habenicht, D. (1994). The Kinetic Family Drawing Technique: A review of the literature. *Journal of Personality Assessment, 63,* 440–464.

Handler, L., & Riethmiller, R. (1998). Teaching and learning the administration and interpretation of graphic techniques. In L. Handler & M. Hilsenroth (Eds.), *Teaching and learning personality assessment* (pp. 267–294), Mahwah, NJ: Lawrence Erlbaum.

Machover, K. (1949). Personality projection in the drawing of the human figure. Springfield, IL: Charles Thomas.

Matto, H. (2007). Drawings in clinical assessment of children. In S. Smith & L. Handler, (Eds.), *The clinical assessment of children and adolescents: A practitioner's handbook* (pp. 207–222). Mahwah, NJ: Lawrence Erlbaum.

SUGGESTED READINGS

Burns, R. (1982). *Self growth in families: Kinetic family drawings (K-F-D) research and application.* New York: Brunner/Mazel.

Camara, W., Nathan, J., & Puente, A. (2000). Psychological test usage: Implications in professional psychology. *Professional psychology: Research and Practice, 31,* 141–154.

Handler, L., Campbell, A., & Martin, B. (2004). Use of graphic techniques in personality assessment: Reliability, validity, & clinical utility. In M. Hilsenroth & D. Segal (Eds.), *Comprehensive handbook of psychological assessment,* Vol. 2 (pp. 387–399). Hoboken, NJ: John Wiley & Sons.

Kissen, M. (1986). Object relations aspects of figure drawings. In M. Kissen (Ed.), *Assessment of object relations phenomena* (pp. 175–191). Madison, CT: International Universities Press.

LEONARD HANDLER
University of Tennessee

See also: **Personality Assessment**

FINLAND, PSYCHOLOGY IN

Not surprisingly, the first Finnish psychologists were trained by Wilhelm Wundt in his Leipzig laboratory. Most promising among them was Hjalmar Neiglick, who prepared his doctoral thesis there and defended it at the University of Helsinki in 1887. Unfortunately, Neiglick's premature death two years afterward put a brake on the development of an independent discipline of psychology, which thereafter remained a subsidiary interest of professors of philosophy. One of them, Eino Kaila, finally emerged as a founding father in psychology as late as 1922, when as a newly appointed professor of philosophy, he established a psychological laboratory in Turku. Kaila was keen on following the up-to-date trends in psychology. Some years earlier, he had defended this thesis "Über die Motivation und die Entscheidung" (On Motivation and Decision Making"). He also published in one of the leading German journals, *Psychologische Forschung,* in the 1920s and by so doing set a standard for his successors. However, a long time elapsed before Kaila's work entered the scene, with the exception that applied psychology was started by Esther Hjelt, who became the head of the State Railways' Psychotechnical Laboratory founded in 1923.

Departments Emerge

The first chair of psychology was founded as late as 1936. What is more, an expansion of the discipline had to wait until the 1950s and 1960s, when the usefulness of the psychological profession was realized by the government, which had to monitor the country through extensive restructuring after World War II. By the beginning of the 1970s, there was a total of six departments. The number of graduated psychologists rose rapidly, and by the 1980s Finland had one of the highest proportional densities of psychologists in the world (Rosenzweig, 1982).

International Influences

International influences were very much needed when psychology started to expand. Kai von Fieandt at the University of Helsinki continued to work along the continental European lines in the area of human perception. Johan von Wright defended his thesis on human learning at Oxford University in 1955. Shortly afterward he was appointed to a chair at the University of Turku and started there a process that later resulted in an early debut of cognitive psychology in Finland. Risto Näätänen was trained in psychophysiology in California in the late 1960s. In subsequent decades he created at the University of Helsinki what has so far been the most successful Finnish research tradition and which is focused on the theme of cognitive neuroscience. In developmental psychology, the University of Jyväskylä has achieved a strong international reputation. International influences have mainly come from the United States, due to an extensive scholarship program started after World War II. Soviet psychology also played a visible role during the 1970s and 1980s, on other than scientific grounds. Its impact on research was centered on few prominent persons (Luria, Sokolov, Vygotsky). Since the beginning of the present millennium, the various European Union programs have gained significance in their influence in Finland.

An Effective Trade Union of Psychologists

There were about 5,000 registered psychologists in Finland (pop. 5.2 million) in the year 2005. The Trade Union of Psychologists is professionally led and plays an active role in the European context. It was also an important factor when the academic psychology was restructured in Finland, as discussed next.

Rising Quantities, Improving Quality

About 200 psychology majors graduate annually, 20 people defend their doctoral theses, and 30 psychologists attain the special psychologist's degree based on a national study program. International scientific publishing has become a standard, and the annual output is about 250 articles that are listed in international databases. The progress has been impressive during the past 30 years, both quantitatively and qualitatively.

A Unique Finnish Solution: Networking the Entire Psychology

The economic recession in the early 1990s put a strain on the Finnish university sector and resulted in budget cuts. A number of departments were closed or reduced in size. Such plans were also made for psychology. However, the six departments, effectively supported by the Trade Union of Psychologists, made a countermove that has proved very useful. They proposed to the Ministry of Education that all of academic psychology function as a network that would be able to deal with challenges that individual departments could not meet. Against the odds, the proposal was well received, and a number of important events followed. Niemi and Hämäläinen (1999) describe these events in detail, and the main points follow.

A decree put forth in 1993 stated that the special psychologist's curriculum can consist of the Master of Arts degree plus two years of professional work experience. The final goal is to provide a special psychologist's degree to about 20% of the work force. The psychological profession was legally protected in 1994, including the professional title. The following year saw the foundation of the National Graduate School of Psychology, the task of which is to organize and administer the doctoral training in psychology. Since the turn of the millennium, an extensive (about 100 hours) common basic course of psychology has been designed. It is sent to all departments in the form of online lectures through the Internet. The participants in a given lecture number 500 to 600. The network has evoked positive attention. It has been nominated twice as a National Center of Excellence in Education, during 1997–1998 and 2004–2006. It was also selected by the European Federation of Professional Psychologists Associations as the best European educational innovation in psychology in 2000.

REFERENCES

Niemi, P., & Hämäläinen, H. (1999). Networking psychology in Finland: New collaboration between research and profession. *International Journal of Psychology, 34*, 469–472.

Rosenzweig, M. R. (1982). Trends in development and status of psychology: An international perspective. *International Journal of Psychology, 17*, 117–140.

PEKKA NIEMI
University of Turku, Finland

FIRESETTING

Intentional firesetting by children and adolescents causes thousands of deaths, serious injuries, more than $300 million in property damage yearly, and numerous other serious consequences for children, families, and communities (Stickle & Kaufman, 2008).

In the United States, children and adolescents set the majority of reported fires, are arrested for arson more than for any other crime, and account for about half of all arson arrests. Prevalence of firesetting is difficult to determine precisely, because many fires are undetected or unreported. Available estimates suggest that in community samples in the United States and Australia, prevalence of fire play and firesetting ranges from 0% to 3% in boys and girls aged four to six years, up to between 6% and 7% in boys aged seven to thirteen years (Achenbach, 1991; Dadds & Fraser, 2006). These estimates are considerably lower than those in clinical and adjudicated samples, in which 20% to 50% of youth set fires. Although firesetting is exhibited across childhood, intentional firesetting appears to be most commonly seen in boys who also exhibit other conduct problem behaviors (Kolko & Kazdin, 1986; Stickle & Blechman, 2002).

Historically, psychological conceptualizations of firesetting among youth have tended to be oversimplified. Early psychological accounts suggested that firesetting behavior represented a unique type of pathology, usually labeled pyromania. According to this psychoanalytically derived conceptualization of firesetting, young people set fires because they found fire arousing, usually sexually. Empirical evidence does not support this conceptualization. Overall, findings from controlled studies suggest that, if what is known as pyromania exists at all, it is likely rare (Geller, Erlen, & Pincus, 1986).

Additionally, clinical observation of a few clinically-referred and troubled youth led some to conclude that, among other things, a so-called "ego triad" of behaviors that include firesetting, enuresis, and cruelty to animals is an identifiable syndrome indicative of severe, persistent, violent pathology. Although each of these behaviors may be associated with severe psychological problems, research findings have failed to demonstrate that these particular behaviors co-occur systematically or indicate a specific psychological profile.

Contemporary psychological conceptualizations of firesetting do indicate that numerous risk factors and circumstances influence risk for firesetting. It is worth noting that the available reliable data indicate that boys who exhibit conduct problems and intentionally set fires are responsible for the majority of intentionally set fires. Although other factors are found to be related to firesetting in some individuals, previous fire play and experimentation, previous firesetting, age of the child, other conduct problems, and to a lesser extent, other mental health problems such as depression and anxiety also increase risk for repeat firesetting.

Boys, children from single-parent homes, and children who have been abused are at increased risk for setting fires (McCarty & McMahon, 2005). In clinical samples, firesetting youth exhibit greater deficits in social adjustment, including inappropriate display of anger and ineffective responses to social problems, compared with nonfiresetting youth. Older youth who set fires are likely to exhibit other antisocial behaviors, such as property destruction and stealing (Kolko & Kazdin, 1986) and aggressive and oppositional behaviors (Stickle & Blechman, 2002).

As with parents of children with conduct problems, parents of firesetting youth display less warmth, engage in more harsh and ineffective discipline, and provide less supervision and monitoring than parents of children without conduct problems. Compared to children without conduct problems, firesetting youth are more likely to live in single-parent homes with absent fathers, have mothers with depression, and to have been abused (Kolko & Kazdin, 1986; McCarty & McMahon, 2005). Children who continue setting fires after early childhood are more likely to have parents with the noted parenting deficits and with mental health and interpersonal problems than are children who stop setting fires (McCarty & McMahon, 2005).

In sum, firesetting is a serious and sometimes persistent behavior pattern related to children's social, cognitive, and behavioral deficits, influenced by their early fire experiences, and by poor parental monitoring and discipline.

Assessment

Because firesetting occurs among a wide age range of youth with differing patterns of presentation and comorbid problems, comprehensive psychological assessment of firesetting youth is particularly important for informing intervention. Assessment should be guided by the principles and practices of evidence-based assessment for children and adolescents. Specifically, assessment procedures and instruments should (1) begin with broad band assessment and focus on narrow band assessment as specific problems are indicated, (2) be appropriate to the age and developmental level of the youth, (3) assess risk factors for differing developmental pathways to particular problems (e.g., age of onset for conduct disorder), (4) have known and strong psychometric properties, (5) have empirical support for their use with particular problems and populations, (6) be comprehensive (i.e., include cognitive, behavioral, emotional, and contextual factors), and (7) use multiple measures and multiple informants (e.g., youth, parent, teacher, behavioral observation). Lastly, fire specific behavior should be assessed as one of the narrow-band areas and incorporated into the comprehensive assessment.

Treatment Overview

Firesetting is frequently associated with conduct problems, and firesetting behavior includes attributes in common with other conduct problems. Therefore, effective treatment shares components of treatment for conduct problems: a cognitive-behavioral focus, parent involvement, and the involvement of community organizations. Treatments for firesetting, however, also address the unique features of firesetting, such as children's curiosity about fire and the damage fire can do. Treatments that combine cognitive-behavioral child therapy and parent management training with fire safety education are often needed to address firesetting. Thus, collaboration between mental health services and community fire services is an important but underutilized strategy.

There are also a few widely used but ineffective treatments that should be avoided. The use of threats and warnings about the potential dangers of fire, such as having the child view injury to persons or property, is ineffective. Satiation, which typically involves having the child light matches for long periods of time, may have negative effects such as increasing the child's sense of control over fire (Sharp, Blackman, Cole, & Cole, 2006).

Parent Management Training and Cognitive Behavioral Therapy

The two psychological treatments found to be most effective in reducing conduct problems and firesetting are parent management training (PMT) and cognitive-behavioral therapy (CBT) for children and adolescents. Research evidence shows that parent management training and child cognitive-behavioral therapy together significantly reduce conduct problems (Kazdin, 2003). Evidence also shows that PMT and CBT together lead to significant decreases in firesetting and matchplay in firesetting youth (Kolko, 2001).

In most cases, reducing firesetting requires effective parental monitoring and discipline combined with reinforcement of alternative behaviors. PMT refers to a set of interventions that addresses parents' expectations and behaviors in order to modify children's conduct problem behaviors. Treatment focuses on changing parental behaviors to increase parents' consistency across occasions and with each other, increase positive behaviors toward their children, and increase effective discipline practices.

In addition, CBT focuses on teaching the youth skills to decrease problem behaviors. For firesetting specifically, skill training typically focuses on learning to identify the antecedents of setting fires, such as feelings of loneliness, boredom, or interpersonal conflicts. Youths learn techniques for evaluating the risks and benefits of firesetting and to identify alternative behaviors, such as self instruction, interpersonal conflict resolution, and increasing prosocial activities.

Psychoeducational Intervention

In addition to these psychological treatments, reducing firesetting may also require fire safety education. Children who set fires exhibit greater curiosity about fire, exposure to people who smoke, and more knowledge about materials that burn, but less competence with fire than nonfiresetters. Effective fire safety education programs include both cognitive or fire science components, such as knowledge of how fires start, and competence or fire safety components, such as how to escape a burning house. Those interventions that involve just a visit with firefighters or to fire stations or a discussion of the dangers of fire, however, have been shown to be ineffective (Kolko, 2001).

Community-based Treatment

The most effective treatments frequently combine mental health and fire service components. Interventions that involve parents and children in the psychological treatments utilizing PMT and CBT with empirically based fire safety education effectively reduce firesetting and behaviors associated with firesetting. With a serious yet covert pattern of behaviors such as firesetting, increased involvement of multiple community agencies should be the aim. Community-based, multidisciplinary teams that include representatives from mental health, human service, law enforcement, and fire service may be able to more effectively increase public awareness and increase the prevention of fires (Sharp et al., 2006), refer firesetters to appropriate interventions, and better implement treatment across settings. From research on conduct problems, it is also clear that the more severe and chronic the problem behaviors, the greater the need for multidisciplinary community services.

REFERENCES

Achenbach, T. M. (1991). *Manual for the Child Behavior Checklist/ 4-18 and 1991 profile.* Burlington, VT: University of Vermont, Department of Psychiatry.

Dadds, M. R., & Fraser, J. A. (2006). Fire interest, fire setting and psychopathology in Australian children: A normative study. *Australian and New Zealand Journal of Psychiatry, 40,* 581–586.

Geller, J. L., Erlen, J., & Pinkus R. L. (1986). A historical appraisal of America's experience with pyromania: A diagnosis in search of a disorder. *International Journal of Law and Psychiatry, 9,* 201–229.

Kolko, D. J. (2001). Efficacy of cognitive-behavioral treatment and fire safety education for children who set fires: Initial and follow-up outcomes. *Journal of Child Psychology and Psychiatry, 42*(3), 359–369.

Kolko, D. J., & Kazdin, A. E. (1986). A conceptualization of firesetting in children and adolescents. *Journal of Abnormal Child Psychology, 14,* 49–61.

McCarty, C. A., McMahon, R. J., & the Conduct Problems Prevention Research Group. (2005). Domains of risk in the developmental continuity of fire setting. *Behavior Therapy, 36,* 185–195.

Sharp, D. L., Blaakman, S. W., Cole, E. C., & Cole, R. E. (2006). Evidence-based multidisciplinary strategies for working with children who set fires. *American Psychiatric Nurses Association, 11*(6), 329–337.

Stickle, T. R., & Blechman, E. A. (2002). Aggression and fire: Antisocial behavior in firesetting and nonfiresetting juvenile offenders. *Journal of Psychopathology & Behavioral Assessment, 24,* 177–193.

Stickle, T. R., & Kaufman, L. (2007). Juvenile firesetting. In M. Hersen & D. Reitman (Eds.), *Handbook of assessment, conceptualization, and treatment, Volume II. Children and adolescents.* New York: John Wiley & Sons.

SUGGESTED READINGS

Kolko, K. J. (2002). *Handbook on firesetting in children and youth,* (pp. 305–336). Amsterdam: Academic Press.

McMahon, R. J., & Forehand, R. L. (2003). *Helping the noncompliant child* (2nd ed). New York: Guilford Press.

TIMOTHY R. STICKLE
University of Vermont

See also: Antisocial Behavior; Conduct Disorder

FITNESS-FOR-DUTY EVALUATIONS

Fitness-for-duty evaluations (FFDEs) involve the application of comprehensive psychological assessment skills to address employer questions about a worker's ability to perform essential job duties safely and effectively. Such evaluations should never be undertaken lightly, as they are of importance for both employers and employees. For employers, FFDEs are often intended to help fulfill their obligation to provide a safe working environment. For employees, FFDEs concern issues related to their livelihood, self-esteem, and privacy. In addition to employers, organizations with service oversight responsibility, such as professional licensing boards or hospitals, may also request FFDEs.

Appropriate referrals for FFDEs occur when specific instances of an employee's behavior raise reasonable question about risk for unsafe or incompetent functioning in the work setting due to psychological factors. It is inappropriate to utilize FFDEs as a means to circumvent disciplinary or other administrative action. FFDE referrals may be prompted by a single significant behavioral event or by a pattern of more minor behavioral events. The situational context of the behavior raising concern also requires consideration. For example, occupations and workplaces differ with regard to the behavioral threshold needed to prompt an FFDE. In general, the behavioral threshold needed for referral is inversely related to job safety-sensitivity, with lower referral thresholds being warranted for high-risk occupations.

An FFDE is a third-party assessment in that the client is the employer requesting evaluation rather than the employee being evaluated. Such assessments require special attention to forensic issues. FFDE evaluators should be knowledgeable about the Americans with Disabilities Act (ADA) and other related federal or state statutes. Beyond disability law, evaluators need to be aware of federal, state, and case law relevant to confidentiality; labor agreements pertinent to the job setting; and federal or state regulations applicable to some occupations (e.g. aviation pilots, law enforcement officers, nuclear power plant personnel).

The fundamental goal of FFDE is to provide a fair, multimethod, objective, and valid appraisal of psychological factors that have raised fitness questions. Police psychology, in particular, has been attentive to evaluation processes for achieving that goal (Decker, 2006; Rostow & Davis, 2004). In fact, the International Association of Chiefs of Police Psychological Services Section (IACP, 2004) has ratified guidelines for conducting FFDEs that have substantial applicability beyond law enforcement.

FFDE methodology varies depending on case circumstances, employer expectations, and evaluator preferences. However, certain core elements and commonly accepted practices can be identified. The evaluator should be a licensed psychologist or psychiatrist possessing specialized knowledge and skills relevant to FFDEs. In order to promote unbiased assessment, the evaluator should have no treatment relationship with the employee either before or after the evaluation.

FFDEs are based on multiple sources of information. Assessment begins with a review of documentation from the employer that includes description of circumstances prompting referral and other background material, such as the employee's job description and job performance history. Upon meeting the employee, the evaluator first secures informed consent by clearly identifying the employer as the client requesting evaluation, explaining the purpose of the evaluation, and detailing confidentiality parameters among other issues. Informed consent should be verified with both written documentation and verbal discussion prior to proceeding with the evaluation. Through the informed consent process, the evaluator conveys respect for the employee and a genuine desire to answer referral questions accurately, which encourages development of a rapport helpful to the assessment process.

FFDEs call for prioritized attention to risk for both suicide and violence. The assessment process should promote the safety of all concerned, including the employee, co-workers, the public, and the evaluator. The evaluator should be skilled in suicide and violence risk assessment methods, especially in regard to workplace violence issues (Kausch & Resnick, 2001; Stock, 2007). Evaluators should also be skilled in substance abuse assessment, since substance misuse is an important safety risk factor that can influence a range of other behavioral problems affecting fitness.

At least one face-to-face clinical interview is presumed to be an essential component of FFDE. It allows the evaluator to listen to, and learn from, the employee's perspective on the referring circumstances. It permits opportunity for behavioral observation and traditional mental status examination. Interviews should also include careful history taking, with particular attention to work history. Psychological testing should not constitute the sole basis for conclusions in the evaluation, but test results provide a unique and important contribution to the assessment's overall database. Typically, psychological testing incorporates, at minimum, an instrument capable of measuring a broad bandwidth of psychopathology in addition to test-taking attitudes, such as defensiveness, that are relevant to understanding the employee's approach to the evaluation.

It is particularly important to seek out information pertinent to fitness questions from collateral sources, such as statements by supervising managers, police reports, psychiatric hospitalization records, and records from therapists and treating physicians. Of course, accessing many collateral sources requires appropriate written authorization by the employee that explicitly identifies the purpose for which information is being sought. Referral for specialty consultation (e.g., medical specialist, neuropsychologist) may be called for on rare occasions if considered essential to FFDE completion.

Finally, FFDE findings are communicated to the employer in the form of a report. The report should be written in clear language intended for the representative of the employer designated to receive it. The report should omit personal or private information irrelevant to the evaluation's purpose. If the employee is found unfit, the report should indicate the work-related functional limitations causing that determination. For such determinations, the report may describe employment restrictions or other accommodations that might be feasible. The report should indicate if functional limitations may improve in the foreseeable future, for example as the result of counseling or treatment. Some reports forwarded to the employer may be limited solely to conclusions and recommendations. In such cases, it is advisable that the evaluator compose a contemporaneous document for the record that describes the assessment data and the associated logic supporting the report's conclusions.

Inevitably, employers will occasionally be confronted with situations that raise questions about an employee's psychological ability to function safely and effectively in the workplace. In answer to such questions, properly conducted FFDEs provide employers expert professional opinion based on empirically supported principles of psychological assessment.

REFERENCES

Decker, K. P. (Ed.). (2006). *Fit, unfit or misfit?: How to perform fitness for duty evaluations in law enforcement professionals.* Springfield, IL: Charles C. Thomas.

IACP Police Psychological Services Section. (2004). *Psychological fitness-for-duty evaluation guidelines.* Alexandria, VA: Author.

Kausch, O., & Resnick, P. J. (2001). Assessment of employees for workplace violence. *Journal of Forensic Psychology Practice, 1*(4), 1–22.

Rostow, C. D., & Davis, R. D. (2004). *A handbook for psychological fitness-for-duty evaluations in law enforcement.* Binghamton, NY: Haworth Reference Press.

Stock, H. V. (2007). Workplace violence: Advances in consultation and assessment. In A. M. Goldstein (Ed.), *Forensic psychology: Emerging topics and expanding roles* (pp. 511–549). Hoboken, NJ: John Wiley & Sons.

SUGGESTED READINGS

Borum, R., Super, J., & Rand, M. (2003). Forensic assessment for high-risk occupations. In I. B. Weiner (Series Ed.) & A. M. Goldstein (Vol. Ed.), *Handbook of psychology: Vol. 11. Forensic psychology* (pp. 133–147). Hoboken, NJ: John Wiley & Sons.

Stone, A. V. (2000). *Fitness for duty: Principles, methods, and legal issues.* Boca Raton, FL: CRC Press.

PATRICK F. LAVIN
Chattanooga, TN

See also: Police Psychology; Psychological Assessment; Violence Risk Assessment

FITTS'S LAW

Fitts's law is a mathematical relationship that captures how speed and accuracy trade off in human movement. Originally formulated by Paul M. Fitts (Fitts, 1954), it predicts the time it takes to move to a target as a function of the target's size and the distance that needs to be covered to attain it. In Fitts's study, people were asked to move a hand-held stylus between two targets as fast as possible without missing them. The targets were of identical width (*W*) and were separated center-to-center by a certain amplitude (*A*). By systematically varying the width of the targets and distance between them, he found that the average movement time (*MT*) to go from one target to the other was specified by the following equation:

$$MT = a + b \cdot \log_2(2A/W),$$

where a and b are empirically defined constants, and the expression $\log_2(2 \cdot A/W)$ was termed the index of difficulty (*ID*) of the movement. Thus *MT* is predicted to increase linearly with *ID*: $MT = a + b \cdot ID$. The index of difficulty is defined such that it increases with the distance that needs to be covered and the narrowness of the targets (required movement accuracy). Moreover, *MT* is predicted to be the same as long as the ratio between movement amplitude and target width (*A/W*) remains unchanged.

Although there are some exceptions, Fitts's relationship is one of the most reliable principles of motor behavior and has consequently become known as a "law." In addition to the cyclical (back-and-forth) movements described above, it has been shown to hold for a variety of actions, such as discrete (one-shot) movements, grasping and transferring objects, and pointing and dragging objects with a mouse on computer displays. Fitts's law has also been demonstrated to apply to various movement contexts (under water or under a microscope), the use of different limbs (fingers, arms, and feet), and many types of people (young, elderly, and patients with motor impairments; for a review of the many circumstances where the law applies, see Plamondon & Alimi, 1997).

More recent research has established that this principle also holds for two other important aspects of human behavior: motor (mental) imagery and action perception. Indeed, when people are asked to imagine themselves performing aimed movements, the duration of those movements conforms with Fitts's law. Furthermore, the maximum speed at which we perceive the movement of others as still being possible also obeys this principle. This has been taken to suggest that motor control, motor imagery, and action perception rely on a common set of cognitive processes. More generally, the robustness and generality of Fitts's law has also led to its use in applied (human factors) research. For example, it has been employed to predict the time it takes to interact with novel graphical interfaces as well as evaluate various types of pointing devices (for a review of applied research and design recommendations, see Soukoreff & MacKenzie, 2004).

Fitts's law is a very powerful principle because it often explains a substantial amount (> 90%) of the variance in movement time data. Fitts's attempt at explaining the functional mechanisms underlying the law were grounded in information theory, which was a popular approach at the time (hence his use of log base 2 and his definition of *ID* in terms of "bits"). Since then, there have been many efforts to find more precise and theory-driven formulations of the law (for a review, see Plamondon & Alimi, 1997). One successful line of thinking has been to focus on the inherent variability of the motor system. In particular, higher movement speeds require the generation of greater muscle forces, which in turn lead to more variability in motor output (e.g., landing positions). Based on these notions, Fitts's law has been shown to be consistent with the minimum movement times that lead to an optimal balance between movement speed (force) and the corresponding amount of movement variability.

REFERENCES

Fitts, P. M. (1954). The information capacity of the human motor system in controlling the amplitude of movement. *Journal of Experimental Psychology, 47*, 381–391.

Plamondon, R., & Alimi, A. M. (1997). Speed/accuracy trade-offs in target-directed movements. *Behavioral and Brain Sciences, 20*, 279–349.

Soukoreff, R. W., & MacKenzie, I. S. (2004). Towards a standard for pointing device evaluation: Perspectives on 27 years of Fitts' law research in HCI. *International Journal of Human-Computer Studies, 61*, 751–789.

Marc Grosjean
Leibniz Research Centre for Working Environment and Human Factors, Dortmund, Germany

See also: **Motor Control**

FIVE-FACTOR MODEL OF PERSONALITY

Personality traits describe individual differences in human beings' typical ways of perceiving, thinking, feeling, and behaving that are generally consistent over time and across situations. Beginning with the work of Allport and Odbert (1936), trait psychologists have attempted to identify a set of basic traits that adequately describe variation in human personality. This effort has employed two strategies: the analysis of descriptive adjectives across human languages (the lexical approach) and the measurement of various traits derived from personality theories (the questionnaire approach). For nearly 50 years, competing sets of fundamental traits (e.g., Cattell, Eysenck, Guilford), typically derived through factor analysis, created disagreement about which traits were basic. However, in the 1980s, a convergence of the lexical and questionnaire strategies generated a consensus among many trait psychologists that five basic broad traits provided an adequate description of individual differences (McCrae & John, 1992). This set of basic traits is referred to as the Five-Factor Model (FFM) of personality.

Contemporary factor-analytic investigations have recovered the FFM traits in diverse languages spoken around the world (McCrae & Costa, 1997) and demonstrated that most traits assessed by personality questionnaires, regardless of their original theoretical roots and applied purposes, can be subsumed by the FFM. The major advantages of this consensus include (1) the provision of a common language for psychologists of different traditions to use in describing individual differences and (2) the ability to focus research on the roles traits play in diverse human phenomena rather than on endless debates over which traits are basic.

Description

Although differences of opinion exist regarding the names of the five basic traits, the labels associated with the most popular articulation of the FFM (Costa & McCrae, 1992) are the following:

Neuroticism vs. Emotional Stability. High neuroticism suggests a proneness to psychological distress and emotional reactivity reflected in chronic experiences of anxiety, depression, self-consciousness, low self-esteem, and ineffective coping. Low neuroticism does not guarantee psychological health but does suggest a calm, even-tempered emotional style.

Extraversion vs. Introversion. High extraversion suggests an interpersonal style marked by preferences for social interaction, high activity levels, and the capacity to experience positive emotions. Low extraversion suggests a preference for solitude and a reserved, quiet, and independent interpersonal style, but not an inherently unhappy or unfriendly individual.

Openness to Experience vs. Closed to Experience. High openness suggests an active pursuit and appreciation of experiences for their own sake, reflecting curiosity, imagination, tolerance of diverse values and beliefs, novelty seeking, and attraction to aesthetic experiences. Low openness suggests a preference for conventional attitudes, conservative tastes, dogmatic views, and little interest in the unfamiliar or markedly different.

Agreeableness vs. Antagonism. High agreeableness suggests a friendly, cooperative, trustworthy, and nurturant interpersonal style. Low agreeableness suggests a cynical, rude, abrasive, suspicious, uncooperative, and irritable interpersonal style.

Conscientiousness vs. Unconscientiousness. This trait describes individual differences in the degree of organization, persistence, control, and motivation in goal-directed behavior. High conscientiousness reflects a tendency to be organized, reliable, hardworking, self-directed, deliberate, ambitious, and persevering. Low conscientiousness reflects a tendency to be disorganized, aimless, lazy, careless, lax, negligent, and hedonistic.

Theory

Although the FFM is empirically derived through factor-analytic investigations of language and personality questionnaires, it is erroneous to conceive of the model as atheoretical. The emerging consensus led to the question, "Why are these five basic traits universal descriptors of human individual differences?" Several theoretical viewpoints have been applied to this question (Wiggins, 1996), including the lexical hypothesis, the dyadic-interactional perspective, socioanalytic personality theory, evolutionary theory, and personality metatheory.

Assessment

The FFM can be assessed through self-reports, observer ratings, and a structured interview. In addition, FFM scales have been derived for many existing self-report instruments originally designed to assess alternative personality and mental health constructs. FFM assessment procedures vary dramatically in length and format. Individuals interested in assessing the FFM should consider important differences among instruments and methods.

Applications

The FFM has been widely applied in diverse domains of psychological science and practice. Clinical psychologists have linked the FFM to both symptom-based psychopathologies and personality disorders (McCrae, 2006; Widiger & Lowe, 2007), as well as demonstrating its advantages for treatment planning and understanding the psychotherapeutic process. Beyond clinical psychology, the FFM has been widely used in industrial and organizational psychology, cross-cultural psychology, health psychology, social psychology, developmental psychology, counseling psychology, and the study of close relationships. These investigations indicate the FFM dimensions are reliable and valid predictors of many everyday behaviors, aspects of relationship functioning, coping styles, and levels of adjustment across childhood, adolescence, adulthood, and even in late life. For example, recent research has demonstrated that the FFM is predictive of occupational preference, performance, and leadership; human motivations and goals; criminal justice processes and outcomes; identity formation and cohesion; and coping with physical and psychological changes associated with aging.

Criticisms

Although the FFM has been successfully applied in diverse areas of psychology, criticisms of the model have been raised. These largely focus on the inherent vulnerabilities of factor analysis, lack of validity scales for most FFM inventories, and the limitations of the descriptive scope of the FFM.

REFERENCES

Allport, G. W., & Odbert, H. S. (1936). Trait names: A psycholexical study. *Psychological Monographs, 47*(1, Whole No. 211).

Costa, P. T., Jr., & McCrae, R. R. (1992). *NEO-PI-R/NEO-FFI professional manual.* Odessa, FL: Psychological Assessment Resources.

McCrae, R. R. (2006). Psychopathology from the perspective of the Five-Factor Model. In S. Strack (Ed.), *Differentiating normal and abnormal personality* (2nd ed., pp. 51–64). New York: Springer.

McCrae, R. R., & Costa, P. T., Jr. (1997). Personality trait structure as a human universal. *American Psychologist, 52,* 509–516.

McCrae, R. R., & John, O. P. (1992). An introduction to the Five-Factor Model and its applications. *Journal of Personality, 60,* 175–215.

Widiger, T. A., & Lowe, J. R. (2007). Five-Factor Model assessment of personality disorder. *Journal of Personality Assessment, 89,* 16–29.

Wiggins, J. S. (1996). *The five-factor model of personality: Theoretical perspectives.* New York: Guilford Press.

SUGGESTED READINGS

Costa, P. T., Jr., & Widiger, T. A. (2002). *Personality disorders and the Five-Factor Model of personality* (2nd ed.). Washington, DC: American Psychological Association.

McCrae, R. R., & Costa, P. T., Jr. (2003). *Personality in adulthood: A five-factor theory perspective* (2nd ed.). New York: Guilford Press.

Wiggins, J. S. (1996). *The five-factor model of personality: Theoretical perspectives.* New York: Guilford Press.

AARON L. PINCUS
Pennsylvania State University

FLOURISHING

Arguing that mental health and mental illness are not merely opposite ends of one single measurement continuum, Keyes (2002, 2005, 2006) proposes that mental health should be viewed as a complete state consisting of two dimensions: (1) the mental illness continuum and (2) the mental health continuum. Furthermore, symptoms of mental health consist of individuals' subjective well-being, which in turn reflects their perceptions and evaluations of their lives in terms of their affective states and their psychological and social functioning.

The instrument utilized by the mental health model represents a taxonomy of mental health symptoms consisting of emotional well-being (i.e., measures of positive affect, happiness, and life satisfaction), functional psychological well-being (i.e., measures of self-acceptance, personal growth, purpose in life, environmental mastery, autonomy, and positive relations with others), and functional social well-being (i.e., measures of social acceptance, social actualization, social contribution, social coherence, and social integration). In the same way that depression is characterized by symptoms of anhedonia, mental health, according to proponents of this perspective, is proposed to consist of symptoms of hedonia, or emotional vitality and positive feelings toward one's life.

To be diagnosed as flourishing, individuals must exhibit high levels on one of three scales of emotional well-being and high levels on six of eleven scales of positive functioning. Flourishing is not only distinct from psychopathology, but also from languishing, which is a state in which an individual is devoid of positive emotion toward life, is functioning poorly psychologically or socially, and has not experienced depression in the past one year. In short, languishers are neither mentally ill nor mentally healthy. To be diagnosed as languishing in life, individuals must exhibit low levels on 6 of the 11 scales of positive functioning. Individuals who are neither flourishing nor languishing—which represent the ends of the mental health continuum—are thereby moderately mentally healthy.

In a national probability sample of adolescents between the ages of 12 and 18, research has shown that flourishing youth reported lower levels of deviance and conduct problems and higher levels of psychosocial assets than moderately mentally healthy or languishing youth. In particular, flourishing youth reported lower rates of having ever been arrested, having ever skipped school, smoking cigarettes or, in the past month, having smoked cigarettes, smoked marijuana, drank alcohol, or sniffed inhalants than moderately mentally health youth, who in turn reported lower rates than languishing youth. Similarly, flourishing youth scored higher on scales measuring positive self-concept, self-determination, integration into school, and closeness to others than moderately mentally healthy youth, who scored higher than languishing youth (Keyes, 2006).

In adults between the ages of 25 and 74, research has also shown that flourishing is an asset, whereas moderate mental health and languishing are liabilities. Recent studies have revealed that completely mentally healthy adults—individuals free of a 12-month mental disorder and flourishing—report the fewest missed days of work, the fewest half-day or greater work cutbacks, the healthiest psychosocial functioning, the lowest risk of cardiovascular disease, the lowest number of chronic physical diseases with age, the fewest health limitations of activities of daily living, and lower healthcare utilization (Keyes, 2002, 2005).

Only 18% of adults between the ages of 25 and 74 fit the criteria for flourishing. Instead, most adults, 65%, were moderately mentally healthy, while 17% were languishing (Keyes, 2005). In contrast, flourishing is more common in adolescents. Between the ages of 12 and 18, 38% of youth were flourishing, 56% were moderately mentally healthy, and 6% were languishing (Keyes, 2006).

REFERENCES

Keyes, C. L. M. (2002). The mental health continuum: From languishing to flourishing in life. *Journal of Health and Social Behavior, 43*, 207–222.

Keyes, C. L. M. (2005). Mental illness and/or mental health? Investigating axioms of the complete state model of health. *Journal of Consulting and Clinical Psychology, 73*, 539–548.

Keyes, C. L. M. (2006). Mental health in adolescence: Is America's youth flourishing? *American Journal of Orthopsychiatry, 76*, 395–402.

Corey L. M. Keyes
Emory University

See also: **Happiness; Positive Psychology; Psychological Health**

FLYNN EFFECT

The term "Flynn Effect" refers to the finding that IQ test scores have increased over time in many countries (Flynn, 2007). Most existing evidence of the effect comes from industrialized nations; however, recent studies suggest that gains are now occurring in developing countries as well. In some northern European countries, the trend appears to have stopped. At present there is no generally agreed-on explanation for the effect.

Any eventual explanation for the trend will have to account for a number of relevant empirical findings, some of which are listed next. Several proposed explanations are also discussed, along with their respective strengths and weaknesses in explaining various findings.

Relevant Findings

Gains in IQ have tended to be larger, in relative terms, on tests of on-the-spot problem solving than on tests that measure previously learned information (Flynn, 2007, p. 5). For example, the typical rate of gain on common test batteries such as the Wechsler Adult Intelligence Scale has been approximately three IQ points per decade, whereas gains on Raven's Progressive Matrices have been as high as seven IQ points per decade.

Gains have been observed in young children, at or before the age when formal schooling begins. Some studies report a decline in the variance of IQ over time, but this is not a universal finding (Flynn, 2007, p. 104). IQ test performance has consistently displayed moderate to high heritability during the many decades that scores have risen. For example, studies of monozygotic twins reared apart have found them to be quite similar in IQ, even in populations that went on to witness large subsequent IQ gains after the study. Within-family studies of the effect of birth order have generally shown no IQ advantage to the younger siblings. This would suggest that IQ has not risen over time within families. It should be emphasized that the results of birth order studies allow only a tentative conclusion, as multiple factors other than those causing Flynn effects could cause IQ differences among siblings. Studies of the effect of inbreeding on IQ report relatively modest effects, approximately three IQ points in the offspring of first cousin unions.

IQ is not the only trait to have undergone large changes over time. Height has increased at about the same relative rate as IQ. Age of menarche has declined, and conditions like asthma and myopia have increased.

Proposed Hypotheses

The following five hypotheses have been put forward to account for the Flynn effect.

Nutrition

The nutrition hypothesis (Lynn, 1998) has the advantage of being able to explain multiple trends. It can also account for the early onset of gains. To the extent that one would expect improved nutrition to benefit those at the bottom of the IQ distribution, the lack of any clear trend in IQ variance is somewhat problematic. The greatest problem for nutrition, however, is the IQ paradox and the related twin paradox, as one would expect differences in nutrition to be considerable at any single point in time, thereby lowering heritability estimates and causing differences among reared-apart twins.

Education

Improved education as a causal factor is problematic for several reasons. Gains are apparent before the age when formal schooling begins. It is unlikely to explain trends in other traits. The high heritability of IQ is a problem. It has also been argued that education-induced gains should be larger on tests of previously learned information rather than on-the-spot problem solving.

The Dickens-Flynn Model

This theoretical model is a specific attempt to resolve the paradox of high IQ heritability (Dickens & Flynn, 2001). It posits change in environmental factors that are highly correlated with IQ genes, as well as an IQ "social multiplier" in which the IQ of individuals is influenced by the mean IQ of the population. It is not clear whether the model resolves the twin paradox, because something in the nature of the interaction between genes and environment must still change over time, but must do so at the same rate in every household. It is unlikely to explain trends in other traits. This explanation is also difficult to test, because the effects of the environmental factors it posits are difficult to distinguish from the effects of the genes with which they are correlated.

Heterosis

The heterosis hypothesis (Mingroni, 2007) posits that urbanization has caused the mixing of previously isolated and genetically distinct communities. This mixing of genes, combined with nonadditive gene interaction, causes IQ gains and changes in other traits. As a genetic hypothesis, heterosis resolves the paradox of high IQ heritability. It explains the finding of no IQ gains within families. It can explain multiple trends. Its main problem is the relatively small effects observed in IQ inbreeding studies, thereby requiring large genetic differences among local communities in the affected populations.

Genomic Imprinting

In this hypothesis, put forward by Storfer (1999), the effects of environmental factors such as visual stimulation are transmitted between generations via the sperm and ultimately affect brain development. Genomic imprinting offers an explanation for trends in IQ, myopia, and brain size, but it does not specifically attempt to explain the height trend. The main problem is that it is very difficult to test.

Although the Flynn Effect was first documented decades ago, basic questions related to the effect remain unanswered, such as whether the effect occurs within families and whether IQ gains have been accompanied by changes in brain physiology. What can be said with reasonable certainty, however, is that finding the cause of Flynn Effect is likely to increase substantially our understanding of human intelligence.

REFERENCES

Dickens, W. T., & Flynn, J. R. (2001). Heritability estimates versus large environmental effects: The IQ paradox resolved. *Psychological Review, 108*, 346–369.

Flynn, J. R. (2007). *What is intelligence? Beyond the Flynn effect.* New York: Cambridge University Press.

Lynn, R. (1998). In support of the nutrition theory. In U. Neisser (Ed.), *The rising curve: Long-term gains in IQ and related measures.* (pp. 207–218). Washington, DC: American Psychological Association.

Mingroni, M. A. (2007). Resolving the IQ paradox: Heterosis as a cause of the Flynn effect and other trends. *Psychological Review, 114*, 806–829.

Storfer, M. (1999). Myopia, intelligence, and the expanding human neocortex: Behavioral influences and evolutionary implications. *International Journal of Neuroscience, 98*, 153–276.

SUGGESTED READINGS

Deary, I. J. (2001). *Intelligence: A very short introduction.* Chapter 6: The lands of the rising IQ. Oxford, UK: Oxford University Press.

Neisser, U. (1998). *The rising curve: Long-term gains in IQ and related measures.* Washington, DC: American Psychological Association.

MICHAEL A. MINGRONI
Newark, DE

See also: Intelligence

FOOD ADDICTION

Food addiction is a topic that has received attention in the psychological literature in part because of the role that it potentially plays in binge eating, obesity, and eating disorders. Food addiction has also received attention as an addiction in its own right, akin to widely known addictive substances and behaviors such as drugs, gambling, and sex. An addiction is defined by the *Diagnostic and Statistical Manual of Mental Disorders* (DSM-IV-TR) as (1) the use of a substance that has mood altering or psychoactive effects, (2) highly controlled or compulsive use of a substance, and (3) the used substance reinforces behavior (American Psychiatric Association, 2000). Other criteria include tolerance and physical dependence. Food addiction specifically is typically characterized by a loss of control over eating certain foods, preoccupation with or craving of certain food or foods, failed attempts to overcome the eating problem despite negative consequences, and use of the food or foods to cope with negative emotions. Food addiction has been tied most often to highly palatable foods such as chocolate, confectionary foods, carbohydrate-rich foods, and foods high in fat content.

Considerable research has been conducted to study the physiological effects of food consumption. The psychoactive effects of food are hypothesized to act through specific neurochemical pathways. Some models propose that certain foods have rewarding effects by stimulating the release of dopamine in the nucleus accumbens and additionally through modifications to the opioid systems in the brain (Avena, Rada, & Hoebel, 2008; Spring et al., 2008). The dopaminergic and opioid pathways seem to be particularly sensitive and responsive to foods high in sugar and rich in fat. Studies with animals have shown that administration of a sugar substance in intermittent periods (i.e., the animal has access to the sugar for a certain period of time and then is deprived of the substance) causes increased dopamine release in the brain, altered opioid receptor function, and delayed release of

the neurotransmitter acetylcholine (Avena et al., 2008). These neurotransmitter systems are the same pathways that are involved in natural reward and in addiction to other drugs. It is believed that when these dopamine and opioid pathways become overstimulated, neurobiological adaptations may be triggered that make the behaviors (i.e., eating) more compulsive and out of control (Volkow & Wise, 2005).

A second neurotransmitter effect implicated in food addiction is the induced synthesis of serotonin by eating foods rich in carbohydrates and poor in protein. The elevated levels of serotonin then interact with the dopaminergic systems to stimulate the experience of reward (Spring et al., 2008). Serotonin plays an important role in the central nervous system in the regulation of mood. Past research and observation have demonstrated that, when people experience depressed mood, they also show increased cravings for carbohydrate rich foods (Rogers & Smit, 2000). These observations have been supported by studies with humans showing that, when women who were identified as "carbohydrate cravers" were in a negative mood state, they blindly chose a carbohydrate-rich drink to alleviate their mood. These women overwhelmingly indicated that the carbohydrate-rich beverage had made them feel better, and mood was indeed significantly elevated in the conditions in which participants had drunk the carbohydrate-rich beverage. These results offer support for the mood-altering effects of carbohydrates and their use in coping with negative mood.

Another characteristic of addiction—compulsive use—manifests itself in the form of intense cravings for food and subsequent binges. A craving is defined as intense desire to eat a specific food. Food cravings are frequently reported during periods of depressed mood and in such disorders and conditions as bulimia nervosa, obesity, premenstrual syndrome, and seasonal affective disorder (Rogers & Smit, 2000). Cravings and binges associated with food addiction may exist in part because of nutritional-physiological mechanisms (Rogers & Smit, 2000). As was stated earlier, one reason for these cravings may be the need to elevate mood by increasing the production of serotonin in the brain through the intake of carbohydrate-rich foods. Cravings for foods rich in sugars are also hypothesized to exist in response to stress, because eating sugary foods helps to stimulate opioid release in the brain. Binges, which are episodes of severe psychopathology accompanied by feelings of being "out of control," also frequently occur during periods of stress and negative affect and have been reported to be characterized by brief elevations in mood, a sense of a "high," or a decrease in negative affect (Engelberg, Steiger, Gauvin, & Wonderlich, 2007).

There are also several psychological explanations and correlates of food craving and binges. Food cravings can be initiated by external cues, such as the sight, smell, taste, or thought of certain foods, as well as a time and place for eating (Rogers & Smit, 2000). Based on a classical conditioning model, these cues are thought to stimulate affective, physiological, and behavioral arousal in food addicts, leading to greater cravings. One study has shown that people who self-identify as food addicts (e.g., chocolate addicts) do indeed become more aroused compared to non-addicts, as evidenced by greater salivation and reported cravings, when presented with a picture of chocolate or even when asked to imagine chocolate (Tuomisto et al., 1999). Additionally, external cues in this study were also associated with more negative affective states, such as anxiety, guilt, depression, and frustration. Therefore, it is important to note that these intense cravings and binges are not necessarily signaled by hunger, but by external and internal cues related to food and emotional states (Rogers & Smit, 2000; Tuomisto et al., 1999).

Dietary restriction may also play an important role in cravings, out of control eating behaviors, and failed attempts to regulate the intake of addictive foods. In current society, certain foods are considered "bad," unhealthy, or forbidden, and dieting practices related to these kinds of food are common. The actual process of restraint and deprivation, though, may be counterproductive and lead to the kinds of cravings experienced in food addiction. Research supports that people who restrain themselves from eating certain foods (e.g., chocolate, carbohydrates) actually consume more of those foods after a period of deprivation or restriction (Polivy, Coleman, & Herman, 2005). The phenomenon of thought suppression is thought to partially explain this link between dieting and an increase in cravings (Hill, 2007). In dieters' efforts not to think about eating certain foods, they actually increase the salience and desirability of the foods they are trying not to eat. However, although this pattern of restraint and craving has been demonstrated in many groups of highly restrained eaters, this explanation for cravings may not be specific to self-identified food addicts. Cravings and restraint, though, do seem to be limited to the highly palatable foods implicated in food addictions.

Individuals who engage in the restriction of highly palatable foods may not only experience greater cravings, but may also be more likely to engage in binge eating behaviors (Rogers & Smit, 2000). Research suggests that people identified as high-restrictors have more episodes of binge eating than people who do not restrict their diets (Polivy & Herman, 1985). In other words, the process of abstaining from certain foods may trigger a binge when the food is consumed again. Rogers and Smit (2000) suggest that disinhibition may be responsible for this result. After the diet is broken by consuming a certain amount of the restricted food or foods, the dieters suspend their self-imposed restraint. Other triggers of binge eating in individuals include emotional events, alcohol consumption, and anticipated overeating (Rogers & Smit, 2000). Therefore, people with food addictions may find it difficult

to break their habit because of the causal connection between dieting and bingeing.

Although food addiction is still being investigated and defined as a phenomenon, we do know that specific neurochemical pathways responsible for drug addiction may play a role in the process of becoming addicted to foods rich in sugar, fat, and carbohydrates. Furthermore, the addiction to certain foods may be reinforced by the connections between affective states, palatable foods, and neurochemical pathways involved in managing stress and negative affect. Other psychological influences of compulsive eating, preoccupation, and trouble restricting include the sensitivity of cravings to external food cues, thought suppression, mood states, and the disinhibition effect of dieting. However, several questions regarding food addiction still remain. No evidence yet exists that food has physically addictive properties, and alternative theories posit instead that self-labeled food addictions are merely the result of attribution errors (Hill, 2007; Rogers & Smit, 2000). In other words, we use the term "addiction" to explain why we have trouble restraining ourselves from eating socially undesirable or "bad" foods. On the other hand, this explanation may not be sufficient to explain the intense psychological states and behaviors surrounding food that are associated with eating disorders such as bulimia nervosa.

REFERENCES

American Psychiatric Association. (2000). *Diagnostic and statistical manual of mental disorders* (4th ed., text rev.). Washington, DC: Author.

Avena, N. M., Rada, P., & Hoebel, B. G. (2008). Evidence for sugar addiction: Behavioral and neurochemical effects of intermittent and excessive sugar intake. *Neuroscience and Behavioral Reviews, 32,* 20–39.

Engelberg, M. J., Steiger, H., Gauvin, L., & Wonderlich, S. A. (2007). Binge antecedents in bulimic syndromes: An examination of dissociation and negative affect. *International Journal of Eating Disorders, 40,* 531–536.

Hill, A. J. (2007). The psychology of food craving. *Proceedings of the Nutrition Society, Aberdeen, 66,* 277–285.

Polivy, J., Coleman, J., & Herman, C. P. (2005). The effect of deprivation on food cravings and eating behavior in restrained and unrestrained eaters. *International Journal of Eating Disorders, 38,* 301–309.

Polivy, J., & Herman, C. P. (1985). Dieting and binging: A causal analysis. *American Psychologist, 40,* 193–201.

Rogers, P. J., & Smit, H. J. (2000). Food craving and food "addiction": A critical review of the evidence from a biopsychosocial perspective. *Pharmacology Biochemistry and Behavior, 66,* 3–14.

Spring, B., Schneider, K., Smith, M., Kendzor, D., Appelhans, B., Hedeker, D., et al. (2008). Abuse potential of carbohydrates for overweight carbohydrate cravers. *Psychopharmacology, 19,* 637–647.

Tuomisto, T., Hetherington, M. M., Morris, M., Tuomisto, M., Turjanmaa, V., & Lappalainen, R. (1999). Psychological and physiological characteristics of sweet food "addiction." *International Journal of Eating Disorders, 25*, 169–175.

Volkow, N., & Wise, R. (2005). How can drug addiction help us understand obesity? *Nature Neuroscience, 8*, 555–560.

SUGGESTED READING

Drenowski, A., & Bellisle, F. (2007). Is sweetness addictive? *Nutrition Bulletin, 32*, 52–60.

JESSIE MENZEL
J. KEVIN THOMPSON
University of South Florida

See also: Eating Disorders; Obesity; Weight Control

FORENSIC ASSESSMENT INSTRUMENTS AND TECHNIQUES

Assessment and evaluation is a key component of the identity and practice of clinical psychologists. The majority of assessment activity in which psychologists engage is best described as *therapeutic assessment*—psychological evaluation that is conducted to facilitate or inform decision making about treatment and other types of interventions. In contrast, *forensic assessment* is conducted during or in anticipation of litigation, for the purpose of providing legal decision makers or others with information about aspects of the examinee's psychological functioning that are relevant to some issue that is in dispute. Many commentators, when discussing this issue, distinguish between "clinical assessment" and "forensic assessment" (or between clinical activities and forensic activities). Such terminology is potentially misleading, however, insofar as all forensic assessment is clinical in nature, and it is psychologists' clinical expertise that leads to the court to seek input and opinions from them.

Grisso's (1986/2003) model is invaluable for conceptualizing any type of forensic psychological assessment and the psychologist's obligations. According to Grisso, the psychologist who is conducting a forensic evaluation must (1) identify the legal issue and standard, (2) define what aspects of the legal issue are psychological in nature, (3) conceptualize the "psycholegal capacities" that are at issue, and (4) choose and employ the appropriate psychological assessment techniques.

In a review of forensic evaluation practice Heilbrun, Rogers, and Otto (2002) offered a typology of assessment techniques that can be utilized by psychologists conducting forensic evaluations. Clinical assessment techniques (CATs) are tools (e.g., tests, interviews, checklists) that assess clinical constructs that may be relevant to understanding a person's functioning as it relates to some legal or psycholegal issue. CATs are standardized measures that are used in clinical evaluations but can also provide relevant psycholegal information about an individual's psychopathology (if any), personality characteristics, intelligence, academic achievement, memory, adaptive behavior, and executive functioning. Among numerous CATs widely used in forensic evaluations are the Minnesota Multiphasic Personality Inventory, the Personality Assessment Inventory-Adolescent Version, the Beck Depression Inventory, the Structured Interview for Personality Disorders, the Diagnostic Interview for Children, the Wechsler Adult Intelligence Scale, and the Wide Range Achievement Test.

Forensically relevant assessment techniques (FRATs) are tests, interviews, and checklists that also assess clinical constructs but focus on particular issues relevant to and commonly arising in forensic contexts and settings. FRATs inform or structure psychologists' judgments about such matters as an examinee's risk for violence (e.g., Structured Assessment for Violence Risk in Youth, Violence Risk Appraisal Guide, Sexual Violence Risk-20), level of psychopathy (e.g., Psychopathy Checklist-Revised, Psychopathic Personality Inventory), and response style (e.g., Validity Indicator Profile, Word Memory Test, Paulhus Deception Scale, Structured Interview of Reported Symptoms).

Forensic assessment techniques (FATs) are tools specifically developed to aid in assessment of a psycholegal construct and, as such, are used only in forensic assessment contexts. These include tools that structure assessment of or provide normative data about a criminal defendant's trial competence (e.g., Fitness Interview Test-Revised, MacArthur Competence Assessment Tool-Criminal Adjudication, Georgia Court Competency Test); about a criminal defendant's mental state at the time of an alleged offense (e.g., Rogers Criminal Responsibility Assessment Scales); about a person's capacity to make important decisions concerning financial, health care, and other matters as they may indicate the need for a guardian (e.g., Independent Living Scales, Florida Guardianship Assessment Procedure); or about a patient's capacity to consent to treatment (MacArthur Competence Assessment Tool-Treatment). Because FATs are designed to assess and inform judgments about what are ultimately legal issues, it can be a challenging task to identify the appropriate variables against which the validity of these measures can be assessed.

The first FAT was developed by Dr. Ames Robey, a psychiatrist. The Checklist of Criteria for Competency to

Stand Trial (Robey, 1965) was an attempt to ensure that mental health professionals, when evaluating a criminal defendant's competence to proceed with the legal process, considered how the examinee's emotional, behavioral, and cognitive functioning affected the relevant psycholegal capacities (i.e., understanding and comprehension of the legal process and capacity to work with counsel). A few FATS and FRATs were developed for this purpose in the 1970s (e.g., Competence Screening Test, Competence Assessment Instrument, Georgia Court Competency Test) and also in the 1980s (e.g., Rogers Criminal Responsibility Assessment Scales, Interdisciplinary Fitness Interview, Instruments for Assessing Understanding and Appreciation of Miranda Rights, Custody Quotient, Bricklin Perceptual Scales). However, it was in the 1990s that development and publication of FATs and FRATs increased considerably (e.g., Victoria Symptom Validity Test, Word Memory Test, M Test, Violence Risk Appraisal Guide, Malingering Probability Scale, Rapid Risk Assessment for Sex Offender Recidivism, Static-99, Computerized Assessment of Response Bias, Test of Memory Malingering, Validity Indicator Profile, Parent Awareness of Skills Survey, Ackerman-Schoendorf Parent Evaluation of Custody Test, Child Abuse Potential Inventory, Level of Service Inventory-Revised). Heilbrun et al. (2002) concluded in this regard that more of these measures were developed during the decade of the 1990s than in any time prior.

More specifically, the 1990s saw a particular increase in two types of assessment tools. One type comprised structured professional judgment tools, as exemplified by the HCR-20, the Fitness Interview Test-Revised, the Sexual Violence Risk-20, the Early Assessment of Risk List for Boys, the Early Assessment of Risk List for Girls, the Structured Assessment of Violence Risk in Youth, the Juvenile Adjudicative Competence Interview, and the Spousal Assault Risk Assessment. All of these tools are rationally derived assessment formats simply designed to structure clinicians' assessments and ensure that they consider variables or factors that have a demonstrated empirical relationship to the issue at hand. The second type of tools were actuarial measures to provide specific probabilities regarding events of interest, typically violence or other offending behavior, and these measures are exemplified by the Violence Risk Appraisal Guide, the Static-99, the Rapid Risk Assessment of Sex Offender Risk, and the Classification of Violence Risk.

As mentioned, CATs aid in assessment of clinical constructs (e.g., psychopathology, intellectual abilities, memory functioning, personality characteristics, academic skills, adaptive behaviors) that can also be minimally or remotely related to the psycholegal or legal issues at hand. In contrast, using FATs and FRATs when conducting forensic examinations is enticing because they assist in structuring or informing judgments about constructs that are more directly related than CATs to the psycholegal or legal issues in dispute. However, psychologists must be wary consumers and be judicious when considering use of FATs and FRATs, in part because of the inverse relationship between the clinical certainty of psychological assessment tools and techniques and their legal relevance (Rogers, 1987). That is, the psychological assessment tools and techniques that are the most researched and best validated, which are the CATs, assess constructs that are often least relevant to issues of interest to the court. In contrast, the psychological assessment tools and techniques that aid in assessment of issues that are of most interest to the court, the FATs and FRATs, are typically the least researched and validated.

This circumstance, in combination with observations that numerous FATs and FRATs have been made available for professional use—both by authors as well as independent test publishers—without adequate research examining their reliability and validity, makes clear that psychologists should select the tools they employ with considerable care (Heilbrun et al., 2002; Otto & Heilbrun, 2002). When considering the use of any assessment tools or techniques, psychologists should consider whether the assessment technique (1) is commercially published and is readily available to the professional community; (2) has a test manual that describes its purpose, use, development, and properties; (3) has acceptable levels of reliability and validity; (4) has received appropriate peer review; and (5) has been reviewed in a positive or negative light by the courts if issues have been raised concerning the admissibility of opinions based in full or in part on the technique.

REFERENCES

Grisso, T. (1986/2003). *Evaluating competencies: Forensic assessments and instruments* (1st and 2nd ed.). New York: Kluwer/Plenum.

Heilbrun, K., Rogers, R., & Otto, R. K. (2002). Forensic assessment: Current status and future directions. In J. R. P. Ogloff (Ed.), *Taking psychology and law into the twenty-first century* (pp. 119–146). New York: Kluwer/Plenum.

Otto R. K., & Heilbrun, K. (2002). The practice of forensic psychology: A look to the future in light of the past. *American Psychologist, 57*, 5–18. Reprinted in Roesch, R., & McLachlan, K. (Eds.). (2007). *Clinical forensic psychology and law*. Hampshire, UK: Ashgate.

Robey, A. (1965). Criteria for competency to stand trial: A checklist for psychiatrists. *American Journal of Psychiatry, 122*, 616–623.

Rogers, R. (1987). Ethical dilemmas in forensic evaluations. *Behavioral Sciences and the Law, 5*, 149–160.

SUGGESTED READINGS

Heilbrun, K. (2001). *Principles of forensic mental health assessment*. New York: Kluwer/Plenum.

Melton, G. B., Petrila, J., Poythress, N., Lyon, P., & Otto, R. K. (2007). *Psychological evaluations for the courts: A handbook for mental health professionals and lawyers* (3rd ed.). New York: Guilford Press.

RANDY K. OTTO
University of South Florida

See also: Forensic Consulting; Psychological Assessment; Psychology and the Law

FORENSIC CONSULTING

Forensic consulting occurs when psychologists support one side's attempts to prevail over another in civil and criminal legal proceedings. Unlike expert witnesses, who are expected to approach each case in an unbiased fashion and to testify about their findings under oath, forensic consultants strive from the very beginning to identify helpful information and winning strategies for the party that retains them, secure in the knowledge that they will never take the witness stand.

The legal system's need for forensic consulting springs from certain limitations in the role of the expert witness. Experts are allowed to tell an attorney what may be useful about the results of their forensic evaluations, but they are required to remain aloof from the "adversary process" typically employed in resolving legal disputes. Becoming a partisan member of a defense or prosecution "team" involves generating material, receiving confidences, and developing a mindset that the other side may investigate and expose during cross-examination, thus eroding the expert's credibility and bringing harm to the attorney's clients. The forensic consultant, by contrast, works behind the scenes to identify and train useful experts, to neutralize the effectiveness of the other side's experts, and to develop a perspective on the relevant scientific literature that attorneys can pursue to their clients' advantage (Shuman, 2007).

Identifying appropriate and effective expert witnesses requires a thorough understanding of the relevant subject matter and access to the names and addresses of the most knowledgeable and respected clinicians and researchers. It also calls for the ability to convey the nature of a legal case to professional colleagues in a concise, accessible, and engaging fashion and to gauge the likely fit between hiring attorneys and specific scientific experts. The attorneys in question may already possess a list of potential expert witnesses, and they may have one or two favorites whom they have employed from time to time. The forensic consultant must be able to weigh potential experts' comparative qualifications and attributes quickly and effectively and to convey these to counsel with economy and tact.

Investigating the other side's expert witnesses relies additionally on investigative skills and the capacity for critical analysis of forensic reports and published scientific research. One of the most important initial tasks is to obtain a copy of the expert's most recent *curriculum vitae*. Does it reveal insufficient experience or controversial viewpoints? Does it contain inflated qualifications or misrepresented publications? Are its contents outdated, referring to employment or committee assignments that lapsed years ago? Does it reflect relevant and respectable board certification, or instead does it refer to "vanity board" credentials that can be obtained—for a price—by anyone with a bare minimum of training or interest?

Reports by the other side's witness may possess a number of negative attributes that judges or juries will find important. Is the report signed by more than one individual? This may signal that the expert is so inexperienced as to require supervision, or that the examination in question was conducted by a student being trained by the expert, such that the expert has never even met the examinee. Multiple authors of a forensic report may possess differing opinions about relevant details, even if they endorse the same broad conclusion. Reports and the test data underlying them—often far more obtainable and understandable by the forensic consultant than by counsel—may reflect scoring errors that undercut the findings and impair the expert's credibility. The expert may have relied on computer-generated interpretations or even have "cut and pasted" excerpts from these into his or her own report, without comprehending their bases in the underlying test data or the logic used to develop them (Drogin, 2007).

Merely advising attorneys of the presence or absence of an opposing expert's errors and other shortcomings is insufficient. Forensic consulting also extends to assisting counsel to construct the avenues of inquiry and specific questions most likely to constitute an effective and revealing cross-examination. In addition, forensic consultants instruct the experts they have located in how to avoid similar pitfalls and how to offer a credible and compelling alternative, since judges and juries will expect more of counsel's painstakingly constructed legal position than incessant criticism of the other side's perspective (Imwinkelried, 2004).

Focusing solely on the other side's alleged shortcomings also fails to utilize the forensic consultant in an important role: that of a participant in brainstorming sessions, in which all members of the legal team contribute notions that may inform counsel's evolving theory of the case. Brainstorming may be a loose, almost free associative process in which ideas are generated without respect to any specific outline. It may also involve complex strategies for soliciting input from each individual team member in a structured and hierarchical fashion. In this context, forensic consultants can contribute a "jurisprudent science" analysis in which relevant aspects of mental health science, mental health practice, and mental health roles are each evaluated in terms of the degree to which these augment or detract from the goals of litigation and the acknowledged values of the legal system (Drogin & Barrett, 2003).

Forensic consultants are uniquely qualified to specify a need for ongoing treatment and follow-up clinical evaluations that largely determines the monetary value of a civil case. Key to this function is an orderly file review that includes such steps as identifying the presence or absence of substantial functional limitations, assessing treatment adequacy, weighing information used to estimate return to work dates, considering the role of secondary gain and exaggeration, analyzing the merits of independent psychological assessments, and distinguishing between personality pathology, work problems, and disability (Hadjistavropoulos & Bieling, 2001). These factors will have a differential impact depending on the forensic consultant's mastery of the various contexts in which they are being reviewed, such as private insurance policies, federal entitlement programs, worker's compensation, or private sector employee benefits, with each subject to a distinct mixture of state and federal statutes and case law (Piechowski, 2006).

In criminal cases, forensic consulting focuses on each expert's understanding and accommodation of the specific elements of the charges that the defendant is facing. Some defenses and mitigating circumstances will prevail in one state, but not another. Does the expert's report rely on doctrines unsupported by local statutes or case law? Licensure and certification requirements are quite different from state to state. Has the expert actually obtained permission to conduct an examination in a state where he or she is not formally licensed or certified? Failing to do so may itself constitute a criminal offense, will naturally undermine the expert's credibility on the witness stand, and may even lead to the expert's disqualification. Following a determination by the United States Supreme Court in *Ake v. Oklahama* (1985) that criminal defendants are entitled to forensic consultation in serious criminal cases, most states now guarantee some level of public funding for these services.

As with other modes of psychological service delivery, what happens during the initial meeting with a client is crucial in establishing the appropriate legal and ethical boundaries for interaction with counsel (Melton et al., 2007). The attorney may, for example, not grasp critical distinctions between the roles of the forensic consultant and the expert witness, particularly after working with representatives of other professions who, unlike psychologists, may not recognize or value such considerations. Sometimes counsel will want to employ the psychologist

as an expert witness and subsequently as a forensic consultant, if the results of the psychologist's evaluation are not going to be helpful to the client. This is acceptable, but counsel must realize that this transformation cannot occur in reverse; forensic consultants ally themselves with attorneys and share the sorts of opinions and confidences that are inconsistent with the unbiased role of the expert witness (Brodsky, 1999).

Forensic consulting is an invaluable resource for trial attorneys in civil and criminal cases, and it is a steadily evolving aspect of psychological practice. Because it draws psychologists directly into the adversarial nature of legal proceedings, it presents ethical challenges that restrict its application to experienced clinicians and researchers. Increasingly sophisticated computerized investigation resources, and the legal profession's growing sense of vulnerabilities in expert psychological testimony, will contribute to an expanding market for forensic consulting in the decades to come.

REFERENCES

Ake v. Oklahoma, 470 U.S. 68 (1985).

Brodsky, S. L. (1999). *The "expert" expert witness: More maxims and guidelines for testifying in court*. Washington, DC: American Psychological Association.

Drogin, E. Y. (2007). The forensic psychologist as consultant: Examples from a jurisprudent science perspective. *The Journal of Psychiatry and Law, 35,* 245–260.

Drogin, E. Y., & Barrett, C. L. (2003). Off the witness stand: The forensic psychologist as consultant. In A. M. Goldstein (Ed.), *Forensic psychology: Emerging topics and expanding roles* (pp. 465–488). Hoboken, NJ: John Wiley & Sons.

Hadjistavropoulos, T., & Bieling, P. (2001). File review consultation in the adjudication of mental health and chronic disability claims. *Consulting Psychology Journal: Practice and Research, 53,* 52–63.

Imwinkelried, E. J. (2004). *The methods of attacking scientific evidence* (4th ed.). Newark, NJ: Matthew Bender.

Melton, G. B., Petrila, P., Poythress, N. G., Slobogin, C., Lyons, P. M., & Otto, R. K. (2007). *Psychological evaluations for the courts: A handbook for mental health professionals and lawyers* (3rd ed.). New York: Guilford Press.

Piechowski, L. D. (2006). Forensic consultation in disability insurance matters. *The Journal of Psychiatry and Law, 34,* 151–167.

Shuman, D. W. (2007). Discovery of consulting and psychiatric and psychological experts. *The Journal of Psychiatry and Law, 35,* 299–324.

SUGGESTED READINGS

Guilmette, T. J., & Hagan, L. D. (1997). Ethical considerations in forensic neuropsychological consultation. *Clinical Neuropsychologist, 11,* 287–290.

Martindale, D. M. (2007). Forensic consultation in litigated custody disputes. *The Journal of Psychiatry and Law, 35,* 281–298.

Posey, A. J., & Wrightsman, L. S. (2005). *Trial consulting.* New York: Oxford University Press.

Eric Y. Drogin
Harvard Medical School

See also: **Forensic Assessment Instruments and Techniques; Forensic Psychologists, Roles and Activities of**

FORENSIC PSYCHOLOGISTS, ROLES AND ACTIVITIES OF

Forensic psychology is an increasingly popular area of practice within psychology. It has been defined as "the application of psychological research, theory, practice, and traditional and specialized methodology (e.g., interviewing, psychological testing, forensic assessment and forensically relevant instruments) to provide information relevant to a legal question" (Goldstein, 2003, p. 4). The American Psychological Association designated forensic psychology as an area of specialization in 2001 (Goldstein, 2003), and it is the subject of a rapidly growing number of books, journals, and professional conferences (Otto & Heilbrun, 2002).

Forensic assessments are requested in a wide variety of legal disputes, including both criminal and civil cases. For example, in a criminal case, a psychologist may be asked to assess whether the defendant is competent to stand trial or meets criteria for an insanity defense. In anticipation of sentencing, a psychologist may be asked to assess whether a person who has been found guilty is likely to be a danger to third parties in the future. In civil cases, forensic psychologists may be asked to evaluate individuals in many types of situations. For example, a psychologist may be asked to evaluate whether a plaintiff has suffered emotional damage as a result of an injury. Parental fitness may be the issue in a custody dispute, and the extent of a person's disability may be the issue in a Social Security proceeding. A person's competency to consent to treatment or handle finances might be challenged in a guardianship proceeding, and a person's fitness for work may be at issue in litigation involving the workplace. In short, a psychologist may be asked to perform a forensic examination in nearly any type of legal proceeding in which the relationship between a person's mental state and a legal question is at issue.

The practice of forensic psychology differs in significant ways from usual clinical practice (Melton, Petrila,

Poythress, & Slobogin, 2007). Four of the most significant differences are noted here. First, the practice of forensic psychology involves the assessment of an individual at the request of a third party (e.g., a judge, an attorney, an employer) rather than for treatment. Although the person's treatment needs may be at issue in some cases as part of the assessment, the provision of treatment is usually not part of forensic practice. Second, the client in a forensic assessment is the party making the referral rather than the individual who is being assessed. In usual clinical practice, the clients are people who have presented themselves for assessment or treatment. Third, whereas individuals in usual practice seek services voluntarily, individuals referred for forensic assessment have typically been requested or required to do so by the referral source. Fourth, in usual practice, the therapist and client are working in common to improve the client's mental health. In forensic practice, however, the answer to the question posed by the referral source (e.g., is this individual dangerous?) may be at odds with the individual's perceived self-interest. As a result, the individual may withhold or distort information, thereby creating threats to the validity of the assessment.

Activities

Although psychologists engaged in forensic practice must have the general skills of any practicing psychologist, forensic assessments differ in significant ways from treatment-oriented assessments. Psychologists who are asked to conduct an assessment must understand the question that has been posed, including its legal contours. For example, if a defense attorney asks an examiner to assess whether a defendant is competent to stand trial, the person performing the examination must know how competency to stand trial is defined in the jurisdiction in which the assessment will occur. The examiner must also be clear about what types of information can be placed in the report that emerges from the assessment. In most jurisdictions, as an example, information about the alleged criminal conduct of a defendant is not to be placed in a report on competency to stand trial, because this information may violate the person's constitutional protection against self-incrimination.

There are three major components to most forensic psychological assessments: an interview, some testing, and a review of third-party or archival information. These same components are present in usual clinical practice, but with different emphases and objectives. The interview in clinical practice has a therapeutic goal, whereas a forensic interview typically will be more investigative in nature, more probing, and more focused on matters other than the therapeutic well-being of the person being interviewed (Craig, 2003). Forensic interviews may also extend over several sessions, depending on the complexity of the issues being considered. Because the person may not be participating in the assessment voluntarily or may be intent on leading the examiner to a particular conclusion, examiners must be alert to different response styles (e.g., open, guarded, malingering) while attempting to establish sufficient rapport with the examinee to obtain the information necessary for answering the query of the referring party. When examinees are refusing to answer or appear to be feigning symptoms, for example, the examiner must be prepared to identify and address such matters (Melton et al., 2007, pp. 56–62).

Forensic assessments often involve the use of tests in addition to an interview. The use of psychological tests is also part of usual practice, but commentators have placed such tests into three categories when they are used in forensic evaluations: clinical assessment instruments (CAIs), which are tests and measures developed for use in therapeutic contexts; forensically relevant instruments (FRIs), which are techniques that assess clinical constructs such as psychopathy or response styles likely to arise in some forensic assessments; and forensic assessment instruments (FAIs), which are instruments designed specifically for use in legal contexts to address such questions as competency to stand trial. Instruments in the last category, in particular, attempt to structure the examiner's inquiry to focus on only those issues relevant to the legal question (Archer, 2006; Heilbrun, Rogers, & Otto, 2002). Although guidelines have been developed to assess the reliability and validity of such tests, not all tests meet those guidelines. Psychologists performing forensic assessments must accordingly be mindful of the strengths and limitations of any instrument they choose for use in the assessment (Grisso, 2002).

Finally, forensic assessments often benefit from third-party and archival information that may not be as relevant in clinical practice. Such information may provide important facts that are not available from the person being interviewed and may shed light on details of that person's life that are relevant to the legal issue at hand. Depending on the legal issue, potentially important third-party information may be obtainable from interviews with family members and other significant individuals in a person's life, from past criminal and treatment histories, and from police reports of a criminal offense that precipitated the forensic assessment.

After the assessment is completed, examiners ordinarily prepare a written report of their findings and conclusions. As with assessments, forensic reports differ in important respects from clinical reports (Melton, et al., 2007, pp. 582–583). For example, forensic reports are written for individuals (attorneys, judges, administrative decision makers) who are often unfamiliar with clinical language and jargon. In addition, a forensic report may become public knowledge through different mechanisms such as a court record. Numerous helpful guides for organizing and writing forensic reports are available in the literature (e.g., Karson, 2005; Weiner, 2006).

Forensic Psychology as a Discrete Specialty

In an influential article in 1987, Grisso argued that forensic practice had to become anchored more rigorously in empirical research and become more standardized. He noted that although numerous psychologists had begun to make forensic practice a full-time enterprise, other practitioners without particular training or experience in forensic work were conducting forensic assessments as an occasional part of their practice and that such assessments were often substandard. By 2002, forensic psychology had become a discrete field, with certification and practice standards (Otto & Heilbrun, 2002). In addition, there are ethical guidelines for forensic practice for both psychiatry (American Academy of Psychiatry and Law, 2005) and psychology (Committee on Ethical Guidelines for Forensic Psychologists, 1991), with new guidelines under consideration for forensic psychology. As the field has become a specialty, it has become increasingly popular with students and with researchers, and in certain areas, such as risk assessment and competency, sophisticated tools have been developed to further structure the forensic assessment.

As forensic psychology grows in popularity, it faces continued challenges in the future. The issues identified by Grisso (1987) and Otto and Heilbrun (2002) still exist. For example, untrained practitioners still perform forensic assessments in many areas, and some instruments designed to structure an inquiry do not have proven reliability and validity. In addition, research findings often come slowly to practice. Whereas those who specialize in forensic practice have more knowledge available than ever before, those for whom forensic assessment is only an occasional area of practice are often unaware of developments in the field. One can anticipate that professional organizations devoted to this area of practice, such as the American Psychology–Law Society and the American Academy of Psychiatry and Law will continue to address these issues through the continued evolution of specialty and ethical guidelines.

REFERENCES

American Academy of Psychiatry and Law. (2005). *Ethics guidelines for the practice of forensic psychiatry*. Retrieved March 9, 2009, from http: //www.aapl.org/ethics.htm.

Archer, R. P. (Ed.). (2006). *Forensic uses of clinical assessment instruments*. Mahwah, NJ: Lawrence Erlbaum.

Committee on Ethical Guidelines for Forensic Psychologists. (1991). Specialty guidelines for forensic psychologists. *Law and Human Behavior, 15,* 655–665.

Craig, R. J. (2003). Assessing personality and psychopathology with interviews. In J. R. Graham, J. A. Naglieri (Vol. Eds.), & I. B. Weiner (Ed.-in-Chief), *Handbook of Psychology: Vol. 10, Clinical Psychology* (pp. 487–508). Hoboken, NJ: John Wiley & Sons.

Goldstein, A. M. (2003). Overview of forensic psychology. In A. M. Goldstein (Vol. Ed.) & I. B. Weiner (Ed.-in-Chief), *Handbook of psychology: Vol. 11. Forensic psychology* (pp. 3–20). Hoboken, NJ: John Wiley & Sons.

Grisso, T. (1987). The economic and scientific future of forensic assessment. *American Psychologist, 42,* 831–839.

Grisso, T. (2002). *Evaluating competencies: Forensic assessments and instruments.* New York: Springer.

Heilbrun, K., Rogers, R., & Otto, R. K. (2002). Forensic assessment: Current status and future directions. In J. R. Ogloff (Ed.), *Taking psychology and law into the 21st century* (pp. 120–147). New York: Springer.

Karson, M. (2005). Ten things I learned about report writing in law school (and the eighth grade). *Clinical Psychologist, 58,* 4–11.

Melton, G., Petrila, J., Poythress, N., & Slobogin, C. (2007). *Psychological evaluations for the courts: A handbook for mental health professionals and lawyers* (3rd ed.). New York: Guilford Press.

Otto, R. K., & Heilbrun, K. (2002). The practice of forensic psychology: A look toward the future in light of the past. *American Psychologist, 57,* 5–18.

Weiner, I. B. (2006). Writing forensic reports. In I. B. Weiner & A. K. Hess (Eds.), *The handbook of forensic psychology* (3rd ed., pp. 631–651). Hoboken, NJ: John Wiley & Sons.

JOHN PETRILA
University of South Florida

See also: Forensic Consulting; Forensic Psychology

FORENSIC PSYCHOLOGY

Forensic psychology refers to the three ways psychology and law interact (A. K. Hess, 2006). Notwithstanding the common association of forensic with autopsies as in forensic medicine, the three ways are (1) psychology by the law, (2) psychology in the law, and (3) psychology of the law.

By the Law

When psychologists practice by the law, they are mindful of the many statutes, regulations, and guidelines that govern their practices. For example, record-keeping guidelines specify how long clinical psychologists must preserve patient records. HIPPA regulations stipulate how securely the records must be handled in storage and when communicated to others, particularly through electronic channels. Child custody evaluations must meet certain standards of care or the psychologist is vulnerable to both ethics complaints and to civil (tort) suits because they might have not lived up to duties imposed by the guidelines issued by the governing professional association. Similarly, authors who use case materials in their writings must know how to disguise writings without distorting the case materials so the

cases are not defamed or harmed (and in fact, it would be best they not recognize themselves to prevent emotional distress). Professors need to know about disability and privacy as well as how to set curricula and their changes so student rights are honored. When psychologists have cases that involve legal questions, then they are practicing in the law.

In the Law

Civil applications. A psychologist might be hired in both civil and criminal cases. Civil cases range from domestic issues such as child custody and adoption suitability (K. D. Hess, 2006a) to competence to assessing damages. The right and ability to marry, parameters of marriage that include privacy and spousal privilege, resolving disputes within marriages, preventing and treating domestic violence are crucial areas in which psychologists labor (K. D. Hess, 2006b). Despite their best efforts, marriages break down at alarming rates. The most contested area that employs psychologists in high-risk work is child custody determination. Advising the courts on parental fitness and on a child's best interests and guiding the custodial arrangements has far-reaching impact on the family, each of its members, and on extended family members (Blau, 1998). Assessing and ameliorating the effects of divorce, particularly on the children, calls for finely honed clinical skills. Checking claims of child neglect and child sexual, physical, and emotional abuse is difficult but critically important as those claims are highly emotional and important in guiding the best interests of the child. Assessing the ability of potential parents for foster care and for adoption can be life-changing for the parenting one and the children. One can think of no more important calling than helping build enriched families.

Second only to the area of family relations, work occupies much of our time. Psychologists often help companies hire and train employees and are called upon to determine an employee's fitness for duty. That is, if an employee is showing signs of distress, that employee might be put on leave, be fit to return from leave, or be fired. Then the psychologist might help out-placing the employee, both a humanistic and a self-protective venture by the company. In police consultation, the psychologist assesses the degree to which the candidate has impulse control as society cedes to police the ability to use deadly force, a status that ought to be accorded only to those with the judgment to use it only as a last resort. In the event of a shooting or other critical incident, procedure in most police agencies calls for psychologists to debrief and even provide counseling services to the officers and, depending on the department, to their families.

Psychologists are employed by agencies responsible for transporting people. For example, the time to process road signs is crucial in their placement. If placed too close to a highway exit, drivers are unable to safely move toward the right-most lane. If signs are placed too far from the exit, drivers might forget as they are processing so much information before exiting. When accidents happen, psychologists might serve as expert witnesses regarding the possible liability in cases such as road sign placement. Whereas 40,000 deaths occur annually on the highways, more than 600,000 victims survive the accidents in an impaired state. Psychologists determine disability in allocating damages and in guiding rehabilitation of functioning so the survivors can have legal and monetary remedies and the most optimal lifelong adjustment with regard to injuries (Walsh, 1978). Similarly, psychologists assess work injuries for disability, and they assess educational disabilities and help plan educational curricula to best meet the learning needs of children in schools.

Language analysis calls for psychologists to evaluate the degree to which material can be understood. Psychologists assess informed consent forms for readability and contracts for misleading language that can cost the consumer dearly. Such analyses involve estimating the intelligence level of consumers while making the language specific and technical enough to assure that all the required legal issues are stated. Also, readability questions involve entry tests for jobs. When a job does not require certain reading levels but an entry test has forbidding language, are the tests prejudicial? Courts have held that to be the case so psychologists are involved in calibrating the appropriate language levels of the test and the job.

Psychologists specializing in motor skills are used for disability determination as well as assigning liability. They help design products such as child car safety seats and also assess products to see whether the product-human interface was reasonably considered and designed. Psychologists have been active in research and consulting regarding the estimation of driver response time and the erosion of attention because of distractions such as cell phones. New cars feature visual displays that compete for the driver's attention to the road. When warnings are ineffective, psychologists have been involved in providing expertise to the courts (Noy & Warkowski, 2005). The internet poses new threats to our children that have involved psychologists in trying to prevent victimization.

Psychologists help courts determine competence in both civil and criminal cases. Whether individuals must be civilly committed due to potential dangerousness, can care for themselves or their children, can make contractual decisions, or even make basic medical decisions are questions of competence about which psychologists render expert opinions (Stone, 1975).

Criminal Applications. Determining mental states is central to insanity and incompetency pleas. If the alleged perpetrator of a crime is unable to reason during the commission of the crime, he or she is liable to be judged insane and in most jurisdictions, is then deemed not guilty by reason of insanity (Beis, 1984; Robinson, 1980). When the accused is unable to meaningfully contribute to his or her own defense, the accused might be held incompetent to stand trial. These controversial findings, of insanity and incompetence, are important to the administration of justice and depend on psychologists' testimony about the mental status of the accused. Competence to understand the Miranda warning and the ability to understand a confession become central issues that psychologists help determine. That is, if a person does not understand the Miranda warning or the confession that he or she may have given or signed, then the judge might find the confession inadmissible.

During criminal trials, questions arise as to witness competence and credibility. For example, what weight can be given a child's testimony, particularly on complex issues? Do cross-racial, cross-gender and cross-ethnic identifications by witnesses have the same accuracy rates as same-race, same-gender and same-ethnic identifications? Was a lineup identification compromised or fairly administered? How does one select an optimal jury? To what degree is an ear witness just as credible as an eye witness? Under what conditions might an eye witness have mis-remembered a face or crucial detail in a felony?

After a conviction, psychologists contribute to assessing the guilty as to the best disposition. Judges and the correctional system need the help of psychologists in placing the convicted on probation, within various institutions from maximum to minimal and even no custodial care, and when and under what conditions to effect a parole.

At every phase in this process, psychologists are concerned with violence potential and with recidivism or re-offending by assaultive and abusive people. This concern includes prevention programs for those likely to offend, as well as rehabilitation and relapse prevention programs for those who have offended and are making efforts not to re-offend. Psychologists help train police, correctional and rehabilitation staff members in recognizing and preventing violence, and in debriefing after violent encounters. In short, for a century, psychologists have been heavily involved beginning with lie detection during the early twentieth century to forensic hypnosis in reconstruction of a crime to enable a witness to recall details and overcome trauma.

Of the Law

Psychologists are trained to conduct research. They use powerful research design and analysis tools to investigate many topics, some of which are essential for the just functioning of law. Simply determining whether a crime has occurred or whether a person ought to press charges are decisions that involve perceptions. Similarly, what charges to pursue and at what levels are decisions that prosecutors make, based on perceptions and likelihood of conviction. The degree to which a witness's recall of a face or of dialogue or can be mistaken weighs heavily on whether

FREUD, SIGMUND (1856–1939)

we justly convict the guilty or falsely convict the innocent (Buckout, 1978; Castelli et al., 2006). Judges and juries, by their nature, are involved in decision making, all of which are subject to biases and have been researched by psychologists (Konecni & Ebbesen, 1982). Psychologists study how jury composition and evidence weighs in to verdicts, and how limits to civil awards or criminal sentencing leads to differing verdicts in civil and criminal cases. Research on lie detection, graphology, voice stress analysis, and hypnosis are duly considered by legislators and judges in guiding standards of admissibility of evidence. Recently, research on a variety of topics such as gun control, limits to tort awards, gender equity in the workplace, and the effects of television violence and pornography on children lead to psychologists' testimony in forums that affect public policy. Advocacy for victims, including domestic abuse and terrorism victims involves psychologists to lobby for legislation ranging from support of shelters, for law enforcement and hospital personnel training in helping rape victims, to support for rehabilitation of torture victims.

In sum, the law concerns people, and psychologists are concerned with people. The synergy between both fields has led to a fruitful collaboration that has seen forensic psychology as the most rapidly growing specialty area in psychology.

REFERENCES

Beis, E. B. (1984). *Mental health and the law*. Rockville, MD: Aspen Publishers.

Blau, T. (1998). *The psychologist as expert witness* (2nd ed.). New York: John Wiley & Sons.

Buckhout, R. (1974). Eyewitness testimony. *Scientific American*, *231*, 23–31.

Castelli, P., Goodman, G. S., Edelstein, R. S., Mitchell, E. B., Paz Alonso, P. M., Lyons, K. E., et al. (2006). Evaluating eyewitness testimony in adults and children. In I. B. Weiner & A. K. Hess (Eds.), *The handbook of forensic psychology*, (3rd ed., pp. 243–304). Hoboken, NJ: John Wiley & Sons.

Hess, A. K. (2006). Defining forensic psychology. In I. B. Weiner & A. K. Hess (Eds.), *The handbook of forensic psychology* (3rd ed., pp. 28–58). Hoboken, NJ: John Wiley & Sons.

Hess, K. D. (2006a). Understanding child domestic law issues: Custody, adoptions and abuse. In I. B. Weiner & A. K. Hess (Eds.), *The handbook of forensic psychology* (3rd ed., pp. 73–97). Hoboken, NJ: John Wiley & Sons.

Hess, K. D. (2006b). Understanding adult domestic law issues: Marriage, divorce, and domestic violence. In I. B. Weiner & A. K. Hess (Eds.), *The handbook of forensic psychology* (3rd ed., pp. 98–123). New York: John Wiley & Sons.

Konecni, V. J., & Ebbesen, E. B. (1982). *The criminal justice system: A social psychlogical analysis*. San Francisco: Freeman.

Noy, Y. I., & Karwowski, W. (Eds.). (2005). *The handbook of human factors in litigation*. Boca Raton, FL: CRC Press.

Robinson, D. N. (1980). *Psychology and law: Can justice survive the social sciences?* New York: Oxford University Press.

Stone, A. A. (1975). *Mental health and the law: A system in transition*. Washington, DC: U. S. Department of Health, Education and Welfare.

Walsh, K. W. (1978). *Neuropsychology: A clinical approach*. New York: Churchill Livingstone.

SUGGESTED READINGS

Bartol, C. R., & Bartol, A. M. *Criminal behavior: A psychosocial approach* (8th ed.). Upper Saddle River, NJ: Pearson/Prentice Hall.

Goldstein, A. M. (Vol. Ed.). (2003). *Forensic psychology*, Vol. 11. In I. B. Weiner (Ed-in-Chief), *Handbook of Psychology*. Hoboken, NJ: John Wiley & Sons.

Stone, A. A. (1976). *Mental health and the law: A system in transition*. Washington, DC: Center of the Studies on Crime and Delinquency, NIMH.

Weiner, I. B., & Hess, A. K. (Eds.). (2006). *The handbook of forensic psychology*, (3rd ed.). Hoboken, NJ: John Wiley & Sons.

ALLEN K. HESS
Auburn University at Montgomery

See also: **Forensic Psychologists, Roles and Activities of; Psychology and the Law**

FREUD, SIGMUND (1856–1939)

Sigmund Freud moved from Moravia to Vienna at age four and lived there for nearly 80 years. He demonstrated an unusual intellectual ability early in life and was encouraged by his family. Freud graduated with distinction from Gymnasium at age 17 and entered the University of Vienna to study medicine and scientific research. Because of his diversified interests in biology, physiology, and teaching, as well as medicine, Freud spent eight years at the university. Finally persuaded to take his medical examinations, he entered private practice as a clinical neurologist in 1881.

Freud's interests in what was to become psychoanalysis began and developed during his association with Josef Breuer in 1884. From Breuer he learned about the "talking cure" and the use of hypnosis for hysterical neuroses. In 1885, Freud spent four and a half months in France studying hypnosis with Jean Charcot, from whom he heard about a sexual basis for patients' problems. The idea stayed in his mind, and by the mid-1890s Freud was convinced that the dominant difficulty in neurosis was inadequate sexual development and gratification.

In 1895, Breuer and Freud published *Studies on Hysteria*, often noted as the formal beginning of psychoanalysis. In 1897, Freud undertook the task of self-analysis. He diagnosed his own neurotic difficulties as anxiety neuroses, which he claimed were caused by an accumulation of sexual tensions. The method of self-analysis that Freud used was dream analysis. This was both a creative period of his life and a time of intense inner turmoil. The analysis continued for about two years and was reported in *The Interpretation of Dreams*, now considered one of Freud's major works.

By 1902 Freud had become interested in promoting psychoanalytic theory and practice. A small number of colleagues, including Alfred Adler, joined him in weekly discussion groups at his home. These early discussions on the problems of neurosis were important to the development of the different theoretical beliefs and applied techniques of the four pillars of depth psychology: Freud, Adler, Otto Rank, and Carl Jung. The group became known as the Vienna Psychological Society; later Freud expanded his efforts to promote psychoanalysis and formed the Vienna Psychoanalytical Association. In 1909 he was invited to America by Stanley G. Hall of Clark University; in this, his first international recognition, he was awarded an honorary doctorate.

As Adler, Jung, and Rank developed their own theories and style, the original psychoanalytic group was disrupted with conflict and disagreement. Adler left the group in 1911; Jung in 1914. The height of Freud's fame was from 1919 to his death in 1939. In the 1920s, Freud developed a personality theory and system for all human motivation that expanded his influence beyond a method of treatment for psychiatric disorders.

Freud's method of treatment in psychoanalysis identified resistance as a form of protection from pain and repression as the way of eliminating pain from conscious awareness. Repression became the fundamental principle of psychoanalysis. Repressed material was uncovered through free association and dream analysis in a long, intensive course of therapy that lasted for months or years. Effective therapeutic work depended on the personal relationship developed between client and therapist, or transference. Freud believed that transference of the client's emotional attitudes from parent figures to therapist was necessary for curing neuroses.

The personality system of psychoanalysis dealt with the driving forces or energies that have been called instincts or urges for self-preservation, and creative forces were called libido. The death instincts were energies directed either inward toward self-destruction, or outward in aggression or hatred. Freud divided psychic mental life of the personality into id, ego, and superego. The id included sexual and aggressive instincts, no value judgments, and energies directed toward immediate satisfaction and tension reduction; it obeyed the pleasure principle. The ego, commonly known as reason or rationality, mediated between the id and the external world, holding under control the pleasure seeking demands of the id; it obeyed the reality principle. The superego—the conscience developed in early childhood—worked toward inhibiting the id completely, and toward actualizing the ego ideal to a state of perfection. The superego repressed the "internalized" community values and standards. Anxiety occurred whenever the ego became overburdened with the triple impact of the psychic energies of the pleasure-seeking id, the need to manipulate reality for tension reduction, and the perfectionistic superego.

Freud's theories and methods have been criticized on several grounds: (1) unsystematic and uncontrolled data collection and interpretation (the theory is largely untestable); (2) overemphasis on biological forces, particularly sex, as the primary influence on personality development; and (3) a deterministic view on the influence of past behavior, with a denial of free will and the role of future goals, dreams, and hopes in personal growth.

Psychoanalysis retains its particular identity today, having been absorbed into general psychological thought. Freud has clearly been among the world's most influential thinkers, with his ideas not only affecting psychotherapy but also art, literature, and even modern entertainment, including movies and the theatre.

SUGGESTED READINGS

Freud, S. (1900). *The interpretation of dreams.* New York: Macmillan.

Freud, S. & Breuer, J. (1895). *Studies on hysteria.* New York: Basic Books.

N. A. HAYNIE

FRIENDSHIPS

Friendships are important relationships in all cultures and throughout the lifespan. Friendships are characterized by several defining features: (1) they are dyadic relationships, (2) there is a reciprocated, affective bond, (3) they are voluntary relationships, (4) they are typically egalitarian in nature, and (5) almost all friendships entail shared activities and companionship. Friendships often meet other functions as well, such as serving as a source of support and providing opportunities for self-disclosure and intimacy.

These features differentiate friendships from several related phenomena. The fact that friendships are dyadic relationships distinguishes them from cliques or groups of peers. (Of course, individuals often have friendships with several members of their cliques). Similarly, having friendships is not the same as being popular. Individuals who are unpopular may still have friendships; and less commonly, a popular person may not have a close friendship. The reciprocal nature of friendship differentiates actual friendships from relationships in which one person thinks or wishes it were a friendship. The criterion of a strong affective bond distinguishes friendships from acquaintanceships. Friends often provide individuals with more emotional and functional support than acquaintances. Friendships typically entail more cooperation, positive social interactions, and affective responsivity than acquaintanceships. Rates of conflict, however, do not differ between friends and acquaintances. Finally, romantic relationships are considered a special form of friendship, and in fact, romantic partners are commonly seen as one's best friend.

Friendship Selection

Who become friends? Two key predictors of friendship formation are proximity and similarity. Friends usually live near one another, attend the same school, or work nearby each other. Proximity means that individuals will have relatively frequent opportunities to interact with each other and to develop a friendship. In addition, contrary to the adage "opposites attract," friends usually share a number of similarities. For example, they tend to be of the same age, gender, socioeconomic and ethnic background. Moreover, friends commonly share interests and tend to develop more similar interests and values over the course of being friends. Individuals who are dissimilar are less likely to remain friends than those who are similar.

Friendships across the Lifespan

Individuals of almost all ages develop friendships. Approximately 75% of preschoolers report having friends, and the percentage increases to over 90% by adulthood. The proportion remains high through adulthood, although about 15% of the elderly report not having friends. It is debatable whether very young children have "true friendships." However, even toddlers prefer some playmates to others. Preschoolers' friendships are typically based on shared activities and tend to be much less long-lasting than friendships later in life. One of the most striking developmental changes in friendships occurs during preadolescence, when children begin to develop "chumships." These relationships are usually with a same-sex peer and involve more support and acceptance than earlier friendships.

In adolescence, teens typically begin to spend more time with their friends than with their families, and friendships become characterized by greater intimacy, self-disclosure, and closeness than in childhood. Other-sex friendships also become more commonplace, and romantic relationships begin to emerge. Adolescents and adults often develop specialized friendships wherein one turns to different friends for different purposes. Throughout adulthood, friendships remain important, although they may not be as central as a romantic relationship.

Friendship and Gender

Friendships develop more often between members of the same gender than between males and females. Other-sex friendships are particularly infrequent during the elementary-school years, accounting for less than 20% of friendships during this time. Other-sex friendships occur less commonly because of structural barriers and cultural norms. Differences also exist in the typical nature of friendships of males and females. For instance, perhaps because of gender differences in the socialization of emotion expression and regulation, female friendships tend to be characterized by more intimacy and self-disclosure than male friendships, and this distinction becomes particularly notable in adolescence.

Adolescent girls and their friends also coruminate more often about their problems, which fosters both closeness as well as potential problems in adjustment when rumination is marked. Closeness in male friendships may occur through shared activities; sometimes experiencing a very stressful event together can also foster closeness. During childhood and adolescence, girls tend to be more exclusive in their friendships than boys are, whereas boys' friendships often develop in the context of a larger group. Additionally, girls' friendships are typically less stable than those of boys.

Developmental Significance of Friendships

Friendships play an important role in development and adjustment in several key ways. Whereas parents ultimately have more power in parent-child relationships, friends are on equal footing. Accordingly, what friends do together or how they behave toward each other is more open to negotiation. As a result, children obtain valuable experience in learning how to express their own wishes and compromise with another person in a way that they can't learn by interacting with a parent or other authority figure. In addition, friendships provide a ready venue for communicating information about peer norms and values, as well as about taboo topics such as sex.

These contrasts between friendships and parent-child relationships do not mean that friends and parents are opposing social influences. In fact, contrary to some depictions in the popular media, friends and parents actually have more similar than opposing influences on youth. Children typically select friends whose values are congruent with their parents' values. Parents and friends are both likely to exert important influences on youths' behavior. For example, the habit of smoking in either friends or parents of adolescents both uniquely influence the likelihood of their choosing to smoke. The strongest clashes between the influences of friends versus parents occur when relationships with parents are strained.

Empirical research has repeatedly found links between healthy adjustment and having friendships. Well-adjusted individuals are more likely to develop friendships, and friendships seem to promote psychological health and well-being. It seems particularly important to have at least one close friendship. Friends can serve to protect children from being victimized by other peers, including bullies. Chronic friendlessness is associated with social timidity, sensitivity, and a lack of social skills. Although friendships are generally thought to have a positive influence on adjustment, the specific effects vary as a function of who the friend is. For instance, having a friend who engages in deviant or antisocial behavior is likely to foster more deviant or antisocial behavior in a young person. Similarly, conflictual, problematic friendships can have deleterious effects on an individual's emotional well-being.

Both having friendships and being accepted by one's peers contribute to well-being. Similarly, the characteristics of relationships with parents and friends both contribute to adjustment and development. In effect, friendships share features with other close relationships, but also have their own unique features and make their own contributions to individuals' lives.

SUGGESTED READINGS

Berndt, T. J. (2002). Friendship quality and social development. *Current Directions in Psychological Science, 11*, 7–10.

Bukowski, W. M., Newcomb, A. F., & Hartup, W. W. (Eds.). (1996). *The company they keep: Friendship during childhood and adolescence.* New York: Cambridge University Press.

Hartup, W. W. (1996). The company they keep: Friendships and their developmental significance. *Child Development, 67*, 1–13.

Newcomb, A., & Bagwell, C. (1995). Children's friendship relations: A meta-analytic review. *Psychological Bulletin, 117*, 306–347.

Rubin, K. H., Bukowski, W., & Laursen, B. (Eds.). (In press). *Peer interactions, relationships, and groups.* New York: Guilford Press.

WYNDOL FURMAN
LAREN B. SHOMAKER
University of Denver

See also: Interpersonal Relationships; Peer Influences

FUNCTIONAL ANALYSIS

Functional analysis is a strategy for the assessment and treatment of mental health problems (or preferably "behavioral problems") with origins in radical behaviorism, and particularly behavior therapy. It is generally viewed as an assessment and treatment strategy within the larger realm of behavioral assessment and behavior therapy. More specifically, functional analysis is a set of procedures that attempts to identify important environmental variables that develop and maintain behavior. The clinical goal of functional analysis is to effectively identify targets of intervention that are alterable, in order that appropriate treatments may be rapidly implemented and evaluated.

History

Historically, functional analysis entered psychology through the influence of B. F. Skinner, who in turn was influenced by Ernst Mach's conceptualizations of functional relationships. Mach attempted to resolve David Hume's proffered puzzle about causation, that is, that causal relationships are never observed, but are just "constant conjunction." Mach suggested that instead of "cause" one focus on functional relationships, that is, relationships (often depicted in Cartesian coordinates as $y = f(x)$) such that the value of one variable is seen as systematically depending on the value of another variable. Skinner agreed with this suggestion, and his cumulative recorder can be viewed as an instrument that attempts to capture and depict functional relationships. Functional analysis becomes the systematic attempt to uncover these functional relationships.

Clinical Applications

When a client seeks psychological or psychiatric intervention for a mental health or behavioral problem, the obvious questions are "What created and maintains the problem?" and "How can the problem be solved?" Assessment procedures are the data-gathering tools that are used to investigate the former question and to inform the latter one. Assessment is sifting through the multitude of variables that comprise a person's life and determining which historical and current aspects are relevant to the development and maintenance of the problem.

Behaviorally oriented clinicians have questioned the usefulness of diagnosis and syndromal classification systems such as the *Diagnostic and Statistical Manual of Mental Disorders* of the American Psychiatric Association (2000) on many grounds. Of particular relevance to functional analysis are the significant varieties in symptom presentation that comprise a single category. A key concern is whether topographical similarities in behavior are useful for postdicting causes or predicting treatment responses. As a result, newer approaches to assessment that consider the function of the behaviors over the topographical form of the behaviors, and that attend more closely to individual differences in behavior, have been explored. The product of this desire to understand behavior functionally and idiographically is functional analysis.

Functional analysis is a term that has been used with some overlap with several others in the behavioral literature, including behavioral analysis, behavioral assessment, functional behavioral analysis, and behavioral case formulation. Compounding the confusion is that just as many terms are used to refer to the same procedures, functional analysis is used to refer to a diversity of procedures in the literature. This phrase has been used to describe any part of the process that includes discovering the variables of which behavior is a function, designing an intervention for the environment or behaviors, implementing the intervention, reevaluating the case conceptualization based on response to treatment, and recycling the process until the problem subsides. Although some behavior analysts focus exclusively on the assessment portion of this intervention process, others consider the whole process to be a complete functional analysis.

Procedures

Functional analysis is derived from basic behavioral principles. It attends to the antecedents, stimuli, responses, consequences, and contingencies that produce and maintain effective or ineffective behaviors. The identification of pertinent, controllable variables in this sequence, and the effective treatment of those variables to produce different outcomes, are its challenges. The basic form of a functional analysis is (1) identify aspects of the client and his or her environment or history that may be relevant to the problem; (2) organize information about potentially relevant variables according to behavioral principles in order to identify possible causal relationships among variables; (3) collect additional detailed information about potential causal variables in order to complete the analysis; (4) identify or create a treatment hypothesized to produce a desired increase in the frequency or intensity of the causal variables based on the case conceptualization of how the variable functions for the individual; (5) implement the intervention for one variable at a time and observe any changes in the problem; (6) if there is no change in the target behavior, remove the original intervention, move to the next suspected causal variable, and implement and evaluate the treatment of that variable; (7) if the problem is not alleviated, return to the case conceptualization to identify alternative variables that may be pertinent or alternative casual relationships and continue with the steps of the functional analysis; and (8) continue to revise the conceptualizations and interventions until the problem is solved.

Strengths and Weaknesses

The strengths of functional analysis are the precisions with which cases may be conceptualized and the direct link to treatment implementation. Instead of relying on imprecise diagnostic categories as heuristics to guide conceptualizations of the problem, both case conceptualizations and treatment planning focus on the unique aspects of the particular problem. These unique aspects of the problem are the points of customized clinical interventions instead of a generic syndrome-level intervention.

The weakness of functional analysis stems from its lack of specificity. Initial variables to be put into the analytic methodology (e.g., parental attention as a maintaining factor for a child's tantrum) are based on clinical judgment or experience, and thus functional analysis remains partly an art. In addition, communication between mental health professionals and replication of assessment, treatment, and treatment evaluations are impeded by the imprecision of functional analysis language and procedures. When different terms are being used for functional analyses, relevant information may not be shared, because it is not identified as belonging to the functional analysis category. Similarly, when functional analysis is used to refer to overlapping or altogether different procedures, miscommunications may occur, because the discussants are working from different assumptions about the procedures that are involved. Moreover, as communication is increasingly removed from direct observations of client behaviors, there are greater opportunities for miscommunications to arise. In addition, functional analysis may be much more expensive (e.g., requiring direct observation in clients' naturalistic environments) than other assessment strategies such as the clinical interview or paper and pencil tests.

A related problem is replication. Functional analysis currently refers to a range of assessment and intervention procedures. Without a standard of practice for the subfield, clinicians may perform different sets of procedures and call each of them a functional analysis. As a result, there is no guarantee that one clinician's conclusions are going to match another clinician's conclusions in the same case. This lack of replicability detracts confidence from the assessment procedures, thereby diluting their effectiveness. Furthermore, if a functional analysis cannot be replicated, doubt is cast on its ability to reliable studies of the phenomenon. This replicability problem ironically renders an assessment and intervention procedure that arose out of the behavioral empirical literature untestable.

Future Directions

The field of behavior analysis lies in acknowledging the strengths and weaknesses of functional analysis and beginning to propose improvements. Suggestions have been made that promote standardizing the definition of functional analysis and the procedures that comprise such an analysis in order to advance communication and replication. Additional proposals have been made to strengthen the communication aspect of the procedure. The development of a nomothetic classification system that is based on functional analysis has been offered. Proposed variations of this taxonomy include expert systems, logical functional analytic systems, and functional diagnostic systems, each based on functional analyses.

In addition to more advanced clinical applications, researchers have segued into an expanded use of functional analysis as a research strategy. Compiling and analyzing functional analytic data within and across clients may contribute to basic understanding of many behaviors and behavior-environment interactions.

SUGGESTED READINGS

Cone, J. (1997). Issues in functional analysis in behavioral assessment. *Behaviour Research and Therapy, 35*, 259–273.

Haynes, S., & O'Brien, W. (1990). Functional analysis in behavior therapy. *Clinical Psychology Review, 10*, 649–668.

Iwata, B., Kahng, S., Wallace, M., & Lindberg, J. (2001). The functional analysis model of behavioral assessments. In J. Austin & J. Carr (Eds). *Handbook of applied behavior analysis* (pp. 61–90). Reno, NV: Context Press.

Kanfer, F., & Saslow, G. (1969). Behavioral diagnosis. In C. M. Franks (Ed.), *Behavior therapy: Appraisal and status* (pp. 412–444). New York: McGraw-Hill.

Sturmey, P. (1996). *Functional analysis in clinical psychology.* Chichester, UK: John Wiley & Sons.

WILLIAM T. O'DONOHUE
University of Nevada Reno

TAMARA PENIX LOVERICH
Eastern Michigan University

See also: Behavioral Assessment; Contextualism

FUGUE (See Amnesia; Dissociative Disorders)

G

GABA RECEPTORS

It is now universally recognized that γ-aminobutyric acid (GABA), synthesized by the two molecular forms of glutamix acid decarboxylase (GAD65 or 67) and expressed in neurons, functions as a key neurotransmitter in creatures ranging from crustaceans to mammals. In the brains of vertebrates, GABA mediates synaptic inhibitory events by binding to specific recognition sites located in various members of a pentameric protein family, including a transmembrane anion channel, which is termed GABA.

GABAA Receptors

When two molecules of GABA bind to a GABA receptor molecule, the opening frequency of the anionic channels increases and, most of the time, negatively charged chloride (Cl−) ions flow inwardly. In 1952, Hodgkin and Huxely suggested that in volgate-separated Na+ and K+ channels, the gating and its ion permeation are two independent processes. The idea that gating opens and closes the channels but pays scant attention to the behavior of fully activated channels might also apply to the GABAA-gated receptor channels. The binding of the two GABA molecules to a GABAA receptor molecule activate that Cl− channel; in contrast, the binding to a positive or negative allosteric modulatory site of hormones (neurosteroids) or endogenous modulatory ligands (endozepines) affects the ohmic behavior of the channel by changing either the open time duration or the opening frequency of the Cl− channels gated by GABA.

Some of these modulatory sites also function as the high-affinity binding sites for important drugs used during surgery to induce anesthesia (barbiturates) or in psychiatry for the treatment of anxiety or mood disorders (benzodiazepines [BZ]). Both drugs amplify the GABA-gated Cl− current intensity and thereby decrease retention of recent memories, reduce learning speed, and induce sedation. Anesthesia is induced by barbiturates and not by BZs because only barbiturates can gate the GABAA receptor channels in the absence of GABA.

GABAB Receptors

The family of metabotropic GABA receptors was identified after the ionotropic GABAA receptor family. The activation of GABAB receptors by GABA decreases the rate of CAMP formation and this metabotropic function differentiates these receptors from ionotropic GABAA receptors. The GABAB receptors were further characterized by their insensitivity to bicuculline inhibition and muscimol stimulation (typical of GABAA receptors) by a specific inhibition by a number of selective antagonists inactive on GABAA receptors and by their selective stimulation by baclofen, which does not stimulate GABAA receptors. Confirmation of the metabotropic nature of their functional association to G proteins has been accomplished by cloning two specific DNA sequences (each encoding for a slightly different 7-transmembrane domain protein) which, functioning as dimmers, inhibit adenylate cyclase or gate K+ channels using various G protein subtypes as second messengers.

The complete structural and functional distinction between GABAA (ionotropic) and GABAB (metabotropic) receptors has a clear parallel to that between nicotinic (ionotropic) and muscarinic (metabotropic) acetylcholine receptors and ionotropic and metabotropic receptors for the transmitter glutamate.

GABAC Receptors

This third family of ionotropic receptors ligated by GABA is insensitive to bicuculline inhibition, baclofen or muscimol stimulation, and positive allosteric modulation by BZs. The ionotropic responses elicited by GABA acting on GABAC receptors are also of the fast type associated with an opening of an anion channel. The GABAC receptor structure results from homomeric assembly of ρ (ρ1, ρ2, ρ3) subunits. The only organ that expresses ρ subunits has a 27% homology to GABAA receptor subunits. However, unlike GABAA receptors, when ρ subunits combine to form GABAC receptors, they form only homomeric receptors. Thus, the function of homomeric ρ receptors sharply differs from that of GABAA receptors because ρ subunits lack the regulatory sites that are expressed in α, β, and γ subunits. The resistance of GABAC receptors to bicuculline inhibition or muscimol stimulation and the absence of allosteric modulation sites for barbiturates and BZs justify maintaining a functional distinction between GABAC and GABAA receptors.

Characterizations of GABAA, Receptor Functional Modifications by Various Anxiolytic Drugs Acting on the BZ Recognition Site

There is considerable interest in the availability of an effective GABAA receptor acting anxiolytic drug that will not share the problems of presently available medications. These problems are tolerance, dependence liability, and several inconvenient side effects such as sedation, induction of recent memory deficit, barbiturate or ethanol potentiation, and ataxia. The high-affinity binding site for BZs located in GABAA receptors has specific structural features. One consists of a binding pocket formed by the contiguity of an α (not present in $\alpha6$ and with low intrinsic activity in $\alpha5$) with a $\gamma2$ or $\gamma3$ subunit (which is not expressed by a $\gamma1$ subunit). These requirements should predict which GABAA receptors are susceptible to positive allosteric modulation by ligands to the BZ recognition sites, that is, subunit isomerism and sequence. Unfortunately, we do not have suitable methods to fulfill either task. It is presently believed that BZs amplify the actions of GABA by facilitating the opening of channels in monoligated GABAA receptors that, in order to open the channels in absence of BZs, require two molecules of GABA bound to the receptor.

New Vistas on the Concept of Partial Agonists in the Mode of Action of Benzodiazepines

As previously discussed, the concept that partial agonists of BZ recognition sites can amplify GABA gated Cl current intensity acting at virtually all GABAA receptor subtypes has been modified based by ongoing studies on the diversity of GABAA receptor signal transduction operative in different regions of the central nervous system.

Functional studies, especially of cortical and hippocampal pyramidal neurons have identified dendritic domains that receive distinct synaptic GABAergic afferents and may express distinct GABAA receptor subtypes (Möhler, Fritschy, Vogt, Crestani, & Rudolph, 2005; Guidotti et al., 2005; Spruston, 2008).

Not every GABAA receptor function is modified by BZs; such responsiveness is characterized by the expression of α_1, α_2, α_3, or α_5 subunit combinations with β, γ in their participation to heteropentameric structures and by the contiguity of an α and β receptor subunit. Möhler et al. (2005) have established that the sedative and amnestic action of commercially available BZs is related to the amplification intensity of GABA action at α_1 GABAA subunit contiguous to a γ_2 subunit, whereas their anxiolytic, anticonvulsant, and antipsychotic actions are presumably mediated by analogous changes occurring at GABAA receptors including α_2, α_3, or α_5 subunits.

Hence, a partial agonist is a drug that acts as (1) a partial positive allosteric modulator of GABAA receptor gated Cl channels at several GABAA receptor subtypes, or (2) a full positive allosteric modulator of the action of GABA at selective populations of GABAA receptor subtypes located in specific central nervous system domains but lacking an intrinsic action on other populations of GABAA receptor subtypes. Thus, pharmacological opportunities for the molecular design of a new generation of ligands for BZ binding sites that are partial agonists but act as full agonist on specifically selective GABAA receptor subtype structures is still under investigation. These new drugs may express reduced tolerance and dependence liability and can be designed to act selectively on certain GABAA receptor subtypes (e.g., α_2, α_3, α_5 expressing GABAA receptors) that may control anxiety, panic, psychotic symptoms in schizophrenia patients without eliciting sedation or amnesia.

A BZ recognition site ligand that is devoid of intrinsic action at $\alpha1$- expressing GABAA receptors but allosterically and maximally increases GABA action at $\alpha5$-expressing GABAA receptors is exemplified by imidazenil. This drug pharmacological profile differs from diazepam and other commercially available BZs because of its ability to elicit potent anticonvulsant and anxiolytic actions at doses that are several orders of magnitude lower than those eliciting sedation or amnesia (Costa et al., 2002, Guidotti et al. 2005).

Imidazenil binds with an insignificant intrinsic activity to GABAA receptors including α_1 β_2 γ_{2s} subunits but acts as a potent full agonist with high intrinsic activity on GABAA receptors including α_5 β_2 γ_{2s} subunits (Costa et al., 2002). Hence, Imidazenil is a partial agonist that never maximizes the intensity of Cl-currents gated by GABA-receptors including α_1 subunits and therefore its pharmacological profile is virtually devoid of sedative and amnestic action. Moreover, as previously discussed with respect to dependence and tolerance to protracted treatment with anxiolytic drugs that bind to BZ recognition sites, imidazenil, unlike diazepam, when it is used protractedly, fails to induce tolerance to its anticonvulsant (rats) or antiamnestic actions (monkeys) also when administered in doses that saturate its recognition sites expressed on GABAA receptors (Costa, Guidotti 1996).

The remarkably unique features of the pharmacological profile of imidazenil (compared with diazepam or alprazolam) warrant the investigation of this drug and other selective positive allosteric modulators as prospective remedies to treat anxiety, panic, and thought disorders, or hallucinations found in schizophrenia, bipolar, or other psychiatric disorders. Recent studies also suggest that imidazenil may be an ideal anticonvulsant and neuroprotective BZ for the prophylaxis and emergency treatment of chemical warfare agents. Imidazenil administered in doses that are devoid of sedative, amnesic, and muscle relaxant effects, potently antagonized chemical warfare agents–induced seizures and lethality in rodents (Auta et al. 2004). If applied to military personnel or civilian who are considered under danger of exposure to nerve agents, the prophylactic use of imidazenil may be particularly significant because not only it guarantees a potent and efficacious protection against various aspects of chemical warfare toxicity but it acts without impairing alertness.

REFERENCES

Costa, E., Auta, J., Grayson, D. R., Matsumoto, K., Pappas, G. D., Zhang, X., et al. (2002). *Neuropharmacology, 43,* 925–937.

Costa, E., & Guidotti, A. (1996). *TIPS, 17,* 192–200.

Guidotti, A., Auta, J., Davis, J. M., Dong, E., Grayson, D. R., Veldic, M., et al. (2005). *Psychopharmacology, 180,* 191–205.

Möhler, H., Fritschy, J. M., Vogt, K., Crestani, F., & Rudolph, U. (2005). *Handbook of Experimental Pharmacology, 169,* 225–247.

Spruston, N. (2008). *Nature Reviews Neuroscience, 9,* 206–221.

SUGGESTED READINGS

Costa, E., Auta, J., & Guidotti, A. (2001). Tolerance and dependence to ligands of the benzodiazepine recognition sites expressed by GABAA receptors. In H. Möhler (Ed.), *Pharmacology of GABA and glycine neurotransmission* (pp. 227–247). Berlin: Springer-Verlag.

Mohler, H. (2001). Functions of GABAA receptors: Pharmacology and pathophysiology. In H. Möhler (Ed.), *Pharmacology of GABA and glycine neurotransmission* (pp. 101–112). Berlin: Springer-Verlag.

ERMINIO COSTA
University of Illinois, Chicago

See also: Neurotransmitters

GAMBLING ADDICTION

The past three decades have witnessed significant increases in legalized gambling opportunities in the United States, with all but two states allowing some form of legalized gambling. These opportunities have been accompanied by record levels of gambling expenditures. For example, Americans spent over $90 billion on legal gambling activities in 2006, which represented a 7.7% increase over record expenditures in 2005 (Christiansen, 2007).

Increasing gambling availability and high rates of involvement have fueled growing concern over those whose gambling causes problems. Over 5% of adults have experienced significant problems related to gambling, and 1% of adults meet criteria for pathological gambling disorder (Shaffer, Hall & Vander Bilt, 1999). Higher rates of problem gambling have been reported among males, youth, college students, African Americans, and individuals with easy access to gambling.

Problems Associated with Excessive Gambling

Excessive gambling diminishes gamblers' finances, leaving them unable to pay for basic necessities. To deal with their debts, problem gamblers often must turn to other sources for money, including family, friends, or criminal activities, such as embezzlement. Their problems are often further compounded because they may wager these monies to "get ahead," believing that a big win will solve their problems. As a result of their financial problems many gamblers file for bankruptcy. Arrest and incarceration due to illegal activities aimed at securing more money are also common.

Problem gamblers are more likely than people in general to suffer from depression or alcohol problems. They report greater than average rates of psychological distress and more use of psychiatric treatment. Problem gamblers often experience serious relationship difficulties. Spouses and family members must cope with the consequences of the gambler's behavior, including absence from the home, distrust of the gambler, and stress over family finances. Divorce rates are elevated among problem gamblers.

Pathological Gambling Disorder

Pathological gambling disorder was officially recognized as an impulse-control disorder by the American Psychiatric Association in 1980. Diagnosis of pathological gambling disorder requires the presence of at least five of the following ten criteria: (1) preoccupation with gambling, (2) wagering larger amounts of money to experience excitement, (3) feelings of withdrawal when trying to control gambling, (4) gambling to escape problems, (5) chasing losses, (6) lying to others to conceal gambling involvement, (7) committing illegal acts to obtain money to gamble, (8) jeopardizing important relationships or opportunities because of gambling, (9) relying on financial assistance from others to pay gambling debts, and (10) unsuccessful efforts to limit gambling (American Psychiatric Association, 2000). These criteria were fashioned after the criteria for substance use disorders and are based on the assumption that gambling may be similar to addictive behaviors.

Models of Problem Gambling: Medical

A variety of explanatory models for problem gambling have been developed. The disease model views problem gambling as a medical illness. Excessive gambling behavior is considered a chronic condition that manifests itself in clear signs and symptoms. Many explanations for the cause of the "disease" have been offered. Psychodynamic theorists have explained that gambling may fulfill an individual's instinctual drives; however, the nature of the psychodynamic position has not allowed researchers to support or refute it.

Research has suggested that problem gamblers may inherit a genetic predisposition to gamble excessively. Although the specific neurophysiological mechanisms responsible for genetic predisposition toward problem gambling remain unclear, initial findings implicate reward and decision-making pathways within the brain. Available evidence suggests that biogenetic factors appear to be only one important component in the development of gambling problems.

Models of Problem Gambling: Psychological

Psychologists have attempted to understand the role of psychological factors in the development of gambling problems. Theorists who have examined the relationship between gambling and personality traits, such as sensation-seeking, extroversion, and locus of control, have generated only limited support for the role of personality in gambling.

Behavioral theorists have used learning models to explain how individuals develop gambling-related problems. According to operant conditioning theory, individuals gamble because they have been reinforced on a variable ratio schedule (Skinner, 1953). Occasional wins serve to maintain the gambling behavior. Behavioral theories have difficulty explaining why some individuals develop gambling problems, while others do not.

In response to exclusively behavioral conceptualizations, more recent problem gambling models have increasingly focused on the role of cognition (Ladouceur, Sylvain, Boutin, & Doucet, 2002). These cognitive models are based on empirical studies that have identified irrational beliefs among problem gamblers. According to cognitive theory, many gamblers hold beliefs that lead them to continue to gamble, despite the odds and their mounting losses. Belief in luck and the ability to control chance events are examples of irrational beliefs that may lead to problematic gambling behavior. Because irrational beliefs are found among problem gamblers and nonproblem gamblers alike, their causal role in problematic gambling remains in question.

Prevention of Problem Gambling

Efforts to address problem gambling have typically focused on treating those who develop gambling-related problems, although there is a growing awareness of the need for prevention programs. Current problem gambling prevention efforts are in the early stages of development and rely primarily on informational strategies. For example, informational programs have been designed to educate young people of the risks of excessive gambling with the hope that such knowledge will reduce problem gambling in the future. Casinos and others in the gambling industry are more vigorously promoting responsible gambling initiatives in an effort to encourage gambling in moderation.

Treatment of Problem Gambling

Individuals who develop gambling problems are unlikely to pursue treatment. For the small number of problem gamblers who seek treatment, the most available option is Gamblers' Anonymous (GA). GA is a self-help group based on the disease model of problem gambling and focused on a 12-step program emphasizing group support, faith, and commitment. GA members share with the group their story about how excessive gambling led to problems. Complete abstinence from gambling is considered the only viable treatment goal in GA, and members are encouraged to be actively involved in the program even after extensive periods of abstinence to avoid relapse. Research has suggested that a small percentage of those who attend GA remain in the program and maintain abstinence (Stewart & Brown, 1988).

The efficacy of pharmacological agents in treating problem gambling has only recently been studied. At this point in time, there are no FDA-approved drug therapies for gambling problems. Recent drug studies have focused on serotonin reuptake inhibitors, opioid antagonists, and mood stabilizers for the treatment of problem gambling. Growing interest in biological views of problem gambling is likely to fuel ongoing studies of such treatments.

Empirically based therapies for problem gambling continue to evolve. Whereas early treatment approaches were based on medical models of problem gambling, more recent treatment strategies have developed from cognitive and behavioral perspectives (Ladouceur et al., 2002; Petry, 2005; Whelan, Steenbergh, & Meyers, 2007). Early therapies emphasized behavioral strategies including aversion therapy, in vivo desensitization, imaginal desensitization, and cue exposure and response prevention. Although most of these programs lacked rigorous evaluation, outcome data generally supported their efficacy.

Therapeutic strategies built on a cognitive model of problem gambling have demonstrated efficacy (e.g., Ladouceur et al., 2002). These treatments use cognitive restructuring techniques designed to change gamblers' irrational beliefs about gambling. Cognitive strategies are often combined with problem-solving skills training and training to identify and cope with situations that present a high risk of relapse.

Brief, motivationally based treatment programs, which have received empirical support as effective alternatives to traditional abstinence-based interventions for alcohol problems (Sobell & Sobell, 1993), have been adapted and appear to be effective in treating problem gamblers (Whelan et al., 2007). These programs represent the latest development in problem-gambling treatment. They provide gamblers feedback on their behavior that is designed to enhance motivation for change. As gamblers commit to change, a functional assessment of their gambling behavior is conducted, situations associated with excessive gambling are identified, and alternative strategies for dealing with those situations are developed. Finally, relapse prevention training is undertaken.

The growing availability of gambling, the recognition of individual and societal problems associated with excessive gambling, and the increasing attention of scientists and clinicians suggest that the area of problem gambling will continue to be a dynamic one.

REFERENCES

American Psychiatric Association. (2000). Diagnostic and statistical manual of mental disorders *(4th ed., text rev.)*. Washington, DC: Author.

Christiansen, E. M. (2007, November). Gross annual wager. *International Gaming & Wagering Business, 28*, pp. 1, 68, 70–72.

Ladouceur, R., Sylvain, C., Boutin, C., & Doucet, C. (2002). *Understanding and treating the pathological gambler*. West Sussex, UK: John Wiley & Sons.

Petry, N. M. (2005). *Pathological gambling: Etiology, comorbidity, and treatment*. Washington, DC: American Psychological Association.

Shaffer, H. J., Hall, M. N., & Vander Bilt, J. (1999). Estimating the prevalence of disordered gambling behavior in the United States and Canada: A research synthesis. *American Journal of Public Health, 89*, 1369–1376.

Skinner, B. F. (1953). *Science and human behavior*. New York: Free Press.

Sobell, M. B., & Sobell, L. C. (1993). *Problem drinkers: Guided self-change treatment*. New York: Guilford Press.

Stewart, R. M., & Brown, I. A. F. (1988). An outcome study of Gamblers Anonymous. *British Journal of Psychiatry, 152*, 284–288.

Whelan, J. P., Steenbergh, T. A., & Meyers, A. W. (2007). *Problem and pathological gambling*. Cambridge, MA: Hogrefe & Huber.

ANDREW W. MEYERS
University of Memphis

TIMOTHY A. STEENBERGH
Indiana Wesleyan University

See also: Addiction

GENDER DIFFERENCES

The study of psychological gender differences (GDs) originated with the earliest studies linking brain structures to differences in behavior, especially in the area of intellectual performance. These lines of research purported to explain sex differences in behavior by comparing brain structures of men and women that were believed to account for them (Shields, 1975). These inquiries represented one facet of the continuing "nature–nurture" debate over the relative impact of genetic heritage and environmental influences as causes of behavior. Present-day neuroscience research has found evidence for neural plasticity that supports a biopsychosocial interactionist view, which is gaining acceptance over earlier monocausal models (Halpern et al., 2007). However, in the presence of ideological and political commitments to differing views of "human nature," debates continue over how much of a difference is a just-noticeable difference, as this depends on who is doing the noticing, and over what is a functionally important difference, as this depends on the function, its context, and its consequences.

After a period of conceptual and terminological confusion, the study of GDs became differentiated from the study of sex differences following Unger's (1979) call for a vocabulary that distinguished explanatory models based on biological determinism from those that implicitly included sociocultural influences. Subsequently, generally accepted usage has identified "sex" as denoting reproductive structures and their related functions, and "gender" as denoting a cultural construct that covaries with, but is not synonymous with, biological sex and may be defined differently in different cultures.

Gender is not a unitary construct, however; scientific understanding has evolved further to differentiate among gender-related constructs that are variously identified with biology, behavior preferences, personal identity, and/or broader sociocultural roles. In the 1980s, with greater awareness of the functional distinctions between sex and gender, familial and occupational role choices ("gender role"—traditional woman's job, traditional man's job) were differentiated from the individual's adoption of a gender-typed self-concept ("gender role identity"—feminine, masculine, androgynous, undifferentiated), from gendered personal identity ("gender identity"—woman, man, transgender, other), from other specifically sexual aspects of physical self-concept ("sexual identity"—female, male, intersexed, transsexual), and from specifically sexual aspects of partner choice and the corollaries thereof ("sexual orientation"—homosexual, heterosexual, bisexual, pansexual, asexual). Thus, an accurate reading of the GDs research literature from previous decades requires identifying first the ways in which the gender-related constructs were conceptualized and measured, and then whether other gender-related constructs were also measured and ruled out as alternative and perhaps more parsimonious explanations of the findings.

To examine the associations among these aspects of gender, Twenge (1999) factor-analyzed gender-related variables in seven content areas and found significant differences between men and women on both mean scores and factor structures (four for men and seven for women; only one, Occupational and Leisure Interests, included the same variables. A further innovation has been the move from classification of individuals into mutually exclusive binary categories to ratings on continuous variables, and from bipolar continua to separate and independent dimensions that may combine in complex ways (Bem, 1981; Twenge, 1999).

These distinctions are important for understanding GDs, because the above constructs often covary with one another and with their assortment of commonly correlated personality characteristics, self-presentations, developed abilities, social circumstances, life experiences, institutional positions, and locations in gendered social roles. Thus, either biological sex or social gender may be marker variables for statistically related but functionally independent causal variables. One confusion in the literature is that theory-driven GD analyses are designed to identify differences due primarily to gender and its proximate causes, whereas others appear only post hoc in demographic analyses of data gathered for other purposes. Attribution to gender as the central "cause" (strongest correlate) of the latter differences is even more scientifically suspect than for most correlational studies.

Further, constructs that describe characteristics of individuals should be distinguished from gender-related social-structural constructs such as dominant versus subordinate occupational roles, financially advantaged versus disadvantaged social status, hours spent in child care, and visible gender display as a stimulus variable that cues stereotyped cognitive schemas and related social perceptions for the beholder (Stewart & McDermott, 2004; Unger, 1979). These more culture-based expectations in turn shape observers' perceptions of biological realities (Shields, 1975). There is now considerable evidence implicating these social variables as influences on both physical development (via role expectations and role-consistent behavior, for example, sports participation; Twenge, 1999) and psychological processes such as assimilation, accommodation, and stereotype formation that link the individual to the biosocial environment and its social categories. Studies using self-report ratings typically find larger GDs that converge with gender stereotypes than do studies using physiological or performance-based measures that are less vulnerable to expectancy effects from both participants and researchers.

Similarly, the content of culturally defined stereotypes for gender role behavior creates differing expectations for women and men, and thus for GDs, which are often specific to social context (e.g., Hyde, 2005). The effects of these expectations are not limited to structural gender discrimination, but may include self-fulfilling prophesies of conformity, especially when the behavior is measured by self-report or is being observed, which further emphasizes the importance of context (Hyde, 2005). Because the behavior considered socially desirable (i.e., role-conforming) may differ by culture and gender in ways that vary among situations, researchers must be alert to possible biases in their measures and experimental conditions that might alter the validity of their findings. For example, stereotype threat describes the tendency of individuals to conform to negative stereotypes about their own social category when that stereotype has been made salient. Early studies showed the impact of stereotype threat for African Americans; more recently, the same effect has been found for women taking difficult mathematics tests (reviewed in Hyde, 2005).

Sex and gender are especially confounded with markers of social power inequality. Thus, it is essential to view the research literature on GDs through the lens of the social structural positions and structural power inherent in the social roles differentially occupied by women and men. In the resulting gender-linked power relations, "maleness signals authority, status, competence, social power and influence, and femaleness signals lack of authority, low status, incompetence, and little power and influence" (Stewart & McDermott, 2004, p. 521). Gendered power relations in face-to-face dyads or small groups are further reinforced by gender-differentiated power relations in the larger institutional or community context, for example, by control of resources, avenues of appeal, rewards, or punishments. Cultures define the points of intersection among the social structures and gendered roles that constitute institutions, the interaction rules for face-to-face behavior among genders, and the facets of individual social identity such as gender that reflect the individual's participation in multiple roles and face-to-face relationships.

Many of these roles and relationships confer differential privileges and rewards on women and men. The term "intersectionality" (Stewart & McDermott, 2004) denotes the analysis of those points of intersection between gender and various other social identities and structural positions not linked to gender that shape the way that gender is experienced and enacted differently by occupants of those identities and roles. Culturally defined differences in expectations for individuals who differ by gender may be further redefined based on the person's other identities and roles, for example, social class, race-identified appearance, sexual orientation, gender traditionality of occupation, or a combination of these.

As culture's role in GDs becomes clearer, cross-national research is examining consistencies and contrasts in how gender-related variables are defined, as well as their empirical correlates (e.g., Wood & Eagly, 2002; Eastwick et al., 2006). For example, a culture's gender ideology may be used to justify its norms for household labor allocation (Eastwick et al., 2006), which in turn produces gender role norms that help to socialize and reinforce gender role identities. Both sexual behavior and gender roles are constructed and enforced by cultures, with sharper gender differentiation in agrarian societies due to the greater survival value of sex-typed physical abilities and continuous child-tending (Wood & Eagly, 2002).

Due to the explosion of theory and research on GDs in the past 30 years, the content of those differences cannot be covered here in any appreciable depth. Even a review of relevant meta-analyses is beyond the scope of this article: a PsycInfo search on "gender differences and meta-analysis" yielded 171 published articles. The reader interested in GDs in psychiatric diagnoses is referred to Grant and Weissman (2007). Similarly, this review must omit much coverage of theory; the reader is referred to Eagly (1987), Maccoby and Jacklin (1974), Stewart and McDermott (2004), Twenge (1999), and Wood and Eagly (2002) for summaries of relevant theoretical positions.

The classical (pre-1970) theories of GDs have received only modest empirical support, and rapid and radical social changes in gender roles have undermined the evidence for others. More recent theories can be described in two classes. General developmental theories explain gender-typed development as a specific example of the theory's general processes (e.g., psychodynamic, evolutionary, cognitive developmental, and social learning theories). Gender-focused theories likewise address general processes, but were developed primarily to understand gender development (Bem's [1981] gender schema theory, Eagly's [1987] social role theory, Wood & Eagly's [2002] biosocial theory). Wood and Eagly (2002) further classify gender-focused theories into two broad theoretical positions: essentialism, which emphasizes stable, biologically based sex differences and is exemplified by evolutionary psychology, and social constructionism, which emphasizes the flexible construction of gender by cultures to suit the varying survival needs dictated by environmental conditions.

The best tested and supported of the newer theories is Eagly's (1987) social role theory, which is examined in several of the meta-analyses reviewed by Hyde (2005). Eagly and colleagues have found support for her theory in their meta-analyses of GDs in leadership, influenceability, helping behavior, aggressive behavior, and in a more recent cross-national study of mate selection preferences (Eastwick et al., 2006). More recent is biosocial theory, which is explicitly cross-cultural, and which shows promising initial support across nonindustrial societies (Wood & Eagly, 2002).

Consistent with the past 30 years of social change in American gender roles, earlier studies (e.g., Maccoby & Jacklin, 1974) found relatively more and larger GDs than have more recent ones; 78% of the effect sizes in Hyde's (2005) review of meta-analyses were classified as near zero or small. Several meta-analyses have reported the same effect of history across the studies they reviewed, with older studies showing larger GDs than more recent ones (reviewed in Hyde, 2005). GDs in self-reported gender role identity decreased from 1973 to 1994 due to increases in women's self-ratings on masculine items; men's feminine self-ratings did not increase (reviewed in Twenge, 1999).

GDs in cognitive abilities have decreased since Maccoby and Jacklin (1974) identified three cognitive ability areas and one behavioral area showing consistent GDs: verbal ability, visual-spatial ability, mathematical ability, and aggressive behavior. In Hyde's (2005) review of meta-analyses, the largest and most consistent areas of difference involved biologically based characteristics: motor performance, sex (masturbation frequency and attitudes toward casual sex), and aggression, especially physical aggression. Hyde explained that even when the genders' means differ significantly, the score distributions for most nonbiologically based variables show considerable overlap.

A recent consensus statement that appraised GDs in the component skills related to successful careers in science and mathematics noted that girls and women perform better on written tasks, whereas the greater relative variability of boys and men on mathematics and visuospatial ability measures means that they more often score at both extremes of the distribution, so that more of the highest scorers are male. Although this is partially consistent with an evolutionary explanation based on known GDs in brain functioning, there is considerable evidence for neural plasticity, meaning that these biological features change with experience of differing environmental performance demands (Halpern et al., 2007).

Three decades ago, researchers focused on chronicling GDs and found little support for the prevailing theories. The range of perspectives from which their data were gathered has enabled theorists to develop new conceptual tools (e.g., Stewart & McDermott, 2004; Wood & Eagly, 2002). Those tools in turn are facilitating new research approaches that connect the study of GDs across cultures and across disciplines.

REFERENCES

Bem, S. L. (1981). Gender schema theory: A cognitive account of sex typing. *Psychological Review, 88*(4), 354–364.

Eagly, A. H. (1987). *Sex differences in social behavior: A social role interpretation.* Hillsdale, NJ/UK: Lawrence Erlbaum.

Eastwick, P. W., Eagly, A. H., Glick, P., Johannesen-Schmidt, M. C., Fiske, S. T., Blum, A. M. B., et al. (2006). Is traditional gender ideology associated with sex-typed mate preferences? A test in nine nations. *Sex Roles, 54*(910), 603–614.

Grant, B. F., & Weissman, M. M. (2007). Gender and the prevalence of psychiatric disorders. In W. E. Narrow, M. B. First, P. J. Sirovatka, & D. A. Regier, *Age and gender considerations in psychiatric diagnosis: A research agenda for DSMV.* (pp. 31–45). Arlington, VA: American Psychiatric Publishing.

Halpern, D. F., Benbow, C. P., Geary, D. C., Gur, R. C., Hyde, J. S., & Gernsbacher, M. A. (2007). The science of sex differences in science and mathematics. *Psychological Science in the Public Interest, 8*(1), 151.

Hyde, J. S. (2005). The gender similarities hypothesis. *American Psychologist, 60*(6), 581–592.

Maccoby, E. E., & Jacklin, C. N. (1974). *The psychology of sex differences.* Stanford University Press, 1974.

Shields, S. (1975). Functionalism, Darwinism, and the psychology of women. *American Psychologist, 30*(7), 739–754.

Stewart, A. J., & McDermott, C. (2004). Gender in psychology. *Annual Review of Psychology, 55*, 519–544.

Twenge, J. M. (1999). Mapping gender: The multifactorial approach and the organization of gender-related attributes. *Psychology of Women Quarterly, 23*(3), 485–502.

Unger, R. K. (1979). Toward a redefinition of sex and gender. *American Psychologist, 34*(11), 1085–1094.

Wood, W., & Eagly, A. H. (2002). A cross-cultural analysis of the behavior of women and men: Implications for the origins of sex differences. *Psychological Bulletin, 128*(5), 699–727.

SHARON RAE JENKINS
University of North Texas

See also: **Femininity; Gender Roles; Masculinity**

GENDER IDENTITY (See Gender Roles)

GENDER IDENTITY DISORDER

Gender identity is a psychological concept that refers to one's subjective sense of being male or female. The intensity of gender identity exists along a continuum and therefore may vary between individuals. Gender identity disorder is a mental disorder in which gender identity is incongruent with anatomical sex (American Psychiatric Association, 2000). As a consequence, individuals with gender identity disorder experience varying degrees of dissatisfaction with their designated anatomical birth sex. In extreme cases (transsexualism) they express and pursue their desire to live and have the body of a person of the opposite sex as well as be viewed socially as a person of the opposite sex.

Gender identity disturbance is often first apparent in early childhood (Zucker, 2005). An affected child may repeatedly express a desire to be, or insist that he or she is, a member of the opposite sex. Boys may cross-dress or simulate female clothing, and girls may wear only masculine clothing and engage in cross-gender roles during games or imaginative play. Such children may also describe revulsion toward their anatomical sex. Boys may insist that their penis will fall off, whereas girls may urinate only from a standing position and be certain that they will grow a penis. During adolescence and early adulthood, many individuals with gender identity disorder increasingly identify with, and behave as, a member of the opposite gender. The task of ridding themselves of primary and secondary sexual characteristics, with visits to physicians to request hormonal therapy and surgical gender reassignment, occupies a substantial proportion of their time. Alternatively, other individuals experience a great amount of shame and distress over the conflict between their anatomical sex and self-identified gender. In response to such distress, they may attempt to suppress these feelings by marrying and having children in order to meet the perceived societal expectations of their anatomical sex.

Etiology

During normal fetal development, the female gender is the default or fundamental gender state for mammals. Normative female anatomical development occurs in the absence of any and all sex steroid hormones. For normal male anatomical sexual development to occur, not only are adequate levels of sex hormones required, but they are also needed at specific critical periods in development. A variety of psychological and biological theories exist regarding the etiology and gender differences in the prevalence of gender identity disorder. Psychodynamic theories have focused on normative psychosexual development and the role of identification with the same sex parent during normal development. Biological theories have considered the role of prenatal androgens with respect to brain masculinization *in utero*. However, theoretical speculation about the etiology of gender identity disorder is substantially limited, first by the level of present understanding regarding how gender identity is normally established, and second by a lack of consistent replication in clinical studies examining the gender identity characteristics of intersex patients, androgen exposure in female to male transsexuals, and neuroanatomical characteristics of transsexual and homosexual subjects (Gooren, 2006).

Diagnosis and Epidemiology

Gender identity disorder may be diagnosed in children, adolescents, and adults. As with other mental disorders, the presence of social, occupational, or functional impairment is central to accurate assessment for both clinical and research purposes, as is the exclusion of other diagnosable, non-psychiatric disorders that, in the case of gender identity disorders, have gender ambiguity or gender identity disturbance as a major component (e.g., intersex conditions such as congenital virilizing adrenal hyperplasia, Turner's syndrome, and androgen insensitivity syndrome). Estimates of the prevalence of gender identity disorder are severely limited by the lack of epidemiologic studies performed in children and the paucity of data derived from adults with gender disturbance.

Using national population data from the Netherlands in the largest epidemiological study of transsexualism conducted to date, the prevalence of transsexualism in adult Dutch males was found to be one in 11,900, while that of adult Dutch females was found to be one in 30,400 (van Kesteren, Gooren, & Megens, 1996). Similarly, the sex ratio for clinically referred male and female patients with gender identity disorders is consistent with adult epidemiological findings indicating a higher male prevalence of gender disturbance. In most childhood clinical programs, the ratio of referred children is four to five boys for each girl (Zucker, 2005), while adult clinical centers report a ratio of three to five male patients for each female patient (van Kesteren, Gooren, & Megens, 1996).

Psychological treatments for gender identity disorder are extraordinarily limited, and there has been little systematic evaluation of their efficacy. However, for some adult individuals, gender reassignment surgery is a treatment option to address gender identity disturbance. Although the modern history of gender reassignment surgery is less than a century old, accounts of surgical procedures designed to alter gender are found in the records of several ancient civilizations (Goddard, Vickery, & Terry, 2007). Selection of patients for gender reassignment involves extensive psychiatric and medical evaluation in addition to the experience of continuously living as a member of the preferred gender, usually with hormonal treatment, for a minimum of one year. For appropriately selected individuals, gender reassignment surgery and aftercare are best conducted with a multidisciplinary team of clinicians to achieve optimal cosmetic, functional, and psychological results (Sohn & Bosinski, 2007).

REFERENCES

American Psychiatric Association (2000). *Diagnostic and statistical manual of mental disorders* (4th ed., text rev.). Washington, DC: Author.

Goddard, J. C., Vickery, R. M., & Terry, T. R. (2007). Development of feminizing genitoplasty for gender dysphoria. *Journal of Sexual Medicine, 4*, 981–989.

Gooren, L. (2006). The biology of human psychosexual differentiation. *Hormones and Behavior, 50*, 589–601.

Sohn, M., & Bosinski, H. A. (2007). Gender identity disorders: Diagnostic and surgical aspects. *Journal of Sexual Medicine, 4*, 1193–207.

van Kesteren, P. J., Gooren, L. J., & Megens, A. J. (1996). An epidemiological and demographic study of transsexuals in The Netherlands. *Archives of Sexual Behavior, 25*, 589–600.

Zucker, K. J. (2005). Gender identity disorder in children and adolescents. *Annual Review of Clinical Psychology, 1*, 467–92.

Kristen A. Burgess
Charles F. Gillespie
Emory University School of Medicine

See also: **Gender Roles; Sexual Orientation and Gender Identity; Transsexualism**

GENDER ROLES

Gender roles are the set of expectations a society has about girls and boys, and women and men. These expectations are multifaceted and generally include specifications about appearances, personality traits, emotions, interests, abilities, and occupations. For example, in Western societies men are expected to be more agentic and less emotional than women, and women are expected to be more communal and less aggressive than men. More commonly, men may be assumed to have paid occupations and to be financially responsible for their families, whereas women are assumed to be homemakers with primary responsibility for the children. Such beliefs serve to define the sets of characteristics and behaviors that are considered appropriate or inappropriate for each sex. In other words, gender roles do more than merely describe the way things are: They describe how things should be.

Gender roles serve both social and intrapsychic functions. With respect to the former function, gender role expectations guide people's judgments and evaluations of others. When one assumes that another person possesses certain characteristics on the basis of her or his sex, one is engaging in *gender stereotyping*. Gender stereotyping is pervasive and can influence judgments in a subtle, nonconscious, and unintended manner (Lenton, Blair, & Hastie, 2001).

Gender roles also influence interpersonal evaluations directly: A person who conforms to the appropriate gender role is likely to be evaluated positively, whereas deviation from that role may result in avoidance, disapproval, or even physical hostility (Rudman & Glick, 2001). Gender roles serve an intrapsychic function by helping people to define themselves as individuals and to guide their behavior (Oswald & Lindstedt, 2006). Importantly, however, people vary in the extent to which they identify with a given gender role. That is, not all men view themselves in traditionally masculine terms, nor do all women identify with a traditionally feminine image. The extent to which one shares the constellation of characteristics associated with a particular gender role is known as *gender role identity*.

The measurement of gender role identity typically focuses on personality traits (e.g., agentic versus communal), with individuals indicating on a paper-and-pencil survey the degree to which each trait provides a true description of themselves. Note, however, that measurement of gender role identity is not without some debate. Initially, masculinity and femininity were thought to be opposite ends of a single continuum (i.e., if you are high in femininity, you must be low in masculinity). Later on, however, masculinity and femininity came to be seen as independent characteristics (i.e., you can be high or low on both dimensions, as well as high on one and low on the other; e.g., Bem, 1974). According to this framework, persons describing themselves as being both strongly masculine and strongly feminine are *androgynous*. The notion of androgyny has been criticized, however, for not adding substantial predictive power over and above that of masculinity and femininity. In other words, its utility as a psychological construct is in question.

There are a number of theories regarding how individuals become gender identified (also known as *gender typed*). One of the earliest formal theories, proposed by Freud, suggested that individuals must pass through a series of stages (oral, anal, phallic, genital, and latency) in order to become appropriately gender typed. Successful gender typing is argued to occur when children learn to identify with their same-sex parent and, in doing so, adopt the qualities and characteristics of that parent. Despite the popular attention paid to this theory, there is little empirical evidence to support it.

More modern theories regarding gender identification generally fall within the nature or nurture traditions. The theory that best represents the biological or nature tradition focuses upon the role of evolution in shaping each gender's interests, traits and behaviors. In particular, this theory suggests that contemporary differences in male and female gender roles are, in effect, carryovers from those interests, traits, and behaviors that had been adaptive for our ancestors. For example, the observed gender difference in the number of desired sexual partners is thought to have originated from gender differences in the sexual strategies that our ancestors found to be successful (Buss, 1985).

On the other hand, the socialization or nurture account argues that parents and other adults influence behavior by rewarding appropriate gender role behavior and punishing inappropriate role behavior. For example, parents may praise obedience and punish aggressiveness in their daughters, and praise risk taking and punish crying in their sons. According to a variant of this theoretical account, *cognition* is an important intervening variable. Thus, children are not merely shaped by external forces; instead social cognitive learning theory (Bussey & Bandura, 1999) argues that the process of receiving reinforcements and punishments for gender-appropriate and gender-inappropriate behavior results in the eventual creation of *cognitive expectancies*, which serve to guide future behavior as well as the understanding and evaluation of other peoples' behavior.

This account still further suggests that receiving reinforcements and punishments is not the only means by which children learn what constitutes gender-appropriate behavior. Significant adults may also impact gender typing by modeling behavior. Children learn to imitate those behaviors they see adults of their same sex performing. Although theories have tended to follow one or the other tradition (nature versus nurture), these two general accounts need not be antagonistic or mutually exclusive. Today, most psychologists who study gender typing recognize that biology and socialization likely work together to shape gendered behavior; it is no longer necessary to decide between nature *or* nurture, but to acknowledge the influence of nature *and* nurture.

Regardless of how they develop, it is important to emphasize that gender roles are neither static within individuals nor invariant across time or culture. With respect to the latter contention, what is considered masculine in one culture may be perceived as feminine in another. For example, in the United States (versus Pakistan), where there are stronger cultural injunctions against men expressing positive emotions such as love and joy, sex differences in the expression of these emotions are greater (see Alexander & Wood, 2000). Again, gender roles also vary over time within a given culture. For instance, within the United States alone, gender roles have changed tremendously in the last 50 years, with far fewer people expecting married women to confine their activities to the home (Diekman & Eagly, 2000). Gender roles also change as we age. Research indicates that younger and middle-aged adults are more likely to ascribe agentic or "masculine" traits to themselves, and middle-aged and older adults are more likely to ascribe communal or "feminine" traits to themselves (Diehl, Owen, & Youngblade, 2004), a pattern that could be explained by either nature (hormones) or nurture (differential role demands).

Scientists have long debated the degree to which females and males differ in their traits, interests, and behavior. Consensus is emerging, however, that observed gender differences must be considered in the context of situational and cultural norms, gender stereotypes, and individual differences in gender identity. Although each individual is unique and, furthermore, there is typically more variation within each sex than between each sex, gender roles exert a powerful influence that should not be ignored in our attempt to understand human behavior.

REFERENCES

Alexander, M. G., & Wood, W. (2000). Women, men and positive emotions. In A. Fischer & A. Manstead (Eds.), *Gender & emotion* (pp. 189–210). Cambridge University Press.

Bem, S. L. (1974). The measurement of psychological androgyny. *Journal of Consulting and Clinical Psychology, 42,* 155–162.

Buss, D. M. (1985). Psychological sex differences: Origins through sexual selection. *American Psychologist, 50,* 164–168.

Bussey, K., & Bandura, A. (1999). Social cognitive theory of gender development and differentiation. *Psychological Review, 106,* 676–713.

Diehl, M., Owen, S. K., & Youngblade, L. M. (2004). Agency and communion in adults' self representations. *International Journal of Behavioral Development, 28,* 1–15.

Diekman, A. B., & Eagly, A. H. (2000). Stereotypes as dynamic constructs: Women and men of the past, present, and future. *Personality and Social Psychology Bulletin, 26,* 1171–1188.

Lenton, A. P., Blair, I. V., & Hastie, R. (2001). Illusions of gender: Stereotypes evoke false memories. *Journal of Experimental Social Psychology, 37*, 3–14.

Oswald, D., & Lindstedt, K. (2006). The content and function of gender self-stereotypes: An exploratory investigation. *Sex Roles, 54*, 447–458.

Rudman, L. A., & Glick, P. (2001). Prescriptive gender stereotypes and backlash toward agentic women. *Journal of Social Issues, 57*, 743–762.

SUGGESTED READINGS

Costa, P. T., Jr., Terracciano, A., & McCrae, R. R. (2001). Gender differences in personality traits across cultures: Robust and surprising findings. *Journal of Personality and Social Psychology, 81*, 322–331.

Lenton, A. P., & Webber, L. (2006). Cross-sex friendships: Who has more? *Sex Roles, 54*, 809–820.

Prentice, D. A., & Carranza, E. (2002). What women and men should be, shouldn't be, are allowed to be, and don't have to be: The contents of prescriptive gender stereotypes. *Psychology of Women Quarterly, 26*, 269–281.

ALISON P. LENTON
University of Edinburgh, Scotland, United Kingdom

See also: **Femininity; Masculinity**

GENERAL ADAPTATION SYNDROME

The General Adaptation Syndrome (GAS) is a cluster of bodily responses to severe, prolonged stressors that was first described by Hans Selye. Selye observed that rats exposed to a wide variety of noxious agents exhibited a nonspecific syndrome consisting of enlargement of the adrenal gland, shrinkage of the thymus, spleen, and lymph glands, and the emergence of ulcers in the stomach and small intestine. This was seen in animals exposed to extreme cold and heat, intense sound or light, forced exercise, injections of various organ extracts or formalin, and other potent biological challenges to homeostasis.

Based on animal studies, Selye suggested that the GAS consists of three phases of response to a stressor. The initial stage is an *alarm reaction* during which the following occurs: (1) the adrenal-cortex enlarges and releases large amounts of the anti-inflammatory hormone, cortisol, into the bloodstream; (2) lymphatic tissues shrink; (3) the number of white blood cells decline; (4) ulcers develop; (5) heart rate and blood pressure increase; and (6) the animals lose weight. During the second stage, the *stage of resistance*, the adrenal cortex remains enlarged, but instead of releasing cortisol, the gland retains the hormone; other tissues and physiological functions appear relatively normal; and

body weight returns to near normal levels. With continued application of the severe stressor, the animals eventually enter a third stage, the *stage of exhaustion*. Similar to the alarm reaction, substantial cortisol is released into the blood, lymphatic tissues shrink, and body weight again falls. This stage ends with the animal's death.

Selye's GAS and the research that followed from this notion of nonspecific response to environmental challenges were extremely important in launching the study of biological stress. Selye borrowed the term "stress" from physics to refer to this syndrome of responses to a noxious agent. However, in his memoir, *The Stress of My Life* (1977), Selye noted that he had insufficient knowledge of the English language when he defined the term "stress" (what would often now be called the stress response), and he suggested that the more correct analogous physical term would have been "strain." More recent studies of the concept of stress have broadened the definition of stressors to include less potent challenges to an organism's normal function, including psychological presses. It is now clear that the GAS does not occur following all events that would reasonably be considered stressors, nor does it occur for all individuals in a given situation. As Selye himself noted, organisms may not experience all three stages of the GAS, and stressors may sometimes only produce limited features of the alarm reaction (e.g., cortisol release without gastric ulceration). Thus, the GAS does not appear to generalize all prolonged and painful stressors and perhaps only generalizes to the most intense of these stressors. Despite these criticisms, Selye's GAS was an important concept in the history of research on stress, because it suggested that in addition to the specific, finely tuned bodily changes induced by aversive physical challenges to homeostasis, there was also a more generalized bodily response that could be elicited by any one of a diverse array of intense stressors that threatened an organism's survival.

SUGGESTED READINGS

Selye, H. (1936). A syndrome produced by diverse nocuous agents. *Nature, 138*, 32.

Selye, H. (1956). *The stress of life.* New York: McGraw-Hill.

Selye, H. (1977). *The stress of my life: A scientist's memoirs.* Toronto: McClelland & Stewart.

Weiner, H. (1992). *Perturbing the organism: The biology of stressful experience.* Chicago: Chicago University Press.

KAREN S. QUIGLEY
Department of Veterans Affairs, New Jersey Healthcare System, East Orange, NJ, and

New Jersey Medical School, University of Medicine and Dentistry of New Jersey

See also: **Homeostasis; Stress Consequences**

GENERALIZED ANXIETY DISORDER

Generalized anxiety disorder (GAD) is a clinical anxiety disorder that is centrally characterized by excessive, pervasive, and chronic worry. Worry is a cognitive activity that involves repeatedly thinking about potential negative future events, such as "What if I can't finish this task?" "What if I never graduate?" "What if I have some type of illness?" According to the *Diagnostic and Statistical Manual of Mental Disorders* (DSM-IV-TR; American Psychiatric Association, 2000), in order to warrant a diagnosis of GAD an individual must experience excessive and uncontrollable worry for at least 6 months, as well as three or more associated symptoms that are present, more days than not, over this time period. These associated symptoms include restlessness, being easily fatigued, difficulty concentrating, irritability, muscle tension, or sleep disturbances (e.g., difficulty falling or staying asleep). Consistent with other DSM-IV diagnostic criteria, both the worry and associated symptoms must cause clinically significant distress or impairment.

Individuals with GAD typically report that the content of their worries is broad and pervasive and spans domains such as interpersonal relationships, physical health, school/work, finances, world events, and minor matters (e.g., punctuality). In addition, these worries cannot solely be accounted for by the presence of another disorder (e.g., worry about having a panic attack in panic disorder, worry about social interactions in social phobia). This is an important diagnostic consideration, as GAD is a highly comorbid disorder and often co-occurs with many anxiety and mood disorders, most commonly major depressive disorder and social phobia (Roemer, Orsillo, & Barlow, 2002).

Recent epidemiological surveys report 12-month and lifetime prevalence rates for GAD of 2.9% and 6.1% respectively (Kessler et al., 2005) with approximately twice as many women as men meeting criteria (Roemer et al., 2002). Further research is needed to determine whether there are any racial and ethnic differences in the prevalence of GAD.

Models of GAD

Behavioral Models of Anxiety

As in other anxiety disorders, behavioral models of GAD posit that individuals learn to associate fear with certain stimuli. This can occur through stimuli being present during a threatening event, modeling of fearful behavior by others, or negative experiences with unpredictable and uncontrollable events in general. Once these fearful associations are formed, they can spread to similar stimuli. In addition, they are maintained by avoidance, because individuals cannot learn that a stimulus is not threatening if they do not come into contact with it. Avoiding

feared stimuli or contexts can become habitual, because the initial reduction in distress that follows it serves as negative reinforcement that increases the frequency of later avoidant responses. As explained next, worry itself might serve such an avoidant function.

Avoidance Theory

As excessive and uncontrollable worry is the central and defining feature of GAD, many researchers have examined the function of worry in order to better understand GAD. Borkovec, Alcaine, and Behar (2004) have proposed that, although worry is itself aversive, it also serves an avoidant function, in that it is associated with reduced somatic arousal, which negatively reinforces its occurrence. In other words, worry seems to damp down physiological arousal and may distract from other sources of distress; this consequence makes worriers engage in worry more often. As Borkovec and colleagues (2004) review in depth, experimental studies have shown that inducing worry is either related to reduced somatic arousal or more gradual increases in activation. Indeed, psychophysiological investigations of individuals with GAD indicate that, unlike other anxiety disorders, it is not associated with increased physiological arousal. Individuals with GAD also report that their worry serves to distract them from more emotional topics (Borkovec et al., 2004). These emotionally avoidant properties of worry may, in fact, prolong distress because they interfere with complete processing of emotional responses.

Cognitive Correlates of GAD and Attempts at Suppression

In addition to the avoidance of somatic activity, there may be a variety of other factors that exacerbate the process of worry in individuals with GAD. Evidence suggests that GAD may be associated with an intolerance of uncertainty. That is, individuals may have a lower threshold for ambiguity, and this may increase the likelihood that they engage in worry in an effort to cope (Dugas, Buhr, & Ladouceur, 2004). In a related concept, individuals may engage in worry in the belief that this helps prepare them for future events. Given the fact that worry is often directed towards events with a low probability of occurrence, the non-occurrence of these feared events can be taken as evidence for the benefits of worry as a preparatory strategy, thereby reinforcing this behavior (Borkovec et al., 2004).

Although individuals with GAD may hold positive beliefs about worrying, they may also develop secondary worries about worrying itself. This "meta-worry" may perpetuate the cycle of worry by increasing anxiety, as individuals worry about their own worries (Wells, 1999). Individuals with GAD often find worry extremely distressing and frequently engage in attempts to stop or suppress their worrisome thoughts. Given the lack of rigid control that we have over our internal experiences (e.g., thoughts, emotions), attempts at suppression are often ineffective, and evidence also suggests that suppression may paradoxically increase the thoughts that one is trying to avoid (Purdon, 1999). Thus, individuals with GAD may be caught in a cycle in which they worry about their own worry and its uncontrollability, but attempts to control the worry actually increase its frequency.

Information Processing Theories

The way that individuals perceive and attend to information in their environment may also contribute to the maintenance of GAD. For example, several studies have demonstrated that individuals with GAD display an attentional bias towards threatening information. That is, they are more likely than individuals without an anxiety disorder to attend to threatening cues in their environment. In addition to this attentional bias, individuals with GAD may also be more likely to interpret ambiguous situations as threatening and believe negative outcomes to be likely (MacLeod & Rutherford, 2004). Given these tendencies, it is not hard to imagine why individuals may find themselves generally anxious and locked in cycles of worry.

Treatment

Cognitive-Behavioral Treatment

Cognitive-behavioral therapy (CBT) is currently the first line psychological intervention for GAD. A variety of randomized control trials indicate that CBT results in statistically and clinically significant changes in GAD symptomatology and yields large effect sizes that are maintained at follow up (Borkovec & Ruscio, 2001). Although researchers have tailored specific aspects of the full CBT package to fit their model (e.g., to target "meta-worry" or intolerance of uncertainty), what we present here is the standard approach with the longest history of empirical validation. The common elements of a CBT package include psychoeducation, monitoring, relaxation training, exposure, and cognitive restructuring.

Most CBT treatments begin with a psychoeducation component (although psychoeducation may be a component of later phases as well). During this phase of treatment, clients are provided with information about the functional nature of fear and anxiety, as well as how these processes can become rigid, habitual cycles that are maladaptive. The cognitive, affective, behavioral, and physiological components of the anxiety and worry cycle are highlighted, with examples drawn from the client's own experiences.

As with all CBT approaches, successful monitoring is an essential component to therapy. Clients are taught how to notice early situational, behavioral, cognitive, or physiological cues to their anxious responding so that they can intervene early on in the worry/anxiety cycle. Monitoring may also allow clients to view their thoughts and emotions as rising and falling, allowing them to be less reactive to their internal experiences. As a consequence, individuals with GAD may be able to observe their worry, rather than worrying more about it. Moreover, consistent monitoring can help clients monitor changes in their mood and anxiety over the course of therapy, thereby reinforcing the benefits of certain interventions.

Clients are also taught various methods of relaxation (e.g., diaphragmatic breathing, progressive muscle relaxation) in session, and are asked to practice these techniques on their own. In addition to developing the skill of relaxation, these techniques may facilitate greater present-moment focus (as worry itself is largely a future or past-focused activity). Gradually, clients are helped to use these relaxation strategies when confronted with fearful situations either imaginally or *in vivo* (i.e., exposure). However, care must be taken to ensure that clients are not using relaxation as another means of avoidance, as this can maintain threatening associations and interfere with learning new, nonthreatening associations.

A variety of methods of cognitive restructuring are also included in order to counter the rigidity characteristic of individuals with GAD. Clients are taught to identify their tendencies to overestimate the probability of feared outcomes or engage in catastrophic thinking, and they are encouraged to consider alternative ways of conceptualizing feared situations. Elements unique to a given model (e.g., meta-worry or intolerance of uncertainty) may also be added. A common emphasis on early cue detection and implementing alternative responses helps clients to develop new habits and increase their flexibility.

Psychopharmacological Interventions

Three basic classes of drugs have been studied for use with GAD. These include benzodiazepines, azapirones, and antidepressants (e.g., SSRIs). The choice as to which type of drug will be most effective is usually based on a particular client's presentation and symptom profile. Compared to azapirones and antidepressants, benzodiazepines are relatively fast acting. However, there exists considerable controversy as to the risks of using fast-acting anxiolytics in the treatment of anxiety disorders. Specifically, there is concern about the possible addictive properties of some fast-acting anxiolytics and their use as a means of avoidance. Inasmuch as certain anxiolytics reduce physiological arousal, chronic use can inhibit activation of the fear network in memory and successful emotional processing. Given the frequent co-occurrence of depression in clients with GAD, and the long-term tolerability of such agents, antidepressants are currently considered the first line pharmacological treatment for GAD (Lydiard & Monnier, 2004). However, it is important to note that interventions that are solely psychopharmacologically based may require individuals to remain on medication over long periods of time, as medication discontinuation can be associated with the return of symptoms.

Newer Treatment Approaches

Despite the efficacy of CBT for GAD, a proportion of those treated continue to experience clinically significant levels of symptoms (Roemer et al., 2002), leading investigators to pursue additional intervention strategies in order to enhance treatment efficacy. Given the paradoxical effects of suppression, and the tendency to avoid internal experiences that appears to be characteristic of individuals with GAD, recent approaches have incorporated acceptance and mindfulness techniques with behavioral principles. Although there is need for further study, recent empirical investigations have yielded promising results (Roemer & Orsillo, 2007).

Researchers have also begun to explore whether the addition of interpersonal and experiential elements enhances treatment effectiveness (Newman, Castonguay, Borkovec, & Molnar, 2004). This approach stems from clinical and research evidence suggesting that GAD is characterized by significant interpersonal problems and emotional avoidance. Therapists use a variety of experiential exercises, as well as the therapeutic relationship, to explore interpersonal concerns and deepen emotional experience. Finally, based on research demonstrating emotion regulation difficulties in individuals with GAD (such as emotional intensity, difficulty understanding emotions, reactivity to one's emotions, and difficulty modulating emotional responses), researchers have begun to develop treatments that specifically target these difficulties (Mennin, 2006). Future research is needed to establish the efficacy of these newer approaches.

REFERENCES

American Psychiatric Association. (2000). *Diagnostic and statistical manual of mental disorders* (4th ed.; text rev.). Washington, DC: Author.

Borkovec, T. D., Alcaine, O. M., & Behar, E. (2004). Avoidance theory of worry and generalized anxiety disorder. In D. S. Mennin, R. G. Heimberg, & C. L. Turk (Eds.), *Generalized anxiety disorder: Advances in research and practice* (pp. 77–108). New York: Guilford Press.

Borkovec, T. D., & Ruscio, A. M. (2001). Psychotherapy for generalized anxiety disorder. *Journal of Clinical Psychiatry, 62,* 37–45.

Dugas, M. J., Buhr, K., & Ladouceur, R. (2004). The role of intolerance of uncertainty in etiology and maintenance. In D. S. Mennin, R. G. Heimberg, & C. L. Turk (Eds.), *Generalized anxiety disorder: Advances in research and practice* (pp. 143–163). New York: Guilford Press.

Kessler, R. C., Brandenburg, N., Lane, M., Roy-Byrne, P., Stang, P. D., Stein, D. J., et al. (2005). Rethinking the duration requirement for generalized anxiety disorder: Evidence from the National Comorbidity Survey Replication. *Psychological Medicine, 35,* 1073–1082.

Lydiard, R. B., & Monnier, J. (2004). Pharmacological treatment. In D. S. Mennin, R. G. Heimberg, & C. L. Turk (Eds.), *Generalized anxiety disorder: Advances in research and practice* (pp. 353–379). New York: Guilford Press.

MacLeod, C., & Rutherford, E. (2004). Information-processing approaches: Assessing the selective functioning of attention, interpretation, and retrieval. In D. S. Mennin, R. G. Heimberg, & C. L. Turk (Eds.), *Generalized anxiety disorder: Advances in research and practice* (pp. 109–142). New York: Guilford Press.

Mennin, D. S. (2006). Emotion regulation therapy: An integrative approach to treatment-resistant anxiety disorders. *Journal of Contemporary Psychotherapy, 36,* 95–105.

Newman, M. G., Castonguay, L. G., Borkovec, T. D., & Molnar, C. (2004). In D. S. Mennin, R. G. Heimberg, & C. L. Turk (Eds.), *Generalized anxiety disorder: Advances in research and practice* (pp. 320–350). New York: Guilford Press.

Purdon, C. (1999). Thought suppression and psychopathology. *Behavior Research and Therapy, 35,* 35–47.

Roemer, L., & Orsillo, S. M. (2007). An open trial of an acceptance-based behavior therapy for generalized anxiety disorder. *Behavior Therapy, 38,* 72–85.

Roemer, L., Orsillo, S. M., & Barlow, D. H. (2002). Generalized anxiety disorder. In D. H. Barlow, *Anxiety and its disorders: The nature and treatment of anxiety and panic* (pp. 477–515). New York: Guilford Press.

Wells, A. (1999). A metacognitive model and therapy for generalized anxiety disorder. *Clinical Psychology and Psychotherapy, 6,* 86–95.

SUGGESTED READINGS

Barlow, D. H. (2002). Anxiety and its disorders: The nature and treatment of anxiety and panic. New York: Guilford Press.

Heimberg, R. G., Turk, C. L., & Mennin, D. S. (2004). Generalized anxiety disorder: Advances in research and practice. New York: Guilford Press.

MICHAEL TREANOR
LIZABETH ROEMER
University of Massachusetts, Boston

See also: Anxiety; Anxiety Disorders

GENETIC COUNSELING

Genetic counseling as a separate and distinct component of medical care was introduced as part of the eugenics movement in the United States during the 1940s. Over time, societal rejection of "eugenic" practices as well as advances in medical technology highlighted the need to consider the psychological effects on the family of a genetic diagnosis (R. G. Resta, 2006). Throughout the 1950s and 1960s genetic counseling evolved from this primarily social and public health perspective, and many different types of health-care professionals—including physicians, nurses, and social workers, as well as research geneticists—provided explanations and social support to individuals and families diagnosed with genetic disorders. Genetic counseling as we know it today benefited from these early practitioners.

As the focus of genetic counseling expanded, the need for formal training in genetic counseling was recognized, and Sarah Lawrence College established the first training program for masters-level, nonphysician genetic counselors in 1969 (Veach, Bartels, & Leroy, 2007). Standards for training as well as clinical competencies are defined and regulated by the American Board of Genetic Counseling. Although the majority of genetic counselors are masters-level persons trained in genetic counseling, there are also training programs for nurses. Social work has also had continued strong interest in supporting families diagnosed with genetic disorders, working in partnership with the genetics team. As of 2008, there are estimated to be only 2,000 or so professionals actively working as clinical genetic counselors. Doctoral training opportunities in genetic counseling are presently limited in North America. The emerging literature about genetic counseling models and practice is often spearheaded by MD- or PhD-level professionals with advanced degrees in other disciplines and includes a large international contingent.

Professional Identity

The majority of genetic counselors are employed at large medical centers as part of an assessment team that includes a physician supervisor. Initially, clients most frequently encountered genetic counselors in prenatal or pediatric settings in the context of either diagnostic or screening testing for a possible condition. Since the mid 1990s, genetic counselors have also become an integral member of cancer care teams where predisposition or presymptomatic testing is commonplace. A recent task force of the National Society of Genetic Counselors defined genetic counseling as follows:

Genetic counseling is the process of helping people understand and adapt to the medical, psychological and familial implications of genetic contributions to disease. This process integrates the following:

- Interpretation of family and medical histories to assess the chance of disease occurrence or recurrence.

- Education about inheritance, testing, management, prevention resources and research

- Counseling to promote informed choices and adaptation to the risk or condition (R. Resta et al., 2006, p. 79).

As genetic information becomes more complex and more integrated into the international perception of medical care, genetic counselors are increasingly acting independently as genetic "experts" in private industry, consumer organizations, and government ventures. In such roles, genetic counselors most frequently focus on the education component of the above definition.

Genetic Counseling Interventions

At present, genetic counseling interventions have built on or borrowed from other medical and psychology disciplines. Specific interventions such as crisis intervention, Rolland's family system illness model, and Lazarus and Folkman's stress and coping model have been adapted and restructured to integrate family history, genetic testing, and/or genetic diagnosis (Rolland & Williams, 2005). As patient encounters are highly variable in terms of family situation, information needs, and medical situation, genetic counselors are likely to continue looking to more developed helping professions to inform different aspects of care. Research into the practice of genetic counseling is stymied by the lack of comprehensive, operationally defined, empirically established models of practice.

Models of Practice

The Rogerian Model

Initial formal instruction in genetic counseling at Sarah Lawrence College emphasized the psychosocial impact of genetics. Coursework relied heavily on Carl Roger's Client-Centered Counseling (later called Person-Centered Counseling) and emphasized the concept of *nondirectiveness* as a mechanism to respect the client's autonomy (Veach et al., 2007). New graduate programs in North America perpetuated this central tenet of genetic counseling through the 1980s and early 1990s, with limited discussion of alternative models. In the late 1990s, as outcomes-based research in genetic counseling expanded, nondirectiveness was criticized as a description of inaction (what *should not* happen during genetic counseling) rather than action (what should characterize the genetic counseling process). Nondirectiveness remains a central tenet of genetic counseling, but it is now acknowledged as one of many tenets and one that may or may not be appropriate for a given medical, family, or social situation (R. G. Resta, 2006; Veach et al., 2007).

The Teaching/Counseling Models

In 1997, Kessler described two primary models of genetic counseling (Kessler, 1997). The first, an "education" model derived from the didactic methods most frequently used in academic medicine, is focused on information sharing. This model highlights the *genetic* component of genetic counseling and often focuses on the large amounts of complex scientific information necessary in the context of medical decision making. Some studies indicate that this model is more prevalent among practicing counselors than the nondirective model. However, it has also been noted that the pedagogical approach of this model has the potential to create an unequal power dynamic between the health-care provider (the genetic counselor) and the client/patient, resulting in information overload, limited understanding, and reduced self-determination.

Kessler's second model, a "counseling" model, is informed by the mental-health professions. This model emphasizes the counseling portion of genetic counseling and focuses on psychological goals, such as creating competency and developing autonomy. In time-limited relationships or in settings where outcomes are focused on test uptake, this model is difficult to evoke.

The Reciprocal-Engagement Model

In 2007 the *Reciprocal-Engagement Model* was the first model developed by genetic counseling professionals for genetic counselors (Veach et al., 2007). This model was developed by North American–based genetic counseling graduate program directors to include previously defined clinical competencies, as well as other prior models of genetic counseling. The reciprocal-engagement model acts a conceptual framework "that puts patients at the core of determining their medical and psychosocial futures" (p. 723). The model highlights the importance of autonomy as well as family resiliency, thereby encouraging the contextualization of the genetic information to the individual family's needs. The key attributes of this model include education, individual patient/family characteristics, the counseling partnership, and shared decision-making, leading to the outcome of positive adaptation to genetic information.

Evolving Practice in Genetic Counseling

Research on the genetic counseling process is expanding knowledge about how genetic information can affect individuals and families as well as about developing counseling interventions to facilitate coping and adjustment to a genetic diagnosis. Additionally, recent work suggests that genetic counseling can improve family communication about risk (Forrest, Burke, Bacic, & Amor, 2008). As the scope of knowledge about genetics moves beyond rare diseases to include more common health-care concerns (e.g., diabetes, cardiovascular disease), the need to understand the interplay between the genetic information, psychosocial adaptation, and family dynamics also grows exponentially.

REFERENCES

Forrest, L. E., Burke, J., Bacic, S., & Amor, D. J. (2008). Increased genetic counseling support improves communication of genetic information in families. *Genetics in Medicine, 10*(3), 167–172.

Kessler, S. (1997). Psychological aspects of genetic counseling: IX. Teaching and counseling. *Journal of Genetic Counseling, 6*(3), 287–295.

Resta, R. G. (2006). Defining and redefining the scope and goals of genetic counseling. *American Journal of Medical Genetics, Part C, Seminars in Medical Genetics, 142*(4), 269–275.

Resta, R., Biesecker, B. B., Bennett, R. L., Blum, S., Estabrooks Hahn, S., Strecker, M. N., et al. (2006). A new definition of genetic counseling: National Society of Genetic Counselors' Task Force Report. *Journal of Genetic Counseling*.

Rolland, J. S., & Williams, J. K. (2005). Toward a biopsychosocial model for 21st-century genetics. *Family Process, 44*(1), 3–24.

Veach, P. M., Bartels, D. M., & Leroy, B. S. (2007). Coming full circle: A reciprocal-engagement model of genetic counseling practice. *Journal of Genetic Counseling, 16*(6), 713–728.

SUGGESTED READINGS

Baker, D. L., Schuette, J. L., & Uhlmann, W. R. (1998). *A guide to genetic counseling*. New York: Wiley-Liss.

McCarth-Veach, P., LeRoy, B. S., & Bartels, D. M. (2003). *Facilitating the genetic counseling process: A practice manual*. New York: Springer-Verlag.

Weil, J. (2000). *Psychosocial genetic counseling* (Vol. 41). New York: Oxford University Press.

Jennifer A. Sullivan
Allyn McConkie-Rosell
Duke University Medical Center

See also: Counseling

GENETICS AND GENERAL INTELLIGENCE

A question that directs many research fields within psychology concerns the origins of observed differences among individuals. Behavioral genetics targets this research question. Quantitative behavioral genetics and molecular genetics are the two methodological approaches within behavioral genetics.

Quantitative behavioral genetics deals with the contributions of nature and nurture to the etiology of individual differences in a certain trait. Because nature and nurture are not distinct categories, examining genetic and environmental determination of individual differences and their development can be very complex. In molecular genetic research, the sequencing of the human genome has been one of the major attainments within the last 10 years. This attainment represents the basis of further studies to identify the etiology of diseases and complex behavioral traits on the level of genes.

We focus on the different methodological approaches in the study of individual differences in general intelligence and aim at providing a concise summary of select research results.

General Cognitive Ability

Over the last 100 years the structure of intelligence was the target of numerous scientific studies. One of the most discussed topics involved the existence of one general factor (g factor) of intelligence: Many studies verified that such a factor accounts for about 40% of variance in various psychometric intelligence tests (Jensen, 1998). Additionally, cognitive ability is one of the most reliable and valid constructs in the psychological science. Besides the correlation with school performance and academic success (Neisser, Boodoo, Bouchard et al., 1996), general cognitive ability is predictive of a large range of real-life criteria, including job success and health (Gottfredson, 2002). Moreover, the stability of individual differences in psychometric intelligence across the lifespan was convincingly demonstrated in the Scottish Mental Survey, which contains data from more than 500 participants who took intelligence tests in 1932 and again in 2000. Deary and colleagues reported a stability of .66 between the two measurement points at ages 11 and 79 (Deary, Whitemann, Starr, Whalley, & Fox, 2004).

Quantitative Behavioral Genetics

The aim of this discipline of psychological research is to apply the methods and knowledge of genetics to the exploration of human behavior. In this research domain, nature (genetics) and nurture (environment) are studied simultaneously as two sources of interindividual differences. Differences in human traits (e.g., general cognitive ability) are attributed to relative proportions of genetic differences and differences in environmental factors that contribute to the phenotypic differences under study. Environmental factors can be biological, social, or cultural in nature. Furthermore, environmental influences are separated into shared and nonshared influences. Shared environmental factors (c) contain influences that make siblings growing up in the same family more similar (such as socioeconomic status, parental style, family climate). Nonshared environmental factors (e) contain influences that make siblings more different (such as peers, illness, preferential treatment by one parent). Both kinds of influences contribute to the variability of a trait. A third source of variance is the heritability (h) of a trait. It describes the proportion of the trait variance in a given population that traces back to genetic differences. This

is equivalent to another definition of heritability as the ratio of two variances: the genetic variance over the total phenotypic variance. As a group statistic, heritability always refers to differences within a population and not to the phenotype of one single person. Apart from genetic and environmental influences, gene-environment interaction and gene-environment correlation can further contribute to interindividual differences. Details regarding these concepts are available in Plomin, DeFries, McClearn, and McGuffin (2008).

Quantitative behavioral genetic research usually uses adoption, family, and twin studies to explore the relative contributions of genetics and environment to interindividual differences in phenotypic trait. A common feature among all these designs is that phenotypic similarities of persons with known genetic and environmental similarities (e.g., monozygotic twins [MZ] and dizygotic twins [DZ] reared together or adopted children and their unrelated siblings) are compared to estimate the variance components described earlier. Twin studies are the most common design in quantitative behavioral genetic research. Because MZ twins share 100% of their genes whereas DZ twins have an average genetic similarity of 50%, the relative importance of genetic and shared as well as nonshared environmental influences can be derived from analyses of phenotypic twin similarities measured as intraclass-correlations (ICC).

Modern quantitative behavioral genetic studies usually use structural equation modeling to estimate the variance components contributing to individual differences in a given trait based on data from groups of relatives with varying genetic and environmental similarity. Introductory literature on methods of quantitative genetics, including a detailed description of twin and adoption designs, is available elsewhere (Plomin et al., 2008). Despite the fact that twin studies are a powerful tool to understand the etiology of traits, it is advantageous to combine twin, family, and adoption samples in simultaneous multigroup analyses of different relatives/kinship groups. This combination can strengthen the robustness and generalizability of findings as well as the statistical power of quantitative-genetic studies.

Molecular Genetics

Quantitative genetic studies can provide a starting point for molecular genetic research as they can help to identify areas of behavior in which genetic influences make important contributions to the variation between individuals. For the most complex psychological traits, such as intelligence, it is safe to assume that many genes are involved and that each gene has only a relatively small effect. These genes are called quantitative trait loci (QTL), indicating that they are a part of a multiple-gene system that contributes to the expression of a trait or disorder. Identifying specific genes will facilitate the understanding of the biological and neurophysiological pathways between genes and observed behavior.

There are two major research strategies within molecular genetics: association studies and linkage analysis. With linkage analysis it is possible to detect linkage between DNA markers and traits with the aim of mapping genes to chromosomes or to specific regions of chromosomes. Whereas traditional linkage studies involved a few large family pedigrees to trace dichotomous disorders, current designs, such as the affected sib-pair linkage design, are able to identify linkages for more complex traits and disorders.

Association studies investigate the correlation between a particular allele and a phenotypic trait. This is a more powerful but also a less systematic approach to find genes for behavior. Allelic association can detect QTLs of small effect sizes. Furthermore, the rapid development of tools such as DNA-chips that can simultaneously analyze 500,000 DNA markers allow for genome-wide association scans (Plomin et al., 2008).

Recent Findings in Quantitative Behavioral Genetics for General Intelligence

General cognitive ability is one of the most extensively studied constructs in behavioral genetic research. Erlenmeyer-Kimling and Jarvik confirmed the convergence of genetic influence on intelligence verified by twin, adoption, and family studies (1963). In their review, Bouchard and McGue (1981) presented an update on the behavior genetic research on g. They reported that genetic influences account for approximately 50% of the variance of g, a result that has been confirmed by newer studies using the model-fit approach (Plomin & Spinath, 2004; Plomin et al., 2008). Shared environment explained about 25%, whereas nonshared environment and measurement error were responsible for the remaining 25% of inter-individual differences. Interestingly, shared environmental factors appear to be more important early in life and in childhood, whereas nonshared environmental influences as well as genetic influences become more important later in early adulthood and later in life. Therefore, the average heritability of 50% is probably an underestimation because studies with older participants are comparatively rare.

Longitudinal genetic analyses focus on genetic and environmental influences on the phenotypic stability over time. Results from the cognitive domain indicate that genetic factors contribute to continuity rather than change, which implies that the set of genes appear to influence intelligence throughout different developmental stages. The increasing importance of genetic factors throughout the life span is a result from both twin and adoption studies (McGue, Bouchard, Iacono, & Lykken, 1993). This rise in heritability can in part be explained by the increasingly active role that individuals play in

selecting and shaping their environments according to their genetic make-up. The fact that MZ twin similarity appears to remain stable over time, whereas DZ twin similarity tends to decrease, could also be viewed as a stronger response to environmentally triggered change from individuals who share fewer genes.

Multivariate genetic analyses can also be used to study the covariance of specific cognitive abilities, such as verbal and spatial abilities. Results from such analyses indicate a significant overlap of genetic influences on diverse cognitive facets. This pattern of results has led to the conclusion that genetic effects on cognitive processes act largely in a global fashion. One further implication is that, quite possibly, the same genes are responsible for cognitive abilities in diverse areas (Kovas & Plomin, 2006).

Recent Findings in Molecular Genetics in General Intelligence

The quest for "intelligence" genes has gone on for more than a decade now. Only a few candidate genes have been identified and replication of positive results has been an even more fruitless endeavor (Butcher, Davis, Craig, & Plomin, 2008). At the same time, genome-wide scans have become an increasingly feasible and appropriate strategy to identify genes so that some researchers in this area consider it to be just a matter of time until the first robust results are found. Genome-wide linkage studies within the normal range of ability are reported and linked with findings from candidate gene studies in clinical samples. An overview can be found in Deary et al. (2006). They reported, among other things, a linkage between the so-called 6p locus and full-scale intelligence scores, suggesting that this region is associated with general cognitive ability. Butcher and colleagues (2008) used a new and extensive genotyping technique to rule out false-positive results. In a multi-stage design, a large number of participants were studied and linkage to 500,000 possible DNA markers (single nucleotide polymorphisms; SNPs) were considered. In the first step, 47 SNPs were nominated, but after the second analysis and correction for false results, only one SNP remained significantly associated with general cognitive ability.

Implications

It is important to address a few misunderstandings in the interpretation of quantitative behavioral genetic results. Heritability is a group statistic that is not applicable to the individual. Heritability represents a proportion of variance and is not a constant. Changes in environmental conditions (e.g., education practice) can lead to a change in the heritability of a trait. Moreover, high heritability scores do not imply lack of malleability at the level of individuals.

At the same time, a better understanding of the importance of environmental influences, and whether these influences tend to contribute to similarities or differences among individuals reared together, can be utilized to sharpen the focus on nongenetic determinants of interindividual differences in a highly important area of psychological functioning. A better understanding of environmental facilitating or constraining factors can be derived from studies with genetically informative data, which is illustrated by the following example of a twin study examining the influence of classroom variables on cognitive abilities: Elementary-school-age twins from the same classrooms who also shared the same teacher were compared to twin children placed in different classrooms and with different teachers. In order to test whether this environmental influence affected cognitive ability, genetic informative data were required. In fact, results indicate that environmental variables associated with same versus different classrooms only had a very small influence on cognitive abilities (Kovas, Haworth, Dale, & Plomin, 2007). Because quantitative genetic studies typically find that nonshared environmental factors contribute meaningfully to the development of difference in general intelligence with increasing age, different peers, differential treatment by parents, or even differential child-perceptions, studies such as these should receive more attention in future research on intelligence.

The above example shows that a behavioral genetic approach can be a useful tool in distinguishing important from less important influences and in pointing researchers to areas of interest within their own fields and beyond. We predict that future research will benefit enormously from interdisciplinary efforts bringing together the traditional educational sciences and behavior genetics. This should lead to a better understanding of the etiology of intelligence in the context of the family, schools, and other learning environments.

REFERENCES

Bouchard, T. J., Jr., & McGue, M. (1981). Familial studies of intelligence: A review. *Science, 212,* 1055–1059.

Butcher L. M., Davis, O. S. P., Craig, I. W., & Plomin, R. (2008). Genomewide QTL association scan of general cognitive ability using pooled DNA and 500k SNP microarrays. *Genes, Brain and Behavior, 7,* 435–446.

Deary, I. J., Spinath, F. M., & Bates, T. C. (2006). Genetics of intelligence. *European Journal of Human Genetics, 14,* 690–700.

Deary, I. J., Whiteman, M. C., Starr, J. M., Whalley, L. J., & Fox, H. C. (2004). The impact of childhood intelligence on later life: Following up the Scottish Mental Surveys of 1932 and 1947. *Journal of Personality and Social Psychology, 86,* 130–147.

Erlenmeyer-Kimling, L., & Jarvik, L. F. (1963). Genetics and intelligence: A review. *Science, 142,* 1477–1479.

Gottfredson, L. S. (2002). *g:* Highly general and highly practical. In R. J. Sternberg & E. L. Grigorenko (Eds.), *The general factor of intelligence: How general is it?* (pp.331–380). Mahwah, NJ: Lawrence Erlbaum.

Jensen, A. R. (1998). *The g Factor: The science of mental ability.* Westport, CT: Praeger.

Kovas, Y., Haworth, C. M. A., Dale, P. S., & Plomin, R. (2007). The genetic and environmental origins of learning abilities and disabilities in the early school years. *Monographs of the Society for Research in Child Development, 72 (Serial No. 288).*

Kovas, Y., & Plomin, R. (2006). Generalist genes: Implications for cognitive sciences. *Trends in Cognitive Science, 10,* 198–203.

McGue, M., Bouchard, T. J. Jr., Iacono, W. G., & Lykken, D. T. (1993). Behavioral genetics of cognitive ability: A life-span perspective. In R. Plomin & G. E. McClearn (Eds.), *Nature, nurture, and psychology* (pp. 59–76). Washington, DC: American Psychological Association.

Neisser, U., Boodoo, G., Bouchard, T. J., Jr., Boykin, A. W., Brody, N., Ceci, S. J., et al. (1996). Intelligence: Knowns and unknowns. *American Psychologist, 51,* 77–101.

Plomin, R., DeFries, J. C., McClearn, G. E., & McGuffin, P. (2008). *Behavioural genetics* (5th ed.). New York: Worth.

Plomin, R., & Spinath. F. M. (2004). Intelligence: Genetics, genes, and genomics. *Journal of Personality and Social Psychology, 86*(1), 112–129.

SUGGESTED READINGS

Deary, I. J., Spinath, F. M., & Bates, T. C. (2006). Genetics of intelligence. *European Journal of Human Genetics, 14,* 690–700.

Plomin, R., DeFries, J. C., McClearn, G. E., & McGuffin, P. (2008). *Behavioural genetics* (5th ed.). New York: Worth.

Plomin, R. & Spinath. F. M. (2004). Intelligence: Genetics, genes, and genomics. *Journal of Personality and Social Psychology, 86*(1), 112–129.

FRANK M. SPINATH
MARION SPENGLER
Saarland University, Saarburcken, Germany

See also: Intelligence

GERIATRIC PSYCHOLOGY

Geriatric psychology, the science and practice of psychology with older adults, is a field experiencing significant growth due to the "age tsunami" that the United States and the world are experiencing. While there are 37 million older Americans today, by 2050 there will be 70 million. Like all geriatric professions, geriatric psychology is focused at its core on function, that is, how to maintain and/or enhance function in adults over the age of 65. Function reflects the convergence of medical, neurocognitive, and behavioral/mental health in older adults. This article first reviews the demographic changes that are fueling our nation's extraordinary population growth of older adults and then reviews how three areas of geriatric function affect geriatric psychology.

In 1900 only 3 million Americans were over the age of 65 years. By 1970 this number had increased to 20 million. This first population growth of older adults in America spurred on the field of gerontology (study of aging and age-related processes), the creation of the interdisciplinary Gerontological Society of America (1955), and some years later the creation by the federal government of the National Institute on Aging (NIA) (1975). The primary responsibility for the NIA, then and now, is the discovery of causes of and effective treatments for Alzheimer's disease (Achenbaum, 1995). Since 1970, there has been even greater growth in the numbers of older adults, with nearly 37 million older adults currently living in America, and it is predicted that 70 million older adults will be over the age of 65 by 2050. The greatest growth is expected to occur in the oldest-old, those over the age of 85 years. Function, medical, neurocognitive, and behavioral/mental health intersect dramatically with advancing age. Alzheimer's disease prevalence statistics may be the most telling in this regard.

The prevalence of Alzheimer's disease doubles every five years from age 60 to 85, with the prevalence increasing from 3% at age 60 to over 30% in those over age 85 and over half of those 100 years old. In 2008, it was estimated that over 5 million older adults suffer from Alzheimer's disease. This number has increased by 10% over the past decade, driven mostly by the increasing number of those over age 85. By 2050 it is expected that there will be over 13 million Americans suffering from Alzheimer's disease (Hebert, Scherr, Bienas, Bennett, & Evans, 2003), with a quadrupling prevalence in those over age 85 years and a doubling of the prevalence in those age 75–84 years. Disability and mental health disorders tend to follow this same pattern, though not as dramatically,

Geriatric psychology requires its practitioners to be knowledgeable about the basic geriatric medicine syndromes of disability, comorbidity, and frailty. The conditions of disability, comorbidity, and frailty, at one time considered to be alike, are now understood as distinct, although overlapping and related, which holds significant implications for geriatric psychology. Perhaps the most familiar concept is disability, defined as difficulty or dependency in carrying out activities essential to independent living. Impairments affecting lower extremity mobility, for example, may curtail a person's independence in transportation and locomotion. Lower-extremity disability, the ability to walk or get around one's community independently, has dramatic implications for health and well-being. Those with lower-extremity disability are more likely to suffer injurious falls, to experience early mortality, to become depressed, and to suffer neurocognitive decline and dementia.

Geriatric psychologists are beginning to assess physical performance as part of their overall assessments. J. M. Guralnik, an NIH investigator, created a Short Physical Performance Battery (SPPB) that can give clinicians and researchers alike a time-efficient method of gaining insight into an older adult's disability status (Guralnik et al., 1994). The SPPB consists of 3 parts; a short, speeded walk test, and a tandem and a semi-tandem balance test. Through a population-based study, some normative data is now available for the test battery.

Frailty describes an aggregate risk of complications for an older patient. Its early definition centered on the compromising of more than one system (e.g., heart, lung, kidney, brain) by disease and disability. More recently, frailty has become more clearly defined in its symptoms and effects on rehabilitation outcomes. Fried et al. (2004) summarized her group's definition as a syndrome with the following elements: decreased appetite and weight loss, gait disturbance and falling, and declining cognition. Some cases also have significant respiratory distress. This constellation of symptoms has an unclear etiology and represents multiple-system failure. Frailty has been linked to significantly increased rates of nursing home placement and mortality. Geriatric psychology is likely to be consulted on cases of frailty. Often there is confusion about the cognitive impairment—where did it come from? What is its cause? Failure to assess the other parts of a frailty syndrome will lead the psychologist to make erroneous conclusions about the nature of the cognitive impairment. The more prominent the syndrome, the more likely it is that the patient is nearing the end of his or her life.

Comorbidity refers to the presence of two or more medically diagnosed diseases in a given individual. Community-dwelling older adults most commonly suffer from arthritis (48%), hypertension (36%), and heart disease (27%), and the prevalence of these conditions increases with age. Many times individuals suffer from more than one of these or other chronic conditions, and are simultaneously being treated for these multiple conditions. Geriatric psychologists will become aware of certain comorbid patterns as significant indicators of overall function. For example, vascular risk factors and depression have become a well-documented pattern of comorbidity. Delirium and dementia is another example of a common comorbidity that geriatric psychologists will recognize. Comorbidity, the combination of these diseases, often has a more significant impact than does a presenting primary diagnosis, such as a hip fracture.

Neurocognitive Functioning and Geriatric Psychology

Normal aging, and in particular cognitive aging, has been the most extensively studied area of gerontology. More recently, with advances in neuroimaging techniques, brain aging and cognition is becoming widely studied. Gross brain changes in normal aging can be generally described as loss of volume and loss of white matter, with the greatest area of loss in the frontal cortex. In the temporal lobe, the hippocampus changes with normal aging and this shrinkage is associated with decreases in memory. Cognitive changes, however, though detectable in older age, are not as dramatic as gross brain changes. The brain appears to show evidence of plasticity into late life and to use more of its resources to reduce the impact of volume loss (Greenwood, 2007). Nevertheless, memory and speeded tasks of problem solving are the more prominent areas of cognitive decline in older adults. These changes, in normal aging, tend to be modest at least until some point in the ninth decade of life. Recently, there has been significant emphasis on the use of training to improve cognitive abilities.

The Advanced Cognitive Training in Vital Elders (ACTIVE) project has provided the largest amount of and the most comprehensive data on cognitive training. Three training techniques were used with each treatment group receiving one of these: speed, problem solving, or memory. Compared to each corresponding control group, treatment participants demonstrated training improvements, although these improvements were limited to the single area of training (Ball et al., 2002). Across time, however, cognitive training was linked to better rates of continuing independence in high-level everyday activities such as driving, medication management, and financial management.

Normal aging studies, including the recent brain-aging studies and ACTIVE project, give insight also into abnormal aging, or cognitive impairment. One recent study of brain aging, for instance, showed that once people were in their older years, only entorhinal cortex shrinkage (and not hippocampal) was associated with memory loss. Entorhinal cortex shrinkage has been linked to early signs of Alzheimer's disease. Those who failed to improve through ACTIVE (i.e., did not benefit from training) were more likely to develop mild cognitive impairment (MCI), a condition that is often a precursor to dementia.

Geriatric psychology is a core part of the diagnostic workup for Alzheimer's disease and related dementias. Geriatric psychology has created or enhanced many assessment methods for detecting Alzheimer's disease or other age-related dementias. Prospective studies from healthy samples indicate that modest decline in cognitive abilities, especially memory, can occur more than a decade before the full dementia symptoms appear. MCI was originally defined by a self-report of memory loss and poor performance on memory testing, in the face of good performance on other types of cognitive tasks. Early cases of dementia when compared to case controls demonstrate significantly reduced memory disturbance. Longitudinal studies of persons with MCI and early dementia demonstrate significant declines and further losses of memory and of every area of cognition.

Neurocognitive or neuropsychological testing is based on a deficit model of measurement. That is, similar to a blood test, an individual's cognitive test scores are compared to a range of normal scores for persons of the same age and educational level. The success of this type of model depends on two factors: (1) how well do the cognitive tests measure the construct, and (2) how accurate is the reference group (i.e., the normative data)? Cognitive testing dates back almost 100 years and has been well validated for younger and older adults. In the past 20 years normative data has become more widely available and there are now volumes devoted to normative data tables for our older adult population.

Neurocognitive test findings should be integrated into the older adult's history and medical and neurological data, and all of these data should be useful for diagnosis and for treatment recommendations. Persons suffering from progressive dementia have the opportunity for early drug treatments (though success is modest at best), and can provide in advance for medical decision making, financial management, and community mobility (i.e., driving). These advanced activities of daily living impact an older adult's sense of identity and their well-being. Understanding how comorbid conditions impact reversible cognitive symptoms is also critical. Delirium, an acute onset attentional disorder due to some underlying medical condition (e.g., infection, dehydration, medication sensitivity) can cause severe declines in persons with mild dementia. When treated, the cognitive declines that are worsened with the delirium onset can be significantly improved, if not reversed.

Increasingly, geriatric psychology is applying itself to the management of dementia symptoms across all stages of the disease. Recent studies suggest that using cognitive rehabilitation strategies for those with early dementia can be beneficial. Prosocial roles and continued cognitive involvement can be enhanced by use of Montessori techniques, as described by Cameron Camp (see Lichtenberg, Murman & Mellow, 2003). Behavioral disturbances, also a part of the unfolding dementia process, are positively affected by nonpharmacological, behavioral techniques.

Behavioral/Mental Health Functioning

Biopsychosocial factors converge in late life, and this may help to explain why depression increases in the oldest old. Whereas about 15% of those ages 65–80 suffer from depression, this rate increases to nearly 25% in those over age 85. Fewer than 5% of these depressive states meet the criteria for a major depression as per DSM IV diagnostic criteria (depressed mood or loss of pleasure and 4 additional symptoms that last at least two weeks and contribute to decline in function), and thus most cases meet the criteria for minor depression. Nevertheless, even more modest symptoms of depression appear to produce similar effects: early disability and mortality. Depression is a syndrome—a constellation of symptoms with multiple etiologies. Several etiologies of depression have been described; the treatments based on these etiologies will be briefly presented (see Skuelty & Zeiss, 2006).

The most common etiology of depression is the neurotransmitter model, particularly some disruption of norepinehphrine, dopamine, and/or serotonin. In the past decade the selective serotonin reuptake inhibitors (SSRI) have become the medication of choice to treat depression; however, their popularity may be greater than their effectiveness. A review of the efficacy studies that were utilized in the FDA approval process for the SSRIs found that efficacy was essentially identical to that of the tricyclic antidepressants (35 to 40% of persons improved significantly), but the SSRI medications had a much lower discontinuation rate due to side effects.

A second etiology is based on activity of daily living (ADL) limitation theory. Briefly, the presence of a disease is linked to depression only when the disease limits the desired activity of the individual. Strong relationships are consistently found between advanced ADL limitations and depressive symptoms in a geriatric rehabilitation population. Accordingly, treatments to improve strength and conditioning (e.g., aerobic and resistance exercise), thereby increasing activity level, have shown promising results in reducing depression.

A third etiology, based on neuron-degeneration, has traditionally focused on poststroke depression with a recent focus on the Vascular Depression Hypothesis. This view postulates that depression is more likely to occur in those who have vascular risk, purportedly through microvascular changes in white matter. Thus comorbid conditions such as hypertension, diabetes, high cholesterol, and atrial fibrillation, for example, can produce higher depression prevalence with more limited success in treatment.

A fourth etiology, the cognitive-behavioral approach, is a better-known psychological theory of depression. While initiating a cognitively-oriented therapeutic approach in a rehabilitation setting may be difficult, incorporating behavioral treatments tends to be easier. Behavioral activation, for example, is structured so as to incorporate pleasant events into the patient's treatment day in an effort to decrease patients' focus on unpleasant events and thereby improve mood.

A fifth etiology of depression involves reaction to loss and grief, such as the effects of loss in widowhood. In the Health and Retirement Survey, depression rates after three years were 3 times higher in those who had been widowed than they were in nonwidowed individuals. Symptoms of depression and normal grief share considerable overlap in early grief (e.g., trouble concentrating, poor sleep, crying, poor appetite, etc.), with 30% of the widowed sample reporting these in the first month after the death of a spouse. After a year, depression prevalence decreased to 12% for the widowed individuals and remained steady for the following two years. Several authors postulate that depression that lasts well into the grieving process is a common factor in complicated grief. The healing process of grief becomes stymied by the presence of depression, making it imperative to treat the depression.

Integrated approaches to depression treatment are becoming more common in settings such as primary and home health care. In these settings, case detection, medication and psychotherapeutic treatments are coordinated within a single practice. Geriatric psychologists have been at the forefront in creating cognitive behavioral, problem solving, and behavioral activation treatments that are the methods most commonly used in integrated care approaches. One integrated care approach has even found that their intervention reduced suicidal ideation in a group of older adult depression patients. Integrated care approaches are usually well received by patients and result in better outcomes than single disciplinary approaches. Geriatric Psychologists will increasingly need to develop better knowledge of and skills within an integrated or interdisciplinary team approach.

Integrated Care for an Aging Population

In 2007 American Psychological Association President Sharon Brehm created an integrated health care task force. The task force's report, Blueprint for Change: Achieving Integrated Care for an Aging Population, was adopted by the APA in early 2008. The report highlights several facets of integrated care, including (1) the growing diversity within the older U.S. population, (2) the need for psychologists to work with or even to create interdisciplinary teams, (3) understanding and respecting the roles of all team members and learning how to share leadership within and across cases, (4) the expanding settings within which geriatric psychology is being practiced, and (5) incorporating the 2003 Geropsychology Practice Guidelines into clinical and research work. The Blueprint put APA in the lead of other geriatric-related professions: An interdisciplinary-focused document of this kind has never before been created by a single professional group. The future effects of geriatric psychology will, in large part, be related to what extent integrated approaches are adopted for our older citizens.

REFERENCES

Achenbaum, W. A. (1995). *Crossing frontiers: Gerontology emerges as a science.* New York: Cambridge University Press.

American Psychological Association (2004). Guidelines for psychological practice with older adults. *American Psychologist, 59,* 236–260.

American Psychological Association (2007). Blueprint for change: Achieving integrated health care for an aging population. Report of the task force on integrated health care. Washington, DC: American Psychological Association.

Ball, K., Berch, D. B., Helmers, K. F., et al. (2002). Effects of cognitive training interventions with older adults: A randomized controlled trial. *Journal of the American Medical Association, 287,* 2271–2281.

Fried, L. P., Ferrucci, L., Darer, J., Williamson, J. D., & Anderson, G. (2004). Untangling the concepts of disability, frailty, and cormorbidity: Implications for improved targeting and care. *Journals of Gerontology: Medical Sciences, 59,* 255–263.

Greenwood, P. M. (2007). Functional plasticity in cognitive aging: Review and hypothesis. *Neuropsychology, 21,* 657–673.

Guralnik, J. M., Simonsick, E. M., Ferrucci, L., Glynn, R. J., Berkman, L. F., Blazer, D. G., et al. (1994). A short physical performance battery assessing lower extremity function: Association with self-reported disability, prediction of mortality and nursing home admission. *Journal of Gerontology, 49*(2), M85–M94.

Lichtenberg, P. A., Murman, D. L., & Mellow, A. M. (Eds.) *Handbook of dementia.* Hoboken, NJ: John Wiley & Sons.

Hebert, L. E., Scherr, P. A., Bienas, J. L., Bennett, D. A., & Evans, D. A. (2003). Alzheimer's disease in the U.S. population. *Archives of Neurology, 60,* 1119–1122.

Skuelty, K. M., & Zeiss, A. (2006). The treatment of depression in older adults in the primary care setting: An evidence-based review. *Health Psychology, 25,* 665–674.

SUGGESTED READINGS

Blazer, D. G. (2003). Depression in late life: Review and commentary. *Journal of Gerontology: Medical Sciences, 58A,* 249–265.

Lichtenberg, P. A. (1999). *Handbook of assessment in clinical gerontology.* New York: John Wiley & Sons.

Raz, N., & Rodrigue, K. M. (2006). Differential aging of the brain: Patterns, cognitive correlates and modifiers. *Science Direct: Neuroscience and Biobehavioral Reviews* (www.science.direct).

PETER A. LICHTENBERG
Wayne University

See also: Adulthood and Aging; Gerontology; Geropsychology

GERMANY, PSYCHOLOGY IN

The history of psychology in German-speaking countries (especially Germany, Austria, and Switzerland) goes back to the nineteenth century, when it began to evolve as an autonomous discipline by separating from philosophy and physiology (see Danziger, 1990; Hothersall, 2004). Typically this is linked to Wilhelm Wundt, who founded the first psychological institute in Leipzig in 1879 and soon launched the first psychological journal in 1883 (*Philosophical Studies*); in 1904 the first German congress was held, and the Society for Experimental Psychology established, later renamed the German Psychological Society (DGPs—*Deutsche Gesellschaft für Psychologie*) in 1929—all hallmarks of an established science. The history of the DGPs and psychology as a discipline is documented in detail in a special issue of its journal *Psychologische Rundschau* (Lukas & Schneider, 2004) on the occasion of its 100th anniversary.

German psychology around 1900 was both international and multidisciplinary (Gundlach, 2004). This is also made evident by Fernberger, who, based on his analyses of publication trends in psychology in 1917, concluded that there is "the extreme necessity for the student of psychology, no matter of what nationality . . . to have a facile and critical reading knowledge of both German and English" (p. 150). From its inception, apart from basic and applied research, "two cultures" (Snow, 1998) are characteristic of scientific approaches in German psychology: humanities (*Geisteswissenschaft*) versus natural science, or understanding versus explanation, their relative influence waxing and waning, the latter mostly predominating thoughout. Interestingly, these topics (international standing, multidisciplinary focus, understanding vs. explanation) are still prevalent preoccupations in critical discourses of academic psychologists (Jüttemann, 2006).

In Germany the traditional divide between academics and practitioners also characterizes the two main organizations of psychology. The German Psychological Society (http://www.dgps.de) is the organization for psychologists working in the academic sector. At present, it has approximately 2,600 members, about 10% of whom are from Austria and Switzerland. Its membership is exclusive, requiring among other credentials a doctorate in psychology. Its aims are to promote and disseminate scientific psychology and to protect and enhance its status in universities. The Association of German Professional Psychologists (BDP—*Bundesverband Deutscher Psychologinnen und Psychologen*) is the largest and most influential organization for professional psychologists (http://www.bdp-verband.org/bdp/verband/englisch.shtml) and is responsible for representing their interests and upholding ethical and occupational standards. At present, the BDP has about 13,000 members, which is about a third of the psychologists working in Germany. Membership requires a diploma in psychology earned at a German university or an equivalent degree from abroad. After its structural reform in 2002, the BDP membership was extended to include persons who graduate with a diploma in an applied branch of psychology at so-called "applied" universities (*Fachhochschulen*).

The DGPs and BDP cooperate at the level of the Federation of German Psychologists Associations, a body in which these two organizations debate and decide on educational and professional matters in a complementary manner, and which represents the interests of German psychologists at a national and international level. However, there is some tension between the two organizations, currently concerning the BDP's decision to establish a psychological institution for postgraduate further education in psychological psychotherapy and traffic psychology. After the reunification of Germany in 1990, members of the East German Society for Psychology, which was established in 1962, had the option of joining the DGPs, if they fulfilled its membership requirements, or alternatively the BDP (for details, including for what follows, see Plath & Eckensberger, 2004). Since the passage of a law regulating professional psychotherapeutic practice in 1999, membership in state chambers of psychological psychotherapists has become mandatory for licensed psychotherapists.

Psychologists are predominantly educated at universities. As admission is restricted, top school grades are required—as high as those for medicine or pharmacy—to study psychology as a major at one of the more than 40 universities, which include over 600 professorships. Students qualify with the *Diplom*, equivalent to a master's degree. About 10% of the approximately 3,000 students annually awarded a diploma continue their studies to the level of a PhD, but fewer than 2% habilitate, the qualification still customary for an academic career in research and teaching. Several continuing education curricula have been established by the DGPs and BDP in various specialties to promote competencies (e.g., forensic, organizational, and clinical psychology), and others were instituted because of legal requirements (e.g., psychological psychotherapy licensure, traffic psychology).

Clinical psychology with all its facets is the field in which most academic and applied psychologists are active, followed (based on the number of annual publications) by general, organizational, educational, and developmental psychology. Outside the academic domain a fairly large proportion of psychologists are self-employed and working in the fields of psychotherapy, counseling, supervision, coaching, and organizational psychology and training. Psychologists are, however, also employed in hospitals and clinics and in the education system, the police force, and the penal and the legal system. Fewer than a fifth of psychologists work at universities or in research centers outside of universities (e.g., Max-Planck-Institutes; Leibniz-Institutes for basic and applied research). Universities and research institutes are governed by international standards, especially with respect to publications and third party funding. The German Research Foundation has a very rigorous reviewing process and is the most prestigious source of funding. This applies to the VW Foundation too. Various ministries also set aside money for applied and contract research projects.

The Center for Psychology Information and Documentation (ZPID) assembles the German equivalent to PsycINFO (http://www.zpid.de). It compiles databases on psychological literature, tests, audiovisual media, and Internet resources published by authors in German-speaking countries. It has been publishing the ZPID-Monitor annually since 1999 to track trends in the internationalization of psychology from German-speaking countries. The proportion of English publications by German-speaking psychologists is growing steadily, amounting to about 26% of their publications in 2006. The highest proportion of English publications is registered in biopsychology and neuropsychology as well as general psychology. Understandably, German is the dominant language of publication in the applied branches of psychology. However, publishing in English does not necessarily mean that the work is recognized by the international community. In 2006 the proportion of documents in the international PsycINFO with an author affiliation of Anglo-American origin was about 85%, those originating from German-speaking countries amounted to about 5%, the proportion of German articles was about 1%, and those in foreign languages as a whole about 5% (Krampen & Shui, in press).

Future trends in German psychology cannot be viewed in isolation. International developments in science and social changes brought about by globalization will have to be taken into account. These circumstances will lead to an intensification of international cooperation and exchange as well as an increase in contextually sensitive and multidisciplinary approaches to theory, research, and practice. Major organizational changes are occurring at universities following the 1999 Bologna Declaration, a pledge by 29 European countries to reform the structures of their higher education systems in a convergent way, through, for example, the adoption of a system of comparable degrees, based on two main cycles (undergraduate and graduate) and the establishment of a system of credits (e.g., ECTS—European credit transfer system). Consequently, German universities have been adapting their psychological courses to conform with the BSc and MSc structure, a process expected to be completed by 2011. In addition, after changes in the law regulating higher education, since 2005 60% of admissions to restricted courses of studies at universities such as psychology have to be conducted by the universities themselves, instead of the central office for the allocation of places to study (ZVS). Another recent trend is the creation of postdoctoral courses to streamline and shorten the time needed to acquire a doctorate. For the same reason, universities are instituting junior professorships, which theoretically should make the habilitation superfluous, but have not had any noticeable effect to date.

Many of these changes have been instituted to improve internationalization, mobility, and networking. English is considered the lingua franca of academic psychology, and students are expected to be able to read and write it (publishing in English being almost equated to quality). In the course of internationalization, even traditionally German journals are being converted into English ones, as exemplified by Hogrefe, one of the most important German publishers of psychological literature. The market for the more than 200 German journals in which psychologists publish remains substantial. German membership in non-domestic editorial boards, psychological associations, and their governing bodies is increasing, as is studying and working overseas, and international visibility and presence is thus on the rise. Yet, it remains an open question whether the Anglo-American dominance is one of quality or one of sheer numbers. When comparing the membership size of the main psychological associations in the United States and Germany, the low proportion of publications originating from the German-speaking sphere is hardly surprising. However, to promote multilateral internationalization, the multilingualism of scholars, ubiquitous in former times, should generally be expected of both English and non-English speaking academic psychologists once again, which would not only allow for more diversity but also more attention to cultural specifics in contexts and approaches.

REFERENCES

Danziger, K. (1990). *Constructing the subject: Historical origins of psychological research.* Cambridge: Cambridge University Press.

Fernberger, S. W. (1917). On the number of articles of psychological interest published in the different languages. *American Journal of Psychology, 28*(1), 141–150.

Gundlach, H. (2004). Die Lage der Psychologie um 1900 [The state of psychology around 1900]. *Psychologische Rundschau, 55,* Suppl. 1, 2–11.

Hothersall, D. (2004). *History of psychology* (4th ed.). Boston: McGraw-Hill.

Jüttemann, G. (Ed.). (2006). *Wilhelm Wundts anderes Erbe* [Wundt's other legacy]. Göttingen: Vandenhoeck & Ruprecht.

Krampen, G., & Schui, G. (in press). ZPID-Monitor 2006 zur Internationalität der Psychologie aus dem deutschsprachigen Bereich: Der Kurzbericht [ZPID-Monitor 2006 on the internationality of psychology from the German-speaking region: Abridged report]. *Psychologische Rundschau, 59*(4).

Lucas, J., & Schneider, W. (Eds.). (2004). Geschichte der Psychologie [History of psychology]. *Psychologische Rundschau, 55,* Suppl. 1.

Plath, I., & Eckensberger, L. H. (2004). Psychology in Germany. In M. J. Stevens & D. Wedding (Eds.), *The handbook of international psychology* (pp. 331–349). New York: Brunner & Routledge.

Snow, C. P. (1998). *The two cultures.* Cambridge: Cambridge University Press.

INGRID PLATH
German Institute for International Educational Research, Frankfort, Germany

LUTZ H. ECKENSBERGER
German Institute for International Educational Research and Johann Wolfgang Goethe University, Frankfort Germany

GERONTOLOGY

Significant improvement in public health and advancement in medical technology in the twentieth century led to increasing life expectancy and remarkable growth in the older adult population. According to the 2000 U.S. Census, 35 million older Americans, 12.4% of the U.S. population, is over the age of 65. With the aging of the baby boom cohort, there will be 70.3 million Americans over age 65 in the year 2030. The rapid growth of the older population and significant changes associated with multiple aging, physical, psychological, and social dimensions suggest that knowledge about gerontology (the scientific study of the process of aging and aging experience) and geriatrics (the branch of medicine studying clinical aspects of aging) will become vital for researchers, clinicians, and policy makers.

Age-Related Disease, Normal Aging, and Successful Aging

There are three distinct categories of aging experiences: age-related disease, normal aging (typical changes without such disease), and successful aging, or aging under optimal conditions. However, any examination of characteristics of older persons should be made with caution. Each age cohort experiences a unique set of historical events, socialization, and education that shapes the experience of aging. Future cohorts of older adults are likely to have higher educational attainment, higher rates of mood and substance-abuse disorders, and more favorable attitudes about mental health services than today's cohort of older persons. Societal changes also produce different contexts for aging, such as changing expectations about retirement and the roles of women. Therefore, the older adults of the future may have very different challenges and resources than are seen at present.

Nevertheless, aging increases risk for many disabling chronic diseases, including osteoarthritis, coronary heart disease, cancer, stroke, and Alzheimer's disease. Even in the absence of significant disease, normal aging is associated with loss of reserve capacity in systems, including cardiovascular, pulmonary, and musculoskeletal systems. This loss of reserve capacity leads to losses of strength, increases in body fat, and poorer aerobic capacity in the absence of sustained efforts to maintain fitness, which in turn increase risk for loss of functioning and independence, especially with illness or trauma. Recent studies of successful aging have shown that older adults who engage in aerobic and strength training can make considerable gains in capacity that are important in maintaining daily functioning. However, even world-class senior athletes, who may be genetically gifted and trained to optimal capacity, do not perform at the level of younger athletes.

In normal aging, many cognitive functions are well maintained, including crystallized intelligence (vocabulary, overlearned information and behaviors, reasoning and judgment), immediate memory, and recognition memory. Aging is associated with declines in fluid intelligence, or the ability to rapidly solve novel problems, with slowing of cognitive functions, and with declines in memory, especially when engaged in difficult tasks requiring the use of recall. However, normal age-related changes in cognition may be of minimal importance in the daily functioning of older persons unless they remain active in extremely demanding occupations. Overall, most older persons find successful ways of compensating for these age changes, or they select activities that suit the changes in their intellectual skills, such as the scientist who transitions into mentoring and administration.

Aging, Stress, and Mental Disorders

With aging, risk for a number of important stressful life events and chronic strains increases, such as declines in health, death of spouse or significant others, and caregiving for impaired family members. As a result, late-life is often viewed negatively as being stressful or unpleasant. However, contrary to such negative perceptions, there is considerable variability in the types and impact of major stressors experienced, and the ways individuals cope with them within and across age groups. For instance, older adults have lower rates of some stressful life events than younger persons because of their retirement status. Recent studies of retirement show no negative effects on health or psychological functioning, once preretirement physical and emotional characteristics are considered. Older persons are also often found to cope as successfully with problems as younger persons, and in some cases better, in part due to their prior experience with adversity, and the fact that certain problems (such as spousal bereavement) are normative in late life. Specifically, compared to young persons, older adults exercise better control over their emotions, especially negative ones, and recuperate from challenging situations more quickly.

Many older adults cope well with challenges unique to late-life. Yet, with increasing age, older adults experience higher risk of developing acute and chronic physical illnesses that often require complex medical care and supportive services. Similarly, older persons are at increased risk for a number of mental disorders, including the dementias (of which Alzheimer's disease is most common), and subsyndromal depressive and anxiety disorders. Mental disorder in older adults is distinct in that it is often comorbid with multiple physical disorders, and complicating social factors. Older persons are often taking multiple medications, and seeing multiple health-care providers. Particularly for older patients with multiple comorbid mental and physical disorders, their ability to cope may

be severely compromised. These unique characteristics and needs of older adults mean that mental health or behavioral health services should be carefully coordinated with medical and social services, through multidisciplinary teams. Family caregivers are also often important for the care of older patients and should be included in treatment planning. The present cohort of older persons has lower rates of major depression, substance abuse, and some other mental disorders than younger cohorts. However, future projections indicate increased prevalence of late-life mental disorders when the baby-boom cohort reaches advanced age, underscoring the need to expand the efforts to accurately assess and treat mental disorders among older adults.

Clinical Assessment and Intervention

Psychological assessment of older adults should identify medical, social, and cultural issues, and clinicians should ensure that assessment instruments are culturally sensitive and appropriately normed for older populations. Without attention to differences in educational attainment, older adults may be inappropriately diagnosed with cognitive and mental disorders. Comorbid medical problems may complicate the assessment process as well. Special measures designed to provide brief and valid assessments of common problems in older adults include the Geriatric Depression Scale, the Mini-Mental State Exam, and the Mattis Dementia Rating Scale.

Past research has demonstrated the effectiveness of a variety of psychological interventions for older persons and their family caregivers, such as geriatric depression, family caregiver distress, managing incontinence, and reducing disruptive behaviors in patients with dementia. With accurately identified needs of older persons and their families, interventions should be tailored to their values and perspectives. For example, the current cohort of older persons tends to fear psychiatric stigma and prefer treatment in medical settings. Innovative approaches that integrate psychological services into primary care and other medical settings hold considerable promise for reaching older adults who would resist referral to traditional psychiatric settings.

Future Issues

Given the projected growth of the older population, mental health professionals should attend to several important issues. First, all professionals providing mental health services to older adults need to receive basic education and training in geriatrics and gerontology with supervised practicum in order to meet the unique and various mental health services needs of future cohorts of older adults. Due to increased rates of disorders in younger cohorts and the aging of the baby-boom population, we must also develop a larger cadre of geriatric specialists in all professions to work with patients with complex problems, conduct research, and train other professionals in the field of aging.

By 2030, over 25% of older Americans will be members of racial and ethnic minority groups. Increasing life expectancy among racial and ethnic minority groups means an increasingly diverse aging population and thus, interventions for older adults should be developed and provided in culturally sensitive and appropriate ways. Clinicians should consider factors such as cohort-specific discrimination and different values concerning caregiving and mental-health issues held among different ethnic minority elderly groups.

Issues regarding reimbursement and public education need more attention as well. While Medicare is the primary insurer of older adults it requires higher co-pays for mental health than for other services. At the same time, many older adults are not aware that psychological services are covered under Medicare. Thus, it is important that the public is educated more about aging and mental-health issues.

Our society is poorly prepared to provide for the growing numbers of older adults who will be increasingly diverse in their demographic and sociocultural characteristics and will also need medical, psychological, social, and long-term care services. Public policy must evolve to find ways to distribute resources to the special needs of older adults and their families while attending to issues of generational equity.

SUGGESTED READINGS

Aldwin, C. M., Park, C. L., & Spiro, A. (2007). *Handbook of health psychology and aging.* New York: Guilford Press.

Knight, B. G., Kaskie, B., Shurgot, G. R., & Dave, J. (2006). Improving the mental health of older adults. In J. E. Birren & W. Schaie (Eds.), *Handbook of psychology and aging.* New York: Academic Press.

WILLIAM E. HALEY
University of South Florida

JUNG KWAK
University of Wisconsin—Milwaukee

See also: Adulthood and Aging; Aging, Physiological and Behavioral Concomitants of; Geriatric Psychology

GEROPSYCHOLOGY

Geropsychology is the "specialized field of psychology concerned with the psychological and behavioral aspects of aging" (Tuleya, 2007). Early uses of the term include a chapter in the *Annual Review of Psychology* in 1970 (Botwinick, 1970) and a book title for the summary of a conference at Duke University in 1974 (Gentry, 1977). Although the conceptual and scientific roots of geropsychology extend back for centuries, the explosion of empirical research that defines the field escalated rapidly during the second half of the twentieth century. The term *geropsychology* was not widely adopted until the latter decades of the twentieth century, however. The *Psychological Literature* database first adopted it as a keyword in 2006 and applied it retrospectively to previous entries (Tuleya, 2007).

The field of geropsychology presumes that aging processes are inherently influenced by biological, psychological, and social factors that occur within particular contexts that influence outcomes and experiences of aging. The period of time encompassed within the term varies, with age 65 primarily referenced because of public policies related to Social Security and Medicare in the United States. More commonly, the psychological processes of aging are viewed within the context of the entire lifespan rather than as a period tightly defined by chronological age, and many geropsychologists adopt an explicitly developmental framework. Aging processes are distinguished from disease and disorder, even those that are age-correlated. Furthermore, geropsychology presumes that aging research focuses on change and thus requires a longitudinal perspective examined across multiple cohorts.

Geropsychologists are interested in a broad range of psychological processes in later life; psychologists whose interests in aging are limited in scope may not identify with the broader field. Various other terms have been used to describe geropsychology historically, including gerontological psychology, adult development and aging, and the psychology of aging, but geropsychology is increasingly recognized as the title of the specialty field. The related but broader discipline of gerontology encompasses aging scholarship and practice across multiple disciplines, including biological, psychological, and social. Geriatric psychology and geriatric mental health focus on medical or pathological sources of discontinuity with earlier life phases.

Professional geropsychology is the term applied to clinical, counseling, and applied psychological work that employs psychological and behavioral research to assess and intervene in the lives of older adults. Included within professional geropsychology are mental health services, consultation, and environmental and community interventions. The field of clinical geropsychology was recognized as a distinct proficiency area by the American Psychological Association in 1994. Guidelines for practice in professional geropsychology and competencies to guide the training of geropsychologists have been established (APA, 2004; Karel, Knight, Hinrichsen, & Zeiss, unpublished manuscript). A model for training professional geropsychologists was formulated recently as the Pikes

Peak model of training in professional geropsychology (Knight, Karel, Hinrichsen, Qualls, & Duffy, unpublished manuscript).

Despite growing clarity about distinct attitudes, knowledge, and skills needed to provide professional geropsychological services, the training pipeline is grossly inadequate to meet needs of the rapidly aging population (Center for Health Workforce Studies, 2005). Predoctoral training programs have not grown in number since the first programs opened in the 1970s, although internship and postdoctoral training opportunities have increased substantially. Post-licensure is a growing area of focus because of its potential to increase the professional geropsychology workforce faster. Indeed, with fewer than 4% of practicing psychologists focusing on work with older adults, new methods of training geropsychologists are critical (Qualls, Segal, Norman, Niederehe, & Gallagher-Thompson, 2002).

Research in geropsychology has expanded in breadth and depth in the past 50 years, aided by a wide venue for publication, including journals focused on aging sponsored by the American Psychological Association (APA; *Psychology of Aging*) and the Gerontological Society of America (*Journal of Gerontology: Psychological Sciences*). Substantive areas within geropsychology are reviewed in a series of handbooks published every five years (most recent, Birren & Schaie, 2006) along with specialty handbooks in more specific topical areas. Geropsychological research also is featured in the mainstream journals of every subdiscipline. The international community of psychologists has embraced geropsychology as well, as represented in books and conferences that summarize work in particular regions. Specialty conferences draw together psychologists interested in aging (e.g., Cognitive Aging Conference; National Clinical Geropsychology Conference), and significant program time is also now available in general psychology and gerontology conferences. In the twenty-first century, geropsychology is considered both mainstream and distinct.

Professional organizations in geropsychology provide identity for the field as well, although some use other names. Within the APA, scientific and professional geropsychologists identify with Division 20, Adult Development and Aging. Clinical geropsychologists formed a section on Clinical Geropsychology within the Society of Clinical Psychology (APA, Division 12, Section II) in 1993 to focus on professional issues. Subgroups of other divisions within APA and the Association for Psychological Science also focus on aging (e.g., APA Division 17, Counseling Psychology, and APA Division 38, Health Psychology). A continuing Committee on Aging and an Office on Aging were formed in APA in 1997 to ensure that older adults receive attention within the policies, education, science, and practice of psychology. A Council of Professional Training Programs in Geropsychology was formed in 2007 at the recommendation of the Pikes Peak

Model conference (Knight et al, unpublished manuscript) to network training programs at all levels.

REFERENCES

American Psychological Association (2004). Guidelines for psychological practice with older adults. *American Psychologist, 59,* 236–260.

Birren, J. E., & Schaie, K. W. (2006). *Handbook of the psychology of aging* (6th edition). San Diego, CA: Academic Press.

Botwinick, J. (1970). Geropsychology. *Annual Review of Psychology, 21,* 239–272.

Center for Health Workforce Studies. (2005). *The impact of the aging population on the health workforce in the United States.* Rensselaer, NY: School of Public Health, University at Albany.

Gentry, W. D. (1977). *Geropsychology.* Cambridge, MA: Ballinger.

Karel, M. J., Knight, B. G., Hinrichsen, G. H., & Zeiss, A. M. (2009). *Attitude, knowledge and skill competencies for practice in professional geropsychology.* Unpublished manuscript.

Knight, B. G., Karel, M. J., Hinrichsen, G. H., Qualls, S. H., & Duffy, M. (2009). *Pikes Peak model for training in professional geropsychology.* Unpublished manuscript.

Qualls, S. H., Segal, D. L., Norman, S., Niederehe, G. N., & Gallagher-Thompson, D. (2002). Psychologists in practice with older adults: Current patterns, sources of training, and need for continuing education. *Professional Psychology: Research and Practice, 33,* 435–442.

Tuleya, L. G. (2007). *Thesaurus of psychological index terms* (11th ed.). Washington, D.C.: American Psychological Association.

SUGGESTED READINGS

Birren, J. E., & Schroots, J. J. F. (2000). *A history of geropsychology in autobiography.* Washington, DC: American Psychological Association.

Fernandez-Ballesteros, R. (Ed.). (2007). *Geropsychology: European perspectives for an aging world.* Ashland, OH: Hogrefe & Huber Publishers.

SARA HONN QUALLS
University of Colorado at Colorado Springs

See also: **Adulthood and Aging; Geriatric Psychology; Gerontology**

GESTALT PSYCHOLOGY

Gestalt psychology refers to the school of psychology that was formed in Berlin by Max Wertheimer (1880–1943), Kurt Koffka (1886–1941), and Wolfgang Köhler (1887–1967) and that continued to have influence throughout the twentieth century at universities where it was particularly practiced, namely the New School for Social Research in New York, Swarthmore College in Philadelphia, the University of Münster in Germany, and the Universities of Padua and Trieste in Italy. After a period of neglect and misunderstanding, the principles of the school are once again central to psychological discussion, especially in perceptual psychology.

The term "Gestalt" entered psychology in 1890 in Christian von Ehrenfels' essay "On Gestalt Qualities" (Smith, 1988). In the case of a melody, transposition in key does not destroy the melody, which is a gestalt quality arising above the individual notes. Most research conducted to solve Ehrenfels' problem—for example the work of Alexius Meinong and his school—was addressed to an overarching quality added to a group of elementary sensations (the individual notes), which was explained by a mental act of integration (Ash, 1995; Smith, 1988). The Berlin variant instead stressed not qualities but wholes. Our experience is not the summation of stimulation plus an integrating factor; rather the experience itself is a strong whole, a Gestalt.

Since Gestalten are emergent entities, new wholes rising above fundamentals but not reducible to them, the whole is literally greater than the sum of its parts. Put another way, the characteristics of a whole are supersummative. The qualities or meaning of a perceptual object, gesture, or statement will change relationally depending on the context. They are parts that have roles in the context of the whole gestalt, and their part-quality also changes when isolated. This is the basis for the Gestalt respect for the total situation.

There was, therefore, a long tradition of solving the "gestalt problem" before Wertheimer and his colleagues began publishing their experiments. Berlin Gestalt psychology emerged as a school with Max Wertheimer's (1921–1961) experiments on stroboscopic motion. In the experiments, Wertheimer was interested in cases where there is no retinal excitation for movement. His novelty was in suggesting a "short circuit" (*Querfunktion*) to explain the movement. Around the same time, Köhler (1913–1971) rejected unnoticed sensations, supposedly built up into a coherent experience (Gestalt) later, arguing that such experience was *sui generis*.

It is sometimes supposed that the Gestaltists were the first to investigate illusory movement, but this is not true. They are also not the first to argue against elementarism. Their achievement lies in taking the objects of phenomenal experience (Gestalten) as basic and normative for psychological explanation and then searching for underlying physiological processes (and not unconscious acts) of a comparable form and complexity to serve as their likely basis.

The Gestaltists provided epochal interpretations of all areas of experimental psychology, from perceptual psychology to memory, learning, and productive thinking (Koffka, 1953; Köhler, 1929, Wertheimer, 1942).

Furthermore, in the work of Kurt Lewin (1890–1947) gestalt ideas were extended to social psychology. By the middle of the twentieth century, a second generation of Gestalt authors had continued to provide important interpretations of perceptual phenomena not only in America (Hans Wallach, Nicholas Pastore, W. C. H. Prentice), but also in Germany (Wolfgang Metzger, Edwin Rausch, Wilhelm Witte) and Italy (Cesare Musatti, Fabio Metelli, Gaetano Kanizsas) and venturing further into social psychology (Fritz Heider, Solomon Asch, Mary Henle) and even art (Rudolf Arnheim), music (Victor Zuckerandl, Leonard Meyer), and philosophy (Aaron Gurwitsch).

Basic Ideas

Gestalt psychology simultaneously recognizes the wisdom of naïve and folk understanding and is rigorously scientific in its standards. This calls for a critical realist attitude in which we balance our experience against our accumulated scientific understanding of the transcendental world (Epstein & Hatfield, 1994). Epistemologically, such a commitment makes gestalt psychologists stress the normativity of perceptual experience. Our experiences—a visual illusion or even a neurosis, for example—are phenomenally primary and require adequate explanation, not the other way around (as in psychoanalysis, where the mechanism is more important).

There is, furthermore, a monistic, naturalistic commitment. Stated briefly, the main tenet of the school is that our perceptual experience is formed by the relational working of neural activity. Because our experience is whole and unified, there must be unified physical processes underlying experience that can account for these phenomenal qualities. This stance is naturalistic, in basing experience on more fundamental factors, and *Naturphilosophische*, in the sense that it monistically unites mind and body. In short, our experience is primary, and, because consciousness must be based on underlying physical processes, these processes must be of a complexity and sophistication to be worthy of serving as the basis for emergent mental activity.

Methodology

Gestalt psychology typically begins with a rigorous phenomenological description of the psychological effect at hand. This includes not only variation of stimuli to find the range of effect, but the very appearance of the stimuli (e.g., "film" versus "surface" color). Since psychological models have to do justice to the phenomenon and not vice versa, premature model building is looked down upon. In fact, many of the important Gestalt phenomena—such as Benary's triangle and the Gelb effect—tell against one simplistic model or another (in these two cases, the theory of antagonistic retinal processes associated with Ewald Hering).

As an example of a typical gestalt explanation of perception, one may look at Karl Duncker's experiments on "induced" movement (Duncker, 1929/1939). Duncker found that a glowing dot that does not move in a dark room can be made to appear to move if its framework, in this case a glowing rectangle around it, moves. Because the framework is hierarchically superior to the dot, the dot appears to move. Such an explanation is based on "relational determination," or organizational factors codified by Wertheimer in his famous laws of perceptual organization (Wertheimer, 1923/1939).

In that paper, Wertheimer identified a number of factors that create unified perceptual objects, among them similarity, size, and good continuation. Wertheimer was interested in a deeper tendency toward "good" form or *prägnanz,* which is extremely difficult to define with precision. But it is clear that the rules were a signature of a more profound organizational capacity of the human mind that is up to the research to discover.

Many Gestalt insights are developed heuristically from the behavior of electromagnetic fields. Thus, perceptual illusions (Müller-Lyer, Poggendorf, etc.) are created "forces" in the perceptual field; the lightness we see on a surface is a higher order ratio among the stimuli equilibrated in the visual field; and as in Duncker's example, frames of reference organize stimuli into hierarchical systems.

Relational determination suggests that perceptual experiences are based on relationships rather than absolute stimulation. This relationism has also been stressed by J. J. Gibson, who was influenced by Koffka when they both taught at Smith College. Indeed, the predictions of Gibson's ecological theory and gestalt psychology are not very different in normal, information-rich environments. The difference is that Gibson chose not to talk about cases of impoverished stimulation like Duncker's example, because it is an artifact of the laboratory and not ecologically valid. Gestalt psychology takes it as a challenge of scientific progress to tackle both these controlled laboratory situations as well as more everyday problems.

Misunderstandings

In the 1960s and 1970s, as the cognitive revolution was taking place, the Gestaltists were popularly regarded to have simply devised some remarkable illusions and the rigorous experimental apparatus behind the discoveries was often overlooked. Nowhere are attitudes toward Gestalt psychology more pronounced than in the reception of Wertheimer's rules for grouping. Most perceptual psychologists were interested in quantifying the factors or making predictions about their relative strength. The rules were tested and interpreted in dozens of ways, but Wertheimer always regarded the rules as an abstraction from a single process.

To American psychology, dominated by a positivistic philosophy of science that equated prediction with explanation, this was a shortcoming. If Wertheimer could not predict which factor would win out over another, was his series of organizational factors merely a list? In its place, information-processing accounts were devised that would attempt to quantify various relationships and yield predictions.

Similarly, Köhler's elaborations of the theory of psychophysical isomorphism—developments of Wertheimer's "short circuit"—were widely dismissed. Köhler had argued on logical grounds that any successful psychophysical theory must find physical processes that bear a structural resemblance (isomorphism) with the supervening experiences. More concretely, he proposed a field theory of electrical activity in the brain that could explain the emergence of percepts and their modification through learning (e.g., after-effects). Köhler was widely misinterpreted to have suggested a "pictures in the head" theory. It was suggested that one simply take the experimental investigations of the Gestaltists without the psychobiological baggage. Most research after Köhler was devoted to discovering single feature detectors in the brain, the aim of which was antithetical to Köhler's holistic solution.

A Recent Revival

From the 1990s on, Gestalt psychology has been treated less as an embarrassment and more sympathetically understood for its naturalistic and monistic spirit. Part of this rehabilitation involves accepting certain beliefs about the philosophy of science. A young science, for example, has to pass through a rigorous phenomenological phase and explain qualitative features first. If psychology today recognizes that it may have prematurely adopted advanced criteria for its model of explanation, it recognizes that the discovery of the features of perceptual organization proceeds *ad hoc,* often without predictive power.

Similarly, in regard to psychophysical isomorphism, many theorists are beginning to understand that there is a large explanatory gap that has to be filled between phenomenal experience and known brain physiology, a gap that Köhler's experiments were intended to address. Armed with findings from chaos and catastrophe theory and synergetics, brain scientists are more apt to recognize the correctness of the overall spirit of Köhler's program, in spite of particular shortcomings (Ehrenstein, Spillmann, & Sarris, 2003). This effort has looked beyond individual feature detectors and to molar percept formation through spatial, harmonic, or temporally bound neural action.

What makes the achievement of the early Gestalt psychologists so impressive is not just the attractive worldview and talented and productive group of researchers.

The Gestaltists were also possessed of a keen sense of the phases that psychology must pass through as a science and thus sought to be the "Newtons" of their field, providing the foundation for later research.

REFERENCES

Ash, M. (1995). *Gestalt psychology in German culture, 1890–1967: Holism and the quest for objectivity*. New York: Cambridge University Press.

Duncker, K. (1929/1939). Über induzierte Bewegung. *Psychologische Forschung, 12*, 180–259; Induced motion. In W. Ellis (Ed.), *A source book of estalt psychology* (pp. 161–172). London: Kegan Paul, Trench, Trubner.

Ehrenstein, W. H., Spillmann, L., & Sarris, V. (2003). Gestalt issues in modern neuroscience: Axiomathes. *An International Journal in Ontology and Cognitive Systems, 13*, 433–458.

Epstein, W., & Hatfield, G. (1994). Gestalt psychology and the philosophy of mind. *Philosophical Psychology, 7*, 163–81.

Köhler, W. (1913). Über unbemerkte Empfindungen und Urteilstäuschungen. *Zeitschrift für Psychologie, 66*, 51–80; On unnoticed sensations and errors of judgment. In M. Henle (Ed.), *Selected papers of Wolfgang Köhler* (pp. 13–39). New York: Liveright.

Koffka, K. (1935). *The principles of Gestalt psychology*. New York: Harcourt, Brace.

Smith, B. (Ed.). (1988). *Foundations of Gestalt theory*. Munich and Vienna: Philosophia.

Wallach, H. (1959). The perception of motion. *Scientific American, 201*, 56–60.

Wallach, H. (1963). The perception of neutral colors. *Scientific American, 208*, 107–116.

Wertheimer, M. (1912/1961). Experimentelle Studien über das Sehen von Bewegung. *Zeitschrift für Psychologie, 61*, 161–265; Studies in the seeing of motion. In *Classics in modern psychology* (pp. 1032–1089). New York: Philosophical Library.

Wertheimer, M. (1923/1939). Untersuchungen zur Lehre von det Gestalt: II. *Psychologische Forschung, 4*, 301–350; Laws of organization in perceptual forms. In W. D. Ellis (Ed.), *A source book of Gestalt psychology* (pp. 71–88). New York: Harcourt, Brace.

Wertheimer, M. (1945). *Productive thinking*. New York: Harper.

SUGGESTED READINGS

Rock, I. (Ed.). (1990). The legacy of Solomon Asch: Essays in cognition and social psychology. Hillsdale, NJ: Lawrence Erlbaum.

Verstegen, I. (2005). Arnheim, Gestalt and art: A psychological theory. Vienna: Springer.

Wertheimer, M., & King, B. (2005). Max Wertheimer and Gestalt psychology. New Brunswick and London: Transaction Publishers.

IAN VERSTEGEN
Philadelphia, Pennsylvania

See also: **Gestalt Therapy; Isomorphism; Visual Illusions**

GESTALT THERAPY

Gestalt therapy is an existential and phenomenological treatment approach that emphasizes the principles of present-centered awareness and immediate experience. To discover how one blocks one's flow of awareness and aliveness, the individual in therapy is directed to fully experience current thoughts, feelings, and body sensations. Gestalt therapy was developed by Frederick S. (Fritz) Perls and his two collaborators, Laura Perls and Paul Goodman. Originally trained in classical Freudian psychoanalysis, Perls incorporated various new cultural and intellectual movements of the 1940s and 1950s, and synthesized them into a new theory and method of therapy. Perl's broad interests in existentialism, Eastern religions, and Gestalt psychology led him away from the Freudian viewpoint to a new humanistic and experiential approach. Perls saw the human being as a unified organism, an integration of mental, physical, emotional, and sensory processes expressed in the present moment.

Gestalt is a German word with no exact English equivalent. It means a configuration or whole, an entity that is more than the sum of its parts. In his first book, Perls presented preliminary outlines of his approach (Perls, 1947). Later works elaborated and extended these early formulations (Perls, Hefferline, & Goodman, 1951; Perls, 1973).

Major Theoretical Concepts

Gestalt theory suggests that a continuing flow of needs and wishes come into awareness, each of which can be thought of as a Gestalt, a figure or focus that emerges out of an undifferentiated background of experience. In healthy functioning, the organism mobilizes to meet each need, making contact with aspects of the environment appropriate to need satisfaction. For this self-regulating process to function, it is essential for the organism to have sufficient *awareness*—that is, to be in touch with thoughts, feelings, and sensations as they occur from moment to moment.

Perls emphasized the importance of accepting responsibility for one's own behavior. Instead of denying, blaming, projecting, and displacing responsibility for one's experience, the individual is encouraged to accept thoughts, feelings, and actions as parts of the self. Another key concept is *unfinished business*, which refers to incomplete situations from the past that are accompanied by unexpressed feelings never fully experienced or discharged. Unfinished business can be resolved by reenacting (either directly or in fantasy) the original situation and allowing the associated affect to be experienced and expressed.

Therapeutic Goals and Role of the Therapist

The Gestalt therapist assists the patient to achieve greater self-acceptance, to assume more personal responsibility, to reintegrate disowned or split-off aspects of personality, and to be more authentic and less manipulative in relating to others. Gestalt therapists bring their own individuality into the encounter and take responsibility for being present in a direct, spontaneous, and self-disclosing manner. Perls summed up the relationship between therapist and patient succinctly in his dictum, "I and Thou, Here and Now."

Techniques of Gestalt Therapy

Gestalt therapists have described a variety of techniques to sharpen direct experience, heighten conflicts and polarities, foster freer expression, or to bring into awareness blocks and avoidance mechanisms. *Continuum of awareness* is a technique that encourages the patient to focus on the now, the ever-shifting midpoint of experience. The Gestalt therapist avoids "why" questions that encourage theorizing, rationalizing, and justifying. Instead, the therapist encourages the patient to "stay with" whatever is in the foreground and bring full awareness to the experience. The resolution of an unpleasant situation lies in experiencing it fully, not trying to avoid it.

In Gestalt therapy as practiced by Fritz Perls, the term *taking the "hot seat"* indicated a person's willingness to engage with the therapist. In this case the hot seat was a chair facing the therapist. An additional empty chair next to the patient might be used to imagine the presence of a significant other or disowned part of self for the purpose of initiating a dialogue. As the interplay between these conflicting parts is heightened and more fully experienced, integration through greater self-acceptance becomes possible.

In the Gestalt method of dream-work, each dream is thought to contain an existential message—an expression of aspects of the dreamer's present state of being. By becoming every object and character in the dream (both animate and inanimate), the dreamer can identify with and thereby reown projections, conflicts, and unfinished situations reflected in the dream.

Applications of Gestalt Therapy

As originally practiced by Fritz Perls, Gestalt therapy was primarily an individual form of treatment. Other Gestaltists have applied the principles to group therapy (e.g., Feder & Ronall, 1980). Going beyond Perls' unique personal style of therapy, the work has been extended to a broad spectrum of client populations. Gestalt work with children, adolescents, and families is described by Resnikoff (1995) and Woldt & Toman (2005). Herman and Korenich's applications to management (1977) further increased the breadth and scope of Gestalt theory and practice. Yontef and Jacobs (2005) summarize recent developments in the theory, practice, and research in Gestalt therapy.

Evaluation and Current Status

Gestalt therapy at its best can be energizing and enlivening through its emphasis on direct contact, expressiveness, focus on feelings, and minimal theorizing and interpreting. Critics, however, have pointed out that this approach can be technique-dependent, overly confrontive, and suitable only to well-motivated, verbal clients.

In the 50 years since its inception, Gestalt therapy has undergone considerable evolution. Yontef (1999) describes a growing movement toward a more relational trend in Gestalt therapy characterized by increased support and greater gender and culture sensitivity, and away from the confrontation, catharsis, and dramatic emphases of the 1960s and 1970s. Gestalt therapy has become truly international with active practitioners, institutes, training centers, and university-based programs throughout the United States and in many other countries. Woldt and Toman (2005) offer a comprehensive Gestalt reference and book list, as well as an international listing of Gestalt professional societies, journals, and newsletters, and university-based research and training programs. Diversity in therapeutic styles, adaptations to varied client populations, and a burgeoning literature all point to Gestalt therapy's continuing vitality and development, as it finds its place in the mainstream of contemporary psychotherapy.

REFERENCES

Feder, B., & Ronall, R. (Eds.). (1980). *Beyond the hot seat: Gestalt approaches to group.* New York: Brunner/Mazel.

Herman, S. M., & Korenich, M. (1977). *Authentic management: A Gestalt orientation to organizations and their development.* Reading, MA: Addison-Wesley.

Perls, F. S. (1947). *Ego, hunger, and aggression.* New York: Vintage.

Perls, F. S. (1973). *The Gestalt approach and eye witness to therapy.* Ben Lomond, CA: Science and Behavior Books.

Perls, F. S., Hefferline, R. F., & Goodman P. (1951). *Gestalt therapy: Excitement and growth in the human personality.* New York: Julian Press.

Resnikoff, R. (1995). Gestalt family therapy. *The Gestalt Journal,* 18(2), 55–75.

Woldt, A. L., & Toman, S. M. (Eds.). (2005). *Gestalt therapy: History, theory and practice.* Thousand Oaks, CA: Sage.

Yontef, G. (1999). Preface to the 1998 edition of *Awareness, dialogue and process. The Gestalt Journal,* 22(1), 9–20.

Yontef, G., & Jacobs, L. (2005). Gestalt therapy. In R. J. Corsini & D. Wedding (Eds.), *Current psychotherapies* (7th ed., pp. 299–336). Belmont, CA: Brooks/Cole-Thomson Learning.

SUGGESTED READING

Korb, M., Gorrell, J., & Van De Reit, V. (1989). *Gestalt therapy: Practice and theory* (2nd ed.). New York: Pergamon Press.

THOMAS A. GLASS
Honolulu, Hawaii

See also: Existential Psychotherapy; Experiential Psychotherapy; Gestalt Psychology; Humanistic Psychotherapies

GIFTEDNESS

In the early and mid 1900s psychologists following in the footsteps of Lewis Terman (1877–1956) equated giftedness with high IQ. This legacy survives to the present day, although a variety of conceptions of giftedness have been suggested by many researchers. These conceptions range from general, broad characterizations to more targeted definitions of giftedness identified by specific actions, products, or abilities within certain domains (Sternberg & Davidson, 2005). Research conducted during the last few decades supports the more broad-based conception of giftedness as a combination of multiple qualities, such as motivation, self-concept, and creativity, in addition to intellectual potential. For example, Joseph Renzulli defines gifted behaviors rather than gifted individuals, as follows:

> Gifted behavior consists of behaviors that reflect an interaction among three basic clusters of human traits—above average ability, high levels of task commitment, and high levels of creativity. Individuals capable of developing gifted behavior are those possessing or capable of developing this composite set of traits and applying them to any potentially valuable area of human performance. (Renzulli, 1978, p. 183)

The U.S. Department of Education also offers a multifaceted approach to giftedness that serves as the basis for many states' definitions of giftedness and talent (Passow & Rudnitski, 1993). The federal definition that follows was initially cited in the Jacob K. Javits Gifted and Talented Students Education Act of 1988, as well as in the most recent national report on the state of gifted and talented education:

> Children and youth with outstanding talent perform or show potential for performing at remarkably high levels of accomplishment when compared with others their age, experience, or environment. These children and youth exhibit high performance capability in intellectual, creative, and/or artistic areas,

possess an unusual leadership capacity, or excel in specific academic fields. They require services or activities not ordinarily provided by schools. Outstanding talents are present in children and youth from all cultural groups, across all economic strata, and in all areas of human endeavor. (U.S. Department of Education, 1993, p. 26)

Though many school districts adopt this or other broad definitions, others continue to pay attention only to "intellectual" ability when both identifying and serving students. Furthermore, even though states have adopted more diverse definitions of giftedness and intelligence today, many students with gifts and talents remain both unrecognized and underserved.

Characteristics of Individuals with High Intellectual Ability or Potential

In research regarding gifted students from diverse backgrounds, Fraiser and Passow (1994) referred to "general/common attributes"—traits, aptitudes, and behaviors consistently identified by researchers as common to all gifted students. They found that the following basic elements of giftedness are similar across cultures (though each is not displayed by every student): motivation, advanced interests, communication skills, problem-solving ability, well-developed memory, inquiry, insight, reasoning, imagination/creativity, sense of humor, and advanced ability to deal with symbol systems.

Each of these common characteristics may be manifested in different ways in different students; educators should be especially careful in attempting to identify these characteristics in students from diverse backgrounds, as behavioral manifestations of the characteristics may vary with context.

Interventions and Programs for Gifted and Talented Students

A comprehensive review of research related to the need for the type of interventions required by gifted and talented students suggests several important points. First, research has demonstrated that the needs of gifted students are generally not met in American classrooms where the focus is most often on struggling learners, and most classroom teachers have not had the training necessary to meet the needs of gifted students (Archambault et al., 1993; Westberg et al., 1003). Second, research documents the benefits of grouping gifted students together for instruction in order to increase achievement for the whole group, and in some cases also finds benefits of grouping for students who are achieving at average and below-average levels (Gentry & Owen, 1999). Grouping students without changing the curriculum after the group has been formed, however, results in far fewer benefits.

A strong research base also demonstrates that the use of acceleration results in higher achievement for gifted and talented learners (Colangelo, Assouline, & Gross, 2004). Similarly, research on the use of enrichment and curriculum enhancement shows that providing these results in higher achievement for gifted and talented learners, as well as other students. During the past decade or so, research has found that differentiation of curriculum and instruction for gifted and talented students in regular classrooms seldom happens, because of a lack of training, resources, and support. However, other research has found that when these resources are provided, teachers can learn to differentiate curriculum and instruction and extend gifted education strategies and pedagogy in their regular classroom.

Gifted programs and strategies have been found effective at serving gifted and high-ability students in a variety of educational settings, including schools serving diverse ethnic and socioeconomic populations, and also in reversing underachievement in these students. Gifted education program and strategies benefit gifted and talented students longitudinally by helping students increase aspirations for college and careers, determining post-secondary and career plans, developing creativity and motivation that is applied to later work, and achieving more advanced degrees.

To challenge gifted and talented learners, educators should develop a continuum of services in each school (Renzulli & Rei, 1997). This continuum of services can challenge the diverse learning and affective needs of gifted and talented students. Services should be targeted for gifted and talented students across all grade levels, and a broad range of services should be defined to ensure that children have access to areas such as curriculum and instructional differentiations. They also need a broad range of enrichment and acceleration opportunities to meet the needs of rapid, advanced learners; opportunities for advanced content to be delivered so that students can continue to make progress in all content areas; and the availability of opportunities for individualized research for students who are highly creative and want to pursue advanced interests. For students who are underachieving or who have gifts and talents but also learning disabilities, counseling and other services are recommended to address these special affective needs.

REFERENCES

Archambault, F. X., Jr., Westberg, K. L., Brown, S., Hallmark, B. W., Emmons, C., & Zhang, W. (1993). *Regular classroom practices with gifted students: Results of a national survey of classroom teachers* (RM93102). Storrs, CT: The National Research Center on the Gifted and Talented, University of Connecticut.

Fraiser, M. M., & Passow, A. H. (1994). *Toward a new paradigm for identifying talent potential*. Storrs, CT: The National Research Center on the Gifted and Talented, University of Connecticut.

Gentry, M. L., & Owen, S. V. (1999). An investigation of the effects of total school flexible cluster grouping on identification, achievement, and classroom practices. *Gifted Child Quarterly*, 43, 224–243.

Renzulli, J. S. (1978). What makes giftedness? Re-examining a definition. *Phi Delta Kappan*, 60, 180–184.

Sternberg, R. J., & Davidson, J. (Eds.). (2005). *Conceptions of giftedness*. (2nd ed.). Boston, MA: Cambridge University Press.

Westberg, K. L., Archambault, F. X., Jr., Dobyns, S. M., & Salvin, T. J. (1993). An observational study of instructional and curricular practices used with gifted and talented students in regular classrooms (RM93104). Storrs, CT: The National Research Center on the Gifted and Talented: The University of Connecticut.

SUGGESTED READINGS

Colangelo, N., Assouline, S., & Gross, M. (Eds). (2004). *A nation deceived: How schools hold back America's brightest students* (pp.109–117). Iowa City, IA: The University of Iowa.

Renzulli, J. S., & Reis, S. M. (1997). *The schoolwide enrichment model: A how-to guide for educational excellence* (2nd ed.). Storrs, CT: Creative Learning Press.

JOSEPH RENZULLI
SALLY M. REIS
University of Connecticut

GREECE, PSYCHOLOGY IN

The notion of psychology in ancient Greece can be traced back to the fifth century B.C.; in the works of Alcmaeon of Croton, Plato, Aristotle, and Hippocrates there are issues mentioned relating to the understanding of human psychological and emotional states (Wolff et al., 1990). In modern Greece, however, psychology is still considered a relatively new academic discipline and profession. Preliminary studies in psychology made their first appearance at the university level in the late 1920s and, for many decades, were closely attached to philosophy studies. Not until 1989 did psychology become recognized as an independent field of study. As a profession, it started to develop to a satisfactory level in the late 1960s.

Academically, the Greek Ministry of Education and Religion is officially responsible for the curricula of university degrees, after accepting the recommendations of the university governing bodies. Currently, there are four university departments in Greece that offer a recognized degree in psychology. These are the National Kapodiastrian University of Athens, the Panteion University of Athens, the Aristotelian University of Thessaloniki, and the University of Crete. These departments admit almost 800 new students yearly (Georgas, 2006). Although there are many private institutes and colleges offering psychology courses throughout Greece, their diplomas are not currently recognized by the State; hence, psychology graduates from such institutions are denied the practice license for psychologists, about which more will be said.

According to Georgas (2006) and the official web site of the Greek Psychology Students' Association (http://www.gpsa.gr), courses in psychology focus primarily on the following topics: fundamental principles of psychology, psychology research, applied psychology, clinical psychology, health psychology, school (educational) psychology, organizational psychology, sports psychology, and industrial psychology. All courses familiarize students with psychotherapeutic approaches, psychometric tests, behavior modification, philosophy, and research methodology. According to their chosen specializations, students also have placements in schools or mental health units. Finally, students are expected to show ability in carrying out research assignments, which are expected to incorporate a literature review, hypothesis testing, experimental design, methodology, statistical analysis of results, and a bibliography.

The duration of psychology courses of study without specialization is usually 4 years and consists mainly of psychology topics and, to a lesser extent, topics in philosophy, sociology, and education. Postgraduate courses usually have a duration of 2–3 years, with at least one year of practice. Currently, there are postgraduate courses in school (educational) psychology, clinical psychology, developmental-cognitive psychology, and organizational-industrial psychology. Doctoral research in different specializations takes place in all universities.

Recently, the Ministry of Health has set up a new committee with the task of refining the current law for professional psychologists and setting up new guidelines for practice, which will also include the minimum training qualifications for clinical psychologists and psychotherapists. While this is in progress, the only law in force was voted by the Greek Parliament in 1979 (Law 991/1979) and was partially amended in 1998 (Law 2646/1998). This law set the criteria for issuing a special practice license for psychologists (PLP) for professional psychologists. Items of the law that warranty professional and educational status state (1) that authorized practice of psychology is granted only to those with a PLP and (2) that PLP applicants should have a university degree in psychology from a Greek university, or from an authorized university abroad, with exceptions are made for applicants who, by the December 31, 1993, have either a philosophy-education-psychology degree with a major in psychology and a two-year postgraduate degree in psychology (or a one-year postgraduate degree in psychology and three years' practice as a psychologist), or an equivalent degree from abroad and five years' practice as a psychologist.

Psychological, psychotherapeutic, and other associated services, both public and private, are widely available in the capital, Athens, and to a lesser extent in all major cities throughout the country. The importance of such services has gradually been recognized and incorporated into the national health and social services, the police, and the armed forces. The main psychotherapeutic approaches in clinical psychology are the psychoanalytic-psychodynamic, systemic, and cognitive-behavioral. The latter is receiving increasing attention and is gradually becoming the approach mostly favored by psychotherapists. In general, the fields of clinical, health, social, and school psychology seem to attract most professional psychologists in Greece, whereas posts in community, engineering, industrial/organizational, or personnel psychology are relatively scarce; this circumstance is predominantly explained by the fact that Greece is still a small country, with a population of just over 10 million people and an economy broadly based on agriculture and tourism.

Finally, Greece has a growing record of showing interest in psychology research. An increasing number of conferences and national/international congresses are hosted in various Greek cities every year. Scientific publications such as journals and periodicals that are exclusively psychology-related are still limited, although many scientific papers are submitted to Greek psychiatric or international journals; examples of scientific journals include the *Hellenic Journal of Psychology, Psychology* (by ELPSE), and *Tetradia psychiatrikis*. On the other hand, the number of Greek scientific, academic, and self-help books has increased considerably in the past 30 years. Various associations have also been founded to represent psychologists of different specializations, such as the Association of Greek Psychologists, the Panhellenic Psychological Association, the Greek Psychological Association (ELPSE), the Greek Association for Behavioral Modification (member of EABCT) and the Greek Psychoanalytic Association.

REFERENCES

Georgas, J. (2006). The education of psychologists in Greece. *International Journal of Psychology, 41*(1), 29–34.

Wolff, H., Bateman, A., & Sturgeon, D. (1990). *UCH textbook of psychiatry.* London: Duckworth.

THOMAS KALPAKOGLOU
Athens, Greece

GRIEF

Grief is usually defined as a person's constellation of responses to bereavement. These include thoughts, feelings, and behaviors that accompany coping with and adjusting to a loss. As a universal human phenomenon, grief has biological, cultural, and uniquely individual components.

Grief's biological aspects can be seen as having roots in the behaviors of animals. Graylag geese were observed by ethologist Konrad Lorenz as having a pattern of restless searching for a lost mate. Bereaved primates such as rhesus monkeys exhibit patterns of depressed behavioral activity, lowered bodily temperature, and whimpering. Elephants have been reported to bury dead animals (including humans). Thus, grief may not be limited to the realm of the human.

Cultural determinants of grief can be seen in the answers to such questions as whether the work of grief should be to detach the person from the lost loved one and get on with a productive life or, conversely, whether grieving should foster a continuing relationship with the deceased. Modern Western cultural norms clearly favor moving on and not ruminating on a loss. Looking through a historical cultural lens, however, there have been many cultural instances in which the maintenance of a relationship with a deceased loved one is a normative grief response.

Individual aspects of grief are the result of many factors in addition to the cultural and biological. These include the personality and coping history of each griever, his or her relationship with the deceased, and the circumstances surrounding the loss. Both cultural and individual differences point to the fact that no single formula exists for successful resolution to grief.

John Bowlby (1980) demonstrated in his work the importance of affectional bonds or attachments. According to Bowlby, we form such bonds through repeated close contact with another. Many of our needs, especially needs for safety and security, are met through our attachments to intimate others. As a result, the death of someone to whom we have been attached is a painful experience. Drawing on the work of Bowlby, several theorists have described grief as occurring in stages or phases. Colin Murray Parkes (1987), for example, described four phases of grieving: shock and numbness (an initial reaction of feeling "dazed"); yearning and searching (protesting the reality of the loss); disorganization and despair (questioning one's sense of self); and reorganization (making sense of one's life and integrating the loss into one's scheme of life).

The experience of losing someone to whom we have been attached occurs on at least four levels, according to thanatologist J. William Worden (2001). Thus grief is normally seen in ways that reflect these levels of experiencing, and knowing that these are "normal" reactions sometimes brings a measure of reassurance to the grieving person. Worden's levels are (1) normal feelings, including sadness (the most common feeling), shock, numbness, yearning, loneliness, guilt, anxiety, helplessness, fatigue, and anger; (2) normal cognitions, including confusion, difficulty concentrating, disbelief, preoccupation, and hallucinations

(thinking one has just seen or heard the deceased); (3) normal behaviors, including crying, sleep disturbance, eating disturbance, restlessness, and searching for, calling out to, or dreaming about the deceased; and (4) normal physical sensations, including oversensitivity to noise, a lump in the throat, tightness in the chest, shortness of breath, dry mouth, lack of energy, and muscle weakness.

Others, notably Corr, Nabe, and Corr (2000), have included two additional levels of normal grief response: (1) social disturbances, including withdrawal, problems in relationships, and problems working in groups (e.g., at work) and (2) spiritual disturbances, including anger with God, a search for meaning, and a sense that previous ways of making sense of life are now inadequate. Among other theorists describing grief and mourning according to a stage or phase model, Rando (1995) delineated a "six R" process consisting of recognizing the loss, reacting to the separation, recollecting the deceased, relinquishing the old attachments, readjusting to move into the new world, and reinventing.

Phase models have considerable face validity, because they describe experiences common to many people. However, their emphasis on sequence may not best describe the process of grieving. It may be more accurate to describe the "phases" as overlapping and often repeating events following a loss. According to research by Attig (1996) and others, for example it is important to recognize that grieving is a process of coping. It is a process that demands energy and presents the grieving person with tasks, choices, and even opportunity for growth. Stroebe and Shut (2001) have emphasized that there are actually two coping processes that constitute the experience of grief and mourning. They point out that bereavement involves two sorts of stressors, loss-oriented and restoration-oriented. Loss-oriented coping involves focusing on and processing aspects of the loss itself and includes such activities as visiting the grave and emoting about the death. Restoration-oriented coping involves focusing on stressors that are secondary to the loss. These may include dealing with diminished financial resources, added household responsibilities, and changes in familiar patterns of communication with family and friends.

The Stroebe and Shut model has come to be known as the Dual Process Model. At its heart is the idea that grieving is an oscillation between the two kinds of coping processes. Both processes are necessary for adaptive coping. An interesting finding of their research has been that men generally tend to cope in more restoration-oriented ways, whereas women tend to cope in more loss-oriented ways. Thus, counseling interventions are best when they are tailored to the type of coping with which an individual person needs help. Men tend to benefit from therapeutic interventions that focus on accepting and expressing their emotions (i.e., working on loss-oriented coping). Women, on the other hand, tend to benefit from interventions focused on problem-solving (i.e., helping them with restoration-oriented coping).

A widely accepted approach to grieving and grief therapy focuses on the individual's reconstruction of meaning. Neimeyer (2000) has articulated this idiographic model, which emphasizes each individual's unique experience of grieving. The revision of one's life story is seen as the central process in grieving, and grief therapy as an opportunity for grieving persons to tell their life stories in ways that will help them make sense of loss and of life.

In this sense, human life can be seen as a process of telling one's story. Through telling and revising their stories, people develop a sense of meaning, purpose, and self. Losses and deaths disrupt our stories. They can threaten assumptions that have given meaning and order to our lives. Significant losses can initiate a search for meaning. Recent studies indicate that at least 70–85% of bereaved persons engage in a search for meaning in their lives. Research by Davis, Nolen-Hoeksema, and Larson (1998) has found that this search usually centers on two kinds of questions. Early questions try to make sense of the loss, as in "Why did this happen?" and "What is the meaning of this loss (death)?" Later questions try to find benefits from the loss: "What can I learn from this experience?" or "What is the meaning of this experience in my life?" Neimeyer has said that such new meanings become part of the grieving person's broad scheme of things. Thus, for most people bereavement can be a time for looking at such existential questions as "What is the purpose of my life?" and "Who am I?"

Grieving can be an active process with opportunities for growth and self-definition. Sanders (1998) has contributed the concept of a "decision point" that most people seem to reach after the early and perhaps more biologically influenced aspects of grieving. She points out that a grieving person makes a decision, sometimes unconsciously, to survive and go on with a new life or to remain in a state of bereavement. We learn about ourselves by observing our own behaviors following a loss, by listening to our own answers to existential questions, and by revising our life stories following the urgent experience of bereavement. A growth outcome of grieving can be increased self-perception and self-definition.

REFERENCES

Attig, T. (1996). *How we grieve: Relearning the world.* New York: Oxford University Press.

Bowlby, J. (1980). *Attachment and loss, Vol. 3. Loss, sadness, and depression.* New York: Basic Books.

Corr, C. A., Nabe, C. M., & Corr, D. M. (2000). *Death and dying, life and living* (3rd Ed.). Belmont, CA: Wadsworth/Thomson Learning.

Davis, C. G., Nolen-Hoeksema, S., & Larson, J. (1998). Making sense of loss and benefiting from the experience: Two construals of meaning. *Journal of Personality and Social Psychology, 75*(2), 561–574.

Neimeyer, R. A. (2000). Searching for the meaning of meaning: Grief therapy and the process of reconstruction. *Death Studies 24*(6), 541–558.

Parkes, C. M. (1987). *Bereavement: Studies of grief in adult life* (2nd ed.). Madison, CT: International Universities Press.

Rando, T. A. (1995). Grief and mourning: Accommodating to loss. In H. Wass & R. A. Neimeyer (Eds.), *Dying: Facing the facts* (pp. 211–241). Washington, DC: Taylor & Francis.

Sanders, C. M. (1998). *Grief the mourning after: Dealing with adult bereavement* (2nd Ed.). New York: John Wiley & Sons.

Stroebe, M. S., & Shut, H. (2001). Meaning making in the dual process model of coping with bereavement. In R. A. Neimeyer (Ed.), *Meaning reconstruction and the experience of loss* (pp. 55–73). Washington, DC: American Psychological Association Press.

Worden, J. W. (2001). *Grief counseling and grief therapy: A handbook for the mental health professional* (3rd Ed.). New York: Springer.

SUGGESTED READINGS

Neimeyer, R. A. (2001). *Meaning reconstruction and the experience of loss.* Washington, DC: American Psychological Association.

Pennebaker, J. W. (1997). *Opening up: The healing power of expressing emotion.* New York: Guilford Press.

ROSTYSLAW W. ROBAK
Pace University, Pleasantville, NY

See also: Attachment and Bonding; Depression

GROSS MOTOR SKILL LEARNING

The acquisition of motor skill, sometimes referred to as *motor learning*, has been the object of a great deal of experimental work. By far the most popular apparatus for such study has been the pursuit rotor or rotary pursuit test.

The most important variable affecting performance during the acquisition of skill is distribution of practice. Typically, performance is very much better with spaced practice than with massed practice. Special procedures employed along with distribution of practice reveal certain other important phenomena. For example, a rest of 10 minutes or more following a series of massed-practice trials produces an increase in performance called *reminiscence*. This spontaneous improvement means that the reduced performance under massed practice is an effect on performance exclusively; massed-practice subjects have learned just as much as distributed-practiced subjects.

Sometimes this last fact is partially obscured by the subjects' need to warm up after the rest following massed practice. The theory that the effects of distribution are on performance rather than on learning is further supported by the data obtained following a test for reminiscence. If the subjects are returned to a massed-practice schedule of trials, their performance decreases. Somewhat surprising, this decrease typically continues until the learning curve has returned approximately to the level where it would have been if no rest period had been introduced; then performance begins to increase. If subjects switch to distributed practice following the rest, their performance shows no trace of the previous experience on massed practice after the necessary warm up.

GREGORY A. KIMBLE
Duke University

See also: **Motor Control**

GROUP COHESIVENESS

Group cohesiveness has been defined in many ways, with no general consensus regarding how to define the term, despite a relatively long history of attempting to reach such a consensus (Yalom, 1985). Leon Festinger (1957) defined the concept in terms of forces that lead an individual to remain in or leave a given group. Credited with developing the concept of cognitive dissonance, a theory that recognizes and, more importantly, explains how individuals become invested in ideas and strongly motivated to maintain those intellectual investments, Festinger and his many students and colleagues contributed much to our understanding of why and how individuals create and maintain groups as well as what causes those groups to fragment. He and others interested in the psychology of groups have taught us that an understanding of group psychology is as important as the study of individual psychology if we wish to fully understand human behavior.

Implicitly or explicitly, every group has a task or set of tasks it seeks to accomplish. Many schemes have been developed for categorizing group tasks. Some approaches have emphasized the unconscious motives harbored by group members. Others have specified aspects of communication among group members. Still others have focused on the content of observed aspects of the work of the group. The extent to which members of a group identify with and work toward a common task can serve as a measure of group cohesiveness

A group's task reflects an important variable affecting the group and its effectiveness. Group tasks can be formally stated and may even convey the reason for the group's existence; for example, a group may be centered around a common interest (e.g., studying and collecting antiques) or around a common need (e.g., a

home-owners association devoted to enhancing the safety of a neighborhood). Many have argued that groups with more commonality of interest are also more cohesive, and the more cohesive the group is, the more effective it becomes in carrying out its tasks. Murrell and Gaertner (1992), for instance, showed that stronger group identity translated into superior performance by college football teams they studied. The authors discussed and contrasted their work with regard to the relationship between common group identity and group cohesion.

What influences group cohesiveness? Rabbie and colleagues (e.g., Rabbie & Horwitz, 1969) have written extensively on the topic of group cohesion and have written about the importance of considering the affect of in-group and out-group variables on group process and effectiveness. Some examples of such variables include between group competition, intergroup cooperation, hostility toward an outside individual or group, and even chance occurrences. Competition between groups, for example, may have no more effect on in-group cohesion than does within group cooperation. On the other hand, hostility toward some outside entity seems to strengthen cohesion within a group. Over time, the study of group phenomena has become increasingly sophisticated from a scientific perspective, yielding information about group process and behavior that earlier in history remained speculative.

Bion (1959) studied in the heyday of psychoanalytic thought, and his substantial contribution to understanding group processes was influenced greatly by psychoanalytic theories. Bion suggested that group tasks, even when stated formally as working toward some specific product, often derived from members' unconscious and primitive needs and expectations. He classified these activities as dependence, fight-flight, and pairing. These activities reflect assumptions shared by all in the group, even though the group members might not be consciously aware of such thinking or that their actions might be tied to these unstated ideas. The three basic assumptions were seen as being part of all group interactions and cohesion centered on cooperative efforts to attend to these assumptions.

To oversimplify somewhat, the task or purpose of the dependent group is to be sustained by a leader. In the fight-flight group the purpose is simply to defend against some threat, either by fighting someone or something or by running away. The desire is for a leader who will effectively rally the group toward that end. In the pairing group the members act as if their purpose is union and some new entity will derive from that unity, a perfect leader, for example, one who will guide the group toward its shared goals, no matter how unrealistic those goals might be. Bion believed that it was necessary to attend to both work and basic aspects of group activity to fully comprehend a given group and such group considerations as cohesiveness.

As is readily apparent from Bion's theories, cohesion is neither good nor bad. Although cohesion may increase the effectiveness of the group, that effectiveness can be in any number of directions, many of which have very little to do with the group's stated purpose. Put another way, a very cohesive group whose stated purpose is to make and sell an industrial product might soon find that they are out of business if their energy is directed away from work and toward one of the basic assumptions listed earlier.

To explain how individuals in a group come together to behave toward some common end, Thomas French developed the concept of focal conflict. Similar ideas have been postulated by other writers as well. In general, such notions refer to a tendency for groups to attend to topics that have relevance, often by reducing anxiety for all members. Many specialties have concerned themselves with group phenomena. Personality and psychotherapy theorists, social and organizational psychologists, anthropologists, and educational specialists are but a few of the professions interested in this topic. Diverse methods and emphases have influenced conclusions. An integration of findings into a universal understanding of group cohesiveness has not yet been achieved.

REFERENCES

Bion, W. R. (1959). *Experiences in group and other papers*. New York: Basic Books.

Festinger, L. (1957). *A theory of cognitive dissonance*. Evanston, IL: Row, Paterson.

Murrell, A. J., & Gaertner, S. L. (1992). Cohesion and sport team effectiveness: The benefit of a common group identity. *Journal of Sport & Social Issues, 16*, 1–14.

Rabbie, J. M., & Horwitz, M. (1969). Arousal of ingroup– outgroup bias by a chance win or loss. *Journal of Personality & Social Psychology, 13*, 269–277.

Yalom, I. D. (1985). *The theory and practice of group psychotherapy*. New York: Basic Books.

STANLEY BERENT
University of Michigan

See also: **Cognitive Dissonance; Conflict Resolution**

GROUP THERAPY

Group therapy is a form of psychosocial therapy that is conducted by one or more trained therapists with a group of patients or clients. Psychosocial therapy involves an extended verbal dialogue among patients and therapists and is believed to operate primarily by means of psychological mechanisms (e.g., insight regarding relationships or positive reinforcement). In contrast, treatment with medication management involves a brief verbal exchange among the parties and is believed to operate primarily by means of physical mechanisms (e.g., increased levels of neurotransmitters).

Group therapy is practiced in a wide range of settings including private offices, outpatient clinics, inpatient wards, and recently on the Internet. It is often used in combination with other treatments (e.g., individual therapy or medication) and encompasses a very wide range of therapist techniques and theoretical orientations. Thus, by itself, the term "group therapy" conveys very little about the nature of techniques and mechanisms associated with specific forms of the treatment. Nevertheless, it is common to hear people make statements such as "She's a group therapist," "He needs group therapy," or "Have you done groups?" Although people do not specify it, they usually have a specific form of group therapy in mind.

In addition to therapy groups, there are support groups and self-help groups. Support groups are made up of people who share a common problem and may be run by peers or trained therapists. They usually provide emotional support and assistance in problem solving with regard to everyday problems. Self-help groups also include people with a common problem. However, they do not include professionally trained therapists. They meet on their own.

A number of basic questions are often raised about group therapy that usually imply a comparison with individual therapy. These include (1) Is group therapy efficacious or effective? (2) Is group therapy time efficient? (3) Does group therapy possess unique therapeutic factors? (4) Are there disadvantages associated with group therapy? (5) Are some problems better treated with group therapy? (6) Are some problems better treated with specific forms of group therapy?

Efficacy

There is considerable evidence in the literature that supports the efficacy of group therapies. In 1980, Smith, Glass, and Miller published an extensive meta-analytic review of 475 controlled outcome studies of psychotherapy. Approximately one-half were studies of group therapy. The evidence clearly indicated that group therapy is effective compared to control conditions and has similar outcomes to individual therapy. More recently in a review of 107 studies and 14 meta-analytic reviews across six disorders and four patient populations of the group therapy outcome literature, Burlingame, MacKenzie, and Strauss (2004) came to similar conclusions.

However, despite the large volume of outcome data collected and the general strength of the methodology of the studies, most studies were subject to the possibility of confounding. For example, in comparisons between the individual and group therapies, the data for the two types of therapy have usually come from separate studies. Thus, differences between the two sets of studies other than the two types of therapy could have been responsible for the reported findings. To control for this possibility, McRoberts, Burlingame, and Hoag (1998) reviewed only the 23 studies in which the two forms of therapy were in the same study. The overall finding of similar positive outcomes for the two forms of therapy did not change.

Efficiency

Given the fact that multiple patients can be treated in a group and outcomes between individual and group are comparable, group therapy appears to be a time-efficient therapy. That is clearly the case for the therapist. For example, rather than schedule eight patients for 50 minutes each, where the total therapist time would be 6 hours and 40 minutes, the therapist can schedule all eight patients for a 90-minute group therapy session. Thus, the total therapist time would be 90 minutes. However, it is important to note that in the case of the patient, a greater commitment of time is associated with group therapy, that is, 90 minutes rather than 50 minutes.

Unique Therapeutic Factors

The encouraging outcome findings reported in the literature require explanation and understanding. Over the years, investigators have suggested a number of therapeutic factors that attempt to explain the positive outcomes of group therapy. Probably the most well known are the 11 "therapeutic factors" described by Yalom and Leszcz (2006). However, four of these factors seem to be present in individual therapy as well as group therapy. In contrast, the remaining eight seem to be unique to group therapy because they rely on the presence of other patients. *Universality* is the recognition that others have similar problems. *Altruism* refers to patients helping each other. *Recapitulation of the family group* refers to the extent to which patients perceive other patients in the group in terms of roles occupied by members of their families. *Socializing techniques* refer to patient attempts to help other patients learn social skills. *Imitative behavior* refers to the processes of modeling and following. *Interpersonal learning* refers to a multistep process where feedback to patients helps them change. *Group cohesiveness* refers to the bonds that unite patients in a group. Although the beneficial results of such factors are quite plausible, definitive research involving experimental manipulation of the factors and observation of their effects on outcome has been lacking.

Therapy groups also differ in whether they are open or closed to the addition of new patients after the group has started. Closed groups are inevitably time-limited and are usually short-term (6 months or less) in duration. Such groups are also usually homogeneous in composition, which facilitates such therapeutic factors as altruism, universality, and cohesiveness.

Therapist Structure

An important feature that distinguishes various forms of group therapy is the extent to which the therapist structures and controls the various activities and processes in the group. Psychodynamically oriented group therapists exert gentle but steady pressure on the patients to decide how to begin each session and what to talk about throughout the session (Rutan & Stone, 2001). To a considerable degree, therapists with an interpersonal orientation (Yalom & Leszcz, 2006) do the same. They believe that under such conditions, patients demonstrate their interpersonal problems in the social microcosm of the group. In contrast, cognitive-behaviorally oriented therapists (Bieling, McCabe, & Antony, 2006) usually have a definite agenda regarding how to begin each session and what tasks should follow. Their technique is regarded as controlling and directive. At most sessions, the therapist works with one patient at a time, while the other patients observe. This format is said to represent individual therapy in a group rather than therapy through the group.

Group Composition

Group composition is a group level feature that similarly distinguishes therapy groups. Groups made up of individuals who share a primary characteristic, such as diagnosis or presenting problem, are called homogeneous groups. Groups made up of individuals who differ on a primary characteristic are called heterogeneous groups. Textbooks advise therapists to consider the composition of a group before deciding if a new patient should join. If a new patient differs on an important characteristic that old members share, there is a danger that the new member may feel isolated or may be rejected by the other members.

Despite the fact that many therapists believe in the importance of group composition, there is a lack of research evidence to support its importance. This is no doubt related to the fact that conducting studies that involve the creation of both homogenous and heterogeneous members is difficult. Requirements include a large patient sample, efficient assessment procedures, standard procedures for assigning patients to groups, a large number of groups, and a substantial number of trained therapists. When such resources can be mobilized, informative composition effects that are consistent with clinical experience can be detected. For example, Piper, Ogrodniczuk, Joyce, Weideman, and Rosie (2007) found that the greater the proportion of patients with a history of mutually satisfying interpersonal relationships, the better the outcome of group therapy for all patients, regardless of the individual's own relationship history.

Group as a Whole

Another distinguishing feature of therapy groups is the extent to which the therapist speaks about (or speaks to) the group as a whole. Therapists from a systems theory orientation believe that group level defenses can be successfully addressed and sometimes reduced in strength through the use of group interventions. Ideally, most therapy groups range in size from 8 to 12 patients, although in closed groups, dropouts often reduce the size to 6 to 8 patients. In partial hospitalization programs (Ogrodniczuk & Piper, 2004) and inpatient wards, which serve a larger and more disturbed population than most outpatient therapy groups, a combination of very different, small therapy groups is typically used, such as art therapy groups and insight-oriented interpretive groups in a day treatment program. The program might also include one or more large groups that include all patients and most of the staff. Such groups may only address administrative issues (e.g., the community group) or may address therapeutic tasks (e.g., the large therapy group). Such combinations of different types of therapy groups represent intensive and powerful treatments that are capable of exerting considerable influence on patients who are difficult to change (e.g., patients with personality disorders).

Disadvantages

Despite having much to offer in its power to highlight and modify problematic behavior, a major disadvantage of group therapy is resistance to participate on the part of both patients and therapists. A number of studies (e.g., Sharp, Power, & Swanson, 2004) have consistently reported that, if offered a choice between individual and group therapy, most patients would choose individual therapy. Preference for individual therapy may be based on perceptions that participation in group therapy involves less control, less individuation, less understanding, less privacy, and less safety. Therapists likely have similar perceptions and concerns. In addition, therapy groups are more difficult for a therapist to assemble and maintain than a set of individual therapy patients. Finally, therapists usually have had far less training and experience with group therapy than with individual therapy (Fuhriman & Burlingame, 2001).

Matching Therapies and Problems

Given that there is considerable evidence that the outcomes of group therapy are similar to the outcomes of group therapy, the question naturally arises, "Are some problems better treated with one or the other of the two types of therapy?" Unfortunately, there is little research evidence to support matching type of therapy (individual vs. group) with type of problem. The same can be said for matching the form of group therapy with type of problem. In contrast, there is a growing body of research suggesting that patients with elevations on certain personality traits, such as their coping style (Beutler et al., 2001) or the

quality of their object relations (Piper, Joyce, McCallum, Azim, & Ogrodniczuk, 2002), do better with one type of therapy than the other.

Underutilization

Considering the number of therapists who have completed some form of training in group therapy, the evidence for the efficacy and effectiveness, and its time efficiency, it is not surprising that some therapists believe that group therapy has been underutilized (Piper, 2008). Accordingly, discovery of more strongly predictive selection criteria, more powerful patient preparation procedures, and more comprehensive therapist training would contribute positively to our knowledge about the mechanisms of group therapy and its effective use.

REFERENCES

Beutler, L. E., Engle, D., Mohr, D., Daldrup, R. J., Bergan, J., Meredith, K., et al. (1991). Predictors of differential response to cognitive, experiential and self-directed psychotherapeutic procedures. *Journal of Consulting and Clinical Psychology, 59,* 333–340.

Bieling, P. J., McCabe, R. E., & Antony, M. M. (2006). *Cognitive-behavioral therapy in groups.* New York: Guilford Press.

Burlingame, G. M., MacKenzie, D., & Strauss, B. (2004). Small group treatment: Evidence for effectiveness and mechanisms of change. In M. J. Lambert (Ed.), *Bergin and Garfield's handbook of psychotherapy and behavioral change* (5th ed., pp. 647–696). Hoboken, NJ: John Wiley & Sons.

Fuhriman, A., & Burlingame, G. M. (2001). Group psychotherapy training and effectiveness. *International Journal of Group Psychotherapy, 51,* 399–416.

McRoberts, C., Burlingame, G. M., & Hoag, M. J. (1998). Comparative efficacy of individual and group psychotherapy: A meta-analytic perspective. *Group Dynamics, 2,* 101–117.

Ogrodniczuk, J. S., & Piper, W. E. (2004). Day treatment of personality disorders. In J. J. Magnavita (Ed.), *Handbook of personality disorder: Therapy and practice* (pp. 356–378). Hoboken, NJ: John Wiley and Sons.

Piper, W. E. (2008). Underutilization of short-term group therapy: Enigmatic or understandable? *Psychotherapy Research, 18,* 127–138.

Piper, W. E., Joyce, A. S., McCallum, M., Azim, H. F., & Ogrodniczuk, J. S. (2002). *Interpretive and supportive psychotherapies: Matching therapy and patient personality.* Washington, DC: American Psychological Association.

Piper, W. E., Ogrodniczuk, J. S., Joyce, A. S., Weideman, R., & Rosie, J. S. (2007). Group composition and group therapy for complicated grief. *Journal of Consulting and Clinical Psychology, 75,* 116–125.

Rutan, J. S., & Stone, W. N. (2001). *Psychodynamic group psychotherapy* (3rd ed.). New York: Guilford Press.

Sharpe, D. M., Power, K. G., & Swanson, V. (2004). A comparison of the efficacy and acceptability of group versus individual cognitive behaviour therapy in the treatment of panic disorder and agoraphobia in primary care. *Clinical Psychology and Psychotherapy, 11*, 73–82.

Smith, M., Glass, G., & Miller, R. (1980). *The benefits of psychotherapy.* Baltimore, MD: John Hopkins University Press.

Yalom, I. D., & Leszcz, M. (2005). *The theory and practice of group psychotherapy* (5th ed.). New York: Basic Books.

WILLIAM PIPER
University of British Columbia

See also: Family Therapy; Psychotherapy

GROWTH CURVE ANALYSIS

Growth curve analysis (GCA) is a statistical technique that assesses change and correlates of change. Although often hailed as a new technique, growth curve analysis actually has long historical roots in slopes-as-outcomes models, repeated measures analysis of variance, mixed and variance components models, time series analysis, random effects models, and empirical Bayes models. It has been only relatively recently, however, that advances in estimation methods and computer technology have made it possible to execute GCA with reasonable facility and considerably more flexibility than its predecessors.

The term *growth curve* refers to a trajectory of some measured variable over time; the shape of the curve may range from straight line to more complex nonlinear functions. Growth curve techniques enable the researcher to test specific hypotheses not only about height and slope of the curves in the population, but also about the correlates of both the height and trajectory (slope) of the shape. Presently, GCA is a special case of a more general model, which has become known synonymously as a multilevel, hierarchical, random coefficient, or mixed model.

The most typical application of GCA involves a variable measured on several occasions over time for a set of individuals. Conceptually, the analysis proceeds by fitting a line of best fit to each individual's set of serial measurements, thus generating a slope (change) and intercept (height of line when time is zero) for each individual. Information involving the degree of fit of the individual regression lines to the individual measures can be generated and ultimately used to inform the estimate of model uncertainty. With only two measurement points for an individual, the regression line can still be generated, but the line will fit perfectly; consequently, no estimate of variability around the line can be generated, nor can any curvilinear form be determined. For these reasons, a minimum of three points of measurement is preferred for GCA.

A key concept in GCA is that the collection of individual slopes and intercepts of the individual lines can be treated in the same way as any random variable. The intercept and slope can be characterized by their mean and variance, yielding estimates of the average intercept and slope for the sample along with the variability around the estimates. It is also possible to determine whether the intercepts and slopes correlate with or can be predicted by other variables. For example, if the data were from an experiment in which an active treatment was compared to a control condition, one might assess whether the average intercept and slope for the treatment differ from the intercept and slope of the control group.

Generalizing from this latter concept, it is possible to estimate the correlation or partial correlation of any variable or condition (e.g., age, depressive symptom score, gender, treatment assignment, etc.) with the slopes and intercepts. In the past, one approach to this problem was a "slopes-as-outcomes" analysis in which individual least squares regressions were conducted for each individual's growth data, and the vector of individual coefficients were subsequently used as the response variable in a new linear regression model with individual background variables as predictors of the individual slopes. The slopes-as-outcomes approach, however, had important shortcomings, the most notable of which was that the standard errors were incorrect (de Leeuw & Kreft, 1986). Modern methods have addressed this shortcoming.

We can formalize the model in the familiar regression or linear model framework. Following the notation of Bryk and Raudenbush (1987), in the simple case where all regression lines are straight, the model for the set of individual growth lines can be written as:

$$y_{it} = \pi_{0i} + \pi_{1i}\text{time}_{it} + R_{it}$$

where y_{it} represents the value of the outcome variable for person i at time t; π_{0i} represents the height of the curve for person i when time is 0, that is, the intercept; π_{1i} represents the slope of the line for person i; *time*$_{it}$ is the observed value of time for measurement occasion t; and R_{it} is the error or residual for person i at occasion t. In other words, this is simply a collection of regression equations, one for each individual, where the outcome variable y is the response variable, and time is a continuous predictor. This model is often described as the within-person or "level one" model, in that it focuses on the trajectory of each individual. The trajectories are modeled as straight lines in the above example, but new parameters can be added to capture nonlinearity in the usual way by including additional nonlinear terms (e.g., polynomials, splines, etc.). In addition, other variables measured repeatedly (i.e., time-varying covariates) over the course of the study can be added as predictors of the outcome.

The within-person model may in and of itself be of interest, but more typically the primary focus is on variables that might correlate with or predict the individual slopes and intercepts. Returning to the example of the experiment with a treatment and a control group, the average intercept and slope for each group could be compared to evaluate the efficacy of the treatment and answer the question, "Did the groups differ on the rate of change on the outcome variable?" This can be achieved in a regression framework, where an indicator variable for treatment can be used to predict the slopes and intercepts.

More generally, we can write the following to represent the prediction of the intercepts and slopes:

predicting intercepts:

$$\pi_{0t} = \beta_{00} + \beta_{01}X_i + U_{0i}$$

predicting slopes:

$$\pi_{1t} = \beta_{10} + \beta_{11}X_i + U_{1i}$$

where π_{0t} and π_{1t} are the intercepts and slopes, also known as growth parameters, from the within-person part of the model, the β's are the weights associated with the observed predictor, X, and U_{1i} is a random error component. Applying the equation to the experiment example, X in the equation above would be the treatment condition indicator, and β_{00} and β_{11} would represent the expected difference between groups on their average intercepts and slopes, respectively.

In simpler terms, these are two regression models, one in which the collection of intercepts is the response variable being predicted by some background variable, X, and the other in which the collection of slopes is the response variable being predicted by the same background variable, X. This part of the model is commonly referred to as the between-person (level two) part of the model. Provided the sample size is adequate, any number of additional background variables can be added to regression equations, with the resulting coefficients interpreted in the usual way for regression equations with multiple predictors.

In practice, the within and between models are combined into a single model. Substituting, a full model might be written as:

$$y_{it} = \beta_{00} + \beta_{01}X_i + \beta_{10}time_{it} + \beta_{11}X_i time_{it} + e_{it}$$

where e_{it} represents the random error components, U_{0i}, $U_{1i} time_{it}$, and R_{it}, from the within and between parts of the model. This full model might now be familiar to those acquainted with conventional repeated measure analysis of variance. The parameter β_{01} is the average intercept of all the individual slopes; β_{01} represents the "main effect" of the background variable on the intercepts (where time = 0); β_{10} is the main effect of time (i.e., the average slope across all individuals); and β_{11} the product interaction between time and the background variable, carrying information about whether the slopes vary by group.

It is usually the interaction term that is of most immediate importance, in that it addresses the question of whether the trajectories vary as a function of the background variable, X. In the experiment example, β_{11} indicates the extent to which the two treatment groups changed at different rates over the course of the study, that is, the difference between the average slope of each group. The numeric coding of the time variable also can be changed so that the intercept (time = 0) falls at any measurement occasion of interest, such as the end of the study; in this case, β_{01} represents the group difference on the outcome means at the end of the trail. Similarly, if a background variable is measured continuously, interpretation is made more sensible by centering that variable prior to analysis (Kreft, de Leeuw, & Aiken, 1995). Unlike the original slopes-as-outcomes approach, which was carried out sequentially, the estimates of the growth parameters and their correlates or predictors are generated simultaneously, usually with the maximum likelihood estimation procedure. In addition to generating estimates, modern growth curve algorithms also offer a number of powerful features. These include the flexibility to test and to relax assumptions about variances and error structures that are usually required with conventional repeated measurement analyses (see Littell, Milliken, Stroup, Wolfinger, & Shabenberger, 2006). In addition, in many of the modern approaches to GCA the measures do not have to be structured across individuals; that is, neither the time of measurement nor the number of measurement occasions has to be identical across individuals. One particularly attractive consequence of this latter feature is that individual cases with incomplete or missing data can still be incorporated into the analysis. This is in contrast to more conventional repeated measures models in which cases with data missing on even a single missing measurement occasion are deleted entirely from the analysis, a practice that can bias results (Little & Rubin, 1987).

The advent of new sophisticated statistical programs dedicated to GCA and related analyses have made it possible to deal with response variables that are measured as continuums, dichotomies, or ordered categories; special adaptations are also available for various distributions, such as Poisson, gamma, negative binomial (Wolfinger & O'Connell, 1993). Growth curve analysis also can be carried out using a structural equation modeling (SEM) framework in the form of latent growth curve modeling, with current software available to handle a wide variety of distributional and variance assumptions (see, e.g., Bollen & Curran, 2006).

REFERENCES

Bollen, K.A., & Curran, P.J. (2006). *Latent curve models: A structural equation approach*. Hoboken, NJ: John Wiley & Sons.

Bryk, A. S., & Raudenbush, S. W. (1987). Application of hierarchical linear models to assessing change. *Psychological Bulletin*, *101*, 142–158.

Burstein, L. (1980). The analysis of multilevel data in educational research and evaluation. *Review of Research in Education, 8,* 158–233.

de Leeuw, J., & Kreft, I. (1986). Random coefficient models for multi-level analysis. *Journal of Educational Statistics, 11,* 57–85.

Kreft, I., de Leeuw, J., & Aiken, L. S. (1995). The effect of different forms of centering in hierarchical linear models. *Multivariate Behavioral Research, 30,* 1–21.

Littell, R. C., Milliken, G. A., Stroup, W. W., Wolfinger, R. D., & Schabenberger, O. (2006). *SAS for mixed models* (2nd ed.). Cary, NC: SAS Institute Inc.

Little, R. J. A., & Rubin, D. B. (1987) *Statistical analysis with missing data.* New York: John Wiley & Sons.

Wolfinger, R., & O'Connell, M. (1993). Generalized linear mixed models: A pseudo-likelihood approach. *Journal of Statistical Computation and Simulation, 4,* 233–243.

SUGGESTED READINGS

Goldstein, H. (2003). *Multilevel statistical models* (3rd ed.). London: Hodder Arnold.

Raudenbush, S. W., & Bryk, A. S. (2002). *Hierarchical linear models: Applications and data analysis methods* (2nd ed.). Thousand Oaks, CA: Sage.

Singer. J. (1998). Using SAS PROC MIXED to fit multilevel models, hierarchical models, and individual growth curve models. *Journal of Educational and Behavioral Statistics, 24,* 323–355.

Michael A. Babyak
Duke University Medical Center

See also: **Time-Series Analysis**

GUILT

Guilt, a notoriously difficult concept to define, is an emotion and a condition that almost everyone experiences. Across all definitions, guilt is related to the violation of a group's or a person's morals. The objective state of guilt refers to a situation in which a person has violated a rule of a religion, a state, a social group, or a community. In this definition a person may be categorized and labeled "guilty." The result usually may involve punishment or censure. This kind of guilt may or may not include subjective or psychological guilt, which is the internal affective state in which a person feels highly anxious, repentant, and regretful. Subjective guilt may result from violating internalized moral standards. Both types of guilt are tied to morality in social contexts or relationships. In most situations, a person categorized as objectively "guilty" is likely to suffer from the internal discomfort of being a transgressor, as well as from the expectation of punishment. When

people are accused of being "guilty," they may suffer from subjective guilt, even when the label has been determined unfairly.

Guilt as a "Self-Conscious" Moral Emotion

Subjective guilt is based on negative reflections about the self in relation to others, associated with violating one's sense of morals (Moll et al., 2008). Another self-conscious emotion, shame, has often been included in discussions of guilt, and even confused or combined with it. Shame is defined as a global, enduring negative evaluation of the self. Both guilt and shame are marked by comparison of the self to others and concerns about relationships with others, and both serve moral and social functions.

Efforts to separate shame and guilt have been confusing. They both involve negative feelings about the self, and they often occur together. If people break a self-imposed or cultural moral rule or standard, or if they do something for which they feel guilty, they may then begin to feel shameful. If people feel shameful, they easily feel guilty across many situations. Psychological guilt involves the belief that one has harmed another, and harming another is shameful if the transgressor views himself or herself as a generally harmful person, meaning immoral. Sometimes the harm done is imaginary, and sometimes it is a real transgression. Sometimes the harm is to a larger social order, and sometimes it is to another person.

Although guilt may take many forms and occur in many situations, it is subjectively an unpleasant emotion that shares features with anxiety. People prone to depression have unusual activity in brain regions connected with guilt (Zahn et al., 2008). When people feel guilty, they attempt restitution and thereby facilitate conflict resolution. When people suffer from feelings of guilt, they search for ways to relieve it.

Evolution of Guilt and Empathy

The capacity to feel guilt is an evolved adaptation to group living and serves the purpose of maintaining social ties and holding social groups together. Guilt is derived from mammalian care-giving behavior, in which animals respond protectively toward conspecifics, particularly infants. In many species, group members are empathic to others in their group, and when group members are suffering, others act to relieve them. This is seen in other primates, and even in rodents (Preston & de Waal, 2002). In order to feel guilt, one must have the capacity for empathy and sympathy and the ability to feel another's distress. In guilt, not only are people able to feel others' discomfort, they also take responsibility for it and try to relieve it. We do not know if other empathic mammals are capable of feeling guilt; this may be a uniquely human emotion.

The system of empathy is built on identifiable neural structures that are present in other mammals (Singer,

2006). When we see another person carrying out an action, we carry out the action ourselves, not in overt action, but in neuronal activity. Neurons that mirror others' actions are called "mirror neurons." When we see other people suffering, we feel it as if it were our own. This leads to thinking that we should do something to relieve the suffering of others. If we fail in our efforts, we experience guilt. From an evolutionary perspective, guilt is a mechanism supported by group selection. In between-group competition, groups with a high percentage of cooperators, who are highly guilt prone, successfully compete against groups with a low percentage of low-guilt low cooperators (Gintis et al., 2003). However, despite the social advantages of guilt, people who are prone to high levels of empathy-based guilt may be likely to suffer from anxiety and depression. This suggests that guilt proneness may not always be beneficial at the level of the individual or within-group competition. Nonetheless, the capacity to feel guilt benefits people as it renders them able to stay in the comfort of their family and group. The link between guilt as a function of group selection and guilt as a function of individual selection serves to connect objective and subjective guilt.

Guilt and Conflict Resolution

Guilt provides a mechanism by which both genetically related and nonrelated people may remain connected. When stable group composition, large group size, and the presence of the pair bond are adaptive forms of social organization, guilt serves to mitigate the effects of within-group competition or conflict between group members. Both objective and subjective guilt also protect each group member. If a person breaks a rule and regrets it, he or she is unlikely to break it again, regardless of the threat of external punishments. If, however, a person feels no guilt over a rule violation (a rare trait found only in psychopathic people), only external punishment will serve to prevent further transgressions.

We need ways to deal with conflicts and events in which we inadvertently or purposefully harm others. People are bound to sometimes harm others. The person who hurts another is at risk of being expelled from the social group so important for life in our species. Social isolation is one of the most damaging punishments that can be endured. However, when a person who has harmed another feels regretful and sorry for the action, the victim tends to be forgiving, the conflict is resolved, and reconciliation is possible. In the wake of a transgression, subjective feelings of guilt serve as social binding; guilt makes it possible for us to make mistakes without losing social group membership altogether.

Adaptive and Maladaptive Guilt

Tangney et al. (1992) studied guilt, defining it as an internal reaction to a real behavioral violation for which

one feels sorry. Here guilt, by definition adaptive, was compared to shame, defined as a self-punishing emotion related to a negative self-evaluation of the whole person, rather than to specific behaviors. Adaptive guilt may be the internal reaction to objective social, legal, or religious rule violation. It may also be the reaction to having done harm to another, or a personal rule violation. Both kinds of adaptive guilt serve significant social and moral functions. This research, however, failed to include guilt in reaction to imaginary crimes or guilt exaggerated far beyond the level warranted by the transgression. Guilt for imaginary crimes is maladaptive, ruminative, and self-punishing. People suffering from maladaptive guilt often inhibit themselves from pursuing normal life goals (O'Connor et al. 2007). People may believe they have violated group morality, for example religious rules, and suffer far more than would be warranted, even by the most stringent leaders of their religion. People may believe they have harmed another, when no harm has been done. Guilt-ridden people may suffer as if they have committed serious crimes. The dark side of guilt may be highly maladaptive. Because the crimes for which one is punished are minor or imaginary, they extend far beyond a discreet behavior and instead become part of a self-definition.

In Freudian theory, "neurotic guilt" was believed to be at the heart of psychopathology. Here it was thought that the crimes for which one is punished involve unconscious wishes to harm another. Of particular importance from the Freudian perspective was the "Oedipal conflict," in which it was believed that a boy, having sexual desire for his mother, wished to kill his father and, as a consequence of this fantasy, became guilt-ridden. Contemporary research has empirically negated the idea of Oedipal wishes, which are no longer considered central to understanding maladaptive guilt. However, the belief that unconscious hostility explains the development of guilt has continued to be popular. Based on the theory that people are driven by self-centered, egocentric motivations, it is believed that people feel pervasive and ruminative guilt because they unconsciously want to harm others. The "new unconscious" discovered by social neuroscience is far more prosocial and altruistic than this. Our view of human nature is changing.

Survivor Guilt: An Example of Altruistic Guilt

Subjective guilt is based on the empathic reaction on witnessing the suffering of others. A witness may feel guilty if he or she cannot help to relieve it. Guilt, then, is connected to a sense of responsibility for others and can be a motive for altruism. In some circumstances, the sense of responsibility for the well-being of others can create guilt over any perceived inequality between oneself and less fortunate others. This has been described as generalized "survivor guilt." Survivor guilt is based on the belief that if one is happy, successful, or merely contented, one makes others suffer by comparison. Both Darwin and Freud noted the guilt that one feels on the death of another.

Survivor guilt was first named and studied as it occurred in survivors of the Holocaust. Neiderland discussed the depression demonstrated in survivors. Modell and Weiss extended survivor guilt to include those who felt similarly in noncatastrophic situations. Highly guilt-prone people who feel survivor guilt may become depressed and anxious, and they may sabotage themselves at work or in the family. Survivor guilt is often below the level of conscious awareness. Although sometimes maladaptive for an individual, survivor guilt may be adaptive at the group level and serve as a means to achieve equality, which is a basic human preference that, with empathy, shows up early in development (Decety et al., 2008; Fehr et al., 2008).

In conclusion, guilt is a complex and unpleasant emotion that serves important positive social functions, including conflict resolution and altruistic behavior. Guilt may be adaptive or maladaptive at the level of the individual. However, even when maladaptive and associated with depression, guilt may, from the perspective of the group, be adaptive.

REFERENCES

Decety, J., Michalska, K. J., & Akitsuki, Y. (2008). Who caused the pain? An fMRI investigation of empathy and intentionality in children. *Neuropsychologia, 46*, 2607–2614.

Fehr, E., Bernhard, H., & Rockenbach, B. (2008). Egalitarianism in young children. *Nature, 454*, 1079–1983.

Gintis, H., Bowles, S., Boyd, R., & Fehr, E. (2003). Explaining altruistic behavior in humans. *Evolution and Human Behavior, 24*, 153–172.

Moll, J., Zahn, R., de Oliveira-Souza, R., Krueger, F., & Grafman, J. (2005). The neural basis of human moral cognition. *Nature Reviews Neuroscience, 6*, 799–809.

O'Connor, L. E., Berry, J. W., Lewis, T., & Mulherin, K. A. (2007). Empathy and depression: The moral system on overdrive. In T. Farrow & P. Woodruff (Eds.), *Empathy and mental illness* (pp. 49–75). London: Cambridge University Press.

Preston, S. D., & de Waal, F. B. M. (2002). The communication of emotions and the possibility of empathy in animals. In S. G. Post, L. G. Underwood, J. P. Schloss, & W. B. Hurlbut (Eds.), *In altruistic love: Science, philosophy, and religion in dialogue* (pp. 284–308). Oxford, UK: Oxford Univeristy Press.

Singer, T. (2006). The neuronal basis and ontogeny of empathy and mind reading: Review of literature and implications for future research. *Neuroscience and Biobehavioral Reviews, 30*, 855–863.

Tangney, J. P., Wagner, P., & Gramzow, R. (1992). Proneness to shame, proneness to guilt and psychopathology. *Journal of Abnormal Psychology, 101*, 469–478.

de Waal, F. B. M. (2008). Putting the altruism back into altruism: The evolution of empathy. *Annual Review of Psychology, 59*, 279–300.

Zahn, R., Moll, J., Paiva, M., Krueger F., Huey, E., & Grafman, J. (2008). The neural basis of human social values: Evidence from functional MRI. *Cerebral Cortex, 10*, 1093 .

LYNN E. O'CONNOR
Wright Institute and University of California, Berkeley

See also: Emotions; Self-Esteem; Shame

GUTHRIE, EDWIN R. (1886–1959)

Edwin R. Guthrie received the PhD from the University of Pennsylvania in 1912. He spent his entire academic career at the University of Washington until his retirement in 1956. In 1958, the year before his death, he was awarded the Gold Medal Award from the American Psychological Foundation.

Like John Watson, Guthrie maintained that psychology should be the study of observable behavior that was measurable and subject to proper experimental procedures. His first book, written in collaboration with Stevenson Smith, was entitled *General Psychology in Terms of Behavior*. Very much in the tradition of behaviorism, Guthrie was a learning theorist. His other books include *The Psychology of Learning, The Psychology of Human Conflict,* and, in collaboration with A. L. Edwards, *Psychology: A First Course in Human Behavior*.

Guthrie is considered one of the most important learning theorists of the twentieth century. His theory was extremely simple and straightforward. He had one basic law of learning: What is being noticed becomes a signal for what is being done. Thus, learning is simply a matter of an S-R (stimulus-response) association by contiguity. Further, a subprinciple states that when an S-R connection occurs, it reaches its full strength on the first trial (one trial learning) and will remain so indefinitely unless some succeeding event occurs to replace or destroy it. He accounts for improvement with practice simply by adding more and more S-R connection to a given performance.

The loss of behavior through either extinction or forgetting is accounted for by associative inhibition, which means that an incompatible response has been learned which interferes with the previous one. Thus no new learning principle is needed. A new S-R connection occurs to replace the previous one. Forgetting is simply a matter of interference by succeeding associations.

Motivation and reward, according to Guthrie, are not essential to the learning process. In animal experimentation deprivation of food merely causes greater activity, thereby allowing for the possibility of more new connections to be established. Reward is useful only because it allows the organism to move away from a situation so that previous learned associations will not be destroyed. Unlike other learning theorists such as B. F. Skinner or Clark Hull, who stressed the crucial role of reinforcement (reward) in the learning process, Guthrie maintained that learning occurs simply because S-R associations are established.

What many consider Guthrie's most important research in support of his theory was a study done with Horton using cats in a puzzle box. They demonstrated that extremely stereotyped responses were established when a cat entered a box, hit a pole, and then left the box via a door opposite the one of entry. They observed that the way in which the cat hit or bumped the pole on the first trial was the same way it would do so on succeeding trials. If differences occurred, the stimulus situation somehow had changed.

Guthrie has been praised for the simplicity of his theory, which did not require numerous postulates, principles, and intervening variables (as did Hull's) to explain the results. It is straightforward and adheres to the observable events. On the other hand, his opponents claim he has tried to explain too much on the basis of too few principles. Furthermore, those who stress the importance of reinforcement (reward) as crucial to learning wonder how Guthrie can set forth a theory where the overwhelming experimental evidence supports a concept of reward. They feel that Guthrie dodged the issue of reward.

SUGGESTED READINGS

Guthrie, E. R. (1949). *Psychology: A first course in human behavior.* New York: Harper & Brothers.

Guthrie, E. R. (1952). *The psychology of learning.* Boston, MA: Harper Brothers.

Guthrie, E. R. (1962). *Psychology of human conflict: The clash of motives within the individual.* New York: Harper & Brothers.

Guthrie, E., & Horton, G. P. (1946). *Cats in a puzzle box.* New York: Rinehart & Company.

Guthrie, E. R., & Stevenson, S. (1921). *General psychology in terms of behavior.* New York: Appleton-Century-Crofts.

RALPH W. LUNDIN
Wheaton, IL

H

HALFWAY HOUSES

Halfway houses, often referred to as group homes or therapeutic communities, are locales where all activities and interactions may be viewed as having potentially healing, rehabilitative, and supportive properties and where all members may consciously or unconsciously contribute to therapy. Residents of these houses are halfway from institutionalization to independence. Halfway houses typically work to prepare individuals to move from institutionalized settings, where they are isolated from the community at large, to becoming able to function independently. It is also the goal of the halfway house to integrate or reintegrate former residents into independent living situations in their communities.

This process is pursued with the aim that residents may live in, interact with, and be contributing members of the community, and be able to gain something from the community experience as well. Halfway houses are commonly affiliated with churches, private organizations, hospitals, or the government, and may differ greatly in the number, gender, and age of residents they serve, as well as in the type of therapeutic approach and environmental conditions they offer residents. One study found that the halfway house integrated patients into the social environment on the basis of outpatient monitoring and created the preconditions for restoration of social status (Litvinenko, 1992).

History

For many years, there have been organizations and individuals that have sought to help people dealing with any number of situations and conditions that interfere with their adjustment to living and being functioning members of society. After World War II, homes were set up to help soldiers make the transition from war to living in their respective communities. During the 1960s, with the emphasis on deinstitutionalization of the mentally ill, advances made with psychotropic medications, and new community mental health legislation, the number of halfway houses increased greatly. As the emphasis on transitional facilities for the mentally ill grew, there was an increased amount of attention paid to helping individuals in the justice system and with substance-abuse problems make the transition from institutional life to

becoming acclimated to the community. Today, there are halfway houses serving a variety of populations with a variety of issues.

Types

Halfway houses serve many different types of individuals coming from various situations and dealing with various conditions. The following is a list of the most frequently served populations within halfway houses.

Mentally Ill

Residents are usually required to attend some type of treatment, whether it is on site or off. The staff ensures that residents take their required prescription medication regularly and properly. A great deal of treatment focus is placed on social and vocational skills, particularly if the individual has been institutionalized for an extended period of time. Such individuals may have forgotten or never learned the skills needed to function independently. In some cases, aftercare for these clients is provided. This provides resources and support for individuals after they leave the house. One study compared the effects of home care and halfway house services on quality of life for patients with schizophrenia. Results show that quality of life in subjects receiving home care programs was significantly higher than those receiving halfway house services (Shu, 2001).

Substance Abusers

Individuals recovering from alcohol or other substance abuse are often sent to halfway houses after they have completed time in a residential treatment facility. Enrollment in a treatment program is mandatory and no drugs or alcohol are allowed to be used by the residents. Many of these residents have little family support, and the halfway house is a tool to facilitate their sobriety, provide support from people with similar problems, and help them to readjust to living in the community.

Criminal Offenders

A research review examining the growth of halfway houses for criminal offenders concluded that halfway houses may be as effective as any other parole program or strategy, and may be more cost effective (Latessa & Allen, 1982). Incarcerated individuals may be sent to halfway houses to serve out the remainder of their sentences if they have had good behavior, or they may be sent to halfway houses after they are released from prison. These homes can be for either adult or youth offenders. There is an emphasis on finding and maintaining a job. Sobriety is also usually required for these residents. One study outlines how sex offenders can be gradually transitioned from a prison program into the community with the use of halfway houses. This study emphasized the importance of this final step in the treatment of sex offenders (Steele, 1995).

Troubled Adolescents

Children with severe behavioral problems, emotional problems, volatile home situations, and other problems are often sent to halfway houses. These children may remain residents until they can be provided with alternative, stable housing, or until their behavior changes. Training children in social skills is a large component of these programs. The halfway house is staffed by personnel around the clock who monitor the children's schoolwork, chores, and recreation. These homes seek to provide children with a consistent, stable environment until more permanent arrangements can be made.

Developmentally Disabled

In halfway houses for the developmentally disabled, staff work to help the residents function independently. Residents learn how to manage their money, cook, clean, and utilize public transportation. Through activities with staff and each other, residents learn to develop more adaptive social behaviors. Some residents attain and maintain jobs while staying at the home. Many of the residents go on to live on their own or to function well with minimal help from others.

Chronically Ill

One solution to the pressing needs of the chronically ill lies in the halfway house. Since its inception in the early 1950s, the halfway homes have facilitated the chronically ill patient's transition from long-term care to community life (Anderson, 1989).

Methods

There are a variety of treatment modalities and techniques used in halfway houses. In fact, two different halfway houses serving the same population may approach the same goal in very different manners. Nevertheless, there are four basic theoretical approaches taken by halfway houses: democratization, communalism, permissiveness,

and reality confrontation. Democratization refers to promoting staff and patients to be involved in the important decisions made in the running of the house. Halfway houses that follow a communalism model encourage staff and residents to take part in the activities of the home together. Houses that follow the permissiveness model allow a greater expression of emotional and behavioral displays than most traditional settings before physical or behavioral restraints are used. In houses that apply the reality confrontation model, patients receive the same response to and consequence for their actions and behaviors that they would in the community.

Halfway house staff members also employ a number of techniques within these modalities to aid in the adjustment of their residents to community life. Group and individual therapy, 12-step programs, social skills training, development of financial management skills, social outings, job training, and moral support are used by many house staff to help foster the independence of their residents. Many houses use some type of reward system, whether a token economy, gaining of privileges as skills are mastered, or acquisition of rewards and privileges with seniority as one moves through the program of the house. These tools are used in many combinations, often depending on the population of residents and the philosophical orientation of the organization, to help the resident develop the skills necessary to become integrated into the community.

Efficacy

The ideals on which the halfway house model is built may seem quite laudable. Nonetheless, the efficacy of such programs has not yet been adequately demonstrated. There has been a wide array of studies producing various results. A critical review of halfway house outcomes studies indicates that the effectiveness of halfway houses in facilitating the independent functioning of psychiatric clients in the community is open to question (Cometa, Morrison, & Ziskoven, 1979). However a study evaluating a halfway house for female criminal offenders found that the halfway house reduced both the number and severity of offenses (Dowell, Klein, & Krichmar, 1985). Several methodological issues, such as no control groups in research and lack of random assignment, have been raised in relation to studies done on halfway houses. Also, due to the various kinds of modalities of treatment and different populations served, it has been difficult to conduct research and determine effectiveness.

A key component of efficacy for the halfway house model is length of stay (LOS). One analysis showed that both resident characteristics and house structure (defined in terms of the number of hours of formal activities each week) contributed significantly to LOS (Ogborne & Cook, 1977). Premature termination of services is viewed as a negative outcome, because generally these individuals are placed in such settings for valid clinical reasons (Hitchcock, Stainback, & Roque, 1995). Another study showed that there was a highly positive relationship between continuing contact with the halfway house and level of adjustment in the community (Holman & Shore, 1978).

REFERENCES

Anderson, L. P. (1989). The halfway house: An often-ignored treatment alternative. *PsychCRITIQUES, 34*(8), 798.

Cometa, M. S., Morrison, J. K., & Ziskoven, M. (1979). Halfway to where? A critique of research on psychiatric halfway houses. *Journal of Community Psychology, 7*, 23–27.

Dowell, D. A., Klein, C., & Krichmar, C. (1985). Evaluation of a halfway house for women. *Journal of Criminal Justice, 13*(3), 217–226.

Hitchcock, H. C., Stainback, R. D., & Roque, G. M. (1995). Effects of halfway house placement on retention of patients in substance-abuse aftercare. *American Journal of Drug and Alcohol Abuse, 21*(3), 379–390.

Holman, T., & Shore, M. F. (1978). Halfway house and family involvement as related to community adjustment for ex-residents of psychiatric halfway house. *Journal of Community Psychology, 6*(2), 123–129.

Latessa, E., & Allen, H. E. (1982). Halfway houses and parole: A national assessment. *Journal of Criminal Justice, 10*(2), 153–163.

Litvinenko, V. I. (1992). Two organizational forms of sheltered residence for mentally ill people who have lost family ties. *Journal of Russian and East Europe Psychiatry, 25*(4), 18–22.

Ogborne, A. C., & Cook, A. C. (1977). Discharge patterns of residents from halfway houses for male alcoholics. *Drug and Alcohol Dependence, 2*(2), 73–79.

Shu, B. C. (2001). Care of patients with chronic mental illness: Comparison of home and halfway house care. *International Journal of Social Psychiatry, 47*(2), 52–62.

Steele, N. (1995). Aftercare treatment programs. In B. K. Schwartz & H. R. Cellini (Eds.), *The sex offender: Corrections, treatment, and legal practice.* Kingston, NJ: Civic Research Institute.

SUGGESTED READINGS

Huberty, D. J. (1978). Innovations in the halfway house concept. *Alcohol Health & Research World, 2*, 13–19.

Moczydlowski, K. (1980). Predictors of success in a correctional halfway house for youthful and adult offenders. *Corrective and Social Psychiatry, 26*, 59–72.

Plotinsky, I. (1985). Conrad house: The halfway house as transitional residential facility. *Psychiatric Annals, 15*, 648–652.

PETER A. DRAKE
R. E. Gutierrez

JOSEPH R. FERRARI
DePaul University

See also: **Community Psychology**

HALL, G. STANLEY (1844–1924)

G. Stanley Hall is honored as the founder and promoter of organized psychology as a science and profession. He founded the American Psychological Association in 1892, was its first president, and in 1887 founded the first psychological journal in America, the *American Journal of Psychology*. He also founded other journals: the *Pedagogical Seminary* (later the *Journal of Genetic Psychology*) in 1894, the *Journal of Religious Psychology* in 1904, and the *Journal of Applied Psychology* in 1917.

After study at Williams College, a year at the Union Theological Seminary, and then a year of study in Germany in which he moved toward physiology, Hall returned to America jobless. To pay off his debts, he tutored children in New York for a year, taught English and foreign languages (among other duties) at Antioch College, and then accepted an instructorship in English at Harvard University. While in that post, he found time to work in the physiological laboratory of Henry P. Bowditch and to study psychology with William James, and he was granted the PhD in psychology under their joint auspices in 1878. It was the first PhD granted at Harvard in all fields of study. Setting off again for Europe, Hall became the first of a succession of American students to work with Wilhelm Wundt at Leipzig, and he was there when Wundt's laboratory was founded.

His American career as a university psychologist began with his professorship in psychology and pedagogics, a title won after his second year at the new Johns Hopkins University, where he had arrived in 1882. During his last years at Hopkins, he had a number of students who became distinguished psychologists, among them W. H. Burnham, J. M. Cattell, John Dewey, Joseph Jastrow, and E. C. Stanford, four of whom were later presidents of the American Psychological Association. The laboratory that Hall founded was second only to a demonstration laboratory that William James had arranged earlier at Harvard.

Hall became president of Clark University, which opened its doors in 1889, and he served until his death in 1924. In the last decade of the nineteenth century, through 1898, of the 54 PhDs that were granted in psychology, 30 were students of Hall. He continued to turn out PhDs—a total of 81 from his department during his active years there. Two of these became presidents of the American Psychological Association: William L. Bryan and Lewis Terman. Other prominent students from Clark days were Arnold Gesell, important in child development, and Henry H. Goddard, known for his studies of mental retardation.

Hall had his hand in many aspects of child development and education and he was widely sought as an adviser for new innovations. A promoter of new views, he invited Sigmund Freud and Carl Jung to come to Clark University for a series of lectures in 1909, giving Freud his first public academic recognition in the U.S. and his only honorary degree.

Hall remains important primarily for what he did for the child study movement, with its many consequences for education and developmental psychology. His theoretical emphasis was upon doctrine of recapitulation as promoted by Haeckel: Ontology recapitulated phylogeny. Although the theory became discredited, it permitted Hall to call attention to adolescence as an important turning point in psychological growth. He thought of childhood essentially as an extension of embryological development. The long period of dependency and of assimilating knowledge and skills in maturing stages leads eventually to the flowering of independence at adolescence. Hall's two-volume *Adolescence* was influential in its day.

The focus on the child and the introduction of questionnaire methods, which soon led to a variety of tests other than merely intellectual ones, are more important contemporary residues from Hall's career than any basic theoretical ideas. His leadership and organizational and promotional skills were needed by the psychology of his day, and contemporary psychology is broader and more viable because of him.

SUGGESTED READINGS

Hall, G. S. (1904). Adolescence: Its psychology and its relations to physiology, anthropology, sociology, sex, crime, religion, and education. New York: Appleton.

Hall, G. S. (1906). Youth: Its education, regiment, and hygiene. New York: Appleton.

ERNEST R. HILGARD
Stanford University

HALLUCINATIONS

Hallucinations are involuntary sensory experiences that are perceived as emanating from the external environment, in the absence of stimulation of relevant sensory receptors. Hallucinations can occur in a variety of contexts but are perhaps most striking and debilitating in the context of schizophrenia, in which they are generally experienced as real and emotionally significant, are related to concurrent delusions, and represent a manifestation of psychosis. Hallucinations can occur in any sensory modality and can involve multiple modalities. Auditory hallucinations are the most common in schizophrenia and other illnesses that are traditionally termed psychiatric, and visual hallucinations are the most common in illnesses termed neurological. Hallucinations can be described at multiple levels of analysis, including cognitive, neurochemical, computational, and social/psychological. This article presents a functional

neuroanatomic approach to hallucinations describing and analyzing them in terms of disorders of sensory input and subcortical (mindbrain/thalamus) and higher brain regions, including cortical sensory, limbic, and frontal regions. It touches also on treatment considerations.

Disorders of Sensory Input Associated with Hallucinations

Hallucinations produced by disorders of the peripheral sensory system appear to result from ongoing cortical sensory processing in the setting of degraded or absent sensory input. In this setting, perception may be dominated by the cortically generated expectations (top-down processing) that interact with peripheral input (bottom-up processing) in the generation of normal perception. Hallucinations of this sort are frequently seen in the visual system, in which case they are termed the *Charles Bonnet Syndrome*. These are usually vivid, colorful representations of people, animals, trees, and so on that appear smaller than normal (Lilliputian) and are often engaged in activities. Notably, the individuals experiencing these hallucinations are aware that they do not represent reality, and generally they have no strong emotional reaction to them. Similar hallucinations can occur in conditions such as stroke that involve destruction of primary visual cortex, as this region provides input to unimodal association areas involved in the generation of complex hallucinations. When lesions are limited to one hemisphere, hallucinations may occur only in the affected contralateral visual field.

In the somatosensory system, a striking example of hallucinations caused by disordered sensory input occurs in the phantom limb syndrome, in which an amputated limb continues to be experienced as present, able to move in space, and able to feel pain or tingling. In the auditory system, individuals with peripheral dysfunction (including deafness) can develop complex hallucinations such as music or voices, or simple hallucinations such as ringing, buzzing, or isolated tones.

Mindbrain/Thalamic Disorders Associated with Hallucinations

Hallucinations similar to those produced by peripheral lesions can occur with lesions of the upper mindbrain and adjacent thalamus. Originally attributed to a lesion in the mindbrain peduncular region, they remain known as *peduncular* hallucinations. Like Charles Bonnet hallucinations, they are usually vivid visual hallucinations, frequently of people or animals, sometimes Lilliputian, often with activities. Unlike those produced by peripheral lesions, peduncular hallucinations are generally associated with disturbances in sleep and arousal and may at times be interpreted as real.

These disturbances in sleep and arousal provide clues to the mechanisms by which hallucinations are generated by midbrain and thalamic lesions. Frequency-specific oscillations in thalamocortical circuits have been associated with the temporal binding of perception and with dreaming—a normal condition involving perception in the absence of external stimuli. During the awake state, thalamic relay nuclei faithfully transmit inputs to the cortex; during dreaming, they do not. Neurotransmitters, notably acetylcholine and serotonin, play an important role in initiating this switch in relay mode. Abnormalities of cholinergic and serotonergic transmission brought on by disease, medication, or drug use are frequently accompanied by hallucinations. Similarly, transitions between states of sleep and wakefulness are associated with hallucinations, usually in the setting of sleep disorders. These are generally multimodal, vivid, and emotionally charged. Common examples are the feeling of being about to fall into a abyss or be attacked, of being caught in fire, or of sensing a presence in the room. Hallucinations in the settings of delirium and sedative drug withdrawal are also associated with disturbances in sleep and arousal. Such hallucinations should be distinguished from illusions, which are misinterpretations of actual sensory stimuli.

Disorders of Higher Brain Regions Associated with Hallucinations

Hallucinations, such as those that occur in migraine, epilepsy, and schizophrenia, may also be associated with primary pathology at higher levels of the brain. In recent years, studies employing functional neuroimaging techniques have implicated a number of higher brain regions in the generation of hallucinations, corresponding to their form, content, and setting.

Cortical Sensory Activity Associated with Hallucinations

Regardless of the mechanism by which they are generated, hallucinations appear to be associated with activity in cortical sensory regions corresponding to their modality and complexity. The hallucinations previously described may be categorized as complex or formed. Noncomplex hallucinations are referred to interchangeably as simple, unformed, or crude. In the visual system, these are known as *photopsias*. These occur most frequently with migraines, and they may also be seen at the onset of partial seizures, for the first few days following an infarction of the central visual system, and with disorders of visual input. Photopsias may consist of colored or colorless glittering spots or of black and white zigzag patterns known as *fortification lines*. They often occur unilaterally, but they may fill the entire visual field. Simple hallucinations are believed to reflect activity in primary sensory or adjacent early unimodal association areas and to correspond, in form, to the area's functional specialization. For example, colored photopsias

would be associated with activity in occipital subregions involved in color processing.

Complex hallucinations are associated with activity in sensory association areas, with or without involvement of primary sensory cortex. As with simple hallucinations, their form and content correspond to the location of activity. For example, in a functional neuroimaging study of an individual experiencing ongoing auditory-visual hallucinations while schizophrenic, we detected activations in association cortices mediating higher-order visual perception, speech perception, and intermodal processing.

Limbic/Paralimbic Activity Associated with Hallucinations

The study just cited included other subjects with schizophrenia, all of whom experienced frequent auditory hallucinations. Although each had a somewhat different pattern of sensory cortical activation, perhaps reflecting differences in the form and content of their hallucinations, group analysis revealed a significant pattern of common activations in thalamic (see earlier discussion), limbic, and paralimbic areas—regions involved in the processing of emotion and memory and their integration with sensory information. Just as abnormal activity in sensory cortex is correlated with the form and content of hallucinations, it is likely that aberrant activity in limbic/paralimbic regions gives rise to marked emotional significances of hallucinations in persons with schizophrenia.

Further evidence of a role for thalamic and limbic system dysfunction in the generation of schizophrenia symptoms is provided by postmortem, neuropsychological, electrophysiologic, and neuroimaging studies that reveal structural and functional abnormalities of thalamic and limbic regions in individuals with schizophrenia, including hyperactivity of temporal regions, left greater than right, associated with psychosis. Additionally, activity of the limbic system is closely interconnected with that of dopamine, a neurotransmitter implicated in the generation of hallucinations and delusions in schizophrenia, medication toxicity, and drug abuse. Recently, dysfunction in the glutamatergic excitatory transmitter system has also been implicated. Hallucinations that arise in the context of severe emotional stress may also involve abnormal limbic activity.

Temporolimbic structures also play a role in the generation of hallucinations associated with epilepsy. The onset of partial seizures can be accompanied by simple hallucinations in any modality, reflecting ictal discharges in primary sensory areas, or by complex hallucinations reflecting discharges in limbic and sensory association areas. Olfactory hallucinations can also be seen in association with epilepsy. These complex hallucinations most often involve temporolimbic regions, including hippocampus and amygdala, which have the lowest seizure thresholds of all brain structures, as well as sensory association areas. Like the hallucinations seen in schizophrenia, these are often emotionally charged. Unlike those seen in schizophrenia, they are more often visual than auditory and are not usually believed by the person experiencing them to represent reality. Individuals who suffer from epilepsy over prolonged periods may also develop hallucinations between seizure episodes. These may resemble more closely those seen in schizophrenia, because they are frequently emotionally charged, accompanied by delusions, and believed to represent reality, and they are as often auditory as visual. As in schizophrenia, they appear to be associated with temporal lobe abnormalities, left more often than right.

Frontal/Executive Activity Associated with Hallucinations

The lack of awareness that hallucinatory experiences do not correspond to reality is a striking feature of schizophrenia. In addition to temporal lobe abnormalities, numerous studies have revealed frontal dysfunction and abnormal frontotemporal connectivity associated with schizophrenia. The frontal lobes, in concert with interconnected regions, mediate the higher, more complex aspects of cognition, termed *executive functions*, that include judgment, insight, and self-monitoring. Although relevant studies have produced mixed results, there is evidence to suggest that frontal dysfunction may contribute to the inability of individuals with schizophrenia to identify the internal origin of their hallucinatory experience and its relation to their illness. Temporal lobe epilepsy may also be accompanied by executive as well as other forms of cognitive dysfunction, and by abnormalities of frontal activity.

Treatment of Hallucinations

For hallucinations accompanying schizophrenia or other primary psychiatric disorders, medications that alter transmission of dopamine and related neurotransmitters (such as serotonin), termed *antipsychotics*, are the mainstay of treatment. In other contexts, the first step in the treatment of hallucinations is to address the condition that underlies their existence. Where this is impossible or ineffective, antipsychotic medications may be tried. However, these tend to be less effective in conditions that do not involve limbic, striatal, or dopaminergic pathology. Fortunately, hallunications in the setting of sensory input disorders, where antipsychotics are least effective, are often less disturbing to those experiencing them, as previously described. Such hallucinations sometimes respond to carbamazepine, a medication used to treat a variety of neuropsychiatric conditions. When hallucinations are distressing and unresponsive to medication, psychological treatments, including cognitive-behavioral and supportive therapies, may be helpful. Future developments in the treatment of hallucinations are likely to be guided by the functional neuroanatomic approach, altering neurotransmission (via medications) or cortical activity (via techniques such as transcranial magnetic stimulation) in specific cerebral regions.

SUGGESTED READINGS

Allen, P., Laroi, F., McGuire, P. K., & Aleman, A. (2008). The hallucinating brain: A review of structural and functional neuroimaging studies of hallucinations. *Neuroscience and Biobehavioral Reviews, 32*(1), 175–191.

Behrendt, R. P. (2003). Hallucinations: Synchronisation of thalamocortical gamma oscillations underconstrained by sensory input. *Consciousness and Cognition, 12*(3), 413–451.

Benke, T. (2006). Peduncular hallucinosis: A syndrome of impaired reality monitoring. *Journal of Neurology, 253*(12), 1561–1571.

Cummings, J. L., & Mega, M. S. (2003). Hallucinations. In *Neuropsychiatry and behavioral neuroscience* (pp. 187–199). New York: Oxford University Press.

Flor, H., Nikolajsen, L., & Staehelin Jensen, T. (2006). Phantom limb pain: A case of maladaptive CNS plasticity? *Nature Reviews Neuroscience, 7*(11), 873–881.

Hobson, J. A., & Pace-Schott, E. F. (2002). The cognitive neuroscience of sleep: Neuronal systems, consciousness and learning. *Nature Reviews Neuroscience, 3*(9), 679–693.

Mocellin, R., Walterfang, M., & Velakoulis, D. (2006). Neuropsychiatry of complex visual hallucinations. *Australian and New Zealand Journal of Psychiatry, 40*(9), 742–751.

DANIEL WEISHOLTZ
JANE EPSTEIN
EMILY STERN
DAVID SILBERSWEIG
Weill Medical College of Cornell University

See also: Brain; Epilepsy; Schizophrenia

HALLUCINOGEN-RELATED DISORDERS

Psychosis is a disturbance in the perception of reality, evidenced by hallucinations (false sensory perceptions), delusions (false beliefs that are not shared with any other people), or disorganized thoughts. Psychotic states brought on by hallucinogen use are often referred to as "trips" by recreational users, and they may be accompanied by agitation, aggression, and other forms of behavioral impairment. Trips generally involve existential experiences, distortions in perception, and synesthesias (blending of the senses).

Hallucinogens alter perceptions without causing any major metabolic changes (Abraham, Aldridge, & Gogia,

1996). They come in many different shapes and forms, ranging from common household items to plant and animal extracts to synthetic derivatives of natural products. The classic hallucinogens include lysergic acid diethylamide, or LSD ("acid"), which is the prototypical hallucinogen, as well as psilocybin ("magic mushrooms") and mescaline ("peyote"). There are three different classes of "designer" drugs (recreational drugs that are derivatives of legal compounds): molecules containing phenylethyl amine scaffolds, synthetic derivatives of opiates, and arylhexylamines such as phencyclidine (PCP). In addition, volatile substances or those that emit vapors (e.g., paint thinners, diethyl ether, gasoline, certain glues, felt tip pens, nitrous oxide, and aerosol containers) can be sniffed, bagged, huffed, or sprayed to induce a hallucinogenic experience (Anderson & Loomis, 2003).

A number of hallucinogens were discovered during the course of routine pharmaceutical research. For example, Albert Hofman first synthesized LSD while investigating the pharmaceutical properties of lysergic acid derivatives, and he subsequently used LSD-induced hallucinations as a model to gain insight into the pathophysiology of schizophrenia. However, the discovery of LSD paved the way for easy synthesis and distribution of hallucinogens to the general public, allowing hallucinogen use to transcend its previous geographical or spiritual boundaries (Abraham, Aldridge, & Gogia, 1996). The affinity of LSD for serotonin receptors, especially the 5-HT$_2$ family of G-protein-coupled receptors, has been well-documented; however, it is still unclear how LSD exerts its effects on perception, mood, and thought processes (Backstrom, Chu, Niswender, & Sanders-Bush, 1999).

Similarly, amphetamine derivatives have their origins in pharmacological research, where it was found that subtle variations of phenylethylamine could produce molecules with properties that ranged from stimulation of the sympathetic nervous system to changes in cognition. Amphetamine, methamphetamine, 3,4-methylenedioxyamphetamine, or MDA, and 3,4-methylenedioxymethamphetamine, or MDMA ("X," "E," "Ecstasy"), have since found their way into recreational use. These drugs can quickly deplete the brain's stores of serotonin through a combination of increased release of serotonin into the synapse with decreased serotonin production and recycling (Britt, 2005).

Another class of designer drugs is the arylhexylamines, which include phencyclidine, or PCP ("angel dust," "peace pill," "whack"), and ketamine ("Special K," "cat valium"). These compounds noncompetitively inhibit the N-methyl-D-aspartate (NMDA) receptor complexes of the central nervous system, leading to increased release of neurotransmitters such as dopamine, serotonin, and norepinephrine in the prefrontal cortex and midbrain. Like the lysergic acid and amphetamine derivatives, arylhexylamines are metabolized in the liver cytochrome

P450 system and excreted by the kidneys (Britt & McCance-Katz, 2005).

Inhalants are readily absorbed through the lungs and rapidly metabolized in the liver cytochrome P450 system. With the exception of nitrates, inhalants are depressants that act directly on the central nervous system, with hypothesized effects on opiate, GABA, and NMDA receptors. Nitrates work to produce sensations of floating by dilating blood vessels and relaxing smooth muscles. Adverse and lethal events related to inhalant abuse are related to their anesthetic and gaseous properties; these include sudden sniffing death syndrome, arrhythmias, asphyxia, and serious accidental injuries. Chronic inhalant abuse can damage the heart, kidneys, liver, bone marrow, and nervous system (Williams & Storck, 2007).

The main purpose of hallucinogen use, regardless of whether it is for recreational purposes or in religion, is to induce the hallucinogenic experience. Religious use by shamans of hallucinogens such as ayahuasca, psilocybin, lysergic acid amide, and peyote has been well documented. Sacramental use of psilocybin can be traced back to the Aztecs, and the use of these mushrooms continues to this day among some indigenous tribes of the Oaxaca region of Mexico. Ayahuasca use has traditionally been located along the Amazon and in Latin America, and its use is in religious ceremonies to help with spiritual cleansing and physical detoxification, such as recovery from alcoholism. Peyote is consumed chiefly in the context of Native American religious ceremonies that either celebrate special occasions such as birthdays or serve a particular purpose such as promoting the health of a loved one or ensuring the safety of church members serving in the military. For those who do not ingest peyote, a few drops of the tea may be placed on the lips as a blessing. Religious use of both ayahuasca and peyote is exempted from prosecution by federal law, which has excited controversy through the intersection of the United States's war on drugs with freedom of religion (Halpern & Sewell, 2005).

Recreationally, hallucinogen use is popular among adolescents and young adults because hallucinogens can produce feelings of euphoria and energy, as well as a desire to socialize, without any withdrawal symptoms or memory impairment. Although hallucinogen abuse dropped off in the 1970s and remained at low levels during the 1980s, there has since been a reemergence in hallucinogen use. This increase is hypothesized to be due to generational forgetting, whereby the current generation of youths has not had opportunities to learn from older peers about bad trips and other adverse consequences of hallucinogen use (Rickert, Siqueira, Dale, & Wiemann, 2003).

Volatile hallucinogen abuse is prevalent among teenagers; almost 20% of teenagers have experimented with inhaled substances. Inhalant abuse can also be found in industrial factory workers who bring home solvents for recreational use. The use of inhalants is equally common among members of both sexes. Non-Hispanic Caucasians are more likely to report inhalant use than are members of other race or ethnic groups (Neumark, Delva, & Anthony, 1998). Inhalant abuse typically causes a euphoric feeling and can become habit-forming (Anderson & Loomis, 2003).

Hallucinogen-induced psychosis is often accompanied by abuse of other drugs, risky or impaired behavior, and physical symptoms such as increased blood pressure, seizures, and balance problems. Flashbacks, a sudden unexpected re-experience of a previous hallucinogen experience, can be common, but they tend to fade over time as long as no additional hallucinogen is taken (Britt & McCance-Katz, 2005). The National Institute on Drug Abuse does not consider classical hallucinogens to be drugs of addiction, because they do not produce compulsive drug-seeking behavior. Over time, most recreational users decrease or completely stop taking hallucinogens (Griffiths, Richards, McCann, & Jesse, 2006).

The acute treatment for hallucinogen and inhalant intoxication revolves around clearing the body of the drugs and their metabolites combined with psychosocial support. Clearance methods depend on the drug abused. For example, inhalant abusers should be placed on supplemental oxygen (Anderson & Loomis, 2003), whereas patients who are intoxicated with PCP should have their urine acidified. Acutely intoxicated patients are in a state of sensory hyperstimulation and are thus easily agitated; treatment should take place in a minimally stimulating environment, such as a quiet, dimly lighted room.

Long-term treatment of hallucinogen abuse and dependence is similar to the treatment of alcohol abuse and includes individual counseling, support groups, and referral to Narcotics Anonymous. The treatment of a prolonged hallucinogen-induced psychotic episode is based around the use of antipsychotic medications for symptom and behavioral management and the promotion of clearance of the hallucinogen from the body of the patient. Treatment of chronic inhalant abuse also relies on support and counseling. Education can help decrease adolescent experimentation with inhalants (Anderson & Loomis, 2003); however, many substance-abuse treatment programs feel that they do not have the resources to address the issues of inhalant abuse or dependence (Beauvais, Jumper-Thurman, Plested, & Helm, 2002).

REFERENCES

Abraham, H. D., Aldridge, A. M., & Gogia, P. (1996). The psychopharmacology of hallucinogens. *Neuropsychopharmacology*, *14*, 285–298.

Anderson, C. E., & Loomis, G. A. (2003). Recognition and prevention of inhalant abuse. *American Family Physician*, *68*, 869–874.

Backstrom, J. R., Chang, M. S., Chu, H., Niswender, C. M., & Sanders-Bush, E. (1999). Agonist-directed signaling of serotonin 5HT$_{2c}$ receptors: Differences between serotonin and lysergic acid diethylamide (LSD). *Neuropsychopharmacology*, *21*, Supplement, 77–81.

Beauvais, F., Jumper-Thurman, P., Plested, B., & Helm, H. (2002). A survey of attitudes among drug user treatment providers toward the treatment of inhalant users. *Substance Use and Misuse*, *37*, 1391–1410.

Britt, G. C., & McCance-Katz, E. F. (2005). A brief overview of the clinical pharmacology of "club drugs." *Substance Use and Misuse*, *40*, 1189–1201.

Griffiths, R. R., Richards, W. A., McCann, U., & Jesse, R. (2006). Psilocybin can occasion mystical-type experiences having substantial and sustained personal meaning and spiritual significance. *Psychopharmacology*, *187*, 268–283.

Halpern, J. H., & Sewell, R. A. (2005). Hallucinogenic botanicals of America: A growing need for focused drug education and research. *Life Science*, *78*, 519–526.

Neumark, Y. D., Delva, J., & Anthony, J. C. (1998). The epidemiology of adolescent inhalant drug involvement. *Archives of Pediatric and Adolescent Medicine*, *152*, 781–786.

Rickert, V. I., Siqueira, L. M., Dale, T., & Wiemann, C. M. (2003). Prevalence and risk factors for LSD use among young women. *Journal of Pediatric and Adolescent Gynecology*, *16*, 67–75.

Williams, J. F., & Storck, M. (2007). American Academy of Pediatrics Committee on Substance Abuse; American Academy of Pediatrics Committee on Native American Child Health (2007): Inhalant abuse. *Pediatrics*, *119*, 1009–1017.

OLIVIA Y. HUNG
CHARLES F. GILLESPIE
Emory University School of Medicine

See also: **Drug Addiction; Psychotic Disorders**

HALSTEAD-REITAN NEUROPSYCHOLOGICAL TEST BATTERY

The Halstead-Reitan Neuropsychological Test Battery consists of a series of individual neuropsychological measures that, in combination, permit a skilled examiner to make detailed inferences about the integrity of the cerebral hemispheres. Because the brain is the organ of adaptive behavior, brain dysfunction is typically observable in some behavioral aberrations. The tests included in the Halstead-Reitan Battery are designed to sample behavior across every possible sphere and assess all major cognitive, sensory, expressive, and motor functions.

Ward Halstead began collecting (and discarding) tests of brain function in the 1930s at his University of Chicago laboratory. His first graduate student, Ralph Reitan, refined the battery, eliminating those tests that failed to discriminate at statistically significant levels. In addition, Reitan began a programmatic series of studies demonstrating the utility of these tests in identifying patients with brain lesions. Since that time, numerous studies have documented the predictive accuracy of the Halstead-Reitan Battery (Horton, 2008).

Many of the subtests included in the Halstead-Reitan Battery are well known and are widely used by other psychologists (e.g., the Wechsler Adult Intelligence Scale [WAIS] or the Henmon-Nelson Test of Mental Ability). Other tests were developed or adapted specifically for the battery. The Category Test, for example, is a visual abstraction and concept formation test that is widely regarded as the single most sensitive measure of cerebral impairment in the Halstead-Reitan Battery. The test consists of a series of 208 stimulus items (slides) that require a manual response from the patient. Positive or negative feedback is given in the form of a bell or buzzer. The test requires that patients deduce abstract principles and use the feedback they receive to regulate their individual responses. This novel learning situation is extremely difficult for the brain-impaired patient, and performance on this test has consistently been shown to be poor in brain-damaged persons (Choca, Laatsch, Wetzel, & Agresti, 1997). The sensitivity of the Category Test may result from the fact that it assesses higher-order cognitive processes, nonverbal abstraction, and problem-solving skills that are diffusely represented across the hemispheres and throughout the cortex (Allen, Strauss, Kemtes, & Goldstein, 2007). The primary drawback to the test is its length, and most patients take approximately an hour to complete this single test.

Another excellent general measure of general cortical function is the Tactual Performance Test (TPT), which requires a person to place 10 different blocks in their proper place on a modified Seguin-Goddard form board using first the dominant hand, then the nondominant hand, and then both hands together. After the third trial, the person is asked to draw the board from memory, and both the number of shapes recalled (memory) and the person's ability to correctly place the shapes (localization) are scored.

Like the Category Test, the Tactual Performance Test is a sensitive measure of overall cortical integrity, perhaps because it simultaneously assesses multiple skills including the integration of tactile and kinesthetic feedback, psychomotor abilities, and spatial memory. The test also provides valuable information about the relative performance of the left and right sides of the body, as well as the ability of the subject to integrate information across the two hemispheres of the brain in order to use both hands in tandem. Its primary drawback is its length; the standard administration allows up to 15 minutes for each trial, although in practice many neuropsychologists limit each trial to 10 minutes.

Other Halstead-Reitan tests include the Speech-Sounds Perception Test (a measure of auditory perception and sustained attention), the Rhythm Test (a measure taken from the Seashore Tests of Musical Talent that measures auditory memory, discrimination of rhythms, and attention),

the Finger Tapping Test (a simple measure of motivation and motor speed), and the Trail Making Test.

The Trail Making Test consists of two separate tests (A and B). Trails A requires the person to draw a continuous line connecting in order 25 consecutively numbered circles scattered across a page. Trails B consists of circles that include both letters and numbers; the person is required to alternately connect numbers and letters (i.e., 1-A-2-B-3-C ...). This test requires visual tracking, sequencing ability, and the ability to rapidly and correctly shift cognitive sets. Trails B has been shown to be one of the best overall indicators of impaired cerebral functioning, and it is widely used as a screening measure.

In addition to the tests described above, sensory-perceptual, lateral dominance, and aphasia examinations are included as part of the battery. Many of these measures are similar to those a neurologist would use when assessing a patient in his or her office or in a hospital. Cutoff scores suggestive of brain impairment are provided for most tests, and the most sensitive tests are included in the calculation of the Halstead Impairment Index, a general measure of cortical dysfunction.

The Halstead Impairment Index provides dichotomous cutoff scores; in contrast, the Average Impairment Index, developed by Philip Rennick, averages the weighted scores of 12 of the most sensitive tests in the battery, to provide a more accurate measure of the magnitude of brain impairment. A similar index developed by Ralph Reitan and Debra Wolfson (1988), known as the General Neuropsychological Deficit Score (GNDS), uses data from 42 separate tests included in the battery to provide a more sensitive measure of global cortical functioning. A variety of other actuarial and statistical approaches to interpretation of Halstead-Reitan results have been developed and are described by Horton (2008).

Most neuropsychologists approach interpretation of the Halstead-Reitan Battery in a standardized fashion. First, the subtests of the Wechsler Adult Intelligence Scale are analyzed to estimate premorbid levels of cognitive functioning. Next, performance on the most sensitive Halstead-Reitan measures is assessed (e.g., the Halstead Impairment Index, the Category Test, Part B of the Trail-Making Test, and the Localization score on the Tactual Performance Test). The next step involves review of the subject's test scores for evidence of lateralization or localization of damage; this requires evaluation of pathognomonic signs, patterns of performance, and comparison of the performance of the left and right sides of the body on a variety of measures. Based on these data, neuropsychologists estimate current levels of impairment, make recommendations about daily activities (e.g., giving up driving after a head injury), and make predictions about a patient's potential for rehabilitation. Some neuropsychologists use Halstead-Reitan data to make inferences about the location of focal lesions and/or the type of pathology that may be present (e.g., a tumor, stroke, head injury, etc.). However, the sophistication of imaging technology has obviated the need for precise lesion localization or speculation about etiology, and the ability to precisely quantify the degree of impairment present, identify functional limitations, and assess a patient's potential for rehabilitation are far more valuable skills for the contemporary neuropsychologist.

Somewhat different tests are included in two other versions of the Halstead-Reitan Battery developed for assessing younger and older children. The children's versions of the battery have not been as well validated as the adult battery.

Reitan's recent work has focused on the development of screening measures that can be applied to large groups of children and adults to identify those individuals who require more detailed neuropsychological assessment. Additional research has focused on head and brain injury, characterizing the types of neuropsychological deficits that occur and identifying the similarities and differences between mild and more severe head injury. Development of knowledge in this area has added to the value of the Halstead-Reitan Battery in both clinical evaluations and in the area of forensic neuropsychology. Finally, a number of researchers are actively looking for ways to shorten the battery without sacrificing predictive validity.

Interest in the Halstead-Reitan Battery continues to grow, spurred by a series of workshops given by Reitan and his colleagues. In addition, graduate students in clinical neuropsychology training programs routinely learn to administer and interpret the Halstead-Reitan Battery. Computer programs have been developed to interpret test results from the battery; these programs typically convert raw test scores into scaled and T scores. Because these programs use exact age and education values in calculating T scores, they may provide data that are more useful for the clinician than raw scores alone. Many researchers and clinicians supplement the traditional Halstead-Reitan Battery with additional tests such as the Boston Diagnostic Aphasia Examination and the Wisconsin Card Sorting Test.

In sum, it appears that the place of the Halstead-Reitan Battery is secure, both in the history of psychology and in the practice of neuropsychology. An indication of the influence of Ralph Reitan and the test battery that he and Ward Halstead developed can be found in the establishment of the Reitan Society in 1993 during a meeting of the National Academy of Neuropsychologists (NAN).

REFERENCES

Allen, D. N., Caron, J. A., Duke, L., & Goldstein, G. (2007). Sensitivity of the Halstead Category Test factor scores to brain damage. *Clinical Neuropsychologist, 21*, 638–652.

Allen, D. N., Strauss, G. P., Kemtes, K. A., & Goldstein, G. (2007). Hemispheric contributions to nonverbal abstract reasoning and problem solving. *Neuropsychology, 21*, 713–720.

Choca, J. P., Laatsch, L., Wetzel, L., & Agresti, A. (1997). The Halstead Category Test: A fifty-year perspective. *Neuropsychology Review, 7*, 61–75.

Heaton, R. K., Grant, I., & Matthews, C. G. (1991). *Comprehensive norms for an expanded Halstead-Reitan Battery: Demographic corrections, research findings, and clinical applications*. Odessa, FL: Psychological Assessment Resources.

Hom, J., & Nici, J. (2004). Forensic neuropsychology. In G. Goldstein, S. R. Beers, & M. Hersen (Eds.), *Comprehensive handbook of psychological assessment: Vol. 1. Intellectual and neuropsychological assessment* (pp. 339–364). Hoboken, NJ: John Wiley & Sons.

Horton, A. M., Jr. (2008). The Halstead-Reitan Neuropsychological Test Battery: Past, present and future. In A. M. Horton & D. Wedding (Eds.), *The neuropsychology handbook* (3rd ed., pp. 251–278). New York: Springer.

Reitan, R. M., & Wolfson, D. (1988). *Traumatic brain injury: Vol. 2. Recovery and rehabilitation*. Tucson, AZ: Neuropsychology Press.

Reitan, R. M., & Wolfson, D. (2001). The Halstead-Reitan Neuropsychological Test Battery: Research findings and clinical applications. In A. S. Kaufman & N. L. Kaufman (Eds.), *Specific learning disabilities and difficulties in children and adolescents* (pp. 308–346). Cambridge, UK: Cambridge University Press.

Reitan, R. M., & Wolfson, D. (2002). Detection of malingering and invalid test results using the Halstead-Reitan Battery. *Journal of Forensic Neuropsychology, 3*, 275–314.

Reitan, R. M., & Wolfson, D. (2004). Theoretical, methodological, and validational bases of the Halstead-Reitan Neuropsychological Test Battery. In G. Goldstein, S. R. Beers, & M. Hersen (Eds.), *Comprehensive handbook of psychological assessment, Vol. 1: Intellectual and neuropsychological assessment* (pp. 105–131). Hoboken, NJ: John Wiley & Sons.

Sweeney, J. E., Slade, H. P., Ivins, R. G., Nemeth, D. G., Ranks, D. M., & Sica, R. B. (2007). Scientific investigation of brain-behavior relationships using the Halstead-Reitan Battery. *Applied Neuropsychology, 14*, 65–72.

Yantz, C. L., Gavett, B. E., Lynch, J. K., & McCaffrey, R. J. (2006). Potential for interpretation disparities of Halstead-Reitan neuropsychological battery performances in a litigating sample. *Archives of Clinical Neuropsychology, 21*, 809–817.

DANNY WEDDING
University of Missouri-Columbia School of Medicine

See also: **Brain Injuries; Neuropsychology**

HAMILTON DEPRESSION RATING SCALE

The Hamilton Depression Rating Scale (HAMD) is a clinician-administered rating scale to assess symptom severity in depressive disorders. First developed by Max Hamilton (1960), it is one of the most widely used outcome measures in antidepressant drug trials, and it is often the criterion measure against which other depression scales are validated. The original scale had 21 items. However, Hamilton later recommended dropping 4 items on account of lack of construct validity, resulting in the standard 17-item scale version. Some continue to use 21 items, and others have expanded the scale to 24 or 28 items. The scale was not designed as a diagnostic instrument; rather, it is intended to be used in patients otherwise diagnosed with depression. Each item is rated on either a 0–4 or 0–2 scale, the latter to be used for items where quantification of severity is difficult, and thus the item is rated as either probably or definitely present.

Hamilton provided brief descriptors of the anchor points, but no probe questions, in the expectation that the information would be gathered during the normal course of an unstructured clinical interview. This brevity led others to develop more fully defined anchor points and semistructured interview guides in an attempt to standardize administration and improve reliability. The Structured Interview Guide for the HAMD (SIGHD) is most commonly used in clinical trials (Williams, 1988). As a result, several different versions of the scale have been developed, creating confusion and sometime conflicting scoring conventions. An attempt to standardize the scoring and administration HAMD was made by a group of academic, government (NIMH), and industry representatives, who developed the GRID HAMD, which uses a gridlike structure to evaluate frequency and severity. Others have developed self-report versions of the HAMD as a way of improving standardization. Both computer-administered (desktop and interactive voice response) and paper-and-pencil versions have been developed.

Several criticisms of the HAMD have been published in recent years. The psychometric properties of the scale have been criticized as not representing a unidimensional index of global depression severity. As a result, the ability of the total scale score to detect changes in classic depressive symptomatology is compromised, because improvement in only a single dimension would have limited impact on the total scale score. Other criticisms include that the items are inconsistent in adequately discriminating between different levels of severity and that the total scale score has a ceiling effect (i.e., fails to differentiate between moderate and severe levels of depression). Others have pointed out that the scale is not in line with modern diagnostic criteria for depression (e.g., *DSM-IV*) and fails to evaluate *DSM* symptoms of overeating, hypersomnia, indecision, and poor concentration. Several investigators have identified a subset of six items that are more responsive to changes due to drug treatment, yielding larger effect sizes than the scale as a whole. The exact symptoms included in this subset vary from study to study but largely overlap; they include depressed mood, guilt, work and interests, psychomotor retardation, psychic anxiety, and general somatic (fatigue). In spite of these shortcomings, the scale continues to be a widely used depression severity measure in treatment outcome studies.

REFERENCES

Hamilton, M. (1960). A rating scale for depression. *Journal of Neurology, Neurosurgery, and Psychiatry, 23*, 56–62.

Williams, J. B. (1988). A structured interview guide for the Hamilton Depression Rating Scale. *Archives of General Psychiatry, 45*, 742–747.

SUGGESTED READING

Williams, J. B., Kobak, K. A., Bech, P., et al. (2008). The GRID-HAMD standardization of the Hamilton Depression Rating Scale. *International Clinical Psychopharmacology, 23*, 120–129.

KENNETH A. KOBAK
MedAvante Research Institute, Hamilton, NJ

HAPPINESS

The study of happiness has long been a playground for philosophical speculation. However, lack of empirical measures of happiness prevented evaluation of the validity of propositions about the matter. In the late twentieth century, survey-research methods introduced by the social sciences brought a breakthrough, in the form of dependable measures of happiness that have provided a significant body of knowledge.

Concept and Components

Originally, the word *happiness* denoted good luck, but nowadays it is used for subjective enjoyment of life and is synonymous with life-satisfaction. A common definition of happiness is "the overall appreciation of one's life-as-a-whole," and psychologists often refer to it as a subjective sense of well-being. With respect to the components of happiness, we draw on two sources of information in evaluating our lives: affective experience and cognitive comparison. The degree to which positive affects outweigh negative ones is called the *hedonic level of affect*. The degree to which our life is seen to meet certain standards we have in mind is called *contentment*. Affective experience typically dominates in the overall evaluation of life.

Measurement

Because happiness is in part something we have in mind, it can be measured using single direct questions. An example of a survey question on overall happiness is "Taken all together, how satisfied or dissatisfied are you currently with your life as a whole?" Respondents are asked to indicate their level of life satisfaction on a 10-point scale from 1

(Dissatisfied) to 10 (Satisfied). Hedonic level of affect can also measured using experience-sampling methods. Available measures of happiness are listed in the item bank of the World Database of Happiness and linked to research findings obtained with them.

How Happy Are We?

In 2005 the average response in the United States to the question about life satisfaction was 7.6 on the 10-point scale. The highest score observed among international samples was an 8.2 in Denmark, and the lowest was a 3.3 in Zimbabwe (3.3). The world average is about 6. So, most people are happy, but not everybody is equally happy—13% of Americans sampled rated their satisfaction at 5 or lower, while 16% rated it at 10. These and related research findings can be found in the collection "Happiness in Nations" of the World Database of Happiness.

What Determines Happiness?

Most of the differences in average happiness across nations are due to the quality of the society. Not surprisingly, people live happier in nations that provide a good material standard of living, safety, freedom, and justice. What may come as a surprise is that people also live happier in modern individualistic societies than in traditional collectivistic societies and that average happiness is not lower in nations where income disparities are great. Together, these societal characteristics explain about 75% of the observed differences in life satisfaction. Social conditions for human happiness are fairly universal.

Social factors explain less of the differences in happiness within modern western societies. Only some 10% of life satisfaction can be attributed to income, education, and social rank. Some 15% seems to be due to strikes of good or bad luck, and about 30% is attributable to genetic make-up. A large part of the difference seems to be in learned art-of-living skills, such as social intelligence. Recent attention to "positive psychology" aims at identifying these aptitudes and finding ways to enhance them. Research results concerning these possible sources of differences in life satisfaction are summarized in the collection "Correlational Findings'" of the World Database of Happiness.

Can Happiness Be Fostered?

Some believe that happiness is relative and that chasing after it will get you as far as a mouse in a treadmill. Others say that happiness is a fixed trait and as such is practically unchangeable. Research shows, however, that happiness can indeed be raised lastingly. Average happiness has gone up in most of the contemporary nations over the last 40 years. On the other hand, long-term follow-up studies have shown that we do not adapt to everything, for example, not to the loss of a child.

Should Happiness Be Fostered?

For some, happiness is the greatest good, and we should aim at greater happiness for the greater number of people. Many religions see this differently and place more value on human suffering. Research into facts cannot determine whether enjoying life is morally better than suffering from it. However, research findings do offer some insight into the consequences of viewpoints and show to what extent seeking happiness meshes with other values. In this connection research has been carried out into the extent to which happiness brings out the good or the bad in people. It appears that happiness does not breed contented cows, but it does activate people. Happiness broadens our scope and helps to build up our resources. Research results indicate that happiness is good for your health and that happy people live longer. Happy people are also better citizens; they need fewer scapegoats, give more of themselves for social organizations and are, perhaps, more sensible voters. In short, fostering happiness achieves more than just a more pleasant life. In a number of ways, subjective happiness can make life objectively better as well.

REFERENCES

Diener, E., Lucas, R. E., Smith, H., & Suh, E. M. (1999). Subjective well-being: Three decades of progress. *Psychological Bulletin*, *125*, 276–301.

Lyubomirsky, S., Diener, E., & King, L. (2005). The benefits of frequent positive affect: Does happiness lead to success? *Psychological Bulletin*, *131*, 803–855.

Veenhoven, R. (2000). The four qualities of life: Ordering concepts and measures of the good life. *Journal of Happiness Studies, 1*, 1–39.

Veenhoven, R. (2008). Healthy happiness: Effects of happiness on physical health and the consequences for preventive health care. *Journal of Happiness Studies, 9*, 449–464.

Veenhoven, R. *World database of happiness: Continuous register of scientific research on subjective enjoyment of life.* Retrieved February 20, 2009, from http://worlddatabaseofhappiness.eur.nl.

RUUT VEENHOVEN
Erasmus University Rotterdam, The Netherlands

See also: Emotions; Flourishing; Quality of Life; Psychological Health

HAPTIC PERCEPTION

The human sense of touch consists of two principal subsystems. One of them, the "cutaneous" or "tactile" system, uses sensory information from mechanoreceptors and thermoreceptors embedded in the skin. The other, known as the "haptic" system, relies on all the sensory inputs used by the tactile system in combination with information from position and movement receptors in joints and muscles and force receptors in tendons. Haptic perception typically involves active manual exploration, although other parts of the body, such as the foot and tongue, may also be used for "touching." When people use their haptic system, they tend to focus on their experiences of the external world of surfaces and objects and their properties (e.g., roughness, compliance, shape, weight, and so forth). In contrast, when their tactile system is passively stimulated, people tend rather to focus on their own internal subjective sensations, such as pressure, vibration, and warmth.

People haptically recognize common objects both quickly and accurately. Research has shown that individuals manually explore multi-attribute objects systematically in order to learn about their most diagnostic properties (Lederman & Klatzky, 1987). The reason that they can haptically recognize objects so well is that they execute a variety of stereotypical hand-movement patterns, known as exploratory procedures, to obtain a wealth of information about many different object properties. Each exploratory procedure has proven to be optimal, even necessary, for obtaining information about one or more specific object properties.

For example, people will typically squeeze or tap an object to see how soft or hard it is, they will trace along its edges to learn the most about its shape, and they will lift it away from a supporting surface to assess its weight. Exploratory procedures differ in several other respects as well: they vary in terms of which other properties are simultaneously available to the observer, how quickly each exploratory procedure is typically performed, and which ones can be co-executed. Researchers have discovered that exploratory procedures that best inform the observer about an object's material properties offer highly precise information; they are also faster to execute and more numerous than the exploratory procedures that best provide geometric information. In contrast, the latter offer relatively imprecise geometric cues, and are very slow to execute.

Researchers have shown that the relative performance characteristics of the exploratory procedures have a number of important consequences for perceiving objects and their properties (Klatzky & Lederman, 2007). First, as a result of the differences just noted with respect to the relative precision and speed with which exploratory procedures provide information about material versus geometric properties, observers are more likely to attend to an object's material features and less likely to attend to its geometric features when using touch, as opposed to vision. Second, because haptic information about material properties is typically better than that provided visually, observers who are required to visually discriminate between common objects along some specific dimension (e.g., texture, shape, and so on) are highly likely to touch the objects in forming judgments based on

material dimensions; however, there is no need, and they do not choose, to do so when geometric dimensions are critical to their judgments.

Other performance characteristics of exploratory procedures lead to two additional consequences. The third is that people typically manually explore objects in a specific sequence. They begin by executing grasp and lift exploratory procedures, both of which provide coarse information about many different object properties quickly and in parallel. If necessary, this initial stage is followed by another stage in which the exploratory procedure that offers the most precise information about the diagnostic property in question is performed. As a fourth consequence, people can and do reduce the time it takes to learn to classify unfamiliar objects by capitalizing on redundant object properties. To accomplish this goal, they typically perform more than one exploratory procedure simultaneously, provided the relevant exploratory procedures are co-executable, that is, motorically or in the same region of the object. To be able to perform more than one relevant exploratory procedure in tandem means that observers gain more "bang for the buck." Thus hand movements are critical for effective haptic perception. Interestingly, the order in which haptic perception of various object properties develops in infants parallels the sequence in which they are first capable of manually executing the associated exploratory procedures (Bushnell & Boudreau, 1991).

People also frequently use their haptic system in conjunction with other sensory modalities, such as vision or audition. How, then, do they coordinate these multiple sensory sources? For some properties common to both modalities (e.g., 2-D geometry, such as found in Braille or raised-line drawings), the sensory inputs initially processed and represented by the inferior modality—in this case, haptics—may be translated into a representation that can then be used by the superior modality (e.g., vision). For other properties, such as 3-D shape and texture, both sources of information may be used, with the inputs from each modality weighted by their relative reliability (Ernst & Banks, 2002). Given what has previously been discussed, in making multimodal judgments about an object's geometric features (e.g., size, shape), people tend to weight the visual information more strongly than the corresponding haptic information; conversely, in multimodal tasks involving surface roughness, they tend to weight the haptic information more strongly than the corresponding visual information.

In addition to haptically perceiving what the observer is touching, it is also important to know where it is located. This requires the construction of a spatial frame of reference. Researchers have shown that although multiple frames of reference may be adopted (e.g., with respect to absolute points in space, or with respect to one's own body), when haptically exploring an object or environment within arm's reach, an egocentric frame of reference (with the origin or egocenter occurring somewhere within the body) tends to be weighted more strongly. For vision, the egocenter has been consistently shown to lie between the eyes, near the bridge of the observer's nose; for audition, it apparently lies inside the head, midway along a line joining the two ears. In contrast, the haptic egocenter is not fixed; rather it varies with the task and exploring limb (e.g., Haggard, Newman, Blundell, & Andrew, 2000).

Knowledge from scientific research on human haptics has contributed to a number of real-world applications, ranging from sensory communication systems for the blind (e.g., tangible graphics displays that are read by hand as opposed to eye), to haptic interfaces that allow the user to feel a real or virtual world at a distance, to "haptic" art (e.g., Burdea, Lin, & Tachie, 2005).

REFERENCES

Burdea, G. C., Lin, M. C., & Tachie, S. (Eds.). (November/December 2005). *IEEE Transactions on Visualization and Computer Graphics.* Special Issue on Haptics, Virtual and Augmented Reality.

Bushnell, E. W., & Boudreau, P. (1991). The development of haptic perception during infancy. In M. Heller & W. Schiff (Eds.), *The psychology of touch* (pp. 139–161). Hillsdale, NJ: Lawrence Erlbaum.

Ernst, M. O., & Banks, M. S. (2002). Humans integrate visual and haptic information in a statistically optimal fashion. *Nature, 415,* 429–433.

Haggard, P., Newman, C., Blundell, J., & Andrew, H. (2000). The perceived position of the hand in space. *Perception & Psychophysics, 68,* 363–377.

Klatzky, R. L., & Lederman, S. J. (2007). Object recognition by touch. In J. Rieser, D. Ashmead, F. Ebner, & A. Corn (Eds.), *Blindness and brain plasticity in navigation and object perception* (pp. 185–207). Mahwah, NJ: Lawrence Erlbaum.

Lederman, S. J., & Klatzky, R. L. (1987). Hand movements: A window into haptic object recognition. *Cognitive Psychology, 19,* 342–368.

SUGGESTED READINGS

Heller, M. A., & Ballesteros, S. (2006). *Touch and blindness: Psychology and neuroscience.* Mahwah, NJ: Lawrence Erlbaum.

Jones, L. A., & Lederman, S. J. (2006). *Human hand function.* New York: Oxford University Press.

Lederman, S. J., & Klatzky, R. L. (Eds.) (2007). *Canadian Journal of Experimental Psychology, 62*(3), Special issue on New Directions in Touch.

Susan J. Lederman
Ryo Kitada
Queen's University, Canada

Dianne Pawluk
Virginia Commonwealth University

See also: Tactile Sensation

HARLOW, HARRY F. (1905–1981)

Harry Frederick Harlow, whose innovative studies of love and family propelled him into both fame and controversy, was born Harry F. Israel in the Iowa farm town of Fairfield. He changed his name to Harlow at the urging of his major professor at Stanford University, Lewis Terman, who told him that the Jewish sound of his name would make it difficult for him to get a job.

By the time he completed his PhD in 1930, the name change was official, and he had a solid job offer, as an assistant professor of psychology at the University of Wisconsin in Madison. He would remain at Wisconsin for more than 40 years, where he built a primate research program that continues today at both the Harlow Primate Laboratory and the Wisconsin Regional Primate Research Center.

Harlow had originally planned to continue rat studies he had begun at Stanford. But when he arrived in Madison, he learned that his department had closed down its rodent laboratory. For several years, he attempted makeshift animal experiments—a tiny rat colony in the basement of the administration building, a series of experiments with cats conducted in a spare room of a campus fraternity—but he finally settled on studying the apes and monkeys housed at Madison's small zoo. His first doctoral student, the humanist psychology pioneer Abraham Maslow, worked with him there and focused his own dissertation on dominance strategies in nonhuman primates.

Harlow eventually persuaded the university to let him create an official primate research facility. Using student labor, his own money, and scavenged supplies, he cobbled together a facility out of an abandoned box factory near the edge of campus. He would later say that the close quarters and small number of monkeys that could be housed there led him to some of his most important discoveries.

In particular, because he was forced to use the same monkeys over and over, repeating the same tasks numerous times, he began to see that the animals were doing more than blind repetition. They showed knowledge from previous tests and applied it to the new ones. They became faster and faster at doing the tests, and quicker to correct themselves when presented with a new challenge. Harlow and his students built an elaborate device, called the Wisconsin General Test Apparatus (WGTA), to test monkeys on everything from shape sorting to pattern recognition. He published a series of papers arguing that this was evidence of cognitive ability—that, effectively, the monkeys learned to learn.

Those results, published in the early 1940s, were at first dismissed by the behavioral psychologists dominating the field. But as other researchers confirmed the results, Harlow began to gain attention as a promising researcher. He became president of the Midwest Psychological Association in 1947 and president of the APA's Division of Experimental Psychology in 1950. By that time, though,

Harlow had turned his attention to the line of research that would eventually bring him national acclaim.

In 1946, Harlow had divorced his first wife, Clara Mears, and then married a fellow faculty member from the educational psychology department, Margaret Kuenne. His second wife strongly encouraged him to explore family relationships in his monkey colony. The timing was excellent; Harlow had become disenchanted by the prevailing behaviorist models. He decided to take on a well-publicized theory that a relationship between mother and child was based mostly on biological drives, a kind of stimulus–response paradigm devoid of emotional connection.

For the first stage of the research, Harlow and his students built two surrogate mothers for comparison, one with a metal-wire body and the other with a soft cloth body, both the same size, both warmed by an electric bulb, and both equipped with a milk-bottle holder. They wanted to find out which surrogate the baby monkeys would prefer and whether what Harlow called "contact comfort" might be as powerful an effect as being fed. The studies showed that the infant monkeys clung almost constantly to the cloth mother, even when an adjacent wire mother held the milk bottle.

Harlow would go on to show that the ability to feel cuddled and comforted—or not—had a profound effect on normal development. In a series of experiments in which young monkeys were placed in a strange room with novel objects, for instance, he found that the "children" of a cloth mother were far more curious and willing to explore than those raised with only a wire substitute. The British psychiatrist John Bowlby credited Harlow's work as some of the most important research to give credibility to his ideas about attachment theory.

Harlow was elected president of the American Psychological Association in 1958 and in a speech titled "The Nature of Love," he urged his colleagues to abandon their resistance to the idea that such relationships were fundamental to human nature. "Psychologists, at least psychologists who write textbooks, not only show no interest in the origin and development of love and affection, but they seem determined to be unaware of its existence," he complained.

For the rest of his career, Harlow worked to change that, focusing his research on the complexities of social relationships and continuing to use the rhesus macaques as a model in his growing laboratory. He looked at peer therapy, that is, whether friendship could help to correct social damage done by a family (the answer was yes), and he compared the social importance of mothers, fathers, siblings, and friends in shaping a developing individual. He publicly crusaded for his ideas, sided with Bowlby in emphasizing the fundamental importance of nuclear family relationships, and declared that no one grows up whole and happy "without a solid foundation of affection." For both his work and his dedication to sharing it with the public, he was honored with the National Medal of Science in 1967.

But Harlow also took his experiments into darker areas of social behavior. He deliberately created abusive surrogate mothers (such as a cloth mother with brass spikes embedded) and studied the effects on child behavior. He also investigated the effects of extreme social isolation, at one point building an inverted pyramid-shaped device he called a "pit of despair," in which he could isolate a young animal for weeks at a time. That work—and his tendency to describe the experiments with graphic precision—led him to become an obvious target for the emerging animal rights movement.

In 1974, Harlow, increasingly besieged by critics, decided to retire from the University of Wisconsin. His wife, Peggy, had died 2 years earlier, and he had remarried his first wife, Clara Mears, who encouraged him to choose a more peaceful life and a warmer climate. The Harlows moved to Tucson, where he took a research professor emeritus position at the University of Arizona. With the help of his wife and a former student, Stephen Bernstein, he worked on a collected volume of his research, published as *The Human Model* in 1979. But while in Arizona, he had been diagnosed with Parkinson's disease, and his health steadily declined. He died December 6, 1981, at the age of 76.

SUGGESTED READINGS

Blum, D. (2002). *Love at Goon Park: Harry Harlow and the science of affection.* Boston: Perseus Books.

Harlow, H. F. (1958). The nature of love. *American Psychologist, 3*(12).

Harlow, H. F., & Mears, C. (1979). *The human model.* New York: John Wiley & Sons.

DEBORAH BLUM
University of Wisconsin–Madison

HEAD START

Head Start is a comprehensive intervention program for young children and their families who live in poverty. It is the largest and longest-running federal program established to prepare this population for a successful entry into elementary school. As such, it has served as a national laboratory for the design, study, and refinement of effective intervention techniques.

Head Start was conceived as part of President Lyndon Johnson's War on Poverty—a national campaign to enable the poor to improve their status through self-help and educational opportunities. Whereas most of the war efforts targeted poor adults, Head Start was envisioned as a program to help poor preschoolers begin school on an equal footing with children from wealthier homes. However, with the exception of a few experimental projects, there was little experience or research evidence to suggest how to bolster their school readiness. Johnson's chief strategist in the war, Sargent Shriver, convened a panel of experts in education, physical and mental health, social work, and developmental psychology to design the new program. The group's professional diversity gave Head Start more than a strictly educational focus.

The committee's recommendations were presented to Shriver in February 1965, just a few months before the program was to open its doors. The planning document was based on a "whole child" philosophy that embraced a variety of objectives related to school readiness. Children were to receive inoculations, physical and dental exams, and follow-up treatment if needed. They would eat hot meals and nutritious snacks, and their parents would be taught to provide healthy diets at home. The preschool education component would be developmentally and culturally appropriate, including language and other academic skills as well as experiences to promote social and emotional development. Parents would volunteer in the classrooms, attend classes of their own, and have a role in program administration. Family needs and goals would be assessed and support services provided through the program and links to community agencies. Head Start would develop community partnerships to enhance the availability and delivery of human services. The need for these components was an educated guess at the time, but has now proved critical to the success of early intervention.

Head Start opened in the summer of 1965, serving over one-half million children and their families. Today the program is housed in the Office of Head Start in the Administration for Children and Families. In Fiscal Year (FY) 2006, over 909,000 children attended Head Start in some 50,000 classrooms nationwide. The majority are three- and four-year-olds whose parents have incomes below the federal poverty line. About 12% are children with disabilities. The FY 2006 budget was $6.7 billion. By law, grantees receive 80% of their funding from the federal government and the rest from other, usually community, sources. The Head Start Act of 2007 (P.L. 110–134), which reauthorized the program after five years of delays, allows Head Start centers to serve a limited number of children from families 130% above the poverty line and expands both the American Indian/Alaskan Native and Migrant Seasonal programs, among other provisions.

Each Head Start center must focus on three major activities: child development services (physical and mental health, nutrition, preschool education); family and community partnerships (including parent involvement and social support services); and program design and management (to improve quality and accountability). Although these components must conform to a national set of performance standards, centers are encouraged to adapt their services to local needs and resources. For example, some programs offer home-based services, and an increasing number are extending hours or collaborating with local childcare providers to accommodate children whose parents work. Thus it is somewhat misleading to think of Head Start as a single intervention because of the variety in local programming.

Head Start's early administrators never believed that a brief preschool experience could end poverty. They dismissed the then-popular "inoculation model," which held that some quick fix could make up for the past and prevent the future effects of growing up in economically disadvantaged conditions. They encouraged the development of dovetailed programs to serve children and families both before and after the preschool years. An example is the Head Start/Public School Early Childhood Transition project, which continued parent involvement and comprehensive services to preschool graduates through third grade. Studies of this and similar programs have shown that extending services into elementary school benefits children's achievement and adaptation (Ramey, Ramey, & Gaines Lanzi, 2004; Reynolds, 2003). All Head Start programs are now mandated to undertake transition-to-school activities at least until the young students are settled in their new environment.

Efforts to serve children before the preschool years also began early in Head Start's mission. Mounting evidence that preventive efforts are more effective than remedial ones, and that waiting until a child is three or four is sometimes too late, spurred political support for interventions for very young children. In 1994, congress authorized Early Head Start for families and children from birth to 3 years. Services begin prenatally and include health care, nutrition, parenting education, and family support activities. In FY 2006, there were 650 such programs serving over 60,000 infants and toddlers. Initial evaluations have shown many developmental benefits to this approach (Love et al., 2005).

Early evaluations of preschool Head Start focused almost entirely on improvements in children's intelligence. This outcome was highlighted both because the project's goals outlined in the planning document were not very specific and because psychologists in the 1960s were enthralled with the possibility that IQ scores could be raised substantially. The results of such research on Head Start and just about every other early intervention arrived at the same conclusion: IQ scores do increase during preschool (a rise that was later found to be caused by better motivation and familiarity with the testing situation), but these gains "fade out" after a few years in elementary school.

When researchers looked at broader outcomes, however, they found more lasting benefits. Quality preschool programs raise school achievement, reduce grade repetition and special education placements, and appear to reduce later juvenile delinquency (Barnett, 2004). A major study currently underway is the Family and Child Experiences Survey (FACES), which is following the progress of former Head Start students and their families as well as analyzing qualities of the preschool programs they attended. Another longitudinal investigation, the Head Start Impact Study, is also looking at key indicators of development and learning and the quality of the preschool and school environments. It is the first nationally representative study in which participants were randomly assigned to Head Start and non–Head Start groups. Results of both efforts thus far suggest that Head Start graduates are ready for kindergarten and better able to benefit from later schooling, and that the Head Start experience closes some of the achievement gap between poor and wealthier children (Administration for Children and Families, 2005, 2006).

Research on Head Start's preschool, demonstrations, and the model programs it inspired has created a large knowledge base on early childhood care and education that did not exist in its founding days. Children who are healthy, have the social and academic skills they need, have parents who are involved in their education, and have families whose basic needs are met are more competent when they arrive at school. To help them attain school readiness, programs must be comprehensive, of high quality, and last long enough to make a meaningful difference (Shonkoff & Phillips, 2000).

The success of Head Start and several smaller interventions has encouraged many states to offer preschool as part of their public education systems (Zigler, Gilliam, & Jones, 2006a). This trend has been supported by economic analyses showing that money invested in the early years of life produces significant later returns (e.g., Ludwig & Phillips, 2007; Reynolds & Temple, 2006). As the preschool movement expands, Head Start will continue its 40-plus year evolution to develop new ways of meeting the needs of at-risk young children, perhaps by focusing on ages zero to three, becoming a therapeutic preschool for children of all income levels with mental health or behavioral problems, and/or providing family support services to strengthen the home environments where children who live in poverty are reared (Zigler et al., 2006b). Each of these functions fills a void and builds on strengths that Head Start has developed over time to address the variety of needs of young children who are at risk of eventual school failure.

REFERENCES

Administration for Children and Families (2005, May). *Head Start impact study: First year findings*. Washington, DC: Author.

Administration for Children and Families. (2006, December). *Head Start FACES findings*. Washington, DC: Author.

Barnett, W. S. (2004). Does Head Start have lasting cognitive effects? The myth of fade-out. In E. Zigler & S. J. Styfco (Eds.), *Head Start debates* (pp. 221–249). Baltimore, MD: Paul H. Brookes.

Love, J. M., Kisker, E., Ross, C., Constantine, J., Boller, K., Chazan-Cohen, R., et al. (2005). The effectiveness of Early Head Start for 3-year-old children and their parents: Lessons for policy and programs. *Developmental Psychology, 41*, 885–901.

Ludwig, J., & Phillips, D. (2007). The benefits and costs of Head Start. *Social Policy Reports, 21*(3), 3–11, 16–18.

Ramey, S. L., Ramey, C. T., & Gaines Lanzi, R. (2004). The transition to school: Building on preschool foundations and preparing for lifelong learning. In E. Zigler & S. J. Styfco (Eds.), *Head Start debates* (pp. 397–413). Baltimore, MD: Paul H. Brookes.

Reynolds, A. J. (2003). The added value of continuing early intervention into the primary grades. In A. J. Reynolds, M. C. Wang, & H. J. Walberg (Eds.), *Early childhood programs for a new century* (pp. 163–196). Washington, DC: CWLA Press.

Reynolds, A. J., & Temple, J. A. (2006). Economic returns of investments in preschool education. In E. Zigler, W. S. Gilliam, & S. M. Jones, *A vision for universal preschool education* (pp. 37–68). New York: Cambridge University Press.

Shonkoff, J., & Phillips, D. (Eds.). (2000). *From neurons to neighborhoods: The science of early childhood development*. Washington, DC: National Academy Press.

Zigler, E., Gilliam, W. S., & Jones, S. M. (2006a). *A vision for universal preschool education*. New York: Cambridge University Press.

Zigler, E., Gilliam, W. S., & Jones, S. M. (with Styfco, S. J.). (2006b). A place for Head Start in a world of universal preschool. In E. Zigler, W. S. Gilliam, & S. M. Jones, *A vision for universal preschool education* (pp. 216–240). New York: Cambridge University Press.

SUGGESTED READINGS

Zigler, E., & Valentine, J. (1997). *Project Head Start: A legacy of the War on Poverty* (2nd ed.). Alexandria, VA: National Head Start Association.

Links to current Head Start practices and research may be found at http://www.acf.dhhs.gov/programs/hsb/

SALLY J. STYFCO
Yale University

See also: Early Childhood Education

HEALTH PSYCHOLOGY

Over 2,500 years have passed since philosophers Plato and Aristotle argued that the human mind or soul could not be found within the material body. Approximately 2,000 years later, René Descartes proposed his own theory about the separation of mind and body, which was rooted in these ancient philosophies and became known as Cartesian dualism. While believing that mental experiences were functions of the soul, which must be separate from the physical, Descartes also believed that the soul and body influenced one another. It has been argued (e.g., Rubin & Wessely, 2001) that perhaps the most important effect of Cartesian dualism is that it placed the body in the domain of physicians and the mind in the domain of philosophers, psychiatrists, and psychologists, leading to the development of modern medicine and psychology. This phenomenon is evident in one of the most common practitioner questions, "Is this problem organic or psychological?" Today, health psychology works within this still influential mind-body dualism to bridge the gap between psychological and physical states.

Health psychology, although a recent area of development and growth within the general field of psychology, has its roots in the philosophies of Descartes and Hippocrates, who viewed health as the balance of physical and emotional factors evidenced through four bodily fluids or humors. The relationship between the psychological and the physical began to receive attention within psychology in the early twentieth century through the growth of psychodynamic and psychophysiological frameworks, two of several early influences on the field. Psychoanalytic theories generated the term *psychosomatic* in their consideration of otherwise unexplained physical illnesses. In the psychophysiological field, researchers began to notice that emotional factors such as stress are related to changes in physiological measures.

The discipline of health psychology experienced significant growth in the mid-1970s. Possible explanations for this growth include (1) inadequate explanation of health and illness by the biomedical model; (2) a growing focus on quality of life and prevention of illness; (3) the growth of chronic illness, over infectious disease, as the major challenge of medicine, with recognition of the influence of lifestyle factors; (4) improved quality and quantity of research in the behavioral sciences; and (5) increasing costs in the healthcare system and a search for alternative approaches (Gentry, 1984). The late 1970s saw the development of several professional organizations and publications dedicated to health psychology and to the more interdisciplinary field of behavioral medicine.

The tradition of mind-body dualism caused skepticism during this growth: Was studying medical patients with medical illnesses really psychology? Just as medicine was often guilty of dismissing the mind, historically psychology was rooted in a dismissal of the body. Despite tremendous growth in the research and practice of health psychology as a discipline, this dualism remains in many administrative and governing structures, including some health insurance policies. Although differences are argued, such terms as behavioral medicine, medical psychology, and psychosomatic medicine are often used interchangeably with health psychology. The primary difference between

behavioral medicine and health psychology is that behavioral medicine is an interdisciplinary field practiced by a variety of health professionals, including physicians, nurses, and social workers, whereas health psychology is discipline-specific to psychology.

Like most areas of psychology, the specialty of health psychology consists of professionals engaged in research, clinical practice, and teaching. In the first concise definition of health psychology, Matarazzo (1980) described it as "the aggregate of the specific educational, scientific, and professional contributions of the discipline of psychology to the promotion and maintenance of health, the prevention and treatment of illness, and the identification of etiologic and diagnostic correlates of health, illness, and related dysfunction" (1980, p. 815).

Developing out of this definition, clinical health psychology merged the focus from clinical psychology on the assessment and treatment of individuals in distress with the academic field of health psychology. Millon (1982) subsequently defined the practice of health psychology as "the application of knowledge and methods from all substantive fields of psychology to the promotion and maintenance of mental and physical health of the individual and to the prevention, assessment, and treatment of all forms of mental and physical disorder in which psychological influences either contribute to or can be used to relieve an individual's distress or dysfunction" (p. 9). Consistent with this merged focus, health psychology has a strong research foundation, both basic and applied. Its theories and interventions are empirically based, and its clinical applications are developed from experimentation and research findings.

Health psychology researchers and practitioners formulate their questions and interventions within a variety of theoretical orientations, including psychodynamic, existential, cognitive social learning theory, behavioral, cognitive-behavioral, and systems approaches (Frantsve, Sledge, Kerns, & Desan, 2008). The biopsychosocial model (Engel, 1977) is commonly used as the most inclusive approach to health through its focus on the complex interactions among biological (e.g., injury, disease), psychological (e.g., depression, anxiety, values, expectations), and social (e.g., family, community, work) factors. The model encourages comprehensive assessment and treatment of health issues, which includes the integration of health psychology with traditional medical care. As a result, health psychologists have the ability to work in a broad variety of health care settings with other health care professionals. This focus on integration and synthesis of factors stands in contrast to the simplistic division of dualism.

Health psychology addresses a broad range of issues through research and practice. These issues include psychological conditions secondary to disease, injury, or disability (e.g., post–myocardial infarction depression and fear of engaging in sexual activities; alteration of body image secondary to burns, amputation, or menopause) and somatic presentations of psychological dysfunction (e.g., chest pain in panic attack, somatization disorders). In addition, psychophysiological disorders (e.g., tension and migraine headache, spastic colitis) and physical symptoms responsive to behavioral interventions (e.g., vasospasms, enuresis, fecal incontinence, anticipatory nausea) are appropriate areas for health psychology.

Health psychologists may also identify psychological presentations of organic disease (e.g., hypothyroidism presenting as depression, steroid-induced psychosis) resulting in appropriate medical treatment. Attending to somatic complications associated with behavioral factors (e.g., mismanagement of diabetes, failure to comply with hypertensive medication) and psychological and behavioral aspects of stressful medical procedures (e.g., pain, lumbar puncture, debriding of wounds, cardiac catheterization) can improve patients' experiences in the health care environment. Health psychologists can help prevent future health problems by addressing behavioral risk factors for disease, injury, and disability (e.g., smoking, excess weight, substance abuse, risk-taking). Problems of health care providers and health care systems (e.g., physician-patient relationships, staff delivery systems) are also areas in which health psychology can intervene (APA Div. 38, 2004).

Health psychologists may work with a variety of specific patient populations. These populations include patients with acute or chronic pain (e.g., burn, low back pain headache, cancer pain), chronic disease (e.g., cardiovascular, pulmonary, gastrointestinal, endocrine, musculoskeletal, hematologic, autoimmune, neurologic, rheumatologic, AIDS), or psychophysiological conditions (e.g., migraine headache). Additionally, common patient populations may be those with traumatic injuries or terminal illness. Other groups might include patients undergoing particular procedures, such as pre- or postsurgical patients or dental patients. Health psychologists may target behavior with patients with risky behavior patterns (e.g., smoking, sedentary lifestyle) or patients with difficulty adhering to treatment recommendations. Finally, physicians, nurses, dentists, and other health-care providers may be the target population for study or intervention (APA Div. 38, 2004).

Potential competence areas for practicing clinical health psychologists reflect the numerous interventions that may be used with these patient populations. Specific competencies will depend on the patient population most frequently encountered by the psychologist. Interventions may be delivered through individual, family, or group psychotherapy or education. Most often, interventions will be short-term, particularly if provided within a health care environment. Clinical health psychologists should be familiar with assessment of specific patient populations (e.g. patients with pain or spinal cord injuries) and neuropsychological assessment. In addition, competence should be developed in major treatment programs (e.g.,

eating disorders, stroke rehabilitation, or pain programs). These treatment programs may require skills in relaxation therapies, behavioral modification techniques, and perhaps biofeedback or hypnosis. Compliance motivation is a necessary area of competence across many patient populations and clinical settings. Clinical health psychologists also use many health promotion and public education skills. Lastly, in working with other health professionals consultation and liaison skills are important (Belar & Deardorff, 2004).

Following are brief examples of research in four health areas commonly addressed by health psychology: pain, insomnia, HIV/AIDS, and smoking and tobacco use. These examples demonstrate the relationship between psychological and physical states and the effectiveness of health psychology interventions to improve health and related issues such as quality of life or coping.

With respect to pain, a meta-analysis of 25 research trials by Morley, Eccleston, and Williams (1999) demonstrated the effectiveness of cognitive-behavioral therapy (CBT; including behavior therapy and biofeedback) in addressing the major impacts of pain. Treatment with CBT interventions resulted in significant improvements in measures of pain experience, mood and affect, cognitive coping and appraisal (increase in positive coping and decrease in negative coping), pain behavior and activity level, and social role functioning compared to patients not receiving a treatment intervention (e.g., a waiting list control group). Compared to patients receiving an alternative intervention (e.g., alternative treatment control group), CBT interventions produced significantly greater changes in pain experience, cognitive coping and appraisal (increase in positive coping), and behavioral expression of pain.

Concerning research on insomnia, Morin and colleagues (2006) reviewed 37 studies published between 1998 and 2004 and found substantial support for the impact of psychological and behavioral therapies on improvement in sleep parameters related to insomnia, both as a primary condition and as a condition secondary to medical or psychiatric disorders. Five techniques were found to meet criteria for empirically supported treatment for insomnia: stimulus control therapy (e.g., getting up at the same time each day, avoiding daytime napping), relaxation, paradoxical intention (e.g., attempting to stay awake rather than sleeping), sleep restriction, and cognitive-behavioral therapy (e.g., addressing faulty beliefs about sleep). Improvements gained through these interventions were maintained over time.

To address the depression and other psychiatric symptoms that often co-occur with HIV/AIDS, Fulk and colleagues (2004) reviewed research on pharmacological, psychological, and complementary or alternative treatments for these symptoms. Both interpersonal therapy (IPT) and CBT were found to be effective for managing the common experiences of depression, anxiety, or fear.

Group and family therapy were also found to be effective interventions. In addition, health psychologists can assist with patient education and motivation about other interventions found to be effective for reducing psychiatric comorbidities, including medication compliance, exercise, and stress management.

Lastly with regard to smoking and tobacco use, the U.S. Public Health Service clinical practice guidelines for treating tobacco use and dependence (2008) were developed through review of more than 8,700 research articles in this area. The guidelines identify several ways in which health psychologists can develop and guide patient efforts to treat tobacco dependence, which is a major cause of illness and mortality. Research demonstrates that a combination of behavioral counseling and medication is more successful than either intervention alone. Brief behavioral interventions are effective, particularly when repeated over time, and the likelihood of success increases with treatment intensity. In particular, interventions aimed at problem solving, skills development, and social support are most effective. Motivational counseling is effective for increasing future attempts to quit in patients who are not yet ready for active treatment. In addition to directly providing interventional services, health psychologists can educate and train other health professionals to provide these empirically based interventions to patients.

Health psychology is a diverse field that has grown substantially during its short history. Due to the increasing depth and breadth of areas within health psychology, increasing subspecialization is occurring within the field. Health psychologists, whether in research or practice, may develop specialization in particular patient groups (e.g., pediatrics, geriatrics, African American patients) or health issues (e.g., diabetes, surgical assessments, obesity). In addition, health psychologists exist across of spectrum of integration with medical practice, from separate private practices specializing in treatment of health issues (minimal integration) to fully collaborative work within a primary care practice (full integration). Although health psychology continues to challenge the historical influence of dualism, the complex relationships among behavior, psychological factors, and physical health are better understood and accepted. This understanding and treatment of the whole patient serves the aims of the discipline, the professional, and the patient to improve health and well-being.

REFERENCES

American Psychological Association (APA) Division 38 (Health Psychology). (2004). *Commission for recognition of specialties and proficiencies in professional psychology (CRSPPP)*. Ashland, VA: Author.

Belar, C. D., & Deardorff, W. W. (2004). *Clinical health psychology in medical settings: A practitioner's guidebook.* Washington DC: American Psychological Association.

Engel, G. L. (1977). The need for a new medical model: A challenge for biomedicine. *Science, 196,* 129–136.

Frantsve, L. M. E., Sledge, W. H., Kerns, R. D., & Desan, P. (2008). Behavioral medicine. In A. Tasman, J. Kay, Lieberman, J. A., First, M. B., & M. Maj (Eds.), *Psychiatry* (3rd ed., pp. 2027–2046). West Sussex, UK: John Wiley & Sons.

Fulk, L. J., Kane, B. E., Phillips, K. D., Bopp, C. M., & Hand, G. A. (2004). Depression in HIV-infected patients: Allopathic, complementary, and alternative treatments. *Journal of Psychosomatic Medicine, 57*(4), 339–351.

Gentry, W. D. (Ed.). (1984). *Handbook of behavioral medicine.* New York: Guilford Press.

Matarazzo, J. D. (1980). Behavioral health and behavioral medicine. *American Psychologist, 35,* 807–817.

Millon, T. (1982). On the nature of clinical health psychology. In T. Millon, C. J. Green, & R. B. Meagher (Eds.), *Handbook of clinical health psychology* (pp. 1–27), New York: Plenum.

Morin, C. M., Bootzin, R. R., Buysse, D. J., Edinger, J. D., Espie, C. A., & Lichstein, K. L. (2006). Psychological and behavioral treatment of insomnia: Update of the recent evidence (1998–2004). *Sleep, 29*(11), 1398–1414.

Morley, S., Eccleston, C., & Williams, A. (1999). Systematic review and meta-analysis of randomized controlled trials of cognitive-behaviour therapy for chronic pain in adults, excluding headache. *Pain, 80,* 1–13.

PHS Guideline Update Panel, Liaisons, and Staff. (2008). Treating tobacco use and dependence: 2008 update U.S. public health service clinical practice guideline executive summary. *Respiratory Care, 53*(9), 1217–1222.

Rubin, G. J., & Wessely, S. (2001). Dealing with dualism. *Advances in Mind Body Medicine, 17*(4), 256–259.

SUGGESTED READINGS

Baum, A., Revenson, T. A., & Singer, J. E. (Eds.). (2001). *Handbook of health psychology.* Mahwah, NJ: Lawrence Erlbaum.

Stone, G. C., Weiss, S. M., Matarazzo, J. D., Miller, N. E., Rodin, J., Belar, C. D., et al. (Eds.). (1987). *Health psychology: A discipline and a profession.* Chicago: University of Chicago Press.

STEPHANIE C. WALLIO
VA Connecticut Healthcare System and University of Kansas

See also: **Occupational Health Psychology**

HEARING LOSS (See Deafness and Hearing Loss)

HEBB, DONALD OLDING (1904–1985)

Donald Olding Hebb was a Canadian born to two physicians in Chester, Nova Scotia, in 1904. He excelled in schoolwork until his reactions to authority led to difficulties in his later teenage years. He completed his undergraduate studies at Dalhousie University receiving a BA degree in 1925. He traveled to the beat of his own drum, engaging in teaching, farming, and common labor while he continued in self-study reading works within the developing field of psychology. In 1928, he enrolled in psychology at McGill university, where he received his MA in 1932. His studies were combined with part-time teaching, and he suffered from health problems and the death of his wife during his graduate studies. After these struggles, he left Canada in 1934 and began serious graduate study with Karl Lashley at the University of Chicago. Lashley left Chicago for Harvard in 1935, and Hebb moved with him. In 1936, at age 32, he received his PhD based on his research on the brains of rats.

After a brief stint teaching first at Radcliffe, Hebb taught for three years at Queens University from 1939 to 1942. In 1942, he moved to Orange Park, Florida, to the Yerkes Laboratories and worked again with Lashley, who had become its director. While at Yerkes he wrote his influential book, *The Organization of Behavior*. In 1947, he moved back to Montreal and to McGill, to study human brain functioning with Wilder Penfield, and he remained until he retired in 1974. He moved back to his undergraduate university, Dalhousie in 1980 and was an Emeritus Professor there until his death in 1985.

Hebb received numerous honors for his enormous contributions to neurophysiology and what is now called neuroscience. He was president of the American Psychological Association in 1960 and received the association's Distinguished Scientific Contribution Award in 1961. The Canadian Psychological Association gives the D. O. Hebb award to those who have made distinguished scientific contributions.

During his time with Penfield and at Queens, Hebb met the problem that determined the course of his later work. Some cases of large loss of brain tissue showed little effect on intelligence as measured by IQ tests or as seen in everyday life. How could one explain a high IQ with a damaged brain? The theory of cell assemblies was proposed as an answer, and this turned out to be relevant to other problems. Experiments confirmed the importance of early experience in the growth of mind and intelligence, and at maturity, the continued need of exposure to a normal sensory environment for mental health.

Perhaps Hebb's most important contribution was his theory of the relationship of neuronal firing and how this affected learning. Hebb's notion of grouping of cells into a processing unit, cell assemblies, and how cell assemblies affect incoming stimuli and learning, was the essence of his theory. His work was extended by his successful doctoral students including Milner, Melzack, and many others.

SUGGESTED READINGS

Hebb, D. O. (1949). *The organization of behavior*. New York: John Wiley & Sons.

Hebb, D. O. (1980). *Essays on mind*. Hillsdale, NJ: Lawrence Erlbaum.

STAFF

HELPLESSNESS (See Learned Helplessness)

HEREDITY (See Nature-Nurture Controversy)

HETEROSEXUALITY

Heterosexualiy is characterized by sexual and/or romantic attraction to the opposite sex and is the most prevalent sexual orientation among humans. The term *heterosexual* can be used to describe an individual's sexual orientation, sexual history, or self-identification. The term *heterosexuality* has been commonly used only since the middle of the nineteenth century, and is usually contrasted with the terms *homosexualilty* and *bisexuality*. Contemporary scientific research indicates that the majority of individuals adhere to a more fluid scale of sexual orientation, exhibiting a range of both same-sex and opposite-sex sexual behaviors or fantasies (Kinsey, Pomeroy, & Martin, 1948; Kinsey, Pomeroy, Martin, & Gebhard, 1953). However, social and cultural pressures have influenced people to self-identify in terms of categories rather than along a spectrum of sexuality.

Sexual Behavior

Human sexual behavior is generally dictated by social norms that are culture-specific and vary widely. Variations in ethnicity, acculturation, religiosity, and socioeconomic status account for great diversity in sexuality. Human sexual behaviors cluster primarily around kissing and touching, masturbation, oral-genital stimulation, and intercourse (vaginal, anal). Sexual behaviors that fall outside this range include noncoercive paraphilias such as fetishism, transvestism, sexual sadism, sexual masochism, and coercive paraphilias such as exhibitionism, voyeurism, frotteurism, necrophilia, and zoophilia. The frequency of sexual intercourse varies widely across individuals and generally declines with age. The average frequency of sexual intercourse for married couples in the United States is 2 to 3 times per week.

Sexual Response

Sexual response refers to the set of physiological and psychological changes that lead up to and follow orgasm.

Aging may affect any stage of sexual response in both men and women and this depends largely on psychological, pharmacological, and illness-related factors.

Sexual Desire

Sexual desire refers to the broad interest in sexual objects or activities and is generally inferred from self-reported frequency of sexual thoughts, fantasies, dreams, wishes, and interest in initiating and/or engaging in sexual activities. Several factors such as attitudes, opportunity/partner availability, relationship issues, mood, and health may make it difficult to define this construct. Of the many hormones that are involved with sexual desire, androgens play a pivotal role. In men, the vast majority of androgens (e.g., testosterone) are produced by the testes, and in women androgens are produced by the ovaries and adrenal glands but in quantities much lower than in men (about 20 to 40 times less) (Rako, 1969). In both men and women, decreased testosterone levels because of, for example, orchidectomy (removal of testes) or oophorectomy (removal of ovaries) have been linked to impaired sexual desire. Women may also display fluctuations in sexual desire that correlate with their menstrual cycle. Many women experience heightened sexual desire in the several days immediately before ovulation, which is attributed to the complex interaction of sex hormones.

Sexual Arousal

Closely connected with desire, sexual arousal consists of both subjective (e.g., sexual pleasure and excitement) and physiological (e.g., genital vasocongestion) changes. The primary markers of sexual arousal in men and women are increased myotonia (muscle tension), heart rate, and blood pressure. Sexual arousal is also distinguished by vasocongestion (blood engorgement), which leads to erection of the penis and engorgement of the clitoris, labia, and vagina (with lubrication).

Physiological sexual arousal in men involves signal input from the central (brain and spinal cord) and peripheral nervous systems, as well as complex interplay between neurotransmitters, vasoactive agents, and endocrine factors. Within the penis is a central artery (corpus cavernosum) and veins that exit and drain blood from the erectile bodies. The muscles that line the sinusoidal spaces and the central artery are contracted during the nonerect state. Erection begins with muscle relaxation that is controlled by autonomic nerves and by the release of nitric oxide (NO) into the corpus cavernosum. Cyclic guanosine monophosphate (cGMP) mediates the effects of NO which causes smooth muscle relaxation, reduces vascular resistance, and allows the erectile bodies to fill with blood (Burnett, Lowenstein, Bredt, Chang, & Snyder, 1992). Once the erectile bodies become engorged, the veins are compressed under the penis's tough fibroelastic covering and blood is trapped in the penis, maintaining its rigidity. Detumescence (loss of erection) usually occurs with the release of catecholamines during orgasm and ejaculation and is initiated by the sympathetic division of the autonomic nervous system.

Physiological sexual arousal in women begins with vasocongestion of the vagina, vulva, clitoris, uterus, and possibly the urethra and can occur within only a few seconds of sexual stimulation. Vaginal lubrication occurs when the blood vessels of the vaginal wall become engorged with blood, causing fluid to pass between the cells of the vaginal epithelium and emerge on the vaginal wall as sweat-like droplets. These droplets can quickly coalesce to form a lubricating film that facilitates vaginal penetration. Estrogens, produced predominantly by the ovaries, help maintain the elasticity of the vaginal lining and assist in vaginal lubrication. A growing body of literature suggests a curvilinear relationship between sympathetic nervous system (SNS) activity and sexual arousal in women, such that moderate levels facilitate, high levels inhibit, and low levels of SNS activation have less of a facilitatory effect on sexual arousal responses (Meston & Gorzalka, 1996).

Orgasm

In both men and women orgasm consists of a peaking of sexual pleasure that is characterized by intense physical pleasure, controlled by the autonomic nervous system. Orgasm is accompanied by quick cycles of rhythmic contractions of the sexual organs and anus, cardiovascular and respiratory changes, and a general euphoric sensation and release of sexual tension. In men, orgasm generally occurs in two stages, emission which refers to rhythmic muscular contractions that force semen into the ejaculatory ducts, and expulsion which is the release of semen through the penis's urethral opening (ejaculation). A female orgasm lasts longer than that of a male and may be induced from stimulation of the vagina (via stimulation of the Gräfenberg spot, accessible through the anterior wall of the vagina), clitoris, or breasts. Additionally, both men and women may experience orgasm from anal stimulation, and/or from psychological arousal alone (sexual fantasy). Contrary to Freud's assertion that clitoral and vaginal orgasms represent qualitatively distinct phenomena, Masters and Johnson (1966) found no physiological differences in orgasm produced by vaginal versus clitoral stimulation. Other researchers note that intensity of orgasm and emotional satisfaction can differ dependent upon the type of stimulation.

Resolution

During the final phase of the sexual response cycle, the body slowly returns to its unaroused state. This phase is marked by a general sense of well-being, enhanced intimacy, and often fatigue. In men, the refractory period is the recovery phase after orgasm during which it is physiologically impossible to achieve additional orgasms. Men may find it difficult or impossible to have an erection, and the penis may be hypersensitive to further stimulation, resulting in discomfort. The length of the refractory period is highly variable between individuals and across species and depends upon a number of factors including age, novelty of the sexual situation, and frequency of sexual intercourse. Some women do not experience a refractory period after orgasm and oftentimes are capable of a rapid return to the orgasm phase with further sexual stimulation, resulting in multiple orgasms.

Sexual Dysfunction

There are many factors that may adversely affect sexual functioning. Diseases of the neurological, vascular, and endocrine systems (e.g., diabetes, cancer, multiple sclerosis) can impair virtually any stage of the sexual response. Medications used to treat depression, high blood pressure, psychiatric disorders, and cancer, as well as numerous recreational drugs (e.g., barbiturates, narcotics, alcohol, tobacco) can interfere with sexual desire, arousal, and orgasm. Psychological factors contributing to impaired sexual function most commonly include anxiety, depression, relationship concerns, negative attitudes about sex, religious inhibition, body image concerns, sexual guilt, and prior sexual abuse, assault, or trauma. Additionally, there may be lifestyle factors that interfere with normal sexual responses such as being very underweight or severely obese.

A deficiency or absence of sexual fantasies or desire for sexual activity (hypoactive sexual desire), is the most common sexual complaint in women, and is also the most common problem for couples who seek sex therapy. In the United States, approximately 32% of women and 15% of men ages 18-59 years report a lack of sexual interest or desire at some point in their lives (Laumann, Paik, & Rosen, 1999). Sexual aversion disorder is a more severe interruption of sexual desire. These individuals actively avoid sexual activity and express fear, anxiety (and often panic attacks), and/or disgust when approached by a sexual partner.

Difficulties with respect to the arousal stage of sexual response include female sexual arousal disorder—inhibition of the vasocongestive/lubrication response—and male erectile disorder. These conditions affect 21% of women and 10% of men at some point during their lifetime (Laumann et al., 1999). Women of all ages may experience difficulty with lubrication, although it tends to be more of a problem associated with hormonal changes caused by pregnancy, breast-feeding, and menopause. Erectile problems may be of organic (e.g., circulatory problems, neurological disorders, hormone imbalances) or psychogenic (e.g., performance anxiety) origin. The ability to have erections

during REM sleep suggests the problem is psychological. Approximately 7% of men ages 18–29 years, and 18% of men ages 50–59 years experience erectile difficulties (Laumann et al., 1999). Dyspareunia, or pain during intercourse, occurs most commonly in women, and generally involves a combination of physical and psychological factors. Dyspareunia has a lifetime prevalence of 3% and 15% for men and women, respectively (American Psychiatric Association, 2000). Vaginismus is characterized by involuntary contractions of the muscles in the outer third of the vagina that interferes with vaginal penetration.

Anorgasmia—the delay in, or absence of, orgasm following sexual arousal—is the second most frequently reported sexual problem in women. Results from large scale surveys indicate that approximately 26% of women ages 18–59 years reported difficulties in achieving orgasm (Laumann et al., 1999). In men, delayed or inhibited orgasm following adequate sexual stimulation is a rare condition, affecting approximately 8% of the male population (Laumann et al., 1999). Premature ejaculation is the most commonly reported sexual disorder in men, affecting approximately 31% of men ages 18–59 years (Laumann et al., 1999). It is defined as the onset of ejaculation and orgasm early on in the sexual scenario and before the person wishes it. Unlike erectile dysfunction, premature ejaculation affects more younger men than older men (Corona et al., 2004).

REFERENCES

American Psychiatric Association. (2000). *Diagnostic and statistical manual of mental disorders* (4th ed., text rev.). Washington, DC: Author.

Burnett, A. L., Lowenstein, C. J., Bredt, D. S., Chang, T. S., & Snyder, S. H. (1992). Nitric oxide: a physiologic mediator of penile erection. *Science, 257*(5068), 401–403.

Corona, G., Petrone, L., Mannucci, E., Jannini, E. A., Mansani, R., Magini, A., et al. (2004). Psycho-biological correlates of rapid ejaculation in patients attending an andrologic unit for sexual dysfunctions. *European Urology, 46,* 615–622.

Kinsey, A. C., Pomeroy, W. B., & Martin, C. E. (1948). *Sexual behavior in the human male.* Philadelphia: W. B. Saunders.

Kinsey, A. C., Pomeroy, W. B., Martin, C. E., & Gebhard, P. H. (1953). *Sexual behavior in the human female.* Philadelphia: W. B. Saunders.

Laumann, E. O., Paik, A., & Rosen, R. C. (1999). Sexual dysfunction in the United States: Prevalence and predictors. *Journal of the American Medical Association, 281,* 537–544.

Masters, W., & Johnson, V. (1966). *Human sexual response.* Boston: Little, Brown.

Meston, C. M., & Gorzalka, B. B. (1996). The effects of immediate, delayed, and residual sympathetic activation on sexual arousal in women. *Behaviour Research and Therapy, 34,* 143–148.

Rako, S. (1969). *The hormone of desire.* New York: Harmony Books.

SUGGESTED READING

Laumann, E. O., Gagnon, J. H., Michael, R. T., & Michaels, S. (1994). *The social organization of sexuality: Sexual practices in the United States.* Chicago: University of Chicago Press.

CINDY M. MESTON
CHRISTOPHER B. HARTE
University of Texas at Austin

See also: Homosexuality; Sexual Desire; Sexual Orientation, Roots of

HIGH-RISK PARTICIPANT STUDIES

In order to improve the efficiency of psychological research concerning etiology, studies may oversample participants who are identified as having high risk for the development of disorders or for the occurrence of adverse outcomes. High-risk participant studies have evolved in the context of "diathesis-stress" developmental models of psychopathology that emphasize the impact of exogenous factors on the vulnerable individual. Such studies are extremely helpful in instances where there is a low population base rate for the presence of a disorder or negative outcome, since few studies conducted by other methods will be able to recruit the number of participants needed to ensure sufficient statistical power. Information obtained from high-risk participant studies may be used to identify vulnerability processes central to the etiology of disorders and to develop preventive intervention programs.

Mednick and McNeil (1968) first offered the use of the "high-risk-group method" as a solution to difficulties encountered in trying to develop etiological hypotheses from two common research paradigms that were used to explore the etiology of schizophrenia. The first research paradigm involved comparison of individuals with or without the disorder. Findings from such studies were difficult to interpret because differences between these groups might just as reasonably be attributed to "epiphenomenal correlates" of the disorder which, according to the authors, might include the effects of being unmarried, lonely, and/or educationally or socially disadvantaged, as well as the long-term effects of institutionalization. Family research carried out in this way might uncover differences that just as reasonably might be attributed as reactions by family members to the presence of the disorder.

The second research paradigm involved retrospective review of childhood records; it had the primary drawback of oversampling a less mobile group of individuals, which was problematic given the relatively high rate of schizophrenia among migrants and the high migrant rate among those with psychiatric disorders. Such studies also resulted in

unsystematic and less-reliable data collection. Although the authors were writing about schizophrenia, they point out in a footnote that the applicability of these criticisms to other mental disorders and correlative research in individual differences and personality development could be envisioned. These authors sought to address these difficulties through a longitudinal study of young children at high risk for schizophrenia (Mednick, 1966; Mednick & Shulsinger, 1965). Children selected as being at "high risk" for schizophrenia had mothers with chronic and severe schizophrenia.

In addition to addressing problems of cross-sectional and retrospective methods in drawing inferences regarding etiology, Mednick and McNeil (1968) indicated that the "high-risk group method" offers other advantages. First, this method systematically obtains unbiased prospective data because neither the child nor the family knows whether the child will develop the disorder. Second, the high-risk participants who either do not develop the disorder or develop other problems are the ideal control group with which to contrast high-risk subjects who do develop schizophrenia. Disadvantages cited by these authors include sample attrition, loss of key personnel, and the risk that long-term longitudinal study may result in dated and trivial data. Because measures and theories that are viewed as central to etiology may become obsolete, it is important that the initial phases of the longitudinal investigation avoid strong theoretical bias. They also need to use procedures that include eclectic measures and recording of basic raw observations and verbalizations wherever possible so that they may be recoded by new methods at a time in the future.

Mednick and McNeil cautioned that high-risk group method studies were difficult to replicate, but they built in a form of replication in the successive analysis of waves of individuals who develop the disorder. They also introduced a cross-sectional comparison of normal controls. They cautioned that, even with this method, it was extremely difficult to identify primary causal agents without experimental manipulation because there is no certainty that correction of any of deviances found in those initially succumbing to the disorder would have been successful in preventing the disorder from occurring. They proposed that the major contribution of the method would be to define premorbid experiential or personal differences that might point to highly specific techniques of remedial preventive intervention.

Since the initial application of the high risk group method to schizophrenia, variations of this design have been employed to identify characteristics of the high-risk group of children of schizophrenic parents (Gooding & Iacano, 1995). However, Bellak and Hersen (1984) point out that, because most adults with schizophrenia do not have a schizophrenic parent, there may be relevant risk factors that have not yet been identified. This illustrates a limitation of the method of identifying risk status through parental psychopathology, because the sample of children of parents who have a particular disorder and progress to development of the disorder may not be representative of all individuals who develop the disorder. Identified risk factors will obviously vary depending upon the disorder or adverse consequence that is the focus of attention.

The high-risk participant method has been conceptually and methodologically refined and applied to a wider range of disorders. Conceptual refinements have primarily centered around attempts to establish relationships among the related constructs of vulnerability, risk, and resilience (Ingram & Price, 2001; Luthar & Zigler, 1991; Rutter, 1987). Ingram and Price pointed out that "risk" and "vulnerability" are empirically related but should be viewed as being conceptually separate. "Risk" refers to the broad array of factors that are statistically associated with an increased probability of the occurrence of a disorder. "Vulnerability" factors are a subset of risk factors that refer to trait-like, endogenous, and causal features. These may be present in individuals who have few signs of the disorder, and they remain stable over the more variable course and statelike appearance of the disorder.

Although vulnerability is viewed as residing within the individual, vulnerability features may be either genetically or environmentally based, vary in their conceptual specificity, are not readily observable, and are difficult to assess. Price and Liento (2001) advise that vulnerability factors need not always be viewed as permanent, particularly when the causal features are psychological in nature. Vulnerability is viewed as existing along a continuum, and the concept of "resilience" has been introduced in various forms (e.g., "protective factors," "competence," and "invulnerability") to describe individuals who have lower probability of experiencing psychopathology in the presence of equivalent levels of stress.

In addition to the inclusion of protective factors or mechanisms of resiliency, methodological refinements to the original high-risk group method have included the introduction of the use of a psychiatric control groups, cautions about generalizations due to "sleeper effects," more sophisticated suggestions regarding how to select high-risk individuals and appropriately balanced control groups (Moffit, Mednick, & Cudeck, 1983), and the use of "experimental-manipulative high-risk research." Because early high-risk studies often had no psychiatric control groups, it was not possible to determine whether differences between offspring of schizophrenic mothers and offspring of nonclinical controls reflected vulnerabilities that were specific to schizophrenia as opposed to more generalized effects of being raised by a disturbed parent. Bellak and Hersen (1984), therefore, recommend the use of psychiatric controls. Moffit and colleagues (1983) also discussed the problem of sleeper effects, which occur when the impact of antecedent factors do not manifest until a later period of life. In order to avoid prematurely dismissing factors that may be contributory, they advise that conclusions regarding the influence of childhood factors in a longitudinal high-risk study should be restricted to their age-specific period.

High-risk studies have evolved to include the presence of experimental-manipulative high-risk research (Moffit, Mednick, et al., 1983). Such programs are part of a shift from single vulnerability factors to a more comprehensive analysis of the interaction between multiple vulnerability and protective factors, environmental stressors, and developmental change. In such programs, early screening techniques are conducted as part of prospective, longitudinal, primary prevention programs. Distinguishing features identified by earlier high-risk studies are used in the process of selecting participants and intervention techniques suggested by the results of the earlier risk project are implemented. A follow-up comparison of intervention groups may then suggest etiological hypotheses. High-risk participant studies or experimental-manipulative high-risk studies have been used increasingly to study participants who are at risk for a variety of disorders (e.g., Conduct Problems Prevention Research Group, 2004; Ingram & Price, 2001; Tarter, 1983).

Issues arise that are not as frequently encountered when conducting other types of clinical research. For instance, one project developed by the National Institute of Mental Health (Fischer Pearson, Kim, & Reynolds, 2002; Pearson, Stanley, King, & Fisher, 2001) outlined ethical responsibilities with individuals at high risk for suicide as including: the need to anticipate and address participants' refusal of treatment; development of plans for referring those in crisis; development of procedures for meaningful consent; and careful use of contrast groups, including "treatment as usual" control groups, which ameliorate comorbid conditions. This work also points out the need to expand the training of those conducting research in the approaches and steps to take when a research participant reports suicidal ideation or planning.

REFERENCES

Bellak, A. S., & Hersen, M. (1984). *Research methods in clinical psychology.* New York: Pergamon Press.

Conduct Problems Prevention Research Group. (2004). The effect of the fast-track program on serious problem outcomes at the end of elementary school. *Journal of Clincial Child and Adolescent Psychology, 33,* 650–651.

Fisher, C., Pearson, J. L., Kim, S., & Reynolds, C. F. (2002). Ethical issues in including suicidal individuals in clinical research. *Ethics & Human Research, 24*(4), 9–14.

Gooding, D. C., & Iacano, W. G. (1995). Schizophrenia through the lens of a developmental psychopathology perspective. In D. Cicchetti & D. J. Cohen (Eds.), *Developmental psychopathology: Theory and methods* (Vol. 2, pp. 535–580). New York: John Wiley & Sons.

Ingram, R. E., & Price, J. M. (2001). *Vulnerability to psychopathology: Risk across the lifespan.* New York: Guilford Press.

Luthar, S. S., & Zigler, E. (1991). Vulnerability and competence: A review of research on resilience in childhood. *American Journal of Orthopsychiatry, 61*, 6–22.

Mednick, S. A. (1966). A longitudinal study of children with a high risk for schizophrenia. *Mental Hygiene, 50*, 522–535.

Mednick, S. A., & McNeil, T. F. (1968). Current methodology in research on the etiology of schizophrenia: Serious difficulties which suggest the use of the high-risk group method. *Psychological Bulletin, 70*(6), 681–693.

Mednick, S. A., & Shulsinger, F. (1965). Longitudinal study of children with a high risk for schizophrenia: A preliminary report. In S. Vandenberg (Ed.), *Methods and goals in human behavior genetics.* New York: Academic Press.

Moffit, T. E., Mednick, S. A., & Cudeck, R. (1983). Methodology of high risk research: Longitudinal approaches. In R.E. Tarter (Ed.), *The child at psychiatric risk* (pp. 54–79). New York: Oxford University Press.

Pearson, J. L., Stanley, B., King, C. A., & Fisher, C. B. (2001). Intervention research with persons at high risk for suicidality: Safety and ethical considerations. *Journal of Clinical Psychiatry, 62*, 17–26.

Price, J. M., & Lento, J. (2001). The nature of child and adolescent vulnerability. In R. E. Ingram & J. M. Price (Eds.), *Vulnerability to psychopathology: Risk across the lifespan.* New York: Guilford Press.

Rutter, M. E. (1987). Psychosocial resilience and protective mechanisms. *American Journal of Orthopsychiatry, 57*, 316–331.

Tarter, R. E. (1983). *The child at psychiatric risk.* New York: Oxford University Press.

JOHN M. STOKES
Pace University

See also: **Experimental Controls; Twin Studies**

HILGARD, ERNEST R. (1905–2001)

Ernest R. Hilgard graduated with honors in chemical engineering at the University of Illinois (1924), and received his PhD (1930) in experimental psychology from Yale upon completing a dissertation on conditioned human eyelid responses under Raymond Dodge. He became a teaching assistant and remained at Yale as an instructor from 1929 to 1933, when he accepted an invitation from Lewis M. Terman to join the faculty at Stanford University. Except for a period during World War II, he spent the rest of his career at Stanford, becoming an Emeritus Professor in 1969. He held a joint appointment in the School of Humanities and the School of Education, served as Executive Head of the Department of Psychology from 1942 to 1950, and was Dean of the Graduate Division from 1951 to 1955.

His early research interests were primarily in psychology of learning and motivation; however, during the years of World War II he turned to social psychology in various agencies as a civilian in Washington. From 1957 to 1979, he headed a laboratory of hypnosis research within the Department of Psychology. He continued publishing and revising his more general books as well as publishing in the field of hypnosis. Later he turned to historical writing; his primary contribution to the field is *American Psychology: A Historical Survey.*

Hilgard was elected President of the American Psychological Association (1949) and was a member of the National Academy of Sciences, the National Academy of Education, the American Academy of Arts and Sciences, and the American Philosophical Society. He received the Gold Medal Award from the American Psychological Foundation in recognition of his lifetime contributions to psychology.

SUGGESTED READINGS

Hilgard, E. R. (1987). *Psychology in America: A historical survey.* San Diego: Harcourt Brace Jovanovich.

Hilgard, E. R., & Atkinson, R. L. (1990). *Introduction to psychology.* New York: Harcourt, Brace, & World.

Hilgard, E. R., & Bower, G. H. (1981). *Theories of learning* (3rd ed.). Englewood Cliffs, NJ: Prentice-Hall.

Hilgard, E. R., Hilgard, J. R., & Barber, J. (1994). *Hypnosis in the relief of pain.* New York: Brunner/Mazel.

STAFF

HIPPOCAMPUS

Ever since Scoville and Milner's 1957 report of the patient H.M., who suffered a profound amnesia following bilateral surgical resection of the medial temporal lobe, it has been clear that the hippocampal region of the brain plays a critical role in memory. There is now considerable knowledge about the anatomical pathways of the hippocampus, about the functional role of the hippocampal region, and about the information encoded by firing patterns of hippocampal neurons.

Anatomy of the Hippocampus

From the perspective of its role in cognition and memory, the hippocampal system is last in a long succession of stages of cortical representation. Neocortical areas that provide information to the hippocampal system include only the highest stages of each neocortical sensory system, plus multimodal and limbic cortical areas and the olfactory cortex. These inputs arrive in three main cortical subdivisions of the parahippocampal region, composed of the perirhinal, parahippocampal, and entorhinal cortices. Superficial layers of parts of the parahippocampal region then project onto the hippocampus itself at each of its main subdivisions. The flow of information into the hippocampus is somewhat segregated, such that information about specific objects originating in the cortical "what" stream is preferentially processed by the perirhinal cortex and lateral entorhinal area, whereas information about spatial and possibly other aspects of context originating in the cortical "what" stream are preferentially processed by the parahippocampal cortex and medial entorhinal area. The information about "what" and "where" then converges within the hippocampus (Burwell et al., 1995).

The main flow of information through the hippocampus involves serial connections from the dentate gyrus to CA3 to CA1, and then to the subiculum (Amaral & Witter, 1989). The intrinsic hippocampal pathway partially preserves the topographical gradients of neocortical input, but there is also considerable divergence and associational connections, particularly at the CA3 step. Outputs of subiculum, and to a lesser extent CA1, are directed back to deep layers of the parahippocampal region, which in turn projects back onto the neocortical and olfactory areas that were the source of cortical inputs. Thus, the hippocampal system is organized for maximal convergence of the final outcomes of cortical "what" and "where" processing, and is positioned to influence the nature of cortical representations based on an architecture ideal for the formation of associations among combinations of what and where information.

Human Amnesia and Animal Models of Hippocampal Function

The early findings on H.M. emphasized the global nature of his impairment, an almost complete failure to learn all sorts of new verbal and nonverbal material (see Corkin, 1984). Yet, H.M.'s remote autobiographical memories and his capacity for short-term memory were completely intact, leading to the initial view that the hippocampal region plays a specific role in the consolidation of short term memories into long term memory.

More recent work with H.M. and other amnesic patients has shown conclusively that the impairment in acquiring long-term memories is also circumscribed to a particular type of memory expression. Thus, amnesiacs can normally acquire new motor, perceptual, and cognitive skills and demonstrate normal sensory adaptations and "priming" of perceptual stimuli, and such implicit learning occurs despite the patients' inability to recall or recognize the learning materials or the events of the learning experience. Based on these distinctions, the kind of memory lost in amnesia has been called "declarative" or "explicit" memory, emphasizing the characteristic capacity for conscious and direct memory expression that is so devastated following damage to the hippocampal region. Conversely, the collection of capacities preserved in amnesia has been called "procedural" or "implicit" memory, emphasizing the finding that hippocampal-independent memories are characteristically revealed by unconscious and indirect means of expression.

Considerable success has been achieved in developing nonhuman primate and rodent models of human amnesia. Following removal of the same medial temporal structures involved in H.M.'s surgery, monkeys are severely impaired on delayed recognition of objects and show poor retention of rapidly acquired object discriminations. Conversely, they have a preserved ability to acquire slowly learned motor skill and pattern discrimination tasks. In addition, hippocampal damage results in impaired retention of object discriminations learned shortly before the lesion, but spares retention of similar discriminations learned long before the damage. In studies on spatial learning, rats with hippocampal damage can learn to localize an important place in an environment when they are allowed to navigate directly to a particular complex of spatial cues. However, rats with hippocampal damage, unlike normal rats, are impaired when they must learn to combine and relate spatial information obtained across different experiences viewing the environment from different perspectives, or when they must express their knowledge of the relevant location from a new perspective. These findings parallel the pattern of impaired and spared memory capacities observed in human amnesic patients.

Further findings from experiments on monkeys and rats focused on more selective damage within the medial temporal lobe suggest that the surrounding parahippocampal region and the hippocampus may play different roles in memory processing. Studies on humans with amnesia and on animals with experimentally created brain damage have shown that different parts of the parahippocampal region play distinct roles in processing and that interactions among these areas and the hippocampus may support conscious recollection.

Thus information about specific objects carried in the "what" cortical stream through the peririnal and lateral entorhinal area may be combined in the hippocampus with information about the context in which events occurred carried in the "where" cortical stream through the parahippocampal cortex and medial entorhinal area, and the hippocampus links these elements of an episodic memory. These linkages are then integrated back into the various cortical areas that represent the details of each type of information. Subsequent recollection may occur when a specific cue passing through the perirhinal-lateral entorhinal area results first in pattern completion in the hippocampus then regeneration of the appropriate context in the parahippocampal cortex and medial entorhinal area.

Information Encoded by Hippocampal Neurons

Complementary evidence on the nature of memory processing accomplished by the hippocampus has been derived from studies of the firing patterns of hippocampal neurons in behaving animals. Consistent with the view that the hippocampus is the ultimate stage of hierarchical processing, the functional correlates of hippocampal cells are "supramodal" in that they appear to encode the abstract stimulus configurations that are independent of any particular sensory input. Most prominent among the functional types of hippocampal principal neurons are "place cells" that fire selectively when a rat is in a particular location in its environment as defined by the spatial relations among multiple and multimodal stimuli (O'Keefe 1976).

In addition, there are many reports of nonspatial behavioral correlates of hippocampal neuronal activity indicating that hippocampal representation is not limited to the encoding of spatial relations among distal cues (e.g., Wood et al., 1999). Even the activity of place cells is influenced by events that are meaningful to the task at hand (e.g., Wood et al., 2000). These findings extend the range of hippocampal coding to reflect the global involvement of the hippocampus in memory indicated by the neuropsychological studies, and serve to reinforce the conclusion that the hippocampus supports relational representations (Eichenbaum et al., 1999). Similarly, in humans, whereas the perirhinal cortex is activated by specific objects and the parahippocampal cortex is activated by views of places, hippocampal activation occurs during the processing of relations between object and context information (Davachi, 2006).

A comprehensive and consensual understanding of the role of the hippocampal system in memory remains elusive. Nevertheless, there is an increasing convergence of evidence indicating that the hippocampus represents and relates specific experiences into a network of memories that support our capacity for declarative memory.

REFERENCES

Amaral, D. G., & Witter, M. P. (1989). The three-dimensional organization of the hippocampal formation: A review of anatomical data. *Neuroscience, 31*, 571–591.

Burwell, R. D., Witter, M. P., & Amaral, D. G. (1995). Perirhinal and postrhinal cortices of the rat: A review of the neuroanatomical literature and comparison with findings from the monkey brain. *Hippocampus, 5*, 390–408.

Corkin, S. (1984). Lasting consequences of bilateral medial temporal lobectomy: Clinical course and experimental findings in H.M. *Seminars in Neurology, 4*, 249–259.

Davachi, L. (2006). Item, context and relational episodic encoding in humans. *Current Opinion in Neurobiology 16*, 693–700.

Eichenbaum, H., Dudchencko, P., Wood, E., Shapiro, M., & Tanila, H. (1999). The hippocampus, memory, and place cells: Is it spatial memory or a memory space? *Neuron, 23*, 209–226.

O'Keefe, J. A. 1976. Place units in the hippocampus of the freely moving rat. *Experimental Neurology, 51*, 78–109.

Scoville, W. B., & Milner, B. (1957). Loss of recent memory after bilateral hippocampal lesions. *Journal of Neurology Neurosurgery and Psychiatry, 20*, 11–12.

Wood, E, Dudchenko, P. A. & Eichenbaum, H. (1999). The global record of memory in hippocampal neuronal activity. *Nature, 397*, 613–616.

Wood, E., Dudchenko, P. Robitsek, J. R., and Eichenbaum, H. (2000). Hippocampal neurons encode information about different types of memory episodes occurring in the same location. *Neuron, 27*, 623–633.

SUGGESTED READINGS

Eichenbaum, H. (2004). Hippocampus: Cognitive processes and neural representations that underlie declarative memory. *Neuron, 44*, 109–120.

Eichenbaum, H., & Cohen, N. J. (2001). *From conditioning to conscious recollection: Memory systems of the brain.* Oxford University Press.

Eichenbaum, H., Yonelinas, A. R., & Ranganath, C. (2007). The medial temporal lobe and recognition memory. *Annual Review of Neuroscience, 20*, 123–152.

HOWARD EICHENBAUM
Boston University

See also: **Episodic Memory and the Hippocampus**

HISTRIONIC PERSONALITY DISORDER

Histrionic Personality Disorder is one of 10 personality disorders listed in the *Diagnostic and Statistical Manual of Mental Disorders* (DSM-IV-TR; American Psychiatric Association, 2000). DSM-IV-TR defines a personality disorder as an enduring pattern of inner experience and inflexible, pervasive, and ultimately self-defeating behavior, which is "stable and of long duration and its onset can be traced back at least to adolescence or early adulthood" (p. 689). Individuals diagnosed with histrionic personality disorder typically display exaggerated attention-seeking behavior, dramatic emotionality, and often sexually seductive or otherwise provocative behavior, all of which are intended to manipulate others to ensure that their childlike dependency needs might be met. One's initial impression of such individuals is that of a rather charming, outgoing, and entertaining person who is often flirtatious and places a great deal of emphasis on his or her physical attractiveness. However, as time passes it becomes evident that this interpersonal style is a superficial façade, calculated to exploit and manipulate others into providing them with excitement and a corresponding, albeit fleeting, sense of self-worth and identity.

DSM-IV-TR summarizes the description of this disorder with eight essential criteria: (1) uncomfortable in situations in which he or she is not the center of attention; (2) interaction with others is often characterized by inappropriate sexually seductive or provocative behavior; (3) displays rapidly shifting and shallow expression of emotions; (4) consistently uses physical appearance to draw attention to self; (5) has a style of speech that is excessively impressionistic and lacking in detail; (6) shows self-dramatization, theatricality, and exaggerated expression of emotion; (7) is suggestible (i.e., easily influenced by others or circumstances); and (8) considers relationships to be more intimate than they actually are.

Clinical Picture

Millon (1999) describes the clinical picture of the histrionic personality across several diagnostic domains to further delineate the DSM-IV criteria. Individuals with this type of personality display a dramatic self-image, by behaving in a theatrical manner that is often impulsive, exhibitionistic, and superficial. They are intolerant of boredom or frustration. Their interpersonal style is attention-seeking and designed to elicit praise and adoration from others. Women, in particular, tend to use seductive tactics to accomplish these goals, but are often surprised and disturbed when men respond with expectations of real sexual intimacy. Histrionic individuals also "market" themselves to others through this engaging and dramatic façade, initially drawing the attention and esteem that they crave, only to lose interest when those around them recognize the shallowness of the relationship and ultimately reject them. Histrionic people will desperately try to adjust their behavior to avoid this rejection by becoming even more "interesting."

Histrionic personalities typically display a very impressionistic, "broad brush" cognitive style. They are so preoccupied with "tuning in" to the external interpersonal world they hope to manipulate that they fail to cultivate the capacity for thoughtful introspection. Their perceptions of the world are based on immediate impressions and "hunches," with poor attention to detail. (Shapiro, 1965; Beck et al., 2003). This cognitive style serves an important psychological function in preventing histrionic individuals from becoming aware of unacceptable conflicts and memories. Histrionic personalities have a gregarious self-image. They view themselves as extroverted, well-liked, and charming in a manner that is attractive and interesting to others. Emotional dependency, anger, and depressive feelings are rarely integrated into this self-image.

Experiencing an impoverished sense of self from which they draw little or no meaning or comfort, individuals with a histrionic personality disorder desperately and chronically crave nourishment from others. Millon (1999) describes the accumulation of superficial memories of their prior relationships and experiences as shallow object-representations. Trying to provide caring and emotional sustenance to people with this condition feels as if one is "pouring water into a bucket with a hole in it." The lack of definition and substance of these "inner templates" requires histrionic individuals to depend almost completely on external validation. The resulting interpersonal pattern invariably leads to disappointment, lack of meaningful relationships, and a constant search for new stimulation. In order to successfully find this stimulation and ultimately the attention and adoration they crave, these individuals avoid focusing on their typically empty inner world. They devote their psychic energy to avoiding unacceptable feelings, conflicts, and memories through what Millon (1999) describes as dissociative regulatory mechanisms that include repression and denial. Unaware of how their thoughts and feelings are related to their behavior, histrionic persons claim innocence when their naïve and inappropriate behavior leads to interpersonal conflict.

Etiology

According to the DSM-IV-TR, the prevalence of histrionic personality disorder is between 2%–3% in the general population and between 10%–15% in mental health settings. The vast majority of individuals with this diagnosis are women; however, the gender differential may be influenced more by sex role stereotypes in our society than by actual occurrence (Belitsky et al., 1998).

The cause of personality disorders in general, and histrionic personality disorder in particular, is controversial and without consistent empirical support for any hypothesis. Although Millon (1999, p. 406) implies that histrionic persons have a biological substrate predisposing them to a "high level of energy and activation and a low threshold for autonomic reactivity," the data relating to a clear biological basis for the disorder are inconclusive. More commonly, the disorder is attributed to early developmental experiences and dysfunctional environments that inhibit the development of healthy, adaptive coping patterns.

For example, parental failures in providing attention and validation, often stemming from marital conflict and schism, can motivate a potential female histrionic to reject a cold, competitive mother and turn toward a more indulgent father. The father in this circumstance will often be superficially supportive, but only in response to his daughter's attention-getting efforts, characterized by flirtatiousness and drama. In adolescence, girls with this histrionic potential will turn to peers for validation, emphasizing their physical attractiveness and seeking attention from those who respond to their seductiveness and charm, while avoiding those individuals who arouse their feelings of jealousy and competition (Dorfman,

2000). Through such a developmental history, according to this explanation, histrionic persons-to-be learn a set of dysfunctional skills and a cognitive belief system that intermittently reinforces and ultimately maintains their self-defeating personality style. Self-statements like "Unless I entertain or impress people, I am nothing" or "If I entertain people, they will not notice my weaknesses," are likely to characterize their belief system (Beck et al., 2003).

Assessment and Diagnosis

Individuals with histrionic personality disorder are extremely unlikely to present to a mental health professional with the goal of altering their attention-seeking and dramatic personality style. Rather, they tend to seek help when they have experienced the failure of an intimate relationship or when they begin to get in touch with the lack of meaning in their lives. These developments will often precipitate significant emotional distress in the form of a clinical depression, a somatoform disorder characterized by complaints of physical symptoms for which there is no organic basis, or a substance-abuse disorder. The clinical symptoms characterizing these disorders are entirely consistent with the histrionic individual's personality and defensive organization. Unconsciously converting psychological conflicts and stress into physical symptoms in conversion or somatization disorders allows histrionic people to avoid awareness of inner struggles and to focus on external physical complaints that elicit attention and concern from their family as well as from physicians. Drugs and alcohol allow histrionic persons to avoid facing life's problems by enhancing the defenses of dissociation, repression, and denial. These drugs permit them to escape from pain and avoid responsibility for their behavior, while bolstering their fragile self-esteem with the grandiosity and omnipotence that often come with intoxication. It is principally when these clinical disorders result in significant emotional and behavioral impairment that the histrionic individual will decide to seek treatment.

Clinicians rely on the clinical evaluation and psychosocial history to make a diagnosis of histrionic personality disorder. Some psychologists additionally utilize objective personality instruments to support the diagnosis. The Minnesota Multiphasic Personality Inventory-2 (Butcher et al., 1989) and the Millon Multiaxial Clinical Inventory (Millon et al., 2006) are two of the most valid and reliable instruments used for this purpose.

Treatment

As noted, typical histrionic personality disorder patients will rarely request treatment for their self-defeating personality style. Instead, the clinician must identify and address the distress or situational stressors that have resulted in the failure of their typical coping style in order to provide the support and reassurance that the histrionic patient craves. Often these situational factors will revolve around interpersonal conflicts, frustrated dependency needs, or difficulties related to substance use and abuse. Time-limited, focused therapeutic interventions with the goal of ameliorating the presenting problems are likely to be most effective. In the process of treating these issues, the clinician will soon become aware of the patient's interpersonal style. Histrionic individuals will interact with the therapist in an emotionally exaggerated, dramatic, and dependent manner. Their complaints will be vague and impressionistic and explained in a manner intended to "interest" the clinician. At this point the clinician must decide whether or how best to address the underlying histrionic personality disorder.

Partly because they are infrequently the basis for seeking help, histrionic personality disorders often prove refractory to treatment. Histrionic persons are, by definition, unable to develop the necessary insight or interest in exploring their unconscious motives and "inner life." Frequently, when their initial stress has been resolved and their depression, anxiety, or external stress has lifted, any motivation they may have had for personality change will dissipate. For some individuals, however, more intensive individual psychotherapy may be helpful in altering their self-defeating style. Cognitive-behavioral approaches and psychodynamic and interpersonal psychotherapies are commonly employed interventions.

Given the complexity of the disorder, it may be most effectively treated using an integrative approach that combines interpersonal, short-term dynamic perspectives that emphasize early developmental influences of childhood and adolescence with a cognitive approach that looks at the histrionic person's resulting belief system and cognitive structures (Beck et al., 2003; Dorfman, 2000; Horowitz, 1995). Therapy focuses on helping these patients to examine their interactions with others and the beliefs that influence these interactions, utilizing the therapy session as a "laboratory" in which these interpersonal and cognitive behaviors are enacted and can be modified. The goal of therapy is rarely characterological restructuring. More realistic and practical goals involve helping histrionic patients to manage emotional distress more effectively, to develop more logical problem-solving skills, and to face painful feelings and conflicts in their lives that their defensive, interpersonal strategies have helped them avoid.

Treatment of histrionic personality disorder patients with psychotropic medication is limited to dealing with their symptoms of depression and anxiety. Anxiolytic and antidepressant medications are helpful in reducing the emotional distress that typically constitutes their presenting problems. Unfortunately, the elimination of psychological distress may eliminate any further motivation for more substantial changes. Furthermore, several sedative medications have a high-abuse potential for histrionic patients, who may use these drugs to continue avoiding their psychological problems.

Treatment of patients with histrionic personality disorder is thus a challenge for any mental health professional. These patients' demand for a "magical cure" and their manipulative and seductive maneuvers, suicidal threats, and needs to be "rescued" by the therapist pose significant challenges in psychotherapy. The mental-health clinician must constantly be on guard for seductive and manipulative behavior and be able and willing to set professional boundaries while maintaining a supportive and empathic stance.

REFERENCES

American Psychiatric Association (2000). *Diagnostic and statistical manual of mental disorders* (4th ed., text rev.). Washington, DC: Author.

Beck, A. T., Freeman, A., & Davis, D. D. (2003). *Cognitive therapy of personality disorders* (2nd ed.). New York: Guilford Press.

Belitsky, C. A., Toner, B. B., Ali, A., Yu, B., Osborne, S. I., & deRooy, E. (1998). Sex-role attitudes and clinical appraisal in psychiatry residents. *Canadian Journal of Psychiatry 41*, 503–508.

Butcher, J. N., Dahlstrom, W. G., Graham, J. R., Tellegen, A., & Kaemmer, B. (1989). *Minnesota Multiphasic Personality Inventory-2 (MMPI-2): Manual for administration and scoring.* Minneapolis: University of Minnesota Press.

Dorfman, W. I. (2000). Histrionic personality disorder. In M. Hersen & M. Biaggio, (Eds.), *Effective brief therapies: A clinician's guide.* San Diego, CA: Academic Press.

Horowitz, M. J. (1995). Histrionic personality disorder. In G. O. Gabbard (Ed.), *Treatment of psychiatric disorders* (pp. 2311–2336). Washington, DC: American Psychiatric Press.

Millon, T. (1999). *Personality-guided therapy.* New York: John Wiley & Sons.

Millon, T., Davis, R., Millon, C., & Grossman, S. (2006). *The Millon Clinical Multiaxial Inventory—III* (3rd ed.). Pearson Assessments.

Shapiro, D. (1965). *Neurotic styles.* New York: Basic Books.

SUGGESTED READINGS

Horowitz, M. J. (Ed.). (1991). *Hysterical personality style and the histrionic personality disorder.* Northvale, NJ: Jason Aronson.

Millon, T., & Davis, R. D. (1996). *Disorders of personality: DSM-IV and beyond.* New York: John Wiley & Sons.

Millon, T., Grossman, S., Millon, C., Meagher, S., & Ramnath, R. (2004). *Personality disorders in modern life* (2nd ed.). New York: John Wiley and Sons.

WILLIAM I. DORFMAN
Nova Southeastern University

See also: **Personality Disorders**

HOARDING

Hoarding has been widely recognized as a serious problem by elder service workers but has been almost completely ignored in the research literature until very recently. Frost and Hartl (1996) defined hoarding as (1) acquisition and failure to discard a large number of possessions; (2) clutter that precludes activities for which living spaces were designed; and (3) significant distress or impairment in functioning caused by acquisition, difficulty in discarding, and clutter. In addition to these primary features, people who hoard tend to be highly perfectionistic, have problems with decision-making, and experience ADHD-like symptoms including extreme disorganization. Hoarding has been associated with impairment in activities of daily living as well as marked problems with occupational and role functioning (Steketee & Frost, 2003). The difficulties caused by hoarding can be extreme and can endanger the health and safety of the individual as well as anyone living nearby. Despite the dearth of information about hoarding, a recent epidemiological survey reported a weighted lifetime prevalence of serious hoarding problems of over 5% (Samuels et al., 2008).

The *Diagnostic and Statistical Manual of Mental Disorders* (DSM-IV-TR; American Psychiatric Association, 2000) lists hoarding as a criterion for Obsessive-Compulsive Personality Disorder (OCPD), defined as the inability "to discard worn-out or worthless objects even when they have no sentimental value" (p. 729). However, close observation of hoarding behavior has revealed that hoarded items include valuable as well as worthless objects, that the items tend to be the same things that most people save, and that many of them are saved for sentimental reasons (Steketee & Frost, 2003). Hoarding is not closely associated with other OCPD criteria other than perfectionism and the preoccupation with details, which has led to the suggestion that it be removed as a diagnostic criterion for OCPD (Saxena, 2008).

Although most studies of hoarding include a larger percentage of female than male participants (Steketee & Frost, 2003), community-based epidemiology research has found a higher percentage of men than women who hoard (5.6% versus 2.6%) (Samuels et al., 2008). Until recently, hoarding was more familiar to elder-service caseworkers than to mental-health practitioners. Samuels et al. (2008) found the prevalence of hoarding to increase with age, and most studies of hoarding include older participants than are included in comparable studies of other anxiety disorders (Steketee & Frost, 2003). However, onset of hoarding occurs between 10–15 years of age, though it typically does not become severe until decades later (Saxena, 2008). Hoarding appears to follow a chronic course with somewhat less fluctuation than is found in other Obsessive-Compulsive Disorder (OCD) subtypes, and people who hoard are more likely to be single or divorced than those who do not hoard (Steketee & Frost, 2003).

Hoarding appears to be familial, with high levels of indecisiveness among relatives of people who hoard (Samuels et al., 2002). Two genetic studies have found suggestive linkage to markers on several chromosomes, although these findings are still preliminary (Saxena, 2008). A cognitive behavioral model of hoarding suggests that it stems from several key deficits or problems. Information-processing deficits include difficulties with attention, categorization, organization, memory, and decision-making. These functions map onto areas of the brain that scanning studies have shown to operate differently among people who hoard (Saxena, 2008). Abnormal attachments to and beliefs about possessions form a second type of deficit seen in hoarding. These attachments include viewing possessions as extensions of the self, as symbols of safety and comfort, as important objects to be responsible for, and as being necessary to preserve one's personal history (Steketee & Frost, 2003). Finally, these attachments lead to approach behaviors (actively saving items) and also to avoidance of distress (avoiding discarding).

Although hoarding appears in the context of several other disorders (e.g., dementia, schizophrenia, Prader Willi syndrome), it has most often been considered a symptom of OCD. Factor and cluster studies of OCD suggest that hoarding occurs in 25–50% of OCD cases. Recent findings challenge the extent to which hoarding is specific to OCD, however. High rates of major depressive disorder, generalized anxiety disorder, and social phobia occur among people who hoard (Samuels et al., 2002), and hoarding frequently occurs in the absence of any other OCD symptoms (Saxena, 2008). Other evidence from neuroimaging studies suggests that hoarding may be neurologically distinct from OCD (Saxena, 2008; Steketee & Frost, 2003).

People who hoard show poorer insight into the nature of the problem than people with other OCD symptoms, which has led researchers to question these persons' motivation for treatment (Steketee & Frost, 2003). Early findings suggested that presence of hoarding symptoms predicted poor response to medication treatment, although one recent study suggests an equal response of hoarders and non-hoarders to paroxetine (Saxena, 2008). Hoarding symptoms have consistently predicted poor response to cognitive behavioral treatments (CBT) for OCD (Steketee & Frost, 2003). However, CBT developed specifically for hoarding has shown promise. In an open trial, Tolin, Frost, and Steketee (2007) found a 28% reduction in hoarding severity among 10 hoarding patients following 26 sessions of CBT for hoarding. At posttest, 50% of treatment completers were rated as "much improved" or "very much improved." In a subsequent wait-list control trial, treated patients were significantly improved compared to a wait-list control after 12 sessions. After treatment, 69% of treatment completers were rated as "much improved" or "very much improved" by independent assessors. Eighty percent of patients who completed treatment rated themselves as "much" or "very much" improved.

REFERENCES

Frost, R. O., & Hartl, T. L. (1996). A cognitive-behavioral model of compulsive hoarding. *Behaviour Research and Therapy, 34,* 341–350.

Samuels, J. F., Bienvenu, O. J., Grados, M. A., Cullen, B. A., Riddle, M. A., Liang, K. Y., Eaton, W. W., & Nestadt, G. (2008). Prevalence and correlates of hoarding behavior in a community-based sample. *Behaviour Research and Therapy, 46,* 836–844.

Samuels, J. F., Bienvenu, O. J., Riddle, M. A., Cullen, B. A., Grados, M. A., Liang, K. Y., Hoehn-Saric, R., & Nestadt, G. (2002). Hoarding in obsessive-compulsive disorder: Results from a case-control study. *Behaviour Research and Therapy, 40,* 517–528.

Saxena, S. (2008). Recent advances in compulsive hoarding. *Current Psychiatry Reports, 10.*

Steketee, G., & Frost, R. O. (2003). Compulsive hoarding: Current status of the research. *Clinical Psychology Review, 23,* 905–927.

Tolin, D. F., Frost, R. O., & Steketee, G. (2007). An open trial of cognitive-behavioral therapy for compulsive hoarding. *Behaviour Research and Therapy, 45,* 1461–1470.

SUGGESTED READING

Steketee, G., & Frost, R. O. (2007). *Compulsive hoarding and acquiring: Therapist guide.* New York: Oxford University Press.

RANDY O. FROST
Smith College

See also: Compulsions; Obsessive-Compulsive Disorder

HOMELESSNESS

Homelessness is a nationwide, major social problem that continues to fester and requires resolution and prevention measures to eradicate. As incomes fall and the cost of living rises, Americans face complicated financial choices in buying food and clothing, securing roofs over their heads, paying for health care, and affording child care and education. Whoever cannot juggle these basic needs may become homeless.

What Is Homelessness?

Homelessness is the absence of a permanent nighttime residence. It is living in a temporary supervised shelter or in any temporary location not intended for sleeping. It also means being cut off from relatives, social groups, and community organizations, and losing a sense of belonging to society.

Who Are the Homeless?

Public perception of the homeless is that of an ADM population: alcoholics, drug abusers, and the mentally disordered. However, the homeless come from all walks of life and can be found among all ages, genders, races, and ethnic backgrounds. Among the homeless are the unemployed as well as the working poor, who are currently facing difficult times with a growing disparity between wages and the cost of living. Nowadays, a minimum-wage worker would need to work over 100 hours each week to afford a two-bedroom apartment (there are only 168 hours in a week).

About half of the homeless are families with children. Approximately 1.35 million children are homeless, and small children are the fastest growing sector of people without a place to live. A large number of the homeless are single adults. About a quarter of the homeless are veterans, who generally have poor access to support networks. There is a smaller percentage of homeless youths and college students (Cunningham & Henry, 2007).

Causes

At the root of homelessness is unemployment, diminished incomes, or other economic factors. Many women suffer domestic abuse, which is the second leading cause of homelessness among women and families. Present-day causes continue to be extreme poverty and the paucity of affordable permanent housing. Urban renewal and gentrification has reduced the number of affordable rental properties, which have been converted into high-priced housing and condominiums. There are many more low-income households in need of housing than there are affordable units available.

Communities have yet to develop sufficient housing and services to care for people with mental disorders. In addition, there are people exiting the criminal justice system who do not have families or homes to which they can return home. There are also homeless sex offenders. Among the homeless are a significant number of women and men who cite gambling as a cause of their situation. Prostitution is another situation that may bring about homelessness (School & Goswami [n.d.]).

Large numbers of the homeless have alcohol or drug-related problems. Substance abuse is not considered to be either the cause or the consequence of homelessness, but rather a preexisting condition exacerbated by loss of housing.

According to the *single calamity hypothesis,* homelessness grows out of a single crisis. Consequently, it would be difficult to predict which characteristics, experiences, and behaviors would lead to an individual's homelessness. A crisis that occurs often to the homeless is a major illness. Thus, the onset of poor health may lead to homelessness and at the same time may also be a consequence of it.

Consequences

Homelessness often leads to stress, which may result in stress-related illnesses. Among the homeless are those who suffer from chronic and infectious diseases. HIV infection is much higher among the homeless than among the general population. The homeless typically lack adequate medical care or treatment, and Medicaid and other welfare benefits are often unattainable.

How Many People Are Homeless?

Since the homeless population is transient, the actual number of homeless people is uncertain. The number cited may be based on *point-in-time data* collected in surveys done by on-the-street interviewers and from counts taken at emergency shelters, soup kitchens, and similar places. A second method is to analyze data from programs for the homeless.

Cunningham and Henry (2007) indicate that 750,000 Americans are homeless on any given night. Of those counted, over half were living in shelters and transitional housing. A surprising 44% were unsheltered. Furthermore there is an alarming increase from 2 million homeless during the course of a year (from days to months) reported in 2004 to 3.5 million homeless reported in 2007.

There are numerous people unaccounted for who manage to live in makeshift locations such as subway caves, shuttered storefronts, cars, motels, empty buildings, public areas, hospitals, and the like. The nation's foreclosure crisis has affected the homeless, according to Sheeran (2008). On any given night, there may be more vacant houses than there are homeless people in some cities. Homeless persons are taking advantage of the opportunity to become squatters. Many view the foreclosure crisis as a chance to find "free" housing.

The Chronic Homeless

The chronic homeless spend long periods of time, often years, living without a permanent address. The typical chronic homeless person likely suffers from a disability, and most have been in treatment programs. Police regularly arrest the chronic homeless for offenses such as loitering, public urination, or public intoxication. From an economic standpoint, it costs the same to provide affordable housing for the chronic homeless as it does to keep that person homeless. For example, Massachusetts spends on the average $3 million per month to house about 5,000 families, and by contrast $1 million per month for 24,000 homeless individuals (Abel, 2008). Living in affordable housing with supportive services reduces the number of vagrant arrests and leads to progress in self-sufficiency and self-efficacy for people who are homeless. The U.S. Department of Housing and Urban Development found that when the chronically homeless were placed in permanent housing, such as apartments, rooms, or halfway houses, and given access to social services, their number dropped significantly between 2005 and 2007 (Swarns, 2008).

Children

Very young children are at greatest risk for the detrimental effects of homelessness, and they suffer the most physical, psychological, and emotional damage. Children are susceptible to infectious and communicable diseases, and their physical development may be delayed because of homelessness.

Behavioral problems have been observed among homeless three- to five-year-olds. Children older than age five frequently act out their anxieties. The greatest danger for homeless children is that they will become virtually trapped in poverty with no escape from homelessness. Thus poverty and homelessness may become a *self-fulfilling prophecy* passed down from one generation to the next.

Bonds between homeless parents and children weaken because parents are likely to assume a diminished role as disciplinarians and nurturers. The potential for child abuse rises when the frustrations of homelessness exceed parental self-control.

Far too many public school pupils are homeless. Teaching often takes a back seat to ensuring that the poorest students are clothed and fed. Homeless children are likely to skip school, fail and repeat grades, perform below the average, test poorly in reading and math, and test as being functionally illiterate.

Youth

Homeless youth are described as abandoned by parents, runaways, and system youth who depart from institutions or foster care. They are living on their own in makeshift places or in shelters. They lack skills of self-sufficiency.

Because their educational backgrounds and job skills are minimal, they become candidates for low-paying jobs. Their salaries are insufficient to cover their basic needs. Homeless youth are beset by issues of poverty, lack of affordable housing, and unemployment. Health and substance-abuse problems are common, as are sexual experiences, which make adolescents vulnerable to hepatitis and AIDS.

Frequently these adolescents come from dysfunctional families in which they are physically and sexually abused.

Large numbers of homeless youth are at risk for depression and suicide. Positive relationships with adults can prevent homelessness among youth and help young people make a good transition into adulthood.

Psychological Trauma

The psychological impact of homelessness can be as detrimental to one's self-esteem and well-being as the physical loss of housing. Homeless people may suffer from extraordinary stresses (e.g., psychological trauma resulting from loss of housing, living in a shelter, or victimization). A symptom of psychological trauma is social disaffiliation, breaking the bonds of *attachment* to significant others and to social institutions. Homelessness leads to distrust of others and isolation.

A second symptom is *learned helplessness*. Traumatized homeless individuals come to believe that they have no control over their lives and that they must depend on others to fulfill their basic needs. Among the homeless who suffer from traumatic victimization are battered women, some of whom report having been abused in childhood. In addition to social disaffiliation and learned helplessness, traumatized women also may display other dysfunctional symptoms, and many are abusive parents.

Suggestions for a Solution

Homelessness impinges on everyone in some way. When food and shelter are lacking, individuals cannot fulfill their need for self-actualization. Human resources that could be applied to improve the quality of their lives remain untapped. Because homelessness results from poverty, the first priorities for helping the homeless include building permanent affordable housing, providing income enhancement, and expanding health care.

Cunningham et al. (2006) found that because federal funding for affordable housing has declined since the 1980s, state and local communities have taken up the challenge. In 2000, The National Alliance to End Homelessness launched local plans with a goal of ending homelessness in 10 years and called "The Ten Year Plan to End Homelessness." By 2006, over 200 communities nationwide created plans to end homelessness and prevent its recurrence. A large number of plans are set up with emergency contingencies, such as assistance with rent, mortgage, and utilities.

Unless local initiatives continue to make progress and more communities join in the endeavor, the financial burden to the public will only increase, as will human suffering. Temporary, overcrowded emergency shelters could become a permanent feature of the American landscape, and the number of homeless people could continue to multiply. Nevertheless, the prospect for ending homelessness in the foreseeable future appears bright, as do the chances for reducing recidivism to homelessness.

REFERENCES

Abel, D. (February 24, 2008). For the homeless, keys to a home. *The Boston Globe.*

Cunningham, M., & Henry, M. (2007). *Homelessness counts.* Washington, D.C.: National Alliance to End Homelessness.

Cunningham, M., Lear, M., Schmitt, E., & Henry, M. (2006). *A new vision: What is in community plans to end homelessness?* Washington, D.C.: National Alliance to End Homelessness.

School, E., & Goswami, S. [n.d.]. *Prostitution: A violent reality of homelessness.* Chicago: The Chicago Coalition for the Homeless.

Sheeran, T. J. (February 18, 2008). Foreclosed homes occupied by homeless. Cleveland: Associated Press.

Swarns, R. L. (July 30, 2008). Number of homeless down 30%. *The Boston Globe.*

SHELDON S. BROWN
*North Shore Community College,
Danvers, MA*

See also: **Learned Helplessness; Self-Efficacy**

HOMEOSTASIS

Complex organisms must maintain relatively stable internal environments to survive and move freely through the changing and often adverse conditions that surround them. "Homeostasis" is the name that was given to this constancy in 1926 by Walter B. Cannon, an American psychologist. Through his work on homeostasis, Cannon created a concept that has become a milestone in the history of ideas. It was the culmination of an approach begun some six decades earlier with the work of Claude Bernard, the French physiologist who is considered to have established the foundations of scientific physiology. Bernard concluded that organisms have evolved toward a greater independence from the changing environment by developing, from the blood of bodily fluids, an *internal environment* that is held stable by its own adjustments (Robin, 1979). Cannon demonstrated that the activities of homeostasis, often simple if each is viewed in isolation, are nevertheless orchestrated by remarkably complex regulatory processes involving the organism across physiological systems and levels of functioning.

In a series of articles first published in 1925 and compiled together by L. L. Langley (1972), Cannon described his findings as instances of the maintenance of steady states in open systems. He named this steady condition "homeostasis" and offered a set of postulates regarding its nature; he expanded on this in 1929 in an overview of homeostasis and the regulatory mechanisms thus far identified. The body, he asserted, was able, through homeostatic reactions, to maintain stability in the fluid matrix surrounding the body cells, thus controlling body temperature, blood pressure, and other aspects of the internal environment necessary for life. Homeostasis was also maintained in the levels of supplies needed directly for cellular activities, including materials for energy and growth (glucose, protein, fat), water, sodium chloride, calcium, oxygen, and certain necessary internal secretions. Regulated by the nervous system and endocrine glands, bodily reactions at all levels of complexity are involved, from the speed with which cell metabolism proceeds and produces heat in cold weather, to increases and decreases in the complex processing giving rise to hunger and thirst, with impact on behaviors affecting energy and water intake.

Cannon's concept of homeostasis emerged as a complex statement regarding the existence, nature, and principles of self-regulating systems. He emphasized that complex living beings are open systems made up of changing and unstable components that are continually subjected to disturbing conditions precisely because they are open to their surroundings in so many ways. Thus, although organisms are continuously tending toward change, they nevertheless must also maintain constancy with regard to the environment, so as to preserve circumstances favorable to life. Adjustments within such systems must be continuous and less than perfect. Homeostasis therefore describes a state that is relatively, rather than absolutely, stable.

The *open system* concept challenged all conventional views regarding the appropriate unit of analysis of an entity. If the heart, lungs, kidneys, and blood, for example, are parts of a self-regulating system, then their actions or functions cannot be understood by studying each alone. Full understanding comes only from knowledge of how each acts with reference to the others. The concept of the open system also challenged all conventional views of causality, substituting complex reciprocal determination for any notion of simple serial or linear causality. Homeostasis therefore offered a new perspective, both for viewing the behavior systems of many sorts and for understanding people as members of open systems.

Homeostasis has served as a cornerstone for a number of subsequent developments involving a system perspective of control and causality. Hans Selye's work with stress and disease, as well as his discovery of the general adaptation syndrome, began with the insight that certain diseases and disorders might arise as the cost of the body's struggle to maintain homeostasis in the face of prolonged disruptive pressure (Selye, 1956/1978). Selye's view of disease as derangement of homeostasis contributed to a view of health in which the role of medicine is to assist the homeostatic processes to return the organism to the relatively constant state. Wiener's *Cybernetic Theory* (1948) offered principles to account for self-regulation across even nonliving systems such as computers, a pursuit construed even more broadly in Ludwig von Bertalanffy's *General System Theory* (1968). In the 1950s, Jackson (1968) began to explore applications of homeostasis to family interaction, identifying family systems in which apparently disturbed behaviors are homeostatic. His concept of family homeostasis provided impetus to the then-emerging field of marital psychotherapy and contributed to such concepts as the double bind.

In recent decades, homeostasis research has continued to stimulate new perceptions by establishing that learning is central to homeostatic regulation of even physiological systems, demonstrating (to select an example of many) that homeostasis is involved in drug tolerance and addiction in complex ways (Poulos & Cappel, 1991). A body of subsequent research demonstrates that the increased levels of drug tolerance developed through repeated drug administrations involve learned homeostatic efforts to restore normal functioning in the presence of many drugs that otherwise disturb normal functioning. With repeated exposure to the drug, the organism learns to produce a pattern of offsetting physiological and/or behavioral responses that counteract its perturbing effects. Once learned, this pattern of homeostatic responses can be elicited in anticipation of the drug that originally evoked it, without the actual presence of that drug (Ramsay & Woods, 1997).

Recent research also addresses the homeostatic role of higher mental processes in decreasing or increasing the effects of pain and disease through exploration of the regulatory processes involved in what is called placebo responding. Placebo responding can reduce pain and promote healing in afflicted persons given placebo medications. Placebo medications are substances whose positive effects appear to derive not from their chemical properties but from processes in the patient's mind and brain that are related to belief of and participation in the trappings of rituals of medical procedures, reinforced by the doctor-patient relationship (Kaptchuk et al., 2008). Although some mental and social variables have been identified as contributing to placebo responding, less is understood about the specific internal regulatory processes, learned and otherwise, by means of which this improvement proceeds. Cannon's powerful concepts, however, continue to play a central role in organizing our efforts to understand the nature of our interactions with our inner and outer environments.

REFERENCES

Bertalanff, L. von. (1968). *General systems theory*. New York: Braziller.

Jackson, D. D. (Ed.). (1968). *Communication, family, and marriage* (Vols. 1, 2). Palo Alto, CA: Science & Behavior Books.

Kaptchuk, T. J., Kelley, J. M., Conboy, L. A., et al. (2008). Components of placebo effect: Randomized controlled trial in patients with irritable bowel syndrome. *British Medical Journal, 336*, 999–1003.

Langley, L. L. (Ed.). (1972). *Homeostasis: Origins of the concept*. Stroudsburg, PA: Dowden, Hutchinson, & Ross.

Poulos, C. X., & Cappell, H. (1991). Homeostatic theory of drug tolerance: A general model of physiological adaptation. *Psychological Review, 98*, 390–408.

Ramsay, D. S., & Woods, S. C. (1997). Biological consequences of drug administration: Implications for acute and chronic tolerance. *Psychological Review, 104*, 170–193.

Robin, E. D. (Ed.). (1979). *Claude Bernard and the internal environment: A memorial symposium*. New York: Dekker.

Selye, H. (1956/1978). *Stress of life*. New York: McGraw-Hill.

Wiener, N. (1948). *Cybernetics: Control and communication in the animal and the machine*. Cambridge, MA: MIT Press.

SUGGESTED READINGS

Bausel, R. R. (2007). A biochemical explanation of the placebo effect. In *Snake oil science: The truth about complementary and alternative medicine*. Oxford: Oxford University Press.

Beishon, J., & Peters, G. (Eds.). (1972). *Systems behaviour*. New York: Open University Press/Harper & Row.

Siegel, S. (1988). State dependent learning and morphine tolerance. *Behavioral Neuroscience, 102*, 228–232.

ROGER E. ENFIELD
*West Central Georgia Regional Hospital,
Columbus, Ohio*

See also: **General Adaptation Syndrome; Perceptual Control Theory**

HOMOSEXUALITY

Homosexuality refers to sexual behaviors, desires, attractions, and relationships among people of the same sex, as well as to the culture, identities, and communities associated with them. The term encompasses at least five phenomena that are often though not always related. First, it is used to describe specific instances of sexual behavior with a person of one's same sex. Second, it refers to ongoing patterns of sexual or romantic attraction to people of one's own sex, which may or may not be expressed behaviorally. Both homosexual and heterosexual behaviors and attractions are common across human societies.

A third aspect of homosexuality is psychological identity, that is, a sense of self defined in terms of one's enduring attractions to members of the same sex. Individuals who identify as homosexual typically refer to themselves as "gay," with many women preferring the term "lesbian." Some use "queer" as a self-descriptive term, thereby transforming a formerly pejorative label into a positive statement of identity. People follow multiple paths to arrive at an adult homosexual identity. Not everyone with homosexual attractions develops a gay identity, and not all people who identify as lesbian or gay engage in homosexual acts.

A fourth component of homosexuality is involvement in same-sex relationships. Many gay and lesbian people are in a long-term intimate relationship and, like heterosexual pairings, those partnerships are characterized by diverse living arrangements, communication styles, levels of commitment, patterns of intimacy, and methods of conflict resolution. Fifth, in the United States and many other societies, homosexuality involves a sense of community membership similar to that experienced by ethnic and religious minority groups. Empirical research indicates that gay people in the United States tend to be better adjusted psychologically to the extent that they identify with and participate in such a community.

The fact that homosexuality has multiple meanings highlights the difficulties of defining who is gay. Moreover, many gay people do not publicly disclose their sexual orientation because they fear discrimination and harassment. Consequently, no accurate estimate exists for the proportions of the U.S. population that are homosexual, heterosexual, and bisexual. In North American and European studies during recent decades, roughly 1–10% of men and 1–6% of women (depending on the survey and the country) reported having had sexual relations with another person of their own sex since puberty (e.g., Laumann, Gagnon, Michael, & Michaels, 1994). Such statistics must be interpreted cautiously because many people who have engaged in same-sex sexual behavior consider themselves bisexual or heterosexual, not gay or lesbian. In addition, many people are reluctant to report such behaviors, even in anonymous surveys, because of the stigma attached to homosexuality.

Relationships and Families

In their psychological dynamics, heterosexual and homosexual relationships are highly similar. For example, no consistent differences have been observed between different- and same-sex relationships in overall psychological adjustment or satisfaction. Nevertheless, homosexual and heterosexual relationships differ in some respects. Perhaps the most significant difference is that antigay stigma denies same-sex couples the tangible benefits and positive social support that heterosexual married couples typically receive, and even forces many same-sex couples to keep their relationship at least partly hidden (Herek, 2006).

In addition, because social norms are lacking for same-sex relationships, there is considerable diversity in the way that such couples define their relationship.

Research suggests that partners in same-sex relationships are less likely than those in heterosexual couples to assume gender-typed roles (i.e., one partner exclusively performing tasks that are stereotypically "men's work" and the other partner doing the "women's work"). Another difference is that same-sex couples appear to be more likely than heterosexual couples to directly discuss and negotiate the issue of sexual monogamy and to distinguish it from emotional fidelity. Lesbian couples appear more likely to be sexually monogamous than heterosexual couples, who in turn are more likely than gay male couples to be sexually exclusive (Peplau & Fingerhut, 2007).

In recent years, growing numbers of lesbians and gay men have chosen to become parents, often in the context of a committed same-sex relationship. Gay parents meet with hostility from conservative segments of society and have even been denied custody of their own children. However, there is no scientific basis for claims that lesbians or gay men are bad parents, or that their children experience more psychological problems than children reared by comparable heterosexual parents (Patterson, 2000).

Behavioral and Social Science Research on Homosexuality

The American mental health profession once regarded homosexuality as a mental illness. Between 1952 and 1973, it was listed in the *Diagnostic and Statistical Manual of Mental Disorders*, the primary diagnostic handbook used by mental health practitioners in the United States. This classification reflected value assumptions and the viewpoints of particular schools of psychiatry rather than findings from empirical data obtained scientifically from nonpatient samples. Its accuracy came into question when behavioral scientists began to systematically study the psychological functioning of homosexuals. Beginning with Hooker's (1957) pioneering research in the 1950s, those studies consistently failed to find an inherent connection between homosexuality and pathology.

In 1973, the weight of empirical data, coupled with changing social mores and the emergence of a politically active gay community in the United States, led the American Psychiatric Association to declare that homosexuality is not an illness (Bayer, 1987). Since then, the mental health professions have recognized that society's continuing prejudice against homosexuality is often a significant source of stress for gay men and women, and sometimes leads to serious psychological distress and maladaptive behaviors (Herek & Garnets, 2007; Meyer, 2003). Consequently, professional associations such as the American Psychological Association and American Psychiatric Association have committed themselves to working actively to remove the stigma historically associated with homosexuality.

When homosexuality was regarded as an illness, its origin or cause was a topic of much speculation. More recently, researchers have recognized that the etiology of heterosexuality is equally puzzling, and scholarly inquiry has now begun to address the broad question of how sexual orientation develops in any given individual. A satisfactory answer to this question has not yet been found. It is possible that scientists will eventually identify multiple ways in which a person comes to be heterosexual, homosexual, or bisexual and will find that biological, psychological, and cultural factors all play a role in this complex process.

Regardless of its origins, a heterosexual or homosexual orientation is experienced by most people in the United States as a deeply rooted and unchangeable part of themselves. Many adults report never having made a conscious choice about their sexual orientation and always having felt sexual attractions to and desires for people of a particular sex. When homosexuality was assumed to be a form of psychopathology, psychiatrists and psychologists often attempted to change homosexual people into heterosexuals. Even today, some counselors and psychotherapists continue this practice. However, such treatments have been rejected by the mainstream mental health profession because they are ethically questionable as well as being usually ineffective and often harmful to the client. Instead, most practitioners working with lesbian and gay clients assist them in developing positive feelings about their sexuality, establishing meaningful intimate relationships, and coping with societal stigma (Herek & Garnets, 2007).

Just as the focus of psychotherapy with gay men and lesbians has changed, so too has the emphasis shifted in empirical research. Increasingly, scientific studies of homosexuality now address the problems and challenges faced by lesbians and gay men as a result of prejudice and discrimination. Researchers have failed to find significant differences between homosexual and heterosexual people on a wide range of characteristics, including their capacity to form and maintain intimate relationships, their ability to be good parents, their likelihood of victimizing children or adults, and their ability to function effectively in work groups and organizations. Perhaps the most important general insight gained from such research is that gay men and lesbians constitute a highly diverse group. Apart from their sexual orientation, they are no more homogeneous than the heterosexual population.

Another significant focus for contemporary empirical research is the social psychology of sexual prejudice, that is, heterosexuals' negative attitudes toward sexual minorities based on the latter's sexual orientation (Herek, 2007). Because such prejudice has many sources and serves differing psychological functions for different individuals, a variety of strategies will probably be needed to change antigay attitudes. One of the most consistently noted sources for heterosexuals' prejudice reduction is having personal contact with a lesbian or gay man, especially when such contact involves open discussion of sexual orientation.

Although psychologists once considered homosexuality to be a form of pathology, this view was discarded in the 1970s. Today homosexuality is understood as an alternative expression of human sexuality, less common than heterosexuality but not inherently problematic for the individual. At the same time, psychologists also recognize that gay men and lesbians continue to face problems as a result of the stigma historically associated with homosexuality.

REFERENCES

Bayer, R. (1987). *Homosexuality and American psychiatry: The politics of diagnosis* (rev. ed.). Princeton, NJ: Princeton University Press.

Herek, G. M. (2006). Legal recognition of same-sex relationships in the United States: A social science perspective. *American Psychologist, 61,* 607–621.

Herek, G. M. (2007). Confronting sexual stigma and prejudice: Theory and practice. *Journal of Social Issues, 63,* 905–925.

Herek, G. M., & Garnets, L. D. (2007). Sexual orientation and mental health. *Annual Review of Clinical Psychology, 3,* 353–375.

Hooker, E. (1957). The adjustment of the male overt homosexual. *Journal of Projective Techniques, 21,* 18–31.

Laumann, E. O., Gagnon, J. H., Michael, R. T., & Michaels, S. (1994). *The social organization of sexuality: Sexual practices in the United States.* Chicago: University of Chicago Press.

Meyer, I. H. (2003). Prejudice, social stress, and mental health in lesbian, gay, and bisexual populations: Conceptual issues and research evidence. *Psychological Bulletin, 129,* 674–697.

Patterson, C. J. (2000). Family relationships of lesbians and gay men. *Journal of Marriage and the Family, 62,* 1052–1069.

Peplau, L. A., & Fingerhut, A. W. (2007). The close relationships of lesbians and gay men. *Annual Review of Psychology, 58,* 405–424.

SUGGESTED READINGS

DeBord, K. A. (Eds.). (2007). *Handbook of counseling and psychotherapy with lesbian, gay, bisexual, and transgender clients* (2nd ed.). Washington, DC: American Psychological Association.

Garnets, L. D., & Kimmel, D. C. (Eds.). (2003). *Psychological perspectives on lesbian, gay, and bisexual experiences* (2nd ed.). New York: Columbia University Press.

Meyer, I. H., & Northridge, M. E. (Eds.). (2007). *The health of sexual minorities: Public health perspectives on lesbian, gay, bisexual and transgender populations.* New York: Springer.

GREGORY M. HEREK
University of California, Davis

See also: **Gender Roles; Heterosexuality; Sexual Desire; Sexual Orientation, Roots of**

HOPE

All humans are goal-directed beings by nature. Whether we seek food, jobs, social connection, relaxation, or better health, much of our behavior is organized around the pursuit of a particular end state. Successful goal attainment requires three elements: a clearly articulated goal, a plan, and motivation to put that plan into action. According to Snyder and colleagues, these three elements constitute hopeful thinking.

The term *hope* generally is used to identify a preferential outcome, although there is some debate as to whether the construct is better classified as a feeling or a thought. Emotion-based theorists (e.g., Mowrer, 1960) describe hope as the feeling that arises from the anticipation that something pleasurable is about to occur. The experience of hoping thus propels us toward goals, as we are motivated to attain the envisioned pleasurable end state. Cognitive-based theorists (e.g., Erikson, 1964; Stotland, 1969) define hopes as an expectation or belief that goals will be attained despite the obstacles encountered in their pursuit; the magnitude of hope is based on the importance of the goal as well as the perceived ability to attain goals.

C. R. Snyder's conceptualization of hope (Snyder, 1994, 1995, 2002) builds on cognitive goal-based theories while acknowledging the role of emotions in propagating motivation to continue goal pursuits. According to Snyder's model, hope is a cognitive set comprising three distinct components: goals, pathways, thinking, and agency thinking. Goals represent the end points for all planful behavior, whereas pathways are the avenues people use to reach their goals, and agency is the energy needed to sustain movement toward those goals. According to this model, goal attainment results in positive emotions, whereas goal blockages produce negative emotions.

Given their central role in guiding and determining intentional behavior, goals are anchors of hope theory. Goals may be smaller, more short-term undertakings (e.g., taking a shower, renting a movie), or they may be long-term endeavors (e.g., writing a book, graduating college). They may stand alone, or they may be subgoals of a larger, more complex enterprise (e.g., learning the Greek alphabet before learning to read or speak Greek). Regardless of their magnitude, the most fulfilling goals are often attainable yet somewhat difficult to achieve (also called "stretch goals"); unattainable goals often produce a sense of demoralization, while easily attainable goals do not engender high energy. Interestingly, individuals with high hope often add an unrequired twist to easily attained goals in order to increase their motivation. For example, people with high hope set shorter time limits for themselves on timed tasks, or they require themselves to select a novel pathway to goal attainment, such as dunking a basketball rather than making a layup.

A critical component of goal attainment is the ability to understand cause–effect relationships and to string together sequential behaviors, as these skills allow the mapping of routes to reach our goals. High "pathways thinkers" are confident of their ability to devise successful pathways and to develop alternative routes in the face of goal blockages. People high in pathways thinking have the ability to visualize a number of methods of solving a problem, and they are not easily discouraged when one pathway is unsuccessful; they merely try the next route they envisioned. High-hope individuals make self-statements such as "I'll find a way to solve this problem" or "I always find a way to get what I want, even when times are tough."

Agency thinking refers to one's perception of the amount of motivation and energy available to pursue goals. Agency thinking of high-hope individuals is often characterized by self-statements such as "I can do this" or "I will succeed." Although agency thinking is important for the initiation of movement toward a goal, it is particularly relevant when an individual encounters an impediment to the goal, as these positive self-statements help the individuals to find a way around the blockage and sustain movement toward the desired end point.

Pathways and agency thinking are processes that build upon one another; that is, increases in pathways thinking tend to produce increases in agency thinking and vice versa. In addition, both components are critical for goal attainment. A goal and a plan with no motivation are as useless as directionless activity. The enterprise of psychotherapy provides an apt illustration for both types of problems. Clients may present for therapy with a goal of "getting better" or achieving emotional stability, but they often cannot generate the ways in which to do so (e.g., a client may not recognize distorted thoughts or know how to reframe them in order to ameliorate a depressed mood). Conversely, many clients come to therapy knowing what it is that will help them feel better, but they are unable to muster the motivation to engage in those behaviors (e.g., a client knows that if she stops drinking and gets more sleep it will help her depressed mood, but she cannot bring herself to do so). Either difficulty is likely to perpetuate negative affect, as failure to attain goals (i.e., goal blockage) is known to do.

Hopeful thinking begins to develop in the first two years of life. Between birth and three months of age, infants learn to identify sensations and perceptions, and they soon are able to understand chronological sequences (e.g., "this follows that"). This comprehension signifies the inception of pathways thinking. Throughout the remainder of the first year of life, children expand upon this learning and develop the ability to point to objects they desire, such as a favorite toy; this denotes the onset of goal-directed thinking. In the second year of life, toddlers become aware of their personhood, and they recognize that they are capable of *initiating* cause-effect sequences, which indicates the beginnings of agency thinking (i.e., "I can make this happen"). Thus, under optimal environmental conditions (e.g., nonabusive, nonneglectful, nurturing parents), the tenets of hopeful thinking have taken root by the beginning of the child's third year of life.

As children grow, they develop a sense of their general ability to set and reach personal goals, which is known as dispositional or trait hope. Interactions with caregivers are crucial during this phase of development. Supportive adults act as coaches, encouraging children to generate solutions to problems and to negotiate obstacles that arise in the pursuit of goals. This mentoring process, along with the positive emotions generated as goals are reached, helps engender in children a sense that "I can."

High hope confers multiple benefits throughout the lifespan. In addition to the aforementioned advantages (i.e., having more well-defined goals, greater confidence in goal mapping, and more positive self-talk), individuals with high hope outperform their low-hope counterparts on multiple domains (for a review, see Snyder, 2002). For example, higher trait hope is related to higher academic achievement. Snyder and colleagues (2002) found that college freshmen with high scores on the Hope Scale (Snyder et al., 1991) had higher overall grade point averages and were more likely to graduate than individuals with low hope, even after controlling for college entrance exam scores. Beyond academics, those with high hope also demonstrate superior athletic outcomes. For instance, Curry and colleagues (1997) found that trait hope predicted athletic outcomes in female track athletes even after athletic ability was taken into account.

Hopeful thinking confers multiple physical health benefits as well. Individuals with high hope tend to demonstrate greater pain tolerance, medication adherence, and overall adjustment following the onset of major illnesses such as spinal cord injuries, breast cancer, blindness, and fibromyalgia. In older adults, high hope is related to greater overall life satisfaction and to greater perceived physical health (Wrobleski & Snyder, 2005). Furthermore, higher hope correlates positively with better psychological and social adjustment as well as better coping. For example, those with high hope are more likely to attribute difficulties in goal achievement to poorly chosen strategies rather than personal weaknesses, and they are more likely to "regoal" in the face of continued goal blockages. In other words, they are more likely than individuals with low hope to reevaluate the importance of the blocked goal and to decide whether continued pursuit is optimal. In addition, Snyder and colleagues posit that hope may be the critical factor predicting change in psychotherapy, particularly in the early stages (Snyder, Ilardi, Michael, & Cheavens, 2000).

Thus, the development and presence of hopeful thinking are highly adaptive in multiple spheres of life. The tenets of hopeful thinking can be taught, and the elegance and simplicity of the model allow for the development of interventions aimed at increasing hope. In doing so, people can learn more clearly to identify and strive for their goals, and they can reconstruct their thinking to maximize energy and motivation. Thus, hopeful thinking is optimal for personal growth and development, and it is attainable for those who seek its benefits.

REFERENCES

Erikson, E. H. (1964). *Insight and responsibility*. New York: W. W. Norton.

Mowrer, O. H. (1960). *Learning theory and behavior*. New York: John Wiley and Sons.

Snyder, C. R. (1994). *The psychology of hope: You can get there from here*. New York: Free Press.

Snyder, C. R. (2002). Hope theory: Rainbows in the mind. *Psychological Inquiry, 13*, 249–275.

Snyder, C. R., Harris, C. Anderson, J. R., Holloran, S. A., Irving, L. M., et al. (1991). The will and the ways: Development and validation of an individual-differences measure of hope. *Journal of Personality and Social Psychology, 60*, 570–585.

Snyder, C. R., Ilardi, S., Michael, S. T., & Cheavens, J. (2000). Hope theory: Updating a common process for psychological change. In C. R. Snyder & R. E. Ingram (Eds.), *Handbook of psychological change: Psychotherapy processes and practices for the 21st century* (pp. 128–153). New York: John Wiley & Sons.

Stotland, E. (1969). *The psychology of hope*. San Francisco: Jossey-Bass.

Wrobleski, K. K., & Snyder, C. R. (2005). Hopeful thinking in older adults: Back to the future. *Experimental Aging Research, 31*, 217–235.

SUGGESTED READINGS

Snyder, C. R. (2000). *Handbook of hope: Theory, measures, and applications*. San Diego, CA: Academic Press.

Snyder, C. R., & Lopez, S. J. (2006). *Positive psychology: The scientific and practical explorations of human strengths*. Thousand Oaks, CA: Sage.

LORIE RITSCHEL
Emory University School of Medicine

HULL, CLARK L. (1884–1952)

Clark L. Hull's most important contribution to psychology lies in his theory of learning, considered one of the most important learning theories of the twentieth century. He received his PhD in 1918 at the University of Wisconsin. Early in his career he was interested in the field of aptitude testing, an area he abandoned because he did not see much future in it. He then turned to the field of hypnosis and suggestibility. In 1929 he accepted an appointment as research professor at Yale University, a post he held until his retirement.

For most of his career Hull devoted himself to the development of a theory of learning along with experimental research to support it. In 1940, with a number of colleagues he published *A Mathematico-Deductive Theory of Rote Learning*. This was considered a masterpiece in theory construction, but it was so complicated that most psychologists failed to understand it. In 1943, he published the first complete statement of his theory of learning, *Principles of Behavior*, of which revisions followed in 1951 and 1952.

Hull's theory was basically an S-R (stimulus-response) theory, but an expanded and complicated one, and it reflected some influences from the behavioristic ideas of John Watson. Hull was also influenced by Ivan Pavlov's work on the conditioned reflex, which he considered to be a simple form of learning on which more complex kinds of learning could be built.

Like B. F. Skinner, Hull stressed the importance of reinforcement if learning was to take place. Reinforcement was successful because it resulted in the reduction of drives. Thus, the concept of drives and their reduction became an important aspect of Hull's theory. He considered the environmental influences on the organism as well: these were input, while the responses the organism made were output.

The formulation of hypothetico-deductive theory of learning involved a series of postulates that should eventually be tested by experimentation. The final formulation of the theory consisted of 18 postulates and 12 corollaries, stated in both mathematical and verbal forms. Hull's theory also included intervening variables, constructs that are assumed but never really subject to direct experimental verification.

Hull's theory was systematic and generated a great deal of research. He insisted on well-controlled experiments and on the quantification of the resulting data. His theory was expanded and modified by Kenneth Spence and was widely taught and studied as the Hull-Spence theory of learning.

SUGGESTED READING

Hull, C. L. (1952). *Principles of behavior: An introduction to behavior theory*. New York: Appleton.

RALPH W. LUNDIN
Wheaton, IL

HUMAN DEVELOPMENT

Theory and research in lifespan psychology rest on the key assumption that human development occurs from conception to death and involves lifelong adaptive processes (Baltes, Lindenberger, & Staudinger, 2006). Thus, human development is the result of biological, psychological, and sociocultural influences that mutually affect each other and shape how individuals develop over the lifespan (Baltes et al., 2006; Li, 2003). With regard to individual development (ontogenesis), lifespan psychologists focus on (1) how single individuals change over time (intraindividual change); (2) differences between individuals during different developmental periods (interindividual differences); (3) differences in individuals' patterns of change over time (interindividual differences in intraindividual change); and (4) how between-person variability in within-person change is brought about as a consequence of biocultural coconstruction (Li, 2003). Moreover, lifespan psychologists agree on a set of core assumptions from which they study human development. These assumptions state that human development is a process that involves continuity and discontinuity, multidirectionality, gains and losses, plasticity, and contextual embeddedness (Baltes et al., 2006).

Continuity and Discontinuity

Theorists of human development have debated two issues with respect to the nature of continuity and discontinuity. The first issue is whether there are certain age periods (e.g., early childhood) that hold primacy in human development, or whether development occurs across the entire lifespan. The second issue is whether human development proceeds in a quantitative and continuous manner or whether it unfolds in a series of qualitative discontinuous stages.

Although certain age periods may have primacy for particular domains of development (e.g., brain development, language acquisition), a review of the literature shows that humans have a capacity for change across the entire lifespan and that no age period holds complete supremacy in regulating the nature of development (Baltes et al., 2006). Moreover, over the course of human development, and at all stages of the lifespan, both continuous (cumulative) and discontinuous (qualitatively different and innovative) processes are at work (Baltes et al., 2006; Lerner, 1984).

Multidimensionality and Multidirectionality

Another core principle of human development concerns its multidimensionality and multidirectionality. Regardless of the domain of development, multiple dimensions are required to capture the complexity of behavioral changes over time. The sequencing of changes, the conditions influencing continuity and change, and the direction of change tend to vary across dimensions within and across behavioral domains. For example, some forms of intelligence remain stable or increase over most of the adult lifespan (e.g., vocabulary), whereas others show normative decline after the age of 60 or earlier (e.g., abstract reasoning). Only by examining multidirectional variations in the trajectories of change over time can the complexity of human development be elucidated.

Gains and Losses in Human Development

Throughout life, development always consists of the joint occurrence of gain (growth) and loss (decline). Human development is not a simple movement toward higher efficiency and growth. In contrast to earlier views of human development that focused solely on processes that increased a person's adaptive capacity, lifespan models of human development assert that in order to gain capacity in one dimension, loss usually occurs in another dimension (Baltes et al., 2006). New adaptive capacities replace or subsume previously functional ones that have been lost. This principle presumes that some dimensions within a system grow and become more efficient and adaptive, whereas others are simultaneously declining and may become less efficient. In the second half of the lifespan and especially in very old age, losses are likely to outpace gains in adaptive capacity, requiring the individual to engage in selective optimization with compensation (Baltes & Baltes, 1990).

Plasticity of Human Development

Plasticity refers to those processes by which individuals develop their capacity to modify their behavior to adjust to, or fit, the demands of a particular context (Lerner, 1984). This principle presumes individuals' capacity to influence their environment and themselves in order to shape the course of development. Structural characteristics of the species both create the potential for, and set the constraints on, behavioral plasticity. Fundamental tasks for developmentalists are to (1) identify the internal and external conditions under which developmental processes can be altered to promote optimal development; (2) examine the range of plasticity (modifiability) in different domains of behavior; and (3) examine developmental changes in the possible range of plasticity across the lifespan (Baltes et al., 2006).

Contextual Embeddedness

Two core assumptions of lifespan psychology are contextual embeddedness and dynamic interaction (Lerner, 1984). Contextual embeddedness refers to the idea that human development occurs at multiple levels (e.g., inner-biological, individual-psychological, social-sociological, cultural-historical, outer-physical/ecological). These levels do not operate independently; rather, variables and processes at all levels influence each other in reciprocal ways. Thus, the task of lifespan psychologists is to describe and explain how different levels interact and influence each other, and to modify the parameters

that affect these interactions to optimize developmental outcomes (Baltes et al., 2006; Lerner, 1984).

Bronfenbrenner and Morris (2006) proposed a theoretical model for examining levels of contextual embeddedness in human development. In this model, development is seen as a joint function of the individual and all levels of the environment. The environment is conceived as a nested structure of four systems including (1) the immediate settings surrounding the individual (microsystems); (2) combinations of microsystems (mesosystem); (3) links between settings that include the individual and settings that affect the individual but do not include the person directly (exosystem); and (4) societal and cultural influences on individuals (macrosystem).

Lifespan theorists have also emphasized that individuals' development may vary considerably due to historical-cultural conditions. Elder's (1974) research on children growing up during the Great Depression showed, for example, how the effects of a major historical event on individual development varied depending on a person's age at the time. Similarly, Schaie (2005) found in a cohort-sequential study of adult intellectual development that important cohort differences existed for different components of human intelligence.

Multidisciplinary Inquiry and Methodological Sophistication

The basic assumptions of lifespan psychology make multidisciplinary inquiry a necessity. Developmental changes across the lifespan can only be explained by examining multiple levels and multiple dimensions of human behavior (Bronfenbrenner & Morris, 2006), making it necessary to examine biological, psychological, social-interpersonal, cultural, and historical influences on development. The dynamic interplay among influences over time can only be understood if multiple disciplines work together and if sophisticated research designs and methods are employed (Hertzog & Nesselroade, 2003).

Although theorists have argued for a long time (Harris, 1957) that developmental research requires observations over the "period of time during which the developmental phenomena of interest are thought to occur" (Schaie, 1983, p. 1), most studies have relied on cross-sectional comparisons of different age groups. Cross-sectional studies are valuable in informing researchers about the possible magnitude and the pattern of age differences in a certain behavior at a given point in time, but they do not permit conclusions about developmental change. Schaie (1983) identified five justifications for the longitudinal study of behavioral development. Specifically, longitudinal studies permit (1) the direct identification of intra-individual change; (2) the identification of inter-individual variability in intra-individual change; (3) the assessment of the interrelationships among different domains of intra-individual change; (4) the analysis of determinants or correlates of intra-individual change; and (5) the analysis of inter-individual variability in the determinants or correlates of intra-individual change.

These justifications have several implications. First, longitudinal studies need, by design, to be multivariate, to draw on multiple data sources, and to include variables from a person's natural environment (Block, 1993). Second, because age is a person attribute that cannot be experimentally assigned, longitudinal studies do not conform to the rules of true experiments. Consequently, longitudinal studies are subject to all the problems inherent in quasi-experimental designs as described by Campbell and Stanley (1967). Third, because longitudinal studies have traditionally been conducted with individuals from a single birth cohort, they confounded time-of-measurement and aging effects and rendered estimates of age effects internally invalid (Schaie, 1983). In order to deal with this confound and with the confound of age and cohort that exists in cross-sectional research, Schaie (1983) has advocated the use of sequential study designs. Lifespan developmental psychologists find cohort-sequential designs of greatest interest because they explicitly differentiate intra-individual change within cohorts from interindividual variability between cohorts (Schaie, 1983). Thus, the use of more complex research designs and the advent of sophisticated methods for the analysis of longitudinal data (Hertzog & Nesselroade, 2003) have given researchers powerful tools to examine human development in appropriate ways across the entire lifespan.

In conclusion, lifespan psychology has made great progress in the description, explanation, and optimization of human development. The use of longitudinal and sequential research designs (Schaie, 1983) in combination with sophisticated methods for analyzing longitudinal data (Hertzog & Nesselroade, 2003) has resulted in elaborate multivariate studies of behavioral development, showing that development occurs at all stages of the human lifespan from conception to death (Baltes et al., 2006). In general, human development is characterized by continuity and discontinuity, multidirectionality, gains and losses, modifiability/plasticity, and contextual embeddedness, and has as the ultimate goal the realization of a person's fullest potential (Baltes et al., 2006; Lerner, 1984).

REFERENCES

Baltes, M. M., & Baltes, P. B. (1990). Psychological perspectives on successful aging: The model of selective optimization with compensation. In P. B. Baltes & M. M. Baltes (Eds.), *Successful aging: Perspectives from the behavioral sciences* (pp. 1–34). New York: Cambridge University Press.

Baltes, P. B., Lindenberger, U., & Staudinger, U. M. (2006). Life-span theory in developmental psychology. In W. Damon (Series Ed.) & R. M. Lerner (Vol. Ed.), *Handbook of child psychology: Vol. 1. Theoretical models of human development* (6th ed., pp. 569–664). Hoboken, NJ: John Wiley & Sons.

Block, J. (1993). Studying personality the long way. In D. C. Funder, R. D. Parke, C. Tomlinson-Keasey, & K. Widaman (Eds.), *Studying lives through time: Personality and development* (pp. 9–41). Washington, DC: American Psychological Association.

Bronfenbrenner, U., & Morris, P. A. (2006). The bioecological model of human development. In W. Damon (Series Ed.) & R. M. Lerner (Vol. Ed.), *Handbook of child psychology: Vol. 1. Theoretical models of human development* (6th ed., pp. 793–828). Hoboken, NJ: John Wiley & Sons.

Campbell, D. T., & Stanley, J. C. (1967). *Experimental and quasi-experimental designs for research.* Chicago: Rand McNally.

Elder, G. H., Jr. (1974). *Children of the Great Depression.* Chicago: University of Chicago Press.

Harris, D. B. (Ed.). (1957). *The concept of development.* Minneapolis, MN: University of Minnesota Press.

Hertzog, C., & Nesselroade, J. R. (2003). Assessing psychological change in adulthood: An overview of methodological issues. *Psychology and Aging, 18,* 639–657.

Lerner, R. M. (1984). *On the nature of human plasticity.* New York: Cambridge University Press.

Li, S.-C. (2003). Biocultural orchestration of developmental plasticity across levels: The interplay of biology and culture in shaping the mind and behavior across the life span. *Psychological Bulletin, 129,* 171–194.

Schaie, K. W. (1983). What can we learn from the longitudinal study of adult psychological development? In K. W. Schaie (Ed.), *Longitudinal studies of adult psychological development* (pp. 1–19). New York: Guilford Press.

Schaie, K. W. (2005). *Developmental influences on adult intelligence: The Seattle Longitudinal Study.* New York: Oxford University Press.

MANFRED DIEHL
HELENA CHUI
LISE M. YOUNGBLADE
Colorado State University

SARA H. QUALLS
University of Colorado—Colorado Springs

See also: Cognitive Development; Developmental Psychology; Emotional Development; Social Cognitive Development

HUMAN FACTORS RESEARCH

Human factors is often used as a superordinate term covering a number of endeavors that share the goal of understanding and improving the interactions of human operators with their technology, work environment, and other domain operators. We all recognize when bad design has not been informed by human factors research: the door you push that is designed to be pulled, instructions that misdirect you, the device that looks elegant but that fails to make clear how it is to be turned on (Norman, 1998).

Many of the disciplines considered in this entry are related by family resemblance, although they do tend to share some common assumptions and the goal of aiding the human operator. The distinctions among endeavors such as engineering psychology, ergonomics, cognitive engineering, cognitive ergonomics, and the like are often subtle, and they need not stand in the way of understanding this family of research efforts. Human factors research includes studying different operators, from the young child working with a computer to the elderly person using a medical reminding system, using a variety of methods—anthropometrics, task analyses, surveys, natural observation, simulations, laboratory experiments, and modeling—in numerous domains—aerospace, transportation, medicine, recreation, and industrial processing, with the hope of improving systems. In the science of human factors there is the added hope of extracting generalizable principles that will be of value in other systems.

We hope to characterize the breadth and diversity of human factors research (see Salvendy, 2005) by presenting a selection of research cases. The reader will note the variety of methods and domains.

Land Mines and Knowledge Elicitation

The impact of land mines as measured in human lives and casualties is huge. Finding and dismantling the weapons is not easy, especially with modern mines. Land-mine detection requires humans using sophisticated hand-held equipment that uses electromagnetic induction to detect metals, and more recently radar, to detect discontinuities in the soil. As late as 1995, the detection rate was quite poor—15% for the M14 mine, for example. As with all tasks, there is variation in performance. Some experts perform at a much higher rate, sometimes 90%. Human factors researchers (Stazewski & Davison, 2000) took advantage of that fact. They elicited the procedural knowledge from experts, by videotaping them and asking them to "think aloud" as they performed the task and then spending hours analyzing the video and verbal protocols. From this, the researchers discerned the skills and strategies relevant to superior performance. They then created an instructional program that was based on the "expert blueprint" and trained new personnel. The new personnel subsequently showed results in the upper 80% range. Insights are being taken from this work to begin developing fully autonomous mine detectors.

Aviation Safety and Natural Observations

In 1978, United Airlines flight 173 ran out of fuel and crashed outside of Portland, Oregon. The flight had actually arrived at its destination much earlier, but the pilot and crew circled the airport for an hour while the tanks emptied. Analysis by the National Transportation Safety board attributed the crash to a failure in communication in the cockpit. Since then a great deal of research on what has come to be known as crew resource management (CRM; Helmreich, Merrit, & Wilhelm, 1999) has taken place and has successfully changed the commercial flight deck from the absolute domain of the captain to a flatter organizational structure in which the copilot can comfortably and effectively bring other perspectives and perceptions to bear. Much of this work developed from natural observations of intact real-world crew interactions. Researchers riding in the jump seat of the flight deck noted characteristics of effective and ineffective communication and cockpit management. Now CRM is part of the routine training of line pilots around the world.

Anesthetic Awareness and Simulation

A woman left her Texas home for a routine surgery. The anesthesiologist applied the usual triplet of drugs to induce paralysis, loss of consciousness, and elimination of pain. Unfortunately, the anesthesiologist had underestimated the dosages, and Jeanette Liska lay on the surgeon's table, paralyzed, but alert and able to feel the cauterizing scalpel cut into her flesh. It is difficult to project cognitively the effectiveness of the three doses on the patient several minutes after administration. Human factors researchers (Drews, Syroid, Agutter, Strayer, & Westenskow, 2006) have developed a system that aids the anesthesiologist in making just such predictions. By incorporating design principles well known to human factors specialists, as well as effective algorithms to make the prediction, the research team was able to create an effective automation aid. Using simulation and laboratory procedures, they were able to confirm that the automation aid allowed more accurate delivery of the three boluses of drugs needed to allow modern surgery.

Traffic Speed

Vehicle speed is a frequent contributor to traffic accidents. Basic knowledge of visual perception was used to reduce vehicle speed and increase safety at traffic circles in Britain (Godley, Fildes, & Triggs, 1997). When objects move at an increasing rate in the optic flow field, drivers perceive that they are accelerating. The Transportation Research Laboratory created an illusion of acceleration by painting transverse lines on a road such that the gap between the lines became increasingly smaller as they approached the traffic circle. Drivers perceived themselves as speeding up and thus decelerated as they entered the traffic circle. As a result of this perceptual countermeasure, there was a 57% reduction in speed-related accidents for two years after the countermeasure, and the reduction in accidents was observed up to seven years later.

Buses and Design Procedures

An information-gathering investigation was undertaken to determine how ergonomics can improve the design of a bus for passenger requirements and preferences (Brooks, 1979). Over 200 disabled and elderly people were surveyed on the problems they encountered while using a bus; anthropometric, physical capabilities, and preferences also were recorded. A wooden model of a bus was used to film and solicit preference ratings of various configurations of step height, hand-rail, and seating. Alternative designs were then evaluated. Finally, levels of acceleration, jerk, and deceleration were measured in service buses, and bus passenger accident data were analyzed over 12 months. The latter showed that over 57% of injuries to bus riders did not involve collisions or other severe vehicle movements, with a disproportionate number involving passengers over 60 years of age. Results indicated that passengers experience particular difficulty getting on and off the bus and led to numerous improvements, including a retractable first step and improved design in doorway handholds.

Video Games and Usability

Developers want to create fun video games. To be fun, the game must appropriately challenge players. Too little challenge will bore players, and too much challenge will frustrate players. However, developers cannot always intuit the appropriate amount of challenge for a given game. Consequently, developers such as Microsoft have begun to user-test their games in order to ensure that they appropriately challenge players (Thompson, 2007). For example, Halo 3 was rigorously user-tested before its release. During testing, hundreds of users played Halo 3 and verbalized what they were thinking as they progressed through the game. In addition, human factors psychologists observed each player and asked questions concerning the user's experience. Based on this information, they identified those portions of the game that inappropriately challenged the players and why. In turn, the researchers conveyed their findings to the developers, along with recommendations for how to more appropriately challenge the game players. As a result, Halo 3 was well-received: It was the top-selling game of 2007 and won numerous awards, including *Time Magazine*'s 2007 "Game of the Year."

Manual Labor and Anthropometrics

Each year, many manual laborers are injured on the job. In some cases, such injuries occur despite the presence of safety equipment. For example, plantation workers who use axes or hatchets to cut plants often cut their own legs, despite wearing leg protectors. Such accidents occur because the leg protectors do not fit properly. To remedy the situation, human factors researchers (Hendrick, 1996) conducted an anthropometric study of plantation worker dimensions. Doing so made it clear that the dimensions of workers' legs varied substantially. In turn, this information was used to redesign the leg protectors. The new leg protectors had improved fasteners, and their dimensions fit workers better. After introducing the new leg protectors into a plantation, ax or hatchet leg injuries were nonexistent. As a result, the plantation saved approximately $250,000 that year in worker-injury compensation. Furthermore, the widespread adoption of these new leg protectors has saved the agricultural industry millions of dollars.

Clearly human factors research is rich in the diversity of its participant populations, its methods, and its application domains. The outcomes are also rich and include new designs, improved training, and general principles.

REFERENCES

Brooks, B. M. (1979). An investigation into aspects of bus design and passenger requirements. *Ergonomics, 22,* 175–188.

Drews, F. A., Syroid, N., Agutter, J., Strayer, D. L., & Westenskow, D. R. (2006). Drug delivery as a control task: Improving patient safety in anesthesia. *Human Factors, 48,* 85–94.

Godley, S. T., Fildes, B. N., & Triggs, T. J. (1997). Perceptual countermeasures to speed-related accidents. In D. Harris (Ed.), *Engineering psychology and cognitive ergonomics, Volume 1. Transportation systems.* Brookfield, VT: Ashgate.

Helmreich, R. L., Merrit, A. C., & Wilhelm, J. A. (1999). The evolution of crew management training in commercial aviation. *International Journal of Aviation Psychology, 9,* 19–32.

Hendrick, H. W. (1996). Good ergonomics is good economics. In *Proceedings of the Human Factors and Ergonomics Society 40th Annual Meeting* (pp. 1–10).

Norman, D. A. (1998). *The design of everyday things.* Cambridge, MA: MIT Press.

Salvendy, G. (2005). *Handbook of human factors and ergonomics* (3rd ed.). Hoboken, NJ: John Wiley & Sons.

Staszewski, J. J., & Davison, A. (2000). Mine detection training based on expert skill. In A. C. Dubey, J. F. Harvey, J. T. Broach, & R. E. Dugan (Eds.), *Detection and remediation technologies for mines and mine-like targets B. Proceedings of SPIE, 4038,* 90–101.

Thompson, C. (2008). Halo 3: How Microsoft Labs invented a new science of play. Retrieved September 6, 2008 from http://www.wired.com/gaming/virtualworlds/magazine/15-09/ff_halo.

SUGGESTED READINGS

Cooke, N. J. (Ed.). (2008). *Human actors, 50th Anniversary Issue, 3,* entire issue.

Cooke, N. J., & Durso, F. (2008). *Stories of modern technology failures and cognitive engineering successes.* Boca Raton: CRC Press.

Wickens, C. D., Lee, J., Liu, Y. D., & Gordon-Becker, S. E. (2004). *An introduction to human factors engineering* (2nd ed.). Upper Saddle River, NJ: Prentice-Hall.

FRANCIS T. DURSO
Georgia Institute of Technology

KEITH S. JONES
PATRICIA R. DELUCIA
Texas Tech University

See also: **Engineering Psychology**

HUMAN LOCOMOTION

In the eighteenth century, the investigation of movement was based on the premise that upright stance and gait, as well as differentiation of hand movements, represented a basic requirement for human cultural development. These movements necessitate that the nervous system must function to automatically balance the body's center of mass over the feet during all motor activities. In other words, every movement must begin and end with a postural adjustment.

Analysis of human gait first became possible toward the end of the nineteenth century with the development of photographic recordings of running movements. Later, the technique for recording of leg muscle electromyographic (EMG) activity during locomotion was developed and applied in cats, and subsequently in human beings.

The relative significance of reflexes on central rhythms and programming in locomotion has been addressed. The central (i.e., spinal) mechanisms involved in locomotion are reflected in a complex pattern of leg muscle activation that is thought to be programmed and inborn in its basic structure (Dietz, 2003). The EMG pattern is assumed to be evoked by a multisensory afferent input and generated by spinal interneuronal circuits that are closely connected with spinal locomotor centers.

It appears that load receptor and hip joint–related afferent input are of crucial importance for evoking a locomotor pattern (Dietz et al., 2002a). The timing of the pattern can, to a limited extent, be modified by afferent inputs. However this has yet to be fully explored. A basic requirement of bipedal locomotion is that both legs act in a cooperative manner; each limb affects the strength of muscle activation and the time/space behavior of the other. There exists some evidence that this interlimb coordination is mediated by spinal interneuronal circuits, which are themselves under supraspinal (e.g., cerebral and cerebellar) control (Dietz, 2003).

With regard to reflex mechanisms, short-latency stretch reflexes in leg extensor muscles are profoundly modulated during gait. This is mainly via presynaptic inhibition group Ia input, but is also influenced to a small degree by fusimotor input. A significant contribution of short-latency stretch reflexes to the compensation of perturbations during walking has not yet been demonstrated. However they may be involved in compensating for small ground irregularities at distinct phases of gait. Compensation for foot displacement during gait is mediated by polysynaptic spinal reflexes, including an activation of synergistic muscle groups of both legs (Dietz, 2002a).

The compensatory EMG responses are thought to be mediated by peripheral information from group Ib (load receptors) and group II afferents (cf. Dietz & Duysens, 2000), converging with different peripheral and supraspinal inputs onto common spinal interneurons in a spinal pathway. These reflexes modulate the basic motor pattern of spinal interneuronal circuits underlying the locomotor task. During recent years, increasing evidence has emerged for the importance of load receptor input in the control of bipedal stance and gait (Dietz & Duysens, 2000); yet we are still only beginning to understand the nature of this input and its interaction with other afferent inputs and control mechanisms.

Vestibular and visual functions are mainly context-dependent and are essential when afferent input from other sources is reduced. Nevertheless, convincing evidence indicates that the amount of proprioceptive feedback from the legs determines the influence of vestibulo-spinal input on body movement. Hence, patients with acute vestibular disorder balance better when running than when standing or walking slowly. Obviously, the automatic spinal locomotor program suppresses destabilizing vestibular input (Brandt et al., 1999)

Furthermore, recent research indicates that interlimb coordination during human locomotion is organized in a similar way to that in cats (Dietz, 2002b). Such a quadrupedal organization is controlled via an excitation of propriospinal neurons by supraspinal centers. This allows a task-dependent neuronal linkage of cervical and thoraco-lumbar propriospinal circuits controlling leg and arm movements during human locomotor activities.

One of the first symptoms of a lesion within the central motor system is *the movement disorder*, which is most obvious during locomotion in patients with spasticity, cerebellar lesions, or Parkinson's disease (Dietz, 2002a). The clinical examination of patients with one of these movement disorders reveals changes in tendon-tap reflexes and muscle tone.

However, today we know that there exists only a weak relationship between the physical signs obtained during the clinical examination in a passive motor condition and the impaired neuronal mechanisms in operation during an active movement (Dietz & Sinkjaer, 2007). For example, after stroke the loss of supraspinal drive is compensated for in a major way by secondarily occurring changes in mechanical muscle fiber properties, which subsequently lead to the spastic movement disorder (Dietz & Sinkjaer, 2007). This enables the patients (e.g., after stroke or spinal cord injury) to support the body during walking. However, the lack of modulated leg muscle activation is associated with a sticklike usage of the legs during locomotion. Exaggerated short-latency reflexes contribute little to the movement disorder.

Only by recording and analyzing electrophysiological and biomechanical parameters during a functional movement, such as locomotion, can the significance of deficits (e.g., impaired reflex behavior or pathophysiology of muscle tone) and their contributions to the movement disorder be reliably assessed. Consequently, adequate treatment of movement disorders should not be restricted to cosmetic therapy and correction of an isolated clinical parameter, but rather should be based on the pathophysiology and significance of the mechanisms underlying the disorder of functional movement that impairs the patient.

REFERENCES

Brandt, T., Strupp, M., & Benson, J. (1999). You are better off running than walking with acute vestibulopathy. *Lancet, 354*(9180), 746.

Dietz, V. (2002a). Do human bipeds use quadrupedal coordination? *Trends in Neurosciences, 25*, 462–467.

Dietz, V. (2002b) Proprioception and locomotor disorders. *Nature Reviews Neuroscience, 3*, 781–790.

Dietz, V. (2003). Spinal cord pattern generators for locomotion (Review). *Clinical Neurophysiology, 114*, 1379–1389.

Dietz, V., & Duysens, J. (2000). Modulation of reflex mechanisms by load receptors (Review). *Gait & Posture, 11*, 102–110

Dietz, V., & Sinkjaer, T. (2007). Divergent aspects of spasticity: Clinical signs and movement disorder (Review). *Lancet Neurology, 6*, 725–733.

SUGGESTED READINGS

Bronstein, A. M., Brandt, T., Woollacott, M. F., & Nutt, J. G. (Eds.) (1996). *Clinical disorders of balance, posture and gait* (2nd ed.). London: Arnold.

Gait Disorders. In E. Ruzicka, M. Hallett, and Z. Jankovic (Eds.). *Advances in neurology, Vol. 87* (pp. 53–63). Philadelphia: Lippincott Williams & Wilkins.

VOLKER DIETZ
University Hospital Balgrit, Zurich, Switzerland

HUMANISTIC PSYCHOTHERAPIES

Humanistic psychotherapies have made a substantial impact on how psychotherapy is conceived and practiced for over 65 years. Beginning with Carl Rogers's seminal contributions in the early 1940s, as part of the third force in psychology, some of the most distinguished psychotherapists of the twentieth century were founders and developers of humanistic psychotherapies. They include Carl Rogers, Art Combs (Person-Centered), Fritz and Laura Perls, Erv and Miriam Polster (Gestalt), Rollo May, R. D. Laing, Ernesto Spinelli, Irv Yalom, Viktor Frankl (Existential), Jim Bugental, Kirk Schneider (Existential-Humanistic), Virginia Satir (Relational), Al Mahrer (Experential), Clark Moustaka (Phenomneological), Eugene Gendlin (Focusing Oriented), and Les Greenberg and Robert Elliot (Emotionally Focused/Process-Experiential). These pioneers and second-generation leaders challenged many of the current views and practices of psychotherapy and offered a different view of the person, psychopathology, and how growth might be promoted in a therapeutic context.

Many humanistic therapeutic values and principles have been incorporated into the practice of almost all therapeutic approaches. Therapists of practically every persuasion acknowledge the constructive impact of the quality of the therapeutic relationship and especially the therapist's communication of the core person-centered conditions of empathy, unconditional positive regard, and congruence articulated by Carl Rogers. In fact, Carl Rogers was identified as the most influential psychotherapist in 1982 in a survey of clinical and counseling psychologists. Twenty-five years later, in a larger survey of over 2,500 psychotherapists of diverse persuasions, Carl Rogers was again identified as the most influential psychotherapist, despite the fact that relatively few of those surveyed identified themselves as client-centered or humanistic psychotherapists. This seeming paradox can be understood, in part, by the sometimes ambivalent relationship between mainstream and humanistic approaches to psychotherapy.

Mainstream psychotherapies (e.g., cognitive, behavioral, psychodynamic, eclectic) tend to embrace a medical model in practice, one in which the client's problem is diagnosed in primarily pathological terms and for which specific treatments are prescribed. In today's zeitgeist, therapeutic approaches are dominated by psychoeducational models emphasizing therapeutic technique despite the fact that only about 15% of the outcome variance can be attributed to therapist technique, while about 70% of the outcome variance is accounted for by client resources and the quality of the therapeutic relationship (Lambert, 1992). In contrast, humanistic psychotherapists tend to reject or minimize the importance of the medical model, preferring instead to view each person as unique and, therefore, not reducible to a diagnostic category. Instead the person in therapy is typically referred to as a client, a designation that suggests that the person is agentic and an active participant in achieving change. Therapeutic goals are oriented toward helping clients tap their resources, move closer to their potential, and achieve a sense of well-being and growth, as opposed to focusing primarily on the alleviation of symptoms and specific mental illnesses. Humanistic psychotherapists believe that, as clients address their basic issues, values, and manner of living in the world, they will also address and alleviate their identified concerns and problems (e.g., depression).

Characteristics and Contributions of Humanistic Psychotherapies

There are a number of humanistic approaches to psychotherapy, the main ones being Person-Centered, Gestalt, Focusing-Oriented, Experiential, Existential, Existential-Humanistic, Process-Experiential, and Relational. These approaches have a number of common characteristics and emphases that distinguish them from nonhumanistic therapies. Several primary and defining characteristics of humanistic therapies can be identified.

View of the Person

Humanistic therapists view persons as *self-actualizing*, endowed with an inherent tendency to develop their potential and as *resilient* in manifesting their natural inclination to survive and grow, even under the most adverse circumstances. Similarly, people are seen as having the capacity to reflect on their experiences in a manner that leads to productive learning, growth, and effective action. There is implicit *optimism* in the humanistic therapist's view of the person's capacity for constructive change. Art Combs, speaking of the person's fundamental drive toward fulfillment or health stated, "clients can, will, and *must* move toward health, *if* the way seems open to them to do so" (1999, p. 14). Tageson believes that the "living organism . . . will always do the best it can to actualize its potentials . . . and it will do so as a *unit* along with all dimensions of its functioning . . . ." (1982, p. 35). Although humanistic therapists acknowledge the extremes of psychopathology that exist in people and their dark and destructive aspects, they are inclined to view most forms of psychopathology as ineffective attempts to cope with life's challenges.

Humanistic therapists view persons as *self aware* and *free to choose* the manner and course of their living and their attitude toward life experiences. Freedom, choice, and the resulting responsibility for one's choices are intertwined. Each choice one makes inevitably means that another choice could not be made. Whatever one's choices, the choosing and the consequences cannot be avoided.

The person is viewed holistically, as an indivisible, interrelated organism that cannot be reduced to the sum of his or her parts, and certainly not to a diagnostic category. All persons are viewed as *embodied* beings, and, consequently, cannot be understood apart from their physical and emotional selves. As Seeman (2002) has articulated, the human organism can be conceived most accurately as composed of interrelated systems. A holistic view also recognizes that persons are always part of a larger field and thus inextricably intertwined with their social and physical environments.

Each person is viewed as a *unique* entity, unlike any other person who has existed or will exist. Consequently, each client is understood in the context of his or her unique experiences, temperament, and personality. Thus, humanistic psychotherapists emphasize ideographic approaches to comprehending the person, while holding nomothetic views as hypotheses that may or may not be of value in understanding a specific individual.

People are *primarily social beings* who have a powerful need to belong, to have a place in their worlds, and to feel valued. Thus, all behaviors are best understood in an interpersonal context.

Humanistic psychotherapists embrace a *phenomenological view* of persons. The basic intent of phenomenology is to describe the structures of experience as they manifest themselves in consciousness. Phenomenological inquiry is atheoretical, nondeductive, and without preconceptions about the client's reality. Its goal is to illuminate the quality of the person's experience and subjective reality.

People are seen as *meaning-making* beings. Meaning is not a given but is constructed from the raw data of life experience, including one's culture, values, perspectives, and personal history. Persons are often troubled by that which eludes their comprehension and, consequently, making sense of experience seems to be a fundamental need of all persons.

Therapeutic Process

Therapeutic Relationship

One of the most fundamental aspects of humanistic psychotherapy is that an *optimal therapeutic relationship* is considered to be primary and foundational as a source of constructive change in the client as well as an ideal atmosphere for intrapersonal and interpersonal learning. A mutually engaged relationship between therapist and client often promotes growth in and of itself. When clients and therapists meet a relational depth, both often have an experience of how one can and might live with others. Through extraordinary moments of contact with the therapist, clients may experience themselves in ways that are rich, fresh, hopeful, and even transformative. As Rogers has eloquently stated, "Individuals have within themselves vast resources for self-understanding, and for altering their self concepts, basic attitudes, and self-directed behavior; these resources can be tapped if a definable climate of facilitative psychological attitudes can be provided" (1980, p. 115). The "definable climate" includes the therapist's genuineness, authenticity, transparency or congruence; acceptance, nonjudgmental caring, liking, prizing, affirmation, unconditional positive regard or nonpossessive warmth; a genuine desire to understand the client's experience and accurate empathic communication of that experience. Other relational qualities and attitudes embraced by humanistic therapists include a collaborative relationship characterized by trust, safety, and support; receptivity to experience; contact and engagement; immersion or indwelling the client's experience; a therapeutic alliance, authentic dialogue; and optimism regarding the client's capacity for constructive change.

Therapeutic goals include the following: (1) enhancing the person's sense of choice, freedom, possibility, autonomy, responsibility, capacity for self-direction, and self-efficacy; (2) increasing receptivity to experience and the capacity to attend to, process, effectively express, and learn from feelings; (3) increasing self-awareness and clarity of perception; (4) increasing sensitivity, vitality, and creativity; (5) enhancing authentic living, greater intimacy with self and others, and greater self-acceptance; (6) discovering one's meaning and purposes; and (7) achieving increasing levels of congruence and integration. In assisting the client to achieve such goals, the therapist often functions as a disciplined improvisational artist who brings forth congruent aspects of self when they are anticipated to have constructive impact. Humanistic therapists may employ a range of response styles and therapeutic methods, but do so with the collaboration of the client in determining how well they fit the client's needs at a given point in therapy. They embrace an egalitarian stance toward clients, believing that they are the best experts on their own experience. Ultimately clients decide what changes to make and how to make them.

The Vital Role of Empathy

Empathy may be conceived as the therapist's desire and endeavor to understand what it is like to be the client and accurately communicate that experience to the client. It is a way of being that is at the heart of humanistic psychotherapies. The therapist's empathy creates a sanctuary for clients. It promotes a sense of "we-ness" and a safe bond that enables clients to listen to themselves in a reflective manner and explore themselves and their relationships with others and the external world. It is a critical factor in accurately illuminating, deepening, and enriching clients' experiences. Clients typically identify "feeling understood" as one of the most important factors in their therapy. Therefore, humanistic therapists strive to focus their attention on the immediate, lived experiences of their clients.

As one of the most powerful facilitators of change and growth, several constructive impacts of therapist empathy are evident. These include (1) increased receptivity, self-exploration, self-discovery, clearer views of the self, and improved self-esteem; (2) greater attunement feelings, which enables clients to better understand their motivations and draw out the implications for more effective living; (3) changes in self concept that often lead to constructive behavioral changes; (4) a greater inclination for clients to listen to and know themselves better, become more self-accepting, feel more grounded and confident in their perceptions and judgment; (5) greater empathy and compassion toward others that often results in more intimate and satisfying relationships; and (6) increased ability for decision-making, self-directed change, and problem solving.

Reality as Subjective and Co-constructed

A central premise of humanistic therapists is that there is a diversity of perspectives on "reality," ranging from the individual to the cultural. There is no assumption of an ultimate or consensual reality but rather a belief that similar experiences may be interpreted in multiple ways. Reality is not a given; it is constructed from the raw data of experiences, tempered by one's collective experiences in interaction with a specific context as a particular moment by a person in a specific psychological state. Therapist empathy plays a role in enabling clients to deconstruct their current worldviews and create more satisfying and functional ones.

As therapist and client engage in a process of exploration and reflection, new ways of perceiving current realities are essentially co-constructed in a collaborative process. In this endeavor, the therapist attempts to suspend all beliefs and preconceptions and to minimize interpretation in the articulation of the client's experience. Therapists view their clients as the ultimate expert on realities and the final arbiters for determining the accuracy of the therapist's understanding.

Meaning Focus

Humanistic psychotherapists strive to assist their clients in making sense of and clarifying the meaning of their experiences and lives. Recognizing that the purpose of clients' lives are often implicit but not clear, humanistic therapists strive to enable their clients to grasp the larger meaning and patterns of their lives. Discovering that there are comprehensible threads of meaning to their lives enables clients to gain a sense of clarity, direction, and groundedness. As meanings and purposes become clear, clients develop a more centered self and system of beliefs and values from which to operate.

Processing Emotion

One of the most distinguishing features of humanistic therapies is their emphasis on the importance of attending to and processing client emotion. Humanistic therapists and researchers have been at the forefront in expanding our understanding of the critical role played by emotion in human behavior. Rather than view emotion primarily as something that interferes with functioning, humanistic therapists have embraced the importance of understanding the adaptive nature of emotion in effective decision-making and effective functioning. Neuroscientist Antonio Damasio, author of *Descartes' Error*, provides compelling evidence that "certain aspects of the process of emotion and feeling are indispensable for rationality [and] ... take us to the appropriate place in a decision-making space, where we may put the instruments of logic to good use" (1994, p. xiii).

The Self

The belief that behavior changes as the self concept is altered has enormous influence in the therapeutic endeavor; this belief alerts therapists and focuses their attention on a client's immediate and ongoing sense of self and the role it plays in mediating their perceptions and behavior. As Mahoney (1991) suggested, "All psychotherapies are psychotherapies of the self" (p. 235). Self-exploration, self-definition, reconstrual of the self, and the development of self-knowledge are primary concerns of the humanistic therapist.

Affirming Freedom and Choice

A fundamental value of humanistic therapists is their belief that people have the right, desire, and ability to determine freely what is best for them and how they will achieve it. Consequently, one of the main endeavors of humanistic therapies is to strengthen a client's belief that she can be the author of her life. As clients are enabled to realize that they are constantly making choices, as opposed to simply being carried along by or reacting to their experiences, they become empowered. They recognize that other paths are available to them. Thus, the existential questions of, "How are you living?" and, "Are you becoming the person you wish to be?" are often integral aspects of humanistic psychotherapy. Humanistic therapists are, therefore, strongly inclined to engage in behaviors that are collaborative and provide optimal freedom from their clients. Conversely, they are disinclined to use methods that are coercive, controlling, or covert, or in guiding, suggesting, or advising their clients how to live.

Research on Humanistic Psychotherapists

More than sixty years of research, both quantitative and qualitative, have demonstrated that humanistic approaches to psychotherapy are as effective or more effective than other established approaches for all major psychological problems. Recent reviews of the research on humanistic psychotherapy (Cain & Seeman, 2002; Elliott, Greenberg, & Lietaer, 2004) indicate that humanistic individual, couples, and group psychotherapy are effective for a wide variety of clients. A meta-analysis of 127 treatment groups showed an average pre-post effect size of .99 for a variety of humanistic therapies (an effect size of .8 is considered large), and the data indicated that clients "maintained or perhaps even increased their post-treatment gains over the past-therapy period" (Elliot, Greenberg, & Lietaer, 2004, p. 502). This body of research continues to expand rapidly and provides ongoing evidence of the effectiveness of all major humanistic psychotherapies.

Research shows that client-rated empathy is strongly and consistently related to good client outcome. Conversely, there is no evidence that empathy is harmful or has a negative impact on constructive outcome. As a value, attitude, skill, behavior, and way of engaging with a client, empathy is arguably the most potent factor in client progress. Evidence from a variety of sources and perspectives consistently shows that the quality of the therapist-client relationship is one of the strongest predictors of therapeutic success. Finally, research on depth of emotional experiencing in psychotherapy has been consistently shown to predict good outcome.

REFERENCES

Cain, D. J., & Seeman, J. (2002). *Humanistic psychotherapies: Handbook of research and practice*. Washington, D.C.: American Psychological Association.

Combs, A. W. (1999). *Being and becoming*. New York: Springer.

Damasio, A. R. (1994). *Descartes' error*. New York: Grosset/Putman.

Elliott, R., Greenberg, L. S., & Lietaer, G. (2004). Research on experiential psychotherapies. In M. J. Lambert (Ed.), *Bergin and Garfield's handbook of psychotherapy and behavior change* (5th ed.) (pp. 493–539). New York: John Wiley & Sons.

Lambert, M. J. (1992). Implications of outcome research for psychotherapy integration. In J. C. Norcross & M. R. Goldfriend (Eds.), *Handbook of psychotherapy integration*. New York: Basic Books.

Mahoney, M. J. (1991). *Human change processes*. New York: Basic Books.

Seeman, J. (2002). Looking back, looking ahead: A synthesis. In D. J. Cain & J. Seeman (Eds.). *Humanistic psychotherapies: Handbook of research and practice* (pp. 617–636). Washington D.C.: American Psychological Association.

Tageson, C. W. (1982). *Humanistic psychology: A synthesis*. Homewood, Illinois: Dorsey Press.

SUGGESTED READINGS

Bohart, A., & Tallman, K. (1999). *How clients make therapy work: The process of active self-healing*. Washington D.C.: American Psychological Association.

Gendlin, E. T. (1996). *Focusing-oriented psychotherapy*. New York: Guilford.

Greenberg, L. S. (2002). *Emotion-focused therapy: Coaching clients to work through their feelings.* Washington, D.C.: American Psychological Association.

Rogers, C. R. (1961). *On becoming a person.* Boston: Houghton Mifflin.

Schneider, K. J., Bugental, J. F., & Pierson, J. F. (2001). *Handbook of humanistic psychology.* Thousand Oaks: Sage.

DAVID J. CAIN
*Alliant International University,
San Diego*

See also: Client-Centered Therapy; Existential Psychotherapy; Experiential Psychotherapy

HYPERACTIVITY

The term *hyperactivity* refers to both a symptom associated with a variety of medical and behavioral disorders and a common psychopathological syndrome. A range of related terms are often treated interchangeably, including *overactivity, hyperkinesis, minimal brain dysfunction, attention deficit disorder* and *attention deficit–hyperactivity disorder.* This discussion addresses hyperactivity as a descriptor, symptom, and syndrome, emphasizing the disorder currently called attention deficit–hyperactivity disorder.

Descriptor

Activity level is an important developmental and temperamental dimension, representing a temporally stable, constitutionally based individual difference among all living beings. Developmental change is expected, as captured in the contrast between a frisky young puppy and a sedentary old dog. Thus, there is a range of behavior considered "within normal limits." Exceeding these limits in either statistical or clinical terms can be called "*overactivity.*" Hyperactivity is a continuous form of movement such as squirming, fidgeting, or foot-tapping, rather than discrete or episodic movement such as a spasm or a tic. Overall "activity level" is one category of temperament: constitutionally based qualities of responsiveness that are evident and relatively stable throughout life. Hyperactivity, as a statistical or clinical extreme, has particular implications for problems in development and adaptation, which can contribute to secondary difficulties for the individual and those around him.

Symptom

A common, often primary symptom, hyperactivity is observed in a variety of medical and behavioral disorders, including bipolar disorder, schizophrenia, autism, developmental disabilities, metabolic disorders, endocrine disorders, toxic exposure (e.g., lead poisoning), and other neurological conditions (brain tumor, encephalitis, Parkinson's disease, etc.). Hyperactivity is not in itself a cause for concern. Instead, it is a nonspecific symptom whose significance depends on demographic and situational factors and the presence of other physiological characteristics or behavioral symptoms.

Syndrome

Despite the heterogeneity of conditions that include motor excess, there appears to be a set of covarying factors, resulting in the identification of a hyperactivity syndrome or disorder. Hyperactivity does not constitute a syndrome in the technical sense of the word; the particular pattern of symptoms or characteristics do not form a unitary cluster, nor is there adequate evidence of common etiology, both *sine qua non* of a true "syndrome." However, the disorder most closely associated with hyperactivity is Attention-Deficit/Hyperactivity Disorder (ADHD; American Psychiatric Association, 2000; Spencer, Biederman, & Nick, 2007), and it is among the most common mental-health disorders of childhood. The core symptoms are inattention, hyperactivity, and impulsivity with onset in childhood but persisting across the lifespan in 30–60% of individuals with the disorder (Wender, Wolf, & Wasserstein, 2001).

Referred to as "hyperkinesis" or "hyperactive child syndrome" in twentieth-century accounts, ADHD has undergone substantial conceptual changes and revisions of diagnostic criteria over the past 30 years. The most current *Diagnostic and Statistical Manual of Mental Disorders* (DSM-IV-TR) emphasizes three behavioral components of the disorder: inattention, distractibility, and hyperactivity/impulsivity. For the diagnosis to be made, six or more symptoms of each component must be present for at least six months, interfering with the child's ability to function in at least two areas of life. These symptoms must be inconsistent with what is typical for the child's developmental level, and may not be better accounted for by another disorder. At least some of the symptoms must be present at a young age (before age seven). Prevalence estimates range from 2–10% of children, with about three times more males than females affected, although the number of females diagnosed has increased since the addition of inattention to ADHD nosology (American Academy of Pediatrics, 2000).

Russell Barkley (2006) has summarized the research and developed a cohesive theory to explain ADHD and the disability it creates. As a chronic developmental disorder, ADHD is present from birth. Symptoms are persistent rather than episodic and often are present across situations. However, children may have more difficulties in certain settings (e.g., unstructured leisure time at home) or tasks (homework or sitting still in class). In addition to the primary symptoms, individuals with ADHD are at increased risk for poor academic progress, school difficulties, and poor interpersonal relationships. ADHD has been associated with a number of comorbid conditions including oppositional defiant disorder, conduct disorder, mood disorders, childhood anxiety disorders, speech and language delays and learning disabilities, tic disorders, and substance abuse. Furthermore, adults with ADHD may have vocational difficulties, increased risk for motor vehicle crashes, and greater marital instability.

Specific etiology of ADHD remains unknown, although professional consensus leans toward biological explanations. Genetic perspectives are supported by the increased incidence of the disorder in relatives of those with ADHD and the overrepresentation of males, although intrafamilial variability does not rule out psychological or behavioral transmission. Organic explanations are supported by observations of similar behavior in individuals with traumatic head injuries and the prevalence of hyperactivity in some metabolic disorders, suggesting that an acquired illness or injury may contribute to the condition.

Recent developments in neuroscience have contributed to our understanding of the biological bases of ADHD, though no clear etiologies have yet been confirmed. A common finding in brain imaging studies shows that children with ADHD exhibit reduced volume of the corpus callosum, frontal lobes, basal ganglia, and cerebellum and total white matter (Castellanos et al., 2002). There is no consensus among scientists as to why the brains of individuals with ADHD differ from typically developing brains or whether their development is abnormal or delayed. Shaw and colleagues (2007) found evidence for the cortical maturation delay hypothesis, reporting the most prominent delays in the lateral prefrontal cortex. The prefrontal hypothesis of ADHD etiology has gained considerable attention, as frontal lobes have been found to play a part in executive functioning and attention, the core deficit observed in ADIID.

Environmental factors associated with ADHD symptoms include pre- and perinatal factors, such as maternal alcohol and cigarette smoking, pregnancy and delivery complications, as well as toxins such as lead and exposure to radiation and specific medications. Although psychological hypotheses such as particular child-rearing patterns or learning patterns are less well accepted than other theories, these factors affect the course and outcome of the disorder. Given the range of factors that may contribute to ADHD and the high prevalence of the disorder, it is likely that the actual etiology is multifactorial. Furthermore, if the notion of multiple syndromes is borne out, multiple etiologies are likely to be revealed.

Consistent with the variation in etiological hypotheses, assessment and treatment of the disorder is wide-ranging and crosses disciplinary lines involving educators, physicians, and mental-health providers. Neurodevelopmental, psychological, psychoeducational, and neuropsychological evaluations all are used to identify the disorder. Several valid and reliable parent and teacher rating scales have been developed for identifying ADHD. Recent attention has turned toward neuropsychological assessment tools that may provide greater sensitivity and specificity; however, none of these has sufficient reliability or validity to be the "gold standard" for diagnosis. Consequently, comprehensive multidisciplinary assessment, incorporating parent and teacher reports, cognitive and behavioral assessment, and norm-based rating scales is particularly desirable in diagnosing ADHD.

Treatment with stimulant medications such as methylphenidate or dextroamphetamine is the most common, most effective, and yet most controversial treatment for ADHD. However, it is generally recognized that medication alone is often insufficient to address either the primary disorder or its disabling effects. Therefore, a variety of cognitive, behavioral, and psychoeducational interventions are necessary adjuncts to medication. A burgeoning international research enterprise seeks to identify evidence-based interventions, including concerns for optimal combinations, cost-effectiveness, and cultural responsiveness (Brown, et al., 2008). In 2001, the American Academy of Pediatrics issued practice guidelines for the diagnosis and treatment of ADHD.

ADHD is now the most frequently diagnosed disorder of childhood. Kelleher and colleagues (2000) have found an increase of over 600% in the identification of ADHD between 1979 and 1996. A chronic illness with a complex biopsychosociocultural etiology and treatment, ADHD represents a serious set of problems. The fundamental shifts in the awareness and acceptance of treatment for ADHD over the past decades are among the primary reasons of the dramatic increase of ADHD diagnoses made by physicians. However, the rates of increase in numbers of children receiving diagnoses and treatment of ADHD have become a public health and economic concern. Calculations by Pelham, Foster, and Robb (2007) suggest that the annual "cost of illness" for ADHD approaches $15,000 per patient, thus making it a $42.5 billion problem.

REFERENCES

American Academy of Pediatrics. (2001). Clinical practice guideline: Diagnosis and evaluation of the child with attention-deficit/hyperactivity disorder. *Pediatrics*, 105, 1158–1170.

American Psychiatric Association. (2000). *Diagnostic and statistical manual of mental disorders* (4th ed., text rev.). Washington, DC: Author.

Barkley, R. A. (2006). *Attention deficit hyperactivity disorder: Handbook for diagnosis and treatment* (3rd ed.). New York: Guilford Press.

Brown, R., et al. (2008). *Childhood mental health disorders: Evidence-base and contextual factors for psychosocial, psychpharmacological, and combined interventions*. Washington, DC: American Psychological Association.

Castellanos, F. X., Lee, P. P., Sharp, W., Jeffries, N. O., Greenstein, D. K., Clasen, L. S., et al. (2002). Developmental trajectories of brain volume abnormalities in children and adolescents with attention-deficit/hyperactivity disorder. *Journal of the American Medical Association, 288*(14), 1740–1748.

Kelleher, K. J., McInerny, T. R., Gardner, W. P., Childs, G. E., & Wasserman, R. C. (2000). Increasing identification of psychosocial problems: 1979–1996. *Pediatrics, 105,* 1313–1321.

Pelham, W., Foster, M., & Robb, J. (2007) The economic impact of ADHD in Children and Adolescents. *Ambulatory Pediatrics, 7*(18), 121–131.

Spencer, T. J., Biederman, J., & Mick, E. (2007). Attention-deficit/hyperactivity disorder: Diagnosis, lifespan, comorbidities, and neurobiology. *Journal of Pediatric Psychology, 32*(6), 631–642.

Wender, P. H., Wolf, L. E., & Wasserstein, J. (2001). Adults with ADHD. An overview. *Annals of the New York Academy of Sciences, 931,* 1–16.

DANTE SPETTER
Harvard University

DONALD WERTLIEB
MYRNA V. VASHCENCKO
Tufts University

See also: Attention-Deficit/Hyperactivity Disorder; Behavior Problems of Childhood and Adolescence

HYPERVENTILATION

Hyperventilation (or hypocapnia) refers to a state of reduced carbon dioxide in the blood. It is usually triggered by breathing too deeply or rapidly, in excess of the metabolic demand. The end result is that alveolar and arterial carbon dioxide (CO_2) pressures decrease and blood pH increases. Sustained hyperventilation produces a variety of adverse changes, including a diminished ability for oxygen to pass from the blood to the organism's cells.

Hyperventilation is associated with a number of physical symptoms such as dizziness or lightheadedness, tingling and numbness in the extremities, and shortness of breath. Counterintuitively, these sensations, in particular shortness of breath or dyspnea, are not a result of a lack of oxygen, but of a reduction of blood CO_2 concentration below a normal level (<37 mmHg). Hyperventilation can lead to a transient reduction in cerebral oxygenation (or cerebral hypoxia) due to vasoconstriction (i.e., narrowing of blood vessels) in the brain. Hyperventilation can lead to fainting if followed by sudden breath holding.

Hyperventilation has been linked experimentally to organ injury and a number of organic illnesses and mental disorders (Laffey & Kavanagh, 1999). Examples include pulmonary diseases such as asthma and chronic obstructive pulmonary disease. It is furthermore associated with worsening of medical conditions such as brain injury and myocardial ischemia. Among the psychiatric disorders, panic disorder is the one most frequently associated with hyperventilation. Dyspnea, accompanied by hyperventilation, may contribute to the development and maintenance of panic disorder (Ley, 1985). A biological vulnerability to CO_2 due to an abnormal brainstem chemoreceptor control mechanism may trigger a false suffocation alarm, resulting in compensatory hyperventilation and panic attacks (Klein, 1993). In addition, hyperventilation may not be limited to the attack itself, but may precede and follow it, giving rise to moderate sustained hypocapnia (Lum, 1987).

Experimental studies (e.g., voluntary hyperventilation test, emotion induction paradigm) have shown that hypocapnia leads to states of panic (as in psychiatric patients) and declines in lung function (as in asthma patients). Hyperventilation may also act as a mediator for asthma exacerbations induced by stress and anxiety states, and it is linked to an overall reduced quality of life (Ritz et al., 2008).

Therapeutic strategies exist to reduce hyperventilation. Biofeedback of expired end-tidal pCO_2 using a portable capnometry device has demonstrated sustained reduction in panic symptoms and normalization of CO_2 into a normal (normocapnic) range (Meuret et al., 2008). Similar effects have been shown for asthma patients, with improved quality of life, normocapnic levels, and reduced airway hyperreactivity (Meuret et al., 2007).

REFERENCES

Laffey, J. G., & Kavanagh, B. P. (1999). Carbon dioxide and the critically ill—too little of a good thing? *Lancet, 354,* 1283–1286.

Meuret, A. E., Wilhelm, F. H., Ritz, T., & Roth, W. T. (2008). Feedback of end-tidal pCO_2 as a therapeutic approach for panic disorder. *Journal of Psychiatric Research, 42,* 560–568.

Ritz, T., Rosenfield, D., Meuret, A. E., Bobb, C., & Steptoe, A. (2008). Hyperventilation symptoms are linked to a lower quality of life in asthma patients. *Annals of Behavioral Medicine, 35,* 97–104.

SUGGESTED READINGS

Meuret, A. E., Ritz, T., Dahme, B., & Roth, W. T. (2004). Therapeutic use of ambulatory capnography. In J. Gravenstein, M. Jaffe, & D. Paulus (Eds.), *Capnography: Clinical aspects.* Cambridge, UK: Cambridge University Press.

Laffey, J. G., & Kavanagh, B. P. (2002). Hypocapnia. *New England Journal of Medicine, 347,* 43–53.

ALICIA E. MEURET
Southern Methodist University

See also: Anxiety; Panic Disorder

HYPNOSIS

From the time of Mesmer, hypnosis has captured the attention of luminaries in psychology including Sigmund Freud, Alfred Binet, William James, Wilhelm Wundt, Clark Hull, and Ernest R. Hilgard. Today, hypnosis is well positioned within the mainstream of psychology. Researchers have debunked common misconceptions about hypnosis and identified important social and cognitive determinants of suggestibility, and clinicians have recognized the promise of hypnosis in treating an array of psychological and medical conditions.

Recognizing the need for a theoretically neutral definition of hypnosis, the American Psychological Association (APA) Division of Psychological Hypnosis (1994) arrived at a consensus definition of hypnosis as a procedure in which a researcher or mental health professional provides suggestions to a participant, client, or patient for changes in sensations, perceptions, thoughts, or behaviors. A decade later, the APA reformulated the definition to encompass self-hypnosis in which individuals self-administer suggestions, usually following practice in responding to hypnotist-facilitated suggestions.

Typically, a hypnosis session begins with a so-called "induction," followed by specific suggestions for a variety of experiences and physical responses such as overt movements, pain relief, and alterations in memory, including amnesia. Many inductions include suggestions for relaxation and deepening of the hypnotic experience, which serve to define the context as hypnosis and increase suggestibility to a small degree—typically 10–15%. Many hypnotic inductions (e.g., hand levitation, eye fixation) can be used interchangeably, including ones that emphasize feeling alert and energized. Moreover, the way suggestions are worded (e.g., explicit versus open-ended, authoritative versus permissive) has little bearing on how people respond. Interestingly, properly motivated awake participants can experience virtually all hypnotic phenomena without a formal hypnotic induction.

People exhibit dramatic differences in hypnotic suggestibility. A variety of well-validated, standardized scales of hypnotic suggestibility have been developed, with laudable psychometric properties that rival those of intelligence tests. Approximately 15–20% of individuals are minimally suggestible (respond to 0–3 suggestions on a 12-item scale), 15–20% are highly suggestible (respond to 9–12 suggestions), and the remainder of the population scores in the medium range (respond to 4–8 suggestions) of hypnotic suggestibility.

Differences in suggestibility can be accounted for largely in terms of people's attitudes, beliefs, and expectancies about hypnosis; their motivation and ability to imagine suggested events; and their ability to respond to waking imaginative suggestions apart from the context of hypnosis. To date, researchers have failed to identify a reproducible physiological signature of a "hypnotic trance." However, suggested experiences (e.g., hallucination of color) have detectable psychophysiological concomitants, often similar to "actual" experiences (e.g., viewing a colored object). Thus, hypnosis can engender vivid and lifelike experiences (Woody & Szechtman, 2000).

Facts about Hypnosis

Movies, the Internet, books, and magazines have fueled the popular imagination, while disseminating myths and misconceptions about hypnosis. Surveys indicate that many college students hold the popular yet mistaken beliefs that hypnotized participants (1) relinquish their free will and cannot resist suggestions; (2) are aware only of what the hypnotist suggests; (3) respond based on the skill of the hypnotist; and (4) can be made to tell the truth about things they would normally lie about.

Research also demonstrates that the following five beliefs do not square with scientific evidence (Nash, 2001):

1. Hypnosis is not a sleeplike state of consciousness. Most people describe their experience as focused attention on suggested events. Moreover, people can respond to hypnotic suggestions when they are wide-awake and while they pedal a stationary bicycle.
2. Most hypnotized people are neither gullible nor faking nor merely complying with suggestions.
3. Spontaneous amnesia for suggested events rarely develops.
4. Hypnosis is not a dangerous procedure when practiced by well-trained professionals.
5. Suggestibility can be increased significantly following training in how to imagine along with and in response to suggestions.

Theoretical Accounts

Historically, hypnosis has been viewed as producing an altered state of consciousness or trance. However, starting in the 1950s, Theodore Sarbin (1950) and later T. X. Barber (1969) contended that a special state or condition is not necessary to account for the behavioral and subjective responses associated with hypnosis. Other sociocognitve theorists, including Spanos, Chaves, Kirsch, Lynn, and Wagstaff, also rejected "trance" as an explanatory concept and argued that hypnotic responses are the product of individuals' abilities, motivations, agendas, attitudes, beliefs, expectancies, attributions, and interpretations of the situation.

Dissociation theories have vied with sociocognitive models for attention and empirical support. According to Ernest Hilgard's (1986) neodissociation theory, multiple cognitive systems or cognitive structures exist in hierarchical arrangement under some measure of control by an "executive ego" that is responsible for planning and monitoring functions of the personality. During hypnosis the hypnotist's suggestions take much of the normal control away from the subject. An amnesic barrier prevents conscious awareness of how a person might bring about a suggested response via imagining, for example, thereby producing the impression of nonvolition that often accompanies hypnotic responses. Other dissociation theorists (e.g., Bowers, Woody) reject the idea of an amnesic barrier and argue that hypnotic suggestions bypass executive controls and directly activate suggested responses.

Paralleling theoretical developments in the broader skein of psychology, theorists have proposed accounts of hypnosis that rely on concepts derived from psychoanalysis (e.g., Fromm, Nash), neuroscience (e.g., Banyai, Gruzelier), cognitive psychology (e.g., Kihlstrom, McConkey, Sheehan), and communication theory (Lankton, Matthews, Yapko, Zeig). Each of these theories has garnered at least a modicum of empirical support.

Clinical Hypnosis

Although theoreticians disagree about the determinants of hypnotic suggestibility, a consensus exists among experts regarding the value of using hypnosis as an adjunct to psychotherapy. Meta-analyses reveal that hypnosis enhances the effectiveness of psychodynamic and cognitive behavioral psychotherapies. Controlled outcome studies also support the usefulness of hypnosis in treating anxiety, depression, and obesity. Moreover, patients who undergo hypnotic treatment for smoking cessation fare better than both patients on a wait list for treatment and patients who receive no treatment, implying that hypnosis can be a valuable intervention in a stepped-care approach to smoking cessation (Lynn, Kirsch, Barabasz, Cardena, & Patterson, 2000).

Hypnosis has been applied in individual and group settings, and with diverse populations including children, athletes, the elderly, marital couples in distress, and patients suffering from a variety of medical conditions. There is considerable support for the effectiveness of hypnosis in the preoperative preparation of surgical patients, the treatment of a subgroup of patients with asthma, and the treatment of patients with dermatological disorders, irritable bowel syndrome, hemophilia, and postchemotherapy nausea and emesis (Covino & Pinnell, in press). Hypnosis has proved to be very effective in alleviating acute and chronic pain, with 75% of the population receiving some benefit regardless of suggestibility level (Montgomery, DuHamel, & Redd, 2000). There is a clear need for additional controlled outcome research that controls for the effects of relaxation and compares hypnotic interventions with a variety of alternative treatments and placebo conditions.

Hypnosis in the Legal Arena

Triers of fact have expressed considerable skepticism about admitting hypnotically elicited testimony to the bar. Court rulings have varied, with 27 states ruling hypnotically elicited recall as per se inadmissible, 4 states with precedents of per se admissibility, and 13 states considering evidence on a case-by-case basis. Many of the reservations concerning hypnosis center on research indicating that increases in accurate recall following hypnosis are often accompanied by even greater increases in inaccurate recollections. Importantly, hypnosis can also increase the confidence that witnesses hold in their memories, independent of the accuracy of the memories recovered. Accordingly, experts and courts have expressed concerns that, when witnesses hold unwarranted confidence in memories, it can render them resistant to cross-examination, thereby corrupting the judicial process. To date, few studies have addressed the issue of cross-examination. However, the available evidence indicates that hypnosis is not a reliable method for improving memory (Lynn, Barnes, & Matthews, in press).

Conclusions

Cognitive and social scientists, as well as mental-health professionals, have made important strides in demystifying hypnosis and mooring it to empirically supported theories, principles, and clinical practices. Our understanding of hypnosis will no doubt be advanced by new technologies, including neuroimaging techniques, that promise to illuminate the neurocognitive underpinnings of suggestions in hypnotic and nonhypnotic contexts. Clinicians can practice with assurance that hypnosis has the potential to enhance the effectiveness of a variety of psychotherapeutic interventions, and they can rely on a burgeoning literature to reassure patients that hypnosis is neither an occult nor a dangerous procedure. Moreover, triers of fact have a sound basis for appreciating the limitations and contraindications of the use of hypnosis for memory retrieval. Whereas the field of hypnosis has surely benefited from advances in psychological science more broadly, the study of hypnosis has the potential to enrich our understanding of how the power of words and communication can radically transform consciousness and behaviors.

REFERENCES

Barber, T. X. (1969). *Hypnosis: A scientific approach.* New York: Van Nostrand Reinhold.

Covino, N., & Pinnell, C. (in press) Medical applications of hypnosis. In S. J. Lynn, Kirsch, I., & J. W. Rhue (Eds.), *Handbook of clinical hypnosis* (2nd ed.). Washington, DC: American Psychological Association.

Hilgard, E. R. (1986). *Divided consciousness: Multiple controls in thought and action* (expanded ed.). New York: John Wiley & Sons.

Lynn, S. J., Barnes, S., & Matthews, A. (in press). Hypnosis and forensic science: Legal decisions and opinions. In C. Edwards (Ed.), *Handbook of forensic science*. New York: Wiley.

Lynn, S.J., Kirsch, I., Barabasz, A., Cardena, E., & Patterson, D. (2000). Hypnosis as an empirically supported adjunctive technique: The state of the evidence. *International Journal of Clinical and Experimental Hypnosis, 48*, 343–361.

Montgomery, G. H., DuHamel, K. N., & Redd, W. H. (2000). A meta-analysis of hypnotically induced analgesia: How effective is hypnosis? *International Journal of Clinical and Experimental Hypnosis, 48*, 138–153.

Nash, M. R. (2001). The truth and hype of hypnosis. *Scientific American, 285*, 46–55.

Sarbin, T. R. (1950). Contributions to role-taking theory: I. Hypnotic behavior. *Psychological Review, 57*, 225–270.

Woody, E., & Szechtman, H. (2000). Hypnotic hallucinations: Toward a biology of epistemology. *Contemporary Hypnosis, 17*, 4–14.

SUGGESTED READINGS

Lynn, S. J., & Kirsch, I. (2006). *Essentials of clinical hypnosis.* Washington, DC: American Psychological Association.

Lynn, S. J., Kirsch, I., & Rhue, J. W. (Eds.). *Handbook of clinical hypnosis* (2nd ed.). Washington, DC: American Psychological Association.

Nash, M. R., & Barnier, A. (in press). *Oxford handbook of hypnosis.* New York: Oxford Press.

STEVEN JAY LYNN
SEAN BARNES
ELZA BOYCHEVA
Binghamton University

HYPOCHONDRIASIS

Hypochondriasis is defined by a preoccupation with the fear of having, or the idea that one has, a serious disease, based on misinterpretation of one or more bodily sensations or changes (American Psychiatric Association [APA], 2000). Fear persists even though the person receives ample reassurance from physicians that there is no evidence of serious disease and despite the fact that frightening bodily changes or sensations the person believes to be symptomatic of disease rarely become progressively worse. People with hypochondriasis usually resist the idea that they are suffering from a psychiatric disorder. To be diagnosed with hypochondriasis, one has to have its symptoms for at least 6 months.

People with hypochondriasis often adopt a sick role, living as invalids and avoiding all effortful activities, and they typically complain persistently about their health to anyone who will listen. This can lead to strained relationships with family, friends, and physicians. Frustration and anger on the part of the physician and patient are not uncommon. Doctor shopping—visiting different physicians in the hope of finding help—is often the result. This puts people with hypochondriasis at risk of unnecessary or repeated medical and surgical treatments, some of which can produce troubling side effects or treatment complications (e.g., scarring).

Hypochondriasis has a lifetime prevalence of 1–5% (APA, 2000), can arise at any age but is most common in early adulthood (APA, 2000), and is equally common in women and men. It typically manifests when the person is under stress, seriously ill or recovering from a serious illness, or has suffered the loss of a family member. The course of hypochondriasis is often chronic, persisting for many years in over 50% of cases, and it frequently co-occurs with mood disorders, anxiety disorders, and somatization disorder (APA, 2000).

Etiology

Preliminary research suggests that genetic factors play a minor role in hypochondriasis and that environmental factors, such as learning experiences, are more important (Taylor, Thordarson, Jang, & Asmundson, 2006). The cognitive-behavioral model of hypochondriasis is the most developed and empirically supported approach, and it has led to effective treatment (Salkovskis, Warwicck, & Deale, 2003). The key concept in this model is that excessive health anxiety (as in hypochondriasis) arises from dysfunctional beliefs about sickness, health, and healthcare, including beliefs that lead the person to misinterpret the significance and dangerousness of benign bodily changes and sensations. Research confirms that people with hypochondriasis, compared to nonanxious controls, are more likely to (1) dwell on their bodily conditions and functions, (2) believe that good health is associated with few or no bodily sensations, (3) interpret bodily sensations as indicators of poor or serious disease, (4) overestimate the likelihood of contracting diseases and the dangerousness of diseases, and (5) regard themselves as being at high risk for developing serious disease (Taylor & Asmundson, 2004).

Among the most important of the maladaptive coping behaviors in hypochondriasis are persistent reassurance seeking (from physicians, friends, or significant others) and other forms of repetitive checking (e.g., bodily checking). Such behaviors appear to persist because they are associated with short-term reduction in anxiety. In the longer term, they can perpetuate health anxiety. By repeatedly turning to others for help, people with elevated health anxiety can train significant others to inquire repeatedly about their health and offer assurance. This fosters helplessness and reinforces the view that the person is weak and vulnerable (Taylor & Asmundson, 2004).

Contemporary Treatments

Until recently, the prognosis of hypochondriasis was considered to be quite poor, and treatments were thought to be of limited value. However, advances over the past few decades have led to empirically supported cognitive-behavioral treatments (CBT). The elements of CBT include education about the nature of hypochondriasis and the cognitive-behavioral model, cognitive restructuring of maladaptive beliefs, behavioral exercises to alter dysfunctional beliefs and to reduce maladaptive coping, and, in some case, behavioral stress management. Recent developments in pharmacotherapies for hypochondriasis—particularly tricyclics antidepressants (e.g., imipramine) and antidepressant serotonergic medications (e.g., fluvoxamine)—have also been promising. Medications are administered in the context of good clinical management, including nonspecific treatment factors (e.g., therapist attention and empathy) and education about the nature of hypochondriasis. Before implementing either CBT or pharmacotherapy for hypochondriasis, it is essential that the patient receive a thorough medical evaluation to rule out general medical conditions that could account for presenting bodily concerns.

Treatment Efficacy

There have been several randomized controlled studies showing that CBT is effective, relative to wait-list controls, in treating hypochondriasis, with gains being maintained at follow-up after a year or longer. There have been comparatively fewer studies of drug treatments for hypochondriasis. These studies have been largely limited to case studies and open (uncontrolled) trials. As of 2008, there has been only one published randomized controlled trial that suggested that fluoxetine is superior to placebo (Fallon et al., 1996; B. A. Fallon, personal communication, September 10, 2002). Meta-analysis of treatments for hypochondriasis suggests CBT and fluoxetine are the most effective treatments, with little difference between the two at post-treatment (Taylor & Asmundson, 2004). Although the benefits of CBT have been shown to persist at follow-up, there is insufficient information to determine whether similar long-term gains are obtained with pharmacotherapy. Despite the encouraging results for these treatments, they are not completely effective for all patients, and about 10–20% of patients drop out of such treatments (Taylor & Asmundson, 2004). The proportion of patients who refuse to enter such treatments is unknown.

In summary, hypochondriasis is a severe and frequently disabling condition. Research supports a cognitive-behavioral mode of this disorder, in which selective attention to one's body, dysfunctional beliefs about health and disease, and maladaptive coping play key roles. Evidence suggests that CBT and serotonergic medications are beneficial but not completely efficacious in treating the disorder. Further research is needed to foster improvements in treatment efficacy and to improve the likelihood that patients will enter and remain in treatment. Much also remains to be learned about the mechanisms of action in these treatments. It is possible that many psychosocial and drug treatments work in much the same way—by reducing the strength of dysfunctional beliefs about bodily changes.

REFERENCES

American Psychiatric Association. (2000). *Diagnostic and statistical manual of mental disorders* (4th ed., text rev.). Washington, DC: Author.

Fallon, B. A., Schneier, F. R., Marshall, R., Campeas, R., Vermes, D., Goetz, D., et al. (1996). The pharmacotherapy of hypochondriasis. *Psychopharmacology Bulletin, 32*, 607–611.

Pennebaker, J. W. (1982). *The psychology of physical symptoms.* New York: Springer.

Salkovskis, P. M., Warwick, H. M., & Deale, A. C. (2003). Cognitive-behavioral treatment for severe and persistent health anxiety (hypochondriasis). *Brief Treatment and Crisis Intervention, 3*, 353–367.

Taylor, S., & Asmundson, G. J. G. (2004). *Treating health anxiety: A cognitive-behavioral approach.* New York: Guilford Press.

Taylor, S., Thordarson, D. S., Jang, K. L., & Asmundson, G. J. G. (2006). Genetic and environmental origins of health anxiety: A twin study. *World Psychiatry, 5*, 47–50.

SUGGESTED READINGS

Asmundson, G. J. G., & Taylor, S. (2005). It's not all in your head: How worrying about your health could be making you sick—and what you can do about it. New York: Guilford Press.

Furer, P., Walker, J. R., & Stein, M. B. (2007). Treating health anxiety and fear of death: A practitioner's guide. New York: Springer.

STEVEN TAYLOR
University of British Columbia, Canada

GORDON J. G. ASMUNDSON
University of Regina, Canada

See also: Somatoform Disorders

HYPOMANIA (See Bipolar Disorder)

HYPOTHESIS TESTING

Statistical hypothesis testing is a formalized decision-making process. It allows one to reach conclusions about the possible value or values of one or more population parameters. These parameters reflect important characteristics of the populations under study that are of interest to the researcher.

The statistical decision-making framework is a form of inferential logic, and not deductive logic. Examples of deductive logic include mathematical proofs and formula derivations. Inferential logic works from the part to the whole. In psychology, a sample from a population is examined and conclusions are based on those observations. For example, one might examine a sample of healthy, normal humans and conclude that all such humans are bipedal. This would represent a correct inference conclusion. If the sample was skewed in some manner, one might conclude that all humans have red hair. That would be an inference error. The critical point is that the sample needs to be representative of the population. Thus, a statistical test result does not prove that a given hypothesis is true or false. Rather, it lends evidence as to the validity of a theory or conjecture.

The profound advantage to statistical hypothesis testing is that one can control, at least approximately, the probability of reaching an inference error. The explicit control of the decision error rates is the primary reason why hypothesis testing has become a standard tool in research. For those new to the study of statistical data analysis, a suitable undergraduate textbook would be Welkowitz, Cohen, and Ewen (2006). A calculus-based graduate-level treatment can be found in Hogg, McKean, and Craig (2005).

In an experimental or observation study, the dependent variable represents those values that are measured from the subjects. The independent variable defines the treatment level or group membership. There is a general structure to hypothesis testing that spans virtually all applications. This can be formulated in an eight-step testing sequence.

Step 1. State the null and alternative hypothesis. The hypotheses are always statements about population parameters, never sample statistics. One of the two hypotheses should exactly match the research claim or question under study. Normally, the hypotheses taken together will cover the entire range of possible parameter values. The equality point is always associated with the null hypothesis. The equality point specifies the location of the null sampling distribution on the number line. The equality point becomes the *Straw Man* model that is tested in the statistical analysis. One starts the analysis assuming that the null hypothesis is correct. If the

evidence from data refutes the null hypothesis, then it is rejected.

Psychological research is unpredictable. One should always be prepared to act on unexpected results. I recommend that two-tail hypothesis tests be used in virtually all applications. One-tail tests should be used only if an outcome in the other direction is completely meaningless and of no interest whatsoever. This is seldom the case in psychology. An unexpected result may be disappointing, but it may indicate a faulty experimental paradigm or the need to correct a behavioral theory. Both of these outcomes are significant conclusions.

Step 2. State the test statistic and sampling distribution that will be used in the testing process. The test statistic is computed from the dependent variable. It is at this point that the statistical assumptions are made and applied.

Step 3. State the Type I error rate. A Type I error is rejecting the null hypothesis when it is true. This is often limited to around 5%. This is a judgment of the decision error risk that the researcher is willing to assume.

Step 4. Determine the decision rules. What values of the test statistic will lead to rejection of the null hypothesis? The decision rule is determined from the probability model and statistical assumptions made for the test.

Step 5. The experimental data are collected under the specified experimental conditions or observational controls. Also note that the quality of the results depends on the quality of the sample taken. Most statistical procedures require the collection of a random sample.

Step 6. Reach your statistical conclusion. Do the results lead to the rejection of the null hypothesis? Do the data fail to reject the null?

Step 7. Compute the statistical power of the test. The power of the experiment is the probability of rejecting the null hypothesis if it is false. Sample data can be used to estimate the various population parameters needed for the power computations, such as the sample variance. The sample results can also help the researcher determine the nature and relevance of the effect size seen in the study. Power analysis is elaborated by Cohen (1988).

Step 8. Interpret the statistical results. How do they reflect on the validity of the research hypotheses and psychological theory in general? Were there confounding events or factors that might have affected the experimental outcomes?

A properly executed power analysis can allow the researcher to test the null hypothesis to a suitable degree of accuracy. For example, the following nutritional statement was found on a milk carton:

According to the EPA, no significant difference has been shown between milk derived from rBST treated and non-rBST treated cows.

rBST is a recombinant bovine growth hormone. In order to provide evidence to support this claim, the hypothesis test needs to be conducted with sufficient sample size to achieve a reasonable statistical power level for a meaningful effect size. Psychological research should achieve a similar level of rigor in the statistical analysis.

REFERENCES

Cohen, J. (1988). *Statistical power analysis for the behavioral sciences* (2nd ed.) Hillsdale, NJ: Lawrence Erlbaum.

Hogg, R. V., McKean, J. W., & Craig, A. T. (2005). *Introduction to mathematical statistics* (6th ed.). Upper Saddle River, NJ: Prentice-Hall.

Welkowitz, J., Cohen, B. H., & Ewen, R. B. (2006). *Introductory statistics for the behavioral sciences* (6th ed.). Hoboken, NJ: John Wiley & Sons.

GLENN W. MILLIGAN
Ohio State University

See also: **Null Hypothesis Significance Testing; Scientific Method**

HYSTERIA (See Somatization Disorder)

I

ICELAND, PSYCHOLOGY IN

Psychologists in Iceland have been trained in various countries. An undergraduate course in psychology was started at the University of Iceland, Reykjavík, in 1971 and at the University of Akureyri in the north of Iceland in 2003. Icelandic psychologists had to go abroad for their post-graduate training in psychology until 1999, when a post-graduate professional training program in psychology at the masters level was begun at the University of Iceland. Initially most Icelandic psychologists completed their training in Denmark, but later they sought their training in other countries, including Norway, Sweden, Germany, France, England, Scotland, the United States, Canada, and Australia.

The Icelandic Psychological Association (IPA) was established in 1954 and has a current membership of 300. Within the association there are three divisions: clinical, school, and rehabilitation psychology. The office of the IPA is based at the Icelandic Academics Union (BHM).

The profession of psychology in Iceland is regulated by law #40/1976, which protects the title and, to some extent, the function of psychologists. The accrediting committee of the Icelandic Psychological Society is consulted by the Directorate of Health, which is the awarding authority of accreditation for psychologists in Iceland by law #41/2007 with amendments #12/2008. Only those who have the right to call themselves psychologists can apply for positions advertised for psychologists. Psychologists are permitted to practice psychotherapy.

There are four specialties recognized within psychology in Iceland regulated by by-law #158/1990: clinical psychology, rehabilitation psychology, educational psychology, and industrial/occupational psychology. Only those who have been accredited by the Directorate of Health to practice as psychologists can embark on training in one of the subspecialties of psychology. The specialist training in psychology lasts four and a half years. During this time trainees have to work under the supervision of a specialist for a stipulated number of months within specified areas. Trainees receive 120 hours of personal supervision from at least two specialists and 40 hours of group supervision (1 hour per week/40 hours per year). A trainee must complete 300 hours of didactic training, conduct a research project, and publish in a refereed journal before becoming recognized as a specialist in one of the four areas just mentioned.

Most of the psychologists in Iceland are employed by the health, social, and school services. There are about 35 psychologists working full time in private practice and 110 working in part-time positions. The services rendered by psychologists and specialists in psychology in private practice are to some extent reimbursed by the national health services, private insurance, or the social services. Patients are either self-referred or referred by a physician or the social services. Many practicing psychologists consult with corporations and industries.

EIRIKUR ORN ARNARSON
Landspitali University Hospital,
Reykjavík, Iceland

IDEALIZATION

The concept of idealization has been elaborated as part of a process that allows for identification and eventual separation from parents during development as well as a part of the therapeutic process. Whereas idealization was once regarded as a homogenous phenomenon, most current psychological approaches consider there to be a variety of kinds of idealization that may serve multiple functions both during development and the therapeutic process.

Within classical psychoanalytic approaches, idealization was sometimes considered part of a defensive process that would protect an individual from awareness of anger and disappointment felt toward loved and needed parents. In particular, the Oedipus complex requires individuals to overcome their rivalry with the same-sexed parent partly through an idealization of power and authority and ultimate identification with such parent in order to vicariously share the parent's success or domination. Melanie Klein (1975) differentiated between good others and idealized others. The good other is a composite of satisfying experiences with others, whereas idealization relates to elaborated fantasies about others, partly compensatory, in order to provide safety and insulate the child from danger. In most of these psychoanalytic formulations, the individual uses idealization of the other in order to augment a sense of power and control.

Heinz Kohut (1977), a psychoanalyst known as the father of a branch of psychoanalysis called *self pychology*, suggested that idealization was a more complex and multifarious phenomenon. Kohut delineated psychological processes organized around the child's need to admire an idealized other. A healthy independent self grows out of a matrix of this relationship, which often involves "mirroring" by the other. This mirroring and responsiveness from the idealized other is a process by which people feel that their presence is noted and welcomed by the other in ways that allow for a kind of self-love and the capacity to love others. Thus idealization was no longer seen only as a defense against hostility, but instead as a part of universal developmental process. Many contemporary infant researchers describe the complex reciprocal processes by which infants gaze at and are registered by their caretakers in processes that relate to the early development of idealization and identification.

Psychotherapists have tried to elaborate a variety of manifestations of idealization within the therapeutic relationship. Some idealization is based on actual therapeutic experiences of the ways that the psychotherapist has provided understanding and been helpful to the patient. A set of concepts construed broadly as therapeutic alliance concepts also refer to the ways that the therapist engenders trust and safety within the therapeutic relationship, often a benevolent authority directed toward a parent. In contrast to these forms of idealization within the therapeutic relationship, there are manifestations of idealization that borrow from defenses against other feelings, such as disappointment. For example, patients who are anxious about being angry toward their psychotherapist might unconsciously gravitate toward a more positive or idealized version of their therapist's behavior in order to avoid or minimize their conflicts about feeling angry.

Once again, Kohut's work on developing more normative developmental processes related to idealization had implications for understanding idealization within the therapeutic process. Kohut suggested that some patients' needs for a healthy kind of idealization of a parent may be manifested in the therapeutic relationship. He further suggested that, with respect to therapeutic technique, the preferred response to this process is to allow the emergence of these forms of idealization, rather than to prematurely assume that all manifestations of idealization are the product of defenses against hostility.

In summary, idealization is now seen as a complex rather than homogeneous phenomenon that involves a number of developmental purposes. It is both part of a healthy developmental trajectory and a defense used to compensate for disappointment felt toward caretakers. Thus in clinical interactions, the meaning and purpose of idealization needs to be determined within particular psychological and interpersonal contexts.

REFERENCES

Beebe, B., Lachmann, F., & Jaffe, J. (1997). Mother-infant interaction structures and presymbolic self- and ego-representations. *Psychoanalytic Dialogues, 7*, 133–182.

Klein, M. (1975). *Envy and gratitude and other works*. New York: Free Press.

Kohut, H. (1977). *The restoration of the self*. New York: International Universities Press.

STEVEN H. COOPER
Harvard Medical School

See also: Defense Mechanisms; Object Relations Theory; Object Splitting

IDENTIFICATION WITH THE AGGRESSOR

In the early 1970s, four Swedish men were held captive in a bank vault for six days during a robbery attempt. The captives reported an emotional bonding with their captors, essentially identifying with their aggressors; this phenomenon was dubbed the Stockholm syndrome.

The original idea of "Identification with the Aggressor" was formulated by Anna Freud (1936/1946) in *The Ego and Mechanisms of Defense*. According to Freud it was a defense mechanism that was used to "protect the self from hurt and disorganization." Prior to that time, the explanation for various forms of psychopathology had remained elusive to our understanding.

Throughout the life cycle, children as well as adults can be faced with an event that produces intense anxiety. It may be a parent who abuses a child, or a priest who violates a child's trust, or an angry police officer who prefers to intimidate rather than educate.

In the military, a drill instructor attempts to scare recruits into believing that they cannot succeed in the service unless they have been terrorized. This overwhelming fear and anxiety is then used at times to ensure that the recruit will morph into the person that they have so feared, thus channeling that fearful and dependent feeling into becoming the person in charge, which is often displayed in an autocratic and intimidating manner. All is justified under the umbrella belief that abuse can lead to effective leadership.

Thus children as well as adults learn to reduce their anxiety by changing from the passive to the active role. This is one possible explanation of why abused children often become abusive adults (Goleman, 1989). Instead of being the object of the ridicule, they become the one causing the terror. The Swedish captives experienced a process whereby their fear changed to relief when they began to identify with their captors. Many argue that knowledge and training can reduce the occurrences of this type of identification. This author believes that under the right set of circumstances, training might reduce the intensity but not eliminate the possible emergence of the syndrome. The most notorious instance of this kind occurred when heiress Patty Hearst was kidnapped by the Symbionese Liberation Army (SLA). After many months of being terrorized by her captors, Hearst redefined herself as "Tanya" and joined their ranks. Thus, what had been labeled the Stockholm syndrome is now sometimes called the Patty Hearst syndrome.

However, not everyone exposed to the same abuse becomes an abuser. A recent *New York Times* article ("Ex-hostages Differ on Captors," Summer 2008) illustrates the point that individuals respond to similar situations in different ways. The "hostages freed last week in Colombia offered vastly different messages about their former captors." Ingrid Betancourt urged Colombia's president to tone down the extremist language of hatred toward the rebels who held her captive for 6 years. But Marc Gonsalves, one of the three American freed hostages, denounced his kidnappers as "terrorists with a capital 'T.'" One possible explanation for these different reactions could be that people respond differently to fear and their own loss of control. The former response could be called identification with the aggressor, and the latter could be righteous indignation.

Presently video games, once only a means of recreation, have become the most ubiquitous manner in which players learn to hurt, intimidate, and kill based upon the dehumanization of their victims. Through observational learning (Bandura, 1977), players watch the action and, because the game is interactive, are able to score points if they can harm fictional characters. Thus the game is also operantly conditioning in that it rewards players when they aim and execute.

Television tends to overrepresent the amount of violence in society. The research of Bandura (1989) shows that people who watch excessive amounts of TV report more fear and anxiety and will use aggressive behavior in response to frustration more often than those who watch less TV. With the multitude of video games and television that condition a person to participate in fictional killing, one has to ask: What are the controls that may be lacking for a person to go the extra distance and commit that terrible crime in reality? Research does show that alcohol and anti-anxiety drugs are disinhibitors (Taylor, 1995) that essentially reduce fear and anxiety. These ingredients added to the mix of aggressive revenge and conditioned behavior can produce deadly results.

REFERENCES

Bandura, A. (1977). *Aggression: A social learning analysis.* Englewood Cliffs, NJ: Prentice-Hall.

Bandura, A. (1986). *Social foundations of thought and action: A social cognitive theory.* Englewood Cliffs, NJ: Prentice-Hall.

Freud, Anna (1946). *The ego and the mechanisms of defense.* New York: International Universities Press. (Original work published in 1936)

Goleman, D. (1989, April 23). The sad legacy of abuse: A search for remedies. *New York Times.*

Taylor, S. (1990). Kent State: Drugs and aggressive behavior in humans. New York: Oxford University Press.

SUGGESTED READING

Melsky, R. (2004). Identification with the aggressor: How crime victims often cope with trauma. *FBI Law Enforcement Bulletin.*

MARTIN M. PARKER
Northwestern University

See also: Aggression

IDENTITY FORMATION

There are numerous theoretical approaches that illuminate certain areas of identity development (e.g., Kagan's constructive-developmental approach or Blos's object relations approach), but Erik Erikson's (1968) psychosocial approach to human development appeals to many professionals because of its utility in many professional arenas, including clinical, theoretical, and empirical. Erikson's seminal work stressed the importance of history (personal and societal) and social contexts in influencing individuals' lives, and he incorporated these ideas into his concept of identity formation in adolescence.

Erik Erikson developed the construct of ego identity as an adaptive response to Freud's focus on neurotic personalities. He was interested in the development of healthy personalities and created a lifespan stage theory that addressed the development of the healthy ego. Obtaining a healthy ego identity evolves through unconscious and conscious mechanisms interacting dynamically in a process of discovering the self. According to Erikson, there are certain key crises inherent in different periods of a person's life, which are a direct reflection of the person's social maturity and societal expectations. The crises are then categorized into distinct psychosocial stages of development at which times certain ego strengths emerge as resolutions of these crises.

A person integrates into his or her ego identity the resolution of the crises for each stage of development. Each stage of psychosocial development culminates in a balance of both syntonic and dystonic outcomes. A syntonic outcome is a positive experience through which the individual strives to attain and consequently maintain the experience in the overall ego structure. Receiving accolades for achievement in school from a significant teacher is an example of a syntonic experience. Conversely, a dystonic outcome is a negative experience whereby the individual strives to avoid and consequently rectify the experience in the overall ego structure. Being the recipient of a disparaging remark from a significant teacher is an example of a dystonic experience. Healthy psychological development occurs when the number of syntonic experiences outweighs the number of dystonic experiences (Waterman, 1993, p. 53).

Adolescence, Erikson's fifth stage of psychosocial development, is the crucial period during which identity formation occurs. It reflects the accumulative syntonic and dystonic outcomes of the prior four stages of development. Identity formation is an integration in the self of the prior outcomes related to earlier stages of development. However, as Erikson noted, the formation of identity does not occur in a vacuum. The culture of society is crucial in how the adolescent integrates the prior stages of development. One's culture is shaped by the contexts in adolescents' lives. Hamachek (1985) uses a metaphor of ego growth rings, much like the growth rings of a tree, to facilitate an understanding of how an adolescent integrates the self in relation to contextual conditions when constructing an identity. Erikson's psychosocial stages of development are embedded in a series of concentric circles such that the width between each ring of development identifies the context, both positive and negative, of growth. Development that is constricted by the environment and made up of mostly dystonic outcomes would show a narrower width in growth for a particular stage, whereas development that is enriched or expanded by the environment and made up of mostly syntonic outcomes would show a broader width in growth for a particular stage.

Identity development mirrors the outcomes achieved in various domains in a person's life. Erikson delineated the identity domains in which this mirroring or self-reflection occurs as consisting of vocation; ideologies (religious, political, and economic); philosophy of life; ethical capacity; sexuality; gender, ethnicity, culture, and nationality; and "an all-inclusive human identity" (Erikson, 1968, p. 42). Through growth and integration in these domains, the adolescent's identity becomes integrated and ideally forms a healthy and stable self.

Marcia (1980) applied Erikson's concepts of ego identity by employing the two operational dimensions of *exploration* and *commitment*.

> *Exploration* refers to a period of struggle or active questioning in arriving at various aspects of personal identity, such as vocational choice, religious beliefs, or attitudes about the role of a spouse or parenting in one's life. *Commitment* involves making a firm, unwavering decision in such areas and engaging in appropriate implementing activities. (Waterman, 1993, p. 56)

Relative to these two dimensions of exploration and commitment, Marcia delineated four identity statuses that exist for an individual in later adolescence: identity diffusion, identity foreclosure, moratorium, and identity achievement. Identity diffused adolescents have not committed to an internally consistent set of values and goals, and exploration is superficial or absent. Identity foreclosed adolescents have committed to a set of values and goals with little or no exploration present. Moratorium adolescents are in the process of committing to a set of values and goals and intensely exploring alternatives to their decisions. Identity achieved adolescents have experienced a period of exploration (as in moratorium) and have come to an autonomous resolution of identity by committing to a set of values and goals (Patterson, Sochting, & Marcia, 1993, pp. 10–12; Marcia, 1993, pp. 10–11). Through the theoretical underpinnings of Erikson and the empirical applications of Marcia and others, it is readily apparent that the earlier stages of psychosocial growth profoundly affect early adolescents' potential to explore and commit to a set of values and goals consistent with their identity.

> For even within a wider identity man meets man always in categories (be they adult and child, man and woman, employer and employee, leader and follower, majority and minority) and "human" interrelations can truly be only the expression of divided function and the concrete overcoming of the specific ambivalence inherent in them: that is why I came to reformulate the Golden Rule as one that commands us to always act in such a way that the identities of both the actor and the one acted upon are enhanced. (Erikson, 1968, p. 316)

Current work on identity formation has expanded empirically and theoretically (Crocetti, Rubini, & Meeus, 2008; Grotevant, 2001). First, the identity statuses include a more fluid or process approach of achieving identity. The process approach to identity includes an interplay among individual and contextual variables in how the self is cognitively perceived. Individual variables could include any number of variables such as sex, race, political affiliation, or even being raised in poverty (Phillips & Pittman, 2003). The complexity of this concept is clearly shown in this recent work while still following along the Eriksonian tradition that society does shape the individual.

REFERENCES

Crocetti, E., Rubini, M., & Meeus, W. (2008). Capturing the dynamics of identity formation in various ethnic groups: Development and validation of a three-dimensional model. *Journal of Adolescence, 31*(2), 207–222.

Erikson, E. H. (1968). *Identity: Youth and crisis.* New York: W. W. Norton & Company.

Grotevant, H. D. (2001). Developing new insights from a process approach to adolescent development. *Human Development, 44,* 55–58.

Hamachek, D. E. (1985). The self's development and ego growth: Conceptual analysis and implications for counselors. *Journal of Counseling and Development, 64,* 136–142.

Marcia, J. E. (1980). Identity in adolescence. In J. Adelson (Ed.), *Handbook of adolescent psychology* (pp. 149–173). New York: John Wiley & Sons.

Marcia, J. E. (1993). The ego identity status approach to ego identity. In J. E. Marcia, A. S. Waterman, D. R. Matteson, S. L. Archer, & J. L. Orlofsky (Eds.). *Ego identity: A handbook for psychosocial research* (pp. 3–21). New York: Springer-Verlag.

Patterson, S. J., Sochting, I., & Marcia, J. E. (1993). The inner space and beyond: Women and identity. In G. R. Adams, T. P. Gullotta, & R. Montemayor (Eds.), *Adolescent identity formation: Vol. 4. Advances in adolescent development* (pp. 9–24). Newbury Park, CA: Sage Publications.

Phillips, T. M., & Pittman, J. F. (2003). Identity processes in poor adolescents: Exploring the linkages between economic disadvantage and the primary task of adolescence. *Identity: An International Journal of Theory and Research, 3*(2), 115–129.

Waterman, A. S. (1993). Identity as an aspect of optimal psychological functioning. In G. R. Adams, T. P. Gullotta, & R. Montemayor (Eds.), *Adolescent identity formation: Vol. 4. Advances in adolescent development* (pp. 50–72). Newbury Park, CA: Sage.

SUGGESTED READINGS

Kroger, J. (2004). *Identity in adolescence: The balance between self and other.* (3rd ed.). New York: Routledge.

Kroger, J. (2007). *Identity development: Adolescence through adulthood.* (2nd ed.). Thousand Oaks, CA: Sage.

Watzlawik, M., & Born, A. (Eds.). (2007). *Capturing identity: Quantitative and qualitative methods.* Lanham, MD: University Press of America.

KATHLEEN MCKINNEY
University of Wyoming

See also: **Adolescent Development; Ego Development; Eriksonian Developmental Stages**

IDIOT SAVANT (See Savant Syndrome)

ILLUSIONS (See Visual Illusions)

IMPLICIT ASSOCIATION TEST

When waiting for a movie to begin, it is common to see advertisements for the soda, popcorn, and candy you passed by (or bought) in the lobby. Whether you are paying attention to the advertisement or are talking to a companion, the pairing of ice-cold containers of soda with other attractive images and sounds establishes an association between "soda" and "good" in your mind. In the theater and beyond, the mind is constantly gathering information from the social environment and creating, revising, and reinforcing associations in memory. The mind is so prolific at forming these associations that it may do so even if you would rather not have them.

The Implicit Association Test (IAT) is a procedure for measuring implicit associations, which are feelings and thoughts that exist outside of conscious awareness or control. The IAT measures the strength of associations that accumulate through everyday experiences, whether or not the person is aware of holding those associations, and whether or not the associations are believed to be valid or true. The IAT is a sorting task predicated on the assumption that it is easier to make the same response to two things when they are related than when they are unrelated. For example, someone who has negative associations about old people might have a more difficult time linking pictures of old people with concepts like "nice," "warm," and "wonderful" compared with concepts like "awful," "terrible," and "horrible."

In an IAT measuring associations with age, participants quickly categorize young and old faces and words whose meanings are "good" or "bad" using two keys on a computer keyboard. In one part of the task, participants categorize pictures of young people and "good" words with one response key and pictures of old people and "bad" words with another key. In a second part of the task, the key assignments change. Participants categorize pictures of old people and "good" words with one response key and pictures of young people and "bad" words with another key. People with more positive associations for young versus old people are able to complete the task more quickly when young and "good" share the same key compared to when old and "good" share a key. Another way of saying this is that they have an automatic preference for young people relative to old people. Importantly, people are not deciding how they feel in the IAT; they are simply categorizing words and faces as quickly as possible. As a consequence, even someone who honestly reports liking old people as much as young people may show evidence of having comparatively negative associations about old people in their memory (try it yourself: https://implicit.harvard.edu/).

The IAT is a flexible tool. The previous example measures age associations, but it can be adapted to measure positive or negative associations about any types of concepts. Also, the evaluative concepts in the IAT can be changed to measure stereotypes and self-concepts. This flexibility has made the IAT a popular tool for a variety of applications, such as measuring fear and threat associations with spiders among people with spider phobia; personality characteristics such as associations of shy with oneself; and positive and negative associations for consumer products, social groups, and political candidates.

Importantly, how people behave is predicted by both automatic associations and self-reported, deliberate thoughts and feelings. For example, a recent review suggests that self-reported feelings, compared to the IAT, are more related to behaviors controlled by the actor (such as what someone says during an interview), whereas the IAT is more predictive than self-reported feelings of relatively uncontrolled behaviors (such as seating position, speaking time, amount of smiling and eye contact in the same interview context). Further, although self-reported feelings in general are important predictors of behavior, the IAT appears to be a better predictor for situations or topics that are socially sensitive, such as racial prejudice and stereotypes.

In just over 10 years after its initial publication, the IAT has been used in more than 500 scientific publications. This has promoted rapid learning and refinement of the IAT's features and limitations. As with any measurement tool, there are extraneous influences that interfere with its effectiveness as a measure of associations. For example, although the IAT is more reliable than related association measures, it is not perfectly reliable. It is somewhat akin to measures of blood pressure by showing some consistency over time but fluctuations from moment-to-moment. Also, some features of the procedure influence performance on the task. The most prominent influence is the order of the categorization tasks (i.e., whether old people and "good" share a response key before or after young people and "good"). The first task performed interferes with performance on the second. Likewise, people who respond more quickly on average tend to show smaller IAT effects than people who respond more slowly. Identification of extraneous influences such as these provides an opportunity to reduce or remove their influence. The "order effect" and "average response time" influences have been reduced with procedural and analytic innovations, respectively. The coming years of research will continue to refine the methodological features of the IAT for association measurement.

There are also a number of open questions about interpreting IAT scores. For example, should mental associations different from a person's expressed beliefs be considered something that belongs to them, or something belonging to their culture? If someone disagrees with associations revealed by their IAT score, does that mean they are lying? The answer to the latter question is "no." People can possess associations that they honestly disagree with, but that still exist in their minds and may even influence their behavior.

The thoughts and feelings that people consciously experience and endorse are integral to understanding human life. However, much of mental processing occurs outside of conscious awareness, and understanding automatic reactions is also important for gaining insight into the workings of the human mind. Tools such as the IAT offer windows into portions of the mind that people are unable

to express, either because they do not want to, or because they do not even know they possess them.

REFERENCES

Gawronski, B., Peters, K. R., & LeBel, E. P. (2008). What makes mental associations personal or extra-personal? Conceptual issues in the methodological debate about implicit attitude measures. *Social and Personality Psychology Compass, 2,* 1002–1023.

Greenwald, A. G., McGhee, D. E., & Schwartz, J. L. K. (1998). Measuring individual differences in implicit cognition: The Implicit Association Test. *Journal of Personality and Social Psychology, 74,* 1464–1480.

Greenwald, A. G., Poehlman, T. A., Uhlmann, E., & Banaji, M. R. (In press). Understanding and using the Implicit Association Test: III. Meta-analysis of predictive validity. *Journal of Personality and Social Psychology.*

Lane, K. A, Banaji, M. R., Nosek, B. A., & Greenwald, A. G. (2007). Understanding and using the Implicit Association Test: IV: What we know (so far) about the method. In B. Wittenbrink and N. Schwarz (Eds.), *Implicit measures of attitudes* (pp. 59–102). New York: Guilford Press.

Nosek, B. A., Greenwald, A. G., & Banaji, M. R. (2006). The Implicit Association Test at age 7: A methodological and conceptual review. In J. A. Bargh (Ed.), *Social psychology and the unconscious: The automaticity of higher mental processes* (pp. 265–292). New York: Psychology Press.

Nosek, B. A., Smyth, F. L., Hansen, J. J., Devos, T., Lindner, N. M., Ranganath, K. A., Smith, C. T., Olson, K. R., Chugh, D., Greenwald, A. G., & Banaji, M. R. (2007). Pervasiveness and correlates of implicit attitudes and stereotypes. *European Review of Social Psychology, 18,* 36–88.

COLIN TUCKER SMITH
BRIAN A. NOSEK
University of Virginia

***See also:* Performance-Based Personality Measures**

IMPRESSION MANAGEMENT

Impression management is a common response style in clinical and work-related settings. It is defined by Rogers (2008, p. 6) as "deliberate efforts to control others' perceptions of an individual; its purposes may range from maximizing social outcomes to the portrayal of a desired identity." In most instances, impression management is perceived in terms of highly positive social outcomes. However, this is not necessarily the case. As a common example, persons involved in business may deliberately cultivate an image of being ruthlessly competitive. More extreme examples include undercover police officers and the tough personas of individuals involved in organized crime.

Impression management, as it relates to positive social outcomes, must be distinguished from two related response styles: defensiveness and social desirability. Of the three, defensiveness is the most narrowly defined as the denial or gross minimization of psychological or physical impairment. In other words, individuals are attempting to avoid the stigmatization and other unwanted consequences of being seen as mentally disordered. In contrast, social desirability is a broader term describing a general tendency for persons to present themselves in a favorable light that reflects the prevailing social norms and mores. Impression management is the broadest term that can encompass both defensiveness and social desirability. It can reflect either a general tendency or a situationally based response, such as portraying a very positive image during the hiring process that is not maintained once the position is secured.

Clinical research has been imprecise in its use of these terms for describing response styles associated with positive social outcomes. For example, the Personality Assessment Inventory (PAI; Morey, 2007) has a Positive Impression Scale (PIM) that is intended to measure "the presentation of a very favorable impression or the denial of relatively minor faults" (p. 30). The initial PIM validation studies involved impression management with college psychology students attempting to impress a potential employer. However, some studies of the PIM scale are more narrowly focused on defensiveness with clinical samples attempting to deny their psychopathology and drug abuse (see Morey, 2007). At question is the generalizability of these studies to the more general construct of impression management.

Impression Management and Assessment Issues

In clinical practice, practitioners need to be able to distinguish between denials of negative attributes (i.e., defensiveness) and efforts at overly positive portrayals (i.e., impression management and social desirability). As a relevant example, clients in contested divorces are likely to simulate adjustment. However, the critical issue is whether they are covering up serious psychopathology or merely exaggerating positive attributes. In conducting child custody evaluations, for instance, the denial of borderline features has very different implications for effective parenting than does the presentation of excessive virtue. Unfortunately, analog studies have not directly compared the experimental conditions of defensiveness and positive presentation (impression management and social desirability). This oversight constrains the usefulness of psychological measures on referral issues where simulated adjustment is expected.

As an exploration between positive attributes and defensiveness, we examined normative data (Bathurst,

Gottfried, & Gottfried, 1997) for the MMPI-2 in child custody cases. According to the original formulation of validity scales (Greene, 2000), Scale L assesses positive presentations whereas Scale K is intended to assess suppressed psychopathology (defensiveness). Using the Bathurst et al. data and Greene's categorization of moderate to marked scores, about half (53.3%) evidenced some positive presentation, whereas approximately two-thirds (68.5%) presented with some defensiveness. These findings suggest that (1) substantial overlap occurs between the two response styles and (2) some parents are likely to exhibit defensiveness alone. Based only on original conceptualization, these findings underscore the pressing need for simulation research that directly compares differences between these response styles on validity scales.

Paulhus (1998) differs from the above conceptualization in his operationalization of impression management on the Paulhus Deception Scales (PDS; Paulhus, 1998) as always being positive. Paulhus contends that impression management, as a factor of socially desirable responding, is part of an individual's pervasive mode of responding in everyday conditions. In high-demand conditions, however, impression management is driven by situational factors and the need to portray a positive image. At present, correlational data suggest impression management on the PDS may be assessing both an exaggeration of virtue and general social desirability (Lanyon & Carle, 2007), and several studies have noted the increase in impression management scores under high-demand situations.

Impression management has been extensively researched in the context of work settings. As a broad and flexible construct, it can be applied to various professions and employment settings. For example, persons involved in sales may wish to present themselves differently depending on their "sizing up" of each customer from a highly confident sales pitch to a very restrained, almost diffident, sales presentation. Impression management techniques may affect both perceived and actual job performance. Studies have become sophisticated in examining impression management as it relates to work roles and corporate structure. More fine-grained studies could be conducted to differentiate impression management for specific roles: creativity and self-initiative might be emphasized in one career, while dependability and consensus building is valued in another.

Impression management is often viewed as an individual's response style without giving due consideration to interactional effects. Beck and Strong (1982) conducted a classic study based on impression management theory. Clinicians offered interpretations of clients' symptoms with either negative or positive connotations. For example, the expression of depressed feelings might be interpreted negatively as a way of making others feel guilty or positively as an awareness of emotions, essential to feeling alive. Marked differences were observed after only two sessions, which likely reflected a combination of actual change and impression management. Clients given positive interpretations exhibited markedly "improved" moods ($d = 2.79$), while those provided with negative interpretations had much "worse" moods ($d = -1.85$) and a greater risk for symptom relapse after termination of treatment. In professional practice, attention must be paid to both clinicians and their clients in determining the various motivations for impression management.

Impression management is one of the most challenging response styles because of its heterogeneity. Individuals may use impression management to create either positive or negative views of themselves. Beyond these broad perspectives, impression management may be used to create desired role assumptions that vary by setting. For example, adolescents with delinquent histories may wish to project a courteous and respectful demeanor in courtroom proceedings and a machismo façade among their delinquent peers. At present, assessment measures are generally useful at evaluating general response styles, such as a positive presentation, which covers defensiveness, social desirability, and positive impression management. Once the general category is identified, clinicians will likely use extensive interviews and corroborative data in their efforts to distinguish impression management from other forms of positive presentation.

REFERENCES

Bathurst, K., Gottfried, A. W., & Gottfried, A. E. (1997). Normative data for the MMPI-2 in child custody litigation. *Psychological Assessment, 9*, 205–211.

Beck, J. T., & Strong, S. R. (1982). Stimulating therapeutic change with interpretations: A comparison of positive and negative connotation. *Journal of Consulting Psychology, 29*, 551–559.

Greene, R. L. (2000). *The MMPI-2: An interpretive manual* (2nd ed.). Boston: Allyn and Bacon.

Lanyon, R. I., & Carle, A. C. (2007). Internal and external validity of scores on the Balanced Inventory of Desirable Responding and the Paulhus Deception Scales. *Educational and Psychological Measurement, 67*, 859–876.

Morey, L. C. (2007). *Personality Assessment Inventory professional manual* (2nd ed.). Odessa, FL: Psychological Assessment Resources.

Paulhus, D. L. (1998). *Paulhus Deception Scales (PDS): The balanced inventory of desirable responding—7*. North Tonawanda, NY: Multi-Health Systems.

Rogers, R. (Ed.) (2008). *Clinical assessment of malingering and deception* (3rd ed.). New York: Guilford Press.

RICHARD ROGERS
CHELSEA E. FIDUCCIA
University of North Texas

See also: **Deception; Malingering**

IMPRINTING

Imprinting is the learning process through which the social preferences of animals of certain species become restricted to a particular object or class of objects. Filial imprinting is involved in the formation, in young animals, of an attachment to, and a preference for, the parent or parent surrogate. Sexual imprinting is involved in the formation of mating preferences that are expressed later in life. Lorenz (1937) gave the phenomenon its name in an influential paper in which he provided a detailed description of imprinting in a number of bird species. Filial imprinting has been studied mostly in precocial birds such as ducklings and domestic chicks. These birds can move about shortly after hatching, and they approach and follow an object to which they are exposed. In a natural situation this object is usually the animal's mother, but inanimate mother surrogates are also effective in eliciting filial behavior (Horn, 1985; Bolhuis, 1991). A chick learns the features of an object during the time the bird is exposed to it, remains close to it, and may run away from novel objects. When given a choice between the familiar stimulus and a novel one, the bird shows a preference for the familiar stimulus.

Filial imprinting and sexual imprinting are two separate (although perhaps partially overlapping) processes. The time of expression of the preferences is different, and so is the period of time during which experience affects preferences, which is up to the time of mating in the case of sexual imprinting. Furthermore, filial preferences may be formed after a relatively short period of exposure to an object, whereas sexual preferences develop as the result of a long period of exposure to and social interaction with the parents as well as the siblings. Normally, sexual imprinting ensures that the bird will mate with a member of its own strain or species. When the young bird is cross-fostered, that is, reared with adults of a different species, it develops a sexual preference for the foster species.

Reversibility and Sensitive Periods

Lorenz suggested that imprinting was irreversible and occurred only during a "sensitive period" (or "critical period"). Subsequent studies have demonstrated that filial preferences can in fact be reversed when the original object is removed and the animal is exposed to a novel object. There is a difference between the memory of the first stimulus and that of subsequent stimuli to which the animal is exposed; under certain circumstances the preference for the first object may return (Bolhuis, 1991). The ability to form filial attachments has been shown to depend on both developmental age and time since hatching. The ability to imprint is related to the development of the animal's sensorimotor abilities. The sensitive period is brought to an end by the learning experience (imprinting) itself; once the bird has formed a preference for a particular object, it avoids novel objects. Consequently, it tends not to be exposed to them for long and so may learn little about them. Thus, the learning process of imprinting does not seem to be restricted to a sensitive period.

Predispositions

Filial preferences are formed not only as a result of learning through exposure, but are also influenced by a predisposition (Horn, 1985; Bolhuis, 1991). This predisposition may be measured in the laboratory by giving chicks (*Gallus gallus domesticus*) a choice between, for example, a rotating stuffed jungle fowl and a rotating red box. Under some conditions the two stimuli are equally attractive. However, if the young chick is given a certain amount of nonspecific experience, such as being handled or allowed to run, the chick prefers the fowl to the box in a subsequent test. In order to be effective, this nonspecific experience must occur within a "sensitive period." It appears that the target stimuli of the predisposition are in the head and neck region but are not species-specific. Once the predisposition has developed, it does not function as a filter that prevents the chick from learning about objects that do not resemble conspecifics; such chicks can learn about other objects by being exposed to them. This and other evidence suggests that the mechanisms underlying the predisposition and those underlying learning influence behavior independently.

Imprinting and Learning

Filial imprinting has been regarded as different from other forms of learning, because it proceeds without any obvious reinforcement such as food or warmth. However, an imprinting object may itself be a reinforcer, that is, a stimulus that an animal finds rewarding. Just as a rat learns to press a pedal to receive a food reward, so a visually naive chick may learn to press a pedal to see an imprinting object. When chicks are exposed to two imprinting stimuli simultaneously, they learn more about the individual stimuli than when they are exposed to the stimuli sequentially, or to only one stimulus. This so-called within-event learning has also been found in conditioning paradigms in rats and humans (Bolhuis & Honey, 1998), and it suggests that conjoint exposure to two stimuli results in the formation of an integrated memory of them. The findings in rats and chicks are consistent with the suggestion that constructing a representation of an object involves the formation of associative links among those elements of an object that reliably co-occur.

Neural Mechanisms of Filial Imprinting

Studies of imprinting in the domestic chick have shown that a restricted brain region, the intermediate and medial part of the mesopallium (IMM), is involved in the recognition memory of imprinting, probably storing information (Horn, 1985, 2004). Imprinting leads to significant changes in the structure of synapses in the IMM. In addition, imprinting results in a significantly increased number of a certain type of glutamate receptors (NMDA receptors) in the IMM that is related to the amount the chicks have learned about the imprinting object. These findings are consistent with the hypothesis that learning leads to an increased efficacy of synaptic transmission. Recently, it was found that a period of sleep immediately after training is necessary for memory consolidation (Jackson et al., 2008).

REFERENCES

Bolhuis, J. J. (1991). Mechanisms of avian imprinting: A review. *Biological Reviews, 66,* 303–345.

Bolhuis, J. J., & Honey, R. C. (1998). Imprinting, learning, and development: From behaviour to brain and back. *Trends in Neurosciences, 21,* 306–311.

Horn, G. (2004). Pathways of the past: The imprint of memory. *Nature Reviews Neuroscience, 5,* 108–120.

Jackson, C., McCabe, B. J., Nicol, A. U., Grout, A. S., Brown, M. W. & Horn, G. (2008). Dynamics of a memory trace: Effects of sleep on consolidation. *Current Biology, 18,* 393–400.

Lorenz, K. (1937) The companion in the bird's world. *Auk, 54,* 245–273.

SUGGESTED READINGS

Gottlieb, G. (1971). *Development of species identification in birds.* Chicago: University of Chicago Press.

Horn, G. (1985). *Memory, imprinting, and the brain.* Oxford, UK: Clarendon Press.

Sluckin, W. (1972). *Imprinting and early learning.* London: Methuen.

JOHAN J. BOLHUIS
Utrecht University, The Netherlands

See also: Learning Theories; Memory Functions

IMPULSE CONTROL DISORDERS (See Firesetting; Gambling Addiction; Intermittent Explosive Disorder; Kleptomania; Trichotillomania)

IMPULSIVITY

The concept of impulsivity has played an important role in psychology. It is included in virtually every theoretical system of human personality. In the field of clinical psychology, it is understood to contribute to many different forms of psychopathology (Whiteside & Lynam, 2001). It is part of borderline personality disorder (a disorder characterized by emotional lability and ill-considered, self-harming acts); antisocial personality disorder (characterized by rash, ill-thought out acts that often harm others); attention deficit/hyperactivity disorder (characterized by difficulty waiting one's turn and persevering on tasks); bulimia nervosa (characterized by binge eating and subsequent purging); alcohol and drug-use disorders; and a whole set of impulse-control disorders, such as kleptomania, pyromania, and intermittent explosive disorder. For many of these forms of psychopathology, impulsivity is understood to contribute to their emergence.

As scientists considered the wide variety of disorders and behaviors characterized as "impulsive," it became clear that the term "impulsivity" was being used by different researchers to mean different things. In the past, some authors had used the term to refer to distractibility and short attention span, others to refer to the need to seek stimulation and novelty, others to susceptibility to boredom, others to acting without forethought, and others to emotionally triggered rash action (Depue & Collins, 1999; Whiteside & Lynam, 2001). In recent years, researchers have begun to clarify the confusing uses of the term. Whiteside and Lynam (2001) examined the interrelationships of several different measures of "impulsivity" and identified four different personality traits related to rash or ill-advised action. Subsequently, Cyders, Smith, Spillane, Fischer, Annus, and Peterson (2007) identified a fifth. The five different personality pathways describe substantively different psychological processes, and they appear to be associated with different kinds of rash action.

Two of these pathways to rash action are emotion-based. *Negative urgency* refers to the tendency to engage in rash acts when experiencing intense, negative emotion, and *positive urgency* refers to the tendency to engage in rash acts when experiencing intense positive emotion. Two other pathways are based on different aspects of low levels of conscientiousness. *Lack of planning* refers to the tendency to act without care or forethought, and *lack of perseverance* refers to a failure to tolerate boredom or remain focused despite distraction. The fifth pathway is *sensation seeking*, or the tendency to seek out novel or thrilling stimulation (Cyders & Smith, 2007; Cyders et al., 2007; Cyders & Smith, in press; Whiteside & Lynam, 2001). These five traits are distinct from each other. There is not an overall psychological trait called "impulsivity," of which each of these traits is a type. Rather, there are five separate pathways to rash, ill-advised action that are only moderately correlated with each other (Cyders & Smith, 2007).

These five different personality pathways are associated with different forms of rash action. Sensation seeking correlates with, and predicts, involvement in highly stimulating risky behaviors (in children, behaviors such as riding roller coasters and jumping out of

trees; in adults, behaviors such as bungee jumping and parachuting) and the frequency with which one engages in risky behaviors such as alcohol use and gambling. Lack of persistence correlates with difficulty paying attention in school, and both it and lack of planning correlate with poor academic performance. The two emotion-based dispositions, negative and positive urgency, correlate with aggressive behavior, and both traits correlate with and predict problematic involvement in risky behaviors, such as problem drinking, risky sexual behavior, drug use, and smoking. Negative urgency correlates with engaging in risky behaviors while in an extremely negative mood, while positive urgency correlates with engaging in risky behaviors when in an extremely positive mood. Negative urgency relates to bulimia nervosa, and both negative and positive urgency relate to alcohol abuse. A summary of the relevant research can be found in Cyders and Smith (in press).

There is at least preliminary evidence that different preventive or treatment interventions may be useful for the different personality pathways to rash action. Researchers have developed prevention programs aimed at adolescents high in sensation seeking, with the goal of reducing their rate of involvement in stimulating but risky activities. The use of media messages with high sensation value that encourage alternative, safe means of seeking stimulation appear to be effective in reducing drug use, particularly among high sensation seekers (Stephenson, 2003).

Very different interventions have been developed that help mitigate emotion-based risky behavior. Common emotion-based risky actions include suicide attempts, heavy drinking, drug use, angry outbursts, risky sexual behavior, and excessive spending (Linehan, 1993). For individuals inclined to engage in acts such as these when emotional, clinicians provide training on how to tolerate their distress or intense emotions. One key component of this training is to learn how to allow the intense emotion to decrease before acting, because once the intensity of the emotion has decreased, one is in a better position to act with one's long-term health and interests in mind. Strategies include distracting oneself through watching a movie, soothing oneself through taking a hot bath, and improving the moment through prayer (Linehan, 1993). To date, there has been little research on interventions to avoid risky behavior when in an extremely positive mood, even though that problem exists. Perhaps strategies that help individuals high in positive urgency maintain awareness of their long-term goals, even when in extremely positive moods, may prove effective.

Perhaps relevant to individuals who tend to act without forethought, there is some evidence that problem-solving interventions that teach individuals to engage in cognitive enterprises before acting may reduce some rash acts (Eyberg, Nelson, & Boggs, 2008). For nonpersistent, highly distractible individuals, it may be the case that stimulant medications such as methylphenidate (e.g., Ritalin) help them maintain focus on the task at hand (Prince & Wilens, 2002).

To date, there have not been systematic studies to determine whether the effectiveness of the different interventions is specific to individuals high on the relevant personality trait, other than the finding that the high sensation intervention is specifically effective for high sensation seekers. That research remains to be done. However, just as it appears to be the case that there are at least five different personality dispositions to rash action, and that those dispositions relate to different forms of rash action, so it may be the case that different clinical interventions are relevant, depending on which disposition is elevated in a given individual.

In conclusion, to understand "impulsivity" as a psychological concept, it is important to appreciate that there appear to be at least five different personality traits that dispose individuals to engage in rash, ill-considered action. Positive and negative urgency refer to dispositions to act rashly when experiencing intense emotion, lack of planning refers to the tendency to act without thinking ahead, lack of perseverance refers to the tendency to be distractible and lose focus on tasks, and sensation seeking refers to the tendency to seek out thrilling or novel stimulation. To speak precisely about the psychology of impulsive acts, one must be clear about the specific personality process one has in mind. The different processes appear to explain different aspects of rash behavior, and there is reason to believe that different clinical interventions may turn out to be most effective for different dispositions. Future research will further clarify these distinctions. One important avenue for researchers is to test the differential effectiveness of different interventions as a function of personality.

REFERENCES

Cyders, M. A., & Smith, G. T. (2007). Mood-based rash action and its components: Positive and negative urgency. *Personality and Individual Differences, 43*, 839–850.

Cyders, M. A., & Smith, G. T. (in press). Emotion-based dispositions to rash action: Positive and negative urgency. *Psychological Bulletin.*

Cyders, M. A., Smith, G. T., Spillane, N. S., Fischer, S., Annus, A. M., & Peterson, C. (2007). Integration of impulsivity and positive mood to predict risky behavior: Development and validation of a measure of positive urgency. *Psychological Assessment, 19*, 107–118.

Depue, R. A., & Collins, P. F. (1999). Neurobiology of the structure of personality: Dopamine, facilitation of incentive motivation, and extraversion. *Behavioral and Brain Sciences, 22*, 491–569.

Eyberg, S. M., Nelson, M. M., & Boggs, S. R. (2008). Evidence-based psychosocial treatments for children and adolescents with disruptive behavior. *Journal of Clinical Child and Adolescent Psychology, 37*, 215–237.

Linehan, M. M. (1993). *Cognitive-behavioral treatment of borderline personality disorder*. New York: Guilford Press.

Prince, J. B., & Wilens, T. E. (2002). Pharmacotherapy of adult ADHD. In S. Goldstein & A. T. Ellison (Eds.), *Clinician's guide to adult ADHD: Assessment and intervention* (pp. 165–186). San Diego, CA: Academic Press.

Stephenson, M. T. (2003). Mass media strategies targeting high sensation seekers: What works and why. *American Journal of Health Behavior, 27*, S233–S238.

Whiteside, S. P., & Lynam, D. R. (2001). The five factor model and impulsivity: Using a structural model of personality to understand impulsivity. *Personality and Individual Differences, 30*, 669–689.

GREGORY T. SMITH
TAMIKA C. B. ZAPOLSKI
JESSICA L. COMBS
REGAN E. FRIEND
University of Kentucky

See also: Sensation Seeking

INCONTINENCE (See Encopresis; Enuresis)

INDIA, PSYCHOLOGY IN

Beginning early in the twentieth century, psychology emerged as one of the most popular professional disciplines in India. It has deep philosophical roots, far more ancient than one might suspect. In the beginning, modern Indian psychology was influenced mainly by the Wundt–Titchener tradition, which was introduced by N. N. Sengupta at Calcutta University in 1915. At about this same time, G. Bose (1886–1953) was instrumental in initiating a postgraduate course of study in psychoanalysis at this very same university. Psychoanalysis subsequently took firm roots in Indian soil when Bose established the Indian Psychoanalytical Society in 1921 in Calcutta. In the south, M. V. Gopalaswamy (1896–1957), a protégé of Spearman, instituted efforts to standardize tests of higher mental functions on the basis of Western constructs. He also spearheaded an independent Department of Clinical Psychology at the All-India Institute of Mental Health in 1955 (AIIMH, now called NIMHANS, Bangalore). In this institute, M. V. Govindaswamy (1904–1961) subsequently brought to bear the rigor of Johns Hopkins University in the United States and the Maudsley Hospital in London in the education and training of qualified clinical psychologists in India.

However, this domination of Western theories of psychology in India was resented and criticized by some as a photocopy approach, adaptology (e.g., Pandey, 2001), and a mismatch of Western psychological constructs with Indian ethos. Thereafter, there was a resurgence of interest in contemporary issues, and prominent psychologists have conducted extensive research and developed some culture-specific insight areas of their specialization, including Durganand Sinha in cross-cultural studies, Ashish Nandy in postcolonial impact, Ramakrishna Rao in parapsychology, Sudhir Kakkar in psychoanalysis, and Udai Pareek and S. K. Chakroborty in innovative models of organizational behavior.

Behavioral constructs from ancient scriptures are now surfacing in the interpretation of behavior. The sociocultural and spiritual repertoire of the Indian psyche is replete with information drawn from its sacred scriptures, such as Upanishads, Vedas (1000 BCE), Bhagwatgita, and Pathanjali's Raja Yoga (300 BCE), which advocated holistic health and emphasized the importance of the mind and consciousness for mental tranquility, peace, and compassion. The function of the mind was analyzed and conceived as *Ahankara* (ego), *Ittcha* (will), and *Budhi* (intellect), and the harmonious action of these three was considered to result in the healthy functioning of the mind. The ideal state of mind is *Satwa*, which is attained by equipoise and harmony. *Atherva Veda* (800 BCE) even mentioned use of psychotherapy (*Atharvani*) as a mode of treatment. Yoga and its practices have been universally lauded for their effectiveness in enhancing cognitive skills, improving visual and perceptual sensitivity, and controlling the autonomic nervous system, as well as being an effective way of coping with stress and anxiety. Yoga psychology has been introduced as a subspecialization in the curriculum of Indian universities.

Current Trends and Challenges

The paradigmatic shift in psychology during the 1960s to consideration of culture-specific and culture-bound issues was a clarion call to examining the process of indigenization (Sinha, 2000). However, the culture-based route to indigenization was blockaded by difficulty in defining and agreeing on what would be culturally appropriate to India, given the size, diversity, and complexity of its populace (1.13 billion people). Nevertheless, this difficulty challenged researchers in psychology to identify common benchmarks for culturally relevant behavioral parameters.

Under the aegis of the University Grants Commission (UGC), psychology picked up considerable momentum in educational institutions, beginning in the 1950s. The psychology departments at Allahabad, Utkal, and Thirupathi universities were accorded special status as centers of advanced studies. A current upgrading of curricular modules, mandated by the UGC's 10th Plan program (2002), ensures uniformity across all the universities with respect to minimum standards of teaching and research in psychology. As for the research output during the years 1998–2002, about 75% of the published studies were empirical in nature and concerned socially relevant topics; however, this body of research reflects a lack of innovative thinking and creativity and a relative absence of indigenous theoretical constructs (Vohra, 2004). This lack of theoretical constructs has spurred some creative reconstruction intended to achieve a more integrative indigenization of the discipline (Sinha, 2000).

Original and innovative contributions to measurement and test construction have taken a back seat, with the exception of one indigenous construct, the tridimensional theory of personality, which measures three *gunas* (constituents): *Sattva* (purity, serenity, and contentment), *Rajas* (love of fame, passion, and power), and *Tamas* (anger, greed, and ignorance). In addition, Jnana Prabhodini, a Pune-based organization, has now embarked on standardizing Indian educational and cognitive tests for schoolchildren.

The published works of Pandey (2000, 2001); Sinha (1986); Kapur (1995); and Rao, Paranjpe, and Dalal (2006) provide a good overview of psychology in India. Systematic compilation and documentation of tests and instruments have been accomplished (Pareek & Rao 1974; Pestonjee, 1988), and a comprehensive status report on standardized intelligence testing (Srivastava, Tripathi, & Misra, 1996) catalogs the standardized tests available to psychologists in India.

Psychology has undeniably made considerable progress in India in evolving as an applied professional discipline. This progress is reflected in the development of psychotherapeutics (including behavior therapy, cognitive behavior therapy, family therapy, and stress management), innovative techniques in human resource management, community psychology (to address devastating disasters), health psychology (to deal with the widespread epidemic of HIV/AIDS and other health hazards), and counseling psychology. Psychologists are now actively involved as counselors by the National AIDS Control Organization, clinical neuropsychology is being applied in forensic medicine, transpersonal psychology in influential in addressing culture-specific problems such as mass hysteria and possession by spirits, and parapsychology is involved in attempting to understand extrasensory perceptions and reincarnation from an Indian perspective.

A prominent shortcoming of psychology in India is a lack of accreditation. The Rehabilitation Council of India, which is a statutory government body, is the only accreditation body in India. The Indian Association of Clinical Psychologists has, however, stipulated minimum criteria for eligibility to be considered a clinical psychologist. There are also concerns about a questionable standard of research and publication and about a gender imbalance, with 95% of psychologists being women. Apprehensions regarding women's long-term commitment to the discipline are voiced, owing to social and family constraints that could eventually foster a gender bias. Among the major referred journals in India are *Indian Journal of Clinical Psychology, Journal of Psychological Research,* and *Indian Journal of Psychological Abstracts and Reviews.*

The twenty-first-century challenge to psychology in India is not only to indigenize but also to Indianize the discipline. This challenge calls for integrated empirical, intuitive, and experiential psychological knowledge to redefine psychology as a science and as a professional discipline in ways that match the cultural milieu and behavioral parameters of the country.

REFERENCES

Kapur, M. (1995). *Mental health of Indian children.* New Delhi: Sage.

Pandey, J. (Ed.). (2000). *Psychology in India revisited: Developments in the discipline: Vol. 1. Physiological foundation and human cognition.* New Delhi: Sage.

Pandey, J. (Ed.). (2001). *Psychology in India revisited: Developments in the discipline: Vol. 2. Personality and health psychology.* New Delhi: Sage.

Pareek, U., & Rao, T. V. (1974). *Handbook of psychological and social instruments.* Baroda, India: Samasthi.

Pestonjee, D. M. (1988). *Second handbook of psychological and social instruments.* New Delhi: Concept Publishing.

Rao, K. R, Paranjpe, A., & Dalal, A. (Eds.). (2008). *Handbook of Indian psychology.* New Delhi: Cambridge University Press.

Sinha, D. (1986). *Psychology in a third world country: The Indian experience.* New Delhi: Sage.

Sinha, J. B. P. (2000). Towards indigenization of psychology in India. *Psychological Studies, 45*(1– 2), 3–13.

Srivastava, A. K., Tripathi, A. M., & Misra, G. (1996). The status of intelligence testing in India: A preliminary analysis. *Indian Educational Review, 31 ,* 1–11.

Vohra, N. (2004). Indigenization of psychology in India: Its unique form and progress. In B. N. Setiadi, A. Supratiknya, W. J. Lonner, & Y. H. Poortinga (Eds.), *Ongoing themes in psychology and culture* (Online Ed.). Retrieved March 31, 2009, from http://www.iaccp.org.

BLANCHE BARNES
Mumbai, India

INDIVIDUALISM

In common usage, individualism is defined as leading one's life in one's own way without regard for others. Individualism involves giving one's own interests precedence over the interests of the state or social group (i.e., egoism or selfishness). It is based on the belief in the primary importance of the individual and in the virtues of self-reliance and personal independence. Individualism may be separated from individuality, which is the sum of the qualities that set one person apart from others. To individualize is to distinguish a person as different from others, whereas to individuate is to make a person individual or distinct. Individualism is also distinct from autonomy, which is the ability to understand what others expect in any given situation and what one's values are, and to be free to choose how to behave based on either or both. Whereas individuality and autonomy are important aspects of healthy psychological development and health, individualism is not. Finally, individualism is often contrasted with collectivism. Collectivism is a moral, political, or social outlook that stresses human interdependence and the importance of communities and societies rather than the importance of separate individuals, thus giving priority to group goals over individual goals. Collectivism requires attention to the well-being of other members of the community and the common good, whereas individualism requires attention to only one's own well-being.

Based on social interdependence theory (Deutsch, 1962; Johnson & Johnson, 1989, 2005), individualism may be defined as believing and behaving as if one's efforts and goal attainments are unrelated to or independent from the efforts toward goal attainment of others. Individualism is usually contrasted with cooperativeness and competitiveness. Cooperativeness may be defined as believing and behaving as if one's efforts and goal attainments are positively related to the efforts and goal attainments of others, or as if one can achieve one's goals if, and only if, the others with whom one is cooperatively linked obtain their goals. Competitiveness may be defined as believing and behaving as if one's efforts and goal attainments are negatively related to the efforts and goal attainments of others, or as if one can achieve one's goals if, and only if, the others with whom one is competitively linked fail to achieve their goals.

There is considerable research comparing the relative effects of individualism, cooperativeness, and competitiveness (Johnson & Johnson, 1989, 2005). Individualism, compared with cooperativeness, tends to be related to problems in interpersonal relationships. Individualism results in less liking for others and more negative interpersonal relationships and the perception that one is relatively disliked and rejected by others who will refuse to provide support and assistance. Individualism results in a lower ability to take the cognitive and affective perspective of others. Individualism results in less seeking of information from others, which leaves one at a disadvantage in coping with difficult situations. Individualism results in lower psychological health, as reflected in greater psychological pathology, delinquency, emotional immaturity, social maladjustment, self-alienation, self-rejection, lack of social participation, basic distrust of other people, pessimism, and inability to resolve conflicts between self-perceptions and adverse information about oneself. Individualism also results in less healthy processes for deriving conclusions about one's self-worth. Finally, individualism results in relatively lower achievement, less intrinsic and continuing motivation, greater orientation toward extrinsic rewards, and less emotional involvement in efforts to achieve one's goals. There has been very little research comparing individualism and competitiveness.

If the direct evidence is relatively unfavorable toward individualism, the writings in personality and clinical psychology are even less so. The solitary human who avoids relationships and coalitions with others is considered abnormal. Humans are basically interdependent beings, biologically and socially. Effective socialization brings with it an awareness that one cannot achieve one's life goals alone; one needs other people's help and resources.

Psychological health requires a realization that one's goals and the goals of others, one's efforts and the efforts of others, and one's success and the success of many different people are all related and interdependent. Accurately perceiving the interdependence between yourself and others involves an awareness of sharing a common fate (both you and your fellow collaborators will receive the same outcome) and of mutual causation (achieving your goals depends on both your own efforts and those of collaborators), and it also involves a long-term time perspective and the skills, information, competencies, and talents of other people as well as oneself. Individuals high on individualism do not have a high degree of such awareness. Individualism often brings with it (1) feelings of alienation, loneliness, isolation, inferiority, worthlessness, depression, and defeat; (2) attitudes reflecting low self-esteem, an emphasis on short-term gratification, and the conviction that no one cares about oneself or one's capabilities; and (3) relationships characterized by impulsiveness, fragmentation, withdrawal, and insensitivity to one's own and other's needs.

Every person needs to establish a coherent and integrated identity that differentiates one as a unique individual separate and distinct from all others. Whereas the ability to act independently, autonomy, and individuality are all important aspects of developing an identity, individualism is not. Paradoxically, it is out of cooperative and supportive relationships that encourage individuality that a mature identity is formed. Self-awareness, self-understanding, differentiating oneself from others, the internalization of values and self-approval, and social sensitivity are all acquired through encouraging and cooperative relationships, not through isolation or leading one's life in one's own way without regard for others.

REFERENCES

Bellah, R. N., Sullivan, W. M., & Madsen, R. (2007). *The habits of the heart: Individualism and commitment in American life.* Los Angeles: University of California Press.

Deutsch, M. (1962). Cooperation and trust: Some theoretical notes. In M. Jones (Ed.), *Nebraska symposium on motivation.* Lincoln: University of Nebraska Press.

Johnson, D. W., & Johnson, R. (1989). *Cooperation and competition: Theory and research.* Edina, MN: Interaction Book Company.

Johnson, D. W., & Johnson, R. (2005). New developments in social interdependence theory. *Psychology Monographs, 131*(4), 285–358.

DAVID W. JOHNSON
ROGER T. JOHNSON
University of Minnesota

See also: Conformity; Social Isolation

INDUSTRIAL AND ORGANIZATIONAL PSYCHOLOGY

Industrial and organizational psychology (I-O) has a long history of research and application in both the United States and abroad. In America, its earliest roots are found in the work of Hugo Munsterberg, a colleague of William James and chair of the Department of Psychology at Harvard at the beginning of the twentieth century. Munsterberg was a pioneer in industrial selection, which is still a core activity of I-O psychologists. He developed tests to hire applicants for jobs such as telephone operator and trolley driver (Landy, 1992). There has been an unbroken development of testing technique and theory for the 100 years since then. Two additional major figures in the early development of I-O psychology (circa 1910–1940) were Walter Dill Scott and Walter Van Dyke Bingham (Landy, 1993, 1997). The early history of I-O psychology was one of application of more general psychological principles, such as learning, without much emphasis on theory development (Viteles, 1932). By 1960, this had changed, and I-O psychology then and to the present day has adopted an integrated scientist-practitioner model for academic training, practice, and research.

I-O psychology is a global knowledge and practice domain. It developed in the United Kingdom (UK) at about the same time as it did in America. In the twenty-first century, some of the strongest non-U.S. homes for I-O psychology include Canada, the UK, the Netherlands, Germany, Romania, Italy, South Africa, Australia, and New Zealand. I-O psychology is also known abroad as work psychology, work and organizational psychology, and occupational psychology.

Three separate areas comprise I-O psychology. The first is the one introduced by Munsterberg, which has been called industrial or personnel psychology and, more recently, human resource (HR) psychology. HR psychology deals with specific subject areas such as selection, training, performance evaluation, and career development. It treats job duties and responsibilities as fixed and people as variable. Thus the goal is to match the attributes of a person (or in the case of training, to modify the attributes of a person) to the demands of a job (Landy & Conte, 2007).

Personnel decision making has received heightened attention since the passage of the Civil Rights Act of 1964. This is because protected classes of employees, as defined by age, race, gender, religion, or national origin, have often alleged that they were disadvantaged by these processes, resulting in large scale lawsuits. Many of these early lawsuits and related research affirmed the discriminatory effect of many early personnel decision-making policies. Although allegations of unfairness are still raised with considerable frequency, I-O psychologists have been at the forefront of creating a fair and unbiased environment for personnel decisions (Guion, 1998).

The second area of I-O psychology is known as organizational psychology and addresses the emotional match or fit between a person and a job. In contrast with HR psychology, organizational psychology assumes that both the nature of work and the individual's characteristics are variable and seeks to optimize the match between work design and human attributes (Greenberg, 2002). It includes issues such as job satisfaction, work motivation, leadership, organizational design, organizational climate and culture, and stress. All of these variables are thought to potentially influence the behavior of workers. Organizational psychologists spend their time looking for ways to adapt both the procedures of the organization and the behavior of the worker to result in an optimal social-emotional environment in the workplace. Organizational psychology was first introduced in the 1930s with emerging theories of job satisfaction, work motivation, and industrial unrest. Elton Mayo, an Australian psychologist who emigrated to the United States in 1922, was largely responsible for the emergence of this area, through his "human relations" approach to work (Trahair, 1984). He was one of the first to actually ask workers about their attitudes toward work.

The third area of I-O psychology is known variously as human factors, human engineering, or applied experimental psychology. Although its roots can be found in research and application beginning in 1910–1915 on time and motion study and a work design system known as "scientific management," it really became a full blown scientific area with the onset of World War II, when military aircraft design began to have an affect on accidents. Unlike HR psychology, human factors psychology assumes that people have fixed characteristics or attributes and that jobs and tasks should be designed around those attributes.

For example, humans have certain limits to what they can see, what they can hear, how much they can lift, and how quickly they can react. The human factors psychologist considers the limitations and capabilities of human beings in the design or modification of job duties. Human factors psychology is often involved in the investigation of accidents and injuries, to determine if the design of jobs

to tasks might have contributed to the accident or injury. The Americans with Disabilities Act of 1992 provided a new opportunity for human factors experts in the redesign of work places and work tasks in order to accommodate to various covered worker disabilities. In recent years, cognitive psychology has become a major scientific foundation for human factors theory, research, and application (Wickens, Lee, Gordon, & Liu, 2004).

As a profession and scientific society, I-O psychology had been an integral part of the American Psychological Association (APA) from its inception, but it was not until 1945 that I-O psychology, along with other specialties, was assigned to its own division. Division 14 of the APA is known as the Division of Industrial and Organizational Psychology and currently has more than 3,000 members. Although the greatest number of APA members is allied with clinical or counseling psychology, I-O psychology is the next largest specialty area in the Association and continues to grow while many other divisions either remain the same size or decline in membership. In 1983, I-O psychology incorporated a new scientific society known as the Society for Industrial and Organizational Psychology (SIOP), which currently has 7,400 members and continues to grow. With its own journals and annual conference, SIOP permits further efficient dissemination of advances in research, theory, and application.

Work in the Twenty-First Century

The nature of work in many organizations has changed substantially since 1980 (Landy & Conte, 2007). Work that was once solitary is now done by teams. Work that was once cognitively simple is now complex. Competition, both for product and service sales and for jobs, is no longer local, but global. The tasks that comprise a job change rapidly, sometimes as frequently as weekly. In earlier years, individuals often retired from the company that gave them their first job. In recent years, 18–24 months with a company before changing employers is not uncommon. American workers often commented on the "foreign worker" in their midst; now "foreign" workers outnumber American workers, signaling an explosion in the multinational nature of work in the United States. Finally, in addition to fewer native born workers, the percentages of older and female workers are increasing rapidly. All of these changes call for I-O theory, research, and application to match the twenty-first century workplace.

Current Theory, Research, and Application in I-O Psychology

HR Psychology

A cornerstone of HR psychology has been job analysis—the deconstruction of jobs into work tasks and required attributes (Brannick, Levine, & Morgeson, 2007).

Although the central role of job analysis has not changed, job analysis methods have. The earlier concentration on observable and individual work behaviors has been enhanced with cognitive task analysis and team behaviors. The earlier concentration on general mental ability or intelligence as the singular predictor of work performance has been enhanced with the addition of personality attributes, interpersonal skills, and the application of formal and procedural knowledge.

Further, rather than a concentration on the prediction of technical task performance, I-O psychologists now include the prediction of nontechnical behavior such as volunteering, persevering, team interaction (called organizational citizenship behavior), counterproductive work behavior (e.g. bullying, sabotage, theft), and adaptive performance (reacting effectively to sudden changes in work demands). In the twentieth century, assessment was accomplished largely with paper and pencil. In the twenty-first century, assessment is often accomplished through local area networks of the employer, or web-based assessment. The face-to-face interview remains popular, as does the use of work sample tests, which are tests that simulate a portion of the job in question, such as a computer-based interaction with a hypothetical "caller" for customer service representative positions.

From 1900 until 1980, the measurement of general mental ability or what is commonly known as intelligence dominated the development of selection systems. Based on both the development of the Big Five theory of personality and the migration of personality measurement and theory from clinical psychology to social psychology, the use of personality assessment for selection and placement has emerged as the twenty-first century challenge to I-O psychology (Mount & Barrick, 1995). Although general mental ability remains an important focus of HR psychology, the role of personality in the prediction of work success has become at least as important.

As has been the case since the passage of the Civil Rights Act of 1964, the issue of fair and nondiscriminatory personnel decisions by organizations has dominated the use of assessment devices for purposes of hiring and promotion. I-O psychologists are commonly called upon to provide expert witness testimony regarding whether assessment practices meet professional, regulatory, and scientific standards (Landy, 2005).

Organizational Psychology

The major topics of interest for I-O psychologists who concentrate on organizational issues include job satisfaction, work motivation, team performance, and leadership. Current thinking and research on job satisfaction integrates work and nonwork experiences. In addition, rather than using attitude surveys administered once a year to capture job satisfaction, measurement has become more specific and time limited, often asking for satisfaction responses on an hourly, daily, or weekly basis. In years past, it was assumed that job satisfaction was a precursor to performance and motivation. It is now more common to think of satisfaction as the result of effective job performance. Nevertheless, job satisfaction does seem to have implications for absenteeism and turnover, as well as for the extent to which individual employees take pride in the organization for which they work.

There is general agreement on the elements of work motivation. These elements include specific hard but achievable work or performance goals, feedback on the progress toward achieving those goals, and high individual self-efficacy, which is the belief of individuals that they actually have the necessary personal and organizational resources to achieve those goals. Applications of work motivation theory usually involve the enhancement of all three of these elements (Locke & Latham, 2002).

Team performance is a particular challenge for I-O psychologists for two reasons: (1) most if not all jobs now involve some team aspect to them, and (2) I-O psychology, unlike social psychology, has traditionally concentrated on differences among individuals in terms of behavior and attributes, not groups of individuals. For that reason, I-O psychologists are now examining work group composition, measures of group and team performance, and the dynamics of team learning and interaction (Salas et al., 2006). An emerging method of analysis, called levels of analysis, looks at the contribution of not only individual attributes, but also group and even organizational attributes in understanding work behavior (Klein & Kozlowski, 2002).

Leadership behavior has been a focal area for research and application in organizational psychology for over five decades (Yukl, 2006). There are several areas of particular interest in the twenty-first century. These areas include the influence of national culture on leadership, the search for a compelling theory of leadership behavior, and the influence of gender on the perception of leadership behavior. There are several efforts ongoing to determine if elements of successful leadership transcend national culture (House, Javidan, & Dorfman, 2001). The answer seems to be yes.

Moreover, these transcendent elements seem to be associated with a theory of leadership known as transformational leadership. Transformational leadership emphasizes the authenticity of the leader and the efforts of that leader to persuade followers to go beyond their individual self-interest to achieve something that serves a greater good, either organizational or social. It appears that transformational leadership has a moral component to it. This theory is in contrast to what is known as transactional leadership. A transactional leader is one who provides rewards and punishments contingent on effective follower behavior. It appears that a transformational leader is more effective than a transactional one, but even transactional leadership can lead to some limited leadership success.

Human Factors Psychology

As work environments become more complex, designing those environments to take into account the capabilities and limitations of workers has become increasingly important. The twenty-first century job is less observable than its twentieth century counterpart, largely because it involves much more thought and much less physical action. This has led to a new form of work analysis known as cognitive task analysis (Goldstein & Ford, 2002). Some examples of cognitive task analysis include asking expert performers to describe each action in a sequence, including the thought that goes into taking that action. Another form of cognitive task analysis is to deconstruct critical incidents (i.e., instances of extraordinary success or failure) through the observation and interview of multiple team members associated with that success or failure.

Human factors research and practice is also implicated in the design of safe working environments and the study of errors and accidents. The design of a work environment that is both safe and that reduces errors that might compromise the well-being of a client population (e.g. hospitals, commercial aviation, nuclear power) has broadened considerably in the twenty-first century to include the study of safety climates in work groups (i.e., the extent to which all levels of the organization from the worker to the CEO share the same values regarding safety and error reduction). Because of the alarming increase in the rate of medical errors, human factors psychologists have become particularly interested in applications in the health care environment.

Based on the description of the three sub-areas of I-O psychology, it may be tempting to see them as independent of each other. However, modern I-O psychology treats them as interdependent and integrated. Most important applications of I-O psychology include considerations of issues related to all three sub-areas. Thus, a "motivating" job requires the selection and training of people with the correct attributes for success, the design of a job that considers limitations and capabilities of a worker, and a leader who helps to set hard but achievable goals and provides feedback with respect to goal accomplishment. Similarly, organizational safety requires individual workers with the requisite abilities, a work and equipment design that safeguards against foreseeable accidents, a system that rewards safe behavior, and leadership that fosters a safety-oriented climate (Landy & Conte, 2007).

Although few I-O psychologists are well versed in all three of these areas, they often call on one another for integrated applications and solutions. Nevertheless, some applications are quite specific, and a single area of expertise is sufficient.

REFERENCES

Brannick, M. T., Levine, E. L., & Morgeson, F. P. (2007). *Job and work analysis*. Thousand Oaks, CA: Sage.

Goldstein, I. L., & Ford, K. J. (2002). *Training in organizations: Needs assessment, development, and evaluation* (4th ed.). Belmont, CA: Wadsworth.

Greenberg, J. (2002). *Managing behavior in organizations* (3rd ed.). Upper Saddle River, NJ: Prentice-Hall.

House, R. J., Javidan, M., & Dorfman, P. (2001). Project GLOBE: An introduction. *Applied Psychology: An International Review, 50*(4), 489–505.

Klein, K., & Kozlowski, S. (2000). *Multilevel theory, research, and methods in organizations: Foundations, extensions, and new directions*. San Francisco: Jossey-Bass.

Landy, F. J. (1992). Hugo Munsterberg: Visionary or victim? *Journal of Applied Psychology, 77,* 787–802.

Landy, F. J. (1993). Early influences on the development of industrial/organizational psychology. In T. Fagan & G. VandenBos (Eds.), *Exploring applied psychology: Origins and critical analyses. Master lectures in psychology.* (pp. 83–118). Washington, DC: American Psychological Association.

Landy, F. J. (1997). Early influences on the development of I/O psychology. *Journal of Applied Psychology, 82*(4), 467–477.

Landy, F. J. (Ed.). (2005). *Employment discrimination litigation: Behavioral, quantitative, and legal perspectives*. San Francisco: Jossey-Bass.

Landy, F. J., & Conte, J. M. (2007). *Work in the 21st century: An introduction to industrial and organizational psychology* (2nd ed.). Boston: Blackwell.

Locke, E. A., & Latham, G. P. (2002). Building a practically useful theory of goal setting and task motivation: A 35-year odyssey. *American Psychologist, 57,* 705–717.

Mount, M. K., & Barrick, M. R. (1998). The Big Five personality dimensions: Implications for research and practice in human resources management. In G. R. Ferris (Ed.). *Research in personnel and human resource management*, Vol. 13. (pp. 153–200). Greenwich, CT: JAI Press.

Salas, E., Rosen, M. A., Burke, C. S., Goodwin, G. F., & Fiore, S. M. (2006). The making of a dream team: When expert teams do best. In K. A. Ericsson, N. Charness, P. J. Feltovich, & R. R. Hoffman (Eds.), *The Cambridge handbook of expertise and expert performance* (pp. 439–453). New York: Cambridge University Press.

Trahair, R. C. S. (1984). *The humanist temper: The life and work of Elton Mayo*. New Brunswick, NJ: Transaction.

Viteles, M. S. (1932). *Industrial psychology*. New York: W.W. Norton.

Wickens, C. D., Lee, J., Gordon, S. E., & Liu, Y. (2004). *Introduction to human factors engineering* (2nd ed.). New York: Prentice-Hall.

Yukl, G. (2006). *Leadership in organizations* (6th ed.). Upper Saddle River, NJ: Pearson Prentice-Hall.

SUGGESTED READINGS

Guion, R. M. (1998). *Assessment, measurement, and prediction for personnel decisions*. Mahwah, NJ: Lawrence Erlbaum.

Koppes, L. (Ed.). (2007). *Historical perspectives in industrial and organizational psychology*. Mahwah, NJ: Lawrence Erlbaum.

FRANK J. LANDY
Baruch College, City University of New York

See also: Human Factors Research; Personnel Selection

INFANTILE AUTISM (See Autistic Disorder)

INFANTILE SEXUALITY (See Psychosexual Stages)

INFERIORITY FEELINGS (See Self-Esteem)

INFORMATION PROCESSING

How does the human mind work? What happens when someone learns or when someone solves a problem? According to the information processing view, the human mind works by forming mental representations and applying cognitive processes to them. This definition has two elements: (1) the content of cognition is mental representations, and (2) the activity of cognition involves cognitive processes. For example, as you read the words in this paragraph, you form a series of mental representations by applying appropriate cognitive processes such as mentally selecting important ideas, mentally organizing them into a coherent cognitive structure, and mentally relating them with prior knowledge. In short, the premise underlying information processing theory is that human mental life consists of building and manipulating mental representations. The information processing view has become a centerpiece of cognitive science—the interdisciplinary study of cognition.

Two Versions of Information Processing Theory

In the history of the information processing approach, there have been two contrasting ways to clarify the nature of mental representations and the nature of cognitive processes—the classical view and constructivist view (Mayer, 1996).

Classical view. The classical view is based on a human-machine metaphor in which (1) information is a commodity that can be transferred from one mind to another as a series of symbols, and (2) processing involves applying an algorithm to information such that a series of symbols is manipulated according to a step-by-step procedure. For example, when given a problem such as

"$x + 2 = 4$, solve for x," a learner forms a mental representation of the problem such as "$x + 2 = 4$," and applies operators such as mentally subtracting 2 from both sides in order to generate a new mental representation, namely "$x = 2$." Two limitations of the classical view concern the characterization of information as an objective commodity and the characterization of processing as the application of symbol-manipulating algorithms.

Constructivist view. The constructivist view is based on the knowledge construction metaphor, in which learners are sense makers who construct knowledge by integrating what is presented with what they already know (Mayer, 1992). Knowledge is a mental representation that exists in a human mind; unlike information, knowledge is a personal construction that cannot be directly moved from one mind to another. Construction involves cognitive processing aimed at sense making, including attending to relevant portions of the presented material, mentally organizing the material into a coherent structure, and mentally integrating the material with relevant existing knowledge. The constructivist approach developed in the 1980s and 1990s, such as in Wittrock's (1990) generative theory, although its earlier proponents include Bartlett's (1932) theory of how people remember stories and Piaget's (1971) theory of how children learn. Although the constructivist view addresses some of the limitations of the classical view, some major limitations of the constructivist view include the need to account for the social and cultural context of cognition and the need to account for the biological and affective bases of cognition.

Major Contributions of Information Processing Theory

Three important contributions of the information processing approach are (1) techniques for analyzing cognitive processing (e.g., "What are the cognitive processes involved in carrying out a cognitive task?"), (2) techniques for analyzing mental representations (e.g., "IIow is knowledge represented in memory?"), and (3) a general description of the architecture of the human cognitive system (e.g., "How does information flow through the human memory system?").

Cognitive Processes: Cognitive Task Analysis. A fundamental contribution of information processing theory is cognitive task analysis—techniques for describing the cognitive processes that a person must carry out to accomplish a cognitive task. For example, suppose a student gives the following answers on an arithmetic test:

234	678	456	545
−156	−434	−327	−295
122	244	131	350

A traditional evaluation would reveal that the student correctly solved 25% of the problems. However, a cognitive task analysis reveals that the student seems to be consistently applying a subtraction procedure that has one incorrect step—that is, one bug—namely, always subtracting the smaller number from the larger number in each column (Brown & Burton, 1978). In specifying the procedure that the student is using, it becomes clear that instruction is needed to help the student replace this smaller-from-larger bug.

Mental Representations: Types of Knowledge. Knowledge is a mental representation: It is mental because it exists only in human minds, and it is a representation because it is intended to denote or signify something. According to the information processing approach, knowledge is at the left of cognition: Learning is the construction of knowledge, memory is the storage of knowledge, and thinking is the logical manipulation of knowledge.

Information processing theorists (Anderson et al., 2001; Mayer, 2008) have identified several types of knowledge (or mental representations): facts, which are simple descriptions of an object or element (such as "apples are red"); concepts, which identify relations among elements within a coherent structure (such as classification hierarchies, cause-and-effect models, explanatory principles, and organizing generalizations); procedures, which involve a step-by-step specification of how to do something (such as the procedure for how to carry out long division); strategies, which are techniques for how to coordinate one's cognitive processing (such as knowing how to monitor the quality of one's essay-writing activity); and beliefs, which are cognitions about how learning and cognitive work (such as seeing oneself as a competent learner). Facts and concepts are knowledge of "what" (i.e., data structures); procedures and strategies are knowledge of "how to" (i.e., processes for manipulating data structures); and beliefs affect one's motivation to engage in information processing.

Cognitive System: Architecture of the Cognitive System. Figure 1 presents a model of the human information processing system, consisting of two channels of knowledge representation (represented as the top and bottom rows), three memory stores (represented as labeled boxes), and five basic cognitive processes (represented as labeled

arrows). The two channels are the auditory/verbal channel (in the top row of Figure 1), in which material enters the cognitive system through the ears and eventually is represented in verbal code, and the visual/pictorial channel (in the bottom row of the figure), in which material enters the cognitive system through the eyes and eventually is represented in pictorial code.

The three memory stores are sensory memory, where sensory input is stored briefly in its original form; working memory, where a limited number of elements of the presented material are stored and manipulated within one's conscious awareness; and long-term memory, where large amounts of knowledge are stored for long periods of time. The five cognitive processes presented in Figure 1 are selecting images—indicated by the arrow from "visual sensation" to "image base"; selecting sounds—indicated by the arrow from "acoustic sensation" to "sound base"; organizing images—indicated by the arrow from "visual base" to "pictorial model"; organizing sounds—indicated by the arrow from "sound base" to "verbal model"; and integration—indicated by arrows among "verbal model," "pictorial model," and "prior knowledge."

On the left side of the figure, spoken words enter the cognitive system through the ears, resulting in a short-lasting acoustic sensation in auditory sensory memory, and graphics and printed words enter the cognitive system through the eyes, resulting in a short-lasting visual sensation in visual sensory memory. If the learner pays attention, parts of the acoustic and visual sensations are transferred to verbal working memory for further processing in the form of a sound base or image base. Images from printed words can be converted into spoken words as indicated by the arrow between image base and sound base. Deeper processing occurs when the learner strives to mentally organize the verbal material into a verbal model and the visual material into a pictorial model, and to mentally integrate the verbal and pictorial models with each other and with prior knowledge activated from long-term memory. Overall, the construction of knowledge requires that the learner select relevant images and sounds from the presented material, organize them into coherent pictorial

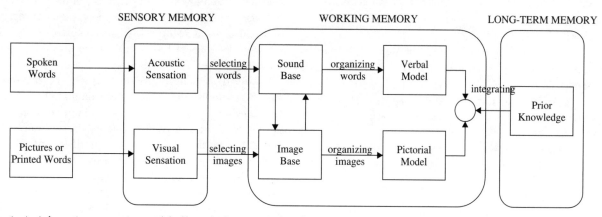

Figure 1. An information-processing model of how the human mind works.

and verbal representations, and integrate the pictorial and verbal representations with each other and with prior knowledge.

The information-processing model presented in Figure 1 is based on three assumptions from the cognitive science of learning: the dual channel assumption, the limited capacity assumption, and the active learning assumption (Mayer, 2001). The dual channel assumption is that humans possess separate information processing channels for visual/pictorial material and auditory/verbal material (Baddeley, 1998; Paivio, 1986). The limited capacity assumption is that only a small amount of material can be processed in a working memory channel at one time (Baddeley, 1998; Sweller, 1999). The active learning assumption is that meaningful learning (or understanding) occurs when learners engage in appropriate cognitive processing during learning—including selecting relevant information, organizing the material into a coherent representation, and integrating incoming visual and verbal material with each other and with prior knowledge (Mayer, 2001, 2008).

According to the information processing approach, human mental life consists of building and manipulating mental representations. Although the information processing view focuses mainly on cognition in individual learners, any complete theory of how the human mind works must incorporate affective, motivational, emotional, social, and biological aspects of cognition. Yet, the information processing approach—now a dominant force in psychology for nearly half a century—also leaves a worthwhile legacy. The information processing approach enabled the rebirth of cognitive psychology by providing an alternative to behaviorism, created a unified framework that stimulated useful research and theory, highlighted the role of mental representations and cognitive processes, and fostered the transition toward studying cognition in more authentic contexts.

REFERENCES

Anderson, L. W., Krathwohl, D. R., Airasian, P. W., Cruickshank, K. A., Mayer, R. E., Pintrich, P. R., et al. (2001). *A taxonomy of learning, teaching, and assessing.* New York: Longman.

Baddeley, A. L. (1998). *Human memory.* Boston: Allyn and Bacon.

Bartlett, F. C. (1932). *Remembering.* Cambridge, UK: Cambridge University Press.

Brown, J. S., & Burton, R. R. (1978). Diagnostic models for procedural bugs in basic mathematical skills. *Cognitive Science, 2,* 155–192.

Mayer, R. E. (1992). Cognition and instruction: On their historic meeting within educational psychology. *Journal of Educational Psychology, 84,* 405–412.

Mayer, R. E. (1996). Learners as information processors: Legacies and limitations of educational psychology's second metaphor. *Educational Psychologist, 31,* 151–161.

Mayer, R. E. (2001). *Multimedia learning.* New York: Cambridge University Press.

Mayer, R. E. (2008). *Learning and instruction.* Upper Saddle River, NJ: Pearson Merrill Prentice-Hall.

Piaget, J. (1971). *Science of education and the psychology of the child.* New York: Viking Press.

Sweller, J. (1999). *Instructional design in technical areas.* Camberwell, Australia: ACER Press.

Wittrock, M. C. (1990). Generative processes of comprehension. *Educational Psychologist, 24,* 345–376.

SUGGESTED READING

Newell, A., & Simon, H. A. (1972). *Human problem solving.* Englewood Cliffs, NJ: Prentice-Hall.

Richard E. Mayer
University of California, Santa Barbara

See also: **Cognitive Neuroscience; Selective Attention**

INFORMED CONSENT

Clinicians have ethical and often legal obligations to obtain consent from clients prior to treatment. This entry provides a brief description of the components of informed consent, the legal and ethical bases of the concept, and the available research on obtaining informed consent.

Description of Informed Consent

Initially, informed consent was a circumscribed medical concept requiring physicians and surgeons to tell patients the type of treatments they would recommend; this was known as the professional standard of informed consent. This concept eventually was expanded, requiring physicians to give patients enough information about available treatments to allow patients to make educated decisions; this was known as the reasonable patient standard of informed consent (Marczyk & Wertheimer, 2001). More recently, the concept has been incorporated into psychology and other disciplines as well.

Informed consent requires clients to be informed of potential benefits and risks of contemplated treatments, the expected prognosis with and without treatment, and any possible alternative treatments. In addition, clients should be informed of therapist qualifications, limits of confidentiality, general client rights, and logistical information, such as scheduling practices and fee structures. Barring exceptions such as emergency treatment, a person cannot be given therapy without informed consent (Koocher & Keith-Spiegel, 2007).

Informed consent is valid only if given intelligently, knowingly, and voluntarily. Intelligence, sometimes referred to as competency, refers to the capacity of clients to comprehend and evaluate information. Knowledge is defined as the ability to appreciate how the given treatment information applies to oneself specifically. Clinicians should question each client's comprehension of the material to assess the person's knowledge. One way of doing this is to ask clients to repeat, in their own words, treatment information that has been presented to them. Finally, the voluntary element suggests that consent may not be coerced or enticed. To ensure the voluntary element necessary for valid consent, clients must be told that they can withdraw from treatment at any time (Appelbaum, 1997; Koocher & Keith-Spiegel, 2007). Obtaining informed consent does not give clinicians permission to perform illegal or unethical acts. For example, therapists cannot justify sexual acts with clients by claiming that informed consent was obtained.

Obtaining informed consent is not a one-time incident; instead, it is an ongoing process throughout treatment. Clinicians should adopt a process rather than event model of informed consent, in which ongoing discussions with clients throughout treatment ensures sufficient opportunities for them to ask questions and have information clarified (Pomerantz, 2005). At a minimum, there are two discrete times during therapy when informed consent should be obtained: at the initiation of therapy and when particular treatments are being proposed. It is imperative for clinicians to document this ongoing process of obtaining informed consent through a written information sheet that is read and signed by the client (Zuckerman, 2003).

In general, only adults are considered legally able to give informed consent. In many states, a minor's consent for treatment must be obtained from a legal guardian. However, some state statutes give minors limited rights to consent to treatment. Regardless of state law, it is important to involve even young children in the process of obtaining consent (known as the nonlegally bound terms of assent) because research has found that even young children may understand and weigh treatment options. If a child does not want to participate in treatment, despite parental consent, ethical principles dictate that the clinician should consider the best interests of the child (Gustofson & McNamara, 1987). Finally, when conducting family or couples therapy, clinicians should pay special attention to obtaining informed consent from all participating members and to unique issues that often arise, such as difficult confidentiality issues faced when more than one client is in the room.

Legal and Ethical Bases of Informed Consent

The first major legal statement of the need for consent occurred in the 1905 case of *Mohr v. Williams*. In this landmark case, the court ruled it unlawful for a physician to perform a surgical operation without the express or implied consent of a patient. In 1914, the case of *Schloendorff v. the Society of New York Hospital* expanded on the requirements for informed consent to include the idea that a patient must be apprised of the potential benefits and major risks of any proposed treatment, as well as the available alternative treatments. A later case, *Canterbury v. Spence* (1972), appeared to support the "reasonable patient" rather than the professional standard of information provision. Since this 1972 case, physicians have been considered to have an affirmative duty to impart as much information as a reasonable patient would require, regardless of whether the patient asks for such information.

Currently, all states have statutes mandating some type of informed consent procedures for physicians and psychiatrists. However, not every state clearly specifies that psychologists or other mental health providers must obtain informed consent for psychological treatments. Clinicians should be aware of the relevant statutes in the states in which they practice.

On the other hand, ethical codes of conduct in psychology dictate that clinicians apply the concept of informed consent with all clients. Standard 3.10 of the American Psychological Association (APA) ethical code (APA, 2002) states that psychologists must obtain informed consent using "language that is reasonably understandable to that person or persons" (p. 1066). Clinicians should be aware that not obtaining valid consent prior to treatment places them in a precarious position. Clients may file ethical complaints with the state licensing board for a clinician's failure to obtain valid consent, potentially resulting in suspension or loss of license to practice psychology in that state (Koocher & Keith-Spiegel, 2007).

Research on Informed Consent Procedures

The limited research that has been conducted on informed consent has addressed the prevalence, optimal methods, and effects on disclosure and attendance. Research has found that not all therapists currently utilize informed consent procedures, believing it may be irrelevant or even harmful to the therapeutic relationship. For example, Somberg, Stone, and Claiborn (1993) found that only 60% of psychologists reported utilizing any type of consent procedure with all clients.

The use of both written forms and ongoing discussions with clients is encouraged. Handelsman and Galvin (1988), and more recently Pomerantz and Handelsman (2004), suggested employing a sheet with common questions as an alternative to detail informed consent forms. In general, research has supported the positive effects of providing more information to the client prior to treatment. For example, two studies conducted by Handelsman in 1990 found that increased information appears to improve client ratings of clinicians. Additionally, Sullivan, Martin, and Handelsman (1993) discovered that combined presentation of oral and written information positively influenced therapist ratings.

In another study in which participants received either a partial or full disclosure at a university counseling center, Dauser, Hedstrom, and Croteau (1995) found no differences between the two conditions in no-show or termination rates during the course of therapy. These results suggested that more information does not negatively affect client attendance. More recently, a study by Pomerantz (2005) supported the process model of obtaining informed consent rather than a single-event model. Although not directly studied, it is possible that providing more information to clients reduces the risk of exploitation of clients by informing them of rights and expectations. In addition, it is possible that utilizing informed consent procedures may align client and clinician expectations of therapy, resulting in a better therapy outcome, as well as fewer lawsuits or ethical complaints for clinicians. Clearly, further research should be conducted on these hypotheses.

It should be noted, however, that research has not been uniformly positive as to the effects of informed consent procedures. When long or complex written materials are utilized, client comprehension suffers. For example, a 1994 study by Mann demonstrated that longer consent forms inhibited the amount of information retained by participants. Additionally, Taube and Elwork (1990) found that disclosure of sensitive material may be inhibited when more information on the limits of confidentiality is provided to clients. Further research on this issue is needed to clarify the extent of client censoring of sensitive materials.

REFERENCES

American Psychological Association. (2002). Ethical principles of psychologists and code of conduct. *American Psychologist, 57,* 1060–1073.

Appelbaum, P. S. (1997). Informed consent to psychotherapy: Recent developments. *Psychiatric Services, 48,* 445–446.

Canterbury v. Spence, 150 U.S. App. DC. 263 (1972).

Dauser, P. J., Hedstrom, S. M., & Croteau, J. M. (1995). Effects of disclosure of comprehensive pretherapy information on clients at a university counseling center. *Professional Psychology: Research and Practice, 26*(2), 190–195.

Gustofson, K. E., & McNamara, J. R. (1987). Confidentiality with minor clients: Issues and guidelines for therapists. *Professional Psychology: Research and Practice, 18*(5), 503–508.

Handelsman, M. M. (1990). Do written consent forms influence clients' first impressions of therapists? *Professional Psychology: Research and Practice, 21*(6), 451–454.

Handelsman, M. M., & Galvin, M. D. (1988). Facilitating informed consent for outpatient psychotherapy: A suggested written format. *Professional Psychology: Research and Practice, 19*(2), 223–225.

Koocher, G. P., & Keith-Spiegel, P. (2007). *Ethics in psychology and the mental health professions: Standards and cases* (3rd ed.). New York: Oxford University Press.

Marczyk, G. R., & Wertheimer, E. (2001). The bitter pill of empiricism: Health maintenance organizations, informed consent, and the reasonable psychotherapist standard of care. *Villanova Law Review, 46,* 33–93.

Mann, T. (1994). Informed consent for psychological research: Do subjects comprehend consent forms and understand their legal rights? *Psychological Science, 5,* 140–143.

Mohr v. Williams, 104 N.W. 12, Supreme Court of Minnesota (1905).

Pomerantz, A. M. (2005). Increasingly informed consent: Discussing distinct aspects of psychotherapy at different points in time. *Ethics & Behavior, 15*(4), 351–360.

Pomerantz, A. M., & Handelsman, M. M. (2004). Informed consent revisited: An updated written question format. *Professional Psychology: Research and Practice, 35*(2), 201–205.

Schloendorff v. Society of New York Hospital, 211 N.Y. 125, 105 N.E. 92 (1914).

Somberg, D. R., Stone, G. L., & Claiborn, C. D. (1993). Informed consent: Therapists' beliefs and practices. *Professional Psychology: Research and Practice, 24*(2), 153–159.

Sullivan, T., Martin, W. L., & Handelsman, M. M. (1993). Practical benefits of an informed consent procedure: An empirical investigation. *Professional Psychology: Research and Practice, 24*(2), 160–163.

Taube, D. O., & Elwork, A. (1990). Researching the effects of confidentiality law on patients' self-disclosures. *Professional Psychology: Research and Practice, 21*(1), 72–75.

Zuckerman, E. L. (2003). *The paper office: Forms, guidelines, and resources to make your practice work ethically, legally, and profitably* (3rd ed.). New York: Guilford Press.

CATHERINE MILLER
COREY ANDERSON
Pacific University

See also: **American Psychological Association Code of Ethics; Ethical Issues in Psychology**

INHALANT-RELATED DISORDERS

Inhalant use is the deliberate ingestion of volatile substances, via a number of methods: (1) "sniffing" or "snorting" fumes from containers; (2) spraying aerosols directly into the nose or mouth; (3) "bagging"—sniffing or inhaling fumes from substances sprayed or deposited inside a plastic or paper bag; (4) "huffing" from an inhalant-soaked rag stuffed in the mouth; or (5) inhaling from balloons filled with nitrous oxide in order to induce a psychoactive or mind-altering effect (National Institute on Drug Abuse, 2005). It constitutes an important public health concern worldwide, particularly among adolescents and socioeconomically disadvantaged populations. Inhalants that are commonly used by adolescents include glue, shoe polish, toluene, gasoline, lighter fluid, spray paints, correction fluid, degreaser, nitrous oxide, and whippets (Wu, Pilowsky, & Schlenger, 2004). In contrast, adult inhalant users are likely to use nitrous oxide, whippets, amyl nitrite, poppers, and rush (Wu & Ringwalt, 2006). Adolescents also tend to use more types of inhalants and have a more frequent pattern of use than do adults (Wu et al., 2004; Wu & Ringwalt, 2006).

Most inhalants are very toxic to organs and, due to a wide variety of substances used for this purpose, inhalant users are at risk for an array of long-lasting adverse or even fatal medical consequences, including substantial cardiac, renal, hepatic, and neurological morbidity and mortality (National Institute on Drug Abuse, 2005). For example, sniffing highly concentrated chemicals in solvents or aerosol sprays can induce irregular and rapid heart rhythms, which can cause heart failure and death within minutes of a session of prolonged sniffing (known as sudden sniffing death). Repeated inhalant use may also lead to serious or irreversible damage to the heart, lungs, liver, and kidneys.

National surveys of adolescents in the United States, such as the Monitoring the Future (MTF) surveys, have found that, after marijuana, inhalants are the second most widely used drugs for eighth- and tenth-graders (Johnston, O'Malley, Bachman, & Schulenberg, 2008). In 2007, 15.6% of eighth-graders, 13.6% of tenth-graders, and 10.5% of twelfth-graders reported a history of inhalant use. Findings from the 2007 National Survey on Drug Use and Health (NSDUH) indicate that approximately 775,000 Americans aged 12 or older had used inhalants for the first time within the past 12 months, and that 66.3% were under age 18 years when they first used them (Substance Abuse and Mental Health Services Administration, 2008). Most (80%) adolescent inhalant users begin their initial use before age 15 (Wu et al., 2004).

Unlike the use of illicit drugs (e.g., marijuana, cocaine, amphetamines, ecstasy, and hallucinogens), inhalant use in youth has been found to decrease with age (Johnston et al., 2008). Probably because of a relatively low rate of inhalant use in adults and because inhalants are often considered as "kids' drugs," inhalant use and particularly inhalant use disorders (i.e., abuse of or dependence on inhalants as defined by the *Diagnostic and Statistical Manual of Mental Disorders* [DSM-IV-TR]; American Psychiatric Association, 2000) among the adult population have received little research attention (Wu & Ringwalt, 2006).

The 12-month prevalence of inhalant use disorders is low among adolescents aged 12–17 (0.4%) and adults (0.04%) nationally (Wu et al., 2004; Wu & Ringwalt, 2006). However, among adolescents aged 12–17 who reported inhalant use in the past year, more than one in ten users exhibit a current inhalant use disorder, of whom 6.3% have an Abuse diagnosis and 4.3% a Dependence diagnosis (Wu et al., 2004). Inhalant use disorders also affect adolescents regardless of gender, age, race/ethnicity, and family income. Among adults aged 18 or older who reported inhalant use in the past year, approximately one in twelve exhibit a current inhalant use disorder: 6.6% have an abuse and 1.1% a dependence diagnosis (Wu et al., 2004). Thus, adult inhalant users have a lower risk for exhibiting inhalant dependence than do adolescent inhalant users.

Finally, recent study findings from the 2001–2002 National Epidemiologic Survey on Alcohol and Related Conditions (NESARC), a large national study of psychiatric comorbidity of adults in the United States, have shown that DSM-IV psychiatric disorders are highly prevalent among adults who reported a history of inhalant use, and that women with such a history have a particularly high rate of multiple psychiatric disorders (Wu & Howard, 2007). Among adults who reported a history of inhalant use, seven in ten (70%) exhibited at least one mood (48%), anxiety (36%), or personality (45%) disorder in their lifetime, and 38% experienced a mood or anxiety disorder in the past year. Compared with male inhalant users, female inhalant users had higher lifetime prevalence rates of dysthymia (24% vs. 16%), any anxiety disorder (53% vs. 30%), panic disorder without agoraphobia (25% vs. 11%), and specific phobia (28% vs. 14%), but a lower prevalence of antisocial personality disorder (22% vs. 36%). Study results also suggest that inhalant users who are poor, less educated, have a history of early onset of inhalant use (i.e., before 13 years old), family histories of psychopathology, or personal histories of substance-abuse treatment are particularly likely to exhibit psychiatric disorders.

REFERENCES

American Psychiatric Association. (2000). *Diagnostic and statistical manual of mental disorders* (DSM-IV, text rev.). Washington, DC: Author.

Johnston, L. D., O'Malley, P. M., Bachman, J. G., & Schulenberg, J. E. (2008). *Monitoring the future: National results on adolescent drug use: Overview of key findings, 2007* (NIH Publication No. 08-6418, 70 pp.). Bethesda, MD: National Institute on Drug Abuse.

National Institute on Drug Abuse. (2005). *NIDA Research Report—Inhalant Abuse: NIH Publication No. 00-3818.* Rockville, MD: National Institute of Health. Retrieved September 23, 2008, from http://www.nida.nih.gov/researchreports/inhalants/Inhalants.html.

Substance Abuse and Mental Health Services Administration, Office of Applied Studies (2008). *Results from the 2007 National Survey on Drug Use and Health: National Findings* (NSDUH Series H-34, DHHS Publication No. SMA 08-4343). Rockville, MD: National Institute on Drug Abuse.

Wu, L. T., & Howard, M. O. (2007). Psychiatric disorders in inhalant users: Results from The National Epidemiologic Survey on Alcohol and Related Conditions. *Drug and Alcohol Dependence, 88*(2–3), 146–155.

Wu, L. T., Pilowsky, D. J., & Schlenger, W. E. (2004). Inhalant abuse and dependence among adolescents in the United States.

Journal of the American Academy of Child and Adolescent Psychiatry, 43(10), 1206–1214.

Wu, L. T., & Ringwalt, C. L. (2006). Inhalant use and disorders among adults in the United States. *Drug and Alcohol Dependence,* 85(1), 1–11.

SUGGESTED READINGS

Sakai, J. T., Hall, S. K., Mikulich-Gilbertson, S. K., & Crowley, T. J. (2004). Inhalant use, abuse, and dependence among adolescent patients: Commonly comorbid problems. *Journal of the American Academy of Child and Adolescent Psychiatry.* 43, 1080–1088.

Williams, J. F., & Storck, M. (2007). American Academy of Pediatrics Committee on Substance Abuse: American Academy of Pediatrics Committee on Native American Child Health. Inhalant abuse. *Pediatrics, 119*(5), 1009–1017.

Li-Tzy Wu
Duke University Medical Center

Christopher L. Ringwalt
Pacific Institute for Research and Evaluation, Chapel Hill, NC

See also: Addiction; Drug Addiction

INSANITY (See Psychotic Disorders)

INSIGHT

Most schools of psychotherapy and psychological treatment recognize the importance of insight as part of what makes psychotherapy effective (Castonguay & Hill, 2007). Insight has been conceptualized in many ways, but the general consensus is that insight provides patients with a new way to understand their inner mental life, their interpersonal conflicts or troubles, or a new understanding of those factors that contribute to an individual's difficulties. The complexities of the construct of insight have been succinctly summarized by Castonguay and Hill: "Insight can vary considerably in terms of content (e.g., links between past and present, links between conscious thoughts and underlying assumptions). Insight also seems to involve several dimensions (e.g., emotional vs. intellectual, explicit vs. implicit, sudden vs. gradual)" (2007, p. 4). Insight is often stereotypically described as when a patient has an "Aha" experience—for instance, the patient may state, "Wow, this is what has been going on! It makes so much sense. This really helps." However, it would be rare to find a psychologist who thinks of insight strictly in this manner. Most psychologists and patients report that insight occurs emotionally rather than intellectually, explicitly and implicitly, as well as gradually—and sometimes, suddenly.

For example, a psychologist treated two women who came to see him separately after they each had recently divorced. In both cases, they had been married to men who seemed narcissistic based on the behaviors each described of her respective husband. Because they assiduously worked to find an explanation for what they had done to lead to the marriage deteriorating, the psychologist read the diagnostic criteria of narcissistic personality disorder to them without telling them what he was reading. The psychologist then asked them to think of whether what he read was characteristically descriptive of their husbands. On both occasions, they agreed with all the criteria. When he explained to them that he was reading the criteria for narcissistic personality disorder, they were amazed. He explained that he did not want to assign a diagnosis to the husbands without ever meeting and evaluating them. However, hearing this helped both women in that particular session and the sessions thereafter. They recognized that their actions were not entirely responsible for the divorce and that the difficulties they had with their husbands reflected some potentially pathological qualities of their spouses. Gradually in the sessions that followed, both women became more aware of ways in which they were drawn to their husbands and what personal needs and desires were met by their former partner. This kind of insight came more slowly, with both emotional and intellectual understanding. Sometimes, they came to the understanding on their own; at other times, the psychologist provided an explanation for them to consider, which they were able to utilize in an effective way.

Insight is often associated with psychoanalysis, psychoanalytic psychotherapy, or psychodynamic psychotherapy. Interestingly, Freud only used the word "insight" when discussing time, and not in the way in which it is typically understood (Messer & McWilliams, 2007). Many ego psychologists credit Strachey (1934) with the implicit introduction of the necessity of insight in treatment. According to Strachey, "insight" comes to the patient by way of the interpretations provided by the therapist. Alternatively, object relations therapists tend to view insight as a product of mutual discovery that arises from the meaningful relationship that develops between the patient and therapist; in this case, both the patient and therapist are considered to have important ideas to share that lead the patient to new ways of thinking about his or her life. Psychodynamically speaking, Messer and McWilliams (2007) provide important criteria by which to determine whether the patient is obtaining insight. These include recognizing patterns of connections; the ability to observe one's own internal processes, personality, or psychopathology; the revision of pathological belief; and recognition of the motives of oneself and others.

Pascual-Leone and Greenberg (2007) have described insight as occurring along two continua that capture an understanding of insight from both an existential and relational perspective. One of these involves the type of mental processing that is involved, which consists of perceptual-emotional or conceptual-relational. The relational involves the nature of the new knowledge, which involves concrete-experiential or abstract relational. Insight that is more "experience near" consists of concrete, experiential, and processing more at the perceptual-emotional level. For instance, this could include the recognition that one's significant other did not mean to harm the patient in a recent argument, and as a result, the patient now feels better about the nature of her interaction. By way of contrast, "experience distant" insight consists of conceptual-relational processing and abstract-relational knowledge. This latter type is what is often considered to be typical of psychodynamic psychotherapy. For instance, a patient comes to a new understanding of how his tendency to be critical of himself is associated with deeply held desires to please his mother, who had been implicitly critical of him during childhood.

Cognitive-behavioral therapists have also begun to recognize and define the concept of insight. Holtforth et al. (2007) define insight as "a learning process (a corrective experience of clarification) in which one consciously perceives connections between two or more mental representations (schemas) that one had not previously viewed as connected or connected in a particular way" (p. 68). In this model, changes in schemas become the focus of attention. Schemas are mental representations of the self and others that are deeply held, some of which are more consciously accessible than others. Much like psychodynamic theories of object relations, schema theory values the importance of recognizing the unique representations of people and experiences in the minds of patients. The patient's schemas occurs through an exploration of the patient's current life experiences and understanding these experiences. Structured activities, such as thought records and homework activities, allow these representations to be identified and understood. By way of contrast, the method of free association, whereby the patient speaks of whatever comes to mind, allows the analytic or dynamic therapist to discover object representations, conflicts, and patterns of defenses that help foster the development of insight.

With insight being such a widely discussed factor in the psychotherapy literature, it is now widely considered that insight is a common factor that accounts for therapeutic change (e.g., Castonguay & Hill, 2007; Wampold, 2001). Stated differently, giving attention to fostering patient insight is often considered a necessary component of psychotherapy. Even with the prevalence and emphasis of empirically supported treatments that focus on particular techniques and skill training, most models of psychotherapy now value the importance and utility of insight in psychotherapy.

REFERENCES

Castonguay, L. G., & Hill, C. E. (Eds.). (2007). *Insight in psychotherapy*. Washington, DC: American Psychological Association.

Holtforth, M. G., Castonguay, L. G., Boswell, J. F., Wilson, L. A., Kakouros, A. A., & Borkovec, T. D. (2007). Insight in cognitive-behavioral therapy. In L. G. Castonguay & C. E. Hill (Eds.), *Insight in psychotherapy* (pp. 57–80). Washington, DC: American Psychological Association.

Messer, S. B., & McWilliams, N. (2007). Insight in psychodynamic therapy: Theory and assessment. In L. G. Castonguay & C. E. Hill (Eds.), *Insight in psychotherapy* (pp. 9–30). Washington, DC: American Psychological Association.

Pascual-Leone, A., & Greenberg, L. S. (2007). Insight and awareness in experiential psychotherapy. In L. G. Castonguay & C. E. Hill (Eds.), *Insight in psychotherapy* (pp. 31–56). Washington, DC: American Psychological Association.

Strachey, J. (1934). The nature of the therapeutic action of psycho-analysis. *International Journal of Psychoanalysis, 15,* 127–159.

Wampold, B. E. (2001). *The great psychotherapy debate: Models, methods, and findings.* Mahwah, NJ: Erlbaum.

SUGGESTED READINGS

Castonguay, L. G., & Hill, C. E. (Eds.). (2007). *Insight in psychotherapy*. Washington, DC: American Psychological Association.

Frank. K. A. (1993). Action, insight, and working through: Outlines of an integrative approach. *Psychoanalytic Dialogues, 3,* 535–577.

Safran, J. D. (1989). Insight and action in psychotherapy. *Journal of Integrative and Eclectic Psychotherapy, 8,* 3–19.

STEVEN K. HUPRICH
Eastern Michigan University

See also: Insight-Oriented Psychotherapy; Psychodynamic Psychotherapy

INSIGHT-ORIENTED PSYCHOTHERAPY

Insight-oriented psychotherapy is not a single method of psychotherapy; rather, it represents a category of psychotherapeutic approaches that share a common assumption about psychopathology and its treatment. These forms of therapy assume that an individual's behavior is disturbed in some way due to a lack of awareness of his or her motivations underlying it. Psychotherapy, then, involves the elucidation of a person's internal motivations and the development of a better sense of awareness and self-understanding, in order to facilitate more adaptive behavior and courses of action in his or her life.

Psychodynamic Psychotherapy and Depth Psychology Origins

The insight-oriented psychotherapies emerged from a field broadly known as "depth psychology," which was initially established by Sigmund Freud in the late nineteenth century. Depth psychology examined the relationship between Freud's concept of the individual's unconscious mind and his or her conscious thought processes and behavior. Freud's (1940) method of treatment was known as psychoanalysis and was the first established form of insight-oriented psychotherapy. Over the years, modifications in the method of psychoanalysis (e.g., frequency of sessions, duration of treatment) have been designated by the terms "psychoanalytic therapy" or "psychodynamic therapy" apart from what has been termed as Freud's "classical psychoanalysis." However, all of these insight-oriented methods are predicated on some form of depth psychology. In addition to these psychodynamic forms of treatment, other approaches to psychotherapy have emerged over the years that can also be classified as insight-oriented treatments (Castonguay & Hill, 2007). Prominent among these are client-centered therapy, existential psychotherapy, interpersonal psychotherapy, and most recently, narrative therapy. Each of these different approaches holds different assumptions about the therapeutic factors that promote insight and change (Scaturo, 2005).

Humanistic Psychology and Client-Centered Therapy

In the evolution of psychotherapy, the psychoanalytic approach to treatment with its focus on the intrapsychic processes of the patient was followed by the influence of behaviorism and behavior therapy, which focused exclusively on the overt behavior of patients and their symptomatology. In turn, a "third force" in the beliefs about treatment that followed behaviorism was known as "humanistic psychology." Humanistic psychotherapy was concerned with ideas that encompassed "human potential," such as love, growth, warmth, autonomy, meaning, insight, and psychological health, in marked contrast to a focus on psychopathology. At the heart of the psychotherapeutic arm of this movement was Carl Rogers's (1951) client-centered therapy, or "nondirective therapy." The client-centered interview was regarded as nondirective, because it was believed that human growth was best able to emerge from an atmosphere in which psychotherapists imposed themselves as little as possible in a client's self-exploration.

Client-centered therapy focuses on the importance of three facilitative conditions that enhance the therapeutic relationship with the client, which are the therapist's degree of genuineness, empathy, and positive regard toward the client. Genuineness involves the therapist's responses to the client being congruent with his or her own honest reactions to the client. Empathy requires a true understanding of the client's subjective reality, such that therapist's words demonstrate an understanding of how the client experiences his or her life circumstances. An uncompromising positive regard for the client consists of the therapist avoiding any verbal or nonverbal behavior that implies personal judgments about the client's experience. The principal method in client-centered therapy is the therapist's reflective mode of therapeutic communication. That is, the therapist attempts to accurately reflect or mirror what the client has said, with perhaps some slight alteration of the response in order to validate the client's perception and also to offer a slightly modified perspective for the client to consider. The reflective method of communication is the means by which nondirective therapists communicate their empathic understanding and validation of a client's perception, worldview, struggles, and emotional suffering.

Existential Psychotherapy and Philosophy

Existential psychotherapy is based on the writings of existential philosophy (Yalom, 1980) and is fundamentally concerned with the emotional issues surrounding existence and non-existence, that is, death. Death anxiety underlies each of the stages of development throughout life and is most noticeable during the middle stage of life. In mid-life, one confronts the disquieting realization that more years in life now lie behind than ahead. The existential psychotherapist's task in treatment is to help the patient examine the question of balance between death's stark reminder that life cannot be postponed, while offering support and optimism that there is still time left for productive living.

Yalom (1980) proposed the following useful equation for therapists' engaging in existentially oriented clinical work: "death anxiety is inversely proportional to life satisfaction" (p. 207). That is to say, if death anxiety is gently confronted with appropriate degrees of reality and support, therapy offers the potential to promote a new perspective on living the remainder of one's life. In therapy, the question concerning the meaning of one's life cannot be productively answered by isolated introspection. Rather, the meaningfulness of one's life is better answered by the process of enhanced social and interpersonal engagement with others, that is, to "immerse oneself in the river of life and let the question [of meaning] drift away" (Yalom, 1980, p. 483).

Interpersonal Psychotherapy and the Therapeutic Foci

Interpersonal psychotherapy (Klerman, Weissman, Rounsaville, & Chevron, 1984) is based on the interpersonal theory of Harry Stack Sullivan (1953), who believed that psychopathology is best understood by the recurrent patterns of interaction that individuals have with others in their interpersonal sphere. The goal of interpersonal therapy is to foster insight into and change in disrupted relationships in the patient's life and to modify any unrealistic expectations about those relationships, and thereby to bring about symptom relief.

The primary therapeutic foci of interpersonal psychotherapy have been distilled into four thematic problem areas: grief, interpersonal disputes, role transitions, and interpersonal skill deficits and sensitivity. Interpersonal losses almost always involve both a grief reaction to the loss of a figure that has provided a sense of safety and security in the world and also one's disrupted beliefs about the relative degree of safety in the world. Interpersonal disputes are likely to involve marital or family conflict, including one's extended family, as well as problematic relationships with close friends or coworkers. Role transitions involve difficulties in transitioning from one phase to another in one's life (e.g., from being a spouse to being a parent). Interpersonal skill deficits and sensitivity to others involve deficiencies that the patient might have in needed social skills, such as assertiveness and responsiveness to the emotional life of others, that serve to create and maintain supportive social relationships.

Narrative Therapy as a Contemporary Insight-Oriented Treatment

Narrative therapy (White & Epston, 1990) is based on the idea that personal problems are constructed within the broader context of one's social and cultural milieu. That is, people experience difficulties in their lives when the stories of their life, as they or significant others in their lives have constructed them, are inconsistent with their own life experience and the subjective meaning they have derived from that experience. The goal of the narrative approach, which is achieved through the use of exploration and narrative construction about one's life, is to assist patients in excavating resources, skills, and abilities through a transformed reconstruction of self.

For example, in the treatment of psychological trauma, the therapist helps survivors of a traumatic life history (e.g., children in alcoholic and abusive families) to move from a sense of "victimization" to a sense of "survivorship" in the personal narratives of their life. Victims become discouraged and incapacitated by the trauma, whereas survivors are able to overcome the traumatic recollections and mobilize themselves to live their lives more fully in the aftermath of such events. In traumatic situations involving interpersonal or existential losses, the overall goal of treatment is regarded as assisting the patient in making this important transformation.

Narrative therapy is most frequently aligned with a range of insight-oriented approaches to treatment, which as noted include psychoanalytic and psychodynamically-oriented approaches as well as existential and humanistic psychotherapies. Narrative therapy appears to represent a resurgence of interest in the psychotherapy patient's view of the value of psychotherapy as a verbal, insight-promoting medium.

The Question of Insight and Behavior Change

The debate over the usefulness of insight into one's behavior and the therapeutic conditions that foster it in the psychodynamic psychotherapies and other insight-oriented approaches (including client-centered therapy), as opposed to the focus on behavior change in the behavioral treatment modalities, has been one of the most vehement discussions in the fields of psychology and psychotherapy. A classic debate on this issue took place in the 1950s between the humanistic psychotherapist Carl Rogers and the founder of behavioral psychology, B. F. Skinner (Rogers & Skinner, 1956). Humanistic psychotherapists have typically depicted behavior therapists with their specific focus on behavior change in therapy as "antihumanistic, Machiavellian manipulators of human behavior" (Bandura, 1969, p. 81). In turn, behavior therapists have criticized humanistic psychotherapy as nothing more than benevolent directionlessness (as the term "nondirective" therapy would imply) with nonspecific therapeutic goals such as "self-actualization," which they typically have viewed as "idealized pretensions" (Bandura, 1969, p. 81). More recent efforts at integrating these two realms of psychotherapy have yielded a more comprehensive understanding of the relative contributions of action and insight in treatment (Wachtel, 1987).

Concerns and Role Functions of the Insight-Oriented Psychotherapist

The revitalization of interest in insight-oriented therapy has been accompanied by a resurgence of concerns about the processes of therapy that have traditionally been the domain of insight-oriented treatment (Scaturo, 2005). These traditional therapeutic issues include (1) a recognition of the importance of the therapeutic alliance, (2) an understanding of the patient's psychosocial history in addition to the contemporary stressors in the patient's life, (3) the role of the therapist's countertransference in psychotherapy, (4) the manner in which directive therapy borrows on the nurturant function of the therapist for the patient, and (5) the moment-to-moment patient-therapist interactions in treatment that require a therapist's ability to exercise clinical judgment.

Clinical Dilemmas in Insight-Oriented Psychotherapy

One of the most prevalent moment-to-moment dilemmas in an insight-oriented psychotherapy session is how much to confront versus how much to support a given patient at a given point in treatment (Scaturo, 2005). Too much confrontation may overwhelm the patient; too much support without any confrontation may yield no change or movement of the patient in therapy. It is the psychotherapist's responsibility to decide how much confrontation a particular patient with a specific psychosocial history and a given diagnosis and defensive structure can tolerate at a particular point in time. Alternatively, how much emotional support is needed throughout this process? This decision is an ongoing one that occurs on a moment-to-moment basis as a result of insight-oriented psychotherapy being a dynamic process in which the status of these considerations is changing constantly throughout the course of treatment.

REFERENCES

Bandura, A. (1969). *Principles of behavior modification*. New York: Holt, Rinehart, & Winston.

Castonguay, L. G., & Hill, C. E. (Eds.). (2007). *Insight in psychotherapy*. Washington, DC: American Psychological Association.

Freud, S. (1964). An outline of psychoanalysis. In J. Strachey (Ed. & Trans.), *The standard edition of the complete psychological works of Sigmund Freud* (Vol. 23, pp. 141–207). London: Hogarth Press. (Original work published 1940)

Klerman, G. L., Weissman, M. M., Rounsaville, B. J., & Chevron, E. S. (1984). *Interpersonal psychotherapy of depression*. New York: Basic Books.

Rogers, C. R. (1951). *Client-centered therapy: Its current practice, implications, and theory*. Boston: Houghton Mifflin.

Rogers, C. R., & Skinner, B. F. (1956). Some issues concerning the control of human behavior: A symposium. *Science, 124*, 1057–1066.

Scaturo, D. J. (2005). *Clinical dilemmas in psychotherapy: A transtheoretical approach to psychotherapy integration*. Washington, DC: American Psychological Association.

Sullivan, H. S. (1953). *The interpersonal theory of psychiatry*. New York: Norton.

Wachtel, P. L. (1987). *Action and insight*. New York: Guilford Press.

White, M., & Epston, D. (1990). *Narrative means to therapeutic ends*. New York: Norton.

Yalom, I. D. (1980). *Existential psychotherapy*. New York: Basic Books.

DOUGLAS J. SCATURO
State University of New York Upstate Medical University and Syracuse VA Medical Center

See also: **Current Psychotherapies; Insight; Psychodynamic Psychotherapy**

INSOMNIA

Insomnia entails a spectrum of complaints reflecting dissatisfaction with the quality, duration, or continuity of sleep. These complaints may involve problems with falling asleep initially at bedtime (initial insomnia), waking up in the middle of the night and having difficulty going back to sleep (middle insomnia), awakening prematurely in the morning with an inability to return to sleep (late insomnia), or a perception of nonrestorative sleep. In order to fulfill the American Psychiatric Association (APA) diagnostic criteria of an insomnia disorder (e.g., Primary Insomnia, Insomnia related to another mental disorder), the sleep disturbance or its daytime consequences (e.g., fatigue) have to cause significant psychological distress or impaired functioning (APA, 2000). More than one third of the adult population reports insomnia symptoms, whereas 6% suffer from an insomnia disorder (Ohayon, 2002).

The International Classification of Sleep Disorders recognizes three different subtypes of primary insomnia (American Academy of Sleep Medicine, 2005). *Psychophysiological insomnia* is the most classic form of insomnia and is the result of conditioned arousal from the repeated pairings of situational (bed/bedroom) and temporal (bedtime) stimuli, normally associated with sleep, with the inability to sleep. *Paradoxical insomnia* involves a genuine complaint of poor sleep that is not corroborated by objective evidence of sleep disturbances. *Idiopathic insomnia* presents an insidious onset during childhood, unrelated to psychosocial stressors or medical disorders, and is very persistent throughout the adult life.

Associated Features

Daytime Consequences

Along with subjective complaints of poor sleep, individuals with insomnia are often distressed about their sleep and report significant fatigue and impairments of their daytime functioning. Common sleep-loss-related daytime problems include difficulties with attention, concentration, memory, completion of tasks, reduced energy, and mood disturbances. Chronic insomnia is also associated with reduced quality of life, decreased productivity, increased absenteeism from work, and increased risk for depression.

Associated Mental Disorders

There is extensive comorbidity between insomnia and psychopathology. The relationship between insomnia and mental disorders is bidirectional: prevalence rates of psychological symptoms and psychopathology are higher among individuals reporting sleep difficulties, and individuals suffering from mental disorders are more likely to report sleep difficulties. For example, sleep difficulties are present in up to 80% of individuals suffering from Major Depressive Disorder and persistent insomnia represents an important risk factor for new onset depression (Ford & Kamerow, 1989). Insomnia is (with fatigue) the most prevalent residual symptom after treatment of depression, and it may represent an important risk factor for future relapse. Insomnia is also very prevalent among individuals suffering from Anxiety Disorders, particularly Generalized Anxiety Disorder and Post-Traumatic Stress Disorder. Overall, insomnia is associated with a mental disorder in at least 35–40% of all cases (Ohayon, 2002).

Theoretical Models

Three types of factors, known as Spielman's 3P model, are involved at different points during the development of chronic insomnia. Predisposing factors are psychological or biological characteristics that increase vulnerability, or predisposition, to sleep difficulties (e.g., female gender, increasing age, family history, anxiety traits, hyperarousal). These factors are not a direct cause of insomnia, but they increase the risk that an individual will develop sleep difficulties. Precipitating factors are the medical, environmental, or psychological factors that trigger insomnia (e.g., divorce, death of a significant other, illness, medication, familial or occupational stress). Perpetuating factors maintain or exacerbate sleep difficulties. They are typically behaviors (e.g., excessive amounts of time spent in bed, naps) and/or beliefs and thoughts (fear of sleeplessness, excessive worries about daytime consequences) that people adopt in response to or in an attempt to cope with sleeplessness, but they may contribute to perpetuating insomnia in the long run.

Figure 1 illustrates how transient insomnia can evolve into persistent insomnia. Everyone presents, to various

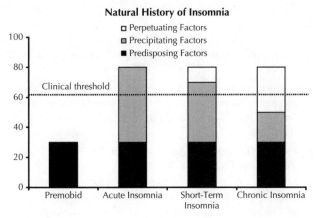

Figure 1. Natural History of Insomnia.
Adapted from Spielman, A. J. & Glovinsky, P. (1991). The varied nature of insomnia. In P. J. Hauri (Ed.). *Case studies in insomnia.* New York, Plenum Press. Reproduced with the permission of Springer Science and Business Media.

degrees, some vulnerability to develop insomnia; this is more or less important depending on individual differences (predisposing factors). Different types of precipitating factors may trigger insomnia, even among those with little vulnerability. Once the initial precipitating event fades away, most people return to normal sleep. For others, perhaps those at greater risk for insomnia, sleep difficulties persist even after the initial precipitating event has been removed or managed. For these people, insomnia develops a life of its own and several psychological and behavioral factors contribute to perpetuate the sleep difficulties over time. Effective management of chronic insomnia must directly target these perpetuating factors.

The Vicious Cycle of Chronic Insomnia

Persistent insomnia may be conceptualized as a vicious cycle (Morin, 1993; see Figure 2). Arousal or activation, whether emotional (anxiety, anger), cognitive (worries, mental images) or physiological (muscle tension, pain), is a central feature of insomnia. It is often the starting point of an insomnia night. Repeated nights of disrupted sleep may lead the person to engage in some practices intended to recuperate or compensate for sleep loss. Some of these strategies may be useful on a short-term basis (e.g., taking a nap or spending more time in bed) but in the long run, they tend to maintain and even exacerbate sleep difficulties (e.g., too much time in bed leads to light and fragmented sleep). After several nights of disturbed sleep, some temporal (bedtime) and situational (bed and bedroom) cues, usually associated with somnolence and sleep among good sleepers, become associated with frustration, anxiety, and a feeling of loss of control over one's own ability to sleep. With time, the very idea of having to go to bed increases tension, worries, and fear of a sleepless night, which, in turn, prevent the occurrence of sleep.

In reaction to worsening sleep difficulties, worries increase, generating more self-monitoring of sleeplessness cues and, hence, more cognitive activation at bedtime and during nocturnal awakenings. People with insomnia will also become more focused on the negative daytime consequences of a bad night's sleep. To avoid these consequences, they may become more apprehensive and develop performance anxiety at bedtime, creating yet another form of activation incompatible with sleep (Harvey, 2002; Morin & Espie, 2003).

Directions for Treatment

Hypnotic Medication

Medication (prescribed and over-the-counter) is the most common treatment used for insomnia. Overall, hypnotic medication (i.e., benzodiazepine-agonist receptors) is a useful therapeutic option to alleviate transient insomnia.

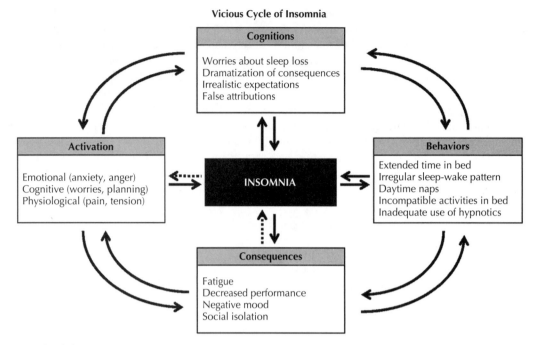

Figure 2. Vicious Cycle of Chronic Insomnia.
Adapted from Morin, C. M. (1993). *Insomnia*. Psychological assessment and management. New York: Guilford Press. Permission pending.

However the role of long-term use of hypnotics is controversial and there is limited evidence at this time to support this clinical practice. Behavioral approaches, alone or combined with brief pharmacotherapy, should be preferred to continuous long-term use of hypnotics to treat chronic insomnia (NIH, 2005).

Cognitive and Behavioral Therapies

The main objective of cognitive and behavioral therapies is to alter those factors that perpetuate or exacerbate sleep disturbances. *Sleep restriction* consists of curtailing the amount of time spent in bed to the actual amount of sleep. *Stimulus control therapy* consists of a set of instructions designed to re-associate temporal (bedtime) and environmental (bed and bedroom) stimuli with sleep. *Relaxation-based interventions* aim at reducing somatic (e.g., muscle tension) and cognitive (worries, intrusive thoughts, racing mind) arousal. *Cognitive therapy* is a psychotherapeutic method that seeks to alter dysfunctional sleep cognitions (e.g., beliefs, expectations, attributions) and maladaptive cognitive processes (e.g., excessive self-monitoring or worrying) in order to reduce distress, improve coping and facilitate sleep. *Sleep hygiene education* is intended to provide information about lifestyle (diet, exercise, substance use) and environmental factors (light, noise, temperature) that may either interfere with or promote better sleep.

Although some of these interventions can be used successfully as single therapies, they can also be effectively combined to optimize outcome. *Cognitive-behavioral therapy*

(CBT) is becoming the standard nonpharmacological approach for treating chronic insomnia. CBT has been shown effective for treating chronic insomnia and one of its greatest benefits is that it produces long-term sleep improvements (Morin et al., 2006; NIH, 2005).

REFERENCES

American Academy of Sleep Medicine. (2005). *International classification of sleep disorders: Diagnostic and coding manual* (2nd ed.). Westchester, IL: American Academy of Sleep Medicine.

American Psychiatric Association. (2000). *Diagnostic and statistical manual of mental disorders* (4th ed., rev.). Washington, DC: American Psychiatric Association.

Breslau, N., Roth, T., Rosenthal, L., & Andreski, P. (1996). Sleep disturbance and psychiatric disorders: A longitudinal epidemiological study of young adults. *Biological Psychiatry, 39,* 411–418.

Ford, D. E., & Kamerow, D. B. (1989). Epidemiologic study of sleep disturbances and psychiatric disorders. An opportunity for prevention? *Journal of the American Medical Association, 262,* 1479–1484.

Harvey, A. G. (2002). A cognitive model of insomnia. *Behaviour Research and Therapy, 8,* 869–893.

Morin, C. M., Bootzin, R. R., Buysse, D. J., Edinger, J. D., Espie, C. A., & Lickstein, K. L. (2006). Psychological and behavioral treatment of insomnia: Update of the recent evidence (1998–2004). *Sleep, 29,* 1398–1414.

National Institutes of Health (2005). National Institutes of Health state of the science conference statement on manifestations and management of chronic insomnia in adults. *Sleep, 28,* 1049–1057.

Ohayon, M. M. (2002). Epidemiology of insomnia: What we know and what we still need to learn. *Sleep Medicine Reviews*, 6, 97–111.

Spielman, A. J. & Glovinsky, P. (1991). The varied nature of insomnia. In P. J. Hauri (Ed.), *Case studies in insomnia*. New York: Plenum Press.

SUGGESTED READINGS

Morin, C. M., & Espie, C. A. (2003). *Insomnia: A clinical guide to assessment and treatment*. New York: Kluwer Academic/Plenum Publishers.

National Institutes of Health (2005). National Institutes of Health state of the science conference statement on manifestations and management of chronic insomnia in adults. *Sleep*, 28, 1049–1057.

The National Sleep Foundation web site, http://www.sleep foundation.org/

GENEVIÈVE BELLEVILLE
University of Quebec at Montreal

CHARLES M. MORIN
Laval University Canada

See also: **Sleep Disorders**

INSTRUMENTAL CONDITIONING

Instrumental conditioning represents a form of behavioral change that depends on the temporal relationship (contingency) between a response and an environmental outcome. The response might correspond to pressing a bar, lifting a leg, turning a wheel, or navigating a maze. In the laboratory, the outcome is typically a biologically relevant event, such as food, water, or a frightening shock. Outside the laboratory, behavior can be modified by a variety of events including social praise, access to a sexual partner, or a stimulus that has acquired value (e.g., money). Outcomes capable of modifying an organism's behavior are sometimes called reinforcers, and the process through which they influence behavior is known as reinforcement. Examples of an instrumental contingency include praising a child for waiting quietly or providing a food pellet to a rat whenever it presses a bar. According to Thorndike's law of effect, these contingencies should bring about a lasting change in behavior, leading the child to stand quietly and increasing the frequency with which the rat presses the bar.

It is clear that the timely application of a reinforcer can bring about a dramatic change in behavior. Anyone who has trained a pet using food as a reward, or attempted to influence a roommate's behavior through

social reinforcement, has employed a form of instrumental conditioning. It is important to remember, however, that instituting a response-outcome relationship can sometimes affect performance in the absence of instrumental learning. For example, stimuli that regularly predict an aversive reinforcer can be associated with the reinforcer through a form of Pavlovian (classical) conditioning. This learning can endow the stimuli with the capacity to produce a conditioned response that affects our target behavior. The problem is that this Pavlovian conditioning can lead us to mistakenly conclude that instrumental (response-outcome) learning has occurred, when in fact the behavioral modification actually reflects the acquisition of a stimulus-outcome relation. Similarly, simple exposure to an outcome alone can cause a response to grow stronger (sensitization) or weaker (habituation) in the absence of an instrumental relation. Demonstrating instrumental learning is at work requires that we discount these alternatives.

Outlining some formal criteria can help us determine whether a behavioral change reflects instrumental conditioning (Grau, Barstow, & Joynes, 1998). At a minimum, the following four conditions must be met: (1) The behavioral modification depends on a form of neural plasticity; (2) the modification depends on the organism's experiential history; (3) the modification outlasts (extends beyond) the environmental contingencies used to induce it; and (4) imposing a temporal relationship between the response and the outcome alters the response.

The first three criteria specify essential conditions for learning. Because performing the response can alter its vigor through a peripheral modification (e.g., muscular exercise or fatigue), it is important to show that the behavioral change is neurally mediated (Criterion 1). Changes attributable to neural development or injury do not count as learning (Criterion 2). Finally, because instituting an environmental contingency can bring about a temporary mechanical modification in the response, we must show that our training regimen has a lasting effect on behavior (Criterion 3).

The fourth criterion specifies the nature of the behavioral change required for instrumental learning: that the behavioral modification depends on the response-outcome relation. Two operations are used to establish this. One involves the inclusion of a yoked control group that receives the reinforcer independent of its behavior. A second technique degrades the essential relation by imposing a temporal gap between the response and the outcome. If the response-outcome relation is essential, both procedures should undermine the response.

Some instrumental behavior is biologically constrained by the organism's evolutionary history (Timberlake & Lucas, 1989). For example, consider the flexion response elicited by an aversive stimulus applied to the base of the foot. Because this response is organized by neurons within the spinal cord, it can be elicited in the absence of feedback from the brain. This reflex can be modified by imposing a response-outcome contingency; if shock is only presented when the limb is extended, the organism quickly learns to maintain its leg in a flexed (up) position. This modification of a reflexive behavior meets the minimum criteria (1–4) for instrumental conditioning. However, learning within the spinal cord appears biologically constrained. Given the same outcome, we cannot arbitrarily train subjects to exhibit either a flexion or an extension. More sophisticated neural systems can support a greater range of flexibility. We could train you to lift or lower your hand using a variety of reinforcers (food, money, or shock). Such advanced forms of instrumental conditioning meet two additional criteria: (5) The nature of the behavioral change is not constrained (e.g., either an increase or decrease in the response can be established); and (6) The nature of the reinforcer is not constrained (a variety of outcomes can be used to produce the behavioral effect).

The term instrumental conditioning has its roots in the reflexive tradition of E. L. Thorndike, J. Konorski, and C. L. Hull. From this perspective, instrumental learning reflects a form of elicited behavior, one that depends on the relationship established between a response and an outcome. An alternative view was suggested by B. F. Skinner, who noted that it is often difficult (or impossible) to specify the eliciting stimulus for advanced forms of instrumental behavior. He referred to this type of behavior as operant conditioning and argued that it is emitted, not elicited.

These historical facts continue to influence how the terms are used within the modern learning literature. Skinnerians focus on the experimental analysis of behavior and generally employ the term operant conditioning. The emphasis is on emitted behavior and rate of responding. Those who follow in the tradition of Hull assume that response-outcome relations can affect elicited responses and that associative processes underlie complex instrumental behavior.

Because both instrumental and operant conditioning depend on the response-outcome relation, they are sometimes treated as synonyms. However, in cases where the target response is elicited, and/or an attempt is made to explain the behavior in terms of associative mechanisms, the term instrumental conditioning is more appropriate.

REFERENCES

Grau, J. W., Barstow, D. G., & Joynes, R. L. (1998). Instrumental learning within the spinal cord. I. Behavioral properties. *Behavioral Neuroscience, 112,* 1366–1386.

Timberlake, W., & Lucas, G. A. (1989). Behavior systems and learning: From misbehavior to general principles. In S. B. Klein & R. R. Mowrer (Eds.), *Contemporary learning theories: Instrumental conditioning theory and the impact of biological constraints on learning* (pp. 237–275). Hillsdale, NJ: Lawrence Erlbaum.

SUGGESTED READING

Hearst, E. (1975). The classical-instrumental distinction: Reflexes, voluntary behavior, and categories of associative learning. In W. K. Estes (Ed.), *Handbook of learning and cognitive processes: Conditioning and behavior theory* (pp. 181–223). Hillsdale, NJ: Lawrence Erlbaum.

JAMES W. GRAU
Texas A&M University

See also: Operant Conditioning; Pavlovian Conditioning

INTEGRAL PSYCHOLOGY

The phrase "integral psychology" was first used in the 1940s by Indra Sen, a student of the Indian philosopher-sage Sri Aurobindo (1872–1950), to describe the synthesis of yoga (karma-, jnana-, and bhakti-yoga) pioneered by Aurobindo. Forty years later, in 1986, Sen published a book in India by that title, *Integral Psychology: The Psychological System of Sri Aurobindo.* On a somewhat parallel track, another student of Aurobindo, Haridas Chaudhuri, further developed an integral yoga psychology based on his teacher's evolutionary philosophy. His approach to integral psychology is explicated in his book *The Evolution of Integral Consciousness* (1977). More recently, Brant Cortright published a book entitled *Integral Psychology: Yoga, Growth, and Opening the Heart* (2007), which explores psychotherapy in the context of the Aurobindo tradition of integral yoga.

Aurobindo's integral yoga psychology consists basically of three systems: (1) the surface/outer/frontal consciousness (typically gross state), consisting of physical, vital, and mental levels of consciousness; (2) a deeper/psychic/soul system "behind" the frontal in each of its levels (inner physical, inner vital, inner mental, and innermost psychic or soul; typically subtle state); and (3) the vertical ascending/descending systems stretching both above the mind (higher mind, illumined mind, intuitive mind, overmind, supermind; including causal/nondual) and below the mind (the subconscient and inconscient)—all nested in Sat-Chit-Ananda, or pure nondual Spirit.

In addition to the Aurobindoian trajectory of yoga psychology as articulated by Sen, Chaudhuri, and Cortright (among others), another integral arc for psychology has been articulated by integral theorist Ken Wilber. Wilber's approach to psychology has revised and expanded upon the insights of the Aurobindoian school of thought. The areas of overlap, as well as the differences, between Aurobindoian and Wilberian integral psychology are many (see Vrinte, 2002). Wilber has drawn on Sri Aurobindo from the beginning of his writing career in 1973 (five years before Chaudhuri published *The Evolution of Integral Consciousness*). Although Wilber's unique approach to psychology has certain roots in Sri Aurobindo's evolutionary synthesis of spiritual practice, its branches reach into new integral skies.

Wilber's integral psychology has been the most influenced by a number of prominent psychologists, such as James Mark Baldwin, Sigmund Freud, Jean Piaget, Norman O. Brown, Abraham Maslow, and Jane Loevinger (as well as many philosophers, theorists, and researchers from dozens of disciplines). In fact, Wilber identifies the great American philosopher and psychologist James Mark Baldwin (1861–1934)—not Aurobindo—as the first integral psychologist.

In addition to drawing on essential insights from individuals from various fields, integral psychology is a true integration of the major schools of psychology: psychoanalytic, humanistic, transpersonal, cognitive, developmental, neuropsychological, cultural, evolutionary, and so forth. As a result of drawing on various psychological traditions, integral psychology emphasizes such things as nested hierarchies of multiple intelligences, developmental dysfunctions, a spectrum of defenses, and combined treatment modalities. Wilber's mature vision of an integral approach to psychology is presented in his book *Integral Psychology: Consciousness, Spirit, Psychology, Therapy* (1999). In this text, Wilber presents his AQAL model (discussed next) and takes a cross-paradigmatic approach in outlining the essential characteristics of an integral psychology. This text is well known for its charts at the end of the book that compare and contrast more than 100 developmental psychologists—West and East, ancient and modern. From this comparison, he created a master template of the full spectrum of human psychology, using each system to fill in any gaps left by the others.

The AQAL Model

One of the defining characteristics of Wilber's integral psychology is its application and use across a myriad of disciplines. In contrast, Aurobindo's approach is largely confined to yoga studies and depth psychology and does not correlate the actual psychological interrelationships between intentional, behavioral, social, and cultural dimensions (i.e., the four quadrants of the AQAL model). Currently, there are professionals in more than 50 fields drawing on the AQAL model of integral psychology to develop their own comprehensive solutions to the complex problems they face. Principles of integral psychology are being applied in environmental studies, community development, urban planning, medicine, art, business, leadership, international development, nursing, education, legal studies, feminist theory, coaching, psychiatry, criminology, future studies, health care management, religious studies, creative writing, political

analysis, mixed-methods research, gender studies, psychotherapy, and sustainability. (See the *Journal of Integral Theory and Practice* for articles that showcase these and other applications.)

As can be seen by its widespread use, integral psychology is supportive to almost any integral endeavor. After all, if you do not have a comprehensive view of psychology, it is hard to have an integral approach to anything that involves humans. Thus, integral psychology serves as a keystone to many integral efforts. At the center of Wilber's approach to integral psychology is integral theory, which he has developed during 40 years through the publication of more than 20 books (see Visser, 2003; Wilber 1999–2000).

There are five elements of integral theory: quadrants, levels, lines, states, and types. These five components, referred to by the acronym AQAL (for "all quadrants, all levels"), represent the intrinsic perspectives that occur at all scales and in all contexts of being human. By including these basic elements, an integral psychologist can be sure of covering the main dimensions of any phenomenon. There is no single ontological or epistemological priority assigned to any of these dimensions, because each aspect is seen as coarising with every other in the seamless fabric of reality in every moment.

Quadrants refer to the four basic irreducible dimension-perspectives of reality (Wilber, 1995). There is, at any given moment, always an individual and a collective aspect, and within each of these, there is also an interior and an exterior aspect. These four domains—the interior and exterior of individuals and collectives—are also described as the domains of (1) intentional ("I": individual-interior, subjective), (2) cultural ("we": collective-interior, intersubjective), (3) behavioral ("it": individual-exterior, objective), and (4) social ("its": collective-exterior, interobjective).

The remaining four elements of the AQAL model all arise as further distinctions within these four basic domains. *Levels* are another way to describe the occurrence of complexity or depth within each quadrant. For example, in the individual-exterior quadrant of behavior, we witness the physical complexity of any given individual organism. A dog is more physically complex than an amoeba and thus is located at a higher level. *Lines* of development are another way to describe the distinct capacities that develop through levels. For example, in the individual-interior quadrant are capacities or lines that develop, including cognitive, emotional, interpersonal, and moral capacities. A graphic representation of an individual's development within his or her major lines is called a psychograph. *States* are the temporary occurrence of any aspect of reality. For example, stormy weather is a state that arises in the collective-exterior quadrant of systems, whereas euphoria is a state that occurs in the individual-interior quadrant. *Types* are the variety of styles that arise in various domains. An example would be a particular kind of religious worldview, like Protestant, in the collective-interior quadrant of culture or the body type of endomorph in the individual-exterior.

As a result of the AQAL model, integral psychology is characterized by at least six main components of human psychology that need to be included in any comprehensive theory: four quadrants of behavior, intention, culture, and social systems; developmental levels or structure-stages of consciousness; developmental lines of psychology; normal and altered states of awareness (e.g., the state-stages of gross, subtle, causal, and nondual); personality and gender types; and the self or self-system.

The Self-System

The self-system has four parts: the proximate self ("I," the observing self), the distal self ("me" or "mine," the observed), the antecedent self ("I-I," the transcendental Witness), and the overall self, the amalgam of all of these selves. The proximate self is the navigator of development with the "I" of one stage becoming the "me" of the next stage. In other words, our sense of "I" is in a continual process of identifying with a new structure-stage, transcending it, and then integrating it into a higher level of psychological organization.

As the central navigator through psychological growth, the self is the locus of such important functions as identification (what is called "I"), will (or choices that are free within the constraints and limitations of its present level), defenses (which are laid down hierarchically in development), metabolism (which converts states into traits), and most important of all, integration (the self is responsible for balancing and integrating whatever elements are present). As the locus of integration, the self is responsible for balancing and integrating all of the quadrants, levels, lines, states, and types in the individual. The self-system can be understood through the metaphor of ladder, climber, and view, where the ladder represents the basic structures of consciousness, the climber is the proximate self, and the view is the perspective the "I" can take from the rung they are on. One of the more important contributions integral psychology makes is pointing out that the self at any level of development (i.e., structure-stages) can have access (temporary or stable) to any state (state-stages) (Wilber, 2006).

A defining characteristic of integral psychology is its use of integral methodological pluralism (IMP) to marshal, coordinate, and assess pertinent perspectives (Wilber, 2006). IMP has three principles: inclusion (consult multiple perspectives and methods impartially), enfoldment (prioritize the importance of findings generated from these perspectives), and enactment (recognize that phenomena are disclosed to subjects through their activity of knowing it). As a result of these commitments, integral psychology is considered to be postmetaphysical (i.e., it avoids postulating a priori structures by highlighting the perspectival

nature of enacted reality). In other words, a particular phenomenon can show itself—and in that sense, be—only within a perspective or worldspace consistent with the features of that phenomenon.

In sum, integral psychology uses a comprehensive, metaperspectival, and postdisciplinary framework for characterizing psychological phenomena, healing wounds, and resolving sociocultural problems. It is comprehensive in that it both draws upon and provides a theoretical scheme for showing the relations among a myriad of different psychological methods, including those at work in the natural and social sciences, as well as in the arts and humanities. The variety and breadth of psychology is astounding: There are currently more than 150 distinct schools of psychology, more than 70 distinct therapies, and more than 40 specializations. Anything less than an approach that takes into consideration the strengths and limits of each of these will fall short of being a truly integral psychology. It is metaperspectival because it unites, coordinates, and mutually enriches knowledge generated from at least four different major perspectives (i.e., the quadrants) and eight foundational methodological families (e.g., phenomenology, hermeneutics, empiricism, and systems theory). Integral psychology is postdisciplinary by virtue of its applicability within, between, and across disciplinary boundaries.

REFERENCES

Chaudhuri, H. (1977). *The evolution of integral consciousness.* Wheaton, IL: Quest Books.

Cortright, B. (2007). *Integral psychology: Yoga, growth, and opening the heart.* Albany: State University of New York Press.

Sen, I. (1986). *Integral psychology: The psychological system of Sri Aurobindo.* Pondicherry, India: Sri Aurobindo Ashram Trust.

Visser, F. (2003). *Ken Wilber: Thought as passion.* Albany: State University of New York Press.

Vrinte, J. (2002). *The perennial quest for a psychology with a soul: An inquiry into the relevance of Sri Aurobindo's metaphysical yoga psychology in the context of Ken Wilber's integral psychology.* Delhi, India: Motilal Banarsidass.

Wilber, K. (1995). *Sex, ecology, spirituality: The spirit of evolution.* Boston: Shambhala.

Wilber, K. (1999). *Integral psychology: Consciousness, spirit, psychology, therapy.* Boston: Shambhala.

Wilber, K. (1999–2000). *The collected works of Ken Wilber* (Vols. 1–8). Boston: Shambhala.

Wilber, K. (2006). *Integral spirituality: A startling new role for religion in the modern and postmodern world.* Boston: Shambhala.

SUGGESTED READINGS

Integral psychology. (2007). [Special issue]. *AQAL: Journal of Integral Theory and Practice, 2*(3).

Integral theory in counseling. (2007). [Special issue]. *Counseling and Values, 51*(3).

Wilber, K. (2000). Waves, streams, states and self. *Journal of Consciousness Studies, 7*(11– 12), 145–176.

SEAN ESBJÖRN-HARGENS
John F. Kennedy University, Pleasant Hill, CA

KEN WILBER
Integral Institute, Boulder, CO

INTELLECTUAL DEVELOPMENT

Intellectual development concerns how individuals develop their higher mental functions, such as understanding abstract ideas, mastering complex skills, formulating logically organized thoughts, and solving novel problems, which allow them to deal effectively with life challenges and lead successful lives. The terms *intellectual development* and *cognitive development* are often used interchangeably. However, it can be argued that the scope of intellectual development should be broader than cognitive development, as it goes beyond the development of specific cognitive structures and functions to encompass issues of the effectiveness, efficiency, and productivity of a living system trying to achieve its goals in a complex and sometimes treacherous environment. Intellectual development is clearly associated with knowledge acquisition through experience and formal instruction, yet intellectual development connotes the growth of a mind that has more pervasive, transferable power than narrowly defined knowledge and skills or expertise.

With intellectual development defined in this way, an adequate theory of it should be able to explain (1) how intellectual apparatus develops from its rudimentary form to a mature, sophisticated form; (2) what endogenous (e.g., biological-constitutional) and exogenous (e.g., nutrition or educational provision) factors contribute to its development; and (3) what causes determine intra-individual as well as interindividual variability in intellectual performances observed in everyday life. Extant theories tend to succeed in some but not all of these aspects of intellectual development.

Jean Piaget (1950) developed what is arguably the first systematic account of how intellect develops during childhood and adolescence. Piaget saw children's thinking as having its own "logic," a logic that is qualitatively different from the logic of adults: at different developmental levels, intellectual functioning has its own unique patterns or organization of thought processes. At a macro-level, intellectual development is engendered by a qualitative shift from situated sensory-motor action schemes (pre-operational) to more sophisticated, symbolic representations of the world (concrete-operational), and it is furthermore marked by a shift to more systematically organized logical thoughts that are not dependent on observable concrete dimensions (formal operational). At a micro-level, intellectual development is characterized as using two complementary modes of functioning to bootstrap a mental model of the world with adequate veracity: using existing cognitive structures to understand the world (assimilation) and changing existing cognitive structures to develop increasingly refined and differentiated mental models (accommodation). This delicate dance is choreographed in accordance with the principle of equilibration, a psychological or biological tendency to maintain or restore order and balance within itself.

Piaget's theory is often juxtaposed with that of Vygostky (1978), whose theory grants a more prominent role to social mediation (e.g., more competent adults or peers) and speech communication in developing higher mental functions (e.g., social speech becoming private speech through internalization). Both Piaget and Vygostky are seen as initiating a tradition of constructivism accounting for sources of knowing and knowledge. Although Piaget's theory gives biological maturation a prominent role in its emphasis on an invariant sequence and timing of developmental milestones, he was by and large an interactionist or constructivist, in that mental structures, representations, and operations are seen as actively constructed and maintained as adapations through the person's functional relations and transactions with the world. However, it is important to note the differences between Piaget and Vygostky. Piaget, given his focus on species-specific genetic (i.e., developmental) epistemology, stressed developmental invariance (orderly changes in cognitive apparatus for all human beings) and treated contextual variables and individual differences as relatively insignificant in shaping developmental course. Vygotsky, with his emphasis on social and cultural mediation, highlighted the contextual and individual variability of intellectual development.

Theoretical developments in the wake of Piaget and Vygotsky echo the traditions set up by these two pioneers. Neo-Piagetian theorists remain loyal to the Piagetian organismic principle and the notion of pervasive developmental changes that have a system-wide impact, while adding new features, such as how cognitive infrastructure (working memory) gives rise to a growth spurt in fashioning complex thought patterns, or how positive and negative affect-regulation gives shape to one's developmental trajectory (e.g., overassimilation or overaccommodation; Labouvie-Vief & Gonzalez, 2004). Neonativists endorse Piaget's doctrine of developmental invariance but refute his notion of the human cognitive system as being unified and domain-general. Neonativists argue that the cognitive apparatus consists of multiple cognitive systems specialized to process specific types of information, and that some of our rudimentary understandings of the world are innate, not learned (e.g., number, force, vitality, and agency). They have not only tried to garner empirical evidence from infant and early childhood research, but have also sought the evolutionary origins of these innate conceptual structures or skeletal principles (Gelman, 1991).

On the other end of the theory spectrum are those who emphasize developmental variability. These include but are not limited to adherents of differential approaches, social-situative approaches, and dynamic systems approaches.

Differential approaches. Differential approaches attempt to account for the apparent vast individual differences in intellectual development, which has been by and large ignored by Piaget and other theorists on child development. These approaches typically consider both biological-constitutional (including genetic) differences and environmental variations as sources of differences in children's development of higher mental functions. Some posit divergent developmental trajectories and pathways at the onset of six years of age due to both genetic and environmental forces (McCall, 1981). Others emphasize proximal processes or transactional experiences with specific environmental contexts, both immediate and mediated, as specifying the nature of interaction between biological predispositions or preparedness and environmental affordances, ultimately responsible for the observed developmental outcomes (Bronfenbrenner & Ceci, 1994). These approaches attempt to integrate differential and developmental theories and research in a theoretically coherent manner.

Socio-situative approaches. Vygotsky's notion of *zone of proximal development* treats intellectual development as fundamentally mediated by socializing agents. Thus, cognitive apprenticeship is indispensible for optimal intellectual development (Rogoff, 1990). Recent socio-situative approaches further posit that thought processes are so deeply influenced by specific functional contexts that it is better to think of knowledge as situated in the person-context interface than as residing in the head. Thus, Brazilian children can perform well on "street math" but do poorly on an equivalent task shaped as "school math"; professional racetrack gamblers are capable of sophisticated reasoning in their domain of expertise but do not perform superbly on standard intelligence tests. They point out the limitations of Piagetian conceptions of knowledge construction as merely a matter of symbolic representations and logical operations, without attention to its roots in action and perception.

The socio-situative approach enables a new understanding of relationships between functioning and development, and learning and development. Intellectual development used to be seen as invariant organization and reorganization of experiences and cognitive/behavioral functions over time; experience and knowledge facilitates this process but does not change its structure; learning, on the other hand, is seen as a process of the acquisition of new knowledge and skills that has little bearing on the cognitive infrastructure. Now, learning is seen an integral part of development. Integrating learning and knowledge into developmental theory entails a more functional, rather than structural, view of intellectual development; in other words, intellectual development is likely more contextual than purely organismic.

Dynamic systems approaches. Like socio-situative approaches, dynamic systems approaches have a distinct flavor of developmental contextualism, in that they treat intellectual development as situated and relational. However, instead of looking at situational experiences for answers to developmental questions, dynamic systems approaches treat the human mind as interacting with multilevel systems (biological, psychological, and socio-cultural) in engendering developmental changes that suit adaptive functions (Fischer & Bidell, 2006). Dynamic systems theorists endorse Piaget's interactionism and constructivism but refute his stage theory, which posits static, enduring cognitive structures as governing daily transactions with the environments. They also see nativism as untenable in assuming invariant, inborn cognitive principles and modules separate from dynamic, functional relations with the world. Different from differential approaches, dynamic systems theories emphasize intra-individual rather than interindividual differences across situations.

In contrast to traditional developmental theories that tend to portray development as acquiring stable, enduring, and often static cognitive structures, and dismiss variability as noise or even nuisance, dynamic systems approaches see behavioral and cognitive variability as fundamentally adaptive and psychological structures as inseparable from behavioral and functional relations with a variety of environmental challenges. For example, cognitive evolution theory of development sees development as parallel to natural variation and selection: ultimately the most effective cognitive strategy will win out, but there is no single cognitive structure calling the shots. Indeed, the more variable one's behavior, the more likely the adaptive outcomes. Treating human living systems as dynamic and forming functional relationships with multiple aspects of the world also highlights the role of "nonintellective" factors that are sensitive to environmental variations and developmentally instigative. In building complexity into the theory of intellectual development, dynamic systems approaches also face the challenge of how to develop coherent accounts of development that stay true to the principle of dynamism, yet still generate sufficient prediction power for research.

It appears that to have an account of intellectual development, not only various nature and nurture forces but also human reflective consciousness and intentionality are essential to consider. This is why using cognitive development and intellectual development interchangeably may reveal an oversight regarding proper levels of analysis. Granted that various "sub-personal" factors impenetrable to human cognition and consciousness are at work in engendering developmental changes in cognitive infrastructure, thinking, particularly of a systematic kind, is an enactive, purposive act and, as such, carries an agentic role.

One does not need to assume a dualistic position in assigning consciousness a special place in a Cartesian fashion. Human consciousness and intentionality can be "naturalized" as reflecting a tendency of human beings to exercise cognitive and metacognitive control over aspects of the environment and, indeed, over their own development (Karmiloff-Smith, 1992). Thus, to follow the tenet of ecological psychology, cognition has no intrinsic value or essence except in allowing us to keep up with the ever-changing world. At the core of intellectual development is action control, and the rest are just more and more refined tools and models, residing in the head or situated in the person-environment interface.

REFERENCES

Bronfenbrenner, U., & Ceci, S. J. (1994). Nature-nurture reconceptualized in developmental perspective: A bio-ecological model. *Psychological Review, 101*, 568–586.

Fischer, K. W., & Bidell, T. R. (2006). Dynamic development of action and thought. In W. Damon & R. M. Lerner (Eds.), *Hoboken handbook of child psychology, Vol. 1. Theoretical model of human development* (pp. 313–399). Hoboken, NJ: John Wiley & Sons.

Gelman, R. (1991). Constraining nativist inferences about cognitive capacities. In S. Carey & R. Gelman (Eds.), *The epigenesis of mind: Essays on biology and cognition* (pp. 293–322). Hillsdale, NJ: Lawrence Erlbaum.

Karmiloff-Smith, A. (1992). *Beyond modularity: A developmental perspective on cognitive science.* Cambridge, MA: MIT Press.

Labouvie-Vief, G., & Gonzalez, M. M. (2004). Dynamic integration: Affect optimization and differentiation in development. In D. Y. Dai & R. J. Sternberg (Eds.), *Motivation, emotion, and cognition: Integrative perspectives on intellectual functioning and development* (pp. 237–272). Mahwah, NJ: Lawrence Erlbaum.

McCall, R. B. (1981). Nature-nurture and the two realms of development: A proposed integration with respect to mental development. *Child Development, 52*, 1–12.

Piaget, J. (1950). *The psychology of intelligence.* London: Routledge.

Rogoff, B. (1990). *Apprenticeship in thinking: Cognitive development in social context.* New York: Oxford University Press.

Vygotsky, L. S. (1978). *Mind in society: The development of higher psychological processes.* Cambridge, MA: Harvard University Press.

SUGGESTED READINGS

Case, R. (1992). *The mind's staircase: Exploring the conceptual underpinnings of children's thought and knowledge.* Hillsdale, NJ: Lawrence Erlbaum.

Ceci, S. J. (1996). *On intelligence: A bio-ecological treatise on intellectual development* (2nd ed.). Cambridge, MA: Harvard University Press.

Siegler, R. S. (1996). *Emerging minds: The process of change in children's thinking.* New York: Oxford University Press.

DAVID YUN DAI
University at Albany, State University of New York

See also: Cognitive Development; Intelligence; Piaget's Theory

INTELLIGENCE

Intelligence is cognition comprising sensory, perceptual, associative, and relational knowledge. A concise definition of intelligence, according to Das, Naglieri, and Kirby (1994), is the ability to plan and structure one's behavior with an end in view. If the end is a social one, then it is the most parsimonious solution to a problem that will best serve the common good. Sternberg (2005) defined intelligence as a number of components that allow one to adapt, select, and shape one's environment. Gardner (1999) defined intelligence as the ability to create an effective product or offer a service that is valued in a culture; in other words, intelligence is a set of skills that make it possible for a person to solve problems in life. The challenge, however, is to devise ways of measuring intelligence by operationalizing the above concepts.

Factors and Abilities

Contemporary theories about intelligence can be divided into two classes: psychometric and cognitive types. The quantitative approach to intelligence is better reflected in psychometric theories, of which Spearman's is an early example. In contrast, cognitive theories are both qualitative and quantitative. Following Spearman and even his predecessor, Galton, A. R. Jensen (2006) is perhaps the chief advocate of general intelligence or "psychometric g" as it is described in current literature. His evidence for "g" goes beyond factor analysis and seeks validity in reaction time studies of elementary mental processes. He is poised to launch a movement for finding a "super G," or an all-inclusive general ability, picking up where Galton left off (Jensen, personal communication, March 2008).

More sophisticated statistical methods have been employed since Spearman, although these are primarily derived from factor analysis for identifying hierarchical strata of mental abilities. For example, Carroll's (1993) theory is a proposal for three such strata: Stratum I (narrow abilities); Stratum II (broad abilities); and Stratum III, a general ability—Jensen's psychometric g is in the third one. Stratum II contains Cattell's fluid (Gf) and crystallized intelligence (Gc) (Hunt, 1997).

Stratum I includes specific skills such as reading words and arithmetic knowledge. However, the usefulness of these statistical results within a diverse cultural context has been questioned because the data sets were based on North American participants who were administered familiar North American tests.

Gf and Gc is a popular way to divide intelligence. As advanced by Cattell, and later by Horn, fluid intelligence is the ability to deal with novel intellectual problems, whereas crystallized intelligence is the ability to apply learned solutions to new problems (Hunt, 1997). The problem, however, is agreeing on a standard battery for fluid and crystallized intelligence.

The psychometric approach to general intelligence has continued to advance. A recent classification of abilities has been proposed. It comprises verbal, perceptual, and image rotation abilities with general intelligence or *g* at its top. However, like all psychometric classification of intelligence, it has a common weakness. "The weakness of psychometric models is related to their strength. They stand on an impressive mathematical model of analysis of a given set of tests, without any clear stance about what the tests should be in the first place" (Hunt, personal communication, April, 2008).

Intelligence as Cognitive Processes

Intelligence as cognitive processing is a common base for cognitive theories of intelligence. Such theories also advance the idea that intelligence has multiple categories. For example, both Sternberg and Gardner view intelligence as neither a single nor biologically determined factor, but as a number of domains that represent the interaction of the individual's biological predispositions with the environment and cultural context. Das's PASS theory is a further advance in this direction (Das et al., 1994).

The theory of multiple intelligences, developed by Gardner (1999), proposes seven separate kinds of intelligences comprising linguistic, logical-mathematical, spatial, musical, bodily-kinesthetic, interpersonal, and intrapersonal domains. There have also been two recent additions: naturalistic and existential intelligence. Although these nine types of intelligence are highly popular outside the community of psychologists because of their intuitive appeal, the proposal seems to lack empirical support. One may wonder why nine should be the limit. Earl Hunt reflects the opinions of many when he remarks that the theory of multiple intelligences cannot be evaluated by the canons of science until it is made specific enough to generate measurement models. Thus, if one cannot operationalize the concept of intelligence, it cannot be evaluated.

Sternberg's triarchic theory (Sternberg, 2005) proposes three components of intelligence. The first relates to the internal world of the individual and specifies the cognitive mechanisms that result in intelligent behavior; its components are concerned with information processing. Learning how to do things (and actually doing them) is the essential characteristic of the second component of Sternberg's theory. This component is also concerned with the way people deal with novel tasks and how they develop automatic routine responses for well-practiced tasks. The third component of the theory is concerned with practical intelligence. More recently, Sternberg has expanded the three dimensions of intelligence, adding to these a measure of creativity. This revision led to his theory of successful intelligence, a theory that is still evolving.

The PASS theory of intelligence (Das et al., 1994) proposes that cognition is organized into three systems and four processes. The first system is the planning system, which involves the executive functions responsible for controlling and organizing behavior, selecting and constructing strategies, and monitoring performance. The second is the attention system, which is responsible for maintaining arousal levels and alertness and ensuring focus on relevant stimuli. The third system is an information processing system that employs simultaneous and successive processing to encode, transform, and retain information.

Simultaneous processing is engaged when the relationship between items and their integration into whole units of information is required. Examples include recognizing figures such as a triangle within a circle versus a circle within a triangle, or the difference between "he had a shower before breakfast" and "he had breakfast before a shower." Successive processing is required for organizing separate items in a sequence, for example, remembering a sequence of words or actions exactly in the order in which they had just been presented. These four processes are functions of four areas of the brain: Planning is broadly located in the front part of our brains, the frontal lobe. Attention and arousal are a function of the frontal lobe and the lower parts of the cortex, although some other parts are also involved in attention as well. Simultaneous processing and successive processing occur in the posterior region, or the back of the brain. Simultaneous processing is broadly associated with the occipital and the parietal lobes, while successive processing is associated with the frontal-temporal lobes.

The four processes of the PASS theory can be assessed in a psychometric test battery, the Das-Naglieri Cognitive Assessment System, published in 1997. These tests have been used for understanding, assessment, and intervention with regard to educational problems (mental retardation, reading disability, autism, and attention-deficit), cognitive changes in ageing, and decision making in management.

There are similarities and differences between the theory of successful intelligence including the triarchic theory and the PASS theory. Both theories have empirical support in several research studies and both have an appeal to practical problems. The theory of successful intelligence attempts to include creativity and broader issues in intelligence but only the PASS theory has a psychometric measure. In keeping with contemporary trends, brain functions are also linked to the PASS processes in some recent studies.

The significance of brain studies awaits further discussion in the broader context of the biology of intelligence. The biology of intelligence is concerned with explaining how intelligence is related to specific areas of the brain and the connections between them. A brain network for general intelligence, involving the parietal and frontal lobes, has been recently suggested by Jung and Haier (2007). Their parieto-frontal integration theory attempts to explain individual differences in reasoning. According to Earl Hunt it also holds much promise for explaining individual differences in intelligence. However, it still considers intelligence as a general ability, and it does not appear to explain how emotions impact reasoning.

Emotional Intelligence

Goleman (1995), the researcher who popularized the term *emotional intelligence*, describes it as including such things as being able to motivate oneself and persist in the face of frustrations; to control impulse and delay gratification; to regulate one's moods; and to keep distress from swamping the ability to think, empathize, and hope. More recently, however, emotional intelligence has been researched within the framework of abilities to carry out accurate reasoning about emotions and the ability to use emotions and emotional knowledge to enhance thought. A four-branch model has been advanced comprising accurate perceiving of emotion, using emotions to facilitate thought, understanding emotion, and managing emotions.

Emotional intelligence is not necessarily a part of intelligence as it is defined in Euro-American psychology. It is not like reasoning about abstract relationships, memory, and processing information. Consider compassion, a term that is commonly used in the East as a desirable emotional trait. Compassion is a blend of friendship and kindness, combined with a feeling of nonenmity. Similar adaptive emotions that promote well-being include an attitude of not expecting a return for kindness, a habit of reflection and detachment, and a belief that nothing is permanent. Such ideas are closer to Goleman's concept of emotional intelligence than the four-branch model.

Understanding Heredity and Environment

It is commonly believed that the contribution of heredity to IQ is between 50% and 80%. However, even identical twins from the same household, reared together, do not have a perfect correlation in regard to IQ, as they should for sharing identical genetic material. Even if one accepts that the correlation is .85, it is high, but not perfect. More importantly, other factors have not been considered, such as literally sharing the same womb, that may have contributed to that high correlation. When other contributing factors, such as home environment (17%) along with maternal environment were included, the estimated contribution of heredity dropped down to 48%. The implication of these previously overlooked influences is important—there is room to intervene and enhance intelligence.

One should not assume while accounting for the percentages of contribution that the effect of environmental factors is unidirectional; that is, it can only add to genetic endowment. As a matter of fact, it works both ways: It is bi-directional. The environment plays an active role in regulating gene expression, an important determinant neglected in previous studies of heritability of IQ. Researchers now know much more about the conditions that favor the expression of only specific genes and about *epigenetic* changes. Epigenetics is about regulation of various gene functions, including gene expression, that are brought about by heritable, but potentially reversible, changes that can occur due to a number of cultural and environmental influences. For example, it helps one to understand why identical (monozygotic) twins may be different concerning health and disease and also why during pregnancy the mother's diet influences epigenetic changes. There could be numerous environmental effects, including maternal behavior, that cause some epigenetic traces.

The earlier research that assigned proportions of genetic and environmental contribution to IQ—nature and nurture—ignores the fact that the influence of one on the other is bidirectional. The correct question to ask is how genes and environment work together to influence not only intelligence, but a host of other conditions associated with diseases, such as Alzheimer's. Simply put, one should accept that functions of genes are altered by environmental influences and vice versa.

Understanding Gene × Environment interactions has progressed rapidly: A handful of genes have shown significant association to intelligence and can actually be measured. Thus, it is feasible to identify those environmental factors that interact with genetic makeup. Generalist genes have been proposed, suggesting that the same genes affect several cognitive abilities and disabilities.

Behavior genetics has changed the parameters of measuring heritability but, in a broader perspective, world events have forced us to look at the sociopolitical problems of IQ testing. Consider the two important cultural factors that lower intelligence: the absence of a literacy environment and inadequate provision of health care for children even in some affluent countries. There is, then, room for intervention to enhance intelligent behavior and a reason to believe that intelligence is malleable.

In this brief presentation on intelligence a few important topics have been excluded. Social intelligence and its failures is an emergent topic; it is explained by using brain-imaging studies that focus on how humans interpret their own and other's desires, intentions, and feelings. Significant difficulties in doing so are observed in autism and schizophrenia, as shown by Chris and Uta Frith.

The identification of gifted individuals, especially in verbal and mathematical ability, has much practical value. Lubinski and Benbow (1992) have shown that based on Scholastic Aptitude Test results obtained at age 13, a majority of those individuals who were in the top 1% have become writers and scientists. This is less surprising than the fact that among them, a "tilt" toward verbal or mathematical ability at that early age has tended to produce writers or scientists, respectively.

Racial and gender differences in intelligence have not been considered in this brief article, although this is an age-old topic that remains controversial. Cross-cultural difference in intelligence is another important consideration now that many countries are concerned with multinational communities and business companies. These differences, however, matter much more in personality and motivation than in the area of academic intelligence. Finally, the Euro-American concept of intelligence needs to be broadened by considering Asian and African cultures. A list of words commonly related to intelligence in many cultures includes acquired knowledge, conscience, and a pragmatic understanding of the self and of the life situation.

REFERENCES

Carroll, J. B. (1993). *Human cognitive abilities: A survey of factor-analytical studies.* New York: Cambridge University Press.

Das, J. P., Naglieri, J. A., & Kirby, J. R. (1994). *Assessment of cognitive processes: The PASS theory of intelligence.* Boston: Allyn & Bacon.

Gardner, H. (1999). *Intelligence reframed: Multiple intelligences for the 21st century.* New York: Basis Books.

Goleman, D. (1995). *Emotional intelligence.* New York: Bantam Books.

Hunt, E. (1997). The status of the concept of intelligence. *Japanese Psychological Research, 39,* 1–11.

Jensen, A. R. (2006). *Clocking the mind: Mental chronometry and individual differences.* Oxford, UK: Elsevier.

Jung, R. E., & Haier, R. J. (2007). The parieto-frontal integration theory (P-FIT) of intelligence: Converging neuroimaging evidence. *Behavioral and Brain Sciences, 30,* 135–187.

Lubinski, D., & Benbow, C. P. (1992). Gender differences in abilities and preferences among the gifted: Implications for the math-science pipeline. *Current Directions in Psychological Science, 1,* 61–66.

Sternberg, R. J. (2005). The triarchic theory of successful intelligence. In D. P. Flanagan & P. L. Harrison (Eds.), *Contemporary intellectual assessment.* New York: Guilford Press.

SUGGESTED READINGS

Das, J. P. (2003). Theories of intelligence. In G. Goldstein & S. Beers (Eds.), *Contemporary handbook of psychological assessment.* Hoboken, NJ: John Wiley & Sons.

Hunt, E. (2004). Information processing and intelligence: Where we are and where we are going. In R. Sternberg (Ed.), *Cognition and intelligence.* Cambridge, UK: Cambridge University Press.

J. P. DAS
University of Alberta, Canada

See also: Emotional Intelligence; Intelligence Quotient; Intelligence Testing

INTELLIGENCE QUOTIENT

What is an intelligence quotient (IQ)? Intelligence is a theoretical construct with many definitions. The definition is further complicated by the belief of many that there are multiple types of intelligence. The IQ forms the most common operational definition as a cognitive and behavioral measure of global intellectual capability. Like intelligence, the IQ is best viewed as a multifaceted construct, but one that can be quantified by summing scores across tasks or subtests that comprise an intelligence test. In this way, the IQ is traditionally considered an index of Spearman's *g*, a general ability factor reflecting that how a person performs one task is likely similar to how well they score on others.

How is IQ measured? Binet and Simon introduced formal intelligence testing in 1905 with scores based on the concept that one's mental age (MA) reflected the age at which one's score on a test was average. Stern subsequently coined the term "IQ" for which the quotient was calculated as one's MA divided by one's chronological age (CA). With his 1916 revised and renamed Stanford-Binet Intelligence Test, Terman multiplied the quotient by 100 (i.e., $IQ = 100 \times MA/CA$), converting it to an integer scale (vs. decimals) with a normative average of 100. Stability of this IQ fails to extend beyond youth because continuous increases in CA (aging) exceed any further MA (ability) increases leading to declining IQs. Introducing the Wechsler-Bellevue scale in 1939, Wechsler eliminated this problem by redefining task scores relative to norms within each of several age groups. The sum of these age-scaled scores across subtests is then transformed to a deviation quotient—that is, a score on a normal (Gaussian) distribution with a mean of 100 ("Average") and a standard deviation of 15 points. This "deviation IQ" remains the modern IQ definition. Note that different tests have different standard deviations, but the Wechsler scales are the most widely used across clinical, research, educational, and vocational settings. Thus, 95% of Wechsler IQ scores in a normative population fall between 70 and 130, with scores above and below representing Very Superior and Extremely Low levels of intellectual functioning, respectively. Reporting of IQs as ranges is recommended to better reflect accompanying errors of measurement.

Several additional issues are worthy of consideration. Given potential impact on individuals and sociocultural populations, IQ testing has met with much controversy. Although both genetic and environmental factors are key contributors to IQ, observations such as the Flynn effect (rapid gains in population-level IQs over time) indicate that the malleability of IQ measurement warrants particular attention. Interpretive caution is demanded by the multifactorial and specific composition of tests, and nonintellectual (individual, situational, societal) factors influence performance.

Beyond *g*, there are multiple theoretical approaches that may be taken into account when interpreting IQ-test performance. Global IQ can establish a benchmark for profile analysis of strengths and weaknesses. Importantly, different tests may be designed for specific practical or theoretical purposes. Thus, one's choice of test, including short forms or brief instruments, should consider the representation of the underlying IQ construct being measured.

SUGGESTED READINGS

Cianciolo, A. T., & Sternberg, R. J. (2004). *Intelligence: A brief history*. Malden, MA: Blackwell.

Eysenck, H. J. (2007). *The structure and measurement of intelligence*. New Brunswick, NJ: Transaction.

Kaufman, A. S., & Lichtenberger, E. O. (2006). *Assessing adolescent and adult intelligence* (3rd ed.). Hoboken, NJ: John Wiley & Sons.

TODD A. GIRARD
Ryerson University, Toronto, Canada

INTELLIGENCE TESTING

The idea of intelligence and intellectual abilities underlying human behavior is neither new nor limited to the Western world. However, this elusive construct has received considerable attention in the last 100 years, particularly from psychologists but also from other disciplines and fields ranging from behavior genetics and cultural anthropology to education and business. Intelligence is essentially a "latent" trait describing a complex set of human characteristics that psychologists and others contend is useful in describing individual differences across many of human behaviors ranging from skill in solving mathematics problems to success in the workplace. Measuring such an abstract construct is a demanding task and draws from theory, research evidence, and professional practice needs. Furthermore, fully understanding intelligence necessitates a multidisciplinary perspective drawing from all fields in the social and biological sciences, and a mixed methods approach to researching intelligence, including longitudinal and cross-sectional, and correlational and experimental strategies.

History of Early Tests

There is good evidence that tests were first used in China several thousand years ago to assess abilities and skills for job placement. There has always been some method used to assess human characteristics such as strength and physical skills (e.g., early Greek Olympics) combined with explanations to account for the observed variability between individuals, such as artistic ability or leadership skills (e.g., the four humors proposed by Greek and Roman philosophers and physicians). In the Middle Ages various indicators were employed for assessing mental retardation, such as posing questions related to common occurrences, simple problems (arithmetic), and the names of people.

The first tests that approximated true measures of intellectual ability were those created by Sir Francis Galton. However, these tests were very specific and most often had little relevance to describing or even predicting more important human characteristics such as school success, job selection, and learning problems. These tests ranged from measuring the strength of grip to discriminating pitch differences. The birth of scientific psychology in the latter part of the nineteenth century saw a continued interest in identifying and measuring intelligence, but again with little initial success; while these tests showed differences between persons, they told researchers and clinicians little more.

At the turn of the twentieth century in France, Binet and Simon created a test that could be used to determine which school children would likely succeed in regular classes and which children would require special education services. This test departed from the Galton-type tests and asked children to respond to problems and tasks that were very much akin to the real world of the classroom, such as defining words, solving arithmetic problems, completing puzzles, and so forth. These tests were so successful that they were brought to the United States and adapted for use in American schools. When the United States entered World War I, it was necessary to screen recruits to determine their eligibility for services. The Army Alpha and Beta tests were developed for this purpose; one test using language and the other relying more on nonverbal questions for those who were less literate or not fluent in English. Again, this effort to assess and measure intelligence was deemed a success. From that point on, both intelligence and its measurement became cornerstones in psychological science and were considered to be of particular importance in various settings including schools. Today, the most common method for assessing intelligence is the well-known intelligence test following the tradition begun with the Binet tests, although there are certainly some differences among many of the currently used tests. About 1912, a method for describing intelligence test scores was developed by the German psychologist, Stern, who proposed the use of the mental quotient that later became the intelligence quotient (IQ), but now has various names reflecting a quantitative summary of a person's performance.

Past and Present Views of Intelligence and Their Influence on the Assessment of Intelligence

In order to measure intelligence and use the results for practical purposes such as selection, placement, diagnosis, prediction, and intervention planning, it is critically important that we define just what intelligence is, including its causes and relationship to other human factors. Psychologists have attempted to define intelligence with the aid of theories or by developing models that can be used to describe and explain just what intelligence is. Without such a theory or model of intelligence, it is essentially impossible to develop a test to measure it.

The earliest theories of the twentieth century considered intelligence to be either a general mental ability (referred to as "g") that subsumed a number of specific but related abilities (Charles Spearman's two-factor theory) or a number of primary and independent abilities (L. L. Thurstone's view of primary mental abilities). Tests were developed to reflect these differing theories. For example, the early Wechsler tests yielded a measure of general mental ability reflected in the Full Scale Intelligence Quotient (FSIQ) together with an estimate of Verbal and Performance (more nonverbal) IQ. Later J. P. Guilford, following the tradition begun by Thurstone, argued that intelligence comprised 120 more abilities, each of which had to be measured independently of the others.

Today, the assessment of intelligence still very much reflects these two views, or at least variations on their

themes. The well-known and often used Wechsler tests for preschool and school children through adulthood yield a FSIQ, but they also tap four important factors of intelligence including verbal comprehension, perceptual reasoning, processing speed, and working memory using various core subtests. The Woodcock-Johnson Cognitive Abilities Test, while also providing a general ability measure, is driven by the Horn-Cattell-Caroll model, which has identified a number of core intelligence factors such as comprehension-knowledge, long-term retrieval, visual-spatial thinking, auditory processing, fluid reasoning, processing speed, and short-term memory.

Other theorists have impacted how we measure and assess intelligence. For example, neo-Piagetian psychologists do not use traditional intelligence tests but rather observe children in natural settings for evidence of the kind of thought processes they use to solve problems and engage in knowledge creation. In addition, they may provide varying amounts of support to the child to facilitate problem solving. While using a test format, the Cognitive Assessment system is based on the neurological studies of Luria who proposed that intelligence should be viewed as a system reflecting attention, simultaneous and sequential processing, and planning abilities.

The Measurement of Intelligence

Contemporary intelligence tests vary in the type and number of tasks utilized, although they can be broadly grouped into novel (e.g., those few individuals have routinely experienced or seen) and more common-type tasks. Novel tasks tend to be nonverbal in nature, involving visual stimuli or materials and/or requiring a psychomotor response such as identifying target items within a complex visual array, constructing block designs, and assembling puzzle pieces to form common objects. An example of a novel task is the commonly used matrices task in which an individual is presented with a series of figures and has to identify the pattern in order to identify correctly the next figure in the series (see Figure 1).

Typically, the design of the stimuli used in novel tasks reduces or eliminates the need for an examinee to provide a verbal response. For example, the matrix task in Figure 1 uses multiple-choice format in which the examinee selects an answer from a set of figures, one of which

Figure 1. Sample matrices task. Point to the one figure from the bottom row that continues the series presented on top.

is correct. Moreover, while instructions and prompts for novel tasks are sometimes given orally, verbal requirements are further minimized within some tests through the use of gestures, modeling, or pictorial directions.

Novel tasks are generally considered to measure more fluid or innate intellectual abilities (as opposed to knowledge obtained through school or culture) and as such are often advanced as equally fair across cultures. There are a number of intelligence tests purported to be "culture-fair" or "nonverbal" measures of intelligence, such as the Universal Nonverbal Intelligence Test and the Wechsler Nonverbal Scale of Ability, that consist largely, if not entirely, of novel tasks.

The most common-type tasks included within intelligence tests typically entail a verbally presented prompt or question and require an oral response such as defining words (What is a "library"?), responding to general knowledge questions (e.g., How many inches are in a foot?), and reasoning about social behaviors (e.g., Why is it wrong to exceed the speed limit?). Success on these tasks is generally considered to be highly influenced by an individual's home, schooling, opportunities to learn, and cultural experiences. Such tasks are generally considered superior to novel tasks in predicting success in such areas as schools or jobs, likely because of the verbal demands of these activities.

Whereas most intelligence tests provide an overall score indicating general ability (e.g., FSIQ), the type and range of tasks included within each particular intelligence test is determined by the specific intelligence factors the test has been designed to measure (e.g., processing speed, working memory). Because an IQ score essentially represents a quantitative summary of an individual's success on the tasks given within a particular instrument, it is possible to obtain different IQ scores using different instruments. Such variation is typically small, however, given the strong

psychometric integrity of most contemporary intelligence tests. Differences in test items between instruments permit the clinician to select intelligence tests based on how well-suited they are for a particular purpose or area of investigation. Alternatively, a cross-battery assessment approach, in which particular tasks are selected from a number of different assessment batteries, can be used to assess a more comprehensive array of cognitive factors. This approach also allows for a more detailed examination of specific processes (e.g., perceptual reasoning, nonverbal problem solving).

The scores obtained on intelligence tests are given meaning by comparing them to the performance of large and appropriate reference groups, called *norms*. Published tests go through extensive standardization studies, in which the tests are administered to a large group of individuals who are similar to those the test is intended for in terms of such variables as age, grade, gender, race, geographic location, and parental education level. The norm groups for many tests often include thousands of individuals, such as the nearly 9,000 subjects included in the Woodcock-Johnson Cognitive Abilities Test. Included in the development and standardization of intelligence tests is the assurance that these tests provide reliable (i.e., accurate and consistent measures of a minimum of measurement error) and valid (i.e., measure intelligence and not some other factors) test scores reflecting intelligence as defined by the particular test.

In general, the scores obtained by a sufficiently large reference group fall within a normal distribution of scores (see Figure 2); with relatively few individuals (approximately 4%) obtaining high or low IQ scores, a moderate number of individuals (approximately 28%) obtaining slightly above or below average scores, and the majority of individuals achieving within the middle or average range (68%). On the tail ends of the distribution

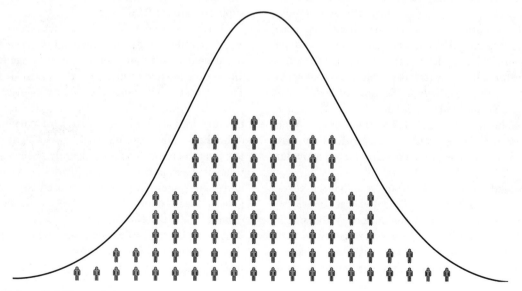

Figure 2. Distribution of intelligence test scores.

would be a very small number of individuals obtaining extremely high or extremely low IQ scores (less than 1%).

To determine an individual's performance on an intelligence test, her raw score can be compared to scores of this norm. For example, an individual obtaining an IQ score of 100 falls exactly at the middle of this distribution, indicating that she scored better than 50% of the individuals in the norm group. It is the comparison of an individual's test score(s) with the results from a group of same-aged peers that assists in identifying an individual's cognitive strengths and weaknesses and can also be used to measure an individual's progress over time.

In order for such norm-referenced comparisons to be valid, the intelligence tests must be administered in a standardized manner, in which test instructions and tasks are given and scored in a consistent manner by every individual who administers such tests (e.g., verbatim instructions, same order of task administration, standard scoring procedures, etc.). Just as it would not be accurate to compare the running time of an individual at sea level to that of an individual at 5,000 meters above sea level, it would be inappropriate to compare the test scores of a child who completes a test independently to one who is given frequent verbal prompts. The standardized administration of intelligence tests also allows a trained clinician to more readily identify behaviors that may influence test performance, such as anxious or inattentive behaviors.

Professional Test Administration and the Use of Results

The level of knowledge and skill required to successfully administer and interpret intelligence tests restricts their use to psychologists or other professionals who have extensive training and understanding in areas such as measurement principles (reliability, validity, test construction, norm groups, types of scores), human development and learning, and test administration and interpretation. These individuals are additionally members of regulatory bodies whose primary purpose is to protect the public's interest and safety, and as such are required to abide by ethical and professional guidelines established for test users and psychologists in general (e.g., the *Standards for Educational and Psychological Testing*). Such standards ensure that psychologists are responsible for selecting tests that have sound technical characteristics and for ensuring they are well-suited for the intended purpose and for a particular individual.

The information obtained from intelligence tests, including both test scores and clinical observations, can be used for a variety of purposes including diagnostic and eligibility decisions (e.g., accessing special school programs or funding for individuals with severe cognitive disabilities), intervention planning, and progress monitoring. Intelligence test scores also contribute to our understanding of intelligence and how it is expressed, what causes it, and how it impacts various aspects of human behavior. For example, intelligence tests can be used to identify impaired areas of cognitive functioning resulting from injuries to particular areas of the brain or can be used to show qualitative differences in the way we think as we age. Assessment instruments designed to measure intelligence historically and currently function not only as the products of theories of intelligence but also as the generators of such theories.

Current Controversies and Support for Intelligence and Intelligence Testing

Despite intelligence being a much-studied area of psychology, the use of intelligence tests to describe both individuals and groups has been an area of ongoing debate and discussion within public, academic, legislative, and judicial arenas. One of the more commonly raised concerns is test bias and fairness. Arguments in this area tend to be concerned with whether intelligence tests measure the same thing, and with the same degree of consistency and accuracy, in groups that differ in terms of cultural background, race, and gender. For example, whereas a quick mind might be equated with intelligence in one culture, careful reflection may be considered indicative of intelligent behavior in another culture.

Two legal challenges that are particularly illustrative of this debate are the commonly cited *Larry P. v. Riles* (1979/1984) and the *PASE v. Hannon* (1980) cases in which intelligence tests were challenged for being the sole criterion for assigning minority children to special education classes for the mentally retarded. Despite substantial similarities between the cases, the use of standardized intelligence tests in educational placement decisions for minority children was enjoined in the *Larry P.* case while supported in the *PASE* case.

Other prominent discussions concern the extent to which testing leads to beneficial treatment outcomes (treatment utility) and the role of intelligence testing in diagnosing particular disorders (e.g., Learning Disability). The argument by some is that intelligence tests do not yield the type of data necessary to develop meaningful instructional strategies or to diagnose particular learning difficulties. For example, while the identification of a learning disability has traditionally been based on a significant discrepancy between an individual's intellectual and achievement abilities, increased attention is being given instead to an individual's responsiveness to specific changes in instruction.

Although such controversy and ongoing debate reflects the complexity of measuring the latent and multifaceted human trait of intelligence, the sophistication of contemporary intelligence measures and assessment practices allows us to better evaluate cognitive factors and processes underlying a wide range of individual differences. Recent improvements in psychometrics and statistical technology have resulted in improved test construction procedures and more sound psychometric integrity of cognitive measures. In general, today's intelligence tests are among the best tools psychologists have to measure individual differences. In fact, psychological tests have been identified as being at least as good as medical tests in the types of information they provide to assist with such clinical tasks as diagnosing emotional, behavioral, and cognitive disorders, identifying treatment needs, and predicting future functioning (Meyer et al., 2001). Furthermore, ongoing research with contributions from specialty areas of psychology such as neuropsychology and pediatric psychology, together with findings from neuroimaging and cross-cultural studies, for example, have provided a compelling foundation supporting the significance of intelligence in describing and understanding individual differences.

At the same time, it is important to acknowledge there are a number of additional intellectual abilities and skills that are not presently assessed by contemporary intelligence tests. For example, Mayer and Salovey's emotional intelligence, Robert Sternberg's practical intelligence, and Howard Gardner's kinesthetic intelligence are not measured in the typical intelligence test such as the Wechsler Intelligence Scale for Children–Fourth Edition or Colin Elliot's Differential Ability Scales–Second Edition. In addition, there are a number of non-cognitive factors, including personality (e.g., extraversion, openness to experience), conative (e.g., motivation, self-efficacy), and family and cultural factors that must be considered when assessing and explaining human behavior. However, when integrated with information collected from other sources and using various methods to tap the full range of human behavior, intelligence tests can serve as a most useful tool in a comprehensive, meaningful, and professionally responsible assessment program.

SUGGESTED READINGS

Deary, I. J. (2001). *Intelligence: A very short introduction.* Oxford, UK: Oxford University Press.

Meyer, G. J., Finn, S. E., Eyde, L. D., Kay, G. G., Moreland, K. L., Dies, R. R., et al. (2001). Psychological testing and psychological assessment: A review of evidence and issues. *American Psychologist, 56,* 128–165.

Prifitera, A., Saklofske, D. H., & Weiss, L. G. (2008). *WISC-IV clinical assessment and intervention.* San Diego: Academic Press.

Sattler, J. (2008). *Assessment of children: Cognitive foundations.* San Diego: Author.

Sternberg, R. J. (2004). *International handbook of intelligence.* New York: Cambridge University Press.

DONALD H. SAKLOFSKE
MICHELLE DREFS
University of Calgary, Canada

See also: Kaufman Assessment Battery for Children; Kaufman Adolescent and Adult Intelligence Test; Stanford-Binet Intelligence Scales; Wechsler Intelligence Tests

INTERAMERICAN SOCIETY OF PSYCHOLOGY

The Interamerican Society of Psychology (www.sipysch.org), known by its acronym in Spanish, SIP, for *Sociedad Interamericana de Psicologia,* is a nonprofit, scientific, and professional organization, serving psychologists in the Americas and beyond. SIP's purposes are twofold: to foster scientific and professional collaboration among persons concerned with psychology and related fields while promoting an understanding and appreciation of cultural similarities and differences in the Americas; and to aid in the development of psychology as a science and as a profession in all of the countries of the Americas. SIP was founded on December 17, 1951, by a group of behavioral scientists who met in Mexico City while attending the meeting of the World Federation of Mental Health.

SIP's organizational affairs are conducted democratically and in accordance to its constitution. A board of directors consisting of 12 elected and appointed officers governs SIP. Elected officers include the President-Elect, the President, the Past President, the Treasurer, the Vice President for South America, the Vice President for Mexico, Central America, and the Caribbean, and the Vice President for Canada and the United States. The appointed officers are the Executive Secretaries for each of the three regions mentioned, the Secretary General, and the editor of SIP's journal. In addition, each SIP member elects a national representative from its country who serves as liaison to SIP's board of directors and the membership. The central office of SIP is housed at the University of Puerto Rico, Rio Piedras campus.

Under the auspices of SIP, the Interamerican Congress of Psychology is currently celebrated every other year in a different country of the Americas. Thirty-one Interamerican Congresses and two Regional Congresses have been convened already. Upcoming Interamerican Congresses are scheduled in Guatemala City, Guatemala (2009), and Medelin, Colombia (2011).

In 1967, SIP began the publication of its *Interamerican Journal of Psychology (IJP)*. With 41 volumes already published, *IJP* is currently published three times a year; printed copies are included in the membership fees. *IJP* reviews and publishes articles in any of SIP's four official languages: Spanish, English, Portuguese, and French. *IJP*'s current editor is Dr. Silvia Koller from Brazil. *IJP* has published several special issues, with a recent one on International Perspectives on AIDS Stigma (Vol. 41 [1], 2007). SIP's commitment to the advancement of open access to the world's scientific literature has resulted in making *IJP* available online, with restrictions.

Started in 1957, SIP has published a newsletter, currently named the *Interamerican Psychology: SIP's Bulletin*, which is edited by Marcelo Urra (Chile). SIP also publishes *iSIP*, which summarizes research projects and findings by SIP members and is edited by Carlos Zalaquett (U.S.). SIP has multiple, active working groups on specific areas of psychology, including clinical, community, economic and consumer, educational, environmental, ethics, health, history, industrial/organizational, students, and training.

Biennially, SIP grants the Interamerican Psychology Award to an English- or French-speaking psychologist and the Rogelio Diaz Guerrero Interamerican Psychology Award to a Spanish- or Portuguese-speaking psychologist. SIP also grants prizes biennially, one to an undergraduate and one to a graduate student. *IJP* confers the Jose Miguel Salazar award biennially to the best article published in the journal within the prior two years.

ANDRES J. CONSOLI
San Francisco State University

INTERESTS

Interests refer to individual difference characteristics of people that influence the types of occupations and leisure activities that they will find attractive, fulfilling, and enjoyable. Interests motivate people to pursue certain activities and not to pursue or persist with others (e.g., Crites, 1999). Lowman (2003) defined interests as follows: "Interests are relatively stable psychological characteristics of people which identify the personal evaluation (subjective attributions of 'goodness' or 'badness,' judged degree of personal fit or misfit) attached to particular groups of occupational or leisure activity clusters" (p. 478).

A Theory of People

The study of interests has one of the longest legacies in the history of psychology. For example, Strong's Vocational Interest Blank (Harmon, Hansen, Borgen, & Hammer,

1994) was developed in the 1920s; another early measure of interests by Kuder dates from the 1940s (Diamond & Zytowski, 2000). Versions of both of these measures are still in use today.

Theorists differ in the extent to which they consider interests to be part of a larger theoretical grouping of psychological characteristics (such as needs or values), but few would challenge the practical utility of interests in predicting career and avocational choices. When interests are measured with well-validated measures early in a person's life, these patterns are very likely to be similar over the lifespan of the person and be consistent with the career and vocational choices made (see Strong, 1955). Indeed, interests are also among the most predictable individual difference variables in all psychology, are markedly stable over time, and can reliably predict choices of college majors, careers, and avocational activities. One reason for this stability and predictability is suggested in research that has found a strong genetic component associated with interests (Gottfredson, 1999).

The Dimensionality of Interests

By most accounts, occupational interests can meaningfully be grouped into four to seven dimensions with two underlying metadimensions. Holland's (1997) six-factor "RIASEC" (realistic, investigative, artistic, social, enterprising, and conventional) interest model has been widely adopted in applied practice and research. Some of the characteristics that have been found, on average, to be associated with each of these factors include the following:

1. *Realistic*: Interest in things versus people; liking mechanical activities, or comfort with the physical world. Typically reserved, conservative, and change avoidant.
2. *Investigative*: Interest in ideas and abstractions; intellectual pursuits. Typically asocial, intelligent, and more motivated by ideas than people or things.
3. *Artistic*: Interest in creativity, innovation, and the arts. Usually favors change and pursuit of new ideas; not motivated by, or conforming with, the traditional or conventional.
4. *Social*: Interest in working with and helping people. Usually extraverted, interpersonally sensitive, nurturing, and open to new ideas.
5. *Enterprising*: Prefers working with people from managerial and leadership positions rather than helping roles. Usually outgoing, influential, and persuasive; counterdependent.
6. *Conventional*: Interest in data and detail. Gravitates to careers involving attention to and manipulation of data and symbols such as numbers or words. Typically reserved and change aversive; supportive of and enjoy enforcing rules.

At the individual level, people are typically assessed in terms of their top three interest factors (Lowman, 1991). This means there are 720 different combinations (e.g., Realistic, Investigative, Conventional) into which people may be classified using the RIASEC model. However, far less research has been done on the significance of differences grouped according to these various dimensions of interest than at the level of a single dimension only.

The commonly assessed six interest variables have shown marked factorial stability across a variety of measures, populations, and contexts. Interests have been demonstrated to be equally valid across racial and cultural groups (Day & Rounds, 1998). Some research (e.g., Einarsdottir & Rounds, 2000) has suggested broader factors underlying the six interest dimensions. The two commonly found and interpreted underlying dimensions are usually seen as relating to (1) concern with people as opposed to things, and (2) concern with data as opposed to ideas.

Relationship of Interests or Other Individual Difference Variables

Research has demonstrated that there are predictable, theoretically relevant overlaps between interests and other characteristics of people, particularly between interests and personality variables (Schinka, Dye, & Curtiss, 1997). For example, social and enterprising interests are usually associated with extraversion, whereas realistic and investigative interests are associated with introversion. Artistic interests are more highly correlated with openness than are realistic and conventional interests.

The relationships between interests and abilities are more complex, but at least some evidence suggests that primary abilities (such as spatial abilities, verbal reasoning, and the like) may be patterned similarly to interests (Ackerman, 1996). This finding is complicated by a large overlap between general mental ability (intelligence) and primary abilities. However, there do appear to be differences in average intelligence among persons in occupations associated with particular interest patterns; these are differences that can be interpreted consistently with interest theory (e.g., investigative occupations and interest patterns are associated with high general intelligence). More research is needed to understand the complex relationships that exist across the domains of interests and abilities. Particularly complex is the relationship of interests, abilities, and personality characteristics, both at the group and individual level (Ackerman, 1996; Lowman, 1991). It is important to assess not just interests alone, but interests in association with measures of abilities and personality, in order to maximize prediction and understanding by individuals of best-fitting career or college majors.

A Theory of Environments

Interests have been studied as characteristics of people and also as characteristics of environments (Gottfredson

& Holland, 1996; Holland, 1997). Environments can be classified in a variety of ways, but these methods typically involve assessing the modal or average interest patterns of people in a particular occupation, college major, avocational activity, corporation, or other circumscribed context. Consistently, people are grouped naturally into such clusters in a manner such that average profiles differ in ways consistent with the theory. For example, the question of goodness of fit to an occupation or college major becomes particularly important when people feel poorly matched with career or employer. Techniques have been developed to match the degree of fit between person and environment. Some evidence exists that misfit of person with career, work, or work environment is associated with negative outcomes.

In many respects, interests seem disarmingly straightforward, but their ease of understanding masks considerable complexity. Interests predict career and avocational choice very well, appear to have substantial (though not exclusive) genetic basis, and are markedly stable over time. The relationship of interests to personality variables is relatively well understood, but the relationship to abilities is less well understood.

REFERENCES

Ackerman, P. L. (1996). A theory of adult intellectual development: Process, personality, interests, and knowledge. *Intelligence, 22,* 227–257.

Crites, J. O. (1999). Operational definitions of vocational interests. In M. L. Savickas & A. R. Spokane (Eds.), *Vocational interests: Meaning, measurement, and counseling use* (pp. 163–170). Palo Alto, CA: Davies-Black Publishing.

Day, S. X., & Rounds, J. (1998). Universality of vocational interest structure among racial and ethnic minorities. *American Psychologist, 53,* 728–736.

Diamond, E. E., & Zytowski, D. G. (2000). The Kuder Occupational Interest Survey. In C. E. Watkins, Jr., & V. L. Campbell (Eds.), *Testing and assessment in counseling practice: Contemporary topics in vocational psychology* (2nd ed., pp. 263–294). Mahwah, NJ: Lawrence Erlbaum.

Gottfredson, G. D., & Holland, J. L. (1996). *Dictionary of Holland occupational codes* (3rd ed.). Odessa, FL: Psychological Assessment Resources.

Gottfredson, L. S. (1999). The nature and nurture of vocational interests. In M. L. Savickas & A. R. Spokane (Eds.), *Vocational interests: Meaning, measurement, and counseling use* (pp. 57–85). Palo Alto, CA: Davies-Black Publishing.

Harmon, L. W., Hansen, J. I. C., Borgen, F. H., & Hammer, A. L. (1994). *Strong Interest Inventory: Applications and technical guide.* Palo Alto, CA: Consulting Psychologists Press.

Holland, J. L. (1997). *Making vocational choices: A theory of vocational personalities and work environments* (3rd ed.). Odessa, FL: Psychological Assessment Resources.

Lowman, R. L. (1991). *The clinical practice of career assessment: Interests, abilities, and personality.* Washington, DC: American Psychological Association.

Lowman, R. L. (2003). Interest. In R. Fernandez-Ballesteros (Ed.), *Encyclopedia of psychological assessment* (pp. 477–481). Thousand Oaks, CA: Sage.

Schinka, J., Dye, D. A., & Curtiss, G. (1997). Correspondence between five-factor and RIASEC models of personality. *Journal of Personality Assessment, 68*, 355–386.

Strong, E. K. (1955). *Vocational interests 18 years after college.* Minneapolis: University of Minnesota Press.

SUGGESTED READING

Lowman, R. L., & Carson, A. D. (2003). Assessment of interests. In I. B. Weiner (Ed.-in-Chief), J. R. Graham & J. A. Naglieri (Eds.), *Handbook of psychology: Vol. 10. Assessment psychology* (pp. 467–485). Hoboken, NJ: John Wiley & Sons.

RODNEY L. LOWMAN
Lake Superior State University

See also: **Occupational Interests; Strong Interest Inventory; Vocational Testing**

INTERFERENCE

One of the earliest and most robust findings of experimental psychology is that two event representations in memory can compete with one another. If training on Task A precedes Task B, subsequent testing on Task B may yield impaired (i.e., proactive interference) or facilitated performance relative to control subjects who were not exposed to Task A. Conversely, subsequent testing on Task A may yield impairment (i.e., retroactive interference) or facilitation relative to control subjects who were not exposed to Task B. Such interference is commonly viewed as evidence of competition between the representations of Tasks A and B. Interference (and facilitation) has been observed across a wide variety of subjects (including humans and nonhuman species) and tasks. Much of the memory research conducted over the past century has attempted to identify relevant variables (for excellent reviews, old but still relevant, see Postman & Underwood, 1973; Underwood, 1957). The following remarks apply equally to proactive and retroactive interference (and facilitation) except where otherwise noted.

Independent Variables

The three most important variables in producing proactive and retroactive interference appear to be (1) the amount of training on each task, (2) the temporal interval between training on the two tasks and between training on each task and testing, and (3) the similarity of the two tasks,

the last of which appears central in determining whether interference or facilitation will be observed.

Not surprisingly, more extensive training on a task makes it more apt to impact performance on another task and less apt to be impacted by training on another task. The closer in time the two tasks are to one another, the more apt they are to interact, producing interference (or facilitation) on the test task. Given a fixed interval between Task A and Task B training, the retention interval can be manipulated. Unlike the effects of most other independent variables on interference, which are symmetric between the proactive and retroactive cases, lengthening the retention interval decreases retroactive interference and enhances proactive interference, presumably because a significant portion of retroactive interference depends on a recency effect, and recency effects wane with increasing retention intervals (Postman, Stark, & Fraser, 1968).

Task similarity appears to be the prime determinant of whether interference or enhancement will be observed. One of the most systematic attempts to summarize these relationships was by Osgood (1949). Although his principles were elegantly logical, research has found that only some of them are consistently supported. Let us conceptualize a task as consisting of an eliciting stimulus and an acquired response to that stimulus (e.g., in paired-associate learning, Task A eliciting stimulus = chair, response = banana; Task B eliciting stimulus = stool, response = car). Obviously, two tasks with the same eliciting stimuli and same responses are identical, reducing the Task A–Task B sequence to additional training on a single task; consequently, facilitation is anticipated and, of course, observed. Conversely, when the two eliciting stimuli are highly dissimilar and the two responses are also highly dissimilar, little interaction is expected and little is observed. The interesting cases are when the eliciting stimuli are similar and the responses are dissimilar (or incompatible), as in the above example from paired associate learning, and when the eliciting stimuli are dissimilar and the responses are similar. In the former case, interference is ordinarily observed. But in the latter case, the outcome can range from interference to facilitation, and we do not yet have a simple rule for anticipating which outcome will occur other than experience with prior similar situations.

Theoretical Mechanisms

Several different theoretical accounts have been proposed to explain interference. Available evidence suggests that no single account will suffice (which is not to suggest that all proposed mechanisms contribute equally or even at all in each case). Accounts appear to fall into one of three categories (Miller, Greco, Marlin, & Balaz, 1985; Runquist, 1975): (1) competition for a limited capacity processing system at the time of acquisition (often called "processing interference"), (2) competition between tasks for representation in long-term memory over the Task B–test retention interval, and (3) competition for retrieval and response generation at the time of testing (often called "trace interference").

Processing interference appears to take place only when the two competing tasks are trained close in time. With this type of interference, task similarity is relatively unimportant. (However, more interference can be expected if the two events use the same sensory modality than in different modalities because the limited processing capacity of organisms appears to be largely segregated by sensory modality.) The second mechanism assumes that the representations of the two task (or event) representations compete for a place in long-term memory rather than co-exist with one another. This mechanism would only be relevant when the two events are contrafactual (e.g., acquisition and extinction, or conditioning and counterconditioning). Many researchers deny that this second interference mechanism occurs at all, preferring to attribute all evidence cited in support of this mechanism to trace interference.

Trace interference has received the greatest amount of attention, and, not surprisingly, theorizing concerning it is most highly developed. The consistent finding concerning this third mechanism is that the greater the similarity between eliciting stimulus of the interfering task (including nominal, contextual, and temporal cues) and the test conditions, relative to the similarity between the eliciting stimulus of the target task and the test conditions, the greater interference will be (e.g., Bouton, 1993; Tulving & Thomson, 1973).

Generally speaking, temporal variables (i.e., processing interference) appear to have their greatest impact when the intervals separating Tasks A, B, and testing are relatively short (measured in seconds, e.g., Peterson & Peterson, 1959), whereas the impact of task similarity variables (trace interference) seems to be greatest at longer intervals (Runquist, 1975). This suggests that these variables act through fundamentally different mechanisms (Miller et al., 1985). Seemingly, most interference with short intervals separating Tasks A and B reflects competition between A and B for access to a limited capacity short-term memory. In contrast, interference with longer intervals reflects competition for retrieval and for response generation. These relationships have been well known for over 30 years. Contemporary research on interference (e.g., Matute & Pineno, 1998) has given rise to a plethora of hypothesized mechanisms, but they all appear to fall within the three families of accounts described above.

Permanence

Interference effects in principle could be due either to a potentially reversible lapse in performance (an expression failure) or an irreversible absence of information (i.e.,

failure to acquire information or loss after acquisition). Each of the three types of mechanisms could in principle yield reversible or irreversible interference. But the three types of mechanisms are commonly thought to diverge sharply in terms of the interference that they produce being reversible or irreversible. The first and second types of interference are generally viewed as resulting in an irreversible absence from memory of the target task representation. In contrast, the third type of interference is usually viewed as yielding a failure to express information that is still retained in memory.

Consistent with this view, interference observed with relatively long intervals between training on the two tasks often can be reversed without additional training on the target task. Spontaneous recovery from retroactive interference is one particularly clear case of this. Priming of one or the other of the tasks and variation in retrieval cues at test are other often successful means of obtaining recovery from interference; however, these demonstrations are less compelling evidence of a lapse rather than an absence of information because they potentially tap into different representations of the target task than that which was assessed (and found wanting) originally.

An Applied Example

Interference theory is applicable to many practical situations. For example, a contemporary (and controversial) application of interference theory is provided by demonstrations that eyewitness accounts of events are subject to retroactive interference, often originating with leading questions from attorneys. One view is that the representation of the original (target) event is irreversibly altered by the (subsequent) interfering event (in our terminology, mechanism type 2; e.g., Loftus, 1975). In contrast, an alternative view is that the representation of the original event is still present in memory but is less readily retrieved because of the interfering event (trace interference; e.g., McCloskey & Zaragoza, 1985).

REFERENCES

Bouton, M. E. (1993). Context, time, and memory retrieval in the interference paradigms of Pavlovian learning. *Psychological Bulletin, 114,* 80–99.

Loftus, E. F. (1975). Leading questions and the eyewitness report. *Cognitive Psychology, 7,* 560–572.

Matute, H., & Pineno, O. (1998). Stimulus competition in the absence of compound conditioning. *Animal Learning & Behavior, 26,* 3–14.

McCloskey, M., & Zaragoza, M. (1985). Misleading postevent information and memory for events: Arguments and evidence against memory impairment hypotheses. *Journal of Experimental Psychology: General, 114,* 3–18.

Miller, R. R., Greco, C., Marlin, N. A., & Balaz, M. A. (1985). Retroactive interference in rats: Independent effects of time and similarity of the interfering event with respect to acquisition. *Quarterly Journal of Experimental Psychology, 37B*, 81–100.

Osgood, C. E. (1949). The similarity paradox in human learning: A resolution. *Psychological Review, 56*, 132–143.

Peterson, L., & Peterson, M. J. (1959). Short-term retention of individual verbal items. *Journal of Experimental Psychology, 58*, 193–198.

Postman, L., Stark, K., & Fraser, J. (1968). Temporal changes in interference. *Journal of Verbal Learning and Verbal Behavior, 7*, 672–694.

Postman, L., & Underwood, B. J. (1973). Critical issues in interference theory. *Memory & Cognition, 1*, 19–40.

Runquist, W. N. (1975). Interference among memory traces. *Memory & Cognition, 3*, 143–159.

Tulving, E., & Thomson, D. M. (1973). Encoding specificity and retrieval processes in episodic memory. *Psychological Review, 80*, 352–373.

Underwood, B. J. (1957). Interference and forgetting. *Psychological Review, 64*, 49–60.

RALPH I. MILLER
State University of New York at Binghamton

INTERMITTENT EXPLOSIVE DISORDER

Intermittent explosive disorder (IED) is a psychiatric diagnosis used to identify individuals who are repeatedly unable to resist angry and aggressive impulses and, as a result, engage in recurrent acts of aggression. As such, IED is the only adult psychiatric disorder for which impulsive aggression is pathognomonic.

History of IED

The diagnostic criteria for IED have undergone several revisions since IED was first classified as a mental disorder in the third version of the *Diagnostic and Statistical Manual of Mental Disorders* (DSM-III) in 1980. In the DSM-III, IED was described as the commission of aggressive acts that resulted in serious assault or property destruction and in which the acts were disproportionate to any provocation. The DSM-III criteria excluded individuals who met criteria for antisocial personality disorder and required that individuals with IED demonstrate periods of non-aggressive behavior between major aggressive outbursts. When the DSM was revised in 1987 (DSM-III revised edition), borderline personality disorder was added as an exclusionary diagnosis.

The diagnostic criteria for IED were again modified in 1994 with the publication of the fourth edition of the DSM (DSM-IV). The earlier criterion excluding chronically aggressive individuals was omitted, as it was shown that impulsively aggressive individuals are often irritable and mildly aggressive between major assaultive episodes. Furthermore, the criterion excluding individuals with comorbid antisocial or borderline personality disorder was softened. Specifically, the DSM-IV criteria for IED (American Psychiatric Association [APA], 2000) require that (1) there are several discrete episodes of failure to resist aggressive impulses that result in serious assaultive acts or destruction of property, (2) the degree of aggressiveness expressed during the episodes is grossly out of proportion to any precipitating psychosocial stressors, and (3) the aggressive episodes are not better accounted for by another mental disorder (e.g., antisocial personality disorder, borderline personality disorder, a psychotic disorder, a manic episode, conduct disorder, or attention-deficit/hyperactivity disorder) and are not due to the direct physiological effects of a substance (e.g., a drug of abuse, a medication) or a general medical condition (e.g., head trauma, dementia of the Alzheimer's type) (p. 667).

Despite the improvements made by the DSM-IV IED diagnosis, it was criticized for, among other things, being simultaneously too vague and too restrictive with regard to the amount and intensity of aggressive behavior. For example, verbal aggression (e.g., screaming, making threats) was not sufficient to meet the aggression criteria for IED. However, individuals who express anger through frequent verbal aggression show the same deficits and level of impairment as individuals with IED (McCloskey, Lee, Berman, Noblett, & Coccaro, 2008). Concerns about the IED diagnostic criteria led to alternate "research" IED criteria that defined pathological aggression as frequent (at least twice weekly) acts of verbal aggression, or less frequent (at least three times yearly) acts of physical aggression (Coccaro, 2003). It is noteworthy that the most recent text revision of the DSM-IV (APA, 2000) now identifies "verbally threatening to physically assault another individual" (p. 663) as an assaultive act.

Prevalence and Course

Although it is described as "rare" in the DSM-IV, recent findings from multiple epidemiological studies show lifetime prevalence rates of 4–7% for IED (Kessler et al., 2006; Ortega, Canino, & Alegria, 2008). Approximately 60% of individuals with IED are male (Coccaro, Posternak, & Zimmerman, 2005; Kessler et al., 2006). The typical age of onset for IED is adolescence, and it may first appear earlier in men than in women (Coccaro, Posternak, & Zimmerman, 2005; Kessler et al., 2006). The disorder takes a chronic, waxing and waning course, lasting on average between 12 and 20 years (Kessler et al., 2006; McElroy, Soutullo, Beckman, Taylor, & Keck, 1998).

Phenomenology

Approximately three-quarters of individuals with IED engage in both physical aggression (assault, property destruction) and frequent verbal aggression. Individuals with IED report engaging, on the average, in 55 acts of lifetime physical aggression resulting in approximately $1,600 in property damage. Furthermore, two to three of the physically aggressive acts require medical attention (Kessler et al., 2006).

Aggressive outbursts in IED typically have a rapid onset. They may occur without a recognizable prodromal period, and they are often experienced by IED patients as "going from 0 to 100." However, chronic irritability and rumination about perceived slights, of which the individual with IED may or may not be fully aware, are also common. Aggressive outbursts are usually short-lived, typically lasting less than 30 minutes (McElroy, Soutullo, Beckman, Taylor, & Keck, 1998). The type of aggression expressed ranges from verbal snapping and arguing to threats, property damage, and physical assault. Most aggressive outbursts are directed toward a close intimate or associate, although aggression towards strangers (e.g., road rage) is not uncommon. The aggressive outburst is usually preceded by a minor provocation to which the individual overresponds. Individuals with IED typically have more frequent verbal and nondestructive property assault in between the less frequent acts of physical assault and/or property destruction (Coccaro, 2003; McElroy, Soutullo, Beckman, Taylor, & Keck, 1998).

Aggressive episodes are associated with substantial distress, troubled relationships, occupational difficulty, and legal or financial problems (McElroy, Soutullo, Beckman, Taylor, & Keck, 1998). Consequently, individuals with IED are more impaired in terms of overall functioning and report a lower level of life satisfaction than healthy volunteers or psychiatric controls (McCloskey, Berman, Noblett, & Coccaro, 2006; McCloskey, Lee, Berman, Noblett, & Coccaro, 2008).

Comorbidity

Approximately 75–80% of individuals with IED also meet criteria for another psychological disorder. Depressive disorders, substance-use disorders, and anxiety disorders all show significant comorbidities with IED (Coccaro, Posternak, & Zimmerman, 2005; Kessler et al., 2006; Ortega, Canino, & Alegria, 2008). This has led some to suggest that IED is a nonspecific symptom of other disorders. However, age-of-onset analyses show that the diagnosis of IED precedes the development of most other disorders, including depressive and substance-use disorders (Coccaro, Posternak, & Zimmerman, 2005). There is also significant comorbidity between IED and personality disorders. Over 30% of general psychiatric outpatients with IED also meet criteria for a personality disorder (Coccaro, Posternak, & Zimmerman, 2005). Other studies suggest that the majority of IED patients meet criteria for a personality disorder.

Biology

Consistent with overall aggression research, there is evidence that IED is associated with impaired serotonin (5-HT) functioning. Individuals with IED show reduced levels of platelet 5-HT (Goveas, Csernansky, & Coccaro, 2004). Furthermore, relative to healthy volunteers, IED subjects demonstrate a diminished hormonal (prolactin) response and reduced frontal cortex activity when receiving a 5-HT agonist (New, Buchsbaum et al., 2004; New, Trestman et al., 2004). Individuals with IED may also have altered patterns of neural activation for tasks that involve processing anger. A functional Magnetic Resonance Imaging study demonstrated that IED subjects, compared to healthy volunteers, showed increased amygdala activation and reduced prefrontal activation when looking at angry faces (Coccaro, McCloskey, Fitzgerald, & Phan, 2007). This deficit was specific to angry faces and was not present when looking at other emotional expressions (e.g., sadness, fear, happiness).

Treatment

Although many interventions both biological and psychological have been used to treat anger and aggression with varying degrees of success, little research has examined the efficacy of interventions for IED. A randomized clinical trial found that, in contrast to placebo, the selective 5-HT reuptake inhibitor fluoxetine decreased aggression and irritability among patients with IED (Coccaro & Kavoussi, 1997). Another placebo-controlled study of IED involving the GABA agonist divalproex reported mixed results, with only a subset of IED subjects (those with a comorbid Cluster B personality disorder) showing decreased aggression in response to divalproex (Hollander et al., 2003).

In terms of psychotherapy, an early study comparing IED and non-IED aggressive drivers who received a brief (four 90-minute sessions) cognitive behavioral therapy (CBT) found that IED subjects tended to be less responsive to treatment (Galovski & Blanchard, 2002). However, a recent psychotherapy outcome study comparing a 12-week, multicomponent CBT to a wait-list control group found that CBT reduced aggression, anger, hostile thinking, and depressive symptoms, while simultaneously improving anger control and quality of life (McCloskey, Noblett, Deffenbacher, Gollan, & Coccaro, in press). The treatment effects were maintained at 3-month follow-up, providing initial support for the efficacy of CBT in the treatment of IED.

IED is a psychiatric disorder characterized by recurrent episodes of angry, aggressive behavior disproportionate to the provocation. IED has a high prevalence, early onset, and long-standing time course, and it is associated with high levels of psychiatric comorbidity and significant impairment. Diagnostic concerns have, in part, limited research on IED; however, the expanding biological and psychosocial profiles of IED have contributed to the development of potentially efficacious pharmacological and psychotherapeutic interventions, especially serotonergic agonists and cognitive behavioral therapies.

REFERENCES

American Psychiatric Association. (2000). *Diagnostic and statistical manual of mental disorders* (4th ed., text rev.). Washington, DC: Author.

Coccaro, E. F., & Kavoussi, R. J. (1997). Fluoxetine and impulsive aggressive behavior in personality-disordered subjects. *Archives of General Psychiatry, 54*(12), 1081–1088.

Coccaro, E. F., McCloskey, M. S., Fitzgerald, D. A., & Phan, K. L. (2007). Amygdala and orbitofrontal reactivity to social threat in individuals with impulsive aggression. *Biological Psychiatry, 62*(2), 168–178.

Coccaro, E. F., Posternak, M. A., & Zimmerman, M. (2005). Prevalence and features of intermittent explosive disorder in a clinical setting. *Journal of Clinical Psychiatry, 66*(10), 1221–1227.

Galovski, T., & Blanchard, E. B. (2002). The effectiveness of a brief psychological intervention on court-referred and self-referred aggressive drivers. *Behavioral Research and Therapy, 40*(12), 1385–1402.

Goveas, J. S., Csernansky, J. G., & Coccaro, E. F. (2004). Platelet serotonin content correlates inversely with life history of aggression in personality-disordered subjects. *Psychiatry Research, 126*(1), 23–32.

Hollander, E., Tracy, K. A., Swann, A. C., Coccaro, E. F., McElroy, S. L., Wozniak, P., et al. (2003). Divalproex in the treatment of impulsive aggression: efficacy in cluster B personality disorders. *Neuropsychopharmacology, 28*(6), 1186–1197.

McCloskey, M. S., Berman, M. E., Noblett, K. L., & Coccaro, E. F. (2006). Intermittent explosive disorder-integrated research diagnostic criteria: Convergent and discriminant validity. *Journal of Psychiatric Research, 40*(3), 231 242.

McCloskey, M. S., Lee, R., Berman, M. E., Noblett, K. L., & Coccaro, E. F. (2008). The relationship between impulsive verbal aggression and intermittent explosive disorder. *Aggressive Behavior, 34*(1), 51–60.

McElroy, S. L., Soutullo, C. A., Beckman, D. A., Taylor, P., Jr., & Keck, P. E. Jr., (1998). DSM-IV intermittent explosive disorder: A report of 27 cases. *The Journal of Clinical Psychiatry, 59*(4), 203–210; quiz 211.

New, A. S., Buchsbaum, M. S., Hazlett, E. A., Goodman, M., Koenigsberg, H. W., Lo, J., et al. (2004). Fluoxetine increases relative metabolic rate in prefrontal cortex in impulsive aggression. *Psychopharmacology (Berl), 176*(3–4), 451–458.

New, A. S., Trestman, R. F., Mitropoulou, V., Goodman, M., Koenigsberg, H. H., Silverman, J., et al. (2004). Low prolactin response to fenfluramine in impulsive aggression. *Journal of Psychiatric Research, 38*(3), 223–230.

Ortega, A. N., Canino, G., & Alegria, M. (2008). Lifetime and 12-month intermittent explosive disorder in Latinos. *American Journal of Orthopsychiatry, 78*(1), 133–139.

SUGGESTED READINGS

Coccaro, E. F. (2003). Intermittent explosive disorder. In E. F. Coccaro (Ed.), *Aggression: Psychiatric Assessment and Treatment* (pp. 149–199). New York: Marcel Dekker.

Kessler, R. C., Coccaro, E. F., Fava, M., Jaeger, S., Jin, R., & Walters, E. (2006). The prevalence and correlates of DSM-IV intermittent explosive disorder in the National Comorbidity Survey Replication. *Archives of General Psychiatry, 63*(6), 669–678.

McCloskey, M. S., Noblett, K. L., Deffenbacher, J. L., Gollan, J. K., & Coccaro, E. F. (In press). Cognitive-behavioral therapy for Intermittent Explosive Disorder: A pilot randomized clinical trial. *Journal of Consulting and Clinical Psychology.*

MICHAEL MCCLOSKEY
KURT L. NOBLETT
EDWARD J. HINES
EMIL R. COCCARO
University of Chicago

See also: Anger; Self-Control

INTERNAL CONSISTENCY (See Alpha Coefficient)

INTERNATIONAL ASSOCIATION OF APPLIED PSYCHOLOGY

The International Association of Applied Psychology (IAAP) was founded in 1920 to advance knowledge about applied psychology, and it is the oldest of the international psychology member associations. The International Union of Psychological Science (IUPsyS) is older, founded in 1889, but it is an international organization of psychological societies. The IAAP is a member organization with over 3,300 individual members from more than 80 countries. In order to sustain an international membership, the organization's dues structure allows for reduced and subsidized dues for individuals from developing countries and those who for other reasons cannot afford the standard dues.

Sixteen divisions provide homes for member interests. These divisions are (1) Work and Organizational Psychology, (2) Psychological Assessment and Evaluation; (3) Psychological and National Development; (4) Environmental Psychology; (5) Educational, Instructional and School Psychology; (6) Clinical and Community Psychology; (7) Applied Gerontology; (8) Health Psychology; (9) Economic Psychology; (10) Psychology and the Law; (11) Political Psychology; (12) Sport Psychology; (13) Traffic and Transportation Psychology; (14) Applied Cognitive Psychology; (15) Psychology Students; and (16) Counseling Psychology.

The organization is governed by a board of directors consisting of the six officers of the association (president, past-president, president-elect, secretary-general, treasurer, and communication officer), the presidents of the sixteen divisions, and 24 to 45 members-at-large. The IAAP sponsors or cosponsors an International Congress of Psychology every four years. Its most recent congresses took place in Kyoto in 1990, Madrid in 1994, San Francisco in 1998, Singapore in 2002, and Athens in 2006. The 2010 meeting will be in Melbourne, Australia. IAAP alternates on a two-year cycle with the IUPsyS in holding international congresses. The most recent IUPsyS congresses were held in Brussels in 1992, Montreal in 1996, Stockholm in 2000, Beijing in 2004, and Berlin in 2008. The IAAP Board of Directors meets every two years at either its own or the IUPsyS congress.

The IAAP publishes a journal and a newsletter. The quarterly journal is titled *Applied Psychology: An International Review*. Three types of articles are published: journal articles describe research findings or theoretical developments on a specific issue; lead articles are reviews of research developments at critical junctures, and they are often supplemented with peer commentaries; and "International Replication Notes" are replication studies in new cultural contexts. The journal emphasizes applied research in different national and cultural contexts. Special issues are occasionally published. The IAAP Newsletter publishes news of the organization from the editor, the president, the board, and divisions and also short articles on relevant topics. Both publications are offered to members online as well as in paper formats.

One of the more significant activities of the IAAP in recent years has been a collaboration with the IUPsyS and the International Association for Cross-Cultural Psychology (IACCP) to develop a Universal Declaration of Ethical Principles for Psychologists. This declaration has as its purpose establishing a common moral framework and generic ethical principles for psychological organizations worldwide. Further information about the declaration and about other IAAP activities can be found on its web site, http://www.iaapsy.org.

LYNN P. REHM
University of Houston

INTERNATIONAL COUNCIL OF PSYCHOLOGISTS

The International Council of Psychologists (ICP), comprised of members from over 35 countries, has been active since 1941. The organization's mission is to strengthen international bonds and improve communication among psychologists throughout the world. Regular Members are psychologists with membership in a national psychological association affiliated with the International Union of Psychological Science (IUPsyS) who have been working in psychology for at least two years. Associate Members lack two years of qualifying experience, or, in countries in which the national psychological association recognizes a higher and lower level of experience, qualify at the lower level. Professional Affiliates are active in a profession allied to psychology. Student Affiliates are working toward a degree in psychology or a related field.

ICP publishes the International Psychologist quarterly, maintains a webpage at www.icpweb.org, and holds annual conferences. ICP also serves as a recognized nongovernmental organization (NGO) in consultative status with the United Nations (UN). Since 1981, designated members represent ICP in supporting resolutions in the UN General Assembly and at conferences sponsored by the UN Council.

The Council began on November 25, 1941, as the National Council of Women Psychologists (NCWP), to assist U.S. war efforts. Rather than disbanding after World War II, the group switched its focus to improving international relations. In 1946, the name changed to the International Council of Women Psychologists (ICWP) when women psychologists from other countries joined. In 1960, men were admitted, and the name was changed to the International Council of Psychologists. ICP was incorporated under this name in 1962 and has remained a constant force since then, committed to using psychology to develop a healthy society and fostering goodwill among psychologists around the world. During its early years, ICP annual meetings were held in conjunction with the American Psychological Association (APA). As international membership expanded, conferences moved to locations around the world. The first conference outside North America was in Israel during 1970. Since 2000, conference sites have included Russia, Greece, Brazil, Canada, the Philippines, the United Kingdom, Mexico, Australia, Italy, and China.

Along with its conference sites becoming more international, the ICP leadership, which was almost exclusively North American up through the 1960s, became representative of the international community. Presidents in recent years have come from Italy, Australia, the United Kingdom, Malaysia, Israel, Austria, the Philippines, Mexico, and France. The ICP Board of Directors is similarly international. The offices of president, vice-president, secretary, and treasurer were used until 1965, at which time vice-president was changed to president-elect. From 1942–1975, presidents served a term of 2 years. Since 1975, they serve 1 year preceded by a year as president-elect and followed by a year as past-president. A 12-member Board of Directors, elected for staggered 3-year terms, assists in governing the organization.

Each year, four new members are elected. Further organizational structure is provided by committees.

The ICP Bylaws, originally based on those of APA, are revised periodically (most recently in 2008) and approved by the membership as a whole. Special interest groups within ICP focus on specific areas of psychology to implement the mission by working with agencies and governments to use psychology to educate all people regarding human rights, well-being, and developing a healthier world.

SHERRI MCCARTHY
Northern Arizona University–Yuma

INTERNATIONAL PSYCHOLOGY

Although modern psychology is often said to have originated with Wilhelm Wundt's laboratory, it actually arose in several Western countries at nearly the same time (i.e., Germany, United Kingdom, United States). Because of these multiple beginnings, psychology was an international discipline from its inception (Brock, 2006; Stevens & Gielen, 2007). Following World War II, with the emigration of prominent psychologists from Germany and Austria and the growth of the American Psychological Association (APA), psychology in the United States advanced rapidly and came to dominate the discipline. Given its preeminence, psychology in the United States became increasingly monocultural and monolingual as well as less responsive to scientific and applied innovations occurring elsewhere in the world (Brock, 2006; David & Buchanan, 2003; Stevens & Gielen, 2007). As a consequence of the insularity and hegemony of U.S. psychology, efforts were undertaken in many countries to develop psychologies of greater relevance to local culture and needs (i.e., indigenization). The internationalization of psychology is also an outgrowth of the broader process of globalization, which has expanded and accelerated the worldwide exchange of information and dialogue among diverse peoples.

International psychology has been described as an emerging branch of psychology with a mission " ... to increase the frequency, broaden the scope, and enhance the meaningfulness of communication and collaboration among psychologists and psychology students with shared interests from diverse countries and cultures" (Stevens & Gielen, 2007, p. 7). International psychology nurtures such communication and collaboration through scholarship, advocacy, education, and networking. As an orientation and process, international psychology encourages multidisciplinary and integrative theorizing, research, applied practice, and pedagogy as well as values the development

of a global consciousness and sense of social responsibility that is tempered by principled ethical reasoning given divergent worldviews. As a substantive domain, international psychology contributes to a science-informed understanding and resolution of pressing concerns that are situated in culture, economics, history, politics, and religion. The scope of international psychology cuts across traditional fields and includes such foci as intergroup conflict and peace building, societal transformation and nation building, environmental degradation and preservation, risks for and prevention of physical and mental illness, and the struggles of at-risk groups (e.g., women, children, migrants and refugees) (Stevens & Gielen, 2007; Stevens & Wedding, 2004).

The term *international psychology* is often used synonymously with global psychology and cross-cultural psychology; although these terms overlap, they possess important distinctions (Stevens & Gielen, 2007; Stevens & Wedding, 2004). Global psychology typically refers to the investigation of psychosocial and sociocultural phenomena from a worldwide perspective, such as evolving gender roles, family systems, and child-rearing practices. By contrast, international psychology not only encompasses aspects of psychological science that may or may not have attained a global footing, but also avoids implying paradigmatic universality which has been severely criticized (Brock, 2006; Stevens & Wedding, 2004). Cross-cultural psychology subsumes the comparative study of behavior and mental processes in different cultures, that is, the identification of culture-specific differentiation as well as patterns of functioning across cultures. Thus, cross-cultural psychology is one element of the broader field of international psychology.

Within psychology, current international trends that are occurring mainly in the industrial and developing worlds, include the sustained growth, specialization, and feminization of psychology; regional revitalization and expansion of the discipline; and the emergence of contextually sensitive paradigms (Stevens & Gielen, 2007; Stevens & Wedding, 2004). The number of psychologists, psychology students, and degree programs in psychology at state and private universities has proliferated. The increased specialization of psychology is revealed by newly formed psychological organizations and discrete sections within established organizations; advanced training programs offered by universities, institutes, and psychological organizations; and the publication of psychological journals and special issues of journals that emphasize disciplinary subfields. Specialization typically reflects the societal needs and goals of a particular country (e.g., economic development, public health), and it is enhanced by access to the Internet. Women have come to dominate psychology, especially in Europe, Latin America, and North America, but also in countries with traditional gender roles, where they constitute the majority of psychologists and undergraduate students in psychology. Female psychologists often work in social service settings (e.g., clinics, schools), whereas male psychologists tend to hold positions in academia, business and industry, and administration; female psychologists are also more likely to be employed part-time and paid lower wages. Due to national and regional economic growth and political stability, psychology is again a dynamic science and profession in Europe and is gaining prominence and influence in East and South Asia. Finally, psychologists worldwide have recognized that the theories, research methods and findings, and applied practices that are situated in the norms and values of Western psychology do not always fit cross-culturally. Consequently, these psychologists have sought to develop indigenous psychologies and other alternatives (e.g., multiculturalism) to the mainstream, reductionistic paradigm. Notable centers of indigenous psychology can be found in Mexico, the Philippines, South Korea, and West Africa.

The internationalization of psychology has made significant inroads in psychological theory, research methodology, applied practice, the psychology curriculum, and professional ethics (Pawlik & d'Ydewalle, 2006; Pawlik & Rosenzweig, 2000; Stevens & Gielen, 2007). There is rekindled interest in conceptual models that can complement the linear, causal tradition. These models stress the primacy of meaning, social construction of reality, and normative description (e.g., Vygotsky). Qualitative research methods have been adapted from allied social sciences to capture psychological phenomena-in-context. Such methods emphasize the unfolding of meaning via interaction, reality as internally derived, and research as value-fused (e.g., discourse analysis), and they are used as a springboard for quantitative inquiry. Clinical practice illustrates the fusion of non-Western and mainstream psychotherapies. These blended innovations address the cultural dimensions of individualism-collectivism, power distance, uncertainty avoidance, and time orientation (e.g., Zikyr Allah in Pakistan) and are designed to improve both individual well-being and sociocultural integration.

Macro-level interventions bring interdisciplinary and multilevel remedies to bear on widespread social problems, and integrate policy development, community empowerment, and group work. Such interventions are systems-based and target government and grassroots leaders and institutions (e.g., integration of former child soldiers into Congolese society). The evolving psychological curriculum is best exemplified by the European Diploma in Psychology (EuroPsy), which is comparable to a master's degree in the United States and requires three years of undergraduate study, a two-year post-graduate certificate, and one year of supervised practice. This standardized curriculum gives diploma holders identical qualifications for licensure and ensures their professional mobility within the European Union (EU). Although many nations have adopted the APA's *Ethical Principles and Code of Conduct*, the European Federation of Psychologists' Associations has crafted a metacode that delineates a common set of standards for psychologists practicing within the EU. The *Universal Declaration of Ethical Principles for Psychologists* was adopted in 2008 by the International Union of Psychological Science (IUPsyS) and International Association of Applied Psychology (IAAP) as a moral framework to guide the development of national codes of ethics. The *Universal Declaration* articulates principles and values shared by the international psychology community. A number of countries do not have laws that regulate the practice of psychology (e.g., Japan, Kuwait, Russia, United Kingdom), although several are pursuing such legislation (e.g., the Philippines).

There are three major international psychological organizations: the IUPsyS, the IAAP, and the International Council of Psychologists (ICP) (David & Buchanan, 2003; Stevens & Gielen, 2007; Stevens & Wedding, 2004). The IUPsyS was founded in 1951 and comprises representatives from the national psychological organizations of 72 countries. The IUPsyS fosters the global development and exchange of ideas and data, and it forms networks among national and international organizations on matters of shared interest. The IAAP was launched in 1920, is the oldest international psychological association, and has more than 3,300 members from over 80 countries. Its goals are worldwide dialogue between psychologists who teach, conduct research, and practice in the various fields of applied psychology. The ICP was established in 1941, with members from over 35 countries. The mission of the ICP is to advance scientific psychology and its global application. In addition to these international organizations, the Division of International Psychology of the APA, which was formed in 1997 and has approximately 1,000 members worldwide, seeks to develop a psychological science and practice that is contextually informed, culturally inclusive, and promotes global perspectives.

Listed below are selected general resources on international psychology:

Conversations with International Psychologists (Gielen, in press) contains interviews with twenty psychologists who have advanced the internationalization of psychological science and practice.

Psychology Concepts: An International Historical Perspective (Pawlik & d'Ydewalle, 2006) unravels the evolving contents and functions of psychological concepts from cross-cultural and historical perspectives.

International Handbook of Psychology (Pawlik & Rosenzweig, 2000) reviews contemporary knowledge in psychological science and practice from an international perspective.

Toward a Global Psychology: Theory, Research, Interventions, and Pedagogy (Stevens & Gielen, 2007) presents the conceptual, methodological, and strategic knowledge relevant to international research, practice, and training.

Handbook of International Psychology (Stevens & Wedding, 2004) surveys the history and scope, education and training, and future challenges of 27 national psychologies in 9 distinct regions across the globe.

Psychology: IUPsyS Global Resource (Wedding & Stevens, 2009) is a cumulative reference tool that contains archival records, bibliographies, directories, annotated listings, surveys, and articles from around the world.

REFERENCES

Brock, A. (2006). *Internationalizing the history of psychology*. New York: New York University Press.

David, H. P., & Buchanan, J. (2003). International psychology. In D. K. Freedheim (Ed.), *Handbook of psychology: History of psychology* (Vol. 1, pp. 509–533). Hoboken, NJ: John Wiley & Sons.

Gielen, U. P. (Ed.). (in press). *Conversations with international psychologists*. Greenwich, CT: Information Age.

Pawlik, K., & d'Ydewalle, G. (Eds.). (2006). *Psychology concepts: An international historical perspective*. Hove, UK: Psychology Press.

Pawlik, K., & Rosenzweig, M. R. (Eds.). (2000). *International handbook of psychology*. Thousand Oaks, CA: Sage.

Stevens, M. J., & Gielen, U. P. (Eds.). (2007). *Toward a global psychology: Theory, research, interventions, and pedagogy*. Mahwah, NJ: Lawrence Erlbaum.

Stevens, M. J., & Wedding, D. (Eds.). (2004). *Handbook of international psychology*. New York: Brunner-Routledge.

Wedding, D., & Stevens, M. J. (Eds.). (2009). *Psychology: IUPsyS global resource* [CD-ROM] (10th ed.). Hove, UK: Psychology Press.

MICHAEL J. STEVENS
Illinois State University

UWE P. GIELEN
St. Francis College, Brooklyn, NY

INTERNATIONAL SOCIETY OF CLINICAL PSYCHOLOGY

The International Society of Clinical Psychology (ISCP) was founded in 1998 in San Francisco, due to the initiative of a group of psychologists led by Donald K. Routh of the University of Miami. The ISCP was established to fill the need for a world organization of clinical psychologists, with the aim of providing a vehicle for global communication among clinicians, intended to foster multicultural understanding in the practice of clinical psychology, to enhance knowledge by cross-cultural research, to support the education and training of clinical psychologists based on a foundational level of knowledge, to encourage the development of a world certification for clinical psychologists, and to collaborate with other world organizations in providing clinical psychology expertise where required.

The need for this kind of organization has been expressed in the past. ISCP has the mission of building bridges between individuals and across cultures, in an effort to understand the complex issues associated with "normal" and "abnormal" behavior at the cultural level and also at the global level. The ISCP has held annual Congresses in San Francisco in 1998; in Salem, Massachusetts, in 1999: in Stockholm in 2000; in London in 2001; in Singapore in 2002; in Toronto in 2003; in Beijing in 2004; in Granada, Spain, in 2005; in Athens in 2006, in Mexico City in 2007; and in Berlin in 2008.

In view of the substantial development of clinical psychology at the international level, the demand for clinical psychological services around the world, the interest of psychologists in working in this area, the concern for appropriate training and ethical responsibility, and the internationalization of psychology as a science and as a profession, it is very likely that an association like the International Society of Clinical Psychology will have a promising future.

RUBEN ARDILA
National University of Colombia

INTERNATIONAL TEST COMMISSION

The International Test Commission (ITC) is a not-for-profit organization dedicated to active promotion of coherent assessment and testing practices around the world. The idea of establishing an international organization that contributes to the improvement of testing practices worldwide was first raised by Professor Jean Cardinet in Switzerland in the late 1960s. Through correspondence with national societies and meetings among interested individuals during international conferences, his initial idea for an organization began to take shape. The International Test Commission was established in 1974 at a general meeting held during the International Association of Applied Psychology (IAAP) meeting in Montreal (Oakland, Poortinga, Schlegel, & Hambleton, 2001).

Currently, most of the industrialized countries' national psychological associations are members of ITC, and the number of associations from developing countries is growing. ITC also includes test publishers, other national and international organizations (testing agencies, university departments), and individual members committed to promoting effective testing and assessment policies, as well as proper development, evaluation, and use of educational and psychological instruments. ITC assists in the exchange of testing information with member and affiliate organizations as well as with nonmember societies, organizations, and individuals who wish to improve their assessment practices. To achieve this goal, ITC carries out the following activities: (1) organizing conferences as well as symposia for regional and international psychology meetings; (2) publishing the *International Journal of Testing* (Taylor & Francis Group), which appears four times a year; (3) publishing a newsletter, *Testing International*, containing testing news and announcements from around the world; (4) encouraging and/or directing research studies, reviews, and projects on important testing issues and topics; and (5) responding to technical queries and helping to put policy-makers in touch with organizations and researchers that can assist them.

ITC has developed, published, and promoted several guidelines related to testing practices. *Guidelines in Adapting Tests* were published in 1994. The objective was to produce a detailed set of guidelines for adapting psychological and educational tests for use in various different linguistic and cultural contexts. These guidelines were featured at two international conferences that ITC organized in Washington, D.C. (1999), and Brussels (2006). A detailed presentation of these guidelines was included in a book published by Hambleton, Merenda, and Spielberger (2005). Subsequently, ITC's *Guidelines on Test Use* was published in 2000. These guidelines provide a common international framework within which specific local standards, codes of practice, qualifications, and user registration criteria could be developed in order to meet local needs. These guidelines have currently been officially translated into 14 languages, all of which are available on the ITC web site (www.intestcom.org). Later, *Guidelines on Computer-Base and Internet-Delivered Testing* was published in 2005, complementing the *Guidelines on Test Use*. These guidelines were needed because of the developments in stand-alone and Internet-delivered computer-based testing that had raised several issues regarding test administration, security of the tests and test results, and control over the testing process. A book presenting these guidelines was published by Bartram and Hambleton in 2006.

REFERENCES

Bartram, D., & Hambleton, R. K. (2006). *Computer-based testing and the Internet*. Hoboken, NJ: John Wiley & Sons.

Hambleton, R. K., Merenda, P. F., & Spielberger, C. D. (2005). *Adapting educational and psychological tests for cross-cultural assessment*. Mahwah, NJ: Lawrence Erlbaum.

Oakland, T., Poortinga, Y. H., Schlegel, J., & Hambleton, R. K. (2001). International test commission: Its history, current status, and future orientations. *International Journal of Testing, 1,* 3–32.

JACQUES GRÉGOIRE
Catholic University of Louvain, Belgium

See also: Psychological Assessment; Test Standardization; Testing Methods

INTERPERSONAL EXPECTANCY EFFECTS (See Pygmalion Effect)

INTERPERSONAL PERCEPTION

In order to function in society, it is crucial that people be able accurately to notice, classify, and predict the behavior of other individuals. This process of perceiving other people and making inferences about what they are like and how they will behave is known as interpersonal perception. Sometimes, perceiving the attributes of others is easy—for example, knowing whether a person is a man or a woman, or knowing the general age of a person. Many of the inferences we form about other people, however, involve difficult-to-see attributes, such as personality traits, as well as other more transitory states such as emotions, goals, and intentions. The process of perceiving these types of attributes in other people can be quite complex. Indeed, perceptions of other people can be influenced by a wide range of factors within both the perceivers and the person being perceived, as well as factors within the immediate social situation.

Many studies of interpersonal perception have focused on two broad phenomena: accuracy and bias (Kenny, 1994). Accuracy refers to the amount of overlap that exists between the inferences drawn about a person and that person's actual traits. For example, a person may be very accurate in judging whether or not his best friend is conscientious but less accurate in judging whether a complete stranger possesses that same trait. Bias, on the other hand, refers to systematic overestimation or underestimation of particular attributes. For example, one person may consistently perceive that other people are more threatening and hostile than they really are, whereas another person may consistently perceive others as friendlier than they might really be. In the following sections we briefly summarize the body of scientific knowledge pertaining to accuracy and bias in interpersonal perception.

Accuracy

Perceivers rarely are perfect in judging the attributes of others, but usually their perceptions do reflect some degree of objective accuracy. Blackman and Funder (1998) integrated several of the factors known to influence interpersonal accuracy into the Realistic Accuracy Model (RAM). According to the RAM, two of the most important factors that increase interpersonal accuracy are (1) the amount of time a person spends observing the behavior of another person and (2) how observable a particular trait is. In one study, for example, participants watched a videotaped person for differing amounts of time between 5 and 30 minutes. As expected, the accuracy of their trait inferences increased as their viewing time increased. However, observers were still significantly less accurate compared to the long-term acquaintances of the videotaped targets, especially on traits that are difficult to detect. Depending on the situation, however, some traits are easier to judge than others. For example, watching someone interact with strangers may provide useful information about that person's level of extraversion or friendliness, but it is unlikely to offer much information about the person's level of conscientiousness.

In some cases, people are very good at making judgments about others based on limited information. Imagine, for example, that you were asked to guess how good a particular teacher is by watching a very short (10-second) video clip of that person in front of a class. Now imagine that the videotape did not even contain sound; all you saw was a visual 10-second clip of the teacher. Many people might guess that, under these circumstances, it would be nearly impossible to know how good a teacher the person is. However, work by Ambady and Rosenthal (1993) showed that people's guesses about the teachers were highly predictive of the teacher's actual student evaluations, and this was true even after viewing only two seconds of silent videotape. It turned out that much of this accuracy was due to observers picking up on subtle cues to the professor's level of extraversion: Teachers who were outgoing were rated highly by students, and observers were able to detect a teacher's level of extraversion based on very thin slices of the teacher's behavior. Studies such as these demonstrate just how attuned to the behavior of others people can be, and how accurate they are when judging traits that are relatively easy to see.

Personality is not the only internal attribute that observers attempt to perceive. Dating back to Darwin, scientists have shown that people are often quite good at detecting the emotions of others, often on the basis of their facial expressions. Ekman (1971) identified six emotions (anger, fear, disgust, joy, sadness, and surprise) that are recognized clearly by people in every culture worldwide. His early studies showed pictures of people pretending to experience these emotions, and nearly everyone was able accurately to link the face with the emotion. Since then, many subsequent studies have identified the specific facial cues that are used to judge people's emotions, such as the furrowed eyebrows of a person experiencing anger. Other researchers have focused on the situational cues that help people distinguish between emotions that have similar facial markers. Imagine a man with a red face, mouth opened, and eyebrows furrowed. Many people would think that the man is angry, but if one were to zoom out and see the crowd of supporters cheering their favorite politician, the similarity between excitement and anger becomes evident. The use of contextual cues thus helps people recognize emotional facial displays that are sometimes ambiguous. Indeed, looking to aspects of the situation can help people discern the emotions, traits, and intentions of people, more broadly.

Bias

Above and beyond people's level of accuracy, there are also systematic biases in perceiving the attributes of others. When asked to rate their romantic partner on a variety of traits such as intelligence and friendliness, for example, people consistently rate their partner very high on the positive traits and relatively low on negative traits (Murray, Holmes, & Griffin, 1996). The ratings of people's romantic partner were much more flattering than ratings supplied by the partners' friends or even by the partners themselves. Seeing one's partner in positive ways can help people achieve their goal of staying committed and satisfied with their relationship (Campbell, 2005). This example illustrates the fact that people's goals, thoughts, feelings, and beliefs can have a profound influence on the way they view other people. As another example, studies suggest that being lonely or wanting to seek out new friends can lead people to see others as friendly and kind; in contrast, being afraid of other people or wanting to avoid rejection can lead people to see others as especially unfriendly and hostile (Maner, DeWall, Baumeister, & Schaller, 2007). Similarly, having low self-esteem can lead people to see others in a negative light, in turn helping the perceiver to feel a bit better about himself or herself. Thus, the way people perceive others can serve important interpersonal and self-esteem goals.

In addition to the goals of the perceiver, interpersonal perception also can be shaped by the perceiver's current emotions. Emotions signal to the observer that particular kinds of threats or opportunities are present in the environment. Emotions can bias the way they perceive other people; for example, being scared can lead people to see others (especially members of other groups) as angry and hostile (Maner et al., 2005). Even general positive and negative moods can affect how we see and pay attention to others. Happy participants attend less to the emotions of others than sad participants do, for example, and this decreased attention sometimes leads to less accurate trait inferences. Happiness is theorized to function as an "all-clear" signal, decreasing attention to potential threats in the environment, whereas sadness signals to the perceiver that he or she ought to attend carefully to other people.

Biases in interpersonal perceptions are especially apparent when people are perceiving members of groups other than their own. For example, people's stereotyped beliefs about what members of certain groups are like can dramatically affect the way members of those groups are perceived. Many studies have demonstrated that perceptions of certain minority groups can become biased by prejudicial beliefs about the groups' traits (e.g., that they are lazy, hostile, or unintelligent). When observing members of stereotyped groups, people often attend to, perceive, and remember things that are consistent with their own stereotypes.

Indeed, people tend to automatically categorize others as "us" and "them" or into the "ingroup" and the "outgroup." People tend to perceive members of their own group more positively than members of other groups, and these positive perceptions apply to almost any trait imaginable—for example, people see members of their own group as smarter, more trusting, and more cooperative than members of other groups (Otten & Moskowitz, 1999; Hewstone, Rubin, & Willis, 2002). This tendency to inflate one's perceptions of one's own group is known as "ingroup favoritism." In contrast, people often taint their perceptions of other groups with negative content, and this tendency has been linked with people's desire to protect themselves from perceived threats posed by members of other groups (e.g., threats to physical safety, economic threats; see Mackie, Devos, & Smith, 2000). In addition to being seen in a more negative light, members of other groups are also seen as being physically and psychologically similar to one another. This tendency of seeing the outgroup as less diverse than the ingroup is known as "outgroup homogeneity effect."

It may seem unfortunate that people sometimes perceive others in systematically biased ways, but although biased interpersonal perceptions can have negative consequences (e.g., racial prejudice), sometimes they can be quite functional. Perceiving another person as hostile, for example, could lead to one becoming interpersonally wary and to avoid a potentially dangerous social encounter. Conversely, seeing others as friendly and welcoming could help us make new friends, and seeing ourselves as attractive could give us the confidence to approach people and ask them out on a date (Haselton & Buss, 2000). Indeed, sometimes seeing others in biased ways can help people achieve their current social goals.

Many of the biases in our perceptions of other people can be mitigated if people try hard to see others in an accurate way (Neuberg, 1989). Some individuals have a general tendency to be concerned with creating accurate impressions of others and try to see others in an objective light. In contrast, other people tend not to worry about being accurate or to use strategies to insure accuracy. People who tend to strive for accuracy, not surprisingly, also tend to form relatively more accurate perceptions of other people. People's level of accuracy can also change from situation to situation; people are more accurate in some situations than others. Simply instructing people to try to form an accurate impression of another person can lead people to form more accurate, less biased, impressions (e.g., Neuberg, 1989). When interacting with a member of a stigmatized group, trying to see that person as an individual rather than simply as a member of a particular group can help reduce interpersonal biases. Nevertheless, to reduce one's biases and to form accurate impressions of others usually requires a far amount of ability and motivation. Things that detract from either of these (e.g., being in a rush, having a lot on one's mind, not being particularly concerned with forming an accurate impression) often set the stage for biased interpersonal perceptions.

In summary, interpersonal perception can be an incredibly complex process. Not only are many of the things we perceive in others difficult to see, but many of them are also in constant flux—the emotions and intentions of others, for example, are constantly changing. Adding to this complexity, interpersonal perceptions can be profoundly influenced by the perceiver's own goals and emotions, as well as by aspects of the immediate social situation. Nevertheless, psychologists have made great strides toward identifying many of the factors that can shape both accuracy and bias in interpersonal perception.

REFERENCES

Ambady, N., & Rosenthal, R. (1993). Half a minute: Predicting teacher evaluations from thin slices of nonverbal behavior and physical attractiveness. *Journal of Personality and Social Psychology, 64,* 431–441.

Blackman, M., & Funder, D. (1998). The effect of information on consensus and accuracy in personality judgment. *Journal of Experimental Social Psychology, 34,* 164–181.

Campbell, L. (2005). Responses to verifying and enhancing appraisals from romantic partners: The role of trait importance and trait visibility. *European Journal of Social Psychology, 35,* 663–675.

Ekman, P., & Wallace, F. (1971). Constants across cultures in the face of emotion. *Journal of Personality and Social Psychology, 17,* 124–129.

Haselton, M., & Buss, D. (2000). Error management theory: A new perspective on biases in cross-sex mind reading. *Journal of Personality and Social Psychology, 78,* 81–91.

Mackie, D., Devos, T., & Smith, E. (2000). Intergroup emotions: Explaining offensive action tendencies in an intergroup context. *Journal of Personality and Social Psychology, 79,* 602–616.

Maner, J., DeWall, N., Baumeister, R., & Schaller, M. (2007). Does social exclusion motivate interpersonal reconnection? Resolving the "porcupine problem." *Journal of Personality and Social Psychology, 92,* 42–55.

Maner, J., Kenrick, D., Becker, D., Robertson, T., Hofer, B., Neuberg, S., et al. (2005). Functional projection: How fundamental social motives can bias interpersonal perception. *Journal of Personality and Social Psychology, 88*, 63–78.

Murray, S., Holmes, J., & Griffin, D. (1996). The benefits of positive illusions: Idealization and the construction of satisfaction in close relationships. *Journal of Personality and Social Psychology, 70*, 79–98.

Neuberg, S. L. (1989). The goal of forming accurate impressions during social interactions: Attenuating the impact of negative expectancies. *Journal of Personality and Social Psychology, 56*, 374–386.

Otten, S., & Moskowitz, G. (2000). Evidence for implicit evaluative in-group bias: Affect-based spontaneous trait inference in a minimal group paradigm. *Journal of Experimental Social Psychology, 36*, 77–89.

SUGGESTED READINGS

Funder, D. C. (1999). *Personality judgment: A realistic approach to person perception.* San Diego: Academic Press.

Kenny, D. A. (1994). *Interpersonal perception: A social relations analysis.* New York: Guilford Press.

Lee, Y-T, McCauley, C., & Draguns, J. (1999). *Personality and person perception across cultures: Personality in culture.* Mahwah, NJ: Lawrence Erlbaum.

ANDREW J. MENZEL
JON K. MANER
Florida State University

See also: **Facial Recognition**

INTERPERSONAL PSYCHOTHERAPY

Interpersonal psychotherapy (IPT) is a time-limited, evidence-based psychotherapy, specified and described in a manual. It was initially developed for patients with major depressive disorder and later adapted for other disorders. Designed for administration by trained mental health professionals, it has been taught to mental-health workers with less professional training. The original manual detailed the empirical and theoretical basis of IPT (Klerman & Weissman, 1984) and was updated in 2000 (Weissman, Markowitz, & Klerman). The most recent manual is oriented to clinicians and contains numerous clinical examples (Weissman, Markowitz, & Klerman, 2007).

IPT has been adapted and tested for acute and maintenance treatment of depression for adolescents and the elderly, for pregnant and postpartum women, for people in developing countries, with primary care patients and the medically ill, and for dysthymic and bipolar patients. It has been delivered in an individual and a group format as well as over the telephone. There are some adaptations for nonmood disorders. IPT has been tested in numerous controlled clinical trials for depression, in which it is compared with psychotropic medication, placebo, other brief psychotherapies, and no psychotherapy. The most recent adaptations and different levels of success in clinical trials are summarized in a review by Weissman and colleagues (2007). Different versions of the IPT manual have been translated into German, Italian, Spanish, French, Korean, Japanese, and, more recently, Portuguese and Danish. IPT has been tested and used in many parts of the world including developing countries such as Uganda, Goa, and Ethiopia.

In the United States, the American Psychiatric Association and the 1993 Primary Care Practice Guidelines included IPT as one of the recommended treatments for adult depressed patients. IPT has been endorsed by the Royal College of Psychiatry for residency training and by the National Institute of Clinical Excellence (NICE) in the United Kingdom as part of evidence-based practice. It is also named in the guidelines for the treatment of depression in The Netherlands. The International Society for Interpersonal Psychotherapy has a website (www.interpersonalpsychotherapy.org) and holds a biannual international meeting that brings clinicians and researchers together from all over the world.

Theoretical and Empirical Studies

IPT is based on theory from the independent work of Adolph Meyer and Harry Stack Sullivan (Klerman, Weissman, Rounsaville, & Chevron, 1984). Meyer and Sullivan put emphasis on the patient's current interpersonal experience and social relationship and viewed the patient's response to environmental change and stress in adulthood as determined by early experience in the family. The general principle is that life events occurring after the early formative years trigger psychopathology. IPT uses this principle in a nonetiological fashion and does not pretend to discern the cause of a depressive episode. The connection between current life events in four problem areas and mood disorders is used to help the patient understand and deal with the onset of the current episode. Adaptations of IPT for other disorders have used the onset of the new disorder as a starting point with variable success.

IPT is also based on a large body of clinical and epidemiologic research demonstrating the relationships between the onset of depression and life events. Recent research integrating life events and modern genetics has shown the influence of life stress as a trigger of the onset of a depressive episode in patients who are genetically vulnerable (Caspi et al., 2003). A functional polymorphism in the promoter region of the serotonin transporter gene has been found to moderate the effect of life events on depression. Patients who come for treatment for depression could be the 60% who have the genetic vulnerability, which includes one or two copies of the short allele of the 5-HTT promoter polymorphism, in the presence of a significant life event. These genetic findings will undoubtedly be updated, However, the IPT model highlights the relevance of a depression treatment that focuses on current life stress in genetically susceptible individuals. In the absence of definitive biological markers, a family history of depression is a reasonable guide.

Another theoretical background for IPT comes from attachment theory by Bowlby (1969). This theory states that the need for attachment is an intrinsic human drive that is biologically grounded and contributes to the survival of the species. Intense human emotions are associated with the formation, maintenance, disruption, and renewal of attachment bonds. Investigations by ethologists applied to mother-child relationships have demonstrated the importance of attachment and social bonds to human functioning. Humans of all ages are vulnerable to impaired interpersonal relations if strong attachment bonds do not develop early, and they are vulnerable to depression when attachment bonds are disrupted.

Attachment theory has stimulated empirical research on the association between interpersonal relationships and depression. This research has covered studies of the onset of depression and grief, social stress, social supports, marital discord, separation, and divorce as well as on the interpersonal and social functioning consequence of depression. IPT does not rely on any one of these theories exclusively. Instead, IPT's emphasis is on understanding the social and interpersonal triggers of a depressive episode in the current "here and now." These triggers are usually the disruption of one or many human attachments.

Description of IPT

IPT is based on the idea that a depressive episode is usually triggered by an event(s): a marriage breaks up, a dispute threatens an important relationship, a spouse has an affair, a job is lost, a move takes place, a loved one dies, a promotion or demotion occurs, a person retires, or a medical illness changes a person's participation in social life. Understanding the social and interpersonal context of a depressive episode may unravel the immediate reasons for the onset of symptoms.

The IPT therapist views depression as having three parts:

1. *Symptoms:* The emotional, cognitive, and physical symptoms of depression including depressed and anxious mood, difficulty concentrating, indecisiveness, pessimism, guilt, sleeping and eating disturbances, loss of interest and pleasure, fatigue, and suicidality.
2. *Social and Interpersonal Functioning:* The ability to get along with others.

3. *Personality:* Enduring patterns that people use to deal with life. How they assert themselves, express their anger and hurt feelings, maintain their self-esteem, and whether they are shy, aggressive, inhibited, or suspicious. These traits may contribute to the development or maintenance of depression.

Some therapists begin by trying to treat a person's personality difficulties and see personality as the underlying cause of depression. The IPT therapist does not treat personality and recognizes that many behaviors that appear to be enduring and lifelong may be a reflection of the depression itself. Patients seem dependent, self-preoccupied, and irritable while acutely depressed, yet when the depression lifts, these supposedly lasting traits may recede.

The thrust of IPT is to try to understand the interpersonal context in which the depressive symptoms arose and how they related to the current social and personal context. The IPT therapist looks for what is currently happening in the patient's life ("here and now" problems) rather than problems from childhood or the past. Coping with these current problems and the development of self-reliance outside of the therapeutic situation is encouraged. The brief time limit of the treatment rules out any major reconstruction of personality. Although IPT has been used for as long as 3 years as a maintenance treatment, in practice most psychotherapy is brief. A renegotiation of the time at the expiration of the acute time-specified treatment as possible. If IPT has not been helpful at the end of its time-limited intervention, it is appropriate to reconsider the treatment plan.

The goals of IPT are (1) to reduce the symptoms of depression (i.e., to improve sleep, appetite, energy, and one's general outlook on life); and (2) to help the patient deal better with the people and life situations associated with onset of symptoms. IPT proceeds in three phases. The first phase, usually one to three sessions, includes diagnostic evaluation and psychiatric history and sets the framework for the treatment. The therapist reviews the symptoms, diagnoses the patient as depressed based on standard criteria, and gives the patient the sick role. The sick role excuses the patient from overwhelming social obligations, but it requires the patient to work in treatment to recover full function. The psychiatric history includes the "interpersonal inventory," a review of the patient's current social functioning and close relationships. The interpersonal inventory is a careful, interpersonally focused medical history as opposed to a semistructured interview. Changes in relationships proximal to the onset of symptoms are elucidated (e.g., death of a loved one, children leaving home, worsening marital strife), and the therapist listens closely for themes that are emotionally charged. The review provides a framework for understanding the social and interpersonal context of the onset of depressive symptoms and defines the problem areas that will become the focus of treatment.

Having assessed the need for medication based on symptom severity, past history, response to treatment, and patient preference, the therapist educates the patient about the disorder under treatment by explicitly discussing the diagnosis, including the constellation of symptoms that define the disorder and what the patient can expect from treatment. Patients are told that the depression is not their fault. The therapist next links the disorder to the patient's interpersonal situation in a formulation that uses as a framework one of four interpersonal problem areas: grief, interpersonal role disputes, role transition, and interpersonal deficits. The therapist and the patient make a choice by weighing which problem area is most closely linked by time and affect to the onset of depression.

In the second or middle phase of IPT, the therapist pursues strategies specific to the chosen interpersonal problem area. These problems areas may change in the course of treatment as new information is obtained, but the switch should be explicit. For grief, defined as complicated bereavement following the death of a loved one, the therapist facilitates the catharsis of mourning and gradually helps the patient to find new activities and relationships to compensate for the loss. Role disputes are conflicts with a significant other. The therapist helps the patient explore the relationship, the nature and phase of the dispute, and the available options for resolution. If these fail, the therapist and patient may conclude that the relationship has reached an impasse and consider ways to change this (renegotiation) or to end the relationship (dissolution).

Role transition includes changes in life status such as beginning or ending a relationship or career, moving, promotion, retirement, graduation, or the diagnosis of a medical illness. The patient learns to deal with the change by mourning the loss of the old role while recognizing positive and negative aspects of the new role and finding ways of dealing with the new situation. Interpersonal deficits, the residual fourth IPT problem area, define the patient as lacking the social skills to initiate or sustain relationships, and helps the patient develop new relationships and skills. This area is the most difficult to deal with in a time-limited treatment.

Sessions open with the question, "How have things been since we last met?" This focuses the patient on recent interpersonal events and moods, which the therapist helps the patient to link. The therapist takes an active, nonneutral, supportive, and hopeful stance to counter the depressed patient's pessimism. The options that exist for change in the patient's life, options that the depression may have kept the patient from seeing or considering fully, are explored. The therapist stresses the need for the patient to test these options to improve his or her life and simultaneously treat the depressive episode. By trying out options

in real life with important others, the patient will learn what fosters mood change and what does not.

In the final phase of IPT, which occupies the last few weeks of treatment (or months, in case of maintenance treatment), the therapist works to support the patient's independence and competence by recognizing and consolidating therapeutic gains. The therapist also helps the patient anticipate and develop ways to identify and counter depressive symptoms should they arise in the future. IPT de-emphasizes termination and defines it as a graduation from treatment. The sadness of parting, if present, is distinguished from depressive feelings. If the patient has not improved, the therapist emphasizes that it is the treatment that has failed, not the patient, and stresses the existence of alternative treatment options.

The adaptations of IPT for different age groups (adolescents and the elderly); formats (group and telephone); locations (medical practices and school-based clinics); mood disorders (dysthymia and bipolar disorder); cultures (Uganda or low-income minorities); and other disorders (drug abuse, social anxiety disorder, etc.), as well as the status of the evidence are described in a review by Weissman and colleagues (2007).

Training

Training programs in psychiatry, psychology, and social work are beginning to incorporate evidence-based psychotherapy, but there is still a long way to go (Weissman et al., 2006). IPT workshops are held regularly in the United States, Canada, and the United Kingdom. The best way to learn about them is through the previously noted international IPT website. In the absence of a convenient program, one way to learn is to read the manuals and obtain clinical supervision from an experienced IPT therapist. Names are available on the IPT website.

REFERENCES

Bowlby, K. (1969). *Attachment*. London: Hogarth Press.

Caspi, A., Sugden, K., Moffitt, T. E., Taylor, A., Craig, I. W., Harrington, H., et al. (2003). Influence of life stress on depression: Moderation by a polymorphism in the 5-HTT gene. *Science, 301(5631)*, 386–389.

Klerman, G. L., Weissman, M. M., Rounsaville, B., & Chevron, E. (1984). *Interpersonal psychotherapy of depression*. New York: Basic Books.

Weissman, M. M., Markowitz, J. C., & Klerman, G. L. (2000). *Comprehensive guide to interpersonal psychotherapy*. New York: Basic Books.

Weissman, M. M., Markowitz, J.C., & Klerman, G. L. (2007). *A clinician's quick guide to interpersonal psychotherapy*. New York: Oxford University Press.

Weissman, M. M., Verdeli, H., Gameroff, M. J., Bledsoe, S. E., Betts, K., Mufson, L., et al. (2006). *National Survey of Psychotherapy Training in Psychiatry, Psychology, and Social Work*. Archives of General Psychiatry, *63*, 925–934.

SUGGESTED READINGS

Mufson, L., Pollack-Dorta, K., Moreau, D., & Weissman, M. M. (2004). *Interpersonal psychotherapy for depressed adolescents* (2nd ed.). New York: Guilford Press.

Verdeli, H., Clougherty, K., Bolton, P., Speelman, L., Lincoln, N., Bass, J., et al. (2003). Adapting group interpersonal psychotherapy for a developing country: Experience in rural Uganda. *World Psychiatry, 2*(2), 114–120.

MYRNA M. WEISSMAN
*College of Physicians and Surgeons and
Mailman School of Public Health,
Columbia University*

See also: **Personality, Interpersonal Theories of;
Psychotherapy; Sullivan's Interpersonal Theory**

INTERPERSONAL RELATIONSHIPS

Although most people like to be alone at times, most also choose to spend the majority of their time involved in relationships with other people. So important are relationships that, when asked about the factors that give their life meaning, participants in one study rated most highly their interpersonal relationships with others (Klinger, 1977). The nature of these relationships can take a number of different forms, including casual acquaintances, friendships, family relationships, working relationships, and romantic relationships. The duration of these relationships may be short-term or long-term. People's intense desire to affiliate and form relationships with others stems from an innate need to belong (Baumeister & Leary, 1995). Much of people's behavior is driven by their desire to be included by others and to avoid being excluded by them. As anyone who has ever been ostracized or excluded can attest, the consequences of being excluded from important interpersonal relationships can be severe and include both psychological and physical problems.

How Relationships Form

Given the importance of interpersonal relationships, what determines who we are attracted to and wish to be included by? Psychologists have identified several factors that determine which of the myriad of people we interact with on a daily basis we choose to form relationships with. Among the factors that have received the most attention are proximity, physical attractiveness, similarity, and interpersonal rewards.

Proximity. Not surprisingly, people who are in close proximity to one another are more likely to form relationships with one another than those who live further away. In a classic study by Festinger, Schachter, and Back (1950), when asked to name their three closest friends, respondents named someone who lived one door away 41% of the time. Only 10% of the time was someone who lived four doors away listed. Relatedly, when asked their opinions about immigrants, Americans who lived in close proximity to them had more favorable opinions of them than those who have little contact with them ("America's Immigration Quandry," 2006). A key reason for the influence of proximity on liking is mere exposure or repeated contact with those individuals. Repeated exposure to others leads to familiarity, which typically leads to liking (Miller, Perlman, & Brehm, 2007). Sometimes, however, familiarity also exposes us to others' annoying idiosyncrasies, which can lead to negative feelings toward those others. Increasing contact with others to whom we already have negative feelings only serves to intensify those feelings.

Technological advances, such as the Internet, have allowed people to have "virtual proximity" to others, thus broadening the potential pool of individuals with whom they may establish interpersonal relationships. This has led researchers to propose that the key factor is interaction accessibility rather than mere physical proximity (Berscheid & Reis, 1998). Thus, with technology, the potential pool of individuals accessible to us on a regular and frequent basis is broader than it once was.

Physical attractiveness. People are attracted to and desire to form relationships with those who are physically attractive, and this pattern begins in childhood. Children who are attractive are more popular among their peers than those who are less attractive. Attractive adults are treated more favorably than less attractive adults (Miller et al., 2007). Physically attractive people are assumed to possess a number of other desirable traits, such as being warm, intelligent, and successful, a phenomenon known as the "what is beautiful is good stereotype." However, in spite of the fact that people are often drawn to the most attractive others, they typically end up forming relationships with those who match or are similar to them in attractiveness.

Similarity. Not only do people form relationships with others who match them in attractiveness, but they also form relationships with people who are similar to them on other dimensions. People who are similar to us validate our thoughts, feelings, and attitudes. As the old adage goes, "birds of a feather flock together." Interactions with people who are similar to us are generally easier and less conflicted than those with dissimilar others, a finding that has led some researchers to suggest that it is not so much that similarity attracts as that dissimilarity "repulses." People avoid forming relationships with those who are too dissimilar to them, unless the dimensions on which they differ are complementary. Internet dating services have made good use of the "similarity attracts" idea by trying to match people up based on similarity.

Interpersonal rewards. People who are similar to us reward us by validating our views and values. In general, people choose to interact with and form relationships with those who provide them with desired rewards. The more rewarding an interaction is with a particular other, the more likely people are to want to have subsequent interactions with that individual.

Attachment

Not everyone approaches relationships, whether friendships or romantic relationships, the same way. Some people actively seek out interpersonal relationships, whereas others seem awkward and uncomfortable when interacting with others. These differences in the nature of people's styles of relating have been observed among children as well as adults. Indeed, people's interpersonal styles as adults can be traced, in part, to their patterns of interacting and attachment in childhood.

Researchers have delineated three attachment styles: secure, anxious-ambivalent, and avoidant (Feeney, Noller, & Roberts, 2000). Securely attached individuals seek out relationships with others, believing that others can be trusted and depended upon. They experience happiness and warmth in their relationships with others. Individuals with an anxious-ambivalent style of attachment desire relationships with others, but are uncertain of how others will respond. They tend to cling to others out of fear that those others will reject or abandon them. Avoidant individuals are untrusting and thus, they do not easily form relationships with others. Unfortunately, these varied styles of attachment can create self-fulfilling prophecies in relationships. Securely attached individuals eagerly seek out relationships with others and respond to others with trust and ease. Anxious-ambivalent individuals, through their clinginess and excessive reassurance-seeking, elicit the very rejection they fear. Avoidant individuals often don't give others a chance to prove that they can be trusted (Feeney et al., 2000).

Importantly, attachment styles do not appear to be determined entirely by temperament. Although certainly an "easy" baby elicits more satisfying responses from a caregiver than a colicky infant, parental behavior toward infants independent of temperament plays a critical role in determining child and adult attachment styles. Parents who respond in a warm, close manner with their children most often have children who, as adults, have secure attachment styles.

Intimate Relationships

Although early research on relationships focused on the factors that determined interpersonal attraction, beginning in the early 1980s researchers began to turn their attention to love and intimate relationships. One of the biggest issues was defining love. Is love simply more liking

(i.e., a quantitative difference), or are liking and love qualitatively different phenomena? A leading researcher in this area, Robert Sternberg, provided support for the qualitative perspective. In his triangular theory of love, Sternberg suggested that love can be classified along three dimensions: intimacy, passion, and commitment. Viewed in this way, some relationships are passionate in nature with little commitment, whereas others may have intimacy, passion, and commitment.

As people initiate and pursue relationships that may become committed relationships, they subject those potential or actual relationships to an evaluative process. According to social exchange theory, people form and maintain friendships and romantic relationships that will allow them to maximize their rewards and minimize their costs (Thibaut & Kelley, 1959). Three variables are involved in the calculation of this reward/cost ratio: comparison level (CL), comparison level for alternatives (CL-alt), and investment. In deciding whether or not to form relationships with others, people use as a guide their comparison level, or the average of all relationship outcomes they have had in the past. People with a high comparison level will be more selective about choosing relationships than those who have low comparison levels.

Additionally, though, they also evaluate what else (or who else) is out there (i.e., CL-alt). People are more selective in choosing friends and relationship partners when they have a number of alternatives to select from. CL-alt also plays a role in determining satisfaction levels with existing relationships. Once in a friendship or relationship, people use investment to determine whether or not they will stay in that relationship. The phrase "too much invested to quit" plays out in many relationships in which people choose to maintain relationships in which they have invested considerable time, money, and effort.

What allows committed relationships in which people have invested a great deal to remain satisfying to those involved? People who maintain long-term, satisfying relationships are able to stop themselves from responding to negative comments with negative comments, a phenomenon referred to as negative reciprocity (Miller et al., 2007). In addition, people in satisfying, long-term relationships are more likely than those in dissatisfying relationships to give their friends and romantic partners the benefit of the doubt. They make more benign attributions for negative behavior and are more likely to reframe or reinterpret the behavior (Miller et al., 2007).

Dark Side of Close Relationships

In spite of our innate need to be in the company of others and the physical and psychological toll exacted when relationships and friendships fail, there is a dark side to ongoing relationships: "On any given day, 44% of us are likely to be annoyed by a close relational partner.... On average, young adults encounter 8.7 aggravating hassles in their romantic relationships each week ... and every seven days *most* young adults will be distressed by different encounters with their lover's (1) criticism, (2) stubbornness, (3) selfishness, and (4) lack of conscientiousness, at least once .... Over time, people are meaner to their intimate partners than to anyone else they know" (Miller, 1997, p. 15).

One of the most common sources of dissatisfaction reported by people entering therapy is their interpersonal relationships (Rook, 1998). Beyond criminal acts, such as domestic violence, people on occasion "behave badly" in relationships; they engage in any of a number of different mundane behaviors that take a toll as well (Kowalski, 2001). Included among these behaviors are teasing, complaining, guilt-induction, jealousy, hurting of feelings, betrayal, breaches of propriety, and gossip, to name a few. All of these behaviors have in common relational devaluation: they convey that others no longer value their relationship with us as much as they once did or as much as we would desire (Leary, Springer, Negel, Ansell, & Evans, 1988). The angst produced by perceived relational devaluation can be seen in the hurt feelings so commonly experienced as a result.

People's innate need to belong leads them to seek out friendships and relationships with others who they believe will be a source of fulfillment and joy. The individuals with whom people form relationships are most often those who are close by and who are similar to them in both values and attractiveness. The manner in which people approach relationships often reflects attachment styles they acquired in childhood, which can lead to trusting or distrusting views on relationships. As humans, not surprisingly, no relationship is without its problems. Although sometimes these problems can be severe, more commonly they reflect annoying behaviors, such as complaining or guilt-induction, that people are more likely to perpetrate on close others than on acquaintances.

REFERENCES

America's immigration quandary. (2006, March 30). The Pew Research Center for the People and the Press. Retrieved August 24, 2008, from http://people-press.org/report/274/americas-immigration-quandary.

Baumeister, R. F., & Leary, M. R. (1995). The need to belong: Desire for interpersonal attachments as a fundamental human motivation. *Psychological Bulletin, 117,* 497–529.

Berscheid, E., & Reis, H. T. (1998). Attraction and close relationships. In D. T. Gilbert, S. T. Fiske, & G. Lindzey (Eds.), *The handbook of social psychology* (Vol. 2, pp. 193–281). New York: McGraw-Hill.

Feeney, J. A., Noller, P., & Roberts, N. (2000). Attachment and close relationships. In C. Hendrick & S. S. Hendrick (Eds.), *Close relationships: A sourcebook* (pp. 185–202). Thousand Oaks, CA: Sage.

Festinger, L., Schachter, S., & Back, K. W. (1950). *Social pressures in informal groups: A study of human factors in housing.* New York: Harper & Brothers.

Klinger, E. (1977). *Meaning and void: Inner experience and the incentives in people's lives.* Minneapolis: University of Minnesota Press.

Kowalski, R. M. (2001). *Behaving badly: Aversive behaviors in interpersonal relationships.* Washington, DC: American Psychological Association.

Leary, M. R., Springer, C., Negel, L., Ansell, E., & Evans, K. (1998). The causes, phenomenology, and consequences of hurt feelings. *Journal of Personality and Social Psychology, 74,* 1225–1237.

Miller, R. S. (1997). We only hurt the ones we love: Aversive interactions in close relationships. In R. Kowalski (Ed.), *Aversive interpersonal interactions* (pp. 11–29). New York: Plenum Press.

Miller, R. S., Perlman, D., & Brehm, S. S. (2007). *Intimate relationships.* Boston: McGraw-Hill.

Rook, K. S. (1998). Investigating the positive and negative sides of personal relationships: Through a lens darkly? In B. H. Spitzberg & W. R. Cupach (Eds.), *The dark side of close relationships* (pp. 369–393). Mahwah, NJ: Lawrence Erlbaum.

Thibaut, J. W., & Kelley, H. H. (1959). *The social psychology of groups.* New York: John Wiley & Sons.

Robin M. Kowalski
Clemson University

See also: Attachment and Bonding; Conflict Resolution; Interpersonal Perception; Mate Selection

INTERROGATION

This article addresses interrogations by police and by military and intelligence agencies.

Interrogations by Police

In criminal cases, three types of confessions have been distinguished from each other (DeClue, 2005). *Self-initiated* confessions occur when a person initiates contact with a law enforcement officer or other person in authority and declares that he or she is guilty of a crime. *First-response* confessions occur when the police approach a person and initiate questioning, and the person's first response is "I did it." *Police-induced* confessions occur when the police approach a person and initiate questioning, and the person's first response is something other than "I did it" (e.g., "I didn't do it"); the police then engage in further conversation with the person, and the person subsequently says

"I did it." The further conversation between police and suspect is police interrogation.

Although the proper goal of police interrogation, like any police investigation, is to determine the truth, accusatory interrogation proceeds systematically with one goal: to obtain a confession from whomever has been selected as a suspect. Police are legally permitted to lie and otherwise deceive a suspect as they encourage the suspect to believe that the evidence of guilt is overwhelming and resistance is futile, that there is nothing to lose by confessing, and that there is something to gain by confessing.

The same process that induces guilty suspects to confess induces some innocent people to give false confessions (Gudjonsson, 2003). The Innocence Project (www.innocenceproject.org/understand/False-Confessions .php) reports that among people who have been exonerated by DNA evidence, more than 25% had falsely confessed. In most criminal cases there is no biological evidence suitable for DNA testing, so if we want to prevent future wrongful convictions we need to study known cases of false confessions and learn what went wrong.

The first step is to keep in mind that a confession in response to police pressure in not the same as a confession offered spontaneously. In *Hopt v. Territory of Utah* the U.S. Supreme Court held that "A confession, if freely and voluntarily made, is evidence of the most satisfactory character. Such a confession is deserving of the highest credit, because it is presumed to flow from the strongest sense of guilt, and therefore it is admitted as proof of the crime to which it refers.... But the presumption upon which weight is given to such evidence, namely, that one who is innocent will not imperil his safety or prejudice his interests by an untrue statement, ceases when the confession appears to have been made [in response to] inducements, threats, or promises."

Hindsight analysis of known cases of false confessions, such as those in the Central Park jogger case, reveal that neither *Miranda* warnings nor a voluntariness test work to keep false confessions out of courtrooms. But there is a solution: "The legacy of the Central Park jogger case is that by extracting five demonstrably false confessions from five innocent young boys, police and prosecutors allowed a violent serial predator to continue robbing, raping, stabbing and, in one case, killing other women before he was finally apprehended and brought to justice. The pretrial reliability test that we propose ... will prevent judges from admitting false confessions into evidence, thus preventing juries from wrongfully convicting the innocent" (Leo, Drizin, Neufeld, Hall, & Vatner, 2006, pp. 537–538).

What is that reliability test? The entire interrogation and confession should be electronically recorded and judges should weigh three factors in deciding whether or not to admit confession evidence at trial: "(1) whether the confession contains nonpublic information that can be independently verified, would only be known by the true perpetrator or an accomplice, and cannot likely be guessed by chance; (2) whether the suspect's confession led the police to new evidence about the crime; and (3) whether the suspect's post-admission narrative 'fits' (or fails to fit) with the crime facts and existing objective evidence" (Leo et al., 2006, p. 530).

Interrogations by Military and Intelligence Agencies

In police interrogations, as just discussed, the goal is typically to discover truth about a crime that has been committed. In contrast, the goal of interrogations by military and intelligence agencies is often to gain information that could help to prevent acts of war or terrorism, or that could help to win a battle. Military and intelligence agencies are not governed by the same rules as domestic police forces, and some people have advocated the use of physical and/or psychological torture to get prisoners to divulge information in spite of international agreements regarding human rights (for example, see www.unhchr.ch/html/menu3/b/h_cat39.htm), in spite of the fact that publicly available evidence does not show that torture or "harsh interrogation" is more effective than nonstressful interrogation techniques (McCoy, 2006).

The federal government of the United States suffered a breakdown of its commitment to human rights following the terrorist acts of September 11, 2001, and government agents employed interrogation techniques that had been outlawed for decades. Recently, the U.S. Army Field Manual (www.army.mil/institution/armypublicaffairs/pdf/ fm2-22-3.pdf) has been revised to clearly exclude torture. At the time of this writing, the U.S. Congress has passed legislation including "No individual in the custody or under the effective control of an element of the intelligence community or instrumentality thereof, regardless of nationality or physical location, shall be subject to any treatment or technique of interrogation not authorized by the United States Army Field Manual on Human Intelligence Collector Operations." That legislation was vetoed by President George W. Bush, thus leaving further action necessary to bring the United States back into the civilized world. As one of his first acts on assuming office, President Barack Obama upheld the commitment of the United States to the Geneva Conventions.

REFERENCES

DeClue, G. (2005). *Interrogations and disputed confessions: A manual for forensic psychological practice.* Sarasota, FL: Professional Resource Press.

Gudjonsson, G. H. (2003). *The psychology of interrogations and confessions: A handbook.* West Sussex, England: John Wiley & Sons.

Hopt v. *Territory of Utah*, 110 U.S. 574, 584–585 (1884).

Leo, R. A., Drizin, S. A., Neufeld, P. J., Hall, B. R., & Vatner, A. (2006). Bringing reliability back in: False confessions and legal safeguards in the twenty-first century. *Wisconsin Law Review, 2006*(2), 479–538.

McCoy, A. W. (2006). *A question of torture: CIA interrogation from the cold war to the war on terror.* New York: Metropolitan Books.

SUGGESTED READINGS

DeClue, G. (2005). *Interrogations and disputed confessions: A manual for forensic psychological practice.* Sarasota, FL: Professional Resource Press.

Leo, R. A. (2008). *Police interrogation and American justice.* Cambridge, MA: Harvard University Press.

McCoy, A. W. (2006). *A question of torture: CIA interrogation from the cold war to the war on terror.* New York: Metropolitan Books.

GREGORY DECLUE
Sarasota, Florida

See also: **Torture**

INTERVENING VARIABLES

The term "intervening variable," as used by behavioral theorists such as Clark Hull and Edward Tolman, describes a variable that mediates the relationship between a stimulus and response (Hilgard, 1958). Behavioral theorists were not consistent in their use of the term *intervening variable* and often disagreed about what even constituted an intervening variable. At the heart of the controversy was whether intervening variables that were hypothetical entities could be considered scientific or whether allowing hypothetical entities threatened the rigor and objectivity of behavioral science. During this time American behavioral scientists wanted psychology to be a natural science and thus aligned themselves (often in name only) with the logical positivists (Smith, 1986). Consequently, ideas that smacked of subjectivity or that allowed for the positing of hypothetical entities that could not be empirically verified were met with resistance and skepticism.

Given the confusion and disagreement among theorists about intervening variables, MacCorquodale and Meehl (1948) entered the debate in an attempt to clarify some of the crucial issues. They distinguished between two kinds of mediating variables: (1) hypothetical constructs and (2) intervening variables. The key distinction is whether the use of a mediating variable suggests the presence of an unseen entity or process or if it does not. The former is a hypothetical construct and the latter an intervening variable.

Intervening variables are shorthand summaries that describe relationships among empirical variables. As MacCorquodale and Meehl (1948) point out, Hull's concept of habit strength is an intervening variable. Habit strength is a function of four quantities: (1) number of reinforcements, (2) delay in reinforcements, (3) amount of reinforcement, and (4) asynchronisms between the discriminative stimuli and the response (p. 98). Habit strength does not have any meaning beyond its relationship to these quantities. In contrast, hypothetical constructs do not simply describe relationships among variables—they have "surplus meaning" (MacCorquodale & Meehl, 1948). That is, hypothetical constructs are often treated as entities (i.e., things in the world) that account for empirical relationships but are not reducible to them. For example, although the construct "schizophrenia" may account for the relationships among the symptoms experienced by a person (e.g., delusions, hallucinations, flat affect), it is not typically thought to be reducible simply to those symptoms. Instead, it is often considered a disease caused by neurological and behavioral dysfunctions that produce the symptoms.

It is unclear how relevant the distinction between intervening variables and hypothetical constructs is in contemporary psychology. This theoretical work was done to clarify ideas in behavioral theories that are largely out of fashion. The distinctions, however, are useful in helping current psychologists to be clear about what they mean when they introduce constructs in their theories.

REFERENCES

Hilgard, E. R. (1958). Intervening variables, hypothetical constructs, parameters, and constants. *The American Journal of Psychology, 71*, 238–246.

MacCorquodale, K., & Meehl, P. E. (1948). On a distinction between hypothetical constructs and intervening variables. *Psychological Review, 55*, 95–107.

Smith, L. D. (1986). *Behaviorism and logical positivism: A reassessment of the alliance.* Stanford, CA: Stanford University Press.

SCOTT A. BALDWIN
ARJAN BERKELJON
Brigham Young University

INTERVIEW ASSESSMENT

Surveys reveal that the clinical interview is the most frequently used assessment method among 95% of psychologists (Watkins, Campbell, Nieberding, & Hallmark, 1995). Although there are general factors that influence the content and structure of a clinical interview, perhaps the single most guiding factor is the theoretical orientation of the psychologist. There are primarily four major theoretical orientations that are popular among psychologists today: psychodynamic, client-centered (which has merged with humanistic and existential orientations), cognitive-behavioral, and family systems approaches.

A psychodynamic orientation argues that much of behavior is guided by unconscious influences and by factors outside of a person's awareness. A psychologist who operates from this frame of reference begins to formulate hypotheses consistent with this way of thinking.

A client-centered or nondirective approach views all of human behavior as oriented towards self-growth and self-actualization. The psychologist's task is to accept the phenomenological world of the client, show unconditional positive regard, use genuineness and accurate empathy as the main therapeutic conditions to advance behavior change, and to use reflection and clarification as the primary intervention tools.

A cognitive-behavioral approach to a clinical interview sees behavior as influenced by contingencies of reinforcement, that is, rewards and punishments levied in contiguity with an environmental influence. Accompanying this system are automatic thoughts that also influence behavior. The psychologist's task in an interview is to determine the environmental factors and rewards and punishments that are controlling a person's behavior, along with the automatic thoughts that accompany them.

A family systems approach views aberrant behavior as a manifestation of a dysfunctional family. The identified patient plays a certain role that is designed to maintain family homeostasis. The task of the psychologist with this orientation is to treat the entire family and not just the identified patient. This is true even when the patient is receiving only individual counseling and the relevant family members are not present in the session.

The reader is encouraged to consult specialized references for further elaboration of these theories, of recommended content of initial interviews from each of these orientations, and of recommended interventions as well (see Craig, 2005a).

Types of Clinical Interviews

A number of different types of clinical interviews have been described in the literature. These include brief screening interviews, case histories, crisis interviews, diagnostic and etiologic interviews, forensic evaluations, follow-up interviews, intake evaluations, mental status exams, motivational interviews, orientation interviews, screening interviews, specialized interviews, and termination interviews. Craig (in press) provides a detailed overview of each of these different types of interviews. More often than not, several of these different types of interviews are combined as elements of a single interview. For example, clinicians typically listen to the presenting problem, take a case history, conduct a mental status exam, and perform a diagnostic evaluation. There are two types of specialized interviews that merit further discussion: forensic interviews and motivational interviews.

Forensic interviews apply knowledge of psychology and psychopathology to legal aspects before the court. They are actually clinical interviews within a legal context. These types of interviews address a wide variety of issues, and the content of these interviews will depend on the specific question before the court. These may include child custody evaluations, screening police applicants, evaluating competency to stand trial or questions of insanity, evaluating sexual predators, evaluating defendants in civil and criminal cases including capital cases, and determining whether adolescents have the intellectual capacity to waive their *Miranda* rights (Craig, 2005b).

Forensic interviews differ in several ways from clinical interviews (Craig, 2005b; Marczyk, Nauss, Kutinsky, DeMatteo, & Heilbrun, 2008). First, they are not confidential and are not protected by legal privilege. The clinician must inform defendants and litigants that anything they say can and will be used in a court of law. Second, whereas a clinical interview tends to be supportive and accepting, the forensic interview is far more probative and investigative in nature. Forensic psychologists usually spend more time evaluating past records (police reports, court documents such as depositions) than do psychologists conducting a clinical interview.

Third, clinicians expect to see the patient over time and hence can afford to take a more longitudinal view of patient progress. However, forensic interviewers may only see the defendant a few times, sometimes only once. Fourth, the purpose of a forensic interview is to assist the decision-maker (i.e., judge, jury) in a civil or criminal trial, whereas the purpose of the typical clinical interview is to provide a diagnosis and treatment recommendations to provide for the mental health needs of the patient. The forensic interview must address not only the mental health needs of the interviewee but also the relevant legal standards in the case.

The standards for writing the final assessment report also differ between these two approaches. The forensic report is more demanding and extensive, requiring detailed information as to fact (Craig, in press). Finally, the person being evaluated may not be the psychologist's "patient" or "client" at all. More often not, the client who requests the forensic assessors services is a referring judge or attorney.

An increasingly popular type of interview is the "motivational interview" (Miller & Rollnick, 2002). The techniques recommended in this type of interview are consistent with current models of how people change (Prochaska & DiClemente, 1983). Although motivational interviewing was developed independent of this model of change, it is consistent with it. Miller and Rollnick argue that patient motivation is ephemeral. It is, in fact, a state of readiness to change that fluctuates, based on conditions, and it is the clinician's style that largely determines whether or not the patient will change. They further believe that change processes can begin even in the initial clinical interview if the clinician uses the proper techniques.

Miller and Rollnick have developed a mnemonic device (FRAMES) that describes six active processes in which clinicians should engage to promote behavior change. These are as follows: give *feedback*; emphasize that it is the patient's *responsibility* to change; give *advice*, in a nonauthoritarian manner; provide a *menu* of treatment choices and change strategies; be *empathic*; and encourage *self-efficacy*. The last of these refers to the belief that patients have the ability to succeed in meeting their change goals. Motivational interviewing has become a mainstream intervention approach in substance abuse treatment and is finding applications in other mental health problems as well.

The Structure and Content of Assessment Interviews

One of the essential differences among interviews is their degree of structure. They range from completely unstructured, as in client-centered interviews, to the rigidly structured clinical interview. In general, a typical initial interview will entail an introduction, in which patients describe their chief complaint or presenting problem, a detailed inquiry, in which the psychologist elicits enough information to make a DSM-IV-TR (American Psychiatric Association, 2000) diagnosis, hypothesis testing, in which a causal hypothesis is formulated and tested with subsequent questions, and a summary, in which treatment goals and a treatment plan are established.

The content of a clinical interview will depend largely on the kind of interview that is being conducted. In general, essential material would include basic demographics, the presenting problem or chief complaint, prior treatment episodes, emotional stability, mental status, substance abuse history, child abuse and/or neglect history, the development of a hypothesis that explains the problem, treatment goals, and a treatment plan. Depending on the nature of the problem, supplemental (optional) material that may be explored include family constellations and relationships, cultural background, ego resources, coping skills, socioeconomic level, legal problems, marital/partner relationships, medical history, and social and work history.

Patient and Clinical Expectations

How might a patient approach a clinical interview? One relevant factor is whether or not the patient is voluntarily coming to the interview. There are many situations and circumstances in which the patient is not there on a voluntary basis. Children and adolescent patients are usually brought to an evaluation by a concerned parent or referred by a concerned teacher. Some patients are referred for psychological evaluations by the court.

Sometimes a patient may seem to be a voluntary patient but actually is there out of coercion. A common example is a couple who come for counseling when a wife threatens to leave her husband unless he comes for help. Many alcoholics come for counseling under such circumstances. Whereas a voluntary patient is likely to be motivated to accept help, an involuntary patient is likely to demonstrate much resistance to the interviewing process.

Clinicians will expect a patient to discuss relevant material pertinent to the presenting problem and to form a working alliance that strives to resolve the conflicts and improve patient functioning. In order to accomplish this, psychologists typically invoke a number of interviewing techniques.

Interviewing Attitudes and Interviewing Techniques

Interviewing techniques differ from interviewing attitudes. The former comprise the various ways to intervene in a session. They are specific things a psychologist can do within the interview to advance the process. The latter represent a way of being with the patient that is evidenced throughout the interview, whatever interviewing technique is being used at the time. Four such important interviewing attitudes are rapport, genuineness and authenticity, a nonjudgmental stance, and empathic behaviors.

Rapport may be defined as a comfortable working relationship between psychologist and patient. Rapport is an important ingredient in any working relationship. It is even more important in a relationship where the patient is expected to discuss personal feelings and material that would not otherwise be discussed outside of the professional relationship.

Genuineness and authenticity are sometimes referred to as congruence and even as "therapist warmth." This means that interviewers are a "real" person with the patient and do not say anything they do not sincerely believe or express any emotions that do not come naturally to them.

Many neophyte students report that it is very difficult to be nonjudgmental with patients who are engaging in heinous behavior, such as domestic abuse, criminal behavior, and the sexual abuse of children. However, patient acceptance does not mean endorsing or approving of a patient's behavior. It means accepting the patient as a worthwhile human being capable of improvement and disapproving the behavior while not disapproving the person.

A long history of psychological research has proved that the provision of accurate empathy is positively associated with psychological growth. In being empathic, clinicians communicate to patients that they understand them from their point of view. Being empathic indicates that the psychologist is sensitive to the patient's needs and problems and is "in synch" with them.

A variety of interviewing techniques have been presented in the literature. These include active listening, clarification, confrontation, exploration, humor, interpretation, normalizing, paraphrasing, probing, questioning, reflection, reframing, restatement, self-disclosure, silence, structuring, and summarizing. These techniques should be employed in concert with the interviewing attitudes that have been shown to be beneficial to people receiving psychotherapy.

Reliability and Validity of Assessment Interviews

Although sometimes done in the past, it is no longer acceptable to discuss interview reliability and validity in general terms. Rather, it is necessary to determine and report on the reliability and validity of specific types of structured clinical interviews. Craig (2003) provides a list of the major structured clinical interviews for which there are research findings. For the most part, published structured interview have shown reliabilities in the .60s and .70s.

Many of the published structured clinical interviews can be computer-administered. These computerized interviews tend to have acceptable reliability, but convergent validity has been somewhat of a problem in selected situations when they are compared to similar instruments. It seems likely that there will be increasing use of computer-assisted screening interviews in the future (Chipman, Hassell, Magnabosco, Nowlin-Finch, Marusak, & Young, 2007). Unfortunately, there are as yet no published studies that compare the incremental validity of assessment interviews with other assessment tools, and such research is clearly needed.

REFERENCES

American Psychiatric Association. (2000). *Diagnostic and statistical manual of mental disorders* (4th ed., text rev.). Washington, DC: American Psychiatric Association.

Chipman, M., Hassell, J., Magnabosco, J., Nowlin-Finch, N., Marusak, S., & Young, A. S. (2007). The feasibility of computerized patient self-assessment at mental health clinics. *Administration and Policy in Mental Health Services Research, 34,* 401–409.

Craig, R. J. (2003). Assessing personality and psychopathology with interviews. In J. Graham & J. Naglieri (Eds.), *Handbook of psychology, Vol. 10: Assessment psychology* (pp. 487–508). New York: John Wiley & Sons.

Craig, R. J. (Ed.). (2005a). *Clinical and diagnostic interviewing* (2nd ed). Lanham, MD: Jason Aronson/Rowman & Littlefield.

Craig, R. J. (2005b). *Personality-guided forensic psychology.* Washington, DC: American Psychological Association.

Craig, R. J. (in press). Clinical interviewing. In J. N. Butcher (Ed.), *Handbook of personality assessment.* New York: Oxford University Press.

Marcyyk, G., Knauss, L., Kutinsky, J., DeMatteo, D., & Heibrun, K. (2008). The legal, ethical, and applied aspects of capital mitigation evaluations: Practice guidance from a principles-based approach. In H. V. Hall (Ed.), *Forensic psychology and neuropsychology for criminal and civil cases* (pp. 41–92). Boca Raton, FL: CRC Press.

Miller, W. R., & Rollnick, S. (2002). *Motivational interviewing: Preparing people to change addictive behavior.* New York: Guilford Press.

Prochaska, J., & DiClemente, C. C. (1983). Stages and processes of self-change of smoking: toward an integrated model of change. *Journal of Consulting and Clinical Psychology, 51,* 390–395.

Watkins, C. E., Campbell, V. L., Nieberding, R., & Hallmark, R. (1995). Contemporary practice of psychological assessment by clinical psychologists. *Professional Psychology: Research and Practice, 26,* 54–60.

SUGGESTED READING

Hersen, M., & Thomas, J. C. (Eds.). (2007). *Handbook of clinical interviewing with adults.* Thousand Oaks, CA: Sage.

ROBERT J. CRAIG
Roosevelt University

See also: **Motivational Interviewing; Structured and Semistructured Interviews**

INTRINSIC MOTIVATION

Little children love to play and to learn. They are active, curious, and eager to engage their environments, and when they do they learn. To some extent adults also love to play and to learn. When people are playing and learning in this eager and willing way, they are intrinsically motivated. Throughout life, when they are in their healthiest states, they are active and interested, and the intrinsically motivated behaviors that result help them acquire knowledge about themselves and their world.

Intrinsic motivation is a type of motivation based in people's natural interest in various activities that provide novelty and challenge. Intrinsically motivated behaviors do not require external rewards; rather, they are an expression of a person's sense of who they are, of what interests them. Intrinsically motivated behaviors have what is referred to in attribution theory as an *internal perceived locus of causality*; people experience the causes of their intrinsically motivated behaviors to be internal to themselves (de Charms, 1968).

Prior to the 1950s, theories of motivation focused on physiological drives such as hunger, thirst, and sex, proposing that all behaviors are motivated by those drives and their derivatives (Freud, 1962/1923; Hull, 1943). However, as various phenomena emerged that could not be explained by drive theories, White (1959) suggested that a full understanding of motivation required considering psychological motivations as the basis for some behaviors. He proposed an intrinsic, psychological motivation for interacting effectively with the environment. Deci and Ryan (1985) subsequently stated that the psychological needs for competence and autonomy underlie intrinsic motivation, which flourishes in contexts that allow satisfaction of those needs.

Whereas drive theories implied that humans seek quiescence and minimal stimulation, intrinsic motivation theories suggest that people desire an optimal level of stimulation. Thus, intrinsic motivation involves an ongoing cycle of finding optimal challenges and interesting activities that provide stimulation and then working to master those activities and challenges and then, perhaps after a bit of quiescence, beginning another cycle. In short, when intrinsically motivated, people seek and conquer optimal challenges.

Behaviors such as reading books, solving puzzles, exploring new areas, looking at paintings, and playing softball are intrinsically motivating for many people, but not necessarily for all, because intrinsic motivation is a property of the interaction between a person and an activity. For people to be intrinsically motivated for an activity, they must be doing it because they find it interesting.

Discussions of intrinsic motivation have typically contrasted it with extrinsic motivation. Extrinsic motivation involves doing an activity because it is instrumental to some separate consequence rather than, as is the case with intrinsic motivation, because the activity is interesting and rewarding in its own right. Thus, people are extrinsically motivated for an activity when they do it in order to earn money, avoid punishment, or comply with social norms.

Since 1971 there has been an enormous amount of research on intrinsic and extrinsic motivation. Numerous studies have confirmed that, relative to extrinsic motivation, intrinsic motivation leads to better conceptual learning, greater creativity, more cognitive flexibility, and enhanced well-being (see Ryan & Deci, 2000). Consequently, there has been great interest in understanding the conditions that enhance versus diminish intrinsic motivation. That is, although intrinsic motivation is inherent to human life, social conditions can help people maintain it or, alternatively, diminish it.

Initial studies on this topic examined how extrinsic rewards affect intrinsic motivation: might they enhance it, undermine it, or leave it unchanged? Thus, if a person were engaged in an intrinsically interesting activity that he or she would be happy to do with no external reward, what would happen to the person's intrinsic interest for the activity if he or she were given an extrinsic reward for doing it? A meta-analysis of 128 experiments examining this question confirmed that tangible extrinsic rewards tend to undermine intrinsic motivation for rewarded activities (Deci, Koestner, & Ryan, 1999). After people are given monetary rewards or prizes for doing an interesting activity, they tend to find the activity less interesting and are less likely to do it spontaneously than they were before they had been rewarded.

Additional studies with young children, teenagers, college students, and adults revealed that other external events, such as directives, surveillance, deadlines, threats of punishment, and negative performance feedback also decrease intrinsic motivation. These extrinsic incentives can control people's behavior, getting them to do the activity, but in the process the people tend to lose interest and persist less. In turn, they are likely to perform less well if the activity requires resourcefulness, deep thinking, or creativity. In contrast, external factors such as offering choice, acknowledging people's feelings, and providing positive performance feedback have been found to enhance their intrinsic motivation, resulting in better performance.

Deci and Ryan (2000) interpreted these results in terms of satisfaction versus thwarting of the basic needs for autonomy and competence. Specifically, people tend to interpret rewards, directives, deadlines, and threats as controllers of their behavior, which thwarts their need for autonomy; in contrast, people tend to experience choice and acknowledgment as support for their autonomy. Similarly, positive feedback tends to satisfy people's basic need for competence, whereas negative feedback tends to thwart that need. When people experience satisfaction of both needs in relation to an activity, they will tend to be highly intrinsically motivated for that activity, whether it is learning, playing baseball, or making a sculpture. When both needs are thwarted they will be very low in intrinsic motivation, and when there is partial satisfaction of the needs, the level of intrinsic motivation will be moderate.

Further studies examined the general interpersonal context or ambience of particular settings, such as classrooms or workgroups. For example, investigators found that teachers who were more supportive of autonomy and created a supportive classroom environment by understanding their students' perspectives, providing choice, encouraging initiations, and refraining from using controlling language, catalyzed their students' intrinsic motivation and desire for challenge. Similarly, managers who supported their subordinates' autonomy promoted greater motivation and satisfaction on the job. In fact, authority figures such as doctors, parents, and coaches have also been found to influence the motivation and behaviors of their patients, children, and athletes, depending on the degree to which they are supportive of autonomy and competence rather than being controlling and critical.

Finally, Deci and Ryan (2000) pointed out that different people may interpret differently the same external events, such as rewards, feedback, and deadlines. That is, many external events such as rewards have both an aspect that *controls* behavior and one that conveys positive competence *information*. If the controlling aspect is more salient, it pressures people toward specific outcomes, thus thwarting their sense of autonomy and undermining their intrinsic motivation. However, if the informational aspect is more salient, it affirms people's competence and enhances their intrinsic motivation. Whether the controlling or informational aspect is more salient depends on both the situation and the person.

When the interpersonal contexts within which rewards or feedback are administered is generally supportive of autonomy, the informational aspect of the rewards or feedback tends to be more salient. For example, studies have shown that, although monetary rewards typically diminish intrinsic motivation, they can maintain or enhance it if they are administered in an autonomy-supportive context.

In addition, some people, due to socialization, are inclined to experience events such as rewards and feedback as more informational, whereas others are inclined to experience them as more controlling. Thus, individual differences can lead different people to experience the same external event differently, so the event will have different effects on the intrinsic motivation of the different people (Deci & Ryan, 2000).

To summarize, intrinsic motivation flourishes when people are able to satisfy their needs for competence and autonomy while doing interesting tasks. Specific events in the interpersonal environment, such as the offer of rewards, the imposition of deadlines, and the provision of performance feedback can directly affect people's need satisfaction and, thus, their intrinsic motivation. The general interpersonal ambience can also impact people's need satisfaction and intrinsic motivation both directly and by influencing how they experience external events. Finally, people differ in their tendencies to interpret events and environments in ways that support versus thwart need satisfaction and intrinsic motivation.

Because intrinsic motivation is relevant in many walks of life and leads to more positive outcomes than extrinsic motivation, it seems important to support the autonomy and competence of our children, students, clients, employees, and patients.

REFERENCES

de Charms, R. (1968). *Personal causation.* New York: Academic Press.

Deci, E. L., Koestner, R., & Ryan, R. M. (1999). A meta-analytic review of experiments examining the effects of extrinsic rewards on intrinsic motivation. *Psychological Bulletin, 125,* 627–668.

Deci, E. L., & Ryan, R. M. (1985). *Intrinsic motivation and self-determination in human behavior.* New York: Plenum.

Deci, E. L., & Ryan, R. (2000). The "what" and "why" of goal pursuits: Human needs and the self-determination of behavior. *Psychological Inquiry, 11,* 227–268.

Freud, S. (1962). *The ego and the id.* New York: Norton. (Original work published 1923)

Hull, C. L. (1943). *Principles of behavior.* New York: Appleton-Century-Crofts.

Ryan, R. M., & Deci, E. L. (2000). Self-determination theory and the facilitation of intrinsic motivation, social development, and well-being.*American Psychologist, 55,* 68–78.

White, R. W. (1959). Motivation reconsidered.*Psychological Review, 66,* 297–333.

EDWARD L. DECI
RICHARD M. RYAN
University of Rochester

INTROVERSION-EXTRAVERSION

Carl Jung coined the terms *introversion* and *extraversion* to refer to two different psychological attitudes. By introversion, Jung meant a turning inward of the libido (psychic energy), whereas extraversion referred to a directing outward of the libido. Note that either term can be spelled with an "o" or an "a" (that is, either as above or as intraversion and extroversion). Although inconsistent, introversion and extraversion are the spellings used with the Myers-Briggs Type Indicator®(MBTI®) instrument, which is a popular personality assessment tool based on Jung's type theory.

An introvert's mind, emotions, attention, and so forth are turned inward toward himself or herself. Jung believed that the introvert directs the libido inward because of inferiority feelings, an idea reminiscent of Alfred Adler. Particularly during stressful periods, introverts tend to withdraw into themselves, to avoid others, and to be self-absorbed. With a bent toward self-sufficiency, the introvert's essential stimulation is from within, from his or her inner world of thoughts and reflections. Introverts are frequently reserved and difficult to get to know, tend to bottle up their emotions, and need privacy. Introverts find that interacting with others drains their energy; for extraverts the opposite is true.

Extraverts orient primarily to the outer world, focusing their perceptions and judgments on people and things. Extraverts draw energy from other people and external experiences; tend to express their emotions; need relationships more than privacy; and are usually friendly, talkative, and easy to get to know. Extraverts may seem shallow to introverts, whereas introverts may seem withdrawn to extraverts. Both attitudes are present in all people, but usually one is preferred over the other.

On the MBTI®instrument, the E-I or Extraversion-Introversion index is one of four dichotomous scales. The other three are Sensing-Intuition (S-N), Thinking-Feeling (T-F), and Judging-Perceiving (J-P). The J-P scale was an addition by the test authors, as Jung did not directly identify this dichotomy.

SUGGESTED READINGS

Jung, C. G. (1971). Psychological types. In *The collected works of C. G. Jung (Vol. 6), Bollinger Series XX*. Princeton, NJ: Princeton University Press.

Myers, I. B., McCaulley, M. H., Quenk, N. L., & Hammer, A. L. (1998). *MBTI Manual: A guide to the Myers-Briggs Type Indicator* (3rd ed.). Palo Alto, CA: Consulting Psychologists Press.

Myers, I. B., & Myers, P. B. (1980). *Gifts differing*. Palo Alto, CA: Consulting Psychologists Press.

B. MICHAEL THORNE
Mississippi State University

See also: Myers-Briggs Type Indicator (MBT)

IQ (See Intelligence Quotient)

IRRATIONAL BELIEFS

Irrational beliefs are rigid, inaccurate, or illogical beliefs that are used to interpret external events. They are self-defeating, unconditional, inconsistent with reality, and unlikely to find empirical support. Conversely, rational beliefs are logical, flexible, and consistent with reality. If a person holds irrational beliefs, negative life events—inevitable in everyone's life—will result in inappropriate negative emotions and dysfunctional behaviors. Irrational beliefs also play a role as predisposing or causal factors in a number of behavior disorders.

Theory

The work of Albert Ellis and the work of Aaron Beck have provided the theoretical underpinnings of most research on irrational beliefs. Ellis (1962) developed rational-emotive therapy (RET), now known as rational emotive-behavior therapy (REBT), in the 1950s. RET was a product of dissatisfaction with the effectiveness of psychoanalysis and the time required for its completion. The main idea behind REBT is that the most important causes of inappropriate and self-defeating behaviors and emotions are the beliefs about the events and not the events themselves. REBT is based on the ABC model of psychopathology in which people experience unpleasant activating environmental events. These events (A) do not cause dysfunctional behavioral and emotional consequences (C); instead, the dysfunctional behaviors and emotional consequences (C) are caused by the distorted or irrational beliefs (B) about the event (A). Initially, Ellis proposed 11 types of irrational beliefs. Subsequent developments in REBT have articulated four categories: demandingness, awfulizing or catastrophizing, low frustration tolerance, and global evaluation or self-downing.

Demandingness is the core irrational belief in REBT. It refers to absolustic requirements that are expressed in terms of "musts," "have to," "shoulds," and "oughts." One common irrational belief noted by Ellis is that people believe that they must be completely competent in everything they do. When an inevitable mistake is made, it becomes catastrophic, as it is a violation of the belief in personal perfection. Awfulizing beliefs refer to the extreme evaluation of a bad event as worse than it should be. Low frustration tolerance is the belief that it is not possible to bear certain circumstances, thereby rendering a situation intolerable. Global evaluation described pervasive negative ratings about the world and oneself. These four irrational beliefs are considered to be fundamental etiological factors in emotional disorders.

Like Ellis, Beck (1976) was disenchanted with psychoanalysis and created another version of the ABC model. Beck, who developed cognitive therapy (CT), believed that many disorders are produced and maintained by negative thinking styles and negative beliefs that people hold about themselves, their circumstances, and their future. These cognitive errors include believing in excessive personal causality for negative events and believing that the worst possible outcome is the most likely to happen. According to Beck, these cognitive fallacies, referred to as distortions, guide a person's interpretation of new experiences and increase the probability of behavioral and emotional disorders.

The cognitive triad of irrational beliefs—negative thoughts about oneself ("I'm not good enough"), the world ("This is an awful place"), and the future ("Something bad will always happen")—are activated by negative life events and produce systematic errors in thinking. Among the most frequent errors are the following: "All or nothing" thinking: (i.e., the tendency to view a negative event in only two ways, as opposed to a continuum); arbitrary inference (i.e., the predisposition to reach negative conclusions without supporting evidence); selective abstraction (i.e., the tendency to pay attention to one negative detail versus the whole picture); magnification/minimization (i.e., unreasonably amplifying the negative and minimizing the positive when evaluating one's situation); and labeling (i.e., the inclination to globally evaluate things negatively and dismiss evidence that supports a less extreme position). Beck believed that deep-seated negative thinking plays a major role in generating depression.

Measurement

For both REBT and CT, it is essential to measure irrational beliefs accurately in order to provide evidence of their scientific status and to assist in treatment. The first objective measures were based on Ellis's (1962) original list of 11 specific irrational ideas. Many early measures appeared to confound negative affect with irrational beliefs; consequently, more recent measures have been designed to maximize discriminant validity by excluding items consisting of emotional statements. Over a dozen questionnaires based on the Ellis model and the Beck model have been developed and tested.

Of the early measures of irrational beliefs, the Irrational Beliefs Test (Jones, 1968) and the Rational Behavior Inventory (Shorkey & Whiteman, 1977) remain in use and are often cited, despite the fact they are based on Ellis's earlier work. The Dysfunctional Attitude Scale (Weissman, 1979) and the Cognitive Error Questionnaire (Lefebvre, 1980), based on the work of Beck, are viewed as valid measures of irrationality and are also frequently cited in the research literature.

Therapy

The goal of REBT is to use cognitive restructuring to eliminate self-defeating irrational beliefs. This is accomplished via the forceful disputation of these beliefs by questioning the client's evidence for the belief. An REBT therapist indicates to clients when they demonstrate an irrational belief and reveals the consequences of these beliefs. Clients are assigned specific behavioral tasks in which they work on changing their emotional and cognitive reactions.

The goal of Beck's CT is to change systematic mistakes in logic or alter misconceptions about events which render a person vulnerable to behavior disorders. Therapeutic intervention is progressively focused on observable behavior, automatic thoughts, cognitive errors, and then on core beliefs. A cognitive therapist prompts clients to maintain a record of distressing thoughts and the resultant negative feelings, followed by demonstrations about how to challenge the validity of these cognitions and substitute rational alternatives. Thus, clients are challenged to provide evidence for their beliefs.

Other therapies, referred to as cognitive-behavior therapies, have since emerged. Therapy aimed at changing irrational beliefs was initially focused on depression, but it is now considered to have a variety of applications. Studies of therapy aimed at changing irrational beliefs have demonstrated its usefulness in treating mood disorders, anxiety disorders, personality disorders, eating disorders, substance-use disorders, and psychotic disorders. Therapies aimed at changing irrational beliefs are considered to be among the most rapid in terms of results; this is due to their instructive nature and the use of homework. This type of therapy has widespread empirical support and has become popular with therapists and consumers.

REFERENCES

Beck, A. T. (1976). *Cognitive therapy and the emotional disorders*. New York: International Universities Press.

Ellis, A. (1962). *Reason and emotion in psychotherapy*. New York: Lyle-Stuart.

Jones, R. (1968). *A factored measure of Ellis irrational beliefs system with personality maladjustment correlates*. Unpublished doctoral dissertation, Texas Technological College.

Lefebvre, M. F. (1980). *Cognitive distortion in depressed psychiatric and low back pain patients*. Unpublished doctoral dissertation, University of Vermont, Burlington.

Shorkey, C. T., & Whiteman, V. L. (1977). Development of the Rational Behavior Inventory: Initial validity and reliability. *Educational and Psychological Measurement, 37*, 527–534.

Weissman, A. N. (1979). *The Dysfunctional Attitude Scale: A validation study*. Unpublished doctoral dissertation, University of Pennsylvania, Philadelphia.

SUGGESTED READINGS

Beck, A. T. (2005). The current state of cognitive therapy: A 40-year retrospective. *Archives of General Psychiatry, 62*, 953–959.

Butler, A. C., Chapman, J. E., Forman, E. M., & Beck, A. T. (2006). The empirical status of cognitive-behavioral therapy: A review of meta-analyses. *Clinical Psychology Review, 26*, 17–31.

Dryden, W., & Ellis, A. (2001). Rational emotive behavior therapy. In K. S. Dobson (Ed.), *Handbook of cognitive behavioral therapies* (2nd ed., pp. 295–348). New York: Guilford Press.

K. ROBERT BRIDGES
RICHARD J. HARNISH
Pennsylvania State University at New Kensington

See also: **Cognitive Therapy; Delusions; Rational Emotive Behavior Therapy**

IRRITABLE BOWEL SYNDROME

Irritable bowel syndrome (IBS) is a complex, multidetermined syndrome involving altered gut reactivity, altered pain perception, and brain-gut dysregulation that is modulated by psychosocial and biological factors (Palsson & Drossman, 2005). The symptomatology of IBS is a combination of abdominal pain or discomfort, rectal distension, and altered bowel habit (i.e., diarrhea or constipation).

Diagnosis

IBS can currently be diagnosed using the Rome II criteria (Thompson, Longstreth, Drossman, Heaton, Irvine, & Muller-Lissner, 2000). The Rome criteria, shown in Table 1, were developed using a consensus-based approach adopted by a panel of international experts and are generally found to be both sensitive and specific for

Table 1. Diagnostic Criteria for IBS (Revised Rome Criteria)

At least 12 weeks or more, which need not be consecutive, in the preceding 12 months of abdominal discomfort or pain that has 2 of 3 features:
Relieved with defecation *and/or*
Onset associated with a change in frequency of stool *and/or*
Onset associated with a change in form (appearance) of stool
Symptoms that cumulatively support the diagnosis of IBS:
Abnormal stool frequency (for research purposes, "abnormal" may be defined as more than 3 bowel movements per day and fewer than 3 bowel movements per week)
Abnormal stool form (lumpy/hard or loose/watery stool)
Abnormal stool passage (straining, urgency, or feeling of incomplete evacuation)
Passage of mucus
Bloating or feeling of abdominal distension

Adapted from Thompson et al. (2000)

the diagnosis of IBS. Recently, Rome III criteria have been developed emphasizing subtyping according to bowel habit (Longstreth, Thompson, Chey, Houghton, Mearin, & Spiller, 2006), but there is not yet a sufficient body of research using the new criteria to determine if the subtyping approach is illuminating.

Prevalence

IBS is a very common disorder, with an overall prevalence estimated between 10–20% of the U.S. population. International studies have documented a fairly constant prevalence across national boundaries and ethnic and racial lines for IBS. Prevalence is higher in individuals in the second to fifth decades of life and declines considerably thereafter. IBS accounts for about 12% of patients seen in primary care practice, although most IBS sufferers do not seek medical treatment (Horwitz & Fisher, 2001).

Patients with IBS, when compared with nonconsulting persons with IBS, have more nongastrointestinal (GI) complaints and consult physicians more for these other symptoms. Those who consult physicians display increased illness behavior, greater psychological distress, and more fears of serious illness than nonconsulters. Conversely, IBS nonconsulters have been found to have better coping capabilities, to view IBS as less disruptive, and to exhibit less denial than patients. Collectively, these studies indicate that psychological factors influence who consults a doctor for IBS symptoms (Johnson, 2008).

IBS is more prevalent in women than in men. The sex ratio for individuals with IBS who do not seek care is 2:1 (female to male). Among individuals who seek care for IBS, the ratio jumps to 4:1 (female to male). Female dominance may reflect the general tendency of females to seek medical care and to have slower gut transit times and higher vigilance and perception regarding sensory input from the pelvic, visceral, and hormonal influences (Chang & Heitkemper, 2003).

Many individuals with IBS also meet criteria for other medically unexplained illnesses. IBS often co-occurs with functional dyspepsia, interstitial cystitis, fibromyalgia, chronic pelvic pain, chronic fatigue syndrome, and temporomandibular joint disorder. These conditions share certain features: they disproportionately affect women, they are stress-related, and they are associated with fatigue, sleep difficulties, anxiety, and depression.

Disability and Quality of Life

IBS is not associated with excess mortality, yet it involves significant levels of disability and impaired quality of life (QOL). Absence from school and work, difficulty in activities of daily living; and the need to modify one's work setting or work fewer hours are common impacts. In this respect, patients with IBS differ significantly from patients with many other chronic medical illnesses. Compared with individuals with rheumatoid arthritis, asthma, diabetes, as well as gastroesophageal reflux disease, IBS patients show significantly lower levels of QOL. Other studies have found that individuals with IBS have more unhealthy days than people with serious chronic diseases such as heart disease and diabetes.

Etiology

Etiologic mechanisms for IBS are not completely understood. Drossman (1998) has proposed that early life factors, including both genetics and environmental exposures, influence the later interaction of psychosocial and physiological functioning with the CNS/enteric nervous system axis, and that this interaction affects the clinical expression IBS and such outcomes as physician visits, functional status, and quality of life.

Pathophysiology

IBS involves both diffuse smooth muscle dysmotility and lower visceral pain thresholds. A finding that IBS patients experience pain and bloating at lower levels of balloon inflation in the rectum and lower bowel than do controls has been replicated in numerous studies, and the concept of "visceral" hypersensitivity has been hypothesized (Johnson, 2008).

Perceptual findings indicate that IBS is associated with hypersensitivity in the upper GI tract and the colon and heightened perception of normal intestinal contractions, but IBS is not associated with a generalized hypersensitivity to noxious somatic stimulation. Further, perception of colonic distensions can be modified by attention, anxiety, and relaxation (Mayer, 2000). Research suggests the possibility of a "brain-gut axis" where peripheral symptoms are processed in the end organ (i.e., the colon), following which neural signals are carried via visceral afferents to the spinal cord and then to the brain, where they are subject to additional processing that can influence descending pathways. Individuals with IBS have been shown to have increased activation of pain pathways involved in this brain-gut axis.

Psychological Issues in IBS

A number of studies have documented high rates of symptomatic mental disorders in people with IBS. In IBS clinic and treatment trial samples being assessed with standardized interview procedures, about half of the patients meet criteria for a diagnosable psychiatric condition. The most common psychiatric diagnoses among these patients are depression, stress reaction, and anxiety. The high rates of psychiatric disorders in IBS have been found mainly in patients who present to referral centers for care, whereas community cohort studies do not find high rates of psychiatric diagnosis (Johnson, 2008). It is the consulters who have an impact on the health care system and are most likely to need psychological treatment.

A number of studies have documented a high prevalence of reported childhood sexual abuse (CSA) in individuals with IBS, finding that generally about 30–50% of women with IBS report a history of having been sexually abused. Individuals with a relatively severe abuse history generally report more symptoms, greater health care use, and worse functional disability than those reports of less severe abuse. Early traumatic stress can lead individuals to develop hypervigilance, which may predispose them to experience symptoms as particularly salient and threatening.

Although various physiologic and psychological mechanisms are implicated in IBS, no one mechanism explains the condition of the majority of patients with IBS. The biopsychosocial model applied to IBS has been explicated in the previously mentioned work of Drossman (1998), who maintains that (1) many factors contribute to symptom development, (2) no one factor is necessary for IBS to develop, and (3) factors will interact in different combinations. Thus in some patients, higher levels of stress predict who develops IBS after a bout of gastroenteritis, while patients with a low sensory threshold will be more susceptible to GI pain in IBS. Research also suggests that people with IBS and comorbid UI have somatization tendencies and a predominantly psychological etiology, whereas those without comorbid conditions and excessive symptoms are more likely to have a physiological etiology for their IBS. The female predominance in IBS is likely due to a number of biopsychosocial factors. Women's higher levels of somatic reporting, higher rates of CSA, different brain-gut axis, and visceral sensitivity could all be important contributors (Johnson, 2008).

REFERENCES

Chang, L., & Heitkemper, M. M. (2003). Gender differences in irritable bowel syndrome. *Gastroenterology, 123,* 1686–1701.

Drossman, D. A. (1998). Presidential address: Gastrointestinal illness and the biopsychosocial model. *Psychosomatic Medicine, 60,* 258–267.

Horwitz, B. J., & Fisher, R. S. (2001). The irritable bowel syndrome. *The New England Journal of Medicine, 334,* 1846–1850.

Johnson, S. K. (2008). *Medically unexplained illness: Gender and biopsychosocial implications.* Washington, DC: American Psychological Association. Longstreth, G. F., Thompson, W. G., Chey, W. D., Houghton, L. A., Mearin, F., & Spiller, R. C. (2006). Functional bowel disorders. *Gastroenterology, 130,* 1480–1491.

Mayer, E. A. (2000). Review: The neurobiology of stress and gastrointestinal disease. *Gut, 47,* 861–869.

Palsson, O. S., & Drossman, D. A. (2005). Psychiatric and psychological dysfunction in irritable bowel syndrome and the role of psychological treatments. *Gastroenterology Clinics of North America, 34,* 281–303.

Thompson, W. G., Longstreth, G. F., Drossman, D. A., Heaton, K. W., Irvin, E. J., & Muller-Lissner, S. A. (2000). Functional bowel disorders and functional abdominal pain. In D. A. Drossman, E. Corazziari, N. J. Talley, W. G. Tompson, & W. E. Whitehead (Eds.), *Rome II: The functional gastrointestinal disorders* (pp. 351–396). McLean, VA: Degnon Associates.

SUSAN K. JOHNSON
University of North Carolina-Charlotte

See also: **Somatoform Disorders**

ISOMORPHISM

In psychology, the term "isomorphism" is identified with the classical Berlin school of Gestalt psychology, which used the word to characterize the Gestaltists' approach to the mind/brain problem. They argued that the objective brain processes underlying and correlated with particular phenomenological experiences are isomorphic with (that is, have functionally the same form and structure as) those subjective experiences.

The etymology of the word "isomorphism" makes the term appropriate for such a theory. The Greek root "iso-" means same, equal, or identical, and "morph-" means form, shape, organization, or structure. What Gestalt psychologists intended to convey with their principle of isomorphism is that the Gestalt properties (the form, shape, organization, and structure) of biophysical, electrochemical processes in the brain that underlie subjective cognitive experiences are identical to the Gestalt properties (the form, shape, organization, and structure) of the experiences themselves. This proposal contrasted with the connectionistic mind/brain theories that prevailed during the first half of the twentieth century, which tended to view the brain as a giant switchboard of interconnected, insulated switches and wires rather than as a dynamic system of interdependent electrochemical biological processes that constitute a complex interactive field.

Because this dynamic field conception of brain function and activity was so different from the more static and mechanistic view of the brain that was implicitly taken for granted by the majority of psychologists at the time, the Gestalt idea of isomorphism was generally not well understood. One Gestalt theorist, Mary Henle (1984, p. 317), wrote, "I know of no concept in psychology that has been more misunderstood, indeed more distorted, than isomorphism."

One reason for this distortion or misunderstanding of *isomorphism* is that the term had been used long before Gestalt theorists adopted it in such fields as chemistry, crystallography, and mathematics, and in a way that typically implied a piecemeal orientation that is inconsistent with the Gestalt conception. In mathematical set theory, for example, two groups of items are isomorphic if there is a perfect one-to-one correspondence between the two sets; that is, each item in the first set can be paired one-for-one with an item in the second set, without remainder in either set.

This kind of one-to-one correspondence between two isomorphic processes or phenomena is foreign to the Gestalt approach. For instance, two dotted circles, one composed of 25 dots along its circumference and another of 27 dots, are isomorphic in that Gestalt sense of having the same functional form; the number of dots composing each circle is immaterial as long as there are enough them to specify the overall shape reasonably clearly. What is crucial is precisely the form or shape or structure itself, not the number of "elements" that happen to make up its "parts." Thinking in terms of one-to-one correspondence of dots on the circumference of the two circles is a piecemeal process that ignores the dynamic characteristics of the continuity of the trajectory of a circle, of the equidistance of each part of the circumference from the center, and so on, that make up the essential Gestalt or configuration of a circle.

Two circles, whatever the number of "elements" composing their circumference and irrespective of their color or size, are isomorphic simply because they are both circles: Both display the same circular shape. Comparably, two squares are isomorphic even if they are made up of different "elements" or are of difference sizes, brightness, or colors. Further, although the notes of a particular melody are all different when the melody is played in a different key, the sequences of notes are isomorphic and still constitute the same melody—and variations on the melody remain isomorphic as long as the basic melody is still recognizable (even if some variations may contain many more or fewer notes than others).

The first reference to brain processes that are isomorphic in the Gestalt sense to perceptual processes occurred in a 1912 paper on apparent motion by Max Wertheimer that is generally considered to have launched the Gestalt School. The reference concerns processes in the visual brain that are presumed to correspond to what Wertheimer called the "phi phenomenon," the illusory perception of motion when in fact there is no motion in the physical stimulus. Assume, say, two short vertical lines X and Y, each about two inches long, separated horizontally by about one inch. If X is exposed for a few seconds then disappears, and a fraction of a second later Y is exposed, it may appear to the observer that what was shown was not two different lines, X and Y, successively exposed, but a single line that moved from location X to location Y. If the sequence is continued, so that a very short time after Y disappears X is exposed again, then Y again followed by X, and so on, as long as the distance and time relationships are appropriate, the result is that a single line is seen moving back and forth in stereoscopic motion. If the time between removal of one line and the appearance of the other is too long, the observer experiences two stationary lines successively exposed; if the time interval is too short (or if there is overlap in the time both lines are exposed), the observer reports two stationary lines being exposed in two different places.

What happens in the brain under the condition in which a single moving line is seen in such an experiment? Wertheimer argued that every mind/brain theory must assume that there is excitation of particular parts of the visual cortex when the observer sees the lines, one area of excitation, x, that corresponds to stimulus X, and another nearby, y, that corresponds to stimulus Y. Furthermore (and here is where Gestalt theory deviated from other mind/brain theories), when motion is perceived, there must be some kind of a "short circuit" between the brain area x corresponding to X and the nearby area y corresponding to Y; this "short circuit" is the brain process that is isomorphic with the experience of a single moving line. The Gestalt properties of the process in the brain must somehow correspond with the Gestalt properties of seeing a single moving line rather than two separate stationary isolated lines.

Wertheimer's theoretical conception was elaborated in much greater detail by two of his Gestalt colleagues, Kurt Koffka (in his major book) and Wolfgang Köhler (in extensive biopsychological and perceptual experiments, 1929). Koehler and his collaborators generated some rather surprising predictions from the theory, and managed to validate many of these predictions experimentally (e.g., Koehler & Wallach, 1944).

Wertheimer and a prominent Harvard psychologist in the structuralist tradition, Edwin G. Boring, engaged in a lengthy and mutually respectful correspondence during the 1930s about the principle of isomorphism, but Wertheimer did not succeed in convincing Boring of the validity of the theory, and indeed Boring admitted that he never did manage to understand "isomorphism" in the way in which the Gestalt theorists were using the term (King & Wertheimer, 2005, pp. 261–267).

A large number of experiments (not only in vision but in other sense modalities such as kinesthesis) made the theory of isomorphism widely discussed by the middle of the twentieth century. In the early 1950s, two illustrious neuroscientists (Karl Lashley, 1951, and Roger Sperry, 1955) and their collaborators performed experiments intended to disprove the theory by inserting insulating material or material with excellent electrical conductivity into the visual brains of animals. They found no evidence of any resulting visual dysfunctions, but Köhler responded by pointing out various serious technical flaws in these experiments.

Interest in the Gestalt isomorphism hypothesis waned during the 1960s and 1970s; discussions of it in books about perception and about physiology psychology or cognitive neuroscience became rare by the 1980s. The predominant views by the late 1980s and early 1990s among neuroscientists about how the brain functions encountered difficulty in trying to accommodate processes as dynamic, interactive, field-theoretical, and systems-oriented as the Gestalt view of isomorphism. The theory was neither definitively proven nor refuted by empirical data; neuropsychological research went on to study other issues instead. Nevertheless, the Gestalt theory of physical processes in the brain that are functionally isomorphic with processes in subjective experience was one of the more influential twentieth-century efforts to come to grips with the recurring and ancient fundamental question of the relation between mind and brain.

REFERENCES

Henle, M. (1984). Isomorphism: Setting the record straight. *Psychological Research, 46*, 317–327.

King, D. B., & Wertheimer, M. (2005). *Max Wertheimer and Gestalt theory*. New Brunswick, NJ, & London: Transaction.

Koffka, K. (1935). *Principles of Gestalt psychology*. New York: Harcourt, Brace.

Köhler, W. (1929). *Gestalt psychology*. New York: Liveright.

Köhler, W., & Wallach, H. (1944). Figural after-effects. Proceedings of the American Philosophical Society, *88*, 269–357.

Lashley, K. S., Chow, K. L., & Semmes, J. (1951). An examination of the electrical field theory of cerebral integration. *Psychological Review, 58*, 123–136.

Sperry, R. W., & Miner, N. (1955). Pattern perception following insertion of mica plates into visual cortex. *Journal of Comparative and Physiological Psychology, 48*, 463–469.

Sperry, R. W., Miner, N., & Myers, R. E. (1955). Visual pattern perception following subpial slicing and tantalum wire implantations in the visual cortex. *Journal of Comparative and Physiological Psychology, 48*, 50–58.

Wertheimer, M. (1912). Experimentelle Studien ueber das Sehen von Bewegung [Experimental studies of seeing motion]. *Zeitschrift fuer Psychologie, 60*, 321–378.

SUGGESTED READING

Pribram, K. H. (1984). What is iso and what is morphic in isomorphism? *Psychological Research, 46*, 329–332.

MICHAEL WERTHEIMER
University of Colorado–Boulder

See also: Gestalt Psychology

ISRAEL, PSYCHOLOGY IN

With repeated experiences of warfare and terror threats and a wide range of social problems, psychology in Israel might be described as linking together general and country-specific science and practice. This description can be found in documents dating back to 1935, when Kurt Lewin negotiated his candidacy for establishing the first academic psychology department in what was then Palestine, at the Hebrew University in Jerusalem.

Basic Foundations of Israeli Psychology

When negotiation with Kurt Lewin failed, an offer to establish the department was made to Joseph Bonaventura, an Italian experimental psychologist. However, the need to mobilize national resources for the foundation of the state, exacerbated by the economic distress of World War II, did not allow the development of research activity within the department, which opened in 1940 as a secondary field. A solid foundation of research began to develop only in 1957, when psychology was fully approved as an independent academic discipline.

Unlike scientific activity, clinical practice emerged initially between the two world wars, when a group of Freud's students arrived in Palestine. At the head of this group was Max Eitingon, a member of the committee that ran the affairs of the psychoanalytic movement. In 1933 he established the Palestine Psychoanalytic Society, followed by the Psychoanalytic Institute, which was accredited in 1936 by the International Psychoanalytic Association.

During the pre-state period, the effect of psychoanalysis on neighboring fields was demonstrated in different social and educational issues, particularly in those related to the collectively oriented ideology of the kibbutz. Psychology as a profession thus took shape at the intersection between the collectivistic-oriented Zionist ideology of those who settled in Palestine and the individualistic psychoanalytic movement. At that period, some additional activities of educational counseling, vocational guidance, and psychometric testing were conducted in the field.

Developmental Lines: Science and Practice

Psychological activity in Israel was proceeding along the basic lines of national development, being invariably related to historical events and geopolitical conditions. The Israeli population in 2008, consisting of more than 7 million people, was about nine times larger than the population in 1948, when the state was established. The ratio of psychologists in proportion to the population, which has increased over time to become the highest of any country in the world, might be understood in the light of the national challenges, particularly those related to mass immigration and constant security threats.

Since the early 1950s, Israel has become the largest immigrant-absorbing nation relative to its population. The heterogeneous groups of immigrants, including Holocaust survivors and newcomers from Asian and African countries, were entering a country with a chaotic social structure. The adaptation problems, intensified by the complexity of intergroup relationships between Jewish and Arab citizens and between religious and non-religious groups, have provided psychological scholars with a very rich research field, while also creating urgent needs for psychological interventions.

Furthermore, Israel has been considered to be a natural research field for studying the impact of constant threats of terror on mentally healthy people. Certainly, this observation warrants a cautious interpretation of any data, so as to distinguish between psychopathological manifestations and what could be defined as a national epidemic of affective disorder. Within the rapidly growing research area of peace psychology, however, the case of Israel often serves as a rich database for exploring a wide range of psychological issues.

Another development related to security problems has emerged in the area of neuropsychology. Israel is one of the first countries to develop national psychological services specifically designed to address the needs of young disabled veterans with severe traumatic brain injury. The modern neuroimaging techniques applied in scientific research, together with extensive rehabilitation services supported by the Israeli Defense Forces (IDF), have resulted in substantial achievements that have gained worldwide recognition.

The IDF, which is a leading agency with respect to recruiting and training psychologists, conducting testing, and providing mental health services, has had notable impact on general developments in the field. Thus, Louis Guttman, one of the most influential psychometricians of the twentieth century, used his experience as the founder of the IDF unit of behavioral sciences to explore his ideas about scale analysis and facet theory. Daniel Kahneman, the first PhD in psychology to receive a Nobel Prize (2002), applied his IDF experience in interviewing combat-unit recruits to developing the construct *illusion of validity*, which points to a complete lack of connection between statistical information and compelling experience.

Current Scientific and Professional Activities

Psychology in Israel has increasingly become both specialized and interdisciplinary. Researchers work together with colleagues from other fields such as mathematics, computer science, biology, and medical sciences to promote scientific achievements that are robustly reflected in international publications, particularly when weighted by population size. According to data provided by Thomson Scientific (2008) from Essential Science Indicators 1997–2007, Israel ranks 14th in its Impact Factor and is among the top 10 nations in the number of published papers and citations in the leading journals of psychiatry and psychology.

Israeli psychological research is notably diverse and is strongly influenced by American scientific activity. Important research is being conducted in a variety of realms including psychobiology, psychophysiology, and cognitive, social, political, developmental, organizational, occupational, educational, and clinical psychology. Although usually oriented toward basic research, the majority of projects also explore practical applications. Prominent among these are studies related to interactions between brain functions and behavior, psychophysiological correlates of information processing, language, visual attention, implicit memory, psychopathological manifestations, judgment and decision-making processes, personality characteristics, and cross-cultural patterns of attitudes and behavior.

The major developments in practice and training also point to substantial effects of American psychology. Israeli clinicians are most frequently psychoanalytically oriented. While initially applying classical and ego-psychology perspectives, Israeli clinical practice is gradually diversifying, absorbing competing conceptual influences of object-relations, self-psychology, relational-intersubjective, and other approaches. Cognitive-behavioral therapy popularity is currently increasing, particularly within the context of crisis interventions.

Psychology offers some of the most highly demanded degree programs by Israeli students. The number of applicants is much higher than available places, particularly in the clinical programs, which are offered by six academic institutions accredited by the Council for Higher Education. Following the submission of the M.A. thesis, graduates of applied fields (clinical, educational, developmental, organizational-occupational, health psychology, and neuropsychology) can enter internship, which provides them with the needed experience for the license examination.

The vast majority of the graduates work as practitioners who are rarely involved in research activity. The lower salary, however, leads many of the practitioners to leave the public service in favor of private practice as soon as they receive credentials as experts.

Controversial Issues

Being extremely applicable to the daily problems of the society, Israeli psychology has gained substantial public recognition. Nonetheless, there exist some conflicts and controversies that might detract from the high regard in which the field is held. These include an increasing engagement of the popular media in giving psychological advice and controversies between psychoanalytically oriented and cognitive-behavioral psychologists and between supporters and critics of different personality assessment tools. There are also ideological gaps and conflicts of interests between the governmental authority, the professional organization of the Israeli Psychological Association (IPA), and the academic institutions that create substantial hurdles. Debates between members of the different IPA divisions, which have different perspectives concerning the needs of specific groups, also frequently slow down professional progress.

One of the most controversial issues in Israel has been related to the positions of psychologists toward the Middle East conflict and its resolution. Political claims, based apparently on professional experience or scientific knowledge, generate public debates regarding the legitimacy of using expertise to support personal attitudes. However, some psychologists, joining their colleagues from different academic disciplines, feel that they are condemned by the international community because of governmental policy with which they do not agree. The gap between research and practice constitutes another controversial issue. Although it is claimed as an academic benchmark, the scientist-practitioner model is often overlooked. Further developments in integrating theoretical ideas and empirical data from science and practice seem to be needed in the field.

SHIRA TIBON
Bar-Ilan University and Academic College of Tel-Aviv Yaffo, Israel

ITEM ANALYSIS

Item analysis refers to a family of techniques for examining characteristics of test items. Most psychological tests consist of a collection of individual items. Test developers use item analysis techniques to evaluate these test items,

eliminate poorly performing items, include nicely performing items, and apprise test users of test features resulting from the selection of items. In formal test development projects, item analysis precedes preparation of the final test. In less formal applications, item analysis may occur only after administration of the final test to indicate quality of the test.

Traditional Item Analysis

Traditional procedures for item analysis, based on classical test theory (CTT), yield two key indexes. The first is item difficulty, often called the p-value. In cognitive tests, the p-value tells the percentage of examinees getting the item right; in noncognitive tests, it tells the percentage answering in a certain direction. The second index in CTT is the discrimination index. It tells the extent to which performance on the item distinguishes examinees with more or less of the trait being measured. In the context of item analysis, the term discrimination has nothing to do with racial, cultural, or gender discrimination.

Defining item discrimination requires definition of who has more or less of the trait. An external criterion such as a clinician's rating of depression might provide such a criterion. We then check the extent to which performance on an item agrees with status on the external criterion. The more common way to define status on the trait involves using the total score on the test itself. After scoring the test, we split the total group into high-scoring and low-scoring subgroups and then contrast the performance of these subgroups on each item. Desirable items show good separation between the high and low subgroups. The item discrimination index is sometimes called the item validity index.

The "high" and "low" groups may comprise the top and bottom 50% of scorers in the item analysis group. However, the most common split uses the top and bottom 27% of scorers. The item discrimination index may be the difference (designated D) in percentage of correct responses between high and low groups. Alternatively, the index may be a point-biserial correlation ($r_{p\text{-}bis}$), the correlation between performance on the item and score on the total test.

Figure 1 shows a typical array of data for traditional item analysis of a multiple-choice item. The high and low groups are top and bottom 27%. Entries in the body of the figure are percentages of examinees selecting each response. An asterisk indicates the correct response.

Item 4	A	B	C	D*			
High	7	7	0	87			
Low	13	31	6	50			
Total	10	20	3	68	$p = .68$	$D = .37$	$r_{p\text{-}bis} = .35$

*indicates correct response

Figure 1. Traditional item analysis data for one item.

Item Analysis in Item Response Theory

Item response theory (IRT) presents another set of item analysis procedures. IRT fits a mathematical function to the interplay between an underlying (latent) trait and responses to individual test items. Parameters of the mathematical function provide the item analysis statistics. The IRT approach features three main models, known by the number of parameters in the model: 1P, 2P, and 3P. The three parameters and their usual letter designations are: discrimination (a), difficulty (b), and guessing (c). The a and b parameters are analogous to the discrimination and difficulty indexes, respectively, in CTT. The difficulty (b) parameter lies on a scale generally ranging from -4 to +4; it maps to the ability scale for examinees. The guessing (or pseudo-guessing) parameter estimates likelihood of answering an item correctly by sheer guessing or other irrelevant influences. The item parameters in IRT are often represented in an item characteristic curve (ICC), a generally S-shaped curve relating status on the theoretical trait or "ability," labeled theta (θ), to the probability of answering an item in the desired direction.

Although considerably more complex than the CTT item analysis procedures, the IRT procedures serve the same purpose: helping to select items that yield a test with desired characteristics and eliminate undesirable items. IRT procedures extend to a considerable variety of applications besides item analysis (e.g., they lie at the heart of computer adaptive testing), but for purposes of item analysis they function much like the CTT procedures. In contemporary practice, test developers use both CTT and IRT statistical methods. IRT procedures require large samples and sophisticated computer programs. CTT procedures, although less powerful, require fewer resources and thus may apply in a greater variety of circumstances. To use item analysis information effectively, the test developer must have in mind the desired features of the final test, for example, its average difficulty and range of coverage.

Differential Item Functioning (DIF)

DIF is a special type of item analysis designed to detect differences in how subgroups respond to an item. DIF procedures select subgroups performing at the same level on the total test (e.g., at score level 16–17) and then examine their performance on individual items. The most common application of DIF involves comparison of groups defined by gender or racial/ethnic group. Items identified as functioning differently between groups may be eliminated.

Factor Analysis as an Item Analysis Technique

Factor analysis of test items, based on intercorrelations among the items, often serves as an item analysis technique, especially for measures of personality and attitudes. Any of the various methods of extracting and rotating factors may be used. The test developer attempts to find items with high loadings on a factor to help define that dimension in a final test.

Nonstatistical Item Review

The term *item analysis* usually implies only statistical analyses, but sometimes encompasses two types of nonstatistical review. First, experts in a professional field relevant to the test content review items for technical correctness. Second, panels of individuals representing cultural minority groups review items to spot potential cultural bias.

SUGGESTED READINGS

Downing, S. M., & Haladyna, T. M. (2006). *Handbook of test development.* Mahwah, NJ: Lawrence Erlbaum.

Hambleton, R. K., & Swaminathan, H. (1985). *Item response theory: Principles and applications.* Boston: Kluwer-Nijhoff.

Hogan, T. P. (2007). *Psychological testing: A practical introduction* (2nd ed.). Hoboken, NJ: John Wiley & Sons.

THOMAS P. HOGAN
University of Scranton

See also: Factor Analysis; Psychometrics

ITEM RESPONSE THEORY (See Item Analysis; Psychometrics)

J

JAMES, WILLIAM (1842–1910)

An American philosopher and psychologist, William James was educated in Europe, England, and America. He was part of a prominent Harvard family of literature professors. Frequent trips abroad gave James a wide knowledge of the world. Although he was supported and encouraged to pursue a scientific education, James suffered physical illness, indecision, and depression throughout his early years. Finally he earned a medical degree from Harvard in 1869 and took a teaching position there in 1872. From 1875 to 1876 James taught the first psychology course in an American university at Harvard. He was given funds for laboratory and demonstration equipment for the course in 1875, about the same time that Wilhelm Wundt established his psychology laboratory at Leipzig.

After 12 years of work, in 1890 James published *The Principles of Psychology*, a major contribution to the field. Dissatisfied with his work, he decided that he had nothing else to offer psychology. He left the Harvard psychological laboratory and the course work to Hugo Munsterberg, and he concentrated on philosophy for the remaining 20 years of his life. In the 1890s James became one of America's leading philosophers.

James is considered among America's greatest psychologists because of the brilliant clarity of his scientific writing and his view of the human mind as consisting of functional, adaptive mental processes, in opposition to Wundt's structural analysis of consciousness into elements. The concept of functionalism in James's psychology became the central principle of American functional psychology: the study of living persons as they adapt to their environment.

James treated psychology as a natural, biological science. He believed mental processes to be functional activities of living creatures attempting to adapt and maintain themselves in a world of nature. The function of consciousness was to guide persons toward adaptation for survival. James emphasized the nonrational aspects of human nature, in addition to the reasonable. He described mental life as always changing—a total experience that flows as a unit, a stream of consciousness. His most famous theoretical contribution concerned emotions. He stated that the physical response of arousal preceded the appearance of emotion—*because of* the bodily change such as increased heart rate or muscle tension, the person experienced emotion. The example of this chain of events was "see the bear, run, and *then* feel afraid." A simultaneous discovery of this theory by Danish physiologist Cal Lange led to its designation as the *James-Lange Theory*.

James believed that mental and emotional activities should be studied as processes and not as the static elements of consciousness being taught by the structural psychologists of that time. Because of the dynamic focus of his theories and views, James's psychology was named *functionalism*. G. Stanley Hall and James M. Cattell anticipated the University of Chicago, which developed the school of functional psychology under John Dewey and James Rowland Angell. James's *The Principles of Psychology* influenced thousands of students. He is generally considered the founder of psychology in the United States.

SUGGESTED READING

James, W. (1890). *Principles of psychology*. New York: Cosimo Classics.

N. A. HAYNIE
Honolulu, Hawaii

JAPAN, PSYCHOLOGY IN

Japan is located in the Pacific Ocean in East Asia, off the east coast of China, Korea, and Russia. Japan's population reached 127,777,000 in 2005. Nearly 76% of high school graduates attend a post-secondary institution of some kind. About 32% of individuals in that age group attend a university. Psychology is one of the most popular majors for both undergraduate and graduate students.

The history of psychology in Japan dates back over 100 years to the pioneering efforts of Yujiro Motora (1858–1912), who trained with G. Stanley Hall at Johns Hopkins University and obtained his PhD in 1888 (Sato & Sato, 2005). Motora became the first professor of psychology in Japan at the Imperial University of Tokyo in 1890. His student, Matataro Matsumoto (1865–1943) obtained his PhD at Yale University in 1899. Matsumoto established Japan's first experimental psychology laboratory at the Imperial University of Tokyo in 1903 and a second one at the Imperial University of Kyoto in 1906. There were a total of 15 university-based psychology laboratories prior to World War II (Japanese Psychological Association, 2002). In the 1930s and 1940s, Japanese psychologists conducted original experimental studies on perceptual problems including those of optical illusions, size constancy, and visual and auditory apparent movements under the influence of German Gestalt psychologists (Oyama, Torii, & Mochizuki, 2005). After World War II, Japanese psychologists were strongly influenced by the neobehaviorism of the American psychologists Clark Hull and B. F. Skinner. In tests and measurement, Kan-ichi Tanaka (1882–1962) published the Tanaka-Binet Intelligence test in 1947, and many followed his path in adapting and standardizing Western-derived intelligence and personality tests. In the 1960s Carl Rogers' client-centered counseling method exerted a major influence on the practice of counseling and psychotherapy in Japan. In social psychology the Lewinian theory of group dynamics was influential in forming the Japanese Group Dynamics Association in 1949 (Misumi & Peterson, 2000).

Early on, a small group of Japanese psychologists attempted to develop an indigenous Japanese field of psychology, but the discipline was soon dominated by Western psychology (Azuma & Imada, 1994). Studies on Zen and psychology, however, have a long history dating back to the beginning of the twentieth century (Kato, 2005). In more recent years, Markus and Kitayama's (1991) call for contextualizing self-construal into the independent versus interdependent orientation in East Asian and Western cultures has sparked empirical psychological research interests in the Japanese self, and has contributed to the development of cultural psychology.

The Japan Society for the Promotion of Science (JSPS) is Japan's leading funding agency. JSPS established the 21st Century COE (Center for Excellence) Program in 2002 and the Global COE Program in 2007 in order to establish world-standard education and research bases in Japan. One such example is the "Center for the Study of Cultural and Ecological Foundations of the Mind, a 21st Century Center of Excellence" headed by the social psychologist, Toshio Yamagishi, at Hokkaido University.

Organizationally, the Japanese Psychological Association (JPA), established in 1927, is the oldest professional psychological association in Japan. The JPA's membership reached 7,265 in 2007. The JPA has five major divisions: (1) perception, physiology, thinking, and learning; (2) development and education; (3) clinical psychology, personality, forensics, and rehabilitation; (4) social, industrial, and cultural; and (5) methodology, principles, history, and general psychology. As main scientific research outlets, the JPA publishes two periodicals: *Japanese Journal of Psychology,* in Japanese; and *Japanese Psychological Research*, in English. In 1999, the leadership of the JPA established the Japanese Union of Psychological Associations (JUPA) in order to coordinate the diverse activities of the growing number of psychological associations. The JUPA included 39 national psychological associations as members in 2007.

Internationally, the JPA has been a national member of the International Union of Psychological Science (IUPsyS) since 1951. The JPA organized the 20th International Congress of Psychology in Tokyo, in 1972, and the 22nd International Congress of Applied Psychology in Kyoto, in 1990. In recent years, the 2004 World Congress of Behavioral and Cognitive Therapies, the 2006 International Congress of Psychotherapy, and the 2008 International Congress of Behavioral Medicine were held in Japan.

As for education and training, nearly 200 universities offer undergraduate and graduate training in psychology in either psychology departments or in related departments of disciplines such as education, sociology, and social welfare (Tanaka-Matsumi & Otsui, 2004). The JPA has developed a standard undergraduate psychology program as part of a certification system for psychologists at the bachelor's level. The program includes courses in both basic and applied psychology, research methodology, and statistics. Japanese graduate programs have begun reorganizing graduate curricula to enable qualified doctoral candidates to earn their PhDs after five years of training.

Professionally, Japanese psychologists typically work in four settings: educational, medical, and social welfare; forensic; and labor and industry. The Japanese Ministry of Education, Culture, Sports, Science, and Technology (MEXT) started the school-counselor system in 1995 in an attempt to resolve the nation's imminent problem of over 130,000 students withdrawing from elementary and middle schools for various adjustment problems.

The professional status of a psychologist is not protected by the licensing law. At the present time, only certification agencies exist. In 1988, the AJCP (Association of Japanese Clinical Psychology) established the Japanese Certification Board for Clinical Psychologists (JCBCP), Inc. The total cumulative number of certified clinical psychologists, with a master's degree, reached 16,732 in April, 2007. The JCBCP also approves graduate programs in clinical psychology. As of May 2007, the JCBCP had approved a total of 156 master's programs in clinical psychology. In 1989, the JPA developed a separate system to certify those who have taken the required undergraduate credits in psychology at a college or university. By 2007, nearly 10,000 individuals qualified for certificates (Japanese Psychological Association, 2002).

As reviewed, psychology in Japan has a history of over 100 years. The future of the science and practice of psychology in Japan will depend on the development of a strong academic undergraduate psychology curriculum, internationally competitive doctoral level education and research bases, and licensing laws for the professional practice of psychology.

REFERENCES

Azuma, H., & Imada, H. (1994). Origins and development of psychology in Japan: The interaction between western science and the Japanese cultural heritage. *International Journal of Psychology, 29,* 707–715.

Japanese Psychological Association. (2002). *Nippon Shinrigakkai 75 nenshi* [A 75-year history of the Japanese Psychological Association]. Tokyo: Japanese Psychological Association.

Kato, H. (2005). Zen and psychology. *Japanese Psychological Research, 47,* 125–136.

Markus, H., & Kitayama, S. (1991). Culture and the self: Implications for cognition, emotion, and motivation. *Psychological Review, 98,* 224–253.

Misumi, J., & Peterson, M. F. (1990). Psychology in Japan. *Annual Review of Psychology, 41,* 213–241.

Oyama, T., Torii, S., & Mochizuki, T. (2005). Pioneering studies on perception in the 1930s on perception: An historical background of experimental psychology in Japan. *Japanese Psychological Research, 47,* 73–87.

Sato, T., & Sato, T. (2005). The early 20th century: Shaping the discipline of psychology in Japan. *Japanese Psychological Research, 47,* 52–62.

Tanaka-Matsumi, J., & Otsui, K. (2004). Psychology in Japan. In M. J. Stevens & D. Wedding (Eds.), *Handbook of international psychology* (pp. 193–210). New York: Brunner-Routledge.

JUNKO TANAKA-MATSUMI
Kansei Gakuin University, Japan

JEALOUSY

Jealousy is typically defined as an emotional response to the threat of losing a valued relationship to a rival. Although it is not considered to be a primary emotion, such as fear, sadness or joy, jealousy reflects a vital emotional process that is clinically and socially relevant to psychologists. Jealousy is found in every culture and has been recorded throughout history as an integral component to human relationships. Although it is neither desired nor essential for healthy relationships, it is nevertheless a common, even ubiquitous response. All people experience jealousy at some point in their lives. Unfortunately, some people's experience of jealousy involves intense psychological turmoil that can lead to aggressive or maladaptive responses. A majority of violent crime involving intimate partners—including murder, stalking or domestic abuse—can be attributed to feelings of jealousy.

Some leading researchers on emotion argue that jealousy is not an emotion at all, but an amalgamation of fluctuating feelings of anger, fear, sadness, or disgust, and that the reaction reflects the dynamics of a social situation. Psychologists generally identify jealousy as a social emotion, in the same class as shame, embarrassment, and envy. Jealousy emerges when a valued relationship with another person is threatened by a rival who appears to be competing for attention, affection, or commitment. Unlike envy, jealousy requires a triangulation. Envy arises when we covet the possession of another, but jealousy occurs when we feel we possess a valued relationship that may be taken by someone else. Both envy and jealousy arise when our self-esteem is diminished, but jealousy is much more likely to evoke an overt response to secure what is believed to be one's own, whereas envy is usually concealed from others. Some people may feel ashamed of envying another person, but a jealous individual may feel righteous and justified in acting deliberately or aggressively in response to the perceived encroachment on the relationship.

In *Othello,* Shakespeare refers to jealousy as a green-eyed monster. It is interesting that the color green is a blending of two primary hues, yellow and blue, just as jealousy is also a blending of emotions. Furthermore, the color green reflects the immature nature of jealousy in the context of love. It is a possessive love that betrays the need for the other person's esteem and good will to compensate for one's own inadequacies. Green is also the color through which the monster sees the world, through a sickened veneer that transforms normal perception into a distorted view of suspicion everywhere the person looks. In this sense jealousy has taken on pathological dimensions in which people feel emotionally sick and distort reality through delusional thoughts about the motives and activities of the one they love and the person who threatens to disrupt the harmony of the relationship.

At the heart of jealousy is the threat to self esteem. The investments and commitments inherent in close interpersonal relationships contain an implicit recognition that one is valued and esteemed by the other. Jealous people have calculated that their status in a valued relationship has been diminished by the possibility that another person may become more important. It is the potential preference of a rival that sparks the jealous response. Jealousy signals a diminishment of status in a relationship in which people once believed they were in a favored position. It is this perceived threat to self-esteem that leads to protective and potentially aggressive responses as a means to eliminating the rival.

Not all experiences of jealousy are pathological. In fact, the absence of jealous feelings in the face of bona fide threats to significant relationships would be abnormal. Normal jealousy, sometimes referred to as reactive jealousy, occurs when there has been a completed and verifiable act of infidelity or transgression of the relationship. In these instances, the jealous person is reacting to an external event and is likely to feel an admixture of anger, fear, and sadness. A second type of jealousy would be considered more pathological, in that it is rooted in the personality and disposition of the jealous individual. Suspicious jealousy is more likely to emerge for individuals who have developmental histories of being insecurely attached or in individuals who have damaged or distorted self-systems. These people are responding more to intrapsychic dynamics in which they feel rejection and abandonment at the slightest provocation, than to actual events in the social world. They defend against feelings of inadequacy through denial and projection. Suspicious jealousy is characterized by internal conflicts, and the emotions of anxiety, doubt, and insecurity predominate.

The field of evolutionary psychology has introduced a new focus to the research on jealousy. According to evolutionary psychologists, jealousy is a remnant of our ancestral past that serves to warn us of potential threats to the integrity of close interpersonal relationships. According to this theory, a man is more likely to feel intense jealousy if his mate cuckolds him, whereas women are more threatened by emotional infidelity. The reason for these sex differences is rooted in reproductive biology. Ancestral women needed the man's emotional commitment to secure vital resources for their offspring, whereas ancestral men could not be assured of their paternity if their mates were sexually active with others. Therefore, evolutionary psychologists maintain that modern men and women are likely to become jealous for different reasons and with varying intensities, depending on whether their partner is engaged in sexual or emotional infidelity. Some researchers suggest, however, that the apparent differences in the responses of modern men and women are a result of faulty methodologies, and that the suggestion of sex differences in jealousy is spurious at best.

Psychologists generally agree that jealousy is a disturbing experience that combines the emotions of anger, anxiety, betrayal, and hurt when one feels that a valued relationship is threatened by a third party. There are different theories about the underlying motives and dynamics that lead to jealous feelings and responses. These competing theories include evolved sex differences, attachment styles or disposition, self-esteem, and learned social and cultural expectations. Future research on jealousy should help to clarify these controversies while addressing the more pragmatic needs of therapists and human service professionals to effectively manage this unsettling and potentially dangerous emotional experience.

REFERENCES

Buss, D. M. (2000). *The dangerous passion: Why jealousy is as necessary as love and sex*. New York: Free Press.

Desteno, D., Piercarlo, V., & Bartlett, M.Y. (2006). Jealousy and the threatened self: Getting to the heart of the green-eyed monster. *Journal of Personality and Social Psychology, 91*, 626–641.

Ekman, P. (2003). *Emotions revealed*. New York: Henry Holt.

Rydell, R. J., & Bringle, R. G. (2007). Differentiating reactive and suspicious jealousy. *Social Behavior and Personality, 35*, 1099–1114.

Walton, S. (2004). *A natural history of human emotions*. New York: Grove Press.

JAMES M. HEPBURN
Waynesburg University

See also: Emotions; Envy; Self-Esteem

JOB STRESS (See Occupational Stress)

JOB STRESS SURVEY

Negative effects of stress in the workplace on the health and well-being of workers have been observed throughout human history. The phrase "mad as a hatter" came into the English language long before anyone knew that mercury in the materials used in making hats affected the central nervous system (Kahn, 1981). In the nineteenth century, descriptions of the "black lung" disease of coal miners recognized a causal link between a hazardous work environment and a particular physical disorder. The World Health Organization has noted that "... occupational health and the well-being of working people are crucial prerequisites for productivity and are of utmost importance for overall socioeconomic and sustainable development" (2000, p. 2). In a recent survey by Northwestern National Life, many employees viewed their jobs as the number one stressor in their lives.

Each year, an estimated 160 million new cases of work-related disorders occur worldwide, including respiration and cardiovascular diseases, cancer, and mental and neurological illnesses (Spielberger & Reheiser, 2005). Work-related injuries and diseases annually kill an estimated 1.1 million people worldwide, including more than 300,000 fatalities from accidents that happen in the workplace. In the United States, nearly 600,000 workers are disabled each year by stress-related psychological disorders, costing $5.5 billion in annual payments to individuals and their families.

The Job Stress Survey (JSS) was designed to assess generic sources of occupational stress encountered by men and women in a wide variety of work settings. The 30 JSS items were adapted from our earlier work on sources of stress experienced by both police officers (Police Stress Survey, PSS) and school teachers (Teacher Stress Survey, TSS). Items included in both the PSS and TSS that described stressors encountered in a wide range of occupations were selected for the JSS.

The 30-item JSS Severity and Frequency scales assess the perceived severity ("intensity") of specific sources of occupational stress and how often each of these stressors was experienced in the work environment during the previous six months. Examinees first rate, on a 9-point scale, the perceived severity of each stressor event as compared to a standard stressor ("Assignment of disagreeable duties"), and they then report how often each stressor occurred during the past six months.

Factor analyses of the 30 JSS Severity and Frequency items have consistently identified two major components of job stress—job pressure (JP) and lack of organizational support (LS)—that are assessed with 10-item JP and LS subscales. Factor analyses of the JSS severity and frequency ratings for large samples of managers and professionals identified work-related conditions and requirements and job duties and responsibilities as the major components of job pressure. Three components of the JSS LS factor were defined by items with content related to lack of support from supervisors and coworkers and to the rules and procedures of the employees' organization. The effects of the job-related stressor events assessed by the JSS on psychological and physical strain and adverse behavioral consequences are mediated by the employee's perception and appraisal of these stressors.

REFERENCES

Kahn, R. L. (1981). *Work and health*. New York: John Wiley & Sons.

Spielberger, C. D., & Reheiser, E. C. (2005). Occupational stress and health. In A. G. Antoniou & C. L. Cooper (Eds.), *Research companion to organizational health psychology* (pp. 441–454). Northampton, MA: Edward Elgar.

Spielberger, C. D., & Vagg, P. R. (1999). *Job stress survey: Professional manual*. Odessa, FL: Psychological Assessment Resources.

World Health Organization (WHO). (2000). Retrieved February 22, 2009, from http://www.who.int/oeh/OCHweb/OCHweb/OSHpages/OSHdocuments /Global/Strategy/GlobalStrategyonOccupationalHealth.htm.

CHARLES D. SPIELBERGER
University of South Florida

See also: **Employee Assistance Programs; Occupational Stress**

JONES, MARY COVER (1896–1987)

Mary Cover Jones was an undergraduate at Vassar and graduated in 1919. She received a PhD from Columbia in 1926. Most of her career was spent at the Institute of Human Development of the University of California at Berkeley. Much of her later work on longitudinal studies of development was in collaboration with her husband, Harold E. Jones, whom she met and married (1920) during graduate school at Columbia. Although best known for her early work on fear conditioning in children, her most lasting contribution was as a pioneer in the design and completion of developmental psychology.

Her name is most prominent as the first researcher to remove a fear in a child, in the case of Peter. On a weekend trip to New York during her last semester at Vassar, she attended a lecture by John Watson in which he discussed and showed movies of the fear conditioning of Little Albert. By the time Jones became a graduate student at Columbia, Watson had been expelled by Johns Hopkins for his sensationally publicized divorce and was working with the J. Walter Thompson Advertising Agency in New York. Since Jones had been a classmate and friend of his second wife, Rosalie Raynor Watson, Jones was able to obtain Watson's advice on most Saturday afternoons throughout the project. The therapeutic experiments were carried on in the children's home where, as it happened, Jones lived with her husband and daughter. The project ended with the article "A Laboratory Study of Fear."

Since a single case study was unacceptable as a dissertation, Jones extended Watson's studies of developmental activities to a larger and more representative sample. Her comparison of observations of 300 normal babies was accepted. In 1936, with Barbara Burks, she published an extended monograph on the topic.

In 1927, she and her husband moved to the Institute for Child Welfare (later the Institute of Child Development). Although Harold Jones was "Professor," Mary Cover Jones, because of nepotism rules, did not receive an academic appointment until 1952. In 1931 she undertook a longitudinal study of adolescents (the Oakland Growth Study) and she followed the development of this group for the remainder of her career. She became a Professor in 1959, just prior to her retirement.

She served as President of the APA Division of Developmental Psychology. In 1968, she received the G. Stanley Hall Award from that Division of APA. Joseph Wolpe, a founder of behavior therapy, referred to her as "the mother of behavior therapy."

SUGGESTED READINGS

Jones, M. C. (1924). A laboratory study of fear: The case of Peter. *Pedagogical Seminary, 31,* 308–315.

Jones, M. C. (1926). The development of early behavior patterns in young children. *Pedagogical Seminary, 33,* 53–85.

Jones, M. C. (1957). The later careers of boys who were early or late maturing. *Child Development, 28,* 113–128.

STAFF

JUNG, CARL (1875–1961)

Carl Jung was a Swiss psychiatrist and psychoanalyst and the founder of analytical psychology. Born and raised in Switzerland in an unhappy family, he learned early to depend upon his own inner resources for guidance and encouragement. He graduated in 1900 with a medical degree from the University of Basel. He was appointed to the University of Zurich psychiatric clinic to work under Eugene Bleuler, noted for his interest in schizophrenia. Jung also studied with Pierre Janet, the French psychiatrist known for his work in hysteria and multiple personality. In 1905, Jung was lecturer in psychiatry at the University of Basel, but after several years he resigned to concentrate on private practice, research, and writing. From 1932 to 1942 he was professor at the Federal Polytechnical University of Zurich. Illness forced his resignation; his last years were spent in writing and publishing books about analytic psychology.

Jung read Sigmund Freud's *The Interpretation of Dreams* in 1900 and met Freud in 1907. In 1909 he accompanied Freud to Clark University in America, at which they both delivered lectures. In 1911 Jung became president of the International Psychoanalytic Association with Freud's complete endorsement. However, Jung's interpretations and theories of psychoanalysis, the unconscious, and the libido differed from Freud's. After Jung published *Psychology and the Unconscious*, dissent and disagreement grew between him and Freud, and in 1914 their relationship ended. Thereafter, Jung's theory and practice were known as analytical psychology.

In 1913, Jung suffered inner turmoil that lasted about three years. Like Freud, he used self-analysis through dream interpretation to resolve emotional distress. It was a time of creativity and growth, leading to Jung's unique approach to personality theory. Jung came to appreciate the myths and symbols of humankind throughout the centuries. He made several field trips in the 1920s to Africa and the southwestern United States, where he studied the myths, folkways, religions, and more of preliterate peoples.

Jung's basic argument with Freud's psychoanalytic theory concerned libido: Freud insisted upon its sexual energy, whereas Jung regarded it as a generalized life energy. A second difference was with Freud's deterministic view of the influences of childhood on personality. Jung believed that personality can change later in life and is shaped by future goals and aspirations.

Jung's personality system included three levels of *psyche*, or mind: (1) the *conscious*, or ego; (2) the *personal unconscious*, forgotten and repressed experiences sometimes formed into complexes; and (3) the deeper, *collective unconscious*, containing the cumulative experiences of previous generations, including animal heritage. The collective or transpersonal unconscious forms the basis of personality and is its most powerful influence. It is a storehouse of universal evolutionary and latent memory traces inherited from man's ancestral past.

The components of the collective unconscious Jung called *archetypes*. There are numerous archetypes, including energy, the hero, the earth mother, death, birth, rebirth, unity, the child, God, and demon. Some archetypes are identified as separate systems within the personality, i.e., the *persona*, or masked public personality; the *anima* and the *animus*, or bisexual characteristics; the *shadow*, or animal-like part of human nature; and the *self*, which, composed of all parts of the unconscious, strives for unity and equilibrium as expressed in the symbol of the circle, the *mandala*. The self attempts to achieve integration, self-actualization, and harmony of the personality.

Jung is probably best known for his descriptions of the orientations of the personality, *extraversion* and *introversion*, published in *Psychological Types* (1921). He also identified four psychology functions: thinking, feeling, sensing, and intuiting. Research has been generated about these dimensions of personality, although scientific psychology has largely ignored Jung's work.

Jung has been influential and inspirational to other disciplines, such as art, literature, filmmaking, religion, anthropology, and history. He published prolifically, but many of his works did not appear in English until after 1965. Only a few days before his death, Jung finished his own chapter and drafts of his disciples' chapters for *Man and His Symbols*, a book that has popularized and explained Jung's use of dream analysis and his theories of universal symbolic representations of man's deeper nature.

SUGGESTED READINGS

Jung, C. G. (1981). *The archetypes and the collective unconscious*. In *The Collected Works of C. G. Jung*: Vol. 9, Part 1 (2nd ed.). Princeton, NJ: Bollingen.

Jung, C. G., & Franz, M. L. (1968). *Man and his symbols*. Garden City, NY: Doubleday.

Jung, C. G., & Jaffe, A. (1962). *Memories, dreams, reflections*. London: Collins.

N. A. Haynie
Honolulu, Hawaii

JUST NOTICEABLE DIFFERENCE

The concept of just noticeable difference (jnd), also known as the difference threshold or difference limen (Latin for threshold), derives from early work in the area of classical psychophysics conducted in the mid-nineteenth century. This work was highlighted by Weber (1795–1878), a German physiologist, whose experimental investigations focused on tactile stimulation and the determination of sensory thresholds. Weber's seminal work in this area was extended and elaborated upon by German philosopher and mathematician Fechner (1801–1878), who coined the term "psychophysics" to refer to this area of experimental psychology and, in 1860, published the first textbook on psychophysics, which laid out the basic goals of this emerging discipline and the scientific methods that were to be employed to advance knowledge in this area (Watson, 1973).

A primary focus of classical psychophysics was on investigating the relationships between different types of physical stimuli and the sensations they evoked in human and animal subjects and in assessing the ultimate sensory capabilities of the organism. Of specific interest was determining thresholds for the detectability of stimuli. Much of the early research in this area focused on the determination of absolute thresholds. Whereas investigators employed various experimental methods, depending on the specific nature of the research, subjects in such studies were typically presented with some stimulus (e.g., auditory, visual, tactile) of very low (and undetectable) intensity. This was then followed by a graded presentation of test stimuli, at increasing levels of stimulus intensity. Presentation of stimuli was continued until a stimulus intensity was reached where the subject reported the stimulus as present. Since subjects in such studies were often found to be variable regarding the level of stimulus intensity required for detectability on different trials, experiments often provided subjects with a number of stimulus presentation trials, with each subject's absolute threshold being considered as that level of stimulation where the subject reported the stimulus as being present 50% of the time.

While experiments like these were designed to determine absolute thresholds (e.g., the smallest amount of sensory stimulation required for detectability), other studies, specifically relevant to the present topic, focused on the issue of difference thresholds. Here, the primary research questions were the following: To what extent must the intensity of one physical stimulus differ from the intensity of a second physical stimulus for subjects to distinguish one from the other? What is the smallest increment in stimulus intensity that is detectable?

Studies of difference thresholds often employed experimental methods similar to those used in determining absolute thresholds. For example, subjects might be provided with a stimulus of a given weight, which could be used for purposes of comparison (the standard stimulus), and then be presented with a graded series of test stimuli that differed from the standard stimulus along the weight dimension. The subject's task would be to indicate whether a test stimulus was the same or heavier (or lighter, depending on the nature of the study) than the standard stimulus. The primary focus of these studies was on determining the smallest increment in weight necessary for subjects to

perceive the test stimulus as different from the standard stimulus (50% of the time). This threshold for the detection of differences in physical stimuli has been referred to by a variety of terms: difference threshold, difference or differential limen, least perceptible difference, and just noticeable difference. The term "just noticeable difference," typically abbreviated "jnd," is the one most widely accepted in the psychophysics literature.

Formally, the jnd can be defined as the magnitude of change in a stimulus necessary for it to be perceived as different from another stimulus, or as the smallest detectable difference between two stimuli (Levine & Shefner, 1981). Early work related to just noticeable differences in sensation was subsequently extended by attempting to characterize, quantitatively, the precise nature of the relationship between increases in the magnitude of physical stimuli and just noticeable differences in detectability. Indeed, one of the first general laws of psychology dealt with the degree to which the intensity of a stimulus must be increased beyond that of a comparison stimulus for the difference between the two to be detectable. Here, Weber's law (which was actually popularized by Fechner) states that the amount of increase in stimulation that results in a just noticeable difference is a constant proportion of the standard stimulus. Thus, a heavy stimulus must be increased by a larger increment in weight for one to notice a difference between the two objects than a lighter stimulus, where a smaller increment in weight may result in the detectability of a difference

It should be noted that remnants of this early interest in the concepts of absolute and difference thresholds are reflected in the psychological literature even today, although the concept of threshold has to some extent fallen into disrepute (apart from its value in assessing the capacity of sensory systems). This is due, in part, to the influence of contemporary cognitive psychology and current views of the individual as an active processor of information. Specifically, it would seem that notions of thresholds have been largely supplanted by concepts derived from signal detection theory (see Green & Swets, 1974), in which it is assumed that detectability of stimuli is determined not only by the sensory capacities of the individual, but also by the nature of the response criteria one adopts in responding to detectability (Levine & Shefner, 1981).

Despite the preceding comments, it can be noted that researchers continue to investigate the concept of just noticeable differences by going beyond studies of sensory perception to include studying thresholds for perceiving behaviors. For example, studies have looked at just noticeable differences in observers' ratings of personality characteristics. This has been followed by finding corresponding changes on relevant measures that can quantify the difference in scores, for example, on a personality measure. This would capture the increment needed for just noticeable difference. Thus, while the field of psychophysics has let just noticeable differences fall out of focus, researchers in other domains continue to investigate its utility as it relates to areas outside of strict human sensory perception.

REFERENCES

Green, D., & Swets, J. A. (1974). *Signal detection theory and psychophysics*. Huntington, NY: Krieger.

Levine, M. W., & Shefner, J. M. (1981). *Fundamentals of sensations and perceptions*. Reading, MA: Addison-Wesley.

Watson, C. S. (1973). Psychophysics. In B. B. Wolman (Ed.), *Handbook of general psychology* (pp. 275–305). New York: John Wiley & Sons.

SUGGESTED READINGS

Iverson, G. J. (2006). Analytical methods in the theory of psychophysical discrimination: I. Inequalities, convexity, and integration of just noticeable differences. *Journal of Mathematical Psychology, 50*, 271–282.

Laming, D. (1997). *The measurement of sensations*. New York: Oxford University Press.

MELISSA K. STERN
JAMES H. JOHNSON
University of Florida

See also: Perception; Weber's Law

JUVENILE DELINQUENCY

Juvenile delinquency generally refers to acts committed by a child or adolescent that would lead to prosecution if committed by an adult (e.g., theft, battery, homicide). Status offenses, which are acts that are illegal for minors but not for adults (e.g., tobacco use, truancy, curfew violations) are often included in research definitions of delinquency. Despite the broad range of delinquent behaviors, a particular emphasis has been placed on addressing the problem of more serious forms of juvenile delinquency, especially youth violence.

Although rates of antisocial and violent behavior have decreased among young people in recent years, they remain at very high levels (Snyder & Sickmund, 2006). Violent Crime Index juvenile arrests increased by 61% between 1988 and 1994 before declining below the levels of the early 1980s (Snyder & Sickmund, 2006). The sharp increase in the late 1980s, coupled with high rates of antisocial and violent behavior in the United States compared with other industrialized nations and dramatic examples of youth violence, led to increased concern about youth crime (Tolan, 2007).

This surge, once recognized, piqued substantial public concern and led policymakers and others to erroneously predict an unprecedented crime wave driven by "super predators"—youth who exhibited excessive rates of crime and violence and for whom rehabilitative efforts would fail. There was a subsequent call for punitive measures, including the use of metal detectors in schools; the charging, trying, and sentencing of youth as adults; and the enactment of legislative measures to curtail opportunities for treatment and supportive interventions with youthful offenders. Although appealing to the public sentiment to "do something," these efforts often were poorly formulated and did little to improve public safety. A second effect of the surge in youth crime was a greater research focus on juvenile delinquency. As a result, over the past 15–20 years a large body of authoritative data has accumulated on rates, patterns, risk and protective factors, and effective interventions to reduce delinquency.

Patterns of Delinquency

At some point during adolescence, nearly all youth engage in some form of criminal behavior; however, most adolescents commit only a few minor illegal acts. The vast majority of delinquent acts, especially severe and violent delinquency, are committed by a small proportion of all adolescents. In addition, delinquent acts are committed by youth from all segments of society; however, higher rates of delinquency are found in inner-city communities characterized by poverty, high rates of exposure to violence, and inadequate neighborhood social processes (Tolan, 2007). This juxtaposition of universality and concentration suggests that delinquency requires a multifaceted focus and may have different causes for high-risk youth than for the general population (Moffitt, 1993).

Risk and Protective Factors for Delinquency

Understanding key risk and protective factors for delinquency is a complex matter. Most research has moved toward a perspective that incorporates multiple factors within a developmental-ecological perspective in which risk factors are organized by system level, from individual to close interpersonal relationships (e.g., family and peers), to less proximal microsystems (e.g., neighborhood conditions), to macrosystem influences of society as a whole (Tolan, Guerra, & Kendall, 1995). Particularly in recent years, the application of neuroscientific advances has made possible the examination of the interplay of various biological, psychological, and social markers of risk.

An exceptionally large literature on risk factors exists, with some representing the most sophisticated methodology and designs in developmental psychopathology (Loeber & Farrington, 1998; Loeber, Slot, & Stouthamer-Loeber, 2006). At the individual level, risk factors include demographic characteristics (e.g., gender and age), social skills (e.g., poor social problem-solving skills, deficient forms of social information processing), cognitive shortcomings (e.g., academic failure), and behavioral problems (e.g., attention deficit hyperactivity disorder). Family factors include poor parent management practices (e.g., overly harsh discipline, poor supervision and monitoring), family conflict, and parental antisocial behaviors. Association with antisocial peers increases risk for involvement in delinquent and antisocial behavior.

Community risk factors include living in impoverished and disorganized neighborhoods (i.e., those with high crime rates, marked violence, and a lack of informal child supervision by adults). In addition to directly affecting residents, life in a chaotic and violent neighborhood also appears to leave children particularly vulnerable to the effects of other risk factors. Risk factors at a societal level can help explain the markedly higher rates of violence in the United States compared with other industrialized nations. Examples of societal risk factors include widespread availability of handguns, tolerance of youth alcohol use, and societal norms that support media violence. Historically, protective factors have been viewed simply as the converse or absence of risk factors (e.g., academic success), although recent work is beginning to investigate a more complex view of protective factors in terms of their ability to mitigate the negative impact of risk factors.

It must be stressed that risk and protective factors reflect complex, dynamic, and reciprocal processes that unfold as individuals interact with their environment over time. Risk factors tend to co-occur, cluster, and interact to compound risk. For example, children facing one risk factor are substantially more likely to face others and, as these factors mount, to engage in more problem behavior than would be predicted by each individual risk factor alone. Also, many of the risk factors are not specific to delinquency and also predict risk for many problems of childhood and adolescence. Therefore, interventions that target and reduce risk for delinquency may also decrease risk for several problem outcomes (Lipsey & Wilson, 1998).

Intervention

Numerous interventions have been implemented to target the problem of juvenile crime and violence. Although many of these interventions lack sufficient evaluation of their impact on juvenile crime, there is a growing body of empirical evidence for interventions that work, as well as for interventions that have either no effects or iatrogenic effects. Meta-analytic reviews (Aos, Miller, & Drake, 2006;

Lipsey & Wilson, 1998) have been used to identify the most successful treatment approaches as well as specific interventions with significant positive effects. Although "get tough" interventions such as "Scared Straight," wilderness camps, and transfer to adult courts and prisons often have wide political appeal, there is actually evidence that these methods may increase juvenile crime. Aos and colleagues (2006) estimated that the negative effects of "Scared Straight" actually cost society an average of nearly $15,000 per participant.

In contrast, research evidence shows positive effects for interventions such as multidimensional treatment foster care (MTFC) and functional family therapy (FFT). MTFC and FFT were estimated to save more than $77,000 and $31,000, respectively, per participant. MTFC and FFT are among 11 model programs identified by Blueprints for Violence Prevention (Mihalic, Fagan, Irwin, Ballard, & Elliott, 2004), a project developed to identify effective violence prevention programs. Each of these programs must meet stringent criteria, including lasting effects and independent replication of effects. Together, the findings from meta-analytic reviews and Blueprints suggest that programs focusing on parenting and family relationships and those that improve cognitive processes in managing interpersonal conflicts and social situations are the most promising.

Unlike treatment interventions that target youth who have already initiated delinquent behaviors and are frequently involved in the juvenile justice system, prevention programs seek to prevent the onset or expansion of delinquency (Tolan & Titus, in press). Promising prevention interventions have emerged across many targets for change. No single intervention targeting a single domain of interest holds the key for preventing antisocial behavior among youth (Tolan & Titus, in press). Instead, a combination of approaches is needed, including large-scale universal (primary prevention) interventions focused on changing the norms and practices of youth behavior and supervision in key social settings; selective interventions targeting at-risk youth and families; and more intensive, indicated interventions to support the families of children with emerging antisocial behavior.

Policy

The political response to the spike in juvenile crime during the late 1980s was characterized by harsh, punitive measures fashioned to "get tough on crime" and take young criminals off the streets. Four major policy and program initiatives were introduced as violence prevention or control strategies during the 1990s: (1) the use of judicial waivers, transferring violent juvenile offenders as young as age 12 into the adult criminal justice system for trial, sentencing, and adult prison terms; (2) longer sentences for violent crimes, exemplified by "three strikes and you're out" legislation; (3) new gun control policies, such as the Brady Handgun Violence Prevention Act (1993); and (4) the creation of "boot camps" or shock incarceration programs for young offenders, designed to instill discipline and respect for authority. Although popular for their "tough on crime" approach, each of these measures except gun control policies have, as previously noted, been shown to be ineffective by empirical study. Intervention and community based alternatives have consistently been shown to have a stronger impact on crime than getting tough, to increase public safety, and to save costs incurred in addressing delinquency.

An important influence in the shift from a punitive response to delinquency to a rehabilitative focus has been the growing appreciation of neurodevelopmental differences between adolescents and adults. Research suggests that adolescents should be evaluated differently from adults, because they lack the adult capacity for judgment, intent, and responsibility. Recently, with the advent of brain-imaging techniques, it has become apparent that substantial change occurs over time in the areas of the brain thought to be the center of judgment and moral decision making (Steinberg & Scott, 2003). This shift marks an important step forward in integrating scientific knowledge of normative development with juvenile justice processes.

In a trend that shows the power of research to shape public policy, there is a growing emphasis toward policies aimed at rehabilitating juvenile offenders and using interventions with strong empirical support. One example of such a change is RECLAIM (reasoned and equitable community and local alternatives to the incarceration of minors) Ohio (Moon, Applegate, & Latessa, 1997). This program was designed to reduce the number of incarcerated youth by giving local jurisdictions the flexibility to choose programs from community agencies as an alternative to incarceration. The community programs are paid with funds that would otherwise be used to pay for detention by the Ohio Division of Youth Services. While there is need for continued efforts to ensure the use of empirically supported interventions by programs such as RECLAIM Ohio, the shift in policy emphasis from incarceration to rehabilitation of young offenders is a promising policy change.

The potential of these policy changes is quite impressive. Based on their cost benefit analysis, Aos and colleagues (2006) estimated that, by increasing the use of evidence-based programs by 20%, the state of Washington could save nearly two billion dollars over the next 22 years. As Aos and colleagues (2006) note, these projections require the needed expansion of the use of evidence-based programs to maintain high standards of program delivery and fidelity to the program models. Despite this limitation, these estimates show the potential for developmentally appropriate, empirically driven, and evidence based programs to significantly improve the national response to delinquency.

REFERENCES

Aos, S., Miller, M., & Drake, E. (2006). *Evidence-based public policy options to reduce future prison construction, criminal justice costs, and crime rates.* Olympia, WA: Washington State Institute for Public Policy.

Lipsey, M. W., & Wilson, D. B. (1998). Effective intervention for serious juvenile offenders: A synthesis of research. In R. Loeber & D. P. Farrington (Eds.), *Serious and violent juvenile offenders: Risk factors and successful interventions* (pp. 313–345). Thousand Oaks, CA: Sage.

Loeber, R., & Farrington, D. P. (1998). *Serious and violent juvenile offenders: Risk factors and successful interventions.* Thousand Oaks, CA: Sage.

Loeber, R., Slot, N. W., & Stouthamer-Loeber, M. (2006). A three-dimensional, cumulative developmental model of serious delinquency. In P-O. Wikström & R. Sampson (Eds.), *The social contexts of pathways in crime: Contexts and mechanisms* (pp. 153–194). Cambridge, UK: Cambridge University Press.

Mihalic, S., Fagan, A., Irwin, K., Ballard, D., & Elliott, D. (2004). *Blueprints for violence prevention.* Washington, DC: Office of Juvenile Justice and Delinquency Prevention.

Moffitt, T. E. (1993). Life-course-persistent and adolescence-limited antisocial behavior: A developmental taxonomy. *Psychological Review, 100,* 674–701.

Moon, M. M., Applegate, B. K., & Latessa, E. J. (1997). RECLAIM Ohio: A politically viable alternative to treating youthful felony offenders. *Crime and Delinquency, 43,* 438–456.

Snyder, H. N., & Sickmund, M. (2006). *Juvenile offenders and victims: 2006 national report.* Washington, DC: U.S. Department of Justice, Office of Justice Programs, Office of Juvenile Justice and Delinquency Prevention.

Steinberg, L., & Scott, E. S. (2003). Less guilty by reason of adolescence: Developmental immaturity, diminished responsibility, and the juvenile death penalty. *American Psychologist, 58*(12), 1009–1018.

Tolan, P. H. (2007). Understanding violence. In D. J. Flannery, A. T. Vazsonyi & I. D. Waldman (Eds.), *The Cambridge handbook of violent behavior and aggression* (pp. 5–18). Cambridge, UK: Cambridge University Press.

Tolan, P. H., Guerra, N. G., & Kendall, P. C. (1995). A developmental-ecological perspective on antisocial behavior in children and adolescents: Toward a unified risk and intervention framework. *Journal of Consulting and Clinical Psychology, 63*(4), 579–584.

Tolan, P. H. & Titus, J. (In press). Therapeutic jurisprudence in juvenile justice. In B. Bottoms, G. Goodman, & C. Najdowski (Eds.), *Child victims, child offenders.* New York: Guilford Press.

SUGGESTED READINGS

Blueprints for Violence and Drug Abuse Prevention. Retrieved February 22, 2009, from http://www.colorado.edu/cspv/index.html.

The Future of Children (2008). *Juvenile justice. 18*(2). Retrieved February 22, 2009, from http://www.futureofchildren.org.

Models for Change initiative. Retrieved February 22, 2009, from http://www.modelsforchange.net/.

Skowrya, K. R., & Cocozza, J. J. (2007). *Blueprint for change: A comprehensive model for the identification and treatment of youth with mental health needs in contact with the juvenile justice system*, National Center for Mental Health and Juvenile Justice.

Retrieved February 22, 2009, from http://www.ncmhjj.com/Blueprint/default.shtml.

MICHAEL E. SCHOENY
PATRICK H. TOLAN
Institute for Juvenile Research and University of Illinois at Chicago

See also: **Behavior Problems of Childhood and Adolescence; Conduct Disorder**

JUVENILE FIRESETTING (See Firesetting)

K

KAGAN, JEROME (1929–)

Jerome Kagan received his bachelor of science degree from Rutgers University in 1950 and the PhD from Yale University in 1954. After a term at Ohio State University, he was inducted into the United States Army during the Korean War. Following discharge from the Army in 1957, Kagan became senior scientist at the Fels Research Institute in Yellow Springs, Ohio, where his major work involved analyzing a large corpus of longitudinal data on children who were followed from birth to adolescence and assessed again when they were young adults. The results of his work, in collaboration with Howard Moss, revealed that preservation of individual differences in this relatively typical middle-class sample did not emerge until after six or seven years of age. A summary of the project was published in a book, entitled *Birth to Maturity*, which won the Hofheimer Prize of the American Psychiatric Association.

Kagan went to Harvard in 1964 as professor of psychology with the hope of building a graduate program in developmental psychology within the Arts and Sciences faculty. After 36 years of teaching at Harvard, Kagan retired in 2000, but he is still an active writer.

Kagan's work at Harvard can be divided into three phases. The first studies probed the maturation of a small number of fundamental human competences that emerge in all children during the first 2 years of life. These include recognition memory at 3 to 4 months, the ability to retrieve the past between 7 and 12 months, awareness of self in the middle of the second year, and, finally, a moral sense which emerges toward the end of the second year. These discoveries were summarized in the books *Change and Continuity in Infancy* and *The Second Year*.

Kagan spent a sabbatical year in 1972–1973 working in an isolated Mayan Indian village in northwest Guatemala. His observations of infants and children in this isolated site motivated him to challenge the view, which was popular among many American developmental psychologists in the early 1970s, that lack of a variety of visual and auditory stimulation during the first year of life could permanently compromise the child's cognitive development. The infants in this village were deprived of a great deal of stimulation because of cultural mores, but the older children were cognitively and affectively competent. This discovery supported Kagan's growing belief that basic human competences mature in all children under all but the most adverse conditions.

The second phase of research involved an extensive study of the effects of daycare on young infants in collaboration with P. Zelzo and R. Kearsley. Because of the large numbers of American mothers with young children entering the workforce, Congress was considering, during the early 1970s, the establishment of daycare centers even though it was not clear whether these institutions would be harmful to young infants. The project revealed minimal differences between infants raised in a daycare center and those raised at home. However, data also revealed the existence of stable temperamental differences among infants, whether they were raised in a daycare center or at home. This finding provided the incentive for the third phase of work at Harvard.

Kagan has been working for over 20 years on the temperamental categories called "behaviorally inhibited" and "behaviorally uninhibited" to the unfamiliar. The evidence has revealed that four-month-old infants who show a combination of vigorous motor activity and irritability to unfamiliar stimulation, presumably due to low thresholds of excitability in limbic areas, are prone to become shy, fearful, timid children. Infants who show the complementary characteristics of minimal motor activity and minimal irritability to stimulation are biased to become sociable, relatively fearless children. These qualities show modest preservation through ten years of age.

Kagan has received a large number of honors, including Distinguished Scientist Award for Research from the American Psychological Association and the Society for Research in Child Development, Kenneth Craik Award of St. Johns College, Cambridge University; Wilbur Cross Medal from Yale University; the C. Anderson Aldrich Award of the American Academy of Pediatrics; and G. Stanley Hall Award given by Division 7 of the American Psychological Association. Kagan is a member of the Institute of Medicine of the National Academy of Sciences and a fellow of the American Academy of Arts and Sciences. Kagan's scholarship is marked by a probing skepticism toward premises that are in accord with the deep ethical biases of Western society but fail the criterion of sound empirical support.

SUGGESTED READINGS

Kagan, J. (1989). *Unstable ideas: Temperament, cognition, and self.* Cambridge, MA: Harvard University Press.

Kagan, J. (1994). *The nature of the child.* New York: Basic Books.

Kagan, J. (1998). *Three seductive ideas.* Cambridge, MA: Harvard University Press.

Kagan, J., & Moss, H. A. (1962). *Birth to maturity: A study in psychological development.* New Haven, CT: Yale University Press.

STAFF

KAPPA COEFFICIENT

The kappa coefficient was introduced by Cohen (1960) as a reliability statistic when two judges are classifying targets into categories on a nominal variable. It is most commonly used to estimate interrater reliability. Cohen (1968) later described weighted kappa, which considers degree of disagreement. For example, two judges classifying individuals on primary diagnosis could receive greater credit if they choose more rather than less similar diagnoses. Weighted kappa is particularly useful when categories are at least ordinally scaled. Another variant is available when there are more than two judges (Fleiss, 1981).

Kappa has been referred to as the chance-corrected agreement rate. Consider a situation in which two teachers must identify intellectually gifted children. If the teachers know that 2% of children are gifted but they have no understanding of how to evaluate for giftedness, they could randomly assign 2% of children to the gifted group and the results would look like this:

		Teacher 1		
		Gifted	**Not**	
Teacher 2	**Gifted**	$p_{11} = (.02 * .02)$ $= .0004$	$p_{12} = (.02 * .98)$ $= .0196$	**.02**
	Not	$P_{21} = (.98 * .02)$ $= .0196$	$P_{22} = (.98 * .98)$ $= .9604$	**.98**
		.02	**.98**	

The proportion of agreement purely by chance would equal $p_C = .0004 + .9604 = .9608$. When the base rates of the categories are very different, proportion of agreement can be very high even with random placement by judges. Kappa is an indicator of the degree to which agreement between two judges exceeds the chance agreement rate. The formula for kappa is

$$\kappa = \frac{P_A - P_C}{1 - p_C}$$

where p_A is the actual agreement rate. Kappa varies between 0 when the actual agreement rate is no better than the chance rate, and 1.0 when the judges agree perfectly.

As a reliability statistic, kappa values below .60 are generally considered undesirable while values of .80 or higher are preferred, though other benchmarks have been suggested. As a practical matter, when the chance agreement rate is high, it is difficult to get an acceptable value for kappa. Furthermore, basing the chance agreement rate on the assumption that the raters are completely random and independent is considered unreasonable by some. These considerations have led to several suggestions for alternatives to kappa, but none has proved successful. Kappa is a true reliability statistic in that it is an estimate of the proportion of observed score variability attributable to true scores. In fact, when judges are rating targets on an ordinal scale, and weighted kappa is used to award partial credit based on the distance between the two judges' ratings, weighted kappa represents a computational form of the intraclass correlation coefficient.

All major statistical software packages provide procedures for the computation of kappa. Significance tests are available for kappa, but the size of kappa is a more important interpretive consideration than rejection of the null hypothesis that judges' ratings are completely random. Methods have also been suggested for the computation of confidence intervals.

REFERENCES

Cohen, J. (1960). A coefficient of agreement for nominal scales. *Educational and Psychological Measurement, 20,* 37–46.

Cohen, J. (1968). Weighted kappa: Nominal scale agreement provision for scaled disagreement or partial credit. *Psychological Bulletin, 70,* 213–220.

Fleiss, J. L. (1971). Measuring nominal scale agreement among many raters. *Psychological Bulletin, 76,* 378–382.

SUGGESTED READINGS

Blackman, N. J., & Koval, J. J. (2000). Interval estimation for Cohen's kappa as a measure of agreement. *Statistics in Medicine, 19,* 723–741.

Maclure, M., & Willett, W. C. (1987). Misinterpretation and misuse of the kappa statistic. *American Journal of Epidemiology, 126,* 161–169.

Mielke, P. W., Berry, K. J., & Johnston, J. E. (2007). The exact variance of weighted kappa with multiple raters. *Psychological Reports, 101,* 655–660.

ROBERT E. MCGRATH
Fairleigh Dickinson University

See also: Psychometrics; Reliability

KAUFMAN ADOLESCENT AND ADULT INTELLIGENCE TEST

The Kaufman Adolescent and Adult Intelligence Test (KAIT) was developed by Alan S. Kaufman and Nadeen L. Kaufman in 1993 and is an individually administered intelligence test for individuals ranging from 11 to 85-plus years of age. It has a strong theoretical base integrating Horn and Cattell's concept of fluid and crystallized intelligence, Luria and Golden's notion of frontal lobe planning ability, and Piaget's construct of formal operational thought (Smith, 2001).

The concepts of crystallized and fluid intelligence are dimensions of general intelligence, as proposed by Charles Spearman. Crystallized intelligence (Gc) is influenced mainly by traditional school learning and acculturation and relies on verbal concepts and knowledge. Gc correlates with abilities that depend on knowledge and experience, such as vocabulary and general information. Fluid intelligence (Gf) is more of a logic-driven form of intelligence that focuses on an individual's ability to solve novel problems and is associated with measures of abstract reasoning and puzzle solving (Smith, 2001). The emphasis on including measures of fluid intelligence in contemporary intelligence tests like the KAIT is important, because it offers good tests of overall intelligence, includes a good number of important cognitive processes, and, most importantly, moves away from culturally-based verbal and factual tasks to a type of subtest that is less influenced by opportunity and specific educational experiences.

Development and Standardization

Alan S. Kaufman was mentored by David Wechsler, the most influential American test developer, whose Wechsler intelligence scales remain the most popular tests worldwide. Alan and Nadeen went on to create their own original Kaufman test series. At the University of Georgia in 1978 to 1979, the research team that they supervised helped develop the original Kaufman Assessment Battery for Children (K-ABC). In the 1980s, the Kaufmans' various research teams began work on the KAIT and other tests, using current intelligence theory and applying it to the next logical progression, that of the adolescent and adult age range. The KAIT normative sample includes 2,000 individuals ranging in age from 11 to 85-plus years. The sample is representative of the U.S. population census for gender, socioeconomic status, geographic region, and race or ethnic group.

Reliability and Validity

With test-retest reliability coefficients ranging from .87 to .97, the KAIT IQ scales are reliable measures of crystallized, fluid, and general intelligence (Kaufman & Kaufman, 1993). When correlated with the WISC-R, WAIS-R, and Stanford-Binet fourth edition, validity coefficients ranged from .57 to .88. Furthermore, both exploratory and confirmatory factor analyses support that the KAIT does indeed measure the two constructs of intelligence across the life span and does, in fact, possess good evidence of construct validity (Smith, 2001).

Structure of KAIT

The KAIT provides a Composite IQ as well as separate IQs for the Crystallized and Fluid Scales, all standard scores with mean = 100 and $SD = 15$. The core battery consists of three crystallized subtest (Auditory Comprehensions, Definitions, and Double Meanings), and three fluid subtests (Logical Steps, Mystery Codes, and Rebus Learning). The expanded battery also includes two measures of delayed memory (Rebus delayed recall and Auditory delayed recall) and two alternate subtests, Memory for block designs and Famous Faces, fluid and crystallized respectively. A supplementary Mental Status subtest is also provided for examinees whose level of cognitive functioning is too low for them to respond effectively to the regular KAIT Gc and Gf subtests. The Core Battery can be typically completed in under an hour, with an additional 30 minutes required for the Expanded Battery (Kaufman & Kaufman, 1993).

Subtest Descriptions

Crystallized Subtests

Definitions: Deciphering words presented with missing letters based on configuration of the letters and a clue about its meaning.

Auditory Comprehension: Listening to a mock news broadcast and then answering factual information about each story.

Double Meanings: Studying two sets of word clues and then thinking of a word that relates both clues.

Famous Faces: Naming current historical and famous individuals based on their photograph and a verbal cue about them.

Fluid Subtests

Rebus Learning: Learning words or concepts associated with particular rebus drawings and then reading sentences or phrases composed of the drawings.

Logical Steps: Understanding logical premises that are presented both visually and orally, and then responding to questions by making use of the premises.

Mystery Codes: Identifying codes associated with pictorial stimuli and figuring out the code by using deductive reasoning.

Memory for Block Designs: Studying a briefly presented printed design and then reproducing that design using six cubes and a tray.

Delayed Recall Subtests

Rebus Delayed Recall: Reading phrases based on rebus drawings they learned 30–45 minutes earlier during the Rebus Learning Subtest.

Auditory Delayed Recall: Answering factual information based on news stories heard 30–45 minutes earlier during the Auditory Comprehension Subtest.

(Kaufman, Kaufman, Kaufman-Singer, & Kaufman, 2005)

The tests of fluid intelligence measure an individual's deductive and inductive reasoning as well as paired-associative learning. The tests of crystallized intelligence measure an individual's vocabulary, factual knowledge, listening comprehension, and ability to solve word problems. The Expanded Battery also measures visual memory, long-term retrieval of learned content, and analysis and synthesis. The Mental Status subtest can be used to classify performance into categories of Average, Below Average, or Lower Extreme. This range of categories is useful for making differential diagnoses depending on the severity of the individual cognitive deficiency (Smith, 2001).

Comparisons to Current Research

A review of the KAIT concluded that it represented advancement in cognitive assessment, but had questionable ability to demonstrate its treatment validity and effectiveness of the resulting diagnosis and intervention (Flanagan & Alfonso, 1994). Current research has used the KAIT as a criterion for establishing the construct validity of newer tests such as the General Ability Measure for Adults (GAMA), a study that also supported the convergent validity of the KAIT (Lassitar, Matthews, Bell, & Maher, 2002). Other research likewise used the KAIT as a criterion measure, which only serves to further the KAIT's acceptance as a construct-valid, theory-based measure of intelligence. The KAIT is an alternative to the Wechsler Scales for the assessment of adolescents and adults and can be used to supplement the Wechsler scales to provide additional information about cognitive abilities, especially in the areas of fluid reasoning and long-term retrieval; the KAIT, therefore, is useful for cross-battery approaches to intelligence assessment. In addition to the American version of the KAIT, this test has been adapted and standardized for the assessment of adolescents and adults in Germany and the Netherlands (e.g., Melchers, Schürmann, & Scholten, 2006).

REFERENCES

Flanagan, D. P., & Alfonso, V. C. (1994). A review of the Kaufman Adolescent and Adult Intelligence Test: An advancement in cognitive assessment? *School Psychology Review, 23*(3), 512–525.

Kaufman, A. S., & Kaufman, N. L. (1993). *Kaufman Adolescent and Adult Intelligence Test.* Circle Pines, MN: American Guidance Service.

Kaufman, J. C., Kaufman A. S., Kaufman-Singer, J., & Kaufman N. L. (2005). The Kaufman Assessment Battery for Children–Second Edition (KABC-II) and the Kaufman Adolescent and Adult Intelligence Test (KAIT). In D. P. Flanagan & P. L. Harrison (Eds.), *Contemporary intellectual assessment: Theories, tests, and issues* (pp. 344–370). New York: Guilford Press.

Lassitar, K., Matthews, T., Bell, N., & Maher, C. (2002). Comparison of the General Ability Measure for Adults and the Kaufman Adolescent and Adult Intelligence Test with college students. *Psychology in the Schools, 39*(5), 497–506.

Melchers, P., Schürmann, S., & Scholten, S. (2006). *Deutschsprachige Fassung des KAIT Kaufman—Adolescent and Adult Intelligence Test (A. S. Kaufman & N .L. Kaufman) Kaufman—Test zur Intelligenzmessung für Jugendliche und Erwachsene Handbuch.* Leiden, the Netherlands: PITS.

Smith, D. K. (2001). Adolescent use of Kaufman Adolescent and Adult Intelligence Test (KAIT) in the new millennium. *U.S. Department of Education* (pp. 203–213). ERIC Document Reproduction Service No. ED 457439.

SUGGESTED READINGS

Kaufman, A. S., & Lichtenberger, E. O. (2006). *Assessing adolescent and adult intelligence* (3rd ed). Hoboken, NJ: John Wiley & Sons.

Lichtenberger, E. O., Broadbooks, D. A., & Kaufman, A. S. (2000). *Essentials of cognitive assessment with the KAIT and other Kaufman measures.* New York: John Wiley & Sons.

RYAN HOLT
DAVID LOOMIS
JAMES C. KAUFMAN
California State University at San Bernardino

ALAN S. KAUFMAN
Yale University School of Medicine

See also: **Intelligence; Intelligence Testing; Kaufman Assessment Battery for Children**

KAUFMAN ASSESSMENT BATTERY FOR CHILDREN

The Kaufman Assessment Battery for Children—Second Edition (KABC-II, Kaufman & Kaufman, 2004) measures the cognitive abilities and mental processing of children and adolescents between the ages of 3 years 0 months and 18 years 11 months. Administered individually, this clinical instrument consists of 16 subtests (plus a Delayed Recall scale) and provides examiners with a Nonverbal scale composed of subtests that can be administered in pantomime and responded to motorically. The Nonverbal Scale is especially useful for children who are hearing impaired or have limited English proficiency (Kaufman, Kaufman, Kaufman-Singer, & Kaufman, 2005).

The KABC-II is grounded in a dual theoretical foundation: Luria's (1973) neuropsychological model, featuring three Blocks or functional units, and the Cattell-Horn-Carroll (CHC) approach to categorizing specific cognitive abilities (Carroll, 1997; McGrew, 2005). The choice of administration between either model is up to the examiner's judgment (Kaufman & Kaufman, 2004), but depends primarily on the child's background. The Luria model emphasizes mental processing and excludes tasks that measure verbal ability and acquired knowledge; it is, therefore, the model of choice when assessing ethnic minority children, bilingual children, and others who may have had limited opportunities for learning and acquisition of knowledge. In contrast, the CHC model, which includes all of the mental processing scales in the Luria model, also features a scale that measures crystallized knowledge, which is the kind of intelligence that is heavily dependent on education and acculturation.

The KABC-II includes both Core and Expanded batteries, with only the Core battery needed to yield the child's scale profile. The KABC-II Expanded battery offers supplementary subtests to increase the breadth of the constructs measured by the Core battery and to follow up hypotheses. Administration time for the Core battery ranges from 30 to 70 minutes, depending on the child's age and whether the examiner administers the CHC model of the KABC-II or the Luria model (Kaufman & Kaufman, 2004).

Model Comparison: Luria to CHC

When interpreted from the Luria model, the KABC-II focuses on mental processing, excludes acquired knowledge to the degree possible, and yields a global standard score called the Mental Processing Index (MPI) with mean = 100 and SD = 15. Like the original K-ABC, the Luria model measures sequential and simultaneous processing, but the KABC-II goes beyond that dichotomy to measure two additional constructs: learning ability and planning ability (Kaufman & Kaufman, 2004).

From the vantage point of the CHC model, the KABC-II Core battery includes all scales in the Luria system, but they are interpreted from an alternate perspective; for example, the scale that measures sequential processing from Luria's theory is seen as measuring the CHC ability of short-term memory (Gsm), and the planning ability scale (Luria interpretation) aligns with Gf or fluid reasoning (CHC interpretation). The CHC model includes one extra scale that is *not* in the Luria model, namely a measure of crystallized ability (Gc) that is labeled Knowledge/Gc. The global standard score yielded by the CHC model is labeled the Fluid-Crystallized Index (FCI), also with a mean of 100 and SD of 15 (Kaufman et al., 2005).

The Kaufmans do not consider one model to be theoretically superior to the other. Both theories are equally important as foundations of the KABC-II. The CHC psychometric theory emphasizes specific cognitive abilities, whereas the Luria neuropsychological theory emphasizes "processes," namely the way children process information when solving problems. Both approaches are valid for understanding how children learn and solve new problems, which is why each scale has two names, one from Luria theory and the other from CHC theory. Regardless of the model of the KABC-II that is *administered* (Luria or CHC), the way in which psychologists *interpret* the scales will undoubtedly be influenced by their theoretical preference (Kaufman et al., 2005).

In general, the CHC model is given priority over the Luria model because the Kaufmans believe that knowledge/Gc is, in principle, an important aspect of cognitive functioning. Therefore, the CHC model (FCI) is preferred for children with known or suspected disabilities in reading, written expression, or mathematics; for children assessed for giftedness or mental retardation; for children assessed for emotional or behavioral disorders; and for children assessed for attentional disorders such as ADHD (Kaufman & Kaufman, 2004). However, as noted, the Luria model is preferred for bilingual children and for ethnic minorities—indeed, for anyone for whom tests of language and acquired knowledge (i.e., the Knowledge/Gc subtests) are likely to provide unfair estimates of their intellectual ability and learning potential.

Subtest Descriptions

Sequential/Gsm Scale includes: *Word Order, Number Recall,* and *Hand Movements*; these require the child to repeat a series of object recognition, number sequences, or various hand movements, respectively.

Simultaneous/Gv Scale includes: *Triangles, Face Recognition, Conceptual Thinking, Rover, Block Counting,* and *Gestalt*

Closure; these emphasize the use of visual processing, spatial reasoning, abstract reasoning, and short-term memory.

Planning/Gf Scale includes: *Pattern Reasoning*, and *Story Completion*; these require the child to first recognize a pattern, and then be able to foresee the next logical step to fill in a missing piece, or arrange items into a logical series of progression. These tasks measure inductive and deductive reasoning.

Learning/Glr Scale includes: *Atlantis, Rebus*, and *Delayed Recall*; these are meant to assess the child's ability to learn new information, store it in long-term memory, and then recall and apply it in a functional manner. The supplementary delayed recall tasks measure the ability to retain information that was learned about 15–25 minutes earlier.

Knowledge/Gc Scale includes: *Riddles, Expressive Vocabulary*, and *Verbal Knowledge*; these are meant to assess the breadth of a child's verbal concepts, vocabulary, and acquired knowledge by assessing the child's ability to recognize or recall the names of pictured objects, or by solving a verbal "riddle."

Standardization Sample

The KABC-II standardization sample is comprised of 3,025 children and adolescents. The sample matched the United States population on the stratification variables of gender, race/ethnicity, SES (parent education), region, and special-education status. Most age groups were comprised of exactly 200 children (Kaufman & Kaufman, 2004).

Reliability

KABC-II global scale (MPI and FCI) split-half reliability coefficients were in the mid-.90s for all age groups (only the value of .90 for the MPI at age 3 was below .94) (Kaufman & Kaufman, 2004).

Validity

Construct validity was given strong support by the results of confirmatory factor analysis (Kaufman & Kaufman, 2004). An independent evaluation of the KABC-II (Reynolds, Keith, Fine, Fisher, & Low, 2007) concluded that: the KABC-II measures the same constructs across its age range of 3–18 years (measurement invariance); the five KABC-II constructs align closely with the corresponding five broad abilities from the CHC theory in school-age children (ages 6–18); some discrepancies do exist in a few subtests, such that some subtests measure more than the single ability specified by the KABC-II manual (i.e., Block Counting and Story Completion).

REFERENCES

Carroll, J. B. (1997). *The three-stratum theory of cognitive abilities*. In D. P. Flanagan, J. L. Genshaft, & P. L. Harrison (Eds.), *Contemporary intellectual assessment: Theories, tests, and issues* (pp. 122–130). New York: Guilford Press.

Kaufman, A. S., & Kaufman, N. L. (2004). Manual for Kaufman Assessment Battery for Children—Second Edition (KABC-II)—Comprehensive Form. Circle Pines, MN: American Guidance Service.

Kaufman, J. C., Kaufman, A. S., Kaufman-Singer, J. L., & Kaufman, N. L. (2005). The Kaufman Assessment Battery for Children—Second Edition (KABC-II) and the Kaufman Adult and Adolescent Intelligence Test (KAIT). In D. P. Flanagan & P. L. Harrison (Eds.), *Contemporary intellectual assessment* (pp. 344–370). New York: Guilford Press.

Luria, A. R. (1973). *The working brain: An introduction to neuropsychology*. London: Penguin.

McGrew, K. S. (2005). The Cattell-Horn-Carroll theory of cognitive abilities: Past, present, and future. In D. P. Flanagan & P. L. Harrison (Eds.), *Contemporary intellectual assessment: Theories, tests, and issues* (2nd ed., pp. 136–181). New York: Guilford Press.

Reynolds, M. R., Keith, T. Z., Fine, J. G., Fisher, M. E., & Low, J. A. (2007). Confirmatory factor structure of the Kaufman Assessment Battery for Children—Second Edition: Consistency with Cattell-Horn-Carroll theory. *School Psychology Quarterly, 22,* 511–539.

SUGGESTED READINGS

Kaufman, J. C., Kaufman, A. S., Kaufman-Singer, J. L., & Kaufman, N. L. (2005). *Essentials of KABC-II assessment.* Hoboken, NJ: John Wiley & Sons.

Lichtenberger, E. O., Mather, N., Kaufman, N. L., & Kaufman, A. S. (2004). *Essentials of assessment report writing.* Hoboken, NJ: John Wiley & Sons.

DAVID LOOMIS
RYAN HOLT
JAMES C. KAUFMAN
California State University at San Bernardino

ALAN S. KAUFMAN
Yale University School of Medicine

See also: Intelligence; Intelligence Testing; Kaufman Adolescent and Adult Intelligence Test

KINETIC FAMILY DRAWING TEST (See Figure Drawing Tests)

KINSEY INSTITUTE

The Kinsey Institute for Research in Sex, Gender, and Reproduction was founded in 1947 by pioneering researcher Alfred C. Kinsey. Located on the campus of Indiana University, the Kinsey Institute's mission is to promote interdisciplinary research and scholarship in the fields of human sexuality, gender, and reproduction. Research scientists conduct studies into sexual health and behavior, and the extensive research collections provide resources for scholars across disciplines in humanities, art, and science.

Historical Publications and Findings

In 1948, Kinsey published *Sexual Behavior in the Human Male*, the first extensive scientific study documenting sexual histories of over 5,500 men in the U.S. population. This publication was followed in 1953 by *Sexual Behavior in the Human Female*. Together, these two books comprise the popularly known "Kinsey Reports." Kinsey and his interview team crossed the country, interviewing over 18,000 men and women. The books included statistics on prevalence of homosexuality, masturbation, premarital sex, infidelity, and other previously understudied behaviors, and they introduced the concept of a continuum of sexual orientation, the Homosexuality-Heterosexuality scale, also known as the "Kinsey Scale."

Although Kinsey was criticized for his nonrepresentative sampling approach, the extensive interviews still represent a unique and comprehensive database on sexual behavior and are accessed by contemporary researchers for reanalysis and comparison with more current studies. In the following decades, the research team, led by Paul Gebhard, continued to analyze and reanalyze the original interview data, releasing books on *Pregnancy, Birth and Abortion* (1958), *Sex Offenders* (1965), and *The Kinsey Data: Marginal Tabulations of the 1938–1963 Interviews Conducted by the Institute for Sex Research* (1979). In 1978, Alan Bell and Martin Weinberg published *Homosexualities: A Study of Diversity Among Men and Women.*

The Kinsey Institute has also convened a number of international workshops on current topics in sex research. Research monographs from these symposia include *The Psychophysiology of Sex* (Janssen, 2007), *Sexual Development in Childhood* (Bancroft, 2003), *The Role of Theory in Sex Research* (Bancroft, 2000), and *Masculinity/Femininity* (Reinisch et al., 1987).

Contemporary Research on Sexual Behavior

Current research at the Kinsey Institute seeks to understand the role of psychological, biological, and cultural factors in sexual behavior and response, including the factors that contribute to sexual health and sexual distress in individuals and couples; the role of mood and emotions in sexual decision making and well-being; gender and sexual orientation differences in sexuality; the role of hormones in sexual response and behavior; and the links between sexual functioning and well-being. Researchers employ a number of methodologies, including questionnaires and surveys, psychophysiological measures (such as fMRI, genital measures, and hormonal assays), and qualitative methods (such as focus groups and in-depth interviews).

Research Highlights

In the 1990s, Kinsey Institute researchers Bancroft and Janssen introduced the dual control model of sexual response, an approach to understanding sexual arousal and behavior, based on the premise that people differ in their propensities for sexual inhibition and excitation. They developed a questionnaire to measure these propensities, and research using this measure has found that sexual inhibition and excitation are relevant to our understanding of sexual dysfunction, sexual risk-taking, sexual aggression, and sexual compulsivity. Other research has focused on condom use and found that condom use errors and problems are much more common than previously assumed. This research applies psychological theory to help identify populations at risk for pregnancy and disease, due to nonuse or incorrect use of condoms. Research with couples explores sexual compatibility and the importance of sex in beginning and long-term relationships. Other research interests include examination of psychological and physiological factors in sexual aggression, the relationship between mood and sexuality, and the relationship of hormones to women's attraction and attention.

Library and Special Research Collections

The Kinsey Institute's research collections include over 105,000 print materials dating back to the 1600s, 10,000 films and videos, and research databases. In addition to scientific and popular books, journals, magazines, pulp fiction, original research papers, newspaper clippings, and ephemera, the archival collections also include personal collections from clinicians, researchers, educators, scientists, and collectors. These rich resources are available to and used by scholars in many disciplines, including history, medicine, anthropology, sociology, and film, art, and literature.

The Kinsey Institute's art and artifacts collection includes original works of commercial, folk, and fine art by both unknown artisans and famous artists. This extensive and growing collection contains approximately 7,000 items from the United States, Europe, South America, Africa, and Asia, and it spans more than 2,000 years of human history. The photography collection contains approximately 48,000 inventoried images dating from the 1870s to the present that come from the United States and Europe (Britain, France, Germany and Italy, primarily). The Kinsey Institute gallery features selections from the collection based on interdisciplinary themes. Recent shows have included Sex Ed, Queer Projections, and the annual Juried Art Show, featuring two- and three-dimensional art from contemporary artists. Publications from The Kinsey

Institute's collections include exhibition catalogues, such as *Feminine Persuasion: Art and Essays on Sexuality* (Stirratt and Johnson, 2003) and *Sex and Humor: Selections from The Kinsey Institute* (Johnson, Stirratt, and Bancroft, 2002).

Education and Collaboration

Undergraduate and graduate students enrolled at Indiana University participate in Kinsey Institute research projects in various ways. The Institute co-sponsors a PhD minor in human sexuality through Indiana University. In addition, The Kinsey Institute welcomes visiting scholars and collaborates with affiliated scholars from around the world on research projects.

Resource for Sexual Behavior

As an international center for the interdisciplinary study of human sexuality, the Kinsey Institute provides online information about sex research and sexual health and behavior. Http://www.Kinseyinstitute.org lists conferences, educational centers, online library catalog, sex research news and current findings, and other resources for scholars, media, and the public. Http://www.Kinseyconfidential.org is a question-and-answer site designed for the college-age population, with information on sexual health and behavior.

REFERENCES

Bancroft, J. (2000). *The role of theory in sex research.* Bloomington: Indiana University Press.

Bancroft, J. (Ed.). (2003). *Sexual development in childhood.* Bloomington: Indiana University Press.

Bell, A., & Weinberg, M. (1978). *Homosexualities: A study of diversity among men and women.* New York: Simon & Schuster.

Gebhard, P. H., Gagnon, J. H., Pomeroy, W. B., & Christenson, C. V. (1965). *Sex offenders: An analysis of types.* New York: Harper-Hoeber.

Gebhard, P. H., & Johnson, A. B. (1979). *The Kinsey data: Marginal tabulations of the 1938–1963 interviews conducted by The Institute for Sex Research.* Philadelphia: W. B. Saunders.

Gebhard, P. H., Pomeroy, W. B., Martin, C. E., & Christenson, C. V. (1958). *Pregnancy, birth and abortion.* New York: Harper-Hoeber.

Janssen, E. (Ed.). (2007). *The psychophysiology of sex.* Bloomington: Indiana University Press.

Johnson, C, Stirratt, B, & Bancroft, J. (2002). *Sex and humor: Selections from the Kinsey Institute.* Bloomington: Indiana University Press.

Kinsey, A. C., Pomeroy, W. B., & Martin, C. E. (1998). *Sexual behavior in the human male.* Bloomington: Indiana University Press. (Original work published in 1948)

Kinsey, A. C., Pomeroy, W. B., Martin, C. E. & Gebhard, P. H. (1998). *Sexual behavior in the human female.* Bloomington: Indiana University Press. (Original work published in 1953)

Reinisch, J. M., Rosenblum, L. A., & Sanders, S. A. (Eds.). (1987). *Masculinity/femininity: Basic perspectives.* New York: Oxford University Press.

Stirratt, B., & Johnson, C. (2003). *Feminine persuasion: Art and essays on sexuality.* Bloomington: Indiana University Press.

SUGGESTED READING

Bancroft, J. (1998). Introduction: Alfred Kinsey's work 50 years later. In A. C. Kinsey, W. B. Pomeroy, C. E. Martin, & P. H. Gebhard, *Sexual activities in the human female.* Bloomington: Indiana University Press.

JENNIFER L. BASS
The Kinsey Institute, Bloomington, IN

See also: Sexual Development

KLEPTOMANIA

Kleptomania is currently defined as an impulse control disorder in which the essential feature is a recurring failure on the part of the individual to resist impulses to steal items, even though those items are not needed for personal use or their monetary value. The individual experiences an increasing sense of tension just prior to the theft and then a release of pressure, gratification, or relief after successfully completing the theft. In order to receive the diagnosis, the stealing should not be committed as an expression of anger or vengeance, should not be done in response to delusions or hallucinations, and cannot better be accounted for by another disorder (American Psychiatric Association, 2000). Thus, the individual's intention prior to and following stealing is important.

Although some researchers and clinicians suggest that kleptomania is simply theft and reject the notion that there are psychological components involved, others categorize kleptomania as an addiction or an "affective spectrum disorder" (e.g., similar to depression and anxiety; McElroy, Hudson, Pope, & Keck, 1991). Persons diagnosed with kleptomania are more likely to be diagnosed with comorbid impulse control disorders (e.g., obsessive compulsive disorder, eating disorders). Historically, wealthy individuals, usually women, have been the bulk of those diagnosed with kleptomania. This may have driven the diagnostic criteria that the stolen items are not needed for personal use or monetary value, which in turn may have unnecessarily restricted the diagnosis to this segment of the population while ostensibly ignoring others (e.g., lower income men or women) who may be kleptomanic (Kohn & Antonuccio, 2002).

Etiology

There is no consensus about the origins and development of kleptomania. Psychoanalytic theorists have posited that the act of stealing is a defensive maneuver, possibly evoked by early traumatic experiences, in which stealing serves to modulate undesirable feelings or emotions or to keep them from being expressed (Goldman, 1991).

Cognitive and behavioral models conceptualize the disorder as being the result of operant conditioning, behavioral chaining, distorted cognitions, and poor coping mechanisms (Kohn & Antonuccio, 2002). Those with cognitive and behavioral views posit that, if the consequence of an individual's stealing behavior is reinforcing (e.g., a reduction in anxiety or tension, an increase in excitement or positive feelings), it is likely that stealing will reoccur in the future under similar circumstances. If negative consequences do not follow the stealing behavior (i.e., punishment), this further increases the likelihood of the stealing reoccurring. As the behavior continues to occur, stronger antecedents or cues become contingently linked with it, in what ultimately becomes a powerful behavioral chain. Both the environment (e.g., advertisements, stressful day at work) and the person (e.g., thoughts, mood) may provide the antecedents to and consequences of the stealing behavior.

The biological theory of kleptomania is based mainly on pharmacological treatment studies examining the use of selective serotonin reuptake inhibitors (SSRIs), mood stabilizers, and opiod receptor antagonists (Dannon, Aizer, & Lowengrub, 2006; Grant & Kim, 2002b). These studies suggest that kleptomania is caused by poor regulation of serotonin, dopamine, and/or natural opioids within the brain. For example, uses of opioid antagonists appear to reduce some people's urges to steal and mute the "rush" typically experienced immediately after stealing (Dannon et al., 2006; Goldman, 1991; Grant & Kim, 2002b). An alternative explanation also based on opioid antagonist studies states that kleptomania is similar to the "self-medication" model, such that stealing serves as a means for stimulating the person's natural opioid system: "The opioid release sooths the patients, treats their sadness, or reduces their anxiety. Thus, stealing is a mechanism to relive oneself from a chronic state of hyperarousal, perhaps produced by prior stressful or traumatic events, and thereby modulate affective states" (Grant & Kim, 2002, p. 354). This latter theory complements the current cognitive behavioral model of kleptomania.

Treatment

Cognitive and behavioral treatments and medication are the most common treatments for kleptomania. SSRIs, antiepileptics, and opiod antagonists have all been used with varying results (Grant & Kim, 2002). However, pharmacological treatments are often accompanied by negative side effects, leading to poor compliance with the medication and possibly higher relapse rates or discontinuation effects (Kohn & Antonuccio, 2002).

A growing body of research suggests the effectiveness of using cognitive and behavioral approaches to treat kleptomania and co-occurring behavioral problems, including such strategies as covert sensitization, shaping, behavioral chaining, problem-solving, cognitive restructuring, and homework. A thorough functional analysis allows for the implementation of techniques like covert sensitization, which pairs an imagined consequence of stealing while desiring to steal with kleptomania-specific consequences (e.g., getting arrested, going to jail, social embarrassment), with high rates of success (Kohn & Antonuccio, 2002). The advantages of this therapy include the absence of side effects and discontinuation effects and the addition of a new skill set that reduces the likelihood of relapse.

In summary, kleptomania is currently considered a disorder that is typified by the lack of malicious intent to steal unnecessary or otherwise affordable items, with a feeling of relief or release of pressure immediately following the theft behavior. This conceptualization may be skewed by historical factors, and this condition is currently best treated by behavioral and cognitive strategies and some medications.

REFERENCES

American Psychiatric Association. (2000). *Diagnostic and statistical manual of mental disorders* (4th ed., text rev.). Washington, DC: Author.

Dannon, P. N., Aizer, A., & Lowengrub, K. (2006). Kleptomania: Differential diagnosis and treatment modalities. *Current Psychiatry Reviews, 2,* 281–283.

Goldman, M. J. (1991). Kleptomania: Making sense of the nonsensical. *American Journal of Psychiatry, 148,* 986–996.

Grant, J. E., & Kim, S. W. (2002). An open-label study of naltrexone in the treatment of kleptomania. *Journal of Clinical Psychiatry, 63,* 349–356.

Kohn, C. S., & Antonuccio, D. O. (2002). Treatment of kleptomania using cognitive and behavioral strategies. *Clinical Case Studies, 1*(1), 25–38.

McElroy, S. L., Hudson, J. I., Pope, H. G., & Keck, P. E. (1991). Kleptomania: Clinical characteristics and associated psychopathology. *Psychological Medicine, 21,* 93–108.

SUGGESTED READING

Kohn, C. S., Kalal, D. M., Kastell, K., & Viera, J. (2006). Kleptomania. In J. E. Fisher & W. O'Donohue (Eds.), *Practitioner's guide to evidence-based psychotherapy*. New York: Kluwer.

CAROLYNN S. KOHN
DEREK D. SZAFRANSKI
University of the Pacific

See also: **Addiction; Compulsions**

KOHLBERG, LAWRENCE (1927–1987)

Lawrence Kohlberg is best known for his research on the moral development of children. He received his BA degree (1948) and the PhD (1958) from the University of Chicago. The following year, he went to Yale University and remained there until 1961. After several interim appointments he joined the Harvard faculty of Education and Social Psychology in 1967. His principal work was *Essays on Moral Development* (two volumes).

Following the lines of Piaget, Kohlberg stated that children followed moral development in three stages: (1) In the preconventional level, children's moral development follows from external standards; (2) in the conventional level, morality is essentially based upon following the correct rules; and (3) in the postconventional level, morality is basically one of the shared standards of rights and duties. Each of these levels comprises three stages of orientation: The first is characterized by obedience and punishment and naïve egoism; the second by "good boy" and authority; the third combines legalism and conscience. Like Piaget's theory, Kohlberg's is one of cognitive development. His results were achieved by 20 years of longitudinal study.

Kohlberg suffered from chronic depression and pain as a result of a parasite-induced disease that began in 1971. In 1987, he apparently drowned of his own choosing in Boston Harbor.

SUGGESTED READINGS

Colby, A., & Kohlberg, L. (1987). *The measurement of moral judgment. Vol. 2: Standard issue scoring manual.* New York: Cambridge University Press.

DeVries, R., & Kohlberg, L. (1987). *Programs of early education: The constructionist view.* New York: Longman.

Kohlberg, L. (1973). *Moral judgment interview and procedures for scoring.* Cambridge, MA: Harvard University Press.

Kohlberg, L. (1981). *Essays on moral development, Vol. 1: The philosophy of moral development.* San Francisco: Harper & Row.

STAFF

KORSAKOFF SYNDROME

Korsakoff syndrome, originally known as Korsakoff's psychosis, is a mental disorder that is characterized by severe and irreversible memory impairments and confabulation behavior in the absence of intellectual decline or attention deficits (Zubaran, Fernandes, & Rodnight, 1997). The syndrome was first described by Sergei Korsakoff in the late nineteenth century, based on observations of brain-lesioned patients with a history of chronic alcoholism. Korsakoff syndrome is associated with chronic alcohol abuse and malnutrition, resulting in a thiamine deficiency that presumably causes brain damage in the diencephalon, notably the mammillary bodies and the thalamus. Lesions in other brain areas, such as the frontal lobes, have also been associated with Korsakoff syndrome (Visser et al., 1999). The syndrome is classified in the *Diagnostic and Statistical Manual of Mental Disorders* (DSM-IV-TR; American Psychiatric Association, 2000) as alcohol-induced persisting amnestic disorder, but Korsakoff syndrome has also been found in patients with chronic thiamine deficiency of nonalcoholic origin, such as anorexia, pregnancy, or dialysis. Typically, it is preceded by a confusional state with a sudden onset in combination with opthalmoplegia and stance and gait ataxia, known as Wernicke's disease or Wernicke's encephalopathy. Since the etiology of both Wernicke's disease and Korsakoff syndrome is the same, they are often taken together as the Wernicke-Korsakoff syndrome or complex, with an estimated prevalence of approximately 1–2% in the general population (Zubaran et al., 1997).

Neuropsychological Findings

Deficits in Memory

A severe memory impairment is the most apparent cognitive deficit in Korsakoff syndrome. It includes amnesia for events that occurred before the syndrome's onset (retrograde amnesia), as well as impaired acquisition of new, episodic information (anterograde amnesia). There is evidence that an inability to store or bind together contextual information, such as spatial or temporal features, is the core of the anterograde amnesia (i.e., a source-memory deficit). In turn, memory for target information isolated from its context is affected to a lesser degree. The retrograde amnesia is characterized by a temporal gradient, indicating that remote memories are better preserved than more recent episodes, that may even extend to semantic, factual memories. Possible explanations for this temporally graded retrograde amnesia in Korsakoff syndrome are a progressive deterioration of the ability to acquire new knowledge in the period before the actual onset of the syndrome due to the chronic alcohol abuse, a role for the diencephalon in the consolidation of memories even 2 to 3 years after their initial acquisition, or the suggestion that continuing reactivation of memory traces results in the formation of multiple traces that facilitate retrieval. Implicit or nondeclarative memory function, such as procedural learning or priming, is generally preserved in Korsakoff syndrome (Kopelman, 2002).

Confabulation Behavior

The confabulation behavior that is associated with Korsakoff syndrome was originally regarded as secondary to the amnesia, that is, seen as the filling in of memory gaps. More recent studies suggest that both spontaneous and provoked confabulations have different neural underpinnings, and different cognitive processes are involved that are unrelated to the amnesia itself, such as impaired source memory, temporal confusion, a reality monitoring deficit, executive dysfunction, or impaired strategic retrieval. Whereas there is some debate whether confabulation behavior is a clinical feature of Korsakoff syndrome or is predominantly related to the more acute Wernicke stage, recent evidence has demonstrated that provoked, episodic confabulations should be regarded as a core feature of the syndrome (Borsutzky, Fujiwara, Brand, & Markowitsch, 2008).

Executive and Neuropsychiatric Dysfunction

Next to the amnesia, executive dysfunction is another clinical feature in most but not all Korsakoff patients. Impairments have been found on task planning, concept shifting, and time management and cognitive estimation, especially on unstructured tasks. These executive deficits can be related to neuroimaging findings showing prefrontal hypometabolism in Korsakoff patients (Van Oort & Kessels, 2008). Moreover, executive control is crucial for strategic retrieval and working-memory function. Consequently, executive dysfunction may enhance the already prominent memory deficits. Neuropsychiatric problems are also prominent in Korsakoff syndrome, specifically impaired social cognitive-functioning. For example, Korsakoff patients have difficulty recognizing emotional expressions in the faces of others, perform poorly on affective prosody recognition, and display impaired social inference ability. Other behavioral symptoms are apathy, disinterest, loss of initiative, and lack of insight. Clearly, these nonmemory cognitive and behavioral deficits may greatly affect everyday life functioning and hamper clinical rehabilitation.

Controversies

Korsakoff syndrome is often debated in the literature, and some controversies exist. First, being a clinical diagnosis, there is no conclusive biomarker to support it. Although group studies and postmortem research consistently show diencephalic lesions to be associated with Korsakoff syndrome, these specific lesions are not visible when examining individual patients with conventional brain-imaging techniques. Since Korsakoff syndrome is associated with chronic alcoholism and malnutrition, self-care in most

patients has often been poor for a long period of time before the syndrome's actual onset, which may have resulted in falls or cerebrovascular events that result in brain injury as well.

Second, the neurotoxic effect of chronic alcohol intake itself, in the absence of thiamine deficiency, should be taken into consideration. There is evidence that chronic and excessive alcohol intake results in cortical and cerebellar atrophy, which is associated with a poorer performance on neuropsychological tests or even dementia. However, the concept of alcohol-related dementia is ill-defined, and proposed criteria for alcohol-related dementia are not very helpful in distinguishing it from Korsakoff syndrome (Oslin, Atkinson, Smith, & Hendrie, 1998). That is, to fulfill these criteria, a history of excessive alcohol intake in combination with a dementia syndrome is required, the latter defined as impairments in memory and one other cognitive domain, resulting in a decline in everyday functioning. Since it is evident that the cognitive impairment in Korsakoff syndrome is not limited to amnesia, but also includes other cognitive domains, most Korsakoff patients would meet these proposed criteria for alcohol-related dementia. However, as Korsakoff syndrome is widely accepted and better defined, and because it is characterized neither by progression of the cognitive impairments nor by intellectual decline, the diagnosis dementia should not be used to classify Korsakoff patients.

REFERENCES

Borsutzky, S., Fujiwara, E., Brand, M., & Markowitsch, H. J. (2002). Confabulations in alcoholic Korsakoff patients. *Neuropsychologia, 46,* 3133–3143.

Kopelman, M. D. (2002). Disorders of memory. *Brain, 125,* 2152–2190.

Oslin, D., Atkinson, R. M., Smith, D. M., & Hendrie, H. (1998). Alcohol related dementia: Proposed clinical criteria. *International Journal of Geriatric Psychiatry, 13,* 203–212.

Van Oort, R., & Kessels, R. P. C. (in press). Executive dysfunction in Korsakoff's syndrome: Time to revise the DSM criteria for alcohol-induced persisting amnestic disorder? *International Journal of Psychiatry in Clinical Practice, 12.*

Visser, P. J., Krabbendam, L., Verhey, F. R. J., Hofman, P. A. M., Verhoeven, W. M. A., Tuinier, S., et al. (1999). Brain correlates of memory dysfunction in alcoholic Korsakoff's syndrome. *Journal of Neurology, Neurosurgery, and Psychiatry, 67,* 774–778.

Zubaran, C., Fernandes, J. G., & Rodnight, R. (1997). Wernicke-Korsakoff syndrome. *Postgraduate Medical Journal, 73,* 27–31.

SUGGESTED READINGS

Fama, R., Marsh, L., & Sullivan, E. V. (2004). Dissociation of remote and anterograde memory impairment and neural correlates in alcoholic Korsakoff syndrome. *Journal of the International Neuropsychological Society, 10,* 427–441.

Postma, A., Van Asselen, M., Keuper, O., Wester, A. J., & Kessels, R. P. C. (2006). Spatial and temporal order memory in Korsakoff patients. *Journal of the International Neuropsychological Society, 12,* 327–336.

Sivolap, Y. P. (2005). The current state of S. S. Korsakov's concept of alcoholic polyneuritic psychosis. *Neuroscience and Behavioral Physiology, 35,* 977–982.

Roy P. C. Kessels
Radboud University Nijmegen, The Netherlands

See also: **Alcohol Use Disorders; Memory Functions; Psychotic Disorders**

KRUSKAL-WALLIS TEST

The Kruskal-Wallis (Kruskal & Wallis, 1952) is a nonparametric statistical test that assesses the differences among three or more independently sampled groups on a single, non-normally distributed continuous variable. Non-normally distributed data (e.g., ordinal or rank data) are suitable for the Kruskal-Wallis test. In contrast, the one-way analysis of variance (ANOVA), which is a parametric test, may be used for a normally distributed continuous variable. The Kruskal-Wallis test is an extension of the two-group Mann-Whitney U (Wilcoxon rank) test. Thus, the Kruskal-Wallis is a more generalized form of the Mann-Whitney U test and is the nonparametric version of the one-way ANOVA.

A typical application of the Kruskal-Wallis test is to assess whether three or more groups differ on a single variable that fails to meet the normality assumptions of ANOVA. Since the variable of interest does not meet normality assumptions, we may not compare group means; instead we compare ranks. The null hypothesis specifies that the groups are subsets from the same population (i.e., H_0: (a, b, c, ... , n) $\subseteq p$). To test the null hypothesis, we combine the groups into a single group and rank the variable of interest. The new rank scores are summed by group (T_a, T_b, ... , T_n) and, along with group sample sizes, can be used to calculate the H statistic (see Equation 1). H reflects the variance in ranks between groups and closely resembles the chi-square distribution. When testing the null, we can use H and refer to a chi-square table with

degrees of freedom equal to n (number of groups) minus 1. If H exceeds a critical value, we may conclude that the groups do not come from the same population; many researchers often conclude that the test is an omnibus test for differences between groups, but many statisticians object to this interpretation:

$$H = N - 1(gn_n\ (t_i - T_i)^2 / gsn_n(t_j - T_i)^2) \qquad (1)$$

where n_n is the sample size of the corresponding group, g is the sum of the group n, sn_n is the sum of the corresponding group n, t_i is the average observed rank sums for the group, t_j is the observed rank for an observation for the corresponding group, and T_i is the observed total average rank sums.

Suppose we are interested in assessing whether the crime rankings from a random sample of 15 U.S. cities from the Northeast, West, and South differ. The original data are as follows: Northeast (U.S. rankings: 2, 5, 89, 203, 241), West (U.S. rankings: 1, 34, 50, 55, 292), and South (U.S. rankings: 6, 12, 19, 22, 356). The procedure reranks the rank data and leaves us with new relative rankings among these 15 cities: Northeast (2, 3, 11, 12, 13), West (1, 8, 9, 10, 14), and South (4, 5, 6, 7, 15). The H statistic for the data above is nonsignificant (H(2) = 0.14, p = .93), and we accordingly fail to reject the null and conclude that the three regions do not differ on crime rankings.

REFERENCE

Kruskal, W. H., & Wallis, W. A. (1952). Use of ranks in one-criterion variance analysis. *Journal of the American Statistical Association, 47,* 583–621.

SUGGESTED READINGS

Cohen, B. H. (2008). *Explaining psychological statistics* (3rd ed.). Hoboken, NJ: John Wiley & Sons.

Gibbons, J. D. (1993). Nonparametric statistics: An introduction (*Quantitative Applications in the Social Sciences, 90*). Newbury Park, CA: Sage.

Hollander, M., & Wolfe, D. A. (1999). *Nonparametric statistical methods* (2nd ed.). New York: John Wiley & Sons.

Patrick E. McKight
Julius Najab
George Mason University

See also: **Mann-Whitney U Test; Nonparametric Statistical Tests**

L

LANGUAGE ACQUISITION

Two basic questions in the field of language acquisition are (1) whether or not some part of language, particularly the structure of the language, is innate or whether it is all learnable from the input, and (2) whether acquisitional mechanisms are domain specific—that is, used only for language—or whether they are domain general—that is, used for learning across a variety of domains.

Some researchers have argued that some part of the knowledge of language structure must be innate, because babies so quickly master such a complex body of information and because there is so little information in the speech stream itself that marks the structural aspects of language. Recent approaches, however, have emphasized the wealth of subtle information that is available in the speech stream and have shown that babies are capable of using this type of information in laboratory experiments. These types of information are often probabilistic rather than definitive in nature; interestingly, children seem better able to pick up consistencies in noisy input than are adults (Singleton & Newport, 2004). Sensitivity to probabilistic cues has also been shown to function across domains, although there may be some interactions with the modality of the stimulus (Conway & Christiansen, 2005).

Language acquisition is an extremely complex task that is accomplished by nearly every human being. Within the first few years of life, babies go from being inarticulate individuals to good comprehenders to fluent speakers of the languages present in their environment. In order for such mastery to take place, learning must occur on multiple levels, including learning about the sound structure of the language, being able to segment the speech stream into words, figuring out what individual words mean, and mastering the grammatical structure. Here we examine the typical pattern of acquisition in these areas and look at the evidence that babies use subtle cues in the speech stream to master these aspects of language.

In their first year of life, infants are engaged in learning about the phonology of their language. Newborns have a preference for speech over other complex sound stimuli (Vouloumanos & Werker, 2007) and, through attending to speech, learn about their native language's sound system. Very early on, even within a few days of birth, they can distinguish their native language from other languages based on prosodic characteristics. Originally, in the first half-year of life, infants are able to distinguish many phonemes, even ones not present in their native language. However, by the end of the second half-year of life, tuning has occurred, such that relevant distinctions are retained, while irrelevant distinctions are largely lost (Jusczyk, 1997).

In this first year, infants are also learning other properties of the sound structure of their language, including properties relevant to parsing words out of the continuous speech stream. Research has shown that infants are able to use properties such as characteristic word stress (e.g., in English, most words start with a strong syllable, so babies posit a boundary before an accented syllable), low frequency of phoneme co-occurrence (e.g., in English, /zt/ is a phonological sequence never found within words, so babies posit a word boundary between the /z/ and the /t/), subtle allophonic and coarticulation differences (e.g., /t/ is pronounced differently in "this tick" than in "this stick"), and familiar words to help posit word boundaries (Jusczyk, 1997).

Perhaps the most abstract property proven to date that infants can use to determine word boundaries is that of the statistical probability of one syllable following another. If the syllable x is usually followed by y, one might posit xy is a word, whereas if the syllable x is only followed by y a low percentage of the time, one might posit a word boundary between x and y. A seminal study by Saffran, Aslin, and Newport (1996) has shown that eight-month-old infants can use this transitional probability information to posit word boundaries after only two minutes of exposure to a speech stream containing nonsense words defined solely by their likelihood of transition.

Speech production in the first year of life starts with cooing and moves to babbling, which begins to capture the prosodic characteristics of the native language. First recognizable spoken words come at the end of the first year, and through a gradual increase in rate of vocabulary acquisition, the number of words a child can produce noticeably increases at around 18 months of age. While some researchers have posited that this vocabulary "spurt" or "explosion" is due to an insight by the child that things have names, a recent simulation has shown that this same word-learning curve can result from a learning mechanism in which all words are gradually acquired, but differences in their difficulty (e.g., frequency of occurrence in the input) cause a sharper increase in number of items mastered after an initial period of slow growth (McMurray, 2007).

One of the major problems in word learning is how children tie a particular word to its meaning. Upon encountering a new word in context, children are able to posit a reasonable guess at its meaning—this process is known as fast mapping. Children seem to be able to use several types of information in helping them determine word meaning, including noticing what the adult is attending to, using the syntactic structure of the sentence to constrain meaning, assuming a new word goes with a novel object, assuming a new word labels a whole object, and a bias to extend word meaning based on shape.

Acquisition of the syntactic and morphological patterns of the native language is evident in comprehension far in advance of children being able to produce grammatical strings of words. In their second year of life, children show the ability to use word-order information to correctly understand sentences and at two, or a bit after, can use syntactic information to distinguish between transitive and intransitive verbs (Hirsh-Pasek & Golinkoff, 1996). Just as children have to figure out what syllables go together to parse words out of the speech stream, they also have to figure out what words go together to parse syntactic clauses out of the speech stream. Children show sensitivity to prosodic cues that mark syntactic or clausal boundaries in the speech stream (Jusczyk, 1997), and recent work also indicates that the same type of information that enabled infants to segment the speech stream into words—transitional probabilities—may also operate on groups of words to enable people to posit clause boundaries (Thompson & Newport, 2007).

Another problem in the acquisition of syntax is figuring out the syntactic class of a word—that is, whether it is a grammatical element (such as a function word) or a content word (such as a noun or verb), and then within these larger classes, being able to distinguish word subclasses (such as nouns and verbs). It turns out there are numerous phonological properties that are probabilistically associated with word classes (e.g., in English, function words tend to have fewer phonemes than content words; nouns tend to have more syllables than verbs), as well as different patterns of co-occurrence (e.g., in English, function words are less likely to precede "and" than content words; nouns are more likely to occur after a possessive pronoun, while verbs are more likely to occur after a personal pronoun), that children could use in combination to determine word class (Monaghan, Christiansen, & Chater, 2007).

Production of grammatical elements follows a fairly predictable pattern. Initial productions are single word utterances. With increasing age, utterances increase in length (measured in terms of number of morphemes), but often are telegraphic in nature (i.e., grammatical elements are left out). Morphemes are acquired in a predictable order. For example, in English, plurals are acquired before past tense. Phonological complexity as well as processing demands may play a role in this order of acquisition. Multiword utterances follow a predictable pattern of mastery of negations, questions, passives and relative clauses. While much of language acquisition is complete by the time a child reaches school age, lexical and syntactic skills continue to develop beyond this age.

REFERENCES

Conway, C. M., & Christiansen, M. H. (2005). Modality-constrained statistical learning of tactile, visual, and auditory sequences. *Journal of Experimental Psychology: Learning, Memory & Cognition, 31*, 24–39.

Hirsh-Pasek, K., & Golinkoff, R. M. (1996). *The origins of grammar.* Cambridge, MA: MIT Press.

Jusczyk, P. W. (1997). *Discovering spoken language.* Cambridge, MA: MIT Press.

McMurray, B. (2007). Defusing the childhood vocabulary explosion. *Science, 317*, 631.

Monaghan, P., Christiansen, M. H., & Chater, N. (2007). The phonological-distributional coherence hypothesis: Cross-linguistic evidence in language acquisition. *Cognitive Psychology, 55*, 259–305.

Saffran, J. R., Aslin, R. N., & Newport, E. L. (1996). Statistical learning by 8-month-old infants. *Science, 274*, 1926–1928.

Singleton, J. L., & Newport, E. L. (2004). When learners surpass their models: The acquisition of American Sign Language from inconsistent input. *Cognitive Psychology, 49*, 370–407.

Thompson, S. P., & Newport, E. L. (2007). Statistical learning of syntax: The role of transitional probability. *Language Learning & Development, 3*, 1–42.

Vouloumanos, A., & Werker, J. F. (2007). Listening to language at birth: Evidence for a bias for speech in neonates. *Developmental Science, 10*, 159–164.

SUGGESTED READINGS

Hall, D. G., & Waxman, S. R. (Eds.). (2004). *Weaving a lexicon.* Cambridge, MA: MIT Press.

Hoff, E., & Shatz, M. (Eds.). (2007). *Blackwell handbook of language development.* Oxford: Blackwell.

Karmiloff, K., & Karmiloff-Smith, A. (2001). *Pathways to language.* Cambridge, MA: Harvard University Press.

JANET L. MCDONALD
Louisiana State University

See also: Language Comprehension; Speech Perception

LANGUAGE COMPREHENSION

The ability to comprehend language comprises a fascinating collection of uniquely human skills. These include our ability to recognize speech and read words, our ability to understand sentences by combining the meanings of the words they contain, and our ability to relate the meanings of sentences to one another in texts, to our beliefs, and to the world around us. We exercise these skills quickly and seemingly effortlessly, but in doing so we use an immense amount of information about the structure of our language, the structure of our recent discourse, and the state of the world.

Consider our ability to recognize words we read or hear and put their meanings together in sentences, a process technically referred to as "composing" sentence meanings from the meanings of the words they contain. Few of us have conscious knowledge of the grammatical principles that guide this compositional process. Nonetheless, we all honor the principles implicitly and quickly bring them to bear in understanding sentences, essentially on a word-by-word basis. When researchers measure where the eyes look as we read (under the well-justified assumption that we look at the word we are processing), they find that the initial fixation the eyes make on a word is lengthened when the word is semantically anomalous (e.g., *They used the pump to inflate the* carrots) or syntactically disruptive (e.g., *While the men hunted the bear* was in *the cave*). These effects can appear within the first quarter-second after looking at the word, putting clear limits on how long it takes to understand a sentence (Clifton, Staub, & Rayner, 2007).

We are sensitive to major aspects of grammar, such as word order in English. We know that *The mouse ate the cat* says something quite unexpected (the psycholinguist Merrill Garrett once wrote that the function of grammar was to let us say surprising things). We are also sensitive to very subtle aspects of grammar. We know that there is a big difference between *They fed his baby cookies* and *They fed him baby cookies*, and between *They helped the child on first base* and *They helped the child to first base*.

This seemingly effortless compositional process hides some important decisions. For instance, a word like *bank* can refer to a riverbank or a money bank, and a word like *duck* can be either a noun or a verb. We use the sentence context to decide between alternatives like these. A phrase like *on the table* in *Put the book on the table* ... can specify a goal or can specify which book you are talking about, depending on whether the sentence continues ... *next to your briefcase* or ... *into your briefcase*. These decisions are guided by a variety of factors. Frequency of experience guides how we interpret ambiguous words; *bank* most often refers to where you put your money. We favor simple sentence structures; it's easier to take *the bear* as the grammatical direct object of *hunt* than to have it start a new clause.

The context in which we hear a word matters; if you are sitting in a restaurant after a pleasant dinner and your companion says *The port was very nice*, you probably think about the wine rather than about where the boats dock. There is lively debate about whether all these factors play a role at one time, or whether specifically linguistic factors (such as grammar) play the main role in making initial decisions about what a sentence means. However, there is no doubt that a great many sources of information are used eventually in understanding a sentence (cf. Altmann, 1998; Frazier, 1995).

Once we compose the meanings of words into a sentence meaning, we often connect that sentence to other sentences in discourse. Definite noun phrases (e.g., *the book*) have to be related to specific referents that were mentioned earlier or that can be assumed to be known to the listener/reader, whereas indefinite noun phrases (e.g., *a book*) can be used to introduce a new entity into a discourse. Pronouns are treated rather like definite noun phrases, but place a higher demand on the "givenness" of their referents. Sometimes inferences have to be made to glue sentences together. If a car has been mentioned in the discourse, one can say *the steering wheel* (but not *the tire*) without having mentioned it before, because listeners make the inference that a car has a single steering wheel. Sometimes these inferences are made as a way of grasping a speaker's goals and intentions, as when you know that you are being asked to close the window when your partner says *It's sure cold in here*. Readers and listeners regularly go beyond the information given and use what they have understood, together with their own knowledge of the topic, to construct a cognitive representation that has been termed a *mental model* or a *situational model*.

Finally, readers and listeners take what they have gleaned from the linguistic input and relate it to the world around them. In the simple, concrete case, they identify the words and phrases with the objects and events they can perceive. How this happens can be quickly reflected in where the eyes are directed. Listeners seem to look, with little delay, at the things that are being talked about, a phenomenon researchers can use to determine what listeners *think* is being said (Tanenhaus & Trueswell, 1995). Sometimes, readers and listeners have to decide that what they have understood is not to be taken literally, but instead should be taken idiomatically or metaphorically. If you hear *Someone broke the ice at the boring party*, you don't look around for the ice. Finally, in the paradigmatic case of effective communication, readers and listeners have to evaluate the truth of what is said and, if believed, add it into their belief structure, and perhaps even act upon it.

REFERENCES

Altmann, G. T. M. (1998). Ambiguity in sentence processing. *Trends in Cognitive Sciences, 2*, 146–152.

Clifton, C. J., Staub, A., & Rayner, K. (2007). Eye movements in reading words and sentences. In R. V. Gompel, M. Fisher, W. Murray, & R. L. Hill (Eds.), *Eye movement research: Insights into mind and brain* (pp. 341–371). New York: Elsevier.

Frazier, L. (1995). Constraint satisfaction as a theory of sentence processing. *Journal of Psycholinguistic Research, 24*, 437–468.

Tanenhaus, M. K., & Trueswell, J. C. (1995). Sentence comprehension. In J. Miller & P. Eimas (Eds.), *Handbook of perception and cognition: Speech, language, and communication* Vol. 11 (2nd ed., pp. 217–262). San Diego: Academic Press.

SUGGESTED READINGS

Gaskell, M. G. (Ed.). (2007). *The Oxford handbook of psycholinguistics.* Oxford: Oxford University Press.

Traxler, M., & Gernsbacher, M. A. (Eds.). (2006). *Handbook of psycholinguistics* (2nd ed.). London: Academic Press.

CHARLES CLIFTON JR.
JANE ASHBY
University of Massachusetts, Amherst

See also: **Language Acquisition; Speech Production**

LANGUAGE, INTERGROUP PARAMETERS OF

Language is an integral element of most multicultural contexts. Take, for example, the resurrection of Hebrew as a lingua franca in multicultural Israel, the role of French in Quebecois separation, and the revival of Catalan in Spain. Yet beyond nationalist and ethnic arenas, forms of language (e.g., dialect, nonverbals, and discourse) play key roles in virtually all intergroup situations—as evident in adolescents' distinctive speech styles, patronizing ways of addressing and referring to older adults and those physically challenged, gay expressions and tone of voice, and so forth (see Clément, 1996). In fact, intergroup processes have become core foci in the social psychology of language, as witnessed by their frequent occurrence across many different chapters of *The New Handbook of Language and Social Psychology* (Robinson & Giles, 2001), and language and communication issues have, in turn, featured prominently in the study of intergroup relations (Kashima, Fielder, & Freytag, 2007; Reid & Giles, 2005).

An important phenomenon that has attracted growing research attention is the linguistic intergroup bias (see Maass, 1999). People vary the linguistic abstraction of terms used to describe prosocial and antisocial behaviors performed by ingroup and outgroup members, and they do so in an ingroup favoring way. An ingroup member who, for example, struck a police officer might be described as *hitting* the officer, whereas an outgroup member performing the same act may be described as *assaulting* the officer; when the act is prosocial, however, the effect reverses. An ingroup member who donates to charity is *generous*, but an outgroup member *gives money*. The use of language to describe social events can often be invoked to maintain favorable views of the ingroup that are differentiated from the more negative images ascribed to a relevant outgroup (for recent work on the linguistic bias, see Sutton & Douglas, 2008).

Much of the research and theory devoted to these issues has its origins in the social identity theory (SIT) of intergroup relations (e.g., Tajfel & Turner, 1979). The latter emerged from European social psychologists' dissatisfaction with reductionist (predominantly North American) approaches that provided explanations of intergroup behavior couched in terms of individual psychology (e.g., frustration-aggression, belief dissimilarity). SIT, in contrast, articulated an explanation in terms of social beliefs about the contextual relations between groups. In particular, it highlighted a social motivation to create or maintain a positive social identity that is realized and constrained by people's beliefs about the place of their ingroup in the status hierarchy. These beliefs concern the legitimacy and stability of intergroup status relations as well as beliefs about the feasibility, or otherwise, of passing into another group. Different combinations of these beliefs encourage different identity enhancement strategies.

One of the most developed products of this approach has, arguably, been its extension into the realm of intercultural communication (e.g., Gudykunst & Ting-Toomey, 1988), one that contributes enormously to our understanding of many language phenomena, including second language learning, code-switching, semilingualism, diglossia, patterns of language attitudes and language shifts, and so forth. A theoretical force here has been ethnolinguistic identity theory that has added further criteria (e.g., "group vitality"), bringing into sharper focus the specific language strategies that might be used in intergroup settings (see Giles & Johnson, 1981). Group vitality articulates the ways that groups differ with respect to institutional support (e.g., via education and the media), demographic representation (e.g., numbers and concentration of group members), and status variables (e.g., economic control and an historic sense of ingroup pride). The more group members perceive their group to possess these facets of vitality, the more likely they are to engage in activities designed to maintain their so-called "psycholinguistic distinctiveness" (via language, dialect, specialized jargon, slang, code words, and so forth). Certain caveats notwithstanding, research around the globe has shown that groups possessing high perceived vitality prosper, while those that do not integrate with dominant groups and or die out in terms of their heritage cultures.

While ethnolinguistic identity theory describes the wider macrosocial processes that frame language use, communication accommodation theory describes the accomplishment of these identity enhancement strategies within microsocial contexts (for a history of the theory, see Gallois, Ogay, & Giles, 2005). Broadly, language can be used to draw out similarities with an interlocutor (called "convergence"), or it can be used to maintain or enhance social distance (i.e., "divergence"). In an interpersonal context, convergence is assumed to reflect a motive to be liked by an interlocutor; convergence indicates similarity to the recipient that, in turn, can foster social attraction. In intergroup contexts, "upward" convergence by a minority group speaker to the dominant group's language can be found (1) when people are not particularly invested in their group identity; (2) when group boundaries are thought to be surmountable; and (3) when the status distinction is considered to be legitimate and stable. Such convergences would be even more likely if such speakers also construed their group vitality to be relatively low.

Other times, and sometimes even in the same intergroup context, "downward" divergence (i.e., the maintenance or accentuation of a subordinate group's language forms, such as with the Hawaiian language movement) can be found in individuals (1) who are strongly committed to their group; (2) consider the social boundaries between it and the dominant group to be impermeable; (3) construe their vitality as relatively high; and (4) believe their status inequality vis-á-vis the outgroup as unstable and illegitimate. By considering these (and other) background conditions, we can see how views about bilingualism—as being additive or subtractive to one or other groups' identities—can evolve in a society. Indeed, émigrés' "failure" to acquire native-like proficiency in their host community's language can, from an intergroup perspective, be reinterpreted as the immigrants' successful retention of their own group's language in the face of a significant threat to its survival in that milieu. Such a position has profound implications for second language pedagogy and the kinds of social factors deemed necessary to address in teaching people bilingual skills.

As alluded to earlier, this general theoretical backdrop has been confirmed, extended, and applied in an ever-growing number of intergroup contexts (see Giles, Reid, & Harwood, in press), notably, between the genders, socioeconomic brackets, different generations, and physical capacities, as well as in the strategic use of language in sustaining, legitimizing, and subverting social power (Harwood & Giles, 2005). Future work in the study of "intergroup language"—that which is regulated by individuals' awareness of their memberships in various relevant social groups (Hindu, neighborhood gang, gay, and so on)—is likely to move beyond SIT by taking into account theoretical developments in self-categorization theory (Turner, Hogg, Oakes, Reicher, & Wetherell, 1987).

This replaces the social motivational mechanism in SIT with a social-cognitive one: Group behavior is driven by a search for a distinctively meaningful identity that seeks to determine how individuals fit into the world. They achieve this by identifying with groups that simultaneously maximize within-group similarities and between-group differences. Self-categorization theory can lead, potentially, to language-based theories of leadership emergence, stereotyping, social influence, and social attraction. What is

more, the same mechanism might be integrated into ethnolinguistic identity and communication accommodation theories, thereby providing a more parsimonious account of language shifts and macro-social conditions that increases our understandings of who in a particular social group uses which language strategies and how, when, with what outcomes, and why.

REFERENCES

Clément, R. (Ed.). (1996). The social psychology of intergroup communication. Special Issue of the *Journal of Language and Social Psychology, 15,* 221–392.

Gallois, C., Ogay, T., & Giles, H. (2005). Communication accommodation theory: A look back and a look ahead. In W. Gudykunst (Ed.), *Theorizing about intercultural communication* (pp. 121–148). Thousand Oaks, CA: Sage.

Giles, H., & Coupland, N. (1991). *Language: Contexts and consequences.* Pacific Grove, CA: Brooks/Cole.

Giles, H., & Johnson, P. (1981). The role of language in ethnic group relations. In J. C. Turner and H. Giles (Eds.), *Intergroup behavior* (pp. 199–243). Oxford: Blackwell.

Giles, H., Reid, S., & Harwood, J. (Eds.). (in press). *The dynamics of intergroup communication.* Berlin & New York: Peter Lang.

Gudykunst, W. B., & Ting-Toomey, S., with Chua, E. (1988). *Culture and interpersonal communication.* Newbury Park, CA: Sage.

Harwood, J., & Giles, H. (Eds.). (2005). *Intergroup communication: Multiple perspectives.* New York & Berlin: Peter Lang.

Kashima, Y., Fiedler, K., & Freytag, P. (Eds.). (2007), *Stereotype dynamics: Language-based approaches to stereotype formation, maintenance, and transformation.* Hillsdale, NJ: Laurence Erlbaum.

Maass, A. (1999). Linguistic intergroup bias: Stereotype perpetuation through language. In M. P. Zanna (Ed.), *Advances in experimental social psychology* (Vol. 31, pp. 79–121). San Diego, CA: Academic Press.

Reid, S., & Giles, H. (Eds.). (2005). Intergroup relations: Its linguistic and communicative parameters. Special Issue of *Group Processes and Intergroup Relations, 8*(3), 211–328.

Robinson, W. P., & Giles, H. (Eds.). (2001). *The new handbook of language and social psychology.* Chichester and New York: John Wiley & Sons.

Sutton, R. M., & Douglas, K. M. (Eds.). (2008). Celebrating two decades of linguistic bias research. Special Issue of the *Journal of Language and Social Psychology, 27*(2).

Tajfel, H., & Turner, J. C. (1979). An integrative theory of intergroup conflict. In W. G. Austin & S. Worchel (Eds.), *The social psychology of intergroup relations* (pp. 33–47). Monterey, CA: Brooks/Cole.

Turner, J. C., Hogg, M. A., Oakes, P. J., Reicher, S. D., & Wetherell, M. S. (1987). *Rediscovering the social group: A self-categorization theory.* Oxford, UK: Blackwell.

HOWARD GILES
SCOTT A. REID
University of California, Santa Barbara

LATE-LIFE FORGETTING

On the basis of a recent literature review of the relationship between subjective memory complaints in older adults and quality of life (Mol et al., 2006), it was concluded that forgetfulness is a serious concern that negatively impacts quality of life. APA guidelines for the evaluation of dementia and age-related cognitive decline (1998) note that the consequences of aging include declines in memory and cognitive abilities. The guidelines suggest that these normal, developmental changes should be labeled as age-consistent memory decline.

The question often arises as to how the general public should view the topic of age-related memory decline. This becomes particularly salient when older adults seek help for making legal transactions. Attorneys who are not trained in the evaluation of older adults are faced with trying to decide whether or not their clients possess sufficient capacity to enter into contracts and whether or not the client possesses the legal capacity to carry out specific legal transactions (American Bar Association Commission on Law and Aging & American Psychological Association, 2005).

Based on their contact with a given client, attorneys can take a number of steps following a preliminary assessment. Thus, attorneys may conclude that their client's capacity is intact, in which case the attorney proceeds normally. If mild problems are suspected, the attorney can proceed normally or consider either medical referral or informal mental health consultation. Another option is to request a formal capacity assessment. Any judgment of more than mild problems warrants great caution or referral. A worksheet for attorneys includes observational signs of diminished capacity. These may be cognitive, emotional, or behavioral, or a combination of these signs. Attorneys are advised to consider mitigating factors which may affect the overall conclusions. These can include educational, cultural and ethnic barriers, as well as hearing and vision loss, medical factors, time of day variability and stress, grief, depression and other events.

For the older adult, memory lapses are often experienced as troubling and anxiety provoking. Late-life forgetting, for many people, is not severe enough to cause impairment in daily life or in social or occupational functioning. Short-term memory shows relatively little age-related decline, while long-term memory does show changes as a result of aging. Changes for recall are greater for recall than for recognition and performance tends to benefit from cueing (APA working group, 1998). Many older adults do develop coping mechanisms, such as using lists, participating in mood and memory workshops, or practicing memory and other cognitive tasks, as well as keeping physically fit.

In an article dealing with age-related memory decline, Small (2001) raises the question of whether or not age-related changes occur equally across all cognitive domains or if memory is especially sensitive to the effects of aging. After all, most older adults complain about not remembering names, forgetting phone numbers, not being able to associate names with faces, and similar memory concerns. Small suggests that age-related memory decline might have a genetic component, and he points out that there is some indirect evidence for this. He also suggests that research evidence supports the notion that memory decline as a function of age is not inevitable and thinks that memory decline should be considered a "clinical entity" (p. 361).

It should be noted that DSM IV-TR includes the addition of a listing titled, "Age-related cognitive decline," which can be found under "other conditions that may be a focus of clinical attention." This condition refers to declines in cognitive functions as a result of the aging process and includes those changes that are within normal limits, considering that person's age. Therefore, while this is considered a clinical entity, it does include changes that are within the normal limits. In the final analysis, it may be more important to assess whether or not the decline interferes with the individual's ability to function, and if so, to what extent. Whether one calls it late-life forgetting or age-associated memory decline, many older individuals are concerned and worried about the state of their memory.

REFERENCES

APA working group on the older adult brochure. (1998). What practitioners should know about working with older adults. *Professional Psychology, 29,* 413–427.

American Bar Association Commission on Law and Aging & American Psychological Association. (2005). *Assessment of older adults and diminished capacity: A handbook for lawyers.* Washington, DC: American Bar Association and American Psychological Association.

American Psychological Association. (1998). *Guidelines for the evaluation of dementia and age-related memory decline.* Washington, DC. Author.

Mol, M., Carpay, M., Ramakers, I., Rozendaal, N., Verhey, F., & Jolles, J. (2006). The effects of perceived forgetfulness on quality of life in older adults: A qualitative review. *International Journal of Geriatric Psychiatry, 22*(5), 393–400.

Small, S. (2001). Age-related memory decline. *Archives of Neurology, 58,* 360–364.

SUGGESTED READINGS

LaRue, A. (1992). Aging and neuropsychological assessment. New York: Plenum.

Zarit, S., & Knight, B. (Eds.). (1996). A guide to psychotherapy and aging. Washington, DC: American Psychological Association.

Norman Abeles
Michigan State University

See also: Alzheimer's Disease; Dementia; Memory Functions

LATE-LIFE PSYCHOSIS

The most common psychoses to appear in the later years of life are those associated with dementia and major depressive disorder with psychotic features, with delusional disorders being much less common. This article provides an overview of recent advances pertinent to each of these major categories of late-life psychosis.

Dementia-Related Psychosis

The most common dementia in the United States is Alzheimer's disease (AD). It is estimated that 4.5 million people were diagnosed with AD in 2000, and these rates are increasing. Clinically, diagnoses of AD account for about 50–75% of dementia cases, followed in frequency by dementia with Lewy bodies at 15–35% and vascular dementia at 5–20%. Most data about the presentation, course, neurobiology, and treatment of dementia-related psychosis derive from studies of individuals with clinically diagnosed AD, and these data form the basis for this review. However, neuropathological studies have shown that most individuals with dementia have a combination of AD and vascular lesions and/or Lewy bodies; that is, there is a high degree of overlap among these diagnostic categories, with most individuals having some degree of AD pathology. Thus, it is likely that information about psychosis in clinically diagnosed AD can be generalized (with limited exceptions that are noted) to these other dementias.

Presentation

The definition of psychotic symptoms in dementia has generally been limited to delusions and hallucinations. Disorganized thought processes are not considered to represent a psychotic thought disorder, but rather they are attributed to cognitive impairments. Persecutory delusions, usually of theft, are the most common symptom. Other common delusions include misidentification of people and surroundings, the belief that deceased individuals are still alive, and a belief that characters on television are present in the room. Hallucinations are less frequent than delusions. Hallucinations can occur in any sensory modality, but visual hallucinations are most common. Well-formed visual hallucinations occurring early in the course of dementia are part of the presentation of Lewy body dementia and are more frequent in this disease, occurring in up to 75% of affected individuals.

Determining the presence of delusions in dementia can be clinically challenging. Many putative delusions (e.g., theft, infidelity) may be accurate interpretations of real events. Delusions must also be distinguished from simple forgetting. A patient with moderate dementia is unlikely to sustain memory of a recent event such as the death of a sibling and may claim that the person is still alive.

Additional characteristics, such as refusal to accept reality and persistence of a false idea over time, are useful in distinguishing delusions.

Course

About 40%–60% of individuals with AD develop psychotic symptoms at some point over the course of their dementia. Given the frequency of dementia itself, it is quickly seen that dementia-related psychosis is one of the most common psychotic syndromes at any age, and easily the most frequent in late life. Most psychotic symptoms emerge in the middle stages of dementia, although in up to 5%–25% of individuals, they may occur during the prodromal or early disease stages. Once present, psychotic symptoms are likely to persist over a period of months to years.

Psychotic symptoms in AD identify a subgroup of individuals with more rapid cognitive and functional decline. Aggressive behaviors are more frequent in those individuals who develop psychosis during dementia. Psychotic symptoms are also associated with increased caregiver distress, and they are often predictive of institutionalization.

Neurobiology

In AD, the occurrence of psychosis aggregates within families; that is, if one member of a family has AD with psychotic symptoms, there is an increased likelihood that other members of their family who develop AD will also develop psychotic symptoms. These findings suggest that the risk of psychosis in AD is likely to be genetically determined. No one genetic variant or chromosomal locus has been firmly established, although there is consistent support from several studies for an effect of genetic variation in the dopamine metabolizing enzyme, catechol-O-methyltransferase (COMT), on the risk of psychosis in AD.

From the point of view of brain systems, functional neuroimaging and postmortem studies suggest that psychosis in AD is likely to be associated with greater impairments distributed throughout the neocortex, with temporal and dorsolateral prefrontal cortex particularly affected. With regard to specific pathologies, there is no evidence of a relationship between amyloid deposition and psychosis in AD, although increases in insoluble microtubule associated tau protein have been reported. There is also an association between the presence of Lewy body pathology and increased risk of visual hallucinations.

Treatment

Not all occurrences of psychosis in dementia require pharmacologic treatment. Nonpharmacologic approaches for psychosis, although without specific evidence of efficacy, derive from fundamentals of clinical practice and include enhancing sensory and social engagement while limiting overstimulating or chaotic environments. Medication is indicated when the psychotic symptoms lead to endangerment of self or others, cause distress, or interfere with functioning or acceptance of care. Second-generation (atypical) antipsychotics have established, if modest, efficacy and are indicated as first-line treatments for psychotic behaviors in dementia. These should only be used with caution, as they are associated with increased rates of stroke and may cause mortality in patients with dementia. First-generation antipsychotics (neuroleptics) are also efficacious, but they induce high rates of parkinsonism and tardive dyskinesia. Selective serotonin reuptake inhibitors have shown efficacy in some studies, although their efficacy for this condition is not firmly established.

Psychotic Major Depression

In acute psychiatric settings, estimates of the frequency of psychotic symptoms in elderly patients experiencing a depressive episode (major depression with psychotic features, MD+P) range from 28% to 45%, rates that may be higher than in midlife. Elderly MD+P patients have been observed to have higher degrees of cognitive impairment than their nonpsychotic peers, are at a higher risk for suicide, and have reduced rates of treatment response after pharmacotherapy. Current clinical guidelines indicate that a combination of antidepressant and antipsychotic medication is indicated for MD+P in the elderly, largely because of observations that monotherapy response rates are suboptimal; however, there are few research studies to support the efficacy of the recommended combination. Alternatively, electroconvulsive therapy has substantial acute efficacy and is safe in the elderly, although optimal maintenance treatment after electroconvulsive therapy is not established.

Delusional Disorders

Delusional disorders, characterized by the presence of nonbizarre delusions in the absence of disorganization, hallucinations, or mood disorder, are an infrequent presentation of psychosis in late life. As such, they have not been subject to systematic study. The most important consideration is careful evaluation for an underlying medical cause, such as a central nervous system lesion or endocrine disturbance. Careful neuropsychological testing to exclude an early dementia is also appropriate. Delusional disorders may respond to antipsychotic treatment. However, treatment acceptance is an issue because of the lack of insight regarding the delusional system, and thus use of injectable medications is often preferable.

SUGGESTED READINGS

Andreescu, C., Mulsant, B. H., Rothschild, A. J., Flint, A. J., Meyers, B. S., & Whyte, E. (2006). Pharmacotherapy of major depression with psychotic features: What is the evidence? *Psychiatric Annals 36(1)*, 31–38.

Ropacki, S. A., & Jeste, D. V. (2005). Epidemiology of and risk factors for psychosis of Alzheimer's disease: A review of 55 studies published from 1990 to 2003. *American Journal of Psychiatry, 162*, 2022–2030.

Rothschild, A. J., Mulsant, B. H., Meyers, B. S., & Flint, A. J. (2006). Challenges in differentiating and diagnosing psychotic depression. *Psychiatric Annals, 36*, 40–46.

Sweet, R. A., & Emanuel, J. E. (2008). Psychosis secondary to Alzheimer disease. In *The spectrum of psychotic disorders: Neurobiology, etiology, and pathogenesis* (pp. 455–471). Cambridge, UK: Cambridge University Press.

Sweet, R. A., Nimgaonkar, V. L., Devlin, B., & Jeste, D. V. (2003). Psychotic symptoms in Alzheimer disease: Evidence for a distinct phenotype. *Molecular Psychiatry, 8*, 383–392.

ROBERT A. SWEET
*University of Pittsburgh and VA
Pittsburgh Healthcare System*

LATENCY STAGE (See Psychosexual Stages)

LATENT CLASS ANALYSIS

Latent class analysis (LCA) is a statistical method for finding subtypes of related cases (latent classes) from multivariate categorical data. Latent classes are the dimensions that structure the cases with respect to a set of observed variables. It is assumed that parameters of a statistical model differ across unobserved subgroups. These subgroups form the categories of a categorical latent variable. In principle, cases of a data set are divided into latent classes, which are so-called conditionally independent classes, meaning that the observed variables are uncorrelated within classes. With the estimated parameters, cases are classified according to their most likely latent class. In applications the LCA can be used to find types of attitude structures from survey responses, consumer segments from preference variables, and examinee subgroups from their answers to test items.

LCA was introduced in 1950 by Lazarsfeld as a type of latent structure analysis to describe the use of mathematical models for characterizing latent variables. Whereas factor analysis is used as a latent structure method to describe the relation between continuous latent and observed variables, LCA can be considered as an analog technique to empirically identify the relations between discrete latent and observed variables. For more than 20 years, estimation approaches of the latent class model were unfeasible. In 1974 Goodman made the model applicable in practice by developing an algorithm for obtaining maximum likelihood estimates of the model parameters.

He also proposed extensions for polytomous manifest variables and multiple latent variables, and he did important work on the issue of model identification. During the same period, Haberman (1979) showed the connection between latent class models and log-linear models for frequency tables with missing cell counts.

Regarding Goodman (1974), the latent class model can be described with the simple case of two observed categorical variables A and B having I ($i = 1, 2, \ldots, I$) and J ($j = 1, 2, \ldots, J$) classes. X is an unobserved categorical variable with T ($t = 1, 2, \ldots, T$) classes. The latent class model can be formulated as follows:

$$\pi_{ijt}^{ABX} = \pi_t^X \pi_{it}^{\bar{A}X} \pi_{jt}^{\bar{B}X} \qquad (1)$$

π_{ijt}^{ABX} is the joint probability that a measurement is in class i on variable A, in class j on variable B, and in class t on variable X. π_t^X denote the unconditional (or latent class) probability that the measurement is in class X while $\pi_{it}^{\bar{A}X}$ and $\pi_{jt}^{\bar{B}X}$ denote the conditional probabilities in class i on variable A and class j on variable B. The sum of the unconditional probabilities over all latent classes T must equal one. The minimum number of identifiable classes is two, because a single latent class is equivalent to the independence among the observed variables.

The latent class model states that variables A and B are conditionally independent of each other, given the class level on the latent variable X:

$$\pi_{ijt}^{\bar{A}BX} = \frac{\pi_{ijt}^{ABX}}{\pi_t^X} \qquad (2)$$

$\pi_{ijt}^{\bar{A}BX}$ is the conditional probability that an observation is in class i on variable A and in class j on variable B, given that the observation is in class t on variable X. The number of conditional probabilities for each of the observed variables is equal to the number of levels measured for that variable. If the observed variable is dichotomous, there will be two conditional probabilities of each class T. Within each of the T latent classes the conditional probabilities for each of the observed variables sum to one:

$$\sum_i \pi_{it}^{\bar{A}X} = \sum_j \pi_{jt}^{\bar{B}X} = 1.0 \qquad (3)$$

The conditional probabilities indicate whether observations in class T are likely or unlikely to have characteristics of each of the observed variables. At least, these parameters enable the possibility to characterize the nature of the latent variable. It should be noted that the latent class model can be extended with more than two observed variables and more than one latent class variable.

The parameters of a latent class model are estimated by means of maximum likelihood using the so-called expectation-maximization (EM) algorithm (Dempster, Laird, & Rubin, 1977). The empirical information of the model consists of the cell entries of the multiway contingency table of the observed variables. Nonzero observed cell entries contribute to the estimation function. Model parameters of the latent class model may be not identified, even if the number of degrees of freedom is larger or equal to zero. This means that different sets of parameter values yield the same maximum of the likelihood function. Usually, an identified model can be obtained with different sets of starting values yielding to the same final parameter estimates.

Model fit is assessed by comparing the observed frequencies of the multiway contingency table to the expected frequencies predicted by the model. The difference is formally assessed with a likelihood ratio (LR) chi-squared statistic. A complication arises with large, sparse tables, such that the number of observed patterns is extremely large. For those tables, the chi-square statistic no longer has a theoretical chi-squared distribution. Thus, statistical assessment by the chi-square statistic is inappropriate. Partly due to this, interest in assessing model fit via so-called information statistics arose. These statistics are based on the log-likelihood of the model, on the number of parameters, and also on the sample size. Given two models with equal log-likelihoods, the model with the fewest parameters is the better one. Common information statistics include the Akaike information criterion (AIC) and the Bayesian information criterion (BIC). For these statistics, smaller values correspond to more parsimonious models. In comparing different models for the same data, models with lower values on these indices are preferred.

Many important extensions of the LCA have been developed since then, such as models containing (continuous) covariates, local dependencies, ordinal variables, several latent variables, and repeated measures. A general framework containing all extensions as well as special cases is proposed by Hagenaars (1990) and Vermunt (1997). The first LCA program (MLLSA) from Clifford Clogg in 1977 was limited to a relative small number of nominal variables. Current programs can handle more variables and other scale types. The program LEM (Vermunt, 1997) provides a command language for latent class models as well as M*plus* (Muthén & Muthén, 2007). Especially developed for LCA is Latent GOLD (Vermunt & Magidson, 2005), which implements the most important types of latent class models and their extensions.

REFERENCES

Dempster, A. P., Laird, N. M., & Rubin, D. B. (1977). Maximum likelihood from incomplete data via the EM algorithm. *Journal of the Royal Statistical Society, B, 39*, 1–38.

Goodman, L. A. (1974). The analysis of systems of qualitative variables when some of the variables are unobservable. Part I: A modified latent structure approach. *American Journal of Sociology, 79*, 1179–1259.

Haberman, S. J. (1979). *Analysis of qualitative data, Vol. 2. New developments.* New York: Academic Press.

Hagenaars, J. A. (1990). *Categorical longitudinal data: Loglinear analysis of panel, trend, and cohort data.* Newbury Park, CA: Sage.

Muthén, L., & Muthén, B. O. (2007). *Mplus: Statistical analysis with latent variables. User's guide.* [Version 5]. Los Angeles, CA: Author.

Vermunt, J. K. (1997). *Log-linear models for event histories.* Thousand Oaks, CA: Sage Publications.

Vermunt, J. K., & Magidson, J. (2005). *Latent GOLD 4.0 user's guide.* Belmont, MA: Statistical Innovations.

SUGGESTED READINGS

Clogg, C. C. (1995). Latent class models. In G. Arminger, C. C. Clogg, & M. E. Sobel (Eds.), *Handbook of statistical modeling for the social and behavioral sciences* (pp. 311–359). New York: Plenum Press.

Hagenaars, J. A., & McCutcheon, A. L. (Eds.). (2002). *Applied latent class analysis.* Cambridge, UK: Cambridge University Press.

Heinen, T. (1996). *Latent class and discrete latent trait models: Similarities and differences.* Thousand Oaks, CA: Sage.

McCutcheon, A. L. (1987). *Latent class analysis.* Beverly Hills, CA: Sage.

Jost Reinecke
University of Bielefeld, Germany

See also: **Principal Component Analysis**

LATENT INHIBITION

Latent inhibition (LI) is demonstrated when a previously exposed, unattended stimulus is less effective in a new learning situation than a novel stimulus. The term "latent inhibition" dates back to Lubow and Moore (1959), who intended to design a classical conditioning analog of latent learning. As such, the LI effect was "latent" in that it was not exhibited in the stimulus pre-exposure phase, but rather in the subsequent test phase. "Inhibition" simply reflected the fact that the effect was manifest as a retardation of learning. Since that first demonstration, there have been hundreds of LI-related experiments. LI is extremely robust, appearing in all mammalian species that have been tested and across many different learning paradigms.

The ubiquitous nature of LI suggests some adaptive advantages. Indeed, LI appears to protect the organism from associating irrelevant stimuli with other events. It helps to partition the important from the unimportant and thus to economize on processing capacity by selectively biasing the organism to more fully process new inputs as opposed to old, inconsequential ones.

Although the term "latent inhibition" is descriptive, the phenomenon has been subject to a number of theoretical interpretations. One class of theory holds that inconsequential stimulus pre-exposure results in reduced associability for that stimulus as compared to a novel stimulus. The loss of associability has been attributed to a variety of mechanisms that reduce attention (see Lubow, 1989, for a review), which then must be reacquired in order for learning to proceed normally.

Alternatively, it has been proposed that LI is a result of retrieval failure rather than acquisition failure. Such a hypothesis advocates that, following stimulus pre-exposure, the acquisition of the new association to the old stimulus proceeds normally (e.g., Escobar, Oberling, & Miller, 2002; Miller, Kasprow, & Schachtman, 1986). However, in the test stage, two competing associations may be retrieved, an earlier stimulus–no consequence association from the pre-exposure stage and/or the stimulus–unconditioned stimulus association of the acquisition stage. In normal LI, the non-pre-exposed group performs better than the pre-exposed group because there is only the second association to be retrieved, whereas the pre-exposed group performs poorly because both the first and second associations, which are in competition, are retrieved.

Among those variables that consistently have been shown to modulate the size of the LI effect, and perhaps the most important one theoretically, is that of context. In virtually all LI studies, the context, unless specifically an experimental variable, remains the same in the stimulus pre-exposure and test phases. However, if context is changed from the pre-exposure to the test phase, then LI is severely attenuated.

The various stimulus pre-exposure-context effects, as reviewed by Lubow and Gewirtz (1995), have been used to develop a theory of the conditioning of inattention and its modulation to account for both LI in healthy subjects and its reduction in persons with Schizophrenia. The theory states that normal LI is manifest when the pre-exposure context reappears in test and sets the occasion for eliciting the stimulus-no consequence association that was acquired during pre-exposure. As such, the context limits the access of the previously exposed irrelevant stimulus to working-memory. In addition, it has been proposed that, in Schizophrenia, there is a breakdown in the relationship between the pre-exposed stimulus and the context, such that the context no longer sets the occasion for the expression of the stimulus–no consequence association. Consequently, working-memory is inundated with experimentally familiar but phenomenally novel stimuli, each competing for the limited resources required for efficient information processing. This description fits well with the positive symptoms of Schizophrenia, particularly high distractibility, as well as with research findings.

The assumption that the same attentional process that produces LI in normal subjects is dysfunctional in schizophrenic persons has stimulated considerable research. Evidence to support this contention comes from several sources, including the parallel effects of dopamine activity associated with Schizophrenia and with LI. There are considerable data to indicate that dopamine agonists and antagonists modulate LI in rats and in normal humans. Dopamine agonists, such as amphetamine, abolish LI, whereas dopamine antagonists, such as haloperidol and other antipsychotic drugs, produce a super-LI effect. In addition, manipulations of putative dopamine pathways in the brain also have the expected effects on LI. Thus, hippocampal and septal lesions interfere with the development of LI, as do lesions in selective portions of the nucleus accumbens (see Weiner, 2003). With human subjects, there is evidence that acute, nonmedicated schizophrenics show reduced LI compared to chronic, medicated schizophrenics and to healthy subjects, while there is no difference in the amount of LI in the latter two groups. Finally, symptomatically normal subjects who score high on self-report questionnaires that measure psychotic-proneness or schizotypality also exhibit reduced LI compared to those who score low on the scales (see Lubow, 2005).

In addition to LI illustrating a fundamental strategy for information processing and providing a useful tool for examining attentional dysfunctions in pathological groups, LI has also been used to explain why certain therapies, such as alcohol aversion treatments, are not as effective as might be expected. On the other hand, LI procedures may be useful in counteracting some of the undesirable side effects that frequently accompany radiation and chemotherapies for cancer, as for example food aversion. Finally, LI research has suggested techniques that may be efficacious in the prophylactic treatment of certain fears and phobias. Lubow (1997) provides a review of such practical applications of LI.

In summary, the basic LI phenomenon represents some output of a selective attention process that results in learning to ignore irrelevant stimuli. It has become an important tool for understanding information processing in general, as well as attentional dysfunctions in Schizophrenia, and it has implications for a variety of practical problems.

REFERENCES

Escobar, M., Oberling, P., & Miller, R. R. (2002). Associative deficit accounts of disrupted latent inhibition and blocking in Schizophrenia. *Neuroscience and Biobehavioral Reviews, 26*, 203–216.

Lubow, R. E. (1989). *Latent inhibition and conditioned attention theory.* New York: Cambridge University Press.

Lubow, R. E. (1997). Latent inhibition and behavior pathology. In W. D. O'Donohue (Ed.), *Learning and behavior therapy* (pp. 107–121). Boston: Allyn & Bacon.

Lubow, R. E. (2005). Construct validity of the animal latent inhibition model of selective attention deficits in Schizophrenia. *Schizophrenia Bulletin, 31*, 139–153.

Lubow, R. E., & Gewirtz, J. (1995). Latent inhibition in humans: Data, theory, and implications for Schizophrenia. *Psychological Bulletin, 117*, 87–103.

Lubow, R. E., & Moore, A. U. (1959). Latent inhibition: The effect of nonreinforced preexposure to the conditioned stimulus. *Journal of Comparative and Physiological Psychology, 52*, 415–419.

Miller, R. R., Kasprow, W. J., & Schachtman, T. R. (1986). Retrieval variability: Sources and consequences. *American Journal of Psychology, 99*, 145–218.

Weiner, I. (2003). The "two-headed" latent inhibition model of Schizophrenia: Modeling positive and negative symptoms and their treatment. *Psychopharmacology, 169*, 257–297.

SUGGESTED READING

Lubow, R. E., & Weiner, I. (Eds.). (2009). *Latent inhibition: Data, theories, and applications to Schizophrenia.* New York: Cambridge University Press.

ROBERT E. LUBOW
Tel Aviv University, Israel

See also: Information Processing; Selective Attention

LATIN SQUARE DESIGN

A Latin square of order p is a $p \times p$ array of ordered letters or symbols in which each letter or symbol appears once in each row and once in each column. An example of a 3×3 Latin square is shown here.

$$
\begin{array}{ccc}
A & B & C \\
B & C & A \\
C & A & B
\end{array}
$$

The name *Latin square* was given to the squares by the famous Swiss mathematician Leonard Euler (1707–1783), who studied them and used Latin letters as symbols in the square.

References to Latin squares appeared as early as the thirteenth century. At the time, followers of Islam believed that Latin squares had magical powers. The followers wore objects depicting Latin squares to ward off evil spirits and bring good fortune. A sketch of a Latin square was found in the margin of a sixteenth-century Arabic medical text. The earliest written reference to a Latin square appeared in 1694 in *Récréations Mathématiques et Physiques* by Jacques Ozanam (1640–1717). The reference concerned the solution to a card puzzle: How many ways can 16 face cards be arranged in a 4 × 4 array so that no row, column, or diagonal contains more than one card of each denomination (ace, king, queen, jack) and suit (clubs, hearts, diamonds, spades)?

The 3 × 3 Latin square shown earlier is called a *standard square* because its first row and first column are ordered alphabetically. Two Latin squares are *conjugate* if the rows of one square are identical to the columns of the other. For example, a 5 × 5 Latin square and its conjugate are

$$
\begin{array}{ccccc}
A & B & C & D & E \\
B & A & D & E & C \\
C & E & A & B & D \\
D & C & E & A & B \\
E & D & B & C & A
\end{array}
\qquad
\begin{array}{ccccc}
A & B & C & D & E \\
B & A & E & C & D \\
C & D & A & E & B \\
D & E & B & A & C \\
E & C & D & B & A
\end{array}
$$

A Latin square is *self-conjugate* if the same square is obtained when its rows and columns are interchanged. The 5 × 5 square is not self-conjugate. However, the 3 × 3 Latin square is self-conjugate as are the 2 × 2 and 4 × 4 squares shown here.

$$
\begin{array}{cc}
A & B \\
B & A
\end{array}
\qquad
\begin{array}{cccc}
A & B & C & D \\
B & A & D & C \\
C & D & B & A \\
D & C & A & B
\end{array}
$$

A *transformation* of a Latin square is any permutation of its rows, columns, or elements. A Latin square can be transformed to obtain $p!(p-1)!$ Latin squares, including the original square. For example, there are $3!(3-1)! = 12$ three-by-three Latin squares. An enumeration of Latin squares of size 2 × 2 through 7 × 7 was made by Fisher and Yates (1934, 1963), Norton (1939), and Sade (1951).

Latin squares are interesting mathematical objects as well as being useful in designing experiments. The person most responsible for promoting the use of experimental designs based on a Latin square was Ronald A. Fisher (1890–1962), an eminent British statistician who worked at the Rothamsted Experimental Station north of London. Fisher showed that a Latin square or combination of squares could be used to construct a variety of complex experimental designs. For a description of these designs, see Kirk (1995, chs. 8, 13, 14, and 15).

A *Latin square design* enables a researcher to test the hypothesis that p population means are equal while isolating the effects of two nuisance variables each having p levels. *Nuisance variables* are undesired sources of variation in an experiment. The effects of the two nuisance variables are isolated by assigning one nuisance variable to the rows of a Latin square and the other nuisance variable to the columns of the square. The p levels of the treatment are assigned to the Latin letters of the square. The isolation

of two nuisance variables often reduces the mean square within cell error and results in increased power.

The use of a Latin square design to isolate two nuisance variables is illustrated in the following experiment. Suppose that a researcher is interested in comparing the effectiveness of three diets in helping obese teenage girls lose weight. The independent variable is the three kinds of diets; the dependent variable is the amount of weight loss three months after going on a diet. Instead of denoting the diets by the letters A, B, and C, the researcher follows contemporary usage and denotes the diets by the lowercase letter a and a number subscript: a_1, a_2, and a_3. The researcher believes that ease in losing weight is affected by the amount that a girl is overweight and by her genetic predisposition to be overweight. A rough measure of the latter variable can be obtained by asking a girl's parents if they were overweight as teenagers: c_1 denotes neither parent overweight, c_2 denotes one parent overweight, and c_3 denotes both parents overweight. This nuisance variable is assigned to the columns of a 3 × 3 Latin square. The other nuisance variable, amount that girls are overweight, is assigned to the rows of the Latin square: b_1 is 20–39 pounds, b_2 is 40–59 pounds, and b_3 is 60 or more pounds. Diagrams of the Latin square for this experiment and the associated Latin square design are shown in Figures 1 and 2, respectively.

The total sum of squares and total degrees of freedom for the diet experiment are partitioned as follows:

$$
\begin{aligned}
SSTOTAL ={}& SSA + SSB + SSC + SSRESIDUAL \\
& + SSWCELL \\
np^2 - 1 ={}& p - 1 + p - 1 + p - 1 + (p-1)(p-2) \\
& + p^2(n-1),
\end{aligned}
$$

where *SSA* denotes the treatment sum of squares, *SSB* denotes the row sum of squares, *SSC* denotes the column sum of squares, *SSRESIDUAL* denotes the residual (interaction components) sum of squares, and *SSWCELL* denotes the within-cell sum of squares. Mean squares are obtained by dividing a sum of squares by its degrees of freedom. The following four null hypotheses can be tested, where μ_{jkl} denotes a population mean for the jth treatment level, kth row, and lth column.

	c_1	c_2	c_3
b_1	a_1	a_2	a_3
b_2	a_2	a_3	a_1
b_3	a_3	a_1	a_2

Figure 1. Three-by-three Latin square, where a_j denotes one of the $j = 1, \ldots, p$ levels of treatment A, b_k denotes one of the $k = 1, \ldots, p$ levels of nuisance variable B, and c_l denotes one of the $l = 1, \ldots, p$ levels of nuisance variable C.

		Treat. Comb.	Dep. Var.
Group$_1$	Participant$_1$	$a_1b_1c_1$	Y_{111}
	$\vdots$	$\vdots$	$\vdots$
	Participant$_n$	$a_1b_1c_1$	Y_{111}
			$\bar{Y}_{\cdot 111}$
Group$_2$	Participant$_1$	$a_1b_2c_3$	Y_{123}
	$\vdots$	$\vdots$	$\vdots$
	Participant$_n$	$a_1b_2c_3$	Y_{123}
			$\bar{Y}_{\cdot 123}$
Group$_3$	Participant$_1$	$a_1b_3c_2$	Y_{132}
	$\vdots$	$\vdots$	$\vdots$
	Participant$_n$	$a_1b_3c_2$	Y_{132}
			$\bar{Y}_{\cdot 132}$
Group$_4$	Participant$_1$	$a_2b_1c_2$	Y_{212}
	$\vdots$	$\vdots$	$\vdots$
	Participant$_n$	$a_2b_1c_2$	Y_{212}
			$\bar{Y}_{\cdot 212}$
$\vdots$	$\vdots$	$\vdots$	$\vdots$
Group$_9$	Participant$_1$	$a_3b_3c_1$	Y_{331}
	$\vdots$	$\vdots$	$\vdots$
	Participant$_n$	$a_3b_3c_1$	Y_{331}
			$\bar{Y}_{\cdot 331}$

Figure 2. Layout for a Latin square design that is based on the Latin square in Figure 1. The experiment requires $n \times 3^2$ girls; n girls are assigned to each $a_jb_kc_l$ combination.

H_0: $\mu_{1\cdot\cdot} = \mu_{2\cdot\cdot} = \mu_{3\cdot\cdot}$ (treatment A population means are equal)

H_0: $\mu_{\cdot 1\cdot} = \mu_{\cdot 2\cdot} = \mu_{\cdot 3\cdot}$ (row, B, population means are equal)

H_0: $\mu_{\cdot\cdot 1} = \mu_{\cdot\cdot 2} = \mu_{\cdot\cdot 3}$ (column, C, population means are equal)

H_0: interaction components $= 0$ (selected $A \times B$, $A \times C$, $B \times C$, and $A \times B \times C$ interaction components equal zero).

The F statistics are

$$F = \frac{SSA/(p-1)}{SSWCELL/[p^2(n-1)]} = \frac{MSA}{MSWCELL}$$

$$F = \frac{SSB/(p-1)}{SSWCELL/[p^2(n-1)]} = \frac{MSB}{MSWCELL}$$

$$F = \frac{SSC/(p-1)}{SSWCELL/[p^2(n-1)]} = \frac{MSC}{MSWCELL}$$

$$F = \frac{SSRESIDUAL/(p-1)(p-2)}{SSWCELL/[p^2(n-1)]} = \frac{MSRESIDUAL}{MSWCELL}$$

The advantage of the Latin square design is the ability to isolate two nuisance variables in order to obtain greater power to reject a false null hypothesis. The disadvantages are (1) the number of levels of treatment A and the two nuisance variables must be the same, a balance that may be difficult to achieve; (2) if there are any interactions among treatment A and the nuisance variables, the test of treatment A is positively biased; and (3) the randomization is relatively complex.

REFERENCES

Fisher, R. A., & Yates, F. (1934). The six by six Latin squares. *Proceedings of the Cambridge Philosophical Society, 30*, 492–507.

Fisher, R. A., & Yates, F. (1963). Statistical tables for biological, agricultural and medical research (6th ed.). Edinburgh: Oliver & Boyd. *Proceedings of the Cambridge Philosophical Society, 30*, 492–507.

Kirk, R. E. (1995). *Experimental design: Procedures for the behavioral sciences* (3rd ed.). Pacific Grove, CA: Brooks/Cole.

Norton, H. W. (1939). The 7 × 7 squares. *Annals of Eugenics, 9*, 269–307.

Sade, A. (1951). An omission in Norton's list of 7 × 7 squares. *Annals of Mathematical Statistics, 22*, 306–307.

SUGGESTED READINGS

Cotton, John W. (1993). Latin square designs. In L. K. Edwards (Ed.), *Applied analysis of variance in behavioral science* (pp. 197–253). New York: Marcel Dekker.

Dénes, J., & Keedwell, A. D. (1974). Latin squares and their applications. New York: Academic Press.

Ryan, Thomas P. (2007). *Modern experimental design*. Hoboken, NJ: John Wiley & Sons.

ROGER E. KIRK
Baylor University

LAW AND PSYCHOLOGY (See Psychology and the Law)

LEARNED HELPLESSNESS

Learned helplessness was discovered when researchers immobilized a dog and exposed it to electric shocks that could neither be avoided nor escaped. Twenty-four hours later, the dog was placed in a situation in which electric shock could be terminated by a simple response. The dog did not make this response; instead, it just sat passively. This behavior was in marked contrast to dogs in a control group that reacted vigorously to the shock and learned to turn it off.

These investigators proposed that the dog had learned to be helpless. When originally exposed to uncontrollable shock, it learned that nothing it did mattered. Shocks came and went independently of behavior. This learning of response-outcome independence was represented as an expectation of future helplessness that was generalized to new situations to produce motivational, cognitive, and emotional deficits. These deficits following uncontrollability have come to be known as *learned helplessness phenomena*, and their cognitive explanation as the *learned helplessness model*.

Much of the early interest in learned helplessness stemmed from its clash with traditional stimulus-response theories of learning. Alternative accounts of learned helplessness were proposed by theorists who saw no need to invoke mentalistic constructs, and these alternatives emphasized an incompatible motor response learned when animals were first exposed to uncontrollability. This response was presumably generalized to the second situation, where it interfered with performance at the test task.

Steven Maier and Martin Seligman (1976) conducted a series of studies testing the learned helplessness model and the incompatible motor response alternative. The most compelling argument for the cognitive account comes from the triadic design, a three-group experimental paradigm that differentiates uncontrollability from trauma. Animals in one group are exposed to shock that they are able to terminate by making some response. Animals in a second group are yoked to those in the first group, exposed to the identical shocks; the only difference is that animals in the first group control their outcome whereas those in the second do not. Animals in the third group are exposed to no shock at all. All animals are then given the same test task. Animals with control over the initial shocks typically show no helplessness when tested. They act just like animals with no prior exposure to shock. Animals without control become helpless.

Also supporting a cognitive interpretation of helplessness are studies showing that an animal can be "immunized" against the effects of uncontrollability by first exposing it to controllable events. Presumably, the animal learns during immunization that events can be controlled, and this expectation is sustained during exposure to uncontrollable events, precluding helplessness. Other studies show that learned helplessness deficits can be undone by exposing a helpless animal to the contingency between behavior and outcome. The animal is forced to make an appropriate response to the test task, by pushing or pulling it into action. After several such trials, the animal responds on its own. Again, the presumed process at work is cognitive. The animal's expectation of response-outcome independence is challenged during the "therapy" experience, and learning occurs.

Psychologists interested in human problems were quick to see the parallels between learned helplessness as produced in the laboratory and maladaptive passivity as it exists in the real world. Thus began several lines of research looking at learned helplessness in people. First, helplessness in people was produced in the laboratory much as it was in animals, by exposing them to uncontrollable events and seeing the effects on their motivation, cognition, and emotion. Unsolvable problems were usually substituted for uncontrollable electric shock, but the critical aspects of the phenomenon remained: Following uncontrollability, people show a variety of deficits similar to those observed among animals. Second, researchers proposed various failures of adaptation as analogous to learned helplessness and investigated the similarity between these failures and helplessness. Especially popular was Seligman's (1975) proposal that depression and learned helplessness shared critical features: causes, symptoms, consequences, treatments, and preventions.

It soon became clear that the original helplessness model was an oversimplification when applied to people, failing to account for the range of reactions that people display following uncontrollability. Some people indeed showed pervasive deficits, as the model hypothesized, that were general across time and situation, whereas others did not. Further, failures of adaptation that the learned helplessness model was supposed to explain, such as depression, were sometimes characterized by a striking loss of self-esteem, about which the model was silent.

In an attempt to resolve these discrepancies, Lyn Abramson, Martin Seligman, and John Tresdale (1978) reformulated the helplessness model as it applied to people. The contrary findings could be explained by proposing that when people encounter an uncontrollable (bad) event, they ask themselves why it happened. Their answer sets the parameters for the helplessness that follows. If their causal attribution is stable ("it's going to last forever"), then induced helplessness is long-lasting. If their causal attribution is global ("it's going to undermine everything"), then subsequent helplessness is manifest across a variety of situations. Finally, if the causal attribution is internal ("it's all my fault"), the individual's self-esteem drops following uncontrollability. These hypotheses comprise the *attributional reformulation* of helplessness theory.

In some cases, the situation itself provides the explanation. In other cases, the person relies on a habitual way of making sense of events that occur, what is called *explanatory style*. Explanatory style is therefore a distal influence on helplessness and the failures of adaptation that involve helplessness. Explanatory style has been studied in its own right, and it has an array of correlates. People who explain bad events with internal, stable, and global causes show passivity; poor problem-solving; depression; anxiety; failure in academic, athletic, and vocational realms; social estrangement; morbidity; and mortality. Explanatory style can be highly stable, sometimes over decades. The self-fulfilling nature of explanatory style—and helplessness per se—explains this stability. At the same time, explanatory style can and does change in response to ongoing life events. Cognitive therapy, for example, can move explanatory style in an optimistic direction.

REFERENCES

Abramson, L. Y., Seligman, M. E. P., & Teasdale, J. D. (1978). Learned helplessness in humans: Critique and reformulation. *Journal of Abnormal Psychology, 87*, 49–74.

Maier, S. F., & Seligman, M. E. P. (1976). Learned helplessness: Theory and evidence. *Journal of Experimental Psychology: General*, *105*, 3–46.

Seligman, M. E. P. (1975). *Helplessness: On depression, development, and death*. San Francisco: Freeman.

CHRISTOPHER PETERSON
University of Michigan

high. This fact accounts for at least some of the end spurts obtained in Vincentized data. These appear as rather sudden increases in the final segment of practice. It now seems that they often occur as criterion artifacts, because the experiment is terminated after a series of unusually good performances.

GREGORY A. KIMBLE
Duke University

LEARNING CURVES

Progress in learning reflects itself in a number of different ways: increase in the rate, probability of occurrence, speed and vigor of responding, decrease in latency (time required to initiate a response), time required to complete a task, and number of errors committed in doing so. These changes in performance are frequently presented in one of a variety of forms called *learning curves*, in which the baseline is most often the number of practice trials but occasionally is time. The vertical axis represents one of the measures just mentioned.

The different measures of learning behave in different ways if the learning involves practice. Amplitude, probability of occurrence, speed of responding, and rate curves show an increase; latencies and other time measures decrease. Probability and percentage of response curves often show a double inflection. Because conditioned responses sometimes do not appear until after several reinforcements, the first portion of the curve may be flat. This portion is followed by a positively accelerated increase, which is soon replaced by a negatively accelerated one as a maximum is approached.

Most learning curves are for groups of subjects, rather than for individuals. For many purposes this creates a problem, especially in experiments where subjects are run to some criterion, such as 100% conditioning in a block of trials. Different subjects will take different numbers of trials to reach the criterion, and it becomes difficult to find a baseline against which to plot the response measures to represent the course of acquisition. One solution to this problem is in the use of the Vincent Curve. The total number of trials required for each subject to reach the criterion is divided into fractional parts such as tenths, and measures are plotted for these portions. This method makes it possible to combine data for subjects whose performances differ widely.

Unfortunately, this and other procedures for combining data may distort the picture of acquisition presented by the learning curve. For one thing, the typical performance of individual subjects in a learning experiment is irregular, showing chance upward and downward excursions. To select the first point at which a subject reaches some arbitrary level as the criterion of learning is very often to stop the learning session at a point that is accidentally

LEARNING DISABILITIES

Learning disabilities (LD) encompass a heterogeneous group of perceptual disorders that impact the development of academic performance is the areas of reading, written language, and mathematics. The most prevalent type of learning disability is a specific reading disability that is commonly referred to as dyslexia, but disorders also exist in written language (dysgraphia) and mathematics (dyscalculia). These disorders are often referred to as "specific" because functioning is only affected in certain, but not all, aspects of academic development and performance. Although LD can co-occur with other disorders, such as Attention Deficit Hyperactivity Disorder (ADHD), these disorders are distinct.

Early History

The early history of the field of LD can be traced back over a century to the late 1800s and early 1900s with case descriptions of children with reading disabilities. One early pioneer was James Hinshelwood, a surgeon at the Glasgow Eye Infirmary. In 1902, Hinshelwood described in detail two cases of what he called congenital word-blindness. He reached the following conclusions that are still pertinent today: (1) particular areas of the brain are involved; (2) the children often have average or above-average intelligence and good memory in other respects; (3) the problem with reading is localized, not generalized to all areas of performance; (4) the children do not learn to read with the same rapidity as other children; (5) the earlier the problem is identified, the better, so as not to waste valuable time; (6) the children need special methods adapted to their difficulties; (7) the sense of touch helps children retain visual impressions; and (8) persistent and persevering attempts will help children improve their reading. Hinshelwood (1902) commented that the diagnosis of word blindness is easy to make because the features of the disorder are so distinct and easily understood. Over a century later, Shaywitz (2003) concurred that the diagnosis of dyslexia is as precise and accurate as any known medical condition and that it is a specific problem in decoding within a "sea of strengths."

The first report on word blindness to appear in the American medical literature was written by Samuel Orton (1925). Orton agreed with Hinshelwood that word blindness (1) was not related to mental retardation, (2) could range from mild to severe, and (3) was caused by physiological deficits in the brain. Thus, with LD, the problem is not a result of generalized low abilities, but a localized problem that does not affect functioning in all domains.

Atypical Patterns of Development

Throughout history, one basic concept that is present in most definitions of LD is the existence of significant intra-individual differences, specific strengths in some abilities but specific weaknesses in others (the learning disabilities). Thus, the person's performance is marked by an uneven pattern of development. For example, in cases of reading disability, a student may have average or even above-average oral language and mathematical abilities, but significant weaknesses in reading and written language.

The factors that appear to affect literacy development are often observed within the cognitive and linguistic abilities of the individual. Many difference correlates of dyslexia exist. For example, relevant underlying abilities that can affect the development of word recognition skill include: phonological awareness, rapid automatized naming (RAN), processing speed, and orthographic awareness. In some cases, poor readers struggle because of limited phonological awareness (Torgesen, Wagner, & Rashotte, 1994). In other cases, poor readers have intact phonological skills but are slow to name common stimuli, as measured by RAN tasks. This slowness in perception then appears to impact their ability to process visual symbols such as letters and words quickly. Other struggling readers have low performance on both RAN and phonological awareness tasks (Wolf & Bowers, 1999), whereas still others have average performance on both. These poor readers may have weaknesses in other abilities, such as processing speed, which requires scanning visual symbols efficiently (Kail & Hall, 1994), or orthographic awareness, the memory and recall of letters of visual spelling patterns (Badian, 2005). Regardless of the specific factors affecting performance, if a multidisciplinary team within a school setting determines that a learning disability exists, students are entitled under federal law to special education services.

Individuals with Disabilities Education Act of 2004 (IDEA 2004)

In the United States, the regulations in IDEA 2004 are often used to help determine eligibility of LD services within school settings. Presently, the eight areas of eligibility for a classification of LD in IDEA 2004 are oral expression, listening comprehension, written expression, basic reading skills, reading fluency skills, reading comprehension, mathematics calculation, and mathematics problem solving. Although IDEA 2004 lists oral expression and listening comprehension as areas of qualification for LD, these types of problems are more accurately classified under the category of speech/language impairments.

The criteria state that the child must be provided with learning experiences and instruction appropriate in these areas. The three standards of comparison specified for determining eligibility are age, state-approved grade-level standards, and intellectual development. The child's age and progress on state-approved grade-level standards are to be considered when teams are using ability-achievement discrepancies and Response to Intervention (RTI) models. The student's unique pattern of intellectual development, or strengths and weaknesses, may also be considered as relevant information.

Ability-Achievement Discrepancy

When the first federal special education regulations for LD were written in 1977, the concept of a "severe discrepancy" was part of the diagnostic criteria. In order to qualify for LD services, students were required to demonstrate a significant discrepancy between their intellectual ability, measured by an intelligence test, and their academic achievement as measured by standardized assessments.

One major problem, however, was that the discrepancy procedure was viewed as a "wait to fail" model because students were declared ineligible for services until a "severe discrepancy" could be demonstrated, making it difficult to provide early interventions. Another problem was that the learning disability was measured within tests of the ability measure (e.g., measures of processing speed or memory) or the obtained test scores reflected the effects of the disability on development (e.g., lowered vocabulary because of limited reading experiences). Thus, the overall intelligence test scores were lowered and students with true LD would not have a significant ability-achievement discrepancy. Because of these concerns, as well as others, the eligibility criteria in IDEA 2004 for LD identification was amended so a determination (1) must not require the identification of a severe discrepancy; (2) must permit the use of a process based on response to scientific, research-based interventions; and (3) may permit the use of other alternative research-based procedures.

Response to Intervention (RTI)

IDEA 2004 expands the eligibility process for LD to include a multitiered service delivery model of quality instruction and support in general education. This model is designed to provide early intervention to children using research-based instruction in varying degrees of intensity. To ensure that the underachievement in a child suspected of having LD is not due to lack of appropriate instruction in reading or math, IDEA 2004 states that RTI models must be provided prior to referral. Failure to make sufficient progress or a lack of responsiveness to an intervention does not, however, mean that a student has LD, but simply that the amount of progress has been judged to be inadequate. A myriad of reasons exist for why a student would not respond adequately to particular interventions with only one of them being LD.

The federal definition also contains exclusionary criteria when evaluating children who do not make sufficient progress based on the requirements of IDEA 2004. Children are not eligible for an LD classification if the lack of progress or the ability-achievement discrepancies are primarily the result of one of the following: (1) a visual, hearing, or motor disability; (2) mental retardation; (3) emotional disturbance; (4) cultural factors; (5) environmental or economic disadvantage; or (6) limited English proficiency.

Pattern of Strengths and Weaknesses

IDEA 2004 § 300.309 (a)(2) (ii) also permits consideration of a pattern of strengths and weakness in performance, achievement, or both, relative to intellectual development. This is determined by a multidisciplinary team to be relevant to the identification of a specific learning disability. This provision is in line with the concept of intraindividual discrepancies that can be most accurately identified through a comprehensive evaluation.

The Role of a Comprehensive Evaluation

Although data collected through an RTI process can provide important information, accurate LD identification usually requires a comprehensive evaluation. One major goal of this evaluation is to determine the specific cognitive and linguistic factors that are affecting academic development. Identification of these specific problems helps support the diagnosis of a specific learning disability. Information regarding a student's unique pattern of strengths and weaknesses can provide insights into the selection of the most appropriate and effective accommodations and interventions.

Elements of Effective Interventions

Most of the research regarding effective interventions focused on methods for enhancing reading performance. Through a meta-analysis, Swanson (1999) identified the most important generalizations in regard to evidence-based effective instructional models, methods, and strategies for teaching word recognition and comprehension. Direct instruction was most effective for teaching reading comprehension. The following six components resulted in the most positive gains: (1) direct response/questioning, (2) controlling task difficulty, (3) elaboration, (4) modeling,

(5) small group instruction, and (6) instruction in the use of strategy cues.

Principles for effective instruction in mathematics address both computation and acquisition of concepts. Fuchs et al. (2008) identified the following seven basic principles: (1) explicit instruction; (2) instruction that is precise, sequenced, and integrated; (3) procedures that include the use of manipulatives; (4) drill and practice; (5) cumulative review; (6) incorporation of motivation techniques and strategies to help regulate attention and reduce stress; and (7) ongoing progress motivation.

For students with handwriting difficulties, the use of assistive technology devices, such as word processors, portable keyboards, and software that enables text to speech and speech to text capability can increase access and support independence. Other effective intervention strategies include: use of multisensory methods for teaching letter formation, automaticity, and fluency; and use of a pencil grip to promote finger positioning. Students with a learning disability in written expression, which can include both difficulty with spelling and putting thought and ideas in written form, can benefit from (1) talking spellers; (2) use of graphic organizers for assistance in planning and organizing writing for different purposes; (3) explicit modeling and instruction in writing sentences, paragraphs, and essays; (4) use of checklists for editing; and (5) specific accommodations to address length of assignments, format of assignments, and use of assistive technology as appropriate (Richards, 1999). Sometimes an accommodation can be as simple as providing the student with more time on assignments and tests.

In summarizing the research on the most effective interventions for students with LD, Fletcher, Lyon, Fuchs, and Barnes (2007) concluded the following: (1) effective instruction is critical; (2) early, intensive interventions are important; (3) instruction must be based upon a student's needs; (4) training in processes without academic content is ineffective; (5) the most effective methods are explicit and intensive; (6) no single approach works with all students; and (7) even "evidence-based" methods fail to work with certain students. Children who have difficulty learning to read or completing math problems will not benefit from more of the same, but rather they require alternative teaching methods to assist their learning (Semrud-Clikeman, 2005).

In summary, despite all that is known about the needs of children with LD, some children still do not receive sufficient interventions to realize their academic potentials. Other children do receive intensive, systematic instruction, but do not progress as anticipated because of other reasons, including English language status or comorbidity of other disorders, such as ADHD. Repeated failures have a devastating impact on children's self-determination, motivation, self-esteem, and future opportunities for success. The fields of school psychology and special education must ensure adequate training and preparation of their school psychologists and teachers so that they can provide bias-free assessments and then plan, implement, and monitor interventions. For students with LD, accurate diagnoses, effective instruction, access to assistive technology, and the provision of appropriate accommodations are all critical factors.

REFERENCES

Badian, N. (2005). Does a visual-orthographic deficit contribute to reading disability? *Annals of Dyslexia, 55*, 28–52.

Fletcher, J. M., Lyon, G. R., Fuchs, L. S., & Barnes, M. A. (2007). *Learning disabilities: From identification to intervention.* New York: Guilford Press.

Fuchs, L. S., Fuchs, D., Powell, S. R., Seethaler, P. M., Cirino, P. T., & Fletcher, J. M. (2008). Intensive intervention for students with mathematics disabilities: Seven principles of effective practice. *Learning Disability Quarterly, 31*, 79–92.

Hinshelwood, J. (1902). *Congenital word-blindness with reports of two cases.* London: John Bale, Sons & Danielsson, Ltd.

Kail, R., & Hall, L. K. (1994). Processing speed, naming speed, and reading. *Developmental Psychology, 30*, 949–954.

Office of Special Education and Rehabilitative Services. (2006). *Identification of specific learning disabilities: Regulations.* Washington, DC: U.S. Department of Education Office of Special Education Programs.

Orton, S. T. (1925). Word-blindness in school children. *Archives of Neurology and Psychiatry, 14*, 581–615.

Richards, R.G. (1999). *When writing's a problem.* Riverside, CA: RET Center Press.

Semrud-Clikeman, M. (2005). Neuropsychological aspects for evaluating learning disabilities. *Journal of Learning Disabilities, 38*, 563–568.

Shaywitz, S. (2003). *Overcoming dyslexia: A new and complete science-based program for reading problems at any level.* New York: Knopf.

Swanson, II. L. (1999). Reading research for students with LD: A meta-analysis of intervention outcomes. *Journal of Learning Disabilities, 32*, 504–532.

Torgesen, J. K., Wagner, R. K., & Rashotte, C. A. (1994). Longitudinal studies of phonological processing and reading. *Journal of Learning Disabilities, 27*, 276–286.

Wolf, M., & Bowers, P. (1999). The "double-deficit hypothesis" for the developmental dyslexias. *Journal of Educational Psychology, 91*, 1–24.

SUGGESTED READINGS

Allsopp, D. H., Kyger, M. M., & Lovin, L. H. (Eds.). (2007). *Teaching mathematics meaningfully: Solutions for reaching struggling learners.* Baltimore: Paul H. Brookes.

Mather, N., & Goldstein, S. (2008). *Learning disabilities and challenging behaviors: A guide to intervention & classroom management* (2nd ed.). Baltimore: Paul H. Brookes.

Minskoff, E. (2005). *Teaching reading to struggling learners.* Baltimore: Paul H. Brookes.

Morris, R., & Mather, N. (Eds.). (2008). *Evidence-based interventions for students with learning and behavioral challenges.* Hillsdale, NJ: Lawrence Erlbaum.

NANCY MATHER
University of Arizona

ANNMARIE URSO
State University of New York College at Geneseo

See also: Alexia/Dyslexia; Reading Disability

LEARNING THEORIES

A theory consists of a set of principles based on observations typically obtained under controlled laboratory conditions. The function of theory is to summarize in a concise fashion observations in a field of study and to enable predictions about future observations in that field. Learning theory is concerned with the variables that produce long-lasting changes in individual behavior and the cumulative effects of those variables acting over time. Although based on laboratory research, often with animals, the principles are intended to apply to all behavior including the behavior of humans.

Development of Learning Theory

Science-based learning theory began in the early 1900s with the work of Ivan Pavlov in Russia and Edward Thorndike in the United States. At its outset, learning theory was an experimentally based extension of prior philosophical work in British associationism and empiricism. In Pavlov's experiments, some environmental event (a *stimulus*) reliably preceded another stimulus that already elicited behavior. For example, a tone would sound for a dog immediately before the presentation of food, which elicited salivation. As a result, an environment-behavior relation was strengthened—the dog salivated when it heard the tone. Pavlov's procedure is known as *classical*, or respondent, conditioning.

In Thorndike's experiments, some behavioral event (a *response*) reliably preceded an eliciting stimulus. For example, a cat would operate a latch that allowed it to escape from a chamber and obtain food. As a result, an environment-behavior relation was strengthened—the cat operated the latch (and presumably salivated) when it saw the latch. Thorndike's procedure is known as *operant* or *instrumental conditioning.* The technical term for the process whereby classical and operant procedures produce changes in the environmental guidance of behavior is *conditioning.* The process is called conditioning because the changes in the environmental guidance of behavior are dependent on (conditional on) the experience of the individual organism and not its evolutionary history alone.

Learning theory that was influenced by findings from the classical procedure tended to emphasize the importance of stimuli; for example, hear-the-tone and taste-the-food. Learning theory that was influenced primarily by findings from the operant procedure stressed the importance of both stimulus and response; for example, see-the-latch and operate-the-latch. In both procedures, the eliciting stimulus served as a *reinforcing stimulus*—or *reinforcer*—because it strengthened an environment-behavior relation. In the 1930s, B. F. Skinner noted that the difference between classical and operant experiments was procedural and did not necessarily have theoretical implications for the nature of the conditioning process (Skinner, 1938).

Skinner also appreciated more keenly than others that Pavlov's procedure limited the behavior that could be learned to responses that were already elicited by the reinforcing stimulus. The dog learned to salivate to the tone and salivation was a response that was already elicited by food. In contrast, Thorndike's procedure opened the possibility of changing the environmental guidance of *any* behavior of which the learner was capable: Select a response and follow it with a reinforcer. More complex behavior could then be strengthened using shaping procedures in which successively closer approximations to the more complex target behavior were reinforced. Skinner referred to the conditioned behavior in the operant procedure as *emitted* instead of elicited because the stimuli that were present when the response was reinforced did not need to be specified.

Until the late 1960s, the only variable upon which all learning theories agreed was *temporal contiguity*. That is, the time between the stimulus and the reinforcer in the classical procedure or between the response and the reinforcer in the operant procedure had to be very brief for conditioning to occur. Some additional variables were proposed—for example, that the reinforcing stimulus had also to reduce a biological drive (Hull, 1943)—but experimental evidence showed that some stimuli could function as reinforcers even if they did not have this effect.

However, evidence began to accumulate that something in addition to contiguity was required for conditioning. When a new stimulus was presented before a reinforcing stimulus in a classical procedure, the new stimulus did not acquire control of behavior if another stimulus was present that already controlled the behavior elicited by the reinforcer (Kamin, 1969). For instance, if a tone was first conditioned with food and later a light occurred together with the tone, then the light did not acquire control of salivating. Prior conditioning to one stimulus (the tone) *blocked* conditioning to the new stimulus (the light) even though the new stimulus was temporally contiguous with the reinforcer. This finding was soon confirmed with an operant procedure (vom Saal & Jenkins, 1970). Based on these and many related findings, a second variable was identified as necessary for conditioning—*discrepancy*. That is, the reinforcing stimulus had to evoke a *change* in activity for conditioning to occur (cf. Rescorla & Wagner, 1972). In nontechnical terms, the learner had to be "surprised" by the eliciting stimulus for it to serve as a reinforcer.

Modern Learning Theory

The view that both temporal contiguity and discrepancy are required for conditioning is now widely accepted by learning theorists (but see Stout & Miller, 2007). Current work is progressing along two primary lines—the neural/cellular processes involved in learning and the implications of basic learning processes for complex human behavior.

Regarding the neural/cellular processes of learning, research indicates that reinforcing stimuli initiate neural activity in a midbrain area (the ventral tegmental area) that sends widespread projections to cortical and subcortical regions. Reinforcers cause these projections to release a neuromodulator dopamine that can alter the strengths of connections (*synaptic efficacies*) between simultaneously activated neurons. In keeping with the behavioral finding of blocking, stimuli do not function as reinforcers when they are accompanied by a stimulus that already evokes the release of dopamine (Schultz, 2001).

Research at the cellular level indicates that when a presynaptic neuron releases the excitatory neurotransmitter glutamate into a synapse and dopamine is introduced soon thereafter, long-lasting changes occur in glutamate receptors on the postsynaptic neuron (Sajikumar & Frey, 2004). These changes make it more likely that release of glutamate by the presynaptic neuron will initiate activity in the postsynaptic neuron. Thus neural and cellular findings are consistent with the behavioral requirements of temporal contiguity and discrepancy. The changes in synaptic efficacies that occur during conditioning can be reproduced in the laboratory. Electrical stimulation of a presynaptic neuron leads to long-lasting changes in glutamate receptors on the postsynaptic neuron. These changes produce *long-term potentiation*, or *LTP*, which is a persistent increase in the responsivity of postsynaptic neurons to glutamate from presynaptic neurons (Bliss & Lømo, 1973).

A fundamental reason that learning theory is concerned with the neural/cellular basis of conditioning is the likelihood of a historical parallel between the acceptance of reinforcement and of natural selection. Reinforcement, like natural selection, is a selection process but one in which synaptic efficacies rather than genes are selected. Darwin's initial proposal of natural selection was not accepted as the key insight into the emergence of complex structure until some 70 years after it was first proposed. Natural selection became accepted only after the discovery of its biological basis—genetics—and the development of quantitative methods to trace its effects over time—population genetics. The general acceptance of selection by reinforcement as the primary insight into the emergence of complex behavior may well follow a similar course. If so, knowledge of the neural/cellular basis of reinforcement and appropriate quantitative methods will be required.

Regarding the implications of learning theory, two complementary paths are being simultaneously pursued—simulation research and applications to real-world problems. Information from behavior and neuroscience is integrated through quantitative research using computer simulations with neural networks. Neural networks are interconnected collections of neuron-like units in which the strengths of connections between units are modified by computations that simulate the reinforcement process. Computer simulation is a technique used in many fields to explore the implications of basic processes for complex phenomena. Neural-network research varies widely with regard to how closely it is informed by neuroscience and behavior concerning the characteristics of units, connections, and reinforcement. Even at this early stage of computational research, however, networks of units whose connections are strengthened by a reinforcement-like process have been shown to simulate a wide range of environment-behavior relations that were previously thought to require higher level (i.e., cognitive) formulations (Rumelhart, McClelland, & the PDP Research Group, 1986).

The validity and power of learning principles are also being explored through applications to complex phenomena. These include language, memory, and problem-solving (Donahoe & Palmer, 2005). Applied behavior analysis is being used to treat dysfunctional behavior (such as phobias and other anxiety disorders), developmental disabilities (such as autism), and to devise more effective educational practices through programmed instruction, personalized systems of instruction and precision teaching. Whether basic learning processes are competent to explain the full range of complex human behavior remains a work in progress.

REFERENCES

Bliss, T., & Lømo, T. (1973). Long-lasting potentiation of synaptic transmission in the dentate area of the anaesthetized rabbit following stimulation of the perforant path. *Journal of Physiology* (London), *232*, 331–356.

Donahoe, J. W., & Palmer, D. C. (2005). *Learning and complex behavior*. Richmond, MA: Ledgetop Publishing (Reprinted from Allyn & Bacon, 1994).

Hull, C. L. (1943). *Principles of behavior*. New York: Appleton-Century-Crofts.

Kamin, L. J. (1969). Predictability, surprise, attention, and conditioning. In B. A. Campbell & R. M. Church (Eds.), *Punishment*

and aversive behavior (pp. 279–296). New York: Appleton-Century-Crofts.

Rescorla, R. A., & Wagner, A. R. (1972). A theory of Pavlovian conditioning: Variations in the effectiveness of reinforcement and non-reinforcement. In A. Black & W. Prokasy (Eds.), *Classical conditioning II: Current research and theory* (pp. 64–99). New York: Appleton-Century-Crofts.

Rumelhart, D. E., McClelland, J. L., & the PDP Research Group (Eds.). (1986). *Parallel distributed processing: Explorations in the microstructure of cognition: Vol. 1. Foundations*. Cambridge, MA: MIT Press.

Sajikumar, S., & Frey, J. U. (2004). Late-associativity, synaptic tagging, and the role of dopamine during LTP and LTD. *Neurobiology of Learning and Memory, 82*, 12–25.

Schultz, W. (2001). Reward signaling by dopamine neurons. *The Neuroscientist, 7*, 293–302.

Skinner, B. F. (1938). *The behavior of organisms*. New York: Appleton-Century-Crofts.

Stout, S. C., & Miller, R. R. (2007) Sometimes-competing retrieval (SOCR): A formalization of the comparator hypothesis. *Psychological Review, 114*, 759–783.

vom Saal, W., & Jenkins, H. M. (1969). Blocking the development of stimulus control. *Learning and Motivation, 1*, 52–64.

JOHN W. DONAHOE
University of Massachusetts

See also: Operant Conditioning; Pavlovian Conditioning

LESBIANISM

Lesbianism denotes a woman's same-sex attraction, behavior, and/or identification. Lesbian is the preferred term for women who self identify as having same-sex preference. Most recently, the term lesbianism has also given way to the use of "lesbian" as an adjective; thus we speak of "lesbian behavior," "lesbian relationships," and "lesbian community."

A great disparity exists in the volume of social science research addressing male and female homosexuality, as exemplified by this being the first edition in which lesbianism is included in this encyclopedia. Recently, social science research has begun to address areas of differences and similarities between male and female homosexuality. For example, whereas the sexual orientation of most lesbians is highly persistent, there appears to be a greater degree of sexual fluidity among women than men. These results, however, may be a by-product of a degree of underestimation of bisexuality. Despite possibilities of fluidity, there is no evidence that efforts to change lesbian orientation through psychotherapy are effective.

Estimated Prevalence

Estimating the prevalence of lesbianism is difficult due to definitional and sampling problems in demographic research. For example, the famed reports by Kinsey, Pomeroy, and Martin (1953) asserted that 2–6% of females and 5–22% of males are more or less exclusively homosexual, but struggled to differentiate between sexual desire, behavior, and identity. More recently, Black and colleagues' (2000) careful review of several large national data sets found a more conservative 3.5% of women having at least one same-sex experience since age 18, 1.4% of women engaging exclusively in same-sex sexual activity over the last year, and 0.6% self-identifying as lesbian. This compared to 4.7% of men having at least one same-sex experience since age 18, 2.5% having engaged in exclusively same-sex sexual experience within the past year, and 1.8% self-identifying as gay. The authors reported other findings (Laumann, Gagnon, & Michael, 1994, as cited in Black, Gates, Sanders, et al., 2000) supporting incidence rates of homosexual desire among 7.5% of women and 7.7% of men.

History of Lesbianism

Lesbian behavior has been documented in all time periods. Until the nineteenth century, there was no term for physical affection between women, and sex was seen only as the purview of men. Since defining lesbianism as a deviant behavior or status, Western societies have debated whether to consider it an abomination, crime, disease, or natural variant of human behavior. The medicalization of homosexuality in the United States was amplified during World War II, when the military developed procedures for discharging soldiers suspected of homosexuality on grounds that their presence would threaten discipline and morale. At the same time, according to historian Allan Berbue (1990), "butch" women occupied a more respected status within the armed forces than effeminate men, because aggressive, masculine traits more comfortably fit the stereotype of the good soldier.

In the 1960s and 1970s, spawned by the civil rights and feminist movements, groups such as the Daughters of Bilitis formed to promote lesbian rights and well-being. At first frowned upon by feminists who believed sexual desire was socially constructed for male pleasure, lesbianism was eventually embraced as being consistent with the feminist perspective (Greene & Herek, 1994). The American Psychiatric Association removed homosexuality from the *Diagnostic and Statistical Manual of Mental Disorders* in 1973. Recent attitude research indicates that younger respondents have more favorable attitudes toward a range of lesbian issues. Lesbians currently have the right to marry in the Netherlands, Belgium, Canada, Spain, South Africa, Massachusetts, and California, and several other states and countries recognize same-sex unions and partnerships.

Origins of Lesbianism

Given the lack of scientific understanding regarding the cause of sexual response, studies of the complex relationship between biological, psychological, social, and cultural influences of homosexuality may help shed light on sexuality in general. Although overly simplistic, there is some merit to the argument that biology has more influence on sexual and gender orientation, and culture and social learning have greater impact on sexual identity and behavior. As with most areas of research, the preponderance of biological studies of homosexuality addresses males.

The argument for a biological influence in homosexuality is supported by studies of genetics, brain structures, and endocrinology. In studies of twins, the concordance rate of sexual orientation in siblings is consistent with a level of genetic influence: lowest in nontwin siblings, second in fraternal twins, and highest in monozygotic twins. There is no evidence, however, of a single "gay" gene. Endocrine studies conducted by Berglund, Lindstrom, and Savic (2006) found that exposure to estrogen in both lesbians and heterosexual men activated pathways of the brain linked to sexual behavior, a response not seen in heterosexual women. There is also evidence that prenatal exposure to extremely high levels of androgens may masculinize and defeminize certain brain structures that are correlated to gender nonconforming behaviors and homosexual behavior. More research is needed to determine if these structural or endocrine differences are casual, byproducts, or indirectly related to sexual and/or gender orientation.

Lesbian Stress and Resilience

Although negative attitudes toward gay men, bisexuals, and lesbians have improved in the past three decades, widespread prejudice, stigma, and violence directed toward them still exist. Originally referred to as "homophobia," prejudice against homosexuals is now referred to as "heterosexism" and "homonegativity." Both negative attitudes and discrimination are seen in the reluctance of many to recognize gay marriage, childrearing, and other legal arrangements. Lesbian, gay, and bisexual individuals may also subscribe to these negative attitudes, a phenomenon that has been termed "internalized homonegativity."

Although women tend to be less stigmatized for gender nonconformity than men, the stress of anti-lesbian violence and victimization often creates psychological distress by making the world seem less predictable and reducing the individual's basic sense of safety and trust. In order to avoid physical or verbal attacks, gay men and lesbians may try to evade threats by remaining hidden or "closeted." The manifestations of this stress are often mistaken as psychopathology due to homosexuality. However, clinical practice and research support explanations that link mental health problems in this population to the stress of being a sexual minority (Garnets & Kimmel, 2003).

Despite these stressors, research indicates that lesbian relationships are not unlike heterosexual relationships in regard to satisfaction, commitment, length, and the types of issues that affect the couple. Research (Garnets & Kimmel, 2003) also suggests that there are no differences between children of lesbian and heterosexual mothers on self-concepts relevant to aggression, intimacy, and self-efficacy. While lesbian mothers report greater stress reactions in their children than heterosexual mothers, children of lesbian mothers report greater overall sense of well-being than children of heterosexual couples. This could reflect better coping abilities or better abilities in expression of both positive and negative feelings, calling into question the discrimination faced by lesbian couples in adoption processes. Further exploration of diversity within sexuality will aid in the promotion of tolerance and understand in today's society.

REFERENCES

Berglund, H., Lindström, P., & Savic, I. (2006). Brain response to putative pheromones in lesbian women. *Proceedings of the National Academy of Sciences of the United States of America, 103*(21), 8269–8274.

Berube, A. (1990). *Coming out under fire: The history of gay men and women in World War Two*. New York: Free Press.

Black, D., Gates, G., Sanders, S., & Taylor, L. (2000). Demographics of gay and lesbian population in the United States: Evidence from available systematic data sources. *Demography, 37*(2), 139–154.

Garnets, L. D., & Kimmel, D. C. (2003). *Psychological perspectives on lesbian, gay, and bisexual experiences* (2nd ed.). New York: Columbia University Press.

Green, B. & Herek, G. M. (1994). *Lesbian and gay psychology: Theory, research, and clinical applications, Vol. 1*. Thousand Oaks, CA: Sage.

Kinsey, A., Pomeroy, W., & Martin, C. (1953). *Sexual behavior in the human female*. Philadelphia: W. B. Saunders.

SUGGESTED READINGS

D'Augelli, A., & Patterson, C. J. (2001). *Lesbian, gay, and bisexual identities and youth: Psychological perspectives*. New York: Oxford University Press.

Omoto, A. M. & Kurtzman, H. S. (2006). *Sexual orientation and mental health: Examining identity and development in lesbian, gay, and bisexual people*. Washington, DC: American Psychological Association.

MALIQUE L. CARR
PETER B. GOLBLUM
Pacific Graduate School of Psychology

See also: Bisexuality; Homosexuality; Sexual Orientation and Gender Identity

LEWIN, KURT (1890–1947)

Kurt Lewin received his PhD from the University of Berlin in 1914. Among his early associates were two of the Gestalt psychologists, Max Wertheimer and Wolfgang Köhler. Some psychologists consider Lewin's system to be an extension of the Gestalt movement. Lewin considered his system to be *topological* and *vectoral psychology*. He took the terms "topology" and "vector" from mathematics. Topology investigates the properties of space. But topology was not enough: he needed a concept of force or vector.

Lewin began his system of psychology with the concept *life space*. This is a psychological field identified as the space in which a person moves. This constitutes the totality of facts that determine the behavior of an individual at any one time. Behavior is a function of life space at any moment. B = fL. "L" is a psychological field and not necessarily a physical one. The life space includes oneself and other people and objects as one perceives them.

The life space is divided into regions by boundaries. Each region might be considered a psychological fact. The boundaries have several dimensions, such as nearness/remoteness. This could be illustrated by a college student wanting to be a physician: the region of setting up practice as a physician is quite remote from the present situation. Other regions that must be passed through might include graduating from college, entering medical school, graduating from medical school, internship/residency, and finally setting up practice. Another dimension of boundaries is firmness/weakness. Some boundaries are weak, or easy to cross, while others, such as passing a qualifying examination, can be anywhere from firm to difficult.

When a person passes from one region to another, movement occurs that has direction. In such movement one follows a pathway. Here Lewin invented a kind of geometry that he called hodological space. The characteristics of a given path varied according to the situation, and the direction depended on the properties of the entire field.

On the dynamic side, Lewin postulated a concept of tension. Tension occurred when needs arose. Needs could be either psychological or physiological.

Objects in the life space also have valences—plus or minus, depending on whether they were attractive or repulsive. Often a life space might contain several regions in which valences exist at the same time. A conflict can occur when a person must choose between objects that both have a positive valence or objects that are both equally repulsive. The vector or force constitutes the push toward or away from a goal. This force correlates with the valence of the object.

In his later years Lewin directed his attention to problems of social psychology. A major research project (Lewin, Lippitt, & White, 1939) studied various social climates and aggression. Lewin also developed the concept of group dynamics, an application to the group that he borrowed from his earlier individual psychology. Just as the person in his life space constitutes the psychological field, so the group and its environment constitute the social field. The group is characterized by a dynamic interdependence of its members. One's status depends on one's region as it relates to other regions (members of the group). The group is subjected to cohesive and disruptive forces. Disruptive forces arise out of too-strong barriers between numbers, which hamper communication. The group constitutes a field of forces and individuals that are attracted or repelled depending on the kinds of valences existing in the group. Lewin's theories and work on group psychology had a major impact on subsequent investigations of this topic.

SUGGESTED READINGS

Lewin, K. (1935). *A dynamic theory of personality*. New York: McGraw-Hill.

Lewin, K. (1936). *Principles of topological psychology*. New York: McGraw-Hill.

Lewin, K. (1951). *Field theory in social sciences: Selected theoretical papers*. D. Cartwright (Ed.). New York: Harper & Row.

RALPH W. LUNDIN
Wheaton, IL

LIBIDO

"Libido is a term used in the theory of the instincts for describing the dynamic manifestation of sexuality." Thus Sigmund Freud began his 1923 encyclopedia article on libido theory. He had used the term *libido* (derived from the Latin for lust and desire) as early as 1894. His major theoretical treatise, *Three Essays on the Theory of Sexuality* (1905/1973, p. 255) placed libido at the center of his theories of development and psychopathology. In his *New Introductory Lectures on Psychoanalysis*, a decade later, he introduced his review and current synthesis of libido theory by noting that "the theory of instincts is so to say our mythology" (Freud (1933/1973, p. 95). Even in Freud's later years, libido remained a central construct in psychoanalytic theory, one side of the basic, pervasive, instinctual dualisms: sex and aggression, life and death. The metapsychology of libido's vicissitudes and reorganizations over the course of development through the psychosexual stages—oral, anal, phallic, latency, and genital—formed the core of early psychoanalytic theories of developmental psychopathology and clinical practice.

Libido theory is among the most far-reaching and controversial notions in psychoanalysis. Now, as then, libido refers to the sexual biological instinct, drive, or psychic energy. Many psychoanalytic institutes and mental health consulting rooms continue to be venues conversant in the theory and its applications. However, whereas libido was not typically discussed in general physicians' offices in Freud's era, modern internists and specialty physicians recognize the importance of healthy sexual functioning as a vital indicator of overall health and quality of life. With the discovery of pharmacologic agents such as Levitra, Cialis, and Viagra at the dawn of the twenty-first century, and successful treatment of erectile dysfunction in men, the term libido, referring to sexual drive and behaviors more generally, enters health care and public conversations with increasing frequency. By 2001, annual sales of the first of these drugs, Viagra, exceeded $1 billion in the United States. Most recently, evidence is emerging that Viagra may help counter sexually dysfunctional side-effects of anti-depressant drugs in women. In today's society, libido is a concept with broad and deep biopsychosociocultural utility and meaning. With few exceptions, contemporary conversations about libido impairment and libido enhancement are only weakly linked to psychoanalysis.

Freud himself had strong allegiance and high hopes for biological causation and explanation, but he still broadened his notion of libido to include the more sensual aspects of life. Nonetheless, the relative emphasis on biological versus psychological or social description still characterizes controversies over libido theory. As early as 1916, Carl Jung, in his *Theory of the Unconscious*, attacked Freud's theory of libido, arguing that sexuality was only a variant of a more primal, undifferentiated form of psychic energy. Furthermore, in Jung's view sexuality emerged and predominated only in puberty, much later than in Freud's theory with its focus on highly salient infant and early childhood manifestations of libidinal expression and development.

Neo-Freudian and post-Freudian scholars have continued this debate. For instance, David Rapaport replaced the libido concept with a more general, nonspecific drive energy as he cast traditional and id-oriented psychoanalysis into more general ego psychology. The growing concern with the bankruptcy of hydraulic, thermodynamic, and drive-discharge models led to the elimination or de-emphasis of libido theory in many modern and post-modern psychoanalytic formulations. George Klein, one of the more recent and influential systematizers of twentieth century psychoanalysis, remarked that "in fact, the uncritical acceptance of libido theory with the newer current of ego psychology brings into sharp relief one of the focal dilemmas confronting psychoanalysis" (Klein, 1976, p. 147). Erik Erikson's enrichment of the theory of psychosexual development with social and cultural contextualization propelled his theory of psychosocial development into a major contribution.

Aside from ongoing debate over what role, if any, libido theory plays in psychoanalytic psychology or in any other theory of behavior or pathology, two abiding domains or concepts derived from libido theory remain useful, especially when their metapsychological nature is appreciated and respected. One of these domains is the qualitative properties of libido (or any instinctual or biological energy) that serve as structure, process, and organization for the so-called drive. Schafer notes that, through variation in degree of anticathexis, cathexis, or hypercathexis of libido, we may posit dreams, symptoms, jokes, rituals, pathology, relationships, therapeutic effects, and so on—the concerns of psychoanalysis. Schafer (1976, pp. 80–81) identifies the qualitative properties of libido as consisting of direction (sexual gratification), urgency or peremptoriness (unremitting pressure for discharge), mobility (readiness to divert itself into indirect channels when direct channels are blocked), dischargeability (its being reduced in quantity, hence in impetus, following certain activities, a loss known as desexualization or deinstinctualization), bindability (its being maintained in a fixed or blocked position, possibly by opposing energy), transformability (loss of its properties of direction, peremptoriness, and probability), and fusability (its capacity to blend with aggressive impulses or energy).

The second domain of useful concepts derived from libido theory are those of the developmental progressions of psychosexuality and object relations. In the theory of infantile sexuality, Freud described the maturation and successive reorganization of libido through the oral stage (birth to about 18 months), anal stage (18–36 months), phallic stage (three to five years), latency stage (middle childhood), and genital stage (adolescence and adulthood). Libidinal gratification was associated with sensuality or activity focused on each of the so-called erotogenic body zones implied in the stage sequence. Particular qualities of character or pathology were associated with successes, failures, or compromises at each mutually influential step of the developmental unfolding. A related progression of libido from autoerotism (gratification through one's own body), through narcissism (love of one's "self"), and to object love (gratification through investment and involvement with other people) complements the psychosexual progression, contributing yet another of the major developmental lines or trajectories that form the framework for psychoanalytic diagnostic classification.

The scientific status of libido theory and its derived constructs remains to be established by empirical research, an effort abandoned by many in the belief that libido theory is not researchable. Greater understanding will undoubtedly emerge with improved conceptualization and technology. Until then, libido theory remains an influential, though controversial girder in the framework that guides a major portion of applied psychology and psychoanalysis.

REFERENCES

Freud, S. (1905/1973). Three essays on the theory of sexuality. In J. Strachey (Ed.), *The standard edition of the complete psychological works of Sigmund Freud*, Vol. 7. London: Hogarth Press.

Freud, S. (1923/1973). Libido theory. In J. Strachey (Ed.), *The standard edition of the complete psychological works of Sigmund Freud*, Vol. 18. London: Hogarth Press.

Freud, S. (1933/1973). New introductory lectures on psychoanalysis. In J. Strachey (Ed.), *The standard edition of the complete psychological works of Sigmund Freud*, Vol. 23. London: Hogarth Press.

Jung, C. (1993). *The basic writings of C. G. Jung.* New York: Modern Library.

Klein, G. S. (1976). *Psychoanalytic theory: An exploration of essentials.* New York: International Universities Press.

Schafer, R. (1976). *A new language for psychoanalysis.* Oxford, England: Yale University Press.

SUGGESTED READING

Nagera, H. (1990). *Basic psychoanalytic concepts on the libido theory.* London: Karnac Books.

DONALD WERTLIEB
Tufts University

See also: **Psychoanalytic Theories**

LIE DETECTION

Because lying often has harmful consequences, it is not surprising that law enforcement and security agencies have long been invested in having a valid lie detector. However, despite almost a century of effort devoted to lie detector development, there remains no fool-proof method for identifying liars.

Polygraph testing represents the most widespread form of applied lie detection, with tens of thousands of tests given annually. Modern polygraph apparatus is computerized and involves recording palmar sweating, respiration, and cardiovascular activity while subjects are queried. Because there is no unique pattern of response associated with lying, polygraph tests involve comparing the magnitude of physiological reactivity to different types of questions. All polygraph tests include relevant or "did you do it?" questions (e.g., "Did you shoot Hockheimer?"). In the relevant-irrelevant test (RIT), the response to relevant questions is compared to the response to truthfully answered irrelevant questions that deal with straightforward facts (e.g., "Are you sitting down?"). Guilt is indicated by stronger responses to relevant questions. The RIT has been largely discredited, because the accusatory relevant question is more likely to be emotionally arousing than the psychologically innocuous irrelevant question even for innocent people, which leads to many false positive (truthful but diagnosed deceptive) outcomes.

To address this problem, the "control" or comparison question test (CQT) was developed. Introduced in the 1940s, the CQT remains the method of choice for testing criminal suspects. In a CQT, the reaction to the relevant question is compared to the response to a "probable lie" control question that covers a likely but denied misdeed from the person's past (e.g., "Have you ever intentionally hurt someone?"). For the innocent, their (presumed) lie to the control question is expected to elicit a stronger response than their truthful denial to the relevant question. For the guilty, the relevant question taps a more serious lie, so it should overshadow the response to the control question. Although the inclusion of the control question appears to add an improvement over the RIT, the accusation in the relevant question is not balanced by a similarly consequential charge in the control question. This again biases the test against innocent people who, even though honest, may be unduly aroused by the threatening relevant question. Also undermining confidence in the CQT is the possibility that guilty people can beat the test by augmenting their response to control questions, something that can be accomplished by lightly biting the tongue or thinking stressful thoughts when asked control questions. Thus it is not surprising that 40% or more of innocent people undergoing real-life CQTs produce false positive results, or that over half of the guilty who augment their responses to control questions pass their tests with their successful use of countermeasures going undetected (Iacono, 2008a).

The most commonly used polygraph tests are administered by law enforcement and security agencies to job applicants and employees whose untrustworthiness could compromise their value as an employee. These screening tests typically resemble an RIT, but with many relevant questions covering a broad array of possible misbehaviors (e.g., use of drugs, breeching security regulations, stealing from employer). Any relevant questions that elicit relatively stronger reactions than others are likely to serve as a basis for interrogation, and, if the employee cannot satisfactorily address concerns raised in the interrogation, the test is failed. Poorly studied and with no known validity, employee screening tests have been harshly condemned by scientists scrutinizing their use (National Research Council, 2003).

Given that polygraph tests have questionable validity, why does their use persist? Polygraph tests are administered by skilled examiners who use the test occasion and the physiological data as leverage to extract admissions and confessions from untruthful people. Often this information could not be obtained using alternative investigative methods. This fact speaks to the utility of polygraph testing (Iacono, 2008a), and there is considerable anecdotal evidence to support its utility in solving crimes and identifying risky employees.

Although lie detection has a shaky foundation, there is a memory-based detection method that has a strong scientific rationale, the guilty knowledge test (GKT). With this technique, multiple-choice questions are formulated about the crime, with the correct answer to each question reflecting knowledge that only the criminal and the police have. Physiological responses are monitored to each of the alternative answers. For the innocent, who do not know the correct answer, only chance determines their responding more to one alternative than another. But the correct alternative will be known by the guilty, and this recognized memory causes the response to the guilty alternative to be enhanced relative to the other alternatives. With a multi-item GKT, the probability of guilt increases as a function of the number of items failed. There is considerable evidence backing the validity of the GKT (Ben-Shakhar & Elaad, 2003), but its routine use is not endorsed by law enforcement, because it is more difficult to construct than a CQT, and it is always possible that a guilty person could pass a GKT due to the test inadequately tapping guilty knowledge.

Although polygraph techniques have relied on autonomic nervous system measures since their inception, advances in brain recording technology have led investigators to develop methods of monitoring brain electrical activity or cerebral blood flow using functional magnetic resonance imaging technology. Although these methods have shown some promise, it is not yet evident that they offer an advantage over autonomic measures. In addition, studies using brain-based measures examine their effectiveness using variations of conventional testing procedures like the CQT or GKT; the limitations of these tests are not overcome simply by recording a different type of physiological signal (Iacono, 2007).

To conclude, despite the development of modern polygraphic interrogation methods like the CQT and RIT over a half-century ago, there is no generally accepted and valid method for detecting lying. The fact that these methods are in common use provides testimony to their utility as investigative tools, not their accuracy. Because the theoretical foundation for these techniques is weak, they are unlikely to be substantially improved. Memory based methods like the GKT, however, because they have a strong scientific basis, are likely to benefit from further development and evaluation (Iacono, 2008b).

REFERENCES

Ben-Shakhar, G., & Elaad, E. (2003). The validity of psychophysiological detection of information with the Guilty Knowledge Test: A meta-analytic review. *Journal of Applied Psychology*, *88*(1), 131–151.

Iacono, W. G. (2007). Detection of deception. In J. Cacioppo, L. Tassinary, & G. Berntson (Eds.), *Handbook of psychophysiology* (3rd ed., pp. 688–703). New York: Cambridge University Press.

Iacono, W. G. (2008a). Effective policing: Understanding how polygraph tests work and are used. *Criminal Justice & Behavior*, *35*, 1295–1308.

Iacono, W. G. (2008b). The forensic application of "brain fingerprinting": Why scientists should encourage the use of P300 memory detection methods. *American Journal of Bioethics*, *8*(1), 30–32; discussion W31– 34.

National Research Council. (2003). *The polygraph and lie detection*. Washington, DC: National Academies Press.

SUGGESTED READINGS

Honts, C. R., Raskin, D. C., & Kircher, J. C. (2006). The case for polygraph tests. In D. L. Faigman, D. H. Kaye, M. J. Saks, J. Sanders, & E. K. Cheng (Eds.), *Modern scientific evidence: The law and science of expert testimony, Vol. 4. Forensics* (pp. 787–831). Eagan, MN: Thomson West.

Iacono, W. G., & Lykken, D. T. (2006). The case against polygraph tests. In D. L. Faigman, D. H. Kaye, M. J. Saks, J. Sanders, & E. K. Cheng (Eds.), *Modern scientific evidence: The law and science of expert testimony, Vol. 4. Forensics* (pp. 831–895). Eagan, MN: Thomson West.

National Research Council. (2003). *The polygraph and lie detection*. Washington, DC: National Academies Press.

WILLIAM G. IACONO
University of Minnesota

See also: **Deception**

LIFESPAN DEPRESSION

In the United States, the word "depression" refers to everything from a transient mood state (feeling down) to the clinically diagnosed disorder known as Major Depressive Disorder (MDD). In order to receive a diagnosis of MDD, a person must experience marked psychological distress as well as a decrease in cognitive and behavioral functioning. In addition, the two weeks prior to diagnosis the patient's life must be characterized by an almost daily occurrence of a dysphoric mood (i.e., sadness) and/or a loss of interest or pleasure in almost all activities (anhedonia). The individual must also experience at least four of the following seven symptoms nearly every day for at least a two-week period: (1) significant weight change or change in appetite; (2) insomnia or hypersomnia; (3) psychomotor agitation or retardation; (4) fatigue or loss of energy; (5) feelings of worthlessness or of excessive or inappropriate guilt; (6) decreased concentration or indecisiveness; and (7) suicidal ideation, plan or attempt (see American Psychiatric Association, 2000). Only three of the above additional symptoms are needed for a diagnosis if dysphoric mood and anhedonia are both present. Other mood disorders related to MDD include Dysthymic Disorder, Bipolar (Manic-Depressive) Disorder, and Cyclothymic Disorder.

Prevalence Rates

MDD is one of the most commonly diagnosed psychiatric disorders among adults, with lifetime prevalence rates of 20–25% for women and 9–12% for men, yielding an overall lifetime prevalence rate of 17–18% of the population (Kessler, Chiu, Demier, & Walters, 2005). At any given time, the prevalence rates are about 6% for women and 3% for men.

MDD is fairly rare among young children (about 1–2%), and there are no gender differences in rates of MDD in the early years. Clinical depression begins to become more frequently manifest beginning at puberty, with clear increases in the disorder by age 15, and this is the time when the previously noted gender differences begin to emerge. The criteria used to diagnose MDD among children and adolescents are the same as those used to diagnose adult depression; however, differential diagnosis is more often a difficult in children and adolescents than in adults because of the presence of co-morbid externalizing problems. Some authorities attribute this difficulty to indications that about 25–30% of persons with bipolar disorder experience their first mood disturbances as a depression rather than as mania or hypomania, even though that some of these symptoms may be evident when bipolar young people present first with a major depression disorder. Furthermore, depressed children and adolescents often have a substantial number of interpersonal and academic problems, and it is not uncommon for depressed youth to present at least initially with these kinds of problems rather than a sad or depressed mood.

In recent years, depression has been diagnosed with increased frequency among young people aged 16 to 25, with approximately 18% of people currently in this age group having already suffered from an episode of major depression. Although depression-related suicide is very low among children, suicide is the tenth leading cause of death among young people aged 10–14 and the second leading second cause among those aged 15–19, exceeded only by road and traffic accidents (WHO/UNICEF, 2008). After late adolescence, the prevalence rate and gender differences in depression remain fairly constant over the human life span; after age 65, however, the prevalence rates for first episodes are equal for men and women. Along with familial environmental and genetic factors that contribute to susceptibility to depressive disorder, events such as breaking up a strong romantic relationship, moving to a new location, and physical injury are other major causes for the development of a depressive episode. A depressive episode can also bring many associated problems with it, such as increased substance abuse and eating disorders, and it frequently increases the risk for long-term use of tobacco products. Finally of note with respect to young people, individuals who suffer from MDD during adolescence are likely to suffer from recurrent episodes of depression as adults; adolescent depression is not a transient difficulty, but is instead a disorder that continues, even if episodically, over the lifespan.

Among adults, depression is generally viewed as an episodic disorder, but recent research suggests that for many individuals it can become a chronic condition. Among adults who have had one episode of depressions, the probability of a second episode is 50%; among those who have had two episodes, the probability of a third episode is 75–80%. After a third episode, the disorder is likely to plague individuals chronically, even though their depressive episodes may abate without treatment (APA, 2000; also see Eaton et al., 2008). The episodes are painful for individuals with the disorder and for those around them. As previously noted, the disorder can interfere with a person's level of functioning in both social and work situations. The costs of this interference, to both the individual and to society, are enormous. MDD is among the top five most costly health problems in the United States, and it is a leading source of disability (Murray & Lopez, 1997).

Depression is likely to be particularly problematic and also difficult to treat in the elderly. Although the rate of new episodes decreases after age 65, many older people suffer from recurrences of previous depressions, which as already mentioned tend to become a chronic disorder. As people get older, MDD may be complicated by other health problems or cognitive deterioration associated with the aging process, especially the onset of other diseases. The best available epidemiological study of depression among the elderly is the Epidemiological Catchment Area study (ECA) reported by Robins and Regier (1991). (The elderly were not included in a more recent epidemiological survey, the National Comorbidity Study, reported by Kessler, Chiu, Demier, and Walter in 2005). The rate of first onset of MDD among the elderly is estimated to be one-third to one-half of that of younger age group cohorts, but the rate is nearly 20 times higher among elderly persons who are medically ill (Koenig, George, Peterson, & Pieper, 1997). Part of this increased rate is due to the difficulty of separating MDD from the commonly comorbid problems of delirium and dementia in the elderly. The lower rates of first onset of MDD among the elderly may also be affected by the following difficulties: memory problems; misclassifications such as dementia; possible cohort effects, with elderly cohorts simply having had lower rates of MDD than younger cohorts; and greater early mortality due to suicide and alcohol abuse related to MDD (see McDonald & Hermida, in press).

Treatments

There are two major approaches to the treatment of MDD: psychopharmacological interventions and psychotherapies. Additionally of note in attempting to alleviate severe and otherwise treatment resistant depression are electroconvulsive therapy (ECT) and transcranial magnetic stimulation (TMS). These therapies can now be conducted on an outpatient basis and tend to work very well, although the relapse rate following treatment is fairly high. Both therapies can have side effects such as memory loss (at least temporarily), and there are also risks associated with anesthesia used with ECT. A surgical procedure called Deep Brain Stimulation (DBS) is also currently being studied as a treatment for severe, recurrent, and treatment-resistant MDD. In DBS, electrodes are implanted into a very specific region of the brain (Broadman's area 25; the subgenual cingulate) to allow for chronic stimulation. Chronic stimulation of this brain region is believed to be the active mechanism in the alleviation of the symptoms of MDD. The DBS success rate for appropriate individuals has been surprisingly good, although the treatment samples to data have been rather small (see Mayberg et al., 2005).

Some clinical research projects have suggested that behavioral marital therapy is an effective treatment for MDD when the depressed individual is a partner in an unhappy marriage. It has been found that 50% of depressed married individuals are in unhappy marriages and that 50% of individuals in unhappy marriages are depressed. Hence behavioral marital therapy may be useful for many married patients suffering from MDD (see Craighead, Hart, Craighead, & Illardi, 2002).

A recent large-scale clinical trial showed that the combination of cognitive behavior therapy (CBT) and an SSRI (fluoxetine; Prozac) was the safest and most effective treatment for depressed adolescents (TADS Team, 2007). This was an important study because of its size and because of recent concerns about the safety of SSRIs when used in treating adolescents.

Treatments for MDD among the elderly are similar to those for younger individuals and most often begin with the SSRI antidepressants. Some studies have found that CBT, interpersonal therapy (IPT), and exercise may be effective interventions for a substantial proportion of the depressed elderly. Because of treatment resistance and complications from the use of antidepressant medications, ECT is used more among the elderly than with younger people in treating MDD. As just mentioned, ECT, especially when administered bilaterally, may cause memory difficulties. However, these difficulties are generally limited to memory for events occurring at or near the time of receiving ECT, and they typically clear up within about 6 months following the treatment. There does not appear to be any brain damage associated with modern ECT methods as currently used with severely depressed and treatment resistant patients (see McDonald & Hermida, in press).

Prevention

Due to the increased rate of MDD as young people enter the 16–25 age range, it is becomes increasingly important at this time to prevent the first episode of depression from occurring and to prevent its recurrence should it arise. Prevention programs targeting individuals experiencing some symptoms of MDD or demonstrating pessimistic cognitive styles have shown some promise. Small studies have also begun to suggest that the combined use of CBT and IPT for individuals who have had a prior episode of MDD, but are not currently depressed, may help decrease the recurrence of MDD.

REFERENCES

American Psychiatric Association (2000). *Diagnostic and statistical manual of mental disorders* (4th ed., text rev.). Washington, DC: Author.

Craighead, W. E., Hart, A. B., Craighead, L. W., & Ilardi, S. S. (2002). Psychosocial treatments for major depressive disorder. In P. E. Nathan & J. M. Gorman (Eds.), *A guide to treatments that work* (2nd ed., pp. 245–261). New York: Oxford University Press.

Eaton, W. W., Shao, H., Nestadt, G., Lee, B. H., Bienvenu, J., & Zandi, P. Population-based study of first onset and chronicity in major depressive disorder. *Archives of General Psychiatry, 65,* 513–520.

Kessler, R. C., Chiu, W. T., Demier, O., & Walters, E. (2005). Prevalence, severity, and comorbidity of 12-month DSM-IV disorders in the National Comobidity Survey replication. *Archives of General Psychiatry, 62,* 617–627.

Koenig, H. G., George, L. K., Peterson, B. L., & Pieper, C. F. (1997). Depression in medically ill hospitalized older adults: Prevalence, characteristics, and course of symptoms according to six diagnostic schemes. *American Journal of Psychiatry, 154,* 1376–1383.

Mayberg H., Lozano A., Voon V., McNeely H., Seminowicz D., Hamani C., Schwalb, J., & Kennedy S. (2005). Deep brain stimulation for treatment-resistant depression. *Neuron, 45,* 651–660.

McDonald, W. M., Hermida, A. P. (In press). Geriatric psychiatry. In K. R. R. Krishnan (Ed.). *Psychiatric disorders: Diagnoses and treatment.* Washington, American Psychiatric Press.

Murray, J. L., & Lopez, A. D. (1997). Global mortality, disability, and the contribution of risk factors: Global Burden of Disease Study. *Lancet, 349,* 1436–1442.

Robins, L. N., & Regier, D. A. (1991). *Psychiatric disorders in America: The Epidemiological Catchment Area Study.* New York: The Free Press.

Tads Team. (2007). The Treatment for Adolescents with Depression Study (TADS): Long-term effectiveness and safety outcomes. *Archives of General Psychiatry, 64,* 1132–1143.

World Health Organization and UNICEF. (December 9, 2008). *World Report on Child Injury Prevention.* Report available from World Health Organization, http://whqlibdoc.who.int/publications/2008/9789241563574_eng.pdf.

SUGGESTED READINGS

Beck, A.T. (1975). *Cognitive therapy and the emotional disorders.* Madison, CT: International Universities Press.

Beck, A. T., Freeman, A., and Davis, D. D. (2003). *Cognitive therapy of personality disorders.* New York: Guilford Press.

Weissman, M. M,, Markowitz, J. C., & Klerman, G. L. (2007). *Clinician's quick guide to interpersonal psychotherapy.* New York: Oxford University Press.

MARGARET C. CRAIGHEAD
Emory University School of Medicine

BENJAMIN H. CRAIGHEAD
Salisbury Pediatrics, Salisbury, NC

W. EDWARD CRAIGHEAD
Emory University School of Medicine

See also: Adolescent Depression; Antidepressant Medications; Depression; Electroconvulsive Therapy; Postpartum Depression

LIKERT SCALES

On a scale of 1 to 5, is this encyclopaedia very useful? Surveys containing questions like this one play a pivotal role in conducting research and making decisions. Likert scales are important to a broad range of disciplines and are used to assess everything from the taste of wine to the efficacy of new anaesthetic techniques. Typically, Likert scales contain five levels of response, ranging from (1) strongly agree, (2) agree, (3) neither agree nor disagree, (4) disagree and (5) strongly disagree. The number of response categories within a question can vary from 5 and 10, apparently with little effect on the construct validity of the question (Dawes, 2008). Sometimes a visual analogue scale is used on which respondents are free to place a mark anywhere along a line between the response extremes.

Although Likert scales provide a useful tool for evaluating opinion and experience, they do suffer from a number of response biases. First, there can be a tendency for participants to respond towards the middle of the scale (central tendency bias). This can be avoided by using a scale with an even number of response items, thus avoiding a central item indicating no decision. Second, there can be social desirability biases, wherein participants respond toward items that are perceived to be positive. The effect of biases like this can be avoided by including questions with a reversed meaning. For example, instead of always asking questions such as "The course suited my academic needs," the question can be reversed to read, "The course did not suit my academic needs." A questionnaire containing roughly equal numbers of positively and negatively oriented questions is ideal. Finally, Likert scales are subject to left and right biases. Nicholls, Orr, Okaho, and Loftus (2006) gave a student satisfaction scale to a large number of students. Half of the questionnaires contained the positive items on the left (e.g., Very satisfied ... Very unsatisfied) while the other half had the reverse order (e.g., Very unsatisfied ... Very satisfied). They found that the students biased their responses toward the categories on the left. Therefore, Likert scales with positive items on the left will receive higher scores compared to scales with positive items on the right. The leftward bias was attributed to an asymmetry in spatial attention, know as pseudoneglect, which makes stimuli on the left appear more salient than those on the right (Jewell & McCourt, 2000). The best way to avoid left/right biases is to give half of the respondents questionnaires with Likert scales arranged left-to-right and the other half with scales arranged right-to-left. By taking an average of the two surveys, an accurate indication of opinion can be obtained. If researchers want to paint a rosy picture, however, they should place the favourable categories on the left.

REFERENCES

Dawes, J. (2008). Do data characteristics change according to the number of scale points used? An experiment using 5-point, 7-point and 10-point scales. *International Journal of Market Research, 50,* 61–77.

Nicholls, M. E. R., Orr, C. A., Okubo, M., & Loftus, A. (2006). Satisfaction guaranteed: The effect of spatial biases on responses to Likert scales. *Psychological Science, 17,* 1027–1028.

Jewell, G., & McCourt, M. E. (2000). Pseudoneglect: A review and meta-analysis of performance factors in line bisection tasks. *Neuropsychologia, 38,* 93–110.

SUGGESTED READINGS

McIver, J. P. & Carmines, E. G. (1981). *Unidimensional scaling.* Beverly Hills, CA: Sage.

Spector, P. E. (1992). *Summated rating scale construction.* Newbury Park, CA: Sage.

MICHAEL E. R. NICHOLLS
University of Melbourne, Australia

See also: **Thurstone Scaling**

LIMBIC SYSTEM

Broca described the "great limbic lobe" of the brain as a large cerebral convolution that lies medially and envelops the brain stem and is common to all mammals (Broca, 1878). The limbic lobe was thought to be important in olfaction due to its dense connections with the olfactory cortex and was often referred to as the *rhinencephalon* (smell brain). Papez, in 1937, proposed that the rhinencephalon was also important in emotional behavior. In 1952, MacLean coined the term *limbic system* to refer to both a medial part of the cortex that enveloped the brain stem and to subcortical structures that were tightly associated with this region. He based this group not only on its anatomic location but also on evidence that this region was well developed only in mammals, was phylogenetically older than the more peripheral neocortex, and appeared to be important in emotional and social behavior (1990). The limbic, or paleomammalian, system of the brain is shown in Figure 1 in relation to higher cortical (or neomammalian) and deep brain (or reptilian) structures. MacLean's subdivisions of the limbic system (1990) include the amygdala, septal, and thalamocingulate divisions shown in Figure 2. Extensive preclinical and clinical observations have suggested that the limbic system is critical in learning, memory, emotions, social behaviors, and autonomic responses. This article will briefly review the definition and anatomy of the limbic system, describe the three limbic subdivisions, and discuss evidence for and against the limbic system construct.

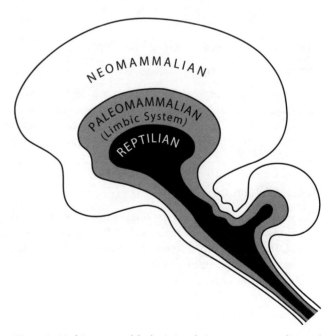

Figure 1. Limbic system of the brain in relation to neomammalian and reptilian structures.

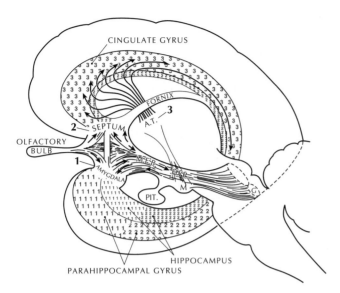

Figure 2. Maclean's subdivisions of the limbic system.

Definition and Anatomy

Although there is no clear consensus, the following regions are generally considered part of the limbic system: The cortical structures include the cingulated gyrus, the subcallosal gyrus, the hippocampus, and the olfactory cortex. Subcortical regions include the amygdala, the septum, the pellucidum, the epithalamus (habenula), the anterior thalamic nuclei, the hypothalamus, and parts of the basal ganglia. In addition, several closely linked cortical structures that appear important in emotional behavior are also considered part of this circuit and are often referred to as paralimbic. These regions include the anterior temporal polar cortex, the medial-posterior orbitofrontal cortex, and the insular cortex (Mesulam & Mufson, 1982).

MacLean's Proposed Limbic Subdivisions

Amygdalar Division

MacLean (1990) emphasizes that this region is involved in self-preservation behaviors such as those required in the search for food, including fighting and self-defense. Stimulation of this area in humans may produce fear and anxiety.

Septal Division

The septal region may subserve behaviors related to sexual function and procreation. MacLean (1990) emphasizes that septal stimulation in humans can produce pleasurable sensations and in animals can elicit social grooming as well as genital tumescence.

Thalamocingulate Division

This region represents the phylogenetically newest subdivision of the limbic system. It is present in mammals but

not in reptiles. Several typical mammalian social behaviors are associated with this area, including extensive mother-infant bonding, infant crying, and play. Lesions of this region in nonhuman mammals often produce social apathy; even mothers will neglect their young (MacLean, 1990). In addition to these social functions, the cingulated, particularly its anterior extent, is believed to be important in selective attention and pain (MacLean, 1990).

Evidence For and Against the Limbic System Construct

Extensive research suggests that limbic structures are important in emotional behavior. What is uncertain is the extent to which limbic regions and associated brain structures alone are critical in emotional regulation and whether the limbic system functions as a unified network. Much of the clinical evidence for the unified network concept has come from studies of psychomotor seizures (Jasper, 1964), although recent functional imaging studies in humans also support the notion of a limbic system concept (George et al., 1995). Critics of the limbic system construct (Kotter & Meyer, 1992; LeDoux, 1996) point out that no two authorities can agree on which structures should be included in the limbic system. Also, limbic structures are connected with virtually all areas of the brain, so critics argue that one should then consider the whole brain the limbic system. Moreover, if the limbic system is defined functionally as that part of the brain involved in emotion, evidence suggests that the neocortex may be important in the regulation and recognition of emotions and that limbic regions such as the hippocampus and cingulated are important in functions other than emotion, such as memory, cognition, and selective attention.

Extensive preclinical and clinical observations have suggested that the limbic system structures are critical in emotional behavior. Limbic structures have also been found to be important in social behavior, cognition, and autonomic responses. The limbic system, however, has extensive direct interconnections with all brain regions, and the extent to which the limbic system functions as a network itself remains to be determined. Perhaps the limbic system concept will lose its heuristic appeal as we improve our definitions of emotional states and the roles of discrete structures and small circuits important in motivation (Kalivas, Churchill, & Romanides, 1999), fear (LeDoux, 1996), and other emotional behaviors. Alternatively, as some imaging studies suggest, we may actually confirm that emotional behaviors do not arise from the activity of single brain regions, but instead emerge from the coordinated action of many connected structures. New techniques in functional imaging and noninvasive regional brain stimulation will allow for direct testing of the limbic system construct in normal function and in psychiatric and medical disorders. Broca's limbic lobe, initially thought to be important by some only in olfaction, is certainly no longer ignored.

REFERENCES

Broca, P. (1878). Anatomie comparee des circonvolutions cerebrales, Le grand lobe limbique et la scissure limbique ans la serie des mammiferes (Comparative anatomy of the cerebral cortex: The limbic lobe and connections in mammalian species). *Review of Anthropology, 1*(2), 456–498.

George, M. S., Ketter, T. A., Praekh, P. I., Horwitz, B., Herscovitch, P., & Post, R. M. (1995). Brain activity during transient sadness and happiness in healthy women. *American Journal of Psychiatry, 152*(3), 341–351.

Jasper, J. J. (1964). Some physiological mechanisms involved in epileptic automatisms. *Epilepsia, 5,* 1–20.

Kalivas, P. W., Churchill, L., & Romanides, A. (1999). Involvement of the pallidal-thalamocortical circuit in adaptive behavior. *Annals of the New York Academy of Sciences, 29*(877), 64–70.

Kotter, R., & Meyer, N. (1992). The limbic system: A review of its empirical foundation. *Behavioral Brain Research, 52,* 105–127.

LeDoux, J. (1996). *The emotional brain.* New York: Simon & Schuster.

MacLean, P. D. (1952). Some psychiatric implications of physiological studies on frontotemporal portion of limbic system (visceral brain). *Electroencephalographic Clinical Neurophysiology, 4,* 407–418.

MacLean, P. D. (1990). *The triune brain in evolution: Role in paleocerebral functions.* New York: Plenum Press.

Mesulam, M. M., & Mufson, E. J. (1982). Insula of the old world monkey: I. Architectonics in the insula-orbito-temporal component of the paralimbic brain. *Journal of Comparative Neurology, 212,* 1–122.

Papez, J. W. (1937). A proposed mechanism of emotion. *Archives of Neurological Psychiatry, 38,* 722–743.

Mark B. Hamner
Jeffrey P. Lorberbaum
Mark S. George
Medical University of South Carolina

See also: Amygdala; Brain; Hippocampus

LINEAR REGRESSION

Linear regression characterizes the relationship of a set of independent variables or *predictors* $X_1, X_2, \ldots X_p$ to a single dependent variable or *criterion Y*. The goals of linear regression are (1) to characterize the overall strength of the relationship of the set of predictors to the criterion and (2) to identify those individual predictors or subsets of predictors that contribute to this overall relationship. Through a multiple regression analysis, all the predictors are combined into a composite *predicted score* $\hat{Y}$ ("Y hat") that has the highest possible linear correlation with the observed criterion Y. The square of this correlation, termed the *squared multiple correlation* $R^2_{Y\hat{Y}}$, is the overall effect size measure for a regression analysis and measures the proportion of variation in the criterion accounted for by the set of predictors. In general, regression analysis, of which linear regression analysis is one example, can be used for (1) description (i.e., to summarize the relationship of predictors to the criterion); (2) prediction (i.e., to make judgments about the future based on the predicted score of an individual); or (3) theory testing (i.e., to examine whether relationships predicted by theory are, in fact, supported).

In regression analysis, a multiple linear regression equation (Equation 1) expresses the predicted score $\hat{Y}$ as a function of a linear combination of the predictors; the weights to form the linear combination are *partial regression coefficients* $b_1, b_2, \ldots b_p$.

$$\hat{Y} = b_1X_1 + b_2X_2 + \ldots + b_pX_p + b_0. \qquad (1)$$

The *regression intercept* b_0 serves to equate the arithmetic means of the predicted and observed criterion scores.

Each partial regression coefficient represents the unique contribution of a predictor to prediction over and above all other predictors in the regression equation; the coefficient indicates the amount of change in the criterion Y associated with a one-unit increase in the predictor, when all other predictors are held constant or partialed out.

Predictors in linear regression analysis may be continuous or categorical. Categorical predictors are entered into regression analysis with special code variables. For example, gender might be represented by *dummy codes* (1 = female, 0 = male), *contrast codes* (.5 = female, −.5 = male), or *unweighted effect codes* (1 = female; −1 = male).

The criterion in linear regression analysis is continuous. Other forms of regression analysis treat a variety of outcome variables, among them, a binary criterion (probit regression, logistic regression), an ordinal criterion (ordinal logistic regression), and a count of events in a particular time period (Poisson regression). In samples in which there is inherent structure that produces clustering of cases (e.g., children drawn from the same family), *random coefficient regression* and *multilevel modeling* are appropriate.

Linear regression is highly flexible. It can be used to assess the extent to which a single predictor or set of predictors contributes to prediction over and above a set of control variables or covariates. Assume that a predictor X_4 is a critical theoretical predictor; $X_1, X_2,$ and $X_3,$ are covariates that should be controlled. In an analysis strategy termed *hierarchical regression*, predictors $X_1, X_2,$ and X_3 are entered into a regression equation, yielding a squared multiple correlation, $R^2_{Y.123}$. Then a second regression equation adds X_4 to predictors $X_1, X_2,$ and $X_3,$ yielding squared multiple correlation $R^2_{Y.1234}$. The *squared semipartial correlation,* $R^2_{Y.4(123)} = R^2_{Y.1234} - R^2_{Y.123}$, the difference

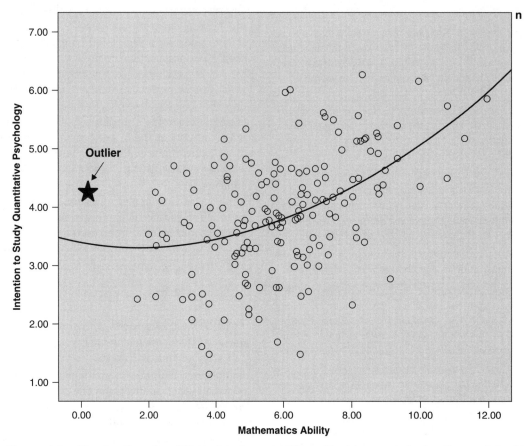

Figure 1. Curvilinear relationship of mathematics ability to intention; when the outlier is removed, the curvilinear relationship is no longer significant.

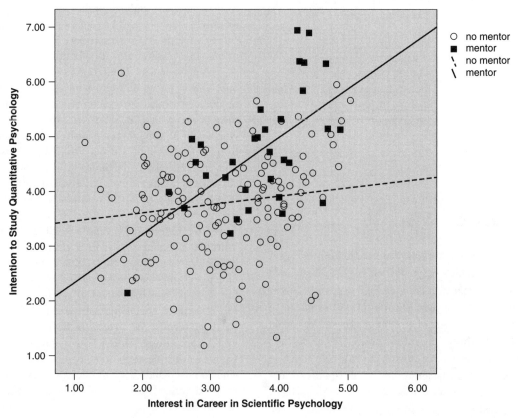

Figure 2. Interaction between interest and having a quantitative mentor in predicting intention to study quantitative psychology. $R^2 = .02$ (no mentor); $R^2 = .36$ (mentor).

Table 1. Regression analysis predicting intention to study quantitative psychology from mathematics ability (ability), squared mathematics ability (abilitysq), interest in a scientific psychology career (interest), presence of a quantitative mentor (mentor), and the interaction between interest and mentor (interest × mentor); simulated data.

Predictor	Unstandardized partial regression coefficient	Standard error of regression coefficient	95% Confidence interval on confidence interval	
			Lower limit	Upper limit
ability	.22**	.03	.15	.28
abilitysq	.03**	.01	.01	.05
interest	.34**	.08	.19	.49
mentor[a]	.44*	.18	.08	.79
Interest x mentor	.75**	.21	.34	1.18
Intercept	3.79**	.08	3.63	3.94

**$p < .01$, *$p < .05$ for test of significance of coefficient.
Note: Higher scores on all variables are associated with greater level on the variable, higher ability, greater interest, having a quantitative mentor. For appropriate estimation of coefficients for the curvilinear and interactive effects, the ability, interest, and mentor predictors are centered (put in deviation form) following Aiken and West (1991).

between two squared multiple correlations, measures the proportion of variation in the criterion accounted for by predictor X_4, above and beyond X_1, X_2, and X_3. A closely related measure, *the squared partial correlation, $R^2_{Y4.123} = [R^2_{Y.1234} - R^2_{Y.123}]/[1 - R^2_{Y.123}]$*, measures the proportion of residual variation in the criterion not accounted for by X_1, X_2, and X_3, that is accounted for by X_4. The target set of variables (here only X_4) may contain multiple predictors; this strategy can be extended to more than two sets of variables.

Linear regression analysis can characterize curvilinear and interactive relationships of predictors to a criterion. The strategy employed is to create a new predictor that is a nonlinear function of the original predictors; the new predictor bears a linear relationship to the criterion. The curvilinear relationship of a predictor X_1 to Y is specified in a *polynomial regression equation*. Equation 2 expresses a quadratic relationship of X_1 to Y, where the new predictor X_1^2, the square of predictor X_1, carries the curvilinear relationship:

$$\hat{Y} = b_1X_1 + b_2X_1^2 + b_0. \qquad (2)$$

The interaction between two continuous predictors X_1 and X_2, or between a continuous and a categorical predictor, is specified by creating the new predictor X_1X_2, the product of the two predictors. In Equation 3 predictor X_1X_2 carries the interaction:

$$\hat{Y} = b_1X_1 + b_2X_2 + b_3X_1X_2 + b_0 \qquad (3)$$

Inspection of Equations 1–3 reveals the nature of linear regression, that the equations are "linear in the coefficients" (i.e., the predictors are simply multiplied by the regression coefficients, making the predicted score a simple linear combination of the predictors).

Individual cases can have a strong impact on the outcome of regression analysis; one case has the potential to change a regression coefficient dramatically (e.g., to produce a significant regression coefficient that disappears if the case is removed). *Regression diagnostics* are *case statistics*, measures calculated for each individual case. Two classes of diagnostic measures, *leverage* and *distance*, characterize the extremity of a case on the predictors and on the criterion, respectively. *Influence* measures the extent to which a case actually changes individual regression coefficients or predicted scores. Examination of regression outcomes with regression diagnostics is critical for valid inference.

A simulated example illustrates concepts presented here. Among 170 undergraduate psychology majors, intention to study quantitative psychology is predicted from mathematics ability, squared mathematics ability (to test for a quadratic relationship), interest in a scientific psychology career, the presence (versus absence) of a mentor who specializes in quantitative psychology, and the interaction between interest and presence of a quantitative mentor. Table 1 provides results. Mathematics ability has a curvilinear relationship to intention (see Figure 1 and the significant regression coefficient for "abilitysq" in Table 1). Intention is positively related to both interest and to the presence of a quantitative mentor. The interaction is also significant: The presence of a mentor greatly enhances the relationship between a general interest in scientific psychology and the intention to become a quantitative psychologist (see Figure 2). The squared semipartial correlation of this interaction with the criterion = .045; an apparently small interaction has a notable effect. Regression diagnostics identifies an outlier that is producing the curvilinear effect of ability to intention (see the star in Figure 1); when this outlier is removed, only the linear relationship remains.

In sum, linear regression analysis provides a broad and flexible approach to understanding the relationships of multiple independent variables to a single outcome.

REFERENCES

Aiken, L. S., & West, S. G. (1991). *Multiple regression: Testing and interpreting interactions.* Newbury Park, CA: Sage.

Aiken, L. S., West, S. G., & Pitts, S. C. (2003). Multiple linear regression. In J. A. Schinka & W. F. Velicer (Eds.), *Research methods in psychology* (pp. 483–508). Vol. 2 in I. B. Weiner (Ed.-in-chief), *Handbook of psychology.* Hoboken, NJ: John Wiley & Sons.

Aiken, L. S, West, S. G., & Taylor, A. B. (2008). Correlation methods/regression Methods. In D. McKay (Ed.), *Handbook of research methods in abnormal and clinical psychology, Section II: Foundations of design and analysis.* Newbury Park, CA: Sage.

Cohen, J., Cohen, P., West, S., & Aiken, L. (2003). *Applied multiple regression/correlation analysis for the behavioral sciences* (3rd ed.). Hillsdale, NJ: Lawrence Erlbaum.

West, S. G., Aiken, L. S., & Krull, J. (1996). Experimental personality designs: Analyzing categorical by continuous variable interactions. *Journal of Personality, 64,* 1–47.

West, S. G., Aiken, L. S., Taylor, A. B., & Wu, W. (2007). Multiple regression: Application of the basics and beyond in personality research. In R. W. Robbins, R. C. Fraley, & R. Krueger (Eds.), *Handbook of research methods in personality psychology* (pp. 573–601). New York: Guilford Press.

LEONA S. AIKEN
STEFANY COXE
Arizona State University

See also: **Logistic Regression**

LINGUISTICS (See Psycholinguistics)

LOEVINGER, JANE (1918–2008)

Jane Loevinger was well known for her work in psychometrics, her theory of ego development, and her widely used assessment instrument, the Washington University Sentence Completion Test. Born February 6, 1918, in St. Paul, Minnesota, Loevinger was the third of five children of Gustavus and Millie (Strause) Loevinger. Her father was a German immigrant who became a district court judge. Her mother was a part-time schoolteacher and amateur pianist. Loevinger finished high school a semester early and enrolled at the University of Minnesota. She went to Jack Darley for vocational counseling and was told that psychology was "too mathematical" for her, whereupon she immediately enrolled in trigonometry and declared psychology as her major. Loevinger graduated magna cum laude in psychology at the age of 19, and a year later earned a Master of Science in psychometrics, also from the University of Minnesota (1939).

The American Psychological Association (APA) held its convention in Minneapolis in 1939, and Loevinger attended Edward Tolman's presidential address on the behavior of rats at choice points. His lively and engaging talk so impressed her that she enrolled in graduate school to study with him at Berkeley. Among her professors were Erik Erikson, Else Frenkel-Brunswik, and Nevitt Stanford, all of whom gave her an appreciation for psychoanalysis, and Jerzy Neyman, who strengthened her statistical skills. Her cohort of graduate students included Donald Campbell, Milton Rokeach, Richard Christie, and Daniel Levinson. She described the experience at Berkeley as being "born again" (Loevinger, 2002).

At Berkeley, Loevinger served as a research assistant for Erik Erikson, who was conducting his famous studies on gender differences in play configurations among young children. Her quantitative and psychometric skills were of little use to Erikson, so she moved into teaching positions in the Bay area, including Stanford and Berkeley. The radiation laboratory at Berkeley attracted a group of outstanding physical science students, and Loevinger came to know many of them. In 1943 she married Sam Weissman, a postdoctoral scientist working with Robert Oppenheimer. Later that year, Oppenheimer left Berkeley with his research team, including Sam Weissman, to establish the weapon design component of the Manhattan Project in Los Alamos, New Mexico.

Loevinger stayed at Berkeley to finish her dissertation, which was a critique of psychometric theory and test reliability. She paid to publish her dissertation in a vanity journal because no peer-reviewed journal at the time would accept her critique. This paper ("Object Tests as Instruments of Psychological Theory," 1957) has since become a citation classic and is widely used in graduate courses. Loevinger then joined her husband at Los Alamos, where their two children were born. Subsequently, her husband accepted a position in the chemistry department at Washington University in St. Louis.

In St. Louis, Loevinger did some part-time teaching for the psychology department at Washington University, plus she worked on various Air Force grants. She described this period as the "dark days" of her career, feeling the disadvantages of her gender in securing professional employment, as well as the social pressures to be a "good" wife and mother. She decided to abandon her unfulfilling part-time work to pursue her own research interests in women's experiences. Loevinger obtained funding from the National Institute of Mental Health to study problems facing mothers and women in general.

Loevinger went on to broaden her research interests into ego development and put forward an influential theory. Her theory proposes that individuals move through a series of nine sequential stages that reflect increasing cognitive complexity and moral maturity. Her use of the term "ego" differs from a Freudian conception, and it is more similar to the work of Erikson and Sullivan. An important aspect of Loevinger's theory is that different people may pass through the stages of ego development at different ages, and that few people ever complete all nine stages. For Loevinger, ego development was a lifelong process whereby people gain an increasingly differentiated perception of themselves, their social world, and the relationship between their own thoughts and feelings and those of others. What starts as the internalization of social rules into personal conscience results in the development of a frame of reference that the person uses to perceive and understand their social world. She held that this frame of reference is an individual construct that can be measured with semi-projective, yet quantitative, assessment devices.

In addition to her theory of ego development, Loevinger also constructed measures of individual differences in the stages of ego development. The most widely used of these is the 36-item Washington University Sentence Completion Test (WUSCT), which is a semi-structured projective instrument. The WUSCT provides respondents with the beginning stems of sentences, and the respondent then completes the sentences in a way that is meaningful to him or her. These responses are then interpreted as indicative of the person's beliefs, motivations, and morals, the basic components of ego development. More than 30 years of accumulated research establishes the construct validity of the test as well (Loevinger, 1998).

The psychology department at Washington University recognized Loevinger's achievements in 1961 when they appointed Loevinger as an associate professor in psychology. In 1973, she was promoted to full professor, and in 1985 she became the inaugural holder of the William R. Stuckenberg Professorship in Human Values and Moral Development. In 1988, Loevinger became Emeritus Professor, though she maintained a research group, continued to publish papers, and kept a hand in professional activities.

Jane Loevinger died unexpectedly on January 4, 2008, in St. Louis, Missouri.

SUGGESTED READINGS

Loevinger, J. (1957). Objective tests as instruments of psychological theory. *Psychological Reports, 3*, 635–694.

Loevinger, J. (1998). *Technical foundations for measuring ego development: The Washington University Sentence Completion Test*. Mahwah, NJ: Lawrence Erlbaum.

Loevinger, J. (2002). Confessions of an iconoclast: At home on the fringe. *Journal of Personality Assessment, 78*, 195–208.

RANDY J. LARSEN
Washington University

LOGICAL POSITIVISM

Logical positivism is an approach to philosophy of science that was developed in the 1920s and 1930s in Vienna and Berlin (for a review, see Suppe, 1974). These philosophers pursued a common goal: to rid philosophy of the excesses of metaphysical idealism by clarifying philosophical language. This project called for strict logical and empirical criteria for assigning meaning to terms and truth value to propositions. The logical criteria were those of deductive logic, and the empirical criteria were appropriated from a misreading of Wittgenstein. Members of the Vienna Circle mistook Wittgenstein's quite imprecise claims about "atomic facts" as implying that science contained a language of facts independent from theoretical assumptions. Bloor (1983) has provided a corrective reading of Wittgenstein.

These philosophers wanted to set philosophy straight by making it conform to deductive logic and the meaning criteria of naïve empiricist epistemology. In order to correct philosophy and set it on "the sure path of science," the positivist movement concluded that it was necessary to justify scientific practice philosophically. The primary concern of philosophy of science was the context of justification where one could show, via a reconstruction of history, that scientist's products (i.e., their theories) changed and developed in a pattern consistent with logical reasoning. From this perspective, science is the set of theoretical and empirical propositions devised by physicists, chemists, and biologists to describe and explain the world. Science differs from nonscience by adhering to both logical and empirical truth.

Overall, the logical positivists were not enthusiastic about psychology. Attempts to base the authority of deductive logic on "natural" habits of mind or psychological processes were rejected as psychologism. In order for the truths of logic and mathematics to command the high philosophical status of clear and certain truth (also transhistorical and universal), it was necessary that these truths be objectively true. By definition and consistent with the Platonic tradition, objective truth meant truth independent of subjective experience. Consequently, any attempt to base the truths of logic and mathematics on a study of cognitive contents and/or processes undermined their privileged status and authority.

Epistemologically speaking, the positivist program assumed that the relationship between human perception and the world was virtually uncomplicated, with "basic facts" being "given" in direct observation. Psychologically speaking, the scientist or at least the collective community of scientists was conceived as a perfect information-processing device capable of isomorphic inputs and outputs. Moreover, the claim was made that the language of science could neatly be bifurcated into distinct and nonoverlapping sets: (1) basic statements about the world or the language of direct observation (e.g., blue, hard, hot) and (2) theoretical terms (e.g., wavelength, density, kinetic energy) that, when introduced, had to be linked to observation terms via various explicit correspondence rules (i.e., operational definition).

The project of logical reconstruction consisted of demonstrating how new scientific knowledge was achieved through the accumulation of more extensive and accurate observations coupled with rigorous application of deductive logic. Scientific theories were reconstructed as if they were axiomatic systems like the postulates of pure geometry, their only difference being that they also had empirical content. In the later form, known as "logical empiricism," the historical picture that emerged was a reconstruction of scientific development in which both rationality (i.e., adherence to deductive logic) and progress (i.e., movement toward ever more comprehensive theories) were inevitable (Feigl, 1970; Hempel, 1965).

The logical positivists and logical empiricists accomplished their reconstruction of science by ignoring many of the particulars of what individual scientists might have done and said. Science, as described by logical positivists and logical empiricists, was an abstraction: a set of propositions often taken out of historical context and only loosely tied to people called scientists.

Whether scientists actually behaved in the manner described by this reconstruction was deemed irrelevant to the paramount task of establishing that science in the abstract somehow proceeded along logical lines and, therefore, made valid claims to "Truth." Thus, by focusing on an abstraction called "science," the project of logical reconstruction could be carried forward without entertaining the sort of evidence that might be provided by detailed sociological and psychological studies of scientists' actual practices. As subsequent work in the history of science has shown, it is a bitter irony that the philosophical movement that promised to rid philosophy of speculative idealism only reinstated a kind of idealism in the logical reconstruction of science without scientists.

Much of psychology itself was judged by the logical positivists to be defective and in need of the purification they offered (Bergmann, 1940; Carnap, 1932/1959). To complicate matters further, the positivist prescriptions for doing philosophy were widely taken as prescriptions for doing science. This was evident in the often tacit but nevertheless dogmatic application of major tenets of positivist philosophy by empirically oriented psychologists (for review, see Koch, 1959–1963), who apparently overlooked the antidogmatic stance of most members of the Vienna Circle. Smith's (1986) study of leading behaviorists in the 1930s and 1940s raises doubts about the direct connection between their views and those of logical positivists, but he also noted that by the 1950s logical empiricism was widely accepted as the standard account of science among psychologists in general. Although some of the logical positivists and logical empiricists advocated types of

behaviorism at times, Smith has shown that it is clearly incorrect to call Skinner a logical positivist.

Within professional psychology, arguments about whether a particular approach is scientific have typically been carried out along the values consistent with and derived from a logical positivist view of what separates science from so-called pseudo-science (Lilienfeld, Lyn, & Lohr, 2003). Whereas positivist ideals for what constitutes science have been largely debunked in science studies (Fuller, 1998), those ideals are very much in vogue among some professional psychologists who appeal to these ideals in American psychology's internal culture wars.

REFERENCES

Bergmann, G. (1940). On some methodological problems of psychology. *Philosophy of Science, 7,* 205–219.

Bloor, D. (1983). *Wittgenstein: A social theory of knowledge.* New York: Columbia University Press.

Carnap, R. (1959). Psychology in physical language. In A. J. Ayer (Ed.), *Logical positivism* (pp. 165–198). New York: Free Press. (Original work published in 1932).

Feigl, H. (1970). The "orthodox" view of theories. In M. Radner & S. Winokur (Eds.), *Minnesota Studies in Philosophy of Science IV* (pp. 3–16). Minneapolis: University of Minnesota Press.

Fuller, S. (1988). *Social epistemology.* Bloomington: Indiana University Press.

Hempel, C. G. (1965). *Aspects of scientific explanation.* New York: Free Press.

Koch, S. (Ed.). (1959–1963). *Psychology: A study of a science* (6 vols.). New York: McGraw-Hill.

Lilienfeld, S. O., Lynn, S. J., & Lohr, J. M. (2003). *Science and pseudoscience in clinical psychology.* New York: Guilford Press.

Smith, L. D. (1986). *Behaviorism and logical positivism: A reassessment of the alliance.* Stanford: Stanford University Press.

Suppe, F. (1974). The search for philosophic understanding of scientific theories. In F. Suppe (Ed.), *The structure of scientific theories* (pp. 3–235). Urbana: University of Illinois Press.

ARTHUR C. HOUTS
University of Memphis

See also: **Psychology and Philosophy**

LOGISTIC REGRESSION

In general, regression modeling is a foundational statistical procedure for studying the functional relationship between two or more variables. The most basic of all cases is the simple linear regression model in which the value of some dependent or outcome variable Y is expressed mathematically as a linear function of a single independent or predictor variable X. Given that values of Y are measured on a continuous scale (interval or ratio), the simple linear relationship between Y and X may be expressed by the following regression model

$$Y_i = \beta_0 + \beta_1 X_i + \varepsilon_i \qquad (1)$$

where Y_i is the observed value of Y for individual i ($i = 1, \ldots, n$), X_i is the observed value of the independent predictor variable for individual i (which may or may not be measured on a continuous scale), β_0 is an intercept term that is equivalent to the expected value of Y_i given that $X_i = 0$, β_1 is a regression weight equivalent to the expected change in Y_i per unit increase in X_i (also known as the slope of the regression equation), and $_i$ is a residual error term equivalent to the deviation of Y_i from its expected value given X_i, β_0, and β_1. It is assumed that the residuals ε_i are normally distributed (i.e., $\varepsilon_i \sim N(\mu, \sigma^2)$. The simple linear regression model in (1) may be expanded to include multiple independent predictor variables.

If Y is measured on a discrete or categorical scale (ordinal or nominal) rather than a continuous scale, then the linear regression model in (1) does not apply. Instead, logistic regression is the appropriate technique for modeling the functional relationship between Y and X. The simplest case of logistic regression arises when Y is measured on a dichotomous scale with binary values 0 and 1. Because Y can take on only two values, the outcome or dependent portion of the logistic regression model is not the observed value Y_i as in (1), but rather the probability that $Y_i = 1$. Specifically, let $\pi_i = P(Y_i = 1)$, which is the probability that the dependent variable $Y = 1$ for individual i. The simple logistic regression model of the functional association between Y and X may be expressed as

$$\pi_i = \frac{\exp(\beta_0 + \beta_1 X_i)}{1 + \exp(\beta_0 + \beta_1 X_i)} \qquad (2)$$

where $Y_i \sim$ Bernoulli(π_i). The logistic regression model in (2) is expressed in its exponential form and, as such, is a nonlinear model. The model may be re-expressed as a linear model, however, by means of a logarithmic transformation such that

$$\ln\left(\frac{\pi_i}{1 - \pi_i}\right) = \beta_0 + \beta_1 X_i \qquad (3)$$

In the model in (3), π_i is transformed via the logit link function, such that the dependent outcome is the natural logarithm of $\frac{\pi_i}{1-\pi_i}$, or the log-odds that $Y_i = 1$. The advantage of the logit expression in (3) over the corresponding exponential expression in (2) is that the portion of the model to the right of the equals sign is a linear model, the parameters of which may be estimated in closed form using conventional maximum likelihood methods. The disadvantage of (3) is that the maximum

likelihood estimates of β_0 and β_1 are expressed on a logit scale and are not directly interpretable as probabilities. The probabilities may be derived, however, simply by substituting the maximum likelihood estimates obtained from (3) into the exponential form of the model in (2).

In the logistic regression model in (3), the parameter β_0 is interpreted as the expected log-odds that $Y_i = 1$ given that $X_i = 0$. The parameter β_1 represents the expected change in the log-odds that $Y_i = 1$ per unit increase in X_i. Values of X_i may be measured on either a continuous or discrete scale. In contrast to the linear regression model in (1), the logistic regression models in (2) and (3) include no explicit error term. This is so because uncertainty in the prediction of Y_i according to the logistic model is already captured in the expression of the dependent outcome as a probability π_i rather than as a fixed value Y_i. Incorporating an error term in the logistic regression model would be a redundant expression of this uncertainty. This redundancy is evident in the formulation of the variance of π_i [$\sigma_i^2 = \pi_i(1 - \pi_i)$] which is a function of π_i itself.

To illustrate the logistic regression model, a fictitious data set was created composed of 500 individuals with observed values on two dichotomous variables X and Y, both of which may take the values 0 or 1. For each individual, a value of X was drawn from a binomial distribution with $n = 1$ and $p = .50$ (i.e., about 50% of the sample had values of $X = 0$ and 50% had values of $X = 1$). Values of Y were simulated to be conditional on X, such that $P(Y = 1 \mid X = 0) = .30$ and $P(Y = 1 \mid X = 1) = .50$. The logistic regression model in (3) was fit to the simulated data. The estimate of the intercept parameter in (3) was $\hat{\beta}_0 = -0.89[SE = 0.14, X^2(1) = 40.22, p < .0001]$. This result indicates that the expected log-odds that $Y = 1$ among individuals with values of $X = 0$ was -0.89. The parameter β_1 in (3) represents the expected difference in the log-odds that $Y = 1$ for individuals with values of $X = 1$ compared to those with $X = 0$. This estimate was $\hat{\beta}_1 = 0.99[SE = 0.19, X^2(1) = 27.69, p < .0001]$. This estimate indicates that the expected log-odds that $Y = 1$ among individuals with values of $X = 1$ is $-0.89 + 0.99 = .10$. The χ^2 test statistics associated with $\hat{\beta}_0$ and $\hat{\beta}_1$ were both statistically significant, suggesting that β_0 and β_1 are different from zero in the population.

The expected log-odds derived from the model in (3) may be translated into conditional probabilities by exponentiating the parameter estimates according to the model in (2). Specifically, the expected conditional probabilities that $Y = 1$ given that $X = 0$ and $X = 1$ may be computed as follows:

$$P(Y = 1 | X = 0) = \frac{\exp(-0.89)}{1 + \exp(-0.89)} = .29$$

and

$$P(Y = 1 | X = 1) = \frac{\exp(-0.89 + 0.99)}{1 + \exp(-0.89 + 0.99)} = .52.$$

Both of these expected conditional probabilities are very close to the corresponding simulated population values of .30 and .50, suggesting the logistic regression model effectively captured the true (i.e., simulated) association between X and Y in the population.

The logistic regression models in (2) and (3) may be expanded to include multiple independent predictor variables. Furthermore, these models may accommodate dependent outcome variables with more than two values. The list of suggested readings that follows provides details on these types of expansions and adaptations as well as other fundamental topics such as evaluating goodness-of-fit and comparisons between alternative models.

SUGGESTED READINGS

Agresti, A. (2002). *Categorical data analysis* (2nd ed.). Hoboken, NJ: John Wiley & Sons.

Hosmer, D. W., & Lemeshow, S. (2000). *Applied logistic regression* (2nd ed.). New York: John Wiley & Sons.

McCullagh, P., & Nelder, J. A. (1989). *Generalized linear models* (2nd ed.). Boca Raton, FL: Chapman & Hall/CRC.

Tabachnick, B. G., & Fidell, L. S. (2007). *Using multivariate statistics* (5th ed.). New York: Allyn & Bacon.

TIMOTHY J. OZECHOWSKI
Oregon Research Institute

See also: Linear Regression

LONELINESS

Loneliness is a feeling of distress that accompanies perceived deficiencies in social relationships. Loneliness often occurs in conjunction with social isolation, but a person can be socially isolated without feeling lonely and can feel lonely without being socially isolated. In contrast with social isolation, loneliness is more closely related to the perceived quality than quantity of social relationships. Historically, emotional loneliness, defined as deficiencies in relationships with a close other such as a spouse, has been distinguished from social loneliness, defined as deficiencies in social networks or feelings of belonging (Weiss, 1973). Recent empirical evidence supports three distinct dimensions of loneliness reflecting perceived deficits in intimate, relational, and collective connections. Thus, not being married, having few friends and relatives and/or little contact with them, and not taking part in any voluntary groups are examples of specific risk factors for intimate, relational, and collective loneliness, respectively (Hawkley, Browne, & Cacioppo, 2005).

Antecedents

Loneliness has a sizeable heritable component, accounting for about half of the variance in loneliness (Boomsma, Willemsen, Dolan, Hawkley, & Cacioppo, 2005). In addition, relatively stable personality characteristics such as lower levels of extraversion, agreeableness, conscientiousness, and sociability, and higher levels of neuroticism and shyness, are associated with higher levels of loneliness (Cacioppo, Hawkley, Ernst et al., 2006).

Loneliness exhibits relatively high temporal stability (r's > .70 over periods as long as 3 years). Variability in loneliness between individuals and within individuals over time has been associated with a variety of demographic and situational factors. Loneliness is associated with age, for example, but the relationship is not linear as might be expected. Rather, the association has the shape of an inverted flattened U, with adolescents and young adults (16–25 years of age) and the oldest old (over 80 years) experiencing the highest levels of loneliness.

The prevalence and intensity of lonely feelings can change due to situational circumstances that influence the number and especially the quality of social interactions. In general, any factor that influences social contact and interaction opportunities may influence loneliness. For example, geographic relocation, death of a spouse, and social rejection experiences (e.g., discrimination) amplify lonely feelings. Similarly, impairments in health that limit social contact can increase feelings of loneliness. Conversely, greater opportunity for social connections afforded by a larger social network protect against loneliness (Cacioppo & Hawkley, 2005).

Consequences

Social cognition

Regardless of which combination of antecedent factors, loneliness, once triggered, generates a defensive form of thinking about the social world. This defensive thinking derives from the heightened sense of insecurity and threat that characterizes lonely individuals and is evident in higher levels of negative mood, anxiety, and anger, and lower levels of optimism, self-esteem, and social support. These socioemotional states are unique to loneliness and independent of personality traits related to loneliness (e.g., extraversion, neuroticism, shyness). Relative to nonlonely individuals, lonely individuals perceive negative interactions and situations as more threatening and distressing, and positive interactions and situations as less uplifting and gratifying. They are aware that their social needs are not being met, but perceive that they have little control over their ability to meet their needs. Lonely individuals fear negative social evaluation and hold negative expectations that result in their tendency to relate to others in negative, anxious, and self-protective ways. These behaviors tend to elicit in others the very behaviors the lonely person fears, thereby confirming the lonely person's negative expectations and perpetuating a self-fulfilling prophecy that culminates in chronic feelings of loneliness (Cacioppo & Hawkley, 2005; Cacioppo, Hawkley, Ernst et al., 2006).

Health

Loneliness has negative implications for mental and physical health. In a prospective study of middle-age adults, loneliness predicted an increase in depressive symptoms over the subsequent 3 years, an effect that was independent of demographic factors (age, gender, ethnicity, socioeconomic status, marital status) and psychosocial factors related to loneliness, including hostility, perceived stress, and poor social support (Cacioppo, Hughes, Waite, Hawkley, & Thisted, 2006). In addition, loneliness in older adults has been associated with lower cognitive ability, a more rapid decline in cognitive function over time, and an increased risk of developing dementia (Wilson et al., 2007).

The effect of loneliness on health outcomes has been theorized to operate through health behaviors and a family of stress-related pathways to influence the rate of physiological decline and the development and progression of disease (Hawkley & Cacioppo, 2007). In terms of health behaviors, some studies have found a greater prevalence of smoking in lonely than nonlonely adults. In addition, loneliness has been associated with higher BMI, at least in samples that cover a wide age range from young to elderly adults. Smoking and overweight-obesity have well-known adverse health implications, indicating that these health behaviors may contribute to loneliness differences in health outcomes.

Other risk factors that may contribute to loneliness differences in health involve stress and individual differences in exposure and responses to stressful events and circumstances. In this conceptualization, loneliness not only influences the experience of stress but is itself a source of stress. Among young adults, loneliness was not associated with differences in the number of objective stressors experienced over the course of daily life, but the lonely perceived the same stressors as more severe. In middle-aged adults, loneliness was associated with both increased likelihood of experiencing chronic stress (e.g., financial, marital, social) and perceptions of greater stress. Lonely individuals also use less effective coping strategies in response to stressors and tend to respond to stressful situations with pessimism and avoidance rather than with optimism and active coping strategies. They seek less emotional and instrumental (practical) support following a stressor, and when they do obtain support from others, they find the support less efficacious than do the nonlonely (Hawkley & Cacioppo, 2007).

In addition to the greater subjective impact of stressors on the lonely, loneliness is associated with dysregulated activity of the hypothalamic-pituitary-adrenocortical (HPA) axis leading to higher levels of circulating cortisol, a stress hormone. For instance, in a three-day diary study among middle-age adults, feelings of loneliness, sadness, threat, and lack of control one day predicted a higher post-awakening increase in salivary cortisol the next day, but the morning cortisol awakening response did not predict experiences of these psychosocial states later the same day, a pattern of results that is consistent with a causal role for loneliness. Cortisol serves to constrain immune responses and inflammation within normal bounds, and elevated levels of circulating cortisol can impair immune functioning and inflammation.

Ironically, loneliness is associated with increased cortisol but also increases risk for inflammation-mediated disease. One possible explanation for inflammation-related disease in individuals with high cortisol levels involves impaired transduction of the cortisol signal. Genome-wide analyses have revealed reduced transcription of glucocorticoid response (GR) genes and increased expression of genes carrying pro-inflammatory elements in lonely relative to nonlonely middle-age adults (Cole et al., 2007). These transcriptional alterations provide a functional genomic explanation for elevated risk of inflammatory disease in individuals who experience chronically high levels of loneliness.

Loneliness has also been associated with differences in blood pressure and its regulation. In young adults, comparable levels of systolic blood pressure (SBP) were reflected in higher vascular resistance among lonely relative to nonlonely individuals. This pattern of blood pressure regulation can lead to elevated SBP over time and indeed, in middle-age adults, loneliness differences in SBP were apparent. Moreover, the association between loneliness and SBP increased with age in this middle-age sample, consistent with an accelerated physiological decline in lonely relative to nonlonely individuals (Hawkley & Cacioppo, 2007).

Restorative processes can offset the costs of stress exposure and response. Sleep is a prototypical example of a restorative behavior, and lonely individuals appear not to derive the same benefit from sleep as do nonlonely individuals. Nonrestorative sleep results not only in physical and intellectual fatigue but also in irritability and daytime impairments in cognition and memory. Quality, rather than quantity, of sleep appears to be the main source of loneliness differences in daytime dysfunction; relative to nonlonely individuals, the lonely exhibit more nightly micro-awakenings and not differences in sleep duration (Hawkley & Cacioppo, 2007).

REFERENCES

Boomsma, D. I., Willemsen, G., Dolan, C. V., Hawkley, L. C., & Cacioppo, J. T. (2005). Genetic and environmental contributions to loneliness in adults: The Netherlands Twin Register Study. *Behavior Genetics, 35*, 745–752.

Cacioppo, J. T., & Hawkley, L. C. (2005). People thinking about people: The vicious cycle of being a social outcast in one's own mind. In Williams, K. D., Forgas, J. P., and von Hippel, W. (Eds.), *The social outcast: Ostracism, social exclusion, rejection, and bullying* (pp. 91–108). New York: Psychology Press.

Cacioppo, J. T., Hawkley, L. C., Ernst, J. M., Burleson, M. H., Berntson, G. G., Nouriani, B., et al. (2006). Loneliness within a nomological net: An evolutionary perspective. *Journal of Research in Personality, 40*, 1054–1085.

Cacioppo, J. T., Hughes, M. E., Waite, L. J., Hawkley, L. C., & Thisted, R. (2006). Loneliness as a specific risk factor for depressive symptoms in older adults: Cross-sectional and longitudinal analyses. *Psychology and Aging, 21*, 140–151.

Cole, S. W., Hawkley, L. C., Arevalo, J. M., Sung, C. Y., Rose, R. M., & Cacioppo, J. T. (2007). Social regulation of gene expression in humans: Glucocorticoid resistance in the leukocyte transcriptome. *Genome Biology, 8*, R189.1–R189.13.

Hawkley, L. C., Browne, M. W., & Cacioppo, J. T. (2005). How can I connect with thee? Let me count the ways. *Psychological Science, 16*, 798–804.

Hawkley, L. C., & Cacioppo, J. T. (2007). Aging and loneliness: Downhill quickly? *Current Directions in Psychological Science, 16*, 187–191.

Weiss, R. S. (1973). *The experience of emotional and social isolation.* Cambridge, MA: MIT Press.

Wilson, R. S., Krueger, K. R., Arnold, S. E., Schneider, J. A., Kelly, J. F., Barnes, L. L., Tang, Y., & Bennett, D. A. (2007). Loneliness and risk of Alzheimer's Disease. *Archives of General Psychiatry, 64*, 234–240.

SUGGESTED READINGS

Caspi, A., Harrington, H., Moffitt, T. E., Milne, B. J., & Poulton, R. (2006). Socially isolated children 20 years later. *Archives of Pediatric Adolescent Medicine, 160*, 805–811.

Pinquart, M., & Sörensen, S. (2003). Risk factors for loneliness in adulthood and old age—A meta-analysis. In S. P. Shohov (Ed.), *Advances in Psychology Research, Volume 19* (pp. 111–143). Hauppauge, NY: Nova Science.

Rotenberg, K. J., Gruman, J. A., & Ariganello, M. (2002). Behavioral confirmation of the loneliness stereotype. *Basic and Applied Social Psychology, 24*, 81–89.

Leah Lavelle
Louise C. Hawkley
University of Chicago

See also: **Interpersonal Relationships; Social Isolation**

LONG-TERM POTENTIATION

Virtually all notions about memory hold dear the central notion that learning relies on the modification of synaptic function. In recent years considerable attention has focused on one particular form of use-dependent synaptic plasticity known as long-term potentiation (LTP). LTP was first discovered by Terje Lomo, who observed that repetitive high-frequency electrical stimulations of the pathway from the cortex to the hippocampus resulted in a steeper rise time of the excitatory synaptic potential as well as recruitment of spike activity from a greater number of cells. Moreover, these changes in synaptic and cellular responses to subsequent single shocks lasted several hours, suggesting the possibility of a lasting memory mechanism.

Two key properties of LTP are most notable: First, LTP is specific to those synapses activated during stimulation. Other neighboring synapses, even on the same neurons, are not altered. This phenomenon parallels the natural specificity of our memories, and would be a key requirement of any useful cellular memory mechanism. The property of specificity may be key to the storage capacity of brain structures because each cell can participate in the representation of multiple memories composed from distinct subsets of its synaptic inputs.

Second, LTP is associative, in that potentiation characteristically occurs across multiple inputs that are stimulated simultaneously. The property of associativity is consistent with Hebb's 1949 postulate that increasing synaptic efficacy requires the repeated activation of a presynaptic element *and* its participation in the success in firing the postsynaptic cell, as indeed occurs in associative LTP when several inputs are simultaneously active.

Considerable evidence has now accumulated revealing the cellular and molecular mechanisms that mediate the properties of different forms of LTP, as well as the cousin synaptic plasticity mechanism called long-term depression (LTD), in both the hippocampus and the neocortex (reviewed in Bliss & Collingridge, 1993; Malenka, 1994).

Molecular Mechanisms

LTP occurs through changes in synaptic strength at contacts involving N-methyl-d-aspartate (NMDA) receptors, which are activated during coactivation of other (AMPA) receptors when multiple inputs arrive at the synapse simultaneously. Subsequently, a series of molecular reactions plays a vital role in fixating the changes in synaptic function that occur in LTP. These molecular events begin with the entry of Ca++ into the synapse, which activates a molecule called cyclic adenosine monophosphate (cAMP). This molecule activates several kinds of kinases, some of which increase the number of synaptic receptors, making the synapse more sensitive to neurotransmitters. In addition, cAMP activates another molecule called cAMP-response element-binding protein (CREB). CREB operates within the nucleus of the neuron to activate a class of genes called early immediate genes, which, in turn, activate other genes that direct protein synthesis. Among the proteins produced is neurotrophin, which activates growth of the synapse and increases the neuron's responsiveness to subsequent stimulation.

In addition to LTP, there is also a mechanism that diminishes the strength of connections at infrequently used synapses, called long-term depression (LTD). LTD involves the same molecular substrates as LTD but occurs with different timing rules of activity at synapses. The combination LTP and LTD allow for a sophisticated reorganization of circuits that create neural representations of information. LTP and LTD occur among all brain structures that are known to participate in different kinds of memory. These cellular and molecular events occur on a timescale of seconds, and minutes are essential for learning to transition from short-term storage to long-term memory. These events occur in every brain structure that participates in memory.

LTP and Memory: Is There a Connection?

As Stevens (1996) once put it, the mechanism of LTP is so attractive that it would be a shame if LTP turned out not to be a memory device. But there should be no doubt about the fact that LTP is not memory; it is a laboratory phenomenon never observed in nature. The best we can hope for is that LTP and memory share some of their physiological and molecular bases. In recent years evidence from two general strategies have emerged to provide supporting connections between LTP and memory.

Behavioral LTP

One strategy is to determine if learning produces changes in synaptic physiology similar to the increases in synaptic and cellular responses that occur after LTP. For example, LeDoux and colleagues (Rogan, Staubli, & LeDoux, 1997) offered some of the most compelling evidence to date that these aspects of LTP are a consequence of natural learning. In this case the circuit under study was the pathway from the medial geniculate nucleus of the thalamus to the lateral amygdala nucleus that is part of the critical circuit for auditory fear conditioning. These investigators found that repeated pairings of auditory stimuli and foot shocks train rats to fear the tones. Furthermore, this learning experience alters evoked sensory responses to the tones in the same way as LTP in that pathway. Other studies have shown a similar pattern of enhanced strength of connections among neurons in the motor cortex of rats trained on a skilled reaching task (Rioult-Pedotti, Friedman, Hess, & Donoghue, 1998) and in the hippocampus, albeit with a distinct pattern characterized by sparseness of the enhanced synapses (Whitlock, Heynen, Shuler, & Bear, 2006).

Blocking LTP and Memory

Perhaps the most compelling and straightforward data on a potential connection between the molecular basis of LTP and memory has come from experiments where a drug is used to block LTP and, correspondingly, prevent learning. We know that the permanent fixation of newly acquired memories depends on this molecular and cellular cascade of events because memory fixation can be halted by treatments given after learning takes place that interfere with the molecules in this cascade (Martin, Grimwood, & Morris, 2000). Many studies have shown that drugs that block NMDA receptors, cAMP, CREB, or other molecules involved in protein synthesis block memory if given before or within minutes after learning, and these drugs are not effective if they are delayed. The general finding of these studies is that the molecular cascade leading to protein synthesis is not essential to initial learning or to maintaining short-term memory; however this cascade is essential for permanent memory fixation. In addition, studies using genetically modified mice have shown that alterations in specific genes for NMDA receptors or CREB can dramatically affect the capacity for LTP in particular brain areas, and the same studies have shown that these molecules are critical to memory fixation (e.g., Silva, Paylor, Wehner, & Tonegawa, 1992: McHugh, Blum, Tsien, Tonegawa, & Wilson, 1996).

REFERENCES

Bliss, T. V. P., & Collingridge G. L. (1993). A synaptic model of memory: Long-term potentiation in the hippocampus. *Nature*, *361*, 31–39.

Malenka, R. C. (1994). Synaptic plasticity in the hippocampus: LTP and LTD. *Cell, 78*, 535–538.

Martin, S. J., Grimwood, P. D., & Morris R. G. M. (2000). Synaptic plasticity and memory: An evaluation of the hypothesis. *Annual Review of Neuroscience, 23*, 649–711.

McHugh, T. J., Blum, K. I., Tsien, J. Z., Tonegawa, S., & Wilson, M. A. (1996). Impaired hippocampal representation of space in CA1-specific NMDAR1 knockout mice. *Cell, 87*, 1339–1349.

Rioult-Pedotti, M.-S., Friedman, D., Hess, G., & Donoghue, J. P. (1998). Strengthening of horizontal cortical connections following skill learning. *Nature Neuroscience. 1*, 230–234.

Rogan, M. T., Staubli, U. V., & LeDoux, J. E. (1997). Fear conditioning induces associative long-term potentiation in the amygdala. *Nature, 390*, 604–607.

Silva, A. J., Paylor, C. F. R., Wehner, J. W., & Tonegawa, S. (1992). Impaired spatial learning in a-calcium-calmodulin kinase II mutant mice. *Science, 257*, 206–211.

Stevens, C. F. (1996). Strengths and weaknesses in memory. *Nature, 381*, 471–472.

Whitlock, J. R., Heynen, A. J., Shuler, M. G., & Bear, M. F. (2006). Learning induces long-term potentiation in the hippocampus. *Science, 313*, 1093–1097.

SUGGESTED READINGS

Bear, M. F. (1996). A synaptic basis for memory storage in the cerebral cortex. *Proceeding of the National Academy of Sciences (PNAS U.S.A.), 93*, 13453–13459.

Hebb, D. O. (1949). *The organization of behavior*. New York: John Wiley & Sons.

Squire, L. R., & Kandel, E. R. (1999). *Memory: From mind to molecules*. New York: Freeman & Co.

HOWARD EICHENBAUM
Boston University

LONGITUDINAL STUDIES

Investigators in psychology use longitudinal research designs to assess changes in participant performance or status over time. Longitudinal studies employ research designs where groups of participants are observed or repeatedly assessed over a fairly lengthy interval—sometimes years. Longitudinal designs represent a very important research approach in psychology and other behavioral science investigations where time-related phenomena are under study. This has particularly been the case in developmental psychology and gerontology where maturation is the focus of an investigation. Often the intent is to examine behavioral, cognitive, or physiological changes that may occur in participants as they grow older.

Two major research approaches have been employed to investigate the time-related change trajectories: cross-sectional and longitudinal designs. *Cross-sectional* studies measure one or more dependent variables (e.g., learning style, recall accuracy) on several different age cohorts, for example, 4, 7, 10, and 12 years old. In this type of study the researcher may measure performance on such different groups to determine the effects of age on a given cognitive task. *Longitudinal* investigations repeatedly assess the dependent variable or variables on the same cohort of subjects over time (e.g., testing or recording data on them when they are 4, 7, 10, and 12 years of age). Narrowly defined, a longitudinal study is any investigation where repeated measurements are recorded on the same subjects over time. However, the term "longitudinal" is typically not used for studies where the time span is less than several months or years.

Longitudinal studies have a long history in various specialties of psychology as well as many other fields ranging from health status to sociological variables. The late nineteenth century is generally viewed as the time when psychology began to seriously employ longitudinal research, although some historians identify individual studies using this approach much earlier. Early work using longitudinal investigations significantly influenced the nature of developmental psychology. During the recent past longitudinal research has been used across the complete lifespan from developmental investigations on the very young through those focusing on elderly people and into the final periods of life.

One major strength of longitudinal designs is that researchers are able to follow the same subjects over the period of the investigation. This permits examination of change in the same individuals as they develop or decline. Consequently, longitudinal investigations permit more direct interpretations regarding development and maturation than cross-sectional studies. Longitudinal studies with multiple-measure administrations, such as the examples noted above (i.e., assessments at ages 4, 7, 10, and 12), are also preferred because of strong statistical analysis power in determining the trajectory of a change over time.

Longitudinal designs also present certain methodological challenges that must receive attention as studies are planned. Because the participants are measured repeatedly, it is possible that changes may be observed that are partially due to the effects of repeated assessment. This might lead one to interpret change as cognitive growth when in part that change was due to participants learning how to take the test. Another challenge or potential weakness in longitudinal research is potential growth or change in participant's scores due to the continuing attention, or Hawthorne effect, over time. Still another potential problem is participant attrition. Because longitudinal studies typically continue for an extended period of time, a certain number of participants may be lost for a variety of reasons (death, moving away, refusal to continue). As with most experimental designs, a majority of the challenges associated with longitudinal studies can be successfully circumvented by inventive researchers. Such studies remain an important research strategy in psychology, although not frequently undertaken because of the time and expense involved.

SUGGESTED READINGS

Binstock, R. H., & George, L. K. (Eds.). (2005). *Handbook of aging and the social sciences* (6th ed.). San Diego, CA: Academic Press.

Creasey, G. L. (2006). *Research methods in lifespan development*. Boston: Allyn & Bacon.

Drew, C. J., Hardman, M. L., & Hosp, J. (2008). *Designing and conducting research in education*. Thousand Oaks, CA: Sage Publications.

Dunn, D. S. (2008). *Research methods for social psychology*. Hoboken, NJ: John Wiley & Sons.

Gelfand, D. M., & Drew, C. J. (2003). *Understanding child behavior disorders* (4th ed.). Belmont, CA: Wadsworth.

Hedeker, D., & Gibbons, R. D. (2006). *Longitudinal data analysis*. Hoboken, NJ: John Wiley & Sons.

CLIFFORD J. DREW
University of Utah

See also: **Developmental Psychology**

LOOSE ASSOCIATIONS

The primary source of data for assessing patients with psychotic disorders is speech behavior during a clinical interview. One critical component of this assessment is the patient's ability to produce coherent conversational discourse.

The *sine qua non* of disrupted discourse coherence consists of loose associations. A synonymous term currently used is "derailment." Loose associations or derailments are identified when the listener has significant difficulty following or tracking continuous, conversational speech. The overall intention or focus of the utterance is left obscure, and the speaker seems to shift idiosyncratically from one frame of reference to another (Andreasen, 1979a). The following is a typical instance of loose associations (Hoffman, Kirstein, Stopek, & Cicchetti, 1982):

Interviewer: Tell me about where you live.
Patient: I live in one place and then another place. They're black and white you know. That's why I love Christmas and stuff because, you know, it's different colors. I used to live in Brooklyn.

The patient seems to respond to the interviewer's prompt but then abruptly switches to a Christmas motif that fails to elaborate on the "where I live" theme and does not, in itself, make a point. Of note is that each of the sentences, when considered separately, is quite ordinary and grammatical. Deviance instead reflects how multiple sentences are combined. A more complex form of loose associations is illustrated by the following (Hoffman, 1986):

Interviewer: Did you ever try to hurt yourself?
Patient: I cut myself once when I was in the kitchen trying to please David. I was scared for life because if David didn't want me then no man would.

Here the patient seems to be talking about two frames of reference in parallel, the first pertaining to cutting herself, presumably while preparing food, and the second pertaining to reasons for being suicidal. Shifts between dual frames of reference are expressed without warning to the listener. In other words, the patient did not state, "I never intentionally hurt myself but I was so upset about David that ... " These verbal cues ordinarily help the listener to make the transition from one frame of reference to another (Hoffman et al., 1982).

Loose associations comprise one manifestation of thought disorder, which is defined roughly along a spectrum, with less severe difficulties such as tangentiality (in which the speaker provides lots of superfluous details and, in the process, loses track of the original point of the remark), to especially severe difficulties such as

"word salad," in which speech is so dysgrammatical and disorganized that there is a near complete breakdown in expressed meaning.

Loose associations are often produced by patients with Schizophrenia. However, some patients with aphasia or brain disturbances secondary to drug intoxication or organic encephalopathy may also produce such language disturbances. A related language difficulty referred to as "flight of ideas" is typically associated with patients with mania or amphetamine-induced states. Some researchers tend not to distinguish flight of ideas from loose associations (Andreasen, 1979a), but there is some empirical evidence that the two terms refer to distinct phenomena (Hoffman, Stopek, & Andreasen, 1986). In the case of flight of ideas, conversational speech yields unannounced and disruptive shifts in frame of reference, but is also accompanied by rapid production of speech. Most importantly, the speaker in the former case seems to retain the ability to flesh out particular themes or topics within a particular frame of reference.

In contrast, loose associations typically expressed by patients with Schizophrenia suggest a sustained inability to fully and coherently elaborate on any theme or topic. Although the presence of loose associations in generating coherent conversational discourse favors some psychiatric diagnoses over others, these occurrences are not diagnostic of a specific disorder. Moreover, analyses of spontaneous speech samples have shown that speakers without a psychiatric or neurological disorder occasionally produce loose associations (Andreasen, 1979b; Hoffman et al., 1986).

There is considerable research exploring the cognitive, linguistic, and neurobiological underpinnings of loose associations. One view is that psychotic speakers fail to take into consideration the needs of the listener when speaking (Rochester & Martin, 1979; Hoffman et al., 1982). It is as if they are talking to themselves—not providing sufficient background information during speaking to allow the listener to fully process intended meaning. This difficulty is at times manifested by a failure to provide enough information to infer the identity of the person referred to by pronoun references such as "he" or "she." Other evidence that the speaker has difficulty in keeping in mind listener needs is that verbal cues that the topic is being switched are not provided. A related experimental finding is that patients with loose associations tend to have impairments in the capacity to understand the perspective and mental state of others at a more global level (Langdon, Coltheart, Ward, & Catts, 2002).

A second approach is reflected in studies of alterations of semantic processing in patients demonstrating loose associations. Some of these studies have suggested that alterations in how concepts are organized relative to each other in "semantic space" may underlie these speech disturbances (Goldberg et al., 1998). Other studies have linked loose associations to indiscriminate spreading activation across semantic networks. The latter refers to a tendency to activate word representations in the brain that are only indirectly related to the meaning of target words during performance of word recognition tasks (Spitzer, 1997; Moritz, Woodward, Kuppers, Lausen, & Schickel, 2003). Indiscriminate semantic activation in theory could cause incorrect word choices and disorganized discourse.

Other research has linked loose associations and other aspects of thought disorder to problems in conceptually sequencing events when performing multistep tasks (Zalla et al., 2006) and other executive functions (Barrera, McKenna, & Berrios, 2005). Studies have also attempted to characterize abnormal brain functions that contribute to loose associations using neuroimaging. For instance, a study of regional cerebral blood flow using positron emission tomography suggested that these speech disturbances arise from an imbalance of regional cerebral activation—with reduced activation in inferior frontal and cingulate brain regions combined with excessive activation in hippocampal regions (McGuire et al., 1998). A functional magnetic resonance imaging study found that patients with Schizophrenia, particularly those with positive thought disorder, show inappropriate increases in activity within inferior prefrontal and temporal cortices when responding to semantic associations (Kuperberg, Deckersbach, Holt, Goff, & West, 2007). Additional research on the neurocognitive basis of loose associations and other aspects of thought disorder is needed.

REFERENCES

Andreasen, N. C. (1979a). Thought, language, and communication disorders: 1. Clinical assessment, definition of terms, and evaluation of their reliability. *Archives of General Psychiatry, 36*, 1315–1321.

Andreasen, N. C. (1979b). Thought, language, and communication disorders: 2. Diagnostic significance. *Archives of General Psychiatry, 36*, 1325–1330.

Barrera, A., McKenna, P. J., & Berrios, G. E. (2005). Formal thought disorder in Schizophrenia: An executive or a semantic deficit? *Psychological Medicine, 35*(1), 121–132.

Goldberg, T. E., Aloia, M. S., Gourovitch, M. L., Missar, D., Pickar, D., & Weinberger, D. R. (1998). Cognitive substrates of thought disorder: I. The semantic system. *American Journal of Psychiatry, 155*, 1671–1676.

Hoffman, R. E. (1986). Verbal hallucinations and language production processes in Schizophrenia. *Behavior and Brain Science, 9*, 503–548.

Hoffman, R. E., Kirstein, L., Stopek, S., & Cicchetti, D. (1982). Apprehending Schizophrenic discourse: A structural analysis of the listener's task. *Brain Language, 15*, 207–233.

Hoffman, R. E., Stopek, S., & Andreasen, N. C. (1986). A comparative study of Manic versus Schizophrenic speech disorganization. *Archives of General Psychiatry, 43*, 831–838.

Kuperberg, G. R., Deckersbach, T., Holt, D. J., Goff, D., & West, W. C. (2007). Increased temporal and prefrontal activity in

response to semantic associations in Schizophrenia. *Archives of General Psychiatry, 64*, 138–151.

Langdon, R., Coltheart, M., Ward, P. B., & Catts, S. V. (2002). Disturbed communication in Schizophrenia: The role of poor pragmatics and poor mind-reading. *Psychological Medicine, 32*(7), 1273–1284.

McGuire, P. K., Quested, D. J., Spence, S. A., Murray, R. M., Frith, C .D., & Liddle, P. F. (1998). Pathophysiology of 'positive' thought disorder in Schizophrenia. *British Journal of Psychiatry 173*, 231–235.

Moritz, S., Woodward, T. S., Kuppers, D., Lausen, A., & Schickel, M. (2003). Increased automatic spreading of activation in thought-disordered Schizophrenic patients. *Schizophrenia Research, 59*(2–3), 181–186.

Rochester, S., & Martin, J. (1979). *Crazy talk: A study of the discourse of Schizophrenic speakers*. New York: Plenum Press.

Spitzer, M. (1997). A cognitive neuroscience view of Schizophrenic thought disorder. *Schizophrenia Bulletin, 23*, 29–50.

Zalla, T., Bouchilloux, N., Labruyere, N., Georgieff, N., Bougerol, T., & Franck, N. (2006). Impairment in event sequencing in disorganised and nondisorganised patients with Schizophrenia. *Brain Research Bulletin, 68*(4), 195–202.

RALPH E. HOFFMAN
Yale University

See also: **Disordered Thinking**

LOVE

Social psychologists distinguish between two kinds of love: *passionate* love and *companionate* love. Passionate love, a potent emotion, is defined as an intense longing for union with the other. It is associated with a confusion of feelings: tenderness and sexuality, elation and pain, anxiety and relief, altruism and jealousy (Hatfield & Rapson, 1993). Companionate love, a cooler emotion, is characterized by affection, intimacy, attachment, and a concern for the welfare of the other (Sternberg, 2006).

Is Passionate Love a Cultural Universal?

Since Darwin's classic treatise on *The Descent of Man and Selection in Relation to Sex*, scientists have debated the universality of romantic love. Once, scientists assumed that passionate love was a Western phenomenon. Today, most assume it to be a cultural universal. In one study, anthropologists selected a sampling of tribal societies from the *Standard Cross-Cultural Sample*. They found that in far-flung societies young lovers talked about passionate love, recounted tales of love, sang love songs, and talked about the longings and anguish of infatuation. When passionate affections clashed with parents' or elders' wishes, young people often eloped. It appears that romantic love is a panhuman characteristic (see Jankowiak, 1997).

Does Culture Influence Men and Women's Views of Love?

Culture has been found to have a significant impact on how men and women view passionate love. In one study, for example, researchers interviewed young people in America, Italy, and the People's Republic of China about their emotional experiences. They found that, although almost all people were aware that passionate love is generally a bittersweet experience, Americans and Italians tended to equate love with joy and happiness, whereas Chinese students had a darker view of passion, associating it with sadness, pain, and heartache.

What Do Men and Women Desire in Romantic Partners, Sexual Partners, and Mates?

Throughout the world, young men and women desire many of the same things in a mate. In one cross-cultural study, Buss and his colleagues asked 10,000 men and women from 37 countries to indicate what they valued in a mate. The cultures represented a tremendous diversity of geographic, cultural, political, ethnic, religious, racial, economic, and linguistic groups. Of utmost importance was love! High on the list of other things men and women cared about were character, emotional stability and maturity, a pleasing disposition, education and intelligence, health, sociability, a desire for home and children, refinement, good looks, and ambition (Buss, 1994).

Scientists have documented that a major determinant of sexual "chemistry" is physical attractiveness (Hatfield & Sprecher, 1986). People tend to fall in love with people who are similar to themselves in attitudes, religious affiliation, values, interests, education, and socioeconomic status (Hatfield & Rapson, 1995).

Do Men and Women Desire the Same Thing in Mates?

Evolutionary psychologists have argued that men and women should differ in what they desire in a mate. According to evolutionary biology, an animal's "fitness" depends on how successful it is in transmitting its genes to subsequent generations. It is to both men's and women's evolutionary advantage to produce as many progeny as possible. But men and women differ in one crucial respect—how much they must invest in their offspring if they are to survive and reproduce. Men need to invest a trivial amount of energy in any one child. (One Saudi ruler claims to have fathered more than 5,000 children). Women, on the other hand, must invest a great deal in their offspring if they

are to survive. In tribal societies, most women are lucky to produce at most five surviving children.

On the basis of this logic, Buss (1994) proposed a "sexual strategies theory" of human mating. Men and women, he argued, are genetically programmed to desire different traits in potential mates. In order to maximize reproductive outcomes, men must seek quantity, women quality in a mate. Men ought to prefer women who are physically attractive, healthy, and young, and they ought to desire sexual encounters with a variety of partners. Women ought to seek out men who possess status, power, and money, who are willing to make a commitment, who are kind and considerate, and who like children.

Many anthropologists, historians, sociologists, and psychologists have sharply criticized the evolutionary approach. They point out that *Homo sapiens* possess an unrivaled ability to adapt—to change themselves and their worlds. Men and women possess different attitudes, these critics continue, not because they are propelled by ancient genetic codes, but because they are responding to different sociocultural realities. For most of human history, men and women who desired romantic and passionate liaisons and/or defied convention were likely to face very different consequences. Is it surprising then, that even today many women are more cautious about taking a chance on love (or engaging in casual sex) than are their male counterparts? (see Hatfield, Rapson, & Martel, 2007, for a summary of this research).

What Does Passionate Love Look Like?

In 2000, two London neuroscientists, Andreas Bartels and Semir Zeki, attempted to identify the brain regions associated with passionate love and sexual desire. The scientists put up posters around London, advertising for men and women who were "truly, deeply, and madly in love." People who answered the advertisement were asked to complete the Passionate Love Scale (PLS). Those who were most in love were selected for the study. Participants were then placed in an fMRI (functional magnetic resonance imagery) scanner. This high-tech scanner constructs an image of the brain such that changes in blood flow (induced by brain activity) are represented as color-coded pixels. The scientists gave each participant a color photograph of their beloved to gaze at, alternating the beloved's picture with pictures of casual friends. They then digitally compared the scans taken while the participants viewed their beloved's picture with those taken while they viewed a friend's picture, creating images that represented the brain regions that became more (or less) active in both conditions. These images, the researchers argued, revealed the brain regions involved when a person experiences passionate love and/or sexual desire.

Bartels and Zeki (2000) discovered that passion sparked activity in the brain areas associated with euphoria and reward, and decreased activity in the areas associated with sadness, anxiety, and fear. Activity seemed to be restricted to foci in the medial insula and the anterior cingulated cortex and, subcortically, in the caudate nucleus, and the putamen, all bilaterally. Most of the regions that were activated during the experience of romantic love were those that are active when people have taken euphoria-inducing drugs such as cocaine. Apparently, both passionate love and those drugs activate a "joyous" circuit in the brain. The anterior cingulated cortex is also active when people are sexually aroused. This makes sense, because passionate love and sexual desire are tightly linked constructs.

Among the regions where activity decreased during the experience of love were zones previously implicated in the areas of the brain controlling critical thought. Such brain areas are also activated when people experience painful emotions such as sadness, anger and fear. The authors argue that once we fall in love with someone, we feel less need to assess critically their character and personality. (In that sense, love may indeed be "blind.") Deactivations were also observed in the posterior cingulated gyrus and in the amygdala and were right-lateralized in the prefrontal, parietal, and middle temporal cortices. As before, the authors found passionate love and sexual arousal to be tightly linked. Fisher (2004) and Hatfield and Rapson (2009) provide reviews of the literature on the neuroscience and neurobiology of passionate love and sexual desire.

REFERENCES

Bartels, A., & Zeki, S. (November 27, 2000). The neural basis of romantic love. *Neuroreport, 11,* 3829–3834.

Buss, D. M. (1994). *The evolution of desire.* New York: Basic Books.

Darwin, C. (1871). *The descent of man and selection in relation to sex.* London: Murray.

Fisher, H. E. (2004). *Why we love: The nature and chemistry of romantic love.* New York: Henry Holt.

Hatfield, E., & Rapson, R. L. (1993). *Love, sex, and intimacy: Their psychology, biology, and history.* New York: HarperCollins.

Hatfield, E., & Rapson, R. L. (1995). *Love and sex: Cross-cultural perspectives.* New York: Allyn and Bacon.

Hatfield, E., & Rapson, R. L. (2009). The neuropsychology of passionate love and sexual desire. In D. Marazziti (Ed.), *Neuropsychology of social relationships.* Nova Science.

Hatfield, E., Rapson, R. L., & Martel, L. D. (2007). Passionate love and sexual desire. In S. Kitayama & D. Cohen (Eds.). *Handbook of cultural psychology,* (pp. 760–779). New York: Guilford Press.

Hatfield, E., & Sprecher, S. (1986). *Mirror, mirror: The importance of looks in everyday life.* New York: State University of New York Press.

Jankowiak, W. (Ed.). (1997). *Romantic passion: A universal experience?* New York: Columbia University Press.

Sternberg R. J., & Weis, K. (Eds.). (2006). *The new psychology of love.* New Haven, CT: Yale University Press.

ELAINE HATFIELD
RICHARD L. RAPSON
University of Hawaii

See also: Attachment and Bonding; Sexual Desire

LSD (See Hallucinogen-Related Disorders)

LURIA, ALEXANDER ROMANOVICH (1902–1977)

Alexander Luria graduated from the University of Kazan, Russia, at the age of 19 in 1921. He entered medical school in the late 1930s and earned degrees of MD, EdD, and DMed from the University of Moscow, where he later became a professor in the Department of Psychology and head of the Department of Neuropsychology. Luria was influenced in the direction of his studies and research by Vygotsky, whom he met in 1924.

Although the locales of Luria's work were dictated by the political shifts in power of his native Russia, there was an overarching guiding framework that unites his contributions. This framework, developed in collaboration with Vygotsky and Leont'ev, is generally labeled a sociohistorical school of psychology. Principles of language learning, writing, and cognitive thought were viewed as an interaction of the developing human within a sociohistorical context. Sometimes Luria had more freedom to pursue topics guided by his own interests, such as early in his career and again in the 1950s when he returned to neuropsychology. At other times he had to manage to study topics of interest within contexts of Marxism and communism, which necessitated that he express his findings and concepts within a Pavlovian framework.

Luria had a broad background in psychology and neurology and carried out research on aphasia, the restoration of functions following brain trauma, speech, and higher cortical functions. He developed theories of language disorders and of the functions of the frontal lobe. He believed that mental functions are complex functional systems that cannot be localized in isolated cell groups or narrow regions of the cortex. Rather, the cell groups must be organized in systems of zones working in concert, each performing its role in the complex system.

Because many of his works have been available in English, Luria is well known in the United States. In the 1920s he studied human conflict, using hand movements and associative responses into which a conflict situation was introduced. This work was summarized in *The Nature of Human Conflicts*.

SUGGESTED READINGS

Luria, A. (1968). *The mind of the mnemonist*. New York: Basic Books

Luria, A. (1972). *The man with the shattered world*. New York: Basic Books.

Luria, A. (1973). *Working brain: An introduction to neuropsychology*. New York: Basic Books.

STAFF

LURIA-NEBRASKA NEUROPSYCHOLOGICAL BATTERY

The Luria-Nebraska Neuropsychological Battery (LNNB) is a neuropsychological assessment battery based on the psychological procedures originated by the Russian neuropsychologist Alexander R. Luria and subsequently reorganized by Charles J. Golden and his associates (Golden, Hammeke, & Purisch, 1978) into a standardized battery of Luria's tests for the purpose of clinical neurodiagnosis. Luria, like the English neurologist J. Hughlings Jackson and his fellow Russian L. S. Vygotsky, believed that brain-behavior relationships could not be explained satisfactorily by either the localizationalist or the equipotentialist theories of brain function. Instead, Luria conceived of behavior as the result of the interactions among all areas of the brain, and he favored the use of simple test procedures that reflected relatively uncomplicated patterns of brain interactions and made possible precise investigation of functional systems of the brain.

Recognition of Luria in the United States came with the publication of *Higher Cortical Functions in Man* (1962) and *The Working Brain* (1973). Detailed information on Luria's test procedures became available with Anne-Lise Christensen's (1979) *Luria's Neuropsychological Investigation*. Luria's testing methods were not immediately accepted by American clinical neuropsychologists because of the absence of a standardized, quantitative scoring system and experimental evidence supporting the validity of the test procedures. In addition, Luria's procedures appeared to rely heavily on clinical judgment rather than objective, verifiable data.

To remedy the psychometric deficits of the Luria techniques, Golden and his colleagues transformed Luria's test items into standardized test procedures with objective scoring systems and a battery that allowed a clinical evaluation on a quantitative level, like most American tests, as well as a qualitative level, as urged by Luria. The standardized version of Luria's tests assesses major areas of neuropsychological performance, including motor, tactile, and visual skills; auditory abilities; expressive and receptive speech functions; reading, writing, and arithmetic abilities; spatial skills; and memory and intelligence.

Description of the Battery

There are 269 items in the standardized Luria battery, initially referred to as the Luria-South Dakota Neuropsychological Test Battery. Each item is a test of a specific aspect of neuropsychological functioning. Subgroups of items emerge that represent performance in the content area implied by the name of the scale, as, for example, the motor functions scale. The names of the scales of the LNNB are Motor functions; Rhythym (acoustic-motor) functions; Tactile (higher cutaneous and kinesthetic) functions; Visual (spatial) functions; Receptive speech; Expressive speech; Writing functions; Reading skills; Arithmetical skills; Memory, and Intellectual processes.

Form II of this battery added a twelfth scale, Intermediate Memory, which assesses delayed recall of 10 of the previously administered Memory items.

There are five summary scales, based on some of the items of the clinical scales: (1) Pathognominic—this scale consists of simple items rarely missed by normal subjects and is highly indicative of brain dysfunction; (2) Right hemisphere—this scale measures the motor and tactile functioning of the left side of the body; (3) Left hemisphere—this scale measures the motor and tactile functioning of the right side of the body; (4) Profile elevation—this scale measures the level of present functioning or degree of behavioral compensation; and (5) Impairment—this scale measures the degree of overall impairment.

Since the original publication of this battery, other scales have been developed, including eight localization scales (Frontal, Sensorimotor, Parietal-Occipital, and Temporal scales for each brain hemisphere) and 28 separate factor scales. A 66-item list of qualitative descriptors of test performance is also provided to aid the examiner in evaluating the nature of performance errors. An impaired performance on any of the scales is determined by comparison with a critical level, which is calculated for each patient with age and education corrections. If a scale exceeds the critical level, the possibility of impairment on that scale is suggested. Two or more scales exceeding the critical level is suggestive of brain damage.

An adaptation for children, the Luria-Nebraska Neuropsychological Battery-Children's Revision, is available for ages 8–12. A short form of this battery, with 141 items, has been developed to be used with elderly patients. The LNNB is administered by psychologists as well as by psychology technicians trained in the administration and scoring procedures of the battery. The testing time averages about two and one-half hours. The scale scores can be hand-scored, but a computerized service by the test battery's publisher is also available.

Neuropsychological Studies

Several validity studies of the LNNB were completed using normal, brain-damaged, and schizophrenic patients. In 1978, Golden, Hammeke, and Purisch reported the first validity study of the LNNB, examining the test items with 50 brain-damaged and 50 control subjects. Of the 269 LNNB items, 252 were found to discriminate significantly at the .05 level or better, with the remaining 17 items significant at the .02 level.

Hammeke, Golden, and Purisch (1978) also studied the 14 scales of the LNNB with 50 brain-damaged subjects and 50 controls. The diagnostic accuracy of the scales with the brain-damaged subjects ranged from 64% for the Arithmetic Scale to 86% for the Expressive Speech Scale. The hit rates with the normal subjects ranged from 74% for the Expressive Speech Scale to 96% for the Memory Scale. A discriminant analysis using the 14 scaled scores correctly classified all 50 control patients and 43 of the brain-damaged patients, yielding an overall hit rate of 93%.

Cross-validation of the LNNB was reported by Golden and colleagues (1981b), utilizing 87 patients with localized lesions and 30 control patients. An LNNB summary score led to a 74% accuracy rate for determining brain damage. The hemisphere scales yielded a lateralization hit rate of 78%, whereas the highest localization scale led to a lateralization hit rate of 92% and a localization hit rate of 84%.

The effectiveness of the LNNB was compared with the Halstead-Reitan Neuropsychological Battery, recognized as the most widely used standardized battery. Both test batteries were administered to 48 brain-damaged and 60 normal subjects. The results showed a high degree of relationship (all rs ≥ .71, p ≤ .05) between the 14 LNNB scale scores and the major 14 scores of the Halstead-Reitan. Discriminant analysis found both batteries equally effective in identifying the brain-damaged subjects, with hit rates over 85% (Golden et al., 1981a).

Critiques of the LNNB have noted that it is comprised of test items from Luria's work but does not necessarily represent Luria's clinical and qualitative methodology of testing hypotheses concerning a patient's neuropsychological functions or deficits. Support for the battery, on the other hand, has identified the standardization and empirical aspects of this battery as its strongest assets (Anastasi, 1982), along with its assets of ease of administration, portability, and brevity (Hogan, 2006). On the other hand, although the validity of the LNNB with neurologically impaired patients has been confirmed by a number of studies by Golden and his associates, others have been unable to replicate these validation findings. A frequent source of diagnostic errors occur with patients experiencing language impairment, evidently due to the highly verbal nature of many of the test items. In addition, the stringent time limits of several items make it difficult to distinguish failed performance due to slowness from failed performance due to specific impaired functions.

The LNNB, along with the Halstead-Reitan Neuropsychological Battery, are the two most widely used fixed neuropsychological test batteries employed by clinical neuropsychologists. A concise review of this battery is presented in Lezak, Howieson, and Loring's (2004) *Neuropsychological Assessment* (4th ed.), with a discussion of concerns about the battery's norms, scale specificity, validation studies, lateralization capabilities, and limitations.

REFERENCES

Anastasi, A. (1982). *Psychological testing* (5th ed.). New York: Macmillan.

Christensen, A.-L. (1979). *Luria's neuropsychological investigation* (2nd ed.). Copenhagen, Denmark: Munksgaard.

Golden, C. J., Hammeke, T. A., & Purisch, A. D. (1978). Diagnostic validity of a standardized neuropsychological battery derived from Luria's Neuropsychological Tests. *Journal of Consulting and Clinical Psychology, 46*, 1258–1265.

Golden, C. J., Kane, R., Sweet, J., Moses, J. A., Cardellino, J. P., Templeton, R., et al. (1981a). Relationship of the Halstead-Reitan Neuropsychological Battery to the Luria-Nebraska Neuropsychological Battery. *Journal of Consulting and Clinical Psychology, 49*, 410–417.

Golden, C. J., Moses, J. A., Fishburne, F. J., Engum, E., Lewis, G. P., Wisniewski, A. M., et al. (1981b). Cross-validation of the Luria-Nebraska Neuropsychological Battery for the presence, lateralization, and localization of brain damage. *Journal of Consulting and Clinical Psychology, 49*, 491–507.

Golden, C. J., Purisch, A. D., & Hammeke, T. A. (1985). *Luria-Nebraska Neuropsychological Battery: Forms I and II*. Los Angeles: Western Psychological Services.

Hammeke, T. A., Golden, C. J., & Purisch, A. D. (1978). A standardized, short, and comprehensive neuropsychological test battery based on the Luria neuropsychological evaluation. *International Journal of Neuroscience, 8*, 135–141.

Hogan, T. P. (2006). *Psychological testing: A practical introduction* (2nd ed.). Hoboken, NJ: John Wiley & Sons.

Lezak, M. D., Howieson, D. B., & Loring, D. W. (2004). *Neuropsychological assessment* (4th ed.). New York: Oxford University Press.

Luria, A. R. (1962). *Higher cortical functions in man*. New York: Basic Books.

Luria, A. R. (1973). *The working brain*. New York: Basic Books.

Moses, J. A., Jr., & Purisch, A. D. (1997). The evolution of the Luria-Nebraska Neuropsychological Battery. In G. Goldstein & T. M. Incagnoli (Eds.), *Contemporary approaches to neuropsychological assessment* (pp. 131–170). New York: Plenum.

WILLIAM T. TSUSHIMA
Straub Clinic and Hospital Honolulu, HI

See also: **Neuropsychology; Psychological Assessment**